We the People

An Introduction to American Politics

THIRD EDITION

TEXAS EDITION

We the People

An Introduction to American Politics

BENJAMIN GINSBERG
The Johns Hopkins University

THEODORE J. LOWI
Cornell University

MARGARET WEIR
University of California at Berkeley

ANTHONY CHAMPAGNE
University of Texas at Dallas

JOHN FORSHEE
San Jacinto College, Central

EDWARD J. HARPHAM
University of Texas at Dallas

THIRD EDITION
TEXAS EDITION

W • W • NORTON & COMPANY • NEW YORK • LONDON

PRINTED IN THE UNITED STATES OF AMERICA

Illustration credits and copyrights are given on page A73, which constitutes an extension of this copyright page.

For information about permission to reproduce selections from this book, write to Permissions, W. W. Norton & Company, Inc., 500 Fifth Avenue, New York, NY 10110.

★

Editor: Stephen Dunn
Associate Managing Editor—College: Jane Carter
Director of Manufacturing—College: Roy Tedoff
Manuscript Editor: Margaret Farley
Project Editor: Christopher Miragliotta
Editorial Assistant & Photo Researcher: Aubrey Anable, Sandhya Gupta
Production Manager: Ruth Dworkin
Text Design: Jack Meserole/Joan Greenfield
Figures: John McAusland
The text of this book is composed in Sabon with the display set in Myriad.
Composition by TSI Graphics
Manufacturing by Quebecor/Hawkins

★

Library of Congress Cataloging-in-Publication Data
Ginsberg, Benjamin.
We the people: an introduction to American politics / Benjamin Ginsberg . . . [et al.].—3rd ed, Texas ed.
p. cm.
Rev. ed. of: We the people / Benjamin Ginsberg. 3rd ed. 2001.
Includes bibliographical references and index.
ISBN 0-393-97714-5
1. United States—Politics and government. I. Ginsberg, Benjamin. We the people.
JK271.G65 2001b
320.473—dc21 2001018004

W. W. Norton & Company, Inc., 500 Fifth Avenue, New York, NY 10110
www.wwnorton.com

W. W. Norton & Company Ltd., 10 Coptic Street, London WC1A 1PU

1 2 3 4 5 6 7 8 9 0

Contents

PART IV

Institutions

Preface

We the People is a milestone in a collaboration that began between Theodore J. Lowi and Benjamin Ginsberg twenty years ago. The first result of that collaboration, *American Government: Freedom and Power,* was first published in 1990. With its most recent edition, we and the publishers feel warranted in expressing satisfaction that its historical/institutional method has been confirmed by its reception among the teachers who have adopted it and the students who have read it.

But unlike political leaders, textbooks should not try to be all things to all people. Endurance is most often ensured by recognition of one's limitations. Lowi and Ginsberg increasingly came to feel that *American Government* needed a sibling to address a number of themes and problems that have become much more central to American politics since *American Government* was conceived in the early 1980s. For a good text should be both timeless and timely: It should present principles whose value goes beyond the immediate events of the day. At the same time, however, it should present students with the principles they need to help elevate their understanding of contemporary events.

We viewed this process as a challenge rather than as a chore. The first step Lowi and Ginsberg took to meet the challenge of developing a new text was to invite a third author to join the enterprise: Margaret Weir, an expert on social policy in the United States and Europe. Weir brought with her a strong background in urban politics as well as the benefit of several years of teaching experience at Harvard and the University of California at Berkeley, where she now teaches.

From the start, the three of us agreed that this younger sibling would be titled *We the People* and would focus on three sets of issues. The first of these is the question of who is and who is not part of the American political community. This question has been the source of enormous conflict throughout American history and has become salient once again as events at home and throughout the world have brightened the light of democracy, exposing for everyone to see the unreasonable restrictions on who are "we the people," how should "we the people" be defined, and what powers, rights, and obligations "we the people" should have. Although the United States has so far experienced comparatively little conflict over the basic institutions and practices of government, and although our institutions have evolved in a roughly democratic direction, the struggle over the scope and inclusiveness of the American political process has often been a bitter one, and neither the struggle nor the bitterness is over.

The original American political community consisted of a rather limited group of white male property holders. Over the ensuing two centuries, "we the people" became a larger and more inclusive body as a result of such forces as the abolitionist movement, the women's suffrage movement, and the civil rights movement. This expansion of the political community was marked by enormous conflicts involving questions of race, gender, social class, and religious identity. Today, these conflicts continue in the form of struggles over such issues as affirmative action, welfare reform, abortion, the gender gap, the political mobilization of religious groups, and the rise and fall of minority voting districts. These themes are raised in Chapter 2 of *We the People* and are explored further throughout the book.

But regardless of our country's spotty record, one American feature has been and remains the envy of the entire world: Expansion of our political community *has* taken place, and it has happened without having to create new institutions, rules, or procedures. Our democracy is no crustacean that has to shed its structure as it grows.

The second set of issues that we focus on concerns American political values. The American nation is defined not only by its form of government but also by a set of shared beliefs and values, the most basic of which are liberty, equality, and democracy. Although these can be located in antiquity, Americans gave them new vitality and credibility in our founding documents—the Declaration of Independence and the Constitution, which transformed ancient and abstract principles into operating structures and rules for the new Republic. Although the path has deviated and wrong turns have been taken, the general direction of America has been one worthy of pride—a pride we authors share with virtually all of the American people. But our job as authors is to recognize the gap between ideals and realities and to treat the gap honestly so that our students come to understand that a good citizen is a critical citizen, one whose obedience is not unconditional. Liberty, equality, and democracy are concepts that link all the chapters of our book. They are also criteria against which to measure and to judge all aspects of governmental and political performance.

Finally, *We the People* addresses a pedagogical question: Why should Americans be engaged with government and politics at all? For the entire first century and more of American history under the Constitution, Americans were relatively heavily involved in political life, as activists or as active spectators. Politics was a kind of entertainment, a defining aspect of community life. Politics in America was interesting even to those who had not yet been made full members of the political community. As the size of all governments, especially the national government, began to grow after World War I, Americans by all appearances still took their politics seriously, and the scope of their interest seemed to expand from campaigns and elections into public policy issues keeping pace with the expansion of government and of government programs.

During the 1960s and 1970s, American students were heavily engaged with politics, many seeing it, quite realistically, as a matter of life and death. Even during the early 1980s, when *American Government: Freedom and Power* was being planned, it was our assumption that political engagement needed guidance—but that it was *there* to be guided. It hardly seemed necessary to explain to students why they should take politics seriously, as observers as well as activists.

But the involvement of the American people in political life has been declining, and students have been increasingly willing to ask why they should be interested in politics at all. We are deeply troubled by this trend and committed this book to its reversal. Our chapters are introduced by discussions that show where students fit into the materials to be addressed by that chapter and why they should take a personal, indeed selfish, interest in the outcomes of government. For example, our discussion of the media opens with the issues of press freedom faced by college newspapers. Our chapter on civil rights begins with an evaluation of affirmative action programs in college admissions. The opening pages of our discussion of federalism deal with interstate differences that affect college students. Our hope is to make politics interesting to students by demonstrating that their interests are at stake—that their forebears were correct in viewing politics as a matter of life and death.

In this Third Edition, we are freshly dedicated to the goal of getting students to see themselves not only as citizens but as citizens in the Greek ideal, where the opposite of citizen was *idiote.* We recognize at the very outset that politics, like economics, is driven by self-interest, but self-interest includes a commitment to the advancement of one's community as well as to one's purse and property.

This inspired us to use more citizen participation narratives in our teaching, and those successes produced a "Get Invovled" section at the conclusion of every chapter. In fact, some of the chapters also begin with case studies on the possibilities of one, a few, or many student-citizens influencing a legislature, an agency, a party, a newspaper, and other such centers of power. It should be added here how often political influence comes from the capacity of dedicated citizens to make a nuisance of themselves—badgering members of Congress, in person or by using the magnificent new citizen-friendly technology of fax, e-mail, and Web. From local consumer and environmental groups to pro-choice and pro-life picketers, nuisance value is an important form of influence—and the measure of that influence is the intensity of complaints you hear from its recipients: the legislators and their staffs. But that's a sign of political health. We didn't elect our representatives to a life of comfort and leisure.

On the other hand, we already knew but have become increasingly aware that student-citizens can see through sentimental or moralistic appeals to participate in politics. Students don't have to know much about politics or society to be aware of the inherent limits of individual efficacy in a Big Society like the United States—or, for that matter, a Big City or on a Big Campus. We'd be laughed out of the classroom if we pulled out the old adage that every citizen can be president, or that the views of every citizen are taken into account in the representative process. "The People" is a collective noun; "we, the individuals" don't count for much. But that does not diminish the validity of the message we convey in each and every chapter. First, we demonstrate in every chapter that the one and the few *can* count. Moreover, those who doubt this are engaging in a self-fulfilling prophecy; that is, to be *in*active as a result of a pessimistic view of the capacity of citizens is to confirm to the fullest that citizen action cannot count.

But there is a second dimension to our message about participation that must be taken seriously by even the most pessimistic person. This is that inherent in the definition of citizenship itself is the obligation to be enlightened. Self-interest will get you nowhere unless it is enlightened, by knowledge of who you are, what you want, and how you can go about getting it. This is no less true in political life than it is in economic life. Actually, enlightenment is all the more important to effective citizenship precisely because direct political action is not always a practical alternative. Go back once again to Greek antiquity, where politics *was* talk:

> To classical political theory, speech, not sight, is the most political of the faculties. . . . But political speech—and, especially, *listening* to political speech—is a skill and pleasure that must be learned; it demands an extended span of attention, the capacity for critical reflection, and that art of hearing that lets us separate meaning from its disguises. Always difficult, that command of rhetoric is harder to cultivate in a society as supersonic as ours, and the electronic media actually undermine the arts of speech and hearing.[1]

Each citizen must have a third ear, and must listen with that third ear to become the best citizen, which, we repeat, is a critical citizen. Criticism *is* speech in action.

In this Third Edition we have tried all the harder to design every chapter to the fullest extent of our ability to show why everyone must for their own sakes be interested in politics. We have tried in every way possible to provide the context, the background, and the origin of every political issue on the American political agenda. And we have tried to deal with each institution in a way that gives its place in the system but also provides a sense of how the one and the few citizens can gain access to it. And we have included what we call a "Greek chorus"—a new "Student Debate," in which the opposing views of students on current issues are presented, as well as other boxes providing student perspectives, drawn from case studies, polls, campaigns, and news stories. Some of these perspectives are profound; some may seem silly. As with the Greeks, our student chorus illustrates the range of enlightenment. It also demonstrates the potential of the one and the few and the many when knowledge is added to talk. Knowledge and talk are a prelude to action. Enlightenment without action can make a difference. Action without enlightenment can be dangerous. We continue to hope that our book will itself be accepted as a form of enlightened political action. This Third Edition is another chance. It is an advancement toward our goal. We promise to keep trying.

[1]Wilson Carey McWilliams, "The Meaning of the Election," in Gerald Pomper, ed., *The Election of 1988—Reports and Interpretations* (Chatham, NJ: Chatham House Publishers, 1989), p. 183.

ACKNOWLEDGMENTS

Our students at Cornell, Johns Hopkins, Harvard, and Berkeley have been an essential factor in the writing of this book. They have been our most immediate intellectual community, a hospitable one indeed. Another part of our community, perhaps a large suburb, is the discipline of political science itself. Our debt to the scholarship of our colleagues is scientifically measurable, probably to several decimal points, in the endnotes of each chapter. Despite many complaints that the field is too scientific or not scientific enough, political science is alive and well in the United States. It is an aspect of democracy itself, and it has grown and changed in response to the developments in government and politics that we have chronicled in our book. If we did a "time line" on the history of political science, it would show a close association with developments in "the American state." Sometimes the discipline has been out of phase and critical; at other times, it has been in phase and perhaps apologetic. But political science has never been at a loss for relevant literature, and without it, our job would have been impossible.

We are especially pleased to acknowledge our debt to the many colleagues who had a direct and active role in criticism and preparation of the manuscript. Our thanks go to

First Edition Reviewers
Sarah Binder, Brookings Institution
Kathleen Gille, Office of Representative David Bonior
Rodney Hero, University of Colorado at Boulder
Robert Katzmann, Brookings Institution
Kathleen Knight, University of Houston
Robin Kolodny, Temple University
Nancy Kral, Tomball College
Robert C. Lieberman, Columbia University
David A. Marcum, University of Wyoming
Laura R. Winsky Mattei, State University of New York at Buffalo
Marilyn S. Mertens, Midwestern State University
Barbara Suhay, Henry Ford Community College
Carolyn Wong, Stanford University
Julian Zelizer, State University of New York at Albany

Second Edition Reviewers
Lydia Andrade, University of North Texas
John Coleman, University of Wisconsin at Madison
Daphne Eastman, Odessa College
Otto Feinstein, Wayne State University
Elizabeth Flores, Delmar College
James Gimpel, University of Maryland at College Park
Jill Glaathar, Southwest Missouri State University
Shaun Herness, University of Florida
William Lyons, University of Tennessee at Knoxville
Andrew Polsky, Hunter College, City University of New York
Grant Reeher, Syracuse University
Richard Rich, Virginia Polytechnic
Bartholomew Sparrow, University of Texas at Austin

Third Edition Reviewers
Amy Jasperson, University of Texas at San Antonio
Loch Johnson, University of Georgia
Mark Kann, University of Southern California
Andrea Simpson, University of Washington
Brian Smentkowski, Southeast Missouri State University
Nelson Wikstrom, Virginia Commonwealth University

We also must pay thanks to the many collaborators we have had on this project. First, we owe a very special thanks to Robert J. Spitzer of the State University of New York at Cortland for preparing the "Policy Debates." We also owe enormous thanks to Mark Kann and Marcella Marlowe of the University of Southern California for their work on the "Get Involved" sections that conclude every chapter. Their success in getting students involved in the communities surrounding the USC campus is evident in the superb quality of these inserts. Thanks also to John Robertson of Texas A&M University for contributing the "American Democracy in Comparative Perspective" boxes to this edition. A comparativist by training, John's vast experience teaching thousands of students the American politics course shows in these thoughtful essays. We would also like to thank Paul Gronke of Duke University for authoring the "Politics on the Web" sidebars. Van Wiginton of San Jacinto College contributed enormous amounts of very thoughtful content to the Web site, in addition to later keeping it as current as this new technology allows for. Finally, we would like to thank Marilyn Mertens of Midwestern State University for her authorship of both the study guide and instructor's manual to accompany the book. Marilyn's teaching experience was a valuable addition to the whole project.

We are also grateful for the talents and hard work of several research assistants, whose contributions can never be adequately compensated. In particular, Mingus Mapps of Cornell, Doug Harris of Johns Hopkins (now an assistant professor at the University of Texas at Dallas), and Ben Bowyer of the University of California at Berkeley put an enormous amount of thought and time into the figures, tables, and study aids that appear in the text. Mingus also kept a close eye on keeping the book as up-to-date as possible.

We would like to give special thanks to Jacqueline Pastore at Cornell University, who not only prepared portions of the manuscript but also helped to hold the entire project together. We especially thank for her hard work and dedication.

Perhaps above all, we wish to thank those at W. W. Norton. For its three editions, our editor, Steve Dunn, has helped us shape the book in countless ways. We thank Aubrey Anable for devoting an enormous amount of time to the Third Edition, especially in finding new photos and selecting pieces for the "Student Debate." For our interactive Web version of the book, Steve Hoge has been an energetic and visionary editor. Margaret Farley, Ann Tappert, Christopher Miragliotta, and Jan Hoeper all contributed to editing the manuscript and keeping on top of myriad details. Ruth Dworkin has been dedicated in managing production for all three editions. Finally, we wish to thank Roby Harrington, the head of Norton's college department.

We are more than happy, however, to absolve all these contributors from any flaws, errors, and misjudgments that will inevitably be discovered. We wish the book could be free of all production errors, grammatical errors, misspellings, misquotes, missed citations, etc. From that standpoint, a book ought to try to be perfect. But substantively we have not tried to write a flawless book; we have not tried to write a book to please everyone. We have again tried to write an effective book, a book that cannot be taken lightly. Our goal was not to make every reader a political scientist or a political activist. Our goal was to restore politics as a subject matter of vigorous and enjoyable discourse, recapturing it from the bondage of the thirty-second sound bite and the thirty-page technical briefing. Every person can be knowledgeable because everything about politics is accessible. One does not have to be a television anchorperson to profit from political events. One does not have to be a philosopher to argue about the requisites of democracy, a lawyer to dispute constitutional interpretations, an economist to debate a public policy. We would be very proud if our book contributes in a small way to the restoration of the ancient art of political controversy.

BENJAMIN GINSBERG
THEODORE J. LOWI
MARGARET WEIR

DECEMBER 2000

We would also like to thank the following reviewers of the "Texas Politics" chapters:

Bruce R. Drury, Lamar University
Andrew I. E. Ewoh, Prairie View A&M University
Robert L. Perry, University of Texas of the Permian Basin
Wayne Pryor, Brazosport College
Elizabeth A. Rexford, Wharton County Junior College

ANTHONY CHAMPAGNE
JOHN FORSHEE
EDWARD J. HARPHAM

DECEMBER 2000

PART I

American Political Life

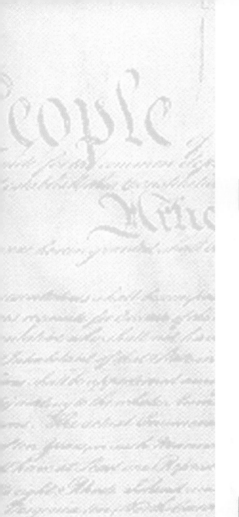

1 American

★ **What Americans Think about Government**

Why has trust in government declined considerably in recent decades?

Why is it important that Americans think that they can influence what the government does?

★ **What Americans Know about Government**

Why is political knowledge the key to effective participation in political life?

★ **Government**

What are the different forms that a government can take?

How did the principle of limited government develop?

How can people participate in politics and influence what the government does?

★ **American Political Culture: Conflict and Consensus**

What are Americans' core political values? What are the meanings of these values?

Does the political system uphold American political values?

How do American political values conflict with one another?

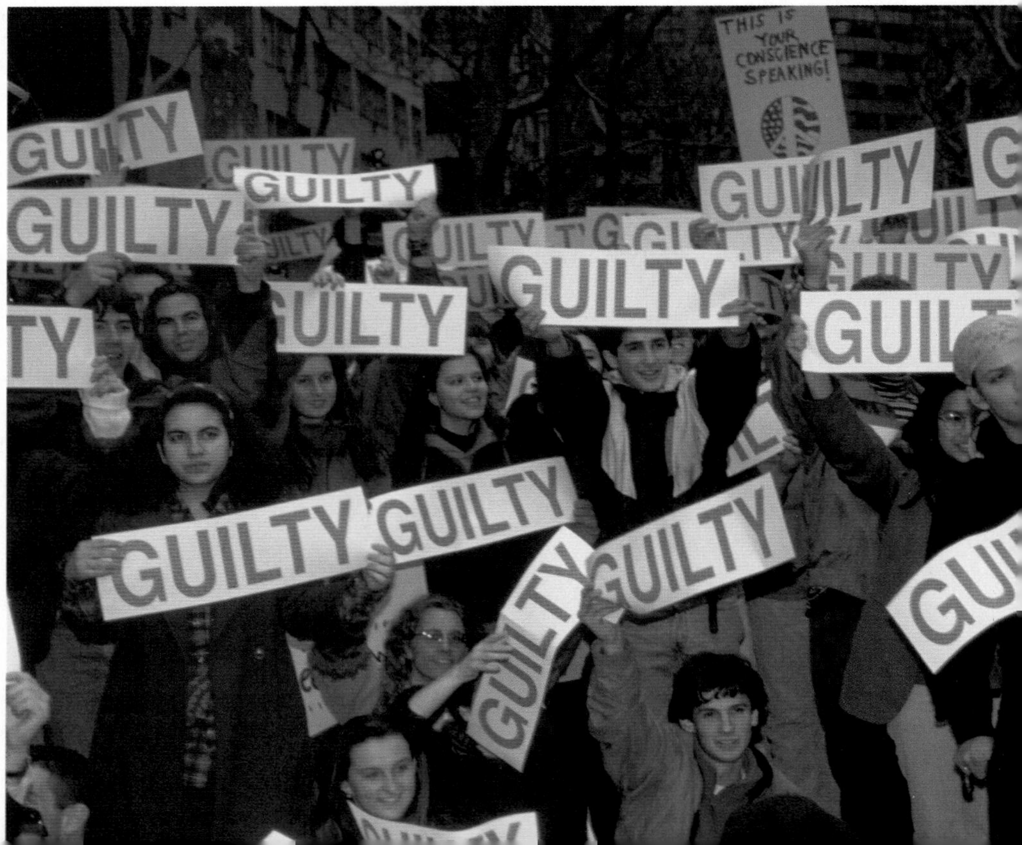

Political Culture

STUDENTS AND POLITICS

ONE of the most striking features of American political life is its openness. Virtually any American citizen who feels strongly about political issues and wants to become involved in the political process can actually do so. The stories of two recent college graduates illustrate this point.

Jim Wilkinson graduated from the University of Texas at Arlington in 1993. During his sophomore year, Jim, a finance major, became convinced that the tax system was unfair and inefficient and needed to be changed. Driven by this conviction, Jim volunteered as an intern in the Arlington, Texas, office of Republican congressional representative Richard Armey, a sharp critic of the current tax structure. Jim had no prior political experience or contacts. Members of Congress, however, are usually happy to put student volunteers to work. Jim worked in Armey's district office for several months, dealing primarily with the problems of people living in Armey's electoral district and learning more about the role and power of a member of Congress. During the summer after his junior year, Jim traveled to Washington, D.C., to work as an unpaid intern in Armey's Capitol Hill office and for Congress's Joint Economic Committee, of which Armey was the senior Republican member.

"That summer changed my life," Wilkinson recalled. "It allowed me to put a face to government." During the course of his internship, Jim worked on education policy and economic policy. He helped to draft a major piece of legislation and, at the same time, had a real chance to act on his conviction that the tax code needed to be overhauled. Jim helped Representative Armey develop a proposal to replace the current tax system with a "flat tax" on all income. Armey's proposal has considerable support among some Republicans and is influencing the current debate over taxation. After graduating from college, Jim became a full-time member of Armey's staff. "I packed up my pickup truck and drove to D.C.," he recalls. Today, Representative Armey holds the powerful position of House majority leader, second in command to the Speaker of the House. Jim Wilkinson served as Armey's press secretary and then took the even more important position of communications director at the National Republican Congressional Committee. Jim says the most important lesson to draw from his political experience is that "in a democracy you have as much right as anyone else to get involved."

Dave Grayson's collegiate political career started more modestly. During his first two years at Villanova University in Pennsylvania, he devoted himself to issues on which students had a general consensus, such as reforming meal-plan spending and converting dorms from single-sex to coeducational. After being voted vice president of the student body for his junior year, however, Grayson started to become a major voice for equality on campus; his supporters campaigned hard for several administrative reforms. Concerned that the

Scholastic Aptitude Test (SAT) discriminates against minorities, Grayson fought for and gained a policy reform in which the admissions office would reduce its reliance on SAT scores. He also worked with the administration to cede to students some authority for appointing speakers at the college. Many of Grayson's reforms and methods—he threatened to hold a sit-in during the most anticipated basketball game of the year—earned him the enmity of some on campus, and even a few death threats in his senior year. Now he leads a more docile existence working toward his Ph.D. in history, but still manages to find the time to edit a newsletter of multicultural events in the Philadelphia area.

Although Jim and Dave are exceptionally talented individuals, their stories are like those of many others. Like Jim, every year thousands of college students work as interns and staffers in the offices of members of Congress, in state and local legislatures, and in various executive agencies. Like hundreds of thousands before them, these students bring their ideals and passions into the American political arena. They "load up their pickup trucks" and come to Washington or to their state capitals, where they can "get involved in history." Like Dave, even more college students are active in campus or local politics. These students choose to get involved by participating in a campus project, helping a community organization, or volunteering for a local election campaign. Though the involvement of these students is closer to home, it is no less important to American political life.

In one important way, however, Jim and Dave are unusual. These two recent college graduates have chosen to get involved in politics; most young Americans, however, have chosen not to. And although "getting involved" can mean many different things, it does not necessarily mean a career in politics. As Dave's story shows, citizen participation is in almost all instances part-time and amateur. Still, few Americans choose to participate. If we measure participation in the political process by whether someone shows up to vote for the president every four years, even then political interest and involvement by Americans is low. College students are no exception to either of these trends. As we will see in later chapters, political involvement in almost all forms is lowest among eighteen- to twenty-four-year-olds. An annual survey of college freshmen shows that fewer than 20 percent of college students considers "influencing the political structure" to be an important life goal. "Participating in a community program" is only slightly more important (see Figure 1.1).

What explains Americans' general lack of interest in politics? The relationship between the American people and American government is a complex one that we will explore here and throughout this textbook. One aspect of this relationship is the increasing presence of government in the lives of all Americans. Yet at the same time, many Americans view government as unresponsive and "out of touch" with their needs. As a result, an increasing number of Americans have grown distrustful of government and opted out of the political process. We will assess the causes and consequences of this phenomenon later in this chapter, but let us say for now that apathy and cynicism need not prevail. The appropriate response to distrust is not passivity but vigilance, which begins with political knowledge and leads to active political participation. Through increased knowledge about government and active involvement in politics, citizens can reconnect with a government that is truly "of, by, and for" the people.

IMPORTANT LIFE GOALS OF COLLEGE FRESHMEN

Figure 1.1

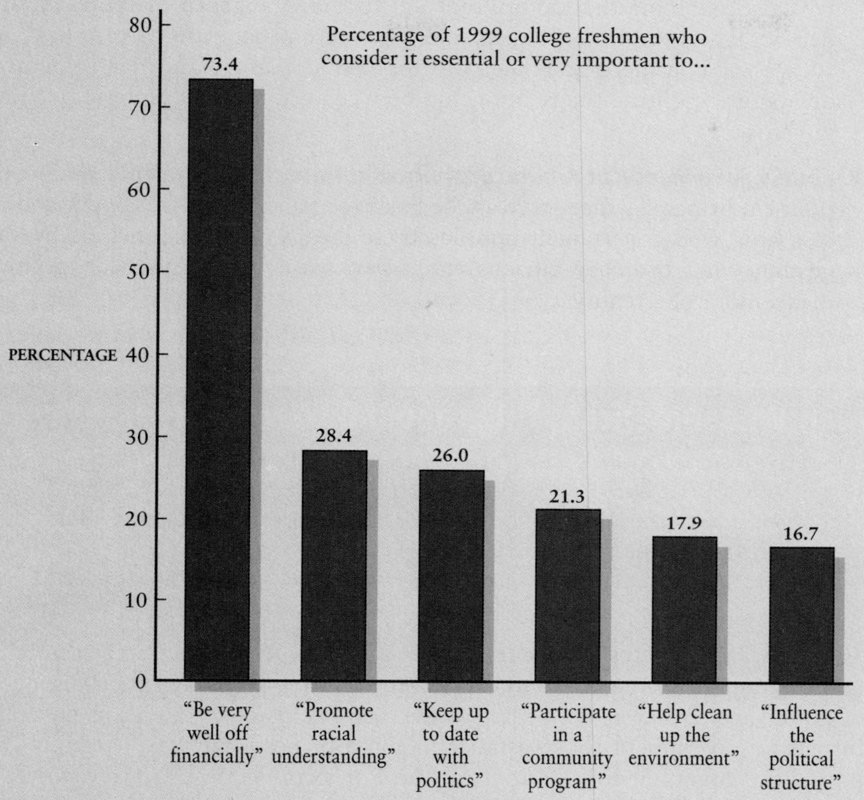

SOURCE: L. J. Sax, A. W. Astin, W. S. Korn, and K. M. Mahoney, *The American Freshman: National Norms for Fall 1999* (Los Angeles: Higher Education Research Institute, UCLA Graduate School of Education, 1999).

Over the past thirty years, college freshmen have been consistently uninterested in political participation. The "American Freshman" polls reveal that students are more interested in their own financial well-being, broader social concerns such as the environment, and the communities in which they live than they are the political system.

- ***In this chapter, we will explore the relationship between the government and the people it governs. First, we will assess what Americans think about their government.*** Although Americans have always been distrustful of governmental power, they rely on government for many of their needs. In recent decades, however, trust in government and the belief that individuals can influence government have both been in decline. These trends have important consequences that we need to examine.
- ***Second, we will explore the principle of democratic citizenship.*** We believe that good citizenship begins with political knowledge—knowledge of government, of politics, and of democratic principles. With this knowledge, citizens can identify their interests and take advantage of their opportunities to influence politics.
- ***Next, we will look at the principles of government and politics.*** The relationship between a government and its citizens is especially dependent on the

form that a government takes. In order to better understand the opportunities that citizens have to influence government, we will look at the alternative forms government can take and the key differences among them. We will also examine the factors that led to the emergence of representative democracy in the United States and elsewhere around the world. In doing so, we will consider one of the most fundamental and enduring problems of democratic politics: the relationship between government and the people it governs.

- ***Finally, we will look at American political culture.*** Here, we will examine the political principles that serve as the basis for American government and assess how well government upholds these ideals. We will conclude by suggesting what ordinary citizens can do to make these American political ideals more of a reality.

What Americans Think about Government

- Why has trust in government declined considerably in recent decades?
- Why is it important that Americans think that they can influence what the government does?

Since the United States was established as a nation, Americans have been reluctant to grant government too much power, and they have often been suspicious of politicians. But over the course of the nation's history, Americans have also turned to government for assistance in times of need and have strongly supported the government in periods of war. For example, in 1933, the power of the government began to expand to meet the crises created by the stock market crash of 1929, the Great Depression, and the run on banks of 1933. Congress passed legislation that brought the government into the businesses of home mortgages, farm mortgages, credit, and relief of personal distress. Today, the national government is an enormous institution with programs and policies reaching into every corner of American life. It oversees the nation's economy; it is the nation's largest employer; it provides citizens with a host of services; it controls the world's most formidable military establishment; and it regulates a wide range of social and commercial activities in which Americans engage.

Citizens are so dependent upon government today that much of what they have come to take for granted—as, somehow, part of the natural environment—is in fact created by government. For example, a college student who drives her car to school may think that she is engaged in a purely private activity. Yet the simple act of driving an automobile is heavily dependent upon a multitude of government initiatives and is surrounded by a host of governmental rules. The roads upon which the student drives were constructed by a local government, probably with the assistance of some fraction of the more than $20 billion in federal highway funds spent each year. The roads are maintained by municipal, county, and state governments. During the winter, snow is removed from the roads by local governments. Traffic is regulated by local governments. Road signs are placed and maintained by local and state governments. The student holds a driver's license issued by her state government, which has also registered her vehicle and inspected it for safety and compli-

THE ROLE OF GOVERNMENT IN YOUR LIFE — Figure 1.2

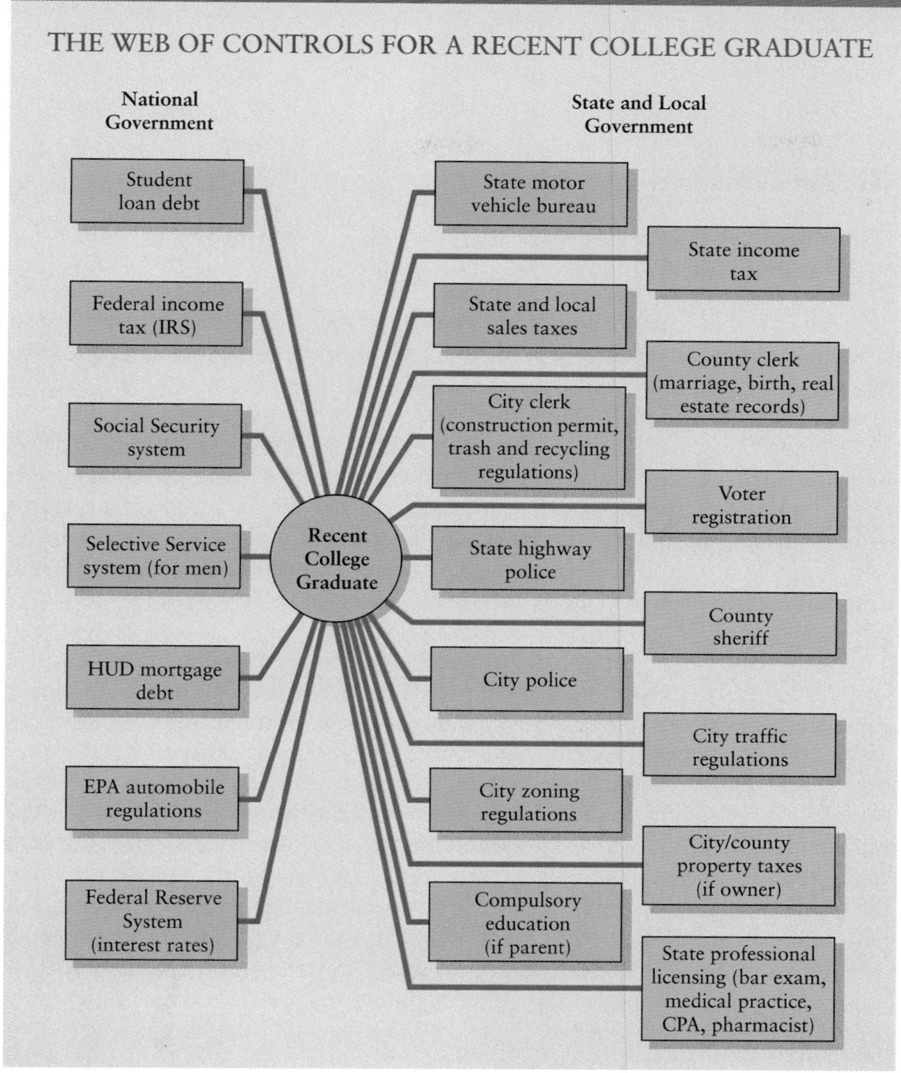

Government is a pervasive force in the lives of all Americans, especially at the state and local level. Think of the many ways in which government affects your life every day.

ance with emissions standards. The vehicle itself has been manufactured to meet safety and emissions standards set by the federal government. The contract under which the student purchased the automobile as well as the loan she signed if she borrowed money for the purchase were both governed by commercial sales and banking regulations established by the state and federal governments. The list goes on.

It might be possible for this student to drive to school without all this government assistance and regulation. In principle, roads could be privately owned, traffic unregulated, and neither drivers nor their autos required to meet any standards. Perhaps our student could still reach her destination in such an environment. Certainly, her driving experience would be markedly different from the current one.

The example of this driver could be applied in endless other situations. Government plays a role in everyone's activities and, by the same token, regulates almost everything we do. Figure 1.2 is a diagram of some of the governmental services received by and controls exerted upon any recent college graduate. Some of these governmental activities are federal, while others are the province of state and local governments.

TRUST IN GOVERNMENT

Ironically, even as popular dependence upon it has grown, the American public's view of government has turned more sour. Public trust in government has declined, and Americans are now more likely to feel that they can do little to influence the government's actions. The decline in public trust among Americans is striking. In the early 1960s, three-quarters of Americans said they trusted government most of the time. By 1994, only one-quarter of Americans expressed trust in government; three-quarters stated that they did not trust government most of the time.[1] Different groups vary somewhat in their levels of trust: African Americans and Latinos actually express more confidence in the federal government than do whites. But even among the most supportive groups, more than half do not trust the government.[2] These developments are important because politically engaged citizens and public confidence in government are vital for the health of a democracy.

Government Performance As distrust in government has grown, so has public dissatisfaction with the performance of government. Opinion polls clearly show that Americans have not been happy with government performance. In a 1996 poll, 81 percent believed that "government is wasteful and inefficient," and 79 percent said that "government spends too much money on the wrong things."[3] There is a broad public sense that the government has spent enormous amounts of money on problems that it has done little to solve and that many such problems have only gotten worse. But in many of the areas where the public believes there has been little progress, such as poverty among the elderly and air pollution, government action has in fact had an important positive impact. Some scholars attribute the negative public perceptions of government performance to the news media, which tend to cover public activities in a negative light and at the same time provide sensational coverage of problems. For example, for many years, ABC News ran a nightly feature called "Your Money," which specialized in finding instances of government waste.[4]

Public views about government are also strongly affected by the national economy. For much of the early 1990s, public assessments about government performance were highly negative, and public anger with government was at an all-time high. By 1998, however, as the economy improved, opinions shifted. For example, in 1995 only 27 percent of those questioned in a poll believed that the country was going in the right direction; two years later, with a booming economy, 44 percent said the country was going in the right direction.[5] Still, even in a period of prosperity, a majority of those polled seemed dissatisfied with government. And some analysts caution that declining anger with government does not mean more public engagement; in fact, declining anger with government is linked with a growing sense of apathy and disconnection.

What Do Young Americans Think about Government? We have already noted that people differ in their views about government. The image commonly portrayed of young people today is that they are among the most cynical and most distrustful of government among all Americans. In fact, however,

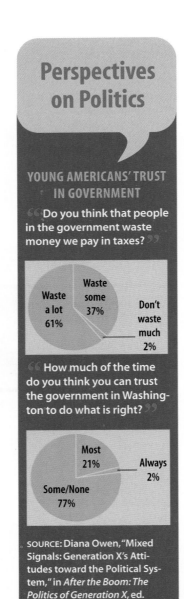

Perspectives on Politics

YOUNG AMERICANS' TRUST IN GOVERNMENT

"Do you think that people in the government waste money we pay in taxes?"

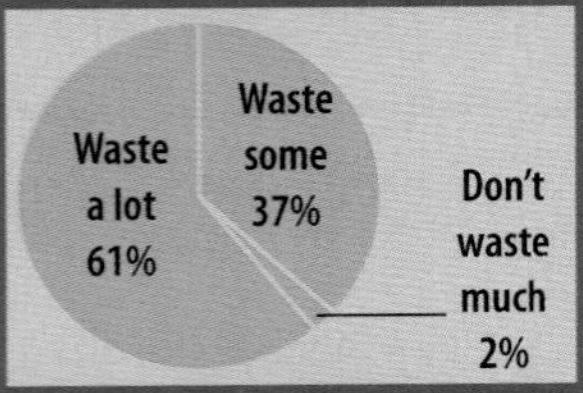

"How much of the time do you think you can trust the government in Washington to do what is right?"

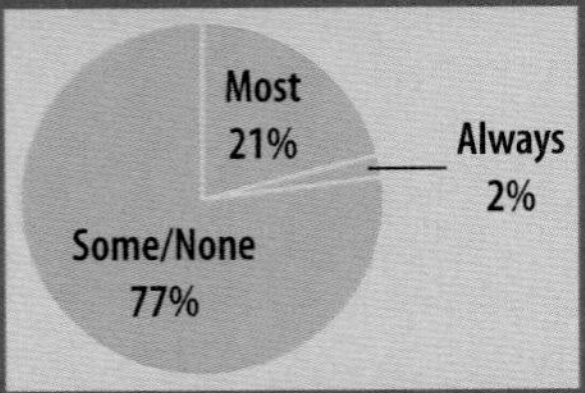

SOURCE: Diana Owen, "Mixed Signals: Generation X's Attitudes toward the Political System," in *After the Boom: The Politics of Generation X*, ed. Stephen C. Craig and Stephen Earl Bennett (Lanham, MD: Rowman and Littlefield, 1997), p. 95.

there is little evidence for this view. If we look at measures of trust, the views of young Americans are very similar to those of the rest of the population. Like most Americans, a majority of young people (77 percent) believe you can trust government only some of the time or none of the time. Young people are even somewhat less likely than their older cohorts to say that government wastes a lot of money. And there are indications that a majority of young people believe that government can play an important role in improving the lives of ordinary people. A 1996 survey, for example, found that 52 percent of young people polled felt that "government can help people, and needs to be made to work for average working families."[6]

Does it matter if large numbers of Americans continue to distrust government? For the most part, the answer is yes. As we have seen, most Americans rely on government for a wide range of services and laws that they simply take for granted. But long-term distrust in government can result in public refusal to pay taxes adequate to support such widely approved public activities. Low levels of confidence may also make it difficult for government to attract talented and effective workers to public service.[7] The weakening of government as a result of prolonged levels of distrust may ultimately harm our capacity to defend our national interest in the world economy and may jeopardize our national security. Likewise, a weak government can do little to assist citizens who need help in weathering periods of sharp economic or technological change.

POLITICAL EFFICACY

Along with growing distrust, another important trend in American views about government has been a declining sense of **political efficacy,** the belief that citizens can affect what government does, that they can take action to make government listen to them. In recent decades, the public belief that government is responsive to ordinary citizens has declined. Today, 66 percent of Americans say that government officials don't care what people think; in 1964, only 36 percent felt so shut out of government. Along with this sense that ordinary people can't get heard is a growing belief—held by 76 percent of the public in 1994—that "government is run by a few big interests looking out only for themselves."[8] These views are widely shared across the age spectrum.

Many young Americans feel that government has ignored their views in particular. They feel that older officials cannot understand the challenges and problems facing the younger generation. For example, 72 percent of young people polled agreed that "our generation has an important voice but no one seems to hear it." But young Americans are not alone in feeling that government doesn't listen to them. In fact, most people of earlier generations feel even more strongly than young Americans that public officials have little interest in what they think.[9] The sense that government is out of touch and the feelings of powerlessness and lack of political efficacy that come with it seem to affect most Americans, regardless of generation.

This widely felt loss of political efficacy is bad news for American democracy. The feeling that you can't affect government decisions can lead to a self-perpetuating cycle of apathy, declining political participation, and withdrawal from political life. Why bother to participate if you believe it makes no difference? Yet, the belief that you can be effective is the first step needed to influence government. Not every effort of ordinary citizens to influence

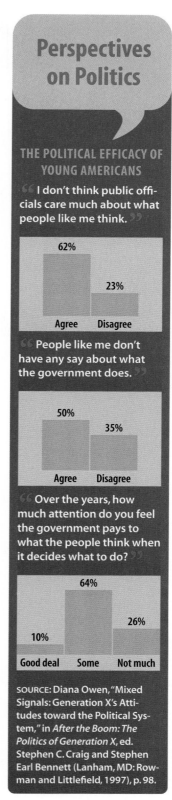

Perspectives on Politics

THE POLITICAL EFFICACY OF YOUNG AMERICANS

"I don't think public officials care much about what people like me think."

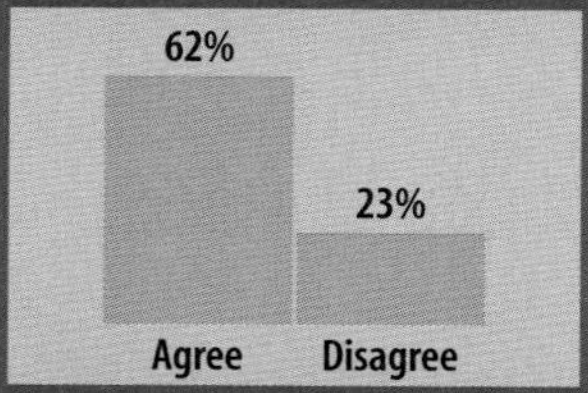

"People like me don't have any say about what the government does."

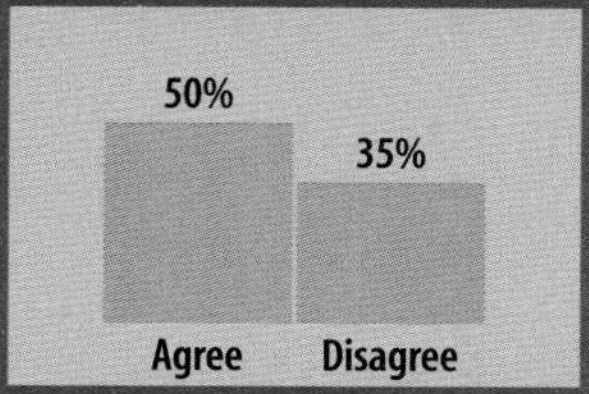

"Over the years, how much attention do you feel the government pays to what the people think when it decides what to do?"

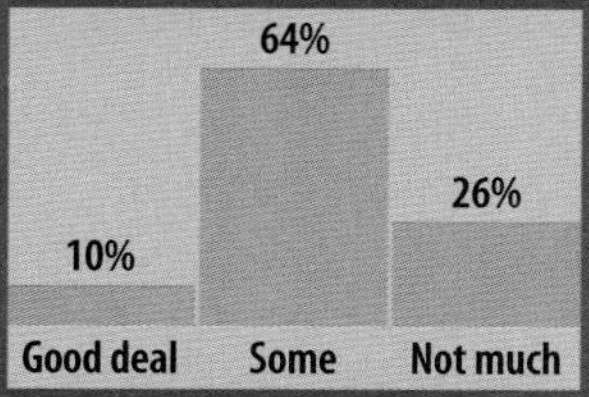

SOURCE: Diana Owen, "Mixed Signals: Generation X's Attitudes toward the Political System," in *After the Boom: The Politics of Generation X,* ed. Stephen C. Craig and Stephen Earl Bennett (Lanham, MD: Rowman and Littlefield, 1997), p. 98.

Box 1.1 THE PRESENCE OF GOVERNMENT IN THE DAILY LIFE OF A STUDENT AT "STATE UNIVERSITY"

Time of Day	Schedule
7:00 AM	Wake up. Standard time set by the national government.
7:10 AM	Shower. Water courtesy of local government, either a public entity or a regulated private company. Brush your teeth with toothpaste, with cavity-fighting claims verified by federal agency. Dry your hair with electric dryer, manufactured according to federal government agency guidelines.
7:30 AM	Have a bowl of cereal with milk for breakfast. "Nutrition Facts" on food labels are a federal requirement, pasteurization of milk required by state law, freshness dating on milk based on state and federal standards, recycling the empty cereal box and milk carton required by state or local laws.
8:30 AM	Drive or take public transportation to campus. Air bags and seat belts required by federal and state laws. Roads and bridges paid for by state and local governments, speed and traffic laws set by state and local governments, public transportation subsidized by all levels of government.
8:45 AM	Arrive on campus of large public university. Buildings are 70 percent financed by state taxpayers.
9:00 AM	First class: Chemistry 101. Tuition partially paid by a federal loan (more than half the cost of university instruction is paid for by taxpayers), chemistry lab paid for with grants from the National Science Foundation (a federal agency) and smaller grants from business corporations made possible by federal income tax deductions for charitable contributions.
Noon	Eat lunch. College cafeteria financed by state dormitory authority on land grant from federal Department of Agriculture.
2:00 PM	Second class: American Government 101 (your favorite class!). You may be taking this class because it's required by the state legislature or because it fulfills a university requirement.
4:00 PM	Third class: Computer lab. Free computers, software, and Internet access courtesy of state subsidies plus grants and discounts from IBM and Microsoft, the costs of which are deducted from their corporate income taxes; Internet built in part by federal government. Duplication of software protected by federal copyright laws.
6:00 PM	Eat dinner: hamburger and french fries. Meat inspected by federal agencies for bacteria.
7:00 PM	Work at part-time job at the campus library. Minimum wage set by federal government, books and journals in library paid for by state taxpayers.
10:00 PM	Go to local bar. Purchase and consumption of alcohol regulated by state law and enforced by city police.
11:00 PM	Go home. Street lighting paid for by county and city governments, police patrols by city government.
11:15 PM	Watch TV. Networks regulated by federal government, cable public-access channels required by city law. Weather forecast provided to broadcasters by a federal agency.
Midnight	Put out the garbage before going to bed. Garbage collected by city sanitation department, financed by "user charges."

government will succeed, but without any such efforts, government decisions will be made by a smaller and smaller circle of powerful people. Such loss of broad popular influence over government actions undermines the key feature of American democracy—government by the people.

political efficacy
the ability to influence government and politics

What Americans Know about Government

▶ Why is political knowledge the key to effective participation in political life?

The first prerequisite to achieving an increased sense of political efficacy is knowledge. Political indifference is often simply a habit that stems from a lack of knowledge about how your interests are affected by politics and from a sense that you can do nothing to affect politics. But political efficacy is a self-fulfilling prophecy: if you think you cannot be effective, chances are you will never try. Most research suggests that people active in politics have a high sense of their efficacy. This means they believe they can make a difference—even if they do not win all the time. Most people do not want to be politically active every day of their lives, but it is essential to our political ideals that all citizens be informed and able to act.

Sadly, the state of political knowledge in the United States today is dismal. Most Americans know little about current issues or debates. A recent survey that tested the knowledge of the institutions and processes of government in the United States found that 70 percent of the respondents answered fewer than 60 percent of the questions correctly (see Table 1.1). In most colleges and universities, below 60 is a failing grade. But, rather than dwell on the widespread political ignorance of many Americans, we prefer to view this as an opportunity for the readers of this book. Those of you who make the effort to become among the knowledgeable few will be much better prepared to influence the political system regarding the issues and concerns that you care most about. Finally, bear in mind that no citizen has to be alone in the effort to influence government. An important aspect of political knowledge is knowing who shares your interests.

WHO KNOWS WHAT? — **Table 1.1**

Question	Percentage answering correctly
What is affirmative action?	31
When was the New Deal?	29
How long is a senator's term?	25
Name two First Amendment rights.	20
What is the Food and Drug Administration?	20
Name all three branches of government.	19
What was the New Deal?	15

SOURCE: Michael X. Delli Carpini and Scott Keeter, *What Americans Know about Politics and Why It Matters* (New Haven, CT: Yale University Press, 1996), pp. 58–94.

CITIZENSHIP: KNOWLEDGE AND PARTICIPATION

Beginning with the ancient Greeks, citizenship has meant membership in one's community. In fact, the Greeks did not even conceive of the individual as a complete person. The complete person was the public person, the *citizen;* noncitizens and private persons were referred to as *idiotés*. Participation in public affairs was virtually the definition of citizenship. Citizenship was never defined as voting. Although voting was not excluded, the essence of citizen participation was talking. As one political philosopher put it, "What counts is argument among the citizens. . . . [T]he citizen who makes the most persuasive argument gets [his or her] way but can't use force, or pull rank, or distribute money; [the citizen] must talk about the issues at hand. . . . Citizens must come into the forum with nothing but their arguments."[10] Involvement in the public debate is the central, quintessential right of citizenship. Following the Greek idea, the First Amendment to the U.S. Constitution makes freedom of speech the primary right of American citizenship.

citizenship
informed and active membership in a political community

Our meaning for **citizenship** derives from the Greek ideal: enlightened political engagement.[11] To be politically engaged in a meaningful way, citizens require resources, especially political knowledge and information. Democracy functions best when citizens are informed.

But to be a citizen in the full sense as understood first by the ancient Greeks requires more than an occasional visit to an election booth. A true citizen must have the knowledge needed to participate in political debate. If you want to be a citizen rather than an *idioté,* it is important that you acquire three forms of political knowledge from this course and this textbook:

1. *Knowledge of government.* Citizens must understand the "rules of the game." From the citizen's perspective, the most important rules concern one's own political rights, which can vary greatly according to the type of government under which one lives. In the United States, these rights are extensive and concrete, and affect every citizen directly.
2. *Knowledge of politics.* We need to understand what is at stake in the political world. This understanding includes the capacity to discern our own interests in the political arena and identify the best means through which to realize them.
3. *Knowledge of democratic principles.* Although politics may divide Americans, democratic ideals hold them together. As citizens, we need to know what forms of political conduct are consistent with democratic principles. Democracy requires that both government and citizens be aware of and respect the constraints upon their political activities.

Political knowledge means more than having a few opinions to offer the pollster or to guide your decisions in a voting booth. It is important to know the rules and strategies that govern political institutions and the principles upon which they are based, but it is more important to know them in ways that relate to your own interests. Citizens need knowledge in order to assess their interests and know when to act upon them. Knowledgeable citizens are more attentive to and more engaged in politics because they understand how and why politics is relevant to their lives.

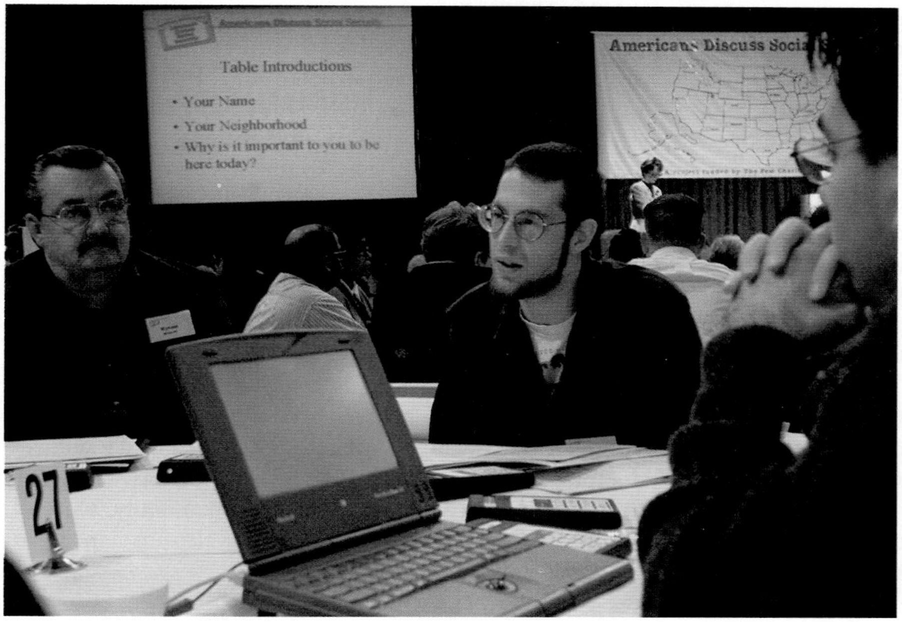

Informed debate is a critical part of citizenship. In 1998, several forums sponsored by the organization Americans Discuss Social Security were held across the United States.

THE NECESSITY OF POLITICAL KNOWLEDGE

Political knowledge is the key to effective participation in political life. Without political knowledge, no citizen can be aware of her interests or stake in a political dispute. In the year preceding the 2000 presidential election, for example, many of the prospective Democratic and Republican candidates presented rather detailed proposals on ways of changing the current American tax system. How many voters paid enough attention to the discussion to be able to meaningfully distinguish among the various proposals and their implications? Did you attempt to ascertain whether you and your family would be better off under the tax system envisioned by Bush or Bradley, Gore or McCain? How could you participate intelligently without this knowledge? Interestingly, various public and private interest groups devote enormous time and energy to understanding alternative policy proposals and their implications so they will know whom to support. Interest groups understand something that every citizen should also understand: Effective participation requires knowledge.

Citizens also need political knowledge to identify the best ways of acting upon their interests. If your road is rendered impassable by snow, what can you do? Is snow removal the responsibility of the federal government? Is it a state or municipal responsibility? Knowing that you have a stake in a clear road does not help much if you do not know that snow removal is a city or county responsibility and cannot identify the municipal agency that deals with the problem. Americans are fond of complaining that government is not responsive to their needs, but is it not possible that many citizens simply lack the information they need to present their problems to the appropriate government officials?

Citizens need political knowledge, as well, to ascertain what they cannot or should not ask of politicians and the government. The famous Scottish economist Adam Smith once observed that in the economic realm the selfish pursuit of private interests improved the general good as if by "an invisible hand." Smith's idea is the basis for our belief in free markets today. It is not so clear, however, that Smith's logic applies as well to political life. One of the reasons that we take part in political life is that many of our most important collective goals, including defense, protection of the environment, and safety from crime, are unlikely to be achieved purely by individual action. We need to cooperate in order to defend our nation, protect our environment, and keep our homes safe. Thus, political knowledge includes knowing the limits upon, as well as the possibilities for pursuing, one's own individual interests through political action. This is, perhaps, the most difficult form of political knowledge to acquire.

The rest of this chapter will look at the forms of political knowledge that we believe are most critical for a citizen to possess. In the next section, we will examine the principles of government and politics. Following that, we will review the democratic principles upon which the United States is based and assess how well American government fulfills these principles. Finally, we will conclude with suggestions of what you and other ordinary citizens can do to become more knowledgeable and more engaged.

Government

- What are the different forms that a government can take?
- How did the principle of limited government develop?
- How can people participate in politics and influence what the government does?

government
institutions and procedures through which a territory and its people are ruled

autocracy
a form of government in which a single individual—a king, queen, or dictator—rules

oligarchy
a form of government in which a small group—landowners, military officers, or wealthy merchants—controls most of the governing decisions

Government is the term generally used to describe the formal institutions through which a land and its people are ruled. To govern is to rule. A government may be as simple as a tribal council that meets occasionally to advise the chief, or as complex as the vast establishments, with their forms, rules, and bureaucracies, found in the United States and the countries of Europe. A more complex government is sometimes referred to as "the state." In the history of civilization, governments have not been difficult to establish. There have been thousands of them. The hard part is establishing a government that lasts. Even more difficult is developing a stable government that is compatible with liberty, equality, and democracy.

FORMS OF GOVERNMENT

Governments vary in their structure, in their size, and in the way they operate. Two questions are of special importance in determining how governments differ: Who governs? And how much government control is permitted?

In some nations, governing is done by a single individual—a king or dictator, for example. This state of affairs is called **autocracy.** Where a small group—perhaps landowners, military officers, or wealthy merchants—controls most of the governing decisions, that government is said to be an **oligarchy.** If more people participate and have some influence over decision making, that government is a **democracy.**

democracy
a system of rule that permits citizens to play a significant part in the governmental process, usually through the election of key public officials

constitutional government
a system of rule in which formal and effective limits are placed on the powers of the government

authoritarian government
a system of rule in which the government recognizes no formal limits but may nevertheless be restrained by the power of other social institutions

totalitarian government
a system of rule in which the government recognizes no formal limits on its power and seeks to absorb or eliminate other social institutions that might challenge it

Governments also vary considerably in terms of how they govern. In the United States and a small number of other nations, governments are limited as to what they are permitted to control (substantive limits), as well as how they go about it (procedural limits). Governments that are so limited are called **constitutional governments,** or liberal governments. In other nations, including many in Europe as well as in South America, Asia, and Africa, though the law imposes few real limits, the government is nevertheless kept in check by other political and social institutions that the government is unable to control and must come to terms with—such as autonomous territories, an organized church, organized business groups, or organized labor unions. Such governments are generally called **authoritarian.** In a third group of nations, including the Soviet Union under Joseph Stalin, Nazi Germany, and perhaps prewar Japan and Italy, governments not only are free of legal limits but also seek to eliminate those organized social groups that might challenge or limit the government's authority. These governments typically attempt to dominate or control every sphere of political, economic, and social life and, as a result, are called **totalitarian.**

Americans have the good fortune to live in a nation in which limits are placed on what governments can do and how they can do it. But such constitutional democracies are relatively rare in today's world; it is estimated that only twenty or so of the world's nearly two hundred governments could be included in this category. And constitutional democracies were unheard of before the modern era. Prior to the eighteenth and nineteenth centuries, governments seldom sought—and rarely received—the support of their ordinary subjects. The available evidence strongly suggests that the ordinary people had little love for the government or for the social order. After all, they had no stake in it. They equated government with the police officer, the bailiff, and the tax collector.[12]

Beginning in the seventeenth century, in a handful of Western nations, two important changes began to take place in the character and conduct of government. First, governments began to acknowledge formal limits upon their power. Second, a small number of governments began to provide the ordinary citizen with a formal voice in public affairs—through the vote. Obviously, the desirability of limits on government and the expansion of popular influence were at the heart of the American Revolution in 1776. "No taxation without representation," as we shall see in Chapter 3, was hotly debated from the beginning of the Revolution through the Founding in 1789. But even before the Revolution, a tradition of limiting government and expanding participation in the political process had developed throughout western Europe. Thus, to understand how the relationship between rulers and the ruled was transformed, we must broaden our focus to take into account events in Europe as well as in America. We will have to divide the transformation into its two separate parts. The first is the effort to put limits on government. The second is the effort to expand the influence of the people through access to government and politics.

LIMITING GOVERNMENT

The key force behind the imposition of limits on government power was a new social class, the bourgeoisie. Bourgeoisie is a French word for freeman of the city, or *bourg*. Being part of the bourgeoisie later became associated with being "middle class" and with being in commerce or industry. In order to gain a share of control of government, joining or even displacing the kings, aristocrats, and gentry who had dominated government for centuries, the bourgeoisie sought to change existing institutions—especially parliaments—into instruments of real political participation. Parliaments had existed for centuries, but were generally aristocratic institutions. The bourgeoisie embraced parliaments as means by which they could exert the weight of their superior numbers and growing economic advantage against their aristocratic rivals. At the same time, the bourgeoisie sought to place restraints on the capacity of governments to threaten these economic and political interests by placing formal or constitutional limits on governmental power.

Although motivated primarily by the need to protect and defend their own interests, the bourgeoisie advanced many of the principles that became the central underpinnings of individual liberty for all citizens—freedom of speech, freedom of assembly, freedom of conscience, and freedom from arbitrary search and seizure. It is important to note here that the bourgeoisie generally did not favor democracy as we know it. They were advocates of electoral and representative institutions, but they favored property requirements and other restrictions so as to limit participation to the middle classes. Yet once these institutions of politics and the protection of the right to engage in politics were established, it was difficult to limit them to the bourgeoisie.

ACCESS TO GOVERNMENT: THE EXPANSION OF PARTICIPATION

The expansion of participation from the bourgeoisie to ever-larger segments of society took two paths. In some nations, popular participation was expanded by the crown or the aristocracy, which ironically saw common people as potential political allies against the bourgeoisie. Thus in nineteenth-century Prussia, for example, it was the emperor and his great minister Otto von Bismarck who expanded popular participation in order to build political support among the lower orders.

In other nations, participation expanded because competing segments of the bourgeoisie sought to gain political advantage by reaching out and mobilizing the support of working- and lower-class groups who craved the opportunity to take part in politics—"lining up the unwashed," as one American historian put it.[13] To be sure, excluded groups often agitated for greater participation. But seldom was such agitation, by itself, enough to secure the right to participate. Usually, expansion of voting rights resulted from a combination of pressure from below and help from above.

This pattern of suffrage expansion by groups hoping to derive some political advantage has been typical in American history. After the Civil War, one of the chief reasons that Republicans moved to enfranchise newly freed slaves was to use the support of the former slaves to maintain Republican control over the defeated southern states. Similarly, in the early twentieth century, upper-middle-class "Progressives" advocated women's suffrage because they believed that women were likely to support the reforms espoused by the Progressive movement. The expansion of participation and the development of the American political community will be discussed in more detail in Chapter 2.

INFLUENCING THE GOVERNMENT THROUGH PARTICIPATION: POLITICS

Expansion of participation means that more and more people have a legal right to take part in politics. Politics is an important term. In its broadest sense, "politics" refers to conflicts over the character, membership, and policies of any organization to which people belong. As Harold Lasswell, a famous political scientist, once put it, politics is the struggle over "who gets what, when, how."[14] Although politics is a phenomenon that can be found in any organization, our concern in this book is more narrow. Here, **politics** will be used to refer only to conflicts and struggles over the leadership, structure, and policies of governments. The goal of politics, as we define it, is to have a share or a say in the composition of the government's leadership, how the government is organized, or what its policies are going to be. Having a share is called **power** or influence.

Politics can take many forms, including everything from sending letters to government officials through voting, lobbying legislators on behalf of particular programs, and participating in protest marches and even violent demonstrations. A system of government that gives citizens a regular opportunity to elect the top government officials is usually called a **representative democracy** or **republic.** A system that permits citizens to vote directly on laws and policies is often called a **direct democracy.** At the national level, America is a representative democracy in which citizens select government officials but do not vote on legislation. Some states, however, have provisions for direct legislation through popular referendum. For example, California voters in 1995 decided to bar undocumented immigrants from receiving some state services.

Groups and organized interests obviously do not vote (although their members do), but they certainly do participate in politics. Their political activities usually consist of such endeavors as providing funds for candidates, lobbying, and trying to influence public opinion. The pattern of struggles among

politics
conflict over the leadership, structure, and policies of governments

power
influence over a government's leadership, organization, or policies

representative democracy/republic
a system of government in which the populace selects representatives, who play a significant role in governmental decision making

direct democracy
a system of rule that permits citizens to vote directly on laws and policies

In George Caleb Bingham's painting, *The Verdict of the People* (1853–54), a jubilant crowd celebrates the outcome of the political process. While the nineteenth century was marked by high levels of political participation, voting was primarily the domain of white men.

pluralism

the theory that all interests are and should be free to compete for influence in the government. The outcome of this competition is compromise and moderation

direct action politics

a form of politics, such as civil disobedience or revolutionary action, that takes place outside formal channels

interests is called group politics, or **pluralism.** Americans have always been ambivalent about pluralist politics. Although the right of groups to press their views is the essence of liberty, Americans often fear that organized groups may sometimes exert too much influence, advancing special interests at the expense of larger public interests. We will return to this problem in Chapter 12.

Sometimes, of course, politics does not take place through formal channels at all, but instead involves direct action. **Direct action politics** can include either violent politics or civil disobedience, both of which attempt to shock rulers into behaving more responsibly. Direct action can also be a form of revolutionary politics, which rejects the system entirely and attempts to replace it with a new ruling group and a new set of rules. In recent years in the United States, groups ranging from animal-rights activists through right-to-life advocates have used direct action and even violence to underline their demands. Direct political action is protected by the U.S. Constitution; violence is not. The country's Founders knew that the right to protest is essential to the maintenance of political freedom, even where the ballot box is available.

American Political Culture: Conflict and Consensus

- What are Americans' core political values? What are the meanings of these values?
- Does the political system uphold American political values?
- How do American political values conflict with one another?

political culture

broadly shared values, beliefs, and attitudes about how the government should function. American political culture emphasizes the values of liberty, equality, and democracy

Underlying and framing political life in the United States are agreements and disagreements over basic political values and philosophies. Philosophical positions and values shape citizens' views of the world and define their sense of what is right and wrong, just and unjust, possible and impossible. If Americans shared no philosophical principles or values, they would have difficulty communicating, much less agreeing upon a common system of government and politics. On the other hand, sharing broad values does not guarantee political consensus. We can agree on principles but disagree over their application.

In fact, differing perspectives can help us understand the patterns of conflict and consensus that have marked the development of American politics. Perhaps the dominant interpretation of U.S. history is that of a success story: as the nation developed, different groups gradually gained equal influence in politics and policy. In this story, the American consensus around a set of basic political ideals provided the framework for the political inclusion of all groups. But today this story of progress is questioned from two different sides, highlighting the continuing significance of conflict. Some critics claim that measures such as affirmative action have not promoted political inclusion and instead have condoned reverse discrimination and a segmented society. Far from fulfilling American ideals, they argue, these policies represent a movement away from our most fundamental values. An opposing perspective questions the progress that has been made in promoting equality. Pointing to the disproportionately high rates of poverty among minorities and continuing evidence of discrimination against women and minorities, this side questions whether Americans are serious about equality. Much of the debate over the role of government has been over what government should do and how far it should go to redress the inequalities within our society and political system.

Even though Americans have disagreed over the meaning of such political ideals as equality, they still agree on the importance of these ideals. Within these conflicts, we can identify shared values, beliefs, and attitudes that form our **political culture** and serve to hold the United States and its people together. These values date back to the time of the founding of the union.

The essential documents of the American Founding—the Declaration of Independence and the Constitution—enunciated a set of political principles about the purposes of the new republic. In contrast with many other democracies, in the United States these political ideals did not just remain words on dusty documents. Americans actively embraced the principles of the Founders and made them central to the national identity. Let us look more closely at three of these ideals: liberty, equality, and democracy.

Patrick Henry delivering his famous "Give me liberty, or give me death" speech. Since the Founding, liberty has been central to the political values of Americans.

LIBERTY

No ideal is more central to American values than liberty. The Declaration of Independence defined three inalienable rights: "life, liberty and the pursuit of happiness." The preamble of the Constitution likewise identified the need to secure "the blessings of liberty" as one of the key reasons for drawing up the Constitution. For Americans, **liberty** means both personal freedom and economic freedom. Both are closely linked to the idea of **limited government.**

The Constitution's first ten amendments, known collectively as the Bill of Rights, above all preserves individual personal liberties and rights. In fact, liberty has come to mean many of the freedoms guaranteed in the Bill of Rights: freedom of speech and writing, the right to assemble freely, and the right to practice religious beliefs without interference from the government. Over the course of American history, the scope of personal liberties has expanded, as laws have become more tolerant and as individuals have successfully used the courts to challenge restrictions on their individual freedoms. Far fewer restrictions exist today on the press, political speech, and individual moral behavior than in the early years of the nation. Even so, conflicts persist over how personal liberties should be extended and when personal liberties violate community norms. For example, one of the most contentious issues in the last thirty years has been that of abortion. Whereas defenders of the right to choose abortion view it is an essential personal freedom for women, opponents view it as murder—something that no society should allow.

In addition to personal freedom, the American concept of liberty means economic freedom. Since the Founding, economic freedom has been linked to capitalism, free markets, and the protection of private property. Free competition, unfettered movement of goods, and the right to enjoy the fruits of one's labor are all essential aspects of economic freedom and American capitalism.[15] In the first century of the Republic, support for capitalism often meant support for the doctrine of laissez-faire. Translated literally as "to leave alone," **laissez-faire capitalism** allowed very little room for the national government to regulate trade or restrict the use of private property, even in the public interest. Americans still strongly support capitalism and economic lib-

liberty
freedom from governmental control

limited government
a principle of constitutional government; a government whose powers are defined and limited by a constitution

laissez-faire capitalism
an economic system in which the means of production and distribution are privately owned and operated for profit with minimal or no government interference

erty, but they now also endorse some restrictions on economic freedoms to protect the public. Federal and state governments now deploy a wide array of regulations in the name of public protection. These include health and safety laws, environmental rules, and workplace regulations. Not surprisingly, fierce disagreements often erupt over what the proper scope of government regulation should be. What some people regard as protecting the public, others see as an infringement of their own freedom to run their businesses and use their property as they see fit.

EQUALITY

The Declaration of Independence declares as its first "self-evident" truth that "all men are created equal." As central as it is to the American political creed, however, equality has been a less well defined ideal than liberty because people interpret "equality" in different ways. Few Americans have wholeheartedly embraced full equality of results, but most Americans share the ideal of **equality of opportunity**—that is, the notion that each person should be given a fair chance to go as far as his or her talents will allow. Yet it is hard for Americans to reach agreement about what constitutes equality of opportunity. Must *past* inequalities be remedied in order to ensure equal opportunity in the *present?* Should inequalities in the legal, political, and economic spheres be given the same weight? In contrast to liberty, which requires limits on the role of government, equality implies an *obligation* of the government to the people.[16]

equality of opportunity
a widely shared American ideal that all people should have the freedom to use whatever talents and wealth they have to reach their fullest potential

Americans do make clear distinctions between political equality and social or economic equality. **Political equality** means that members of the American political community have the right to participate in politics on equal terms. Beginning from a very restricted definition of political community, which originally included only propertied white men, the United States has moved much closer to an ideal of political equality that can be summed up as "one person,

political equality
the right to participate in politics equally, based on the principle of "one person, one vote"

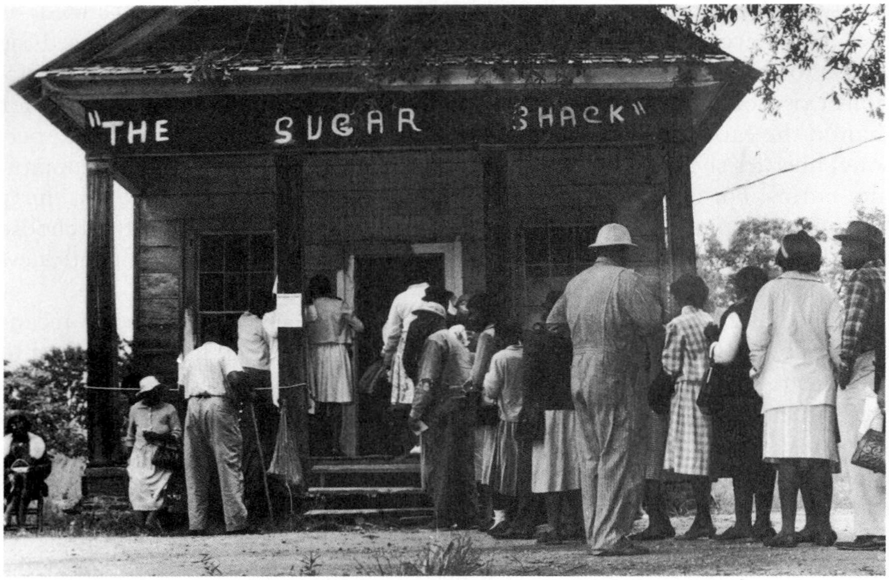

Residents of rural Wilcox County, Alabama, lining up to vote in 1966. Prior to the passage of the Voting Rights Act of 1965, Wilcox County had no registered black voters.

one vote." Broad support for the ideal of political equality has helped expand the American political community and extend the right to participate to all. Although considerable conflict remains over whether the political system makes it harder for some people to participate and easier for others and about whether the role of money in politics has drowned out the public voice, Americans agree that all citizens should have equal rights to participate and that government should enforce that right.

In part because Americans believe that individuals are free to work as hard as they choose, they have always been less concerned about social or economic inequality. Many Americans regard economic differences as the consequence of individual choices, virtues, or failures. Because of this, Americans tend to be less supportive than most Europeans of government action to ensure equality. Yet when major economic forces, such as the Great Depression of the 1930s, affect many people or when systematic barriers appear to block equality of opportunity, Americans support government action to promote equality. Even then, however, Americans have endorsed only a limited government role designed to help people get back on their feet or to open up opportunity.

DEMOCRACY

The essence of democracy is the participation of the people in choosing their rulers and the people's ability to influence what those rulers do. In a democracy, political power ultimately comes from the people. The idea of placing power in the hands of the people is known as **popular sovereignty.** In the United States, popular sovereignty and political equality make politicians accountable to the people. Ideally, democracy envisions an engaged citizenry prepared to exercise its power over rulers. As we saw earlier, the United States is a representative democracy, meaning that the people do not rule directly but instead exercise power through elected representatives. Forms of participation in a democracy vary greatly, but voting is a key element of the representative democracy that the American Founders established.

popular sovereignty
a principle of democracy in which political authority rests ultimately in the hands of the people

American democracy rests on the principle of **majority rule** with **minority rights.** Majority rule means that the wishes of the majority determine what government does. The House of Representatives—a large body elected directly by the people—was designed in particular to ensure majority rule. But the Founders feared that popular majorities could turn government into a "tyranny of the majority" in which individual liberties would be violated. Concern for individual rights has thus been a part of American democracy from the beginning. The rights enumerated in the Bill of Rights and enforced through the courts provide an important check on the power of the majority.

majority rule/minority rights
the democratic principle that a government follows the preferences of the majority of voters but protects the interests of the minority

DOES THE SYSTEM UPHOLD AMERICAN POLITICAL VALUES?

Clearly, the ideals of liberty, equality, and democracy are open to diverse interpretations. Moreover, the ideals can easily conflict with one another in practice. When we examine American history, we can see that there have been large gaps between these ideals and the practice of American politics. We can also see that some ideals have been prized more than others at different historical moments. But it is also clear that as Americans have engaged in political conflict about who should participate in politics and how political institutions

AMERICAN DEMOCRACY IN COMPARATIVE PERSPECTIVE

Freedom and Democracy in the World

How common is democracy as a form of government throughout the world? How unique are the general freedoms that Americans enjoy and that underscore our rich democratic traditions? Foremost among those who specialize in monitoring the extent of democracy and freedom in the world is an organization known as Freedom House. It was founded in 1941 and remains a nonprofit, nonpartisan American organization dedicated to protecting freedom and liberty around the world. Since the 1950s, the organization has sent survey teams to various countries to analyze and compare the structure of their governments and content of their laws and then assigned a standard score representing the degree of freedom found in that country.

For the past twenty-six years Freedom House has presented a widely respected and utilized annual report on the degree of freedom and democracy in countries around the world. Freedom House assesses a country's freedom along two critical dimensions: political rights enjoyed by the citizenry (for example, fair, free, and competitive elections) and the extent of civil liberties extended to the population (for example, diverse opportunities for and different forms of cultural expression, such as religion). While specific scores are assigned to each country, Freedom House also organizes all countries of the world into three general categories based on the extent of their political rights and civil liberties: "free," "partly free," or "not free."

Many democracies that allow free elections and tolerate political opposition nevertheless practice various forms of human rights violations or have populations that are caught in the middle of internal wars and terrorism. Thus, in 1999, Freedom House reported that 117 countries were electoral democracies, yet only 76 of these "electoral democracies" were classified as "free." Forty of these democracies were "partly free" (including Brazil, Turkey, Paraguay, Colombia, Russia, and Ukraine) and one country—Bosnia-Herzegovina—was "not free."

The most "free" countries were those with perfect scores on civil liberties and political rights. Twenty-six independent countries were in this category, including some whose names are probably quite familiar to most students—the United States, Switzerland, Australia, Canada, Denmark, Finland, Luxembourg, the Netherlands, New Zealand, Ireland, Norway, and Sweden.

Also within this "elite" group are countries whose names may be less familiar to many students, including San Marino, Dominica, Barbados, Andorra, Belize, Tuvalu, the Marshall Islands, and Kiribati. Among the fifty countries of the world that Freedom House ranks as "not free" are Egypt, Yugoslavia, Belarus, China, Kenya, Algeria, Laos, Kazakhstan, Tajikistan, and Rwanda. Thirteen countries have populations that are denied virtually any of the basic freedoms and rights found in other countries. These include Afghanistan, Burma, Cuba, Iraq, North Korea, Saudi Arabia, Syria, and Vietnam.

Overall, while only a minority of the world's population live in "free" countries, Freedom House has documented a steady increase over time in the degree of freedom and the foundations for democracy across the globe. In 1988, sixty-one countries (representing 38.9 percent of the world's population) were "free," thirty-nine were "partly free" (21 percent of the world's population), and sixty-eight were "not free" (42 percent of the world's population). Today approximately 40 percent of the world's population is "free" and only 34 percent is "not free." In 1989, there were sixty-nine democracies in the world that were democratic, only about half of what exists today.

SOURCE: Adrian Karatnycky, "The Comparative Survey of Freedom 1998–1999: A Good Year for Freedom" (on the Internet at http://freedomhouse.org/survey99/essays/karat.html).

should be organized, they have called upon these ideals to justify their actions. Now let's reexamine these ideals, noting key historical conflicts and current controversies about what they should mean in practice.

Liberty The central historical conflict regarding liberty in the United States was the enslavement of blacks. The facts of slavery and the differential treat-

The proper scope of governmental regulation of citizens' behavior is the subject of ongoing debate. During 1997 and 1998, the U.S. government took action to ban or limit advertising by tobacco companies, pitting tobacco companies and farmers against health and children's advocates.

ment of the races has cast a long shadow over all of American history. In fact, scholars today note that the American definition of freedom has been formed in relation to the concept of slavery. The right to control one's labor and the right to receive rewards for that labor have been central elements of our definition of freedom precisely because these freedoms were denied to slaves.[17]

Concerns about the meaning of liberty also arise in connection with government regulation of economic and social activity. Economic regulations imposed to ensure public health and safety are often decried by the affected businesses as infringements on their freedom. For example, in 1994, the Occupational Safety and Health Administration (OSHA) of the national government prepared to issue regulations intended to protect workers from repetitive stress injuries. Such injuries, which affect 700,000 workers a year, are caused by long hours on the assembly line or at the computer. OSHA's regulations would have required employers to provide specified work breaks and proper furniture and other equipment. Although such regulations might have been welcomed by workers, employers viewed them as intrusive and extremely costly. In the face of strong opposition from employers, OSHA backed down and decided not to issue the regulations.[18]

Social regulations prompt similar disputes. Some citizens believe that government should enforce certain standards of behavior or instill particular values in citizens. Examples of such activity abound: welfare rules that once denied benefits to women who were found with a "man in the house," the practice of saying prayers in school, laws that require parents to pay child support for their children even if those children no longer live with them, and laws that require citizens to wear seat belts are just a few examples. Deciding the proper scope of economic and social regulation is a topic of great concern and much conflict among Americans today.

Equality Because equality is such an elusive concept, many conflicts have arisen over what it should mean in practice. Americans have engaged in three kinds of controversies about the public role in addressing inequality. The first is determining what constitutes equality of access to public institutions. In 1896, the Supreme Court ruled in *Plessy v. Ferguson* that "separate but equal" accommodations for blacks and whites were constitutional. In 1954, in a major legal victory for the civil rights movement, the Supreme Court overturned the separate but equal doctrine in *Brown v. Board of Education* (see Chapter 6). Today, new questions have been raised about what constitutes equal access to public institutions. Some argue that the unequal financing of public schools in cities, suburbs, and rural districts is a violation of the right to equal education. To date, these claims have not been supported by the federal courts, which have rejected the notion that the unequal economic impacts of public policy outcomes are a constitutional matter.[19] Lawsuits arguing a right to "economic equal protection" stalled in 1973 when the Supreme Court ruled that a Texas school-financing law did not violate the Constitution even though the law affected rich and poor students differently.[20]

A second debate concerns the public role in ensuring equality of opportunity in private life. Although Americans generally agree that discrimination should not be tolerated, people disagree over what should be done to ensure equality of opportunity (see Table 1.2). Controversies about affirmative action programs reflect these disputes. Supporters of affirmative action claim that such programs are necessary to compensate for past discrimination in order to obtain true equality of opportunity today. Opponents maintain that affirmative action amounts to reverse discrimination and that a society that espouses true equality should not acknowledge gender or racial differences. The question of the public responsibility for private inequalities is central to gender issues. The traditional view, still held by many today, sees the special responsibilities of women in the family as something that falls outside the range of public concern. Indeed, from this perspective, women's role within families is essential to the functioning of a democratic society. In the past twenty years, especially, these traditional views have come under fire, as advocates for women have argued that women occupy a subordinate place within the family and that such private inequalities *are* a topic of public concern.[21]

A third debate about equality concerns differences in income and wealth. Unlike in other countries, income inequality has not been an enduring topic of

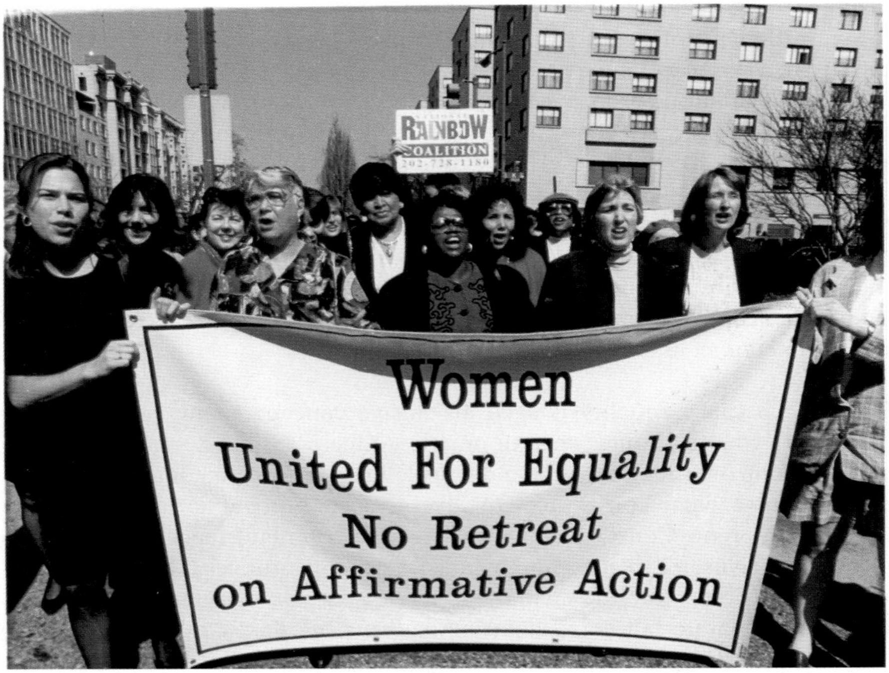

Equality, particularly equal opportunity and equal pay for equal work, has been a primary concern of the women's movement. Here, women's advocates march to the White House to urge the president not to weaken affirmative action programs.

AMERICAN ATTITUDES ABOUT EQUALITY, 1996 AND 1998 — Table 1.2

Statement	Percentage who agree
Our society should do whatever is necessary to make sure that everyone has an equal opportunity to succeed.	82
We have gone too far in pushing equal rights in this country.	45*
One of the big problems in this country is that we don't give everyone an equal chance.	48
It is not really that big a problem if some people have more of a chance in life than others.	37
The country would be better off if we worried less about how equal people are.	53
If people were treated more equally in this country, we would have many fewer problems.	83*

SOURCE: Based on data from the American National Election Studies, conducted by the University of Michigan, Center for Political Studies, and provided by the Inter-University Consortium for Political and Social Research, Ann Arbor, Michigan.
*Indicates 1998 data.

political controversy in the United States, which currently has the largest gap in income and wealth between rich and poor citizens of any developed nation. But Americans have generally tolerated great differences among rich and poor citizens, in part because of a pervasive belief that mobility is possible and that economic success is the product of individual effort.[22] At times, however, concern about economic inequalities emerges, often around the issue of fair taxation. Some analysts today warn that the growing division between rich and poor may invigorate a politics of class and polarize political debate along income lines.[23]

Democracy Despite Americans' deep attachment to the *ideal* of democracy, many questions can be raised about our *practice* of democracy. The first is the restricted definition of the political community during much of American history. The United States was not a full democracy until the 1960s, when African Americans were at last guaranteed the right to vote. Property restrictions on the right to vote were eliminated by 1828; in 1870, the Fifteenth Amendment to the Constitution granted African Americans the vote, although later exclusionary practices denied them that right; in 1920, the Nineteenth Amendment guaranteed women the right to vote; and in 1965, the Voting Rights Act finally secured the right of African Americans to vote.

Just securing the right to vote does not end concerns about democracy, however. The organization of electoral institutions can have a significant impact on access to elections and on who can get elected. During the first two decades of the twentieth century, states and cities enacted many reforms that made it harder to vote, including strict registration requirements and scheduling of elections. The aim was to rid politics of corruption but the consequence was to reduce participation. Other institutional decisions affect which candidates stand the best chance of getting elected (see Chapter 11).

A further consideration about democracy concerns the relationship between economic power and political power. Money has always played an important role in elections and governing in the United States. Many argue that the pervasive influence of money in American electoral campaigns today undermines democracy. With the decline of locally based political parties that depended on party loyalists to turn out the vote, and the rise of political action committees, political consultants, and expensive media campaigns, money has become the central fact of life in American politics. Money often determines who runs for office; it can exert a heavy influence on who wins; and, some argue, money affects what politicians do once they are in office.[24]

A final consideration that must be raised about democracy is the engagement of the citizenry. Low turnout for elections and a pervasive sense of apathy and cynicism characterize American politics today. Many people say that it does not matter if they participate because their votes will not make any difference. This disillusionment and sense of ineffectiveness undermines the vitality of democracy, which in turn reduces the accountability of the rulers to the ruled.

VALUES AND GOVERNMENT

Many of the most important dilemmas of American political life involve conflicts among fundamental political values as those values are put into operation. For example, Americans strongly value both liberty and equality, but often programs designed to promote one may impose restraints upon the other. Thus, affirmative action programs or statutes designed to prevent discrimination against the handicapped, such as the Americans with Disabilities Act, may promote equality but may also infringe upon the liberty of employers to hire whomever they wish. In a similar vein, democratic political processes may sometimes produce results that can challenge both liberty and equality. After all, Adolf Hitler and the Nazis came to power in Germany in the 1930s partly through democratic means. Even in America, political extremists who oppose both liberty and equality have been elected to office. As recently as 1991, a white supremacist, David Duke, was very nearly elected governor of Louisiana.

Conversely, in the name of equality or liberty, courts often hand down verdicts that undo decisions of democratically elected legislatures and even decisions reached in popular referenda. Principles that seem incontrovertible in the abstract become more problematic in operation. In the process of resolving conflicts among core beliefs, America's political principles change and evolve. Even core values should be understood as works in progress rather than immutable facts.

In principle, conflicts among liberty, equality, and democracy can be reconciled. In practice, however, over time, democracy poses a fundamental threat to liberty. This is so because, over time, democracy promotes strong government, often to promote equality, and, over time, strong government inevitably threatens liberty. And with issues of social policy such as affirmative action, what some see as guaranteeing equality, others view as an infringement of liberty. But as we shall see, in the United States, the institutions of democratic government have been critical in guaranteeing both liberty and equality.

Politics on the Web

Many people believe that the Internet is a profound boost to democracy, because it enables anyone and everyone to voice their concerns, frustrations, and aspirations; it gives equal political voice to each person. Already, web sites exist for every conceivable cause, and start-up costs for new web sites are minimal. For these reasons, the Internet will revolutionize politics.

But for real change to occur, the voices on the Internet *must* affect government policy. And so far, it is unclear whether the government is, or can be, listening. There is absolutely no way for a political system, even a democratic one, to address all the opinions that the Internet generates.

The distance between the opportunity for political expression on the Internet and the government's inability to deal with that expression may help perpetuate the cynicism, distrust of government, and, ultimately, apathy about politics that characterizes so many Americans today. If this is the case, then the biggest irony of the Internet is that it was the federal government that built it in the first place.

www.wwnorton.com/wtp3e

Martin Luther King, Jr., the civil rights leader, shakes the hand of President Lyndon B. Johnson following the signing of the Voting Rights Act of 1965, a milestone in assuring political equality for African Americans.

The Citizen's Role

This chapter began with the stories of two recent college graduates, Jim Wilkinson and Dave Grayson. Their interests in issues led them to become politically involved, one at the national level and one at the local level.

Jim and Dave are intelligent, ambitious, and believe passionately in their important, albeit very different, political causes. What made it possible for both these individuals to begin to make their views count was some knowledge of politics and a strong sense of political efficacy. Jim knew from reading and following the news that Representative Dick Armey shared his own doubts and concerns about the U.S. tax code. Dave knew from his study of current issues and political history how to assess the political and social concerns most important to him and how to work effectively on their behalf.

We have seen that knowledge is the first requisite of democratic citizenship. Armed with a modicum of knowledge, any citizen can find ways to influence the political process. Some may take the path illustrated by Jim Wilkinson or Dave Grayson. Others may pursue the variety of paths described at the conclusion of each chapter of this book. There are many paths to political influence. Each path, however, is effectively blocked by a door that can be unlocked only by those possessing some measure of political knowledge. Furthermore, without an understanding of at least the broad outlines of the political process, political interests, concerns, and passions are largely irrelevant. Only those with some understanding of government and politics can know how to take part in any meaningful way.

Testing Political Waters

You may not be interested in politics. You probably distrust politicians. You certainly have other priorities. Why bother with politics? After all, there is not much you can do about children's access to guns or mounting tensions in the Middle East.

Before you decide that public life is strictly for other people, consider several factors. First, political involvement can be fascinating. It may put you at the center of challenging issues that have important effects on many people's lives. Should Americans promote environmental safeguards that protect some people's health but cost other people jobs? Should Americans spend scarce public resources on prenatal care for poor women or build libraries that provide Internet access to all community members?

Second, political engagement can be energizing. Imagine how it feels to be the person who organizes a group that gives voice to the concerns of elderly people who had previously been ignored or neglected. Consider how exciting it would be to participate in a coalition that places a referendum to save wildlife reserves on the state ballot, to feel the tension of campaign volunteers as the first election returns trickle in.

Third, political activism can produce political efficacy—the sense that you can make a difference. If you do nothing, you cannot be part of the solution. When you get involved, you can continue the efforts of those who precede you, try innovative approaches to old problems, and create a legacy for those who will follow. You may ease existing dilemmas and contribute to their resolution. Occasionally, one determined person does make a significant difference.

Accordingly, before you say no to political participation, consider the potential fascination, energy, and accomplishments that await you. Do more than consider. Test political waters. Here are a few easy ways to see if political involvement can be meaningful and fulfilling to you.

- **Assess your political interests.**
  Read a newspaper or a weekly news magazine. Watch national or local news on television. Listen to a political talk show. What issues catch your eye? Which ones seem important to you? How do any of them affect your life? Identify one or two issues and follow them for a week or so. You may discover that political knowledge generates interest.
- **Initiate a discussion with family members, friends, or classmates.**
  Ask a few people what they think about an issue that interests you. Do they care? Are they knowledgeable? Do they have a position on the issue? If so, how do they defend their position? Do you agree or disagree with them? The point here is to *listen* to and *learn* from other people's political viewpoints.
- **Articulate your own views on the issue.**
  Experiment with expressing your own views on the issue. Are they clear? coherent? cogent? Now see if you can articulate your views with enough force that other people take you seriously but also with sufficient civility to keep up the attention and interest of people who disagree with you.

- **Write a letter to the editor of a campus or community newspaper.**
  Write a letter to the editor expressing your view. Make the letter short, direct, and civil. That will increase the likelihood that it will be selected for publication. A few readers may answer your letter by submitting written responses to it.
- **Call in to a radio talk show.**
  State your point clearly and succinctly to the person who screens callers. If you get on air, state your main point, present your key arguments, and invite a response from the host or the call-in audience.

Democracy begins with discussion. Adopt an experimental attitude and join the discussion. It is not important to persuade other people that you are right. People change their minds very slowly. Instead, aim at expressing yourself clearly and knowledgeably so that your views will be communicated effectively. Often, it is as important to be taken seriously as it is to be heeded.

Summary

Despite the relative openness of American political life, fewer and fewer Americans are choosing to take part in the political process. Some speculate that Americans' general lack of interest in politics results from their declining trust in government and their decreasing belief that they can influence what government does. As more and more citizens withdraw from political life, democracy suffers.

The citizen's role in political life begins with information and knowledge. A citizen's knowledge should include knowledge of government, of politics, and of democratic principles. Knowledgeable citizens are better able to identify and act upon their political interests. In short, knowledgeable citizens better understand how and why politics and government influences their lives.

The form that a government takes affects citizens because it determines who governs and how much governmental control is permitted. Americans live in a constitutional democracy, where limits are placed on what governments can do and how they can do it. Americans are also given access to government through legal rights to political participation. Through politics, Americans are able to struggle over the leadership, structure, and policies of governments.

Although politics may divide Americans from one another, the core values of American political culture—liberty, equality, and democracy—hold the United States and its people together. Although these values have been important since the time the United States was founded, during much of American history there have been large gaps between these ideals and the practice of American politics. Moreover, liberty, equality, and democracy often conflict with one another in American political life.

FOR FURTHER READING

Craig, Stephen C., and Stephen Earl Bennett, eds. *After the Boom: The Politics of Generation X.* Lanham, MD: Rowman and Littlefield, 1997.

Dahl, Robert. *Democracy and Its Critics.* New Haven, CT: Yale University Press, 1989.

Delli Carpini, Michael X., and Scott Keeter, *What Americans Know about Politics and Why It Matters.* New Haven, CT: Yale University Press, 1996.

Hochschild, Jennifer L. *Facing Up to the American Dream: Race, Class, and the Soul of the Nation.* Princeton, NJ: Princeton University Press, 1995.

Huntington, Samuel P. *American Politics: The Promise of Disharmony.* Cambridge, MA: Harvard University Press, 1981.

Lasswell, Harold. *Politics: Who Gets What, When, How.* New York: Meridian Books, 1958.

McClosky, Herbert, and John Zaller. *The American Ethos: Public Attitudes toward Capitalism and Democracy.* Cambridge, MA: Harvard University Press, 1984.

Nie, Norman H., Jane Junn, and Kenneth Stehlik-Barry. *Education and Democratic Citizenship in America.* Chicago: University of Chicago Press, 1996.

Nye, Joseph S., Jr., Philip D. Zelikow, and David C. King, eds. *Why People Don't Trust Government.* Cambridge, MA: Harvard University Press, 1997.

Putnam, Robert. *Making Democracy Work: Civic Traditions in Modern Italy.* Princeton, NJ: Princeton University Press, 1993.

de Tocqueville, Alexis. *Democracy in America.* Trans. Phillips Bradley. New York: Knopf, Vintage Books, 1945; orig. published 1835.

STUDY OUTLINE

What Americans Think about Government

1. In recent decades, the public's trust in government has declined considerably. Some Americans believe that government has grown too large and that government programs do not benefit them. As public distrust of government has increased, so has public dissatisfaction with the government's performance.
2. Americans today are less likely to think that they can influence what the government does. This view has led to increased apathy and cynicism among the citizenry.

What Americans Know about Government

1. Informed and active membership in a political community is the basis for citizenship. Citizens require political knowledge in order to be aware of their interests in a political dispute, to identify the best ways of acting upon their interests, and to know what political action can and cannot achieve. However, today many Americans have little political knowledge.

Government

1. Governments vary in their structure, in their size, and in the way they operate.
2. Beginning in the seventeenth century, two important changes began to take place in the governance of some Western nations: governments began to acknowledge formal limits on their power, and governments began to give citizens a formal voice in politics through the vote.
3. Political participation can take many forms: the vote, group activities, and even direct action, such as violence or civil disobedience.

American Political Culture: Conflict and Consensus

1. Three important political values in American politics are liberty, equality, and democracy.
2. At times in American history there have been large gaps between the ideals embodied in Americans' core values and the practice of American government.
3. Many of the important dilemmas of American politics revolve around conflicts over fundamental political values. One such conflict involves the ideals of liberty and democracy. Over time, democracy promotes stronger, more active government, which may threaten liberty.

PRACTICE QUIZ

1. Political efficacy is the belief that
   a) government operates efficiently.
   b) government has grown too large.
   c) government cannot be trusted.
   d) one can influence what government does.

2. The famous political scientist Harold Lasswell defined politics as the struggle over
   a) who gets elected.
   b) who gets what, when, how.
   c) who protests.
   d) who gets to vote.
3. What is the basic difference between autocracy and oligarchy?
   a) the extent to which the average citizen has a say in government affairs
   b) the means of collecting taxes and conscripting soldiers
   c) the number of people who control governing decisions
   d) They are fundamentally the same thing.
4. According to the authors, good citizenship requires
   a) political knowledge.
   b) political engagement.
   c) a good education.
   d) both a and b
5. The principle of political equality can be best summed up as
   a) "equality of results."
   b) "equality of opportunity."
   c) "one person, one vote."
   d) "equality between the sexes."
6. Which of the following is an important principle of American democracy?
   a) popular sovereignty
   b) majority rule/minority rights
   c) limited government
   d) All of the above are important principles of American democracy.
7. Which of the following is not related to the American conception of "liberty"?
   a) freedom of speech
   b) free enterprise
   c) freedom of religion
   d) All of the above are related to liberty.
8. Which of the following is *not* part of the American political culture?
   a) belief in equality of results
   b) belief in equality of opportunity
   c) belief in individual liberty
   d) belief in free competition
9. Which of the following does not represent a current discrepancy between the ideal and practice of democracy in America?
   a) the use of property restrictions for voting in three remaining states
   b) the influence of money in electoral politics
   c) the low voter turnout in American elections
   d) All of the above represent discrepancies between the ideal and practice of democracy in modern America.
10. Americans' trust in their government
    a) has declined steadily since the early 1960s.
    b) declined during Watergate, but rose again during the 1980s.
    c) has risen since 1990.
    d) rose during the 1970s and 1980s, but has declined since 1992.

CRITICAL THINKING QUESTIONS

1. What type of government does the United States have? Is it the most democratic government possible? Do citizens make the decisions of government or do they merely influence them?
2. Think of some examples that demonstrate the gaps between the ideals of America's core political values and the practice of American politics. Describe how such gaps were reconciled in the past. Identify one current gap between Americans' values and their political practices. How might this discrepancy be reconciled?

KEY TERMS

authoritarian government (p. 15)
autocracy (p. 14)
citizenship (p. 12)
constitutional government (p. 15)
democracy (p. 15)
direct action politics (p. 18)
direct democracy (p. 17)
equality of opportunity (p. 20)
government (p. 14)
laissez-faire capitalism (p. 19)
liberty (p. 19)
limited government (p. 19)
majority rule/minority rights (p. 21)
oligarchy (p. 14)
pluralism (p. 18)
political culture (p. 19)
political efficacy (p. 9)
political equality (p. 20)
politics (p. 17)
popular sovereignty (p. 21)
power (p. 17)
representative democracy (or republic) (p. 17)
totalitarian government (p. 15)

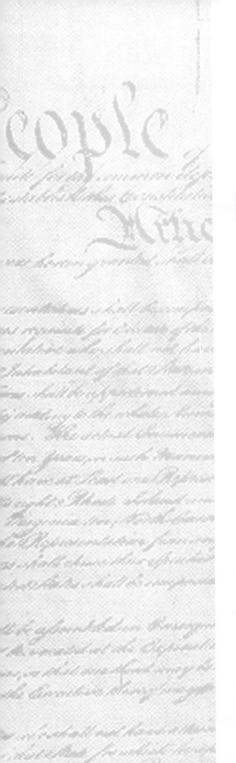

2 The American

- ★ **Expanding the American Political Community**
  - How has the American political community expanded since the time of the Founding?
  - How have racial and ethnic differences, gender, class, and religious affiliation affected the right to participate in the political process throughout America's history?
  - How successfully have social groups such as white ethnics, African Americans, Latinos, Asian Americans, women, and religious groups realized the right to full political participation?
  - What tactics did these groups employ to gain full access to the political process?
- ★ **Participation in the American Political Community: The Citizen's Role**

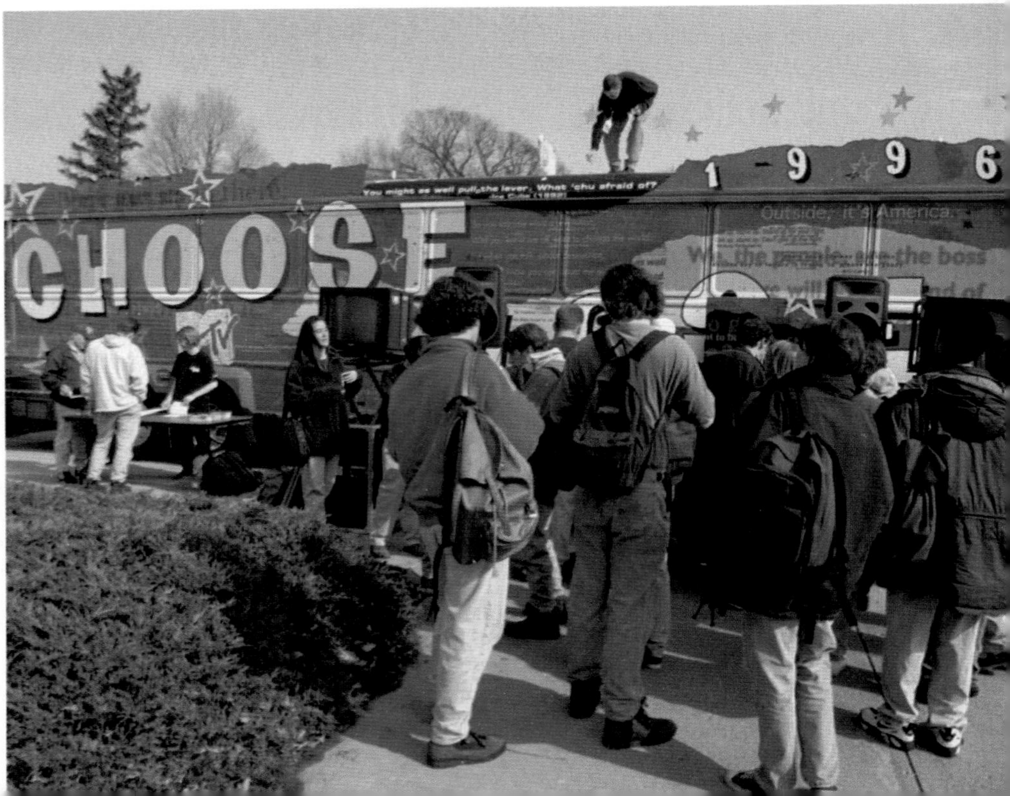

Political Community

STUDENTS AND POLITICS

IN 1971, the Twenty-sixth Amendment to the Constitution enlarged the electorate by nearly 27 million voters when it granted eighteen-, nineteen-, and twenty-year-old Americans the right to vote.[1] This formal expansion of the American political community confirmed what many politicians already knew: young people were an active political force and they had had a wide-ranging impact on politics over the preceding decade. Young people left a lasting imprint on American politics as they took the lead on major issues, including civil rights, antiwar activism, gender discrimination, and the effort to open up political parties to more grassroots influence.

The formal inclusion of young people repeated a process that has occurred over and over again throughout American history. Groups such as women and African Americans, who were in the past formally excluded from the political community, nonetheless found ways to make their views known and to press for full inclusion in the political system. Formally excluded groups and other groups who have felt their views to be insufficiently recognized in politics have won influence through a wide range of activities. They have expressed their views in newspaper editorials and letters, made speeches, circulated and signed petitions, initiated legal challenges in the courts, and protested. Armed with the promises inherent in the American ideals of liberty, equality, and democracy and with their own determination to make the political system respond to them, culturally and socially distinct groups have changed American politics. In so doing they have helped to make the United States one of the most diverse modern democracies. Cultural and social diversity has made American politics a vibrant and often challenging experience, as groups clash over often very different views about what government should do—and should not do—to live up to our national ideals. Such widespread and varied forms of participation have caused the government to abandon some practices and to institute new policies that reflect changing perspectives of our core values of liberty and equality.

- ***In this chapter we will consider the forms of participation and the kinds of access to the political system that groups of different social backgrounds and cultural beliefs fought for and have subsequently enjoyed.*** We will examine the ways that groups with distinctive racial and ethnic, class, gender, and religious backgrounds have used participation to change government policies that mattered to them. We will also see that such identities do not always provide the basis for shared political activity.

- ***We end by considering how citizens can become more involved in politics in order to reinvigorate American democracy and make government reflect their views of liberty and equality.***

Expanding the American Political Community

- How has the American political community expanded since the time of the Founding?
- How have racial and ethnic differences, gender, class, and religious affiliation affected the right to participate in the political process throughout America's history?
- How successfully have social groups such as white ethnics, African Americans, Latinos, Asian Americans, women, and religious groups realized the right to full political participation?
- What tactics did these groups employ to gain full access to the political process?

American political community
citizens who are eligible to vote and participate in American political life

The original **American political community** restricted membership to white men who owned property. Many of the elite merchants and planters who launched the American Revolution did not envision a broad-based democracy. Instead, they presumed that American democracy would encompass a small, homogeneous group. Ethnically, the earliest members of the American political community were white Anglo-Saxon Protestants (WASPs), who shared a common ancestry and culture. But this narrow membership did not last long. By the 1830s, property restrictions had been abandoned and in the next decades the pressure to expand the American political community launched the nation on a path that would ultimately lead to the diverse community we have today.

Groups with distinctive social and cultural identities have often played pivotal roles in changing American politics. Conflicts over their inclusion have tested Americans' understanding of liberty, equality, and democracy. Establishing access to the political system for these groups has expanded the definition of the political community and has often provoked important institutional changes as well. Moreover, the ongoing participation of such groups has transformed politics, altering political coalitions and changing political debates. This section will examine the experiences of four kinds of cultural and social groups in American politics: racial and ethnic, class, gender, and religious. It asks to what extent members of these particular groups have recognized common interests and have sought to act politically on those interests. We will pay particular attention to the forms of mobilization these groups used to build political strength and what strategies they employed to gain access to the political system. The story of their fight for political equality and fundamental liberties is a tribute to the creativity and persistence of these groups, but also to the resilience of the American political system.[2]

ETHNICITY AND RACE

Ethnic and racial identities are the most politically significant social identities in the United States. This great diversity has distinguished the United States from most European nations, which for most of modern history have been much more ethnically and racially homogeneous. As we examine the process of political inclusion of different groups, we shall see that American politics encouraged racial and ethnic identification even as it has excluded many groups on the basis of race or national origin.

White Ethnics The term **"white ethnic"** encompasses a wide range of groups who for most of American history did not identify as a single group. In fact, some of these groups—Italians, for example—were not always identified as "white" when they entered this country.

white ethnics
white immigrants to the United States whose culture differs from that of WASPs

European immigration was the central fact of American life from the colonial period until the 1920s, when Congress sharply cut off immigration. In peak years nearly a million new immigrants entered the country. The colonists came overwhelmingly from the British Isles, particularly from England; a smattering were German or Dutch. The first postcolonial wave of immigration came in the 1840s, when the Irish began to outnumber all other immigrants; Germans and Scandinavians came in the greatest numbers between 1880 and 1890. Finally, between 1890 and 1910, a huge wave of immigration from eastern and central Europe brought Italians, Slavs, and eastern European Jews to the country.[3] The results of these waves of European immigration are reflected in America today: as Figure 2.1 indicates, whites of European origin comprise 73 percent of the total U.S. population.

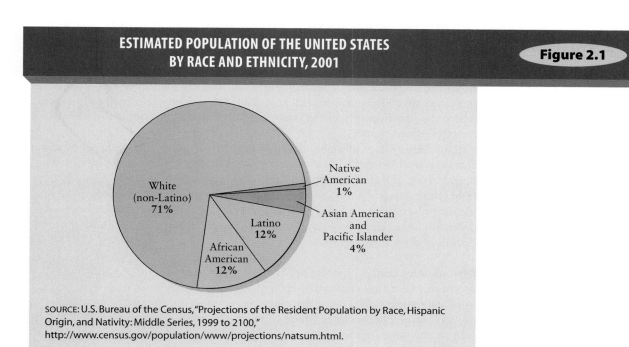

ESTIMATED POPULATION OF THE UNITED STATES BY RACE AND ETHNICITY, 2001 — **Figure 2.1**

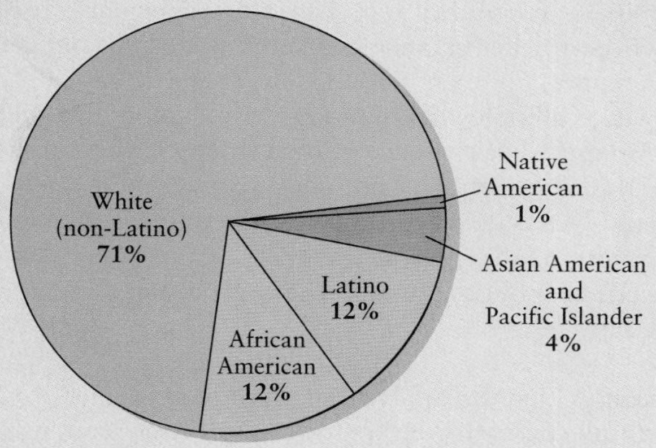

SOURCE: U.S. Bureau of the Census, "Projections of the Resident Population by Race, Hispanic Origin, and Nativity: Middle Series, 1999 to 2100," http://www.census.gov/population/www/projections/natsum.html.

Although the American story is often told as one of assimilation, in fact American politics acknowledged and encouraged the maintenance of ethnic identities. The openness of the political system encouraged politicians to recognize ethnic groups and to mobilize them—as a group—into politics.

For most of American history, citizenship and political equality came to white ethnics without a struggle. Despite the sometimes virulent anti-immigrant sentiment and the eventual restrictions imposed on immigration, the political rights of white immigrants were never in serious peril. They were eligible to become naturalized citizens after five years of residence; rates of naturalization varied from 45.6 percent of all foreign-born residents in 1910 to 67.9 percent by 1950.[4] Many of America's big cities were governed by **political machines,** which were party organizations that controlled local politics by nominating candidates for office and mobilizing voters to elect those candidates. These machines realized that the votes of the newly arrived immigrants could help particular candidates win office and, consequently, saw to it that immigrants quickly became citizens. In New York, the most important political machine, called Tammany Hall, filled out citizenship applications for immigrants and paid the necessary application fees. In the two weeks before elections in New York, Philadelphia, and Baltimore, naturalization rates increased sharply.[5] In addition, many states and territories allowed noncitizens to vote and enjoy other rights of citizenship.

political machines
local party organizations that controlled local politics in the late nineteenth and early twentieth centuries through patronage and control of nominations

Once immigrants became citizens, their ethnic identifications remained important political guideposts. In cities, political machines appealed to voters along ethnic lines and parceled out patronage on the basis of ethnic group membership. Precinct captains spoke the language of the immigrants and acted as a link to the broader world. Thus, although ethnic neighborhoods were insulated, they were not isolated. Ethnic concerns entered politics around such issues as the prohibition of alcohol, Sunday closing laws (a way to preserve Sunday as a day for religious observance by prohibiting businesses from opening on Sunday), and language instruction in the public schools.

Even after white ethnic groups had become assimilated into a broader American culture—which itself was altered by their inclusion—ethnic appeals remained prominent in political life. This was particularly true in big cities, where the practice of ticket balancing ensured that slates of candidates bore a range of ethnic names. For example, in New York City in 1961, a Republican slate of Lefkowitz, Gilhooley, and Fino faced a Democratic lineup of Wagner, Screvane, and Beame.[6] The presence of Irish (Irish-German in the case of Wagner), Italian, and Jewish names on both tickets reflected the need to cover multiple ethnic bases. In recent years, however, the political significance of ethnic identities has begun to fade. Even in New York City, where ethnicity was once a central concern in politics, white ethnic groups no longer fall into predictable voting blocs.

African Americans For African Americans, the central fact of political life has been a denial of full citizenship rights for most of American history. By accepting the institution of slavery, the Founders embraced a system fundamentally at odds with the "Blessings of Liberty" promised in the Constitution. Their decision set the stage for two centuries of African American struggles to achieve full citizenship. In the course of these battles, African Americans built organizations and devised political strategies that transformed American politics.

The vast majority of enslaved blacks had few means for organizing to assert themselves. Their hopes for achieving full citizenship rights initially seemed fulfilled when three constitutional amendments were adopted after the Civil War: the Thirteenth Amendment abolished slavery; the Fourteenth Amendment guaranteed equal protection under the law; and the Fifteenth Amendment guaranteed voting rights for blacks. Protected by the presence of federal troops, African American men were able to exercise their political rights immediately after the war. During Reconstruction, blacks were elected to many political offices: two black senators were elected from Mississippi and a total of fourteen African Americans were elected to the House of Representatives between 1869 and 1877. African Americans also held many state-level political offices. As voters and public officials, black citizens found a home in the Republican Party, which had secured the ratification of the three constitutional amendments guaranteeing black rights. After the war, the Republican Party continued to reach out to black voters as a means to build party strength in the South.[7]

This political equality was short-lived, however. The national government withdrew its troops from the South and turned its back on African Americans in 1877. In the Compromise of 1877, southern Democrats agreed to allow the Republican candidate, Rutherford B. Hayes, to become president after a disputed election. In exchange, northern Republicans dropped their support for the civil liberties and political participation of African Americans. After that, southern states erected a tight system of social, political, and economic inequality that made a mockery of the promises in the Constitution. These years marked the beginning of a long process in which African Americans built organizations and devised strategies for asserting their constitutional rights.

One such strategy sought to win political rights through political pressure and litigation. This approach was championed by the NAACP, established by a group of black and white reformers in 1909. Among the NAACP's founders was W. E. B. DuBois, one of the most influential and creative thinkers on racial issues of the twentieth century. Because the northern black vote was so small in the early decades of the twentieth century, the organization primarily relied on the courts to press for black political rights. After the 1920s, the NAACP built a strong membership base, with some strength in the South, which would be critical when the civil rights movement gained momentum in the 1950s.

W. E. B. DuBois, a founder of the NAACP and a prominent American thinker throughout the twentieth century.

The great migration of blacks to the North beginning around World War I enlivened a protest strategy. Although protest organizations had existed in the nineteenth century, the continuing migration of blacks to the North made protest an increasingly useful tool. Black labor leader A. Philip Randolph forced the federal government to address racial discrimination in hiring practices during World War II by threatening a massive march on Washington. The federal government also grew more attentive to blacks as their voting strength increased as a result of the northward migration. By the 1940s, the black vote had swung away from Republicans, but the Democratic hold on black votes was by no means absolute.

These strategies—political and legal pressure and protest—all played a part in the modern civil rights movement, which took off in the 1950s. The movement drew on an organizational base and network of communication rooted in black churches, the NAACP, and black colleges.

The nonviolent protest tactics adopted by local clergy members, including

STUDENTS AND POLITICS

Rev. Martin Luther King, Jr., eventually spread across the South and brought national attention to the movement. The clergy organized into a group called the Southern Christian Leadership Conference (SCLC). Students also played a key role. The most important student organization was the Student Nonviolent Coordinating Committee (SNCC). In 1960, four black students sat down at the lunch counter of the Greensboro, North Carolina, Woolworth's department store, which like most southern establishments did not serve African Americans. Their sit-in was the first of many. Through a combination of protest, legal action, and political pressure, the civil rights movement compelled a reluctant federal government to enforce black civil and political rights. The 1964 Civil Rights Act and the 1965 Voting Rights Act were the great legislative victories of the movement; the end of legal segregation and the beginning of black political power were the results.[8]

Martin Luther King, Jr., addressed the crowd during the 1963 March on Washington, where he delivered his famous "I have a dream" speech.

The victories of the civil rights movement made blacks full citizens and stimulated a tremendous growth in the number of black public officials at all levels of government, as blacks exercised their newfound political rights. Yet despite these successes, racial segregation remains a fact of life in the United States, and new problems have emerged. Most troubling is the persistence of black urban poverty, now coupled with deep social and economic isolation.[9] These conditions raise new questions about African American political participation. One question concerns black political cohesion: Will blacks continue to vote as a bloc, given the sharp economic differences that now divide a large black middle class from an equally large group of deeply impoverished African Americans? A second question concerns the benefits of participation: How can political participation improve the lives of African Americans, especially of the poor?

Public opinion and voting evidence indicate that African Americans continue to vote as a bloc despite their economic differences.[10] Surveys of black

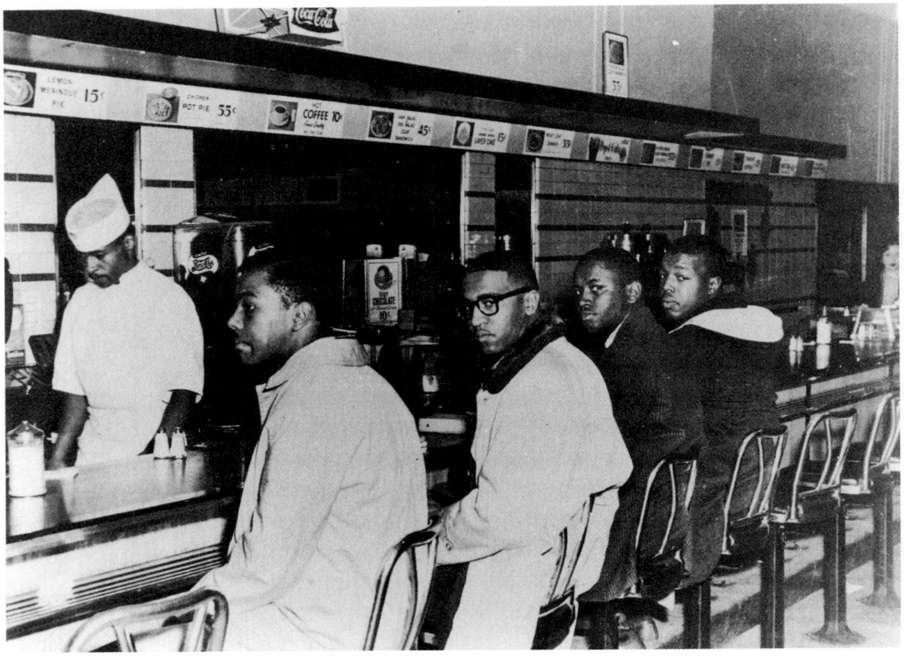

The Woolworth lunch counter sit-in in Greensboro, North Carolina, started a wave of sit-ins throughout the South.

voters show that blacks across the income spectrum believe that their fates are linked because of their race. This sense of shared experience and a common fate has united blacks at the polls and in politics.[11] Since the 1960s, blacks have overwhelmingly chosen Democratic candidates and black candidates have sought election under the Democratic banner. In recent years, however, a small number of black Republicans has been elected to the House of Representatives. Evidence that affluent black Americans are less likely than poorer African Americans to support traditional policies that assist the poor suggests that this trend could continue in the future. However, Republican hostility to affirmative action and other programs of racial preference is likely to sharply check any large-scale black migration to the Republican Party.

At the same time, however, the black community and its political leadership has been considerably frustrated about the benefits of loyalty to the Democratic Party. Some analysts argue that the structure of party competition makes it difficult for African Americans to win policy benefits through political participation. Because Republicans have not sought to win the black vote and Democrats take it for granted, neither party is willing to support bold measures to address the mounting problems of poor African Americans.

Thus, concerns about strategy and organization remain very much on the African American political agenda. In the face of unfavorable political and legal outcomes, interest in self-help has grown, as evidenced by the gathering of hundreds of thousands of black men in Washington in 1995 for the Million Man March. Yet many black Americans continue to search for new ways to induce the government to address their distinctive concerns. These questions and problems now confront a new generation of African Americans.

Latinos The labels "Latino" and "Hispanic" encompass a wide range of groups with diverse national origins and distinctive cultural identities. The experiences of these groups in the American political system have often been very different from one another as well. Mexican Americans, Puerto Ricans, Cubans, and Central Americans have used varying strategies and organizational forms to gain access to American politics. As we will see, their struggles for political equality often differed according to when they entered the United States, in what region of the country they lived, and how racial considerations affected white views of whether they could become full citizens.

Mexican Americans are the largest group of Latinos in the United States today; their population is estimated

Students and Politics

Thirty years after the civil rights movement, the NAACP is making a renewed push for political activism on college campuses.

"This generation really realizes that the civil rights battle isn't over," said Mark Sanders, president of a new student chapter at Stanford. "It's an ongoing battle and now is the time to pick it up."

The National Association for the Advancement of Colored People has always been active in the fight for civil rights, but it hasn't been as effective as it was during the civil rights era, said Tom Massey, faculty adviser of the Stanford chapter. Now, the NAACP is putting a greater emphasis on youth, helping them to understand the legacy of the NAACP.

The new chapter at Stanford and another at Harvard are the results of that new emphasis.

Massey said the NAACP is working hard to revive student interest in the organization because the future depends on them.

Harvard and Stanford have diverse student bodies and the NAACP chapters will provide healthy debate with other campus organizations, Massey said. Organizers said it will make all races more aware of problems facing minority communities.

At Stanford, Massey said students felt a need to be connected to a national civil rights organization instead of just a student organization on campus.

Students began to create a chapter last spring. Sanders said there was interest both on and off campus to start a student chapter.

Both the Harvard and Stanford chapters have specific goals they wish to accomplish in their inaugural years.

Edwards said she hopes the Harvard chapter will unify the campus and be supportive of student's civil rights. The chapter will serve as a forum to express concerns for all students of every ethnicity.

"In three words, my goal for this chapter is purposes, plans, and pursuits," Latham said.

At Stanford, Massey would like to see increased membership, liaisons with other student groups and more awareness of politics and civil rights.

Sanders plans to educate and register minority voters, working not only at Stanford, but in the community as well.

SOURCE: Rebecca Orbach, "NAACP Opens New Chapters, Emphasizes Youth Involvement," *Daily Northwestern* (Northwestern University), October 20, 1998.

at 18.8 million.[12] The Mexican American experience with political equality has been diverse and changing, because the experiences of Mexican Americans range from a people conquered in the middle of the nineteenth century to immigrants who arrived yesterday. The first Mexican Americans did not immigrate to the United States; the United States came to them when it annexed Texas in 1845 and defeated Mexico in 1848. The land that today makes up the states of New Mexico, California, Nevada, Utah, Colorado, Arizona, and Texas, all once part of Mexico, was added to American territory in those years.

The early political experiences of Mexican Americans were shaped by race and by region. In 1898, Mexican Americans were given formal political rights, including the right to vote. In many places, however, and especially in Texas, Mexican Americans were segregated and prevented from voting through such means as the white primary and the poll tax.[13] Region made a difference too. In contrast to the northeastern and midwestern cities to which most European ethnics immigrated, the Southwest did not have a tradition of ethnic mobilization associated with machine politics. Particularly after the political reforms enacted in the first decades of the twentieth century, city politics in the Southwest was dominated by a small group of Anglo elites. In the countryside, when Mexican Americans participated in politics, it was often as part of a political organization dominated by a large white landowner, or *patron.*

The earliest Mexican American independent political organizations, the League of United Latin American Citizens (LULAC) and the GI Forum, worked to stem discrimination against Mexican Americans in the years after World War II. By the late 1950s, the first Mexican American was elected to Congress, and four others followed in the 1960s. In the late 1960s a new kind of Mexican American political movement was born. Inspired by the black civil rights movement, Mexican American students launched boycotts of high school classes in East Los Angeles, Denver, and San Antonio. Students in colleges and universities across California joined in as well. Among their demands were bilingual education, an end to discrimination, and more cultural recognition. In Crystal City, Texas, which had been dominated by Anglo politicians despite a population that was overwhelmingly Mexican American, the newly formed La Raza Unida Party took over the city government.[14]

Since that time, Mexican American political strategy has developed along two tracks. One is a traditional ethnic-group path of voter registration and voting along ethnic lines. The second is a legal strategy using the various civil rights laws designed to ensure fair access to the political system. The Mexican American Legal Defense Fund (MALDEF) has played a key role in designing and pursuing the latter strategy. The two strategies are often used to reinforce one another, but at times they come into conflict.

Like that of the Mexicans, the Puerto Rican experience of the United States began with the experience of conquest. Puerto Rico became an unincorporated territory of the United States in 1898, after the Spanish-American War. In 1917, Puerto Ricans were made American citizens, although their island did not become a state. In the 1950s, Puerto Ricans began migrating to the mainland in large numbers, settling mainly in cities on the eastern seaboard—New York in particular.

Although they migrated to cities that had active traditions of ethnic group political participation, Puerto Ricans did not become politically mobilized until the late 1960s. In New York State, the requirement that voters be literate in English barred the majority of Puerto Ricans from registering in the 1950s.[15] By the 1960s, Puerto Ricans had become more politically mobilized and voted predominantly for Democratic candidates. Nevertheless, as one of the poorest ethnic groups in the United States, Puerto Ricans tend to have relatively low rates of political participation.

The Cuban experience with American politics has been quite different from those of Mexicans and Puerto Ricans. The vast majority of Cuban immigrants have come to the United States since the early 1960s as refugees from communist Cuba. In contrast to Puerto Rican and Mexican immigrants, many of the Cubans who came to the United States were middle class. Because they were granted refugee status, they also received federal government assistance in their settlement process. A central feature of Cuban American politics is a resolute anticommunism, which has led Cuban Americans to favor the Republican Party. Cuban political participation has also been shaped by the great concentration of Cubans in southern Florida. This concentration has allowed Cubans to become a major political force in Miami, and in Florida more broadly. The first Cuban American was elected to Congress from Florida in 1989.

Although Mexican Americans, Puerto Ricans, and Cubans make up the majority of Latinos in the United States, in the last decade substantial numbers of Spanish-speaking immigrants and refugees from the Caribbean, Central America, and South America have entered the country. During the 1980s, 23 percent of all legal immigrants to the United States came from these other Latin American countries.[16] These groups have altered the ethnic composition of Latinos in many cities, but they have not yet begun participating in politics in significant numbers.

The experience of Latinos in winning political equality stands between those of African Americans and white immigrants. In some regions of the country, restrictions on participation limited political equality until the 1960s. Even though Latinos have secured formal political equality, as a group Latinos have a relatively low level of political mobilization. Many analysts have called the Hispanic vote "the sleeping giant" because it has not yet realized its potential influence. Two important reasons for the low mobilization levels among Latinos are the low rates of voter registration and low rates of naturalization.

A Latino voter registration drive in Texas. Increasing rates of naturalization and voter registration will make the Latino vote a powerful force in American politics.

Among those who are eligible to vote, registration and turnout rates are relatively low. Of the 11.2 million Latinos eligible to vote in the 1996 presidential election, only 59 percent were registered and only 38 percent actually voted.[17] Yet the Latino vote has grown more important and has attracted considerable attention from politicians in recent years. In 1996 and 1998 Latino voters registered and voted in unprecedented numbers. Latinos played an important role in electing Democrats to political office in California in 1998. This high level of Latino political mobilization was widely seen as a backlash against the anti-immigrant stance associated with former Republican governor Pete Wilson. Yet, in other states, such as Texas and Florida, Latinos tended to split their votes between Democrats and Republicans.[18] The growing numbers of Latino voters and the uncertainty of their party attachment made them a critical target for politicians who hoped to win office in 2000.

Asian Americans As with Latinos, Asian Americans are a diverse group with many different national backgrounds. The majority of Asian immigrants have come to the United States in the past thirty years, but people from China began arriving on the West Coast in the 1850s.

The early Asian experience in the United States was shaped by a series of naturalization laws dating back to 1790, the first of which declared that only white aliens were eligible for citizenship. Chinese immigrants had begun arriving in California in the 1850s, drawn by the boom of the Gold Rush, but they were immediately met with hostility. The virulent antagonism toward Chinese immigrants in California led Congress to declare Chinese immigrants ineligible for citizenship in 1870. In 1882, the first Chinese Exclusion Act suspended the entry of Chinese laborers.

At the time of the Exclusion Act, the Chinese community was composed predominantly of single male laborers, with few women and children. The few Chinese children in San Francisco were initially denied entry to the public schools; only after parents of American-born Chinese children pressed legal action were the children allowed to attend public school. Even then, however, they were segregated into a separate Chinese school. American-born Chinese children could not be denied citizenship, however; this right was confirmed by the Supreme Court in 1898, when it ruled in *United States v. Wong Kim Ark* that anyone born in the United States was entitled to full citizenship.[19] Still, new Chinese immigrants were barred from the United States until 1943, after China had become a key wartime ally and Congress repealed the Chinese Exclusion Act and permitted Chinese residents to become citizens. As discrimination eased, Chinese Americans ventured out of Chinatowns to take jobs in a variety of wartime industries.[20]

The early Japanese experience in the United States mirrored that of the Chinese. When Japanese immigration to California began to increase in the early 1900s, it set off a wave of hysteria. Whites formed the Asiatic Exclusion League, demanding that immigration be stopped. Fears of the "Yellow Peril" were explicitly racial.

With the advent of World War II and the bombing of Pearl Harbor by the Japanese government in 1941, anti-Japanese sentiment once again flourished, particularly on the West Coast. Several months later Congress passed a law that authorized the military to exclude from designated areas any person it deemed to be a threat. Under this law, more than 110,000 Japanese people—

Thousands of Japanese Americans were confined to "relocation camps" during World War II, even though they were American citizens.

two-thirds of them American citizens—were rounded up and sent to "relocation camps." There they were kept for up to three years, deprived of their property, their jobs, and their freedom.

After the war, Japanese Americans began to challenge the laws that restricted their rights in the United States. In 1952 the McCarran-Walter Act finally rescinded the 1790 law allowing only white aliens to become citizens. A later generation of Japanese Americans revived the issue of reparations for those who had been interned during World War II. In 1988 they succeeded in winning passage of a federal law that issued a formal apology and promised a payment of $20,000 to each of the survivors of the camps.

Asian immigration climbed rapidly after the 1965 Immigration Act, which lifted discriminatory quotas on Asian immigration. During the 1980s, 37 percent of new immigrants arrived from a wide range of Asian countries, including the Philippines, China, Korea, and Vietnam. Many Cambodians and Vietnamese entered the country as refugees during these years as well.[21] Asian Americans are widely dispersed throughout the United States, but nearly 40 percent live in California.[22]

The very diversity of national backgrounds among Asian Americans has impeded the development of group-based political power. No one national group dominates among the Asian American population. But in recent years there have been efforts to mobilize a more united Asian American political presence. In 1997 controversy erupted over illegal donations to President Clinton's re-election campaign by a Chinese American named John Huang. Many Asian Americans felt that the attention to this matter unfairly cast suspicion on all Asian Americans who participated in political fund-raising. This experience prompted the formation of several organizations aiming to enhance the power of the Asian vote. In Los Angeles, a group called Vision 21 formed in order to register Asian American voters and to highlight the importance of their vote. In addition, a new effort called the 80/20 initiative was formed to persuade Asian Americans to support the candidate who promises the most to Asian voters. The goal is to have 80 percent of the Asian vote support the candidate who best addresses the interests of Asian Americans. By encouraging Asians to vote as a bloc, the organization hopes to expand group power.[23] Nonetheless, the geographic dispersion of Asian Americans and their diverse backgrounds and experiences raise questions about whether such strategies to build a common interest will succeed.

The Native Americans who occupied Alcatraz Island in 1969 claimed it as Indian property. Their dramatic action brought national attention to the American Indian Movement.

Native Americans Today there are approximately two million Native Americans in the United States. When Europeans first came to North America, the "American Indian" population was estimated at three to seven million. Spread across the continent, they represented several hundred distinct cultural groups or tribes. For the first century after the Founding, the experience of Native Americans with the American government was like that between warring nations. It was a war that the United States government won. For the next hundred years, the relationship was that of a conquered people and their conquerors. Not until the 1960s did a movement representing all tribes assert the rights of Native Americans within the American political system.

The political status of Native Americans was left unclear in the Constitution. But by the early 1800s, the courts had defined each of the Indian tribes as a nation. As members of an Indian nation, Native Americans were declared noncitizens of the United States. The political status of Native Americans changed in 1924, when congressional legislation granted citizenship to those who had been born in the United States. A variety of changes in federal policy toward Native Americans during the 1930s paved the way for a later resurgence of their political power. Most important was the federal decision to encourage Native Americans on reservations to establish local self-government.[24]

The Native American political movement gathered force in the 1960s, as Native Americans began to use protest, litigation, and assertion of tribal rights to improve their situation. In 1968, Dennis Banks cofounded the American Indian Movement (AIM), the most prominent Native American protest organization. AIM won national attention in 1969 when two hundred of its members, representing twenty different tribes, took over the famous prison island of Alcatraz in San Francisco Bay, claiming it for Native Americans. In 1971, AIM members took over the town of Wounded Knee, South Dakota, the site of the last major battle between Native Americans and the U.S. Army, in which a Sioux village had been massacred. The federal government responded to the rise in Indian activism with the Indian Self-Determination and Education Assistance Act, which began to give Indians more control over their own land.[25]

In recent years, Native Americans have used their increasing autonomy to promote economic development on reservations, where deep poverty remains widespread. The biggest moneymaker for reservations has been casino gambling. The Supreme Court paved the way for casino gambling in a 1987 ruling that Indian tribes, as sovereign nations, are exempt from most state gambling regulations. An estimated ninety tribes have opened casinos, which bring in a total income of over $1 billion. They have been able to use the money from gambling to build housing and schools and to establish a base from which to diversify into other forms of economic development. Rather than leasing their lands to non-Indian companies, many tribes are now setting up their own businesses.[26]

IMMIGRATION AND THE AMERICAN POLITICAL COMMUNITY

Immigration raises several questions about our national unity. The first is how many and which immigrants should be allowed in (see the Policy Debate on p. 49). The growing numbers of immigrants have made many Americans uneasy and have prompted calls to restrict immigration. A 1995 poll showed that 65 percent of those questioned believed that immigration levels were too high. When questioned, most Americans pointed to the burden that immigrants place on public services and competition for jobs as the main reasons for limiting immigration.[27] However, some prominent analysts argue that further immigration should be restricted because it changes the racial balance of the country. Peter Brimelow, author of a widely discussed book, argued that "Americans have the right to insist the government stop shifting the racial balance."[28]

A second important issue concerns the rights of noncitizens. The Supreme Court has ruled that illegal immigrants are eligible for education and medical care but can be denied other social benefits; legal immigrants are to be treated much the same as citizens. But growing immigration—including an estimated 300,000 illegal immigrants per year—and mounting economic insecurity have undermined these practices. Groups of voters across the country now strongly support drawing a sharper line between immigrants and citizens. Not surprisingly, the movement to deny benefits to noncitizens began in California, which experienced sharp economic distress in the early 1990s and has the highest levels of immigration of any state. In 1994, Californians voted in favor of Proposition 187, denying illegal immigrants all services except emergency medical care. Supporters of the measure hoped to discourage illegal immigration and to pressure illegal immigrants already in the country to leave. Opponents contended that denying basic services to illegal immigrants risked creating a subclass of residents in the United States whose lack of education and poor health threaten all Americans. In 1994 and in 1997, a federal court declared most of Proposition 187 unconstitutional, affirming previous rulings that illegal immigrants should be granted public education. A booming economy helped to reduce public concern about illegal immigration, but supporters of Proposition 187 promised to reintroduce similar measures in the future.

The question of the rights of legal immigrants poses an even tougher problem. Congress has the power to deny public benefits to this group but doing so would go against long-standing traditions in American political culture. Legal immigrants have traditionally enjoyed most of the rights and obligations (such as paying taxes) of citizens. As constitutional scholar Theodore Bikel points out, the Constitution begins with "We the People of the United States"; likewise the Bill of Rights refers to the rights of *people,* not citizens.[29]

Those who want to retain benefits for legal immigrants and provide some services to illegals worry that we will create a two-tiered society that will hurt all Americans if we deny basic services and traditional social benefits to legal immigrants. They fear that establishing such distinctions simply makes immigrants scapegoats for national economic problems and will make integration of immigrants into American society more difficult. One side effect of the movement to restrict the benefits of immigrants may be to move us back to the higher rates of naturalization that characterized earlier waves of immigration. Unlike the political machines of the 1800s, the Immigration and Naturalization Service has traditionally done little to encourage immigrants to become citizens. But in 1996, the Clinton administration launched Citizenship USA, a

POLICY DEBATE

Should Immigration Be Restricted?

America is a nation of immigrants, yet Americans have always had mixed feelings about who and how many people from other countries should be allowed to become citizens. In the mid-nineteenth century, for example, when millions of Irish immigrants settled in America, their arrival sparked fierce anti-Irish and anti-Catholic sentiment. From 1870 to 1920, more than twenty-six million immigrants came to America. This tide was stemmed by law in 1924. More recently, new tides of Latino and Asian immigrants have spurred pressure to tighten restrictions. In 1996, California passed Proposition 187, which blocked all state assistance to illegal immigrants. In 1997, the federal government imposed new financial support and minimum income requirements on those sponsoring immigrants.

Those who seek to restrict immigration argue that America simply cannot afford to throw open, or even keep open, its gates. Current restrictions do not prevent millions of legal and illegal immigrants from coming to this country. During the 1980s, for example, more than ten million legal and illegal immigrants entered the United States—a record high, eclipsing the nearly nine million immigrants who entered America during the first decade of the twentieth century. A disproportionate number of these newcomers use social services, the educational system, the health care system, and the criminal justice system. The attendant service drain and overall cost places an ever-greater burden on taxpayers, especially in states that receive most new immigrants, including California (whose population has increased by a third in a little more than a decade), Florida, Texas, and New York. Furthermore, immigrants may displace American workers because they are willing to accept lower pay and to work without union protection. The immigrant flood visibly contributes to urban overcrowding and the related problems of energy consumption, waste generation, and environmental degradation. Polls reveal that most Americans favor tougher immigration restrictions.

One remedy, an immigration moratorium, would serve several useful purposes. It would encourage existing immigrant communities to assimilate, a trend that is otherwise impeded by the constant influx of new immigrants. It would allow overburdened public agencies and institutions a chance to improve or rebuild their services. And it would allow for a more measured public dialogue on the future of immigration. Restrictions are a matter of simple necessity, proponents argue, because existing law allows recent immigrants to sponsor family members, who account for a major proportion of the new immigrant population.

Opponents of immigration restriction point out, first, that the stereotypical picture of the illegal, unskilled, crime-prone, welfare-seeking immigrant is a far cry from the actual immigrant population. About three-quarters of all immigrants enter the United States legally. These immigrants are, on average, better-educated and more highly skilled than the average citizens of the countries they leave. While immigrants do provide an important source for manual labor in agriculture and garment work, for example, immigrants also provide critical skills for important industries. California's "Silicon Valley," home to many high-tech industries, relies heavily on skilled immigrant labor. Immigrants also generate jobs. Many Korean immigrants, for example, start small businesses that generate jobs, a significant fact, given that small businesses employ more workers in America than do large businesses.

As for the social service burden imposed by immigrants, this has been exaggerated, according to restriction opponents. According to the 1990 census, 7 percent of foreign-born persons receive social service benefits, compared to 6 percent of native-born citizens and less than 5 percent of illegal immigrants. Much of the opposition to immigration, opponents say, has less to do with economics or crime, and more to do with racial hatred and a generalized fear that new immigrant groups will exert greater political and social influence. But racial and ethnic diversity ought not be feared. Instead, new cultures should be celebrated and embraced precisely for the differences they bring.

program to speed up the naturalization process for immigrants, some of whom had been waiting for two years to become citizens. As a result of the program the number of new citizens each year more than doubled. The program drew critics, however, who charged that the citizenship drive was an effort by Democrats to attract immigrant votes. Moreover, congressional investigators found that in the effort to register so many new citizens so fast, improper screening may have allowed unqualified people, including those with criminal backgrounds, to become citizens.[30]

A final issue concerns the assimilation of immigrants into American culture. Many Americans now worry that immigrants are not assimilating into the broader culture. Such fears have given rise to the "English only" movement, which seeks to prevent public services from offering assistance in languages other than English and to allow voter ballots only in English. Fear that immigrants are not assimilating also underlies many calls to restrict immigration. Despite the growing visibility of distinctive immigrant cultures and languages as immigration has increased, there is no evidence that today's immigrants are any less likely to assimilate than those of earlier generations. A 1995 poll found that 59 percent of immigrants questioned believed they should blend into American society even if it means giving up some of their own culture.[31] Evidence suggests that today's second- and third-generation immigrants are in fact learning English and becoming Americanized.[32]

The debate about immigration today reflects both older themes and new concerns. Fears about the ethnic composition of the new immigrants echo sentiments from the nineteenth century, as do efforts to ensure that immigrants are assimilated. Yet changes in the past one hundred years pose new questions about immigration: with the frontier gone and major cities struggling, can we afford to welcome new immigrants, especially those with few resources? What are the implications for American democracy if identifiably different groups have unequal access to public resources?

Students and Politics

Although California's Proposition 187 passed by a wide margin in a 1994 referendum, many students and faculty members expressed concern that the initiative would unfairly hinder minorities from receiving an equal education. The initiative, which would have forced beneficiaries of public assistance, grants, or medical coverage to provide documentation of their citizenship, contained a clause covering public education: "Commencing with the first term or semester . . . each public postsecondary educational institution shall verify the status of each person enrolled. . . ." Some opponents worried that minority students would be singled out for inspection based on their ethnicity. Protest against the initiative was widespread on campuses across the state. Students at California State University, Chico, led by Student Body President Oscar de la Torre, gathered approximately 2,000 signatures protesting the implementation of Proposition 187 at their university.* At Irvine Valley College, faculty and 300 students gathered to protest the law, saying that it played on the public's paranoia about immigrants. "We want to change the way people look at immigration," said student Angel Cervantes, leader of the Four Winds Student Movement, an organization devoted to fighting the proposition. "This is more of a human rights issue than a legal issue."† Students at the rally circulated a petition of noncompliance with the law.

A federal judge declared part of Proposition 187 unconstitutional in 1998, including the clause dealing with higher education.

*"CSU won't enforce Proposition 187," *Orion*, Wednesday, November 30, 1998.

†"Educators, Students Hammer Proposition 187 at 'Teach-In'," *Los Angeles Times*, November 23, 1994.

CLASS

If asked what economic class they belong to, most Americans reply that they are in the middle class. The relative weakness of class in the United States stems in part from the American ideals of equality and individual liberty. But it is also a product of the American political system. For it is not just values but also the experiences—both positive and negative—of workers with the American political system that have prevented class from becoming a significant category of political action in the United States.

STUDENT DEBATE

Should Immigration Be Restricted?

Yes

Of the many issues facing America and our economy, immigration should not be overlooked. In its present form, immigration, both legal and illegal, continues to harm—rather than help—our country. The crisis does not stem from the immigrants' ethnicity, but from their sheer numbers.

Every year, about one million people immigrate into our nation—a number rivaling the last great wave of immigrants around the turn of the century. The first wave began in the 1840's and lasted until right before the Civil War. During that period, millions of Northern Europeans, Irish and Germans made the long voyage to the New World. A large influx of Eastern and Southern Europeans followed, from around 1900 until World War I. For the next 40 years, the nation kept its immigration levels low. In 1965, a new law opened America's doors to people worldwide. Since then, a steadily growing number of immigrants from Asia, Africa and Latin America have come to our nation's shores to find better lives. But now, it's time to again reduce the number of immigrants to reasonable levels.

The rationale for this change is grounded in economics, not racism. In 1994, a four-year college grad made only slightly more than a high school grad did in 1973. Last year, *The Wall Street Journal* reported that 40 percent of math jobs in 1996 went to immigrants, mostly Russian and Chinese. The unemployment rate among math Ph.Ds is now five times higher than it was just a few years ago. These problems can be partly attributed to the abundance of labor created by our open immigration policy.

Too many workers and too few jobs result in falling wages and weakening bargaining power for workers. Proponents of massive immigration argue immigrants take jobs Americans don't want. This is misleading. Americans would take these menial jobs if they paid more. If the immigrants didn't take the jobs, employers would have two options—either raise wages to an acceptable level or find innovative ways to complete the jobs without human labor. The first option raises wages, and the second increases productivity; both benefit society. But, in the short term, it's cheaper for employers to exploit immigrant labor. Wages stagnate and fall. Productivity stalls.

This effect would occur regardless of immigrants' ethnicity—people from poor, third-world countries will work for remarkably little. But it's arguable that if these industrious immigrants stayed put, they could make their own countries prosperous. The countries these immigrants come from—Mexico, Vietnam, Zaire—are not barren of resources or wealth. They simply lack the political organization to demand a more equitable distribution of jobs and capital that leads to a higher standard of living.

Historically, immigrants have become the scapegoats for many cultures' problems. Yet we should not let that obscure the very real and devastating effect massive immigration has on jobs and wages. The answer is not to hate immigrants, but to limit their number to reasonable levels. Keeping the number of immigrants who come into our country equal to the number of people who leave our country each year—about 200,000—would provide a better situation for all.

SOURCE: Donyel McCollister, "Massive Immigration Lowers Wages," *Daily Texan* (University of Texas-Austin), April 1, 1997.

No

Does anyone out there remember having to memorize the preamble of the Constitution in order to pass eighth grade? I know I do. That was probably the hardest test of what it means to be American ever given to me.

I think I'm one among many who simply stored that sort of information in their short-term memories so they could pass the history tests and move on. I'm openly admitting my ignorance. However, I also plan to educate myself.

My parents were privileged because they came here when educational and career opportunities were offered to them and not because they were escaping a bad situation in their country of origin. I have a different experience from other people who were born here because I'm first-generation American, but like many people I know, I have taken for granted the fact that I have never had to prove myself as an American citizen.

Ever since I had to help my grandparents go through the process of naturalization in the last year, I've decided it's crucial to appreciate all that comes with my citizenship.

I was shocked when I saw how much historical knowledge they had to know in such a short amount of time. Imagine having to learn eight years of history in a month's time. Now imagine having to be tested on that history in another language in which you're not very fluent. There is a written test, a diction test and an oral test. Although naturalization regulations are supposed to give exceptions for people 65 years and older, they are still given oral exams, which ask a long list of questions about their political involvement and their moral character. Some of the moral questions were "Are you a drunkard?" "A polygamist?" "A gambler?" Some of the questions were ridiculous. In a twisted way, they reminded me of the beliefs in eugenics during World War II which consisted of compulsory immigration laws for immigrants who were believed to have "bad moral genes" that they were likely to pass down to their children. All in all, if the same questions being asked to immigrants were asked to American-born citizens, plenty of people would probably be deported.

However, the hardest part of the naturalization process wasn't even the exam but the long and frustrating lines in the immigration office, the fingerprinting, the endless paperwork, the money spent on fees and trying to get any sort of help from the overworked and rude government employees who, in most cases, only speak English.

Then the wait for the letter telling you when you are scheduled to be tested, which may take months or even a year. From there, it's time to study. If there is even the slightest discrepancy in the forms or the information given, you have to start the whole process again—from the beginning. I don't know how anyone applying for citizenship these days would feel at all welcome in this country.

* * *

Yet these people, whose sweat and whose tears have been so beneficial for our country and who do not benefit from their own work, get kicked in the face with things such as Proposition 187, whose function was to deny health care to illegal alien children and other laws attempting to deny a public education to alien children. Often they do not have health insurance and must be treated at clinics, which are often, and sadly, unsanitary and overcrowded. When people come here with no resources at all, they are blatantly exploited by companies that are more than willing to take advantage of the fact that these immigrants speak little or no English, have little or no education and have no rights since they are not American citizens.

* * *

Our history started with pilgrims who were escaping religious and political persecution. The pilgrims of today are the immigrants who come to the United States—whether legally or even illegally because they are so desperate to improve the condition of their lives. It is sad to see that the United States closes [its borders] because it claims we don't have enough resources to share with everybody. Yet we take and we take and we take, and when we don't need anymore, we throw it away.

SOURCE: Katherinne Bardales, "Where Have All the Pilgrims Gone?" *Daily Illini* (University of Illinois), November 20, 1998.

The 1886 convention of the Knights of Labor. The organization accepted large numbers of black and female workers as members.

A glance at American history shows that there were times when class organization was very important. In the early years of the Republic, workers—mainly skilled artisans—formed political parties in more than sixty cities and towns. They demanded the ten-hour workday, free public schooling, and democratic political reforms. After the Civil War, the Knights of Labor became the first mass organization of the working class. In the 1880s, local elections featured Knights of Labor political tickets in more than two hundred state and local elections. Fueling this political activity was deep discontent with the emergence of big corporations, the factory system, and the degradation of work in general. In addition, deep economic depressions in the 1870s threw people out of work in unprecedented numbers. These conditions lay behind the massive labor strikes in the late nineteenth century. In fact, it is often forgotten that the United States has the most violent labor history of any industrialized nation.

If we look at the demands these workers made, we see that they were very much in tune with the key values of a thriving democracy. In fact, workers often drew on these values to support their positions. For example, workers assailed the emergence of the large corporation as antidemocratic. They defended a shorter working day and adequate wages as essential for workers to exercise the rights and responsibilities of citizenship. They argued that workers needed time to spend with their families and to attend public lectures. Labor organizations at this time had quite a broad notion of who was a member of the working class; for example, anyone except a capitalist or a lawyer could become a member of the Knights of Labor.[33]

Despite all this working-class activity, workers' parties never managed to last in the United States, and national politics did not organize along class lines. The American Federation of Labor (AFL), the largest labor federation to survive into the twentieth century, turned its back on politics. Instead of formally aligning with a political party, the AFL remained aloof from politics and instead practiced "business unionism"—it would fight for workers' rights but it would not enter the political arena to do so.

The closest Americans have come to having a class-based politics in this century was during the New Deal of the 1930s. President Franklin Roosevelt changed American politics with legislation that assisted workers and their families: work relief, the Social Security Act, and the right to organize labor unions, for instance. Roosevelt used explicit class imagery to retain the political support of working-class voters and spoke of the need to equalize the distribution of wealth in the United States. His policies cemented working-class support for the Democratic Party, and the Republican Party became increasingly identified with business interests. These divisions were by no means absolute, however. The Democratic Party had plenty of supporters in the business community. Furthermore, the southern attachment to the Democratic Party had little to do with class; it was based more on the Democratic Party's refusal to challenge the political and economic inequality of blacks in the South. This loose class alignment characterized American politics until the 1960s, when racial and cultural divisions, along with a growing distrust of all politicians, began to diminish the expression of class in politics.

What are the prospects of reviving a class orientation in politics today? If we simply look at what Americans say about class, it does not look promising. Polls show that 93 percent of all Americans identify themselves as middle class; only 1 percent say they are in the upper class.[34] Nonetheless, some analysts argue that trends in the distribution of income and wealth over the past two decades have laid the groundwork for class politics. Since 1970, while incomes in the United States have remained stagnant, inequality has grown (see Figure 2.2). In fact, the United States has the greatest inequality in income and

INCOME INEQUALITY IN THE UNITED STATES, 1970–97 **Figure 2.2**

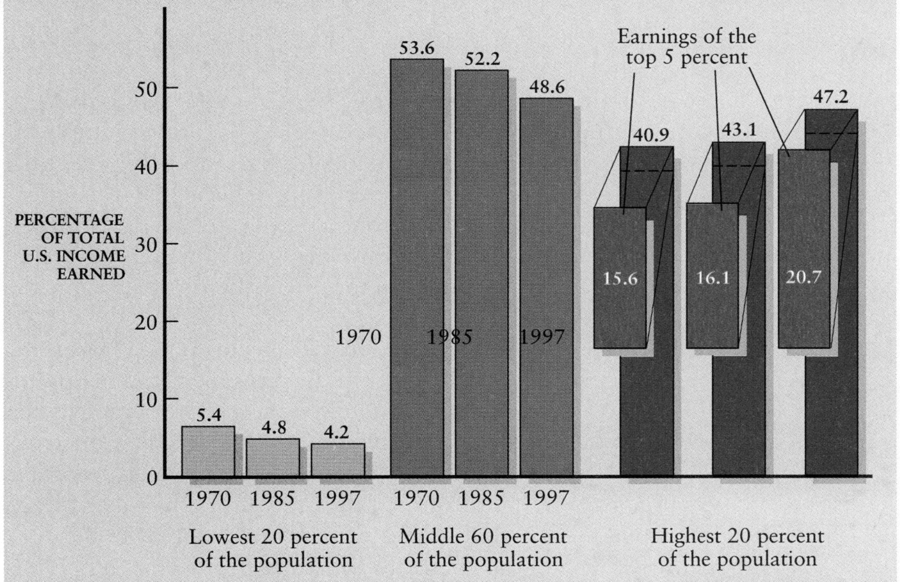

SOURCE: U.S. Bureau of the Census, *Statistical Abstract of the United States 1999* (Washington, DC: Government Printing Office, 1999), p. 479.

Over the last thirty years, America's lower and middle classes have been growing relatively poorer, while the upper classes have been growing wealthier. In 1997, the top 5 percent of the population took home more than 20 percent of the income in the United States.

wealth of any industrial nation.[35] In recent years, Democratic candidates have sought to highlight these realities to revive a politics of class. But, aware of the weakness of class identity in the United States, they embrace only a loose definition of class. For example, Democrats attacked the tax policies of Presidents Ronald Reagan and George Bush as unfair to middle-class Americans. Republicans reject these arguments, however, saying that their policies create economic growth, which benefits all Americans. Thus, Republicans claim, there is a shared interest across classes, not opposing interests. Republicans also charge that class appeals are un-American. For example, President Bush defended himself against Democratic attacks by remarking that class is "for European democracies or something else—it isn't for the United States of America. We are not going to be divided by class."[36]

The recent Democratic efforts reveal the difficulty of trying to organize politics around class. Since most people feel they are in the middle class, Democrats face the challenge of deciding how and where to draw the line between the middle class and the rich. Moreover, the impact of the new inequality has been especially felt by the poor; assisting them requires taxing the upper end of the middle class. Yet upper-middle-class taxpayers participate the most and are the most vocal in American politics. They mounted such vigorous opposition to the income tax increase signed by President Bill Clinton in 1993 that most Americans ended up thinking that their taxes had been raised, when in fact the increase affected only those at the very top of the income distribution.

Democrats also face another problem: to win support from voters on the lower half of the income spectrum, Democrats have to show that they can enact policies that will reduce economic inequality. With an electorate deeply mistrustful of politicians, this is a tall order. Nonetheless, even in times of economic prosperity, public concern about jobs and income suggests that politicians will continue to invoke the themes of class.

GENDER

Until 1920, electoral politics was a decidedly masculine world. Not only were women barred from voting in national politics, but electoral politics was closely tied to such male social institutions as lodges, bars, and clubs. Yet the exclusion of women from this political world did not prevent them from engaging in public life. Instead, women carved out a "separate sphere" for their public activities. Emphasizing female stewardship over the moral realm, women became important voices in social reform well before they won the right to vote.[37]

Women played leading roles in two key groundswells of social reform: the abolitionist movement prior to the Civil War and the movement against political corruption and urban social squalor beginning in the 1880s. Some women pressed for the right to vote immediately after the Civil War, when male ex-slaves won the franchise. Politicians in both parties rejected women's suffrage as disruptive and unrealistic. Barred from voting, women found other means of participating in public life. For one thing, they formed their own clubs; as the nineteenth century ended, the General Federation of Women's Clubs boasted 495 affiliates throughout the country. These clubs provided female fellowship, but they also sought to bring women's distinctive perspectives into the public sphere. Women, they believed, had a special mission to bring morality into public life. Thus, women fought to prohibit alcohol consumption through the Woman's Christian Temperance Union; worked in urban charity organizations; sought to abolish child labor and to establish laws protecting public health; and led movements to reform education and schools in cities across the country.

At the same time, women began organizing to win the right to vote. Women formally started to press for the vote in 1867 when a state referendum to give women the vote in Kansas failed. Scattered efforts over the next decades took organizational form when the National American Woman Suffrage Association (NAWSA) formed in 1890. Many states granted women the right to vote before the national government did; Western states with less-entrenched political systems opened politics to women earliest. When Wyoming became a state in 1890, it was the first state to grant full suffrage to women. Colorado, Utah, and Idaho all followed suit in the next several years. Suffrage organizations grew—NAWSA claimed two million members by 1917—and staged mass meetings, parades, petitions, and protests. NAWSA organized state-by-state efforts to win the right to vote. A more militant group, the National Woman's Party, staged pickets and got arrested in front of the White House to protest President Wilson's opposition to a constitutional amendment granting women the right to vote. Finally in 1920, the Nineteenth Amendment was ratified, guaranteeing women the right to vote.

The consequences of gaining the vote proved disappointing, however, especially to feminists, who wanted equality between men and women. The earliest advocates of women's rights had favored equality in all spheres of life. By contrast, the mainstream of the suffrage movement stressed "women's special

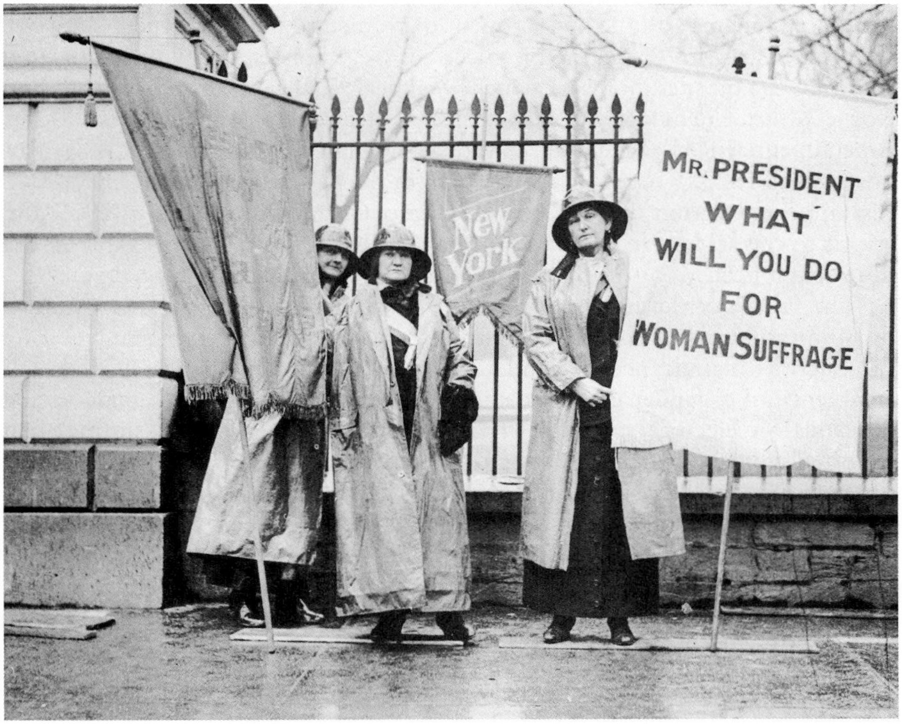

Suffragettes on the sidewalk in front of the White House in 1920. That year, after decades of political mobilization and state-level victories, women won a constitutional amendment guaranteeing them the right to vote.

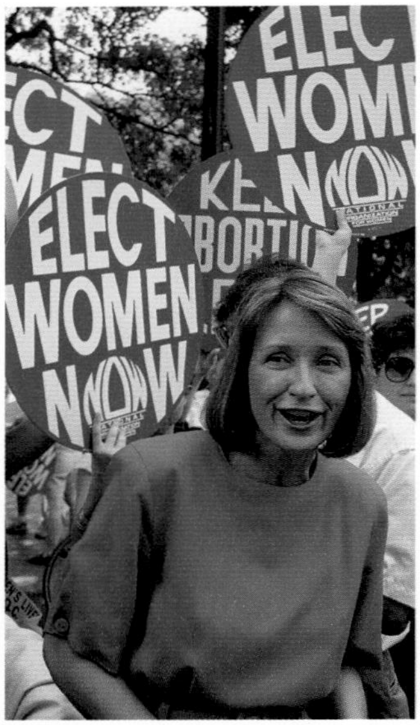

Patricia Ireland, president of the National Organization for Women (NOW), leads a women's rights demonstration in Washington, D.C. NOW is one of many women's rights organizations that seek to increase the number of women in elected office

sphere"—the realm of morality, social reform, and family. Politics proved somewhat more amenable to the latter vision because it accorded better with widely held cultural beliefs. The idea of a separate women's sphere also built on institutions and initiatives that had begun before women had the vote. For example, Democrats responded to the women's vote by establishing the Women's Bureau within the Labor Department. Once granted the franchise, however, women did not vote as a group, and many of them did not vote at all. Thus, hopes that women would achieve equality through the vote or that their votes would make some distinctive impact on politics diminished. In this context, the National Woman's Party's legislation for an Equal Rights Amendment stood little chance of success when it was submitted to Congress in 1923. Even legislation premised on women's "special sphere"—such as maternal and child health care reform—was abandoned by the end of the 1920s. Not until the 1960s did a broad movement for women's equality reemerge. The initial impetus for its revival was growing concern about inequality in the world of work.

Armed with new legal tools that outlawed discrimination in employment and wages, women formed a set of organizations dedicated to fight for equality for women in many different spheres. Among the new organizations were the National Organization for Women (NOW), the Women's Equity Action League (WEAL), and the National Women's Political Caucus (NWPC). NOW used protest tactics to combat the unequal treatment of women. It picketed the Equal Employment Opportunity Commission for refusing to ban sex-segregated employment ads and filed charges against *The New York Times* for publishing such ads. WEAL focused on legal action around a wide range of sex discrimination issues, including lawsuits against law and medical schools for discriminatory admissions policies. The NWPC promoted the election of female candidates and the appointment of women to political office.

By the early 1970s, legislative successes were bolstered by important legal victories, the most stunning of which was the 1973 legalization of abortion in *Roe v. Wade*. The movement next turned its efforts to passing an Equal Rights Amendment (ERA), which the National Woman's Party had regularly proposed since 1923. Buoyed by the strength of the new women's movement, success appeared within reach. Congress approved the amendment in 1972 and sent it to the states for ratification. But the ERA fell three states short of the thirty-eight needed for ratification and, by 1982, it was dead.

The failure of the ERA was a defeat for the feminist organizations, but it by no means marked the end of gender politics. Three developments indicate the ongoing significance of gender issues in American politics. First is the emergence of a **gender gap**—a distinctive pattern of male and female voting decisions—in electoral politics. Although proponents of women's suffrage had expected women to make a distinctive impact on politics as soon as they won the vote, not until the 1980s did voting patterns reveal a clear difference between male and female votes. In 1980, men voted heavily for Republican candidate Ronald Reagan; women divided their votes between Reagan and the incumbent Democratic president, Jimmy Carter. Since that election, gender differences have emerged in congressional and state elections, as well. Women tend to vote in higher numbers for Democratic candidates, while Republicans win more male votes. Behind these voting patterns are differing assessments of

gender gap

a distinctive pattern of voting behavior reflecting the differences in views between men and women key policy issues. For one thing, more women than men take liberal positions on political issues; women are more likely than men to oppose military activities and support social spending. For example, 54 percent of women approved of the U.S. decision to send troops to Saudi Arabia in 1991, compared to 78 percent of men. On social spending, these trends reverse: 69 percent of women favor increased spending on Social Security, compared to 57 percent of men; 83 percent of women favor improving the nation's health care, compared to 76 percent of men; 72 percent of women advocate more spending on programs for the homeless, compared to 63 percent of men.[38] It is important to note that these differences do not mean that all women vote more liberally than all men. In fact, the voting differences between women who are homemakers and women who are in the workforce are almost as large as the differences between men and women. The sharpest differences are found between married men and single women, with single women tending to take the most liberal positions.[39]

The second key development in gender politics in recent years is the growing number of women in political office (see Figure 2.3). Journalists dubbed 1992 the "Year of the Woman" because so many women were elected to Con-

INCREASE IN NUMBER OF WOMEN IN ELECTIVE OFFICE, 1975–97 **Figure 2.3**

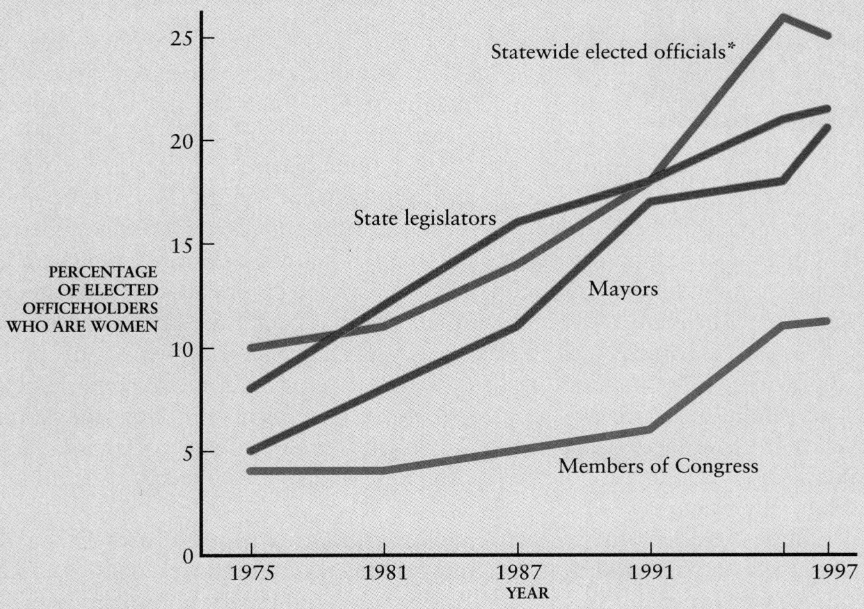

*Governors, attorneys general, etc.

SOURCE: Cynthia Costello, Shari Miles, and Anne J. Stone, eds., *The American Woman, 1999–2000* (New York: W. W. Norton, 1998), p. 361.

Students and Politics

California's 1996 battle over Proposition 209, which outlawed affirmative action programs in state and local governments, created a firestorm of debate on campuses across the state. The National Organization for Women (NOW) began several grassroots campaigns to defeat the measure, including at the Claremont Colleges near Los Angeles. Students there made a big effort to get out the vote, organizing marches on the campuses and in the community. A speech by NOW president Patricia Ireland helped spark the movement. Despite the passage of Proposition 209, the students' efforts helped to form the Action Coalition of the Claremont Colleges, a progressive alliance. NOW's intervention and assistance provided a cohesion that had not existed before the election. "The 209 campaign is really what clicked for us," said Amy Drayer, copresident of Scripps NOW. "It is the issue that mobilized our efforts." NOW Action Vice President Rosemary Dempsey agreed: "This kind of organizing doesn't have to focus only on major elections, like the presidential election," she said. "Campus organizing is an effective tool for any kind of issue, particularly issues NOW focuses on, like affirmative action, reproductive rights, and fighting racism."

gress: women doubled their numbers in the House and tripled them in the Senate. By 2000 women held 12.9 percent of the seats in the House of Representatives and 9 percent in the Senate; 22.5 percent of state legislators in 2000 were women.[40] Organizations supporting female candidates have worked to encourage more women to run for office and have supported them financially. In addition to the bipartisan NWPC, the Women's Campaign Fund and EMILY's List provide pro-choice Democratic women with early campaign financing, which is critical to establishing electoral momentum (the acronym of the latter group stands for Early Money Is Like Yeast). Recent research has shown that the key to increasing the numbers of women in political office is to encourage more women to run for election. Women are disadvantaged as candidates not because they are women but because male candidates are more likely to have the advantage of incumbency.[41] Although women in public office by no means take uniform positions on policy issues, surveys show that, on the whole, women legislators are more supportive of women's rights, health care spending, and children's and family issues.[42]

The third way in which women affect politics today is through the continuing salience of policy issues of special concern to women. Before the women's movement, many issues of deep concern to women were simply not on the political agenda. Today, however, issues such as abortion, sexual harassment, and comparable worth, and the concerns of families and children are often central to political debate. In 1991 the issue of sexual harassment burst into public consciousness when University of Oklahoma law professor Anita Hill accused Supreme Court nominee Clarence Thomas of sexual harassment. As Figure 2.4 shows, the number of sexual harassment complaints rose sharply after the hearings. The spectacle of the hearings—in which an all-male Senate Judiciary Committee harshly questioned Hill—also galvanized many women politically. In the words of pollster Celinda Lake, "Anita Hill has become a metaphor for something a lot broader than sexual harassment. She has become a symbol for a system that's failed, that's become distorted and out of touch."[43] The salience of sexual harassment and abortion as political issues contributed to the electoral gains of female candidates in 1992.

Since the 1960s the women's movement has helped to transform the place of women in society and the economy, it has brought unprecedented numbers of women into public office, and it has altered the national political agenda. Although women's opinions diverge widely on many political issues, the emergence of a gender gap in voting and the growing numbers of women in political office ensure that gender issues will continue to influence American politics.

INCREASE IN SEXUAL HARASSMENT COMPLAINTS IN THE UNITED STATES, 1990–99 Figure 2.4

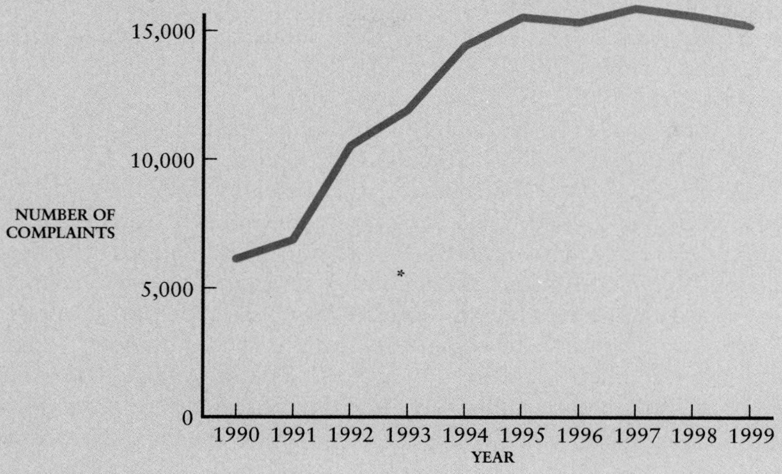

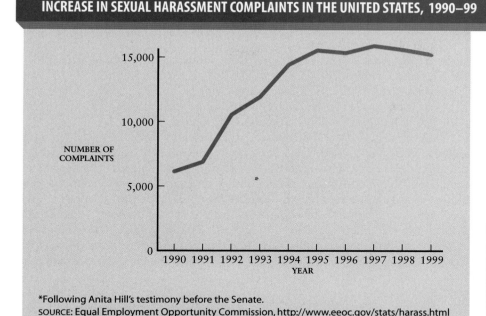

*Following Anita Hill's testimony before the Senate.
SOURCE: Equal Employment Opportunity Commission, http://www.eeoc.gov/stats/harass.html

The number of sexual harassment complaints reported to the Equal Employment Opportunity Commission has increased dramatically since the early 1990s.

RELIGION

Religion has always played an important role in American politics and public life. Religious freedom was a central tenet of the new nation. The people who first settled the American colonies sought the freedom to practice their religious beliefs. The central role that religion played in their lives made it likely that religious beliefs would spill over into politics and debates about how to organize public life. Thus, despite the formal separation of church and state established by the Constitution, religious groups have regularly entered the political arena, often provoking heated debate about the proper role of government in enforcing moral values and in protecting the personal freedoms of those with different values.

Religion continues to play an important role in American life. For some people, religious groups provide an organizational infrastructure for participating in politics around issues of special group concern. Black churches, for example, were instrumental in the civil rights movement, and black religious leaders continue to play important roles in national and local politics. Jews have also been active as a group in politics, but less through religious bodies than through a variety of social action agencies. Such agencies include the American Jewish Congress, the Anti-Defamation League, and the American Jewish Committee.

For most of American history, religious values have been woven deeply into the fabric of public life. Public school students began the day with prayers or Bible reading; city halls displayed crèches during the Christmas season. Practices that were religiously proscribed—most notably abortion—were also forbidden under law. But over the past thirty-five years, a variety of court decisions greatly reduced this kind of religious influence on public life. In 1962, the Supreme Court ruled in *Engel v. Vitale* that prayer in public schools was unconstitutional—that government should not be in the business of sponsoring official prayers. Bible reading was prohibited the following year. By 1973, with *Roe v. Wade,* the Court had made abortion legal.[44]

These decisions drew the condemnation of many Catholic and Protestant leaders. They also helped to spawn a countermovement of religious activists seeking to roll back these decisions and to find a renewed role for religion in public life. The mobilization of religious organizations and other groups that aim to reintroduce their view of morality into public life has been one of the most significant political developments of the past two decades. Some of the most divisive conflicts in politics today, such as that over abortion, hinge on differences over religious and moral issues. These divisions have become so significant and so broad that they now constitute a major clash of cultures with repercussions throughout the political system and across many different areas of policy.

'96 Christian Coalition
VOTER GUIDE
NEW YORK
U.S. Congress, District 19
Republican & Conservative Primary Election

Joe DioGuardi	ISSUES	Sue Kelly
Supports	Balanced Budget Amendment	Supports
Opposes	Abortion on Demand	Supports
Opposes	Taxpayer Funding of Abortion	Supports
Supports	Partial-Birth Abortion Ban	Opposes
Opposes	Federal Funding of Planned Parenthood	Supports
Supports	Religious Freedom Amendment	Undecided
Supports	Abolish the National Endowment for the Arts	Opposes
Supports	Reverse "Don't Ask, Don't Tell" Gays in Military Policy	Undecided
Supports	Abolish the Legal Services Corporation	Opposes
Supports	Term Limits for Congress	Supports

*Each candidate was sent a 1996 Federal Issues Survey by certified mail or facsimile machine. When possible, positions of candidates on issues were verified or determined using voting records and/or public statements.

Paid for and authorized by the Christian Coalition, Post Office Box 1990; Chesapeake, Virginia 23327-1990. The Christian Coalition is a pro-family citizen action organization. This voter guide is provided for educational purposes only and is not to be construed as an endorsement of any candidate or political party.

★ Vote on September 10 ★

Religious organizations have emerged as a strong influence on voters' choices concerning issues and candidates. The Christian Coalition produces voter guides for every state and distributes them by the millions each election year.

Politically, one of the most significant elements of this new politics has been the mobilization of evangelical Protestants into a cohesive and politically shrewd organization aligned with the Republican Party. The Moral Majority, the first broad political organization of evangelical Christians, showed its political muscle in the 1980 election, when it aligned with the Republican Party, eventually backing Ronald Reagan for president. Over the next few years, evangelicals strengthened their movement by registering voters and mobilizing them with sophisticated, state-of-the-art political techniques. Their success was evident in the 1984 election, when 80 percent of evangelical Christian voters cast their ballots for Reagan. The 1988 election was a turning point in the political development of the Christian Right. Televangelist Pat Robertson ran for president and, although his candidacy was unsuccessful, his effort laid the groundwork for future political strength. Robertson's supporters gained control of some state Republican parties and won positions of power in others. With this new organizational base and sharply honed political skills, Robertson formed a new organization, the Christian Coalition. This organization has become one of the most important groups in American politics today because of its ability to reach and mobilize a large grassroots base. It is now part of a growing number of loosely connected organizations dedicated to similar goals.[45]

The rise of the Christian Coalition has raised important challenges for both political parties. Republicans, who have benefited enormously from their alliance with this new political base, face the dilemma of retaining the support of the Christian Right without losing more moderate voters. Democrats, in turn, face the challenge of holding on to their liberal base while at the same time acknowledging the widespread fears of social and moral decay so successfully raised by the Christian Right. The sophisticated organization of the Christian Right and the deep divisions among the American people on a range of cultural concerns ensure that such issues will have a prominent place in future politics.

Participation in the American Political Community: The Citizen's Role

As we have seen, the American political community has become much more diverse than it was at the nation's founding. Yet the active participation of all citizens is needed to ensure that our politics accurately reflect this diversity. Without such participation, politics may reflect only the values and interests of a part of the American political community. And in recent years, concern has mounted that our political institutions do not help ensure that all Americans participate.

What can ordinary citizens do to make politics fit their vision of what liberty, equality, and democracy should mean today? Some people answer this question with a defeated cynicism that says not much can be done through the political system. Others express an enthusiasm for participation that is often unrealistic and pays little attention to the question of what constitutes effective participation. Our view of the citizen's role in politics highlights the importance of knowledge, not just about the workings of government but about how politics and policy affect *you*. It also stresses the importance of learning how to be politically effective. What can students do to learn both about how actions of the government affect them and about how to be effective themselves?

The road to knowledge can be a rocky one because it is often hard to know how government is affecting you or how its current policies may affect you in the future. The challenge of identifying your interests among all the different things that government does requires a critical stance toward information. This means being focused enough to sift through the mountain of information easily available today; it also means asking where information is coming from. Is the information really an effort to instill in you one view of the world and to convince you about what your interests are? There is nothing wrong with that, but it is important to know if that is what is going on. For example, the Concord Coalition, which argues that controlling federal spending is the biggest problem facing the country, has sought to publicize this particular view among students, arguing that they will be stuck paying off the debt of the country if spending is not dramatically curbed. Yet an alternative view argues that the debt is not such a big problem and that it is most important to use public resources today to build a productive and educated workforce for the future. From this perspective, cutting spending is a false economy that may actually harm us in the future. To make sense of such divergent views requires a perspective that welcomes debate and looks for connections among issues that may not be apparent at first glance. But the judgment about the right answer is up to the individual.

In Chapter 1, we stressed that most people approach the political system from a perspective of self-interest. This does not mean that they care only about themselves but rather that they want politics to address the things they care about. People may care passionately about things that will not fatten their own wallets but that might push the world a little closer to their vision of how things should be. Most people, in fact, care about both their wallets and their

Politics on the Web

The Internet could contribute to American democracy by expanding the avenues of political communication and participation available to underrepresented segments of the population. Various interest groups representing minority populations, such as the National Association for the Advancement of Colored People, can use the Internet to present information about themselves and their aims, and to recruit members and solicit contributions on-line. Moreover, racial, ethnic, and religious minorities can use the Internet to disseminate their own perspectives on political events, providing a vast array of alternatives to the "mainstream" view.

However, these hopeful predictions rest on a much more equal distribution of Internet access than currently exists in America. Right now, whites use the Internet more than blacks and Latinos, men more than women, the rich more than the poor, the young more than the old. Only as these disparities lessen will the Internet realize its full potential as an equalizing force in American politics.

www.wwnorton.com/wtp3e

visions of the world. This double orientation is evident, for example, in the activities of the United States Student Association (USSA), the oldest national organization of students. Among its central goals, the USSA seeks to increase the maximum Pell grant to help pay college expenses. The organization also pushes to boost funding for GEAR UP, an early-intervention/mentorship program for low-income youth. The ability to identify your own political interests and to locate organizations working toward those interests that you can join is a key component of political knowledge.

Many students do want to be engaged with issues that concern them but they—like many other Americans—simply are not that interested in politics. In a 1997 survey a large majority of freshmen—72 percent—revealed that they had performed volunteer work in the past year, 10 percent more than in 1989. At the same time, however, only about 30 percent said they considered it "very important" to keep up with current events.[46] How does such volunteer activity connect to more political forms of civic engagement? Is it a substitute for politics or does it help people become more politically active? Supporters of "service learning," which engages students in public-service volunteer activities as part of their curriculum, argue that learning firsthand about diverse people and problems prepares students to be better citizens. Some supporters argue that through such volunteer activities, students may be drawn into politics, as they learn about how political decisions affect such issues as care for the elderly, homelessness, or public education. By itself, however, service learning is not likely to help students understand how politics affects their volunteer activities or to draw them into politics. Such connections are often not obvious and it is not easy to see how an individual can affect a political issue. Service learning must be combined with attention to politics and with information about how politics affects a variety of social issues.[47]

STUDENTS AND POLITICS

As a freshman, University of Pennsylvania student Noah Bilenker arrived on campus with an urge to help the homeless in West Philadelphia. Through his fraternity, he contacted a local soup kitchen and offered to set up tables and clean once each week. "I felt guilty seeing homeless people on the street," he says. "But I was told never to give them money, and with good reason. So I started working with the soup kitchen." As time passed, Bilenker also began to participate in student government, and he realized that the University of Pennsylvania, as the largest employer in Philadelphia, could also serve as a resource to the community in dealing on a much larger scale with some of the problems that he had encountered. During his junior year, Bilenker joined the 40th Street Committee, an organization of students, administration, and faculty that planned ways that the university could aid the surrounding areas, such as helping with soup kitchens. After he graduates, Bilenker plans to continue with both community service and political activism. "I want to continue to do both," he says. "With community [service], you can see a more immediate impact, but politics gives bigger results."[48]

An important lesson of civic education is that it is possible to be effective. At a minimum, effectiveness requires developing basic skills, including how to find information, how to bring people together, how to run meetings, how to speak publicly, and how to express your views in writing. Such skills do not guarantee political success, but it is certain that you cannot be politically successful without them.

AMERICAN DEMOCRACY IN COMPARATIVE PERSPECTIVE

Contrasting Types of Democracy

One of the most crucial challenges to a democratic society is the need to forge a balance between the instinct to be inclusive, that is, to design government institutions so as to include as many voices as possible in decisions, and the competing instinct to be exclusive, that is, to design institutions so as to exclude as many voices as possible. This challenge becomes all the more real when a society is heterogeneous, with a diversity of races, ethnicities, religious affiliations, and linguistic groups, and when historical conflicts over issues such as wealth and socioeconomic status divide the population.

In Chapter 1, we placed the American democracy into a comparative context by briefly surveying the range and extent of civil liberties and political rights among nations of the world. Another important question to consider is how American institutions of government are contoured to accommodate a community of diverse social interests. In other words, what are the broader institutional patterns in America that balance inclusiveness and exclusiveness in government decisions, and how do these compare to other democracies?

One of the leading students of democracy, Arend Lijphart, has developed and refined a classification scheme for democracies with this challenge of inclusion an exclusion in clear focus. His scheme distinguishes between two broader types of democratic governments: those that are predominately majoritarian in nature, and those that are predominately consensual in nature. In fact, among the freest democracies of the world today, none exhibits a "pure" form of either majoritarian or consensual institutional patterns.

All democracies reflect a mix or blend of traditions, yet, there are clear differences among countries with respect to this blend. Majoritarian democracies tend to reflect a preference for restricting the amount of voices and interests that may actively involve themselves in shaping the policy agenda. Their institutions tend to make it more difficult for groups to have an immediate impact on decision making. Consensual democracies, on the other hand, reflect a preference for including a wide array of voices and interests in the policy agenda process. Their institutions tend to provide many different ways for groups to have an immediate impact on decision making. The United Kingdom, New Zealand, and to a lesser extent France and Greece are examples of contemporary majoritarian democracies. Switzerland, Austria, India, Germany, the United States, Australia, and Canada are examples of predominately consensual democracies. Belgium, Denmark, Israel, Sweden, Italy, the Netherlands, Ireland, Japan, Colombia, Venezuela, Spain, and Norway are examples of countries that exhibit institutions of government that roughly blend equal parts of consensual and majoritarian patterns.

The dominant features that distinguish a majoritarian democracy from a consensual democracy include:

1. having only two major political parties, not many (see Chapter 10);
2. having an electoral system that requires a bare majority to elect one clear winner in an election, as opposed to a proportional electoral system that distributes seats to political parties according to the rough share of votes received in the election (see Chapter 11);
3. a strong executive (president or prime minister) and cabinet that together are largely independent of the legislature when it comes to exercising the executive's constitutional duties, in contrast to an executive and cabinet that are politically controlled by the parties in the legislature and therefore unable to exercise much influence when proposing policy initiatives (see Chapter 14);
4. a tradition of competitive and largely uncoordinated competition between organized interest groups and associations in society rather than interest groups that are organized into highly centralized, national organizations that limit their independence and competition (see Chapter 12);
5. decentralized (non-federal) government rather than nationalized government (see Chapter 4);
6. a tradition of having effective political power within the legislature concentrated in one chamber rather than divided between two (see Chapter 13);
7. the absence of judicial review by an independent judiciary, rather than a powerful judiciary that can review the constitutionality of either laws passed by the national legislature or policy actions of the executive (see Chapter 16).

Is one type of democracy "better" than the other? That, of course, depends upon one's values and priorities. For instance, should power and policy making be concentrated and free from a wide array of group influence, or should it be subject to the pressure of intense scrutiny and competition? Should society have a government that can "quickly" and perhaps more "efficiently" make policy, or should it have a more "accountable" and pliable policy process? It should be apparent that while all democracies face varying degrees of pressure from social diversity within their society, no single pattern of government is clearly dominant among the world's freest nations.

SOURCE: Arend Lijphart, *Patterns of Democracy: Government Forms and Performance in Thirty-Six Countries* (New Haven: Yale University Press, 1999).

Becoming a Citizen . . . Being a Citizen

Citizenship may be defined as knowledgeable, active membership in the American political community. What do we expect members of our community to know? We are forced to think about these expectations when we establish requirements for immigrants to become citizens.

The U.S. Immigration and Naturalization Service administers tests to all immigrants who apply for U.S. citizenship. Here are some typical test questions (with the answers in italics):

- What is the date of Independence Day? *July 4th*
- What country did we fight during the Revolution? *England*
- Who elects the president of the United States? *the electoral college*
- What are the three branches of our government? *legislative, executive, and judicial*
- Name the two U.S. senators from your state. *insert local information*
- How many representatives are in Congress? *435*
- What is the Bill of Rights? *the first ten amendments of the U.S. Constitution*
- Who is the Chief Justice of the U.S. Supreme Court? *William Rehnquist*
- Who becomes president of the United States if the president and the vice president should die? *Speaker of the House of Representatives*
- What is the minimum age for voting in the United States? *eighteen*
- What was the purpose of the Emancipation Proclamation? *free many slaves*
- Where is the White House located? *Washington, D.C.*
- In what month do we vote for the president? *November*
- In what month is the new president inaugurated? *January*
- Name one purpose of the United Nations. *for countries to discuss and resolve world problems, to provide economic aid to many countries*

Becoming a citizen involves learning some U.S. history, the U.S. Constitution and structure of U.S. government, and current events. In additional, new citizens must understand and adopt general political values such as liberty, equality, and democracy. While we do not test the political knowledge or norms of native-born citizens, we do require schools to teach them U.S. history, government, and civic values.

Being a citizen allows you to claim certain rights, including the right to vote, sit on juries, and serve in the military. Citizenship also enables you to claim unrestricted residence in this country, a U.S. passport, eligibility for federal employment, and preference for bringing noncitizen relatives to come live here.

Many Americans agree that being a citizen entrails assuming an obligation to be an active participant in public life. The most common way that citizens fulfill this obligation is by registering to vote and then actually voting on election days. However, many avenues of active participation are open to you.

- ***Research your family's "public" history.*** What knowledge and values give meaning to the idea of "political community"? Explore your own family's history. When did your ancestors come to the United States? When did they acquire citizenship? Why did they seek it? How did they get it? What do your family members think should be the basic requirements for citizenship? Do they believe citizens have obligations as well as rights? How active are they in public life?
- ***Organize a forum on campus citizenship.*** Organize and publicize a forum about membership in the campus community. You might tackle questions such as: Do separate student groups for African Americans, Latinos, and Asian Americans contribute to community or fragment the student body? Are women students given equal respect and opportunity in college classrooms? What ideas and values should be expected of all members of the campus community?
- ***Volunteer to work with a community organization.*** Does your community contain homeless people? Does it have immigrant enclaves where few people are involved in public life? Does it contain poor families with great health and education needs? Find the telephone number of nearby churches or social service organizations. Call one of them and volunteer your time, energy, and enthusiasm.

Notice that you can participate at different levels of the American political community. Explore the relationship between your family and the community, consider your campus as your community, or focus on your neighborhood, city, and state as well as the nation as arenas for citizen action. Notice also that your commitment may vary. Researching your family's public history will likely take less time than organizing a forum. Working with a community agency may be more or less demanding. It is easy to be an active citizen because you have so many options.

Summary

Some of the most contentious political issues in the United States today concern conflicts that stem from social differences such as ethnicity and gender. Such struggles reveal the important role that the national government plays in forming and enforcing policies that aim to ensure equality for all groups. Government efforts at guaranteeing equality may create new problems, however, because they often entail restricting the liberties of some citizens. It is through such conflicts that Americans put the core ideals of liberty, equality, and democracy into practice.

The first section of this chapter examined the efforts of groups who had been denied political equality to gain access to the American political system. Throughout much of the country's history, racial and ethnic differences were used as a basis to deny some groups full political equality. White ethnics experienced discrimination, but their rights to political equality were never in serious doubt. For African Americans, the struggle to eliminate slavery and the quest for full political equality after slavery was abolished have constituted the most far-reaching political struggles in all of American history. Over the past decade, the rapidly growing number of new immigrants has raised many new questions about the rights of immigrants and the impact of immigration on American life. Gender differences have also had an important impact on American politics. It took decades of mobilization and a constitutional amendment to grant women the right to vote. For women and racial minorities alike, efforts to achieve political equality did not stop with winning the right to vote. Groups continued to struggle to win political office and to make their voices heard in the political arena.

Class and religion are two other important bases of social difference that were examined in this chapter. Class has never been as important in the American context as it has been elsewhere in the world because Americans believe in individual mobility. Religion, on the other hand, has always played a role in public life in the United States, where religious freedom was a central tenet of the Founders. Today, the mobilization of religious groups has had an important impact on politics.

The last section of the chapter examined how ordinary citizens can take a more active role in our democracy. Gaining knowledge of how politics and policy affect them is the first important step. Political effectiveness also requires learning basic skills, such as how to bring people together and how to run meetings.

FOR FURTHER READING

Dawson, Michael C. *Behind the Mule: Race and Class in African-American Politics.* Princeton, NJ: Princeton University Press, 1994.

Edsall, Thomas B., and Mary D. Edsall. *Chain Reaction: The Impact of Race, Rights, and Taxes on American Politics.* New York: Norton, 1992.

de la Garza, Rodolfo O., and Louis DeSipio, eds. *Awash in the Mainstream: Latino Politics in the 1996 Elections.* Boulder, CO: Westview, 1999.

Hero, Rodney E. *Latinos and the U.S. Political System: Two-Tiered Pluralism.* Philadelphia: Temple University Press, 1992.

Klein, Ethel. *Gender Politics.* Cambridge, MA: Harvard University Press, 1984.

McClain, Paula D., and Joseph Stewart, Jr. *"Can We All Get Along?" Racial and Ethnic Minorities in American Politics.* Boulder, CO: Westview, 1995.

Mansbridge, Jane J. *Why We Lost the ERA.* Chicago: University of Chicago Press, 1986.

Sonenshein, Raphael J. *Politics in Black and White: Race and Power in Los Angeles.* Princeton, NJ: Princeton University Press, 1993.

Takaki, Ronald T. *A Different Mirror: A History of Multicultural America.* Boston: Little, Brown, 1993.

Tate, Katherine. *From Protest to Politics: The New Black Voters in American Elections.* Cambridge, MA: Harvard University Press, 1993.

STUDY OUTLINE

Expanding the American Political Community

1. Americans hold conflicting perspectives about how to reconcile our core national values of liberty, equality, and democracy with our history of social discrimination and political exclusion.
2. Racial and ethnic identities are the most politically significant social identities in the United States.
3. Although the American story is often told as one of group assimilation, in fact American politics acknowledged and encouraged ethnic identities by providing an

incentive for politicians to recognize ethnic groups and mobilize them into politics.

4. For African Americans, the central fact of political life has been a denial of full citizenship rights for most of American history.
5. Several strategies of mobilization emerged to guide African Americans' quest for equality, including political pressure, legal strategies, and protest.
6. The labels "Latino" or "Hispanic" encompass a wide range of groups with diverse national origins, distinctive cultural identities, and disparate political experiences in America.
7. In recent years, Latino political organizations have attempted to mobilize members of their community. This effort, if successful, would tap a "sleeping giant" of political influence.
8. The diversity of national backgrounds among Asian Americans has impeded the development of group-based political power. Furthermore, the geographical dispersion of Asian Americans and their diverse experiences raise questions about whether Asian Americans will ever form a cohesive political bloc.
9. For much of their history, the relationship of Native Americans to the U.S. government has been that of a warring, then a conquered, people.
10. In the 1960s, using protest, litigation, and the assertion of tribal rights, the Native American political movement gained strength, which helped tribes achieve self-government and economic development.
11. The relative weakness of class in the United States stems from the ideals of equality and liberty, as well as from the positive and negative experiences of workers within the American political system.
12. The closest Americans have come to having a class-based politics in this century was during the New Deal.
13. Because most Americans consider themselves to be middle class, mobilizing citizens on class-based appeals is difficult.
14. Although women were barred from electoral politics for much of American history, they were important voices in social reform movements, such as the abolitionist movement and the movements against political corruption and urban squalor.
15. Although women gained the vote in 1920, their political power was still thwarted for decades. Not until the 1960s did a broad movement for women's equality emerge.
16. The ongoing significance of gender issues in American politics is indicated by three trends: the gender gap, the increase in the number of women holding public office, and the continued importance of political issues of special concern to women.
17. Religion has always played an important role in American politics. Despite the formal separation of church and state, religious groups have regularly entered the political arena.
18. A significant element of modern religious politics has been the mobilization of evangelical Protestants into a cohesive and politically active organization aligned with the Republican Party.

PRACTICE QUIZ

1. Which of the following has (have) been the most politically significant social identities in American politics?
   a) class
   b) race and ethnicity
   c) gender
   d) religion
2. Which of the following statements best describes the impact of Reconstruction on African American political involvement?
   a) It was immediate, but short-lived.
   b) It sustained African American dominance.
   c) It actually hurt African American participation.
   d) It had little impact.
3. Which of the following helps to explain the relatively low level of Latino political participation?
   a) low rates of voter registration
   b) low rates of naturalization
   c) both a and b
   d) neither a nor b
4. What has impeded the group power of Asian Americans?
   a) the corruption of group leaders
   b) a lack of economic resources
   c) organized attempts to keep Asian Americans from participating
   d) heterogeneity
5. In which of the following eras was class *least* salient in American politics?
   a) the early years of the republic
   b) after the Civil War
   c) during the New Deal
   d) in the 1980s
6. What percentage of Americans identify themselves as upper class?
   a) 1 percent
   b) 5 percent
   c) 10 percent
   d) 18 percent

7. Which of the following helps to explain the ongoing significance of gender issues in American politics?
   a) the similarity of male and female voting trends
   b) the increase in the number of women holding public office
   c) the decline of party politics
   d) the increasing professionalization of state legislatures

8. Voting rights for black males were guaranteed by the
   a) U.S. Constitution.
   b) Bill of Rights.
   c) Fifteenth Amendment.
   d) Nineteenth Amendment.

9. Which of the following would policy makers most likely use if they wanted to control who immigrated into the United States?
   a) open immigration
   b) free trade agreements
   c) formal recognition of a nation by the United Nations
   d) a quota system based on national origin

10. Which of the following best explains the lack of support for socialism in the United States?
    a) lack of a class consciousness
    b) lack of a history of working-class activity in the United States
    c) the absence of labor unions in America
    d) the absence of a violent labor history in the United States

CRITICAL THINKING QUESTIONS

1. Trace the development of the "American political community." Describe the evolution of this community in terms of the opportunities for various groups for participation and inclusion in political affairs. Describe one group's struggle for inclusion. What were the obstacles the group's members faced? What strategies did they use to overcome those obstacles? To what extent have they succeeded in their quest for participation and inclusion? How did they succeed?

2. Describe the ways in which the ideals of liberty and equality have come into conflict in terms of the politics of ethnicity, class, gender, and religion. Looking at various laws, court cases, social movements, and political behaviors, describe how liberty has, at times, prevented equality. Might the quest for equality preempt liberty?

KEY TERMS

American political community (p. 34)
gender gap (p. 54)
political machines (p. 36)
white ethnics (p. 35)

PART II

Foundations

3 The Founding

★ **The First Founding: Interests and Conflicts**

What conflicts were apparent and what interests prevailed during the American Revolution and the drafting of the Articles of Confederation?

★ **The Second Founding: From Compromise to Constitution**

Why were the Articles of Confederation unable to hold the nation together?

In what ways is the United States Constitution a marriage of interest and principle? How did the framers of the Constitution reconcile their competing interests and principles?

★ **The Constitution**

What principles does the Constitution embody? Why did the framers of the Constitution establish the legislative, executive, and judicial branches?

What limits on the national government's power are embodied in the Constitution?

★ **The Fight for Ratification**

What sides did the Federalists and the Antifederalists represent in the fight over ratification?

Over what key principles did the Federalists and the Antifederalists disagree?

★ **The Citizen's Role and the Changing Constitution**

Why is the Constitution difficult to amend?

What purposes do the amendments to the Constitution serve?

★ **Reflections on Liberty, Equality, and Democracy**

Did the framers value liberty, equality, and democracy? Why or why not?

and the Constitution

STUDENTS AND POLITICS

"No taxation without representation" were words that stirred a generation of Americans long before they even dreamed of calling themselves Americans rather than Britons. Reacting to new British attempts to extract tax revenues to pay for the troops that were being sent to defend the colonial frontier, protests erupted throughout the colonies against the infamous Stamp Act of 1765. This act created revenue stamps and required that they be affixed to all printed and legal documents, including newspapers, pamphlets, advertisements, notes and bonds, leases, deeds, and licenses. To show their displeasure with the act, the colonists conducted mass meetings, parades, bonfires, and other demonstrations throughout the spring and summer of 1765. In Boston, for example, a stamp agent was hanged and burned in effigy. Later, the home of the lieutenant-governor was sacked, leading to his resignation and that of all of his colonial commission and stamp agents. By November 1765, business proceeded and newspapers were published without the stamp; in March 1766, Parliament repealed the detested law. Through their protest, the nonimportation agreements that the colonists subsequently adopted, and the Stamp Act Congress that met in October 1765, the colonists took the first steps that ultimately would lead to war and a new nation.

The people of every nation tend to glorify their own history and especially their nation's creation. Americans are no exception. To most contemporary Americans, the Revolutionary period represents a heroic struggle by a determined and united group of colonists against British oppression. The Boston Tea Party, the battles of Lexington and Concord, the winter at Valley Forge—these are the events that are emphasized in American history. Similarly, the American Constitution—the document establishing the system of government that ultimately emerged from this struggle—is often seen as an inspired, if not divine, work, expressing timeless principles of democratic government. These views are by no means false. During the Founding era, Americans did struggle against misrule. Moreover, the American Constitution did establish the foundations for more than two hundred years of democratic government.

The story of the Founding and the Constitution is generally presented to students as a fait accompli: the Constitution, which established the best of all possible forms of government, was adopted without much difficulty and its critics and doubters were quickly proven wrong. In reality, though, the constitutional period was precisely the era in American history when *nothing* was a given. Nothing was simple. The proposed new system of government faced considerable opposition. The objections raised by opponents of the proposed constitution—who called themselves Antifederalists—were profound and important. The Antifederalists thought that the state governments would be able to represent the people much better than the national government could. They also were concerned that the officials of a large and powerful government would inevitably abuse their authority. The Antifederalists understood the basic problem of freedom and power and feared that the powers given to the national government to do good would sooner or later be turned to evil purposes.

One noted authority has asserted that the Federalists won the great debate over the Constitution because their ideas were better.[1] The jury, however, may still be out on whether the Constitution's opponents were proven wrong. The Federalists presented some very powerful ideas, and the Constitution they wrote became so well established as to seem part of the natural political environment today. Nevertheless, the issues raised by the Antifederalists should be pondered by every student of American politics, because they provide an essential perspective from which to view and evaluate the American system of government.

The story of the Founding is not so much the morality tale that is usually presented to students as it is a study of political choices. And because Americans continue to make choices about the constitutional framework, the debates of the Founding period are as relevant today as they were then. During the 1980s, proponents of adding an "equal rights amendment" to the Constitution raised important questions about equal representation. In the 1990s, both friends and foes of a proposed "balanced budget amendment" were forced to confront questions of tyranny and governmental power. If we limit the government's power, are we striking a blow for liberty or merely restricting the government's capacity to serve its citizens? The great questions Americans confronted at the close of the eighteenth century are not so different from those faced at the end of the twentieth.

The Founding era was also the period during which Americans first confronted the great question of who was to be included and who was to be excluded from full citizenship. The answer given by the Founders—all white men were entitled to full citizenship rights—was an extremely democratic position for its time. America was one of the few nations that extended citizenship so broadly. Yet the Founding generation did not resolve the question once and for all. Over the ensuing two hundred years, as we shall see, the question of who is and who is not a full citizen of the United States has been debated many times and has never been completely resolved.

- ***In this chapter, we will first assess the political backdrop of the American Revolution, which led to the Declaration of Independence and the establishment of a governmental structure under the Articles of Confederation.***

- ***We will then consider the conditions that led to the Constitutional Convention of 1787 and the great issues that were debated by the framers.*** To fully understand the character of the Founding and the meaning of the Constitution, it is essential to look beyond the myths and rhetoric and to explore the conflicting interests and forces at work during the period.

- ***Next, we will examine the Constitution that ultimately emerged as the basis for the national government.*** Although the Constitution was the product of a particular set of political forces, the principles of government it established have had long-lasting significance. The framers sought to create a powerful national government, but guarded against possible misuse of that power through the separation of powers, federalism, and the Bill of Rights.

- ***We will then examine the first hurdle that the Constitution faced, the fight for ratification.*** Two sides, the Federalists and the Antifederalists, vigorously debated the great political issues and principles at stake. The resolution of this debate created the framework for a national government that has lasted more than two hundred years.
- ***We will then look at how the Constitution has changed over the past two centuries.*** The framers designed an amendment process so that the Constitution could change, but the process has succeeded only on rare occasions.
- ***Finally, we will ask what liberty, equality, and democracy meant to the framers of the Constitution.*** Although the framers established a system of government that would eventually allow each of these political values to thrive, they championed liberty as the most important of the three.

The First Founding: Interests and Conflicts

▶ What conflicts were apparent and what interests prevailed during the American Revolution and the drafting of the Articles of Confederation?

Competing ideals and principles often reflect competing interests, and so it was in Revolutionary America. The American Revolution and the American Constitution were outgrowths and expressions of a struggle among economic and political forces within the colonies. Five sectors of society had interests that were important in colonial politics: (1) the New England merchants; (2) the southern planters; (3) the "royalists"—holders of royal lands, offices, and patents (licenses to engage in a profession or business activity); (4) shopkeepers, artisans, and laborers; and (5) small farmers. Throughout the eighteenth century, these groups were in conflict over issues of taxation, trade, and commerce. For the most part, however, the southern planters, the New England merchants, and the royal office and patent holders—groups that together made up the colonial elite—were able to maintain a political alliance that held in check the more radical forces representing shopkeepers, laborers, and small farmers. After 1750, however, by seriously threatening the interests of New England merchants and southern planters, British tax and trade policies split the colonial elite, permitting radical forces to expand their political influence, and set into motion a chain of events that culminated in the American Revolution.[2]

BRITISH TAXES AND COLONIAL INTERESTS

Beginning in the 1750s, the debts and other financial problems faced by the British government forced it to search for new revenue sources. This search rather quickly led to the Crown's North American colonies, which, on the whole, paid remarkably little in taxes to their parent country. The British government reasoned that a sizable fraction of its debt was, in fact, attributable to the expenses it had incurred in defense of the colonies during the recent French and Indian wars, as well as to the continuing protection that British forces were giving the colonists from Indian attacks and that the British navy was providing for colonial shipping. Thus, during the 1760s, England sought to impose new, though relatively modest, taxes upon the colonists.

Like most governments of the period, the British regime had limited ways in which to collect revenues. The income tax, which in the twentieth century has become the single most important source of governmental revenues, had not yet been developed. For the most part, in the mid-eighteenth century, governments relied on tariffs, duties, and other taxes on commerce, and it was to such taxes, including the Stamp Act, that the British turned during the 1760s.

The Stamp Act and other taxes on commerce, such as the Sugar Act of 1764, which taxed sugar, molasses, and other commodities, most heavily affected the two groups in colonial society whose commercial interests and activities were most extensive—the New England merchants and the southern planters. Under the famous slogan "no taxation without representation," the merchants and planters together sought to organize opposition to these new taxes. In the course of the struggle against British tax measures, the planters and merchants broke with their royalist allies and turned to their former adversaries—the shopkeepers, small farmers, laborers, and artisans—for help. With the assistance of these groups, the merchants and planters organized demonstrations and a boycott of British goods that ultimately forced the Crown to rescind most of its new taxes.

From the perspective of the merchants and planters, however, the British government's decision to eliminate most of the hated taxes represented a victorious end to their struggle with the mother country. They were anxious to end the unrest they had helped to arouse, and they supported the British government's efforts to restore order. Indeed, most respectable Bostonians supported the actions of the British soldiers involved in the Boston Massacre. In their subsequent trial, the soldiers were defended by John Adams, a pillar of Boston society and a future president of the United States. Adams asserted that the soldiers' actions were entirely justified, provoked by "a motley rabble of saucy boys, Negroes and mulattos, Irish teagues and outlandish Jack tars." All but two of the soldiers were acquitted.[3]

Despite the efforts of the British government and the better-to-do strata of colonial society, it proved difficult to bring an end to the political strife. The more radical forces representing shopkeepers, artisans, laborers, and small farmers, who had been mobilized and energized by the struggle over taxes, continued to agitate for political and social change within the colonies. These radicals, led by individuals like Samuel Adams, a cousin of John Adams, asserted that British power supported an unjust political and social structure within the colonies, and began to advocate an end to British rule.[4]

POLITICAL STRIFE AND THE RADICALIZING OF THE COLONISTS

The political strife within the colonies was the background for the events of 1773–74. In 1773, the British government granted the politically powerful East India Company a monopoly on the export of tea from Britain, eliminating a lucrative form of trade for colonial merchants. To add to the injury, the East India Company sought to sell the tea directly in the colonies instead of

In many ways, the British helped provoke the Boston Tea Party by providing the ailing East India Company with a monopoly on the tea trade with the American colonies. But the colonists feared British monopolies would hurt colonial merchants' business; they protested by throwing the East India Company's tea into Boston Harbor.

working through the colonial merchants. Tea was an extremely important commodity in the 1770s, and these British actions posed a mortal threat to the New England merchants. Together with their southern allies, the merchants once again called upon their radical adversaries for support. The most dramatic result was the Boston Tea Party of 1773, led by Samuel Adams.

This event was of decisive importance in American history. The merchants had hoped to force the British government to rescind the Tea Act, but they did not support any demands beyond this one. They certainly did not seek independence from Britain. Samuel Adams and the other radicals, however, hoped to provoke the British government to take actions that would alienate its colonial supporters and pave the way for a rebellion. This was precisely the purpose of the Boston Tea Party, and it succeeded. By dumping the East India Company's tea into Boston Harbor, Adams and his followers goaded the British into enacting a number of harsh reprisals. Within five months after the incident in Boston, the House of Commons passed a series of acts that closed the port of Boston to commerce, changed the provincial government of Massachusetts, provided for the removal of accused persons to England for trial, and most important, restricted movement to the West—further alienating the southern planters, who depended upon access to new western lands. These acts of retaliation confirmed the worst criticisms of England and helped radicalize Americans. Radicals like Samuel Adams and Christopher Gadsden of South Carolina had been agitating for more violent measures to deal with England. But ultimately they needed Britain's political repression to create widespread support for independence.

Thus, the Boston Tea Party set into motion a cycle of provocation and retaliation that in 1774 resulted in the convening of the First Continental Congress—an assembly of delegates from all parts of the country—that called for a total boycott of British goods and, under the prodding of the radicals, began to consider the possibility of independence from British rule. The eventual result was the Declaration of Independence.

THE DECLARATION OF INDEPENDENCE

In 1776, the Second Continental Congress appointed a committee consisting of Thomas Jefferson of Virginia, Benjamin Franklin of Pennsylvania, Roger Sherman of Connecticut, John Adams of Massachusetts, and Robert Livingston of New York to draft a statement of American independence from British rule. The Declaration of Independence, written by Jefferson and adopted by the Second Continental Congress, was an extraordinary document in both philosophical and political terms. Philosophically, the Declaration was remarkable for its assertion that certain rights, called "unalienable rights"—including life, liberty, and the pursuit of happiness—could not be abridged by governments. In the world of 1776, a world in which some kings still claimed to rule by divine right, this was a dramatic statement. Politically, the Declaration was remarkable because, despite the differences of interest that divided the colonists along economic, regional, and philosophical lines, the Declaration identified and focused on problems, grievances, aspirations, and principles that might unify the various colonial groups. The Declaration was an attempt to identify and articulate a history and set of principles that might help to forge national unity.[5]

THE ARTICLES OF CONFEDERATION

Articles of Confederation
America's first written constitution; served as the basis for America's national government until 1789

Having declared their independence, the colonies needed to establish a governmental structure. In November of 1777, the Continental Congress adopted the **Articles of Confederation and Perpetual Union**—the United States's first written constitution. Although it was not ratified by all the states until 1781, it was the country's operative constitution for almost twelve years, until March 1789.

The Articles of Confederation was a constitution concerned primarily with limiting the powers of the central government. The central government, first of all, was based entirely in a Congress. Since it was not intended to be a powerful government, it was given no executive branch. Execution of its laws was to be left to the individual states. Second, the Congress had little power. Its members were not much more than delegates or messengers from the state legislatures. They were chosen by the state legislatures, their salaries were paid out of the state treasuries, and they were subject to immediate recall by state authorities. In addition, each state, regardless of its size, had only a single vote.

The Congress was given the power to declare war and make peace, to make treaties and alliances, to coin or borrow money, and to regulate trade with the Native Americans. It could also appoint the senior officers of the United States army. But it could not levy taxes or regulate commerce among the states. Moreover, the army officers it appointed had no army to serve in because the nation's armed forces were composed of the state militias. Probably the most unfortunate part of the Articles of Confederation was that the central government could not prevent one state from discriminating against other states in the quest for foreign commerce.

confederation
a system of government in which states retain sovereign authority except for the powers expressly delegated to the national governments

In brief, the relationship between the Congress and the states under the Articles of Confederation was much like the contemporary relationship between the United Nations and its member states, a relationship in which virtually all governmental powers are retained by the states. It was properly called a **confederation** because, as provided under Article II, "each state retains its sovereignty, freedom and independence, and every Power, Jurisdiction and right, which is not by this confederation expressly delegated to the United States, in Congress assembled." Not only was there no executive, there also was no judicial authority and no other means of enforcing the Congress's will. If there was to be any enforcement at all, it would be done for the Congress by the states.[6]

The Second Founding: From Compromise to Constitution

- Why were the Articles of Confederation unable to hold the nation together?
- In what ways is the United States Constitution a marriage of interest and principle?
- How did the framers of the Constitution reconcile their competing interests and principles?

The Declaration of Independence and the Articles of Confederation were not sufficient to hold the new nation together as an independent and effective nation-state. From almost the moment of armistice with the British in 1783, moves were afoot to reform and strengthen the Articles of Confederation.

INTERNATIONAL STANDING AND BALANCE OF POWER

There was a special concern for the country's international position. Competition among the states for foreign commerce allowed the European powers to play the states off against one another, which created confusion on both sides of the Atlantic. At one point during the winter of 1786–87, John Adams of Massachusetts, a leader in the independence struggle, was sent to negotiate a new treaty with the British, one that would cover disputes left over from the war. The British government responded that, since the United States under the Articles of Confederation was unable to enforce existing treaties, it would negotiate with each of the thirteen states separately.

At the same time, well-to-do Americans—in particular the New England merchants and southern planters—were troubled by the influence that "radical" forces exercised in the Continental Congress and in the governments of several of the states. The colonists' victory in the Revolutionary War had not only meant the end of British rule, but also significantly changed the balance of political power within the new states. As a result of the Revolution, one key segment of the colonial elite—the royal land, office, and patent holders—was stripped of its economic and political privileges. In fact, many of these individuals, along with tens of thousands of other colonists who considered themselves loyal British subjects, left for Canada after the British surrender. And while the pre-Revolutionary elite was weakened, the pre-Revolutionary radicals were now better organized than ever before and were the controlling forces in such states as Pennsylvania and Rhode Island, where they pursued economic and political policies that struck terror into the hearts of the pre-Revolutionary political establishment. In Rhode Island, for example, between 1783 and 1785, a legislature dominated by representatives of small farmers, artisans, and shopkeepers had instituted economic policies, including drastic currency inflation, that frightened business and property owners throughout the country. Of course, the central government under the Articles of Confederation was powerless to intervene.

THE ANNAPOLIS CONVENTION

The continuation of international weakness and domestic economic turmoil led many Americans to consider whether their newly adopted form of government might not already require revision. In the fall of 1786, many state leaders accepted an invitation from the Virginia legislature for a conference of representatives of all the states. Delegates from five states actually attended. This conference, held in Annapolis, Maryland, was the first step toward the second founding. The one positive thing that came out of the Annapolis Convention was a carefully worded resolution calling on the Congress to send commissioners to Philadelphia at a later time "to devise such further provisions as shall appear to them necessary to render the Constitution of the Federal Government adequate to the exigencies of the Union."[7] This resolution was drafted by Alexander Hamilton, a thirty-four-year-old New York lawyer who had played a significant role in the Revolution as George Washington's secretary and who would play a still more significant role in framing the Constitution and forming the new government in the 1790s. But the resolution did not necessarily imply any desire to do more than improve and reform the Articles of Confederation.

In the winter of 1787, the Massachusetts legislature levied heavy taxes that hit the poor particularly hard. Daniel Shays led a makeshift army against the federal arsenal at Springfield in protest. Shays's group was easily routed, but they did get the legislature to grant some of their demands.

SHAYS'S REBELLION

It is quite possible that the Constitutional Convention of 1787 in Philadelphia would never have taken place at all except for a single event that occurred during the winter following the Annapolis Convention: Shays's Rebellion.

Daniel Shays, a former army captain, led a mob of farmers in a rebellion against the government of Massachusetts. The purpose of the rebellion was to prevent foreclosures on their debt-ridden land by keeping the county courts of western Massachusetts from sitting until after the next election. The state militia dispersed the mob, but for several days Shays and his followers terrified the state government by attempting to capture the federal arsenal at Springfield, provoking an appeal to the Congress to help restore order. Within a few days, the state government regained control and captured fourteen of the rebels (all were eventually pardoned). In 1787, a newly elected Massachusetts legislature granted some of the farmers' demands.

Although the incident ended peacefully, its effects lingered and spread. Washington summed it up: "I am mortified beyond expression that in the moment of our acknowledged independence we should by our conduct verify the predictions of our transatlantic foe, and render ourselves ridiculous and contemptible in the eyes of all Europe."[8]

The Congress under the Confederation had been unable to act decisively in a time of crisis. This provided critics of the Articles of Confederation with precisely the evidence they needed to push Hamilton's Annapolis resolution through the Congress. Thus, the states were asked to send representatives to Philadelphia to discuss constitutional revision. Delegates were eventually sent by every state except Rhode Island.

THE CONSTITUTIONAL CONVENTION

Delegates selected by the state governments convened in Philadelphia in May 1787, with political strife, international embarrassment, national weakness, and local rebellion fixed in their minds. Recognizing that these issues were symptoms of fundamental flaws in the Articles of Confederation, the delegates soon abandoned the plan to revise the Articles and committed themselves to a second founding—a second, and ultimately successful, attempt to create a legitimate and effective national system of government. This effort occupied the convention for the next five months.

A Marriage of Interest and Principle Scholars have for years disagreed about the motives of the Founders in Philadelphia. Among the most controversial views of the framers' motives is the "economic interpretation" put forward by historian Charles Beard and his disciples.[9] According to Beard's account, America's Founders were a collection of securities speculators and property owners whose only aim was personal enrichment. From this perspective, the Constitution's lofty principles were little more than sophisticated masks behind which the most venal interests sought to enrich themselves.

Contrary to Beard's approach is the view that the framers of the Constitution *were* concerned with philosophical and ethical principles. Indeed, the framers sought to devise a system of government consistent with the dominant philosophical and moral principles of the day. But, in fact, these two views belong together; the Founders' interests were reinforced by their principles. The convention that drafted the American Constitution was chiefly organized by the New England merchants and southern planters. Although the delegates representing these groups did not all hope to profit personally from an increase in the value of their securities, as Beard would have it, they did hope to benefit in the broadest political and economic sense by breaking the power of their radical foes and establishing a system of government more compatible with their long-term economic and political interests. Thus, the framers sought to create a new government capable of promoting commerce and protecting property from radical state legislatures. At the same time, they hoped to fashion a government less susceptible than the existing state and national regimes to populist forces hostile to the interests of the commercial and propertied classes.

The Great Compromise The proponents of a new government fired their opening shot on May 29, 1787, when Edmund Randolph of Virginia offered a resolution that proposed corrections and enlargements in the Articles of Confederation. The proposal, which showed the strong influence of James Madison, was not a simple motion. It provided for virtually every aspect of a new government. Randolph later admitted it was intended to be an alternative draft constitution, and it did in fact serve as the framework for what ultimately became the Constitution. (There is no verbatim record of the debates, but Madison was present during virtually all of the deliberations and kept full notes on them.)[10]

Virginia Plan
a framework for the Constitution, introduced by Edmund Randolph, which called for representation in the national legislature based upon the population of each state

New Jersey Plan
a framework for the Constitution, introduced by William Paterson, which called for equal state representation in the national legislature regardless of population

Great Compromise
the agreement reached at the Constitutional Convention of 1787 that gave each state an equal number of senators regardless of its population, but linked representation in the House of Representatives to population

The portion of Randolph's motion that became most controversial was called the **Virginia Plan.** This plan provided for a system of representation in the national legislature based upon the population of each state or the proportion of each state's revenue contribution to the national government, or both. (Randolph also proposed a second branch of the legislature, but it was to be elected by the members of the first branch.) Since the states varied enormously in size and wealth, the Virginia Plan was thought to be heavily biased in favor of the large states.

While the convention was debating the Virginia Plan, additional delegates were arriving in Philadelphia and were beginning to mount opposition to it. Their resolution, introduced by William Paterson of New Jersey and known as the **New Jersey Plan,** did not oppose the Virginia Plan point for point. Instead, it concentrated on specific weaknesses in the Articles of Confederation, in the spirit of revision rather than radical replacement of that document. Supporters of the New Jersey Plan did not seriously question the convention's commitment to replacing the Articles. But their opposition to the Virginia Plan's scheme of representation was sufficient to send its proposals back to committee for reworking into a common document. In particular, delegates from the less-populous states, which included Delaware, New Jersey, Connecticut, and New York, asserted that the more populous states, such as Virginia, Pennsylvania, North Carolina, Massachusetts, and Georgia, would dominate the new government if representation were determined by population. The smaller states argued that each state should be equally represented in the new regime regardless of that state's population.

The issue of representation was one that threatened to wreck the entire constitutional enterprise. Delegates conferred, factions maneuvered, and tempers flared. James Wilson of Pennsylvania told the small-state delegates that if they wanted to disrupt the union they should go ahead. The separation could, he said, "never happen on better grounds." Small-state delegates were equally blunt. Gunning Bedford of Delaware declared that the small states might look elsewhere for friends if they were forced. "The large states," he said, "dare not dissolve the confederation. If they do the small ones will find some foreign ally of more honor and good faith, who will take them by the hand and do them justice." These sentiments were widely shared. The union, as Oliver Ellsworth of Connecticut put it, was "on the verge of dissolution, scarcely held together by the strength of a hair."

The outcome of this debate was the Connecticut Compromise, also known as the **Great Compromise.** Under the terms of this compromise, in the first branch of Congress—the House of Representatives—the representatives would be apportioned according to the number of inhabitants in each state. This, of course, was what delegates from the large states had sought. But in the second branch—the Senate—each state would have an equal vote regardless of its size; this provision addressed the concerns of the small states. This compromise was not immediately satisfactory to all the delegates. Indeed, two of the most vocal members of the small-state faction, John Lansing and Robert Yates of New York, were so incensed by the concession that their colleagues had made to the large-state forces that they stormed out of the convention. In the end, however, both sets of forces preferred compromise to the breakup of the Union, and the plan was accepted.

The Question of Slavery: The Three-Fifths Compromise The story so far is too neat, too easy, and too anticlimactic. If it were left here, it would only contribute to American mythology. After all, the notion of a **bicameral** (two-chambered) legislature was very much in the air in 1787. Some of the states had had bicameral legislatures for years. The Philadelphia delegates might well have gone straight to the adoption of two chambers based on two different principles of representation even without the dramatic interplay of conflict and compromise. But a far more fundamental issue had to be confronted before the Great Compromise could take place: the issue of slavery.

bicameral
having a legislative assembly composed of two chambers or houses

Many of the conflicts that emerged during the Constitutional Convention were reflections of the fundamental differences between the slave and the nonslave states—differences that pitted the southern planters and New England merchants against one another. This was the first premonition of a conflict that would almost destroy the Republic in later years. In the midst of debate over large versus small states, Madison observed,

> The great danger to our general government is the great southern and northern interests of the continent, being opposed to each other. Look to the votes in Congress, and most of them stand divided by the geography of the country, not according to the size of the states.[11]

More than 90 percent of the country's slaves resided in five states—Georgia, Maryland, North Carolina, South Carolina, and Virginia—where they accounted for 30 percent of the total population. In some places, slaves outnumbered nonslaves by as much as ten to one. If the Constitution were to embody any principle of national supremacy, some basic decisions would have to be made about the place of slavery in the general scheme. Madison hit on this point on several occasions as different aspects of the Constitution were being discussed. For example, he observed,

> It seemed now to be pretty well understood that the real difference of interests lay, not between the large and small but between the northern and southern states. The institution of slavery and its consequences formed the line of discrimination. There were five states on the South, eight on the northern side of this line. Should a proportional representation take place it was true, the northern side would still outnumber the other: but not in the same degree, at this time; and every day would tend towards an equilibrium.[12]

Northerners and Southerners eventually reached agreement through the **Three-fifths Compromise.** The seats in the House of Representatives would be apportioned according to a "population" in which five slaves would count as three free persons. The slaves would not be allowed to vote, of course, but the number of representatives would be apportioned accordingly.

Three-fifths Compromise
the agreement reached at the Constitutional Convention of 1787 that stipulated that for purposes of the apportionment of congressional seats, every slave would be counted as three-fifths of a person

The issue of slavery was the most difficult one faced by the framers and nearly destroyed the Union. Although some delegates believed slavery to be morally wrong, an evil and oppressive institution that made a mockery of the ideals and values espoused in the Constitution, morality was not the issue that caused the framers to support or oppose the Three-fifths Compromise. Whatever they thought of the institution of slavery, most delegates from the northern states opposed counting slaves in the distribution of congressional seats.

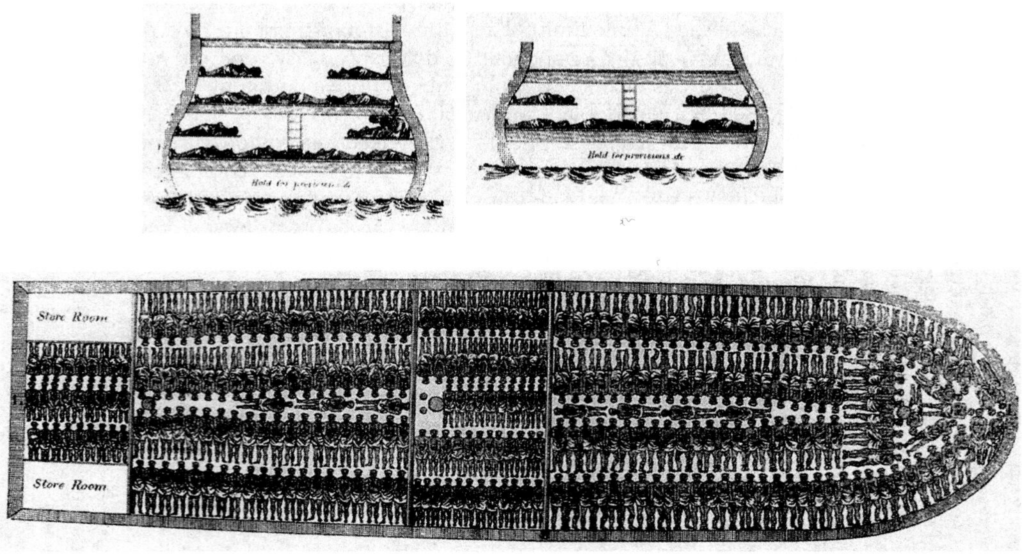

These cross-sectional views of a slave ship show the crowded conditions that Africans endured on the passage to America. The Constitution explicitly prevented Congress from banning the slave trade until at least 1808. Even though the trade was banned on January 1 of that year, illegal traffic in slaves continued.

Wilson of Pennsylvania, for example, argued that if slaves were citizens they should be treated and counted like other citizens. If, on the other hand, they were property, then why should not other forms of property be counted toward the apportionment of representatives? But southern delegates made it clear that if the northerners refused to give in, they would never agree to the new government. William R. Davie of North Carolina heatedly said that it was time "to speak out." He asserted that the people of North Carolina would never enter the Union if slaves were not counted as part of the basis for representation. Without such agreement, he asserted ominously, "the business was at an end." Even southerners like Edmund Randolph of Virginia, who conceded that slavery was immoral, insisted upon including slaves in the allocation of congressional seats. This conflict between the southern and northern delegates was so divisive that many came to question the possibility of creating and maintaining a union of the two. Pierce Butler of South Carolina declared that the North and South were as different as Russia and Turkey. Eventually, the North and South compromised on the issue of slavery and representation. Indeed, northerners even agreed to permit a continuation of the odious slave trade to keep the South in the union. But, in due course, Butler proved to be correct, and a bloody war was fought when the disparate interests of the North and the South could no longer be reconciled.

The Constitution

- What principles does the Constitution embody?
- What were the intents of the framers of the Constitution regarding the legislative, executive, and judicial branches?
- What limits on the national government's power are embodied in the Constitution?

The political significance of the Great Compromise and the Three-fifths Compromise was to reinforce the unity of the mercantile and planter forces that sought to create a new government. The Great Compromise reassured those who feared that the importance of their own local or regional influence would be reduced by the new governmental framework. The Three-fifths Compromise temporarily defused the rivalry between the merchants and planters. Their unity secured, members of the alliance supporting the establishment of a new government moved to fashion a constitutional framework consistent with their economic and political interests.

In particular, the framers sought a new government that, first, would be strong enough to promote commerce and protect property from radical state legislatures such as Rhode Island's. This became the constitutional basis for national control over commerce and finance, as well as for the establishment of national judicial supremacy and the effort to construct a strong presidency. Second, the framers sought to prevent what they saw as the threat posed by the "excessive democracy" of the state and national governments under the Articles of Confederation. This led to such constitutional principles as bicameralism (division of the Congress into two chambers), **checks and balances,** staggered terms in office, and indirect election (selection of the president by an **electoral college** rather than by voters directly). Third, the framers, lacking the power to force the states or the public at large to accept the new form of government, sought to identify principles that would help to secure support. This became the basis of the constitutional provision for direct popular election of representatives and, subsequently, for the addition of the **Bill of Rights** to the Constitution. Finally, the framers wanted to be certain that the government they created did not pose even more of a threat to its citizens' liberties and property rights than did the radical state legislatures they feared and despised. To prevent the new government from abusing its power, the framers incorporated principles such as the **separation of powers** and **federalism** into the Constitution. Let us assess the major provisions of the Constitution's seven articles (listed in Box 3.1) to see how each relates to these objectives.

checks and balances
mechanisms through which each branch of government is able to participate in and influence the activities of the other branches. Major examples include the presidential veto power over congressional legislation, the power of the Senate to approve presidential appointments, and judicial review of congressional enactments

electoral college
the presidential electors from each state who meet after the popular election to cast ballots for president and vice president

Bill of Rights
the first ten amendments to the U.S. Constitution, ratified in 1791; they ensure certain rights and liberties to the people

separation of powers
the division of governmental power among several institutions that must cooperate in decision making

federalism
a system of government in which power is divided, by a constitution, between a central government and regional governments

THE LEGISLATIVE BRANCH

The Constitution provided in Article I, Sections 1–7, for a Congress consisting of two chambers—a House of Representatives and a Senate. Members of the House of Representatives were given two-year terms in office and were to be elected directly by the people. Members of the Senate were to be appointed by the state legislatures (this was changed in 1913 by the Seventeenth Amendment, which instituted direct election of senators) for six-year terms. These terms were staggered so that the appointments of one-third of the senators would expire every two years. The Constitution assigned somewhat different tasks to the House and Senate. Though the approval of each body was required for the enactment of a law, the Senate alone was given the power to ratify treaties and approve presidential appointments. The House, on the other hand, was given the sole power to originate revenue bills.

The character of the legislative branch was directly related to the framers' major goals. The House of Representatives was designed to be directly responsible to the people in order to encourage popular consent for the new Constitution and to help enhance the power of the new government. At the same time, to guard against "excessive democracy," the power of the House of Representatives was checked by the Senate, whose members were to be appointed by the states for long terms rather than be elected directly by the people. The

Box 3.1 THE SEVEN ARTICLES OF THE CONSTITUTION

1. The Legislative Branch

House: two-year terms, elected directly by the people.

Senate: six-year terms (staggered so that only one-third of the Senate changes in any given election), appointed by state legislature (changed in 1913 to direct election).

Expressed powers of the national government: collecting taxes, borrowing money, regulating commerce, declaring war, and maintaining an army and a navy; all other power belongs to the states, unless deemed otherwise by the elastic ("necessary and proper") clause.

Exclusive powers of the national government: states are expressly forbidden to issue their own paper money, tax imports and exports, regulate trade outside their own borders, and impair the obligation of contracts; these powers are the exclusive domain of the national government.

2. The Executive Branch

Presidency: four-year terms (limited in 1951 to a maximum of two terms), elected indirectly by the electoral college.

Powers: can recognize other countries, negotiate treaties, grant reprieves and pardons, convene Congress in special sessions, and veto congressional enactment.

3. The Judicial Branch

Supreme Court: lifetime terms, appointed by the president with the approval of the Senate.

Powers: include resolving conflicts between federal and state laws, determining whether power belongs to the national government or the states, and settling controversies between citizens of different states.

4. National Unity and Power

Reciprocity among states: establishes that each state must give "full faith and credit" to official acts of other states, and guarantees citizens of any state the "privileges and immunities" of every other state.

5. Amending the Constitution

Procedure: requires approval by two-thirds of Congress and adoption by three-fourths of the states.

6. National Supremacy

The Constitution and national law are the supreme law of the land and cannot be overruled by state law.

7. Ratification

The Constitution became effective when approved by nine states.

purpose of this provision, according to Alexander Hamilton, was to avoid "an unqualified complaisance to every sudden breeze of passion, or to every transient impulse which the people may receive."[13] Staggered terms of service in the Senate, moreover, were intended to make that body even more resistant to popular pressure. Since only one-third of the senators would be selected at any given time, the composition of the institution would be protected from changes in popular preferences transmitted by the state legislatures. This

Delegates to the Constitutional Convention gather to sign their names to the Constitution on September 17, 1787.

would prevent what James Madison called "mutability in the public councils arising from a rapid succession of new members."[14] Thus, the structure of the legislative branch was designed to contribute to governmental power, to promote popular consent for the new government, and at the same time to place limits on the popular political currents that many of the framers saw as a radical threat to the economic and social order.

The issues of power and consent were important throughout the Constitution. Section 8 of Article I specifically listed the powers of Congress, which include the authority to collect taxes, to borrow money, to regulate commerce, to declare war, and to maintain an army and navy. By granting Congress these powers, the framers indicated very clearly that they intended the new government to be far more influential than its predecessor. At the same time, by defining the new government's most important powers as belonging to Congress, the framers sought to promote popular acceptance of this critical change by reassuring citizens that their views would be fully represented whenever the government exercised its new powers.

As a further guarantee to the people that the new government would pose no threat to them, the Constitution implied that any powers not listed were not granted at all. This is the doctrine of **expressed power.** The Constitution grants only those powers specifically expressed in its text. But the framers intended to create an active and powerful government, and so they included the **elastic clause,** sometimes known as the necessary and proper clause, which signified that the enumerated powers were meant to be a source of strength to the national government, not a limitation on it. Each power could be used with the utmost vigor, but no new powers could be seized upon by the national government without a constitutional amendment. In the absence of such an amendment, any power not enumerated was conceived to be "reserved" to the states (or the people).

expressed powers
specific powers granted to Congress under Article I, Section 8, of the Constitution

elastic clause
Article I, Section 8, of the Constitution (also known as the "necessary and proper" clause), which enumerates the powers of Congress and provides Congress with the authority to make all laws "necessary and proper" to carry them out

THE EXECUTIVE BRANCH

The Constitution provided for the establishment of the presidency in Article II. As Alexander Hamilton commented, the presidential article aimed toward "energy in the Executive." It did so in an effort to overcome the natural tendency toward stalemate that was built into the bicameral legislature as well as into the separation of powers among the three branches. The Constitution afforded the president a measure of independence from the people and from the other branches of government—particularly the Congress.

In line with the framers' goal of increased power to the national government, the president was granted the unconditional power to accept ambassadors from other countries; this amounted to the power to "recognize" other countries. The president was also given the power to negotiate treaties, although their acceptance required the approval of the Senate. The president was given the unconditional right to grant reprieves and pardons, except in cases of impeachment. And the president was provided with the power to appoint major departmental personnel, to convene Congress in special session, and to veto congressional enactments. (The veto power is formidable, but it is not absolute, since Congress can override it by a two-thirds vote.)

The framers hoped to create a presidency that would make the federal government rather than the states the agency capable of timely and decisive action to deal with public issues and problems. This was the meaning of the "energy" that Hamilton hoped to impart to the executive branch.[15] At the same time, however, the framers sought to help the president withstand excessively democratic pressures by creating a system of indirect rather than direct election through a separate electoral college.

THE JUDICIAL BRANCH

In establishing the judicial branch in Article III, the Constitution reflected the framers' preoccupations with nationalizing governmental power and checking radical democratic impulses while guarding against potential interference with liberty and property from the new national government itself.

Under the provisions of Article III, the framers created a court that was to be literally a supreme court of the United States, and not merely the highest court of the national government. The most important expression of this intention was granting the Supreme Court the power to resolve any conflicts that might emerge between federal and state laws. In particular, the Supreme Court was given the right to determine whether a power was exclusive to the national government, concurrent with the states, or exclusive to the states. In addition, the Supreme Court was assigned jurisdiction over controversies between citizens of different states. The long-term significance of this provision was that as the country developed a national economy, it came to rely increasingly on the federal judiciary, rather than on the state courts, for the resolution of disputes.

Judges were given lifetime appointments in order to protect them from popular politics and from interference by the other branches. This, however, did not mean that the judiciary would remain totally impartial to political considerations or to the other branches, for the president was to appoint the judges, and the Senate to approve the appointments. Congress would also have the power to create inferior (lower) courts, to change the jurisdiction of the federal courts, to add or subtract federal judges, and even to change the size of the Supreme Court.

judicial review
the power of the courts to declare actions of the legislative and executive branches invalid or unconstitutional. The Supreme Court asserted this power in *Marbury v. Madison*

No direct mention is made in the Constitution of **judicial review**—the power of the courts to render the final decision when there is a conflict of interpretation of the Constitution or of laws between the courts and Congress, the courts and the executive branch, or the courts and the states. The Supreme Court eventually assumed the power of judicial review. Its assumption of this power, as we shall see in Chapter 16, was based not on the Constitution itself but on the politics of later decades and the membership of the Court.

NATIONAL UNITY AND POWER

Various provisions in the Constitution addressed the framers' concern with national unity and power, including Article IV's provisions for comity (reciprocity) among states and among citizens of all states. Each state was prohibited from discriminating against the citizens of other states in favor of its own citizens, with the Supreme Court charged with deciding in each case whether a state had discriminated against goods or people from another state. The Constitution restricted the power of the states in favor of ensuring enough power to the national government to give the country a free-flowing national economy.

The framers' concern with national supremacy was also expressed in Article VI, in the **supremacy clause,** which provided that national laws and treaties "shall be the supreme law of the land." This meant that all laws made under the "authority of the United States" would be superior to all laws adopted by any state or any other subdivision, and the states would be expected to respect all treaties made under that authority. The supremacy clause also bound the officials of all state and local as well as federal governments to take an oath of office to support the national Constitution. This meant that every action taken by the United States Congress would have to be applied within each state as though the action were in fact state law.

supremacy clause
Article VI of the Constitution, which states that laws passed by the national government and all treaties are the supreme law of the land and superior to all laws adopted by any state or any subdivision

AMENDING THE CONSTITUTION

The Constitution established procedures for its own revision in Article V. Its provisions are so difficult that Americans have availed themselves of the amending process only seventeen times since 1791, when the first ten amendments were adopted. Many other amendments have been proposed in Congress, but fewer than forty of them have even come close to fulfilling the Constitution's requirement of a two-thirds vote in Congress, and only a fraction have gotten anywhere near adoption by three-fourths of the states. Article V also provides that the Constitution can be amended by a constitutional convention. Occasionally, proponents of particular measures, such as a balanced-budget amendment, have called for a constitutional convention to consider their proposals. Whatever the purpose for which it were called, however, such a convention would presumably have the authority to revise America's entire system of government.

RATIFYING THE CONSTITUTION

The rules for the ratification of the Constitution were set forth in Article VII. Nine of the thirteen states would have to ratify, or agree upon, the terms in order for the Constitution to pass.

CONSTITUTIONAL LIMITS ON THE NATIONAL GOVERNMENT'S POWER

As we have indicated, although the framers sought to create a powerful national government, they also wanted to guard against possible misuse of that power. To that end, the framers incorporated two key principles into the Constitution—the separation of powers and federalism. A third set of limitations, in the form of the Bill of Rights, was added to the Constitution to help secure its ratification when opponents of the document charged that it paid insufficient attention to citizens' rights.

The Separation of Powers No principle of politics was more widely shared at the time of the 1787 founding than the principle that power must be used to balance power. The French political theorist Baron de la Brède et de Montesquieu (1689–1755) believed that this balance was an indispensable defense against tyranny, and his writings, especially his major work, *The Spirit of the Laws,* "were taken as political gospel" at the Philadelphia Convention.[16] The principle of the separation of powers is not stated explicitly in the Constitution, but it is clearly built on Articles I, II, and III, which provide for the following:

1. Three separate and distinct branches of government (see Figure 3.1);
2. Different methods of selecting the top personnel, so that each branch is responsible to a different constituency. This is supposed to produce a "mixed regime," in which the personnel of each department will de-

Figure 3.1 THE SEPARATION OF POWERS

Executive	Legislative	Judicial
Enforces laws Commander in chief of armed forces Makes foreign treaties Proposes laws Appoints Supreme Court justices and federal court judges Pardons those convicted in federal court	Passes federal laws Controls federal appropriations Approves treaties and presidential appointments Regulates interstate commerce Establishes lower court system	Reviews lower court decisions Decides constitutionality of laws Decides cases involving disputes between states

The Constitution provides for the separation of powers to ensure that no one branch of American government holds too much power.

CHECKS AND BALANCES

Figure 3.2

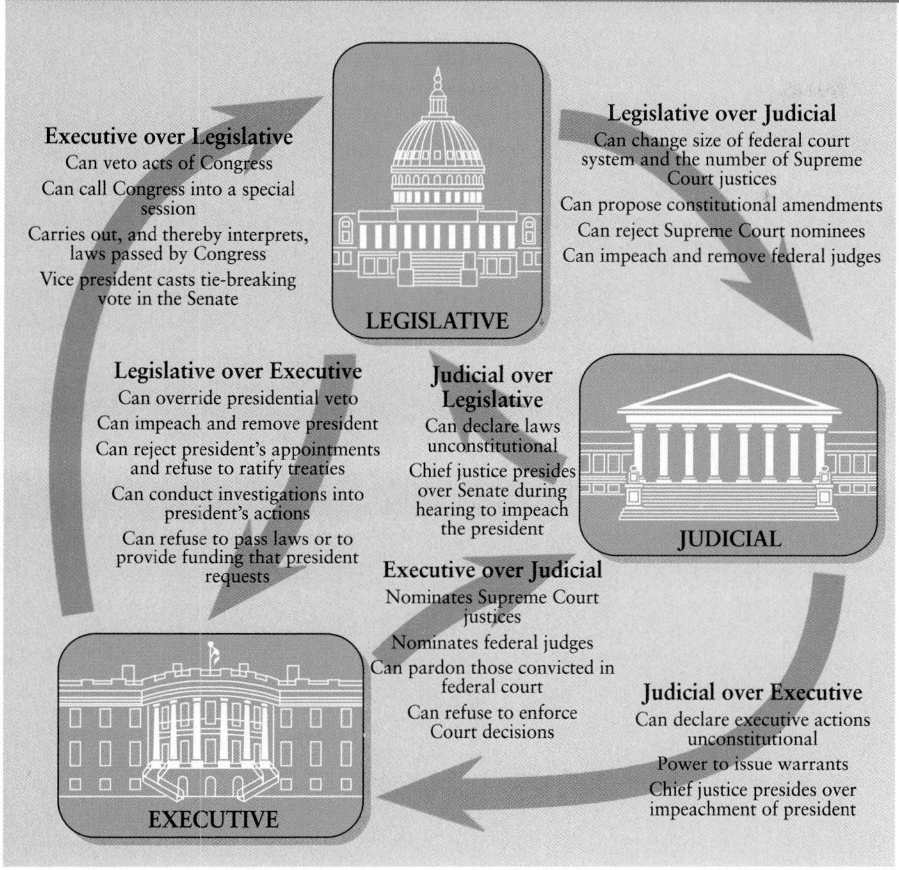
LEGISLATIVE
Executive over Legislative
Can veto acts of Congress
Can call Congress into a special session
Carries out, and thereby interprets, laws passed by Congress
Vice president casts tie-breaking vote in the Senate
Legislative over Judicial
Can change size of federal court system and the number of Supreme Court justices
Can propose constitutional amendments
Can reject Supreme Court nominees
Can impeach and remove federal judges
Legislative over Executive
Can override presidential veto
Can impeach and remove president
Can reject president's appointments and refuse to ratify treaties
Can conduct investigations into president's actions
Can refuse to pass laws or to provide funding that president requests
Judicial over Legislative
Can declare laws unconstitutional
Chief justice presides over Senate during hearing to impeach the president
JUDICIAL
Executive over Judicial
Nominates Supreme Court justices
Nominates federal judges
Can pardon those convicted in federal court
Can refuse to enforce Court decisions
Judicial over Executive
Can declare executive actions unconstitutional
Power to issue warrants
Chief justice presides over impeachment of president
EXECUTIVE

velop very different interests and outlooks on how to govern, and different groups in society will be assured some access to governmental decision making; and

3. Checks and balances—a system under which each of the branches is given some power over the others. Familiar examples are the presidential veto power over legislation, the power of the Senate to approve presidential appointments, and judicial review of acts of Congress (see Figure 3.2).

One clever formulation of the separation of powers is that of a system not of separated powers but of "separated institutions sharing power,"[17] and thus diminishing the chance that power will be misused.

Federalism Compared to the confederation principle of the Articles of Confederation, federalism was a step toward greater centralization of power. The delegates agreed that they needed to place more power at the national level, without completely undermining the power of the state governments. Thus, they devised a system of two sovereigns—the states and the nation—with the hope that competition between the two would be an effective limitation on the power of both.

The Bill of Rights Late in the Philadelphia Convention, a motion was made to include a list of citizens' rights in the Constitution. After a brief debate in which hardly a word was said in its favor and only one speech was made against it, the motion was almost unanimously turned down. Most delegates sincerely believed that since the federal government was already limited to its expressed powers, further protection of citizens was not needed. The delegates argued that the states should adopt bills of rights because their greater powers needed greater limitations. But almost immediately after the Constitution was ratified, there was a movement to adopt a national bill of rights. This is why the Bill of Rights, adopted in 1791, comprises the first ten amendments to the Constitution rather than being part of the body of it. We will have a good deal more to say about the Bill of Rights in Chapter 5.

The Fight for Ratification

- What sides did the Federalists and the Antifederalists represent in the fight over ratification?
- Over what key principles did the Federalists and the Antifederalists disagree?

The first hurdle faced by the Constitution was ratification by state conventions of delegates elected by the people of each state. This struggle for ratification was carried out in thirteen separate campaigns. Each involved different people, moved at a different pace, and was influenced by local as well as national considerations. Two sides faced off throughout the states, however, calling themselves Federalists and Antifederalists (see Table 3.1 on page 92). The **Federalists** (who more accurately should have called themselves "Nationalists," but who took their name to appear to follow in the revolutionary tradition) supported the Constitution and preferred a strong national government. The **Antifederalists** opposed the Constitution and preferred a federal system of government that was decentralized; they took their name by default, in reaction to their better-organized opponents. The Federalists were united in their support of the Constitution, while the Antifederalists were divided over what they believed the alternative to the Constitution should be.

Federalists
those who favored a strong national government and supported the constitution proposed at the American Constitutional Convention of 1787

Antifederalists
those who favored strong state governments and a weak national government and who were opponents of the constitution proposed at the American Constitutional Convention of 1787

During the struggle over ratification of the Constitution, Americans argued about great political issues and principles. How much power should the national government be given? What safeguards were most likely to prevent the abuse of power? What institutional arrangements could best ensure adequate representation for all Americans? Was tyranny to be feared more from the many or from the few?

FEDERALISTS VS. ANTIFEDERALISTS

During the ratification struggle, thousands of essays, speeches, pamphlets, and letters were presented in support of and in opposition to the proposed Consti-

POLICY DEBATE

Religious Freedom and School Prayer

The first two rights enshrined in the First Amendment bar the government from establishing a state religion and from inhibiting the free exercise of religion by individuals. Thus, the government is barred from breaching the "wall of separation" between church and state, so that religious liberty may find full expression. Yet is that wall breached if individuals wish to express their religious beliefs in schools? At first glance, the answer would appear to be yes. In the 1962 case of *Engel v. Vitale,* the Supreme Court barred government-organized and -led religious prayer. Since then, proponents of prayer in school have marshaled much support for a more flexible approach, arguing in part that courts have misunderstood the framers' intent. Proponents have also pushed for a constitutional amendment guaranteeing free religious expression in public schools.

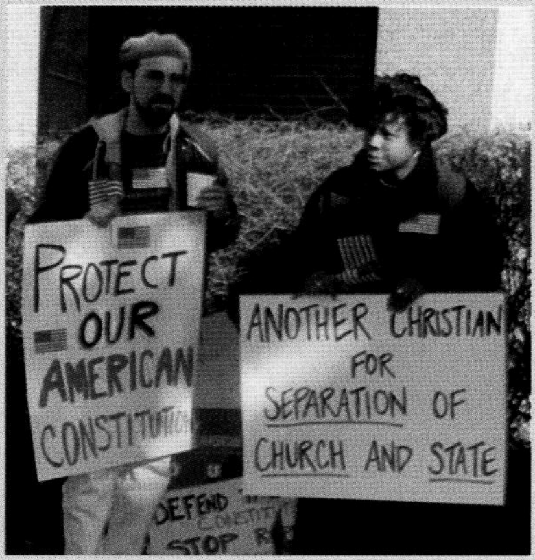

Proponents of prayer in school argue that the Constitution's framers were pious men who were not out to drive religion from schools or other aspects of public life. Thomas Jefferson, for example, who wrote of maintaining a "wall of separation" between church and state, also wrote of the importance of religious training as an integral part of education. Every congress since the Founding has opened its daily session with a prayer. Supreme Court sessions begin with the words "God save the United States and this Honorable Court." Schoolchildren have prayed in public schools for most of the country's history. By now shunning any form of religious expression at a time when children seem increasingly in need of moral and spiritual guidance, schools are sending the wrong message to the nation's children. Moreover, the absence of school religion implicitly encourages another belief system—secularism. The elimination of all religious teachings elevates a secular ideology that, in the minds of many, amounts to little more than state-sponsored atheism. Thus, some argue, schools that ignore or deny the existence of God and religion are promoting another belief—that there is no God.

School prayer need not be led by teachers or administrators, nor need it be required. Voluntary prayer led by students would pose no threat to the First Amendment. Instead, it would reflect the proper extension of religious liberty into schools. In short, an enlightened approach to school prayer requires neither a government stamp of approval nor any form of coercion.

Opponents of school prayer argue that both the First Amendment and American respect for individual freedom require that schools avoid any role in religious teaching, instruction, or prayer. They point out the important fact that prayer is not barred from any school, as any student may pray at any time. It is organized prayer, they assert, that must be avoided. Government meddling in religion drove many European settlers to America, and the Founders understood that keeping government out of religious matters was not an expression of hostility to religion, but a simple acknowledgment that both government and religion were better off if the former let the latter alone.

Although most Americans hold some form of religious belief, the range of those beliefs is wide and growing, meaning that any form of religious teaching or prayer is bound to offend the sensibilities of some religious groups. Moreover, the rights of nonbelievers are equal to those of believers. School actions that ostracize, penalize, or stigmatize nonbelievers violate their right to equal treatment and their right not to be subjected to religious teachings in what is a public and secular institution.

The desire to teach moral values in schools is not limited to, or by, religion. Moral and ethical training does not require the infusion of religion. Moral problems related to drugs and sex, for example, already receive considerable attention in public school curricula. Finally, the teaching of religious beliefs is best left to professionals—churches and their clergy—and to families.

STUDENT DEBATE

Should School Prayer Be Allowed?

Yes

There has been much said and written in the past few months in the wake of the Columbine High School shootings regarding religion's place in the public schools of this country.

One of the victims who was murdered in the Littleton, Colo. high school was asked whether she believed in God before she was executed. Since the tragedy that claimed thirteen innocent lives, many have begun to question whether prayer should be allowed to take place in public schools.

Students across the country have been prohibited from leading prayers on school grounds on the basis that by doing so, the separation of church and state would be violated.

In addition, allowing time for prayer supposedly discriminates against those who don't practice religion or would isolate those who are not of a religion shared by the majority of a particular school's student body.

Stephanie Vega, a student at Santa Fe High School in Texas, had decided that she would not lead her fellow students in a prayer before each home football game after she was threatened with expulsion from the school system. (*Washington Post*, Aug. 27 [1997])

School Superintendent Richard Ownby stated that any student who leads a prayer at a football game "would be disciplined as if they had cursed."

For anyone, especially a school official, to place prayer in the same category as cursing is not only outlandish, but it is sad. Since this country's birth, religion has helped to solidify the moral foundation with which this country was founded.

Cursing, of course, is downright improper in school settings and should not be tolerated. Prayer, on the other hand, brings peace, hope, self-assurance and a host of other positives. It is difficult to understand why so many liberals in this country are against allowing students to pray in school.

These same people will not even tolerate allowing students to observe a moment of silence or hold a quiet time of a minute or two when a student or teacher can pray or meditate.

Perhaps it is because liberals believe the proper way for the young to build motivation and self-esteem is not through prayer and religion, but to consult some quack psychiatrist.

As religion has decreased its influence on children in the past couple of decades, there has been an explosion in the number of people diagnosed as having some psychological psychobabble disorder.

It is amazing what is allowed in today's public school systems. In a school project, the two Columbine murderers showed off collections of weapons and discussed violence against others. They walked around in "cult-like" wardrobe. The school officials tolerated this as freedom of expression.

Put a Bible in their hand, however, and they would have been escorted to the principal's office and told that carrying a Bible around the school was unacceptable. Something is wrong with this anti-religious attitude, but liberals can't see it.

It is reasonable for the courts to prevent public schools from forcing students to pray, but not allowing students to have a quiet minute at the beginning of the school day or not allowing students to lead prayers at their own discretion infringes on the rights of those students to express themselves.

SOURCE: Brian Stora, "School Prayer Is the Answer to Violence Epidemic," *The Collegiate Times* (Virginia Tech), October 6, 1999.

No

There is a famous story about a scientist who removes all of the legs from a frog and asks it to jump. When the frog, inevitably, does not jump, the scientist writes in his notebook, "With no legs, frog is deaf."

A similar phenomenon has been occurring among Republicans lately. In the wake of the Littleton shootings the one point of agreement between the left and the right has been the lack of easy explanations, which hasn't stopped the Republicans from suggesting one.

Newt Gingrich stated it bluntly in a recent speech to the Republican Women Leaders Forum. "When Al Gore talks about God and faith, is he for voluntary school prayer or isn't he? Does he want to bring God back in or does he want to give us a psychobabble?"

Absent from all of this Republican invective is even the slightest shred of evidence that any of the recent school shootings are connected to the absence of religious instruction in public schools. And without such evidence, the Republicans are in danger of looking as foolish as our frog scientist.

It is a tautology to say the Littleton murderers have no values. The problem comes in linking values to God. Indeed, the shooters in the recent Arkansas and Kentucky incidents both came from families that attended church regularly. They were no strangers to God and his message. Early reports out of Littleton indicated that one of the two shooters had attended a seder in the weeks leading up to the massacre (but in the minds of many moral majoritarians, Judaism doesn't count). Also unmentioned is the virtual lack of violent crime in many European countries. These are countries whose secular culture differs from ours primarily in the strictness of their gun laws, and in their taboos against violence.

Equally irritating is Republican vagueness about what, exactly, they want. Gingrich wants "to bring God back in," but what does that mean? Does he want a special class devoted to religious training? And whose God? He calls for "voluntary school prayer," but that is precisely what we have now. Any student can pray whenever he or she feels like it. Does Gingrich want teachers to lead students in prayer? Does it matter to him what religion the teacher practices? Perhaps he only wants a nebulous moment of silence, but surely he doesn't think that would be sufficient to guard against all future shootings? Gingrich and his ilk really want Christianity to be taught in the schools, but they know this idea would be unpalatable to most people. So they couch their rhetoric in terms like "values" and "prayer" that generally garner a more favorable reaction.

Even here I might be inclined to take Gingrich seriously, if his hypocrisy were not so blazingly evident. Elsewhere in his speech he says, "And [Bill Bradley and Al Gore] can set a standard and say that we are only going to do fundraisers with producers and stars that do decent films." It doesn't seem to bother him that Republicans take money from Arnold Schwarzenegger, Bruce Willis, and Sylvester Stallone, perpetrators of some of the most violent movies ever made. Of course, these movies usually show a macho American super-patriot delivering a rousing, red-white-and-blue butt-kicking to some ill-mannered foreigners. By Republican standards, this is a good moral message to be teaching our kids. Gingrich, incidentally, goes on to say, "And I am not using that just to make a partisan point."

If teaching values means instructing our kids about racial equality, the perils of crime and drugs, the importance of hard work and discipline, and respect for the people around you then I'm all for it. These are good, sound values regardless of whether there's a spirit in the sky watching over us or not. But the answer to Littleton does not lie in Republican simple-mindedness. Using God as some sort of three-letter bogeyman for scaring kids into line is an idea that should be offensive to all genuinely religious people. Our "core American values" include things like freedom of religion and tolerance of others. It would be foolish to allow the latest crop of Republican theocrats to sully these values in the name of righteousness or morality or God.

SOURCE: Jason Rosenhouse, "Teach Values, Not God," *The Dartmouth* (Darthmouth College), May 19, 1999.

Table 3.1 FEDERALISTS VS. ANTIFEDERALISTS

	Federalists	Antifederalists
Who were they?	Property owners, creditors, merchants	Small farmers, frontiersmen, debtors, shopkeepers
What did they believe?	Believed that elites were best fit to govern; feared "excessive democracy"	Believed that government should be closer to the people; feared concentration of power in hands of the elites
What system of government did they favor?	Favored strong national government; believed in "filtration" so that only elites would obtain governmental power	Favored rentention of power by state governments and protection of individual rights
Who were their leaders?	Alexander Hamilton James Madison George Washington	Patrick Henry George Mason Elbridge Gerry George Clinton

tution. The best-known pieces supporting ratification of the Constitution were the eighty-five essays written, under the name of "Publius," by Alexander Hamilton, James Madison, and John Jay between the fall of 1787 and the spring of 1788. These **Federalist Papers,** as they are collectively known today, defended the principles of the Constitution and sought to dispel fears of a national authority. The Antifederalists published essays of their own, arguing that the new Constitution betrayed the Revolution and was a step toward monarchy. Among the best of the Antifederalist works were the essays, usually attributed to New York Supreme Court justice Robert Yates, that were written under the name of "Brutus" and published in the *New York Journal* at the same time the Federalist Papers appeared. The Antifederalist view was also ably presented in the pamphlets and letters written by a former delegate to the Continental Congress and future U.S. senator, Richard Henry Lee of Virginia, using the pen name "The Federal Farmer." These essays highlight the major differences of opinion between Federalists and Antifederalists. Federalists appealed to basic principles of government in support of their nationalist vision. Antifederalists cited equally fundamental precepts to support their vision of a looser confederacy of small republics.

Federalist Papers
a series of essays written by James Madison, Alexander Hamilton, and John Jay supporting the ratification of the Constitution

Representation One major area of contention between the two sides was the question of representation. The Antifederalists asserted that representatives must be "a true picture of the people, . . . [possessing] the knowledge of their circumstances and their wants."[18] This could be achieved, argued the Antifederalists, only in small, relatively homogeneous republics such as the existing states. In their view, the size and extent of the entire nation precluded the construction of a truly representative form of government. As Brutus put it, "Is it practicable for a country so large and so numerous . . . to elect a representation that will speak their sentiments? . . . It certainly is not."[19]

Federalists, for their part, saw no reason that representatives should be precisely like those they represented. In the Federalist view, one of the great advantages of representative government over direct democracy was precisely the possibility that the people would choose as their representatives individuals possessing ability, experience, and talent superior to their own. In Madison's words, rather than serve as a mirror or reflection of society, representatives must be "[those] who possess [the] most wisdom to discern, and [the] most virtue to pursue, the common good of the society."[20]

James Madison, the "father" of the Constitution, was a prominent Federalist.

Although the terms of discussion have changed, this debate over representation continues today. Some argue that representatives must be very close in life experience, race, and ethnic background to their constituents to truly understand the needs and interests of those constituents. This argument is made by contemporary proponents of giving the states more control over social programs. This argument is also made by proponents of "minority districts"—legislative districts whose boundaries are drawn so as to guarantee that minorities will be able to elect their own representative to Congress. Opponents of this practice, which we will explore further in Chapter 11, have argued in court that it is discriminatory and unnecessary; blacks, they say, can be represented by whites and vice versa. Who is correct? It would appear that this question can never be answered to everyone's complete satisfaction.

Tyranny of the Majority A second important issue dividing Federalists and Antifederalists was the threat of **tyranny**—unjust rule by the group in power. Both opponents and defenders of the Constitution frequently affirmed their fear of tyrannical rule. Each side, however, had a different view of the most likely source of tyranny and, hence, of the way in which the threat was to be forestalled.

tyranny
oppressive and unjust government that employs cruel and unjust use of power and authority

From the Antifederalist perspective, the great danger was the tendency of all governments—including republican governments—to become gradually more and more "aristocratic" in character, wherein the small number of individuals in positions of authority would use their stations to gain more and more power over the general citizenry. In essence, the few would use their power to tyrannize the many. For this reason, Antifederalists were sharply critical of those features of the Constitution that divorced governmental institutions from direct responsibility to the people—institutions such as the Senate, the executive, and the federal judiciary. The latter, appointed for life, presented a particular threat: "I wonder if the world ever saw . . . a court of justice invested with such immense powers, and yet placed in a situation so little responsible," protested Brutus.[21]

The Federalists, too, recognized the threat of tyranny, but they believed that the danger particularly associated with republican governments was not aristocracy, but instead, majority tyranny. The Federalists were concerned that a popular majority, "united and actuated by some common impulse of passion, or of interest, adverse to the rights of other citizens," would endeavor to "trample on the rules of justice."[22] From the Federalist perspective, it was precisely those features of the Constitution attacked as potential sources of tyranny by the Antifederalists that actually offered the best hope of averting the threat of oppression. The size and extent of the nation, for instance, was for the Federalists a bulwark against tyranny.

limited government
a government whose powers are defined and limited by a constitution

Governmental Power A third major difference between Federalists and Antifederalists was the issue of governmental power. Both the opponents and proponents of the Constitution agreed on the principle of **limited government.** They differed, however, on the fundamentally important question of how to place limits on governmental action. Antifederalists favored limiting and enumerating the powers granted to the national government in relation both to the states and to the people at large. To them, the powers given the national government ought to be "confined to certain defined national objects."[23] Otherwise, the national government would "swallow up all the power of the state governments."[24] Antifederalists bitterly attacked the supremacy clause and the elastic clause of the Constitution as unlimited and dangerous grants of power to the national government.[25] Antifederalists also demanded that a bill of rights be added to the Constitution to place limits upon the government's exercise of power over the citizenry.

Federalists favored the construction of a government with broad powers. They wanted a government that had the capacity to defend the nation against foreign foes, guard against domestic strife and insurrection, promote commerce, and expand the nation's economy. Antifederalists shared some of these goals but still feared governmental power. Hamilton pointed out, however, that these goals could not be achieved without allowing the government to exercise the necessary power. Federalists acknowledged that every power could be abused but argued that the way to prevent misuse of power was not by depriving the government of the powers needed to achieve national goals. Instead, they argued that the threat of abuse of power would be mitigated by the Constitution's internal checks and controls. As Madison put it, "the power surrendered by the people is first divided between two distinct governments, and then the portion allotted to each subdivided among distinct and separate departments. Hence, a double security arises to the rights of the people. The different governments will control each other, at the same time that each will be controlled by itself."[26] The Federalists' concern with avoiding unwarranted limits on governmental power led them to oppose a bill of rights, which they saw as nothing more than a set of unnecessary restrictions on the government.

The Federalists acknowledged that abuse of power remained a possibility, but felt that the risk had to be taken because of the goals to be achieved. "The very idea of power included a possibility of doing harm," said the Federalist John Rutledge during the South Carolina ratification debates. "If the gentleman would show the power that could do no harm," Rutledge continued, "he would at once discover it to be a power that could do no good."[27] This aspect of the debate between the Federalists and the Antifederalists, perhaps more than any other, continues to reverberate through American politics. Should the nation limit the federal government's power to tax and spend? Should Congress limit the capacity of federal agencies to issue new regulations? Should the government endeavor to create new rights for minorities, the disabled, and others? What is the proper balance between promoting equality and protecting liberty? Though the details have changed, these are the same great questions that have been debated since the time of the Founding.

Contrasting Approaches to Constitutional Democracy

Constitutions are, in effect, the codification of the basic rules and procedures designed to regulate and control the balance between mathematical minorities and majorities within society.

There are generally three critical characteristics of the constitutional tradition of a country (whether that constitution is formally written or not). These three characteristics provide the comparative perspective by which students of contitutional theory may evaluate the constitutional tradition within the broader political culture of a country. These three characteristics are (1) the *determination* of the actual content of the constitutional rules; (2) the *distinctiveness* of the constitution's structure; and (3) the degree to which the specific rules and codes within the constitution are *entrenched* aspects of the political culture.

Being a majoritarian democracy (see Chapter 2), the British have a constitution that is characterized by *indeterminate content, indistinct structure,* and an *unentrenched constitutional process.* With respect to content, the Queen's Stationary Office published the Official Revised Edition of the statutes in force within Britain. This consists in part of 138 acts of Parliament dating from 1297 through the present, including the Parliamentary Acts of 1911 and 1949, as well as an additional 32 statutes dealing with the "rights of the subjects," including what is left of the Magna Carta.

In contrast to the British "constitution," it is hard to miss the determining content of the American constitution. Its Preamble, seven articles, and 27 amendments are written in an explicit document. Similarly, the German constitution (commonly referred to as the Basic Laws or *Grundgesetz*) is clearly and explicitly written for strict interpretation. It consists of a preamble and 141 articles. Even the content of the French Constitution (of the current Fifth Republic, formed in October 1958) is rather explicit: It consists of the famous Declaration of the Rights of Man and the Citizen drafted in 1789, specifying the general principles of human liberties, including 17 specific Rights of Man and the Citizen; the preamble to the French Fourth Republic (1946–1958); and the Fifth Republic's own preamble and 93 articles.

The British constitution is also indistinct in structure: It consists, in effect, of a miscellany of statutes of Parliament (which, in English law, consists of the monarch and two chambers of the British legislature—the House of Lords and the House of Commons), a variety of "legal conventions," and a series of special laws passed by Parliament. This contrasts with the clear and sharply defined targets found in the articles of the American, French, and German constitutions. Thus, the American Supreme Court has a distinct body of articles to evaluate in the event it examines the constitutionality of an act of Congress.

Finally, the British constitutional tradition is clearly unentrenched in the political process of government because there are no formal requirements for enacting or amending the norms of the unwritten constitution. In other words, there is no special procedure to establish British constitution principles: Its enactment is, in effect, ongoing and is indistinguishable from the way any ordinary statute or law is promulgated in Parliament. The unwritten British constitution, therefore, stands vulnerable to the political will of a bare majority within the House of Commons. This contrasts sharply with the American, French, and German written constitutions, each of which specify strict rules and procedures by which the constitution may be amended. Such amendments and enactments require special voting procedures (both for ratification and amendment) as well as complicated popular referendums (in the case of the French Fifth Republic).

The American, French, and German constitutions were each drafted during difficult and trying times for their respective democracies, thus reflecting the anxieties among majorities and minorities within each society (revolution in America, attempted military coup d'état in France, and the painful memories and lessons of the Third Reich, as well as the rise of the Cold War in Germany). Britain's constitution reflects a tradition of gradual compromise and stability achieved over several centuries, thereby nurturing public tolerance for a constitution less distinct, less structured, and less entrenched than that found in the more recent American, French, and German constitutional democracies. Constitutions, while often overlooked and ignored by many modern students of political science, are invaluable windows into the political culture and formal power structure of any democracy, consensual or majoritarian.

SOURCE: S. E. Finer, Vernon Bogdanor, and Bernard Rudden, *Comparing Constitutions.* Oxford: Clarendon Press, 1995.

New York was the scene of a great celebration following the ratification of the Constitution. The federal ship *Hamilton* leads this parade.

REFLECTIONS ON THE FOUNDING

The final product of the Constitutional Convention would have to be considered an extraordinary victory for the groups that had most forcefully called for the creation of a new system of government to replace the Articles of Confederation. Antifederalist criticisms forced the Constitution's proponents to accept the addition of a bill of rights designed to limit the powers of the national government. In general, however, it was the Federalist vision of America that triumphed. The Constitution adopted in 1789 created the framework for a powerful national government that for more than two hundred years has defended the nation's interests, promoted its commerce, and maintained national unity. In one notable instance, the national government fought and won a bloody war to prevent the nation from breaking apart. And despite this powerful government, the system of internal checks and balances has functioned reasonably well, as the Federalists predicted, to prevent the national government from tyrannizing its citizens.

Although they were defeated in 1789, the Antifederalists present us with an important picture of a road not taken and of an America that might have been. Would the country have been worse off if it had been governed by a confederacy of small republics linked by a national administration with severely limited powers? Were the Antifederalists correct in predicting that a government given great power in the hope that it might do good would, through "insensible progress," inevitably turn to evil purposes? Two hundred years of government under the federal Constitution are not necessarily enough to definitively answer these questions. Time must tell.

The Citizen's Role and the Changing Constitution

- Why is the Constitution difficult to amend?
- What purposes do the amendments to the Constitution serve?

The Constitution has endured for more than two centuries as the framework of government. But it has not endured without change. Without change, the Constitution might have become merely a sacred text, stored under glass.

AMENDMENTS: MANY ARE CALLED, FEW ARE CHOSEN

The need for change was recognized by the framers of the Constitution, and the provisions for **amendment** incorporated into Article V were thought to be "an easy, regular and Constitutional way" to make changes, which would occasionally be necessary because members of Congress "may abuse their power and refuse their consent on that very account . . . to admit to amendments to correct the source of the abuse."[28] Madison made a more balanced defense of the amendment procedure in Article V: "It guards equally against that extreme facility, which would render the Constitution too mutable; and that extreme difficulty, which might perpetuate its discovered faults."[29]

amendment
a change added to a bill, law, or constitution

Experience since 1789 raises questions even about Madison's more modest claims. The Constitution has proven to be extremely difficult to amend. In the history of efforts to amend the Constitution, the most appropriate characterization is "many are called, few are chosen." Between 1789 and 1996, more than 11,000 amendments were formally offered in Congress. Of these, Congress officially proposed only twenty-nine, and twenty-seven of these were eventually ratified by the states. But the record is even more severe than that. Since 1791, when the first ten amendments, the Bill of Rights, were added, only seventeen amendments have been adopted. And two of them—Prohibition and its repeal—cancel each other out, so that for all practical purposes, only fifteen amendments have been added to the Constitution since 1791. Despite vast changes in American society and its economy, only twelve amendments have been adopted since the Civil War amendments in 1868.

Four methods of amendment are provided for in Article V:

1. Passage in House and Senate by two-thirds vote; then ratification by majority vote of the legislatures of three-fourths (thirty-eight) of the states.
2. Passage in House and Senate by two-thirds vote; then ratification by conventions called for the purpose in three-fourths of the states.
3. Passage in a national convention called by Congress in response to petitions by two-thirds of the states; ratification by majority vote of the legislatures of three-fourths of the states.
4. Passage in a national convention, as in (3); then ratification by conventions called for the purpose in three-fourths of the states.

Figure 3.3 FOUR WAYS THE CONSTITUTION CAN BE AMENDED

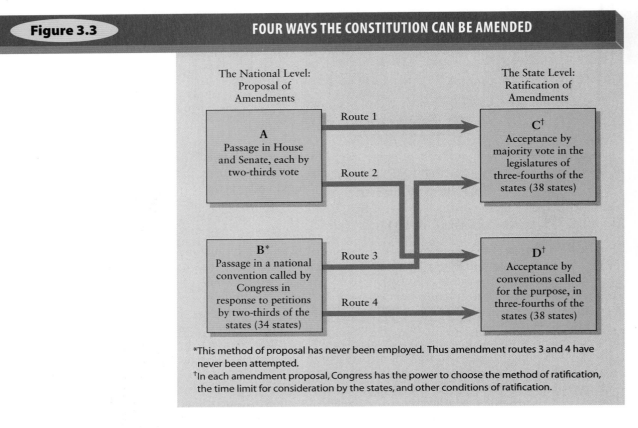

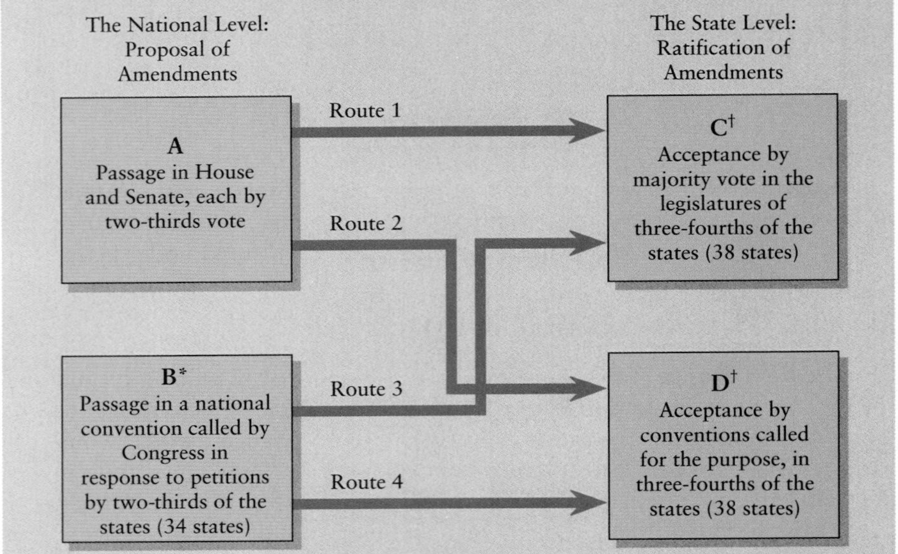

*This method of proposal has never been employed. Thus amendment routes 3 and 4 have never been attempted.

†In each amendment proposal, Congress has the power to choose the method of ratification, the time limit for consideration by the states, and other conditions of ratification.

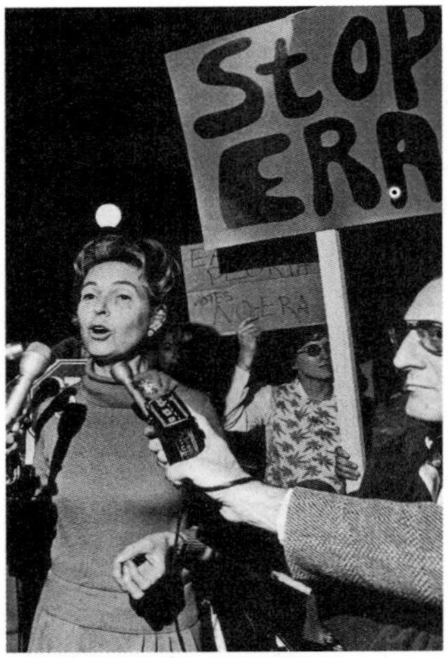

Phyllis Schlafly, leader of the group Stop ERA, argued that the ERA was unnecessary and even harmful to women.

(Figure 3.3 illustrates each of these possible methods.) Since no amendment has ever been proposed by national convention, however, methods (3) and (4) have never been employed. And method (2) has only been employed once (the Twenty-first Amendment, which repealed the Eighteenth, or Prohibition, Amendment). Thus, method (1) has been used for all the others.

Now it should be clear why it has been so difficult to amend the Constitution. The requirement of a two-thirds vote in the House and the Senate means that any proposal for an amendment in Congress can be killed by only 34 senators or 136 members of the House. What is more, if the necessary two-thirds vote is obtained, the amendment can still be killed by the refusal or inability of only thirteen state legislatures to ratify it. Since each state has an equal vote regardless of its population, the thirteen holdout states may represent a very small fraction of the total American population.

THE CASE OF THE EQUAL RIGHTS AMENDMENT

The Equal Rights Amendment (ERA) is a case study of a proposed amendment that almost succeeded. In fact, the ERA is one of the very few proposals that got the necessary two-thirds vote in Congress yet failed to obtain the ratification of the requisite thirty-eight states.

On October 12, 1971, the U.S. House of Representatives approved the Equal Rights Amendment by the required two-thirds majority; the Senate followed suit on March 22, 1972. The amendment was simple:

> Sec. 1. Equality of rights under the law shall not be denied or abridged by the United States or by any State on account of sex.
> Sec. 2. The Congress shall have the power to enforce, by appropriate legislation, the provisions of this article.
> Sec. 3. This amendment shall take effect two years after the date of ratification.

The congressional resolution provided for the accustomed method of ratification through the state legislatures rather than by state conventions—route (1) rather than route (2) in Figure 3.3—and that it had to be completed within seven years, by March 22, 1979.

Since the amendment was the culmination of nearly a half-century of efforts, and since the women's movement had spread its struggle for several years prior to 1971, the amendment was ratified by twenty-eight state legislatures during the very first year. But opposition forces quickly organized into the "Stop ERA" movement. By the end of 1974, five more states had ratified the amendment, but three states that had ratified it in 1973—Idaho, Nebraska, and Tennessee—had afterwards voted to rescind their ratification. This posed an unprecedented problem: whether a state legislature had the right to rescind its approval. The Supreme Court refused to deal with this question, insisting that it was a political question to be settled by Congress. If the ERA had been ratified by the thirty-eight-state minimum, Congress would have had to decide whether to respect the rescissions or to count them as ratifications.

This point was rendered moot by events. By the end of 1978, thirty-five state legislatures had ratified the ERA—counting the three rescinding legislatures as ratifiers. But even counting them, the three additional state ratifications necessary to reach thirty-eight became increasingly difficult to get. In each of the remaining fifteen states, the amendment had already been rejected at least once. The only hope of the ERA forces was that the 1978 elections would change the composition of some of those state legislatures. Pinning their hopes on that, the ERA forces turned back to Congress and succeeded in getting an extension of the ratification deadline to June 30, 1982. This was an especially significant victory, because it was the first time Congress had extended the time limit since it began placing time restrictions on ratification in 1917. But this victory in Washington failed to impress any of the fifteen holdout

Students and Politics

Few students know that the Bill of Rights as proposed by Madison consisted of twelve amendments, not ten. The states did not ratify two of the proposed amendments, one of which would have prohibited Congress from voting itself a salary raise to take effect before the next election.

That proposed amendment had remained dormant for almost two hundred years when Gregory Watson, a student at the University of Texas at Austin, unearthed it while researching a paper for a political science class. Watson argued that sentiment and viability for the amendment remained, although his professor did not agree; he received a C. Shocked by the poor grade for his hard work, Watson spent the next ten years on a crusade to champion the amendment, including soliciting the support of sympathetic members of Congress and sifting through an immense amount of constitutional scholarship. Finally, despite powerful detractors in the academic and political communities, the measure went before the states, where it gained the necessary number of ratifications to go before Congress, which subsequently voted it the Twenty-seventh Amendment, also known as the Madison/Watson amendment.

SOURCE: "Profile in Constitutional Courage," http://webusers. anet-stl.com/~hvmlr/mf_hon2.html.

Gloria Steinem, one of the founders of the National Organization for Women (NOW), helped organize state-by-state campaigns to persuade state legislatures to pass the ERA.

legislatures. June 30, 1982, came and went, and the ERA was, for the time being at least, laid to rest. It was beaten by the efforts of Stop ERA and by the emergence of conservatism generally, which had culminated in Ronald Reagan's election as president.[30]

WHICH WERE CHOSEN? AN ANALYSIS OF THE TWENTY-SEVEN

There is more to the amending difficulties than the politics of campaigning and voting. It would appear that only a limited number of changes needed by society can actually be made through the Constitution. Although we shall see that the ERA fits the pattern of successful amendments, most efforts to amend the Constitution have failed because they were simply attempts to use the Constitution as an alternative to legislation for dealing directly with a public problem. A review of the successful amendments will provide two insights: First, it will give us some understanding of the conditions underlying successful amendments; and second, it will reveal a great deal about what constitutionalism means.

The purpose of the ten amendments in the Bill of Rights was basically structural, to give each of the three branches clearer and more restricted boundaries. The First Amendment clarified the jurisdiction of Congress. Although the powers of Congress under Article I, Section 8, would not have justified laws regulating religion, speech, and the like, the First Amendment made this limitation explicit: "Congress shall make no law. . . ." The Second, Third, and Fourth amendments similarly spelled out specific limits on the executive

Table 3.2 THE BILL OF RIGHTS: ANALYSIS OF ITS PROVISIONS

Amendment	Purpose
I	*Limits on Congress:* Congress is not to make any law establishing a religion or abridging speech, press, assembly, or petition freedoms.
II, III, IV	*Limits on Executive:* The executive branch is not to infringe on the right of people to keep arms (II), is not to arbitrarily take houses for a militia (III), and is not to engage in the search or seizure of evidence without a court warrant swearing to belief in the probable existence of a crime (IV).
V, VI, VII, VIII	*Limits on Courts:* The courts are not to hold trials for serious offenses without provision for a grand jury (V), a petit (trial) jury (VII), a speedy trial (VI), presentation of charges (VI), confrontation of hostile witnesses (VI), immunity from testimony against oneself (V), and immunity from trial more than once for the same offense (V). Neither bail nor punishment can be excessive (VIII), and no property can be taken without just compensation (V).
IX, X	*Limits on National Government:* All rights not enumerated are reserved to the states or the people.

AMENDING THE CONSTITUTION TO EXPAND THE ELECTORATE — **Table 3.3**

Amendment	Purpose	Year proposed	Year adopted
XV	Extended voting rights to all races	1869	1870
XIX	Extended voting rights to women	1919	1920
XXIII	Extended voting rights to residents of the District of Columbia	1960	1961
XXIV	Extended voting rights to all classes by abolition of poll taxes	1962	1964
XXVI	Extended voting rights to citizens aged 18 and over	1971	1971*

*The Twenty-sixth Amendment holds the record for speed of adoption. It was proposed on March 23, 1971, and adopted on July 5, 1971.

branch. This was seen as a necessity given the abuses of executive power Americans had endured under British rule.

The Fifth, Sixth, Seventh, and Eighth amendments contain some of the most important safeguards for individual citizens against the arbitrary exercise of government power. And these amendments sought to accomplish their goal by defining the judicial branch more concretely and clearly than had been done in Article III of the Constitution. Table 3.2 analyzes the ten amendments included in the Bill of Rights.

Five of the seventeen amendments adopted since 1791 are directly concerned with the expansion of the electorate and, thus, political equality (see Table 3.3). The Founders were unable to establish a national electorate with uniform voting qualifications. They decided to evade it by providing in the final draft of Article I, Section 2, that eligibility to vote in a national election would be the same as "the Qualification requisite for Elector of the most numerous branch of the state Legislature." Article I, Section 4, added that Congress could alter state regulations as to the "Times, Places, and Manner of holding Elections for Senators and Representatives." Nevertheless, this meant that any important *expansion* of the American electorate would almost certainly require a constitutional amendment.

Six more amendments are also electoral in nature, although they are not concerned directly with voting rights and the expansion of the electorate (see Table 3.4 on the following page). These six amendments are concerned with the elective offices themselves (the Twentieth, Twenty-second, and Twenty-fifth) or with the relationship between elective offices and the electorate (the Twelfth, Fourteenth, and Seventeenth). One could conclude that one effect was the enhancement of democracy.

Another five amendments serve to expand or limit the power of government (see Table 3.5 on the following page).[31] The Eleventh Amendment

Table 3.4 AMENDING THE CONSTITUTION TO CHANGE THE RELATIONSHIP BETWEEN ELECTED OFFICES AND THE ELECTORATE

Amendment	Purpose	Year proposed	Year adopted
XII	Provided separate ballot for vice president in the electoral college	1803	1804
XIV	(Part 1) Provided a national definition of citizenship*	1866	1868
XVII	Provided direct election of senators	1912	1913
XX	Eliminated "lame duck" session of Congress	1932	1933
XXII	Limited presidential term	1947	1951
XXV	Provided presidential succession in case of disability	1965	1967

*In defining *citizenship,* the Fourteenth Amendment actually provided the constitutional basis for expanding the electorate to include all races, women, and residents of the District of Columbia. Only the "eighteen-year-olds' amendment" should have been necessary, since it changed the definition of citizenship. The fact that additional amendments were required following the Fourteenth suggests that voting is not considered an inherent right of U.S. citizenship. Instead it is viewed as a privilege.

Table 3.5 AMENDING THE CONSTITUTION TO EXPAND OR LIMIT THE POWER OF GOVERNMENT

Amendment	Purpose	Year proposed	Year adopted
XI	Limited jurisdiction of federal courts over suits involving the states	1794	1798
XIII	Eliminated slavery and eliminated the right of states to allow property in persons	1865*	1865
XIV	(Part 2) Applied due process of Bill of Rights to the states	1866	1868
XVI	Established national power to tax incomes	1909	1913
XXVII	Limited Congress's power to raise its own salary	1789	1992

*The Thirteenth Amendment was proposed January 31, 1865, and adopted less than a year later, on December 18, 1865.

protected the states from suits by private individuals and took away from the federal courts any power to take suits by private individuals of one state (or a foreign country) against another state. The other three amendments in Table 3.5 are obviously designed to reduce state power (Thirteenth), to reduce state power and expand national power (Fourteenth), and to expand national power (Sixteenth). The Twenty-seventh put a limit on Congress's ability to raise its own salary.

The one missing amendment underscores the meaning of the rest: the Eighteenth, or Prohibition, Amendment. This is the only instance in which the country tried to *legislate* by constitutional amendment. In other words, it is the only amendment that was designed to deal directly with some substantive social problem. And it was the only amendment ever to have been repealed. Two other amendments—the Thirteenth, which abolished slavery, and the Sixteenth, which established the power to levy an income tax—can be said to have had the effect of legislation. But the purpose of the Thirteenth was to restrict the power of the states by forever forbidding them to treat any human being as property. As for the Sixteenth, it is certainly true that income tax legislation followed immediately; nevertheless, the amendment concerns itself strictly with establishing the power of Congress to enact such legislation. The legislation came later; and if down the line a majority in Congress had wanted to abolish the income tax, they could also have done this by legislation rather than through the arduous path of a constitutional amendment repealing the income tax.

Students and Politics

The 1996 elections marked the twenty-fifth anniversary of the Twenty-sixth Amendment to the Constitution, which lowered the national voting age from twenty-one to eighteen. Although various political leaders throughout U.S. history had advocated lowering the voting age, and some states (especially in the South) had enfranchised their young citizens, the movement for a national lowering of the voting age did not begin in earnest until the late 1960s. During the Vietnam War, students staged massive protests that occasionally turned violent, including the infamous confrontation between students and the National Guard at Ohio's Kent State University, which left three students dead, and the melee at the Democratic National Convention in Chicago in 1968. In a move to help pacify what seemed like a student rebellion, Congress passed and the states ratified the amendment. Students and congressional leaders argued that those who were conscripted to fight for national interests should have a voice in what those interests were. Furthermore, Congress wished to provide an alternative form of participation to the student protesters. Today, although the turnout of eighteen- to twenty-four-year-old voters remains the lowest of any age group, the 1996 elections saw the highest turnout percentage among voters in that age group since the ratification of the Twenty-sixth Amendment.

All of this points to the principle underlying the twenty-five existing amendments: All are concerned with the structure or composition of government. This is consistent with the dictionary, which defines *constitution* as the makeup or composition of something. And it is consistent with the concept of a constitution as "higher law," because the whole point and purpose of a higher law is to establish a framework within which government and the process of making ordinary law can take place. Even those who would have preferred more changes in the Constitution would have to agree that there is great wisdom in this principle. A constitution ought to enable legislation and public policies to take place, but it should not determine what that legislation or those public policies ought to be.

For those whose hopes for change center on the Constitution, it must be emphasized that the amendment route to social change is, and always will be, extremely limited. Through a constitution it is possible to establish a working structure of government, and through a constitution it is possible to establish basic rights of citizens by placing limitations on the powers of that government. Once these things have been accomplished, the real problem is how to extend rights to those people who do not already enjoy them. Of course, the

Constitution cannot enforce itself. But it can and does have a real influence on everyday life because a right or an obligation set forth in the Constitution can become a cause of action in the hands of an otherwise powerless person.

Private property is an excellent example. Property is one of the most fundamental and well-established rights in the United States; but it is well established not because it is recognized in so many words in the Constitution, but because legislatures and courts have made it a crime for anyone, including the government, to trespass or to take away property without compensation.

A constitution is good if it produces the cause of action that leads to good legislation, good case law, and appropriate police behavior. A constitution cannot eliminate power. But its principles can be a citizen's dependable defense against the abuse of power.

Reflections on Liberty, Equality, and Democracy

▶ Did the framers value liberty, equality, and democracy? Why or why not?

The Constitution's framers placed individual liberty ahead of all other political values. Their concern for liberty led many of the framers to distrust both democracy and equality. They feared that democracy could degenerate into a majority tyranny in which the populace, perhaps led by a rabble-rousing demagogue, would trample on liberty. As to equality, the framers were products of their time and place; our contemporary ideas of racial and gender equality would have been foreign to them. The framers were concerned primarily with another manifestation of equality: they feared that those without property or position might be driven by what some called a "leveling spirit" to infringe upon liberty in the name of greater economic or social equality. Indeed, the framers believed that this leveling spirit was most likely to produce demagoguery and majority tyranny. As a result, the basic structure of the Constitution—separated powers, internal checks and balances, and federalism—was designed to safeguard liberty, and the Bill of Rights created further safeguards for liberty. At the same time, however, many of the Constitution's other key provisions, such as indirect election of senators and the president, as well as the appointment of judges for life, were designed to limit democracy and, hence, the threat of majority tyranny.

By championing liberty, however, the framers virtually guaranteed that democracy and even a measure of equality would sooner or later evolve in the United States. For liberty inevitably leads to the growth of political activity and the expansion of political participation. In James Madison's famous phrase, "Liberty is to faction as air is to fire."[32] Where they have liberty, more and more people, groups, and interests will almost inevitably engage in politics and gradually overcome whatever restrictions might have been placed upon participation. This is precisely what happened in the early years of the American Republic. During the Jeffersonian period, political parties formed. During the Jacksonian period, many state suffrage restrictions were removed and popular participation greatly expanded. Over time, liberty is conducive to democracy.

Liberty does not guarantee that everyone will be equal. It does, however, reduce the threat of inequality in one very important way. Historically, the greatest inequalities of wealth, power, and privilege have arisen where governments have used their power to allocate status and opportunity among individuals or groups. From the aristocracies of the early modern period to the *nomenklatura* of twentieth-century despotisms, the most extreme cases of inequality are associated with the most tyrannical regimes. In the United States, however, by promoting a democratic politics, over time liberty unleashed forces that militated against inequality. As a result, over the past two hundred years, groups that have learned to use the political process have achieved important economic and social gains.

When the framers chose liberty as the basis for a constitution, it wasn't such a bad place to start.

GET INVOLVED Become a Framer

Constitutions are "higher law." They spell out general principles and procedures for how people should interact, make dicisions, and enforce them. Like the U.S. Constitution and the fifty state constitutions, they also structure politics. The U.S. Constitution outlines three major branches of government, limits their powers, and reserves authority for the states. State constitutions set up state institutions and processes, delegating some authority to regional and local governments. These constitutions declare or imply that the courts should interpret and enforce higher law to ensure that all government actions are consistent with it.

Very few people found new nations or frame constitutions; relatively few people propose and promote amendments to constitutions. However, students and citizens can and do get involved in setting forth general principles, establishing decision-making procedures, and structuring institutions on their campuses and in their communities.

For example, many college campuses have "principles of community" that are very much like constitutions. They articulate the aspirations and values that bind faculty, staff, alumni, and students into a cohesive community. Typically, principles of community highlight the educational mission of the institution and call on all members to show respect for people with diverse racial/ethnic backgrounds, religious beliefs, abilities and disabilities, and so forth. The principles may prohibit activities (such as the use of racial slurs) and outline processes for adjudicating and punishing infractions.

Organizations often frame "bylaws" that are similar to constitutions. Bylaws might include "mission statements," outline organization arrangements, detail procedures for choosing officers, specify decision-making processes, and set down the frequency and timing of meetings. Some colleges require student groups to establish bylaws in order to be eligible for funding. And many groups voluntarily frame bylaws to focus and structure their activities.

Common variations on constitutions are "charters." A state may share its power with city governments by approving city charters that authorize local officials to engage in a range of decision making without requiring explicit state approval. A local government may create an agency by issuing a charter

Politics on the Web

Even though most of our Founding documents were written on parchment, we need not travel to Washington, D.C., to see and learn about them. The Web has become an essential source for information and analysis on important issues and documents. Need to read Article II of the Constitution or find out when each amendment was passed? Need to access the Federalist Papers? These can be found on the Internet. The Library of Congress—the biggest library in the world, may also be the biggest site for interactive lessons on early American life. For instance, its "Learning Page" provides students and educators with a variety of "showcases" on the Founding.

The World Wide Web is most often thought of as a source of fast-breaking news and on-line commerce. But as libraries, archives, and scholars enter text, scan documents, and build a variety of web sites, the Web will also become a valuable resource for historical research. Where else can you peruse a signed copy of the Declaration of Independence from the comfort of your dorm room?

www.wwnorton.com/wtp3e

that specifies the new agency's goals, structure, personnel, and timeline. Similarly, a college may approve the charter of a student organization to authorize it to exercise discretionary authority in distributing student-generated funds for a variety of campus activities.

Here are some possibilities for you to become a framer of "constitutions" on your campus and in your community.

- Identify a general problem on your campus. Perhaps administrators ignore student voices, tolerate long lines for financial aid, and serve poor quality food in cafeterias. Working with a few classmates or an appropriate student organization, discuss, develop, circulate, and promote a "Student Bill of Rights" that expresses principles that protect students from abuse and promotes student voices on campus.
- If you are starting a group, such as a campus chapter of Human Rights Watch, consider drafting bylaws to focus and structure the group as well as to initiate a conversation about its goals and strategies. When you invite other students to be group founders and bylaw framers, they are likely to develop a sense of ownership that strengthens their commitment and loyalty to the group.
- If you are a member of a group, whether it is Campus Republicans or a youth service group, consider raising "constitutional" questions. Does the group have bylaws? If not, would they be useful? If so, perhaps current bylaws should be re-examined and amended. Take the constitutional pulse of your group.
- Perhaps you are working on a student government or community political campaign. Is the campaign inefficient, disorganized, and chaotic? Do workers and volunteers grumble because little is being accomplished? Many groups hit a low point marked by morale problems. To prevent or resolve morale problems, you might suggest that members draft a "mission statement." The drafting process encourages individuals to strengthen commitment, identifies sources of cohesion, and prods folks to set aside minor complaints to achieve major goals.

By articulating shared principles, framing and rethinking bylaws, or drafting mission statements, you do not directly accomplish group goals. However, you do clarify goals, establish processes, and set up structures that empower group members to collaborate and cooperate more effectively.

Summary

Political conflicts between the colonies and Britain, and among competing groups within the colonies, led to the first founding as expressed by the Declaration of Independence. The first constitution, the Articles of Confederation, was adopted one year later (1777). Under this document, the states retained their sovereignty and the central government had few powers and no means of enforcing its will. The national government's weakness led to the Constitution of 1787, the second founding.

The Constitution's framers sought, first, to fashion a new government sufficiently powerful to promote commerce and protect property from radical state legislatures. Second, the framers sought to bring an end to the "excessive democracy" of the state and national governments under the Articles of Confederation. Third, the framers introduced mechanisms that helped secure popular consent for the new government. Finally, the framers made certain that their new government would not itself pose a threat to liberty and property.

The struggle for the ratification of the Constitution pitted the Antifederalists, who thought the proposed new government would be too powerful, against the Federalists, who supported the Constitution and were able to secure its ratification after a nationwide political debate.

This chapter also sought to gain an appreciation of constitutionalism itself. In addition to describing how the Constitution is formally amended, we analyzed the twenty-seven amendments in order to determine what they had in common, contrasting them with the hundreds of amendments that were offered but never adopted. We found that with the exception of the two Prohibition amendments, all amendments were oriented toward some change in the framework or structure of government. The Prohibition Amendment was the only adopted amendment that sought to legislate by constitutional means.

FOR FURTHER READING

Beard, Charles. *An Economic Interpretation of the Constitution of the United States.* New York: Macmillan, 1913.

Cohler, Anne M. *Montesquieu's Politics and the Spirit of American Constitutionalism.* Lawrence: University Press of Kansas, 1988.

Farrand, Max, ed. *The Records of the Federal Convention of 1787.* 4 vols. New Haven, CT: Yale University Press, 1966.

Hamilton, Alexander, James Madison, and John Jay. *The Federalist Papers.* Edited by Isaac Kramnick. New York: Viking, 1987.

Jensen, Merrill. *The Articles of Confederation.* Madison: University of Wisconsin Press, 1963.

Lipset, Seymour M. *The First New Nation: The United States in Historical and Comparative Perspective.* New York: Basic Books, 1963.

McDonald, Forrest. *The Formation of the American Republic.* New York: Penguin, 1967.

Main, Jackson Turner. *The Social Structure of Revolutionary America.* Princeton, NJ: Princeton University Press, 1965.

Rossiter, Clinton. *1787: Grand Convention.* New York: Macmillan, 1966.

Storing, Herbert, ed. *The Complete Anti-Federalist.* 7 vols. Chicago: University of Chicago Press, 1981.

Wills, Gary. *Explaining America.* New York: Penguin, 1982.

Wood, Gordon S. *The Creation of the American Republic.* New York: Norton, 1982.

STUDY OUTLINE

The First Founding: Interests and Conflicts

1. In an effort to alleviate financial problems, including considerable debt, the British government sought to raise revenue by taxing its North American colonies. This energized New England merchants and southern planters, who then organized colonial resistance.
2. Colonial resistance set into motion a cycle of provocation and reaction that resulted in the First Continental Congress and eventually the Declaration of Independence.
3. The Declaration of Independence was an attempt to identify and articulate a history and set of principles that might help to forge national unity.
4. The colonies established the Articles of Confederation and Perpetual Union. Under the Articles, the central government was based entirely in Congress, yet Congress had little power.

The Second Founding: From Compromise to Constitution

1. Concern over America's precarious position in the international community coupled with domestic concern that "radical forces" had too much influence in Congress and in state governments led to the Annapolis Convention in 1786.
2. Shays's Rebellion in Massachusetts provided critics of the Articles of Confederation with the evidence they needed to push for constitutional revision.
3. Recognizing fundamental flaws in the Articles, the delegates to the Philadelphia Convention abandoned the plan to revise the Articles and committed themselves to a second founding.
4. Conflict between large and small states over the issue of representation in Congress led to the Great Compromise, which created a bicameral legislature based on two different principles of representation.
5. The Three-fifths Compromise addressed the question of slavery by apportioning the seats in the House of Representatives according to a population in which five slaves would count as three persons.

The Constitution

1. The new government was to be strong enough to defend the nation's interests internationally, promote commerce and protect property, and prevent the threat posed by "excessive democracy."
2. The House of Representatives was designed to be directly responsible to the people in order to encourage popular consent for the Constitution. The Senate was designed to guard against the potential for excessive democracy in the House.
3. The Constitution grants Congress important and influential powers, but any power not specifically enumerated in its text is reserved specifically to the states.
4. The framers hoped to create a presidency with energy—one that would be capable of timely and decisive action to deal with public issues and problems.
5. The establishment of the Supreme Court reflected the framers' preoccupations with nationalizing governmental power and checking radical democratic impulses while guarding against potential interference with liberty and property from the new national government itself.
6. Various provisions in the Constitution addressed the framers' concern with national unity and power. Such provisions included clauses promoting reciprocity among states.
7. Procedures for amending the Constitution are provided in Article V. These procedures are so difficult that amendments are quite rare in American history.
8. To guard against possible misuse of national government power, the framers incorporated the principles of the separation of powers and federalism, as well as a Bill of Rights, in the Constitution.
9. The separation of powers was based on the principle that power must be used to balance power.
10. Although the framers' move to federalism was a step toward greater centralization of national government power, they retained state power by devising a system of two sovereigns.
11. The Bill of Rights was adopted as the first ten amendments to the Constitution in 1791.

The Fight for Ratification

1. The struggle for ratification was carried out in thirteen separate campaigns—one in each state.
2. The Federalists supported the Constitution and a stronger national government. The Antifederalists, on the other hand, preferred a more decentralized system of government and fought against ratification.
3. Federalists and Antifederalists had differing views regarding issues such as representation and the prevention of tyranny.
4. Antifederalist criticisms helped to shape the Constitution and the national government, but it was the Federalist vision of America that triumphed.

The Citizen's Role and the Changing Constitution

1. Provisions for amending the Constitution, incorporated into Article V, have proven to be difficult criteria to meet. Relatively few amendments have been made to the Constitution.
2. Most of the amendments to the Constitution deal with the structure or composition of the government.

Reflections on Liberty, Equality, and Democracy

1. The Constitution's framers placed individual liberty ahead of all other political values. But by emphasizing liberty, the framers virtually guaranteed that democracy and equality would evolve in the United States.

PRACTICE QUIZ

1. In the Revolutionary struggles, which of the following groups was allied with the New England merchants?
   a) artisans
   b) southern planters
   c) western speculators
   d) laborers

2. How did the British attempt to raise revenue in the North American colonies?
   a) income tax
   b) taxes on commerce
   c) expropriation and government sale of land
   d) government asset sales
3. The first governing document in the United States was
   a) the Declaration of Independence.
   b) the Articles of Confederation and Perpetual Union.
   c) the Constitution.
   d) none of the above.
4. Which state's proposal embodied a principle of representing states in the Congress according to their size and wealth?
   a) Connecticut
   b) Maryland
   c) New Jersey
   d) Virginia
5. Where was the execution of laws conducted under the Articles of Confederation?
   a) the presidency
   b) the Congress
   c) the states
   d) the expanding federal bureaucracy
6. Which of the following was *not* a reason that the Articles of Confederation seemed too weak?
   a) the lack of a single voice in international affairs
   b) the power of radical forces in the Congress
   c) the impending "tyranny of the states"
   d) the power of radical forces in several states
7. What mechanism was instituted in the Congress to guard against "excessive democracy"?
   a) bicameralism
   b) staggered Senate terms
   c) appointment of senators for long terms
   d) all of the above
8. Which of the following best describes the Supreme Court as understood by the Founders?
   a) the highest court of the national government
   b) arbiter of disputes within the Congress
   c) a figurehead commission of elders
   d) a supreme court of the nation and its states
9. Which of the following were the Antifederalists most concerned with?
   a) interstate commerce
   b) the protection of property
   c) the distinction between principles and interests
   d) the potential for tyranny in the central government
10. The draft constitution that was introduced at the start of the Constitutional Convention was authored by
    a) Edmund Randolph.
    b) Thomas Jefferson.
    c) James Madison.
    d) George Clinton.

CRITICAL THINKING QUESTIONS

1. In many ways, the framers of the Constitution created a central government much stronger than the government created by the Articles of Confederation. Still, the framers seem to have taken great care to limit the power of the central government in various ways. Describe the ways in which the central government under the Constitution was stronger than the central government under the Articles. Describe the ways in which the framers limited the national government's power under the Constitution. Why might the framers have placed such limits on the government they had just created?
2. Recount and explain the ideological, geographical, social, and political conflicts both at the time of the American Revolution and at the time of the writing of the United States Constitution. What experiences and interests informed the forces involved in each of these conflicts? How did the framers resolve these conflicts? Were there any conflicts left unresolved?

KEY TERMS

amendment (p. 97)
Antifederalists (p. 88)
Articles of Confederation (p. 74)
bicameral (p. 79)
Bill of Rights (p. 81)
checks and balances (p. 81)
confederation (p. 74)
elastic clause (p. 83)
electoral college (p. 81)
expressed powers (p. 83)
federalism (p. 81)
Federalist Papers (p. 92)
Federalists (p. 88)
Great Compromise (p. 78)
judicial review (p. 84)
limited government (p. 94)
New Jersey Plan (p. 78)
separation of powers (p. 81)
supremacy clause (p. 85)
Three-fifths Compromise (p. 79)
tyranny (p. 93)
Virginia Plan (p. 78)

4 Federalism

★ **The Federal Framework**

How does federalism limit the power of the national government?

How strong a role have the states traditionally had in the federal framework?

★ **Who Does What? The Changing Federal Framework**

Why did the balance of responsibility shift toward the national government in the 1930s?

What means does the national government use to control the actions of the states?

How has the relationship between the national government and the states evolved over the last several decades?

What methods have been employed to give more control back to the states?

★ **Federalism and American Political Values**

How do changes in American federalism reflect different interpretations of liberty, equality, and democracy?

STUDENTS AND POLITICS

If you live in Huntington, West Virginia, you might decide to spend a Saturday night cruising in a friend's new car; in Fargo, North Dakota, the same weekend plans would get you a ticket. And if you decide to take your car out to the highway, in Montana, during the day, you could go as fast as you like, but if you live in New York State, you would risk getting a speeding ticket if you drove over 65 miles per hour.

Driving is just one of the many areas in which where you live affects what you can do and what the government does. If you lose your job in New Hampshire, the highest level of unemployment insurance benefits you can get is $228 per week; in neighboring Massachusetts, you could receive as much as $543 per week. By giving the states power to set benefit levels on such social policies as unemployment insurance and welfare, the American system of federalism allows substantial inequalities to exist across the country. Likewise, what kinds of classes are offered in high schools, the taxes citizens pay for public schools, and the tuition you pay if you attend a state university or college are all affected by where you live. In fact, most of the rules and regulations that Americans face in their daily lives are set by state and local governments.[1]

State and local governments play such important roles in the lives of American citizens because the United States is a federal system in which other levels of government are assigned considerable responsibility. The enduring significance of state and local governments reflects the Founders' mistrust of centralized power and the long-standing preference of Americans for local self-government as the best form of democracy. Such local self-government has meant that personal liberty has varied substantially from state to state. As we saw in Chapter 2, before the 1960s, southern states used their powers of local self-rule to deny basic freedoms to their black citizens. In the two hundred years since the Founding, struggles to realize the ideas of liberty and equality for all citizens have expanded the power of the federal government and reduced the powers of the states. Especially since the New Deal in the 1930s, the national government has played a much more prominent role in protecting liberty and promoting equality. In recent years, however, citizens have become more mistrustful of government, and especially of the national government. Once again we are facing questions about whether the national government is too powerful and whether the institutions of government in Washington should step aside and let the states take on more responsibility. This is an old debate in American politics; it traces back to the Founding, when the Federalists argued in favor of a stronger national government and the Antifederalists opposed them.

The debate about "who should do what" remains one of the most important discussions in American politics. Much is at stake in how authority is divided up among the different levels of government. The debate about how responsibilities should be divided is often informed by conflicting principles and differing evaluations about what each level of government is best suited to do. For example, many people believe that the United States needs national goals and standards to ensure equal opportunities for citizens across the nation; others contend that state and local governments can do a better job at most things because they are closer to the people. For this reason the states have been called "laboratories of democracy": they can experiment with different policies to find measures that best meet the needs of their citizens.

But decisions about who should do what are also highly political. Groups that want government to do more to promote equality frequently prefer a stronger national role. After all, it was the national government that first implemented the civil rights policies in the 1960s and guaranteed civil liberties in all states. Groups that want less government, on the other hand, often favor shifting power to the states or localities. Many conservatives oppose a strong national role because they believe that nationwide regulations infringe on individual liberties. Furthermore, different interest groups argue for placing policy responsibilities at the level of government that they find easiest to influence. And politicians in national, state, and local governments often have quite different views about which level of government should be expected to do what.

Thus, both political principles and interests influence decisions about how power and responsibility should be sorted out across the levels of government. At various points in history, Americans have given different answers to questions about the appropriate role of national, state, and local governments. National power increased as the national government initiated new social and regulatory policies during the New Deal of the 1930s and the Great Society of the 1960s. But in the 1970s and 1980s, states began to claim more authority over these policies. The effort to increase state responsibility and reduce the national role received a boost when the Republicans took over Congress in 1995. With the support of a growing number of Republican governors, congressional Republicans advocated a strategy of devolution, in which the national government would grant the states more authority over a range of policies. For the most part, Republicans did not deliver on their promise to devolve more responsibility to state and local governments; in some areas, they actually increased federal control.

- ***In this chapter, we will first look at how federalism was defined in the Constitution.*** The framers sought to limit national power with the creation of a separate layer of government in opposition to it. For the first 150 years of American government, the states were most important in governing the lives of American citizens. Over time, however, the Supreme Court interpreted the principle of federalism in a way that gave the national government more expansive powers.

- ***We will then examine how the federal framework has changed in recent years, especially in the growth of the national government's role.*** After the 1930s, the national government began to expand, yet the states maintained most of their traditional powers.

- ***We will then assess how changes in federalism reflect the changes in how Americans perceive liberty, equality, and democracy.*** American federalism has always been a work in progress. As federal, state, and local governments change, questions about the relationship between American political values and federalism continue to emerge.

- ***Finally, we will discuss how political participation by citizens at the local, state, and national levels affects the federal system.***

The Federal Framework

- How does federalism limit the power of the national government?
- How strong a role have the states traditionally had in the federal framework?

The Constitution has had its most fundamental influence on American life through federalism. **Federalism** can be defined with misleading ease and simplicity as the division of powers and functions between the national government and the state governments. Governments can organize power in a variety of ways. One of the most important distinctions is between unitary and federal governments. In a **unitary system,** the central government makes the important decisions, and lower levels of government have little independent power. In such systems, lower levels of government primarily serve to implement decisions taken by the central government. In France, for example, the central government was once so involved in the smallest details of local activity that the minister of education boasted that by looking at his watch he could tell what all French schoolchildren were learning at that time because the central government set the school curriculum. In a **federal system,** by contrast, the central government shares power or functions with lower levels of government, such as regions or states. Nations with diverse ethnic or language groupings, such as Switzerland and Canada, are most likely to have federal arrangements. In federal systems, lower levels of government often have significant independent power to set policy in some areas, such as education and social programs, and to impose taxes. Yet the specific ways in which power is shared vary greatly: no two federal systems are exactly the same.

federalism
a system of government in which power is divided, by a constitution, between a central government and regional governments

unitary system
a centralized government system in which lower levels of government have little power independent of the national government

federal system
a system of government in which the national government shares power with lower levels of government, such as states

FEDERALISM IN THE CONSTITUTION

The United States was the first nation to adopt federalism as its governing framework. With federalism, the framers sought to limit the national government by creating a second layer of state governments. American federalism recognized two sovereigns in the original Constitution and reinforced the principle in the Bill of Rights by granting a few **"expressed powers"** to the national government and reserving all the rest to the states.

expressed powers
specific powers granted to Congress under Article I, Section 8, of the Constitution

The Powers of the National Government As we saw in Chapter 3, the "expressed powers" granted to the national government are found in Article I, Section 8, of the Constitution. These seventeen powers include the power to collect taxes, to coin money, to declare war, and to regulate commerce (which, as we will see, became a very important power for the national government). Article I, Section 8, also contains another important source of power for the national government: the **implied powers** that enable Congress "to make all Laws which shall be necessary and proper for carrying into Execution the foregoing Powers." Not until several decades after the Founding did the Supreme Court allow Congress to exercise the power granted in this **necessary and proper clause,** but, as we shall see later in this chapter, this doctrine allowed the national government to expand considerably the scope of its authority, although the process was a slow one.

implied powers
powers derived from the "necessary and proper" clause of Article I, Section 8, of the Constitution. Such powers are not specifically expressed, but are implied through the expansive interpretation of delegated powers

necessary and proper clause
from Article I, Section 8, of the Constitution, it provides Congress with the authority to make all laws "necessary and proper" to carry out its expressed powers

The Powers of State Government One way in which the framers sought to preserve a strong role for the states was through the Tenth Amendment to the Constitution. The Tenth Amendment states that the powers that the Constitution does not delegate to the national government or prohibit to the states are "reserved to the States respectively, or to the people." The Antifederalists, who feared that a strong central government would encroach on individual liberty, repeatedly pressed for such an amendment as a way of limiting national power. Federalists agreed to the amendment because they did not think it would do much harm, given the powers of the Constitution already granted to the national government. The Tenth Amendment is also called the **reserved powers** amendment because it aims to reserve powers to the states.

reserved powers
powers, derived from the Tenth Amendment to the Constitution, that are not specifically delegated to the national government or denied to the states

The most fundamental power that is retained by the states is that of coercion—the power to develop and enforce criminal codes, to administer health and safety rules, to regulate the family via marriage and divorce laws. The states have the power to regulate individuals' livelihoods; if you're a doctor or a lawyer or a plumber or a barber, you must be licensed by the state. Even more fundamentally, the states had the power to define private property—private property exists because state laws against trespass define who is and is not entitled to use a piece of property. If you own a car, your ownership isn't worth much unless the state is willing to enforce your right to possession by making it a crime for anyone else to drive your car. These are fundamental matters, and the powers of the states regarding these domestic issues are much greater than the powers of the national government, even today.

A state's authority to regulate these fundamental matters is commonly referred to as the **police power** of the state and encompasses the state's power to regulate the health, safety, welfare, and morals of its citizens. Policing is what states do—they coerce you in the name of the community in order to maintain public order. And this was exactly the type of power that the Founders intended the states to exercise.

police power
power reserved to the government to regulate the health, safety, and morals of its citizens

In some areas, the states share **concurrent powers** with the national government, wherein they retain and share some power to regulate commerce and to affect the currency—for example, by being able to charter banks, grant or deny corporate charters, grant or deny licenses to engage in a business or practice a trade, and regulate the quality of products or the conditions of labor. This issue of concurrent versus exclusive power has come up from time to time in our history, but wherever there is a direct conflict of laws between the federal and the state levels, the issue will most likely be resolved in favor of national supremacy.

concurrent powers
authority possessed by *both* state and national governments, such as the power to levy taxes

AMERICAN DEMOCRACY IN COMPARATIVE PERSPECTIVE

Different Forms of Federalism

Federalism is an institutional feature central to the logic of consensual democracy. A federal form of government is most commonly found in countries that have geographically concentrated population pockets, which exhibit distinctly different cultures (based on languages, religions, races, or ethnic features that distinguish the groups from the national majority) and which wish to preserve their distinctiveness by having some autonomy over their defined geographical region. For countries with histories of ethnic and religious conflict, federalism allows power to be shared among different major cultural groups and, in so doing, may effectively reduce tensions and animosities between different cultures within a democracy, which otherwise would find it difficult or impossible to cooperate.

Since 1800, federalism has been an institutional device associated not merely with democracy but with nationalism. Nationalism is a cultural group's awareness that it is distinct, that it deserves its own institutions to preserve its culture, and that any central or "alien" power trying to impose laws and policies will lack legitimacy because the majority power may not fully appreciate or understand the local culture. Indeed, there may be deep historical animosities and even hatred among the different cultures. In 1800, according to data collected by Ted Robert Gurr and his colleagues, there were four federal political systems in the world, one of which was the United States. There were none in Europe. By 1994, of the 151 countries for which Gurr and his associates have data, only 18 were strong federal systems (separate, sovereign regional governments, with some linguistic religious or racial/ethnic distinctiveness, and authority over local fiscal and cultural affairs). Within the Americas, the United States, Canada, Trinidad, Mexico, Venezuela, and Brazil were strong federal systems. In Europe, Germany, Belgium, Switzerland, and Russia were classified as strong federal governments, with Spain, Austria, Yugoslavia, Ukraine, Georgia, and Azerbaijan classified as intermediate, or weak, federal governments.

Despite the numerous institutional similarities in the broad structural outlines common to federal democracies as well as certain institutional features common to federal nation-states (such as a bicameral legislature—with the upper chambers usually reserved for territorial representation—and a written constitution that is determinate in content, distinct in structure, and entrenched within the political process—see Chapter 3), the specific nature and features of the federal process found within each country varies greatly among democracies.

Compared to many federal democracies, the American political system is relatively free from sharp cultural tensions that define the relationship between the national and subnational units in other federal democracies. In the case of Canada, French-speaking Quebec stands apart from the other nine provinces (all of which are predominately English-speaking) because of a belief among many in Quebec that became entrenched following a Canadian Supreme Court ruling in 1988. The ruling held that Quebec's "French-only" sign law violated Canada's Charter of Human Rights. In 1995, separatists within the province campaigned for a referendum to secede from the Canadian federal democracy, coming within an eyelash of winning.

The federal "experiment" among democracies, which began with the American constitutional system, remains a very powerful and attractive institutional device for nations that have had historically centralized governments. For instance, complicated pressures associated with the European Union—an emerging federal structure in its own right, which now competes directly with national governments for authority over the domestic laws of member countries of the Union—have prompted the British national government (a nonfederal democracy) to recently extend a form of limited autonomy to its historical subnational regions of Scotland and Wales. These two regions now have their own separately elected parliamentary bodies with a wide range of policy autonomy (excluding of course, foreign policy and defines). This reform, however, is having an unintended consequence for Great Britain: It is causing some in England (the third major geographical region of Great Britain) to argue that the British constitution should be wholly revamped to create something akin to an American federal structure in order to allow the degree of representation of English interests to be equal to that afforded the citizens of Scotland and Wales.

SOURCES: The Council for Canadian Unity (http://www.ccu-cuc.ca/en/op/archives); *The Polity Data Archive* (http://k-gleditsch.socsi.gla.ac.uk/Polity.html); and Sanford Lakoff, *Democracy: History, Theory Practice* (Boulder: Westview Press, 1996).

State Obligations to One Another The Constitution also creates obligations among the states. These obligations, spelled out in Article IV, were intended to promote national unity. By requiring the states to recognize actions and decisions taken in other states as legal and proper, the framers aimed to make the states less like independent countries and more like parts of a single nation.

Article IV, Section I, calls for "Full Faith and Credit" among states, meaning that each state is normally expected to honor the "public Acts, Records, and judicial Proceedings" that take place in any other state. So, for example, if a couple is married in Texas—marriage being regulated by state law—Missouri must also recognize that marriage, even though they were not married under Missouri state law.

full faith and credit clause
provision from Article IV, Section 1, of the Constitution, requiring that the states normally honor the public acts and judicial decisions that take place in another state

This **full faith and credit clause** has recently become embroiled in the controversy over gay and lesbian marriage. In 1993, the Hawaii Supreme Court prohibited discrimination against gay and lesbian marriage except in very limited circumstances. Many observers believed that Hawaii would eventually fully legalize gay marriage. In fact, after a long political battle, Hawaii passed a constitutional amendment in 1998 outlawing gay marriage. However, in December 1999, the Vermont Supreme Court ruled that gay and lesbian couples should have the same rights as heterosexuals. The Vermont legislature responded with a new law that allowed gays and lesbians to form "civil unions." Although not legally considered marriages, such unions allow gay and lesbian couples most of the benefits of marriage, such as eligibility for the partner's health insurance, inheritance rights, and the right to transfer property. The Vermont statute could have broad implications for other states. More than thirty states have passed "defense of marriage acts" that define marriage as a union between men and women only; whether these states have to recognize Vermont's civil unions under the full faith and credit clause is still unclear.

The attempt to legalize marriage for gays and lesbians in Hawaii ended when the state passed a constitutional amendment restricting marriage to a union between a man and a woman. In April of 2000 Vermont became the first state to approve a legal union—defined as a civil union, not marriage—for gays and lesbians.

Anxious to show its disapproval of gay marriage, Congress passed the Defense of Marriage Act in 1996, which declared that states will *not* have to recognize a same-sex marriage, even if it is legal in one state. The act also said that the federal government will not recognize gay marriage—even if it is legal under state law—and that gay marriage partners will not be eligible for the federal benefits, such as Medicare and Social Security, normally available to spouses.[2] For a further discussion of gay and lesbian marriage, see Chapter 6.

Because of this controversy, the extent and meaning of the full faith and credit clause is sure to be considered by the Supreme Court. In fact, it is not clear that the clause requires states to recognize gay marriage because the Court's past interpretation of the clause has provided exceptions for "public policy" reasons: if states have strong objections to a law, they do not have to honor it. In 1997 the Court took up a case involving the full faith and credit clause. The case concerns a Michigan court order that prevented a former engineer for General Motors from testifying against the company. The engineer, who left the company on bad terms, later testified in a Missouri court about a car accident in which a woman died when her Chevrolet Blazer caught fire. General Motors challenged his right to testify, arguing that Missouri should give "full faith and credit" to the Michigan ruling. The Supreme Court ruled that the engineer could testify and that the court system in one state cannot hinder other state courts in their "search for the truth."[3]

Article IV, Section 2, known as the "comity clause," also seeks to promote national unity. It provides that citizens enjoying the **"Privileges and Immunities"** of one state should be entitled to similar treatment in other states. What this has come to mean is that a state cannot discriminate against someone from another state or give special privileges to its own residents. For example, in the 1970s, when Alaska passed a law that gave residents preference over nonresidents in obtaining work on the state's oil and gas pipelines, the Supreme Court ruled the law illegal because it discriminated against citizens of other states.[4] This clause also regulates criminal justice among the states by requiring states to return fugitives to the states from which they have fled. Thus, in 1952, when an inmate escaped from an Alabama prison and sought to avoid being returned to Alabama on the grounds that he was being subjected to "cruel and unusual punishment" there, the Supreme Court ruled that he must be returned according to Article IV, Section 2.[5] This example highlights the difference between the obligations among states and those among different countries. Recently, France refused to return an American fugitive because he might be subject to the death penalty, which does not exist in France.[6] The Constitution clearly forbids states from doing something similar.

privileges and immunities clause
provision from Article IV, Section 2, of the Constitution, that a state cannot discriminate against someone from another state or give its own residents special privileges

Local Government and the Constitution Local government occupies a peculiar but very important place in the American system. In fact, the status of American local government is probably unique in world experience. First, it must be pointed out that local government has no status in the American Constitution. *State* legislatures created local governments, and *state* constitutions and laws permit local governments to take on some of the responsibilities of the state governments. Most states amended their own constitutions to give their larger cities **home rule**—a guarantee of noninterference in various areas of local affairs. But local governments enjoy no such recognition in the Constitution. Local governments have always been mere conveniences of the states.[7]

home rule
power delegated by the state to a local unit of government to manage its own affairs

Table 4.1 87,504 GOVERNMENTS IN THE UNITED STATES

Type	Number
National	1
State	50
County	3,043
Municipal	19,372
Townships	16,629
School districts	13,726
Other special districts	34,683

SOURCE: *Statistical Abstract of the United States, 1999* (Washington, DC: U.S. Government Printing Office, 1999), p. 309.

Local governments became administratively important in the early years of the Republic because the states possessed little administrative capability. They relied on local governments—cities and countries—to implement the laws of the state. Local government was an alternative to a statewide bureaucracy (see Table 4.1).

RESTRAINING NATIONAL POWER WITH DUAL FEDERALISM, 1789–1937

As we have noted, the Constitution created two layers of government: the national government and the state governments. The consequences of this **dual federalism** are fundamental to the American system of government in theory and in practice; they have meant that states have done most of the fundamental governing. For evidence, look at Table 4.2. It lists the major types of public policies by which Americans were governed for the first century and a half under the Constitution. We call it the "traditional system" because it prevailed for three-quarters of American history and because it closely approximates the intentions of the framers of the Constitution.

Under the traditional system, the national government was quite small by comparison both to the state governments and to the governments of other Western nations. Not only was it smaller than most governments of that time, it was actually very narrowly specialized in the functions it performed. The national government built or sponsored the construction of roads, canals, and bridges (internal improvements). It provided cash subsidies to shippers and shipbuilders and distributed free or low-priced public land to encourage western settlement and business ventures. It placed relatively heavy taxes on imported goods (tariffs), not only to raise rev-

Students and Politics

In 1984, the national government passed legislation that denied highway funds to states that failed to raise the legal drinking age to twenty-one. The last bastion of eighteen-year-old drinking, Louisiana, capitulated in 1996. Louisiana students reacted swiftly to the legislation. Protests at the state capitol were led by Louisiana State University sophomore Jonathan Doro, who argued that eighteen-year-olds were deemed responsible as adults in every other way, including the obligation to fight in war and the right to vote. Newspapers covered the issue extensively; several national newspapers and a few national television programs ran feature stories on the Louisiana battle. The State Supreme Court ruled the new law violated the state constitution; the state legislature, however, succeeded in passing an amendment to the constitution raising the drinking age to twenty-one. Recent events, such as the death of a Louisiana student due to excessive drinking, have slowed the movement to repeal the amendment.

enues but to protect "infant industries" from competition from the more advanced European enterprises. It protected patents and provided for a common currency, also to encourage and facilitate enterprises and to expand markets.

What do these functions of the national government reveal? First, virtually all its functions were aimed at assisting commerce. It is quite appropriate to refer to the traditional American system as a "commercial republic." Second, virtually none of the national government's policies directly coerced citizens. The emphasis of governmental programs was on assistance, promotion, and encouragement—the allocation of land or capital where they were insufficiently available for economic development.

Meanwhile, state legislatures were actively involved in economic regulation during the nineteenth century. In the United States, then and now, private property exists only in state laws and state court decisions regarding property, trespass, and real estate. American capitalism took its form from state property and trespass laws, as well as from state laws and court decisions regarding contracts, markets, credit, banking, incorporation, and insurance. Laws

dual federalism
the system of government that prevailed in the United States from 1789 to 1937, in which most fundamental governmental powers were shared between the federal and state governments

THE FEDERAL SYSTEM: SPECIALIZATION OF GOVERNMENTAL FUNCTIONS IN THE TRADITIONAL SYSTEM (1800–1933)

Table 4.2

National government policies (domestic)	State government policies	Local government policies
Internal improvements	Property laws (including slavery)	Adaptation of state laws to local conditions ("variances")
Subsidies	Estate and inheritance laws	Public works
Tariffs	Commerce laws	Contracts for public works
Public lands disposal	Banking and credit laws	Licensing of public accommodations
Patents	Corporate laws	Assessible improvements
Currency	Insurance laws	Basic public services
	Family laws	
	Morality laws	
	Public health laws	
	Education laws	
	General penal laws	
	Eminent domain laws	
	Construction codes	
	Land-use laws	
	Water and mineral laws	
	Criminal procedure laws	
	Electoral and political parties laws	
	Local government laws	
	Civil service laws	
	Occupations and professions laws	

concerning slavery were a subdivision of property law in states where slavery existed. The practice of important professions, such as law and medicine, was and is illegal, except as provided for by state law. Marriage, divorce, and the birth or adoption of a child have always been regulated by state law. To educate or not to educate a child has been a decision governed more by state laws than by parents, and not at all by national law. It is important to note also that virtually all criminal laws—regarding everything from trespass to murder—have been state laws. Most of the criminal laws adopted by Congress are concerned with the District of Columbia and other federal territories.

All this (and more, as shown in the middle column of Table 4.2) demonstrates without any question that most of the fundamental governing in the United States was done by the states. The contrast between national and state policies, as shown by Table 4.2, demonstrates the difference in the power vested in each. The list of items in the middle column could actually have been made longer. Moreover, each item on the list is a category of law that fills many volumes of statutes and court decisions.

This contrast between national and state governments is all the more impressive because it is basically what the framers of the Constitution intended. Since the 1930s, the national government has expanded into local and intrastate matters, far beyond what anyone would have foreseen in 1790, 1890, or even in the 1920s. But this significant expansion of the national government did not alter the basic framework. The national government has become much larger, but the states have continued to be central to the American system of government.

Here lies probably the most important point of all: The fundamental impact of federalism on the way the United States is governed comes not from any particular provision of the Constitution but from the framework itself, which has determined the flow of government functions and, through that, the political development of the country. By allowing state governments to do

State laws govern the minimum age for drivers. Shelly Larson, of Bridgewater, South Dakota, testified in favor of increasing the minimum driving age in South Dakota after her fourteen-year-old son, Erich, died after his truck rolled over on a gravel road.

In 1815, President James Madison called for a federally funded program of "internal improvements," which during the first half of the nineteenth century was one of the few policy roles for the national government. By improving transportation through the construction of roads and canals, the government fostered the growth of the market economy.

most of the fundamental governing, the Constitution saved the national government from many policy decisions that might have proven too divisive for a large and very young country. There is no doubt that if the Constitution had provided for a unitary rather than a federal system, the war over slavery would have come in 1789 or 1809 rather than in 1860; and if it had come that early, the South might very well have seceded and established a separate and permanent slaveholding nation.

In helping the national government remain small and aloof from the most divisive issues of the day, federalism contributed significantly to the political stability of the nation, even as the social, economic, and political systems of many of the states and regions of the country were undergoing tremendous, profound, and sometimes violent, change.[8] As we shall see, some important aspects of federalism have changed, but the federal framework has survived two centuries and a devastating civil war.

FEDERALISM AND THE SLOW GROWTH OF THE NATIONAL GOVERNMENT'S POWER

Having created the national government, and recognizing the potential for abuse of power, the states sought through federalism to constrain the national government. The "traditional system" of a weak national government prevailed for over a century despite economic forces favoring its expansion and despite Supreme Court cases giving a pro-national interpretation to Article I, Section 8, of the Constitution.

That article delegates to Congress the power "to regulate commerce with foreign nations, and among the several States and with the Indian tribes." This **commerce clause** was consistently interpreted *in favor* of national power by the Supreme Court for most of the nineteenth century. The first and most important case favoring national power over the economy was *McCulloch v. Maryland*.[9] This case involved the question of whether Congress had the power to charter a national bank, since such an explicit grant of power was nowhere to be found in Article I, Section 8. Chief Justice John Marshall answered that the power could be "implied" from other powers that were expressly delegated to Congress, such as the "powers to lay and collect taxes; to borrow money; to regulate commerce; and to declare and conduct a war."

commerce clause
Article I, Section 8, of the Constitution, which delegates to Congress the power "to regulate commerce with foreign nations, and among the several States and with the Indian tribes." This clause was interpreted by the Supreme Court in favor of national power over the economy

By allowing Congress to use the necessary and proper clause to interpret its delegated powers expansively, the Supreme Court created the potential for an unprecedented increase in national government power. Marshall also concluded that whenever a state law conflicted with a federal law (as in the case of *McCulloch v. Maryland*), the state law would be deemed invalid since the Constitution states that "the Laws of the United States . . . shall be the supreme Law of the Land." Both parts of this great case are pro-national, yet Congress did not immediately seek to expand the policies of the national government.

Another major case, *Gibbons v. Ogden* in 1824, reinforced this nationalistic interpretation of the Constitution. The important but relatively narrow issue was whether the state of New York could grant a monopoly to Robert Fulton's steamboat company to operate an exclusive service between New York and New Jersey. Chief Justice Marshall argued that New York State did not have the power to grant this particular monopoly. In order to reach this decision, it was necessary for Marshall to define what Article I, Section 8, meant by "commerce among the several states." He insisted that the definition was "comprehensive," extending to "every species of commercial intercourse." He did say that this comprehensiveness was limited "to that commerce which concerns more states than one," giving rise to what later came to be called "interstate commerce." *Gibbons* is important because it established the supremacy of the national government in all matters affecting interstate commerce.[10] But what would remain uncertain during several decades of constitutional discourse was the precise meaning of interstate commerce.

Article I, Section 8, backed by the implied powers decision in *McCulloch* and by the broad definition of "interstate commerce" in *Gibbons,* was a source of power for the national government as long as Congress sought to facilitate commerce through subsidies, services, and land grants. But later in the nineteenth century, when the national government sought to use those powers to *regulate* the economy rather than merely to promote economic development, federalism and the concept of interstate commerce began to operate as restraints on, rather than sources of, national power. Any effort of the national government to regulate commerce in such areas as fraud, the production of impure goods, the use of child labor, or the existence of dangerous working conditions or long hours was declared unconstitutional by the Supreme Court as a violation of the concept of interstate commerce. Such legislation meant that the federal government was entering the factory and the workplace—local areas—and was attempting to regulate goods that had not passed into commerce. To enter these local workplaces was to exercise police power—the power reserved to the states for the protection of the health, safety, and morals of their citizens. No one questioned the power of the national government to regulate businesses that intrinsically involved interstate commerce, such as railroads, gas pipelines, and waterway transportation. But well into the twentieth century, the Supreme Court used the concept of interstate commerce as a barrier against most efforts by Congress to regulate local conditions.

This aspect of federalism was alive and well during an epoch of tremendous economic development, the period between the Civil War and the 1930s. It gave the American economy a freedom from federal government control that closely approximated the ideal of free enterprise. The economy was never entirely free, of course; in fact, entrepreneurs themselves did not want complete freedom from government. They needed law and order. They needed a stable currency. They needed courts and police to enforce contracts and prevent trespass. They needed roads, canals, and railroads. But federalism, as interpreted by the Supreme Court for seventy years after the Civil War, made it possible for business to have its cake and eat it, too. Entrepreneurs enjoyed the benefits of national policies facilitating commerce and were protected by the courts from policies regulating commerce.[11]

All this changed after 1937, when the Supreme Court threw out the old distinction between interstate and intrastate commerce, converting the commerce clause from a source of limitations to a source of power for the national government. The Court began to refuse to review appeals challenging acts of Congress protecting the rights of employees to organize and engage in collective bargaining, regulating the amount of farmland in cultivation, extending low-interest credit to small businesses and farmers, and restricting the activities of corporations dealing in the stock market, and many other laws that contributed to the construction of the "welfare state."[12]

In 1916, the national government passed the Keating-Owen Child Labor Act, which excluded from interstate commerce goods manufactured by children under fourteen. The act was ruled unconstitutional by the Supreme Court on the grounds that the regulation of interstate commerce could not extend to the conditions of labor. The regulation of child labor remained in the hands of state governments until the 1930s.

THE CHANGING ROLE OF THE STATES

As we have seen, the Constitution contained the seeds of a very expansive national government—in the commerce clause. For much of the nineteenth century, federal power remained limited. The Tenth Amendment was used to bolster arguments about **states' rights,** which in their extreme version claimed that the states did not have to submit to national laws when they believed the national government had exceeded its authority. These arguments in favor of states' rights were voiced less often after the Civil War. But the Supreme Court continued to use the Tenth Amendment to strike down laws that it thought exceeded national power, including the Civil Rights Act passed in 1875.

states' rights
the principle that the states should oppose the increasing authority of the national government. This principle was most popular in the period before the Civil War

In the early twentieth century, however, the Tenth Amendment appeared to lose its force. Reformers began to press for national regulations to limit the power of large corporations and to preserve the health and welfare of citizens. The Supreme Court approved of some of these laws but it struck others down, including a law combating child labor. The Court stated that the law violated the Tenth Amendment because only states should have the power to regulate conditions of employment. By the late 1930s, however, the Supreme Court had approved such an expansion of federal power that the Tenth Amendment appeared irrelevant. In fact, in 1941, Justice Harlan Fiske Stone declared that the Tenth Amendment was simply a "truism," that it had no real meaning.[13]

Yet the idea that some powers should be reserved to the states did not go away. Indeed, in the 1950s, southern opponents of the civil rights movement revived the idea of states' rights. In 1956, ninety-six southern members of Congress issued a "Southern Manifesto" in which they declared that southern states were not constitutionally bound by Supreme Court decisions outlawing racial segregation. They believed that states' rights should override individual rights to liberty and formal equality. With the triumph of the civil rights movement, the slogan of "states' rights" became tarnished by its association with racial inequality.

Recent years have seen a revival of interest in the Tenth Amendment and important Supreme Court decisions limiting federal power. Much of the interest in the Tenth Amendment stems from conservatives who believe that a strong federal government encroaches on individual liberties. They believe such freedoms are better protected by returning more power to the states

devolution
a policy to remove a program from one level of government by delegating it or passing it down to a lower level of government, such as from the national government to the state and local governments

through the process of **devolution.** In 1996, Republican presidential candidate Bob Dole carried a copy of the Tenth Amendment in his pocket as he campaigned, pulling it out to read at rallies.[14] The Supreme Court's ruling in *United States v. Lopez* in 1995 fueled further interest in the Tenth Amendment. In that case, the Court, stating that Congress had exceeded its authority under the commerce clause, struck down a federal law that barred handguns near schools. This was the first time since the New Deal that the Court had limited congressional powers in this way. In 1997, the Court again relied on the Tenth Amendment to limit federal power in *Printz v. United States.*[15] The decision declared unconstitutional a provision of the Brady Handgun Violence Prevention Act that required state and local law enforcement officials to conduct background checks on handgun purchasers. The Court declared that this provision violated state sovereignty guaranteed in the Tenth Amendment because it required state and local officials to administer a federal regulatory program. The Court also limited the power of the federal government over the states in a 1996 ruling that prevented Native Americans from the Seminole tribe from suing the state of Florida in federal court. A 1988 law had given Indian tribes the right to sue a state in federal court if the state did not negotiate in good faith over issues related to gambling casinos on tribal land. The Supreme Court's ruling appeared to signal a much broader limitation on national power by raising new questions about whether individuals can sue a state if it fails to uphold federal law.[16] It remains to be seen whether these rulings signal a move toward a much more restricted federal government in future Supreme Court decisions, or whether they will simply serve as a reminder that federal power is not infinite.[17]

The expansion of the power of the national government has not left the states powerless. The state governments continue to make most of the fundamental laws; the national government did not expand at the expense of the states. The growth of the national government has been an addition, not a redistribution of power from the states. No better demonstration of the continuing influence of the federal framework can be offered than the fact that the middle column of Table 4.2 is still a fairly accurate characterization of state government today.

Who Does What? The Changing Federal Framework

- Why did the balance of responsibility shift toward the national government in the 1930s?
- What means does the national government use to control the actions of the states?
- How has the relationship between the national government and the states evolved over the last several decades?
- What methods have been employed to give more control back to the states?

Questions about how to divide responsibilities between the states and the national government first arose more than two hundred years ago, when the framers wrote the Constitution to create a stronger union. But they did not solve the issue of who should do what. There is no "right" answer to that question; each generation of Americans has provided its own answer. In recent years, Americans have grown distrustful of the federal government and have supported giving more responsibility to the states.[18] Even so, they still want the federal government to set standards and promote equality.

Political debates about the division of responsibility often take sides: some people argue for a strong federal role to set national standards, while others say the states should do more. These two goals are not necessarily at odds. The key is to find the right balance. During the first 150 years of American history, that balance favored state power. But the balance began to shift toward Washington in the 1930s. In this section, we will look at how the balance shifted, and then we will consider current efforts to reshape the relationship between the national government and the states.

EXPANSION OF THE NATIONAL GOVERNMENT

The New Deal of the 1930s signaled the rise of a more active national government. The door to increased federal action opened when states proved unable to cope with the demands brought on by the Great Depression. Before the Depression, states and localities took responsibility for addressing the needs of the poor, usually through private charity. But the extent of the need created by the Depression quickly exhausted local and state capacities. By 1932, 25 percent of the workforce was unemployed. The jobless lost their homes and settled into camps all over the country, called "Hoovervilles," after President Herbert Hoover. Elected in 1928, the year before the Depression hit, Hoover steadfastly maintained that there was little the federal government could do to alleviate the misery caused by the Depression. It was a matter for state and local governments, he said.

A "Hooverville" in Seattle, Washington, in 1933. The residents of this Hooverville elected a mayor and city council to govern their "town."

Yet demands mounted for the federal government to take action. In Congress, some Democrats proposed that the federal government finance public works to aid the economy and put people back to work. Other members of Congress introduced legislation to provide federal grants to the states to assist them in their relief efforts. None of these measures passed while Hoover remained in the White House.

When Franklin D. Roosevelt took office in 1933, he energetically threw the federal government into the business of fighting the Depression. He proposed a variety of temporary measures to provide federal relief and work programs. Most of the programs he proposed were to be financed by the federal government but administered by the states. In addition to these temporary measures, Roosevelt presided over the creation of several important federal programs designed to provide future economic security for Americans.

FEDERAL GRANTS

grants-in-aid
programs through which Congress provides money to state and local governments on the condition that the funds be employed for purposes defined by the federal government

For the most part, the new national programs that the Roosevelt administration developed did not directly take power away from the states. Instead, Washington typically redirected states by offering them **grants-in-aid,** whereby Congress appropriates money to state and local governments on the condition that the money be spent for a particular purpose defined by Congress.

The principle of the grant-in-aid can be traced back to the nineteenth-century land grants that the national government made to the states for the improvement of agriculture and farm-related education. Since farms were not in "interstate commerce," it was unclear whether the Constitution permitted the national government to provide direct assistance to agriculture. Grants made to the states, but designated to go to farmers, presented a way of avoiding the question of constitutionality while pursuing what was recognized in Congress as a national goal.

During the 1950s, the national government funded 90 percent of the cost of building more than 42,500 miles of interstate highways. State governments paid for the remaining 10 percent.

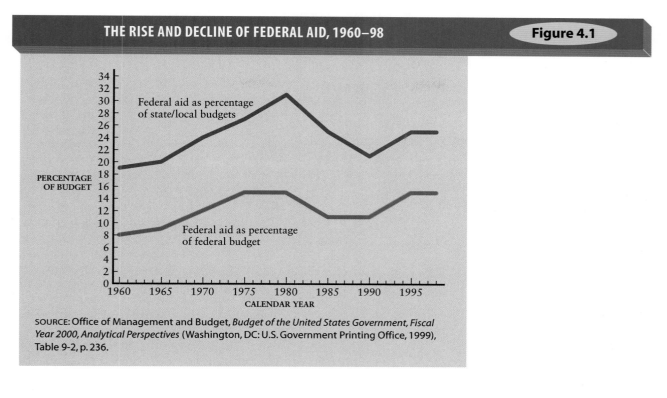

THE RISE AND DECLINE OF FEDERAL AID, 1960–98 **Figure 4.1**

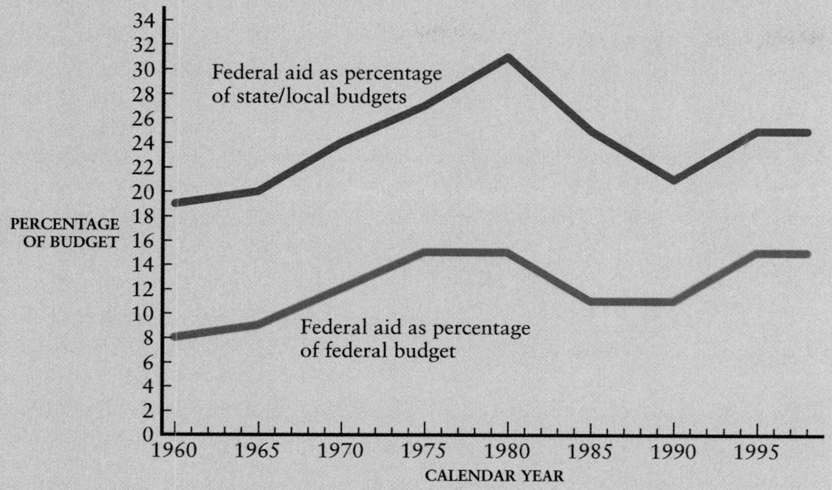

SOURCE: Office of Management and Budget, *Budget of the United States Government, Fiscal Year 2000, Analytical Perspectives* (Washington, DC: U.S. Government Printing Office, 1999), Table 9-2, p. 236.

Franklin Roosevelt's New Deal expanded the range of grants-in-aid into social programs, providing grants to the states for financial assistance to poor children. Congress added new grants after World War II, creating new programs to help states fund activities such as providing school lunches and building highways. Sometimes the national government required state or local governments to match the national contribution dollar for dollar, but in some programs, such as the development of the interstate highway system, the congressional grants provided 90 percent of the cost of the program.

These types of federal grants-in-aid are also called **categorical grants**, because the national government determines the purposes, or categories, for which the money can be used. For the most part, the categorical grants created before the 1960s simply helped the states perform their traditional functions.[19] In the 1960s, however, the national role expanded and the number of categorical grants increased dramatically (see Figure 4.1). For example, during the Eighty-ninth Congress (1965–66) alone, the number of categorical grant-in-aid programs grew from 221 to 379.[20] The grants authorized during the 1960s announced national purposes much more strongly than did earlier grants. Central to that national purpose was the need to provide opportunities to the poor.

Many of the categorical grants enacted during the 1960s were **project grants,** which require state and local governments to submit proposals to federal agencies. In contrast to the older **formula grants,** which used a formula (composed of such elements as need and state and local capacities) to distribute funds, the new project grants made funding available on a competitive basis. Federal agencies would give grants to the proposals they judged to be

categorical grants
congressional grants given to states and localities on the condition that expenditures be limited to a problem or group specified by law

project grants
grant programs in which state and local governments submit proposals to federal agencies and for which funding is provided on a competitive basis

formula grants
grants-in-aid in which a formula is used to determine the amount of federal funds a state or local government will receive

the best. In this way, the national government acquired substantial control over which state and local governments got money, how much they got, and how they spent it.

COOPERATIVE FEDERALISM

cooperative federalism
a type of federalism existing since the New Deal era in which grants-in-aid have been used strategically to encourage states and localities (without commanding them) to pursue nationally defined goals. Also known as "intergovernmental cooperation"

The growth of categorical grants created a new kind of federalism. If the traditional system of two sovereigns performing highly different functions could be called dual federalism, historians of federalism suggest that the system since the New Deal could be called **cooperative federalism.** The most important student of the history of American federalism, Morton Grozdins, characterized this as a move from "layer-cake federalism" to "marble-cake federalism,"[21] in which intergovernmental cooperation and sharing have blurred a once-clear distinguishing line, making it difficult to say where the national government ends and the state and local governments begin (see Figure 4.2).

For a while in the 1960s, however, it appeared as if the state governments would become increasingly irrelevant to American federalism. Many of the new federal grants bypassed the states and instead sent money directly to local governments and even to local nonprofit organizations. The theme heard repeatedly in Washington was that the states simply could not be trusted to carry out national purposes.[22]

One of the reasons that Washington distrusted the states was because of the way African American citizens were treated in the South. The southern states' forthright defense of segregation, justified on the grounds of states' rights, helped to tarnish the image of the states as the civil rights movement took hold. The national officials who planned the War on Poverty in the 1960s pointed to the racial exclusion practiced in the southern states as a reason for bypassing state governments. Political scientist James Sundquist described how the "Alabama syndrome" affected the War on Poverty: "In the drafting of the Economic Opportunity Act, an 'Alabama syndrome' developed. Any suggestion within the poverty task force that the states be given a role in the administration of the act was met with the question, 'Do you want to give that kind of power to [Alabama governor] George Wallace?' "[23]

Figure 4.2 EVOLVING FEDERALISM

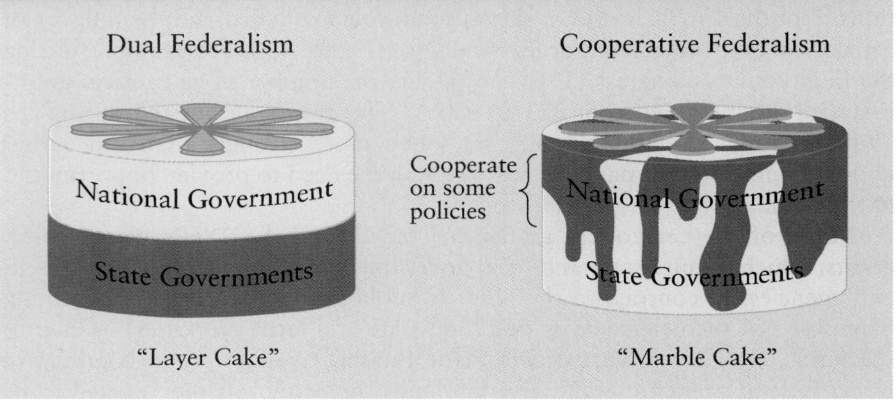

In marble-cake federalism, national policies, state policies, and local policies overlap in many areas.

Governor George Wallace of Alabama stood in defiance as he turned back U.S. Attorney General Nicholas Katzenbach, who was trying to enroll two black students at the University of Alabama at Tuscaloosa in 1963. Wallace, who proclaimed "segregation now, segregation tomorrow, segregation forever," was a vocal advocate of states' rights.

Yet, even though many national policies of the 1960s bypassed the states, other new programs, such as Medicaid—the health program for the poor—relied on state governments for their implementation. In addition, as the national government expanded existing programs run by the states, states had to take on more responsibility. These new responsibilities meant that the states were playing a very important role in the federal system.

REGULATED FEDERALISM AND NATIONAL STANDARDS

The question of who decides what each level of government should do goes to the very heart of what it means to be an American citizen. How different should things be when one crosses a state line? In what policy areas is it acceptable to have state differences and in what areas should states be similar? Supreme Court decisions about the fundamental rights of American citizens provide the most important answers to these questions. Over time, the Court has pushed for greater uniformity across the states. In addition to legal decisions, the national government uses two other tools to create similarities across the states: grants-in-aid and regulations.

Grants-in-aid, as we have seen, are a little like bribes: Congress gives money to state and local governments if they agree to spend it for the purposes Congress specifies. But as Congress began to enact legislation in new areas, such as environmental policy, it also imposed additional regulations on states and localities. Some political scientists call this a move toward **regulated federalism.**[24] The national government began to set standards of conduct or required the states to set standards that met national guidelines. The effect of these national standards is that state and local policies in the areas of environmental protection, social services, and education are more uniform from coast to coast than are other nationally funded policies.

Some national standards require the federal government to take over areas of regulation formerly overseen by state or local governments. Such **preemption** occurs when state and local actions are found to be inconsistent with

regulated federalism
a form of federalism in which Congress imposes legislation on states and localities, requiring them to meet national standards

preemption
the principle that allows the national government to override state or local actions in certain policy areas

federal requirements. If this occurs, all regulations in the preempted area must henceforth come from the national government. In many cases, the scope of the federal authority to preempt is decided by the courts. For example, in 1973 the Supreme Court struck down a local ordinance prohibiting jets from taking off from the airport in Burbank, California, between 11 P.M. and 7 A.M. It ruled that the Federal Aeronautics Act granted the Federal Aviation Administration all authority over flight patterns, takeoffs, and landings and that local governments could not impose regulations in this area. As federal regulations increased after the 1970s, Washington increasingly preempted state and local action in many different policy areas. This preemption has escalated since 1995, when Republicans gained control of Congress. Although the Republicans came to power promising to grant more responsibility to the states, they have reduced state control in many areas by preemption. For example, in 1998 Congress passed a law that prohibits states and localities from taxing Internet commerce for the next three to six years. The 1996 Telecommunications Act reduced local control by giving broadcasters and digital companies broad discretion over where they could erect digital television and cellular phone towers even if local citizens objected. [25]

unfunded mandates

regulations or conditions for receiving grants that impose costs on state and local governments for which they are not reimbursed by the federal government

The growth of national standards has created some new problems and has raised questions about how far federal standardization should go. One problem that emerged in the 1980s was the increase in **unfunded mandates**—regulations or new conditions for receiving grants that impose costs on state and local governments for which they are not reimbursed by the national government. The growth of unfunded mandates was the product of a Democratic Congress, which wanted to achieve liberal social objectives, and a Republican president, who opposed increased social spending. Between 1983 and 1991, Congress mandated standards in many policy areas, including social services and environmental regulations, without providing additional funds to meet those standards. Altogether, Congress enacted twenty-seven laws that imposed new regulations or required states to expand existing programs.[26] For example, in the late 1980s, Congress ordered the states to extend the coverage provided by Medicaid, the medical insurance program for the poor. The aim was to make the program serve more people, particularly poor children, and to expand services. But Congress did not supply additional funding to help states meet these new requirements; the states had to shoulder the increased financial burden themselves.

States and localities quickly began to protest the cost of unfunded mandates. Although it is very hard to determine the exact cost of federal regulations, the Congressional Budget Office estimated that between 1983 and 1990, new federal regulations cost states and localities between $8.9 and $12.7 billion.[27] States complained that mandates took up so much of their budgets that they were not able to set their own priorities.

These burdens became part of a rallying cry to reduce the power of the federal government—a cry that took center stage when a Republican Congress was elected in 1994. One of the first measures the new Congress passed was an act to limit the cost of unfunded mandates, the Unfunded Mandate Reform Act (UMRA). Under this law, Congress must estimate the cost of any proposal it believes will cost more than $50 million. It must then vote to approve the regulation, acknowledging the expenditure. Since 1996, the Congressional Budget Office has examined close to 1,800 bills and amendments for unfunded mandates and found that 197 of them contained intergovermental mandates. Twenty-five of them included mandates that exceeded the $50-million threshold. Among these were such measures as an increase in the federal minimum wage, mandated use of Social Security numbers on driver's licenses, requirements to upgrade airport runway safety equipment, and prohibition of gambling over the Internet. Only two of these bills—the increased minimum wage and a reduction in federal funding for the administrative expenses of the Food Stamp program—were ultimately enacted in a form that will impose costs of $50 million a year more on state and local governments. [28]

As indicated by its operation to date, the effect of UMRA will not be any kind of revolution in federalism. The act does not prevent congressional members from passing unfunded mandates, but only makes them think twice before they do. Moreover, the act exempts several areas of regulation. States must still enforce antidiscrimination laws and meet other requirements to receive federal assistance. But on the other hand, UMRA does represent a serious effort to move the national/state relationship a bit further to the state side.

NEW FEDERALISM AND STATE CONTROL

In 1970, the mayor of Oakland, California, told Congress that there were twenty-two separate employment and training programs in his city but that few poor residents were being trained for jobs that were available in the local labor market.[29] National programs had proliferated as Congress enacted many small grants, but little effort was made to coordinate or adapt programs to local needs. Today many governors argue for more control over such national grant programs. They complain that national grants do not allow for enough local flexibility and instead take a "one size fits all" approach.[30] These criticisms point to a fundamental problem in American federalism: how to get the best results for the money spent. Do some divisions of responsibility between states and the federal government work better than others? Since the 1970s, as states have become more capable of administering large-scale programs, the idea of devolution—transferring responsibility for policy from the federal government to the states and localities—has become popular.

Proponents of more state authority have looked to **block grants** as a way of reducing federal control. Block grants are federal grants that allow the states considerable leeway in spending federal money. President Nixon led the first push for block grants in the early 1970s, as part of his **New Federalism.** Nixon's block grants consolidated programs in the areas of job training, community development, and social services into three large block grants. These grants imposed some conditions on states and localities for how the money should be spent, but not the narrow regulations contained in the categorical grants. In addition, Congress approved a fourth block grant called **revenue sharing.** Revenue sharing provided money to local governments and counties with no strings attached; localities could spend the money as they wished. Reagan's version of new federalism also looked to block grants. Like Nixon, Reagan wanted to reduce the national government's control and return power to the states. In all, Congress created twelve new block grants between 1981 and 1990.[31]

Another way of letting the states do more is by having the national government do less. When Nixon implemented block grants he increased federal

block grants
federal grants-in-aid that allow states considerable discretion in how the funds are spent

New Federalism
attempts by Presidents Nixon and Reagan to return power to the states through block grants

revenue sharing
the process by which one unit of government yields a portion of its tax income to another unit of government, according to an established formula. Revenue sharing typically involves the national government providing money to state governments

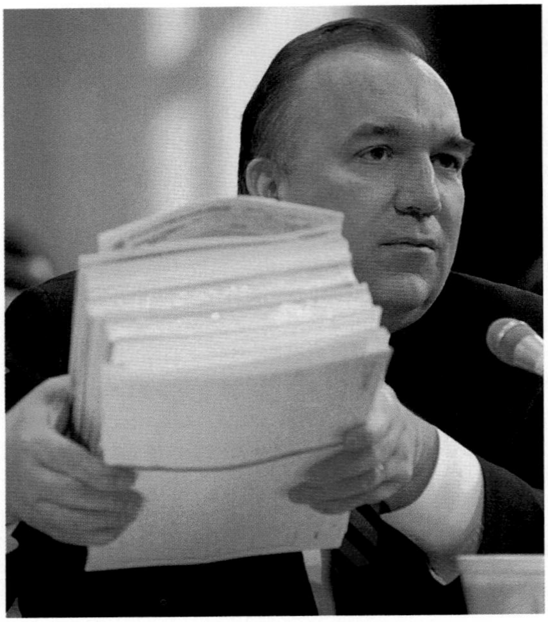

Michigan Governor John Engler, a prominent suppoerter of block grants, holds a stack of welfare regulations as he testifies before the House Budget Committee. Welfare reform became a salient issue for block grant proponents in the mid-1990s as a way to argue for greater flexibility at the state level in the administration of such programs.

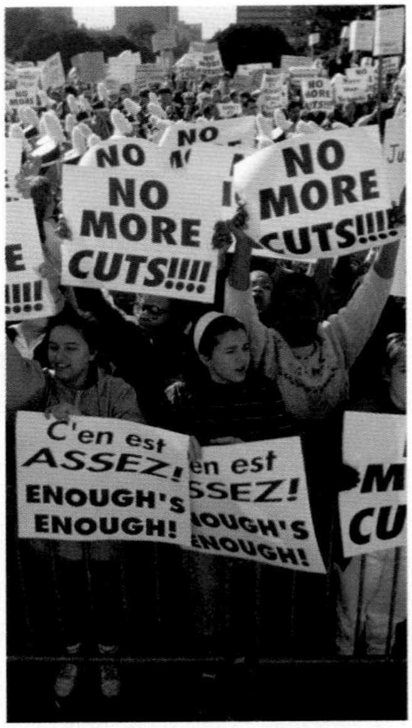

Cuts in federal funding have had a big impact on universities. These Louisiana State University students are protesting proposed funding cuts.

spending. But Reagan's block grants cut federal funding by 12 percent. His view was that the states could spend their own funds to make up the difference, if they chose to do so. The Republican Congress elected in 1994 took this strategy even further, supporting block grants as well as substantial cuts in federal programs. The states' governors were divided over how far these changes should go. Some Republican governors, such as John Engler of Michigan, worked with the Congress; they were willing to accept less federal money in exchange for greater state flexibility in administering programs. Other governors feared that turning existing programs into block grants with less money would leave the states with too large a financial burden.[32]

But neither block grants nor reduced federal funding have proven to be magic solutions to the problems of federalism. For one thing, there is always a trade-off between accountability, that is, whether the states are using funds for the purposes intended, and flexibility. Accountability and proper use of funds continue to be troublesome issues. Even after block grants were created, Congress reimposed regulations in order to increase the states' accountability. If the objective is to have accountable and efficient government, it is not clear that state bureaucracies are any more efficient or more capable than national agencies. In Mississippi, for example, the state Department of Human Services spent money from the child care block grant for office furniture and designer salt and pepper shakers that cost $37.50 a pair. As one Mississippi state legislator said, "I've seen too many years of good ol' boy politics to know they shouldn't [transfer money to the states] without stricter controls and requirements."[33] Both liberals and conservatives have charged that block grants are a way for politicians to avoid the big, controversial policy questions. Instead of facing problems head-on, these critics say, the federal government uses block grants to kick the problem down to the states.[34]

Reduced federal funding may leave states with problems that they do not

Table 4.3

FEDERAL AID AS A PERCENTAGE OF GENERAL ANNUAL EXPENDITURE, 1977 AND 1995

City	1977	1995	City	1977	1995
Chicago	20%	8%	Houston	13%	5%
Cleveland	29	10	Indianapolis	21	6
Denver	14	1	Los Angeles	22	12
Detroit	31	12	San Antonio	28	4
Honolulu	30	8	Seattle	23	3

SOURCE: Department of Commerce, *Statistical Abstract of the United States, 1999* (Washington, DC: U.S. Government Printing Office, 1999), Tables 504 and 506; *Statistical Abstract,* 1998, Tables 525 and 526.

have the resources to solve. During the 1980s, many states had to raise taxes in order to make up for some of the cuts in federal funding. (The impact of these cuts can be seen in Table 4.3.) And in the early 1990s, when a recession hit, states had to cut back services because they were short of funds even after raising taxes. More recently, the economic boom has left many states with budget surpluses. Some of the surplus has been used to make up for past spending cuts and to bolster state spending, particularly in the field of education. For example, in Virginia, the legislature agreed to reduce state college tuition by 20 percent in 1999, and Republican legislators in California proposed a 50 percent cut in fees at state colleges. But in most states a significant portion of the surplus has also gone to tax reduction. In Wisconsin, for example, the state cut income taxes and property taxes in 1999. The state also enacted an unusual sales tax rebate, which promised to send checks averaging $271 to 2.5 million Wisconsin residents.[35]

As states are expected to take on greater responsibility, they will become even more important political arenas, where different interests fight to see their vision of the proper role of government implemented.

IS THERE A RIGHT ANSWER?

Some students of federalism say that states are best at doing some things and the national government is better at doing others. They argue that rather than share responsibility for funding, as many programs now do, each level of government should be fully responsible for the things that it does best.

In 1985, the Robb-Evans Commission, a bipartisan group, proposed a comprehensive approach to the division of responsibility. It argued that the national government should leave all economic development programs to the states and that the national government should take responsibility for programs that serve the poor. The commission built on the ideas of many economists and political scientists who maintain that states and localities should not be in charge of **redistributive programs,** that is, programs that are primarily for the benefit of the poor. These scholars argue that because states and local governments have to compete with one another, they do not have the incentive

redistributive programs
economic policies designed to control the economy through taxing and spending, with the goal of benefiting the poor

to spend their money on the needy people in their areas. Instead, they want to keep taxes low and spend money on things that promote economic development.[36] In this situation, states might engage in a "race to the bottom": if one state cuts assistance to the poor, neighboring states will institute similar or deeper cuts both to reduce expenditures and to discourage poorer people from moving into their states. As one New York legislator put it, "The concern we have is that unless we make our welfare system and our tax and regulatory system competitive with the states around us, we will have too many disincentives for business to move here. Welfare is a big part of that."[37]

In 1996, when Congress enacted a major welfare reform law, it followed a different logic. By changing welfare from a combined federal-state program into a block grant to the states, Congress gave the states more responsibility for programs that serve the poor. One argument in favor of this decision was that states can act as "laboratories of democracy," by experimenting with many different approaches to find ones that best meet the needs of their citizens.[38] As states have altered their welfare programs in the wake of the new law, they have indeed designed diverse approaches. For example, Minnesota has adopted an incentive-based approach that offers extra assistance to families that take low-wage jobs. Other states, such as California, have more "sticks" than "carrots" in their new welfare programs. In the years since the passage of the law, welfare rolls have declined dramatically. On average they have declined by 47 percent from their peak in 1994; in six states the decline was 70 percent or higher. Politicians have cited these statistics to claim success for their programs, yet analysts caution that we do not yet know enough about the fate of those who have left welfare to judge the effect of welfare reform. Most studies have found that the majority of those leaving welfare remain in poverty. And even though many states have increased services to welfare recipients, they have also funneled savings on welfare expenditures into tax cuts for the nonpoor. Critics charge that by cutting taxes and limiting spending, states have missed a historic opportunity provided by reduced welfare rolls and budget surpluses to devise new ways to assist low-income residents.[39]

As the case of welfare shows, assessments about "the right way" to divide responsibility in the federal system change over time. The case of speed limits, discussed in the beginning of this chapter, provides another example. Speed limits have traditionally been a state and local responsibility. But in 1973, at the height of the oil short-

Students and Politics

The clicking sound of dress shoes ricocheted off the walls of the state Capitol, as Cal Poly students raced to lobby legislators for educational funding.

The students organized into groups of three and four, read a list of senators and assemblymen they would meet with, and set off to petition state government for additional funding.

* * *

College of Engineering Board of Directors member Nick Dwork believes the lobbying was worthwhile.

"I think we made an extraordinary impact," he said.

It was easy for Dwork to pinpoint the aspects that surprised him the most.

"The realization of how far away each individual is from the actual decision-making process was very educational," he said.

Agribusiness senior Andy Clarke said he lobbied because he is a "concerned student."

Clarke said he expected to meet more with the delegates than the staff, but observed the important role staff plays.

"The staff is truly the backbone of the system," he said.

Clarke said legislators turned the tables on students asking students to give opinions on upcoming pieces of legislation.

"The best aspect of the trip was actually seeing our legislative government in action," Clarke said.

Campaign organizer Hopper was thrilled with the lobbying.

"I was really impressed with how quickly the students caught on to what the issues were," she said. "They took the initiative to educate themselves."

"I think it was a really productive day," she said. "We definitely met our goals."

Hopper plans on getting more students to sign letters to their district representatives. She said she would also be willing to go back to Sacramento to secure the funds the CSU system so desperately needs.

SOURCE: Dina Chatman, "California Poly State U. Students Lobby for State Funds," *Mustang Daily* (California Poly State University), May 5, 1999.

POLICY DEBATE

Welfare Reform

President Franklin D. Roosevelt's New Deal effort to improve America's social and economic condition established the modern social welfare state, inaugurated with the enactment of the Social Security Act of 1935. This act provided income benefits for retired workers, the disabled, and the unemployed. In the 1960s, social welfare programs were expanded to improve conditions for the nation's poor. In the 1980s, Presidents Ronald Reagan and George Bush won cuts in programs like food stamps, Aid to Families with Dependent Children (AFDC), and job programs. President Bill Clinton also seized on what is now called welfare reform, promising to reorganize and streamline these programs. Congress approved legislation to end AFDC and give the money to the states to run their own welfare programs, limit benefits eligibility to five years, and insist on work requirements for welfare recipients. Yet these and other proposed changes continue to be controversial.

Supporters of welfare reform argue that the federal welfare system has spiraled out of control. Spending on all social welfare programs has topped $300 billion a year in the 1990s, at a time when government resources are shrinking. Despite this vast spending, poverty persists. The United States today supports a self-perpetuating culture of poverty that discourages able-bodied people from working. Welfare tears the fabric of society by producing generations of young people who are ignorant of the work ethic; it encourages unwed motherhood among a rising number of teenagers (three-fourths of all teenage mothers land on welfare within five years); it spawns rising rates of crime. Furthermore, the welfare system is expensive because it is inefficiently run. Too many able-bodied or ineligible people continue to receive government benefits.

Welfare reform seeks not only to weed out those who cheat the system, but to break the cycle of welfare dependency. Proponents of reform argue that the states are in the best position to decide how to handle poverty, since patterns vary widely from state to state. Beyond this, they assert, greater emphasis needs to be placed on the work ethic, so that those who *can* work *do*. "Deadbeat dads," men who fail to support the children they father, should be forced to support their families. The values of family life need to be emphasized to help break the cycle of unmarried teenage motherhood and dependency. Educational opportunities provide a vital route for the poor to acquire the skills they need to lead self-supporting, productive lives. Private charities and the spirit of voluntarism should replace government largesse. A good example of this is the private program Habitat for Humanity, which helps the poor build and occupy their own homes. In short, government welfare may not be ended, but the poor can be aided more cheaply and more effectively through private means.

Opponents of welfare reform argue that a governmental welfare safety net is necessary, and that welfare-related spending levels and problems have been greatly exaggerated. For example, the argument that increases in welfare benefits have encouraged unwed teenage motherhood is not borne out by most studies of the matter. The biggest cause of poverty is economic dislocation and shifts in the nature and demands of the workplace—factors over which individuals have no control. The primary "welfare" programs, including AFDC, food stamps, rent subsidies, and school lunches, comprised only about 5 percent of the 1995 national budget. The most expensive social programs are aimed mostly at the middle class, including Social Security and Medicare, which took up over 30 percent of the 1995 budget. Government spending for AFDC and similar programs has declined by over 40 percent, in real dollars, since the start of the 1980s.

Many of the social and behavioral problems associated with poverty arise from the fact that the government spends far less per capita on its poor than do most other industrialized nations. This keeps the poor at a subsistence level that makes it even more difficult for them to improve their situation. The culture of poverty idea is also greatly exaggerated, as six-sevenths of those who receive AFDC leave the benefits system within five years. Rather than stigmatizing and berating the poor, the government needs to emphasize constructive measures to assist those in need, so that they may get the child care, education, and other support necessary to break out of poverty. Only the federal government can ensure a consistent and fair level of support to those most in need.

STUDENT DEBATE

Does Welfare Reform Help the Poor?

Yes

[In 1996], the passage of the landmark welfare reform bill was met with significant hue and cry about the government abandoning those who needed help the most. Some of the more dire prognostications included an Urban Institute study that predicted that the new law would impoverish 2.6 million people, including 1.1 million children. If you haven't noticed, this apocalyptic rhetoric has been curiously absent in the last few months.

And the reason for this silence is a darn good one. Welfare reform is working. The results of the first year under the bill have started to come in, and the numbers tell a convincing story. By early September, one year after Clinton signed the bill into law, welfare caseloads had been reduced by approximately two million, a whopping 18 percent.

According to Bruce Reed, a Clinton assistant, in the Sept. 1 [1997] edition of *The New Republic,* these numbers "are totally unprecedented in the history of welfare." And, more importantly, most former welfare recipients are not turning to crime or going hungry; instead, they are defying the nay-sayers and becoming contributing members of society. Corporations and local governments are taking the lead, instituting welfare to work programs which feature job training tailored to the needs of those who haven't worked recently. Even the Urban Institute has conceded the success of the bill, calling its results "significantly different than predicted."

It would, however, be an oversimplification to attribute the decrease in welfare roles solely to the change in welfare law. A bustling economy is the most obvious factor; but no other economic boom has been accompanied by results nearly as significant as these. In fact, caseloads have fallen by more than 250,000 in a single year only twice in the history of welfare.

Another possible contributor to the startling results is the 1988 Family Support Act, which allowed states to institute work requirement programs for welfare recipients. This earlier measure surely got the ball rolling in the right direction, but the truly prodigious results didn't occur until last year.

Thus much, if not most of the credit, must go to the visionary initiative worked out between Clinton and the Republican Congress—an initiative that ended the spurious notion of welfare as a cash entitlement and brought the mushrooming program one step closer to the emergency relief measure that it was created to be. It admitted that the big government solution is not always the best one—giving much of the power to decide who did and did not deserve aid back to the states.

Despite its traditionally untouchable status, the modern welfare system must be held accountable for helping to create the self-perpetuating triad of unemployment, crime and illegitimate births which have reduced our inner cities to pockets of despair. Any criticism of welfare, though, was seen as insensitive—attacks on welfare were misconstrued as attacks on the poor.

In reality, critics chide the mechanics of a system that fosters a sense of entitlement and dependency among its recipients and places too much control in the hands of a federal bureaucracy far removed from the differing realities of each community. When the reform bill passed, many Democrats worried about provisions allowing states to apply for waivers enabling them to stop giving food stamps to unemployed adults. They fell victim to one of the great fallacies of America's modern consciousness: If the federal government doesn't do something, no one will. What the success of this bill has proved is that state governments, local churches, businesses and individuals are actually capable of doing more than take orders from Washington. No one, not even conservatives and state politicians, wants to see people starve to death.

Despite all of this success, we are not quite out of the woods yet. A forgotten demographic is the rural poor, which compose 25 percent of the nation's poor and lack the resources and opportunities of their urban counterparts. One former welfare recipient found work in a faraway town, but because her town's welfare office has only one bus, she must wait 6 hours after her shift for her carpool-mates to finish their shifts. She takes home $20 for a 16 hour day.

While stories like these suggest that the system definitely needs some tweaking, they should not take away from the resounding success of a measure that has encouraged two million Americans to get off the couch and into the workplace, and in the process restored the endangered concept of individual accountability.

SOURCE: Parker Stanberry, "Contrary to Predictions, Welfare Reform Helps Nation's Poor," *The Chronicle* (Duke University), November 12, 1997.

No

Officials around the country are heralding the recent drop in welfare recipients as a bureaucratic and social victory. But the corresponding drop in food-stamp recipients points to some disturbing trends on just how poorly the poor are treated.

Welfare rolls are shrinking around the country, with states opting for more stringent regulations on those who receive public aid. Iowa's welfare requests have dropped by nearly 45 percent, and the state's monthly payouts have plummeted from $14.5 million to $7.1 million since April 1994, when welfare requests were at their peak.

Nationally, the food-stamp program's operating costs have dropped from $24.5 billion to $18.9 billion during the same period. Food stamps are a form of public assistance separate from welfare and directed by the Department of Agriculture to promote healthy diets and nutritional assistance. The recent drop in use of these funds has many officials worried that the recent public backlash against welfare programs and recipients has scared eligible and needy people from applying for this assistance.

A large part of the welfare drop-off has been accredited to stricter regulations by welfare offices and a much stronger push for recipients to participate in job search and workfare programs. Requirements for food stamps, on the other hand, are much more lenient and accessible, though many poor people fail to recognize that they are still eligible for food stamps even if they have been turned away from welfare.

Moving people from welfare to jobs is an important goal—but so is keeping people from going hungry. In our zeal to squeeze every dollar out of welfare programs, poor people have been shamed into passing on food stamps—something they would normally be eligible for.

Food stamps provide an important way to make sure families are well-fed, regardless of economic status. There is no reason people should continue to be malnourished in this country when such a program is in place.

Tightening the welfare system may be merely masking poverty as joblessness. The poor have every right to federal food stamps and should not be discouraged by overzealous public officials from accepting the assistance. Shaming and confusing the poor into hunger is not the right way to trim budgets. The federal and state governments need to look at genuine ways of getting people back to work, rather than simply making public assistance increasingly difficult to obtain.

SOURCE: Greg Flanders, "Welfare Drop Signals Unsafe Trend," *The Daily Iowan* (University of Iowa), March 4, 1999.

age, Congress passed legislation to withhold federal highway funds from states that did not adopt a maximum speed limit of 55 miles per hour (mph). The lower speed limit, it was argued, would reduce energy consumption by cars. Although Congress had not formally taken over the authority to set speed limits, the power of its purse was so important that every state adopted the new speed limit. As the energy crisis faded, the national speed limit lost much of its support, even though it was found to have reduced the number of traffic deaths. In 1995, Congress repealed the penalties for higher speed limits, and states once again became free to set their own speed limits. Many states with large rural areas raised their maximum to 75 mph; Montana set unlimited speeds in the rural areas during daylight hours. Early research indicates that numbers of highway deaths have indeed risen in the states that increased the limits.[40]

It is unlikely that American federalism will ever exhibit a strict or simple division of responsibility between the states and the federal government. As new evidence becomes available about public problems, such as welfare and highway deaths, it provides fuel for ongoing debates about what are properly the states' responsibilities and what the federal government should do. Moreover, the temptation is ever present for federal politicians to limit state discretion in order to achieve their own policy objectives. Indeed, the "devolution revolution" promised by congressional Republicans created much more rhetoric than action. Despite the complaints of Republican governors, Congress has continued to use its power to preempt state action and impose mandates on states.

Perspectives on Politics

THE EFFICIENCY OF DIFFERENT LEVELS OF GOVERNMENT

Responses of eighteen- to twenty-four-year-olds to the question, "From which level of government do you feel you get the most for your money?"

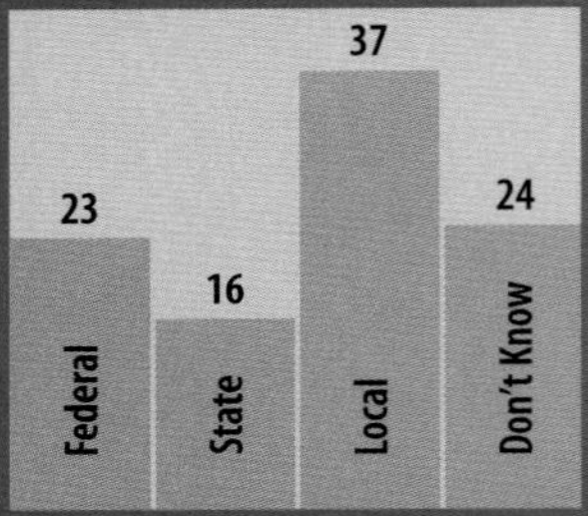

SOURCE: 1993 U.S. Advisory Commission on Intergovernmental Relations survey, reported in Susan A. MacManus, *Young v. Old: Generational Combat in the 21st Century* (Boulder, CO: Westview, 1996), p. 185.

Federalism and American Political Values

▶ How do changes in American federalism reflect different interpretations of liberty, equality, and democracy?

American federalism has changed substantially over the course of our history. The framers would never have dreamed of a federal government with as many powers as ours has today. The changes in American federalism reflect the different ways that we, as a nation, interpret the meanings of liberty, equality, and democracy at different times in our history. They also reflect our changing beliefs about which American institutions can best realize these values. But even today, there is no single consensus on how responsibilities should be organized within the federal system to make our fundamental values come alive. Indeed, a brief look at values and federalism reveals that some of the sharpest tensions among liberty, equality, and democracy are visible in debates over federalism.

The Constitution limited the power of the federal government in order to promote liberty. This decision reflected the framers' suspicions of centralized power, based on their experience with the British Crown. The American suspicion of centralized power lives on today in widespread dislike of "big government," which generally evokes a picture of a bloated federal government. But over the course of our history we have come to realize that the federal government is also an important guarantor of liberty. As we'll see in Chapter 5, it took enhanced federal power to ensure that local and state governments adhered to the fundamental constitutional freedoms in the Bill of Rights.

One of the most important continuing arguments for a strong federal government is its role in ensuring equality. A key puzzle of federalism is deciding when differences across states represent the proper democratic decisions of the states and when such differences represent inequalities that should not be tolerated. Sometimes a decision to eliminate differences is made on the grounds of equality and individual rights, as in the Civil Rights Act of 1964, which outlawed legal segregation. At other times, a stronger federal role is justified on the grounds of national interest, as in the case of the oil shortage and the institution of a 55 mph speed limit in the 1970s. Advocates of a more limited federal role often point to the value of democracy. Public actions can more easily be tailored to fit distinctive local or state desires if states and localities have more power to make policy. Viewed this way, variation across states can be an expression of democratic will.

In recent years, many Americans have grown disillusioned with the federal government and have supported efforts to give the states more responsibilities. A 1997 poll, for example, found that Americans tended to have the most confidence in governments that were closest to them. Thirty-eight percent expressed "a great deal" of confidence in local government, 32 percent in state government, and 22 percent in the federal government. Nearly two-thirds of those polled believed that shifting some responsibility to states and localities would help achieve excellence in government. But the same survey also revealed reluctance to significantly change the division of responsibilities among the levels of government. When asked what should be done, 54 percent called for improving management and only 32 percent called for passing responsibility to states and localities.[41]

Students and Politics

"I was never into politics," says John Potbury describing his youth in Flushing, Michigan. "I just watched some *Nightline* and read the local papers, but never anything in campaigns. . . . I couldn't even identify myself as a Republican or Democrat." A few years later, John's activism had increased significantly. The spark came while in high school, when he and three classmates journeyed to Washington, D.C., to participate in Close Up, a program that brings students from all fifty states together for a week of seminars and behind-the-scenes visits to the legislative, judicial, and executive branches of government. "The air of Washington was really inspiring," he says. "There was so much going on, more than anything I had expected or could imagine from my hometown. I had a new appreciation for the national government." Potbury's Close Up experience prompted him to do more at the local level by winning election to the city council of Flushing, and by working to promote business interests in the area. Today, although he no longer sits on the city council, he divides his time between national Republican Party activities (he worked with the advance teams for Bob Dole's 1996 presidential campaign) and local community service projects, such as bringing professionals into local schools to speak with students about careers. Despite his fascination with the federal government, Potbury still appreciates his time on the city council: "I did things at the local level that must be done at the local level."

American federalism remains a work in progress. As public problems shift and as local, state, and federal governments change, questions about the relationship between American values and federalism naturally emerge. The different views that people bring to this discussion suggest that concerns about federalism will remain a central issue in American democracy.

The Citizen's Role: Participation at Different Levels of the Federal System

How can citizens contribute to the ongoing design of American federalism? To be effective participants in a federal system, citizens must first understand how responsibilities are divided among the different levels of government. They also need to be aware of how decisions taken at one level of government may affect the possibilities for public action at other levels. In other words, if citizens are to be politically effective they must understand the connections among the levels of the federal system and target their activities where they will be most effective.

One of the striking features of political participation in the United States is the preference for engaging in politics at the state and local levels. One study of political participation found that 92 percent of Americans who participated beyond voting—by campaigning, contacting public officials, or sitting on a governing board, for example—engaged in an activity focused on state and local activity. Fifty-one percent of those questioned engaged only in state and local action, while 41 percent added some form of national participation to their state and local activities.[42] This pattern of participation makes sense because politics at these levels—especially the local level—is more personal and often easier to get involved in. Moreover, many of the things that people care most about are close to home, such as their schools and their neighborhoods.

But to be broadly effective, citizens must be able to engage in political activity at different levels of the federal system. For example, in the 1970s, community groups frustrated in their efforts to revitalize inner-city neighborhoods lobbied Congress to pass the Community Reinvestment Act, which requires banks to invest in the neighborhoods where they do business. With this federal law behind them, community organizations have been much more effective in promoting investment in the 1980s and 1990s. But it is often not easy for groups of citizens to focus their activity at different levels of government as needed. Often they do not have the expertise or the contacts or the information to be effective in a different setting.

In recent years, as states have taken on a greater role in making public policy, it has become more important for citizens to become effective participants in state politics. Moreover, the media coverage of state politics is generally not as deep or informative as coverage of national politics. Citizens need a better knowledge of what states do today and more information about state politics simply as a first step to being effective participants in our federal system.

The federal system makes American democracy a flexible form of government for a large and diverse nation. But citizens must be knowledgeable about how public actions across the federal system are connected and they must be able to act at different levels if federalism is to be an effective and representative form of government.

Politics on the Web

As anyone who has ordered clothing from J. Crew can tell you, mail-order shopping has one great advantage: you may avoid sales tax. Internet shopping may further erode state sales tax revenues, but increasing computerization of commerce may finally allow states to capture taxes on mail-order purchases.

Who will regulate Internet commerce? The states or the federal government? Although state and federal powers overlap in many areas of commerce, it is most likely that the federal government will have to regulate all aspects of the Internet. States may claim the power to regulate Internet commerce, but, as in the past, they have no power to regulate corporations located in other states. Unlike a factory or a store, it is fast and easy to "relocate" a web site to another city, state, or even country. Only the federal government can set national standards for companies that can easily shift services and production across state lines.

www.wwnorton.com/wtp3e

GET INVOLVED: Participating in Local Politics

Many of the laws and policies that most directly affect you are made at the local level. What happens in the government offices of your county, city, or town often determines who is eligible for government programs, where commercial or residential buildings will stand, if neighborhood streets will be smooth and traffic uncongested, where and when you can walk the streets safely, and what kind of public education will be available to you and your children.

The good news is that citizens usually have easy access to local officials. They work (and live) close to home and serve a relatively limited constituency. Furthermore, local jurisdictions often provide residents numerous opportunities to participate in government by speaking at public hearings, serving on citizen commissions, and volunteering time at city-sponsored events. Here are two local arenas that may attract your interest.

1. *Public education.* State governments mandate the general requirements for curricula and minimal requirements for graduation, but these state mandates are administered by local school districts. In turn, local school districts are managed by superintendents who have considerable discretion in shaping elementary, middle, high school, and sometimes community college education. Most school districts and superintendents are accountable to local school boards. School board members are usually selected by voters in competitive elections in the same way that mayors or council members are chosen. Here are some ways to get involved in school politics.

- School boards meet regularly and hold public meetings. Attend a board meeting or two, look over the agenda, and consider which issues interest you. School boards usually provide opportunities for public comment. If you have an issue that you think should be addressed, speak up.
- School boards and superintendents often set up community advisory committees and appoint local residents to serve on those committees. Check with the office at a nearby public school, or call information, city hall, the superintendent's office, or school board staff to find out who you should speak to in order to volunteer to serve on an advisory committee.
- Citizens who serve on advisory committees get connected to people who are involved with local education issues. Conceivably, you can build a network of contacts and allies to consider running for a seat on the school board. This often is a good starting point for a political career.

2. *Law enforcement.* Most states have several different police agencies, for example, state police or highway patrol, county sheriffs, and city or town peace officers. Other state and local officials may have police powers, too. We do not necessarily think of lifeguards or forest rangers as police personnel, but they often are.

Many police agencies practice community policing. Rather than simply react to crime, they try to prevent crime by promoting a local environment conducive to law-abiding behavior. They may sponsor after-school programs for at-risk youth; they may provide mediation services to settle domestic disputes; or they may host community forums aimed at easing racial tensions and promoting interracial cooperation. Here are some ways to participate in local law enforcement issues.

- Call up a local law enforcement agency to see if it has any volunteer programs. These programs may range from exposing youth or citizens to policing efforts or organizing citizen patrol groups to helping officers promote Neighborhood Watch programs or other public service activities. If any of these interest you, volunteer.

- Law enforcement officials are often accountable to citizen review commissions. Members of these commissions may be appointed or elected. Contact city hall and find out how you can get involved in these commissions.
- In some localities, citizen groups exercise informal oversight over police officials. Civil rights groups often express concern about the misuse of police authority. They publicize and protest incidents of police brutality and engage in litigation to punish and prevent such incidents. To identify and contact such groups, watch for coverage of them in the news, do an Internet search, or telephone a major civil rights organization such as the American Civil Liberties Union or the National Association for the Advancement of Colored People for relevant information.

Many local governments establish citizen committees and commissions to provide citizen input into various aspects of public life. In some cases, local governments are mandated by law to seek citizen participation in functional areas such as city planning. Other areas that typically invite citizen participation include environmental, traffic, recreation, libraries, and public art issues. A good first contact point is your local city hall. Inquire about what types of citizen committees exist and request information on procedures for filling vacancies.

Summary

In this chapter, we have examined one of the central principles of American government—federalism. The Constitution divides powers between the national government and the states, but over time national power has grown substantially. Many aspects of expanded federal power stem from struggles to realize the ideals of liberty and equality for all citizens.

The aim of federalism in the Constitution was to limit national power by creating two sovereigns—the national government and the state governments. The Founders hoped that this system of dual federalism would ensure the liberty of citizens by preventing the national government from becoming too powerful. But during the 1930s, American citizens used the democratic system to change the balance between federal and state governments. The failure of the states to provide basic economic security for citizens during the Great Depression led to an expansion of the federal government. Most Americans were supportive of this growing federal power because they believed that economic power had become too concentrated in the hands of big corporations and the common person was the loser. Thus, the ideal of equality—in this case, the belief that working people should have a fighting chance to support themselves—overrode fears that a strong federal government would abridge liberties. Expanded federal powers first took the form of grants-in-aid to states. Later, federal regulations became more common.

In recent years, many Americans have come to believe that the pendulum has swung too far in the direction of expanded federal power. A common charge is that the federal government is too big and, as a result, has encroached on fundamental liberties. State and local governments complain that they cannot govern because their powers have been preempted or because they have to use their own funds to fulfill unfunded mandates imposed by the federal government. The move to devolve more powers to the states has been called "New Federalism." Advocates of reduced federal power believe that states can protect liberty without creating unacceptable inequalities. Others continue to believe that a strong central government is essential to ensuring basic equalities. They argue that economic competition among the states means that states cannot ensure equality as well as the federal government can. Such questions about how federalism affects the goals of liberty and equality are not easily settled and will remain a continuing task of American democracy.

FOR FURTHER READING

Bensel, Richard. *Sectionalism and American Political Development: 1880–1980.* Madison: University of Wisconsin Press, 1984.

Bowman, Ann O'M., and Richard Kearny. *The Resurgence of the States.* Englewood Cliffs, NJ: Prentice-Hall, 1986.

Donahue, John D. *Disunited States.* New York: Basic Books, 1997.

Dye, Thomas R. *American Federalism: Competition among Governments.* Lexington, MA: Lexington Books, 1990.

Elazar, Daniel. *American Federalism: A View from the States,* 3rd ed. New York: Harper & Row, 1984.

Grodzins, Morton. *The American System.* Chicago: Rand McNally, 1974.

Kelley, E. Wood. *Policy and Politics in the United States: The Limits of Localism.* Philadelphia: Temple University Press, 1987.

Kettl, Donald. *The Regulation of American Federalism.* Baltimore: Johns Hopkins University Press, 1987.

Peterson, Paul E. *The Price of Federalism.* Washington, DC: Brookings, 1995.

STUDY OUTLINE

The Federal Framework

1. In an effort to limit national power, the framers of the Constitution established a system of dual federalism, wherein both the national and state governments would have sovereignty.
2. The Constitution granted a few "expressed powers" to the national government and, through the Tenth Amendment, reserved all the rest to the states.
3. The Constitution also created obligations among the states in the "full faith and credit" and "privileges and immunities" clauses.
4. Federalism and a restrictive definition of "interstate commerce" limited the national government's control over the economy.
5. Federalism allows a great deal of variation between states.
6. Under the traditional system of federalism, the national government was small and very narrowly specialized in its functions compared with other Western nations. Most of its functions were aimed at promoting commerce.
7. Under the traditional system, states rather than the national government did most of the fundamental governing in the country.
8. The system of federalism limited the expansion of the national government despite economic forces and expansive interpretations of the Constitution in cases such as *McCulloch v. Maryland* and *Gibbons v. Ogden.*
9. For most of U.S. history, the concept of interstate commerce kept the national government from regulating the economy. But in 1937, the Supreme Court converted the commerce clause from a source of limitations to a source of power for the national government.
10. Recent years have seen a revival of interest in returning more power to the states through devolution.

Who Does What? The Changing Federal Framework

1. The rise of national government activity after the New Deal did not necessarily mean that states lost power directly. Rather, the national government paid states through grants-in-aid to administer federal programs.
2. Some federal programs bypass the states by sending money directly to local governments or local organizations. The states are most important, however; they are integral to federal programs such as Medicaid.
3. The national government also imposed regulations on states and localities in areas such as environmental policy in order to guarantee national standards.
4. Under President Nixon, many categorical grants were combined into larger block grants that offered greater flexibility in the use of the money. The Nixon administration also developed revenue sharing that was not tied to any specific programs.
5. As states have become more capable of administering large-scale programs, the idea of devolution has become popular.

Federalism and American Political Values

1. Some of the sharpest tensions among liberty, equality, and democracy are visible in debates over federalism.
2. The Constitution limited the power of the national government as a safeguard for liberty, but over the course of American history, a strong national government has been an important guarantor of liberty.
3. A key puzzle of federalism is deciding when differences across states represent the proper democratic decisions of the states and when such differences represent inequalities that should not be tolerated.

PRACTICE QUIZ

1. Which term describes the sharing of powers between the national government and the state governments?
   a) separation of powers
   b) federalism
   c) checks and balances
   d) shared powers
2. The system of federalism that allowed states to do most of the fundamental governing from 1789 to 1937 was
   a) home rule.
   b) regulated federalism.
   c) dual federalism.
   d) cooperative federalism.
3. Which of the following resulted from the federal system?
   a) It limited the power of the national government in relation to the states.
   b) It restrained the power of the national government over the economy.
   c) It allowed variation among the states.
   d) all of the above
4. The overall effect of the growth of national policies has been
   a) to weaken state government.
   b) to strengthen state government.
   c) to provide uniform laws in the nation.
   d) to make the states more diverse culturally.
5. Which amendment to the Constitution stated that the powers not delegated to the national government or prohibited to the states were "reserved to the states"?
   a) First Amendment
   b) Fifth Amendment
   c) Tenth Amendment
   d) Twenty-sixth Amendment
6. The process of returning more of the responsibilities of governing from the national level to the state level is known as
   a) dual federalism.
   b) devolution.
   c) preemption.
   d) home rule.
7. One of the most powerful tools by which the federal government has attempted to get the states to act in ways that are desired by the federal government is by
   a) providing grants-in-aid.
   b) requiring licensing.
   c) granting home rule.
   d) defending states' rights.
8. The form of regulated federalism that allows the federal government to take over areas of regulation formerly overseen by states or local governments is called
   a) categorical grants.
   b) formula grants.
   c) project grants.
   d) preemption.

9. To what does the term "New Federalism" refer?
   a) the national government's regulation of state action through grants-in-aid
   b) the type of federalism relying on categorical grants
   c) efforts to return more policy-making discretion to the states through the use of block grants
   d) the recent emergence of local governments as important political actors

10. A recent notable example of the process of giving the states more responsibility for administering government programs is
   a) campaign finance reform.
   b) prison reform.
   c) trade reform.
   d) welfare reform.

CRITICAL THINKING QUESTIONS

1. The role of the national government has changed significantly from the Founding era to the present. In what ways and to what extent do you think the framers of the Constitution would recognize modern American federalism? Do you think they would be pleased by the current balance of power between the sovereign national government and the sovereign state governments? In what ways did the system of federalism perform its intended functions? In what ways did it not?
2. Should states be required to implement unfunded mandates? Are Americans better off or worse off as a result of devolution?

KEY TERMS

block grants (p. 131)
categorical grants (p. 127)
commerce clause (p. 121)
concurrent powers (p. 114)
cooperative federalism (p. 128)
devolution (p. 124)
dual federalism (p. 118)
expressed powers (p. 113)
federal system (p. 113)
federalism (p. 113)
formula grants (p. 127)
full faith and credit clause (p. 116)
grants-in-aid (p. 126)
home rule (p. 117)
implied powers (p. 114)
necessary and proper clause (p. 114)
New Federalism (p. 131)
police power (p. 114)
preemption (p. 129)
privileges and immunities clause (p. 117)
project grants (p. 127)
redistributive programs (p. 133)
regulated federalism (p. 129)
reserved powers (p. 114)
revenue sharing (p. 131)
states' rights (p. 123)
unfunded mandates (p. 130)
unitary system (p. 113)

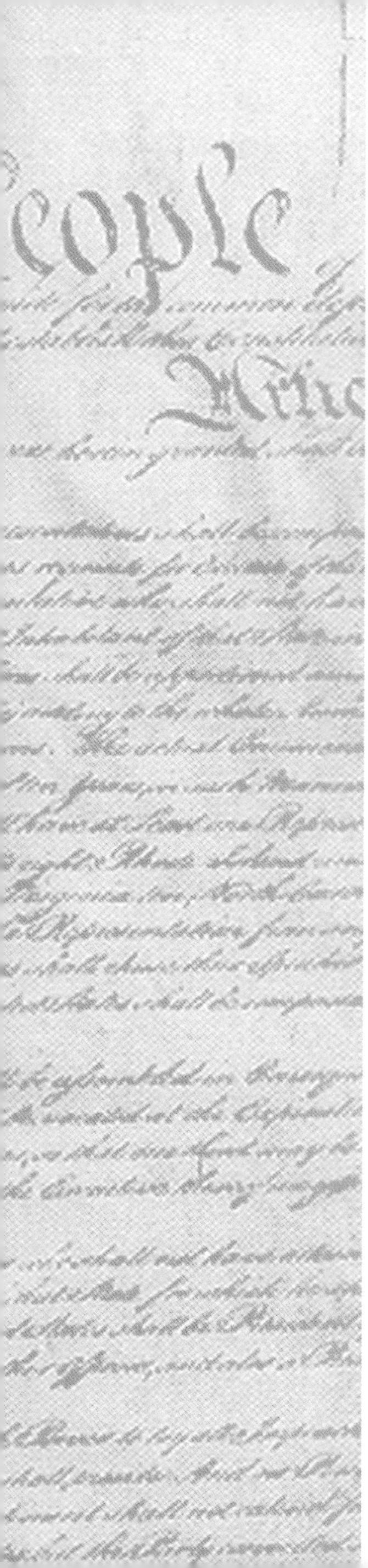

5 Civil Liberties

★ **The Bill of Rights: A Charter of Liberties**

How does the Bill of Rights provide for individual liberties?

What are the differences between the substantive and procedural restraints contained within the Bill of Rights? What are some examples of each?

★ **Nationalizing the Bill of Rights**

Does the Bill of Rights put limits only on the national government or does it limit state governments as well?

How and when did the Supreme Court nationalize the Bill of Rights?

★ **The First Amendment and Freedom of Religion**

How does the First Amendment guarantee the nonestablishment and free exercise of religion?

In what way has the free exercise of religion become a recent political issue?

★ **The First Amendment and Freedom of Speech and the Press**

What forms of speech are protected by the First Amendment? What forms are not protected?

★ **The Second Amendment and the Right to Bear Arms**

Is the right to bear arms guaranteed by the Bill of Rights? How is its exercise restricted?

★ **Rights of the Criminally Accused**

What is due process?

How do the Fourth, Fifth, Sixth, and Eighth Amendments provide for the due process of law?

★ **The Right to Privacy**

What is the right to privacy? How has it been derived from the Bill of Rights? What forms does the right to privacy take today?

★ **The Future of Civil Liberties**

What is the likelihood that the Supreme Court will try to reverse the nationalization of the Bill of Rights?

STUDENTS AND POLITICS

THE first ten amendments of the United States Constitution, together called the **Bill of Rights,** are the basis for the freedoms we enjoy as American citizens. These freedoms include the right to free speech, the right to the free exercise of religion, prohibitions against unreasonable searches and seizures, guarantees of due process of law, and the right to privacy, including a woman's right to have an abortion. Today, we may take the liberties contained within the Bill of Rights for granted. Few citizens of other countries can make such a claim. In fact, few people in recorded history have enjoyed such protections, including American citizens before the 1960s. For more than 170 years after its passage in 1789, the Bill of Rights meant little to most Americans. As we shall see in this chapter, guaranteeing the liberties articulated in the Bill of Rights to all Americans required a long struggle. As new challenges to the Bill of Rights arise, this struggle will likely continue.

Bill of Rights
the first ten amendments to the Constitution, which guarantee certain rights and liberties to the people

As recently as the early 1960s many of the freedoms we enjoy today were not guaranteed. At that time, abortion was illegal everywhere in the United States, criminal suspects in state cases did not have to be informed of their rights, some states required daily Bible readings and prayers in their public schools, and some communities regularly censored reading material that they deemed to be obscene. Since the early 1960s, the Supreme Court has expanded the scope of individual freedoms considerably. But since these liberties are constantly subject to judicial interpretation, their provisions are fragile and need to be vigilantly safeguarded. Nevertheless, the Bill of Rights is available and can make a difference.

In recent years, a new challenge has confronted the Bill of Rights—one that may be of special interest to college students. The controversy involves the persistent and widespread efforts to regulate the Internet. Questions about how much power the national government should have over cyberspace were first answered in 1996, when Congress passed the Communications Decency Act, which prohibited the deliberate transmission of "obscene or indecent . . . or patently offensive" material to persons under eighteen years of age. The constitutionality of the act was immediately challenged by a number of interest groups, ranging from the liberal, pro–free speech American Civil Liberties Union (ACLU); to educational groups like the American Library Association; to groups with an economic interest in an unregulated Internet, such as the American Booksellers Association, Microsoft Corporation, and America Online; to groups with a cultural or lifestyle interest, such as Queer Resources Directory. The case challenging the act, *Reno v. ACLU*, reached the Supreme Court in 1997 and by a unanimous vote, the act was overturned.[1]

Cyberspace has become the new frontier of civil liberties and, as with the crossing of all previous frontiers, a long and difficult process lies ahead: that of

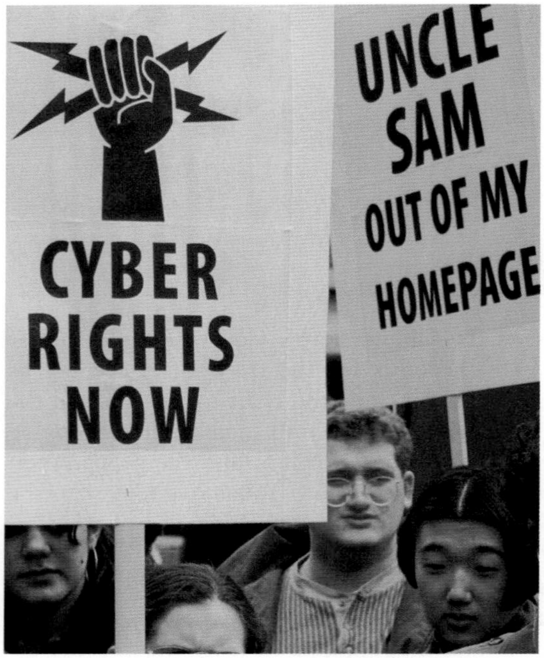

College students have been vocal advocates for free speech on the Internet.

defending the civil liberties of all citizens by protecting the most obnoxious exercises of freedom. Lines of battle were forming as the Supreme Court was filing out of the courtroom after the *Reno v. ACLU* decision. Conservatives were alarmed over what appeared to them to be a trend of more and bolder on-line pornography, and civil liberties groups were equally alarmed at the prospect that regulations proposed by their opponents would not just protect minors but "create virtual gated communities," where members can screen out "inappropriate" messages.[2]

One such civil liberties group formed in the summer of 1996, when a group of college and high school students from around the nation started Peacefire, an interest group founded "to represent students' and minors' interests in the debate over freedom of speech on the Internet." Today, the group, which includes 3,300 members, focuses on anti-censorship legislation and on curtailing the power of home-censorship programs such as CYBERsitter and Cyber Patrol, which sometimes deny minors access to civil rights pages, including several gay-rights, gun-rights, and environmental-protection sites. Web pages blocked by CYBERsitter have included those of the National Organization for Women, the International Gay and Lesbian Human Rights Commission, and Peacefire itself.

The efforts of Peacefire have raised the ire of CYBERsitter employees, one of whom told the organizers via e-mail, "Get a life! Go hang out at the mall with the other kids or something." Supporters fired back, charging CYBERsitter with barring children from intellectual forums; one parent expressed fears "that today's young people will be greatly victimized, often without even knowing it, by use of [CYBERsitter] software." Amid this firestorm, Peacefire cofounder Bennett Haselton and others continue to monitor potential and actual abuses of minors' civil liberties, including censoring programs and legislation. "Kids do not have enough clout in proportion to their numbers," says

Haselton, a senior at Vanderbilt University. Peacefire works to ensure that they do.[3]

Many Americans view companies such as CYBERsitter as infringing on individual liberties. Others argue that parents have the choice not to buy the software in the first place and that they can best regulate their own children's viewing habits. The fundamental liberty at stake is that of free speech, an issue often hotly debated on college campuses. This and the other liberties guaranteed by the Bill of Rights will be the focus of this chapter.

- ***In this chapter, our first task is to define the Bill of Rights and establish its relationship to personal liberty.*** As we shall see, it is through the Bill of Rights that Americans are protected from government.
- ***We then turn to the process by which the Bill of Rights was applied, not only to the national government, but also to the state governments.*** This nationalizing process has been long and selective in applying only certain provisions of the Bill of Rights.
- ***The bulk of this chapter is an analysis of the state of civil liberties today, beginning with the First Amendment and the freedom of religion.*** Questions over the meaning of this First Amendment guarantee continue to be a focal point of judicial interpretation of the Bill of Rights.
- ***We then turn to the other First Amendment rights regarding the freedoms of speech and of the press.*** Although freedom of speech and freedom of the press are critical for a democracy, some forms of speech are only conditionally protected.
- ***After briefly reviewing the Second Amendment right to bear arms, we move on to the rights of those accused of a crime.*** These rights, contained in the Fourth, Fifth, Sixth, and Eighth Amendments, make up the due process of law, a concept that the Supreme Court continues to reinterpret.
- ***We then turn to a right that has become increasingly important in recent decades, the right to privacy.*** This right takes many forms and, like the freedoms found directly in the Bill of Rights, has been subject to new judicial interpretations.
- ***We conclude by pondering the future of civil liberties in the United States.*** As we emphasize throughout this chapter, the Bill of Rights is constantly subject to the interpretations of the Supreme Court. Will the Court try to limit the extent of civil liberties in the near future?

PEACEFIRE
Youth Alliance Against Internet Censorship

Peacefire's logo has become a symbol for free speech on the Internet. See www.peacefire.org for more information.

The Bill of Rights: A Charter of Liberties

- How does the Bill of Rights provide for individual liberties?
- What are the differences between the substantive and procedural restraints contained within the Bill of Rights? What are some examples of each?

When the first Congress under the newly ratified Constitution met in late April of 1789 (having been delayed since March 4 by lack of a quorum because of

Table 5.1 RIGHTS IN THE ORIGINAL CONSTITUTION (NOT IN THE BILL OF RIGHTS)

Clause	Right Established
Article I, Sec. 9	guarantee of *habeas corpus*
Article I, Sec. 9	prohibition of **bills of attainder**
Article I, Sec. 9	prohibition of **ex post facto laws**
Article I, Sec. 9	prohibition against acceptance of titles of nobility, etc., from any foreign state
Article III	guarantee of trial by jury in state where crime was committed
Article III	treason defined and limited to the life of the person convicted, not to the person's heirs

bills of attainder
laws that decree a person guilty of a crime without a trial

ex post facto laws
laws that declare an action to be illegal after it has been committed

bad winter roads), the most important item of business was the consideration of a proposal to add a bill of rights to the Constitution. Such a proposal by Virginia delegate George Mason had been turned down with little debate in the waning days of the Philadelphia Constitutional Convention in 1787, not because the delegates were against rights, but because, as the Federalists, led by Alexander Hamilton, later argued, it was "not only unnecessary in the proposed Constitution but would even be dangerous."[4] First, according to Hamilton, a bill of rights would be irrelevant to a national government that was given only delegated powers in the first place. To put restraints on "powers which are not granted" could provide a pretext for governments to claim more powers than were in fact granted: "For why declare that things shall not be done which there is no power to do?"[5] Second, the Constitution was to Hamilton and the Federalists a bill of rights in itself, or contained provisions that amounted to a bill of rights without requiring additional amendments (see Table 5.1). For example, Article I, Section 9, included the right of **habeas corpus,** which prohibits the government from depriving a person of liberty without an open trial before a judge.

habeas corpus
a court order demanding that an individual in custody be brought into court and shown the cause for detention

Despite the power of Hamilton's arguments, when the Constitution was submitted to the states for ratification, Antifederalists, most of whom had not been delegates in Philadelphia, picked up on the argument of Thomas Jefferson (who also had not been a delegate) that the omission of a bill of rights was a major imperfection of the new Constitution. The Federalists conceded that in order to gain ratification they would have to make an "unwritten but unequivocal pledge" to add a bill of rights that would include a confirmation (in what became the Tenth Amendment) of the understanding that all powers not expressly delegated to the national government or explicitly prohibited to the states were reserved to the states.[6]

"After much discussion and manipulation . . . at the delicate prompting of Washington and under the masterful prodding of Madison," the House of Representatives adopted seventeen amendments; of these, the Senate adopted twelve. Ten of the amendments were ratified by the states on December 15, 1791; from the start these ten were called the Bill of Rights (see Box 5.1).[7]

The Bill of Rights might well have been entitled the "Bill of Liberties," because the provisions that were incorporated in the Bill of Rights were seen as

THE BILL OF RIGHTS **Box 5.1**

Amendment I: Limits on Congress
Congress cannot make any law establishing a religion or abridging freedoms of religious exercise, speech, assembly, or petition.

Amendments II, III, IV: Limits on the Executive
The executive branch cannot infringe on the right of the people to keep arms (II), cannot arbitrarily take houses for militia (III), and cannot search for or seize evidence without a court warrant swearing to the probable existence of a crime (IV).

Amendments V, VI, VII, VIII: Limits on the Judiciary
The courts cannot hold trials for serious offenses without provision for a grand jury (V), a trial jury (VII), a speedy trial (VI), presentation of charges and confrontation by the accused of hostile witnesses (VI), and immunity from testimony against oneself and immunity from trial more than once for the same offense (V). Furthermore, neither bail nor punishment can be excessive (VIII), and no property can be taken without "just compensation" (V).

Amendments IX, X: Limits on the National Government
Any rights not enumerated are reserved to the state or the people (X), but the enumeration of certain rights in the Constitution should not be interpreted to mean that those are the only rights the people have (IX).

defining a private sphere of personal liberty, free of governmental restrictions.[8] As Jefferson had put it, a bill of rights "is what people are entitled to against every government on earth. . . ." Note the emphasis—citizen *against* government. **Civil liberties** are *protections of citizens from* improper government action. Thus, the Bill of Rights is a series of "thou shalt nots"—restraints imposed upon government (see Table 5.2). Some of these restraints are **substantive liberties,** which put limits on *what* the government shall and shall not have power to do—such as establishing a religion, quartering troops in private homes without consent, or seizing private property without just compensation.

civil liberties
areas of personal freedom with which governments are constrained from interfering

substantive liberties
restraints on what the government shall and shall not have the power to do

CIVIL LIBERTIES IN THE BILL OF RIGHTS **Table 5.2**

Amendment	Example
I	"Congress shall make *no* law ..."
II	"The right ... to bear Arms, shall *not* be infringed"
III	"*No* soldier shall ... be quartered ..."
IV	"*No* Warrants shall issue, but upon probable cause ..."
V	"*No* person shall be held to answer for a ... crime, unless on a presentment or indictment of a Grand Jury ..."
VIII	"Excessive bail shall *not* be required ... *nor* cruel and unusual punishments inflicted."

The Bill of Rights accentuates the negative.

procedural liberties
restraints on how the government is supposed to act; for example, citizens are guaranteed the due process of law

due process of law
the right of every citizen against arbitrary action by national or state governments

civil rights
legal or moral claims that citizens are entitled to make upon the government

Other restraints are **procedural liberties,** which deal with *how* the government is supposed to act. These procedural liberties are usually grouped under the general category of **due process of law,** which first appears in the Fifth Amendment provision that "no person shall be . . . deprived of life, liberty, or property, without due process of law." For example, even though the government has the substantive power to declare certain acts to be crimes and to arrest and imprison persons who violate criminal laws, it may not do so without meticulously observing procedures designed to protect the accused person. The best known procedural rule is that an accused person is presumed innocent until proven guilty. This rule does not question the government's power to punish someone for committing a crime; it questions only the way the government determines who committed the crime. Substantive and procedural restraints together identify the realm of civil liberties.

In contrast, **civil rights** as a category refers to the obligations imposed on government to *take positive action* to protect citizens from any illegal actions of government agencies as well as of other private citizens. Civil rights did not become part of the Constitution until 1868, with the adoption of the Fourteenth Amendment, which sought to provide for each citizen "the equal protection of the laws." The easiest and clearest way to understand the distinction between civil liberties and civil rights is to remember that civil liberties issues arise under the "due process" clause in the original Bill of Rights, while civil rights issues arise under the "equal protection" clause that came into play only after the adoption of the Fourteenth Amendment.

Although we will look first at civil liberties because the struggle for freedom against arbitrary and discriminatory action by governments has the longest history, we should not lose sight of the connection in the real world between civil liberties and civil rights and, generally, between liberty and equality. The history of immigration to America, the American colonial experience, and the American Revolution built deeply into the American character and the American culture a commitment to individual liberty and a fear of government intrusions on that liberty. These sentiments have in turn given Americans a love/hate relationship with their government. The 1990s were an era of particularly strong antagonism toward government interference into personal liberty, which continues today. Yet the other side of that love/hate equation is also important, because the individual must recognize that the need to be protected *from* government is forever coupled with the need for an *active and positive* government to protect and to advance each individual's opportunity to enjoy liberty.[9]

Nationalizing the Bill of Rights

- Does the Bill of Rights put limits only on the national government or does it limit state governments as well?
- How and when did the Supreme Court nationalize the Bill of Rights?

The First Amendment provides that "Congress shall make no law. . . ." But this is the only amendment in the Bill of Rights that addresses itself exclusively to the national government. For example, the Second Amendment provides that "the right of the people to keep and bear Arms, shall not be infringed." And the Fifth Amendment says, among other things, that "no person shall . . . be twice put in jeopardy of life or limb" for the same crime. Since the First Amendment is the only part of the Bill of Rights that is explicit in its intention to put limits on Congress and therefore on the national government, a fundamental question inevitably arises: Do the remaining provisions of the Bill of Rights put limits only on the national government, or do they limit the state governments as well?

The Supreme Court first answered this question in 1833 by ruling that the Bill of Rights limited only the national government and not the state governments.[10] But in 1868, when the Fourteenth Amendment was added to the Constitution, the question arose once again. The Fourteenth Amendment reads as if it were meant to impose the Bill of Rights upon the states:

> No *State* shall make or enforce any law which shall abridge the privileges or immunities of citizens of the United States; nor shall any *State* deprive any person of life, liberty, or property, without due process of law; nor deny to any person within its jurisdiction the equal protection of the laws [emphasis added].

This language sounds like an effort to extend the Bill of Rights in its entirety to all citizens, wherever they might reside.[11] Yet this was not the Supreme Court's interpretation of the amendment for nearly a hundred years. Within five years of ratification of the Fourteenth Amendment, the Court was making decisions as though the amendment had never been adopted.[12]

The only change in civil liberties during the first sixty years following the adoption of the Fourteenth Amendment came in 1897, when the Supreme Court held that the due process clause of the Fourteenth Amendment did in fact prohibit states from taking property for a public use without just compensation.[13] However, the Supreme Court had selectively "incorporated" into the Fourteenth Amendment only the property protection provision of the Fifth Amendment and no other clause of the Fifth or any other amendment of the Bill of Rights. In other words, although according to the Fifth Amendment "due process" applied to the taking of life and liberty as well as property, only property was incorporated into the Fourteenth Amendment as a limitation on state power.

No further expansion of civil liberties via the Fourteenth Amendment occurred until 1925, when the Supreme Court held that freedom of speech is "among the fundamental personal rights and 'liberties' protected by the due process clause of the Fourteenth Amendment from impairment by the states."[14] In 1931, the Court added freedom of the press to that short list protected by the Bill of Rights from state action; in 1939, it added freedom of assembly.[15]

But that was as far as the Court was willing to go. As late as 1937, the Supreme Court was still unwilling to nationalize civil liberties beyond the First Amendment. The Constitution, as interpreted as late as 1937 by the Supreme Court in *Palko v. Connecticut*, left standing the framework in which the states had the power to determine their own law on a number of fundamental issues. *Palko* established the principle of **selective incorporation**, by which the provisions of the Bill of Rights were to be considered one-by-one and selectively applied as limits on the states through the Fourteenth Amendment.[16] In order to

selective incorporation
the process by which different protections in the Bill of Rights were incorporated into the Fourteenth Amendment, thus guaranteeing citizens protection from state as well as national governments

make clear that "selective incorporation" should be narrowly interpreted, Justice Benjamin Cardozo, writing for an 8-to-1 majority, asserted that although many rights have value and importance, not all are of the same value and importance:

> [Not all rights are of] the very essence of a scheme of ordered liberty. To abolish them is not to violate a "principle of justice so rooted in the traditions and conscience of our people as to be ranked as fundamental." What is true of jury trials and indictments is also true . . . of the immunity from compulsory self-incrimination [as in *Palko*]. . . . This too might be lost, and justice still be done. . . . If the Fourteenth Amendment has absorbed [for example, freedom of thought and speech] the process of absorption has had its source in the belief that neither liberty nor justice would exist if they were sacrificed.

Palko left states with most of the powers they had possessed even before the adoption of the Fourteenth Amendment, including the power to pass laws segregating the races—a power in fact that the thirteen former Confederate states chose to continue to exercise on into the 1960s, despite *Brown v. Board of*

Table 5.3 INCORPORATION OF THE BILL OF RIGHTS INTO THE FOURTEENTH AMENDMENT

Selected provisions and amendments	Not "incorporated" until	Key case
Eminent domain (V)	1897	*Chicago, Burlington, and Quincy R.R. v. Chicago*
Freedom of speech (I)	1925	*Gitlow v. New York*
Freedom of press (I)	1931	*Near v. Minnesota*
Free exercise of religion (I)	1934	*Hamilton v. Regents of the University of California*
Freedom of assembly (I)	1939	*Hague v. CIO*
Freedom from unnecessary search and seizure (IV)	1949	*Wolf v. Colorado*
Freedom from warrantless search and seizure (IV) ("exclusionary rule")	1961	*Mapp v. Ohio*
Freedom from cruel and unusual punishment (VIII)	1962	*Robinson v. California*
Right to counsel in any criminal trial (VI)	1963	*Gideon v. Wainwright*
Right against self-incrimination and forced confessions (V)	1964	*Mallory v. Hogan* *Escobedo v. Illinois*
Right to privacy (III, IV, & V)	1965	*Griswold v. Connecticut*
Right to remain silent (V)	1966	*Miranda v. Arizona*
Right against double jeopardy (V)	1969	*Benton v. Maryland*

Education in 1954. The constitutional framework also left states with the power to engage in searches and seizures without a warrant, to indict accused persons without a grand jury, to deprive accused persons of trial by jury, to deprive persons of their right not to have to testify against themselves, to deprive accused persons of their right to confront adverse witnesses, and to prosecute accused persons more than once for the same crime.[17] Few states chose to use these kinds of powers, but some states did, and the power to do so was available for any state whose legislative majority or courts so chose.

So, until 1961, only the First Amendment and one clause of the Fifth Amendment had been clearly incorporated into the Fourteenth Amendment as binding on the states as well as on the national government.[18] After that, one by one, most of the important provisions of the Bill of Rights were incorporated into the Fourteenth Amendment and applied to the states. Table 5.3 shows the progress of this revolution in the interpretation of the Constitution.

But the controversy over incorporation lives on. Since liberty requires restraining the power of government, the general status of civil liberties can never be considered fixed and permanent. Every provision in the Bill of Rights is subject to interpretation, and in any dispute involving a clause of the Bill of Rights, interpretations will always be shaped by the interpreter's interest in the outcome. As we shall see, the Court continually reminds everyone that if it has the power to expand the Bill of Rights, it also has the power to contract it.[19]

The best way to examine the Bill of Rights today is the simplest way—to take each of the major provisions one at a time. Some of these provisions are settled areas of law, and others are not. Any one of them can be reinterpreted by the Court at any time.

The First Amendment and Freedom of Religion

- How does the First Amendment guarantee the nonestablishment and free exercise of religion?
- In what way has the free exercise of religion become a recent political issue?

> Congress shall make no law respecting an establishment of religion, or prohibiting the free exercise thereof; or abridging the freedom of speech, or of the press; or the right of the people peaceably to assemble, and to petition the Government for a redress of grievances.

The Bill of Rights begins by guaranteeing freedom, and the First Amendment provides for that freedom in two distinct clauses: "Congress shall make no law [1] respecting an establishment of religion, or [2] prohibiting the free exercise thereof." The first clause is called the "establishment clause," and the second is called the "free exercise clause."

SEPARATION BETWEEN CHURCH AND STATE

establishment clause
the First Amendment clause that says that "Congress shall make no law respecting an establishment of religion." This law means that a "wall of separation" exists between church and state

The **establishment clause** has been interpreted quite strictly to mean that a virtual "wall of separation" exists between church and state. The separation of church and state was especially important to the great numbers of American colonists who had sought refuge from persecution for having rejected membership in state-sponsored churches. The concept of a "wall of separation" was Jefferson's own formulation, and this concept has figured in all of the modern Supreme Court cases arising under the establishment clause.

Despite the absolute sound of the phrase "wall of separation," there is ample room to disagree on how high the wall is or of what materials it is composed. For example, the Court has been consistently strict in cases of school prayer, striking down such practices as Bible reading,[20] nondenominational prayer,[21] and even a moment of silence for meditation.[22] In each of these cases, the Court reasoned that school-sponsored observations, even of an apparently nondenominational character, are highly suggestive of school sponsorship and therefore violate the prohibition against establishment of religion. On the other hand, the Court has been quite permissive (and some would say inconsistent) about the public display of religious symbols, such as city-sponsored Nativity scenes in commercial or municipal areas.[23] And although the Court has consistently disapproved of government financial support for religious schools, even when the purpose has been purely educational and secu-

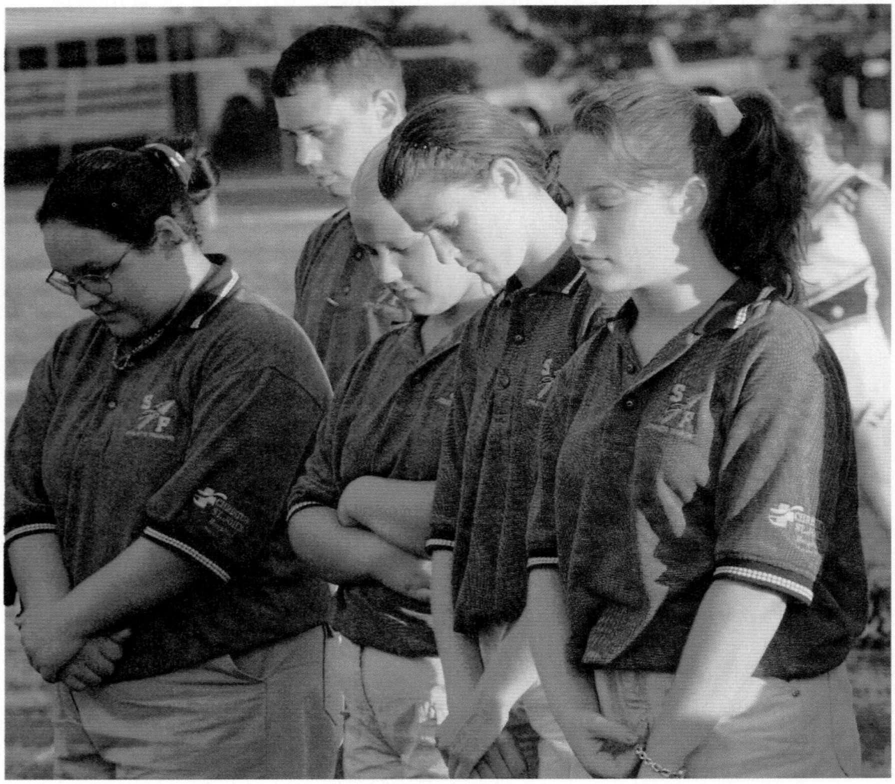

In June of 2000 the Supreme Court ruled against Texas school officials in *Santa Fe Independent School District v. Doe.* The Court rejected the school officials' claim that student-initiated prayer is "private speech" and ruled that pre-game prayer at public schools violates the establishment clause of the First Amendment.

lar, the Court has permitted certain direct aid to students of such schools in the form of busing, for example. In 1971, after thirty years of cases involving religious schools, the Court attempted to specify some criteria to guide its decisions and those of lower courts, indicating, for example, in a decision invalidating state payments for the teaching of secular subjects in parochial schools, circumstances under which the Court might allow certain financial assistance. The case was *Lemon v. Kurtzman;* in its decision, the Supreme Court established three criteria to guide future cases, in what came to be called the ***Lemon* test.** The Court held that government aid to religious schools would be accepted as constitutional if (1) it had a secular purpose, (2) its effect was neither to advance nor to inhibit religion, and (3) it did not entangle government and religious institutions in each other's affairs.[24]

***Lemon* test**

a rule articulated in *Lemon v. Kurtzman* that government action toward religion is permissible if it is secular in purpose, does not lead to "excessive entanglement" with religion, and neither promotes nor inhibits the practice of religion

Although these restrictions make the *Lemon* test a hard test to pass, imaginative authorities are finding ways to do so, and the Supreme Court has demonstrated a willingness to let them. For example, in 1995, the Court narrowly ruled that a student religious group at the University of Virginia could not be denied student activities funds merely because it was a religious group espousing a particular viewpoint about a deity. The Court called the denial "viewpoint discrimination" that violated the free speech rights of the group. Dissenting members of the Court argued that since the message was not scholarly discourse but "the evangelists' mission station and the pulpit," any state aid violated the First Amendment's prohibition against the establishment of a religion.[25] This led two years later to a new, more conservative approach to the "separation of church and state." In 1997, the Court explicitly recognized a change in its interpretation of the establishment clause, and then went on to reverse an important 1985 decision that had forbidden the practice of sending public school teachers into parochial schools to provide remedial education to disadvantaged children.[26] In the aftermath of the 1985 case, teachers from the public schools had to hold their classes in vans parked across the street from the parochial schools. This had added greatly to the cost of the remedial education and had led to a request for relief from the 1985 decision. The Court provided that relief in 1997 and went beyond that to assert that such cooperation between public school teachers and parochial schools was not an "entanglement" that amounted to public support (i.e., establishment) of a religion. More recently, the establishment clause has been put under pressure by the school voucher and charter school movements. The Supreme Court last year declined to clarify the constitutional question when it refused to review a Wisconsin Supreme Court decision upholding the nation's most enduring school voucher program.

Vouchers financed by public revenues are supporting student tuitions at religious schools, where common prayer and religious instruction are known parts of the curriculum. In addition, many financially needy church schools are actively recruiting students with tax-supported vouchers, considering them an essential source of revenue to keep their schools operating. In both these respects, vouchers and charter schools are creating the impression that public support is aiding the establishment of religion.[27] Yet, the Supreme Court has refused to rule on the constitutionality of these programs. All of these developments represent quite a change in the prevailing view of the establishment clause.

FREE EXERCISE OF RELIGION

free exercise clause
the First Amendment clause that protects a citizen's right to believe and practice whatever religion he or she chooses

The **free exercise clause** protects the right to believe and to practice whatever religion one chooses; it also protects the right to be a nonbeliever. The precedent-setting case involving free exercise is *West Virginia State Board of Education v. Barnette* (1943), which involved the children of a family of Jehovah's Witnesses who refused to salute and pledge allegiance to the American flag on the grounds that their religious faith did not permit it. Three years earlier, the Court had upheld such a requirement and had permitted schools to expel students for refusing to salute the flag. But the entry of the United States into a war to defend democracy coupled with the ugly treatment to which the Jehovah's Witnesses children had been subjected induced the Court to reverse itself and to endorse the free exercise of religion even when it may be offensive to the beliefs of the majority.[28]

This Native American holy man performed a "cedar ceremony" outside the Supreme Court prior to the Court's decision against two Native Americans who argued that smoking peyote was a religious sacrament protected by the free exercise clause.

Although the Supreme Court has been fairly consistent and strict in protecting the free exercise of religious belief, it has taken pains to distinguish between religious beliefs and *actions* based on those beliefs. In one case, for example, two Native Americans had been fired from their jobs for smoking peyote, an illegal drug. They claimed that they had been fired from their jobs illegally because smoking peyote was a religious sacrament protected by the free exercise clause. The Court disagreed with their claim in an important 1990 decision,[29] but Congress supported the claim and it went on to engage in an unusual controversy with the Court, involving the separation of powers as well as the proper application of the separation of church and state. Congress literally reversed the Court's 1990 decision with the enactment of the Religious Freedom Restoration Act of 1993 (RFRA), forbidding any federal agency or state government from restricting a person's free exercise of religion unless the federal agency or state government demonstrates that its action "furthers a compelling government interest" and "is the least restrictive means of furthering that compelling governmental interest." One of the first applications of the RFRA was to a case brought by St. Peter's Catholic Church against the city of Boerne, Texas, which had denied permission to the church to enlarge its building because the building had been declared an historic landmark. The case went to federal court on the argument that the city had violated the church's religious freedom as guaranteed by Congress in RFRA. The Supreme Court declared RFRA unconstitutional, but on grounds rarely utilized, if not unique to this case: Congress had violated the separation of powers principle, infringing on the powers of the judiciary by going so far beyond its lawmaking powers that it ended up actually expanding the scope of religious rights rather than just enforcing them. The Court thereby implied that questions requiring a balancing of religious claims against public policy claims was reserved strictly to the judiciary.[30]

The *City of Boerne* case did settle some matters of constitutional controversy over the religious exercise and the establishment clauses of the First Amendment but left a lot more unsettled. What about polygamy, a practice allowed in the Mormon faith? What about snake worship? Or the refusal of Amish parents to send their children to school beyond eighth grade because exposing their children to "modern values" would undermine their religious commitment? In this last example, the Court decided in favor of the Amish and endorsed a very strong interpretation of the protection of free exercise.[31]

The First Amendment and Freedom of Speech and the Press

▶ What forms of speech are protected by the First Amendment? What forms are not protected?

> "Congress shall make no law . . . abridging the freedom of speech, or of the press. . . ."

Because democracy depends upon an open political process and because politics is basically talk, freedom of speech and freedom of the press are considered critical. For this reason, they were given a prominence in the Bill of Rights equal to that of freedom of religion. In 1938, freedom of speech (which in all important respects includes freedom of the press) was given extraordinary constitutional status when the Supreme Court established that any legislation that attempts to restrict these fundamental freedoms "is to be subjected to a more exacting judicial scrutiny . . . than are most other types of legislation."[32]

What the Court was saying is that the democratic political process must be protected at almost any cost. This higher standard of judicial review came to be called **strict scrutiny.** Strict scrutiny implies that speech—at least some kinds of speech—will be protected almost absolutely. But as it turns out, only some types of speech are fully protected against restrictions (see Figure 5.1 on the following page). As we shall see, many forms of speech are less than absolutely protected—even though they are entitled to strict scrutiny. This section will look at these two categories of speech: (1) absolutely protected speech, and (2) conditionally protected speech.

strict scrutiny
test, used by the Supreme Court in racial discrimination cases and other cases involving civil liberties and civil rights, which places the burden of proof on the government rather than on the challengers to show that the law in question is constitutional

ABSOLUTELY PROTECTED SPEECH

There is one and only one absolute defense against efforts to place limitations on speech, oral or in print: the truth. The truth is protected even when its expression damages the person to whom it applies. And of all forms of speech, political speech is the most consistently protected.

Political Speech Political speech was the activity of greatest concern to the framers of the Constitution, even though they found it the most difficult provision to observe. Within seven years of the ratification of the Bill of Rights in 1791, Congress adopted the infamous Alien and Sedition Acts, which, among other things, made it a crime to say or publish anything that might tend to defame or bring into disrepute the government of the United States. Quite clearly, the acts' intentions were to criminalize the very conduct given absolute protection by the First Amendment (see also Chapter 10). Fifteen violators—including several newspaper editors—were indicted, and a few were actually convicted before the relevant portions of the acts were allowed to expire.

The first modern free speech case arose immediately after World War I. It involved persons who had been convicted under the federal Espionage Act of

Figure 5.1 THE PROTECTION OF FREE SPEECH BY THE FIRST AMENDMENT

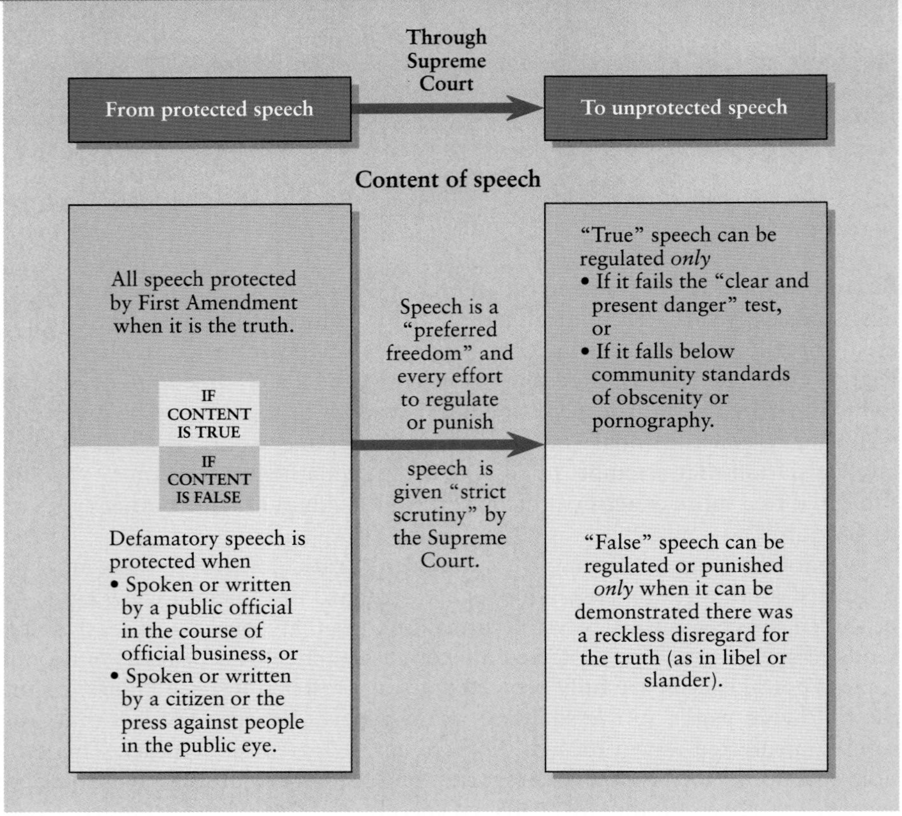

1917 for opposing U.S. involvement in the war. The Supreme Court upheld the Espionage Act and refused to protect the speech rights of the defendants on the grounds that their activities—appeals to draftees to resist the draft—constituted a **"clear and present danger"** to security.[33] This is the first and most famous "test" for when government intervention or censorship could be permitted.

"clear and present danger" test
test to determine whether speech is protected or unprotected, based on its capacity to present a "clear and present danger" to society

It was only after the 1920s that real progress toward a genuinely effective First Amendment was made. Since then, political speech has been consistently protected by the courts even when it has been deemed "insulting" or "outrageous." Here is the way the Supreme Court put it in one of its most important statements on the subject:

> The constitutional guarantees of free speech and free press do not permit a State to forbid or proscribe advocacy of the use of force or of law violation *except where such advocacy is directed to inciting or producing imminent lawless action and is likely to incite or produce such action* [emphasis added].[34]

This statement was made in the case of a Ku Klux Klan leader, Charles Brandenburg, who had been arrested and convicted of advocating "revengent" action against the president, Congress, and the Supreme Court, among others, if they continued "to suppress the white, Caucasian race. . . ." Although Brandenburg was not carrying a weapon, some of the members of his audience were. Nevertheless, the Supreme Court reversed the state courts and freed Brandenburg while also declaring Ohio's Criminal Syndicalism Act unconstitutional because it punished persons who "advocate, or teach the duty, necessity, or propriety [of violence] as a means of accomplishing industrial or political reform . . ."; or who publish materials or "voluntarily assemble . . . to teach or advocate the doctrines of criminal syndicalism." The Supreme Court argued that the statute did not distinguish "mere advocacy" from "incitement to imminent lawless action." It would be difficult to go much further in protecting freedom of speech.

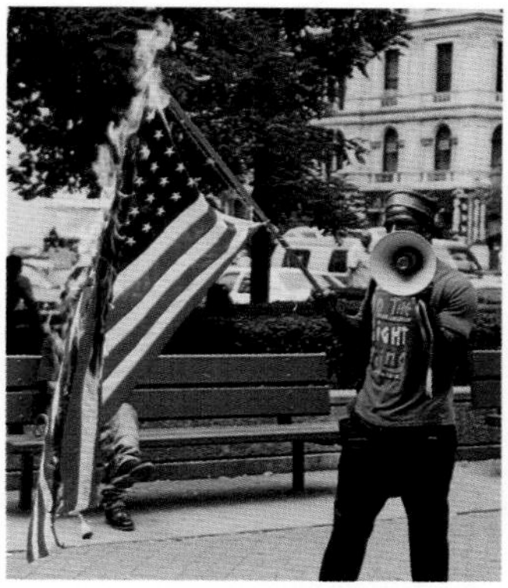

Burning the American flag is a constitutionally protected form of symbolic speech.

Symbolic Speech, Speech Plus, and the Rights of Assembly and Petition
The First Amendment treats the freedoms of assembly and petition as equal to the freedoms of religion and political speech. Freedom of assembly and freedom of petition are closely associated with speech but go beyond it to speech associated with action. Since at least 1931, the Supreme Court has sought to protect actions that are designed to send a political message. (Usually the purpose of a symbolic act is not only to send a direct message but to draw a crowd—to do something spectacular in order to draw spectators to the action and thus strengthen the message.) Thus the Court held unconstitutional a California statute making it a felony to display a red flag "as a sign, symbol or emblem of opposition to organized government."[35] Although today there are limits on how far one can go with actions that symbolically convey a message, the protection of such action is very broad. Thus, although the Court upheld a federal statute making it a crime to burn draft cards to protest the Vietnam War on the grounds that the government had a compelling interest in preserving draft cards as part of the conduct of the war itself, it considered the wearing of black armbands to school a protected form of assembly for symbolic action.

A more contemporary example is the burning of the American flag as a symbol of protest. In 1984, at a political rally held during the Republican National Convention in Dallas, Texas, a political protester burned an American flag in violation of a Texas statute that prohibited desecration of a venerated object. In a 5-to-4 decision, the Supreme Court declared the Texas law unconstitutional on the grounds that flag burning was expressive conduct protected by the First Amendment.[36] Congress reacted immediately with a proposal for a constitutional amendment reversing the Court's Texas decision, and when the amendment failed to receive the necessary two-thirds majority in the Senate, Congress passed the Flag Protection Act of 1989. Protesters promptly violated this act and their prosecution moved quickly into the federal district court, which declared the new law unconstitutional. The Supreme Court, in another 5-to-4 decision, affirmed the lower court decision.[37] A renewed effort began in Congress to propose a constitutional amendment that would reverse the Supreme Court and place this form of expressive conduct outside the realm of protected speech or assembly.

Closer to the original intent of the assembly and petition clause is the category of **"speech plus"**—following speech with physical activity such as picketing, distributing leaflets, and other forms of peaceful demonstration or

speech plus
speech accompanied by conduct such as sit-ins, picketing, and demonstrations; protection of this form of speech under the First Amendment is conditional, and restrictions imposed by state or local authorities are acceptable if properly balanced by considerations of public order

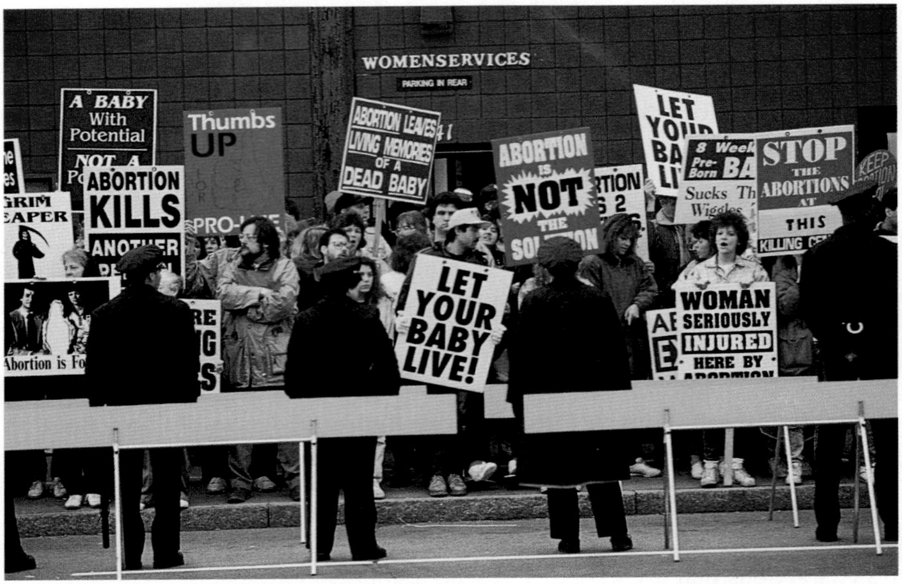

Antiabortion demonstrators protest outside the Buffalo, N.Y., GYN Womenservices clinic. The Supreme Court has recognized the right of assembly for antiabortion protesters but has allowed the preservation of a "buffer zone" between demonstrators and abortion clinics.

assembly. Such assemblies are consistently protected by courts under the First Amendment; state and local laws regulating such activities are closely scrutinized and frequently overturned. But the same assembly on private property is quite another matter and can in many circumstances be regulated. For example, the directors of a shopping center can lawfully prohibit an assembly protesting a war or supporting a ban on abortion. Assemblies in public areas can also be restricted under some circumstances, especially when the assembly or demonstration jeopardizes the health, safety, or rights of others. This condition was the basis of the Supreme Court's decision to uphold a lower court order that restricted the access abortion protesters had to the entrances of abortion clinics.[38]

What of voting and other forms of electoral participation? Are these practices protected as free speech under the First Amendment? In 1999, the Supreme Court came down with a firm but somewhat limited affirmative. The state of Colorado had enacted laws imposing some fairly restrictive conditions on soliciting signatures for initiatives to place referendum items on election ballots. The Court left some of those restrictions in place but did reject as unconstitutional restraints on free speech requirements that petition circulators had to be registered voters, had to wear identification badges, and had to file financial reports identifying the amount of money they were paid to circulate petitions.[39]

prior restraint

an effort by a governmental agency to block the publication of material it deems libelous or harmful in some other way; censorship. In the United States, the courts forbid prior restraint except under the most extraordinary circumstances

FREEDOM OF THE PRESS

For all practical purposes, freedom of speech implies and includes freedom of the press. With the exception of the broadcast media, which are subject to federal regulation, the press is protected under the doctrine against **prior restraint.** Beginning with the landmark 1931 case of *Near v. Minnesota,* the U.S. Supreme Court has held that, except under the most extraordinary circumstances, the First Amendment of the Constitution prohibits government agencies from seeking to prevent newspapers or magazines from publishing whatever they wish.[40] Indeed, in the case of *New York Times v. U.S.*, the so-called *Pentagon Papers* case, the Supreme Court ruled that the government could not even block publication of secret Defense Department documents furnished to *The New York Times* by an opponent of the Vietnam War who had obtained the documents illegally.[41] In a 1990 case, however, the Supreme Court upheld a lower-court order restraining Cable News Network (CNN) from broadcasting tapes of conversations between former Panamanian dictator Manuel Noriega and his lawyer, supposedly recorded by the U.S. government. By a vote of 7 to 2, the Court held that CNN could be restrained from broadcasting the tapes until the trial court in the Noriega case had listened to the tapes and had decided whether their broadcast would violate Noriega's right to a fair trial. This case would seem to weaken the "no prior restraint" doctrine. But whether the same standard will apply to the print media has yet to be tested in the courts. In 1994, the Supreme Court ruled that cable television systems were entitled to essentially the same First Amendment protections as the print media.[42]

CONDITIONALLY PROTECTED SPEECH

At least four forms of speech fall outside the absolute guarantees of the First Amendment and therefore outside the realm of absolute protection. Since they do enjoy some protection, they qualify as "conditionally protected" types of speech: (1) libel and slander, (2) obscenity and pornography, (3) fighting words, and (4) commercial speech. It should be emphasized once again that these four types of speech still enjoy considerable protection by the courts.

Libel and Slander Some speech is not protected at all. If a written statement is made in "reckless disregard of the truth" and is considered damaging to the victim because it is "malicious, scandalous, and defamatory," it can be punished as **libel.** If an oral statement of such nature is made, it can be punished as **slander.**

Today, most libel suits involve freedom of the press, and the realm of free press is enormous. Historically, newspapers were subject to the law of libel, which provided that newspapers that printed false and malicious stories could be compelled to pay damages to those they defamed. In recent years, however, American courts have greatly narrowed the meaning of libel and made it extremely difficult, particularly for politicians or other public figures, to win a libel case against a newspaper. In the important 1964 case of *New York Times v. Sullivan*, the Court held that to be deemed libelous a story about a public official not only had to be untrue, but also had to result from "actual malice" or "reckless disregard" for the truth.[43] In other words, the newspaper had to *deliberately* print false and malicious material. In practice, it is nearly impossible to prove that a paper deliberately printed maliciously false information and, as conservatives discovered in the 1980s, it is especially difficult for a politician or other public figure to win a libel case. Libel suits against CBS News by General William Westmoreland and against *Time* magazine by Israeli general Ariel Sharon, suits that were financed by conservative legal foundations that hoped to embarrass the media, were both defeated in court because they failed to

libel
a written statement made in "reckless disregard of the truth" that is considered damaging to a victim because it is "malicious, scandalous, and defamatory"

slander
an oral statement, made in "reckless disregard of the truth," which is considered damaging to the victim because it is "malicious, scandalous, and defamatory"

show "actual malice." In the 1991 case of *Masson v. New Yorker Magazine*, this tradition was again affirmed when the Court held that fabricated quotations attributed to a public figure were libelous only if the fabricated account "materially changed" the meaning of what the person actually said.[44] Essentially, the print media have been able to publish anything they want about a public figure.

However, in at least one recent case, the Court has opened up the possibility for public officials to file libel suits against the press. In 1985, the Court held that the press was immune from libel only when the printed material was "a matter of public concern." In other words, in future cases a newspaper would have to show that the public official was engaged in activities that were indeed *public*. This new principle has made the press more vulnerable to libel suits, but it still leaves an enormous realm of freedom for the press. For example, Reverend Jerry Falwell, the leader of the Moral Majority, lost his libel suit against *Hustler* magazine even though the magazine had published a cartoon of Falwell showing him having drunken intercourse with his mother in an outhouse. A unanimous Supreme Court rejected a jury verdict in favor of damages for "emotional distress" on the grounds that parodies, no matter how outrageous, are protected because "outrageousness" is too subjective a test and thus would interfere with the free flow of ideas protected by the First Amendment.[45]

Politics on the Web

The Internet is now a crucial forum for battles over civil liberties. The World Wide Web allows any group, regardless of ideology or doctrine, to reach an audience of millions. Because of the low cost of establishing a site, groups that many consider reprehensible are able easily to spread their views all across the country. Whether a neo-Nazi, a pornographer, or a member of an antigovernment militia, anyone can voice his or her beliefs over the Internet. For example, since the 1995 bombing of the federal building in Oklahoma City, the Internet has been blamed for providing bomb-making instruction to those who could not otherwise get such information. This raises a fundamental constitutional issue: Should limitations on free expression exist? If a child can go on the Internet to a site run by a militia group and learn how to make a bomb, whose responsibility is it to protect that child? It is these issues that must be faced by the Congress and the courts and that will ultimately complicate any proposed Internet legislation.

www.wwnorton.com/wtp3e

Obscenity and Pornography If libel and slander cases can be difficult because of the problem of determining the truth of statements and whether those statements are malicious and damaging, cases involving pornography and obscenity can be even more sticky. It is easy to say that pornography and obscenity fall outside the realm of protected speech, but it is impossible to draw a clear line defining exactly where protection ends and unprotected speech begins. Not until 1957 did the Supreme Court confront this problem, and it did so with a definition of obscenity that may have caused more confusion than it cleared up. Justice William Brennan, in writing the Court's opinion, defined obscenity as speech or writing that appeals to the "prurient interest"—that is, books, magazines, films, etc. whose purpose is to excite lust as this appears "to the average person, applying contemporary community standards. . . ." Even so, Brennan added, the work should be judged obscene only when it is "utterly without redeeming social importance."[46] Brennan's definition, instead of clarifying the Court's view, actually caused more confusion. In 1964, Justice Potter Stewart confessed that, although he found pornography impossible to define, "I know it when I see it."[47]

All attempts by the courts to define pornography and obscenity have proved impractical, because each instance required courts to screen thousands of pages of print material and feet of film alleged to be pornographic. The vague and impractical standards that had been developed meant ultimately that almost nothing could be banned on the grounds that it was pornographic and obscene. An effort was made to strengthen the restrictions in 1973, when the Supreme Court expressed its willingness to define pornography as a work which (1) as a whole, is deemed prurient by the "average person" according to "community standards"; (2) depicts sexual conduct "in a patently offensive way"; and (3) lacks "serious literary, artistic, political, or scientific value." This definition meant that pornography would be determined by local rather than national standards. Thus, a local bookseller might be prosecuted for selling a volume that was a best-seller nationally but that was deemed pornographic locally.[48] This new definition of standards did not help much either, and not long after 1973 the Court began again to review all such community antipornography laws, reversing most of them.

Consequently, today there is a widespread fear that Americans are free to publish any and all variety of intellectual expression, whether there is any "redeeming social value" or not. Yet this area of free speech is far from settled.

In recent years, the battle against obscene speech has been against "cyberporn"—pornography on the Internet. Opponents of this form of expression argue that it should be banned because of the easy access children have to the Internet. Where obscenity and pornography are concerned, Internet technology has simply made the line between free speech and regulated speech impossible to draw. The Supreme Court tried to draw such a line in its 1973 opinion in *Miller v. California,* providing that "contemporary community standards" should be used to determine whether a law restricting pornographic and obscene materials is appropriate. But such a rule can no longer be applied, for the obvious reason that Internet communication is nationwide—and worldwide. It is no longer a matter of what to do about *Playboy* on the shelves of the local newsstand.

The first major effort to regulate the content of the Internet occurred on February 1, 1996, when the 104th Congress passed major telecommunications legislation. Attached to the Telecommunications Act was an amendment, called the Communications Decency Act (CDA), that was designed to regulate the on-line transmission of obscene material. On the same day that President Clinton signed the Telecommunications Act, and the CDA, into law the constitutionality of the CDA was challenged in court by a coalition of interests led by the ACLU. In June a panel of federal judges ruled that the CDA violated the First Amendment to the Constitution. The Department of Justice, citing the

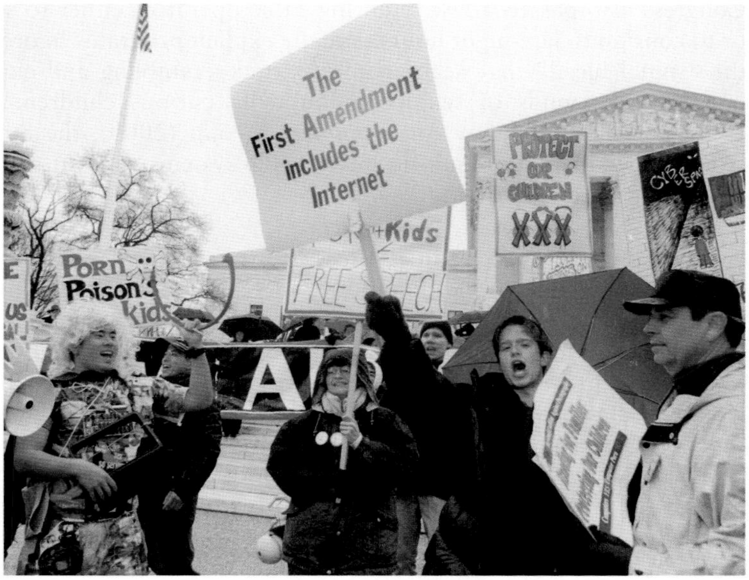

Demonstrators both for and against the 1996 Communications Decency Act gather outside the Supreme Court. The Court unanimously struck down the act, which would have made it a crime to make "indecent" or "patently offensive" works or pictures available on-line, where they can be accessed by children.

need to protect America's children from explicit sexual material on the Internet, appealed the decision to the Supreme Court. In the ensuing case, *Reno v. ACLU,* the Court heard oral arguments on both sides of the issue. In a broad endorsement of free speech on the Internet, the Court struck down the CDA, ruling that it suppressed speech that "adults have a constitutional right to receive." The Court gave several reasons for its decision. First, the CDA's "indecent transmission" and "patently offensive display" were too broad and vague to meet the strict scrutiny of the First Amendment's free speech provisions. Second, the language was too broad and therefore protected children at the price of suppressing speech that adults have a right to send and receive. Governments, as the court argued, may not limit the adult population to messages that are fit for children. "The level of discourse reaching the mailbox simply cannot be limited to that which would be suitable for a sandbox." Moreover, "odds are slim" that a user would enter a sexually explicit site by accident; unlike communications received by radio or television, "the receipt of information on the Internet requires a series of affirmative steps more deliberate and directed than merely turning a dial. A child requires some sophistication and some ability to read to retrieve material and thereby to use the Internet unattended." In other words, factors that permit the regulation of radio or television—such as setting the "time, place and manner" of certain speech—"are not present in cyberspace." The Internet, the Court argued, is not as "invasive" as radio or television because communications do not appear on one's computer screen "unbidden"; and users rarely encounter Internet content "by accident." The implication of the Court's argument is that parents can control what their children receive, and, in any case, software for more effective parental protection of their own children "will soon be widely available."[49]

Although *Reno v. ACLU* is the most important First Amendment case to reach the Supreme Court in many years, the issue is far from settled. After the Communications Decency Act was invalidated by the Supreme Court, Congress promptly enacted the Children Online Protection Act (COPA), prohibiting speech that a federal prosecutor might consider "harmful to minors." Congress also passed a law requiring cable operators either to scramble fully or to consign to late-night hours sexually explicit programs in order to prevent the "signal bleed" that accompanies partial scrambling and exposes fleeting images and sounds of sex to undoubtedly curious children. However, in *United States v. Playboy Entertainment Group* (2000), the Supreme Court struck down the law requiring many cable systems to limit sexually explicit channels to late-night hours.[50]

fighting words
speech that directly incites damaging conduct

Fighting Words Speech can also lose its protected position when it moves toward the sphere of action. "Expressive speech," for example, is protected until it moves from the symbolic realm to the realm of actual conduct—to direct incitement of damaging conduct with the use of so-called **fighting words.** In 1942, the Supreme Court upheld the arrest and conviction of a man who had violated a state law forbidding the use of offensive language in public. He had called the arresting officer a "goddamned racketeer" and "a damn Fascist." When his case reached the Supreme Court, the arrest was upheld on the grounds that the First Amendment provides no protection for such offensive language because such words "are no essential part of any exposition of ideas."[51] This case was reaffirmed in a much more famous and important case decided at the height of the cold war, when the Supreme Court held that "there is no substantial public interest in permitting certain kinds of utterances: the lewd and obscene, the profane, the libelous, and the insulting or 'fighting' words—those which by their very utterance inflict injury or tend to incite an immediate breach of the peace."[52]

Since that time, however, the Supreme Court has reversed almost every conviction based on arguments that the speaker had used "fighting words." But again, that does not mean that this is an absolutely settled area. In recent years, the increased activism of minority and women's groups has prompted a movement against words that might be construed as offensive to members of a particular group. This movement has come to be called, derisively, "political correctness." In response to this movement, many organizations have attempted to impose codes of etiquette that acknowledge these enhanced sensitivities. These efforts to formalize the restraints on the use of certain words in public are causing great concern over their possible infringement of freedom of speech. But how should we determine what words are "fighting words" that fall outside the protections of the freedom of speech?

One category of conditionally protected speech is the free speech of high school students in public schools. In 1986, the Supreme Court backed away from a broad protection of student free-speech rights by upholding the punishment of a high school student for making sexually suggestive speech. The Court opinion held that such speech interfered with the school's goal of teaching students the limits of socially acceptable behavior.[53] Two years later, the Supreme Court took another conservative step and restricted student speech and press rights even further by defining them as part of the educational process not to be treated with the same standard as adult speech in a regular public forum.[54]

In addition, scores of universities have attempted to develop speech codes to suppress utterances deemed to be racial or ethnic slurs. What these universities find, however, is that the codes produce more problems than they solve. The University of Pennsylvania learned this when it first tried to apply its newly written "Harassment Code." Around midnight in January of 1993, Eden Jacobowitz and several other students trying to study yelled from their dorm windows at a noisy group of partying black sorority members: "Shut up, you water buffaloes." Other students also made rude comments, including racial and sexual slurs, but Jacobowitz was the only one who actually came forward and admitted to having yelled. Born in Israel and fluent in Hebrew, Jacobowitz explained that "water buffalo" loosely

Student Perspectives

The American Civil Liberties Union filed a suit this month [March 1999] against the University of California at San Diego for punishing a student who displayed a sign in his dorm room window containing a vulgar word.

Ryan Shapiro, a freshman National Merit Scholar, placed a sign in his window that read "Fuck Netanyahu and Pinochet," referring to the Israeli Prime Minister and the former Chilean dictator.

* * *

The ACLU stepped in to protect Shapiro's First Amendment Rights and stop the university from suppressing his political views.

The organization claims the university's policy is unconstitutional because it restricts posting notices which contain "offensive" materials and "fighting words." Other notices are allowed if the university approves.

They claim banning only this type of language restricts a student's right to express his political views and personal thoughts.

* * *

These types of regulations are needed so the university remains at a professional decor for all campus residents and visitors to the campus.

The university does not want vulgarity and profanity portrayed to those who visit the campus as potential students, employees, or donators.

The University of California had every right to ask the student to remove his sign. The student is a resident in the dormitory, but the building is owned by the university.

The resident can control the appearance of the inside of the room, but the exterior of the building is under the control of the institution. By hanging his sign, Shapiro lessened the appearance of the building and the university had the right to remove it.

The First Amendment guarantees the freedom of speech. But, it does not give individuals the right to degrade or devalue the property of others.

This is what Shapiro's sign did. It degraded the appearance of the university.

SOURCE: Staff Editorial, "Vulgar Signs," *The Collegiate Times* (Virginia Tech), March 3, 1999.

translated from Hebrew means "rude person." Nevertheless, the University of Pennsylvania brought Jacobowitz before a campus judicial inquiry board and charged him with racial harassment in violation of the new code. The black women at whom he had yelled also brought civil charges of racial harassment against Jacobowitz. Five months after the incident, all charges were dropped—both the civil charges and those brought by the university. After reviewing the matter, Penn officials confessed that the university's harassment code "contained flaws which could not withstand the stress of intense publicity and international attention."[55]

Such concerns are not limited to universities, although universities have probably moved furthest toward efforts to formalize "politically correct" speech guidelines. Similar developments have taken place in large corporations, both public and private, in which many successful complaints and lawsuits have been brought, alleging that the words of employers or their supervisors create a "hostile or abusive working environment." These cases arise out of the civil rights laws and will be addressed in more detail in Chapter 6. The Supreme Court has held that "sexual harassment" that creates a "hostile working environment" includes "unwelcome sexual advances, requests for sexual favors, and other *verbal* or physical conduct of a sexual nature" (emphasis added).[56] There is a fundamental free speech issue involved in these regulations of hostile speech. So far, the assumption favoring the regulation of hostile speech in universities and other workplaces is that "some speech must be shut down in the name of free speech because it tends to silence those disparaged by it,"[57] even though a threat of hostile action (usually embodied in "fighting words") is not present. The United States is on something of a collision course between the right to express hostile views and the protection of the sensitivities of minorities and women. The collisions will end up in the courts, but not before a lot more airing in public and balancing efforts by state legislatures and Congress.

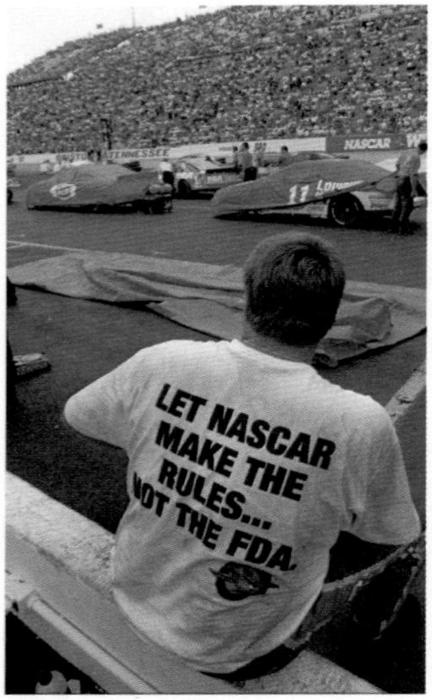

The government has taken steps to curb tobacco advertising, including a 1997 ban on all advertising in sporting events. This auto racing crew member wears a shirt that voices the displeasure felt by those in a sport that depends on tobacco advertising.

Commercial Speech Commercial speech, such as newspaper or television advertisements, does not have full First Amendment protection because it cannot be considered political speech. Initially considered to be entirely outside the protection of the First Amendment, commercial speech has made gains during the twentieth century. Some commercial speech is still unprotected and therefore regulated. For example, the regulation of false and misleading advertising by the Federal Trade Commission is an old and well-established power of the federal government. The Supreme Court long ago approved the constitutionality of laws prohibiting the electronic media from carrying cigarette advertising.[58] The Court has also upheld a state university ban on Tupperware parties in college dormitories.[59] It has also upheld city ordinances prohibiting the posting of all signs on public property (as long as the ban is total, so that there is no hint of censorship).[60] And the Supreme Court, in a heated 5-to-4 decision written by Chief Justice William Rehnquist, upheld Puerto Rico's statute restricting gambling advertising aimed at residents of Puerto Rico.[61]

However, the gains far outweigh the losses in the effort to expand the protection commercial speech enjoys under the First Amendment. "In part, this reflects the growing appreciation that commercial speech is part of the free flow of information necessary for informed choice and democratic participation."[62]

For example, the Court in 1975 struck down a state statute making it a misdemeanor to sell or circulate newspapers encouraging abortions; the Court ruled that the statute infringed upon constitutionally protected speech and upon the right of the reader to make informed choices.[63] On a similar basis, the Court reversed its own earlier decisions upholding laws that prohibited dentists and other professionals from advertising their services. For the Court, medical service advertising was a matter of health that could be advanced by the free flow of information.[64] In 1983, the Supreme Court struck down a congressional statute that prohibited the unsolicited mailing of advertisements for contraceptives. And in 1996 the Supreme Court struck down Rhode Island laws and regulations banning the advertisement of liquor prices as a violation of the First Amendment.[65] These instances of commercial speech are significant in themselves, but they are all the more significant because they indicate the breadth and depth of the freedom existing today to direct appeals broadly to a large public, not only to sell goods and services but also to mobilize people for political purposes.

The Second Amendment and the Right to Bear Arms

▶ Is the right to bear arms guaranteed by the Bill of Rights? How is its exercise restricted?

> A well regulated Militia, being necessary to the security of a free State, the right of the people to keep and bear Arms, shall not be infringed.

The Second Amendment may seem to some to be the product of a long-ago, quaint era, but it is very much alive in spirit and has emerged as one of America's most pressing contemporary public issues.

The point and purpose of the Second Amendment is the provision for militias; they were to be the backing of the government for the maintenance of local public order. "Militia" was understood at the time of the Founding to be a military or police resource for state governments, and militias were specifically distinguished from armies and troops, which came within the sole constitutional jurisdiction of Congress. Under Article I, Section 8, Congress was given the power

> To declare war; . . . To raise and support Armies; . . . To provide and maintain a Navy; . . . To provide for calling forth the Militia to execute the Laws of the Union, suppress Insurrections and repel Invasions; . . . [and] to provide for organizing, arming, and disciplining, the Militia, and for governing such Part of them as may be employed in the Service of the United States, reserving to the States respectively . . . the Authority of training the Militia according to the discipline prescribed by Congress.

Article I, Section 10, made it quite explicit that "no State shall, without the Consent of Congress . . . keep Troops, or Ships of War in time of Peace, . . . or engage in War." The Supreme Court went even further, in the turbulent year of 1939, with the holding that

> the Militia which the States were expected to maintain and train is set in contrast with Troops which they were forbidden to keep without the consent of Congress. The sentiment of the time strongly disfavored standing armies; the common view was that adequate defense of country and laws could be secured through the Militia—civilians primarily, soldiers on occasion.[66]

Thus, there seems to be no question that the right of people to bear arms is based upon and associated with participation in a state militia. Nevertheless, individuals do have a constitutional right to bear arms, as is provided in the second half of the amendment. The experience of Americans with colonial military rule pointed the Founders and their supporters to the need of every citizen for some kind of personal self-defense. One of the fundamental requirements of a strong government is that it have a monopoly on the use of force. Broad distribution of guns in the hands of citizens does in fact weaken the government, for better or for worse. When confronted with the issue in those terms, few Americans would be likely to approve of an American government possessing a monopoly on force, with a totally disarmed citizenry. The fundamental right of Americans to own weapons is promoted by one of America's biggest and most influential contemporary interest groups, the National Rifle Association (NRA).

But the line drawn between owning weapons as part of a militia or army, on the one hand, and as individuals, on the other, raises some complex questions, for which neither the NRA nor its adversaries have good answers. For example, can clear boundaries be drawn around technologies, separating weapons for defense of home and hearth from offensive weapons of massive destructive power? Can a distinction be made between arms necessary for participation in a "well regulated militia" and for individual antipersonnel defense, on the one hand, and weapons used as part of an individual's participation in *private* militias not sponsored or regulated by government, on the other? And, given the absoluteness of the Second Amendment—that "the

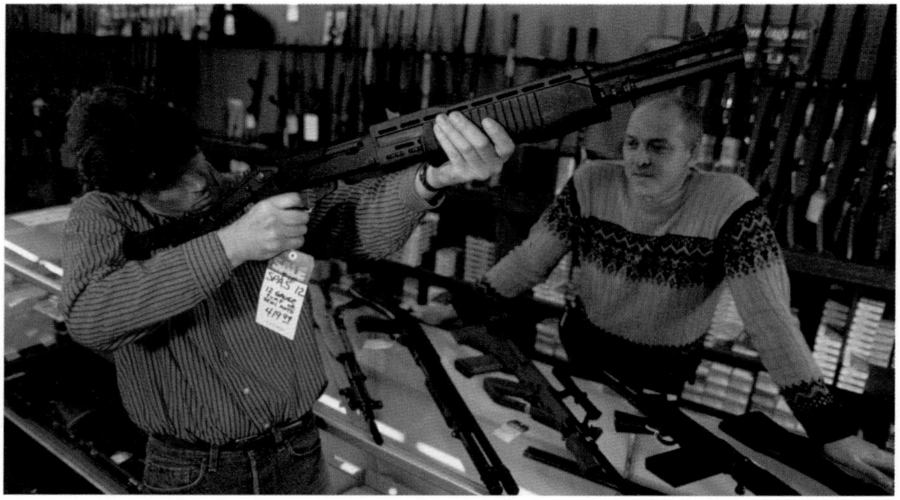

The right to bear arms seems unquestionable, although states are allowed to regulate the sale of weapons by requiring a waiting period or a background check on the purchaser.

right of the people to keep and bear Arms, shall not be infringed"—does any government have any authority to draw the boundaries alluded to above?

Part of the answer to these questions can be found in the amendment itself. A "well regulated" militia implies that the state governments *do* have power to regulate the arms as well as the arms bearers. And in Article I, Section 8, clauses 15 and 16, the Constitution seems to be unmistakably clear: Congress is given the power of "calling forth the Militia to execute the Laws of the Union, . . ." and the power "to provide for organizing, arming, and disciplining, the Militia, and for governing such Part of them as may be employed in the Service of the United States. . . ." The Constitution then reinforces the power of the States by granting them the power to appoint the officers and provide for the training of the militia "according to the discipline prescribed by Congress."

Congress tried to exercise its power in 1993 with adoption of the Brady Handgun Violence Prevention Act (Brady Act), as an amendment to the Gun Control Act of 1968. The law took its name from James S. Brady, an aide to President Ronald Reagan who was disabled in the 1981 assassination attempt on the president. Among its provisions was the requirement that state and local law enforcement officials conduct background checks on prospective handgun purchasers. Two local law enforcement officers sued in court, questioning the constitutionality of the Brady Act on the grounds that Congress has no authority to require state and local officials to implement federal laws. Moreover, they claimed that as an "unfunded federal mandate" the law imposed unfair burdens on them and unfair diversions of resources from their other responsibilities to maintain law and order in their communities. The Supreme Court, in a close decision, agreed with the plaintiffs.[67] This case is a small but significant step back toward a pre–New Deal concept of federalism, making a national program of handgun regulation a lot more difficult. But it in no way gives handgun owners a constitutional right to buy, sell, and possess weapons completely free of federal, state, and local regulation.

Thus American citizens unquestionably have a right to bear arms, but the exercise of this right can be regulated by both state and federal law. Within this well-designed domain, however, are no rules for what is wise and what is foolish legislation, or what is appropriate and what is inappropriate regulation. Issues such as these have to be settled through the political process, not by courts—and certainly not by arms, even if Americans do have a right to bear them.[68]

Former presidential press secretary James Brady salutes the crowd at the Democratic National Convention. Brady supported a congressional bill to establish a waiting period for the purchase of handguns so that background checks could be made on the purchaser. The Supreme Court declared part of the law to be in violation of the Second Amendment.

Rights of the Criminally Accused

- What is due process?
- How do the Fourth, Fifth, Sixth, and Eighth Amendments provide for the due process of law?

Except for the First Amendment, most of the battle to apply the Bill of Rights to the states was fought over the various protections granted to individuals who are accused of a crime, who are suspects in the commission of a crime, or who are brought before the court as a witness to a crime. The Fourth, Fifth, Sixth, and Eighth Amendments, taken together, are the essence of the due process of law, even though this fundamental concept does not appear until the very last words of the Fifth Amendment. Even the Supreme Court itself has admitted that "due process of law" cannot be given a precise and final definition or explanation. In lieu of an outright definition, the Court maintains the position it took over a century ago: it prefers to rely on "the gradual process of judicial inclusion and exclusion" to indicate the meaning of "due process."[69]

Because most criminal laws in the United States exist at the state level, most of the questions over due process have concerned state laws as applied by state police, state prosecutors, and state courts. In the next sections we will look at specific cases that illuminate the dynamics of this important constitutional issue. The procedural safeguards that we will discuss may seem remote to most law-abiding citizens, but they help define the limits of government action against the personal liberty of every citizen.

In all court matters involving crime, "the state" is the plaintiff, or the party charging an individual with the crime: "*New York v. Jones,*" "*New Jersey v. Smith,*" or "*The People of the State of California v. Orenthal James Simpson.*" The idea of the entire power of a state being arrayed against a defendant is pretty imposing; it seems unequal even if the accused has the resources to hire renowned attorneys for his or her defense—as O. J. Simpson did, for example. Few defendants have the resources that Simpson did, and therefore the requirements of due process are an attempt to equalize the playing field between an accused individual and the all-powerful state.

Many Americans believe that "legal technicalities" are responsible for setting many actual criminals free. In many cases, that is absolutely true. In fact, setting defendants free is the very purpose of the requirements that constitute due process. One of America's traditional and most strongly held juridical values is that "it is far worse to convict an innocent man than to let a guilty man

The O.J. Simpson trials illustrated the differences between the evidence needed to convict in criminal vs. civil cases. During his criminal trial, Simpson's dramatic difficulty in donning a glove found at the scene of the crime helped to establish "a reasonable doubt" in the jurors' minds. In the later civil case against Simpson, however, the prosecution needed only "the preponderance of the evidence" (a strong probability of guilt) for conviction.

go free."[70] In civil suits, verdicts rest upon "the preponderance of the evidence"; in criminal cases, guilt has to be proven "beyond a reasonable doubt"—a far higher standard. The provisions for due process in the Bill of Rights were added in order to improve the probability that the standard of "reasonable doubt" will be respected.

THE RIGHTS OF THE ACCUSED FROM ARREST TO TRIAL

- No improper searches and seizures (4th Amendment)
- No arrest without probable cause (4th Amendment)
- Right to remain silent (5th Amendment)
- No self-incrimination during arrest or trial (5th Amendment)
- Right to be informed of charges (6th Amendment)
- Right to counsel (6th Amendment)
- No excessive bail (8th Amendment)
- Right to grand jury (5th Amendment)
- Right to open trial before a judge (Article 1, Section 9)
- Right to speedy and public trial before an impartial jury (6th Amendment)
- Evidence obtained by illegal search not admissible during trial (4th Amendment)
- Right to confront witnesses (6th Amendment)
- No double jeopardy (5th Amendment)
- No cruel and unusual punishment (8th Amendment)

THE FOURTH AMENDMENT AND SEARCHES AND SEIZURES

> The right of the people to be secure in their persons, houses, papers, and effects, against unreasonable searches and seizures, shall not be violated, and no Warrants shall issue, but upon probable cause, supported by Oath or affirmation, and particularly describing the place to be searched, and the persons or things to be seized.

The purpose of the Fourth Amendment is to guarantee the security of citizens against unreasonable (i.e., improper) searches and seizures. In 1990 the Supreme Court summarized its understanding of the Fourth Amendment brilliantly and succinctly: "A search compromises the individual interest in privacy; a seizure deprives the individual of dominion over his or her person or property."[71]

But how are we to define what is reasonable and what is unreasonable? Generally, in the administration of justice in the United States, the decision about whether a search is reasonable is in the hands of judges and courts. First of all, it is the courts that issue a warrant before a search or arrest can be made. If a court has issued a warrant for a search, that search is considered reasonable. But in some circumstances, the time or opportunity may not be available for a court-issued warrant to be obtained. For example, a police officer has the authority to ask a person on the street to give "credible and reliable" identification and to account for his or her presence. But if that person refuses to cooperate and the officer has to take additional steps to get a response, the Fourth Amendment comes into play. The officer must have "probable cause," or reasonable suspicion that the person may be involved in a crime, to detain him or her for further inquiry. Whether such "probable cause" exists is another decision made by a judge or court.

When a crime has occurred and the investigation of it begins, the police often face a thicket of unknowns, and they are always operating on the verge of trampling valuable evidence or violating the rights of suspects and witnesses. The O. J. Simpson case is illustrative. Without eyewitnesses or videotapes to indicate who had committed two murders, the police had to search for clues. In the hysteria following the public revelation of such a scandal involving an extraordinary celebrity, the murder scene was trampled, potentially valuable evidence was mishandled, accounts of events were inconsistent, and expert reports and lab results from samples of blood, clothing, grass, and soil were inconclusive or uncertain. Should a person's fate hang (pardon the pun) on such evidence?

Often the American public expresses frustration when a jury delivers an acquittal in a case involving a prominent suspect or a seemingly solid presentation of evidence. But, as with freedom of speech and the press, if Americans genuinely support the right to a fair trial, they must also support the acquittal of the accused when the police or the courts fail to adhere to due process.

exclusionary rule
the ability of courts to exclude evidence obtained in violation of the Fourth Amendment

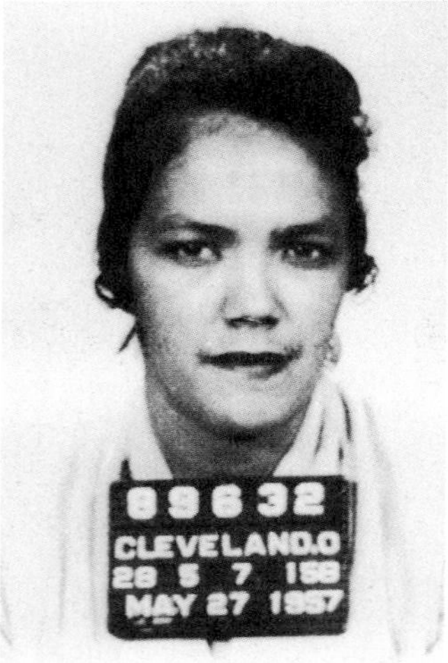

Dollree Mapp's lawsuit against the Cleveland Police Department went to the Supreme Court and nationalized the exclusionary rule.

The 1961 case of *Mapp v. Ohio* illustrates the beauty and the agony of one of the most important procedures that have grown out of the Fourth Amendment—the **exclusionary rule,** which prohibits evidence obtained during an illegal search from being introduced in a trial. Dollree (Dolly) Mapp was "a Cleveland woman of questionable reputation" (by some accounts), the ex-wife of one prominent boxer, and the fiancée of an even more famous one. Acting on a tip that Dolly Mapp was harboring a suspect in a bombing incident, several policemen forcibly entered Ms. Mapp's house claiming they had a warrant to look for the bombing suspect. The police did not find the bombing suspect but did find some materials connected to the local numbers racket (an illegal gambling operation) and a quantity of "obscene materials," in violation of an Ohio law banning possession of such materials. Although the warrant was never produced, the evidence that had been seized was admitted by a court, and Ms. Mapp was charged and convicted for illegal possession of obscene materials.

By the time Ms. Mapp's appeal reached the Supreme Court, the issue of obscene materials had faded into obscurity, and the question before the Court was whether any evidence produced under the circumstances of the search of her home was admissible. The Court's opinion affirmed the exclusionary rule: under the Fourth Amendment (applied to the states through the Fourteenth Amendment), "all evidence obtained by searches and seizures in violation of the Constitution . . . is inadmissible."[72] This means that even people who are clearly guilty of the crime of which they are accused must not be convicted if the only evidence for their conviction was obtained illegally.

The exclusionary rule is the most severe restraint ever imposed by the Constitution and the courts on the behavior of the police. The exclusionary rule is a dramatic restriction because it rules out precisely the evidence that produces a conviction; it frees those people who are *known* to have committed the crime of which they have been accused. Because it works so dramatically in favor of persons known to have committed a crime, the Court has since softened the application of the rule. In recent years, the federal courts have relied upon a discretionary use of the exclusionary rule, whereby they make a judgment as to the "nature and quality of the intrusion." It is thus difficult to know ahead of time whether a defendant will or will not be protected from an illegal search under the Fourth Amendment.[73]

Another recent issue involving the Fourth Amendment is the controversy over mandatory drug testing. Such tests are most widely used on public employees, and in an important case the Supreme Court has upheld the U.S. Customs Service's drug-testing program for its employees.[74] The same year the Court approved drug and alcohol tests for railroad workers if they were involved in serious accidents.[75] After Court approvals of those two cases in 1989, more than forty federal agencies initiated mandatory employee drug tests. The practice of drug testing was reinforced by a presidential executive order widely touted as the "campaign for a drug-free federal workplace." These growing practices gave rise to public appeals against the general practice of "suspicionless testing" of employees. Regardless of any need to limit the spread of drug abuse, working in this manner through public employees seemed patently unconstitutional, in violation of the Fourth Amendment. A 1995 case, in which the Court upheld a public school district's policy requiring all students participating in interscholastic sports to submit to random drug tests, surely contributed to the efforts of federal, state, and local agencies to initiate random and suspicionless drug and alcohol testing.[76] The most recent major case suggests, however, that the Court is beginning to consider limits on the war against drugs. In a decisive 8-to-1 decision, the Court applied the Fourth Amendment as a shield against "state action that diminishes personal privacy" when the officials in question are not performing high-risk or safety-sensitive tasks.[77] Using random and suspicionless drug testing as a symbol to fight drug use was, in the Court's opinion, carrying the exceptions to the Fourth Amendment too far.

These high school band members were searched for weapons before a football game in Birmingham, Alabama. A reasonable search?

THE FIFTH AMENDMENT

> No person shall be held to answer for a capital, or otherwise infamous crime, unless on a presentment or indictment of a Grand Jury, except in cases arising in the land or naval forces, or in the Militia, when in actual service in time of War or public danger; nor shall any person be subject for the same offence to be twice put in jeopardy of life or limb; nor shall be compelled in any criminal case to be a witness against himself, nor be deprived of life, liberty, or property, without due process of law; nor shall private property be taken for public use, without just compensation.

Grand Juries The first clause of the Fifth Amendment, the right to a **grand jury** to determine whether a trial is warranted, is considered "the oldest institution known to the Constitution."[78] Grand juries play an important role in federal criminal cases. However, the provision for a grand jury is the one important civil liberties provision of the Bill of Rights that was not incorporated by the Fourteenth Amendment to apply to state criminal prosecutions. Thus, some states operate without grand juries. In such states, the prosecuting attorney simply files a "bill of information" affirming that there is sufficient evidence available to justify a trial. If the accused person is to be held in custody, the prosecutor must take the available information before a judge to determine that the evidence shows probable cause.

grand jury
jury that determines whether sufficient evidence is available to justify a trial; grand juries do not rule on the accused's guilt or innocence.

Double Jeopardy "Nor shall any person be subject for the same offence to be twice put in jeopardy of life or limb" is the constitutional protection from **double jeopardy,** or being tried more than once for the same crime. The protection from double jeopardy was at the heart of the *Palko* case in 1937, which, as we saw earlier in this chapter, also established the principle of selective incorporation of the Bill of Rights. In that case, the state of Connecticut had indicted Frank Palko for first-degree murder, but a lower court had found him guilty of only second-degree murder and sentenced him to life in prison. Unhappy with the verdict, the state of Connecticut appealed the conviction to its highest court, won the appeal, got a new trial, and then succeeded in getting Palko convicted of first-degree murder. Palko appealed to the Supreme Court on what seemed an open and shut case of double jeopardy. Yet, although the majority of the Court agreed that this could indeed be considered a case of double jeopardy, they decided that double jeopardy was *not* one of the provisions of the Bill of Rights incorporated in the Fourteenth Amendment as a restriction on the powers of the states. It took more than thirty years for the Court to nationalize the constitutional protection against double jeopardy.

double jeopardy
the Fifth Amendment right providing that a person cannot be tried twice for the same crime

Palko was eventually executed for the crime, because he lived in the state of Connecticut rather than in some state whose constitution included a guarantee against double jeopardy.

Self-Incrimination Perhaps the most significant liberty found in the Fifth Amendment, and the one most familiar to many Americans who watch television crime shows, is the guarantee that no citizen "shall be compelled in any criminal case to be a witness against himself. . . ." The most famous case concerning self-incrimination is one of such importance that Chief Justice Earl Warren assessed its results as going "to the very root of our concepts of American criminal jurisprudence."[79] Twenty-three-year-old Ernesto Miranda was sentenced to between twenty and thirty years in prison for the kidnapping and rape of an eighteen-year-old girl. The girl had identified him in a police lineup, and, after two hours of questioning, Miranda confessed, subsequently signing a statement that his confession had been made voluntarily, without threats or promises of immunity. These confessions were admitted into evidence, served as the basis for Miranda's conviction, and also served as the basis of the appeal of his conviction all the way to the Supreme Court. In one of the most intensely and widely criticized decisions ever handed down by the Supreme Court, Ernesto Miranda's case produced the rules the police must follow before questioning an arrested criminal suspect. The reading of a person's "Miranda rights" (see Figure 5.2) became a standard scene in every police station and on virtually every dramatization of police action on television and in the movies. *Miranda* advanced the civil liberties of accused persons by expanding not only the scope of the Fifth Amendment clause covering coerced confessions

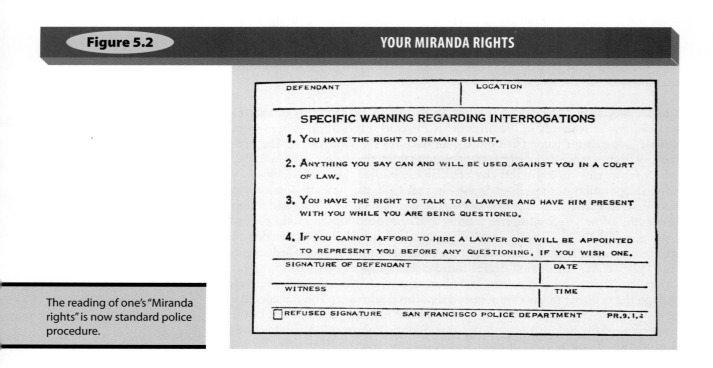

Figure 5.2 **YOUR MIRANDA RIGHTS**

DEFENDANT | LOCATION

SPECIFIC WARNING REGARDING INTERROGATIONS

1. YOU HAVE THE RIGHT TO REMAIN SILENT.
2. ANYTHING YOU SAY CAN AND WILL BE USED AGAINST YOU IN A COURT OF LAW.
3. YOU HAVE THE RIGHT TO TALK TO A LAWYER AND HAVE HIM PRESENT WITH YOU WHILE YOU ARE BEING QUESTIONED.
4. IF YOU CANNOT AFFORD TO HIRE A LAWYER ONE WILL BE APPOINTED TO REPRESENT YOU BEFORE ANY QUESTIONING, IF YOU WISH ONE.

SIGNATURE OF DEFENDANT | DATE

WITNESS | TIME

☐ REFUSED SIGNATURE SAN FRANCISCO POLICE DEPARTMENT PR.9.1.4

The reading of one's "Miranda rights" is now standard police procedure.

Ernesto Miranda was arrested for kidnapping and rape. At first he denied his guilt, but eventually he confessed to the crimes. Since he was never told that he was not required to answer police questions, his case was appealed on the grounds that his right against self-incrimination had been violated.

and self-incrimination, but also by confirming the right to counsel (discussed later). The Supreme Court under Burger and Rehnquist has considerably softened the *Miranda* restrictions, making the job of the police a little easier, but the ***Miranda* rule** still stands as a protection against egregious police abuses of arrested persons. The Supreme Court reaffirmed *Miranda* in *Dickerson v. United States* (2000).

***Miranda* rule**
the requirement, articulated by the Supreme Court in *Miranda v. Arizona*, that persons under arrest must be informed prior to police interrogation of their rights to remain silent and to have the benefit of legal counsel

Eminent Domain The other fundamental clause of the Fifth Amendment is the "takings clause," which extends to each citizen a protection against the "taking" of private property "without just compensation." Although this part of the Fifth Amendment is not specifically concerned with protecting persons accused of crimes, it is nevertheless a fundamentally important instance where the government and the citizen are adversaries. The power of any government to take private property for a public use is called **eminent domain.** This power is essential to the very concept of sovereignty. The Fifth Amendment neither invents eminent domain nor takes it away; its purpose is to put limits on that inherent power through procedures that require a showing of a public purpose and the provision of fair payment for the taking of someone's property. This provision is now universally observed in all U.S. principalities, but it has not always been meticulously observed.

eminent domain
the right of government to take private property for public use

Take the case of Mr. Berman, who in the 1950s owned and operated a "mom and pop" grocery store in a run-down neighborhood on the southwest side of the District of Columbia. In carrying out a vast urban redevelopment program, the city government of Washington, D.C., took Mr. Berman's property as one of a large number of privately owned lots to be cleared for new housing and business construction. Mr. Berman, and his successors after his death, took the government to court on the grounds that it was an unconstitutional use of eminent domain to take property from one private owner and eventually to turn that property back, in altered form, to another private owner. Berman and his successors lost their case. The Supreme Court's argument was a curious but very important one: the "public interest" can mean virtually anything a legislature says it means. In other words, since the overall slum clearance and redevelopment project was in the public interest, according to the legislature, the eventual transfers of property that were going to take place were justified.[80]

THE SIXTH AMENDMENT AND THE RIGHT TO COUNSEL

> In all criminal prosecutions, the accused shall enjoy the right to a speedy and public trial, by an impartial jury of the State and district wherein the crime shall have been committed, which district shall have been ascertained by law, and to be informed of the nature and cause of the accusation; to be confronted with the witnesses against him; to have compulsory process for obtaining witnesses in his favor, and to have the Assistance of Counsel for his defence.

Like the exclusionary rule of the Fourth Amendment and the self-incrimination clause of the Fifth Amendment, the "right to counsel" provision of the Sixth Amendment is notable for freeing defendants who seem to the public to be patently guilty as charged. Other provisions of the Sixth Amendment, such as the right to a speedy trial and the right to confront witnesses before an impartial jury, are less controversial in nature.

Gideon v. Wainwright is the perfect case study because it involved a disreputable person who seemed patently guilty of the crime for which he was convicted. In and out of jails for most of his fifty-one years, Clarence Earl Gideon received a five-year sentence for breaking and entering a poolroom in Panama City, Florida. While serving time in jail, Gideon became a fairly well qualified "jailhouse lawyer," made his own appeal on a handwritten petition, and eventually won the landmark ruling on the right to counsel in all felony cases.[81]

The right to counsel has been expanded rather than contracted during the past few decades, when the courts have become more conservative. For example, although at first the right to counsel was met by judges assigning lawyers from the community as a formal public obligation, most states and cities now have created an office of public defender; these state-employed professional defense lawyers typically provide poor defendants with much better legal representation. And, although a defendant does not have the right to choose any private defense attorney, defendants do have the right to appeal a conviction on the grounds that the counsel provided by the state was deficient. Moreover, the right to counsel extends beyond serious crimes to any trial, with or without jury, that holds the possibility of imprisonment. In other words, the Sixth Amendment provides a right that is seriously intended to be implemented.[82]

THE EIGHTH AMENDMENT AND CRUEL AND UNUSUAL PUNISHMENT

The Eighth Amendment prohibits "excessive bail," "excessive fines," and "cruel and unusual punishment." Virtually all the debate over Eighth Amendment issues focuses on the last clause of the amendment: the protection from "cruel and unusual punishment." One of the greatest challenges in interpreting this provision consistently lies in the fact that what is considered "cruel and unusual" varies from culture to culture and from generation to generation. And,

POLICY DEBATE

The Death Penalty

Since the Supreme Court gave a green light to the reenactment of death penalty laws in 1976, most states have embraced capital punishment as a "get-tough" signal to criminals. Between 1976 and 1996, states executed 328 people. Most of those executions occurred in southern states, with Texas leading the way. As of 1997, thirty-eight states had adopted some form of capital punishment, a move approved of by about three-quarters of all Americans.

Despite the fact that virtually all criminal conduct is regulated by the states, Congress has also jumped on the bandwagon, imposing capital punishment for more than fifty federal crimes. Despite the seeming popularity of the death penalty, the debate has become, if anything, more intense. In 1997, for example, the American Bar Association passed a resolution calling for a halt to the death penalty until concerns about its fairness—that is, whether its application violates the principle of equality—and about ensuring due process are addressed.

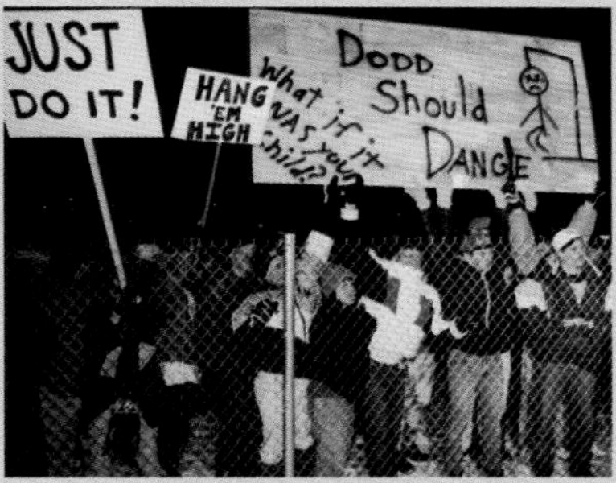

Many death penalty supporters trumpet its deterrent effects on other would-be criminals. Although studies of capital crimes usually fail to demonstrate any direct deterrent effect, that may be due to the lengthy delays—typically years and even decades—between convictions and executions. A system that eliminates undue delays would surely enhance deterrence. And deterring even one murder or other heinous crime, proponents argue, is more than ample justification for such laws.

Beyond this, the death penalty is seen as a proper expression of retribution, echoed in the biblical phrase "an eye for an eye." People who commit vicious crimes deserve to forfeit their lives in exchange for the suffering they have inflicted. If the world applauded the execution of Nazis after World War II, for example, how could it deny the right of society to execute a serial killer?

Constitutional objections to the death penalty often invoke the Eighth Amendment's protection against punishments that are "cruel and unusual." Yet the death penalty can hardly be considered a violation of this protection, say supporters, since the death penalty was commonly used in the eighteenth century and was supported by most early American leaders. And while the poor, males, and blacks and Latinos are more likely to find themselves sitting on death row, this fact reflects the painful reality that these categories of individuals are more likely to commit crimes.

Death penalty opponents are quick to point out that the death penalty has not been proven to deter crime, either in the United States or abroad. In fact, America is the only Western nation that still executes criminals. The fact that American states execute criminals debases, rather than elevates, society, by extolling vengeance. If the government is to serve as an example of proper behavior, say foes, it has no business sanctioning killing when incarceration will similarly protect society.

As for the Constitution, most of the Founders surely supported the death penalty. But, foes note, they also countenanced slavery, and lived at a time when society was both less informed about, and more indifferent to, the human condition. Modern Americans' greater civility should be reflected in how it defines individual rights.

Furthermore, according to death penalty foes, execution is expensive—more expensive than life imprisonment—precisely *because* the government must make every effort to ensure that it is not executing an innocent person. Curtailing legal appeals would make the possibility of a mistake too great. And although most Americans do support the death penalty, people also support life without the possibility of parole as an alternative. Race also intrudes in death penalty cases: people of color (who are more likely to face economic deprivation) are disproportionately more likely to be sentenced to death, whereas whites charged with identical crimes are less likely to be given the ultimate punishment. Such disparity of treatment violates the principle of equal protection. And finally, according to opponents, a life sentence may be a worse punishment for criminals than the death penalty.

STUDENT DEBATE

Is the Death Penalty Fair Punishment?

Yes

There are many misconceptions about the death penalty. A fresh look may be helpful.

* * *

Recently, there has been much discussion regarding the innocent sentenced to death. In the first 48 cases of "innocence" reviewed within a report by Rep. Don Edwards, D-Calif., it was specified that legal and factual innocence claims were both included, as they still are in the recent updates.

After a review of the case descriptions, as prepared by anti–death penalty sources, it appears that about half of the then-75 or so identified as innocent had proof of factual innocence. That is about 0.4 percent of those sentenced to death since 1973, and they have all been released, based on the unchallenged and hardly objective claims of anti–death penalty organizations.

It is important to recall when we heard that 23 "innocents" had been executed in the United States from 1900 to 1984. Within a year of that 1987 study being released, the authors of that study, in response to criticism of their work, stated in *The Risk of Executing the Innocent*: "We agree with our critics that we have not proved these executed defendants to be innocent; we never claimed that we had."

* * *

All murderers do not qualify for execution; specific aggravating factors are necessary to qualify as "death eligible." In observing the class or wealth of defendants, no one disputes the logic that murderers who have more wealth should have an advantage over their poorer ilk in avoiding the death penalty. However, financial gain capital murders, such as those involving robbery, burglary, car jacking, etc., make up a substantial portion of capital crimes. And the capital murders of policemen are often committed in the pursuit of those who commit such financial gain crimes.

Wealthier capital murderers are very unlikely to be involved in such crimes. In that context, and knowing that only 0.1 percent of all murderers have been executed since 1973, is there any evidence that wealthier capital murderers are less likely to be executed than their poorer ilk? Not according to *The New York Times* [1/16/97] article.

What of racism and the death penalty? Since 1973, white murderers have been executed at twice the rate as black murderers, according to this same article. Furthermore, white murderers are also executed 17 months faster than black murderers as reported by the Bureau of Justice Statistics last year.

* * *

There will always be some variables of race, ethnicity and class within any study of criminal justice practices. Based on historic, as well as current prejudices, we can never lower our guard. Because all studies are subject to poor protocols, bias and misinterpretation, we must make reasoned judgments based on as many respected considerations as we may have at our disposal. As the U.S. Supreme Court stated in *McCleskey* [*v. Kemp* (1987)], "Where the discretion that is fundamental to our criminal justice process is involved, we decline to assume that what is unexplained [by measured factors] is invidious." (481 US at 313).

That appears to be good advice.

SOURCE: Dudley Sharp, "Dispelling Death Penalty Myths," *The Diamondback* (University of Maryland), November 11, 1999.

No

White Supremacist John William King was recently sentenced to death for dragging James Byrd, an African-American, by a pickup truck last June, decapitating and mutilating his body. An admitted racist, King was convicted and sentenced by an almost entirely white jury.

King should and will pay dearly for his crime. However, one death does not right another. Byrd will still be dead and hate crimes will still exist. Capital punishment is a morally laden form of retribution that should be abolished due to its ineffectiveness at addressing the core problem of violent crimes.

The logistics of capital punishment reveal its weaknesses. The first mistake is letting states decide whether or not to put capital punishment into effect. This inevitably leads to disproportional application of the death penalty.

The states which employ the death penalty spend too much money and time killing convicted felons. By the time the appeals process is exhausted, killing someone ends up costing more than keeping someone alive. Ironically, most criminals sentenced to death row die from old age before they even make it to the death chamber.

Money would be better spent if directed toward more maximum security prisons and rehabilitation. Society needs to start owning up to its role in violent offenders' actions. If people continue to kill each other, we must question what is wrong or needs to be improved in society.

The demographics show an unequal application, as well. Members of minority groups have a higher chance of receiving the death penalty, and a middle-class man will be more likely to escape the sentence compared to a poor man. It's no mistake that I say "man," either; capital punishment is rarely applied and carried out with women.

It's also proven that the death penalty is not the all powerful crime deterrent it is set up to be. Society needs to see that violence cannot be cured by more violence. The state is teaching its citizens that murder is unacceptable unless it's carried out by the government. The "Do as I say, not as I do," method of social conditioning is ineffective.

Finally, it's barbarous to consider that additional deaths allow the victim's family members to achieve closure. The tragedy must be relived through the media and the highly publicized execution. Studies have shown that months afterward, those affected by the death have found no comfort in knowing a loved one's murder was avenged.

This leads us to the moral implications of capital punishment. Putting someone to death is much more serious than life sentencing. The death penalty cannot be applied objectively and fairly due to people's values, beliefs, and experiences that will inevitably color their judgments.

As long as people are deciding other's fates, their judgments and prejudices will color their abilities to objectively assess the situation at hand. O.J. Simpson showed that being African American, rich, and well known was enough to be declared not guilty. No one has the ability to look beyond superficial exteriors and dollar signs to judge the worth of our lives.

The judicial system was designed to be above stereotypes, generalizations, and prejudices. Ideally, if the due process is applied, truth and justice will prevail. One need only look at ignorant court rulings in the past to see the falseness of this assertion. Oppression of minorities and women stain our history books today; fifty years from now it will be saddening to read that lethal injections and the gas chamber were acceptable means of punishment.

The basis of capital punishment rests too heavily on Old Testament thinking. Separation of church and state is what the government strives for; but how can that be possible when "In God We Trust" covers our currency, the pledge invokes a higher being, and retribution is the main justification for killing a murderer?

Emotions are talking when capital punishment is enforced, not the judicial system.

SOURCE: Kelly Zeigler, "The Death Penalty Is No Solution," *Daily Utah Chronicle* (University of Utah), March 2, 1999.

unfortunately, it also varies by class and race. A sentence of ten years in prison for robbing a liquor store is not considered excessive, yet embezzlement or insider trading involving millions of dollars merits only three years of community service. Are "white-collar" crimes less serious than "working-class" crimes? Consider the 1995 action by Congress to mandate a five-year minimum sentence for offenses involving five or more grams of crack cocaine. The same five-year mandatory sentence for *powdered* cocaine, however, kicks in only when the amount involved is *five hundred* grams or more. As one black member of the House put it, "crack cocaine happens to be used by poor people, mostly black people, because it's cheap. Powdered cocaine happens to be used by wealthy white people."[83]

By far the biggest issue of class and race inconsistency as constituting cruel and unusual punishment arises over the death penalty. In 1972, the Supreme Court overturned several state death penalty laws, not because they were cruel and unusual, but because they were being applied in a capricious manner—i.e., blacks were much more likely than whites to be sentenced to death, and the poor more likely than the rich, and men more likely than women.[84] Very soon after that decision, a majority of states revised their capital punishment provisions to meet the Court's standards.[85] Since 1976, the Court has consistently upheld state laws providing for capital punishment, although the Court also continues to review numerous death penalty appeals each year.

The Right to Privacy

▶ What is the right to privacy? How has it been derived from the Bill of Rights? What forms does the right to privacy take today?

Some of the people all of the time and all of the people some of the time would just like to be left alone, to have their own private domain into which no one—friends, family, government, church, or employer—has the right to enter without permission.

Many Jehovah's Witnesses felt that way in the 1930s. They risked serious punishment in 1940 by telling their children not to salute the flag or say the "Pledge of Allegiance" in school because of their understanding of the First Commandment's prohibition of the worship of "graven images." They lost their appeal, the children were expelled, and the parents were punished.[86] However, the Supreme Court concluded that the 1940 decision was "wrongly decided."[87] These two cases arose under the freedom of religion provisions of the First Amendment, but they were also the first cases to confront the possibility of another right that is not mentioned anywhere in the Constitution or the Bill of Rights: the right to be left alone. When the Court began to take a more activist role in the mid-1950s and 1960s, the idea of a **right to privacy** was revived. In 1958, the Supreme Court recognized "privacy in one's association" in its decision to prevent the state of Alabama from using the membership list of the National Association for the Advancement of Colored People in the state's investigations.[88]

right to privacy
the right to be let alone, which has been interpreted by the Supreme Court to entail free access to birth control and abortions

Birth Control The sphere of privacy was drawn in earnest in 1965, when the Court ruled that a Connecticut statute forbidding the use of contraceptives violated the right of marital privacy. Estelle Griswold, the executive director of the Planned Parenthood League of Connecticut, was arrested by the state of Connecticut for providing information, instruction, and medical advice about contraception to married couples. She and her associates were found guilty as accessories to the crime and fined $100 each. The Supreme Court reversed the lower court decisions and declared the Connecticut law unconstitutional because it violated "a right of privacy older than the Bill of Rights—older than our political parties, older than our school system."[89] Justice William O. Douglas, author of the majority decision in the *Griswold* case, argued that this right of privacy is also grounded in the Constitution, because it fits into a "zone of privacy" created by a combination of the Third, Fourth, and Fifth Amendments. A concurring opinion, written by Justice Arthur Goldberg, attempted to strengthen Douglas's argument by adding that "the concept of liberty . . . embraces the right of marital privacy though that right is not mentioned explicitly in the Constitution [and] is supported by numerous decisions of this Court . . . and *by the language and history of the Ninth Amendment*" (emphasis added).[90]

Abortion The right to privacy was confirmed and extended in 1973 in the most important of all privacy decisions, and one of the most important Supreme Court decisions in American history: *Roe v. Wade*. This decision established a woman's right to seek an abortion and prohibited states from making abortion a criminal act.[91] The Burger Court's decision in *Roe* took a revolutionary step toward establishing the right to privacy. It is important to emphasize that the preference for privacy rights and for their extension to include the rights of women to control their own bodies was not something invented by the Supreme Court in a vacuum. Most states did not regulate abortions in any fashion until the 1840s, at which time only six of the twenty-six existing states had any regulations governing abortion at all. In addition, many states had begun to ease their abortion restrictions well before the 1973 *Roe* decision, although in recent years a number of states have reinstated some restrictions on abortion.

By extending the umbrella of privacy, this sweeping ruling dramatically changed abortion practices in America. In addition, it galvanized and nationalized the abortion debate. Groups opposed to abortion, such as the National Right to Life Committee, organized to fight the new liberal standard, while abortion rights groups sought to maintain that protection. In recent years, the legal standard shifted against abortion rights supporters in two key Supreme Court cases.

In *Webster v. Reproductive Health Services* (1989), the Court narrowly upheld (by a 5-to-4 majority) the

Students and Politics

In recent years, the National Right to Life Party has developed college outreach programs. One of the more active chapters has been at the University of Notre Dame, where Catriona Wilkie and others have led activism both in South Bend, Indiana, and on the national level. As a fourteen-year-old, Wilkie was the only minor to testify before the Texas state legislature on a proposed law that would require parental consent for a minor to obtain an abortion. The passionate speakers that day, she says, "made me realize how hard you have to fight; most people would have been scared away." Wilkie's responsibilities at Notre Dame Right to Life include participating in a national march in Washington, fund-raising for the local and national branches, and educating local youth groups and schools about the group's position on abortion. "The strongest voice is always one that is close to their own," she says, referring to her speaking engagements with audiences of her age and younger. "We stay away from slogans and stick to information. People appreciate that."

SOURCE: Catriona Wilkie, interview by author, February 3, 1998.

constitutionality of restrictions on the use of public medical facilities for abortion.[92] And in the 1992 case of *Planned Parenthood v. Casey,* another 5-to-4 majority of the Court upheld *Roe* but narrowed its scope, refusing to invalidate a Pennsylvania law that significantly limits freedom of choice. The Court's decision defined the right to an abortion as a "limited or qualified" right subject to regulation by the states as long as the regulation does not constitute an "undue burden."[93] More recently, the Court had another opportunity to rule on what constitutes an undue burden. In the 2000 case of *Stenberg v. Carhart,* the Court, by a vote of 5 to 4, struck down Nebraska's ban on partial-birth abortions because the law had the "effect of placing a substantial obstacle in the path of a woman seeking an abortion."[94]

Homosexuality In the last two decades, the right to be left alone began to include the privacy rights of homosexuals. One morning in Atlanta, Georgia, in the mid-1980s, Michael Hardwick was arrested by a police officer who discovered him in bed with another man. The officer had come to serve a warrant for Hardwick's arrest for failure to appear in court to answer charges of drinking in public. One of Hardwick's unknowing housemates invited the officer to look in Hardwick's room, where he found Hardwick and another man engaging in "consensual sexual behavior." He was then arrested under Georgia's laws against heterosexual and homosexual sodomy. Hardwick filed a lawsuit against the state, challenging the constitutionality of the Georgia law. Hardwick won his case in the federal court of appeals. The state of Georgia, in an unusual move, appealed the court's decision to the Supreme Court. The majority of the Court reversed the lower court decision, holding against Mr. Hardwick, on the grounds that "the federal Constitution confers [no] fundamental right upon homosexuals to engage in sodomy," and that therefore there was no basis to invalidate "the laws of the many states that still make such conduct illegal and have done so for a very long time."[95] The Court majority concluded its opinion with a warning that it ought not and would not use its power to "discover new fundamental rights embedded in the Due Process Clause." In other words, the Court under Chief Justice Rehnquist was expressing its determination to restrict quite severely the expansion of the Ninth Amendment and the development of new substantive rights. The four dissenters argued that the case was not about a fundamental right to engage in homosexual sodomy, but was in fact about "the most comprehensive of rights and the right most valued by civilized men, [namely,] the right to be let alone."[96] It is unlikely that many states will adopt new laws against consensual homosexual activity or will vigorously enforce old laws of such a nature already on their books. But it is equally clear that the current Supreme Court will refrain from reviewing such laws and will resist expanding the Ninth Amendment as a source of new substantive rights.

The Right to Die Another area ripe for litigation and public discourse is the so-called right to die. A number of highly publicized physician-assisted suicides in the 1990s focused attention on whether people have a right to choose their own death and to receive assistance in carrying it out. Can this become part of the privacy right or is it a new substantive right? A tentative answer came in 1997, when the Court ruled that a Washington state law establishing a ban on "causing" or "aiding" a suicide did not violate the Fourteenth

Amendment or any clauses of the Bill of Rights incorporated in the Fourteenth Amendment.[97] Thus, if a state can constitutionally adopt such a prohibition, there is no constitutional right to suicide or assisted suicide. However, the Court left open the narrower question of "whether a mentally competent person who is experiencing great suffering has a constitutionally cognizable interest in controlling the circumstances of his or her imminent death."[98] "Americans are engaged in an earnest and profound debate about the morality, legality, and practicality of physician-assisted suicide. Our holding permits this debate to continue, as it should in a democratic society."[99] Never before has the Supreme Court more openly invited further litigation on a point.[100]

The Future of Civil Liberties

▶ What is the likelihood that the Supreme Court will try to reverse the nationalization of the Bill of Rights?

The next and final question for this chapter is whether the current Supreme Court, with its conservative majority, will try to reverse the nationalization of the Bill of Rights after a period of more than thirty-five years. Although such a move is possible, it is not certain. First of all, the Rehnquist Court has not actually reversed important decisions made by the Warren or Burger Courts, but instead has given narrower and more restrictive interpretations of earlier Court decisions. For example, in 1997, the Court made it easier for the police to search cars for drugs or other contraband when the cars have been pulled over only for traffic violations. Activists such as Justices Rehnquist, Antonin Scalia, and Clarence Thomas, who would prefer to overturn many of the Court's decisions from the 1960s and 1970s, do not yet command a majority on the Court. The most recent sign of the times is a case regarding the constitutionality of the 1994 Drivers' Privacy Protection Act. The purpose of the act was to protect privacy rights in general and the safety of women in particular by barring states from disclosing without consent the personal information contained in motor vehicle and driving license records. By selling these lists of registrants to anyone willing to buy them, information can be gained, by stalkers as well as by telemarketers, that many people go to great lengths to keep confidential. Justice Stephen Breyer observed that if the Court overturned this statute, it could on principle overturn "the entire body of law under which the authority of Congress to regulate interstate commerce has been understood to place corresponding limits on state authority." In a unanimous decision the Court rejected the states' rights challenge to the Drivers' Privacy Protection Act. Chief Justice William Rehnquist wrote the *Reno v. Condon* (2000) decision.

Meanwhile, the resurgence of federalism will play itself out in judicial territory. One certain trend in the Court that is likely to continue is its commitment to giving more discretion to the states, returning some of the power to state legislatures that was taken away during the "nationalization" of the Bill of Rights. But what if the state legislatures begin using their regained powers in

BANNED BOOKS

One of the more visible issues of free speech in recent years has been the banning of books in public schools. The following books were the most censored of 1999, with the reasons for which they were banned:

1. *Harry Potter* series, J. K. Rowling: wizardry and magic

2. *Alice* series, Phyllis Reynolds Naylor: offensive language and unsuited to age group
3. *The Chocolate War,* Robert Cormier: offensive language and unsuited to age group
4. *Blubber,* Judy Blume: offensive language and unsuited to age group
5. *Fallen Angels,* Walter Dean Meyers: offensive language and unsuited to age group
6. *Of Mice and Men,* John Steinbeck: offensive language and unsuited to age group
7. *I Know Why the Caged Bird Sings,* Maya Angelou: explicit portrayal of rape and other sexual abuse
8. *The Handmaid's Tale,* Margaret Atwood: sexual content
9. *The Color Purple,* Alice Walker: sexual content and offensive language
10. *Snow Falling on Cedars,* David Guterson: sexual content and offensive language

SOURCE: American Library Association

AMERICAN DEMOCRACY IN COMPARATIVE PERSPECTIVE

The Difficult Partnership: Democracy and Civil Liberties

According to the basic principles of the Universal Declaration of Human Rights of 1948, people should be free from "fear and want." At the core of this principle are civil liberties. Yet even among democracies these liberties are often lacking. As we saw earlier in Chapter 1, of the 191 countries and sovereign territories in the world, 117 countries were classified as electoral democracies in 1999; of these, 88 were classified as "free," and 29 as "partly free."

Freedom House's classification scheme is based on the combined score of a country's *political rights* (essentially the ability of a country's citizens to participate freely in the political process via voting and other forms of political activity, and to trust that elected officials will be responsive to the public in the making of public policy) and *civil liberties* (the ability of citizens to develop independent political views, the availability of open and competitive political institutions, and a sense of personal autonomy free from the direction and inference of the state).

Scores for civil liberties across nation-states of the world as of 1999 are based on Freedom House's coding and assessment. A value of 1 is a "perfect" score, indicating the highest degree of civil liberties possible, while a value of 7 reflects the fewest possible civil liberties.

If we focus on the civil liberties of electoral democracies alone, we find that of the 117 electoral democracies in the world, as of 1999 only 28 (24 percent of the electoral democracies and less than 15 percent of all the countries and sovereign territories) had a perfect score for civil liberties. Freedom House examines four general rights to determine a country's degree of civil liberties: (1) freedom of expression and belief, (2) association and organization rights, (3) rule of law and human rights, and (4) personal autonomy and economic rights. These 28 electoral democracies possess institutions that best represent the ideals of civil liberties. This group includes, among others, the United States, Canada, Belgium, Norway, Dominica, New Zealand, Kiribati, Monaco, Marshall Islands, and Sweden.

However, 23 of the 88 electoral democracies that were classified as "free" by Freedom House had some shortcomings in all major categories of a citizen's general rights. None of these countries had *less* than a value of "3" on civil rights. Thus, while these countries are electoral democracies with a generally higher degree of overall freedom, they have not granted their citizens the full measure of civil liberties. This group of electoral democracies include Argentina, Bolivia, Bulgaria, Greece, India, Israel, Philippines, Thailand, and Venezuela.

Amnesty International, which, like Freedom House, is a widely respected nongovernmental organization that monitors the freedoms and rights of citizens around the world, has listed a number of civil liberty violations frequently seen in the world. These include the denial of rights to women and children, including forcing them to work in slave-labor conditions and often subjecting them to indignities, such as prostitution and drug trafficking; torture of suspects and prisoners; arbitrary imprisonment; denial of trial; and religious persecution.

Among those countries that are classified as electoral democracies but that exhibit sharp civil liberty violations are Turkey (rated 5—an applicant to membership in the European Union and a member of NATO) and Pakistan (rated 5—an electoral democracy until October 1999). Turkey's civil liberties violations stem largely from the Kurdish minority separatist insugency (PKK) that plagues the southeast regions of the country. In January 1999 the government of Turkey confirmed that a government-sanctioned execution squad had killed as many as 5,000 Kurds between 1993 and 1996. Furthermore, the Turkish army, in accordance with emergency laws in effect at the time, forcibly "depopulated"—by murder and torture—thousand of villages and hamlets in the region. In Pakistan, the penal code was revised in 1979 regarding sexual offenses. According to Amnesty International, many women have been imprisoned for alleged extramarital sexual intercourse. These imprisonments are often based on false allegations by their husbands. Rape victims must meet strict legal requirements to prove the crime, or they can be charged with adultery. Even among the freest electoral democracies of the world, laws on political asylum and citizenship prevent countries such as the United Kingdom, Germany, France, and Italy from receiving perfect scores.

SOURCES: Freedom House: *Freedom in the World: The Annual Survey of Political Rights and Civil Liberties, 1998–1999,* on the Web at: http://www.freedomhouse.org/survey/1999/; Amnesty International (United Kingdom), Report 1999, on the Web at: http://www.amnesty.org.uk/library/annrep.shtml.

ways they had used them before the nationalization of the Bill of Rights? What would be the reaction when states pass laws imposing further criminal restrictions on abortion? Permitting more religious practices in the public schools? Spreading the application of capital punishment to new crimes? Imposing stricter sentences on white-collar crimes? Terminating the use of buses to maintain desegregated schools? A great deal will depend upon the three or even four appointments the next president of the United States will be able to make as vacancies are produced by an aging Court membership. When that occurs, what would a majority on the Court do? Would the Court be equally respectful of state-level democracy then?

The Citizen's Role

The civil liberties that Americans enjoy today have been won by the struggles of ordinary citizens. The Bill of Rights offers Americans who have been denied their civil liberties a remedy through the judicial system. Individuals such as Dolly Mapp, Ernesto Miranda, and Clarence Earl Gideon fought to defend their fundamental liberties, and through their efforts all Americans now possess a more clearly defined and protected right to the due process of law. The most central aspect of a woman's right to privacy started with the difficulties of a poor, high school dropout in Texas. Norma McCorvey was a twenty-one-year-old pregnant, divorced carnival worker with a five-year-old daughter. McCorvey lived regularly on the edge of poverty, and as a high school dropout, her prospects were poor, all the poorer in Texas, where the carnival had moved, because Texas had prohibited abortion unless necessary to save the mother's life. "I found one doctor who offered to abort me for $500. Only he didn't have a license, and I was scared to turn my body over to him. So there I was—pregnant, . . . alone and stuck."

McCorvey bore her child and gave it up immediately for adoption, but in the process she was introduced to two recent graduates of the University of Texas Law School, Sarah Weddington and Linda Coffey. These three women decided to challenge the Texas abortion statute. In order to avoid any stigma attached to such an emotionally charged case, Norma McCorvey's name was changed to Jane Roe in the court documents. Her case alleged that "she was unmarried and pregnant; that she wished to terminate her pregnancy by an abortion . . . ; [and] that she was unable to get a 'legal' abortion because her life did not appear to be threatened by the continuation of her pregnancy. . . ." The Court's ruling in *Roe v. Wade* subsequently prohibited states from making abortion illegal.[101]

STUDENTS AND POLITICS

In 1995, a student group at the University of Virginia scored a dramatic legal victory before the U.S. Supreme Court. The university had refused to provide support from the student activities fund for *Wide Awake,* a magazine published by a Christian student group. Although other student publications received subsidies from the activities fund, university policy prohibited grants to religious groups. Ronald Rosenberger, a Virginia undergraduate and an editor of the magazine, and his fellow editors filed suit in federal court, charging, among other things, that the university's refusal to fund their magazine because of its religious focus violated their First Amendment right to freedom of speech. A federal district court ruled in favor of the university on the grounds that funding for a religious newspaper by a state university would violate the Constitution's prohibition against government support for religion. Rosenberger and his colleagues appealed, but lost again when the district court's decision was affirmed by the Fourth Circuit Court of Appeals, which said that the Constitution mandated a strict separation of church and state. Undeterred, the student editors appealed the circuit court's decision to the Supreme Court. As we saw earlier in this chapter, the Supreme Court ruled in favor of the student group, holding that the university's policies amounted to state support for some ideas but not others. This, said the Court, represented a fundamental violation of the First Amendment.[102] The *Rosenberger* decision represents a potential loosening of the Court's long-standing opposition to any government support for religious groups or ideas, and it demonstrates how much influence can be exerted by a determined group of students.

In every sense of the word, the American judiciary is the most accessible branch to the least-represented and the least-organized citizens. The judicial branch has the power to give citizenship its full meaning. The sad news in all of this is that citizens, including many of the most educated citizens, have very little appreciation of their own fundamental liberties, which they don't defend unless under threat. Liberty, like art and enterprise, is strengthened, not worn out, by use.

GET INVOLVED Defending Liberty

"Liberty" has been a rallying call that has united Americans from the Revolution to the present. It is a treasure that we have inherited from our ancestors, one that we feel obligated to defend, extend, and bequeath to our children. When we suspect that our liberty is threatened, we often mobilize our energies and, if necessary, take up arms to protect it against enemies.

"Civil liberties" are areas of personal freedom that we want to protect against government intervention. They include religious freedom, freedom of speech, a free press, the right to bear arms, privacy rights, and protections for the criminally accused. A remarkably strong consensus exists among Americans that our fundamental civil liberties should be protected from overzealous political groups and politicians who want to restrict personal freedom and force their own particular values or lifestyles on citizens. However, this consensus breaks down as the issues become more specific and focused.

Consider the area of free speech. Should we limit free speech on campus by prohibiting racial or sexual slurs that create a hostile environment for some students? Should we protect free speech on the Internet and thereby expose our children to an onslaught of cyber-pornography? Or consider privacy rights. Do women have a constitutional right to choose abortions? Do individuals have a legitimate claim to physician-assisted suicide? Do governments abuse their authority when they attempt to regulate sexual practices among consenting adults? Civil liberty issues often generate passionate feelings and political controversy because they deal with highly personal, complex matters.

One way to become politically involved is to seize on a civil liberties issue that stimulates your emotions and start a campus group to defend your position on the issue. Precisely because civil liberties issues generate strong feelings, there is a good chance that you can identify a small core of committed students who are willing to lend their support, commitment, and time to the group. Talk to classmates and friends. Circulate your ideas around the dormitory. Ask for a few minutes to speak to campus Democrats or Republicans or whatever groups might be sympathetic to your position. With only three or four initial members, you can launch your group.

Most college campuses have a central student board that handles funding for student groups. If so, consider applying for funding. Money widens your options for action. However, even without funding, you can go far. You might announce an organization meeting in your political science class or in the upcoming events section of the student newspaper. Contact the campus radio station (if you have one) or post flyers on campus bulletin boards. Even if just a few people show up, here are some of the kinds of activities and events you can organize.

- Hold informal gatherings where members and interested people can brainstorm possible activities around your civil liberties issue.
- Host prominent speakers who will talk about your issue and address questions from the audience.
- Plan or participate in debates with students or campus groups that have different views on the issue.
- Invite professors and students to participate in a "roundtable discussion" about your civil liberties issue.
- Set up card tables in high-traffic locations at lunch time to disseminate information or to gather signatures for a petition relevant to your issue.
- Make contact with national political groups that share your position. They may be able to provide you materials for dissemination and other resources.

Starting a campus group is a great way to get involved, encourage others to become more politically active, and at the same time focus your energy on an issue that is important to you. You may be surprised to discover that a relatively small but entrepreneurial group can make a difference on campus and beyond.

Summary

The provisions of the Bill of Rights seek to protect citizens from improper government action. Civil liberties ought to be carefully distinguished from civil rights, which did not become part of the Constitution until the Fourteenth Amendment and its provision for "equal protection of the laws."

During its first century, the Bill of Rights was applicable only to the national government and not to the state governments. The Fourteenth Amendment (1868) seemed to apply the Bill of Rights to the states, but the Supreme Court continued to apply the Bill of Rights as though the Fourteenth Amendment had never been adopted. For sixty years following the adoption of the Fourteenth Amendment, only one provision was "incorporated" into the Fourteenth Amendment and applied as a restriction on the state governments: the Fifth Amendment "eminent domain" clause, which was incorporated in 1897. Even as recently as 1961, only the eminent domain clause and the clauses of the First Amendment had been incorporated into the Fourteenth Amendment and applied to the states. After 1961, one by one, most of the provisions of the Bill of Rights were finally incorporated and applied to the states, although a conservative Supreme Court tried to reverse this trend during the 1980s and 1990s. The status of the First Amendment seems to have been least affected by this conservative trend. Protection of purely political speech remains close to absolute. The categories of conditionally protected speech include "speech-plus," libel and slander, obscenity and pornography, fighting words, and commercial speech. Nevertheless, the realm of free speech in all these areas is still quite broad.

Of the other amendments and clauses in the Bill of Rights, the ones most likely to receive conservative interpretations are the religious clauses of the First Amendment, illegal search and seizure cases arising under the Fourth Amendment, and cases involving the Eighth Amendment cruel and unusual punishment clause.

Where the Bill of Rights will go as the American people approach the end of the century is very unclear.

FOR FURTHER READING

Abraham, Henry J. *Freedom and the Court: Civil Rights and Liberties in the United States.* 6th ed. New York: Oxford University Press, 1994.

Bryner, Gary C., and A. Don Sorensen, eds. *The Bill of Rights: A Bicentennial Assessment.* Albany: State University of New York Press, 1993.

Eisenstein, Zillah. *The Female Body and the Law.* Berkeley: University of California Press, 1988.

Friendly, Fred W. *Minnesota Rag: The Dramatic Story of the Landmark Supreme Court Case that Gave New Meaning to Freedom of the Press.* New York: Vintage, 1982.

Glendon, Mary Ann. *Rights Talk: The Impoverishment of Political Discourse.* New York: Free Press, 1991.

Hentoff, Nat. *The First Freedom: The Tumultuous History of Free Speech in America.* New York: Basic Books, 1994.

Levy, Leonard. *Legacy of Suppression: Freedom of Speech and Press in Early American History.* New York: Harper, 1963.

Lewis, Anthony. *Gideon's Trumpet.* New York: Random House, 1964.

Meyer, Michael J., and William A. Parent. *The Constitution of Rights: Human Dignity and American Values.* Ithaca, NY: Cornell University Press, 1992.

Minow, Martha. *Making All the Difference: Inclusion, Exclusion, and American Law.* Ithaca, NY: Cornell University Press, 1990.

Silverstein, Mark. *Constitutional Faiths.* Ithaca, NY: Cornell University Press, 1984.

Stone, Geoffrey R., Richard A. Epstein, and Cass R. Sunstein, eds. *The Bill of Rights in the Modern State.* Chicago: University of Chicago Press, 1992.

STUDY OUTLINE

The Bill of Rights: A Charter of Liberties

1. Despite the insistence of Alexander Hamilton that a bill of rights was both unnecessary and dangerous, adding a list of explicit rights was the most important item of business for the First Congress in 1789.
2. The Bill of Rights would have been more aptly named the "Bill of Liberties," because it is made up of provisions that protect citizens from improper government action.
3. Civil rights did not become part of the Constitution until 1868 with the adoption of the Fourteenth Amendment, which sought to provide for each citizen "the equal protection of the laws."

Nationalizing the Bill of Rights

1. In 1833, the Supreme Court found that the Bill of Rights limited only the national government and not state governments.
2. Although the language of the Fourteenth Amendment seems to indicate that the protections of the Bill of Rights apply to state governments as well as the national government, for the remainder of the nineteenth century the Supreme Court (with only one exception) made decisions as if the Fourteenth Amendment had never been adopted.
3. As of 1961, only the First Amendment and one clause of the Fifth Amendment had been "selectively incorporated" into the Fourteenth Amendment. After 1961, however, most of the provisions of the Bill of Rights were incorporated into the Fourteenth Amendment and applied to the states.

The First Amendment and Freedom of Religion

1. The "establishment clause" of the First Amendment has been interpreted to mean the strict separation of church and state.
2. The "free exercise clause" protects the right to believe and to practice whatever religion one chooses; it also involves protection of the right to be a nonbeliever.

The First Amendment and Freedom of Speech and the Press

1. Although freedom of speech and freedom of the press hold an important place in the Bill of Rights, the extent and nature of certain types of expression are subject to constitutional debate.
2. Among the forms of speech that are absolutely protected are the truth, political speech, symbolic speech, and "speech plus," which is speech plus a physical activity such as picketing. The forms of speech that are currently only conditionally protected include libel and slander; obscenity and pornography; fighting words; and commercial speech.

The Second Amendment and the Right to Bear Arms

1. Constitutionally, the Second Amendment unquestionably protects citizens' rights to bear arms, but this right can be regulated by both state and federal law.

Rights of the Criminally Accused

1. The purpose of due process is to equalize the playing field between the accused individual and the all-powerful state.
2. The Fourth Amendment protects against unreasonable searches and seizures.
3. The Fifth Amendment requires a grand jury for most crimes, protects against double jeopardy, and provides that you cannot be forced to testify against yourself.
4. The Sixth Amendment requires a speedy trial and the right to witnesses and counsel.
5. The Eighth Amendment prohibits cruel and unusual punishment.

The Right to Privacy

1. In the case of *Griswold v. Connecticut,* the Supreme Court found a right of privacy in the Constitution. This right was confirmed and extended in 1973 in the case of *Roe v. Wade.*

The Future of Civil Liberties

1. Under Chief Justice William Rehnquist, the Court has somewhat restricted civil liberties without actually overturning any of the important decisions from the 1960s and 1970s that established many of the liberties enjoyed today.

PRACTICE QUIZ

1. From 1789 until the 1960s, the Bill of Rights put limits on
   a) the national government only.
   b) the state government only.
   c) both the national and state governments.
   d) neither the national nor the state governments.
2. The amendment that provided the basis for the modern understanding of the government's obligation to protect civil rights was the
   a) First Amendment.
   b) Ninth Amendment.
   c) Fourteenth Amendment.
   d) Twenty-second Amendment.
3. The so-called *Lemon* test, derived from the Supreme Court's ruling in *Lemon v. Kurtzman,* concerns the issue of
   a) school desegregation.
   b) aid to religious schools.
   c) prayer in school.
   d) obscenity.
4. The process by which some of the liberties in the Bill of Rights were applied to the states (or nationalized) is known as
   a) selective incorporation.
   b) judicial activism.
   c) civil liberties.
   d) establishment.
5. Which of the following provided that all of the protections contained in the Bill of Rights applied to the states as well as the national government?
   a) the Fourteenth Amendment
   b) *Palko v. Connecticut*
   c) *Gitlow v. New York*
   d) none of the above
6. Which of the following protections are not contained in the First Amendment?
   a) the establishment clause
   b) the free exercise clause
   c) freedom of the press
   d) All of the above are First Amendment protections.
7. Which of the following describes a written statement made in "reckless disregard of the truth" that is considered damaging to a victim because it is "malicious, scandalous, and defamatory"?
   a) slander
   b) libel
   c) fighting words
   d) expressive speech
8. The Fourth, Fifth, Sixth, and Eighth Amendments, taken together, define:
   a) due process of law.
   b) free speech.
   c) the right to bear arms.
   d) civil rights of minorities.
9. In what case was a right to privacy first found in the Constitution?
   a) *Griswold v. Connecticut*
   b) *Roe v. Wade*
   c) *Baker v. Carr*
   d) *Planned Parenthood v. Casey*
10. Which famous case deals with Sixth Amendment issues?
    a) *Miranda v. Arizona*
    b) *Mapp v. Ohio*
    c) *Gideon v. Wainwright*
    d) *Terry v. Ohio*

CRITICAL THINKING QUESTIONS

1. In many ways it seems that the Bill of Rights is an ambiguous document. Choose one protection offered in the Bill of Rights and explain how it has been interpreted in various ways. What does this say about the role of politics and the Constitution in defining the limits of governmental power? What does it say about the power of the Supreme Court in American politics?
2. Recount the history of the constitutional "right to privacy." How has this right affected American politics since the 1960s? How has this right interacted with the other rights in the Bill of Rights? Read the Third, Fourth, Fifth, and Ninth Amendments. In your opinion, do American citizens have a right to privacy?

KEY TERMS

bills of attainder (p. 150)
Bill of Rights (p. 147)
civil liberties (p. 151)
civil rights (p. 152)
"clear and present danger" test (p. 160)
double jeopardy (p. 175)
due process of law (p. 152)
eminent domain (p. 177)
establishment clause (p. 156)
ex post facto laws (p. 150)
exclusionary rule (p. 174)
fighting words (p. 166)
free exercise clause (p. 158)
grand jury (p. 175)
habeas corpus (p. 150)
***Lemon* test** (p. 157)
libel (p. 163)
***Miranda* rule** (p. 177)
prior restraint (p. 162)
procedural liberties (p. 152)
right to privacy (p. 182)
selective incorporation (p. 153)
slander (p. 163)
speech plus (p. 161)
strict scrutiny (p. 159)
substantive liberties (p. 151)

6 Civil Rights

★ **Civil Rights**

What is the legal basis for civil rights?

How has the equal protection clause historically been enforced?

What is the critical Supreme Court ruling in the battle for equal protection?

How has Congress tried to make equal protection a reality?

In what areas did the civil rights acts seek to provide equal access and protection?

★ **The Universalization of Civil Rights**

What groups were spurred by the provision of the Civil Rights Act of 1964 outlawing discrimination in employment practices based on race, religion, and gender, to seek broader protection under the law?

What is the politics of the universalization of civil rights?

★ **Affirmative Action**

What is the basis for affirmative action? What forms does it take?

How does affirmative action contribute to the polarization of the politics of civil rights?

How does the debate about affirmative action reflect the debate over American political values?

STUDENTS AND POLITICS

In 1960, four black students from North Carolina A&T made history: the four freshmen sat down at Woolworth's whites-only lunch counter in Greensboro, North Carolina, challenging the policies of segregation that kept blacks and whites in separate public and private accommodations across the South. Day after day the students sat at the counter, ignoring the taunts of onlookers, determined to break the system of segregation. Their actions and those of many other students, clergy members, and ordinary citizens finally did abolish such practices as separate white and black park benches, water fountains, and waiting rooms; the end of segregation meant opening access to public and private institutions on equal terms to all. But the victories of the civil rights movement did not come cheaply: many marchers, freedom riders, and sit-in participants were beaten; some were murdered.

Today, the Greensboro lunch counter is a part of history, on display at the Smithsonian Institution in Washington, D.C. Many goals of the civil rights movement that aroused such controversy in 1960 are now widely accepted as the proper expression of the American commitment to equal rights. But the question of what is meant by "equal rights" is hardly settled. While most Americans reject the idea that government should create equal outcomes for its citizens, they do widely endorse government action to prohibit public and private discrimination and they support the idea of equality of opportunity. However, even this concept is elusive. When past denial of rights creates unequal starting points for some groups, should government take additional steps to ensure equal opportunity? What kinds of groups should be specially protected against discrimination? Should the disabled receive special protection? Should gays and lesbians? Finally, what kinds of steps are acceptable to remedy discrimination, and who should bear the costs? These questions are at the heart of contemporary debates over **civil rights.**

civil rights
legal or moral claims that citizens are entitled to make upon government

Consider the role of race in university admissions. During the 1970s, in an effort to boost minority enrollment, many universities began to consider an applicant's racial background in their admissions decisions. The University of California (U.C.) system was at the forefront of this process. In 1995, however, the regents of the U.C. system voted to abandon race-based admissions practices. Governor Pete Wilson of California argued that affirmative action trampled on individual rights by admitting unqualified students and denying admission to qualified students. Supporters contended that taking race into account in admissions decisions does not mean accepting unqualified students. Instead, they argued, it means expanding acceptance criteria to include other considerations in addition to grades and test scores. In any event, they argued, merit (defined as test scores) has never been the sole criterion for admission at many universities. Private universities, for example, have long admitted substantial numbers of "legacies"—children of alumni who donate money to the institution—with little attention to grades and test scores. The president of the University of California defended affirmative action in broader public terms: "We are a public institution in the most demographically diverse state in the union. Our affirmative action and other diversity programs more than any other single factor have helped us prepare California for its future. . . ."[1]

What is the proper government action here? How can broad public goals be weighed against individual rights? Is there an individual right to admission to a public university based on test scores and grades? Are twenty-five years of affirmative action sufficient to remedy past inequalities based on race? Why should individuals today be required to pay a price for past discrimination?

In the United States, the history of slavery and legalized racial discrimination against African Americans coexists uneasily with a strong tradition of individual liberty. Indeed, for much of our history Americans have struggled to reconcile such exclusionary racial practices with our notions of individual rights. With the adoption of the Fourteenth Amendment in 1868, civil rights became part of the Constitution, guaranteed to each citizen through "equal protection of the laws." These words launched a century of political movements and legal efforts to press for racial equality. The African American quest for civil rights in turn inspired many other groups, including members of other racial and ethnic groups, women, the disabled, and gays and lesbians, to seek new laws and constitutional guarantees of their civil rights.

- ***First we review the legal developments and political movements that have expanded the scope of civil rights since the Fourteenth Amendment was adopted in 1868.*** In this section, we look at the establishment of legal segregation in the South and the civil rights movement that overthrew it.
- ***Second we trace the broad impact that civil rights legislation has had on American life.*** The Civil Rights Act of 1964 was especially critical in guaranteeing the "equal protection of the laws" set forth in the Fourteenth Amendment almost one hundred years earlier.
- ***We then explore how other groups, including women, Native Americans, Latinos, the disabled, and gays and lesbians, formed movements to win active protection of their rights as well.*** This universalization of civil rights has become the new frontier of the civil rights struggle.
- ***Next we turn to the development of affirmative action and the controversies surrounding it.*** The debate over affirmative action has intensified in recent years, revealing the ways in which Americans differ over the meaning of equality.
- ***Finally, we review the role that citizens play in determining the meaning of civil rights.*** As we see, students have often been in the forefront of the civil rights debate.

Civil Rights

- What is the legal basis for civil rights?
- How has the equal protection clause historically been enforced?
- What is the critical Supreme Court ruling in the battle for equal protection?
- How has the equal protection clause historically been enforced?
- How has Congress tried to make equal protection a reality?
- In what areas did the civil rights acts seek to provide equal access and protection?

Congress passed the Fourteenth Amendment and the states ratified it in the aftermath of the Civil War. Together with the Thirteenth Amendment, which abolished slavery, and the Fifteenth Amendment, which guaranteed voting rights for black men, it seemed to provide a guarantee of civil rights for the newly freed black slaves. But the general language of the Fourteenth Amendment meant that its support for civil rights could be far-reaching. The very simplicity of the **"equal protection clause"** of the Fourteenth Amendment left it open to interpretation:

equal protection clause
provision of the Fourteenth Amendment guaranteeing citizens "the equal protection of the laws." This clause has served as the basis for the civil rights of African Americans, women, and other groups

> No State shall make or enforce any law which shall . . . deny to any person within its jurisdiction the equal protection of the laws.

But in the very first Fourteenth Amendment case to come before the Supreme Court, the majority gave it a distinct meaning:

> . . . it is not difficult to give meaning to this clause ["the equal protection of the laws"]. The existence of laws in the States . . . which discriminated with gross injustice and hardship against [Negroes] as a class, was the evil to be remedied by this clause, and by it such laws are forbidden.[2]

Beyond that, contemporaries of the Fourteenth Amendment understood well that private persons offering conveyances, accommodations, or places of amusement to the public incurred certain public obligations to offer them to one and all—in other words, these are *public* accommodations, such that arbitrary discrimination in their use would amount to denial of equal protection of the laws—unless a government took action to overcome the discrimination.[3] This puts governments under obligation to take positive actions to extend to each citizen the opportunities and resources necessary to their proper enjoyment of freedom. A skeptic once observed that "the law, in its majestic equality, forbids the rich as well as the poor to sleep under bridges, to beg in the streets, and to steal bread."[4] The purpose of civil rights principles and laws is to use government in such a way as to give equality a more substantive meaning than that.

Discrimination refers to the use of any unreasonable and unjust criterion of exclusion. Of course, all laws discriminate, including some people while excluding others; but some forms of discrimination are considered unreasonable. For example, it is considered reasonable to use age as a criterion for legal

discrimination
use of any unreasonable and unjust criterion of exclusion

drinking, excluding all persons younger than twenty-one. But is age a reasonable distinction when seventy (or sixty-five or sixty) is selected as the age for compulsory retirement? In the mid-1970s, Congress answered this question by making old age a new civil right; compulsory retirement at seventy is now an unlawful, unreasonable, discriminatory use of age.

PLESSY V. FERGUSON: "SEPARATE BUT EQUAL"

Following its initial decisions making "equal protection" a civil right, the Supreme Court turned conservative, no more ready to enforce the civil rights aspects of the Fourteenth Amendment than it was to enforce the civil liberties provisions. The Court declared the Civil Rights Act of 1875 unconstitutional on the grounds that the act sought to protect blacks against discrimination by *private* businesses, while the Fourteenth Amendment, according to the Court's interpretation, was intended to protect individuals from discrimination only against actions by *public* officials of state and local governments.

In 1896, the Court went still further, in the infamous case of *Plessy v. Ferguson,* by upholding a Louisiana statute that *required* segregation of the races on trolleys and other public carriers (and by implication in all public facilities, including schools). Plessy, a man defined as "one-eighth black," had violated a Louisiana law that provided for "equal but separate accommodations" on trains and a $25 fine for any white passenger who sat in a car reserved for blacks or any black passenger who sat in a car reserved for whites. The Supreme Court held that the Fourteenth Amendment's "equal protection of the laws" was not violated by racial distinction as long as the facilities were equal, thus establishing the **"separate but equal" rule** that prevailed through the mid-twentieth century. People generally pretended that segregated accommodations were equal as long as some accommodation for blacks existed. The Court said that although "the object of the [Fourteenth] Amendment was undoubtedly to enforce the absolute equality of the two races before the law, . . . it could not have intended to abolish distinctions based on color, or to enforce social, as distinguished from political, equality, or a commingling of the two races upon terms unsatisfactory to either."[5] What the Court was saying in effect was that the use of race as a criterion of exclusion in public matters was not unreasonable.

"separate but equal" rule
doctrine that public accommodations could be segregated by race but still be equal

RACIAL DISCRIMINATION AFTER WORLD WAR II

The shame of discrimination against black military personnel during World War II, plus revelations of Nazi racial atrocities, moved President Harry S. Truman finally to bring the problem to the White House and national attention, with the appointment in 1946 of the President's Commission on Civil Rights. In 1948, the commission submitted its report, *To Secure These Rights,* which laid bare the extent of the problem of racial discrimination and its consequences. The report also revealed the success of experiments with racial integration in the armed forces during World War II to demonstrate to southern society that it had nothing to fear. But the committee recognized that the national government had no clear constitutional authority to pass and implement civil rights legislation. The committee proposed tying civil rights legislation to the commerce power, although it was clear that discrimination was not itself part of the flow of interstate commerce.[6] The committee even suggested using the treaty power as a source of constitutional authority for civil rights legislation.[7]

As for the Supreme Court, it had begun to change its position on racial discrimination before World War II by being stricter about the criterion of equal facilities in the "separate but equal" rule. In 1938, for example, the Court rejected Missouri's policy of paying the tuition of qualified blacks to out-of-state law schools rather than admitting them to the University of Missouri Law School.[8]

After the war, modest progress resumed. In 1950, the Court rejected Texas's claim that its new "law school for Negroes" afforded education equal to that of the all-white University of Texas Law School. Without confronting the "separate but equal" principle itself, the Court's decision anticipated its future civil rights rulings by opening the question of whether *any* segregated facility could be truly equal.[9]

But the Supreme Court, in ordering the admission of blacks to all-white state law schools, did not directly confront the "separate but equal" rule because the Court needed only to recognize the absence of any *equal* law school for blacks. The same was true in 1944, when the Supreme Court struck down the southern practice of "white primaries," which legally excluded blacks from participation in the nominating process. Here the Court simply recognized that primaries could no longer be regarded as the private affairs of the parties but were an integral aspect of the electoral process. This made parties "an agency of the State," and therefore any practice of discrimination against blacks was "state action within the meaning of the Fifteenth Amendment."[10] The most important pre-1954 decision was probably *Shelley v. Kraemer,* in

Separate and *equal?* This 1941 photograph of a school for black students in rural Georgia shows the unequal conditions that African Americans faced in schools and other public accommodations.

Thurgood Marshall (at right), as head of the NAACP's legal staff, led the fight against segregation in cases like that of Autherine Lucy (center), who was denied admission to the University of Alabama because of her race. The NAACP sued to force the university to admit black students. At left is Roy Wilkins, the executive secretary of the NAACP.

which the Court ruled against the widespread practice of "restrictive covenants," whereby the seller of a home added a clause to the sales contract requiring the buyer to agree not to sell the home later to any non-Caucasian, non-Christian, etc. The Court ruled that although private persons could sign such restrictive covenants, they could not be judicially enforced since the Fourteenth Amendment prohibits any organ of the state, including the courts, from denying equal protection of its laws.[11]

Although none of those pre-1954 cases confronted "separate but equal" and the principle of racial discrimination as such, they were extremely significant to black leaders in the 1940s and gave them encouragement enough to believe that there was at last an opportunity and enough legal precedent to change the constitutional framework itself. Much of this legal work was done by the Legal Defense and Educational Fund of the National Association for the Advancement of Colored People (NAACP). Formed in 1909 to fight discrimination against black people, the NAACP was the most important civil rights organization during the first half of the twentieth century. It set up its Legal Defense Fund to support an ongoing challenge to the legal edifice of segregation. Until the late 1940s, lawyers working for the Legal Defense Fund had concentrated on winning small victories within that framework. Then, in 1948, the Legal Defense Fund upgraded its approach by simultaneously filing suits in different federal districts and through each level of schooling from unequal provision of kindergarten for blacks to unequal sports and science facilities in all-black high schools. After nearly two years of these mostly successful equalization suits, the lawyers decided the time was ripe to confront the "separate but equal" rule head-on, but they felt they needed some heavier artillery to lead the attack. Their choice to lead this attack was African American lawyer Thurgood Marshall, who had been fighting, and often winning, equalization suits since the early 1930s. Marshall was pessimistic about the readiness of the Supreme Court for a full confrontation with segregation itself and the constitutional principle sustaining it. But the unwillingness of Congress after the 1948 election to consider fair employment legislation seems to have convinced Marshall that the courts were the only hope.

The Supreme Court must have come to the same conclusion because, during the four years following 1948, there emerged a clear impression that the Court was willing to take more civil rights cases on appeal. Yet, this was no guarantee that the Court would reverse *on principle* the separate but equal precedent of *Plessy v. Ferguson*. All through 1951 and 1952, as cases were winding slowly through the lower-court litigation maze, intense discussions and disagreements arose among NAACP lawyers as to whether a full-scale assault on *Plessy* was good strategy or whether it might not be better to continue with specific cases alleging unequal treatment and demanding relief with a Court-imposed policy of equalization.[12] But for some lawyers like Marshall, these kinds of victories could amount to a defeat. South Carolina, for example, under the leadership of Governor James F. Byrnes, a former Supreme Court justice, had undertaken a strategy of equalization of school services on a large scale in order to satisfy the *Plessy* rule and to head off or render moot litigation against the principle of separate but equal.

A nine-year-old Linda Brown in 1952.

In the fall of 1952, the Court had on its docket cases from Kansas, South Carolina, Virginia, Delaware, and the District of Columbia challenging the constitutionality of school segregation. Of these, the case filed in Kansas became the chosen one. It seemed to be ahead of the pack in its district court, and it had the special advantage of being located in a state outside the Deep South.[13]

Oliver Brown, the father of three girls, lived "across the tracks" in a low-income, racially mixed Topeka neighborhood. Every school-day morning, Linda Brown took the school bus to the Monroe School for black children about a mile away. In September 1950, Oliver Brown took Linda to the all-white Sumner School, which was closer to home, to enter her into the third grade in defiance of state law and local segregation rules. When they were refused, Brown took his case to the NAACP, and soon thereafter ***Brown v. Board of Education*** was born. In mid-1953, the Court announced that the several cases on their way up would be reargued within a set of questions having to do with the intent of the Fourteenth Amendment. Almost exactly a year later, the Court responded to those questions in one of the most important decisions in its history.

Brown v. Board of Education
the 1954 Supreme Court decision that struck down the "separate but equal" doctrine as fundamentally unequal. This case eliminated state power to use race as a criterion of discrimination in law and provided the national government with the power to intervene by exercising strict regulatory policies against discriminatory actions

In deciding the *Brown* case, the Court, to the surprise of many, basically rejected as inconclusive all the learned arguments about the intent and the history of the Fourteenth Amendment and committed itself to considering only the consequences of segregation:

> Does segregation of children in public schools solely on the basis of race, even though the physical facilities and other "tangible" factors may be equal, deprive the children of the minority group of equal educational opportunities? We believe that it does. . . . We conclude that in the field of public education the doctrine of "separate but equal" has no place. Separate educational facilities are inherently unequal.[14]

The *Brown* decision altered the constitutional framework in two fundamental respects. First, after *Brown,* the states no longer had the power to use race as a criterion of discrimination in law. Second, the national government from then on had the power (and eventually the obligation) to intervene with strict regulatory policies against the discriminatory actions of state or local governments, school boards, employers, and many others in the private sector.

CIVIL RIGHTS AFTER *BROWN V. BOARD OF EDUCATION*

Brown v. Board of Education withdrew all constitutional authority to use race as a criterion of exclusion, and it signaled more clearly the Court's determination to use the **strict scrutiny** test in cases related to racial discrimination. This meant that the burden of proof would fall on the government—not on the challengers—to show that the law in question *was* constitutional.[15] Although the use of strict scrutiny in cases relating to racial discrimination would give an advantage to those attacking racial discrimination, the historic decision in *Brown v. Board of Education* was merely a small opening move. First, most states refused to cooperate until sued, and many ingenious schemes were employed to delay obedience (such as paying the tuition for white students to attend newly created "private" academies). Second, even as southern school boards began to cooperate by eliminating their legally enforced (**de jure**) school segregation, there remained extensive actual (**de facto**) school segregation in the North as well as in the South, as a consequence of racially segregated

strict scrutiny
test, used by the Supreme Court in racial discrimination cases and other cases involving civil liberties and civil rights, which places the burden of proof on the government rather than on the challengers to show that the law in question is constitutional

de jure
literally, "by law"; legally enforced practices, such as school segregation in the South before the 1960s

de facto
literally, "by fact"; practices that occur even when there is no legal enforcement, such as school segregation in much of the United States today

housing that could not be reached by the 1954–55 *Brown* principles. Third, discrimination in employment, public accommodations, juries, voting, and other areas of social and economic activity were not directly touched by *Brown*.

School Desegregation, Phase One Although the District of Columbia and some of the school districts in the border states began to respond almost immediately to court-ordered desegregation, the states of the Deep South responded with a carefully planned delaying tactic commonly called "massive resistance" by the more demagogic southern leaders and "nullification" and "interposition" by the centrists. Either way, southern politicians stood shoulder-to-shoulder to declare that the Supreme Court's decisions and orders were without effect. The legislatures in these states enacted statutes ordering school districts to maintain segregated schools and state superintendents to terminate state funding wherever there was racial mixing in the classroom. Some southern states violated their own long traditions of local school autonomy by centralizing public school authority under the governor or the state board of education and by giving states the power to close the schools and to provide alternative private schooling wherever local school boards might be tending to obey the Supreme Court.

Most of these plans of "massive resistance" were tested in the federal courts and were struck down as unconstitutional.[16] But southern resistance was not confined to legislation. For example, in Arkansas in 1957, Governor Orval Faubus mobilized the Arkansas National Guard to intercede against enforcement of a federal court order to integrate Central High School of Little Rock, and President Eisenhower was forced to deploy U.S. troops and literally place the city under martial law. The Supreme Court considered the Little Rock confrontation so historically important that the opinion it rendered in that case was not only agreed to unanimously but was, unprecedentedly, signed personally by each and every one of the justices.[17] The end of massive

Resistance to school desegregation in the South during the 1950s was dramatized by events at Little Rock Central High School in 1957, when an angry mob of white students prevented black students from entering the school. As a result, the federal government sent troops to protect the black students and to uphold the desegregation plan.

PEACEFUL CIVIL RIGHTS DEMONSTRATIONS, 1954–68 **Table 6.1**

Year	Total	For Public Accommodations	For Voting
1954	0	0	0
1955	0	0	0
1956	18	6	0
1957	44	9	0
1958	19	8	0
1959	7	11	0
1960	173	127	0
1961	198	122	0
1962	77	44	0
1963	272	140	1
1964	271	93	12
1965	387	21	128
1966	171	15	32
1967	93	3	3
1968	97	2	0

NOTE: This table is drawn from a search of the *New York Times Index* for all references to civil rights demonstrations during the years the table covers. The table should be taken simply as indicative, for the data—news stories in a single paper—are very crude. The classification of the incident as peaceful or violent and the subject area of the demonstration are inferred from the entry in the *Index,* usually the headline from the story. The two subcategories reported here—public accommodations and voting—do not sum to the total because demonstrations dealing with a variety of other issues (e.g., education, employment, police brutality) are included in the total.
SOURCE: Jonathan D. Casper, *The Politics of Civil Liberties* (New York: Harper & Row, 1972), p. 90.

resistance, however, became simply the beginning of still another southern strategy, "pupil placement" laws, which authorized school districts to place each pupil in a school according to a whole variety of academic, personal, and psychological considerations, never mentioning race at all. This put the burden of transferring to an all-white school on the nonwhite children and their parents, making it almost impossible for a single court order to cover a whole district, let alone a whole state. This delayed desegregation a while longer.[18]

Social Protest and Congressional Action Ten years after *Brown,* fewer than 1 percent of black school-age children in the Deep South were attending schools with whites.[19] A decade of frustration made it fairly obvious to all observers that adjudication alone would not succeed. The goal of "equal protection" required positive, or affirmative, action by Congress and by administrative agencies. And given massive southern resistance and a generally negative national public opinion toward racial integration, progress would not be made through courts, Congress, or federal agencies without intense, well-organized support. Table 6.1 shows the increase in civil rights demonstrations for voting rights and public accommodations during the fourteen years following *Brown.* It shows that organized civil rights demonstrations began to mount slowly but surely after *Brown v. Board of Education.* By the 1960s, the

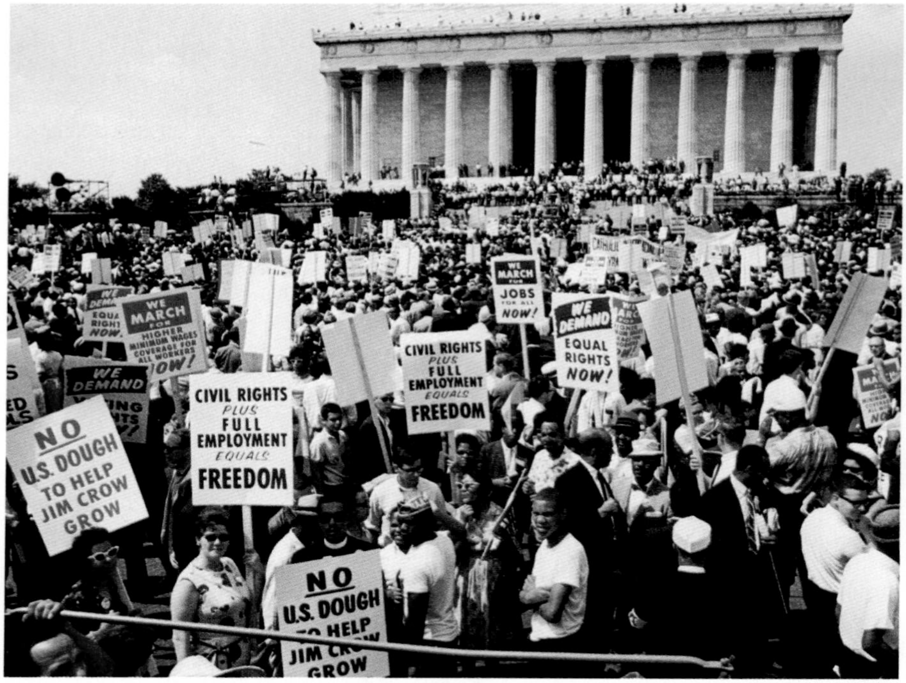

Hundreds of thousands of demonstrators gathered in the March on Washington in March 1963 to demand civil rights for African Americans.

many organizations that made up the civil rights movement had accumulated experience and built networks capable of launching massive direct-action campaigns against southern segregationists. The Southern Christian Leadership Conference, the Student Nonviolent Coordinating Committee, and many other organizations had built a movement that stretched across the South. The movement used the media to attract nationwide attention and support. In the massive March on Washington in 1963, the Reverend Martin Luther King, Jr., staked out the movement's moral claims in his famous "I Have a Dream" speech. The image of protesters being beaten, attacked by police dogs, and set upon with fire hoses did much to win broad sympathy for the cause of black civil rights and to discredit state and local governments in the South. In this way, the movement created intense pressure for a reluctant federal government to take more assertive steps to defend black civil rights.

The first modern effort to legislate in the field of civil rights was made in 1957, but the law contained only a federal guarantee of voting rights, without any powers of enforcement, although it did create the Civil Rights Commission to study abuses. Much more important legislation for civil rights followed, especially the Civil Rights Act of 1964. It is important to observe here the mutual dependence of the courts and legislatures—not only do the legislatures need constitutional authority to act, but the courts need legislative and political assistance, through the power of the purse and the power to organize administrative agencies to implement court orders, and through the focusing of political support. Consequently, even as the U.S. Congress finally moved into the field of school desegregation (and other areas of "equal protection"), the courts continued to exercise their powers, not only by placing court orders against recalcitrant school districts, but also by extending and reinterpreting aspects of the "equal protection" clause to support legislative and administrative actions (see Figure 6.1).

CAUSE AND EFFECT IN THE CIVIL RIGHTS MOVEMENT

Figure 6.1

Judicial and Legal Action	Political Action
1954 *Brown v. Board of Education*	
1955 *Brown* II—Implementation of *Brown* I	**1955** Montgomery, Alabama, bus boycott
1956 Federal courts order school integration, especially one ordering Autherine Lucy admitted to University of Alabama, with Governor Wallace officially protesting	
1957 Civil Rights Act creating Civil Rights Commission; President Eisenhower sends paratroops to Little Rock, Arkansas, to enforce integration of Central High School	**1957** Southern Christian Leadership Conference (SCLC) formed, with Martin Luther King, Jr., as president
1960 First substantive Civil Rights Act, primarily voting rights	**1960** Student Nonviolent Coordinating Committee formed to organize protests, sit-ins, freedom rides
1961 Interstate Commerce Commission orders desegregation on all buses and trains, and in terminals	
1961 JFK favors executive action over civil rights legislation	
1963 JFK shifts, supports strong civil rights law; assassination; LBJ asserts strong support for civil rights	**1963** Nonviolent demonstrations in Birmingham, Alabama, lead to King's arrest and his "Letter from the Birmingham Jail"
	1963 March on Washington
1964 Congress passes historic Civil Rights Act covering voting, employment, public accommodations, education	
1965 Voting Rights Act	**1965** King announces drive to register 3 million blacks in the South
1966 War on Poverty in full swing	Late 1960s Movement dissipates: part toward litigation, part toward Community Action Programs, part toward war protest, part toward more militant "Black Power" actions

Political action and government action spurred each other to produce dramatic changes in American civil rights policies.

THE CIVIL RIGHTS ACTS

The right to equal protection of the laws could be established and, to a certain extent, implemented by the courts. But after a decade of very frustrating efforts, the courts and Congress ultimately came to the conclusion that the federal courts alone were not adequate to the task of changing the social rules, and that legislation and administrative action would be needed.

Three civil rights acts were passed during the first decade after the 1954 Supreme Court decision in *Brown v. Board of Education.* But these acts were of only marginal importance. The first two, in 1957 and 1960, established that the Fourteenth Amendment of the Constitution, adopted almost a century earlier, could no longer be disregarded, particularly with regard to voting. The third, the Equal Pay Act of 1963, was more important, but it was concerned with women, did not touch the question of racial discrimination, and had no enforcement mechanisms.

By far the most important piece of legislation passed by Congress concerning equal opportunity was the Civil Rights Act of 1964. It not only put some teeth in the voting rights provisions of the 1957 and 1960 acts but also went far beyond voting to attack discrimination in public accommodations, segregation in the schools, and at long last, the discriminatory conduct of employers in hiring, promoting, and laying off their employees. Discrimination against women was also included, extending the important 1963 provisions. The 1964 act seemed bold at the time, but it was enacted ten years after the Supreme Court had declared racial discrimination "inherently unequal" under the Fifth and Fourteenth Amendments. And it was enacted long after blacks had demonstrated that discrimination was no longer acceptable. The choice in 1964 was not between congressional action or inaction but between legal action and expanded violence.

The Civil Rights Act of 1964 helped stop some of the most overt discrimination in public accommodations.

Public Accommodations After the passage of the 1964 Civil Rights Act, public accommodations quickly removed some of the most visible forms of racial discrimination. Signs defining "colored" and "white" rest rooms, water fountains, waiting rooms, and seating arrangements were removed and a host of other practices that relegated black people to separate and inferior arrangements were ended. In addition, the federal government filed more than 400 antidiscrimination suits in federal courts against hotels, restaurants, taverns, gas stations, and other "public accommodations."

Many aspects of legalized racial segregation—such as separate Bibles in the courtroom—seem like ancient history today. But the issue of racial discrimination in public settings is by no means over. In 1993, six African American Secret Service agents filed charges against the Denny's restaurant chain for failing to serve them; white Secret Service agents at a nearby table had received prompt service. Similar charges citing discriminatory service at Denny's restaurants surfaced across the country. Faced with evidence of a pattern of systematic discrimination and numerous lawsuits, Denny's paid $45 million in damages to plaintiffs in Maryland and California in what is said to be the largest settlement ever in a public accommodation case.[20] The Denny's case shows how effective the Civil Rights Act of 1964 can be in challenging racial discrimination. In addition to the settlement, the chain vowed to expand employment and management opportunities for minorities in Denny's restaurants. Other forms of racial discrimination in public accommodations are harder to challenge, however. For example, there is considerable evidence that taxicabs often refuse to pick up black passengers.[21] Such practices may be common, but they are difficult to prove and remedy through the law.

In 1993, after the Denny's restaurant chain was charged with racial discrimination, Denny's restaurants were boycotted by protesters such as these from the Labor Black Struggle League.

School Desegregation, Phase Two The 1964 Civil Rights Act also declared discrimination by private employers and state governments (school boards, etc.) illegal, then went further to provide for administrative agencies to help the courts implement these laws. Title IV of the act, for example, authorized the executive branch, through the Justice Department, to implement federal court orders to desegregate schools, and to do so without having to wait for individual parents to bring complaints. Title VI of the act vastly strengthened the role of the executive branch and the credibility of court orders by providing that federal grants-in-aid to state and local governments for education must be withheld from any school system practicing racial segregation. Title VI became the most effective weapon for desegregating schools outside the South, because the situation in northern communities was more subtle and difficult to reach. In the South, the problem was segregation by law coupled with overt resistance to the national government's efforts to change the situation. In contrast, outside the South, segregated facilities were the outcome of hundreds of thousands of housing choices made by individuals and families. Once racial residential patterns emerged, racial homogeneity, property values, and neighborhood schools and churches were defended by realtors, neighborhood organizations, and the like. Thus, in order to eliminate discrimination nationwide, the 1964 Civil Rights Act (1) gave the president through the Office for Civil Rights of the Justice Department the power to withhold federal education grants,[22] and (2) gave the attorney general of the United States the power to initiate suits (rather than having to await complaints) wherever there was a "pattern or practice" of discrimination.[23]

In the decade following the 1964 Civil Rights Act, the Justice Department brought legal action against more than five hundred school districts. During the same period, administrative agencies filed actions against six hundred school districts, threatening to suspend federal aid to education unless real desegregation steps were taken.

Busing One step taken toward desegregation was busing children from poor urban school districts to wealthier suburban ones. In 1971, the Supreme Court held that state-imposed desegregation could be brought about by busing children across school districts, even where relatively long distances were involved:

> If school authorities fail in their affirmative obligations judicial authority may be invoked. Once a right and a violation have been shown, the scope of a district court's equitable powers to remedy past wrongs is broad. . . . Bus transportation [is] a normal and accepted tool of educational policy.[24]

But the decision went beyond that, adding that under certain limited circumstances even racial quotas could be used as the "starting point in shaping a remedy to correct past constitutional violations," and that pairing or grouping of schools and reorganizing school attendance zones would also be acceptable.

Three years later, however, this principle was severely restricted when the Supreme Court determined that only cities found guilty of deliberate and de jure racial segregation would have to desegregate their schools.[25] This ruling had the effect of exempting most northern states and cities from busing because school segregation in northern cities is generally de facto segregation that follows from segregated housing and from thousands of acts of private discrimination against blacks and other minorities.

Boston provides the best illustration of the agonizing problem of making further progress in civil rights in the schools under the constitutional framework established by these decisions. Boston school authorities were found guilty of deliberately building school facilities and drawing school districts "to

Court-ordered busing divided Boston's black and white communities. In 1976, a mob of protesters outside the Boston federal courthouse sought to impale this innocent black bystander, a lawyer on his way to his office. This Pulitzer Prize–winning photograph shows the tension and conflict resulting from the struggle for equal rights for African Americans.

increase racial segregation." After vain efforts by Boston school authorities to draw up an acceptable plan to remedy the segregation, federal judge W. Arthur Garrity ordered an elaborate desegregation plan of his own, involving busing between the all-black neighborhood of Roxbury and the nearby white, working-class community of South Boston. Opponents of this plan were organized and eventually took the case to the Supreme Court, where *certiorari* (the Court's device for accepting appeals; see Chapter 16) was denied; this had the effect of approving Judge Garrity's order. The city's schools were so segregated and uncooperative that even the conservative administration of President Richard Nixon had already initiated a punitive cutoff of funds. But many liberals also criticized Judge Garrity's plan as being badly conceived, because it involved two neighboring communities with a history of tension and mutual resentment. The plan worked well at the elementary school level but proved so explosive at the high school level that it generated a continuing crisis for the city of Boston and for the whole nation over court-ordered, federally directed desegregation in the North.[26]

Additional progress in the desegregation of schools is likely to be extremely slow unless the Supreme Court decides to permit federal action against de facto segregation and against the varieties of private schools and academies that have sprung up for the purpose of avoiding integration. The prospects for further school integration diminished with a Supreme Court decision handed down on January 15, 1991. The opinion, written for the Court by Chief Justice William Rehnquist, held that lower federal courts could end supervision of local school boards if those boards could show compliance "in good faith" with court orders to desegregate and could show that "vestiges of past discrimination" had been eliminated "to the extent practicable."[27] It is not necessarily easy for a school board to prove that the new standard has been met, but this was the first time since *Brown* and the 1964 Civil Rights Act that the Court had opened the door at all to retreat.

That door of retreat was opened further by a 1995 decision in which the Court ruled that the remedies being applied in Kansas City, Missouri, were improper.[28] In accordance with a lower court ruling, the state was pouring additional funding into salaries and remedial programs for Kansas City schools, which had a history of segregation. The aim of the spending was to improve student performance and to attract white students from the suburbs into the city schools. The Supreme Court declared the interdistrict goal improper and reiterated its earlier ruling that states can free themselves of court orders by showing a good faith effort. This decision indicated the Court's new willingness to end desegregation plans even when predominantly minority schools continue to lag significantly behind white suburban schools.

Outlawing Discrimination in Employment Despite the agonizingly slow progress of school desegregation, there was some progress made in other areas of civil rights during the 1960s and 1970s. Voting rights were established and fairly quickly began to revolutionize southern politics. Service on juries was no longer denied to minorities. But progress in the right to participate in politics and government dramatized the relative lack of progress in the economic domain, and it was in this area that battles over civil rights were increasingly fought.

The federal courts and the Justice Department entered this area through Title VII of the Civil Rights Act of 1964, which outlawed job discrimination by all private and public employers, including governmental agencies (such as fire and police departments), that employed more than fifteen workers. We have already seen (in Chapter 4) that the Supreme Court gave "interstate commerce" such a broad definition that Congress had the constitutional authority to cover discrimination by virtually any local employers.[29] Title VII makes it unlawful to discriminate in employment on the basis of color, religion, sex, or national origin, as well as race.

Title VII delegated some of the powers to enforce fair employment practices to the Justice Department's Civil Rights Division and others to a new agency created in the 1964 act, the Equal Employment Opportunity Commission (EEOC). By executive order, these agencies had the power of the national government to revoke public contracts for goods and services and to refuse to engage in contracts for goods and services with any private company that could not guarantee that its rules for hiring, promotion, and firing were nondiscriminatory. Executive orders in 1965, 1967, and 1969 by Presidents Johnson and Nixon extended and reaffirmed nondiscrimination practices in employment and promotion in the federal government service. And in 1972, President Nixon and a Democratic Congress cooperated to strengthen the EEOC by giving it authority to initiate suits rather than wait for grievances.

But one problem with Title VII was that the complaining party had to show that deliberate discrimination was the cause of the failure to get a job or a training opportunity. Rarely does an employer explicitly admit discrimination on the basis of race, sex, or any other illegal reason. Recognizing the rarity of such an admission, the courts have allowed aggrieved parties (the plaintiffs) to make their case if they can show that an employer's hiring practices had the *effect* of exclusion. A leading case in 1971 involved a "class action" by several black employees in North Carolina attempting to show with statistical evidence that blacks had been relegated to only one department in the Duke Power Company, which involved the least desirable, manual-labor jobs, and that they had been kept out of contention for the better jobs because the employer had added attainment of a high school education and the passing of specially prepared aptitude tests as qualifications for higher jobs. The Supreme Court held that although the statistical evidence did not prove intentional discrimination, and although the requirements were race-neutral in appearance, their effects were sufficient to shift the burden of justification to the employer to show that the requirements were a "business necessity" that bore "a demonstrable relationship to successful performance."[30] The ruling in this case was subsequently applied to other hiring, promotion, and training programs.[31]

A student volunteer oversees an older woman registering to vote in Mississippi following passage of the Voting Rights Act in 1965. The percentage of African Americans registered to vote in Mississippi increased from about 7 percent in 1965 to more than 62 percent in 1972.

Voting Rights Although 1964 was the *most* important year for civil rights legislation, it was not the only important year. In 1965, Congress significantly strengthened legislation protecting voting rights by barring literacy and other tests as a condition for voting in six southern states,[32] by setting criminal penalties for interference with efforts to vote, and by providing for the replacement of local registrars with federally appointed registrars in counties designated by the attorney general as significantly resistant to registering eligible blacks to vote. The right to vote was further strengthened with ratification in 1964 of the Twenty-fourth Amendment, which abolished the poll tax, and in 1975 with legislation permanently outlawing literacy tests in all fifty states and mandating bilingual ballots or oral assistance for Spanish, Chinese, Japanese, Koreans, Native Americans, and Eskimos.

REGISTRATION BY RACE AND STATE IN SOUTHERN STATES COVERED BY THE VOTING RIGHTS ACT

Table 6.2

	Before the Act*			After the Act* 1971–72		
	White	Black	Gap†	White	Black	Gap†
Alabama	69.2%	19.3%	49.9%	80.7%	57.1%	23.6%
Georgia	62.6	27.4	35.2	70.6	67.8	2.8
Louisiana	80.5	31.6	48.9	80.0	59.1	20.9
Mississippi	69.9	6.7	63.2	71.6	62.2	9.4
North Carolina	96.8	46.8	50.0	62.2	46.3	15.9
South Carolina	75.7	37.3	38.4	51.2	48.0	3.2
Virginia	61.1	38.3	22.8	61.2	54.0	7.2
TOTAL	73.4	29.3	44.1	67.8	56.6	11.2

*Available registration data as of March 1965 and 1971–72.
†The gap is the percentage point difference between white and black registration rates.
SOURCE: U.S. Commission on Civil Rights, *Political Participation* (1968), Appendix VII: Voter Education Project, Attachment to Press Release, October 3, 1972.

In the long run, the laws extending and protecting voting rights could prove to be the most effective of all the great civil rights legislation, because the progress in black political participation produced by these acts has altered the shape of American politics. In 1965, in the seven states of the Old Confederacy covered by the Voting Rights Act, 29.3 percent of the eligible black residents were registered to vote, compared to 73.4 percent of the white residents (see Table 6.2). Mississippi was the extreme case, with 6.7 percent black and 69.9 percent white registration. In 1967, a mere two years after implementation of the voting rights laws, 52.1 percent of the eligible blacks in the seven states were registered, comparing favorably to 79.5 percent of the eligible whites, a gap of 27.4 points. By 1972, the gap between black and white registration in the seven states was only 11.2 points, and in Mississippi the gap had been reduced to 9.4 points. At one time, white leaders in Mississippi attempted to dilute the influence of this growing black vote by **gerrymandering** districts to ensure that no blacks would be elected to Congress. But the black voters changed Mississippi before Mississippi could change them. In 1988, 11 percent of all elected officials in Mississippi were black. This was up one full percentage point from 1987 and closely approximates the size of the national black electorate, which at the time was just over 11 percent of the American voting-age population. Mississippi's blacks had made significant gains (as was true in other Deep South states) as elected state and local representatives, and Mississippi was one of only eight states in the country in which a black judge presided over the highest state court. (Four of the eight were Deep South states.)[33]

gerrymandering
apportionment of voters in districts in such a way as to give unfair advantage to one racial or ethnic group or political party

Housing The Civil Rights Act of 1964 did not address housing, but in 1968, Congress passed another civil rights act specifically to outlaw housing discrimination. Called the Fair Housing Act, the law prohibited discrimination in the sale or rental of most housing—eventually covering nearly all the nation's housing. Housing was among the most controversial of discrimination issues because of deeply entrenched patterns of residential segregation across the United States. Such segregation was not simply a product of individual choice. Local housing authorities deliberately segregated public housing, and federal guidelines had sanctioned discrimination in Federal Housing Administration mortgage lending, effectively preventing blacks from joining the exodus to the suburbs in the 1950s and 1960s. Nonetheless, Congress had been reluctant to tackle housing discrimination, fearing the tremendous controversy it could arouse. But, just as the housing legislation was being considered in April 1968, civil rights leader Martin Luther King, Jr., was assassinated; this tragedy brought the measure unexpected support in Congress.

Although it pronounced sweeping goals, the Fair Housing Act had little effect on housing segregation because its enforcement mechanisms were so weak. Individuals believing they had been discriminated against had to file suit themselves. The burden was on the individual to prove that housing discrimination had occurred, even though such discrimination is often subtle and difficult to document. Although local fair-housing groups emerged to assist individuals in their court claims, the procedures for proving discrimination proved a formidable barrier to effective change. These procedures were not altered until 1988, when Congress passed the Fair Housing Amendments Act. This new law put more teeth in the enforcement procedures and allowed the Department of Housing and Urban Development (HUD) to initiate legal action in cases of discrimination. With vigorous use, these provisions may prove more successful than past efforts at combating housing discrimination.[34]

Other avenues for challenging residential segregation also had mixed success. HUD tried briefly in the early 1970s to create racially "open communities" by withholding federal funds to suburbs that refused to accept subsidized housing. Confronted with charges of "forced integration" and bitter local protests, however, the administration quickly backed down. Efforts to prohibit discrimination in lending have been somewhat more promising. Several laws passed in the 1970s required banks to report information about their mortgage lending patterns, making it more difficult for them to engage in **redlining**, the practice of refusing to lend to entire neighborhoods. The 1977 Community Reinvestment Act required banks to lend in neighborhoods in which they do business. Through vigorous use of this act, many neighborhood organizations have reached agreements with banks that, as a result, have significantly increased investment in some poor neighborhoods.

redlining
a practice in which banks refuse to make loans to people living in certain geographic locations

The Universalization of Civil Rights

- What groups were spurred by the provision of the Civil Rights Act of 1964, outlawing discrimination in employment practices based on race, religion, and gender, to seek broader protection under the law?
- What is the politics of the universalization of civil rights?

Even before equal employment laws began to have a positive effect on the economic situation of blacks, something far more dramatic began happening—

the universalization of civil rights. The right not to be discriminated against was being successfully claimed by the other groups listed in Title VII of the 1964 Civil Rights Act—those defined by sex, religion, or national origin—and eventually by still other groups defined by age or sexual preference. This universalization of civil rights has become the new frontier of the civil rights struggle, and women have emerged with the greatest prominence in this new struggle. The effort to define and end gender discrimination in employment has led to the historic joining of women's rights to the civil rights cause.

As gender discrimination began to be seen as an important civil rights issue, other groups arose demanding recognition and active protection of their civil rights. Under Title VII, any group or individual can try, and in fact is encouraged to try, to convert goals and grievances into questions of rights and of the deprivation of those rights. A plaintiff must establish only that his or her membership in a group is an unreasonable basis for discrimination—i.e., that it cannot be proven to be a "job-related" or otherwise clearly reasonable and relevant decision. In America today, the list of individuals and groups claiming illegal discrimination is lengthy.

WOMEN AND GENDER DISCRIMINATION

Title VII provided a valuable tool for the growing women's movement in the 1960s and 1970s. In fact, in many ways the law fostered the growth of the women's movement. The first major campaign of the National Organization for Women (NOW) involved picketing the Equal Employment Opportunity Commission for its refusal to ban sex-segregated employment advertisements. NOW also sued *The New York Times* for continuing to publish such ads after the passage of Title VII. Another organization, the Women's Equity Action League (WEAL), pursued legal action on a wide range of sex discrimination issues, filing lawsuits against law schools and medical schools for discriminatory admission policies, for example.

Building on these victories and the growth of the women's movement, feminist activists sought an "Equal Rights Amendment" (ERA) to the Constitution. The proposed amendment was short: its substantive passage stated that

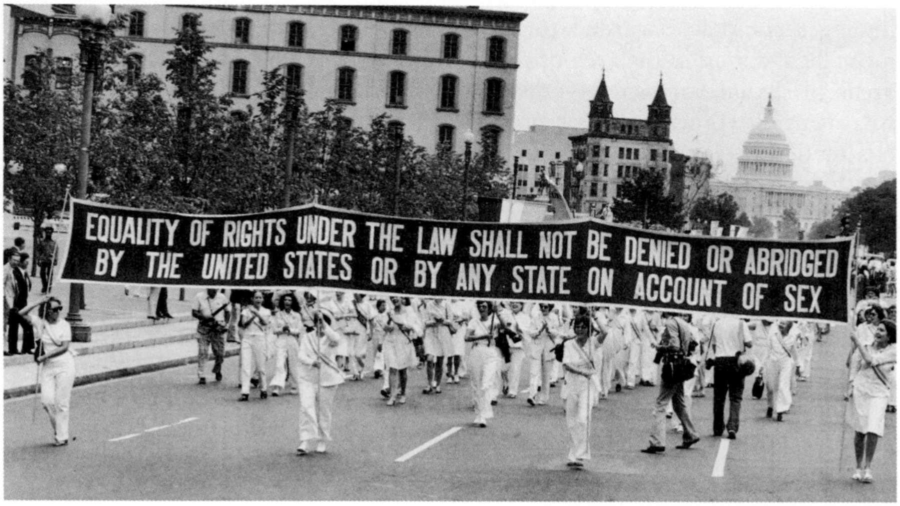

Even though the Equal Rights Amendment seemed a simple declaration of equal opportunity for women, opposition both inside and outside the women's movement prevented its passage.

Students and Politics

Connecticut College, like an increasing number of colleges in the country, allows its students to establish policy on many issues, including minor legal infractions, sexual harassment, and assault. Dan Thompkins has served on several committees to work with students and faculty in forging policies that are acceptable to all parties. "Lots of what we do is educational," he says. "Conducting forums, things like that—moving beyond the freshman seminars on sexual harassment and date rape into an ongoing dialogue." Thompkins has also served on the college's judiciary board, helping to judge alleged infractions, such as contraband in rooms and vandalism. His experience with his college's decision-making process has translated into an interest in public policy, particularly local politics and issues of civil rights. "I want to remain politically active after school," he says. "Maybe start a local interest group. If I think something needs to happen, and I can do it, why not?"

SOURCE: Dan Thompkins, interview with author, January 27, 1998.

"equality of rights under the law shall not be denied or abridged by the United States or by any State on account of sex." The amendment's supporters believed that such a sweeping guarantee of equal rights was a necessary tool for ending all discrimination against women and for making gender roles more equal. Opponents charged that it would be socially disruptive and would introduce changes—such as coed rest rooms—that most Americans did not want. The amendment easily passed Congress in 1972 and won quick approval in many state legislatures, but it fell three states short of the thirty-eight needed to ratify the amendment by the 1982 deadline for its ratification.[35]

Despite the failure of the ERA, gender discrimination expanded dramatically as an area of civil rights law. In the 1970s, the conservative Burger Court (under Chief Justice Warren Burger) helped to establish gender discrimination as a major and highly visible civil rights issue. Although the Burger Court refused to treat gender discrimination as the equivalent of racial discrimination,[36] it did make it easier for plaintiffs to file and win suits on the basis of gender discrimination by applying an "intermediate" level of review to these cases.[37] This **intermediate scrutiny** is midway between traditional rules of evidence, which put the burden of proof on the plaintiff, and the doctrine of strict scrutiny, which requires the defendant to show not only that a particular classification is reasonable but also that there is a need or compelling interest for it. Intermediate scrutiny shifts the burden of proof partially onto the defendant, rather than leaving it entirely on the plaintiff.

intermediate scrutiny
test, used by the Supreme Court in gender discrimination cases, which places the burden of proof partially on the government and partially on the challengers to show that the law in question is constitutional

One major step was taken in 1992, when the Court decided in *Franklin v. Gwinnett County Public Schools* that violations of Title IX of the 1972 Education Act could be remedied with monetary damages.[38] Title IX forbade gender discrimination in education, but it initially sparked little litigation because of its weak enforcement provisions. The Court's 1992 ruling that monetary damages could be awarded for gender discrimination opened the door for more legal action in the area of education. The greatest impact has been in the areas of sexual harassment—the subject of the *Franklin* case—and in equal treatment of women's athletic programs. The potential for monetary damages has made universities and public schools take the problem of sexual harassment more seriously. Colleges and universities have also started to pay more attention to women's athletic programs. In the two years after the *Franklin* case, complaints to the Education Department's Office for Civil Rights about unequal treatment of women's athletic programs nearly tripled. In several high-profile legal cases, some prominent universities have been ordered to create more women's sports programs; many other colleges and universities have begun to add more women's programs in order to avoid potential litigation.[39] In 1997, the Supreme Court refused to hear a petition by Brown University challenging a lower court ruling that the university establish strict sex equity in its athletic programs. The Court's decision meant that in colleges and

AMERICAN DEMOCRACY IN COMPARATIVE PERSPECTIVE

Political Rights and Enabling of Citizens within Democracies

In Chapter 5, we discussed Freedom House's civil rights ratings of countries; it also assigns a political rights score to each country based upon a specific checklist of features built mainly around free elections and the right to form political parties and organizations.

However, these criteria do not fully capture the broader meaning of rights. From a global perspective, the ability of citizens within a country to make a moral or legal claim on government requires more than political and institutional opportunities.

The United Nations' Development Program argues that rights in a global perspective should be understood within the context of human development: *the process of creating an enabling environment for citizens within a country, which permits the people to enjoy long, healthy, and creative lives.* How are people enabled? How are their broader human rights maximized and sustained? People are enabled through political participation and through the application of their talents, which both depend upon their well-being and the range of opportunities for active engagement in the politics and economy of their country.

The United Nations produces an annual assessment of the progress of human development. Their *Human Development Report* records for each country the degree of human development, the degree of gender development, and the degree of gender empowerment. The composite measure for human development (the Human Development Index, or HDI) combines scores on life expectancy within the country, adult literacy rates, educational enrollment among the population, and the per capita income for citizens within the country. The score ranges from 0 (the lowest degree of human development) to 1.000 (the highest degree). The Gender Development Index (GDI) is based on the same measures as the HDI, except that it separates each measure for men and women. The higher the score, the greater the degree of female development within the country. By comparing the GDI to the HDI, one can gauge the extent to which a country has been successful or unsuccessful in sustaining the development of its women relative to the whole population. The Gender Empowerment Measure (GEM) reflects the degree of gender inequality in key areas of political participation and decision making (for instance, the number of female legislators and heads of state, etc.). Again, the maximum score is 1.000, with 0 representing the lowest possible degree of female empowerment.

By comparing the GEM to the HDI and GDI, one can achieve yet another measure of the relative gap within a country between what is possible and what in fact may be achieved by women. In 1999, the average HDI was .680. This is lower than the development level for the thirty-one countries that comprise the most industrialized countries of the world, and lower than the level for Western European nations (.898) or the eighty-five "free" electoral democracies that were also characterized as having perfect or near-perfect political rights scores (.787). The gap between overall human development and gender development is noticeably wide among those thirty-two electoral democracies that were classified by Freedom House as only "partly free" and that had more numerous political rights deficiencies (GEM = .359, HDI = .622). Based on UN data, women within electoral democracies generally enjoy more development capabilities than men, as evidenced by a GDI score (.743) larger than the HDI score (.739), though gender equality has a way to go before it matches the more general capabilities measurers (GEM = .496). This trend is also shown among electoral democracies in Eastern Europe (Poland, Czech Republic, Romania, etc.) and among the former republics of the Soviet Union (the CIS—Commonwealth of Independent States—such as Ukraine). Generally, broad measures of human development, including gender empowerment and development, are shown to be higher among electoral democracies and among European and industrialized democracies (including Japan, Australia, Canada, and the United States) and lower as one moves from the highest forms of democracy and political rights. The values for HDI, GDI, and GEM for the United States are .927, .926, and .708, respectively. These scores ranked second (behind Canada), second (behind Canada), and eighth (behind Norway, Sweden, Denmark, Canada, Finland, and Iceland, in descending order), respectively, among all countries of the world.

SOURCE: Amartya Sen, *Development As Freedom,* Knopf, 1999.

College athletics programs have been affected by gender discrimination battles. In recent years, colleges and universities have added more women's sports programs to comply with government orders.

universities across the country, varsity athletic positions for men and women must now reflect their overall enrollment numbers.[40]

In 1996, the Supreme Court made another important decision about gender and education by putting an end to all-male schools supported by public funds. It ruled that the policy of the Virginia Military Institute not to admit women was unconstitutional.[41] Along with the Citadel, another all-male military college in South Carolina, VMI had never admitted women in its 157-year history. VMI argued that the unique educational experience it offered—including intense physical training and the harsh treatment of freshmen—would be destroyed if women students were admitted. The Court, however, ruled that the male-only policy denied "substantial equality" to women. Two days after the Court's ruling, the Citadel announced that it would accept women. VMI considered becoming a private institution in order to remain all-male, but in September 1996, the school board finally voted to admit women. The legal decisions may have removed formal barriers to entry, but the experience of the new female cadets at these schools has not been easy. The first female cadet at the Citadel, Shannon Faulkner, won admission in 1995 under a federal court order but quit after four days. Although four women were admitted to the Citadel after the Supreme Court decision, two of the four quit several months later. They charged harassment from male students, including attempts to set the female cadets on fire.[42]

Courts began to find sexual harassment a form of sex discrimination during the late 1970s. Although sexual harassment law applies to education, most of the law of sexual harassment has been developed by courts through interpretation of Title VII of the Civil Rights Act of 1964. In 1986, the Supreme Court recognized two forms of sexual harassment—the quid pro quo type, which involves sexual extortion, and the hostile environment type, which involves sexual intimidation.[43] Employers and many employees have worried that hostile-environment sexual harassment is too ambiguous. When can an employee bring charges? When is the employer liable? In 1986, the Court said that sexual harassment may be legally actionable even if the employee did not suffer tangible economic or job-related losses in relation to it. In 1993, the Court said that sexual harassment may be legally actionable even if the employee did not suffer tangible psychological costs as a result of it.[44] In two 1998 cases, the Court further strengthened the law when it said that whether or not sexual harassment results in economic harm to the employee, an employer is liable for the harassment if it was committed by someone with authority over the employee—by a supervisor, for example. But the Court also said that an employer may defend itself by showing that it had a sexual harassment prevention and grievance policy in effect.[45]

In 1993, Teresa Harris won a unanimous Supreme Court decision in her sexual harassment suit against her employer. The Court's decision made it easier for individuals to prove sexual harassment in the workplace.

The development of gender discrimination as an important part of the civil rights struggle has coincided with the rise of women's politics as a discrete movement in American politics. As with the struggle for racial equality, the relationship between changes in government policies and political action suggests that changes in government policies to a great degree produce political action. Today, the existence of a powerful women's movement derives in large measure from the enactment of Title VII of the Civil Rights Act of 1964 and from the Burger Court's vital steps in applying that law to protect women. The recognition of women's civil rights has become an issue that in many ways transcends the usual distinctions of American political debate. In the heavily partisan debate over the federal crime bill enacted in 1994, for instance, the section of the bill that enjoyed the widest support was the Violence Against Women Act, whose most important feature was that it defined gender-biased violent crimes as a matter of civil rights, and created a civil rights remedy for women who have been the victims of such crimes. But since the act was ruled unconstitutional by the Supreme Court in 2000, the struggle for women's rights will likely remain part of the political debate.

Students and Politics

In 1992, Amy Cohen sued Brown University over the proposed demotion of women's gymnastics, a team to which Cohen belonged, from an official school-funded sport to a partially funded school club. Also to be cut were women's volleyball, men's golf, and men's water polo. Cohen and her fellow plaintiffs charged the school with violation of Title IX of the Education Amendments of 1972, which states that "no person in the U.S. shall, on the basis of sex, be excluded from participation in, or denied the benefits of, or be subjected to discrimination under any educational program or activity receiving federal aid." The suit claimed that the university had not provided equal opportunities for women to compete in intercollegiate athletics. Though Brown defended its action, saying that 60 percent of those affected by its cuts were male, Federal District Court Judge Raymond J. Pettine agreed with the plaintiffs, forcing Brown to implement a plan of equal athletic opportunity between men and women. *Cohen v. Brown University* was a landmark case in requiring schools to provide opportunities to both female and male athletes.

LATINOS AND ASIAN AMERICANS

Although the Civil Rights Act of 1964 outlawed discrimination on the basis of national origin, limited English proficiency barred many Asian Americans and Latinos from full participation in American life. Two developments in the 1970s, however, established rights for language minorities. In 1974, the Supreme Court ruled in *Lau v. Nichols,* a suit filed on behalf of Chinese students in San Francisco, that school districts have to provide education for students whose English is limited.[46] It did not mandate bilingual education but it established a duty to provide instruction that the students could understand. The 1970 amendments to the Voting Rights Act permanently outlawed literacy tests in all fifty states and mandated bilingual ballots or oral assistance for those who speak Spanish, Chinese, Japanese, Korean, Native American languages, or Eskimo languages.

Asian Americans and Latinos have also been concerned about the impact of immigration laws on their civil rights. Many Asian American and Latino organizations opposed the Immigration Reform and Control Act of 1986 because it imposed sanctions on employers who hire undocumented workers. Such sanctions, they feared, would lead employers to discriminate against Latinos and Asian Americans. These suspicions were confirmed in a 1990 report by the General Accounting Office that found employer sanctions had created a "widespread pattern of discrimination" against Latinos and others who appear foreign.[47] Latinos and Asian Americans have established organizations modeled on the NAACP's Legal Defense Fund, such as the Mexican-American Legal Defense Fund (MALDEF) and the Asian Law Caucus, to monitor and challenge such discrimination. These groups have turned their attention to the rights of legal and illegal immigrants, as anti-immigrant sentiment has grown in recent years.

NATIVE AMERICANS

As a language minority, Native Americans were affected by the 1975 amendments to the Voting Rights Act and the *Lau* decision. The *Lau* decision established the right of Native Americans to be taught in their own languages. This marked quite a change from the boarding schools once run by the Bureau of Indian Affairs, at which members of Indian tribes had been forbidden to speak their own languages. In addition to these language-related issues, Native Americans have sought to expand their rights on the basis of their sovereign status. Since the 1920s and 1930s, Native American tribes have sued the federal government for illegally seizing land, seeking monetary reparations and land as damages. Both types of damages have been awarded in such suits, but only in small amounts. Native American tribes have been more successful in winning federal recognition of their sovereignty. Sovereign status has, in turn, allowed them to exercise greater self-determination. Most significant economically was a 1987 Supreme Court decision that freed Native American tribes from most state regulations prohibiting gambling. The establishment of casino gambling on Native American lands has brought a substantial flow of new income into desperately poor reservations.

DISABLED AMERICANS

In 1998, Casey Martin sued the Professional Golfers' Association (PGA) under the Americans with Disabilities Act of 1990 for the right to use a golf cart in tour events. Martin, who has a degenerative blood disorder in his leg, won the suit.

The concept of rights for the disabled began to emerge in the 1970s as the civil rights model spread to other groups. The seed was planted in a little-noticed provision of the 1973 Rehabilitation Act, which outlawed discrimination against individuals on the basis of disabilities. As in many other cases, the law itself helped give rise to the movement demanding rights for the handicapped.[48] Modeling itself on the NAACP's Legal Defense Fund, the disability movement founded a Disability Rights Education and Defense Fund to press their legal claims. The movement achieved its greatest success with the passage of the Americans with Disabilities Act (ADA) of 1990, which guarantees equal employment rights and access to public businesses for the disabled. Claims of discrimination in violation of this act are considered by the Equal Employment Opportunity Commission. The impact of the law has been far-reaching, as businesses and public facilities have installed ramps, elevators, and other devices to meet the act's requirements.[49] In 1998, the Supreme Court interpreted the ADA to apply to people with HIV. Until then, ADA was interpreted as covering people with AIDS but not people with HIV. The case arose out of the refusal of a dentist to fill a cavity of a woman with HIV except in a hospital setting. The woman sued, and her complaint was that HIV had already disabled her because it was discouraging her from having children. (The Act prohibits discrimination in employment, housing, and in health care.) Although there have been widespread concerns that the ADA was being expanded too broadly and the costs were becoming too burdensome, corporate America did not seem to be disturbed by the Court's ruling. Stephen Bokat, General Counsel of the U.S. Chamber of Commerce, said businesses in general had already been accommodating people with HIV as well as with AIDS and that the case presented no serious problem.[50]

THE AGED

Age discrimination in employment is illegal. The 1967 federal Age Discrimination in Employment Act (ADEA) makes age discrimination illegal when practiced by employers with at least twenty employees. Many states have added to the federal provisions with their own age discrimination laws, and some such state laws are stronger than the federal provisions. Age discrimination—especially in hiring—is widespread, and it is all the more pressing a problem because of Americans' significantly increased life expectancy. They are a much older population than they used to be. The idea of reduced psychological and physical capacity at age fifty, once prehaps reasonable, seems ridiculous today; and forcible retirement at sixty-five is looking sillier every year. Reasonable people will continue to disagree over the merits of laws against age discrimination. But one thing is clear: the major lobbyist for seniors, the American Association of Retired Persons (AARP, see Chapter 12), with its claim to over thirty million members, will maintain its vigilance and its influence to keep these laws on the books and to make sure that they are vigorously implemented.

GAYS AND LESBIANS

In less than thirty years, the gay and lesbian movement has become one of the largest civil rights movements in contemporary America. Beginning with street protests in the 1960s, the movement has grown into a well-financed and sophisticated lobby. The Human Rights Campaign Fund is the primary national political action committee (PAC) focused on gay rights; it provides campaign financing and volunteers to work for candidates endorsed by the group. The movement has also formed legal rights organizations, including the Lambda Legal Defense and Education Fund.

Gay and lesbian rights drew national attention in 1993, when President Bill Clinton confronted the question of whether gays should be allowed to serve in the military. As a candidate, Clinton had said he favored lifting the ban on homosexuals in the military. The issue set off a huge controversy in the first months of Clinton's presidency. After nearly a year of deliberation, the administration enunciated a compromise: their "Don't ask, don't tell" policy. This policy allows gays and lesbians to serve in the military as long as they do not openly proclaim their sexual orientation or engage in homosexual activity. The administration maintained that the ruling would protect gays and lesbians against witch-hunting investigations, but many gay and lesbian advocates expressed disappointment, charging the president with reneging on his campaign promise.

But until 1996, there was no Supreme Court ruling or national legislation explicitly protecting gays and lesbians from discrimination. The first gay rights case that the Court decided, *Bowers v. Hardwick,* ruled against a right to privacy that would protect consensual homosexual activity.[51] After the *Bowers* decision, the gay and lesbian rights movement sought suitable legal cases to test the constitutionality of discrimination against gays and lesbians, much as the black Civil Rights movement did in the late 1940s and 1950s. As one advocate put it, "lesbians and gay men are looking for their *Brown v. Board of Education.*"[52] Among the cases tested were those stemming from local ordinances restricting gay rights (including the right to marry), job discrimination, and family law issues such as adoption and parental rights. In 1996, the Supreme Court, in *Romer v. Evans*, explicitly extended fundamental civil rights protections to gays and lesbians, by declaring unconstitutional a 1992 amendment to the Colorado state constitution that prohibited local governments from passing ordinances to protect gay rights.[53] The decision's forceful language highlighted the connection between gay rights and civil rights as it declared discrimination against gay people unconstitutional.

Whatever the future of Court rulings in this area, gay and lesbian Americans will continue to press their cases against the many laws they view as discriminatory. In response to the recent legalization of gay and lesbian marriage in Vermont, for example, they are likely to push for observance of the *full faith and credit clause,* as discussed in Chapter 4. But the Defense of Marriage Act of 1996, declaring that states do not have to recognize same-sex marriage, and the efforts of many states to adopt state laws to put same-sex marriage off limits, means that the gay and lesbian struggle against discrimination will follow that of other minorities, using the federal equal protection clause.[54]

Affirmative Action

- What is the basis for affirmative action? What forms does it take?
- How does affirmative action contribute to the polarization of the politics of civil rights?
- How does the debate about affirmative action reflect the debate over American political values?

affirmative action
government policies or programs that seek to redress past injustices against specified groups by making special efforts to provide members of these groups with access to educational and employment opportunities

Not only has the politics of rights spread to increasing numbers of groups in American society since the 1960s, it has also expanded its goal. The relatively narrow goal of equalizing opportunity by eliminating discriminatory barriers developed toward the far broader goal of **affirmative action**—compensatory action to overcome the consequences of past discrimination. An affirmative action policy tends to involve two novel approaches: (1) positive or benign discrimination in which race or some other status is actually taken into account, but for compensatory action rather than mistreatment; and (2) compensatory action to favor members of the disadvantaged group who themselves may never have been the victims of discrimination. Quotas may be but are not necessarily involved in affirmative action policies.

President Lyndon Johnson put the case emotionally in 1965: "You do not take a person who, for years, has been hobbled by chains . . . and then say you are free to compete with all the others, and still just believe that you have been completely fair."[55] Johnson attempted to inaugurate affirmative action by executive orders directing agency heads and personnel officers to pursue vigorously a policy of minority employment in the federal civil service and in companies doing business with the national government. But affirmative action did not become a prominent goal of the national government until the 1970s.

Affirmative action also took the form of efforts by the agencies in the Department of Health, Education, and Welfare to shift their focus from "desegregation" to "integration."[56] Federal agencies—sometimes with court orders and sometimes without them—required school districts to present plans for busing children across district lines, for pairing schools, for closing certain schools, and for redistributing faculties as well as students, under pain of loss of grants-in-aid from the federal government. The guidelines issued for such plans literally constituted preferential treatment to compensate for past discrimination, and without this legislatively assisted approach to integration orders, there would certainly not have been the dramatic increase in black children attending integrated classes. The yellow school bus became a symbol of hope for many and a signal of defeat for others.

Affirmative action was also initiated in the area of employment opportunity. The Equal Employment Opportunity Commission often has required plans whereby employers must attempt to increase the number of their minority employees, and the office of Federal Contract Compliance in the Department of Labor has used the threat of contract revocation for the same purpose.

THE SUPREME COURT AND THE BURDEN OF PROOF

Efforts by the executive, legislative, and judicial branches to shape the meaning of affirmative action today tend to center on a key issue: What is the appropriate level of review in affirmative action cases—that is, on whom should the burden of proof be placed, the plaintiff or the defendant? The issue of qualification versus minority preference was addressed formally by the Supreme Court in the case of Allan Bakke. Bakke, a white male, brought suit against the University of California at Davis Medical School on the grounds that in denying him admission the school had discriminated against him on the basis of his race (that year the school had reserved 16 of 100 available slots for minority applicants). He argued that his grades and test scores had ranked him well above many students who had been accepted at the school and that the only possible explanation for his rejection was that those others accepted were black or Latino while he was white. In 1978, Bakke won his case before the Supreme Court and was admitted to the medical school, but he did not succeed in getting affirmative action declared unconstitutional. The Court rejected the procedures at the University of California because its medical school had used both a quota *and* a separate admissions system for minorities. The Court agreed with Bakke's argument that racial categorizations are suspect categories that place a severe burden of proof on those using them to show a "compelling public purpose." The Court went on to say that achieving "a diverse student body" was such a public purpose, but the method of a rigid quota of student slots assigned on the basis of race was incompatible with the equal protection clause. Thus, the Court permitted universities (and presumably other schools, training programs, and hiring authorities) to continue to take minority status into consideration, but limited severely the use of quotas to situations in which (1) previous discrimination had been shown, and (2) it was used more as a guideline for social diversity than as a mathematically defined ratio.[57]

Allan Bakke at his graduation ceremony from the medical school of the University of California at Davis.

For nearly a decade after *Bakke,* the Supreme Court was tentative and permissive about efforts by corporations and governments to experiment with affirmative action programs in employment.[58] But in 1989, the Court returned to the *Bakke* position that any "rigid numerical quota" is suspect. In *Wards Cove v. Atonio,* the Court backed away further from affirmative action by easing the way for employers to prefer white males, holding that the burden of proof of unlawful discrimination should be shifted from the defendant (the employer) to the plaintiff (the person claiming to be the victim of discrimination).[59] This decision virtually overruled the Court's prior holding.[60] That same year, the Court ruled that any affirmative action program already approved by federal courts could be subsequently challenged by white males who allege that the program discriminates against them.[61]

In 1991, Congress enacted a piece of legislation designed to undo the effects of the decisions limiting affirmative action. Under the terms of the Civil Rights Act of 1991, the burden of proof in employment discrimination cases was shifted back to employers. In addition, the act made it more difficult to mount later challenges to consent decrees in affirmative action cases. Despite Congress's actions, however, the federal judiciary will have the last word as cases under the new law reach the courts. In a 5-to-4 decision in 1993, the Supreme Court ruled that employees had to prove their employers intended discrimination, again placing the burden of proof on employees.[62]

In 1995, the Supreme Court's ruling in *Adarand Constructors v. Pena* further weakened affirmative action. This decision stated that race-based policies, such as preferences given by the government to minority contractors, must survive strict scrutiny, placing the burden on the government to show that such affirmative action programs serve a compelling government interest and are narrowly tailored to address identifiable past discrimination.[63] President Clinton responded to the *Adarand* decision by ordering a review of all government affirmative action policies and practices. Although many observers suspected that the president would use the review as an opportunity to back away from affirmative action, the conclusions of the task force largely defended existing policies. Reflecting the influence of the Supreme Court's decision in *Adarand,* President Clinton acknowledged that some government policies would need to change. But on the whole, the review found that most affirmative action policies were fair and did not "unduly burden nonbeneficiaries."[64]

Although Clinton sought to "mend, not end" affirmative action, developments in the courts and the states continued to restrict affirmative action in important ways. One of the most significant was the *Hopwood* case, in which white students challenged admissions practices in the University of Texas Law School, charging that the school's affirmative action program discriminated against whites. In 1996, a federal court (the U.S. Court of Appeals for the Fifth Circuit) ruling on the case stated that race could never be considered in granting admissions and scholarships at state colleges and universities.[65] This decision effectively rolled back the use of affirmative action permitted by the 1978 *Bakke* case. In *Bakke,* as discussed earlier, the Supreme Court had outlawed quotas but said that race could be used as one factor among many in admissions decisions. Many universities and colleges have since justified affirmative action as a way of promoting racial diversity among their student bodies. What was new in the *Hopwood* decision was the ruling that race could *never* be used as a factor in admissions decisions, even to promote diversity.

In 1996, the Supreme Court refused to hear a challenge to the *Hopwood* case. This meant that its ruling remains in effect in the states covered by the Fifth Circuit—Texas, Louisiana, and Mississippi—but does not apply to the rest of the country. The impact of the *Hopwood* ruling is greatest in Texas because Louisiana and Mississippi are under conflicting court orders to desegregate their universities. In Texas, in the year after the *Hopwood* case, minority applications to Texas universities declined. Concerned about the ability of Texas public universities to serve the state's minority students, the Texas legislature quickly passed a new law granting students who graduate in the top 10 percent of their classes automatic admission to the state's public universities. It is hoped that this measure will ensure a racially diverse student body.[66]

The weakening of affirmative action in the courts was underscored in a case the Supreme Court agreed to hear in 1998. A white schoolteacher in New Jersey who had lost her job had sued her school district, charging that her layoff was racially motivated: a black colleague hired on the same day was not laid off. Under President George Bush, the Justice Department had filed a brief on her behalf in 1989, but in 1994 the Clinton administration formally reversed course in a new brief supporting the school district's right to make distinctions based on race as long as it did not involve the use of quotas. Three years later, the administration, worried that the case was weak and could result in a broad decision against affirmative action, reversed course again. It filed a brief with the Court urging a narrow ruling in favor of the dismissed worker. Because the school board had justified its actions on the grounds of preserving diversity, the administration feared that a broad ruling by the Supreme Court could totally prohibit the use of race in employment decisions, even as one factor among many designed to achieve diversity. But before the Court could issue a ruling, a coalition of civil rights groups brokered and arranged to pay for a settlement. This unusual move reflected the widespread fear of a sweeping negative decision. Cases involving dismissals, as the New Jersey case did, are generally viewed as much more difficult to defend than cases that concern hiring. In addition, the particular facts of the New Jersey case—two equally qualified teachers hired on the same day—were seen as unusual and unfavorable to affirmative action.[67]

Students and Politics

In 1996, a federal court followed the precedent set by *Bakke v. Regents of the University of California* by banning affirmative action in public university admissions; the decision was handed down in *Hopwood v. Texas,* which Texas attorney general Dan Morales broadened to include scholarships and other financial aid. While the *Hopwood* decision had already polarized many students at the various University of Texas campuses, Lino Graglia, a professor at the University of Texas at Austin's law school, created a firestorm when he told the Austin *American-Statesman,* "I don't know that it's good for whites to be with the lower classes. I'm afraid it may actually have deleterious effects on their views because they will see people from situations of economic deprivation usually behave less attractively." Reaction on the campus was swift, led by the newly formed Students for Access and Opportunity (SAO). Hundreds of people gathered for a rally against the perceived racism of Graglia's comments and the *Hopwood* decision. Civil rights leader Jesse Jackson joined selected student speakers in promoting affirmative action in light of Graglia's comments. The battle continues between SAO and its student opposition, the Students for Equal Opportunity (SEO).

SOURCE: Sue Anne Pressley, "Rally Is Urged to Make Law Professor a 'Pariah,'" *The Washington Post,* September 17, 1997, p. A3.

REFERENDUMS ON AFFIRMATIVE ACTION

The courts have not been the only center of action: challenges to affirmative action have also emerged in state and local politics. One of the most significant state actions was the passage of the California Civil Rights Initiative, also known as Proposition 209, in 1996. Proposition 209 outlawed affirmative action programs in the state and local governments of California, thus prohibiting state and local governments from using race or gender preferences in their decisions about hiring, contracting, or university admissions. The political battle over Proposition 209 was heated, and supporters and defenders took to the streets as well as the airwaves to make their cases. When the referendum was held, the measure passed with 54 percent of the vote, including 27 percent of the black vote, 30 percent of the Latino vote, and 45 percent of the Asian American vote.[68] In 1997, the Supreme Court refused to hear a challenge to the new law.

Student Perspectives

COLLEGE FRESHMEN BACK ADMISSIONS FOR RACE, BUT NOT AFFIRMATIVE ACTION

A 1995 survey of 240,082 students revealed that a large majority supports the use of race as a criterion for college admissions, but fewer are committed to the principle of "affirmative action." Seventy percent of the respondents said that the race of an applicant should be given some special consideration for admissions. On the other hand, about 50 percent thought that "affirmative action" in admissions should be eliminated. This discrepancy reveals both the ambiguity of Americans' views on the topic as well as the political significance of the term "affirmative action."

Surveys trying to measure these kinds of attitudes are so sensitive that the response depends mightily on the way the question is posed. For example, asking students their attitude toward college admissions policies that avoid such code words as "preferential treatment" get entirely different responses than those that employ such code words. Political scientist Carol Swain, who has studied this issue in depth, has concluded that although black and white students "are not enthusiastic about racial preference programs," they can agree on some aspects of affirmative action "once we move beyond the racially inflammatory code words found all too often in existing surveys."

SOURCE: Tamara Henry, "Freshmen Back Admissions for Race, Not Affirmative Action," *USA Today*, January 8, 1996, p. A1. Data from the UCLA Higher Education Research Institute and William Julius Wilson, "Affirming Oportunity," *The American Prospect*, September–October 1999, p. 64.

Many observers predicted that the success of California's ban on affirmative action would provoke similar movements in states and localities across the country. But the political factors that contributed to the success of Proposition 209 in California may not exist in many other states. In contrast to California Republican governor Pete Wilson, who strongly opposed affirmative action, other Republican governors, such as New Jersey's Christine Todd Whitman, are strong supporters. Moreover, because public opinion on the issue is very conflicted, the outcome of efforts to roll affirmative action back depends greatly on how the issue is posed to voters. California's Proposition 209 was framed as a civil rights initiative: "the state shall not discriminate against, or grant preferential treatment to, any individual or group on the basis of race, sex, color, ethnicity, or national origin." Different wording can produce quite different outcomes, as a 1997 vote on affirmative action in Houston revealed. There, the ballot initiative asked voters whether they wanted to ban affirmative action in city contracting and hiring, not whether they wanted to end preferential treatment. Fifty-five percent of Houston voters decided in favor of affirmative action.[69]

Affirmative action will continue to be a focus of controversy in coming years, as several other cases challenging affirmative action reach the Supreme Court. There are now several suits similar to the *Hopwood* case working their way through the lower courts, including one against the University of Michigan's affirmative action program. If the Supreme Court decides to hear these cases, the future of affirmative action in universities and colleges will be on the line. Affirmative action is also sure to remain prominent in state and local politics across the country. Efforts to ban affirmative action are under way in a number of states, including Washington, Colorado, Michigan, Massachusetts, Arizona, Arkansas, Ohio, North Dakota, and Oregon.

AFFIRMATIVE ACTION AND AMERICAN POLITICAL VALUES

Affirmative action efforts have contributed to the polarization of the politics of civil rights. At the risk of grievous oversimplification, we can divide the sides by two labels: liberals and conservatives.[70] The conservatives' argument against affirmative action can be reduced to two major points. The first is that rights in the American tradition are *individual* rights, and affirmative action violates this concept by concerning itself with "group rights," an idea said to be alien to the American tradition. The second point has to do with quotas. Conservatives would argue that the Constitution is "color-blind," and that any discrimination, even if it is called positive or benign discrimination, ultimately violates the equal protection clause.

POLICY DEBATE

Affirmative Action

The sweeping civil rights laws enacted in the 1960s officially ended state-sanctioned segregation. They did not, however, end racism, or erase stark inequities between the races in such areas as employment and education. As a consequence, affirmative action policies were enacted to ensure some equality between the races. In the 1978 case of *Regents of the University of California v. Bakke,* the Supreme Court upheld "race-conscious" policies in educational admissions—meaning that race could be used as an admissions criterion—but barred the use of specific, numerical racial quotas. In recent years, a more conservative Supreme Court has chipped away at the scope of such programs—which, incidentally, have become increasingly unpopular among Americans—suggesting that affirmative action programs might be further restricted or eliminated entirely. In 1997, for example, the Court let stand California's Proposition 209, a statewide referendum passed in 1996 that barred the consideration of race or gender in state hiring and school admissions.

Proponents of affirmative action cite the continued need for such programs, especially for African Americans, because of the nation's long history of discrimination and persecution. Racism was institutionalized throughout most of the country's history; indeed, the Constitution specifically recognized, and therefore countenanced, slavery. For example, it rewarded slaveowners with the Three-fifths Compromise, giving slaveowners extra representation in the House of Representatives, a provision excised from the Constitution only after the Civil War. Moreover, few would deny that racism still exists in America. Given these facts, it follows that equal treatment of unequals perpetuates inequality. Programs that give an extra boost to traditionally disadvantaged groups offer the only sure way to overcome structural inequality.

To take the example of university and college admissions, affirmative action opponents argue that admissions decisions should be based on merit, not race. Yet affirmative action does not disregard merit, and in any case, admissions does not operate purely based on merit, however defined, for any college or university. Institutions of higher education rely on such measures as grade point average, board scores, and letters of recommendation. But they also consider such nonmerit factors as region, urban vs. rural background, family relationship to alumni and wealthy donors, athletic ability, or other specialized factors unrelated to the usual definition of merit. The inclusion of race as one of these many admissions criteria is as defensible as any other; moreover, it helps ensure a more diverse student body, which in itself is a laudable educational goal. Moreover, such programs do not guarantee educational success, but simply assure that individuals from disadvantaged groups have a chance to succeed, an idea most Americans support. Affirmative action programs have in fact succeeded in providing opportunity to millions who would not otherwise have had the chance.

Opponents of affirmative action argue that such programs, while based on good intentions, do more harm than good. The belief that persons who gain employment or college admission from such programs did not earn their positions stigmatizes those who are supposed to benefit, creating self-doubt among the recipients and mistrust from others. In the realm of education, students admitted to colleges and universities under these special programs have lower graduation rates. Affirmative action also violates the fundamental American value of equality of opportunity. Although all may not possess the same opportunity, the effort expended to provide special advantages to some would be better directed toward making sure that the principles of equal opportunity and merit are followed.

America's history of discrimination, though reprehensible, should not be used as a basis for employment for educational decisions, because it is unreasonable to ask Americans today to pay for the mistakes of their ancestors. Moreover, the track record of affirmative action programs reveals another problem: the groups that have benefited most are middle-class African Americans and women. If anything, preferential programs should focus on *economic* disadvantage, regardless of race, and better education early in life. Good intentions notwithstanding, there are limits to what government social engineering can accomplish, and most Americans favor the abandonment of race-based preference programs.

STUDENT DEBATE

Is Affirmative Action Fair?

Yes

In a recent episode of *Law and Order*, a defense lawyer contended that affirmative action caused his client to commit manslaughter. While this particular alleged drawback to affirmative action has yet to make it into the widespread communal consciousness, affirmative action, in the past five years, has been blamed for everything from minority inferiority complexes to the downfall of American education.

Play the word association game with the phrase affirmative action and you will hear words like: quotas, preferential treatment, under or unqualified applicants, reverse discrimination. These mental combinations have become automatic short cuts in the public debate on affirmative action, based on anecdotal evidence and prevailing winds of media opinion. In the current climate of affirmative action backlash, the mainstream media perpetuates sadly superficial discussions on affirmative action that rely more on offended sensibilities than any examination of concrete data.

* * *

The fact remains that in American society, significant economic and educational disparities exist among racial and gender (yes, gender—affirmative action's largest beneficiary has been women) lines. The White House review of affirmative action found that 50 percent fewer African Americans and Latinos had college degrees than whites. The average income for a college-educated Latina is the same as the average income of a white male high school graduate. One can differ on how best to address these inequalities, but those who insist that the long way we've come is a long enough way are living in their own universe of frosting and lollipops.

The tragedy is that with the advent of knee-jerk rhetoric, what could have been a thoughtful and reasoned assessment of affirmative action's flaws and successes has become an emotional vendetta pursued by a few, and accepted by many. Even Proposition 209, which was hailed as proof that California voters had rejected affirmative action, passed only 54 percent to 46 percent, hardly a resounding dismissal. Affirmative action is an imperfect policy for an imperfect world, but sloppy rhetoric does no one any good, least of all those who suffer from inequality of opportunity.

We've all heard or know stories about highly qualified white (or Asian) applicants to college, law school, McKinsey, etc., who were rejected, and the minority applicant who just didn't have the grades, test scores, etc., who was accepted purely on the basis of his or her race. We might even believe that we were those rejected people.

"That's unfair!" the peanut gallery cries as we forget the fact that application processes are always subjective, always based on nebulous evaluations of future potential, on activities and community leadership, on the qualitative and not the quantitative. We consider race and its attendant experiences as a factor but not the only factor in recruiting and accepting students, just as athletic ability and legacy status is also considered. To stand outside of the admissions office and pontificate with certainty why a certain person was accepted or rejected is to engage in a useless guessing game.

There are those who charge that affirmative action perpetuates racism by even considering race as a factor, and assert that a color-blind society will only come from color-blind policies. Just as calling anti-affirmative action legislation in California the Civil Rights Initiative appropriates the language of the civil rights movement without following the principles, calling for color-blind admissions in the university sounds good while actually disadvantaging minorities and women.

Because such policies do not take into account previous advantages or inequalities, color-blind admissions ends up only reinforcing already existing racial injustices. In such circumstances, talk about color-blind admissions is disingenuous.

SOURCE: Annie Koh, "Debunking the Affirmative Action Myth," *Yale Daily News* (Yale University), February 24, 1999.

No

Check one: __ American Indian/Alaskan Native __ Asian/Pacific Islander __ Black/African American __ Chicano/Mexican American __ Puerto Rican __ Hispanic __ White __ Other

Like a game of Russian Roulette, the correct answer to such a question could result in a big payoff—acceptance at a top college or graduate school, a scholarship offering big bucks or a job at a high-profile company.

The wrong answer could destroy those same hopes. And more and more these days, saying that you are white is the wrong answer. Indeed, affirmative action—the widespread effort to put all races on an equal footing—has had just the opposite effect, elevating certain races to privileged status at the expense of others.

Regrettably, as they stand now, affirmative action policies are morally questionable—and perhaps illegal.

The *St. Paul Pioneer Press*, the newspaper serving St. Paul, Minn., offers a summer internship, for example, that is available only to minorities.

No matter how qualified an applicant is, if he's white, he's out. Budding Bob Woodwards and Carl Bernsteins need not apply.

Nor could they apply to the many other newspapers or companies in other fields that restrict their applicant pools to minorities only. Where exactly is the equal opportunity in that?

Indeed, affirmative action sharply rejects the widely held American belief promulgated in the Declaration of Independence that all men are created equal. Instead, racial preferences put some Americans on a higher, more distinguished level.

For that reason, the Center for Individual Rights—a public policy and legal center based in Washington, D.C.—has rightly challenged institutions like Penn to eliminate racial preferences in admissions decisions.

[I agree that] the University's use of race in admissions decisions is troubling.

Why does being in a minority make you better than someone who isn't in a minority? Admissions decisions should be based on merit, not on skin color. And merit should be based on things that you have accomplished and achieved, not something that you're born with.

As such, the University should eliminate the offensive racial classification question from its applications. Such a move would equalize race in the admissions process, ensuring that applicants are neither admitted nor rejected based on the color of their skin.

At the same time, it would protect Penn from accusations of racial discrimination. With a blind eye, the University could turn its back on criticism from members of all races, who would be unable to prove that they were rejected because of their ethnicity.

Most importantly, the University could focus more of its attention on the intellectual qualities of its applicants, guaranteeing an academically rich and varied student body.

Already, public institutions are justly feeling the constitutional pressure put on affirmative action. In *Hopwood v. State of Texas*, successfully tried by the CIR, a federal appeals court ruled in 1996 that Texas, Louisiana, and Mississippi are barred from considering race in college admissions. Proposition 209 gave the same mandate in California in 1996. It seems only a matter of time until affirmative action will justifiably be wiped out at public institutions across the country.

But only societal outrage seems likely to lead private institutions to abandon similar policies. With the aid of Penn students racial preferences can at the very least be done away with on this campus.

SOURCE: Mark Fiore, "Reward Merit, Not Skin Color," *Daily Pennsylvanian* (University of Pennsylvania), February 9, 1999.

The liberal side agrees that rights ultimately come down to individuals, but argues that, since the essence of discrimination is the use of unreasonable and unjust criteria of exclusion to deprive *an entire group* of access to something valuable the society has to offer, then the phenomenon of discrimination itself has to be attacked on a group basis. Liberals can also use Supreme Court history to support their side, because the first definitive interpretation of the Fourteenth Amendment by the Court in 1873 stated explicitly that

> [t]he existence of laws in the state where the newly emancipated Negroes resided, which discriminated with gross injustice and hardship against them *as a class,* was the evil to be remedied by this clause [emphasis added].[71]

Liberals also have a response to the other conservative argument concerning quotas. The liberal response is that the Supreme Court has already accepted ratios—a form of quota—that are admitted as evidence to prove a "pattern or practice of discrimination" sufficient to reverse the burden of proof—to obligate the employer to show that there was *not* an intent to discriminate. Liberals can also argue that benign quotas often have been used by Americans both to compensate for some bad action in the past or to provide some desired distribution of social characteristics—sometimes called diversity. For example, a long and respected policy in the United States is that of "veteran's preference," on the basis of which the government automatically gives extra consideration in hiring to persons who have served the country in the armed forces. The justification is that ex-soldiers deserve compensation for having made sacrifices for the good of the country. And the goal of social diversity has justified "positive discrimination," especially in higher education, the very institution where conservatives have most adamantly argued against positive quotas for blacks and women. For example, all of the Ivy League schools and many other private colleges and universities regularly and consistently reserve admissions places for some students whose qualifications in a strict academic sense are below those of others who are not admitted. These schools not only recruit students from minority groups, but they set aside places for the children of loyal alumni and of their own faculty, even when, in a pure competition solely and exclusively based on test scores and high school records, many of those same children would not have been admitted. These practices are not conclusive justification in themselves, but they certainly underscore the liberal argument that affirmative or compensatory action for minorities who have been unjustly treated in the past is not alien to American experience.

If we think of the debate about affirmative action in terms of American political values, it is clear that conservatives emphasize liberty, whereas liberals stress equality. Conservatives believe that using government actively to promote equality for minorities and women infringes on the rights of whites. Lawsuits challenging affirmative action often cite this "reverse discrimination" as a justification. Liberals, on the other hand, traditionally have defended affirmative action as the best way to achieve equality. In recent years, however, the debate over affirmative action has become more complex and has created divisions among liberals. These divisions stem from growing doubts among some liberals about whether affirmative action can be defended as the best way to achieve equality and about the tensions between affirmative action and democratic values. One recent study of public opinion found that many self-identified liberals were angry about affirmative action.[72] These liberals felt

Politics on the Web

The Internet has become a battleground for disputes over civil rights. California's battle over affirmative action illustrated the medium's new role, with groups from both sides arguing their case on the Web. The American Civil Liberties Union (ACLU), for example, published a detailed "briefing paper" in favor of continued racial preferences, while the Center for Individual Rights provided arguments against affirmative action legislation, citing Supreme Court decisions in support. Not surprisingly, plenty of less-thoughtful sites also express opinions on this issue. As a result, private groups such as the Anti-Defamation League, as well as law enforcement agencies, monitor the Internet for extremist organizations expressing racist or misogynist opinions. Despite the fact that the Internet provides a forum for neo-Nazis, white supremacists, and conspiracy theorists, the Web makes it easy for all to have their voices heard, and it compels opponents to provide reasons for their opposition.

www.wwnorton.com/wtp3e

AMERICANS' OPINIONS ON AFFIRMATIVE ACTION — Table 6.3

	Blacks	Whites
Should government make every effort to improve conditions of blacks and minorities, or	59%	34%
Should government not make any special effort, they should help themselves	30	59

SOURCE: The Gallup Poll, "Black/White Relations in the U.S.," June 10, 1997; http://www.gallup.com/poll/socialaudits/sa970610.asp.

Responses to the question "What should government's role be in improving the conditions for blacks and minorities?"

that in the name of equality, affirmative action actually violates norms of fairness and equality of opportunity by giving special advantages to some. Moreover, it is argued, affirmative action is broadly unpopular and is therefore questionable in terms of democratic values. Because our nation has a history of slavery and legalized racial discrimination, and because discrimination continues to exist (although it has declined over time), the question of racial justice, more than any other issue, highlights the difficulty of reconciling our values in practice.

Although the problems of rights in America are agonizing, they can be looked at optimistically. The United States has a long way to go before it constructs a truly just, "equally protected" society. But it also has come very far in a relatively short time. Groups pressing for equality have been able to use government to change a variety of discriminatory practices. The federal government has become an active partner in ensuring civil rights and political equality. All explicit de jure barriers to minorities have been dismantled. Many de facto barriers have also been dismantled, and thousands upon thousands of new opportunities have been opened. Deep and fundamental differences have polarized many Americans (see Table 6.3), but political and governmental institutions have proven themselves capable of maintaining balances between them. This kind of balancing can be done without violence so long as everyone recognizes that policy choices, even about rights, cannot be absolute.

The Citizen's Role

STUDENTS AND POLITICS

Citizens have played the leading role in determining the meaning of civil rights, and students have often been in the forefront of conflicts about civil rights. As we saw in the introduction to this chapter, students played a pivotal role in the Civil Rights movement in the 1960s. When the movement seemed to be at an impasse in 1960, students helped to reenergize it with their sit-in at the Woolworth's lunch counter. Sit-ins had been used by labor unions seeking recognition in the 1930s, but it was students who first applied this tactic in civil rights struggles. Likewise, "Freedom Summer," a movement launched in 1964 to register southern blacks to vote, was run by students, four of whom lost their lives registering people to vote that summer.

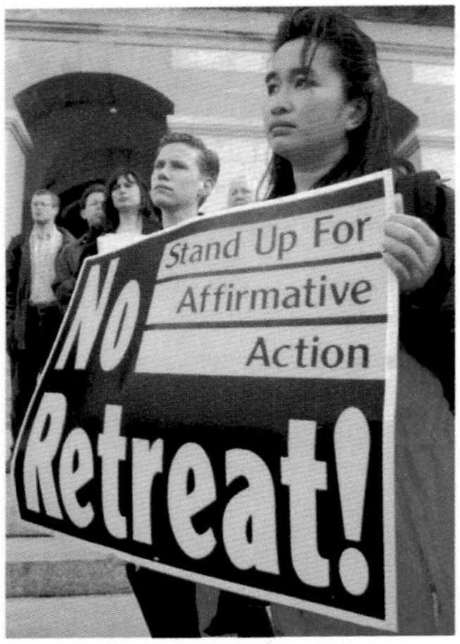

Many University of California students actively defended affirmative action programs, which came under fire during the 1996 debate over Proposition 209. The initiative, which passed as a statewide referendum, prohibits state or local governments from using race or gender as a basis in hiring, education, or contracting.

How have students been involved in civil rights issues in more recent years? Reflecting the conflicting views about what civil rights should mean today, students have been actively involved on both sides of the issue. Students across California were active in the debate about Proposition 209, staging protests and other efforts to persuade voters to reject or support the measure. Since the *Hopwood* decision, students in Texas have held rallies and teach-ins to inform other students about the issues involved. They hope to create a national movement to reinstate affirmative action. Students opposing affirmative action have been less visibly active, but their voices, too, have been heard. For example, the student newspaper at the University of California at Berkeley, *The Californian*, endorsed Proposition 209. Many students on both sides of the issue attended events with speakers presenting arguments for and against affirmative action. Participating in such public events and developing informed opinions is an important kind of political activity.

The range of activities undertaken by supporters of affirmative action raises questions about what is effective political action. On the one hand, protests, such as sit-ins and building takeovers, as occurred after the passage of Proposition 209 and the *Hopwood* decision in Texas, can publicize the views of the protesters. Major newspapers across the country carried accounts of the protests in California. Such protests may spur administrators and politicians to find ways to meet at least some of the goals of affirmative action through different means, since the courts have outlawed current practices. But whether protests can help to change the law or build support for alternatives is an open question. Protests can alienate other students and citizens who may be ambivalent about affirmative action, effectively losing support for the cause. In California, supporters of affirmative action stole copies of the student newspaper that endorsed Proposition 209, making the paper unavailable to readers. Given the commitment to free speech in this country, it is unlikely that such actions generate favorable public opinion, win over new supporters, or put effective pressure on administrators. Decisions about what is effective political action involve thinking hard about the desired outcome and about what actions will help achieve that outcome. These are calculations that every effort to be politically active must make. Often there is no single right answer: effective political action can be learned only by trying many different routes.

GET INVOLVED: Struggling for Civil Rights

Struggles for civil rights often involve mobilizing large numbers of people to get both citizens and government to recognize their claims to rights, prevent the discrimination that betrays those rights, and foster greater inclusiveness to extend those rights throughout society. These mobilizations often focus on issues involving race, ethnicity, religion, gender, disability, and sexual orientation.

They generally aim at influencing public opinion and political officials' ideas and actions. Sometmes, civil rights activists turn to groups such as the American Civil Liberties Union and the Mexican American Legal Defense Fund to engage in litigation as a means to shape government actions. Successful civil rights struggles produce public awareness and popular support, new laws, favorable court rulings, and government agencies to prevent and punish discrimination as well as to take affirmative action to ensure equitable treatment of historically disadvantaged Americans.

It is probable that struggles for civil rights are currently taking place on your college campus. Many higher education institutions have student groups organized around specific identities, for example, African American students, Jewish students, women students, gay and lesbian students, and so forth. These identity groups often seek to promote rights and opportunities for their members by appealing for student support and lobbying campus officials to prohibit some activities (such as racist speech) and promote other activities (such as Black History Month). Also, many colleges have campus affiliates of national or international civil rights organizations such as Amnesty International and Human Rights Watch. Numerous campuses have opened up administrative offices aimed at protecting and advancing the civil rights of particular student populations. For example, your school might have a Student Disabilities Office that monitors campus compliance with the Americans with Disabilities Act of 1990.

One way to get involved in the struggle for civil rights is to join a student identity group or volunteer to work in a relevant campus office. Once you have established your presence and membership, consider several ways to help the group become more effective in achieving its goals.

You might suggest that group members conduct a "needs assessment." Members might investigate how effectively the group is contesting discrimination and how successfully it is protecting the rights of students. The assessment might determine what more could be done to strengthen mutual respect, cooperation, and even solidarity among diverse student groups on campus. What does your group have to gain from conducting a needs assessment? Members are likely to develop a better sense of what needs to be done, how the group could become more influential, and why coalitions with other organizations might be advantageous. Moreover, a needs assessment could renew members' energy and revive their commitment to the struggle.

Consider the range of activities that your group might organize to further the struggle for civil rights. Suppose that your group's immediate goal is to raise campus awareness of civil rights issues. Here are some activities that student groups use to achive that goal.

- Sponsor a gay and lesbian rights parade.
- Conduct a "Take Back the Night" march opposing violence against women.
- Organize a noon rally to protest the lack of a Latino Studies department.
- Set up a photographic display of human rights violations around the world.
- Hold campus forums designed to facilitate multiracial dialogue and cooperation.

When you plan events, be clear about your goals and match them to appropriate means. Accordingly, you may want to orchestrate highly publicized events to build public support, but you may consider quiet negotiations to work out new policies with campus administration. Finally, learn from the past. Think back to the civil rights struggles of the 1950s and 1960s, study the creative strategies that were used to build a national movement, and then update those strategies and innovate on them to build a foundation for civil rights in the new millennium.

Summary

The constitutional basis of civil rights is the "equal protection" clause. This clause imposes a positive obligation on government to advance civil rights, and its original motivation seems to have been to eliminate the gross injustices suffered by "the newly emancipated Negroes . . . as a class." Civil rights call for the expansion of governmental power rather than restraints upon it. This expanded power allows the government to take an active role in promoting equality. But there was little advancement in the interpretation or application of the "equal protection" clause until after World War II. The major breakthrough came in 1954 with *Brown v. Board of Education,* and advancements came in fits and starts during the succeeding ten years.

After 1964, Congress finally supported the federal courts with effective civil rights legislation that outlawed a number of discriminatory practices in the private sector and provided for the withholding of federal grants-in-aid to any local government, school, or private employer as a sanction to help enforce the civil rights laws. From that point, civil rights developed in two ways. First, the definition of civil rights was expanded to include other, nonblack victims of discrimination. Second, the definition of civil rights became increasingly positive; affirmative action has become an official term. Judicial decisions, congressional statutes, and administrative agency actions all have moved beyond the original goal of eliminating discrimination, toward creating new opportunities for minorities and, in some areas, compensating today's minorities for the consequences of discriminatory actions not directly against them but against members of their group in the past. Because compensatory civil rights action has sometimes relied upon quotas, Americans have engaged in intense debate over the constitutionality as well as the desirability of affirmative action, part of a broader debate over American political values. Citizens' involvement in the civil rights movement played a leading role in determining the meaning of civil rights, although recent conflicts over affirmative action have raised questions about what is effective political action.

The story has not ended and is not likely to end. The politics of rights will remain an important part of American political discourse.

FOR FURTHER READING

Baer, Judith A. *Equality under the Constitution: Reclaiming the Fourteenth Amendment.* Ithaca, NY: Cornell University Press, 1983.

Garrow, David J. *Bearing the Cross: Martin Luther King and the Southern Christian Leadership Conference: A Personal Portrait.* New York: Morrow, 1986.

Glendon, Mary Ann. *Rights Talk: The Impoverishment of Political Discourse.* New York: Free Press, 1991.

Greenberg, Jack. *Crusaders in the Courts: How a Dedicated Band of Lawyers Fought for the Civil Rights Revolution.* New York: Basic Books, 1994.

Massey, Douglas S., and Nancy A. Denton. *American Apartheid: Segregation and the Making of the Underclass.* Cambridge, MA: Harvard University Press, 1993.

Nava, Michael. *Created Equal: Why Gay Rights Matter to America.* New York: St. Martin's, 1994.

Rosenberg, Gerald N. *The Hollow Hope: Can Courts Bring About Social Change?* Chicago: University of Chicago Press, 1991.

Thernstrom, Abigail M. *Whose Votes Count? Affirmative Action and Minority Voting Rights.* Cambridge, MA: Harvard University Press, 1987.

STUDY OUTLINE

Civil Rights

1. From 1896 until the end of World War II, the Supreme Court held that the Fourteenth Amendment's equal protection clause was not violated by racial distinction as long as the facilities were equal.
2. After World War II, the Supreme Court began to undermine the separate but equal doctrine, eventually declaring it unconstitutional in *Brown v. Board of Education.*
3. The *Brown* decision marked the beginning of a difficult battle for equal protection in education, employment, housing, voting, and other areas of social and economic activity.
4. The first phase of school desegregation was met with such massive resistance in the South that, ten years after *Brown,* fewer than 1 percent of black children in the South were attending schools with whites.
5. In 1971, the Supreme Court held that state-imposed desegregation could be brought about by busing children across school districts.
6. Title VII of the Civil Rights Act of 1964 outlawed job discrimination by all private and public employers, including governmental agencies, that employed more than fifteen workers.
7. In 1965, Congress significantly strengthened legislation protecting voting rights by barring literacy and other tests as a condition for voting in southern states. In the long run, the laws extending and protecting voting rights could prove to be the most effective of all civil rights legislation, because increased political participation by minorities has altered the shape of American politics.

The Universalization of Civil Rights

1. The protections won by the African American civil rights movement spilled over to protect other groups as well, including women, Latinos, Asian Americans, Native Americans, disabled Americans, and gays and lesbians.

Affirmative Action

1. By seeking to provide compensatory action to overcome the consequences of past discrimination, affirmative action represents the expansion of the goals of groups championing minority rights.
2. Affirmative action has been a controversial policy. Opponents charge that affirmative action creates group rights and establishes quotas, both of which are inimical to the American tradition. Proponents of affirmative action argue that the long history of group discrimination makes affirmative action necessary and that efforts to compensate for some bad action in the past are well within the federal government's purview. Recent conflicts over affirmative action have raised questions about what is effective political action.

PRACTICE QUIZ

1. When did civil rights become part of the Constitution?
   a) in 1789 at the Founding
   b) with the adoption of the Fourteenth Amendment in 1868
   c) with the adoption of the Nineteenth Amendment in 1920
   d) in the 1954 *Brown v. Board of Education* case
2. Which civil rights case established the "separate but equal" rule?
   a) *Plessy v. Ferguson*
   b) *Brown v. Board of Education*
   c) *Bakke v. Regents of the University of California*
   d) *Adarand Constructors v. Pena*

3. "Massive resistance" refers to efforts by southern states during the late 1950s and early 1960s to
   a) build public housing for poor blacks.
   b) defy federal mandates to desegregate public schools.
   c) give women the right to have an abortion.
   d) bus black students to white schools.

4. Which of the following organizations established a Legal Defense Fund to challenge segregation?
   a) the Association of American Trial Lawyers
   b) the National Association for the Advancement of Colored People
   c) the Student Nonviolent Coordinating Committee
   d) the Southern Christian Leadership Council

5. Which of the following made discrimination by private employers and state governments illegal?
   a) the Fourteenth Amendment
   b) *Brown v. Board of Education*
   c) the 1964 Civil Rights Act
   d) *Bakke v. Board of Regents*

6. In what way does the struggle for gender equality most resemble the struggle for racial equality?
   a) There has been very little political action in realizing the goal.
   b) Changes in government policies to a great degree produced political action.
   c) The Supreme Court has not ruled on the issue.
   d) No legislation has passed adopting the aims of the movement.

7. Which of the following is *not* an example of an area in which women have made progress since the 1970s in guaranteeing certain civil rights?
   a) sexual harassment
   b) integration into all-male publicly supported universities
   c) more equal funding for college women's varsity athletic programs
   d) the passage of the Equal Rights Amendment

8. Which of the following civil rights measures dealt with access to public businesses and accommodations?
   a) the 1990 Americans with Disabilities Act
   b) the 1964 Civil Rights Act
   c) neither a nor b
   d) both a and b

9. Which of the following cases represents the *Brown v. Board of Education* case for lesbians and gay men?
   a) *Bowers v. Hardwick*
   b) *Lau v. Nichols*
   c) *Romer v. Evans*
   d) There has not been a Supreme Court ruling explicitly protecting gays and lesbians from discrimination.

10. In what case did the Supreme Court find that "rigid quotas" are incompatible with the equal protection clause of the Fourteenth Amendment?
   a) *Bakke v. Board of Regents*
   b) *Brown v. Board of Education*
   c) *United States v. Nixon*
   d) *Immigration and Naturalization Service v. Chadha*

CRITICAL THINKING QUESTIONS

1. Supporters of affirmative action argue that it is intended not only to compensate for past discrimination, but also to level an uneven playing field in which discrimination still exists. What do you think? To what extent do we have a society free from discrimination? What is the impact of affirmative action on society today? What alternatives to affirmative action policies exist?

2. Describe the changes in American society between the *Plessy v. Ferguson* and the *Brown v. Board of Education* decisions. Using this as an example, explain how changes in society can lead to changes in civil rights policy or other types of government policy. How might changes in society have predicted the changes in civil rights policy in America since the *Brown* case? How might the changes in civil rights policy have changed American society?

KEY TERMS

affirmative action (p. 220)
Brown v. Board of Education (p. 201)
civil rights (p. 195)
de facto (p. 202)
de jure (p. 202)
discrimination (p. 197)
equal protection clause (p. 197)
gerrymandering (p. 211)
intermediate scrutiny (p. 214)
redlining (p. 212)
"separate but equal" rule (p. 198)
strict scrutiny (p. 201)

PART III

Politics

7 Public Opinion

★ **Political Values**

In what ways do Americans agree on fundamental values but disagree on fundamental issues?

How are political values and beliefs formed? What influences individuals' political beliefs?

What do the differences between liberals and conservatives reveal about American political debate?

★ **How We Form Political Opinions**

What influences the way we form political opinions?

How are political issues marketed and managed by the government, private groups, and the media?

★ **Measuring Public Opinion**

How can public opinion be measured?

What problems arise from public opinion polling?

★ **Public Opinion and Democracy**

How responsive is the government to public opinion?

STUDENTS AND POLITICS

DEMOCRATIC government assumes an informed, interested public. Knowledgeable citizens participate in the political process more than do less-knowledgeable citizens because the former have a better understanding of why politics is relevant to their lives. Political knowledge is also important because it promotes a broader acceptance of democratic values. Thus, political knowledge serves the interests of both the individual and the nation as a whole. But, as we saw in Chapter 1, many Americans have little political knowledge or interest. In many respects, college students are among the least politically interested and aware of all Americans. A 1996 national survey of more than 300,000 college freshmen, sponsored by the American Council of Education and conducted by the University of California at Los Angeles, found that only about one-fourth of the students surveyed thought "keeping up with political affairs" was important. Only 13 percent said that they frequently discussed political issues. Few students had any interest in civic activism. Less than one-fifth, for example, said that it was important to "participate in programs to help clean up the environment." Less than one-third thought that it was important to "help promote racial understanding." Most students seemed far more concerned with grades, school expenses, and job prospects than with political matters.[1]

It is, of course, perfectly reasonable for individuals to focus more intently on their own immediate concerns than upon national political issues. The former are real and concrete, while the latter seem abstract and distant. Moreover, students can do something about their grades and job prospects, but issues of government and politics often seem utterly beyond their control. As John Muffo, director of academic assessment at Virginia Polytechnic University, said, "There seems to be a growing sense [among students] of, 'Well, there's nothing you can really do about changing politics, so why bother?' "[2]

Nevertheless, if most citizens have no interest in politics and government, how can popular government or the "self-government" so often invoked by the Founders exist? Fortunately, most citizens do have opinions about government and politics and, indeed, may take an interest in the political process when they feel that it affects them. Even apathetic college students can be mobilized to protest, march, and demonstrate to make their opinions known to those in power.

In the spring of 1999, for example, hundreds of students at the University of California at Berkeley rallied to protest what they saw as the adminstration's lack of attention to the school's ethnic studies programs. Six students conducted a ten-day hunger strike outside Berkeley Chancellor Robert Berdahl's office. The students' fasts ended after the university agreed to fund eight faculty positions in ethnic studies and to support a multicultural student

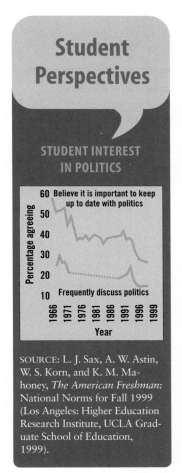

Student Perspectives

STUDENT INTEREST IN POLITICS

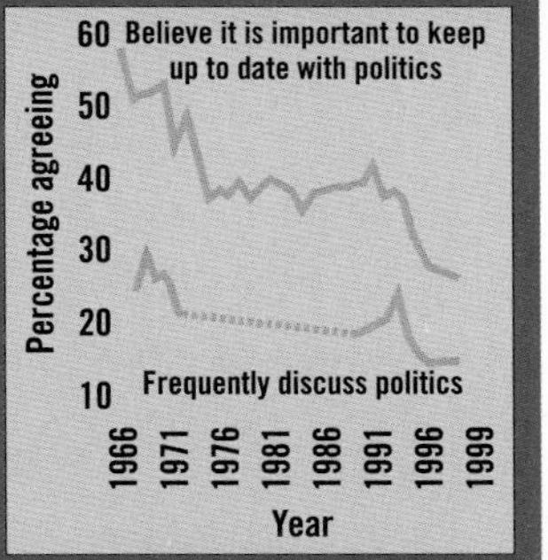

SOURCE: L. J. Sax, A. W. Astin, W. S. Korn, and K. M. Mahoney, *The American Freshman:* National Norms for Fall 1999 (Los Angeles: Higher Education Research Institute, UCLA Graduate School of Education, 1999).

public opinion
citizens' attitudes about political issues, leaders, institutions, and events

values (or beliefs)
basic principles that shape a person's opinions about political issues and events

political ideology
a cohesive set of beliefs that form a general philosophy about the role of government

attitude (or opinion)
a specific preference on a particular issue

center. "We won," declared striker Alison Harrington, who had to be hospitalized for dehydration after her fast. "This is the best class I have ever taken at Cal." she said.[3]

Public opinion is the term used to denote the values and attitudes that people have about issues, events, and personalities. Although the terms are sometimes used interchangeably, it is useful to distinguish between values and beliefs on the one hand, and attitudes or opinions on the other. **Values** (**or beliefs**) are a person's basic orientations to politics. Values represent deep-rooted goals, aspirations, and ideals that shape an individual's perceptions of political issues and events. Liberty, equality, and democracy are basic political values that most Americans hold. Another useful term for understanding public opinion is *ideology*. **Political ideology** refers to a complex set of beliefs and values that, as a whole, form a general philosophy about government. As we shall see, liberalism and conservatism are important ideologies in America today.

For example, the idea that governmental solutions to problems are inherently inferior to solutions offered by the private sector is a belief held by many Americans. This general belief, in turn, may lead individuals to have negative views of specific government programs even before they know much about them. An **attitude** (**or opinion**) is a specific view about a particular issue, personality, or event. An individual may have an opinion about Bill Clinton or an attitude toward American policy in Bosnia. The attitude or opinion may have emerged from a broad belief about Democrats or military intervention, but an attitude itself is very specific. Some attitudes may be short-lived.

This chapter will examine the role of public opinion in American politics.

- ***First, we will examine the political values and beliefs that inform how Americans perceive the political process.*** After reviewing the most basic American political values, we analyze how values and beliefs are formed and how certain processes and institutions influence their formation. We conclude this introductory section by looking at how a person's set of values and beliefs relates to political ideology.
- ***Second, we turn to the process of how political opinions are formed.*** We begin by assessing the relative importance of ideology in this process. We then look at the roles that one's knowledge of politics and influence of political leaders, private groups, and the media have on the formation of political views.
- ***Third, we view the science of gathering and measuring public opinion.*** The reliability of public opinion is directly related to the way in which it is gathered. Despite the limitations of public opinion polls, they remain an important part of the American political process.
- ***Finally, we conclude with an assessment of the implications of public opinion on American democracy.*** Is government responsive to public opinion? Should it be?

Political Values

- In what ways do Americans agree on fundamental values but disagree on fundamental issues?
- How are political values and beliefs formed? What influences individuals' political beliefs?
- What do the differences between liberals and conservatives reveal about American political debate?

When we think of opinion, we often think in terms of differences of opinion. The media are fond of reporting and analyzing political differences between blacks and whites, men and women (the so-called gender gap), the young and old, and so on. Certainly, Americans differ on many issues, and often these differences do seem to be associated with race, religion, gender, age, or other social characteristics. Today, Americans seem sharply divided on truly fundamental questions about the role of government in American society, the proper place of religious and moral values in public life, and how best to deal with racial conflicts.

FUNDAMENTAL VALUES

As we review these differences, however, it is important to remember that Americans also agree on a number of matters. Indeed, most Americans share a common set of values, including a belief in the principles—if not always the actual practice—of liberty, equality, and democracy. **Equality of opportunity** has always been an important theme in American society. Americans believe that all individuals should be allowed to seek personal and material success. Moreover, Americans generally believe that such success should be linked to personal effort and ability, rather than to family "connections" or other forms of special privilege. Similarly, Americans have always voiced strong support for the principle of individual **liberty.** They typically support the notion that governmental interference with individuals' lives and property should be kept to the minimum consistent with the general welfare (although in recent years Americans have grown accustomed to greater levels of governmental intervention than would have been deemed appropriate by the founders of liberal theory). And most Americans also believe in **democracy.** They presume that every person should have the opportunity to take part in the nation's governmental and policy-making processes and to have some "say" in determining how they are governed.[4] Figure 7.1 on the next page offers some indication of this American consensus on fundamental values: 95 percent of those polled believed in equal opportunity, 89 percent supported free speech regardless of the views being expressed, and 95 percent supported majority rule.

equality of opportunity
a widely shared American ideal that all people should have the freedom to use whatever talents and wealth they have to reach their fullest potential

liberty
freedom from government control

democracy
a system of rule that permits citizens to play a significant part in the governmental process, usually through the election of key public officials

One indication that Americans of all political stripes share these fundamental political values is the content of the acceptance speeches delivered by Al Gore and George W. Bush upon receiving their parties' presidential nominations in 2000. Gore and Bush differed on many issues and policies. Yet the political visions they presented reveal an underlying similarity. A major

Figure 7.1 AMERICANS' SUPPORT FOR FUNDAMENTAL VALUES

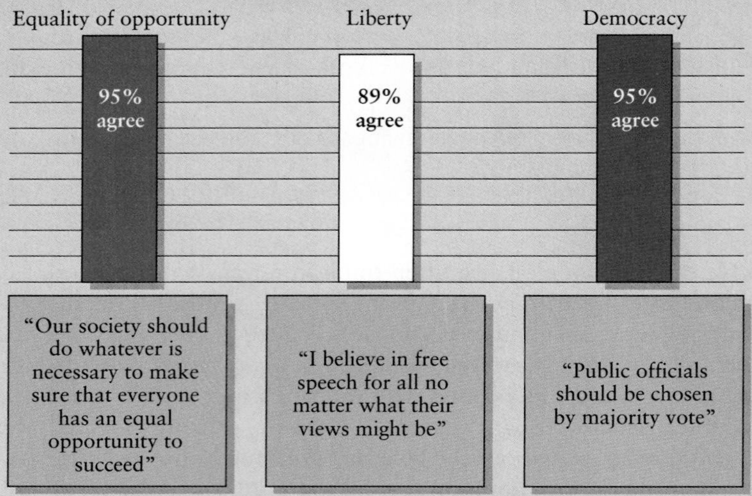

SOURCES: 1992 American National Election Studies; Herbert McCloskey and John Zaller, *The American Ethos: Public Attitudes toward Capitalism and Democracy* (Cambridge, MA: Harvard University Press, 1984), p. 25; and Robert S. Erikson, Norman R. Luttbeg, and Kent L. Tedin, *American Public Opinion: Its Origins, Content, and Impact,* 4th ed. (New York: Macmillan, 1991), p. 108.

emphasis of both candidates was equality of opportunity. Gore referred frequently to opportunity in his speeches, as in this poignant story about his own parents' efforts to make better lives for themselves and their children:

> My father grew up in a small community named Possum Hollow in Middle Tennessee. When he was just eighteen he went to work as a teacher in a one-room school. . . . He entered public service to fight for the people. My mother grew up in a small farming community in northwest Tennessee. She went on to become one of the first women in history to graduate from Vanderbilt Law School. . . . Every hard-working family in America deserves to open the door to their dream.

Bush struck a similar note in his acceptance speech:

> We will seize this moment of American promise. . . . And we will extend the promise of prosperity to every forgotten corner of this country. To every man and woman, a chance to succeed. To every child, a chance to learn. To every family, a chance to live with dignity and hope.

Thus, however much the two candidates differed on means and specifics, their understandings of the fundamental goals of government were quite similar.

Agreement on fundamental political values, though certainly not absolute, is probably more widespread in the United States than anywhere else in the Western world. During the course of Western political history, competing economic, social, and political groups put forward a variety of radically divergent

PROFILE OF A LIBERAL: JESSE JACKSON

Box 7.1

Advocates increasing taxes for corporations and for the wealthy.
Advocates a "Right to Food Policy" to make available a nutritionally balanced diet for all U.S. citizens.
Advocates the establishment of a national health care program for all citizens.
Advocates higher salaries for teachers, more college grants and loans, and a doubling of the federal education budget.
Favors increasing the minimum wage.
Advocates the use of $500 billion in pension funds to finance public works programs, including the construction of a "national railroad."
Favors foreign assistance programs designed to wipe out hunger and starvation throughout the world.
Advocates dramatic expansion of federal social and urban programs.

federal social services, and more vigorous efforts on behalf of the poor, minorities, and women, as well as greater concern for consumers and the environment. In social and cultural areas, liberals generally support abortion rights, are concerned with the rights of persons accused of crime, support decriminalization of drug use, and oppose state involvement with religious institutions and religious expression. In international affairs, liberal positions are usually seen as including support for arms control, opposition to the development and testing of nuclear weapons, support for aid to poor nations, opposition to the use of American troops to influence the domestic affairs of developing nations, and support for international organizations such as the United Nations. Of course, liberalism is not monolithic. For example, among individuals who view themselves as liberal, many support American military intervention when it is tied to a humanitarian purpose, as in the case of America's military action in Kosovo in 1998–99.

PROFILE OF A CONSERVATIVE: PAT BUCHANAN

Box 7.2

Wants to trim the size of the federal government and transfer power to state and local governments. Wants to diminish government regulation of business.
Favors prayer in the public schools.
Opposes gay rights legislation.
Supports programs that would allow children and parents more flexibility in deciding what school to attend.
Supports strict regulation of pornography.
Favors making most abortions illegal.
Would eliminate some environmental regulations.
Supports harsher treatment of criminals.
Opposes affirmative action programs.
Opposes allowing women to serve in military combat units.
Opposes U.S. participation in international organizations.
Opposes the North American Free Trade Agreement (NAFTA).

conservative

today this term refers to those who generally support the social and economic status quo and are suspicious of efforts to introduce new political formulae and economic arrangements. Conservatives believe that a large and powerful government poses a threat to citizens' freedom

By contrast, the term **conservative** today is used to describe those who generally support the social and economic status quo and are suspicious of efforts to introduce new political formulae and economic arrangements. Conservatives believe strongly that a large and powerful government poses a threat to citizens' freedom. Thus, in the domestic arena, conservatives generally oppose the expansion of governmental activity, asserting that solutions to social and economic problems can be developed in the private sector. Conservatives particularly oppose efforts to impose government regulation on business, pointing out that such regulation is frequently economically inefficient and costly and can ultimately lower the entire nation's standard of living. As to social and cultural positions, many conservatives oppose abortion, support school prayer, are more concerned for the victims than the perpetrators of crimes, oppose school busing, and support traditional family arrangements. In international affairs, conservatism has come to mean support for the maintenance of American military power. Like liberalism, conservatism is far from a monolithic ideology. Some conservatives support many government social programs. Republican George W. Bush calls himself a "compassionate conservative" to indicate that he favors programs that assist the poor and needy. Other conservatives oppose efforts to outlaw abortion, arguing that government intrusion in this area is as misguided as government intervention in the economy. Such a position is sometimes called "libertarian." In a similar vein, Pat Buchanan has angered many fellow conservatives by opposing most American military intervention in other regions. Many conservatives charge Buchanan with advocating a form of American "isolationism" that runs counter to contemporary conservative doctrine. The real political world is far too complex to be seen in terms of a simple struggle between liberals and conservatives.

To some extent, contemporary liberalism and conservatism can be seen as differences of emphasis with regard to the fundamental American political values of liberty and equality. For liberals, equality is the most important of the core values. Liberals are willing to tolerate government intervention in such areas as college admissions and business decisions when these seem to result in high levels of race, class, or gender inequality. For conservatives, on the other hand, liberty is the core value. Conservatives oppose most efforts by the government, however well intentioned, to intrude into private life or the marketplace. This simple formula for distinguishing liberalism and conservatism, however, is not always accurate, because political ideologies seldom lend themselves to neat or logical characterizations. Often political observers search for logical connections among the various positions identified with liberalism or with conservatism, and they are disappointed or puzzled when they are unable to find a set of coherent philosophical principles that define and unite the several elements of either of these sets of beliefs. On the liberal side, for example, what is the logical connection between opposition to U.S. government intervention in the affairs of foreign nations and calls for greater intervention in America's economy and society? On the conservative side, what is the logical relationship between opposition to governmental regulation of business and support for a government ban on abortion? Indeed, the latter would seem to be just the sort of regulation of private conduct that conservatives claim to abhor.

Frequently, the relationships among the various elements of liberalism or of conservatism are political rather then logical. One underlying basis of lib-

Student Perspectives

THE AMERICAN FRESHMAN

"How would you describe your political orientation?"

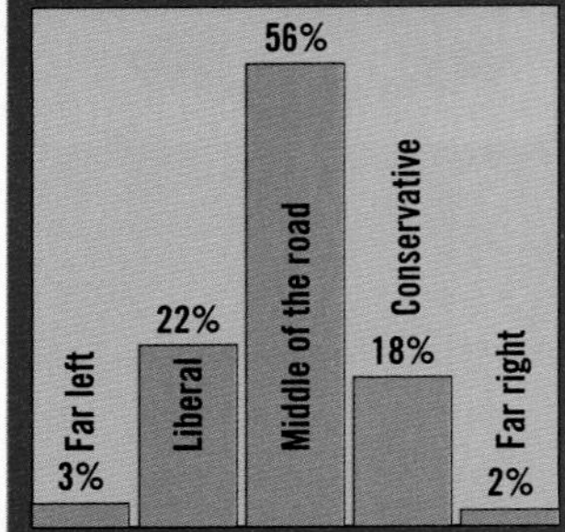

SOURCE: L. J. Sax, A. W. Astin, W. S. Korn, and K. M. Mahoney, *The American Freshman: National Norms for Fall 1999* (Los Angeles: Higher Education Research Institute, UCLA Graduate School of Education, 1999).

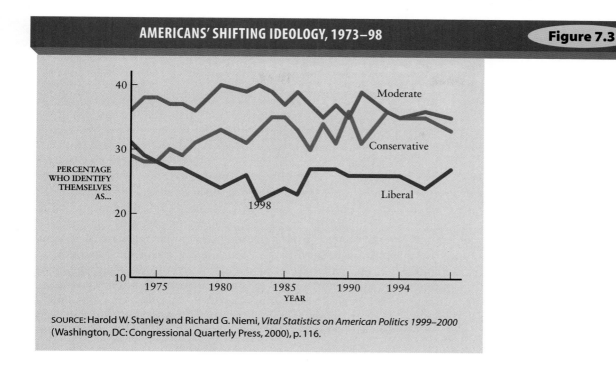

AMERICANS' SHIFTING IDEOLOGY, 1973–98

Figure 7.3

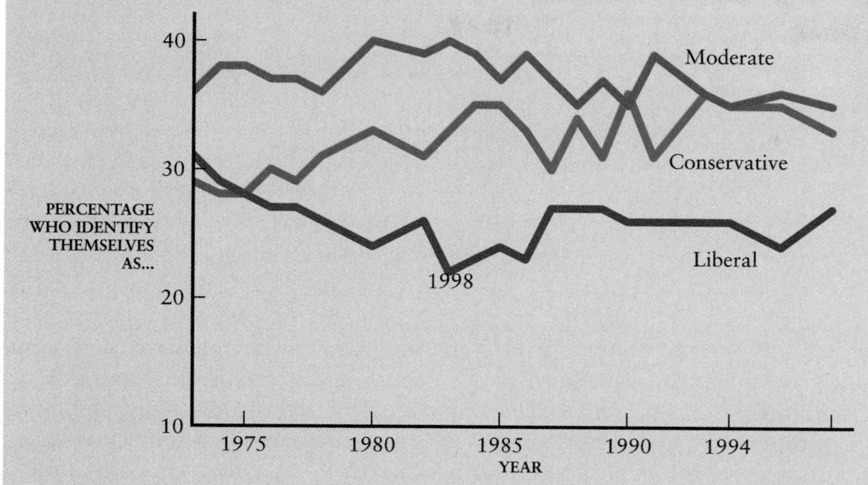

SOURCE: Harold W. Stanley and Richard G. Niemi, *Vital Statistics on American Politics 1999–2000* (Washington, DC: Congressional Quarterly Press, 2000), p. 116.

eral views is that all or most represent criticisms of or attacks on the foreign and domestic policies and cultural values of the business and commercial strata that have been prominent in the United States for the past century. In some measure, the tenets of contemporary conservatism represent this elite's defense of its positions against its enemies, who include organized labor, minority groups, and some intellectuals and professionals. Thus, liberals attack business and commercial elites by advocating more governmental regulation, including consumer protection and environmental regulation, opposing new military weapons programs, and supporting expensive social programs. Conservatives counterattack by asserting that governmental regulation of the economy is ruinous and that new military weapons are needed in a changing world, and they seek to stigmatize their opponents for showing no concern for the rights of "unborn" Americans.

Of course, it is important to note that many people who call themselves liberals or conservatives accept only part of the liberal or conservative ideology. During the 1980s, many political commentators asserted that Americans were becoming increasingly conservative. Indeed, it was partly in response to this view that the Democrats in 1992 selected a presidential candidate, Bill Clinton, drawn from the party's moderate wing. Although it appears that Americans have adopted more conservative outlooks on some issues, their views in most areas have remained largely unchanged or even have become more liberal in recent years. Thus, many individuals who are liberal on social issues are conservative on economic issues. There is nothing illogical about these mixed positions. They simply indicate the relatively open and fluid character of American political debate. As Figure 7.3 indicates, Americans are often apt to shift their ideological preferences.

How We Form Political Opinions

- What influences the way we form political opinions?
- How are political issues marketed and managed by the government, private groups, and the media?

An individual's opinions on particular issues, events, and personalities emerge as he or she evaluates these phenomena through the lenses of the beliefs and orientations that, taken together, comprise his or her political ideology. Thus, if a conservative is confronted with a plan to expand federal social programs, he or she is likely to express opposition to the endeavor without spending too much time pondering the specific plan. Similarly, if a liberal is asked to comment on conservative former president Ronald Reagan, he or she is not likely to hesitate long before offering a negative view. Underlying beliefs and ideologies tend to automatically color people's perceptions and opinions about politics.

Opinions on particular issues, however, are seldom fully shaped by underlying ideologies. Few individuals possess ideologies so cohesive and intensely held that they will automatically shape all their opinions. Indeed, when we occasionally encounter individuals with rigid worldviews, who see everything through a particular political lens, we tend to dismiss them as "ideologues," or lacking common sense.

Although ideologies color our political perspectives, they seldom fully determine our views. This is true for a variety of reasons. First, as noted earlier, most individuals' ideologies contain internal contradictions. Take, for example, a conservative view of the issue of abortion. Should conservatives favor outlawing abortion as an appropriate means of preserving public morality, or should they oppose restrictions on abortion because these represent government intrusions into private life? In this instance, as in many others, ideology can point in different directions.

Second, individuals may have difficulty linking particular issues or personalities to their own underlying beliefs. Some issues defy ideological characterization. Should conservatives have supported or opposed the 1999 "Patient's Bill of Rights" that made it easier for individuals to file suit against the widely unpopular health maintenance organizations (HMOs), which came to dominate American health care in the 1990s? What should liberals think about America's 1998–99 bombing campaign against Serbia and continued bombing of Iraq? Each of these policies combines a mix of issues and is too complex to be viewed through simple ideological lenses.

Finally, most people have at least some conflicting underlying attitudes. Most conservatives support *some* federal programs—defense, or tax deductions for businesses, for example—and wish to see them, and hence the government, expanded. Many liberals favor American military intervention in other nations for what they deem to be humanitarian purposes, but generally oppose American military intervention in the affairs of other nations.

Thus, most individuals' attitudes on particular issues do not spring automatically from their ideological predispositions. It is true that most people have underlying beliefs that help to shape their opinions on particular issues, but two other factors are also important: a person's knowledge of political issues, and outside influences on that person's views.

POLITICAL KNOWLEDGE

As we have seen, general political beliefs can guide the formation of opinions on specific issues, but an individual's beliefs and opinions are not always consistent with one another. Studies of political opinion have shown that most people don't hold specific and clearly defined opinions on every political issue. As a result, they are easily influenced by others. What best explains whether citizens are generally consistent in their political views or inconsistent and open to the influence of others? The key is knowledge and information about political issues. In general, knowledgeable citizens are better able to evaluate new information and determine whether it is relevant to and consistent with their beliefs and opinions. As a result, better-informed individuals can recognize their political interests and act consistently on behalf of them.

One of the most obvious and important examples of this proposition is voting. Despite the predisposition of voters to support their own party's candidates (see Chapter 10 for a discussion of party identification), millions of voters are affected by the information they receive about candidates during a campaign. During the 1996 presidential campaign, for instance, voters weighed the arguments of Bill Clinton against those of Bob Dole about who was better fit to run the U.S. economy based on what they (the voters) knew about the country's economic health. Many Republican voters actually supported Bill Clinton because they approved of the economic policies followed during his first term in office. Thus citizens can use information and judgment to overcome their predispositions. Without some political knowledge, citizens would have a difficult time making sense of the complex political world in which they live.

This point brings up two questions, however. First, how much political knowledge is necessary for one to act as an effective citizen? And second, how is political knowledge distributed throughout the population? In a recent study of political knowledge in the United States, political scientists Michael X. DelliCarpini and Scott Keeter found that the average American exhibits little knowledge of political institutions, processes, leaders, and policy debates. For example, in a 1996 poll, only about half of all Americans could correctly identify Newt Gingrich as the Speaker of the House of Representatives.[16] Does this ignorance of key political facts matter?

Another important concern is the character of those who possess and act upon the political information that they acquire. Political knowledge is not evenly distributed throughout the population. As we saw in Chapters 1 and 2, those with higher education, income, and occupational status and who are members of social or political organizations are more likely to know about and be active in politics. An interest in politics reinforces an individual's sense of **political efficacy** and provides more incentive to acquire additional knowledge and information about politics. Those who don't think they can have an effect on government tend not to be interested in learning about or participating in politics. As a result, individuals with a disproportionate share of income and education also have a disproportionate share of knowledge and influence and are better able to get what they want from government.

political efficacy
the ability to influence government and politics

THE INFLUENCE OF POLITICAL LEADERS, PRIVATE GROUPS, AND THE MEDIA

When individuals attempt to form opinions about particular political issues, events, and personalities, they seldom do so in isolation. Typically, they are confronted—sometimes bombarded—by the efforts of a host of individuals and groups seeking to persuade them to adopt a particular point of view. Someone trying to decide what to think about Bill Clinton, Colin Powell, or Newt Gingrich could hardly avoid an avalanche of opinions expressed through the media, in meetings, or in conversations with friends. The **marketplace of ideas** is the interplay of opinions and views that takes place as competing forces attempt to persuade as many people as possible to accept a particular position on a particular event. Given constant exposure to the ideas of others, it is virtually impossible for most individuals to resist some modification of their own beliefs. For example, as we saw earlier, African Americans and white Americans disagree on a number of matters. Yet, as political scientists Paul Sniderman and Edward Carmines have shown, considerable cross-racial agreement has evolved on fundamental issues of race and civil rights.[17]

The marketplace of ideas has created a common ground on which the discussion of issues is encouraged, based on common understandings. Despite the many and often sharp divisions that exist in the twentieth century—between liberals and conservatives or different income groups—most Americans see the world through similar lenses. This idea market makes it possible for ideas of all sorts to compete for attention and acceptance.

Few ideas spread spontaneously. Usually, whether they are matters of fashion, science, or politics, ideas must be vigorously promoted to become widely known and accepted. For example, the clothing, sports, and entertainment fads that occasionally seem to appear from nowhere and sweep the country before being replaced by some other new trend are almost always the product of careful marketing campaigns by some commercial interest, rather than spontaneous phenomena. Like their counterparts in fashion, successful—or at least widely held—political ideas are usually the products of carefully orchestrated campaigns by government or by organized groups and interests, rather than the results of spontaneous popular enthusiasm. In general, new ideas are presented in ways that make them seem consistent with, or even logical outgrowths of, Americans' more fundamental beliefs. For example, proponents of affirmative action generally present the policy as a necessary step toward racial equality. Or opponents of a proposed government regulation will vehemently assert that the rule is inconsistent with

Student Perspectives

NEW POLL CONFIRMS POLITICAL APATHY AMONG COLLEGE STUDENTS

College-age people are less trusting of politicians and less engaged in politics than are people over twenty-five, according to a report released Monday by political awareness group Project Vote Smart.

Project Vote Smart, a nonpartisan political research group, surveyed respondents divided into a group of 18- to 25-year-olds and a group of people over 25.

Only 22 percent of the younger group said they pay "a lot" of attention to national affairs, versus 37 percent of the older group. Twenty-four percent of the younger group said they did not trust any level of government.

Planned participation in the 2000 election also was lower among the younger set.

Only 45 percent of younger people said they definitely would vote in the 2000 elections, while 64 percent of the older respondents said they would.

They study also shows that the younger group gets news from the Internet more than older people do.

Kristina Saleh, Project Vote Smart assistant director of public information, said the younger group's use of the Internet provides them with more objective information than other sources offer.

"Just because young people aren't coming out in droves to vote doesn't mean that we're not voting smart," Saleh said. "We're voting smarter than the older crowd simply because we're not looking at one source for information."

marketplace of ideas
the public forum in which beliefs and ideas are exchanged and compete

liberty. Both supporters and opponents of campaign finance reform seek to wrap their arguments in the cloak of democracy.[18]

Three forces that play important roles in shaping opinions are the government, private groups, and the news media.

Government and the Shaping of Public Opinion All governments attempt, to a greater or lesser extent, to influence, manipulate, or manage their citizens' beliefs. But the extent to which public opinion is actually affected by governmental public relations efforts is probably limited. The government—despite its size and power—is only one source of information and evaluation in the United States. Very often, governmental claims are disputed by the media, by interest groups, and at times by opposing forces within the government itself. Often, too, governmental efforts to manipulate public opinion backfire when the public is made aware of the government's tactics. Thus, in 1971, the United States government's efforts to build popular support for the Vietnam War were hurt when CBS News aired its documentary "The Selling of the Pentagon," which purported to reveal the extent and character of governmental efforts to sway popular sentiment. In this documentary, CBS demonstrated the techniques, including planted news stories and faked film footage, that the government had used to misrepresent its activities in Vietnam. These revelations, of course, undermined popular trust in all governmental claims.

A hallmark of the Clinton administration was the steady use of techniques like those used in election campaigns to bolster popular enthusiasm for White House initiatives. The president established a political "war room," similar to the one that operated in his campaign headquarters, where representatives from all departments meet daily to discuss and coordinate the president's public relations efforts. Many of the same consultants and pollsters who directed the successful Clinton campaign were also employed in the selling of the president's programs.[19]

Indeed, the Clinton White House made more sustained and systematic use of public-opinion polling than any previous administration. For example, during his presidency Bill Clinton relied heavily on the polling firm of Penn & Schoen to help him decide which issues to emphasize and what strategies to adopt. During the 1995–96 budget battle with Congress, the White House commissioned polls almost every night to chart changes in public perceptions about the struggle. Poll data suggested to Clinton that he should present himself as struggling to save Medicare from Republican cuts. Clinton responded by launching a media attack against what he claimed were GOP efforts to hurt the elderly. This

Student Perspectives (cont.)

[S]tudent leaders said they deplore what they view as marginal interest in political issues among most students at the University [of Virginia].

In the fall of 1997, Ben Seisler helped found Students v. Apathy, a University organization dedicated to informing students and promoting political activity.

Seisler said the lack of student participation in politics is unfortunate.

"The average student doesn't seem to be overly concerned with what's going on at Capitol Hill," he said.

He added that providing information is a good way to spark interest.

"If you inform people, that will encourage them to be more politically active," Seisler said.

College Republicans Chairman John Blair also said educating people was key to increasing the numbers of younger voters, which he said is at an "unacceptably low level.

"I think the survey results show that there is a need for better high-school history, government, and civics classes to educate young people," Blair said.

Politicians also bear some responsibility for low turnout among the college-age group, University Democrats President Rhodes Ritenour said.

"A lot of politicians don't articulate to people why they are important," Ritenour said. "That's what will get people out to the polls."

SOURCE: Clark Williams, *Daily Cavalier* (University of Virginia), September 15, 1999.

Bill Clinton was often criticized for relying too extensively on public opinion polling results to shape his political agenda.

proved to be a successful strategy and helped Clinton defeat the Republican budget.[20] Similarly, in 1999, poll data convinced Clinton that the public would support his position during his struggle with congressional Republicans over the budget. Republicans sought to use projected budget surpluses to fund more than $700 billion in tax cuts over a five-year period. Clinton argued that the projected revenues should be used for what he called investments in education, technology, the environment, and health care for the elderly, and he promised to veto the Republican bill.[21] First Lady Hillary Rodham Clinton has also made extensive use of polling to guide her political actions. For example, Mrs. Clinton's July 1999 remarks suggesting that her husband had been guilty of marital infidelities because he was a "victim" of childhood conflicts between his mother and grandmother were linked to poll data suggesting that she needed to raise and dispose of the issue well before the start of her planned New York senate bid.[22] The administration, however, has asserted that it uses polls only as a check on its communications strategy.[23]

Of course, at the same time that the Clinton administration worked diligently to mobilize popular support, its opponents struggled equally hard to mobilize popular opinion against the White House. A host of public and private interest groups opposed to President Clinton's programs crafted public relations campaigns designed to generate opposition to the president. For example, in 1994, while Clinton campaigned to bolster popular support for his health care reform proposals, groups representing small businesses and segments of the insurance industry, among others, developed their own publicity campaigns that ultimately convinced many Americans that Clinton's initiative posed a threat to their own health care. These opposition campaigns played an important role in the eventual defeat of the president's proposal.

Private Groups and the Shaping of Public Opinion As the story of the health care debate may suggest, political issues and ideas seldom emerge spontaneously from the grass roots. We have already seen how the government tries to shape public opinion. But the ideas that become prominent in political life are also developed and spread by important economic and political groups searching for issues that will advance their causes. One example is the "right-to-life" issue that has inflamed American politics over the past twenty years.

The notion of right-to-life, whose proponents seek to outlaw abortion and overturn the Supreme Court's *Roe v. Wade* decision, was developed and heavily promoted by conservative politicians who saw the issue of abortion as a means of uniting Catholic and Protestant conservatives and linking both groups to the Republican Party. These politicians convinced Catholic and evangelical Protestant leaders that they shared similar views on the question of abortion, and they worked with religious leaders to focus public attention on the negative issues in the abortion debate. To advance their cause, leaders of the movement sponsored well-publicized Senate hearings, where testimony, photographs, and other exhibits were presented to illustrate the violent effects of abortion procedures. At the same time, publicists for the movement produced leaflets, articles, books, and films such as *The Silent Scream* to highlight the agony and pain ostensibly felt by the "unborn" when they were being aborted. All this underscored the movement's claim that abortion was nothing more or less than the murder of millions of innocent human beings. Finally, Catholic and evangelical Protestant religious leaders were organized to denounce abortion from their church pulpits and, increasingly, from their electronic pulpits on the Christian Broadcasting Network (CBN) and the various other television forums available for religious programming. Religious leaders also organized demonstrations, pickets, and disruptions at abortion clinics throughout the nation.[24] Abortion rights remain a potent issue; it even influenced the debate over health care reform.

Typically, ideas are marketed most effectively by groups with access to financial resources, public or private institutional support, and sufficient skill or education to select, develop, and draft ideas that will attract interest and support. Thus, the development and promotion of conservative themes and ideas in recent years has been greatly facilitated by the millions of dollars that conservative corporations and business organizations such as the Chamber of Commerce and the Public Affairs Council spend each year on public information and what is now called in corporate circles "issues management." In addition, conservative business leaders have contributed millions of dollars to such conservative institutions as the Heritage Foundation, the Hoover Institution, and the American Enterprise Institute.[25] Many of the ideas that helped those on the right influence political debate were first developed and articulated by scholars associated with institutions such as these.

Although they do not usually have access to financial assets that match those available to their conservative opponents, liberal intellectuals and professionals have ample organizational skills, access to the media, and practice in creating, communicating, and using ideas. During the past three decades, the chief vehicle through which liberal intellectuals and professionals have advanced their ideas has been the "public interest group," an institution that relies heavily on voluntary contributions of time, effort, and interest on the part of its members. Through groups like Common Cause, the National Organization for Women, the Sierra Club, Friends of the Earth, and Physicians for

Social Responsibility, intellectuals and professionals have been able to use their organizational skills and educational resources to develop and promote ideas.[26] Often, research conducted in universities and in liberal "think tanks" such as the Brookings Institution provides the ideas on which liberal politicians rely. For example, the welfare reform plan introduced by the Clinton administration in 1994 originated with the work of former Harvard professor David Ellwood. Ellwood's academic research led him to the conclusion that the nation's welfare system would be improved if services to the poor were expanded in scope but limited in duration. His idea was adopted by the 1992 Clinton campaign, which was searching for a position on welfare that would appeal to both liberal and conservative Democrats. The Ellwood plan seemed perfect: It promised liberals an immediate expansion of welfare benefits, yet it held out to conservatives the idea that welfare recipients would receive benefits only for a limited period of time. The Clinton welfare reform plan even borrowed phrases from Ellwood's book *Poor Support*.[27]

Journalist and author Joe Queenan has correctly observed that although political ideas can erupt spontaneously, they almost never do. Instead, he says,

> issues are usually manufactured by tenured professors and obscure employees of think tanks. . . . It is inconceivable that the American people, all by themselves, could independently arrive at the conclusion that the depletion of the ozone layer poses a dire threat to our national well-being, or that an immediate, across-the-board cut in the capital-gains tax is the only thing that stands between us and the economic abyss. The American people do not have that kind of sophistication. *They have to have help.*[28]

The Media and Public Opinion The communications media are among the most powerful forces operating in the marketplace of ideas. As we shall see in Chapter 8, the mass media are not simply neutral messengers for ideas developed by others. Instead, the media have an enormous impact on popular attitudes and opinions. Over time, the ways in which the mass media report political events help to shape the underlying attitudes and beliefs from which opinions emerge.[29] For example, for the past thirty years, the national news media have relentlessly investigated personal and official wrongdoing on the part of politicians and public officials. This continual media presentation of corruption in government and venality in politics has undoubtedly fostered the general attitude of cynicism and distrust that exists in the general public.

At the same time, the ways in which media coverage interprets or frames specific events can have a major impact on popular responses and opinions about these events.[30] As we shall see in Chapter 8, the media presented the 1996 budget battle between President Clinton and then Speaker of the House Newt Gingrich in a way that served Clinton's interests. By forcing the closing of a number of government agencies, Gingrich hoped that the media would point out how smoothly life could proceed with less government involvement. Instead, the media focused on the hardships the closings inflicted on out-of-work government employees in the months before Christmas. The way in which the media framed the discussion helped turn opinion against Gingrich and handed Clinton an important victory.

Measuring Public Opinion

- How can public opinion be measured?
- What problems arise from public opinion polling?

As recently as fifty years ago, American political leaders gauged public opinion by people's applause and by the presence of crowds at meetings. This direct exposure to the people's views did not necessarily produce accurate knowledge of public opinion. It did, however, give political leaders confidence in their public support—and therefore confidence in their ability to govern by consent.

Abraham Lincoln and Stephen Douglas debated each other seven times in the summer and autumn of 1858, two years before they became presidential nominees. Their debates took place before audiences in parched cornfields and courthouse squares. A century later, the presidential debates, although seen by millions, take place before a few reporters and technicians in television studios that might as well be on the moon. The public's response cannot be experienced directly. This distance between leaders and followers is one of the agonizing problems of modern democracy. The media send information to millions of people, but they are not yet as efficient at getting information back to leaders. Is government by consent possible where the scale of communication is so large and impersonal? In order to compensate for the decline in their ability to experience public opinion for themselves, leaders have turned to science, in particular to the science of opinion polling.

It is no secret that politicians and public officials make extensive use of **public opinion polls** to help them decide whether to run for office, what policies to support, how to vote on important legislation, and what types of appeals to make in their campaigns. President Lyndon Johnson was famous for carrying the latest Gallup and Roper poll results in his pocket, and it is widely believed that he began to withdraw from politics because the polls reported losses in public support. All recent presidents and other major political figures have worked closely with polls and pollsters.

public opinion polls
scientific instruments for measuring public opinion

CONSTRUCTING PUBLIC OPINION FROM SURVEYS

The population in which pollsters are interested is usually quite large. To conduct their polls they first choose a **sample** of the total population. The selection of this sample is important. Above all, it must be representative; the views of those in the sample must accurately and proportionately reflect the views of the whole. To a large extent, the validity of the poll's results depends on the sampling procedure used (see Box 7.3 on the next page).

sample
a small group selected by researchers to represent the most important characteristics of an entire population

The degree of reliability in polling is a function of sample size. The same sample is needed to represent a small population as to represent a large population. The typical size of a sample ranges from 450 to 1,500 respondents. This number, however, reflects a trade-off between cost and degree of precision desired. The degree of accuracy that can be achieved with even a small sample can be seen from the polls' success in predicting election outcomes. The chance

Box 7.3 METHODS OF MEASURING PUBLIC OPINION

Interpreting Mass Opinion from Mass Behavior and Mass Attributes

Consumer behavior: predicts that people tend to vote against the party in power during a downturn in the economy

Group demographics: can predict party affiliation and voting by measuring income, race, and type of community (urban or rural)

Getting Public Opinion Directly from the People

Person-to-person: form impressions based on conversations with acquaintances, aides, and associates

Selective polling: form impressions based on interviews with a few representative members of a group or groups

Bellwether districts: form impressions based on an entire community that has a reputation for being a good predictor of the entire nation's attitudes

Constructing Public Opinion from Surveys

Quota sampling: respondents are chosen because they match a general population along several significant dimensions, such as geographic region, sex, age, and race

Probability sampling: respondents are chosen without prior screening, based entirely on a lottery system

Area sampling: respondents are chosen as part of a systematic breakdown of larger homogeneous units into smaller representative areas

Haphazard sampling: respondents are chosen by pure chance with no systematic method

Systematically biased sampling: respondents are chosen with a hidden or undetected bias toward a given demographic group

that the sample used does not accurately represent the population from which it is drawn is called the *sampling error* or *margin of error.* A typical survey of 1,500 respondents will have a sampling error of approximately 3 percent. When a preelection poll indicates 51 percent of voters surveyed favor the Republican candidate and 49 percent support the Democratic candidate, the outcome is too close to call because it is within the margin of error of the survey. A figure of 51 percent means that between 54 and 48 percent of voters in the population favor the Republicans, while a figure of 49 percent indicates that between 52 and 46 percent of all voters support the Democrats. Thus, in this example, 52-to-48 percent Democratic victory would still be consistent with polls predicting a 51-to-49 percent Republican triumph.

Table 7.3 shows how accurate two of the major national polling organizations actually have been in predicting the outcomes of presidential elections. While pollsters have been mostly correct in their predictions, the 2000 election proved to be an exception. Before the election, their results were a statistical dead heat—within the margin of error of the poll—but most predicted that Bush would get slightly more votes. This erroneous prediction most likely resulted from last-minute changes of mind among voters.

Even with reliable sampling procedures, problems can occur. Validity can be adversely affected by poor question format, faulty ordering of questions,

TWO POLLSTERS AND THEIR RECORDS (1948–2000) — Table 7.3

	Harris	Gallup	Actual outcome
2000			
Bush	47%	48%	48%
Gore	47	46	49
Nader	5	4	3
1996			
Clinton	51%	52%	49%
Dole	39	41	41
Perot	9	7	8
1992			
Clinton	44%	44%	43%
Bush	38	37	38
Perot	17	14	19
1988			
Bush	51%	53%	54%
Dukakis	47	42	46
1984			
Reagan	56%	59%	59%
Mondale	44	41	41
1980			
Reagan	48%	47%	51%
Carter	43	44	41
Anderson		8	
1976			
Carter	48%	48%	51%
Ford	45	49	48
1972			
Nixon	59%	62%	61%
McGovern	35	38	38
1968			
Nixon	40%	43%	43%
Humphrey	43	42	43
Wallace	13	15	14
1964			
Johnson	62%	64%	61%
Goldwater	33	36	39
1960			
Kennedy	49%	51%	50%
Nixon	41	49	49
1956			
Eisenhower	NA	60%	58%
Stevenson		41	42
1952			
Eisenhower	47%	51%	55%
Stevenson	42	49	44
1948			
Truman	NA	44.5%	49.6%
Dewey		49.5	45.1

All figures except those for 1948 are rounded. NA = Not asked.

SOURCE: Data from the Gallup Poll and the Harris Survey (New York: Chicago Tribune–New York News Syndicate, various press releases 1964–2000). Courtesy of the Gallup Organization and Louis Harris Associates.

Box 7.4 IT DEPENDS ON HOW YOU ASK

The public's desire for tax cuts can be hard to measure. Pollsters asking what should be done with the nation's budget surplus got different results depending on the specifics of the question.

The Question

President Clinton has proposed setting aside approximately two-thirds of an expected budget surplus to fix the Social Security system. What do you think the leaders in Washington should do with the remainder of the surplus?

Variation 1

Should the money be used for a tax cut, or should it be used to fund new government programs?

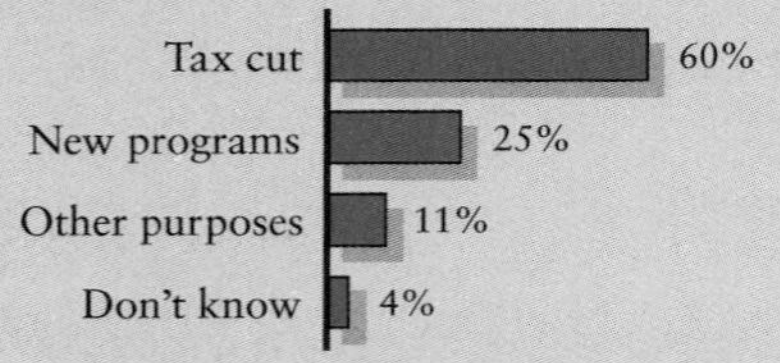

Variation 2

Should the money be used for a tax cut, or should it be spent on programs for education, the environment, health care, crime-fighting, and military defense?

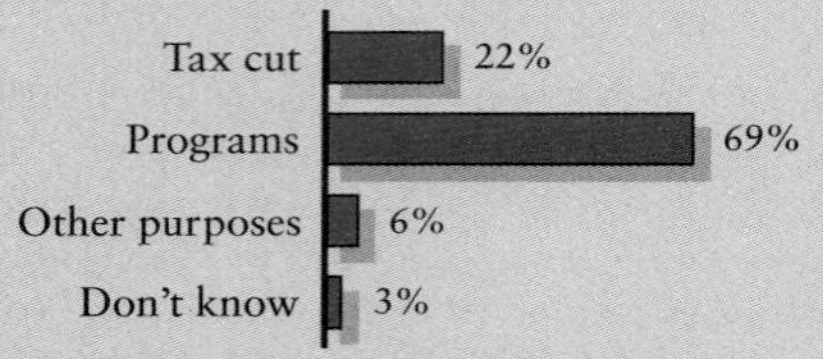

SOURCE: Pew Research Center, reported in *The New York Times,* January 30, 2000, p. WK 3.

inappropriate vocabulary, ambiguity of questions, or questions with built-in biases. Often, seemingly minor differences in the wording of a question can convey vastly different meanings to respondents and thus produce quite different response patterns (see Box 7.4). For example, for many years the University of Chicago's National Opinion Research Center has asked respondents whether they think the federal government is spending too much, too little, or about the right amount of money on "assistance for the poor." Answering the question posed this way, about two-thirds of all respondents seem to believe that the government is spending too little. However, the same survey also asks whether the government spends too much, too little, or about the right amount for "welfare." When the word "welfare" is substituted for "assistance for the poor," about half of all respondents indicate that too much is being spent.[31]

In the early days of a political campaign when voters are asked which candidates they do, or do not, support, the answer they give often has little significance, because the choice is not yet important to them. Their preferences may change many times before the actual election. This is part of the explanation for the phenomenon of the postconvention "bounce" in the popularity of presidential candidates, which was observed after the Democratic and Republican national conventions in 1992 and 1996.[32] Respondents' preferences reflected the amount of attention a candidate had received during the conventions rather than strongly held views.

Salient interests are interests that stand out beyond others, that are of more than ordinary concern to respondents in a survey or to voters in the electorate. Politicans, social scientists, journalists, or pollsters who assume something is important to the public, when in fact it is not, are creating an **illusion of saliency.** This illusion can be created and fostered by polls despite careful controls over sampling, interviewing, and data analysis. In fact, the illusion is strengthened by the credibility that science gives survey results.

salient interests
attitudes and views that are especially important to the individual holding them

illusion of saliency
the impression conveyed by polls that something is important to the public when actually it is not

The problem of saliency has become especially acute as a result of the proliferation of media polls. The television networks and major national newspapers all make heavy use of opinion polls. Increasingly, polls are being commissioned by local television stations and local and regional newspapers as well.[33] On the positive side, polls allow journalists to make independent assessments of political realities—assessments not influenced by the partisan claims of politicians.

At the same time, however, media polls can allow journalists to make news when none really exists. Polling diminishes journalists' dependence upon news makers. A poll commissioned by a news agency can provide the basis for a good story even when candidates, politicians, and other news makers refuse to cooperate by engaging in newsworthy activities. Thus, on days when little or nothing is actually taking place in a political campaign, poll results, especially apparent changes in candidate popularity margins, can provide exciting news.

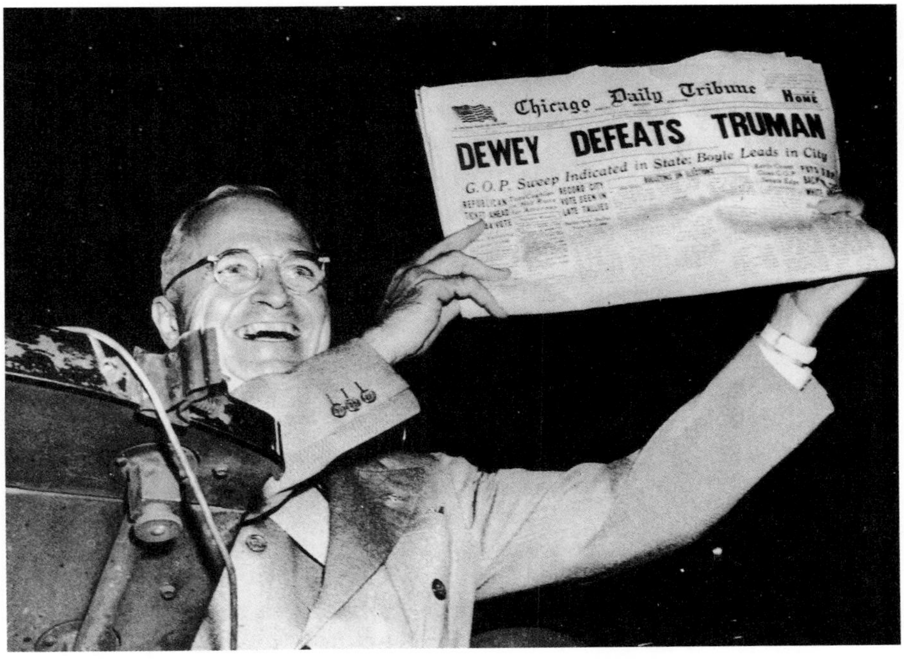

In probably the most famous instance of pollsters getting it wrong, Gallup predicted that Thomas E. Dewey would defeat Harry S. Truman in the 1948 presidential election. Truman, pictured here, won easily. The Gallup organization subsequently changed its polling methods.

Several times during the 2000 presidential campaign, for example, small changes in the relative standing of the Democratic and Republican candidates produced banner headlines around the country. Stories about what the candidates actually did or said often took second place to reporting the "horse race."

Interestingly, because rapid and dramatic shifts in candidate margins tend to take place when voters' preferences are least fully formed, horse-race news is most likely to make the headlines when it is actually least significant.[34] In other words, media interest in poll results is inversely related to the actual salience of voters' opinions and the significance of the polls' findings. However, by influencing perceptions, especially those of major contributors, media polls can influence political realities.

bandwagon effect
a shift in electoral support to the candidate that public opinion polls report as the front-runner

The most noted, but least serious, of polling problems is the **bandwagon effect,** which occurs when polling results influence people to support the candidate marked as the probable victor. Some scholars argue that this bandwagon effect can be offset by an "underdog effect" in favor of the candidate who is trailing in the polls.[35] However, a candidate who demonstrates a lead in the polls usually finds it considerably easier to raise campaign funds than a candidate whose poll standing is poor. With these additional funds, poll leaders can often afford to pay for television time and other campaign activities that will cement their advantage. For example, Bill Clinton's substantial lead in the polls during much of the summer of 1992 helped the Democrats raise far more money than in any previous campaign, primarily from interests hoping to buy access to a future President Clinton. For once, the Democrats were able to outspend the usually better-heeled Republicans. Thus, the *appearance* of a lead, as shown by the polls, helped make Clinton's lead a reality.

In 1996, some major polls were quite wrong in their predictions of the popular vote divisions in both the presidential and congressional races. For example, the *New York Times*/CBS News poll taken two days before the election predicted that Clinton would defeat Dole by a 53 to 35 percent margin (the actual margin was 49 to 41 percent). Similarly, most polls predicted that Democratic House candidates would defeat their GOP rivals by a margin of ten points on a national basis. On election day, however, Republican candidates out-polled the Democrats. The most striking polling error made in 1996 occurred in New Hampshire, where exit polls showed Democratic senatorial candidate Dick Swett defeating Republican senator Bob Smith by a solid 52 to 47 percent. Smith assumed he had lost until early the next morning when actual election results gave him a narrow victory. Some analysts believe that these poll errors are a subtle form of "liberal bias." Since voters often feel that the media have a liberal and Democratic slant, individuals who support the Republicans are slightly more reluctant to confess their true preferences to interviewers. Indications of this phenomenon have appeared in a number of Western democracies whose major media are deemed to be liberal in their political orientation.[36]

In 1998, Jesse Ventura's victory in the Minnesota gubernational election totally confounded the pollsters and revealed another weakness of preelection polling. A poll conducted by the *Minneapolis Star Tribune* just six weeks before the election showed Ventura running a distant third to Democratic candidate Hubert Humphrey III, who seemed to have the support of 49 percent of the electorate, and the Republican Norm Coleman, whose support stood at 29 percent. Only 10 percent of those polled said they were planning to vote for

Pre-election polling failed to account for Jesse Ventura's appeal among first-time voters who, thanks to Minnesotta's same-day voter registration rule, swept Ventura into office.

Ventura. On election day, of course, Ventura out-polled both Humphrey and Coleman. Analysis of exit-poll data showed why the preelection polls had been so wrong. In an effort to be more accurate, preelection pollsters' predictions often take account of the likelihood that respondents will actually vote. This is accomplished by polling only people who have voted in the past or correcting for past frequency of voting. The *Star Tribune* poll was conducted only among individuals who had voted in the previous election. Ventura, however, brought to the polls not only individuals who had not voted in the last election but many people who had never voted before in their lives. Twelve percent of Minnesota's voters in 1998 said they came to the polls only because Ventura was on the ballot. This surge in turnout was facilitated by the fact that Minnesota permits same-day voter registration (See Chapter 11 for a discussion of the consequences of registration rules). Thus, the pollsters were wrong because Ventura changed the composition of the electorate.[37]

In 2000, the use of daily tracking polls by the major news organizations provided a picture of day-to-day shifts in the electorate's mood. The polls revealed that many voters—nearly 10 percent of the electorate—remained undecided until Election Day. This high level of indecision apparently resulted from voters' lack of enthusiasm for both major party candidates. In the end, the tracking polls proved misleading. Most polling organizations seemed to show a narrow lead for Bush up until Election Day, but when the actual votes were counted, Gore won a razor-thin popular plurality.

Interestingly, network exit polls also led to a major error on election night. After Florida polls closed, television networks declared Gore the winner in Florida on the basis of exit poll results. Two hours later, the networks revised their estimates on the basis of actual vote counts and declared Florida too close to call. Furious Republicans asserted that the pollsters' errors might have persuaded GOP supporters that the race was hopeless and discouraged voting on the part of Republicans in western states where polls were still open. At 2 A.M., the networks proclaimed Bush the winner in Florida and, as a result, of the national election. Within one hour, however, they withdrew their projections and announced it was again too close to call. Ultimately, of course, the Florida results were not known until after a lengthy statewide recount and litigation by both presidential hopefuls.

push polling
a polling technique in which the questions are designed to shape the respondent's opinion

In recent years, a new form of bias has been introduced into surveys by the use of a technique called **push polling.** This technique involves asking a respondent a loaded question about a political candidate designed to elicit the response sought by the pollster and, simultaneously, to shape the respondent's perception of the candidate in question. For example, during the 1996 New Hampshire presidential primary, push pollsters employed by the campaign of one of Lamar Alexander's rivals called thousands of voters to ask, "If you knew that Lamar Alexander had raised taxes six times in Tennessee, would you be less inclined or more inclined to support him?"[38] More than one hundred consulting firms across the nation now specialize in push polling.[39] Calling push polling the "political equivalent of a drive-by shooting," Representative Joe Barton (R-Tex.) launched a congressional investigation into the practice.[40] Push polls may be one reason that Americans are becoming increasingly skeptical about the practice of polling and increasingly unwilling to answer pollsters' questions.[41]

Public Opinion and Democracy

▶ How responsive is the government to public opinion?

In democratic nations, leaders should pay heed to public opinion, and the evidence suggests that indeed they do. There are many instances in which public policy and public opinion do not coincide, but in general the government's actions are consistent with citizens' preferences. One recent study, for example, found that between 1935 and 1979, in about two-thirds of all cases, significant changes in public opinion were followed within one year by changes in government policy consistent with the shift in the popular mood.[42] Other studies have come to similar conclusions about public opinion and government policy at the state level.[43] Some recent studies, however, have suggested that the responsiveness of government to public opinion has been declining, reaching an all-time low during President Clinton's first term. These findings imply that, contrary to popular beliefs, elected leaders don't always pander to the results of public opinion polls, but instead use polling to sell their policy proposals and shape the public's views.[44]

In addition, areas of disagreement always arise between opinion and policy. For example, the majority of Americans favored stricter governmental control of handguns for years before Congress finally adopted the modest

AMERICAN DEMOCRACY IN COMPARATIVE PERSPECTIVE

Opinions and the Foundations of Democracy and Markets in the "New Europe"

Since the collapse of the Soviet Union in 1991, the study of public opinion in former communist nations has exploded. For the first time in the history of the region, the people of Central and East Europe have been targets of pollsters seeking their opinions on issues similar to those of interest to their West European counterparts. Of particular concern to students of public opinion are the effects of three intense pressures that have gripped the European continent—both east and west.

First, among the more established democracies of West Europe, the public has come to feel the full force of the European Union, a new political and economic system of power that is daily reminding average citizens of just how much their lives have changed in a few years. With its own sovereign currency and a powerful complement of financial, executive, judicial, and legislative institutions, the European Union is increasingly regulating the lives of citizens in fifteen countries of West Europe. The membership of the Union will soon expand to include several former communist countries of Central and East Europe. By 2002 this set will probably include Poland, Hungary, the Czech Republic, and Slovenia. Within a few more years, it will likely expand to include Estonia, Latvia, Lithuania, Romania, and Slovakia.

Second, with the collapse of the Soviet Union and its communist form of government, the market has now entered the daily lives of virtually all citizens of Central and East Europe. The effect is to subject the average family to not only a change of lifestyle (often meaning a decline in their standard of living) but also the anxieties of uncertainty, at least in the near term, as workers and employers alike must learn to live with global economic competition and the realities of capitalism.

Third, the realities of democracy have now set in and, in many cases, only seem to compound the anxiety and fears of citizens in Central and East Europe. Any one of these changes would be a serious challenge to policy makers and citizens. Combined and compressed by the relentless pressures of globalization and financial competition, the impact of these reforms presses hard against the economic and political institutions of the region, raising the specter of instability, conflict, and social unrest. The reforms also, of course, offer the prospect of a truly revolutionary transformation of the continent—a European Union from the Atlantic to the Urals, from the Artic to the Mediterranean Sea.

A sampling of public opinion among the citizens of the four major West European democracies that are the leaders of the European Union underscore (at least as of 1996 and 1998) the arguments of those who have expressed warnings about lower levels of political efficacy; lower levels of satisfaction with democracy, the European Union (EU), and life in general; a decline in citizens' engagement in society's political discourse (opinion leadership); and the presence of political ideologists that still value the active role of the state in the economy and that run counter to the instincts of open, global economic competition (left ideology). This general trend is, to some degree, mirrored by the data from Central and East Europe, which reveals a general pattern of dissatisfaction with democracy, disenchantment with market capitalism, and concerns for the lack of human rights. For those countries that are indeed likely to be admitted into the European Union during the next few years, the public generally favors such a move. A minority of citizens see the United States as being the most closely tied to the future success and properity of their own country.

The "New Europe" may be more free now than its immediate predecessor. It still confronts, however, the memories of its past, the uncertainties of its future, and the relentless threats and pressures of globalization and the American engine of technological innovation and entrepreneurial zeal. Americans may find it difficult to imagine why some people, even many people within the most democratic European nation-states, do not share the zest for capitalist competition and individualism that so characterizes the political culture of the United States. But the reality is that while Europe's future has the hope of a greater prosperity and deeper freedoms than ever before in its history, this region, so critical to American interests, has not yet settled its mind on how far it wishes to go, or how it wishes to get there.

SOURCES: Elizabeth Pond, *The Rebirth of Europe*, Brookings Institution Press, 1999. John Newhouse, *Europe Adrift: The Conflicting Demands of Unity, Nationalism, Economic Security, Political Stability, and Military Readiness Now Facing a Europe Seeking to Redefine Itself*, Pantheon, 1997.

restrictions on firearms purchases embodied in the Brady bill and the Violent Crime Control Act, passed in 1993 and 1994, respectively. Similarly, most Americans—blacks as well as whites—oppose school busing to achieve racial balance, yet such busing continues to be used in many parts of the nation. Most Americans are far less concerned with the rights of the accused than the federal courts seem to be. Most Americans oppose U.S. military intervention in other nations' affairs, yet such interventions continue to take place in such regions as Bosnia and Haiti, where American troops are currently stationed, and often win public approval after the fact.

Several factors can contribute to a lack of consistency between opinion and governmental policy. First, the nominal majority on a particular issue may not be as intensely committed to its preference as the adherents of the minority viewpoint. An intensely committed minority may often be more willing to commit its time, energy, efforts, and resources to the affirmation of its opinions than an apathetic, even if large, majority. In the case of firearms, for example, although the proponents of gun control are by a wide margin the majority, most do not regard the issue as one of critical importance to themselves and are not willing to commit much effort to advancing their cause. The opponents of gun control, by contrast, are intensely committed, well organized, and well financed, and as a result are usually able to carry the day.

A second important reason that public policy and public opinion may not coincide has to do with the character and structure of the American system of government. The framers of the American Constitution, as we saw in Chapter 3, sought to create a system of government that was based upon popular consent but that did not invariably and automatically translate shifting popular sentiments into public policies. As a result, the American governmental process includes arrangements such as an appointed judiciary that can produce policy decisions that may run contrary to prevailing popular sentiment—at least for a time.

When all is said and done, however, there can be little doubt that in general the actions of the American government do not remain out of line with popular sentiment for very long. One could take these as signs of a vital and thriving democracy.

Politics on the Web

The Internet is an unparalleled source for political information. No other medium has such a variety of political, economic, and social views so readily available. As a learning tool, the Internet holds great promise. As a tool for expression of public opinion, the Internet presents a more mixed picture. On the one hand, individuals have the ability to articulate their opinions through an on-line democratic debate, where one's ideas can be distributed to millions of computer users worldwide. This is empowering. But on the Internet, no intermediaries evaluate and filter these opinions. Direct democracy becomes mob rule. And those with the most time on their hands to post opinions can easily dominate a discussion, which leads to great difficulties in measuring public opinion via the Internet. The Internet is dominated by white, well-off, educated men—not a representative sample of the population. But despite these limitations, the Internet will continue to grow as a way for individuals to learn about politics.

www.wwnorton.com/wtp3e

The Citizen's Role

In a democracy, one central role of the citizen is to be informed and knowledgeable. Many eighteenth- and nineteenth-century political theorists believed that popular government required an informed, aware, and involved citizenry, and wondered whether this condition could be met. The Frenchman, Alexis de Tocqueville, writing in the early nineteenth century, asserted that to participate in democratic politics ordinary citizens needed to be aware of their own interests and understand how those interests might be affected by contemporary issues. De Tocqueville and others have feared that participation by the unenlightened might be worse than no participation at all, since the ignorant could easily be swayed by demagogues to support foolish or even evil causes.

Contemporary public opinion research indicates that better-informed citizens are considerably better able than their uninformed counterparts to exert influence in the political arena. Knowledge, indeed, seems to be power.[45]

Fortunately, the most basic element of citizenship is also one of the simplest to achieve. Viewed correctly, reading a daily newspaper is an important political act! Watching a television news or discussion program is an important form of political participation. For some, visiting and comparing the Web sites of several candidates is a way of becoming politically involved, albeit in cyberspace.

Those who use newspapers, magazines, television, and the computer to become politically knowledgeable and aware have taken a huge first step toward becoming politically influential. Those who limit their newspaper reading to the sports page and their television viewing to situation comedies are also abdicating the responsibilities and opportunities inherent in democratic citizenship. If a person opts to be indifferent or cynical about politics, his or her decision must be based on an informed indifference or cynicism to be truly meaningful.

GET INVOLVED Tapping Public Opinion

Why is public opinion important? Why do the media conduct exit polls during elections, report on the percentage of Americans who favor gun control, or announce the current approval rating of the president of the United States? Why do people in politics care about what most Americans think?

In a democracy, we expect citizens to play a significant role in governmental processes. Public opinion is one important way that citizens express their needs and convey their desires to government officials. It is "the voice of the people." Furthermore, interest groups seeking to influence government decisions have a great deal to gain if they can claim that public opinion is on their side. Favorable public opinion may attract recruits and money, add legitimacy to groups' policy preferences, and enhance their efforts to influence decision makers.

Meanwhile, candidates, politicians, and policy makers usually want to stay attuned to public opinion and to figure out the best way to accomplish their goals. Candidates need citizens' votes to be elected. Politicians need public support to achieve their legislative agendas. Policy makers need sufficient legitimacy to ensure that their decisions will receive public compliance rather than citizen resistance. Accordingly, political players regularly hire professional pollsters to conduct scientific surveys of public opinion on important issues. Based on survey outcomes, political players may proceed with earlier plans, reshape their strategies, alter their proposals, or even drop some of them.

When you participate in a campus group or a community organization, you are likely to be concerned with what particular publics think of your group and its goals. For example, it may be important for you to find out if other students know that your group exists. If not, it will be awfully tough to recruit new members. You also may want to know if most students think your group's ideas are important and if they agree with them. And it might be advantegeous to consider whether underplaying some issues will help you to build greater support for efforts on behalf of other issues.

How could you discover public opinion? Here are two ways to research public opinion on issues important to your group or organization. The first way is survey research. Either on paper or in person, you ask people a series of questions about "who they are" and "how they feel" about the issues in question. The "who they are" questions ask for standard "demographical" information regarding people's age, residence, education, family income, and so forth. This information will enable you to learn, for example, if people from high-income families feel one way about your issues while folks from low-income families have different opinions about your issues. The "how they feel" questions may focus on people's general views on your issues and how intensely they hold their views. Informal surveys are quite easy to construct, conduct, and analyze. Note, however, that scientific surveys tend to be intricate, rigorous affairs.

Focus groups are another tool for tapping public opinion. In focus groups, you sit down with a small group of people and ask them relatively open-ended questions. Your goal is to get people to talk freely about the issues at hand so that you can develop a more nuanced or deeper understanding of their views, why they hold them, and perhaps the circumstances under which they might change them. Unlike surveys, which are usually quite brief, focus groups tend to require a significant time investment for both you and your interviewees.

Once you choose your strategy and frame your questions, the next challenge is to find people who are willing to participate in your survey or focus group. Providing participants a modest incentive (such as snacks or promotional items) may be helpful for getting a few minutes of their time. Here are a few other ways to attract participants.

- With your professor's permission, announce your project and call for volunteers in class.
- Talk to people who you know personally. Ask them to participate and ask them to suggest other people who might participate.
- Set up a card table in a high traffic area during lunchtime. Attach an attention-grabbing sign to the front of the table and ask passers-by for a few minutes of their time.
- Advertise in your school newspaper.
- Work with other groups that have similar interests. They may be willing to help you recruit participants for your public opinion research.

When you have completed your survey or finished conducting your focus group, evaluate the results. Consider whether your sample is representative of the people whose opinions concern you. See if they support, oppose, or have mixed views on your issues. If you can, assess the reasons for their opinions. Finally, consider how your public opinion evaluation should influence the practices and policies of your group.

Summary

Americans disagree on many issues, but they nevertheless share a number of important values, including liberty, equality of opportunity, and democracy. Although factors such as race, education, gender, and social class produce important differences in outlook, Americans probably agree more on fundamental values than do the citizens of most other nations.

Most people acquire their initial orientation to political life from their families. Subsequently, political views are influenced by interests, personal experiences, group memberships, and the conditions under which citizens are first mobilized into politics. Opinions on particular issues may also be influenced by political leaders and the mass media. The media help determine what Americans know about politics.

Most governments, including the U.S. government, endeavor to shape their citizens' political beliefs. In democracies, private groups compete with government to shape opinion.

Public opinion is generally measured by polling. However, polls can also distort opinion, imputing salience to issues that citizens care little about or creating the illusion that most people are moderate or centrist in their views.

Over time, the government's policies are strongly affected by public opinion, although there can be lags and divergences, especially when an intense minority confronts a more apathetic majority.

FOR FURTHER READING

Gallup, George. *The Pulse of Democracy.* New York: Simon and Schuster, 1940.

Ginsberg, Benjamin. *The Captive Public: How Mass Opinion Promotes State Power.* New York: Basic Books, 1986.

Herbst, Susan. *Numbered Voices: How Opinion Polling Has Shaped American Politics.* Chicago: University of Chicago Press, 1993.

Herbst, Susan. *Reading Public Opinion: How Political Actors View the Democratic Process.* Chicago: University of Chicago Press, 1998.

Jacobs, Lawrence R., and Robert Y. Shapiro. *Politicians Don't Pander: Political Manipulation and the Loss of Democratic Responsiveness.* Chicago: University of Chicago Press, 2000.

Key, V. O. *Public Opinion and American Democracy.* New York: Knopf, 1961.

Lippman, Walter. *Public Opinion.* New York: Harcourt, Brace, 1922.

Mayer, William G. *The Changing American Mind: How and Why American Public Opinion Changed between 1960 and 1988.* Ann Arbor: University of Michigan Press, 1992.

Mutz, Diana C. *Impersonal Influence: How Perceptions of Mass Collectives Affect Political Attitudes.* New York: Cambridge University Press, 1998.

Neuman, W. Russell. *The Paradox of Mass Politics: Knowledge and Opinion in the American Electorate.* Cambridge, MA: Harvard University Press, 1986.

Page, Benjamin I., and Robert Y. Shapiro. *The Rational Public: Fifty Years of Trends in Americans' Policy Preferences.* Chicago: University of Chicago Press, 1992.

Rinehart, Sue Tolleson. *Gender Consciousness and Politics.* New York: Routledge, 1992.

Schuman, Howard, Charlotte Steeh, and Lawrence Bobo. *Racial Attitudes in America.* Cambridge, MA: Harvard University Press, 1990.

Traugott, Michael, and Paul Lavrakas. *The Voter's Guide to Election Polls.* 2nd ed. New York: Chatham House, 2000.

STUDY OUTLINE

Political Values

1. Although Americans have many political differences, they share a common set of values, including liberty, equality of opportunity, and democracy.
2. Agreement on fundamental political values is probably more widespread in the United States than anywhere else in the Western world.
3. Often for reasons associated with demographics, Americans' opinions do differ widely on a variety of issues.

4. Most people acquire their initial orientation to politics from their families.
5. Membership in both voluntary and involuntary social groups can affect an individual's political values through personal experience, the influence of group leaders, and recognition of political interests.
6. One's level of education is an important factor in shaping political beliefs.
7. Conditions under which individuals and groups are recruited into political life also shape political orientations.
8. Many Americans describe themselves as either liberal or conservative in political orientation.

How We Form Political Opinions

1. Although ideologies shape political opinions, they seldom fully determine one's views.
2. Political opinions are influenced by an individual's underlying values, knowledge of political issues, and external forces such as the government, private groups, and the media.

Measuring Public Opinion

1. In order to construct public opinion from surveys, a polling sample must be large and the views of those in the sample must accurately and proportionately reflect the views of the whole.

Public Opinion and Democracy

1. Government policies in the United States are generally consistent with popular preferences. There are, however, always some inconsistencies.
2. Disagreements between opinion and policy come about because on some issues, such as gun control, an intensely committed minority can defeat a more apathetic majority. Moreover, the American system of government is not designed to quickly transform changes in opinion into changes in government programs.

PRACTICE QUIZ

1. The term "public opinion" is used to describe
   a) the collected speeches and writings made by a president during his term in office.
   b) the analysis of events broadcast by news reporters during the evening news.
   c) the beliefs and attitudes that people have about issues.
   d) decisions of the Supreme Court.
2. Variables such as income, education, race, gender, and ethnicity
   a) often create differences of political opinion in America.
   b) have consistently been a challenge to America's core political values.
   c) have little impact on political opinions.
   d) help explain why public opinion polls are so unreliable.
3. Which of the following is an agency of socialization?
   a) the family
   b) social groups
   c) education
   d) all of the above
4. When men and women respond differently to issues of public policy, they are demonstrating an example of
   a) liberalism.
   b) educational differences.
   c) the gender gap.
   d) party politics.
5. The process by which Americans learn political beliefs and values is called
   a) brainwashing.
   b) propaganda.
   c) indoctrination.
   d) political socialization.
6. In addition to one's basic political values, what other two factors influence one's political opinions?
   a) ideology and party identification
   b) political knowledge and the influence of political leaders, private groups, and the media
   c) the gender gap and the education gap
   d) sample size and the bandwagon effect
7. Which of the following is (are) *not* an important external influence on how political opinions are formed?
   a) the government and political leaders
   b) private interest groups
   c) the media
   d) the Constitution
8. Which of the following is the term used in public opinion polling to denote the small group representing the opinions of the whole population?
   a) control group

b) sample
c) micropopulation
d) respondents

9. When politicians, pollsters, journalists, or social scientists assume something is important to the public when in fact it is not, they are creating
a) an illusion of saliency.
b) an illusion of responsibility.
c) a gender gap.
d) an elitist issue.

10. A familiar polling problem is the "bandwagon effect," which occurs when
a) the same results are used over and over again.
b) polling results influence people to support the candidate marked as the probable victor in a campaign.
c) polling results influence people to support the candidate who is trailing in a campaign.
d) background noise makes it difficult for a pollster and a respondent to communicate with one another.

CRITICAL THINKING QUESTIONS

1. In the American system of government, public opinion seems to be an important factor in political and governmental decision making. In what ways does the public, through opinion, control its political leaders? In what ways do political leaders control public opinion? What are the positive and negative consequences of governing by popular opinion?

2. Describe the differences between liberal and conservative ideologies in American politics. Using one social or demographic group as an example, describe some of the factors that may have shaped the ideological orientation of that particular group. What factors may explain inconsistencies in that group's political ideology or issue positions?

KEY TERMS

agencies of socialization (p. 246)
attitude (or opinion) (p. 238)
bandwagon effect (p. 268)
conservative (p. 254)
democracy (p. 239)
equality of opportunity (p. 239)
gender gap (p. 249)
illusion of saliency (p. 267)
liberal (p. 252)
liberty (p. 239)
marketplace of ideas (p. 258)
political efficacy (p. 257)
political ideology (p. 238)
political socialization (p. 243)
public opinion (p. 238)
public opinion polls (p. 263)
push polling (p. 270)
salient interests (p. 267)
sample (p. 263)
values (or beliefs) (p. 238)

8 The Media

★ **The Media Industry and Government**

How has the nationalization of the news media contributed to the nationalization of American politics?

How is the media regulated by the government? How does this regulation differ between the broadcast media and the print media?

★ **News Coverage**

How are media content, news coverage, and bias affected by the producers, subjects, and consumers of the news?

★ **Media Power in American Politics**

How do the media shape public perceptions of events, issues, and institutions?

What are the sources of media power?

★ **Media Power and Democracy**

Are the media too powerful and thus in need of restriction, or are a free media necessary for democracy?

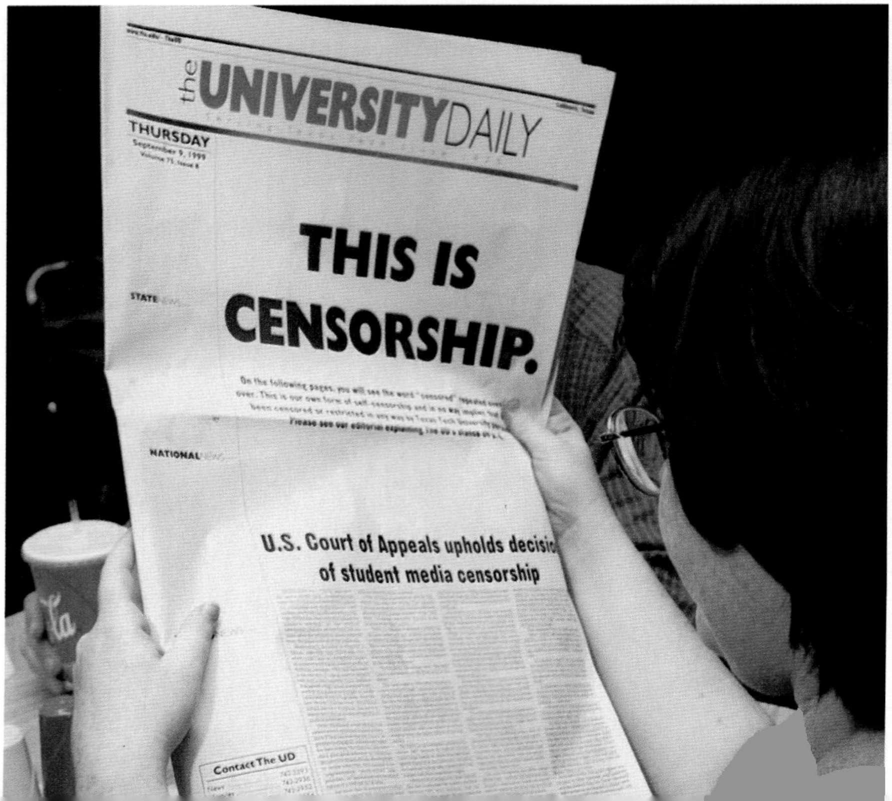

STUDENTS AND POLITICS

It is impossible to imagine democratic politics without a vigorous media. The public depends upon the news media to publicize and assess the claims of political candidates. We depend upon the media to examine government policies and programs. We depend upon the media to reveal wrongdoing on the part of government agencies and public officials. Without the information provided by the media, the public could not possibly know enough to play any role in the political process. Freedom of the press definitely belongs in the First Amendment as one of the first principles of democratic government. This freedom gives the media considerable power. Given this substantial freedom, what prevents the media from abusing its power? In a democracy, to whom are the media accountable—to the people?

Virtually all Americans believe in the principle of freedom of the press. Yet it is interesting to see how quickly groups that champion freedom when the press attacks *their enemies* can become advocates of censorship when the press turns and attacks *them*. In recent years, for instance, newspapers on many college campuses have come under attack by groups that object to their coverage. Traditionally, of course, school administrators sought to influence the content of student newspapers. Today, because of court decisions protecting college papers from the actions of school authorities, most college administrations maintain a hands-off policy toward the campus press. In a number of recent cases, however, student groups that differ politically with a campus paper have sought to prevent the paper's publication and distribution, often by stealing thousands of copies of the paper before other students could read it.

In spring 1997, for example, a group of angry students burned hundreds of copies of the *Cornell Review,* the university's conservative student newspaper, which had printed what many students and faculty saw as an offensive parody of courses offered at Cornell's Africana studies center. Ying Ma, former president of the *Review* was prevented from speaking at a rally organized by protestors when a basket of burning *Reviews* was thrown at her.[1] At Pennsylvania State University, more than 6,000 copies of a conservative student paper, the *Lionheart,* were stolen after the paper published a cartoon that offended feminist groups. One Penn State professor reportedly defended the thefts, arguing that they were justified because of the paper's "misogynistic" views.[2] At the University of California at Berkeley, more than 6,500 copies of the student-run *Daily Californian* were stolen from news racks in October 1997 after the paper published an editorial criticizing a group called the Coalition to Defend Affirmative Action by Any Means Necessary. This theft was the seventh such incident on the Berkeley campus in less than a year.[3] At Clark University in Worcester, Massachusetts, the editor of the *Wheatbread,* an alternative student newspaper, charged that an administrator had stolen and destroyed 500 copies of an edition of the paper that used obscene language to criticize college officials. University administrators reportedly confirmed that the theft had occurred.[4] At the University of Virginia, a food service official confessed to stealing 4,000 copies of the student newspaper after it criticized the cafeteria food for containing "spore, molds and fungi."[5] At a number of other campuses, including Brandeis, Penn, Dartmouth, San Francisco State, Butler, the University of Texas, George Washington, the University of Wisconsin, Trenton State University, the University of Illinois, and Southeastern Louisiana University (SLU), thousands of copies of student newspapers have been stolen by groups objecting to the views the papers presented. At SLU, the theft of 2,000 copies of the *Lion's Roar* allegedly was perpetrated by an officer of the school's student government who wanted to prevent fellow students from reading an article that criticized his organization. All told, hundreds of thousands of student newspapers have been stolen on college campuses in the last decade.[6]

Attempts to silence or discredit the opposition press have a long history in America. The infamous Alien and Sedition Acts were enacted by the Federalists in an attempt to silence the Republican press. In more recent times, during the McCarthy era of the 1950s, right-wing politicians used charges of communist infiltration to intimidate the liberal news media. During President Richard Nixon's administration, the White House attacked its critics in the media by threatening to take action to bar the television networks from owning local affiliates, as well as by illegally wiretapping the phones of government officials suspected of leaking information to the press. In the early 1980s, conservative groups financed a series of libel suits against CBS News, *Time* magazine, and other media organizations, in an attempt to discourage them from publicizing material critical of Reagan administration policies.[7] In 1998, President Clinton's political allies accused the national news media of engaging in tabloid journalism and invading the president's privacy in order to discredit him by publicizing the intimate details of Clinton's sexual relationship with former White House intern Monica Lewinsky. In all these instances, attempts to silence the press failed.

- ***In this chapter we will examine the place of the media in American politics. First, we will look at the organization and regulation of the American news media.*** The media industry continues to grow larger and more centralized, resulting in little variety in what is reported about national issues. Despite the central importance of freedom of the press in the United States, the media are still subject to some regulation by the government.

- ***Second, we will discuss the factors that help to determine "what's news."*** The agenda of issues and type of coverage that the media provide are affected most by those who create the news and those who consume the news.

- ***Third, we will examine the scope of media power in politics.*** What the media report can have far-reaching effects on public perceptions of political events, issues, leaders, and institutions.

- ***Finally, we will address the question of responsibility: to whom, if anyone, are the media accountable for the use of their formidable power?*** The answer to this question has great implications for American democracy.

The Media Industry and Government

- How has the nationalization of the news media contributed to the nationalization of American politics?
- How is the media regulated by the government? How does this regulation differ between the broadcast media and the print media?

The American news media are among the world's most vast and most free. Americans literally have thousands of available options to find political reporting. This wide variety of newspapers, newsmagazines, and broadcast media regularly present information that is at odds with the government's claims, as well as editorial opinions sharply critical of high-ranking officials. The freedom to speak one's mind is one of the most cherished of American political values—one that is jealously safeguarded by the media. Yet although thousands of media companies exist across the United States, surprisingly little variety appears in what is reported about national events and issues.

TYPES OF MEDIA

Americans get their news from broadcast media (radio, television), print media (newspapers and magazines), and, increasingly, the Internet. Each of these sources has distinctive characteristics. Television news reaches more Americans than any other single news source (see Figure 8.1 on the next page). Tens of millions of individuals watch national and local news programs every day. Television news, however, covers relatively few topics and provides little depth of coverage. Television news is more like a series of newspaper headlines connected to pictures. It serves the extremely important function of alerting viewers to issues and events, but provides little more than a series of "sound bites," brief quotes and short characterizations of the day's events. Because they are aware of the character of television news coverage, politicians and other newsmakers often seek to manipulate the news by providing the media with sound bites that will dominate news coverage for at least a few days. George Bush's famous 1988 sound bite, "Read my lips, no new taxes," received a great deal of media coverage. Two years later he was, in effect, bitten by his own sound bite when he signed legislation that included new taxes.

Radio news is also essentially a headline service, but without pictures. In the short time—usually five minutes per hour—they devote to news, radio stations announce the day's major events without providing much detail. In major cities, all-news stations provide a bit more coverage of major stories, but for the most part these stations fill the day with repetition rather than detail. All-news stations like Washington, D.C.'s WTOP or New York's WCBS assume that most listeners are in their cars and that, as a result, the people in the audience change markedly throughout the day as listeners reach their destinations. Thus, rather than use their time to flesh out a given set of stories, they repeat the same stories each hour to present them to new listeners. In recent years, radio talk shows have become important sources of commentary

Politics on the Web

Most mainstream media Web sites are simply new conduits for conventional reporters. The most important effect of the Internet has instead occurred through unconventional outlets. The Web has proven itself to be the greatest rumor mill of all time. Alternative news Web sites publish unverified stories that the mainstream media will not. Sometimes, however, a rumor becomes too important for the mainstream media to ignore. In early 1998, for example, *Newsweek* had information that President Clinton may have had sexual relations with a White House intern. The source of the information was suspect, however, and the reporter lacked corroborating sources, so *Newsweek* chose not to print the story. The next day, Matt Drudge, a self-styled Internet political maven, scooped *Newsweek* on his Web site, "The Drudge Report." Within a day, *Newsweek* had posted a response on its Web site, *The Wall Street Journal* had picked up the story, and Monica Lewinsky entered American political lore.

www.wwnorton.com/wtp3e

Figure 8.1 AMERICANS' PRIMARY MEDIA SOURCES OF NEWS

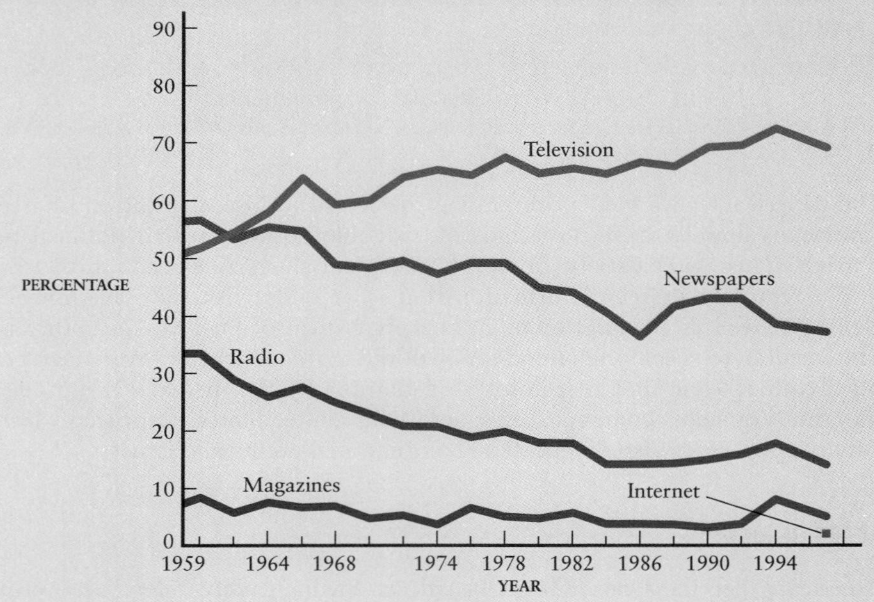

Note: Multiple responses permitted
SOURCE: *America's Watching: Public Attitudes toward Television* (New York: Roper Starch Worldwide, 1995), p. 17, and 1997 Roper Starch Worldwide poll.

and opinion. A number of conservative radio hosts such as Rush Limbaugh and Dr. Laura Schlesinger have huge audiences and have helped to mobilize support for conservative political causes and candidates. Liberals have been somewhat slower to recognize the potential impact of talk radio.

The most important source of news is the old-fashioned newspaper. Newspapers remain critically important even though they are not the primary news source for most Americans. The print media are important for two reasons. First, as we shall see later in this chapter, the broadcast media rely upon leading newspapers such as *The New York Times* and *The Washington Post* to set their news agenda. The broadcast media engage in very little actual reporting; they primarily cover stories that have been "broken," or initially reported, by the print media. For example, sensational charges that President Bill Clinton had an affair with a White House intern were reported first by *The Washington Post* and *Newsweek* before being trumpeted around the world by the broadcast media. It is only a slight exaggeration to observe that if an event is not covered in *The New York Times,* it is not likely to appear on the *CBS Evening News.* The print media are also important because they are the prime source of news for educated and influential individuals. The nation's economic, social, and political elites rely upon the detailed coverage provided by the print media to inform and influence their views about important public matters. The print media may have a smaller audience than their cousins in broadcasting, but they have an audience that matters.

A relatively new source of news is the Internet. Every day, several million Americans scan one of many news sites on the Internet for coverage of current events. For the most part, however, the Internet provides electronic versions of coverage offered by print sources. One great advantage of the Internet is that it allows frequent updating. It potentially can combine the depth of coverage of a newspaper with the timeliness of television and radio, and probably will become a major news source in the next decade. As on-line access becomes simpler and faster, the Internet could give Americans access to unprecedented quantities of up-to-the-minute information. If only computers could also give Americans the ability to make good use of that information!

ORGANIZATION AND OWNERSHIP OF THE MEDIA

Media Organization The United States boasts more than one thousand television stations, approximately eighteen hundred daily newspapers, and more than nine thousand radio stations. The majority of these enterprises (20 percent of which are devoted to news, talk, or public affairs)[8] present a good deal of news and many features with a distinctly local flavor. For example, for many months, viewers of the Syracuse, New York, evening news were informed that the day's "top story" concerned the proposed construction of a local garbage-burning steam plant. Similarly, in Seattle, Washington, viewers were treated to years of discussion about the construction of a domed athletic stadium, and audiences in Baltimore, Maryland, watched and read about struggles over downtown redevelopment. In all these cases, as in literally thousands of others, the local media focused heavily on a matter of particular local concern, providing local viewers, readers, and listeners with considerable information and viewpoints.

Yet, however much variation the American news media offer in terms of local coverage, there is far less diversity in the reporting of national events and issues. More than three-fourths of the daily newspapers in the United States are owned by large media conglomerates such as the Hearst, Knight Ridder, or Gannett corporations; thus the diversity of coverage and editorial opinion in American newspapers is not as broad as it might seem. Much of the national news that is published by local newspapers is provided by one wire service, the Associated Press, while additional coverage is provided by services run by several major newspapers like *The New York Times* and the *Chicago Tribune*. More than five hundred of the nation's television stations are affiliated with one of the four networks and carry

Student Perspectives

THE MESSAGE IS MONOPOLY

"The medium is the message," media critic Marshall McLuhen has said of the media's power in constructing and transmitting cultural values. The January 10 merger between America Online (AOL) and Time Warner is further evidence of the shrinking diversity of media sources. Having eliminated competition, a once free press is being compromised by commercial interests.

As other media corporations seek to compete with the AOL Time Warner media conglomerate, the public can expect to see more mergers and a continued narrowing of independent media services. When media power is so concentrated, conflicts of interest and bias increase; the lack of competition removes the media's accountability to the public.

***

The knotty news/advertisement/media relationships that arise from mega-mergers like the AOL/Time Warner deal and past media marriages between Disney and ABC or Microsoft and NBC can create conflicts of interest when the news must be critical of its corporate sponsors.

Erring on the side of sycophancy, television networks sometimes sacrifice journalistic integrity to please their sponsors, such as when CBS refused to air a *60 Minutes* interview with a critic of a tobacco company because of the relationship between the network and the company in question. As the media grows to global proportions, commercially viable news has become more monopolistic.

When the medium and the message are both about commercial viability, the true message of news media gets lost. For all the blustering about how the merger is really an opportunity to expand communication to the Internet, the AOL/Time Warner merger actually narrows the spectrum of news. The centerpiece of these media outlets, we must remember, is commerce not information.

Staff Editorial, *Columbia Daily Spectator* (Columbia University), January 21, 2000.

that network's evening news reports. Dozens of others carry PBS (Public Broadcasting System) news. Several hundred local radio stations also carry network news or National Public Radio news broadcasts. At the same time, although there are only three truly national newspapers, *The Wall Street Journal, The Christian Science Monitor,* and *USA Today,* two other papers, *The New York Times* and *The Washington Post,* are read by political leaders and other influential Americans throughout the nation. Such is the influence of these two "elite" newspapers that their news coverage sets the standard for virtually all other news outlets. Stories carried in *The New York Times* or *The Washington Post* influence the content of many other papers as well as of the network news. Note how often this text, like most others, relies upon *New York Times* and *Washington Post* stories as sources for contemporary events.

National news is also carried to millions of Americans by the three major newsmagazines—*Time, Newsweek,* and *U.S. News & World Report.* Thus, even though the number of TV and radio stations and daily newspapers reporting news in the United States is enormous, and local coverage varies greatly from place to place, the number of sources of national news is actually quite small—several wire services, four broadcast networks, public radio and television, two elite newspapers, three newsmagazines, and a scattering of other sources such as the national correspondents of a few large local papers and the small independent radio networks. Beginning in the late 1980s, Cable News Network (CNN) became another major news source for Americans. The importance of CNN increased dramatically after its spectacular coverage of the Persian Gulf War. At one point, CNN was able to provide live reports of American bombing raids on Baghdad, Iraq, after the major networks' correspondents had been forced to flee to bomb shelters. Even the availability of new electronic media on the Internet has failed to expand news sources. Most national news available on the World Wide Web, for example, consists of electronic versions of the conventional print media.

Media Ownership Since the enactment of the 1996 Telecommunications Act, which opened the way for further consolidation in the media industry, a wave of mergers and consolidations has further reduced the field of independent media across the country. Since that time, among the major news networks, ABC was bought by the Walt Disney corporation, CBS was bought by Westinghouse Electric and later merged with

Students and Politics

People ages twenty-six and older use television as their main source of information about politics, while 70 percent of eighteen- to twenty-five-year-olds turn to the World Wide Web, according to a study released this week by Project Vote Smart.

***

While the Internet was the main source of political information for the younger group, 79 percent of people in that group said they needed to find a more trustworthy source for information on candidates' backgrounds and issue positions.

***

"We found that people ages eighteen to twenty-five are fairly disillusioned with the government and don't trust it very much," said Kristina Saleh, a Project Vote Smart spokeswoman. "They have issues and concerns that they don't think are heavily addressed. This leads them, in turn, to be uninterested in government altogether."

***

The study is the first stage in a national program that Project Vote Smart is implementing for the 2000 presidential election. The project's goal is to provide younger people with information that will inform them about the political process and encourage them to vote.

Michigan State U. College Republicans President Chase Wade, 22, said to gain trust back from the younger people, politicians need to be honest with their public.

Wade, an international relations senior, said if citizens became involved in politics they would learn that most of their elected officials do care about their concerns.

"A lot of people have become disconnected with the government because they think nobody cares about their concerns," he said. "There's no simple solution. These are the pitfalls of democracy."

***

Criminal justice sophomore Steven Taylor, a registered voter, said the media make politicians less than trustworthy.

"But the media isn't the whole problem," he said. "Young people should just want to get involved in order to make a difference."

Rebekah Amos, "Age Plays Factor in Political Priorities," *The State News* (Michigan State), September 16, 1999.

CNN's live coverage of the Persian Gulf War captivated American television viewers and brought the war into their homes.

Viacom, the owner of MTV and Paramount Studios, and CNN was bought by Time Warner. NBC has been owned by General Electric since 1986. Australian press baron Rupert Murdoch owns the Fox network plus a host of radio, television, and newspaper properties around the world. A small number of giant corporations now controls a wide swath of media holdings, including television networks, movie studios, record companies, cable channels and local cable providers, book publishers, magazines, and newspapers. These developments have prompted questions about whether enough competition exists among the media to produce a diverse set of views on political and corporate matters.[9]

In early 2000, America Online acquired Time Warner, the world's largest media and entertainment company, for $166 billion in stock. The union of the two companies is considered to be the biggest corporate merger ever and has fueled the debate over the effects of concentrated media ownership.

NATIONALIZATION OF THE NEWS

In general, the national news media cover more or less the same sets of events, present similar information, and emphasize similar issues and problems. Indeed, the national news services watch one another quite carefully. It is very likely that a major story carried by one service will quickly find its way into the pages or programming of the others. As a result, in the United States a rather centralized national news has developed, through which a relatively similar picture of events, issues, and problems is presented to the entire nation.[10] The nationalization of the news began at the turn of the century, was accelerated by the development of radio networks in the 1920s and 1930s and by the creation of the television networks after the 1950s, and has been further strengthened by the recent trends toward concentrated media ownership. This nationalization of news content has very important consequences for the American political system.

Nationalization of the news has contributed greatly to the nationalization of politics and of political perspectives in the United States. Prior to the development of the national media and the nationalization of news coverage, news traveled very slowly. Every region and city saw national issues and problems primarily through a local lens. Concerns and perspectives varied greatly from region to region, city to city, and village to village. Today, in large measure as a result of the nationalization of the media, residents of all parts of the country share a similar picture of the day's events.[11] They may not agree on everything, but most see the world in similar ways.

The exception to this pattern can be found with those Americans whose chief source of news is something other than the "mainstream" national media. Despite the nationalization and homogenization of the news, in some American cities, alternative news coverage is available. Such media markets are known as "news enclaves." For example, some African Americans rely upon newspapers and radio stations that aim their coverage primarily at black audiences. As a result, these individuals may interpret events differently than white Americans and even other blacks do.[12] The existence of a black-focused media helps to explain why many African Americans and white Americans reacted differently to the 1995 trial of O. J. Simpson in Los Angeles. While national media outlets generally portrayed Simpson as guilty of the murder of his former wife, African American media outlets depicted Simpson as a victim of a racist criminal justice system. This latter view came to be held by a large number of African Americans.

In a similar vein, some radio stations and print media are aimed exclusively at religious and social conservatives. These individuals are also likely to develop and retain a perception of the news that is quite different from that of "mainstream" America. For example, the rural Midwesterners who rely upon the ultraconservative People's Radio Network for their news coverage may become concerned about the alleged efforts of the United Nations to subordinate the United States in a world government, a viewpoint unfamiliar to most Americans.

Internet newsgroups are another form of news enclave. Newsgroups are informal and tend to develop around the discussion of a particular set of issues. Individuals post their views for others to read; comments are also posted. In some instances, posted comments are attacked by other members of the community. In general, users seem to seek out and exchange postings with those who share their opinions. On a recent day in 2000, the political topics being discussed in the more than 50,000 postings under the heading alt.politics included such conventional subjects as "Clinton," "Bush," "Gore," "corruption," "equality," "media," "libertarianism," and "Democrats and Republicans," as well as racist and neofascist topics that receive little attention from the mass media. While some postings were followed by hostile comments, for the most part responses to postings seemed to come from those who agreed with the position put forth. For example, most of those posting under the heading "libertarianism" seemed to be libertarians, while most of the messages appearing under the heading "white power" put forward racist views.

These and other newsgroups serve as meeting places for the like-minded from all across the nation. Perhaps the long-term significance of the Internet is that it will increasingly allow contacts among individuals with unconventional viewpoints who are geographically dispersed and might otherwise be unaware of the existence of others who share their views. In the mid-1990s, Internet newsgroups played a role in the mobilization of "antigovernment" fringe groups.

The same principle seems to hold for another form of discussion on the Internet, known as a chat room. Chat rooms are on-line forums in which anonymous individuals form groups spontaneously and converse with one another. The topics change often as participants leave and are replaced by newcomers. Although chat rooms sometimes are the scenes of angry arguments, for the most part the groups that congregate in these on-line forums seem to share similar views. On a recent day, "rooms" in America Online's popular chat area included "From the Left," where liberal views were discussed, and "From the Right," where the discussion revolved around more conservative opinions. In the conservative chat room, participants discussed tax credits and conservative politicians. All the participants favored more tax credits to promote business activity. Several felt that Republicans were too willing to compromise with their Democratic foes. Not a single participant questioned the conservative climate of opinion in the room. In the liberal chat room, on this same day, participants were concerned with what many saw as the undue political influence of "big business" and "big money" in the political process. Not a single participant in this chat group presented views that might have been considered conservative. Thus, like newsgroups, chat rooms seem to function as opinion enclaves where like-minded individuals from across the nation can congregate and reinforce one another's views.

REGULATION OF THE BROADCAST MEDIA

In some countries, the government controls media content. In other countries, the government owns the broadcast media (e.g., the BBC in Britain) but it does not tell the media what to say. In the United States, the government neither owns nor controls the communications networks, but it does regulate the broadcast media.

In the United States, the print media are essentially free from government interference, but the broadcast media are subject to federal regulation. American radio and television are regulated by the Federal Communications Commission (FCC), an independent regulatory agency established in 1934. Radio and TV stations must have FCC licenses that must be renewed every five years. Licensing provides a mechanism for allocating radio and TV frequencies to prevent broadcasts from interfering with and garbling one another. License renewals are almost always granted automatically by the FCC. Indeed, renewal requests are now filed by postcard.

For more than sixty years, the FCC also sought to regulate competition in the broadcast industry, but in 1996 Congress passed the Telecommunications Act, a broad effort to do away with most regulations in effect since 1934. The act loosened restrictions on media ownership and allowed for telephone companies, cable television providers, and broadcasters to compete with one another for telecommunication services. Following the passage of the act, several mergers between telephone and cable companies and between different segments of the entertainment media produced an even greater concentration of media ownership.

The Telecommunications Act of 1996 also included an attempt to regulate the content of material transmitted over the Internet. This law, known as the Communications Decency Act, made it illegal to make "indecent" sexual material on the Internet accessible to those under eighteen years old. The act was immediately denounced by civil libertarians and brought to court as an infringement of free speech. The case reached the Supreme Court in 1997 and the act was ruled an unconstitutional infringement of the First Amendment's right to freedom of speech (see Chapter 5).

Although the government's ability to regulate the content of the electronic media on the Internet has been questioned, the federal government has used its licensing power to impose several regulations that can affect the political content of radio and TV broadcasts. The first of these is the **equal time rule,** under which broadcasters must provide candidates for the same political office equal opportunities to communicate their messages to the public. If, for example, a television station sells commercial time to a state's Republican gubernatorial candidate, it may not refuse to sell time to the Democratic candidate for the same position.

equal time rule
the requirement that broadcasters provide candidates for the same political office an equal opportunity to communicate their messages to the public

The second regulation affecting the content of broadcasts is the **right of rebuttal,** which requires that individuals be given the opportunity to respond to personal attacks. In the 1969 case of *Red Lion Broadcasting Company v. FCC,* for example, the U.S. Supreme Court upheld the FCC's determination that a radio station was required to provide a liberal author with an opportunity to respond to an attack from a conservative commentator that the station had aired.[13]

right of rebuttal
a Federal Communications Commission regulation giving individuals the right to have the opportunity to respond to personal attacks made on a radio or television broadcast

For many years, a third important federal regulation was the **fairness doctrine.** Under this doctrine, broadcasters who aired programs on controversial issues were required to provide time for opposing views. In 1985, however, the FCC stopped enforcing the fairness doctrine on the grounds that there were so many radio and television stations—to say nothing of newspapers and newsmagazines—that in all likelihood many different viewpoints were already being presented without having to require each station to try to present all sides of an argument. Critics of this FCC decision charge that in many media markets the number of competing viewpoints is small. Nevertheless, a congressional effort to require the FCC to enforce the fairness doctrine was blocked by the Reagan administration in 1987.

fairness doctrine
a Federal Communications Commission (FCC) requirement for broadcasters who air programs on controversial issues to provide time for opposing views. The FCC ceased enforcing this doctrine in 1985

News Coverage

▶ How are media content, news coverage, and bias affected by the producers, subjects, and consumers of the news?

Because of the important role the media can play in national politics, it is vitally important to understand the factors that affect media coverage.[14] What accounts for the media's agenda of issues and topics? What explains the character of coverage—why does a politician receive good or bad press? What factors determine the interpretation or "spin" that a particular story will receive? Although a host of minor factors plays a role, three major factors are important: (1) the journalists, or producers of the news; (2) the sources or topics of the news; and (3) the audience for the news.

POLICY DEBATE

Internet Regulation: The Communications Decency Act

When Congress, with the support of President Clinton, passed the Communications Decency Act (CDA) as one part of the Telecommunications Act of 1996, it sought to regulate the spread of indecent materials on the Internet—the vast electronic communications network now available to millions of Americans through computers and telephone transmission lines. The CDA sought to bar the transmission of obscene or indecent communications to anyone under the age of eighteen. The constitutionality of the CDA was immediately challenged by Internet service providers and civil liberties groups as an improper infringement of First Amendment liberties. In a sweeping 1997 decision, the Supreme Court ruled in *Reno v. American Civil Liberties Union* that such regulations are a violation of the First Amendment. More important, the Court established that the Internet is a form of communication entitled to the maximum degree of constitutional protection, analogous to newspapers, books, and magazines (electronic media, such as television and radio, may be more strictly regulated by the government). Yet this ruling has not ended the dispute between those favoring and opposing stricter Internet controls.

Supporters of Internet regulation argue that children must be protected from the vast amount of offensive material to be found on the Internet. More than 10,000 Web sites are devoted to some form of pornography. Given the proliferation of obscene materials and sites, and given that the Internet is unregulated, government must be able to intervene to protect children. Despite the Supreme Court's ruling, the Internet is very different from newspapers and other printed media, in that there are no reporters, editors, publishers, or others who control the content of Internet communications.

Even more alarming, sexual predators have used Internet connections not only to expose children to obscene material, but to lure children to dangerous in-person meetings. For example, a California man was convicted of luring a thirteen-year-old girl from Kentucky to a meeting with him, the purpose of which was illegal sexual conduct. From 1995 to 1997, the FBI arrested thirty-five adults seeking to solicit sex from minors via the Internet. Apart from barring children from all Internet use, parents find themselves nearly powerless to protect their children, who often possess far more knowledge of computer technologies than their parents. Some limitation on liberty is necessary to protect America's children.

Those who oppose Internet regulation argue that the total harm done by regulations like the CDA far outweighs the benefits. In constitutional terms, the Internet is a vast electronic forum for speech, expression, and education. Although some harm is likely to accompany the unfettered expression of thoughts and ideas, such expression is central to a democracy and to the fundamental liberties of its citizens. Efforts to regulate Internet content in the name of protecting children too easily restrict legitimate expression. For example, during the brief time that the CDA was in effect, messages with the word "breast" in them were banned from the Internet by some providers. Such bans blocked not only obscene references, but also sites dealing with breast cancer, for example. Efforts to regulate indecent and obscene materials inevitably exclude useful information, and would have a chilling effect on many forms of legitimate communication, such as online support groups dealing with AIDS, child abuse, rape, and the like. Other information having legitimate scientific, artistic, literary, or other social value is too easily suppressed by regulations like the CDA.

Concerned parents can always monitor Internet use by their children. They can obtain software that filters out objectionable materials. Above all, parents should have primary control over what their children do and do not see.

SOURCE: Amy Harmon, "Ruling Leaves Vexing Burden for Parents," *The New York Times,* June 27, 1997.

STUDENT DEBATE

Should the Internet Be Regulated?

Yes

Helping my ten-year-old cousin with her fifth-grade final project was not the breeze I had anticipated it to be. With an ambitious assignment: to write about "The American Government," our first recourse was on-line research. My cousin insisted on typing, eager to show off her Internet proficiency to the big kid sitting next to her. As her pudgy fingers hunted and pecked for a Web site, I watched as the phrase "whitehouse.com" appeared on the screen. Then I watched as the image of a woman in a suit jacket and not much else followed, also beckoning from the screen. I quickly covered my cousin's face, muffling her questioning about the meaning of "foxy chicks" beneath my hands.

Who knew that the innocent replacement of .com for .gov would generate an NC-17 Web site? Certainly not my little cousin, who still pesters me about what "foxy chicks" means today. With new laws being passed in Virginia to ban pornography and other inappropriate content on the Web, shouts of First Amendment violations predictably blare like a foghorn. Numerous Virginia groups, like PSINet (an Internet development company in Herndon), the Comic Book Legal Defense Fund, and Lambda Rising Bookstores, the nation's largest specialty retailer of gay and lesbian materials, tout the law as an attempt to reduce cyberspace to a realm suitable only for juveniles. Civil rights advocates who are currently filing a federal suit against the Commonwealth claim that it limits the Internet as an open forum for communication and information.

To some extent, these protests are justified. A complete ban on public information undoubtedly is a violation of free speech. But one has to wonder what really is being protected in the defense of propagation of material harmful to children—the freedom of press on the Internet, or the industry that profits from it?

The argument against censorship always has been "If the government limits you in one way, who's to say it will not limit you in others?" As another generation raised on a healthy diet of rallies, marches, and sit-ins, however, we are all well aware that Americans are as patient with injustice as a cranky baby is about its bottle. Limiting explicit material on the Internet will not lead to a domino effect of limitations. Groups like People for the American Way, which currently is protesting the Virginia law, and other almost militantly active freedom-of-speech groups will continue to exist. And they will continue to yelp about how the government stepped on the nation's democratic foot to protect us.

Instead of being the revolutionary turning point it is feared as, Internet censorship will be another practical exception to the First Amendment rule. No, you can't yell fire in a crowded movie theater, even if there is free speech. No, you can't print libel even if there is free press. The above are dangerous, and they exceed the dangers of violating the First Amendment. For the same reason—no, you can't sell or display pornography on-line in a manner that is accessible to children.

Completely prohibiting access to explicit sites would be a blatant denial of rights. But prohibiting pornography's dissemination to minors is just another reasonable exception to the First Amendment, and not the Black Death of liberty, as civil rights activists diagnose it. In this case, those who defend free speech do it more for their own sake rather than the sake of the common good. They do not consider how much more harm they are bringing than good.

***

A noteworthy argument against the Virginia ban on explicit material is that, for all practical purposes, it is useless, considering how ineffective a single state law would be in curbing the entire World Wide Web. While this is true, this is also not the purpose of the law. It will not be the single finger that is wagged at explicit Web material, but a part of the larger hand that is doing the smacking. It is the Internet version of *Brown v. the Board of Education*, in that it has the potential to start a chain of events protecting innocent eyes from inappropriate material.

And that's nice to know, because when it comes down to it, who really wants to have to explain what "foxy chicks" means anyway?

Diya Gullapalli, "Limiting Web Makes Surfing Safer," *Cavalier Daily* (University of Virginia), October 13, 1999.

No

On August 1, a Michigan law will be able to stretch far across the country—if Gov. John Engler and certain state legislators have their way. The law, which was sponsored by Sen. Beverly Hammerstrom (R-Temperance), makes knowingly transmitting obscene material to minors over the Internet punishable by up to two years in prison and a $10,000 dollar fine. It is an extension of a 1978 law prohibiting making sexually explicit material available to minors.

The American Civil Liberties Union filed a suit in United States District Court in Detroit on behalf of the AIDS Partnership of Michigan, a marriage counselor who publishes a web site discussing sexual issues, a gay and lesbian book shop, and a company publishing a Web site for artists. The basis of the suit is that the law violates the U.S. Constitution's Commerce Clause—the law would require an individual in another state with an Internet site to publish according to Michigan standards.

On face, the law may seem appropriate, but as with all attempts to legislate content on the Internet, it is fraught with peril and sets a horrible precedent for the passage of similar laws in other states.

The law is a clear attempt on the part of government to legislate morality, and does not acknowledge the rights of individuals and parents to decide what they wish themselves or their children to view. The type of material falling under the law is "obscenity," which has yet to be adequately legally defined, rather than material [that] could potentially be used to hurt others—such as bomb-making instructions.

Even worse, the law could potentially make it illegal for anyone to make available information widely regarded as medically or culturally valid. On-line discussions or postings regarding birth control or sexually transmitted diseases, or literature along the lines of *The Catcher in the Rye* or even the Bible could be become illegal by the law.

Increasing cultural diversity in America has also [led] to increasing moral diversity as well. It is naive to believe that, because it is generally regarded as useful or enriching, certain information could not be banned under the law.

Even if the courts were to vindicate Internet publishers who provide "acceptable" content, the legal process would undoubtedly take time and money and may lead some legitimate content providers to believe that publishing a site on the Internet is simply not worth the risk.

The open and democratic nature of the Internet relies on the free flow of information between individuals. Even if one accepts the precarious argument that obscenity is harmful, it would be very difficult to prove that the potential harms of viewing such material outweigh those of regulating the Internet's content—especially with the advent of software and on-line services empowering parents to prevent their children from viewing such material.

Since the middle of the 1990s, there have been many attempts on the part of lawmakers to regulate content on the Internet and they have all run into the same problems that always arise with anti-obscenity laws. At best, the line between the obscene and the non-obscene is very thin, add into the equation a population with often conflicting values and the destructive futility of regulating content on the Internet becomes readily obvious.

Staff Editorial, "Regulating Obscenity Is Counterproductive," *Michigan Daily* (University of Michigan), June 28, 1999.

$50,000 REWARD.—WHO DESTROYED THE MAINE?—$50,000 REWARD.

EDITION FOR GREATER NEW YORK

NEW YORK JOURNAL

AND ADVERTISER.

DESTRUCTION OF THE WAR SHIP MAINE WAS THE WORK OF AN ENEMY.

$50,000!

$50,000 REWARD!

For the Detection of the Perpetrator of the Maine Outrage!

Assistant Secretary Roosevelt Convinced the Explosion of the War Ship Was Not an Accident.

The Journal Offers $50,000 Reward for the Conviction of the Criminals Who Sent 258 American Sailors to Their Death. Naval Officers Unanimous That the Ship Was Destroyed on Purpose.

$50,000!

$50,000 REWARD!

For the Detection of the Perpetrator of the Maine Outrage!

NAVAL OFFICERS THINK THE MAINE WAS DESTROYED BY A SPANISH MINE.

Hidden Mine or a Sunken Torpedo Believed to Have Been the Weapon Used Against the American Man-of-War---Officers and Men Tell Thrilling Stories of Being Blown Into the Air Amid a Mass of Shattered Steel and Exploding Shells---Survivors Brought to Key West Scout the Idea of Accident---Spanish Officials Protest Too Much---Our Cabinet Orders a Searching Inquiry---Journal Sends Divers to Havana to Report Upon the Condition of the Wreck.

Was the Vessel Anchored Over a Mine?

BY CAPTAIN E. L. ZALINSKI, U. S. A.

(Captain Zalinski is the inventor of the famous dynamite gun, which would be the principal factor in our coast defence in case of war.)

Assistant Secretary of the Navy Theodore Roosevelt says he is convinced that the destruction of the Maine in Havana Harbor was not an accident.

The Journal offers a reward of $50,000 for exclusive evidence that will convict the person, persons or Government criminally responsible for the destruction of the American battle ship and the death of 258 of its crew.

The suspicion that the Maine was deliberately blown up grows stronger every hour. Not a single fact to the contrary has been produced.

Captain Sigsbee, of the Maine, and Consul-General Lee both urge that public opinion be suspended until they have completed their investigation. They are taking the course of tactful men who are convinced that there has been treachery.

Washington reports very late that Captain Sigsbee had feared some such event as a hidden mine. The English cipher code was used all day yesterday by the naval officers in cabling instead of the usual American code.

The *New York Journal*'s sensationalistic coverage of the sinking of the *Maine* in Havana harbor inflamed the American public and edged the United States toward war with Spain.

JOURNALISTS

Media content and news coverage are inevitably affected by the views, ideals, and interests of those who seek out, write, and produce news and other stories. At one time, newspaper publishers exercised a great deal of influence over their papers' news content. Publishers such as William Randolph Hearst and Joseph Pulitzer became political powers through their manipulation of news coverage. Hearst, for example, almost single-handedly pushed the United States into war with Spain in 1898 through his newspapers' relentless coverage of the alleged brutality employed by Spain in its efforts to suppress a rebellion in Cuba, at that time a Spanish colony. The sinking of the American battleship *Maine* in Havana harbor under mysterious circumstances gave Hearst the ammunition he needed to force a reluctant President McKinley to lead the nation into war. Today, few publishers have that kind of power. Most publishers are concerned more with the business operations of their newspapers than with editorial content, although a few continue to impose their interests and tastes on the news. For example, Martin Peretz, owner and publisher of the weekly magazine, *The New Republic* is a staunch backer of Democratic Vice President Al Gore. Peretz fired *New Republic* editor Andrew Sullivan after Sullivan wrote several unflattering pieces about Gore. In a similar vein, conservative publisher Rupert Murdoch provided the financial support that enabled William Kristol, who had been chief of staff to former Republican Vice President Dan Quayle, to launch his conservative news magazine, the *Weekly Standard*.

More important than publishers, for the most part, are the reporters. Those who cover the news for the national media generally have a good deal of discretion or freedom to interpret stories and, as a result, have an opportunity to interject their views and ideals into news stories. For example, the personal friendship and respect that some reporters felt for Franklin Roosevelt or John Kennedy helped to generate more favorable news coverage for these presidents. Likewise, the dislike and distrust felt by many reporters for Richard Nixon was also communicated to the public. In the case of Ronald Reagan, the disdain that many journalists felt for the president was communicated in stories suggesting that he was often asleep or inattentive when important decisions were made. Conservatives have long charged that the liberal biases of reporters and journalists result in distorted news coverage.

A 1996 survey of Washington newspaper bureau chiefs and correspondents seems to support this charge.[15] The study, conducted by the Roper Center and the Freedom Forum, a conservative foundation, found that 61 percent of the bureau chiefs and correspondents polled called themselves "liberal" or "liberal to moderate." Only 9 percent called themselves "conservative" or "conservative to moderate." In a similar vein, 89 percent said they had voted for Democrat Bill Clinton in 1992, while only 7 percent indicated that they had voted for Republican George Bush. Fifty percent said they were Democrats, and only 4 percent claimed to be Republicans.[16]

The linkage between substantial segments of the media and liberal interest groups is by no means absolute. Indeed, over the past several years a conservative media complex has emerged in opposition to the liberal media. This complex includes two major newspapers, *The Wall Street Journal* and *The Washington Times*, several magazines such as the *American Spectator*, and a host of conservative radio and television talk programs. The emergence of this conservative media complex has meant that liberal policies and politicians are virtually certain to come under attack even when the "liberal media" are sympathetic to them.

Probably more important than ideological bias is a selection bias in favor of news that the media view as having a great deal of audience appeal because of its dramatic or entertainment value. In practice, this bias often results in

Student Perspectives

MEDIA SPOTLIGHT SHINES ON UNIMPORTANT ISSUES

If there is one thing Bill Bradley has always been aware of, it is the ticker.

As a basketball star at Princeton and later with the New York Knicks, the presidential hopeful was mindful of how much time remained in his battles. And although he no longer mans the Madison Square Garden hardwood, he still has to be mindful of his ticker.

Because if he is not, the media will not let him forget about it.

The media have set their sights on the former U.S. Senator from New Jersey, circling his presidential campaign like vultures after they learned of his heart ailment.

His heart condition is not mind-blowing news—it's just a case of arrhythmia.

Yet the media sensationalize his condition, vaguely claiming it can cause strokes in some instances and using it to question his ability to run the country.

***

What the media forget all too often during campaigns is what they should cover in the first place—the issues.

It is the issues which effect the course of the election and it is the issues which will be the platform on which this country stands as it enters the new millennium. It's not which candidate failed out of school his freshman year, it's not which candidate smoked marijuana (and even if they inhaled or not), and it's not which candidate has an impotency problem.

Rather it is important to determine which candidate will reform campaign finance, health care, and taxes.

This is what is pertinent to the media's audience because it shapes their lives, has meaning, and it is how they determine their vote to make an educated decision.

Staff Editorial, *Daily Collegian* (Pennsylvania State University), February 3, 2000.

news coverage that focuses on crimes and scandals, especially those involving prominent individuals, despite the fact that the public obviously looks to the media for information about important political debates. For example, even though most journalists may be Democrats, this partisan predisposition did not prevent an enormous media frenzy in January 1998 when reports surfaced that President Clinton may have had an affair with White House intern Lewinsky. Once a hint of blood appeared in the water, partisanship and ideology were swept away by the piranhalike instincts often manifested by journalists.

Students and Politics

Sam Dealey had not always held views on the Right of the American ideological spectrum. But when he arrived at Cornell University, he says, "I had not really thought out what I believed. I took some courses in college and proceeded to become a raving libertarian." Dealey's activism started when he worked on political campaigns in his native Texas, including that of Senator Kay Bailey Hutchison in 1993. In 1996, Dealey's interest in politics peaked as he interned with the *National Review*, a conservative political magazine that focuses on investigative journalism. While there, he wrote an article titled "New Girls' Network," about the alleged liberal bias of the Department of Housing and Urban Development in awarding contracts, and which caused a stir in Washington. Currently, Dealey works as assistant managing editor at the *American Spectator*, another major right-of-center political magazine.

SOURCE: Sam Dealey, interview by author, February 12, 1998.

SOURCES OF THE NEWS

News coverage is also influenced by the individuals or groups who are subjects of the news or whose interests and activities are actual or potential news topics. All politicians, for example, seek to shape or manipulate their media images by cultivating good relations with reporters as well as through news leaks and staged news events. For example, during the lengthy investigation of President Clinton conducted by Special Counsel Kenneth Starr, both the Office of the Special Counsel and the White House frequently leaked information to the press designed to bolster their respective positions in the struggle. Starr admitted speaking to reporters on a not-for-attribution basis about aspects of his investigation of the president. One journalist, Steven Brill, accused a number of prominent reporters of serving as "lap dogs" for the Special Counsel by reporting as fact the information fed to them by Starr.[17] Some politicians become extremely adept image makers—or at least skilled at hiring publicists who are skillful image makers. Indeed, press releases drafted by skillful publicists often become the basis for reporters' stories. A substantial percentage of the news stories published every day were initially drafted by publicists and later rewritten only slightly, if at all, by busy reporters and editors.

Furthermore, political candidates often endeavor to tailor their images for specific audiences. For example, to cultivate a favorable image among younger voters during his 1992 campaign, Bill Clinton made several appearances on MTV, and he continued to grant interviews to MTV after his election. His MTV forays came to an end, however, when he was severely criticized for discussing his preferred type of underwear with members of an MTV audience.

The capacity of news sources and subjects to influence the news is hardly unlimited. Media consultants and issues managers may shape the news for a time, but it is generally not difficult for the media to penetrate the smoke screens thrown up by news sources if they have a reason to do so.

Occasionally, however, a politician proves incredibly adept at surviving repeated media attacks. Bill Clinton, for example, was able to survive repeated revelations of sexual improprieties, financial irregularities, lying to the public, and illegal campaign fund-raising activities. Clinton and his advisers crafted what *The Washington Post* called a "toolkit" for dealing with potentially damaging media revelations. This toolkit includes techniques such as chiding the press, browbeating reporters, referring inquiries quickly to lawyers who will not comment, and acting quickly to change the agenda. These techniques helped Clinton maintain a favorable public image despite the Monica Lewinsky scandal and even the humiliation of a formal impeachment and trial.

THE POWER OF CONSUMERS

The print and broadcast media are businesses that, in general, seek to show a profit. This means that like any other business, they must cater to the preferences of consumers. This has very important consequences for the content and character of the news media.

Catering to the Upscale Audience In general, and especially in the political realm, the print and broadcast media and the publishing industry are not only responsive to the interests of consumers generally, but they are particularly responsive to the interests and views of the more "upscale" segments of their audience. The preferences of these audience segments have a profound effect on the content and orientation of the press, of radio and television programming, and of books, especially in the areas of news and public affairs.[18]

Entertainment shows have become a popular means for candidates to reach the public. For instance, 2000 Republican presidential candidate George W. Bush appeared on *The Tonight Show with Jay Leno.* During that campaign, candidates also appeared on *The Late Show with David Letterman, The Oprah Winfrey Show,* and other such programs.

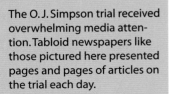

The O. J. Simpson trial received overwhelming media attention. Tabloid newspapers like those pictured here presented pages and pages of articles on the trial each day.

Newspapers, magazines, and the broadcast media depend primarily upon advertising revenues for their profits. These revenues, in turn, depend upon the character and size of the audience that they are able to provide to advertisers for their product displays and promotional efforts. From the perspective of most advertisers and especially those whose products are relatively expensive, the most desirable audiences for their ads and commercials consist of younger, upscale consumers. What makes these individuals an especially desirable consumer audience is, of course, their affluence and their spending habits. Although they represent only a small percentage of the population, individuals under the age of fifty whose family income is in the eightieth percentile or better account for nearly 50 percent of the retail dollars spent on consumer goods in the United States. To reach this audience, advertisers are particularly anxious to promote their products in the periodicals and newspapers and on the radio and television broadcasts that are known or believed to attract upscale patronage. Thus, advertisers flock to magazines like *The New Yorker, Fortune, Forbes, Architectural Digest,* and *Time*. Similarly, the pages of elite newspapers like *The New York Times* and *The Washington Post* are usually packed with advertisements for clothing, autos, computer equipment, stereo equipment, furs, jewelry, resorts and vacations, and the entire range of products and services that are such integral parts of the lifestyles of the well-to-do business and professional strata.

Although affluent consumers do watch television programs and read periodicals whose contents are designed simply to amuse or entertain, the one area that most directly appeals to the upscale audience is that of news and public affairs. The affluent—who are also typically well educated—are the core audience of newsmagazines, journals of opinion, books dealing with public affairs, such newspapers as *The New York Times* and *The Washington Post,* and broadcast news and weekend and evening public-affairs programs. Although other segments of the public also read newspapers and watch television news, their level of interest in world events, national political issues, and the like is closely related to their level of education. As a result, upscale Americans are overrepresented in the news and public-affairs audience. The concentration of these strata in the audience makes news, politics, and public affairs potentially very attractive topics to advertisers, publishers, radio broadcasters, and television executives. As a result, topics in which the middle class is interested, such as the stock market, scientific and literary affairs, and international politics, receive extensive coverage.

At the same time, however, entire categories of events, issues, and phenomena of interest to lower-middle- and working-class Americans receive scant attention from the national print and broadcast media. For example, trade-union news and events are discussed only in the context of major strikes or revelations of corruption. No network or national periodical routinely covers labor organizations. Religious and church affairs receive little coverage. The activities of veterans', fraternal, ethnic, and patriotic organizations are also generally ignored. Certainly, interpretations of economic events tend to reveal a class bias. For example, an increase in airline fares—a cost borne primarily by upper-income travelers—is usually presented as a negative development. Higher prices for commodities heavily used by the poor, such as alcohol and cigarettes, on the other hand, are generally presented as morally justified.

The upscale character of the national media's coverage stands in sharp contrast to the topics discussed by radio and television talk shows and the small number of news tabloids and major daily newspapers that seek to reach a blue-collar audience. These periodicals and programs feature some of the same events described by the national media. But from the perspective of these outlets and their viewers and readers, "public affairs" includes healthy doses of celebrity gossip, crime news, discussions of the occult, and sightings of UFOs. Also featured are ethnic, fraternal, patriotic, and religious affairs and even demolition derbies. Executives, intellectuals, and professionals, as well as the journalists and writers who serve them, may sneer at this blue-collar version of the news, but after all, are the stories of UFOs presented by the decidedly downscale *New York Post* any more peculiar than the stories of the UN told by the almighty *New York Times?*

The Media and Protest While the media respond most to the upscale audience, groups who cannot afford the services of media consultants and issues managers can publicize their views and interests through protest. Frequently, the media are accused of encouraging protest and even violence as a result of the fact that they are instantly available to cover it, providing protesters with the publicity they crave. Clearly, protest and even violence can be important vehicles for attracting the attention and interest of the media, and thus may provide an opportunity for media attention to groups otherwise lacking the financial or organizational resources to broadcast their views. During the 1960s, for example, the media coverage given to civil rights demonstrators and particularly to the violence that southern law enforcement officers in cities such as Selma and Birmingham directed against peaceful black demonstrators at least temporarily increased white sympathy for the civil rights cause. This was, of course, one of the chief aims of Dr. Martin Luther King's strategy of nonviolence.[19] In subsequent years, the media turned their attention to antiwar demonstrations and, more recently, to antiabortion demonstrations, antinuclear demonstrations, and even to acts of international terrorism designed specifically to induce the Western media to publicize the terrorists' causes. But while protest, disorder, and even terrorism can succeed in drawing media attention, these methods ultimately do not allow groups from the bottom of the social ladder to compete effectively in the media.

While demonstrating in Birmingham, Alabama, civil rights protesters were sprayed with fire hoses by the order of Police Commissioner Bull Conner. Images like this one were seen around the world and helped increase pressure on the United States to uphold its claims of being a nation of "liberty and justice for all."

Typically, upper-class protesters—student demonstrators and the like—have little difficulty securing favorable publicity for themselves and their causes. Upper-class protesters are often more skilled than their lower-class counterparts in the techniques of media manipulation. That is, they typically have a better sense—often as a result of formal courses on the subject—of how to package messages for media consumption. For example, it is important to know what time of day a protest should occur if it is to be carried on the evening news. Similarly, the setting, definition of the issues, character of the rhetoric used, and so on, all help to determine whether a protest will receive favorable media coverage, unfavorable coverage, or no coverage at all. Moreover, upper-middle-class protesters can often produce their own media coverage through "underground" newspapers, college papers, student radio and television stations, and, now, over the Internet. The same resources and skills that generally allow upper-middle-class people to publicize their ideas are usually not left behind when segments of this class choose to engage in disruptive forms of political action. This helps to explain why small groups of demonstrators in Seattle, Washington were able to garner enormous media coverage in the winter of 1999 for their protests against the World Trade Organization.

Media Power in American Politics

- How do the media shape public perceptions of events, issues, and institutions?
- What are the sources of media power?

The content and character of news and public affairs programming—what the media choose to present and how they present it—can have far-reaching political consequences. Media disclosures can greatly enhance—or fatally damage—the careers of public officials. Media coverage can rally support for—or intensify opposition to—national policies. The media can shape and modify, if not fully form, public perceptions of events, issues, and institutions.

SHAPING EVENTS

In recent American political history, the media have played a central role in at least three major events. First, the media were a critically important factor in the civil rights movement of the 1950s and 1960s. Television photos showing peaceful civil rights marchers attacked by club-swinging police helped to generate sympathy among northern whites for the civil rights struggle and greatly increased the pressure on Congress to bring an end to segregation.[20] Second, the media were instrumental in compelling the Nixon administration to negotiate an end to American involvement in the Vietnam War. Beginning in 1967, the national media portrayed the war as misguided and unwinnable and, as a result, helped to turn popular sentiment against continued American involvement.[21] So strong was the effect of the media, in fact, that when Walter Cronkite told television news viewers that the war was unwinnable, Johnson himself was reported to have said, "If I've lost Walter, then it's over. I've lost Mr. Average Citizen."[22]

Finally, the media were central actors in the Watergate affair, which ultimately forced President Richard Nixon, landslide victor in the 1972 presidential election, to resign from office in disgrace. It was the relentless series of investigations launched by *The Washington Post, The New York Times,* and the television networks that led to the disclosures of the various abuses of

Media images of the Vietnam War were seen by millions of Americans and helped turn public sentiment against U.S. involvement in the war. In this famous photo, terrified children flee from a Napalm bomb attack.

which Nixon was guilty and ultimately forced Nixon to choose between resignation and almost certain impeachment.

THE SOURCES OF MEDIA POWER

agenda setting
the power of the media to bring public attention to particular issues and problems

Agenda Setting The power of the media stems from several sources. The first is **agenda setting,** which means that the media help to set the agenda for political discussion. Groups and forces that wish to bring their ideas before the public in order to generate support for policy proposals or political candidacies must somehow secure media coverage. If the media are persuaded that an idea is newsworthy, then they may declare it an "issue" that must be confronted or a "problem" to be solved, thus clearing the first hurdle in the policymaking process. On the other hand, if an idea lacks or loses media appeal, its chance of resulting in new programs or policies is diminished.

For example, in 2000, Democratic presidential candidate Bill Bradley sought to make poverty the central issue of his bid for office. Bradley appeared at numerous events to speak out against poverty and offered a plan that he said would "end child poverty as we know it." Bradley also promised to raise the minimum wage and increase tax credits for the working poor.[23] While this topic was popular among some liberal and labor groups, the national media seemed to regard it as old hat and did not make Bradley's plan a central theme in its coverage of the presidential race. Other candidates ignored the Bradley effort since the media failed to label it as a major issue in the race.

On the other hand, Democrats were able to persuade the media that regulation of health maintenance organizations (HMOs) was an issue worthy of discussion. During well-publicized congressional hearings in the fall of 1999, Democrats presented many witnesses who testified that their HMOs had prevented them from receiving adequate treatment. Democrats called for a "Patient's Bill of Rights" to allow HMO physicians more autonomy and to permit unhappy patients redress in the courts. Republicans initially charged that the Democrats were simply doing the bidding of the trial lawyers, major contributors to the Democratic party, who saw HMOs as rich targets for litigation. Media coverage of the disgruntled HMO patients, however, made it impossible for Republicans to dismiss the issue from the agenda and led eventually to the enactment of legislation close to the Democratic proposal.

In many instances, the media serve as conduits for agenda-setting efforts by competing groups and forces. Occasionally, however, journalists themselves play an important role in setting the agenda of political discussion. For example, whereas many of the scandals and investigations surrounding President Clinton were initiated by his political opponents, the Watergate scandal that destroyed Nixon's presidency was in some measure initiated and driven by *The Washington Post* and the national television networks.

framing
the power of the media to influence how events and issues are interpreted

Framing A second source of the media's power, known as **framing,** is their power to decide how political events and results are interpreted by the American people. For example, during the 1995–96 struggle between President Clinton and congressional Republicans over the nation's budget—a struggle that led to several partial shutdowns of the federal government—the media's interpretation of events forced the Republicans to back down and agree to a budget

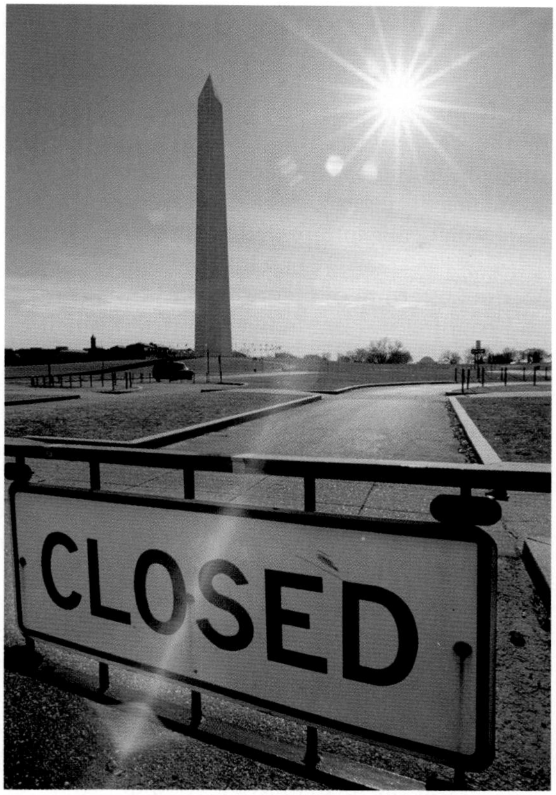

The shutdown of the federal government in 1995–96 closed all national parks and tourist sites, including the Washington Monument. The media helped direct popular opinion against the Republican-controlled Congress during the budget impasse that led to the shutdown.

on Clinton's terms. At the beginning of the crisis, congressional Republicans, led by then House Speaker Newt Gingrich, were confident that they could compel Clinton to accept their budget, which called for substantial cuts in domestic social programs. Republicans calculated that Clinton would fear being blamed for lengthy government shutdowns and would quickly accede to their demands, and that once Americans saw that life went on with government agencies closed, they would support the Republicans in asserting that the United States could get along with less government.

For the most part, however, the media did not cooperate with the GOP's plans. Media coverage of the several government shutdowns during this period emphasized the hardships imposed upon federal workers who were being furloughed in the weeks before Christmas. Indeed, Newt Gingrich, who was generally portrayed as the villain who caused the crisis, came to be called the "Gin*grinch*" who stole Christmas from the children of hundreds of thousands of federal workers. Rather than suggest that the shutdown demonstrated that America could carry on with less government, media accounts focused on the difficulties encountered by Washington tourists unable to visit the capital's monuments, museums, and galleries. The woes of American travelers whose passports were delayed were given considerable attention. Thus, the "dominant frame" became the hardship and disruption caused by the Republicans. The GOP's "competing frame" was dismissed.[24] This sort of coverage eventually convinced most Americans that the government shutdown was bad for the country. In the end, Gingrich and the congressional Republicans were forced to surrender and to accept a new budget reflecting many of Clinton's priorities. The Republicans' defeat in the budget showdown contributed to the unraveling of the GOP's legislative program and, ultimately, to the Republicans' poor showing in the 1996 presidential elections and 1998 congressional races. The character of media coverage of an event thus had enormous repercussions for how Americans interpreted it.

Media Coverage of Elections and Government The media's agenda-setting and framing powers may often determine how people perceive political candidates. In 1968, despite the growing strength of the opposition to his Vietnam War policies, the incumbent president, Lyndon Johnson, won two-thirds of the votes cast in New Hampshire's Democratic presidential primary. His rival, Senator Eugene McCarthy, received less than one-third. The broadcast media, however, declared the outcome to have been a great victory for McCarthy, who was said to have done much better than "expected" (or at least expected by the media). His "defeat" in New Hampshire was one of the factors that persuaded Johnson to withdraw from the 1968 presidential race.

The media also have a good deal of power to shape popular perceptions of politicians and political leaders. Most citizens will never meet Bill Clinton or Al Gore or George Bush. Popular perceptions and evaluations of these individuals are often based solely upon their media images. Obviously, through public relations and other techniques, politicians seek to cultivate favorable media images. But the media have a good deal of discretion over how individuals are portrayed or how they are allowed to portray themselves.

In the case of political candidates, the media have considerable influence over whether or not a particular individual will receive public attention, whether or not a particular individual will be taken seriously as a viable contender, and whether the public will perceive a candidate's performance favorably. Thus, if the media find a candidate interesting, they may treat him or her as a serious contender even though the facts of the matter seem to suggest otherwise. In a similar vein, the media may declare that a candidate has "momentum," a mythical property that the media confer upon candidates they admire. Momentum has no substantive meaning—it is simply a media prediction that a particular candidate will do even better in the future than in the past. Such media prophecies can become self-fulfilling as contributors and supporters jump on the bandwagon of the candidate possessing this "momentum." In 1992, when Bill Clinton's poll standings surged in the wake of the Democratic National Convention, the media determined that Clinton had enormous momentum. In fact, nothing that happened during the remainder of the race led the media to change its collective judgment. In 1996, the national media portrayed Bob Dole's candidacy as hopeless almost from the very beginning. Coverage of the Republican convention and the presidential debates emphasized Clinton's "insurmountable" lead. The media's coverage of Dole's campaign became a self-fulfilling prophecy of his defeat.

During the 2000 presidential contest, the national media initially accepted Republican candidate George W. Bush's claim that his nomination was a foregone conclusion. At first, their consensus made it difficult for Bush's rivals to attract support or raise money, thus forcing other candidates, such as Elizabeth Dole, out of the race.[25] However, Senator John McCain of Arizona was able to use his Senate committee chairmanship to raise enough money to mount a challenge to Bush. In reality, McCain had little chance of defeating the front-runner. Seeing the possibility of a "horse race," however, the media gave McCain a great deal of generally positive coverage and helped him mount a noisy, if brief, challenge to Bush. McCain's hopes were dashed, though, when he was trounced by Bush in a series of primaries, including those held in South Carolina and other GOP strongholds.

At the same time that the media were promoting McCain's candidacy, the networks and major newspapers were questioning Democratic Vice President Al Gore's status as a front-runner for the Democratic nomination even though Gore seemed to have as strong an early lead on the Democratic side as Bush did on the Republican side. When former New Jersey senator Bill Bradley announced his candidacy, the national media gave close attention to what was now deemed to be a horse race between the two men. Daily articles throughout 1999 declared one or the other to be gaining or losing momentum even though the race had barely begun. This horse-race coverage helped Bradley attract money and support and temporarily turned what had seemed a futile effort into a real contest, which Gore won handily.

The media's power to shape images is not absolute. Throughout the last decade, politicians implemented new techniques for communicating with the public and shaping their own images. For instance, Bill Clinton pioneered the use of town meetings and television entertainment programs as means for communicating directly with voters in the 1992 election. During the 2000

SOURCES OF MEDIA POWER

Setting the Agenda for Political Discussion

Groups wishing to generate support for policy proposals or political candidacies must secure media coverage. The media must be persuaded that an item is newsworthy.

Framing

The media's interpretation or evaluation of an event or political action can sometimes determine how people perceive the event or result.

Shaping Perceptions of Leaders

Most citizens will never meet their political leaders, but will base opinions of these leaders on their media images. The media has a great deal of control over how a person is portrayed or whether an individual even receives public attention. The media are also able to shape how a policy issue is perceived by the public.

During the 2000 presidential race, the media seemed particularly smitten with Republican candidate Senator John McCain. The media/McCain love affair resulted in excessive coverage of minor events in McCain's campaign and often uncritical acceptance of the Senator's spin on his image problems.

In recent years, the town meeting has become a favorite media forum among candidates who wish to reach the public without sacrificing control of the agenda to moderators or journalists. Bill Clinton thrived in this type of forum and John McCain used town meetings in New Hampshire as a showcase for his "straight-talk," anti–Washington insider persona.

presidential race between Bush and Gore, both candidates made use of town meetings, as well as talk shows and entertainment programs like *The Oprah Winfrey Show, The Tonight Show with Jay Leno,* and *Saturday Night Live,* to reach mass audiences. During a town meeting, talk show, or entertainment program, politicians are free to craft their own images without interference from journalists.

In 2000, George W. Bush was also able to shape his image by effectively courting the press through informal conversation and interaction. Bush's "charm offensive" was successful. Journalists concluded that Bush was a nice fellow, albeit inexperienced, and refrained from subjecting him to harsh criticism and close scrutiny. Al Gore, on the other hand, seemed to offend journalists by remaining aloof and giving an impression of disdain for the press. Journalists responded by portraying Gore as "stiff." The result was unusually positive coverage for the Republican candidate and unusually negative coverage for the Democratic candidate.

Because politicians, interest groups, and other forces seeking positive news coverage know that the media look for drama and entertainment value, erstwhile newsmakers will typically seek to package their message in a format that the media will deem interesting, controversial, or entertaining. Among federal agencies, the one most adept at using the media to burnish its image and strengthen its claims on tax dollars is the National Aeronautics and Space Administration (NASA). In recent years, NASA has initiated a number of projects of dubious scientific value but high news appeal to generate positive press coverage. For example, NASA sent former astronaut turned senator John Glenn on a space mission for no reason other than the enormous publicity that Glenn's dramatic return to space would produce. Of course, one NASA publicity effort, sending a teacher into space, ended in tragedy with the crash of the *Challenger* spacecraft in 1986.

THE RISE OF ADVERSARIAL JOURNALISM

The political power of the news media vis-à-vis the government has greatly increased in recent years through the growing prominence of "adversarial journalism"—a form of reporting in which the media adopt a hostile posture toward the government and public officials.

During the nineteenth century, American newspapers were completely subordinate to the political parties. Newspapers depended upon official patronage—legal notice and party subsidies—for their financial survival and were controlled by party leaders. (A vestige of that era survived into the twentieth century in such newspaper names as the *Springfield Republican* and the *St. Louis Globe-Democrat.*) At the turn of the century, with the development of commercial advertising, newspapers became financially independent. This made possible the emergence of a formally nonpartisan press.

Franklin Delano Roosevelt used radio addresses, called "fireside chats," to reach millions of listeners and build support for his New Deal programs.

Presidents were the first national officials to see the opportunities in this development. By communicating directly to the electorate through newspapers and magazines, Theodore Roosevelt and Woodrow Wilson established political constituencies for themselves, independent of party organizations, and strengthened their own power relative to Congress. President Franklin Roosevelt used the radio, most notably in his famous fireside chats, to reach out to voters throughout the nation and to make himself the center of American politics. FDR was also adept at developing close personal relationships with reporters that enabled him to obtain favorable news coverage despite the fact that in his day a majority of newspaper owners and publishers were staunch conservatives. Following Roosevelt's example, subsequent presidents have all sought to use the media to enhance their popularity and power. For example, through televised news conferences, President John F. Kennedy mobilized public support for his domestic and foreign policy initiatives.

During the 1950s and early 1960s, a few members of Congress also made successful use of the media—especially television—to mobilize national support for their causes. Senator Estes Kefauver of Tennessee became a major contender for the presidency and won a place on the 1956 Democratic national ticket as a result of his dramatic televised hearings on organized crime. Senator Joseph McCarthy of Wisconsin made himself a powerful national figure through his well-publicized investigations of alleged communist infiltration of key American institutions. These senators, however, were more exceptional than typical. Through the mid-1960s, the executive branch continued to generate the bulk of news coverage, and the media served as a cornerstone of presidential power.

The Vietnam War shattered this relationship between the press and the presidency. During the early stages of U.S. involvement, American officials in Vietnam who disapproved of the way the war was being conducted leaked information critical of administrative policy to reporters. Publication of this material infuriated the White House, which pressured publishers to block its release—on one occasion, President Kennedy went so far as to ask *The New York Times* to reassign its Saigon correspondent. However, the national print and broadcast media—the network news divisions, the national newsweeklies, *The Washington Post,* and *The New York Times*—discovered that there was an audience for critical coverage among segments of the public skeptical of administration policy. As the Vietnam conflict dragged on, critical media coverage fanned antiwar sentiment. Moreover, growing opposition to the war among liberals encouraged some members of Congress, most notably Senator J. William Fulbright, chair of the Senate Foreign Relations Committee, to break with the president. In turn, these shifts in popular and congressional sentiment emboldened journalists and publishers to continue to present critical news reports. Through this process, journalists developed a commitment to adversarial journalism, while a constituency emerged that would rally to the defense of the media when it came under White House attack.

This pattern, established during the Vietnam War, endured through the 1970s and into the 1980s. Political forces opposed to presidential policies, many members of Congress, and the national news media began to find that their interests often overlapped. Liberal opponents of the Nixon, Carter, Reagan, and Bush administrations welcomed news accounts critical of the conduct of executive agencies and officials in foreign affairs and in such domestic areas as race relations, the environment, and regulatory policy. In addition, many senators and representatives found it politically advantageous to champion causes favored by the antiwar, consumer, or environmental movements because, by conducting televised hearings on such issues, they were able to mobilize national constituencies, to become national figures, and in a number of instances to become serious contenders for their party's presidential nomination.

During the 1990s, to be sure, conservative political forces rushed to the defense of their media allies. For example, when First Lady Hillary Clinton declared that the charges of sexual impropriety being levied against her husband were outgrowths of a "vast right-wing conspiracy," conservatives defended such publications as the *Weekly Standard, The Washington Times,* and *American Spectator* that had published numerous articles critical of the president.

For their part, aggressive use of the techniques of investigation, publicity, and exposure allowed the national media to enhance their autonomy and carve out a prominent place for themselves in American government and politics. The power derived by the press from adversarial journalism is one of the reasons that the media seem to relish opportunities to attack political institutions and to publish damaging information about important public officials. Increasingly, media coverage has come to influence politicians' careers, the mobiliza-

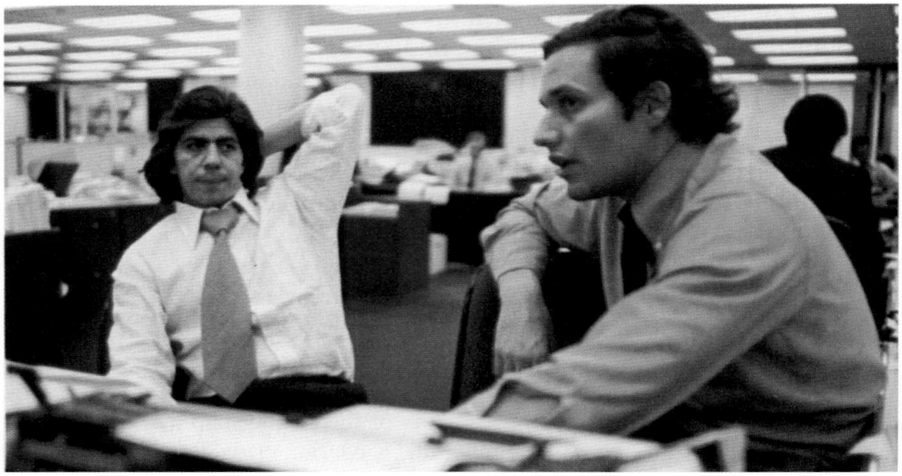

Washington Post reporters Robert Woodward and Carl Bernstein played an important role in uncovering the Watergate conspiracy, which eventually led to the resignation of President Richard M. Nixon.

tion of political constituencies, and the fate of issues and causes. Inasmuch as members of Congress and groups opposed to presidential policies in the 1970s and 1980s benefited from the growing influence of the press, they were prepared to rush to its defense when it came under attack. This constituency could be counted upon to denounce any move by the White House or its supporters to curb media influence as an illegitimate effort to manage the news, chill free speech, and undermine the First Amendment. It was the emergence of these overlapping interests, more than an ideological bias, that often led to a de facto alliance between liberal political forces and the national news media.

Media Power and Democracy

▶ Are the media too powerful and thus in need of restriction, or are a free media necessary for democracy?

The free media are an institution absolutely essential to democratic government. Ordinary citizens depend upon the media to investigate wrongdoing, to publicize and explain governmental actions, to evaluate programs and politicians, and to bring to light matters that might otherwise be known to only a handful of governmental insiders. In short, without free and active media, popular government would be virtually impossible. Citizens would have few means through which to know or assess the government's actions—other than the claims or pronouncements of the government itself. Moreover, without active—indeed, aggressive—media, citizens would be hard-pressed to make informed choices among competing candidates at the polls. Often enough, the media reveal discrepancies between candidates' claims and their actual records, and between the images that candidates seek to project and the underlying realities. Of course, by continually emphasizing deceptions and wrongdoing on the part of political figures, the media encourage the public to become cynical and distrustful, not only of the people in office, but of the government and political process themselves. A widespread sense that all politics is corrupt or deceptive can easily lead to a sense that nothing can be done. In this way, the media's adversarial posture may contribute to the low levels of political participation seen in America today.

At the same time, the declining power of party organizations (as we will see in Chapter 10) has made politicians ever more dependent upon favorable media coverage. National political leaders and journalists have had symbiotic relationships, at least since FDR's presidency, but initially politicians were the senior partners.

Students and Politics

In 1995 Philip Lefebvre founded America the Younger, an organization devoted to finding and publicizing nonviolent forms of protest. The group evolved from an idea, to a producer of venues at which youth leaders were brought together to discuss ideas, and finally to a publication, the *Compass*, a monthly journal that allows contributors to discuss a given issue each week from the perspective of the younger generation. Recent issues have focused on youth in politics and women's rights. "It only takes me about twenty hours each week," says Lefebvre. The *Compass* started as a shoestring operation: "It was pretty modest," says the editor-in-chief, publisher, and production manager. "A circulation of two hundred, and most of that was at local coffee shops and campuses. It's still small, but it's a good starting point for me, with lofty goals: we intend nothing less than the complete reversal of how our generation is perceived."

SOURCE: Philip Lefebvre, interview by author, January 30, 1998.

AMERICAN DEMOCRACY IN COMPARATIVE PERSPECTIVE

Free Press and Democracy

One of the oldest maxims of politics holds that one's freedom depends on the access one has to information about politics and the political process. To John Stuart Mill, democracy's success was measured by its tolerance for a free press. In an age of instant communication and the Internet, how common is a free press? Article 19 of the Universal Declaration of Human Rights (1948) asserts that everyone has the right "to receive and impart information and ideas through any media regardless of frontiers."

Guided by this premise, Freedom House periodically surveys the extent of free press across the globe. Its researchers survey and measure the following factors: (1) the extent of laws and administrative decisions taken by government to restrict media content; (2) political influences and controls over media content; (3) economic influences that restrict media content; and (4) acts of violence and overt physical threats against members of the media.

In 1999, one in five people on the globe lived in the sixty-eight countries that Freedom House described as having a "free press." More refined measures reveal that only 8.5 percent live in what Freedom House considers "very free press" countries. This group of nineteen countries includes the United States, Australia, Denmark, Norway, Netherlands, and Switzerland. Forty percent of the world's population (sixty-six countries) live in countries where the press is "not free." This group includes twenty-four countries (with 20 percent of the world's population) that have virtually no semblance of a free press of any sort. These worst cases include Afghanistan, China, Myanmar (formerly Burma), Cuba, Saudi Arabia, Sierra Leone, Sudan, North Korea, Yugoslavia, Iraq, and Iran.

In general, the industrialized nations of the world enjoy a high degree of press freedom, while Arab and sub-Saharan African nations have the greatest degree of restriction on free press. Across the globe, political restrictions on content are the most pressing threat to free press, while overt acts of terrorism and threats to members of the media are relatively rare, especially among members of the broadcast media. However, even among the twenty-four industrialized electoral democracies of the world, serious restrictions on free press are common, reducing the full effects of the media as a check and balance on concentrated political power.

Perhaps the most alarming and increasingly common threat to content freedom in the media of industrialized electoral democracies is the concentration of broadcast and print media in the hands of a few large conglomerates, often headed by single individuals. In Italy, this trend is reflected in the amassed power of Silvio Berlusconi and his massive Mondadori media conglomerate. Berlusconi owns three national television networks, which control 90 percent of Italian television advertising revenue and serve 45 percent of the Italian television audience (giving his companies a decisive advantage in pricing both commercial and political advertisements in Italy). In addition, his conglomerate owns two large daily newspapers and the country's largest weekly news magazine, and it controls 30 percent of the book trade in Italy. Berlusconi is also head of Italy's largest political party (Forza Italia) and for seven months in 1994 served as Prime Minister of Italy, using his political power to appoint his friends and business associates to key government posts that control rules and regulations of broadcast media. Similar patterns of media concentration are found throughout the industrailized electoral democracies, for instance in Great Britain (Ruppert Murdoch's News International Corporation) and in Germany (Thomas Middlehoff's Bertelsmann).

SOURCES: Freedom House, *Press Freedom Survey 1999* (available online at http://freedomhouse.org/pfs99/); "Emperor of the Air," by Alexander Stille, *The Nation*, November 29, 1999.

They benefited from media publicity, but they were not totally dependent upon it as long as they could still rely upon party organizations to mobilize votes. Journalists, on the other hand, depended upon their relationships with politicians for access to information and would hesitate to report stories that might antagonize valuable sources for fear of being excluded from the flow of information in retaliation. Thus, for example, reporters did not publicize potentially embarrassing information, widely known in Washington, about the personal lives of such figures as Franklin Roosevelt and John F. Kennedy.

With the decline of party organizations, the balance of power between politicians and journalists has been reversed. Now that politicians have become heavily dependent upon the media to reach their constituents, journalists no longer need fear that their access to information can be restricted in retaliation for negative coverage.

Such freedom gives the media enormous power. The media can make or break reputations, help to launch or to destroy political careers, and build support for or rally opposition to programs and institutions.[26] Wherever there is so much power, there exists at least the potential for its abuse or overly zealous use. All things considered, free media are so critically important to the maintenance of a democratic society that Americans must be prepared to take the risk that the media will occasionally abuse their power. The forms of governmental control that would prevent the media from misusing their power would also certainly destroy freedom.

The Citizen's Role

In their relationship to the media, most Americans adopt a passive stance. They read, they watch, or they listen to media accounts of events. However, it is relatively easy to become an active rather than a passive media user. One way to become an active media user is through letter-writing. Every newspaper and newsmagazine, and some television programs as well, provides a forum for citizen commentary. Letter writers have an opportunity to object to editorials with which they disagree, correct errors in news coverage, and even respond to other letter writers.

On one particular day, for example, *The New York Times* published eleven letters from readers. Several objected to the paper's editorial views, two asserted that news stories published in the paper had misrepresented important facts, and others commented on issues discussed in the paper. On the same day, *The Washington Post* published three long letters objecting to facts alleged in prior *Post* stories on German politics and on global warming. Obviously, a few letters cannot completely counterbalance all the errors or biases that may affect a newspaper's coverage. But if a newspaper or magazine were truly biased, it probably would not publish letters pointing out its biases.

Most newspapers and magazines feel some obligation to publish letters critical of their published materials. Even more important, letters can make editors aware of significant errors and omissions in the paper's coverage, perhaps leading them to admonish or reassign the journalists responsible. Letters to the

STUDENTS AND POLITICS

editor can even compel college newspapers to correct errors in news coverage. In November 1997, for example, the University of Buffalo's student newspaper published an apology and retraction after letter writers pointed out significant errors in a news story.[27] This seems to be a far better approach than stealing the newspaper! Letters can also indicate to a newspaper or television station that its viewers are unhappy. As commercial enterprises, the media are very eager to maintain a high level of customer satisfaction.

Citizens must also learn to be critical consumers of the media. It is very important to be alert to the possible biases or hidden messages in any news story. First, when watching the news or reading a story, be alert to the author or reporter's implicit assumptions. For example, the media tend to be naive about the motives of any group claiming to work on behalf of the "public interest" or "citizens" and to take the claims of such groups at face value, especially if the group is criticizing business or the government. You should think carefully about the claims and facts being presented. Second, watch for stereotypes. Most newspapers and radio and television stations make an effort to avoid the racial and gender stereotypes that were once common. However, many other stereotypes are prevalent in the news. For example, some government programs such as the space program enjoy "good press" and generally receive positive coverage despite the often dubious claims made by their backers. Other programs, such as public-assistance programs and the highway program, are treated as "wasteful" or "pork-barrel projects," despite the good they may do. Critical consumers need to make up their own minds rather than allow media stereotypes to color their judgment.

Third, take note of news sources. Very often, reporters rely upon the views of a small number of top officials or influential figures who make it their business to cultivate journalists. When Henry Kissinger was secretary of state, he was such a successful manipulator of the media that most news about American foreign policy reflected his views. Often, politicians and interest groups retain public relations firms to contact journalists and disseminate their views. Always ask yourself whose interests might be served by a particular story. Often, those interests turn out to be the source of the story.

Finally, it is important to rely upon more than one source of news. The best approach is to make use of news sources with disparate ideological perspectives. For example, residents of Washington, D.C., sometimes read both the liberal *Washington Post* and the conservative *Washington Times.* Anyone can subscribe to both a liberal magazine, such as *The Public Interest,* and a conservative one, such as the *Weekly Standard,* that often cover the same topics. The importance of using such disparate news sources is to obtain different perspectives on the same events. This, in turn, will help you see more than one possibility and, ultimately, to make up your own mind.[28]

GET INVOLVED Attracting Media Attention

How can you get attention focused on your group, its major causes, or key issues? Today, students have access to several media as mechanisms for attracting attention from other students, members of the community, and beyond. Here are several of them.

The Internet The Internet is the fastest growing venue in the world for disseminating information as well as for retrieving information. The good news is that college campuses generally provide easy access to the Internet and offer students the opportunity to publish their own Web pages. In addition, commercial Internet service providers now offer relatively low-cost access to the Internet and Web publishing. Meanwhile, innovations in software for creating Web pages and publishing them has made it relatively simple for students to create their own Web pages. Overall, this means that you should be able to set up a Web site to disseminate information about your group, persuade people to join you, and gain greater support, more recruits, and needed resources for your political activities. Indeed, you can do precisely what the Democratic and Republican parties, as well as innumerable other political organizations, have already done to gain widespread publicity.

The bad news is that the explosion of Internet users and Web sites in recent years means that your own Web site will be buried among millions of Web sites already on the Internet. Accordingly, once you have created a Web site, you must face the challenge of getting people to know about your Web site and visit it. You might try targeted advertising (for example, post flyers in dormitories). You might see if allied groups are willing to provide a link from their Web site to your Web site if you are willing to do the same. Nonetheless, unless you invest a great deal of money, expect relatively few "hits" on your Web site at first.

Newpapers Local newspapers may be very interested in covering the activities of student activists, especially newspapers that have a public interest section. Look through your local newspaper to determine where a story about your group's activities might fit. Identify the reporter or reporters who write for that section. Once you have a name, telephone the reporter and make a pitch as to why he or she should cover your group and its activities. Note also that some newspapers have a community calendar section where upcoming events are listed free of charge. You can submit notification of your meetings and events there.

Campus newspapers regularly cover student politics. However, if you are not part of the Student Senate or if you are affiliated with a lesser-known, controversial group, you may need to be a bit entrepreneurial to get coverage. Get to know student reporters. Ask them about what kinds of items they find newsworthy. Prepare news releases and fact sheets that will enable them to write about your group without spending much time researching it. Persevere. Even if you have trouble sparking interest at first, reporters and editors will face slow days when they will run your story if only for lack of options.

Radio Radio offers three options for publicity. First, you can call in to politically oriented talk shows to inform listeners about your group and discuss your issues. Second, you can contact radio talk shows that are not explicitly oriented to politics but nevertheless may be willing to do a quick interview or mention your activities on air. Third, radio stations often have free community calendars or run free public service announcements. When you call a radio station, be prepared to make a brief clear request and provide a succinct justification for your request.

Television While television may be the most effective way to capture people's attention, unfortunately, buying time on commercial television (even on local television) can be extremely expensive. You do have choices. Cable stations often provide a public access channel where local individuals and groups can provide programming. Relatedly, some cities have a government access channel that provides citizens some air time for discussing public matters. Call your local cable company regarding public access channels and call your local city hall for information about government access channels.

Another way to get television coverage is to stage a public action—a well-known speaker, a protest march, a symbolic burial of the Bill of Rights, and so forth. Notify local television stations ahead of time that your group or coalition will be holding a rally to protest an injustice or organizing a demonstration to show support for a proposed piece of legislation. You may want to appoint media liaisons to keep pressure on television stations to send reporters and camera operators, provide pointed interviews when the press arrives, or produce large signs and banners to provide the visual images so important to television news.

Depending on the size and nature of your campus, you may have access to a student-run Internet station, or radio station, or television station as well as a student newspaper. Investigate your media options and choose the most effective strategy for your purposes. Remember, it is a lot easier to achieve most political goals when a lot of people know about your cause, support it, and ultimately join in it. The media are crucial conduits between potential supporters and your group.

Summary

The American news media are among the world's most free. The print and broadcast media regularly present information and opinions critical of the government, political leaders, and policies.

The media help to determine the agenda or focus of political debate in the United States, to shape popular understanding of political events and results, and to influence popular judgments of politicians and leaders.

Over the past century, the media have helped to nationalize American political perspectives. Media coverage is influenced by the perspectives of journalists, the activities of news sources, and, most important, by the media's need to appeal to upscale audiences. The attention that the media give to protest and disruptive activities is also a function of audience factors.

Free media are an essential ingredient of popular government.

FOR FURTHER READING

Ansolabehere, Stephen, and Shanto Iyengar. *Going Negative: How Attack Ads Shrink and Polarize the Electorate.* New York: Free Press, 1995.

Bagdikian, Ben. *The Media Monopoly.* 5th ed. Boston: Beacon, 1997.

Cook, Timothy. *Governing with the News: The News Media as a Political Institution.* Chicago: University of Chicago Press, 1997.

Davis, Richard, and Diana Owen. *New Media and American Politics.* New York: Oxford University Press, 1998.

Graber, Doris, et al. *The Politics of News, The News of Politics.* Washington, DC: Congressional Quarterly Press, 1998.

Hallin, Daniel C. *The Uncensored War.* Berkeley and Los Angeles: University of California Press, 1986.

Hart, Roderick. *Seducing America: How Television Charms the Modern Voter.* New York: Oxford University Press, 1994.

Hess, Stephen. *Live From Capitol Hill: Studies of Congress and the Media.* Washington, DC: Brookings, 1991.

Kurtz, Howard. *Spin Cycle: Inside the Clinton Propaganda Machine.* New York: Free Press, 1998.

Sparrow, Bartholomew H. *Uncertain Guardians: The News Media as a Political Institution.* Baltimore, MD: Johns Hopkins University Press, 1998.

West, Darrell. *Air Wars: Television Advertising in Election Campaigns, 1952–1992.* Washington, DC: Congressional Quarterly Press, 1993.

STUDY OUTLINE

The Media Industry and Government

1. Americans obtain their news from radio, television, newspapers, magazines, and the Internet. Even though television news reaches more Americans than any other single news source, the print media are still important because they often set the agenda for the broadcast media and because they reach a more influential audience.
2. Since the passage of the Telecommunications Act of 1996, a wave of mergers and consolidations in the media industry has reduced the number of independent media in the United States.
3. The nationalization of the American news media, through which a relatively uniform picture of events, issues, and problems is presented to the entire nation, has contributed greatly to the nationalization of politics and of political perspectives in the United States.
4. Despite the widespread nationalization of news in America, news enclaves exist in which some demographic and ideological groups receive alternative news coverage.
5. Part of the Telecommunications Act of 1996, known as the Communications Decency Act, attempted to regulate the content of material transmitted over the Internet, but the law was overruled by the Supreme Court in the 1997 case *Reno v. American Civil Liberties Union.*
6. Under federal regulations, broadcasters must provide candidates seeking the same political office equal time to communicate their messages to the public.
7. Regulations also require that individuals be granted the right to rebut personal attacks.
8. Although recently diminished in importance, the fairness doctrine for many years required that broadcasters who aired programs on controversial issues provide time for opposing views.

News Coverage

1. Media content and news coverage are inevitably affected by the views, ideals, and interests of the journalists who seek out, write, and produce news stories.
2. News coverage is also influenced by the individuals or groups who are subjects of the news or whose interests and activities are actual or potential news topics.
3. Because the print and broadcast media are businesses that generally seek to show a profit, they must cater to the preferences of consumers.
4. The print and broadcast media, as well as the publishing industry, are particularly responsive to the interests and views of the upscale segments of their audiences.
5. Protest is one way that groups who cannot afford the services of media consultants and "issues managers" can publicize their views and interests.

Media Power in American Politics

1. In recent political history, the media have played a central role in the civil rights movement, the ending of American involvement in the Vietnam War, and in the Watergate investigation.

2. The power of the media stems from several sources, all of which contribute to the media's great influence in setting the political agenda, shaping electoral outcomes, and interpreting events and political results.
3. The political power of the news media has greatly increased in recent years through the growing prominence of investigative reporting.

Media Power and Democracy

1. Because the media provide the information citizens need for meaningful participation in the political process, they are essential to democratic government.
2. The decline of political parties has given the media enormous power, which creates a great potential for abuse.

PRACTICE QUIZ

1. The nationalization of the news has been influenced by which of the following trends in ownership of the media?
   a) the purchase of influential newspapers by foreign corporations
   b) the fragmentation of ownership of all media in the United States
   c) the wave of mergers and consolidations following the passage of the 1996 Telecommunications Act
   d) the purchase of the major news networks by the national government
2. Which of the following best describes national news in the United States?
   a) fragmented and localized
   b) nationalized and centralized
   c) centralized but still localized
   d) none of the above
3. Which of the following Supreme Court cases overruled the government's attempt to regulate the content of the Internet?
   a) *Near v. Minnesota*
   b) *New York Times v. United States*
   c) *Red Lion Broadcasting Company v. FCC*
   d) *Reno v. American Civil Liberties Union*
4. How do journalists compare to the general public in their political attitudes?
   a) Journalists are more conservative than the general public.
   b) The two groups' views are about the same.
   c) Journalists are more liberal than the general public.
   d) Journalists tend to be more Republican than the general public.
5. Which of the following have an impact on the nature of media coverage of politics?
   a) reporters
   b) political actors
   c) news consumers
   d) all of the above
6. Which of the following is a strategy available to poor people to increase their coverage by the news media?
   a) protest
   b) media consultants
   c) television advertising
   d) newspaper advertising "time sharing"
7. The media's powers to determine what becomes a part of the political discussion and to shape how political events are interpreted by the American people are known as
   a) issue definition and protest power.
   b) agenda setting and framing.
   c) the illusion of saliency and the bandwagon effect.
   d) the equal time rule and the right of rebuttal.
8. Which of the following can be considered an example of a news enclave?
   a) Internet chat groups
   b) letters to the editor
   c) readers of *The New York Times*
   d) people who watch CNN
9. Which of the following exemplifies the liberal bias in the news media?
   a) talk radio programs
   b) *The Wall Street Journal*
   c) the *American Spectator*
   d) none of the above
10. The newspaper publisher William Randolph Hearst was responsible for encouraging U.S. involvement in which war?
    a) the Spanish-American War
    b) the Vietnam War
    c) the U.S. war with Mexico
    d) the Gulf War

CRITICAL THINKING QUESTIONS

1. If the public receives most of its information about politics from the media, how accurate is its knowledge of government and politics? How does the media itself distort political reality? How do politicians use the media for their own purposes? What are the consequences for American democracy when the electorate is informed through such a filter? How might the quality of political information in America be improved?

2. There is a great deal of talk about the liberal bias of the media in American politics. To what extent is the media liberal? To what extent, do you think, is it biased? Considering the growing importance of conservative talk radio and news enclaves that support conservative causes, describe the ways in which discussions of a liberal bias in the media should be qualified. What other factors might mitigate the liberalism of the media?

KEY TERMS

agenda setting (p. 300)
equal time rule (p. 288)
fairness doctrine (p. 288)
framing (p. 300)
right of rebuttal (p. 288)

9 Political

★ **Political Participation**

In what different ways do Americans participate in politics? Why is voting the most important form of political participation?

What is the history of suffrage in the United States? How does the government influence voters' attitudes about participation?

★ **Explaining Political Participation**

What explains levels of participation? Why has participation declined over time?

What roles do political institutions play in promoting participation and fulfilling American political values? Have attempts to increase participation succeeded? Why or why not? What are the implications for democracy?

Participation and Voting

STUDENTS AND POLITICS

SINCE the ratification of the Twenty-sixth Amendment in 1971, lowering the voting age to eighteen, millions of college students have voted in American national elections. Hundreds of thousands more have taken part in political campaigns, lobbied on behalf of political and social causes, and even demonstrated or protested to assert their views.

In recent years, however, American politics seems to have lost some of its vitality, as growing numbers of citizens have turned away from politics. Participation in most kinds of political activities—with the exception of contributing money—is declining. Instead of a distinctively American optimism, a sense of pessimism pervades our politics. Individuals express a sense of powerlessness, frustration, and disengagement from the political system. Among youth such feelings are especially strong. Many students feel that the political system is not relevant to their lives and that politics will not solve the problems in the world. Only about one in five eighteen- to twenty-year-olds vote, and political organizations that aim to represent the views of young people have a hard time staying afloat.[1] Why is this? What can be done to counteract this disturbing trend?

One solution that has been implemented in many areas of the country is "service learning." Though we generally conceive participation to connote voluntarism, in some areas of the country young people are actually being required to participate in community or civic affairs. For example, the state of Maryland now mandates fulfillment of a "student service learning" requirement as a condition for high school graduation. Students must sign up for public service jobs with charitable, civic, and public interest groups. These jobs, usually undertaken in conjunction with class work, include work with public interest groups such as the Sierra Club, positions in hospitals and nursing homes, shopping for the elderly, caring for abandoned animals, teaching ecology lessons to small children, and demonstrating eighteenth-century farm crafts, including yo-yo making.[2] Students who fail to complete the requisite number of service hours are not allowed to graduate. In 1998, thirty Maryland high school students were denied diplomas because they did not meet their obligation to provide seventy-five hours of community service over four years.[3] Other states are beginning to follow the Maryland example.

At the college level, the presidents of fifty-one American colleges and universities signed a declaration of their commitment to civic responsibility and community participation in July 1999. The declaration called upon colleges to encourage their students to learn about and engage in politics and community srvice. The declaration came at a conference sponsored by Campus Compact, a fifteen-year-old organization based at Brown University and composed of more than 540 college and university presidents who support the integration of public and community service into academic studies.[4] At the same time, California governor Gray Davis proposed that community service be made a mandatory requirement for graduation from California's public colleges and universities. It remains to be seen whether these efforts will solve America's crisis of declining political participation.

- ***In this chapter, we shall examine the role of citizen participation in American politics. We will first examine patterns of contemporary political participation, discussing the different forms that participation can take. We will then consider the reasons for declining participation in recent decades.*** We will see that individual beliefs, such as a sense of efficacy, are important, but that most significant is the failure of our institutions to mobilize people into politics.

Political Participation

- In what different ways do Americans participate in politics? Why is voting the most important form of political participation?
- What is the history of suffrage in the United States? How does the government influence voters' attitudes about participation?

political participation
political activities, such as voting, contacting political officials, volunteering for a campaign, or participating in a protest, whose purpose is to influence government

Political participation makes the ideals of liberty and equality come alive. But by many measures, Americans are participating less and less. For example, in the 1996 presidential election only 49 percent of eligible voters cast ballots, the lowest percentage in a presidential election in more than seventy years. In 2000, voter turnout rose only slightly to 50.7 percent. Citizens can, however, participate in ways other than voting. In this section we will examine the different ways that Americans participate in politics. We will look for changes in rates and methods of participation over time and describe the differences in participation among groups. In the second half of the chapter, we will explore the causes for the patterns we observe. Two questions in particular will concern us: Why has participation declined? Why do people with higher levels of education and wealth participate most? Finally, we will consider the role that political institutions play in promoting participation.

FORMS OF PARTICIPATION

Today, voting has come to be seen as the normal or typical form of citizen political activity. Yet, ordinary people took part in politics long before the advent of the election or any other formal mechanism of popular involvement in political life. If there is any natural or spontaneous form of popular political participation, it is the riot rather than the election. The urban riot and the rural uprising were common in both Europe and America prior to the nineteenth century and not entirely uncommon even in the twentieth century. Urban riots played an important role in American politics in the 1960s and 1970s. Even as recently as 1999, riots during the Seattle, Washington, meeting of the World

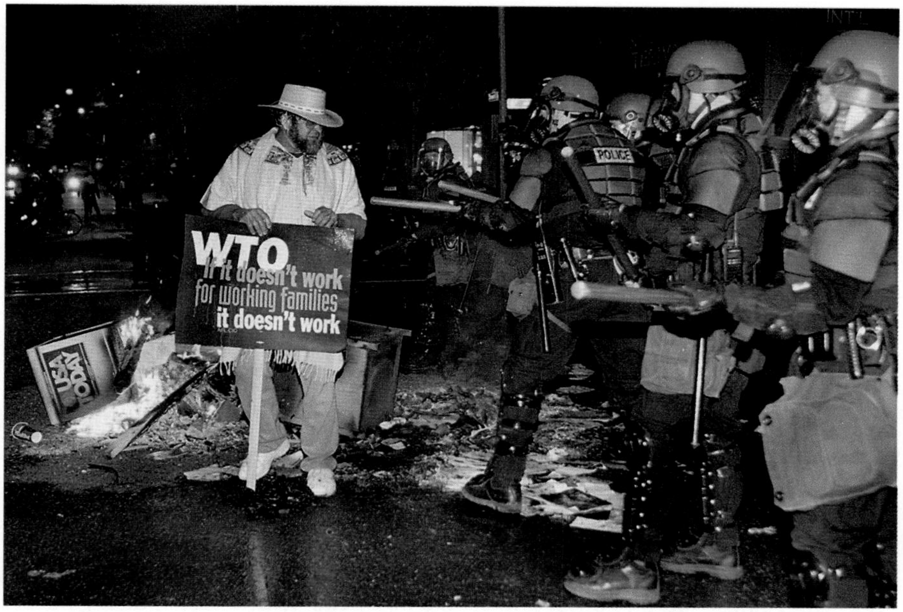

The recent World Trade Organization protests in Seattle are examples of one of the earliest and most spontaneous forms of popular involvement in political life: the riot.

Trade Organization helped labor unions and other opponents of trade liberalization to slow the pace of change in the rules governing world trade.

Most Americans would not consider taking part in a riot. Yet, in recent years, growing numbers of Americans have not been exercising their right to vote. Participation in presidential elections has dropped significantly over the past forty years. In 1960, 64 percent of eligible voters cast ballots; in 1996, less than half of the electorate turned out. Voting in midterm elections is typically lower, on the order of one-third of eligible voters. It took the votes of less than a quarter of the electorate to catapult the Republicans to power in Congress in 1994 because fewer than 39 percent of eligible voters showed up at the polls. Turnout for local elections is usually even lower.[5]

Signing a petition is an easy way to express your opinion to elected officials.

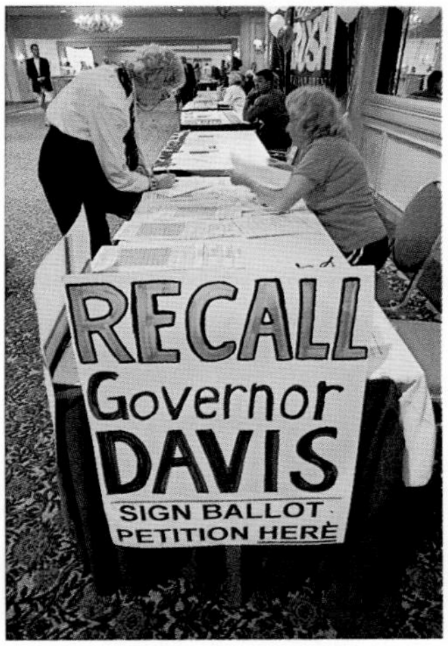

Fortunately, voting and rioting are not the only forms of participation available to Americans. Citizens can contact political officials, sign petitions, attend public meetings, join organizations, give money to a politician or a political organization, volunteer in a campaign, write a letter to the editor or write an article about an issue, or participate in a protest or rally. Such activities differ from voting because they can communicate much more detailed information to public officials than voting can. Voters may support a candidate for many reasons but their actual votes do not indicate specifically what they like and don't like, nor do they tell officials how intensely voters feel about issues. A vote can convey only a general sense of approval or disapproval. By writing a letter or engaging in other kinds of political participation, people can convey much more specific information, telling public officials exactly what issues they care most about and what their views on those issues are. For that reason these other political activities are often more satisfying than voting. And citizens who engage in these other activities are more likely to try to influence state and local politics rather than national politics; in voting, people find the national scene more interesting than state and local politics.[6]

While nonelectoral political activity takes many forms, some of the most prominent in recent years include *lobbying, public relations, litigation,* and *protest.*

lobbying
a strategy by which organized interests seek to influence the passage of legislation by exerting direct pressure on members of the legislature

Lobbying is an effort by groups or individuals to take their case directly to elected or appointed officials. By voting, citizens seek to determine who will govern. By lobbying, citizens attempt to determine what those in power will do. As we shall see in Chapter 12, many interest groups employ professional lobbyists to bring their views to lawmakers. At the same time, however, thousands of volunteers lobby Congress and the bureaucracy each year on behalf of citizen groups like the National Organization for Women, the Sierra Club, and the Home School Legal Defense Fund.[7] The hundreds of thousands of citizens who call or write members of Congress each year, seeking to influence their votes, are also engaged in lobbying.

public relations
an attempt, usually through the use of paid consultants, to establish a favorable relationship with the public and influence its political opinions

Public relations is an effort to sway public opinion on behalf of an issue or cause. Corporations and interest groups typically employ professional public relations firms to produce print, radio, and television advertising in support of their goals. For example, in 1999 public relations firms employed by a group of defense contractors produced a series of highly charged radio ads trumpeting the need for the construction of the F-22 fighter plane. During the same year, firms employed by competing segments of the health-care indistry developed print and broadcast ads for and against different bills purporting to protect patients from abuse by health maintenance organizations (HMOs). At the same time, public relations tactics are also used by numerous citizen groups to promote issues and causes dear to them. A favorite tactic of citizen groups is the press release designed to shape news coverage. In 1999, for example, citizen groups favoring affirmative action released data purporting to show that affirmative action programs were successful. Groups opposing affirmative action released data purporting to show the opposite. The same pattern was manifest in debates about gun control, capital punishment, policy toward the homeless, and the use of school vouchers. In each of these issue areas citizen groups conducted political warfare through public relations.

litigation
a lawsuit or legal proceeding; as a form of political participation, an attempt to seek relief in a court of law

Litigation is an attempt to use the courts to achieve a goal. In recent years, the federal courts have been used more and more frequently by citizen groups and even individuals to affect public policy. Using the so-called citizen-suit provisions of a number of federal statutes, citizen groups play an active role in shaping policy in such areas as air and water quality, preservation of endangered species, civil rights, and the rights of persons with disabilities. Use of the courts by citizen groups is encouraged by federal and state fee-shifting provisions that allow plaintiffs (those bringing a case in court) to recover legal fees from the government or defendant, as well as by class-action rules that allow an individual to bring suit on behalf of large groups. We will learn more about this form of participation in Chapter 16.

protest
participation that involves assembling crowds to confront a government or other official organization

Though most Americans reject violent **protest** for political ends, peaceful protest is generally recognized as a legitimate and important form of political activity and is protected by the First Amendment. During the 1960s and 1970s, hundreds of thousands of Americans took part in peaceful protests that helped bring an end to legalized racial segregation. In recent years, peaceful marches and demonstrations have been employed by a host of groups. While protests can occur anywhere, favorite spots for demonstrations include the park in front of the White House and the members' parking lot in front of the Capitol. During the past year, these two areas have been the sites of demonstrations by large groups of Native Americans, by proponents and opponents of abortion rights, by veterans's groups, and by the handicapped. Occasionally, protests by unpopular groups lead to counterprotests by others. For example, in 1999, planned rallies in New York and Washington by a handful of Ku Klux Klan members led to counterdemonstrations by tens of thousands of people protesting the Klan's presence in their city. Thousands of police officers were mobilized to protect the Klan members and to safeguard their First Amendment rights.

Alternative forms of political action generally require more time, effort, or money than voting does. It is not surprising, then, that far fewer people engage in these forms of political participation than vote. A recent study of participation, for example, found that about a third of those questioned said they had contacted a public official; a quarter reported that they had made a campaign contribution; and fewer than 10 percent said they had been active in a political campaign (see Figure 9.1). Nearly half, however, said they were involved in an organization that took positions on political issues.[8] In contrast to the sharp decline in voting, involvement in these other activities has not fallen off nearly so much and, by some measures, has actually increased. For example, Americans are more likely to contribute money to political organizations

POLITICAL PARTICIPATION: HOW MUCH? ABOUT WHAT? — Figure 9.1

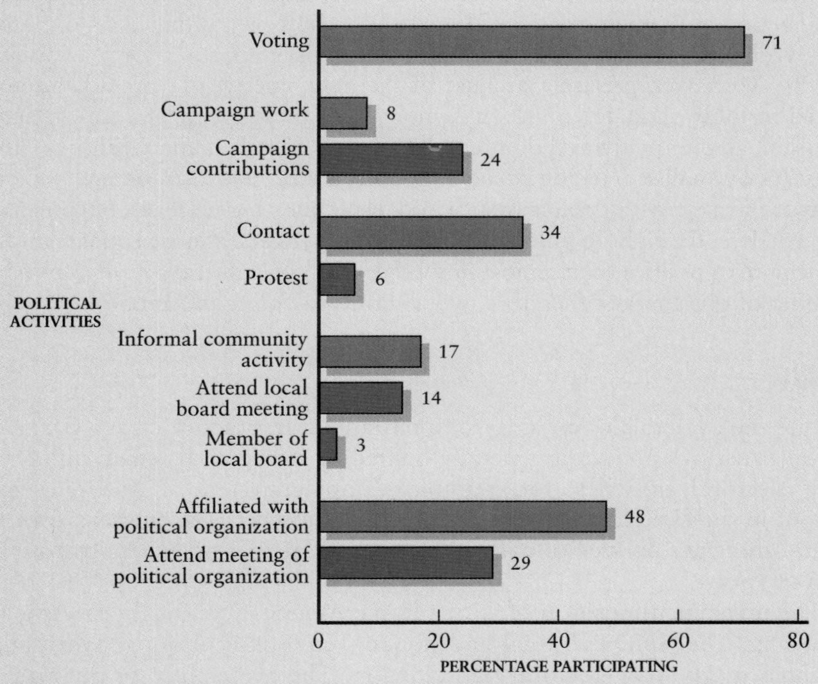

SOURCE: Sidney Verba, Kay Lehman Schlozman, and Henry E. Brady, *Voice and Equality: Civic Voluntarism in American Politics* (Cambridge, MA: Harvard University Press, 1995), p. 51.

This group of disabled persons has assembled in front of the White House, a popular site for peaceful demonstrations.

and campaigns than in the past, but they are less likely to belong to political organizations.[9]

Whether or not voting is as effective or satisfying as these other forms of political action is an open question. What is clear, however, is that for most Americans voting remains the most accessible and most important form of political activity. Moreover, precisely because of the time, energy, and money often required to lobby, litigate, and even demonstrate, these forms of political action are often, albeit not always, dominated by better educated and wealthier Americans. As we shall see, voting participation in American is also somewhat biased in favor of those with greater wealth and, especially, higher levels of education. Nevertheless, the right to vote gives ordinary Americans a more equal chance to participate in politics than almost any other form of political activity. In the remainder of this chapter, therefore, we will turn to voting in America.

VOTING

Despite the available of an array of alternatives, in practice citizen participation in American politics is generally limited to voting and a small number of other electoral activities (for example, campaigning). It is true that voter turnout in the United States is relatively low. But when, for one reason or another, Americans do seek to participate, their participation generally takes the form of voting.

The preeminent position of voting in the American political process is not surprising. The American legal and political environment is overwhelmingly weighted in favor of electoral participation. The availability of the right to vote, or **suffrage,** is, of course, a question of law. And civic eduction, also to a large extent mandated by law, encourages citizens to believe that electoral participation is the appropriate way to express opinions and grievances.

suffrage

the right to vote; also called franchise

After passage of the Voting Rights Act of 1965, the national government intervened in areas where African Americans were denied the right to vote. As a result, thousands of new black voters were registered.

Voting Rights In principle, states determine who is eligible to vote. During the nineteenth and early twentieth centuries, voter eligibility requirements often varied greatly from state to state. Some states openly abridged the right to vote on the basis of race; others did not. Some states imposed property restrictions on voting; others had no such restrictions. Most states mandated lengthy residency requirements, which meant that persons moving from one state to another sometimes lost their right to vote for as much as a year. In more recent years, however, constitutional amendments, federal statutes, and federal court decisions have limited states' discretion in the area of voting rights. Individual states may establish brief residency requirements, generally fifteen days, for record-keeping purposes. Beyond this, states have little or no power to regulate suffrage.

Today in the United States, all native-born or naturalized citizens over the age of eighteen, with the exception of convicted felons, have the right to vote. During the colonial and early national periods of American history, the right to vote was generally restricted to white males over the age of twenty-one. Many states also limited voting to those who owned property or paid more than a specified amount of annual tax. Property and tax requirements began to be rescinded during the 1820s, however, and had generally disappeared by the end of the Civil War.

By the time of the Civil War, blacks had won the right to vote in most northern states. In the South, black voting rights were established by the Fifteenth Amendment, ratified in 1870, which prohibited denial of the right to vote on the basis of race. Despite the Fifteenth Amendment, the voting rights of African Americans were effectively rescinded during the 1880s by the states of the former Confederacy. During this period, the southern states created what was called the "Jim Crow" system of racial segregation. As part of this system, a variety of devices, such as **poll taxes** and literacy tests, were used to prevent virtually all blacks from voting. During the 1950s and 1960s, through the civil rights movement led by Dr. Martin Luther King, Jr., and others, African Americans demanded the restoration of their voting rights. Their goal was accomplished through the enactment of the 1965 Voting Rights Act, which provided for the federal government to register voters in states that discriminated against minority citizens. The result was the reenfranchisement of southern blacks for the first time since the 1860s.

poll tax
a state-imposed tax upon voters as a prerequisite for registration. Poll taxes were rendered unconstitutional in national elections by the Twenty-fourth Amendment, and in state elections by the Supreme Court in 1966

Women won the right to vote in 1920, with the adoption of the Nineteenth Amendment. This amendment resulted primarily from the activities of the women's suffrage movement, led by Elizabeth Cady Stanton, Susan B. Anthony, and Carrie Chapman Catt during the late nineteenth and early twentieth centuries. The "suffragettes," as they were called, held rallies, demonstrations, and protest marches for more than half a century before achieving their goal. The cause of women's suffrage was ultimately advanced by World War I. President Woodrow Wilson and members of Congress were convinced that women would be more likely to support the war effort if they were granted the right to vote. For this same reason, women were given the right to vote in Great Britain and Canada during World War I.

The most recent expansion of the suffrage in the United States took place in 1971, during the Vietnam War, when the Twenty-sixth Amendment was ratified, lowering the voting age from twenty-one to eighteen. Unlike black suffrage and women's suffrage, which came about in part because of the demands of groups that had been deprived of the right to vote, the Twenty-sixth Amendment was not a response to the demands of young people to be given the right to vote. Instead, many policy makers hoped that the right to vote would channel the disruptive protest activities of students involved in the anti–Vietnam War movement into peaceful participation at the ballot box.

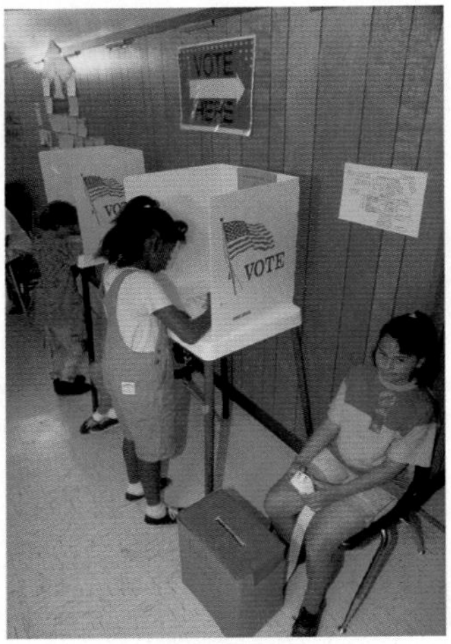

Voting is by no means a natural phenomenon. Civic education starts early and instills a preference for voting over other means of political expression.

Voting and Civic Education Laws, of course, cannot completely explain why most people vote rather than riot or lobby. If public attitudes were completely unfavorable to elections, it is doubtful that *legal* remedies alone would have much impact.

Positive public attitudes about voting do not come into being in a completely spontaneous manner. Americans are taught to equate citizenship with electoral participation. Civic training, designed to give students an appreciation for the American system of government, is a legally required part of the curriculum in every elementary and secondary school. Although it is not as often required by law, civic education usually manages to find its way into college curricula as well.

In the elementary and secondary schools, through formal instruction and, more subtly, through the frequent administration of class and school elections, students are taught the importance of the electoral process. By contrast, little attention is given to lawsuits, direct action, organizing, parliamentary procedures, lobbying, or other possible modes of participation. For example, the techniques involved in organizing a sit-in or protest march are seldom part of an official school course of study. [10]

The New York State first-grade social studies curriculum offers a fairly typical case study of the training in political participation given very young children. The state Education Department provides the following guidelines to teachers:

> To illustrate the voting process, present a situation such as: Chuck and John would both like to be the captain of the kickball team. How will we decide which boy will be the captain? Help the children to understand that the fairest way to choose a captain is by voting.
>
> Write both candidates' names on the chalk board. Pass out slips of paper. Explain to the children that they are to write the name of the boy they would like to have as their captain. Collect and tabulate the results on the chalk board.
>
> Parallel this election to that of the election for the Presidency. Other situations which would illustrate the election procedure are voting for:
>
> a game
> an assignment choice
> classroom helpers.[11]

Although secondary-school students periodically elect student government representatives rather than classroom helpers and are given more sophisticated illustrations than kickball team elections, the same principle continues to be taught, in compliance with legal requirements. College students are also frequently given the opportunity to elect senators, representatives, and the like to serve on the the largely ornamental representative bodies that are to be found at most institutions of higher learning. Obviously, civic education is not always completely successful. Rather than relying on the electoral process, people continue to demonstrate, sit in, and picket for various political causes.

AMERICAN DEMOCRACY IN COMPARATIVE PERSPECTIVE

Election Turnout Rates

When comparing electoral turnout in general elections (that is, national elections for the country's main legislative body and, where relevant, the country's principal head of state) among western democracies, one notes that the United States stands apart from the crowd. The average turnout rate (electoral turnout as a proportion of total eligible voters) for general elections in this set of countries during the period 1990–1997 was 73.4 percent across two general elections. In contrast, across the four general elections held in the United States between 1990 and 1997, the average turnout rate was 44.9 percent. Only Switzerland, with an average turnout rate of 37.7 percent for only one election in seven years, had lower electoral participation in general elections (see Figure 9.3).

Former communist countries of the Soviet Union and Eastern Europe (CIS-EE) recorded average turnout rates of nearly 70 percent following the collapse of European communism, while Asia and Latin America also recorded relatively high average turnout rates during the 1990s (68.5 percent and 66.3 percent, respectively). Sub-Saharan Africa and Arab nations have seen average turnout rates during the same period approaching only 50 percent, with less frequent general elections.

While observing aggregate electoral turnout patterns across countries is important in its own right, we might also inquire as to what may account for differing turnout rates among the most free and democratic countries of the world. In a recent comparative study, Mark Franklin has presented credible evidence linking four factors directly to differing turnout rates among the twenty-five or so wealthiest democracies. These are (1) the saliency of the election—are the stakes of the election high and the issues important? (2) compulsive voting—e.g., it is illegal to not vote in Australia, (3) the degree of proportionality—will voting for a loser be seen as wasting the voter's ballot because only one candidate wins and the votes for the loser are discarded? and (4) the rules of the election—do the polls remain open for more than one day (such as in India, where they are open for four days), and are the polls open on days when people have free time to vote (such as Sundays and holidays, as is customary throughout much of Europe)? Together, Franklin shows that these factors can account for nearly 80 percent of the differences in electoral turnout rates among the more advanced industrial democracies of the world.

Although a number of factors are clearly associated with global patterns of voting, a more interesting question may be why people chose not to vote when the option is available to them. In recent surveys of citizens in various democracies of Europe (and Japan), ineligibility and registration restrictions were the most common explanation offered for failing to vote. Poor knowledge of issues and candidates and a lack of interest in the election were the other reasons offered by nonvoters.

Scholars have debated the importance of voting in democracies. Certainly, large-scale apathy cannot be a healthy aspect of democracy. However, as Richard Rose, a renowned student of democracies, has noted, there is no threshold of turnout rates that one can identify as the point below which the quality of democracy declines. While a few of those who said they are not eligible to vote may be foreigners within the country, this alone cannot account for this factor being the most common reason given for not voting. Across all of the democracies of the world, with few exceptions, registration efforts have reached the voting age population. Within any democracy, a certain proportion are simply not going to vote (indeed, approximately 5 percent of those who did not vote say they never vote for reasons of conscience). Achieving turnout rates higher than three-quarters of the voting-age population may not be either possible or cost-effective. Furthermore, as most scholars have concluded with respect to Japan, Switzerland, and the United States, alternative means to voting as a vehicle of political participation and citizen involvement in civic affairs would seem to account for most nonvoting activity in countries where freedoms are the greatest and the roots of liberal democracy the deepest.

SOURCES: Richard Rose, "Evaluating Election Turnout," in *Voter Turnout from 1945–1997: A Global Report on Political Participation* (Stockholm: International Institute for Democracy and Electoral Assistance, 1997), pp. 35–47; and Mark Franklin, "Electoral Participation," in Lawrence LeDuc, Richard Niemi, and Pippa Norris, eds., *Comparing Democracies: Elections and Voting in Global Perspective* (Thousand Oaks, CA: Sage, 1996), pp. 216–235.

Civic education, of course, does not end with formal schooling. Early training is supplemented by a variety of mechanisms, ranging from the official celebration of national holidays to the activities of private patriotic and political organizations. Election campaigns themselves are occasions for the reinforcement of training to vote. Campaigns and political conventions include a good deal of oratory designed to remind citizens of the importance of voting and the democratic significance of elections. Parties and candidates, even if for selfish reasons, emphasize the value of participation, of "being counted," and the virtues of elections as instruments of popular government. Exposure to such campaign stimuli appears generally to heighten citizens' interest in and awareness of the electoral process.

turnout
the percentage of eligible individuals who actually vote

Voter Participation Although the United States has developed a system of civic education and a legal basis for nearly universal suffrage, America's rate of voter participation, or **turnout,** is very low. About 50 percent of those eligible participate in national presidential elections, while barely one-third of eli-

Figure 9.2

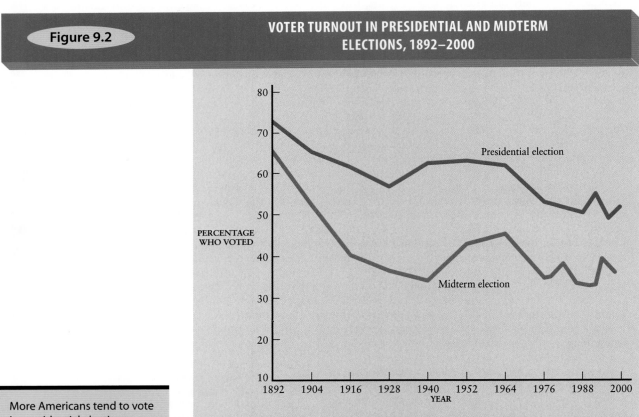

VOTER TURNOUT IN PRESIDENTIAL AND MIDTERM ELECTIONS, 1892–2000

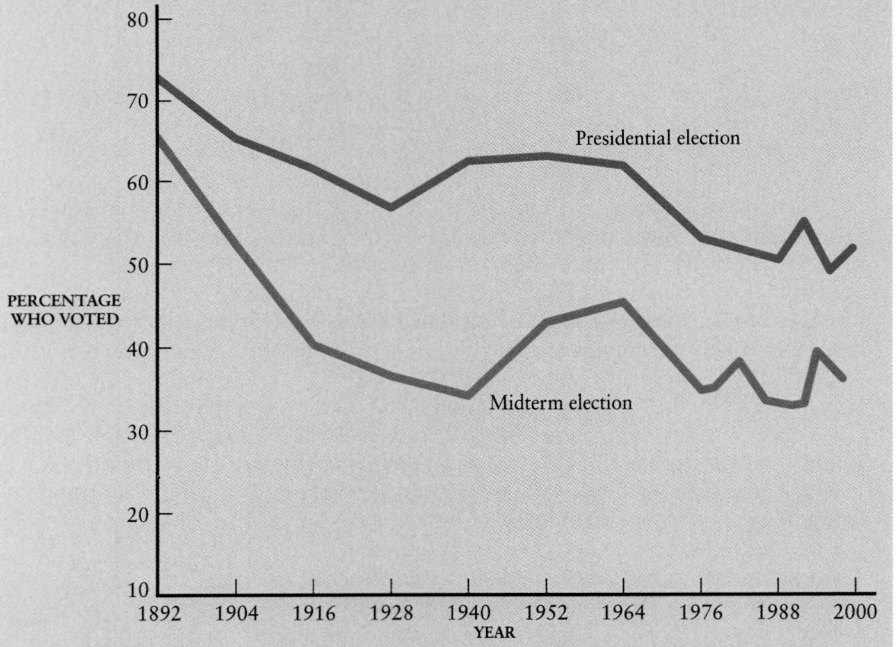

SOURCES: 1892–1958: Erik Austin and Jerome Clubb, *Political Facts of the United States since 1789* (New York: Columbia University Press, 1986), pp. 378–79; 1960–96. U.S. Bureau of the Census, *Statistical Abstract of the United States: 1997* (Washington, DC: Government Printing Office, 1997), p. 289.

More Americans tend to vote in presidential election years than in years when only congressional and local elections are held.

VOTER TURNOUT IN COMPARATIVE PERSPECTIVE*

Figure 9.3

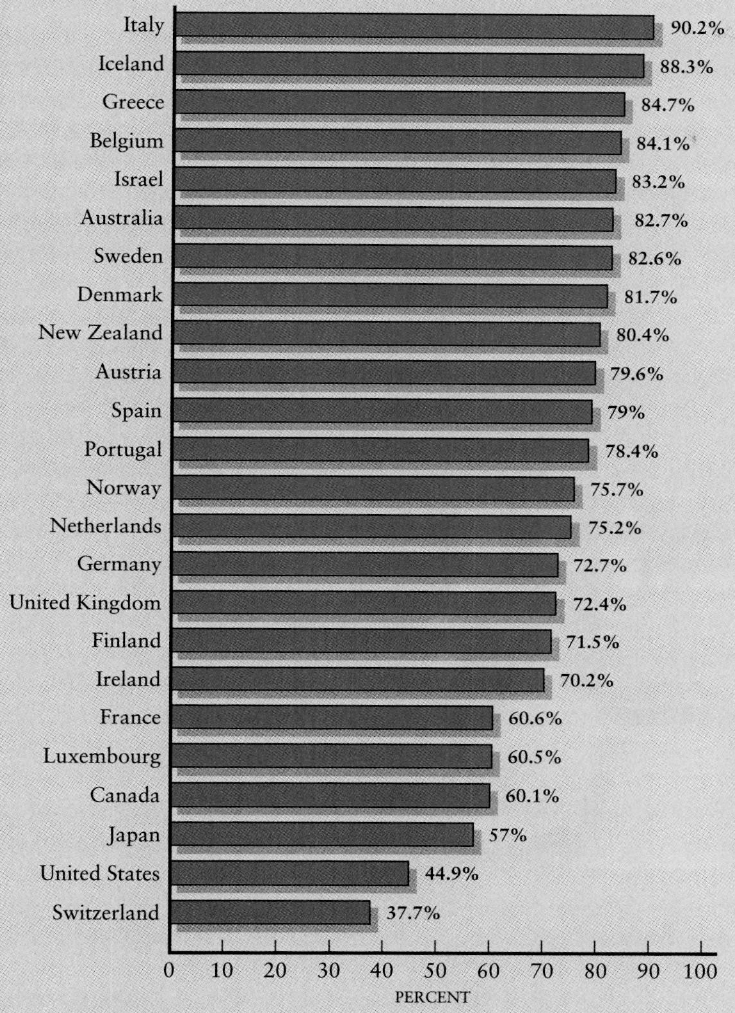

SOURCE: *Institute for Democracy and Electoral Assistance Classification,* "Voter Turnout from 1945 to 1997: A Global Report on Political Participation," 1997.

*Average turnout rate in general elections from 1990–97.

gible voters take part in midterm congressional elections (see Figure 9.2). Turnout in state and local races that do not coincide with national contests is typically even lower. In most European countries and other western democracies, by contrast, national voter turnout is usually between 70 and 90 percent[12] (see Figure 9.3).

POLICY DEBATE

Does Higher Voter Participation Really Matter?

One of the great contradictions of American politics is the fact that our elections—the hallmark of democracy—are plagued by low, and declining, voter turnout. From a high point of about 65 percent turnout in 1960 to a seven-decade low of 49 percent in the 1996 presidential election, Americans are staying away from the polls in record numbers. By comparison, voter turnout in virtually every other democratic nation of the world is significantly higher, typically in the range of 70 to 90 percent in their comparable national elections. But is this anything to worry about?

Yes, say many. Part of the problem lies in the tangle of rules that regulate voting, which are more complicated than those found in almost any other nation. Most of these rules were enacted decades ago to discourage "undesirables"—African Americans, immigrants, the poor—from voting. In many nations, voting is easier because citizens are automatically registered to vote, do not have to worry about local residency requirements, and elections are held on the weekends. A government that cares about its elections should certainly do more to make the act of voting easier. Turnout matters to campaigns, because those who run for office tailor their campaign issues and strategies to those who are likely to vote. Thus, the needs and concerns of the nonvoters—generally those with lower incomes and less education and members of disadvantaged groups—are likely to be ignored, with the result that policy fails to address the nation's most pressing needs. Two states have experimented with making voting easier. In Texas, citizens have been allowed since 1991 to vote any time during the two weeks prior to election day. In Oregon, turnout has risen since the state made balloting by mail easy, more than a decade ago. In 2000, Arizona began experimenting with voting via the Internet. These pioneering efforts demonstrate that the government could do more to make voting easier, and should do so, many argue, because the ever-declining percentage of voting casts a shadow over the very legitimacy of the government that is elected. How can a president, or other elected leaders, claim a mandate to govern when less than a quarter of eligible voters cast ballots for the winner?

Skeptics counter these arguments by asserting that the negative consequences of nonvoting have been greatly overstated. In 1993, Congress passed the "Motor Voter" law, which allowed citizens to register to vote when they applied for a driver's license. Even though millions of new voters registered by this means, it had little or no effect on voting rates, suggesting that existing election laws may have little to do with voting rates. Further, research has demonstrated that there is often less difference between voters and nonvoters than many assume. As study of the 1988 election, for example, showed that, contrary to expectations, nonvoters would have supported the winning presidential candidate, George Bush, over challenger Michael Dukakis. This and similar research supports the idea that the interests of nonvoters are not so different from those of voters. Beyond this, nonvoting is not necessarily a sign of alienation from the political system. To some extent at least, it can be interpreted as citizen satisfaction with the overall course of the country's affairs. While indifference is a less than noble sentiment, it can at least be taken as a green light for the nation's political leaders. When crises have arisen in the past, from the Great Depression to the Gulf War, Americans have turned close attention to their political leaders. Finally, voting is only one method of political expression, and citizens with concerns ranging from race to abortion to guns increasingly express their views through means other than the ballot box, from interest group activity to the Internet. Voting is still the most frequent political activity, but citizens are free to express themselves in an ever-wider array of methods.

Explaining Political Participation

- What explains levels of participation? Why has participation declined over time?
- What roles do political institutions play in promoting participation and fulfilling American political values? Have attempts to increase participation succeeded? Why or why not? What are the implications for democracy?

Given the decline in voting, concern has mounted that Americans are disengaging from the political system and that participation is skewed toward those with more money. To understand these current patterns we must go back to a basic question: Why do people participate in politics? Simple as it seems, there are different ways to answer this question.

SOCIOECONOMIC STATUS

The first explanation for participation points to the characteristics of individuals. One of the most important and consistent results of surveys about participation is that Americans with higher levels of education, more income, and higher-level occupations—what social scientists call **socioeconomic status**—participate much more in politics than do those with less education and less income. Education level alone is the strongest predictor of most kinds of participation, but income becomes important—not surprisingly—when it comes to making contributions. In addition to education and income, other individual characteristics also affect participation. For example, African Americans and Latinos are less likely to participate than are whites, although when differences in education and income are taken into account, both groups participate at the same or higher levels than do whites. Finally, young people are far less likely to participate in politics than are older people. When eighteen-, nineteen-, and twenty-year-olds won the right to vote in 1971, participation dropped off substantially in the next election. But even more important, the proportion of young people that votes has declined in almost every single election since 1972.[13]

socioeconomic status
status in society based on level of education, income, and occupational prestige

Although they give us a picture of who participates and who does not, explanations based on individual characteristics leave many questions open. One of the biggest questions is why the relationship between education and participation—so strong in surveys—does not seem to hold true over time. As Americans have become more educated, with more people finishing high school and attending college, we would expect to see more people participating in politics. Yet participation has declined, not increased.[14] In the nineteenth century, participation in presidential elections was 20 percent higher than current levels. Moreover, politics was a much more vibrant and encompassing activity: large numbers of people joined in parades, public meetings, and electioneering.[15] This puzzle about declining participation suggests that we need to look beyond the characteristics of individuals to the larger social and political setting to understand changes in patterns of participation over time.

STUDENT DEBATE

Should Voter Registration Be Easier?

Yes

I have an embarrassing secret. I am a political science major; I keep up with current events; and I closely follow local and national elections. However, I am not, and have never been, registered to vote.

I do take responsibility for this. As I was running to a class in Willard Building last week, someone passed me a voter registration form. I actually filled it out in class, with every intention of sending the form in, but I am a college student. I have lots to do, and they do tend to slip my mind. As I write this now, it looks as though I missed the deadline for voter registration once again.

At the risk of sounding lazy, I feel that the current system of voter registration is cumbersome and discourages large segments of the population from voting. I am not alone in this view. In the 1996 November elections, only 66 percent of the population registered to vote, according to the U.S. Census Bureau. This was at its lowest point since 1968.

Despite the National Voter Registration Act that went into effect in 1995, which allows citizens to mail in forms, register when renewing a driver's license, or register when applying for Medicare, numbers didn't improve. I don't blame this on public apathy alone. People are busy these days, and the government doesn't make registration easy on them.

There are four ways a person can register to vote in Pennsylvania—in person at the State Election Office, by renewing a driver's license, at government agenices, or by mail, according to the Pennsylvania Department of State's Web site. Because registering is probably not at the top of a typical person's list of priorities, this could be much easier. Why can't a registration card be automatically sent to your home? Or why can't we simply use our social secutity cards to register? Every American citizen has one, and with the computer technology available today vast systems of databases could be compiled in a way that keeps an individual from voting twice.

Not only is registering to vote something that slips people's minds, but I know adults that purposely do not register just to ensure that they are not called for jury duty. I am not contesting the legitimacy of jury duty, and of course it is important, but the voting system is set up in such a way that it deters some people from even registering.

I was in Scotland in May during the regional elections, and I spent election day traveling between various voting centers. There was no registration card. Every citizen was eligible. Each voting area was organized by what street the citizens lived on. People who did not realize it was election day until the evening could just stroll in and cast their vote. How's that for democracy?

I realize that to completely transform the voting system in the United States is a drastic measure. I am suggesting that it could be structured in a better way that would encourage voting and make it easier.

Young people like me, those in their mid-twenties, are the least likely to vote. Only slightly more than half of this segment of the population was even registered in the 1996 election. This is due to our transient nature. Many young people attend college in a state different than their own and move around a lot. Registering becomes even more complex.

Millions of citizens do register to vote. Next time I hope to be one of them.

SOURCE: Shannon Frankel, *Daily Collegian* (Pennsylvania State University), October 13, 1999.

No It's finally over. All this task about voting and election day is done. We can rest assured that we will not be bombarded with requests to fill out a voter registration card as we hurry across the West Mall or receive telephone calls at least four times a day from political party representatives reminding us to cast a ballot, at least until next November.

While this registration effort seems noble and appears to fulfill a basic tenet of democracy, it does nothing to improve the system and may even yield negative results. Just because a person is registered and votes, that doesn't mean he or she has a clue about the implications of casting a ballot.

The event occurs every year: Political parties deputize members to register voters, and civic organizations engage in massive campaigns in an attempt to get people to the polls. This year UT Student Government, University Democrats, and College Republicans distributed over 10,000 voter registration cards to people on our campus alone.

In 1998, Minnesota boasted the highest election turnout of any state in the nation. An overwhelming 60.4 percent of Minnesota voters went to the polls and 37 percent of them voted for Jesse "The Body" Ventura, giving him the win. College-age voters went in droves to cast ballots for this ex-wrestler who made a campaign stop at the University of Minnesota to recite lines from the movie *Predator.* ("This stuff will make you a goddamned sexual Tyrannosaurus Rex, just like me.")

Young voters especially said they appreciated Ventura's "straight talk" on the issues, but were they listening to what he was saying? During his campaign and throughout the past few months Ventura has vocally opposed state funding for higher education. The governor told college students that if they are smart enough to get into college, they are smart enough to find a way to pay for it.

Was Ventura truly the best candidate to represent the ideals of those college students who voted for him? The answer: Not likely, unless they dream to be reincarnated as a 36-DD bra, as the governor told *Playboy* in a recent interview.

This past Tuesday in Texas, many voters went to the polls asking, "Who are we voting for?" No major candidates were up for election this year so the ballot was dedicated to seventeen proposed amendments to the Texas Constitution. The propositions included a move to reallocate money from the Permanent University Fund, firmly establish a line of succession for the governor, and provide bonds for college loans.

Only 6 percent of registered voters turned out in Austin, just below the 7.7 percent state average. In spite of a major election drive at the University, absentee and election day voter turnout numbers were even low at polling places on campus. Can anyone really be blamed for the low turnout?

The Texas Constitution requires public approval on state constitutional amendments. Unfortunately, the document makes the public vote on technical, legalistic measures that could seemingly be resolved by legislators who at least have a clue about the issues. For this reason, seventeen items were up for ratification this past Tuesday, and some were difficult to understand, even for an informed voter. For example, Proposition 2 related "to the making of advances under a reverse mortgage and payment of a reverse mortgage." Does anyone have a clue what that means? Seeing this proposition while at the ballot box would give any voter the inclination to call a real-estate lawyer or tax consultant for some last minute advice on how to vote.

The 92 percent of registered voters who stayed home may have done themselves a favor by not subjecting themselves to the anxiety of punching the ballot or leaving a few spaces blank.

Yes, voting is the cornerstone of a democracy and many groups try to encourage all registered voters to go to the polls, but that democracy will fail if voters do not cast educated votes. The steps to reach this goal are threefold: technical issues should be left off the ballot, voting campaigns should stress educated voting, and most important, voters should pay attention.

SOURCE: Adrian Rodriguez, *Daily Texan* (University of Texas-Austin), November 5, 1999.

Students and Politics

They are found nestled in almost every American community and are used by millions every year. But they've received little attention so far in political campaigns. They are community colleges.

While many people automatically associate college students with four-year institutions, almost half of all U.S. undergraduates attend a community college. These students represent as many as 10.4 million young voters, but they say many politicians overlook the issues that are relevant to them.

"We don't get as much attention as we should," said Charles Errico, a professor at Northern Virginia Community College in Woodbridge, Virginia. "Our students represent the rank and file of American people."

But if politicians overlook these students, the students return the lack of interest. Faced with busy lives, often spent juggling school, work, and young families, these students say there is no time left to follow politics.

"I'm just so busy," said Kim Soo, a twenty-two-year-old student at City College of San Francisco. "I have no clue what's going on."

After attending classes full-time, working part-time, and taking care of her mother, she said she does not have time to listen to the radio or watch television, let alone follow politics.

"There's too much on their plate to be concerned about [politics]," Errico said.

Frances Powell of Montgomery College in Takoma Park, Maryland, agreed that her students were too busy with jobs and schoolwork to be very involved in politics, but added that it is unfortunate students do not realize the impact their votes would have.

"They don't quite [recognize] what a potential political force they could be," echoed Philip Day, chancellor of City College of San Francisco.

Errico said many of his daytime students, who are between the ages of eighteen and twenty-one, are mainly concerned with getting a college education and earning enough to finance their studies.

But their lack of interest in politics is due to more than the demands of work and school: Politicians do not make an effort to reach out to this group of students, he said.

And this lack of attention by politicians to their "real-life" issues is the reason many community college students say they are not involved in politics.

SOURCE: Nicole Maestri, "Politicians Not Attracting Busy Community College Students," *Medill News Service,* May 11, 2000.

CIVIC ENGAGEMENT

The social setting can affect political participation in a variety of ways. One recent study argued that participation depends on three elements: resources (including time, money, and know-how), **civic engagement** (are you concerned about public issues and do you feel that you can make a difference?), and recruitment (are you asked to participate, especially by someone you know?).[16] Whether a person has resources, feels engaged, and is recruited depends very much on his or her social setting—what his parents are like, who she knows, what associations she belongs to. In the United States, churches are a particularly important social institution in helping to foster political participation. Through their church activities people learn the civic skills that prepare them to participate in the political world more broadly. It is often through church activities that people learn to run meetings, write newsletters, or give speeches and presentations. Churches are also an important setting for meeting people and creating networks for recruitment, since people are more likely to participate if asked by a friend or an acquaintance.

As this model suggests, if fewer people belong to social organizations, they may be less likely to participate in politics. The United States has often been called a nation of joiners because of our readiness to form local associations to address common problems. As early as the 1830s, the Frenchman Alexis de Tocqueville singled out this tendency to form associations as a most distinctive American trait.[17] There is evidence, however, that Americans no longer join organizations as much as they did in the past. This declining membership raises concerns that the civic engagement that ordinary Americans once had is deteriorating. These concerns are magnified by declining levels of social trust, which further contribute to the tendency to pull back from public engagement.[18] There are many possible reasons for the decline in organizational membership and social trust, and consequently in civic engagement. Television, for example, keeps people in their houses and away from meetings or other, more civic, engagements.[19] Crime can also reduce civic engagement by reducing social trust, making people suspicious and unwilling to take part in neighborhood activities.

Another way to explain the decline in civic engagement is to look at how the experiences of different generations might make them more or less oriented toward civic engagement. The generation that came of age during the Great Depression and World War II has been called the "long civic generation" because this group tends to participate in politics and associational life much more than previous or later generations. During the 1930s people looked to government to help them with economic hardships, and in the 1940s, the same generation fought World War II, a popular war in which the entire country pulled together.[20] Later generations have not experienced such popular common causes to bring them together in the public sphere: their wars have been less popular and their great social causes more divisive. In addition, political life has seemed much less inspiring, filled with accusations of wrongdoing and constant investigations into possible scandal. Such a generational perspective makes sense because people form habits and beliefs in their early years that are very important in how they participate later in life. A generational perspective also helps explain why participation did not decline during the twentieth century, but instead started out low in the early 1900s, rose from the 1930s through the 1960s, and then began to fall once again.

civic engagement
a sense of concern among members of the political community about public, social, and political life, expressed through participation in social and political organizations

Arguments about declining public trust and generational effects don't pay enough attention to the political setting in which participation takes place. The organization of politics itself plays a key role in channeling participation in particular directions and in encouraging or discouraging people from participating. Participation depends on whether there are formal obstacles in the political system, what people think political engagement has to offer them, and most important, whether political parties and politicians try to mobilize people into politics.

FORMAL OBSTACLES

Formal obstacles can greatly decrease participation. As we saw earlier in the chapter, in the South prior to the 1960s, the widespread use of the poll tax and other measures such as the **white primary** essentially deprived black Americans (and many poor whites) of the right to vote during the first part of this century. This system of legal segregation meant that there were few avenues for black Americans in the South to participate in politics. With the removal of

white primary
primary election in which only white voters are eligible to participate

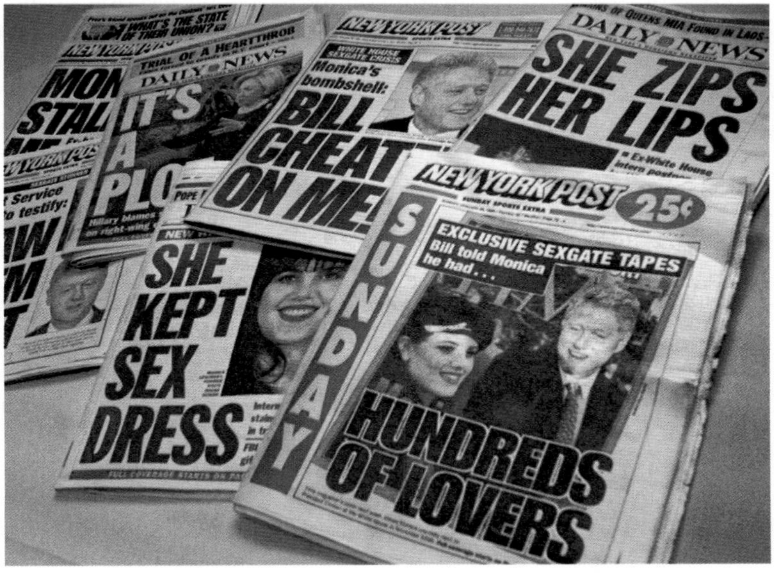

Some analysts have speculated that the constant scandals surrounding politics, such as that which arose in 1998 over President Clinton and former White House intern Monica Lewinsky, have distanced the public from politics.

these legal barriers in the 1960s, black political participation shot up, with rates of turnout approaching those of southern whites, as early as 1968.[21]

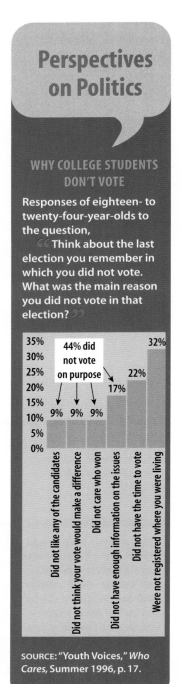

Another important political factor reducing voter turnout in the United States is our nations' peculiar registration rules. In every American state but North Dakota, individuals who are eligible to vote must register with the state election board before they are actually allowed to vote. Registration requirements were introduced at the end of the nineteenth century in response to the demands of the Progressive movement. Progressives hoped to make voting more difficult both to reduce multiple voting and other forms of corruption and to discourage immigrant and working-class voters from going to the polls. When first introduced, registration was extremely difficult and, in some states, reduced voter turnout by as much as 50 percent.

Registration requirements particularly depress the participation of those with little education and low incomes because registration requires a greater degree of political involvement and interest than does the act of voting itself. To vote, a person need be concerned only with the particular election campaign at hand. Requiring individuals to register before the next election forces them to make a decision to participate on the basis of an abstract interest in the electoral process rather than a simple concern with a specific campaign. Such an abstract interest in electoral politics is largely a product of education. Those with relatively little education may become interested in political events once the issues of a particular campaign become salient, but by that time it may be too late to register. Young people tend to assign a low priority to registration even if they are well educated. As a result, personal registration requirements not only diminish the size of the electorate but also tend to create an electorate that is, on average, better educated, higher in income and social status, and composed of fewer young people, African Americans, and other minorities than the citizenry as a whole (see Figure 9.4). In Europe, there is typically no registration burden on the individual voter; voter registration is handled automatically by the government. This is one reason that voter turnout rates in Europe are higher than those in the United States.

As might be expected, in states that do not require registration (North Dakota) or that allow registration on the day of the election (Minnesota) voter turnout is not only higher than average, but younger and less affluent voters turn out in larger percentages.[22] Minnesota's same-day rule played an important role in the surprise 1998 gubernatorial victory of colorful former wrestler Jesse Ventura. Ventura won the votes of many young men who had not been registered until they came to the polls on election day. Without same-day registration, Ventura's electoral chances would have been considerably lessened.

Over the years, voter registration restrictions have been modified somewhat to make registration easier. But the removal of formal obstacles is not enough to ensure that people participate, as the example of the National Voter Registration Act passed in 1993 shows. Popularly known as the Motor Voter Act, the law aimed to increase participation by making it easier to register to vote. The cumbersome process of registering (and staying registered after moving) has often been singled out as a barrier to participation. The new law aimed to remove this obstacle by allowing people to register when they apply for a driver's license and at other public facilities. Although voter registration increased, turnout did not. An estimated 3.4 million people registered to vote as a result of the Motor Voter Act, but turnout in the 1996 election—the first

Perspectives on Politics

WHY COLLEGE STUDENTS DON'T VOTE

Responses of eighteen- to twenty-four-year-olds to the question,

"Think about the last election you remember in which you did not vote. What was the main reason you did not vote in that election?"

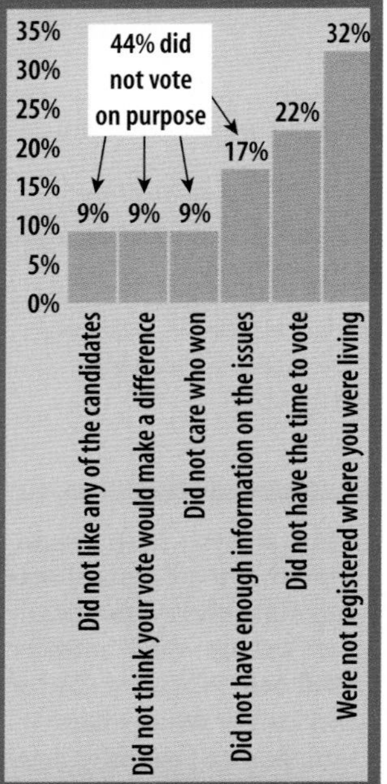

SOURCE: "Youth Voices," *Who Cares,* Summer 1996, p. 17.

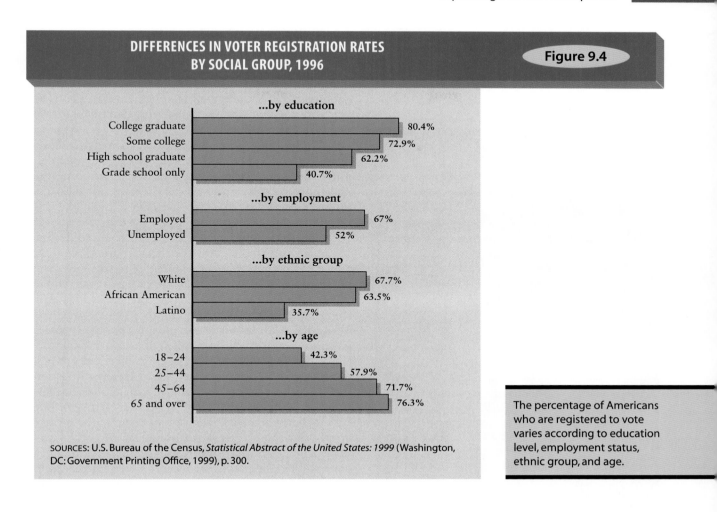

DIFFERENCES IN VOTER REGISTRATION RATES BY SOCIAL GROUP, 1996

Figure 9.4

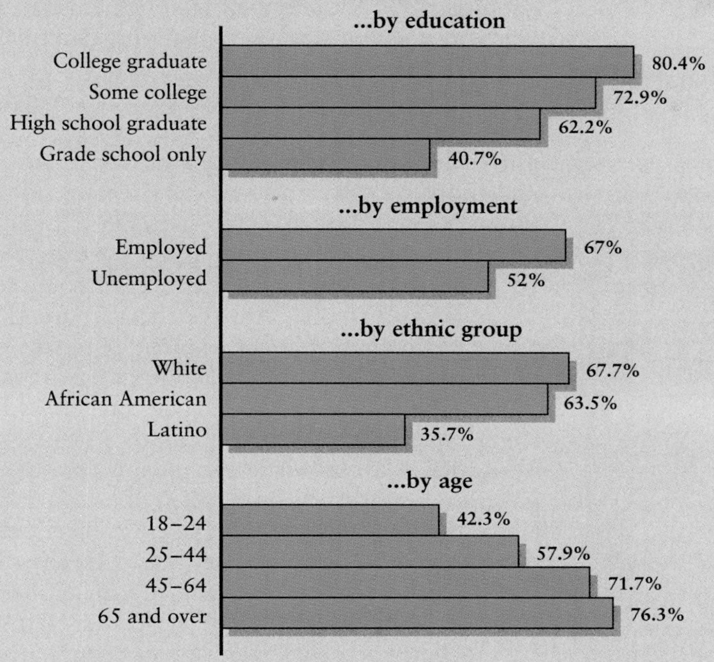

SOURCES: U.S. Bureau of the Census, *Statistical Abstract of the United States: 1999* (Washington, DC: Government Printing Office, 1999), p. 300.

The percentage of Americans who are registered to vote varies according to education level, employment status, ethnic group, and age.

presidential election held after the law went into effect—actually declined by 6 percent from that in 1992.[23] The very limited success of the Motor Voter Act suggests that people need motivation to participate, not simply the removal of barriers.

POLITICAL MOBILIZATION

The political setting can play an important role in motivating people to vote. When elections are closely contested, more people tend to vote. And in political settings where they think their input will make a difference, people are more likely to participate. One study of black political participation, for example, found that blacks were more likely to vote, participate in campaigns, and contact public officials in cities run by a black mayor. Their greater attention to city politics and their belief that city government is more responsive to their concerns helps to spark participation.[24]

But the most significant factor affecting participation is whether people are mobilized by parties, candidates, interest groups, and social movements. A recent comprehensive study of the decline in participation in the United

mobilization

the process by which large numbers of people are organized for a political activity

States found that fully half of the drop-off could be accounted for by reduced **mobilization** efforts.[25] People are much more likely to participate when someone—preferably someone they know—asks them to get involved. In previous decades that is precisely what political parties, organizations, and social movements did.

As we will see in Chapter 10, during the nineteenth century, American political party machines employed hundreds of thousands of workers to organize and mobilize voters as well as to bring them to the polls. The result was an extremely high rate of turnout, typically more than 90 percent of eligible voters.[26] But political party machines began to decline in strength in the beginning of the twentieth century and by now have, for the most part, disappeared. Without party workers to encourage them to go to the polls and even to bring them there if necessary, many eligible voters will not participate.

Rather than mobilizers of people, political parties have largely become fund-raising and advertising organizations. The experience of a Connecticut woman during the 1996 election is typical. Hoping to participate in the campaign, she sent a check to the Democratic Party and asked how she could volunteer. She subsequently received many more requests to donate money but she was never informed of any other way to become involved.[27] For the most part, candidates are left on their own to mobilize voters. In the 2000 Senate race in New Jersey, Democrat Jon Corzine paid "volunteers" to help him get out the vote. In that year's presidential election, both parties did work to mobilize their supporters in a few key "battleground" states like Florida, Michigan, Wisconsin, and Pennsylvania. But not only were these efforts limited to only a handful of important swing states, they were also impersonal political advertisements disguised as "personalized" letters, phone calls, and e-mails from the candidates. For most people, politics consists of little more than irritating intrusions into their lives that become more numerous around election time.

Interest groups have also reduced their efforts at direct mobilization. Although the number of interest groups has grown dramatically in recent years, the connection that most interest-group members have to these groups often extends no further than their checkbook. Rather than being a means for contact by a friend or an acquaintance to take part in a political activity, belonging to an organization is likely to bring requests through the mail for donations. And, rather than providing a

Students and Politics

"With the support of musical artists such as Madonna, Queen Latifah, R.E.M., and Sheryl Crow—and with donated airtime on MTV for public service announcements—Rock the Vote is perhaps the most well known of young voter programs. In 1992, the organization helped to turn out a record number of young people following its unprecedented and much-publicized campaign. [In 1996] Rock the Vote [was] back in force, with PSAs [public service announcements] running on MTV and other stations, an interactive Web site where young people [could] register to vote on-line, a [toll-free] phone number for voter registration, and a lively presence at both the Democratic and Republican national conventions.

"According to [Rock the Vote organizer] Mark Strama, in the first four weeks of a [1996] register-by-phone campaign, Rock the Vote received 75,000 calls on its [toll-free] number. The organization also registered 10,000 young people at Lollapolooza—bringing its total to more than 100,000 voters registered this year. And both parties' youth contingents are doing their share to inspire young voters, with a College Democrats' bus touring the country and the Young Republicans' Victory Train running from Iowa to New Mexico."

"In 1992 and 1996 alone, Rock the Vote and the [MTV] 'Choose or Lose' campaign together helped register more than 850,000 young voters and hope[d] to register even more during [the 2000] election cycle. . . .

"2000 will be an incredibly busy, exciting year for Rock the Vote. In addition to our brand new Web site and the new media campaigns, this summer we're heading out on a 25-city bus tour that will mobilize young voters to make their voices heard on Election Day,' says Rock the Vote campaign director, Alison Byrne Fields."

SOURCES: Joshua Wolf Shenk, "What Youth Politics?" *Who Cares* (Fall 1996), pp. 25–26 and http://www.rockthevote.org/press.html. Reprinted with permission.

venue for meeting new people and widening your circle of engagement, organizational membership is more likely to land your name on yet another mailing list, generating still more requests for funds. Likewise, past social movements, such as the labor movement in the 1930s and the civil rights movement of the 1960s, played an important role in mobilizing people into politics. As such movements have ebbed, nothing has replaced their mobilizing energy. As a result, participation rates drop the most among poorer and less-educated citizens. Because of the absence of strong political parties, the American electorate is smaller and skewed more toward the middle class than the population of all those potentially eligible to vote.

Participation and American Political Values

Over the course of our history, as we have seen, the American political community has expanded to make our politics more closely match our fundamental values of liberty, equality, and democracy. But more recently, our **political institutions** have ceased to mobilize an active citizenry. Furthermore, our uneven pattern of political participation is at odds with our notions of equality and democracy. These problems highlight the tension among our basic values and raise questions about whether our institutions could help provide a better balance among them.

political institution
an organization that connects people to politics, such as a political party, or a governmental organization, such as the Congress or the courts

In a democratic polity, the selection and removal of major public officials is tied closely to popular participation. Through their votes, ordinary citizens should be able to decide who will—and will not—govern. The events of recent years, however, seem to fly in the face of this simple democratic principle.

PARTICIPATION AND DEMOCRACY

During the political struggles of the past decades, politicians have sought to disgrace one another on national television, force their competitors to resign from office, and, in a number of cases, send their opponents to prison. Remarkably, one tactic that has not been so widely used is the mobilization of the electorate. Of course, Democrats and Republicans have contested each other and continue to contest each other in national elections. However, neither side has made much effort to mobilize *new* voters, to create strong local party organizations, or in general, to make full use of the electoral arena to defeat its enemies.

Voter mobilization is hardly a mysterious process. It entails an investment of funds and organizational effort to register voters actively and bring them to the polls on election day. Occasionally, politicians demonstrate that they *do* know how to mobilize voters if they have a strong enough incentive. For example, a massive get-out-the-vote effort by Democrats to defeat neo-Nazi David Duke in the 1991 Louisiana gubernatorial election led to a voter turnout of over 80 percent of those eligible—twice the normal turnout level for a Louisiana election. And in the 1990s it was the GOP, through its alliance with conservative religious leaders, that made the more concerted effort to

Figure 9.5

THE PERCENTAGE OF AMERICANS WHO VOTED, 1976–96

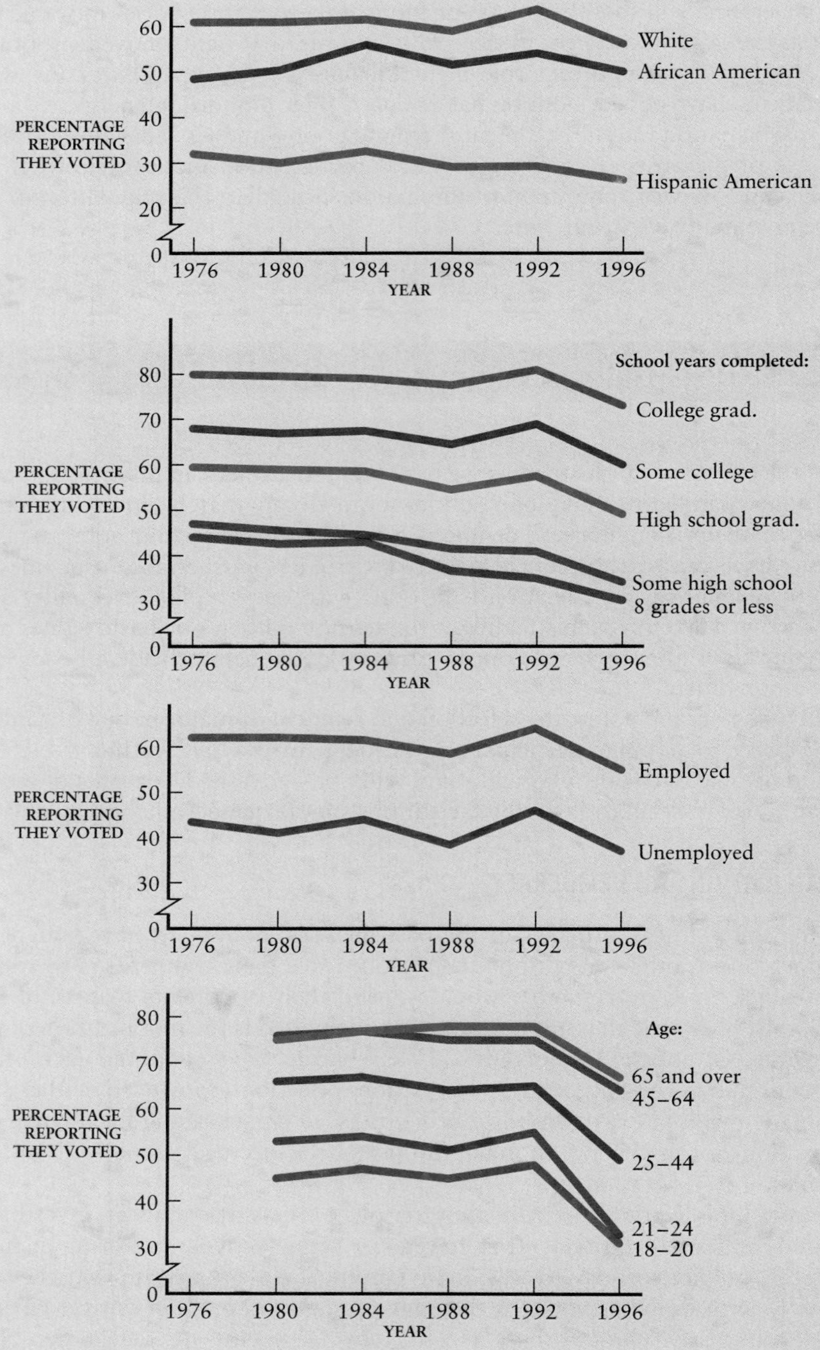

SOURCES: U.S. Bureau of the Census, *Statistical Abstract of the United States: 1994* (Washington, DC: Government Printing Office, 1994), p. 283; and http://www.census.gov/population/socdemo/voting/history/vot23.txt.

Whether or not Americans are likely to vote depends in part on their ethnic group, education level, employment status, and age.

bring new voters into the electorate. This effort was limited in scope, but it played an important part in the Republican Party's capture of both houses of Congress in 1994. The GOP's gains from this limited strategy of mobilization demonstrate what could be achieved from a fuller mobilization of the national electorate. In 1996, many conservative Republican activists were unhappy with Bob Dole and did not vigorously mobilize their followers. As a result, turnout fell below 50 percent.

How extraordinary, then, that politicians stop short of attempting to expand the electorate to overwhelm their foes in competitive elections. Why is this? A large part of the answer to this question is that the decline of political party organizations over the past several decades strengthened politicians in both camps who were linked with and supported by the middle and upper-middle classes. Party organization is an especially important instrument for enhancing the political influence of groups at the bottom of the social hierarchy—groups whose major political resource is numbers. Parties allowed politicians to organize the energies of large numbers of individuals from the lower classes to counter the superior financial and institutional resources available to those from the middle and upper classes.

The decline of party organization that resulted, in large measure, from the efforts of upper- and middle-class "reformers" over the years has undermined politicians such as union officials and Democratic and Republican "machine" leaders who had a stake in popular mobilization, while it has strengthened politicians with an upper-middle- or upper-class base. Recall the effects of registration laws that were discussed earlier in this chapter. As a result of these reforms, today's Democratic and Republican parties are dominated by different segments of the American upper-middle class. For the most part, contemporary Republicans speak for business and professionals from the private sector, while Democratic politicians and political activists are drawn from and speak for upper-middle-class professionals in the public and not-for-profit sectors.

Both sides give lip service to the idea of fuller popular participation in political life. Politicians and their upper-middle-class constituents in both camps, however, have access to a variety of different political resources—the news media, the courts, universities, and interest groups, to say nothing of substantial financial resources. As a result, neither side has much need for or interest in political tactics that might, in effect, stir up trouble from below. Both sides prefer to compete for power without engaging in full-scale popular mobilization. Without

Students and Politics

While some young adults cast their first ballots in New Hampshire's presidential primary, others said they deliberately withheld their votes Tuesday because their issues were ignored or they didn't want to participate in a political process they felt had been corrupted. And a few said they simply didn't know how to vote.

* * *

In the 1996 presidential election, about 32 percent of voters ages eighteen to twenty-four cast ballots.

Walking along a downtown Manchester Street, Ronda Partney, 24, said she deliberately chose not to vote as the way to make her political statement.

"This is the second time I haven't voted since I've been of age," Partney said, who attends the Massachusetts Institute of Technology but is still a New Hampshire resident.

"I just don't feel any connection personally [with the candidates]. They don't really address the issues of concern to me. I think it's a lot of, what they would say down South, 'the good ol' boy network.' And I feel like it's really keeping women out of office." Partney said the candidates barely touched on issues concerning women and minorities.

* * *

Some nonvoters said they had nothing against the candidates or the process, but simply weren't familiar with the registration process.

"I don't know if I register at city hall or at the place I'm suppose to vote at," said Cynthia St. Onge, 19, a bill collector who was taking a cigarette break in the cold winter sun in Manchester.

Ironically, New Hampshire has one of the easiest registration procedures, which allows residents to register the day of the election.

Residents only need to show proof of age, U.S. citizenship, and a piece of mail verifying that they live in New Hampshire. "I think that they should at least set up something like an information booth so that people who don't know can find out," St. Onge said. "If I knew how to register, I would be voting. I think it's important to vote."

SOURCE: Brian Peters, "Some Young Adults Choose Not to Vote in N.H. Primary," *Medill News Service/Y Vote 2000* (Northwestern University), February 2, 2000.

mobilization drives that might encourage low-income citizens or minorities to register and actually to vote, the population that does vote tends to be wealthier, whiter, and better educated than the population as a whole. Figure 9.5 on page 338 shows the marked differences in voter turnout linked to ethnic group, education level, and employment status. This trend has created a political process whose class bias is so obvious and egregious that, if it continues, Americans may have to begin adding a qualifier when they describe their politics as democratic. Perhaps the terms "semidemocratic," "quasidemocratic," or "neodemocratic" are in order to describe a political process in which ordinary voters have as little influence as they do in contemporary America.

PARTICIPATION AND EQUALITY

In a quasidemocratic political process, those who do not participate are inherently unequal. It is because of the quasidemocratic character of American politics that both political parties today focus more on the middle-class concerns of deficits and taxes and far less on the working-class concern of unemployment. Is it not because of these quasidemocratic politics that the two parties argue about how much to cut social programs to balance the budget while barely mentioning the various tax deductions enjoyed by upper-middle-income voters?

Politics on the Web

If the Internet can change American democracy, it can do so most profoundly in the arena of elections. The convenience of Internet-based communication could make registering to vote, casting a ballot, and reporting vote tallies dramatically easier. Once citizens can fill out and submit voter registration forms electronically, at any hour of the day, the barriers to registration will be substantially reduced. Already, a site called "Rock the Ages," cosponsored by MTV's Rock the Vote, MCI, and the American Association of Retired Persons, will submit completed voter registration forms based on information entered via the Internet. In the future, citizens will cast ballots electronically from their home or workplace, significantly reducing the costs of voting and thereby increasing political participation. Although these possibilities pose serious challenges in guarding against fraud and protecting the integrity of the electoral process, the Internet clearly has tremendous potential to expand the pool of citizens participating in American elections.

www.wwnorton.com/wtp3e

The Citizen's Role

In a sense, the role of the citizen in a democracy is obvious. Citizens have a right to participate. If citizens do not participate, then liberty, equality, and democracy become meaningless terms. To make democracy more vital and effective, however, citizens need to do more than vote. There are many opportunities for citizens, including college students, to become actively involved in the political process. Political parties and political campaigns are eager to sign on volunteer workers. Usually, the addresses and phone numbers of campaign offices are well publicized before elections. In addition, information about how to become involved with campaigns is available on the Internet from candidates' Web sites. Political work can be fun and rewarding. Campaign workers can make a real difference in bolstering voter turnout and even in persuading undecided voters one way or the other.

In some instances the effectiveness of citizens' political particpation is easy to discern. Lobbying and demonstrations by members of the American Association for Retired Persons (AARP) has had direct and immediate effects upon legislation affecting Social Security and health care for the elderly. By writing letters and making phone calls, individuals frequently secure the assistance of members of Congress with immigration problems. Student "sit-ins" often force college administrators to revise their policies. Lobbying and demonstrating, however, are activities in which most citizens seldom, if ever, engage. Voting is the form of political participation that engages the energy of the largest number of Americans on a routine basis.

There can be little doubt that the electorate's choices can have significant implications for government and policy in the United States. When, for example, Americans elected Ronald Reagan to the presidency in 1980, they were choosing a president who promised to cut taxes, expand military spending, and limit social spending. Reagan worked successfully to implement all those promises. By the same token, when voters chose Bill Clinton in 1992, they knew they were opting for a president who would work to undo some of the consequences of Reaganism and seek to expand the role of government in the provision of social services. Clinton worked to accomplish this goal, though achieving only mixed success. In both these cases, though, citizens' participation had important implications for America's political leadership and public policies.

GET INVOLVED Becoming a Voter

The most common way for U.S. citizens to get involved in politics is to cast a vote in elections. Many political scientists believe that voting in competitive elections is the most important form of political participation in a democracy. It is the main means by which citizens give their consent to government, choose their governors, and hold them accountable for their actions. Furthermore, voting links people to every level of government. Citizens may be called on to cast ballots for local propositions; school board and city council members; county district attorneys and judges; state governors and treasurers; and federal officials such as the president and U.S. senators. Often, voters' choices for several levels of government are consolidated into one ballot and take place on the same day; other times, elections for different issues and levels of government are put on separate ballots and held at different times of the year.

If you are a U.S. citizen who is eighteen years old or older, you are *eligible* to vote, but you must *register* to vote with the federal government. Registration is not automatic, but it is a fairly painless process. Voter registration forms are usually available at federal government offices and many local government offices, too. U.S. Post Offices, motor vehicle departments, and public libraries often distribute voter registration forms. You can call your local city hall to find out where you can get one. Prior to elections, you are likely to find groups on campus conducting voter registration drives. They make the forms readily accessible to you and, if you need assistance, they may help you fill out the form.

Once you have the form, completing it is fairly straightforward. You must provide general identification information such as name, address, date of birth, and so forth. The form will also ask you to declare your political party affiliation. You can list a specific political party or you can check "no party" if you do not wish to have a party affiliation. In some states, it is important to designate your party preference because that makes you eligible to vote in the primary election of your designated party. In other states, however, all registered voters are eligible to vote for all candidates running in primary elections.

Students and Politics

For those interested in taking action and bringing about change in the voting process within the United States, a Montana- and Boston-based organization is offering internship positions that politically active students may want. Project Vote Smart offers students who are interested in the voting process the chance to take an active part during election times.

"Everything about the political world is at your fingertips," said Kristina Saleh, assistant director of public information for Project Vote Smart, regarding the knowledge that the organization makes available to both interns and people simply interested in finding out more about candidates and elections.

"Our interns can expect to do work such as stuffing envelopes to conducting key research on important issues for both reporters and citizens who want information on voting," said Saleh. "Interns also answer phones for our hotline, helping people out from both the right and the left who want to know about candidates in state and national elections."

Saleh explained the purpose of Project Vote Smart, which is to deliver unbiased information on candidates around the country and to help voters make a more well-grounded judgment on the candidates that they choose. Also, the organization hopes to eliminate votes made based on campaign ads and strategies as well.

"A vote counts more when there's knowledge to back it up," added Saleh. In the mid-1980s, Project Vote Smart began as the grassroots effort of several citizens who were concerned with the way campaigns were run through commercials. To the organizers of Project Vote Smart, these commercials were ultimately influencing the decisions that people were making in the voting booth.

"In looking at this trend, the founders of Project Vote Smart decided that easily accessible information about candidates would help to solve this problem," said Saleh. "In essence, it's a one-stop-shop for election information." Saleh said that because it's a fact-finding type of organization, Project Vote Smart has the ability to inform citizens about how their congressman voted on an education issue within their state to what a presidential candidate's platform is.

"Being a Project Vote Smart intern definitely opens your eyes to the information that's out there," said Saleh, a former intern herself in 1998.

SOURCE: Chandra Broadwater, "Project Vote Smart Gives Students a Chance to Get Involved," *The Daily Athenaeum* (West Virginia University), March 8, 2000.

When you have filled out the voter registration form, mail it to the address shown on the form or return it to the people conductng the voter registration drive. Note that different states have different deadlines regarding when you must be registered in order to be eligible to vote in an upcoming election.

After you are registered to vote, there is a strong probability that you will receive multiple campaign mailings from interest groups, political action committees, direct mail professionals, political parties, and candidates as an election approaches. These mailings may consist of a lot of junk; however, they sometimes contain useful information to help you think through your position on important issues or choose among the competing candidates. For even more information, log on to the Internet, put an issue, a political party, or a candidate's name into a search engine, and see what you can find. Increasingly, interest groups, parties, and candidates are using the Internet as part of their campaign outreach strategies.

Prior to an election, you should receive a sample ballot, which will lay out all of the offices and choices in the election. The sample ballot will tell you where your polling place is (where you vote on Election Day). It will also have a form on it that you can use to request an absentee ballot (if you are unable to appear at your polling place on Election Day). You may also receive information from both government sources and private sources about propositions that may appear on the ballot, the pros and cons of the propositions, and perhaps the costs (if any) to taxpayers should the propositions pass.

Assuming that you do not cast an absentee ballot, you need to go to your polling place on election day. Depending on where you vote, you will encounter one of the five voting systems currently used in the United States. One involves putting check marks next to your preferences on a paper ballot. A second lists all options and requires you to pull a mechanical lever next to your choices. A third system requires that you punch holes in a card to indicate your choices. A fourth system has you darken circles or rectangles beside your choices. A fifth voting method, called Direct Recording Electronic (DRE), asks you to use a touch-screen or push buttons to indicate your preferences. Regardless of the system, your polling place will be staffed by community volunteers who will answer questions about how to cast your votes.

The Federal Elections Commission has launched a Web site containing a wealth of additional detailed information related to voting. You can access that site at http://www.fec.gov.

Summary

Political participation can take many forms, including lobbying, public relations, litigation, protest, and voting. Voting is the most common and important form of participation. At the time of America's founding, the right to vote was generally limited to white males over the age of twenty-one. Many states also limited voting rights to those who owned property. Over the years, voting rights were expanded to give all adult Americans the right to participate in elections. Despite this, only about half of all American citizens over the age of eighteen actually vote in presidential elections.

An individual's socioeconomic status is the most important characteristic determining whether he or she participates in politics. But the efforts of political institutions to mobilize people are especially significant if we wish to understand patterns of participation over time. In recent decades political institutions, such as parties, have done less to mobilize people to participate in politics. The fact that many Americans do not participate gives the American political process a quasidemocratic character.

FOR FURTHER READING

Drew, Elizabeth. *The Corruption of American Politics: What Went Wrong and Why.* New York: Birch Lane, 1999.

Eliasoph, Nina. *Avoiding Politics: How Americans Produce Apathy in Everyday Life.* Cambridge, Eng.: Cambridge University Press, 1998.

Frantzich, Stephen E. *Citizen Democracy: Political Activists in a Cynical Age.* New York: Rowman and Littlefield, 1999.

Miller, Warren, and J. Merrill Shanks. *The New American Voter.* Cambridge, MA: Harvard University Press, 1996.

Putnam, Robert D. *Bowling Alone: The Collapse and Revival of American Community.* New York: Simon & Schuster, 2000.

Rosenstone, Steven J, and John Mark Hansen. *Mobilization, Participation and Democracy in America.* New York: Macmillan, 1993.

Schudson, Michael. *The Good Citizen: A History of American Civic Life.* New Yrok: Free Press, 1998.

Verba, Sidney, Kay Lehman Schlotzman, and Henry Brady. *Voice and Equality: Civic Voluntarism in American Politics.* Cambridge, MA: Harvard University Press, 1995.

STUDY OUTLINE

Political Participation

1. Political participation can take many forms. The most common today are lobbying, public relations, litigation, protest, and, most important, voting.
2. Throughout American history, there has been a progressive, if uneven, expansion of suffrage to groups such as African Americans, women, and youths.
3. Americans are taught to equate citizenship with electoral participation.
4. Though the United States now has a system of universal suffrage, voter turnout continues to be low.

Explaining Political Participation

1. Several factors explain political participation. They include socioeconomic status, levels of civic engagement, formal obstacles, and efforts by political institutions to mobilize people. The most significant political factor affecting participation is whether people are mobilized by parties, candidates, interest groups, and social movements.
2. In recent decades, political institutions have ceased to mobilize an active citizenry. As a result, the ties between elected leaders and members of the upper and middle classes, who tend to vote more regularly, have been strengthened.
3. The quasidemocratic features of the American electoral system reveal its inherent inequality.

PRACTICE QUIZ

1. Which of the following is *not* a form of political participation?
   a) volunteering in a campaign
   b) attending an abortion-rights rally
   c) contributing to the Democratic Party
   d) watching the news on television

2. What is the most common form of political participation?
   a) lobbying
   b) contributing money to a campaign
   c) protesting
   d) voting

3. Which of the following best describes the electorate in the United States prior to the 1820s?
   a) landowning white males over the age of twenty-one
   b) all white males
   c) all literate males
   d) "universal suffrage"

4. Women won the right to vote in _________ with the adoption of the _________ Amendment.
   a) 1791; Fifth
   b) 1868; Fourteenth
   c) 1920; Nineteenth
   d) 1971; Twenty-sixth

5. Civic education takes place during
   a) elementary school.
   b) high school.
   c) election campaigns.
   d) all of the above

6. Which of the following negatively impacts voter turnout in the United States?
   a) registration requirements
   b) weak parties
   c) neither a nor b
   d) both a and b

7. Of all the factors explaining political participation, which is the most important?
   a) the mobilization of people by political institutions
   b) socioeconomic status
   c) civic engagement
   d) level of education

8. Which of the following are examples of obstacles to political participation for African Americans?
   a) mobilization and levels of civic engagement
   b) the Civil Rights Acts of 1957 and 1964
   c) poll taxes and white primaries
   d) churches and community centers

9. After passage of the Motor Voter Act in 1993, participation in the 1996 elections
   a) increased dramatically.
   b) increased somewhat.
   c) declined somewhat.
   d) was not affected, since few people registered to vote as a result of the act.

10. Americans who do vote tend to be _________ than the population as a whole.
    a) wealthier
    b) whiter
    c) more educated
    d) all of the above

CRITICAL THINKING QUESTIONS

1. Describe the expansion of suffrage in the United States since the Founding. Why might the government have denied participation to so many for so long? What forces influenced the expansion of voting rights?

2. Why is voter turnout so low in the United States? What are the consequences of low levels of voter turnout? Some critics charge that the United States cannot claim to be a democracy when so few of its citizens actually vote. Is there any basis to this charge?

KEY TERMS

civic engagement (p. 333)
litigation (p. 320)
lobbying (p. 320)
mobilization (p. 336)
political institutions (p. 337)
political participation (p. 318)
poll tax (p. 323)
protest (p. 320)
public relations (p. 320)
socioeconomic status(p. 329)
suffrage (p. 322)
turnout (p. 326)
white primary (p. 333)

10 Political Parties

★ **What Are Political Parties?**
How have political parties developed in the United States?

★ **The Two-Party System in America**
How do parties form? What are the historical origins of today's Democratic and Republican parties?
What is the history of party politics in America?
What has been the historical role of third parties in the United States?

★ **Party Organization**
How are political parties organized? At what levels are they organized?

★ **Parties and the Electorate**
What ties do people have to political parties?

★ **Parties and Elections**
What are the important electoral functions of parties?

★ **Parties and Government**
How do the differences between Democrats and Republicans affect Congress, the president, and the policy making process?

★ **Parties and Democracy**
Do parties help or hinder democracy?

STUDENTS AND POLITICS

In many parts of the world, college students are associated with the most radical political parties and often spearhead riots, demonstrations, and other forms of political violence. In the Persian Gulf kingdom of Bahrain, for example, thousands of Shiite Muslim students clashed in late 1994 with police as part of a Shiite-supported party's effort to overthrow the Bahraini government. A number of police officers and students were killed.[1] In Bangladesh, a national student party led a general strike against the government. During the course of their protest, student demonstrators had a violent clash with police that led to more than eighty-five casualties.[2]

In the United States, by contrast, relatively few students belong to any political party, much less radical parties. During the 1960s, the Democratic Party appealed for the support of politically active students by sponsoring the Twenty-sixth Amendment, which lowered the voting age to eighteen. The Democrats also gave students an opportunity to play a greater role in party affairs by requiring state-level party organizations to make certain that young people were represented throughout the presidential nominating process, including in the state's delegation to the national presidential convention. These efforts do not seem to have borne much fruit, however. To be sure, young people (eighteen- to twenty-nine-year-olds) are slightly more likely to identify with the Democratic Party than with the Republicans. The strength of their attachment to the Democrats (or any other party), however, is generally weak, and many young people believe that candidates should run for office as individuals rather than as members of political parties.[3]

When American students engage in protest activities, they seem to focus more on matters of immediate concern or interest than on larger political or social issues. For example, in 1999, University of California at Berkeley students protested the university's failure to fund an ethnic studies center. In 1998, other Berkeley students marched to demand the expulsion of a sophomore who had witnessed, but failed to stop or report a heinous crime. During the same year, 3,000 Michigan State University students protested a ban on drinking at Munn Field, a favorite campus spot to celebrate football victories. In 1997, Utah State University students protested cuts in the university's athletic budget. Students at Los Angeles's Mission College protested financial aid cuts. Students at the University of Alabama's New College protested an administration move to merge their college with the university's College of Arts and Sciences. Stanford University students called for a boycott of *U.S. News & World Report* after their school had dropped one notch in that magazine's annual college ratings. A student at Moravian College in Pennsylvania handcuffed himself to the door of the administration building to protest his school's physical education requirement.

One major reason that American college students are less inclined toward radical politics is the relationship between education and access in American society. Higher education is probably the most important route of access to economic success and social status in the United States. Although a college or postgraduate degree is not an absolute guarantee of affluence, for the most part, graduates of American colleges and universities can look forward to meaningful careers in which they will have the opportunity to use and profit from their academic credentials. This expectation, as much as anything else, works against political militancy on the part of American college and university students. Why would students participate in radical attacks upon a political and social order that promises to reward them?

Today's generation of young Americans is little different from earlier ones, which were also relatively indifferent to party politics. Over time, earlier generations began to recognize how differences between the two major parties affected their interests and began to show a greater interest in party politics. Today's generation will likely do the same.

The relationship between political parties and constituent social groups is never simple. Groups that in one social setting or time period are associated with radical parties may, in another place and time, be pillars of conservatism. Groups initially mobilized by one party may shift their allegiance to another as circumstances change. As we will see later in this chapter, during periods of electoral realignment in the United States, enormous blocs of voters have migrated from one party to the other, with major consequences for public policy and political power.

At the same time, the role of parties in political processes is more complex than we sometimes think. In modern history, political parties have been the chief points of contact between governments, on the one side, and groups and forces in society, on the other. In organized political parties, social forces can gain some control over governmental policies and personnel. Simultaneously, governments often seek to organize and influence important groups in society through political parties. All political parties have this dual character: they are instruments through which citizens and governments attempt to influence one another. In some nations, such as the People's Republic of China, the leading political party serves primarily the interests of the government. In others, such as the United States, political parties force the government to concern itself with the needs of its citizens.

The idea of political parties was not always accepted in the United States. In the early years of the Republic, parties were seen as threats to the social order. In his 1796 "Farewell Address," President George Washington warned his countrymen to shun partisan politics:

> Let me warn you in the most solemn manner against the baneful effects of the spirit of party generally. This spirit exists under different shapes in all government, more or less stifled, controlled, or repressed, but in those of the popular form it is seen in its greater rankness and is truly their worst enemy.

Often, those in power viewed the formation of political parties by their opponents as acts of treason that merited severe punishment. Thus, in 1798, the Federalist Party, which controlled the national government, in effect sought to outlaw its Jeffersonian Republican opponents through the infamous Alien and Sedition Acts, which, among other things, made it a crime to publish or say anything that might tend to defame or bring into disrepute either the president

Perspectives on Politics

STRENGTH OF PARTY IDENTIFICATION

Percentage of Americans responding yes to the question, "Do you feel a strong attachment to either the Democratic or Republican parties?"

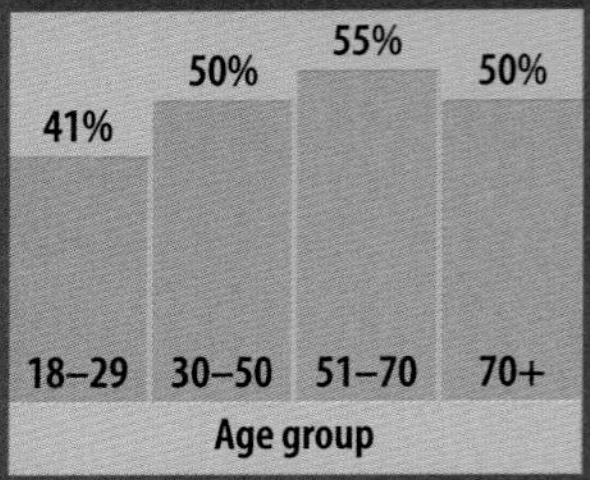

SOURCE: Adapted from American National Election Studies data reported in Jack Dennis and Diana Owen, "The Partisanship Puzzle: Identification and Attitudes of Generation X," in *After the Boom: The Politics of Generation X*, ed. Stephen C. Craig and Stephen Earl Bennett (Lanham, MD: Rowman and Littlefield, 1997), p. 46.

or the Congress. Under this law, fifteen individuals—including several Republican newspaper editors—were arrested and convicted.[4]

Obviously, over the past two hundred years, Americans' conception of political parties has changed considerably—from subversive organizations to bulwarks of democracy. In this chapter, we will examine the realities underlying these changing conceptions.

- ***We begin by explaining why political parties exist.*** In answering this, we will see that parties play a significant role in key aspects of the political process.
- ***We then examine the history of the American two-party system.*** As we will see, the history of parties has followed an interesting pattern that has had important consequences for governance.
- ***In the next three sections, we look at parties as organizations, parties in the electorate, and the role of parties in the campaign process.*** We will see that although party organizations remain strong, the electorate's identification with parties and the role of parties in the electoral process have been declining in recent decades.
- ***We then assess the impact of parties on government and the policymaking process.*** We will see that the differences between the two major parties can and do have an effect on policy.
- ***Finally, we conclude with an evaluation of the importance of political parties to democracy.*** Healthy political parties are extremely important for maintaining American political values.

What Are Political Parties?

▶ How have political parties developed in the United States?

Political parties, like interest groups, are organizations seeking influence over government. Ordinarily, they can be distinguished from interest groups on the basis of their orientation. A party seeks to control the entire government by electing its members to office and thereby controlling the government's personnel. Interest groups usually accept government and its personnel as a given and try to influence government policies through them.

political parties
organized groups that attempt to influence the government by electing their members to important government offices

OUTGROWTHS OF THE ELECTORAL PROCESS

Political parties as they are known today developed along with the expansion of suffrage and can be understood only in the context of elections. The two are so intertwined that American parties actually take their structure from the electoral process. The shape of party organization in the United States has followed a simple rule: for every district where an election is held, there should be some kind of party unit. Republicans failed to maintain units in most counties of the southern states between 1900 and 1952; Democrats were similarly unsuccessful in many areas of New England. But for most of the history of the United States, two major parties have had enough of an organized presence to oppose each other in elections in most of the nation's towns, cities, and counties. This makes the American party system one of the oldest political institutions in the history of democracy.

Compared with political parties in Europe, parties in the United States have always seemed weak. They have no criteria for party membership—no cards for their members to carry, no obligatory participation in any activity. Today, they seem weaker than ever; they inspire less loyalty and are less able to control nominations. Some people are even talking about a "crisis of political parties," as though party politics were being abandoned. But there continues to be at least some substance to party organizations in the United States.

OUTGROWTHS OF THE POLICYMAKING PROCESS

Political parties are also essential elements in the process of making policy. Within the government, parties are coalitions of individuals with shared or overlapping interests who, as a rule, will support one another's programs and initiatives. Even though there may be areas of disagreement within each party, a common party label in and of itself gives party members a reason to cooperate. Because they are permanent coalitions, parties greatly facilitate the policy making process. If alliances had to be formed from scratch for each legislative proposal, the business of government would slow to a crawl or halt altogether. Parties create a basis for coalition and thus sharply reduce the time, energy, and effort needed to advance a legislative proposal. For example, in January 1998 when President Bill Clinton considered a series of new policy initiatives, he met first with the House and Senate leaders of the Democratic Party. Although some congressional Democrats disagreed with the president's approach to a number of issues, all felt they had a stake in cooperating with Clinton to burnish the party's image in preparation for the next round of national elections. Without the support of a party, the president would be compelled to undertake the daunting and probably impossible task of forming a completely new coalition for each and every policy proposal—a virtually impossible task. As political scientist John Aldrich has noted, no group of politicians in our democracy has ever come up with a way to achieve their goals without political parties.[5]

The Two-Party System in America

- How do parties form? What are the historical origins of today's Democratic and Republican parties?
- What is the history of party politics in America?
- What has been the historical role of third parties in the United States?

two-party system
a political system in which only two parties have a realistic opportunity to compete effectively for control

Although George Washington, and in fact many other leaders of his time, deplored partisan politics, the **two-party system** emerged early in the history of the new Republic. Beginning with the Federalists and the Jeffersonian Republicans in the late 1780s, two major parties would dominate national politics, although which particular two parties they were would change with the times and issues. This two-party system has culminated in today's Democrats and Republicans (see Figure 10.1).

HOW THE PARTY SYSTEM EVOLVED

Figure 10.1

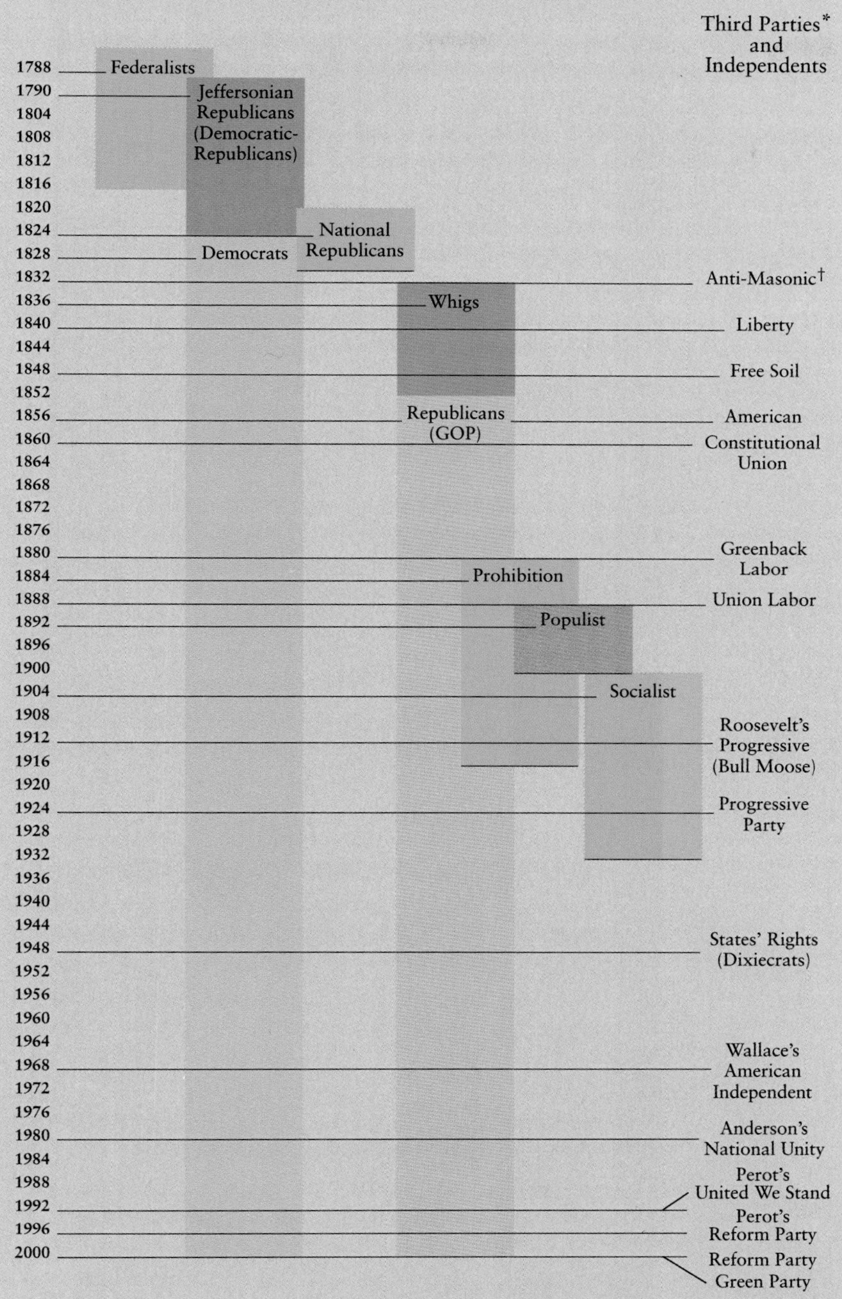

*Or in some cases, fourth party; most of these parties lasted through only one term.

†The Anti-Masonics had the distinction not only of being the first third party, they were also the first party to hold a national nominating convention and the first to announce a party platform.

HISTORICAL ORIGINS

Historically, parties form in one of two ways. The first, which could be called "internal mobilization," occurs when political conflicts break out and government officials and competing factions seek to mobilize popular support. This is precisely what happened during the early years of the American Republic. Competition in the Congress between northeastern mercantile and southern agrarian factions led first the southerners and then the northeasterners to attempt to organize popular followings. The result was the foundation of America's first national parties—the Jeffersonians, whose primary base was in the South, and the Federalists, whose strength was greatest in the New England states.

The second common mode of party formation, which could be called "external mobilization," takes place when a group of politicians outside the established governmental framework develops and organizes popular support to win governmental power. For example, during the 1850s, a group of state politicians who opposed slavery, especially the expansion of slavery in America's territorial possessions, built what became the Republican Party by constructing party organizations and mobilizing popular support in the Northeast and West.

America's two major parties now, of course, are the Democrats and the Republicans. Each has had an important place in U.S. history.

The Democrats When the Jeffersonian Party splintered in 1824, Andrew Jackson emerged as the leader of one of its four factions. In 1830, Jackson's group became the Democratic Party. This new party had the strongest national organization of its time and presented itself as the party of the common man. Jacksonians supported reductions in the price of public lands and a policy of cheaper money and credit. Laborers, immigrants, and settlers west of the Alleghenies were quickly attracted to this new party.

Andrew Jackson's election to the presidency in 1828 was considered a victory for the common people and for the Democratic Party. Jackson's inauguration celebration on the White House lawn lasted several days. This engraving satirized Jackson's popular following.

From 1828, when Jackson was elected president, to 1860, the Democratic Party was the dominant force in American politics. For all but eight of those years, the Democrats held the White House. In addition, a Democratic majority controlled the Senate for twenty-six years and the House for twenty-four years during the same time period. These nineteenth-century Democrats emphasized the importance of interpreting the Constitution literally, upholding states' rights, and limiting federal spending.

In 1860, the issue of slavery split the Democrats along geographic lines. In the South, many Democrats served in the Confederate government. In the North, one faction of the party (the Copperheads) opposed the war and advocated negotiating a peace with the South. Thus, for years after the war, Republicans denounced the Democrats as the "party of treason."

The Democratic Party was not fully able to regain its political strength until the Great Depression. In 1933, Democrat Franklin D. Roosevelt entered the White House and the Democrats won control of Congress as well. Roosevelt's New Deal coalition, composed of Catholics, Jews, blacks, farmers, intellectuals, and members of organized labor, dominated American politics until the 1970s and served as the basis for the party's expansion of federal power and efforts to remedy social problems.

The Democrats were never fully united. In Congress, southern Democrats often aligned with Republicans in the "conservative coalition" rather than with members of their own party. But the Democratic Party remained America's majority party, usually controlling both Congress and the White House, for nearly four decades after 1932. By the 1980s, the Democratic coalition faced serious problems. The once-Solid South often voted for the Republicans, along with many white, blue-collar northern voters. On the other hand, the Democrats increased their strength among African American voters and women. The Democrats maintained a strong base in the bureaucracies of the federal government and the states, in labor unions, and in the not-for-profit sector of the economy. During the 1980s and 1990s, moderate Democrats were able to take control of the party nominating process and sought to broaden middle-class support for the Democrats. This helped the Democrats elect a president in 1992. In 1994, however, growing Republican strength in the South led to the loss of the Democrats' control of both houses of Congress for the first time since 1946. Although President Clinton, a Democrat, was able to win re-election to the White House in 1996 over the weak opposition of Republican Bob Dole, Democrats were unable to recapture control of either house of Congress. Some Democrats argued that the party needed to move even further to the political right and abandon its traditional support for social programs and affirmative action. Others argued that the party should redouble its efforts to appeal to poor and working-class Americans.

Employing a strategy his aides called "triangulation," President Clinton sought to pursue a moderate course that placed him midway between the positions of conservative Republicans and liberal Democrats. This strategy helped Clinton and the Democratic Party as a whole, which gained strength and nearly regained control of the House of Representatives in the 1998 national elections. After the 1998 elections, Clinton survived an effort by Republicans to impeach him after his admission of an inappropriate sexual relationship with White House intern Monica Lewinsky. Clinton was impeached in the House on a party-line vote but acquitted in the Senate (where a two-thirds majority is needed for conviction) on another party-line vote. As the two parties licked their wounds from this bruising struggle, they began preparations for the 2000 national presidential elections. Vice President Al Gore was the obvious front-runner, but he was seriously challenged by former senator Bill Bradley. Bradley's campaign appealed to the Democratic Party's most liberal constituencies, promising them renewed efforts in the realm of social spending. Gore, like Clinton, sought to keep his campaign and the Democratic Party firmly anchored in the political center. Late in the presidential race, in which he was trailing in the polls, Gore shifted course and sought to appeal to the party's liberal, African American, and union-based wing. This strategy may have cost Gore some support among moderate Democrats. Despite the lessons of Clinton's "triangulation," the Democratic Party has not yet found a way to firmly unite its liberal and more moderate wings.

The Republicans The 1854 Kansas-Nebraska Act overturned the Missouri Compromise of 1820 and the Compromise of 1850, which had barred the expansion of slavery in the American territories. The Kansas-Nebraska Act gave each territory the right to decide whether or not to permit slavery. Opposition to this policy galvanized antislavery groups and led them to create a new party, the Republicans. It drew its membership from existing political groups—former Whigs, Know-Nothings, Free Soilers, and antislavery Democrats. In 1856, the party's first presidential candidate, John C. Fremont, won one-third of the popular vote and carried eleven states.

The early Republican platforms appealed to commercial as well as antislavery interests. The Republicans favored homesteading, internal improvements, the construction of a transcontinental railroad, and protective tariffs, as well as the containment of slavery. In 1858, the Republican Party won control of the House of Representatives; in 1860, the Republican presidential candidate, Abraham Lincoln, was victorious in a four-way race.

The 1860 Republican Convention at Chicago, at which Abraham Lincoln received the presidential nomination.

For almost seventy-five years after the North's victory in the Civil War, the Republicans were America's dominant political party, especially after 1896. Between 1860 and 1932, Republicans occupied the White House for fifty-six years, controlled the Senate for sixty years, and the House for fifty. During these years, the Republicans came to be closely associated with big business. The party of Lincoln became the party of Wall Street.

The Great Depression ended Republican hegemony, however. The voters held President Herbert Hoover responsible for the economic catastrophe, and by 1936, the party's popularity was so low that Republicans won only eighty-nine seats in the House and seventeen in the Senate. The Republican presidential candidate in 1936, Governor Alfred M. Landon of Kansas, carried only two states. The Republicans won only four presidential elections between 1932 and 1980, and they controlled Congress for only four of those years (1947–49 and 1953–55).

The Republican Party has widened its appeal over the last four decades. Groups previously associated with the Democratic Party—particularly white, blue-collar workers and white southern Democrats—have been increasingly attracted to Republican presidential candidates (for example, Dwight D. Eisenhower, Richard Nixon, Ronald Reagan, and George Bush). Yet Republicans generally did not do as well at the state and local levels and, until recently, had little chance of capturing a majority in either the House or the Senate. In 1994, however, the Republican Party finally won a majority in both houses of Congress, in large part because of the party's growing strength in the South.

During the 1990s, conservative religious groups, who had been attracted to the Republican camp by its opposition to abortion and support for school prayer, made a concerted effort to expand their influence within the party. This effort led to conflict between these members of the "religious Right" and more traditional "country-club" Republicans, whose major concerns were matters such as taxes and federal regulation of business. The coalition between these two wings won control of both houses of Congress in 1994 and was able to retain control of both houses in 1996, despite President Clinton's re-election. In 1998, however, severe strains began to show in the GOP coalition. After the GOP lost several House seats in the 1998 congressional elections, Speaker Newt Gingrich resigned and was eventually replaced by a relatively unknown Illinois congressman, Dennis Hastert. With their razor-thin majority and inexperienced leadership, congressional

Students and Politics

Brown University's student body has developed an indelible reputation for espousing liberal politics and discouraging conservative—which makes the accomplishments of Parker Hamilton '99 all the more surprising.

In July, Hamilton was named National Field Director of the College Republican National Committee. "I am running an expansion of College Republicans—the largest in 20 years," said Hamilton, a native of Saratoga Springs, New York.

Hamilton supervises a number of full-time representatives, who travel the country recruiting and training students for the College Republicans. The initiative, called the Field Program, is expected to greatly increase the number of College Republicans nationwide.

"The College Republicans have not grown recently," said Hamilton. "We hope to have doubled the number of College Republicans in the country by the 2000 Presidential elections."

Hamilton said that the job is "fantastic."

"It's great to be around people who are excited about the political process," she said.

The College Republican National Committee is located on Capitol Hill, just a few blocks away from the Republican National Committee, according to Hamilton.

Hamilton found her political inspiration away from her home. "My dad is a Republican, my mom is a liberal, but neither are particularly politically active," Hamilton said.

Hamilton attributes her conservative beliefs to her high school experience. "I went to a very liberal all-girls school. I guess I just reacted against that. I like being in the minority for some perverse reason," she said.

Hamilton said that the stereotype of the liberal college student is frustrating to her. "Most of the active students I know are Republican. There is nothing antithetical [in the Republican party] to young people or students. I think a lot of students now are rejecting the excesses of their parents' years," she said.

Hamilton cited "divorce and related turmoil" as repercussions of student activism in the 1960s.

Hamilton, who currently lives in Washington, D.C., is looking forward to the 2000 Presidential elections by gathering a student contingent for the Republican National Convention.

SOURCE: Dara Cohen, "Brown U. Student Named College Republican National Field Director," *Brown Daily Herald* (Brown University), September 9, 1999.

Republicans could do little more than fight the Democrats to a stalemate. In the meantime, like their Democratic rivals, Republicans prepared for the 2000 national elections. Texas governor George W. Bush, son of the former president, was the early front-runner. Bush raised an enormous amount of money and, like Bill Clinton, avoided taking positions that would upset any of his party's factions. At the same time, charging that Republicans had lost their ideological soul, commentator Pat Buchanan left the Republican Party to seek the Reform Party nomination. Republicans worried that Buchanan might draw conservative votes from the GOP ticket and help the Democrats win the election. In the end, Buchanan drew little support for his cause and was irrelevant to the outcome of the election. Bush sought to unite the party's centrist and right wings behind a program of tax cuts, education reform, military strength, and family values. Bush avoided issues that divided the GOP camp, like abortion. Most Republicans were very comfortable with Bush's message, but not with the messenger. Bush was seen, even by GOP stalwarts, as inexperienced and lacking some of the personal qualities needed for the presidency. Even so, Republicans enthusiastically supported his ticket. Bush's candidacy boded well for the future of the GOP insofar as Bush was able to find a political formula that could unite the party. Republicans hoped that future candidates might apply this formula to restore the GOP to its glory years.

ELECTORAL ALIGNMENTS AND REALIGNMENTS

American party history has followed a fascinating pattern (see Figure 10.2). Typically, the national electoral arena has been dominated by one party for a period of roughly thirty years. At the conclusion of this period, the dominant party has been supplanted by a new party in what political scientists call an **electoral realignment.** The realignment is typically followed by a long period in which the new party is the dominant political force in the United States—not necessarily winning every election but generally maintaining control of the Congress and usually of the White House as well.[6]

electoral realignment
the point in history when a new party supplants the ruling party, becoming in turn the dominant political force. In the United States, this has tended to occur roughly every thirty years

Although there are some disputes among scholars about the precise timing of these critical realignments, there is general agreement that at least five have occurred since the Founding. The first took place around 1800 when the Jeffersonian Republicans defeated the Federalists and became the dominant force in American politics. The second realignment occurred in about 1828, when the Jacksonian Democrats took control of the White House and the Congress. The third period of realignment centered on 1860. During this period, the newly founded Republican Party led by Abraham Lincoln won power, in the process destroying the Whig Party, which had been one of the nation's two major parties since the 1830s. During the fourth critical period, centered on the election of 1896, the Republicans reasserted their dominance of the national government, which had been weakening since the 1880s. The fifth realignment took place during the period 1932–36, when the Democrats, led by Franklin Delano Roosevelt, took control of the White House and Congress and, despite sporadic interruptions, maintained control of both through the 1960s. Since that time, American party politics has been characterized primarily by **divided government,** wherein the presidency is controlled by one party while the other party controls one or both houses of Congress.

divided government
the condition in American government wherein the presidency is controlled by one party while the opposing party controls one or both houses of Congress

ELECTORAL REALIGNMENTS

Figure 10.2

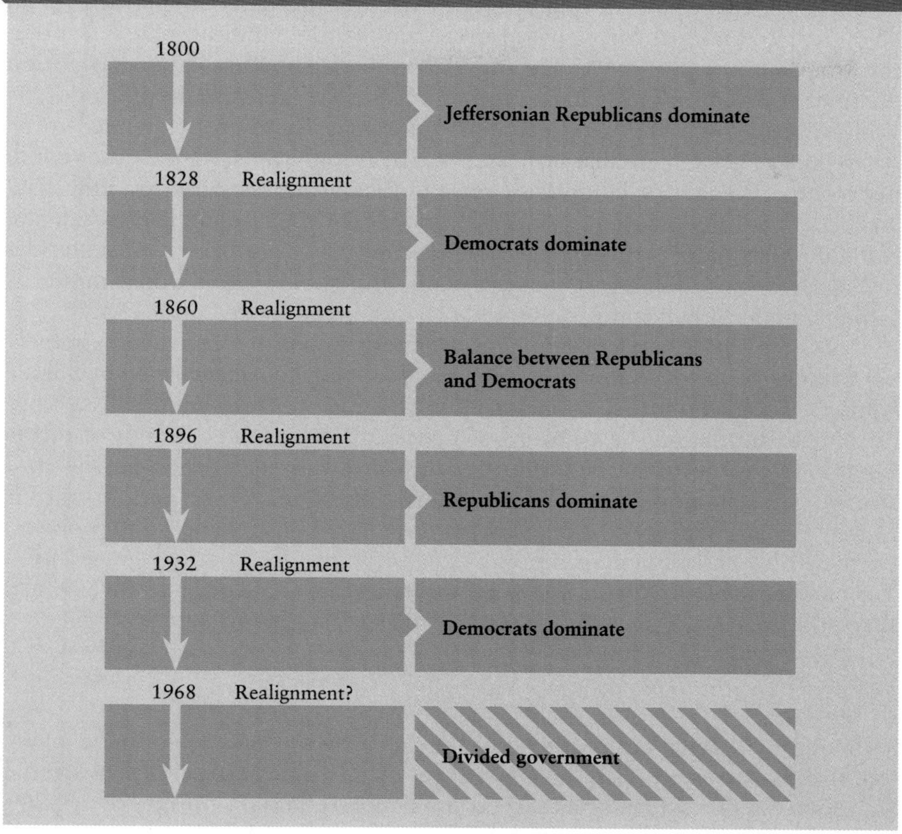

Political scientists disagree over whether electoral alignments occurred in 1968, because no one party clearly dominated the national government after that election.

Historically, realignments occur when new issues combined with economic or political crises mobilize new voters and persuade large numbers of voters to reexamine their traditional partisan loyalties and permanently shift their support from one party to another. For example, during the 1850s, diverse regional, income, and business groups supported one of the two major parties, the Democrats or the Whigs, on the basis of their positions on various economic issues, such as internal improvements, the tariff, monetary policy, and banking. This economic alignment was shattered during the 1850s. The newly formed Republican Party campaigned on the basis of opposition to slavery and, in particular, opposition to the expansion of slavery into the territories. The issues of slavery and sectionalism produced divisions within both the Democratic and the Whig parties, ultimately leading to the dissolution of the latter, and these issues compelled voters to reexamine their partisan allegiances. Many northern voters who had supported the Whigs or the Democrats on the basis of their economic stands shifted their support to the Republicans as slavery replaced tariffs and economic concerns as the central item on the nation's political agenda. Many southern Whigs shifted their support to the Democrats. The new sectional alignment of forces that emerged was solidified by the trauma of the Civil War and persisted almost to the turn of the century.

In 1896, this sectional alignment was at least partially supplanted by an alignment of political forces based on economic and cultural factors. During the economic crises of the 1880s and 1890s, the Democrats forged a coalition consisting of economically hard-pressed midwestern and southern farmers, as well as small-town and rural economic interests. These groups tended to be native-stock, fundamentalist Protestants. The Republicans, on the other hand, put together a coalition comprising most of the business community, industrial workers, and city dwellers. In the election of 1896, Republican candidate William McKinley, emphasizing business, industry, and urban interests, defeated Democrat William Jennings Bryan, who spoke for sectional interests, farmers, and fundamentalism. Republican dominance lasted until 1932.

Such periods of party realignment in American politics have had extremely important institutional and policy results. Realignments occur when new issue concerns coupled with economic or political crises weaken the established political elite and permit new groups of politicians to create coalitions of forces capable of capturing and holding the reins of governmental power. The construction of new governing coalitions during these realigning periods has effected major changes in American governmental institutions and policies. Each period of realignment represents a turning point in American politics. The choices made by the national electorate during these periods have helped shape the course of American political history for a generation.[7]

AMERICAN THIRD PARTIES

Although the United States is said to possess a two-party system, the country has always had more than two parties. Typically, **third parties** in the United States have represented social and economic interests that, for one or another reason, were not given voice by the two major parties.[8] Such parties have had a good deal of influence on ideas and elections in the United States. The Populists, a party centered in the rural areas of the West and Midwest, and the Progressives, spokesmen for the urban middle classes in the late nineteenth and early twentieth centuries, are the most important examples in the past hundred years. More recently, Ross Perot, who ran in 1992 as an independent and in 1996 as the Reform Party's nominee, impressed voters with his folksy style; he garnered almost 19 percent of the votes cast in the 1992 presidential election. Table 10.1 shows a listing of all the parties that offered candidates in one or more states in the presidential election of 2000, as well as independent candidates who ran. With the exception of Ralph Nader, the third-party and independent candidates together polled only 1.02 million votes. They gained no electoral votes for president, and most of them disappeared immediately after the presidential election. The significance of Table 10.1 is that it demonstrates the large number of third parties running candidates and appealing to voters. Third-party candidacies also arise at the state and local levels. In New York, the Liberal and Conservative parties have been on the ballot for decades. In 1998, Minnesota elected a third-party governor, former professional wrestler Jesse Ventura.

Minnesota governor Jesse Ventura was elected as a Reform Party candidate, becoming the Reform Party's highest elected official. Ventura quit the Reform Party in February of 2000 and the state party followed shortly after, changing their name to the Independence Party.

Although the Republican Party was only the third American political party ever to make itself permanent (by replacing the Whigs), other third parties

PARTIES AND CANDIDATES IN 2000 — Table 10.1

Candidate	Party	Vote total*	Percentage of vote*
Al Gore	Democratic	49,307,315	48
George W. Bush	Republican	49,093,218	48
Ralph Nader	Green	2,706,947	3
Pat Buchanan	Reform	438,665	0
Harry Browne	Libertarian	375,265	0
Howard Phillips	Constitution	98,486	0
John Hagelin	Natural Law	88,088	0
James Harris	Socialist Workers	10,589	0
L. Neil Smith	Libertarian	5,195	0
Monica Moorehead	Workers World	4,372	0
David McReynolds	Socialist	3,962	0
Cathy Brown	Independent	1,636	0
Denny Lane	Grass Roots	1,052	0
Louie Youngkeit	Independent	739	0
Randall Venson	Independent	547	0
Earl Dodge	Prohibition	207	0
Jim Wright	None	23	0
Joe Schriner	None	0	0
Gloria Strickland	None	0	0
None of the above	—	3,315	0

*With 99 percent of votes tallied.
SOURCE: www.washingtonpost.com/wp-srv/onpolitics/elections/2000/results/whitehouse Accessed November 14, 2000.

In the 2000 presidential election, in addition to the Democratic and Republican nominees, at least seventeen candidates appeared on the ballot in one or more states. Ralph Nader came the closest to challenging the major-party candidates with almost 3 percent of the popular vote. The remaining sixteen candidates shared about 1 percent of the votes cast with numerous write-ins.

have enjoyed an influence far beyond their electoral size. This was because large parts of their programs were adopted by one or both of the major parties, who sought to appeal to the voters mobilized by the new party, and so to expand their own electoral strength. The Democratic Party, for example, became a great deal more liberal when it adopted most of the Progressive program early in the twentieth century. Many Socialists felt that President Roosevelt's New Deal had adopted most of their party's program, including old-age pensions, unemployment compensation, an agricultural marketing program, and laws guaranteeing workers the right to organize into unions.

This kind of influence explains the short lives of third parties. Their causes are usually eliminated by the ability of the major parties to absorb their programs and to draw their supporters into the mainstream. There are, of course, additional reasons for the short duration of most third parties. One is the usual limitation of their electoral support to one or two regions. Populist support, for example, was primarily midwestern. The 1948 Progressive Party, with Henry Wallace as its candidate, drew nearly half its votes from the state of New York.

third parties
parties that organize to compete against the two major American political parties

The American Independent Party polled nearly 10 million popular votes and 45 electoral votes for George Wallace in 1968—the most electoral votes ever polled by a third-party candidate. But all of Wallace's electoral votes and the majority of his popular vote came from the states of the Deep South.

Americans usually assume that only the candidates nominated by one of the two major parties have any chance of winning an election. Thus, a vote cast for a third-party or independent candidate is often seen as a vote wasted. Voters who would prefer a third-party candidate may feel compelled to vote for the major-party candidate whom they regard as the "lesser of two evils" to avoid wasting their vote in a futile gesture. Third-party candidates must struggle—usually without success—to overcome the perception that they cannot win. Thus, in 1996, many voters who favored Ross Perot gave their votes to Bob Dole or Bill Clinton on the presumption that Perot was not really electable.

During the year prior to the 2000 national elections, Perot struggled with Minnesota governor Jesse Ventura for control of the Reform Party. Perot backed Pat Buchanan as the party's presidential nominee while Ventura promoted the candidacy of real-estate tycoon Donald Trump. Buchanan ultimately won the Reform Party's nomination, but only after a bitter convention battle that prompted many delegates to storm out of the convention hall. The winner of the nomination was not only guaranteed a spot on the ticket in most states, but also received approximately $12 million in federal campaign funds. Under federal election law, any minor party receiving more than 5 percent of the national presidential vote is entitled to federal funds, though considerably less than the major parties receive. The Reform Party qualified by winning 8.2 percent in 1996. Ralph Nader, the Green Party candidate in 2000, hoped to win the 5 percent of the vote that would entitle the Green Party to federal funds. Though Nader may have drawn enough liberal votes in New Hampshire and Florida to give those states—and the national election—to the GOP, hopes of achieving the 5 percent threshold were dashed.

As many scholars have pointed out, third-party prospects are also hampered by America's **single-member-district** plurality election system. In many other nations, several individuals can be elected to represent each legislative district. This is called a system of **multiple-member districts.** With this type of system, the candidates of weaker parties have a better chance of winning at least some seats. For their part, voters are less concerned about wasting ballots and usually more willing to support minor-party candidates.

Reinforcing the effects of the single-member district, the **plurality system** of voting (see Chapter 11) generally has the effect of setting what could be called a high threshold for victory. To win a plurality race, candidates usually must secure many more votes than they would need under most European systems of **proportional representation.** For example, to win an American plurality election in a single-member district where there are only two candidates, a politician must win more than 50 percent of the votes cast. To win a seat from a European multiple-member district under proportional rules, a candidate may need to win only 15 or 20 percent of the votes cast. This high American threshold discourages minor parties and encourages the various political factions that might otherwise form minor parties to minimize their differences and remain within the major-party coalitions.[9]

However, it would be incorrect to assert (as some scholars have) that America's single-member plurality election system is the major cause of its historical

single-member district
an electorate that is allowed to select only one representative from each district; the normal method of representation in the United States

multiple-member district
an electorate that selects all candidates at large from the whole district; each voter is given the number of votes equivalent to the number of seats to be filled

plurality system
a type of electoral system in which, to win a seat in the parliament or other representative body, a candidate need only receive the most votes in the election, not necessarily a majority of votes cast

proportional representation
a multiple-member district system that allows each political party representation in proportion to its percentage of the total vote

AMERICAN DEMOCRACY IN COMPARATIVE PERSPECTIVE

Political Party Systems

The nature of competition among political parties for public support and ultimately electoral victory is the defining characteristic of a *party system*. When we speak of a party system, we are referring not merely to the nature and characteristic of individual parties within a country but to the balance of power and diversity of those parties. Essentially, there are two types of party system in the world today: *single-party systems* and *competitive-party systems*. The least common is the single-party system. In 1945, there were approximately seventy-seven sovereign countries, of which twenty-three had only one political party dominating the political system. Most of these countries were communist (the Soviet Union and its East European satellite countries such as Czechoslovakia, Poland, Hungary, and the German Democratic Republic) or noncommunist but authoritarian and dictatorial in nature. Since the end of World War II, single-party noncommunist political systems became increasingly common throughout Africa and Asia as the colonial empires of West European nation-states began to collapse.

By the second half of the 1990s, of the 180 or so sovereign countries of the world, roughly 39 (approximately 21 percent) were dominated by a single political party, meaning, in effect, the competition for political values and the distribution of economic and social resources in those countries were largely monopolized by one set of values: those of the dominant single party. These countries include Afghanistan, Mexico, Cuba, Egypt, Taiwan, Madagascar, China, and Singapore.

The most common form of party system is a competitive-party system, which consists of more than a single dominant party. This second type of party system operates in approximately 58 percent of the countries in the world today. (The remaining countries have no parties at all but are governed by traditional patrons and clans, such as Saudi Arabia and other Gulf states, Afghanistan, and Libya. Others are governed by military dictatorships and allow no political parties, as in Myanmar, Nigeria, and Sudan.)

Competitive-party systems may, as in the case of the United States, have only two major political parties, or there may be two major political parties and one or two smaller parties that continually receive small but politically important electoral support. The United Kingdom, New Zealand, and Germany have this version of a *two-party system*. A two-party system is one of the institutional features of a political system associated with a majoritarian democratic logic. In other words, one party wins a disproportionate share of resources, while the losing party awaits another electoral contest to redress the balance.

However, the very stable and distinct two-party system is not the norm among the family of industrialized democracies of North America, West Europe, and its various global "outposts," such as Australia, New Zealand, Japan, and Israel. The common pattern found among these highly developed industrialized democracies is a *multi-party system*. They are characterized by at least three political parties that are roughly proportionally balanced with respect to the percentage of votes they receive in national elections. In this group of nations we find Norway, Sweden, Denmark, Belgium, Netherlands, Switzerland, Italy, and recently Canada. These countries usually have some form of distinctive ethnic/linguistic (Belgium, Switzerland, and Canada) or religious (Netherlands) conflict, which has historically divided the public into well-defined and unique issue-communities. This circumstance has thereby reinforced a strong bond between the competing issue-communities and various political parties. The parties have come to both protect and represent the issue-communities in a relatively balanced political struggle in society. In Italy, regional conflict (north versus south) has coincided with sharp socioeconomic distinctions among the public, which has served to undergird the multi-party system, at least until recently. Whatever the specific reasons, multi-party systems reflect a preference for more sharply defined political differences between issue-communities within society. Political parties in these systems serve to channel and mitigate conflict and thereby ensure a necessary balance of power between issue-communities that might otherwise render peaceful democratic governance impossible.

Multi-party systems are strongly associated with consensual democratic logic. The nature of historical conflict between distinct issue-communities in these countries requires political institutions, such as political parties, that can ensure the inclusion of many more interests in the policy process than is necessary within majoritarian democracies. Since the collapse of the Soviet Union and the end of the Cold War, former communist countries in East and Central Europe have also adopted multi-party systems.

SOURCE: Jean Blondel, *Comparative Government: An Introduction*, 2nd ed. (Prentice-Hall, 1995).

two-party pattern. All that can be said is that American election law depresses the number of parties likely to survive over long periods of time in the United States. There is nothing magical about two. Indeed, the single-member plurality system of election can also discourage second parties. After all, if one party consistently receives a large plurality of the vote, people may eventually come to see their vote *even for the second party* as a wasted effort. This happened to the Republican Party in the Deep South before World War II.

Party Organization

▶ How are political parties organized? At what levels are they organized?

party organization
the formal structure of a political party, including its leadership, election committees, active members, and paid staff

caucus (political)
a normally closed meeting of a political or legislative group to select candidates, plan strategy, or make decisions regarding legislative matters

national convention
a national party political institution that serves to nominate the party's presidential and vice presidential candidates, establish party rules, and write and ratify the party's platform

In the United States, **party organizations** exist at virtually every level of government (see Figure 10.3 on page 366). These organizations are usually committees made up of a number of active party members. State law and party rules prescribe how such committees are constituted. Usually, committee members are elected at local party meetings—called **caucuses**—or as part of the regular primary election. The best known examples of these committees are at the national level—the Democratic National Committee and the Republican National Committee.

NATIONAL CONVENTION

At the national level, the party's most important institution is the quadrennial **national convention.** The convention is attended by delegates from each of the states; as a group, they nominate the party's presidential and vice presidential candidates, draft the party's campaign platform for the presidential race, and approve changes in the rules and regulations governing party procedures. Before World War II, presidential nominations occupied most of the time, energy, and effort expended at the national convention. The nomination process required days of negotiation and compromise among state party leaders and often required many ballots before a nominee was selected. In recent years, however, presidential candidates have essentially nominated themselves by winning enough delegate support in primary elections to win the official nomination on the first ballot. The actual convention has played little or no role in selecting the candidates.

The convention's other two tasks, determining the party's rules and its platform, remain important. Party rules can determine the relative influence of competing factions within the party and can also increase or decrease the party's chances for electoral success. In 1972, for example, the Democratic National Convention adopted a new set of rules favored by the party's liberal wing. Under these rules, state delegations to the Democratic convention were required to include women and members of minority groups in rough proportion to those groups' representation among the party's membership in that state. Liberals correctly calculated that women and African Americans would

POLICY DEBATE

Are More Parties Better Than Two Parties?

Despite occasionally strong performances by third parties, America is one of the few nations of the world that has maintained an enduring two-party political system, beginning with the Federalist and Anti-Federalist parties in the post-colonial period. Today's Democratic Party is the world's oldest viable party; the younger Republican Party dates from the 1850s. America's stubborn loyalty to its two parties has been complicated by persistent criticisms of those two parties, including charges that they are little different from each other and that they monopolize political power, choke off new ideas, and restrict the influx of new leaders with different ideas.

These and other criticisms have produced support for the idea of a multiple-party system (any political system with three or more active parties is considered a multi-party system). American history supports the idea that third parties can help the political process. First, new parties can raise new and important issues ignored by the two major parties. In the pre–Civil War era, the Liberty and Free Soil parties advanced the cause of slavery abolition when the dominant Democratic and Whig parties were unable to come to grips with the issue. Early in the twentieth century, the Progressive Party advanced a vast array of social and political reforms eventually embraced by Democrats and Republicans. Ross Perot's Reform Party moved issues like deficit spending and budgetary responsibility to center stage in 1992. Second, as these examples suggest, a third-party option gives voters more choices among candidates and issues, addressing a persistent voter complaint. Third, most democratic nations of the world have a multi-party system, showing that the idea is not only viable, but is a routine part of the workings of democracy. Fourth, new parties might spark renewed voter interest in an electoral system that now attracts fewer than half of the eligible adult electorate to the voting booth. And fifth, states like Minnesota and New York have maintained an active multiple-party tradition (although in these states, the two major parties still dominate), suggesting that some version of the idea could indeed work on a national level.

Supporters of two-partyism argue that the virtues of the existing system are taken for granted. First and foremost, a two-party system produces automatic majorities, for the obvious reason that one will always receive over 50 percent of the vote. In a nation as large and diverse as America, governance could easily become impossible, or at least far more difficult, if multiple parties produced a bevy of candidates with no clear winner, or if American legislatures were populated with representatives from many different parties, barring any one party from organizing power. A second and related point is that the compromises that produce two candidates from two large parties also generally encourage moderation, compromise, and stability. Multiple parties might well heighten polarization and paralysis in America in a way that would make contemporary political gridlock seem tame by comparison. And while many democracies have multi-party systems, politics in those nations is often polarized and unstable. The Italian multi-party system, for example, produced over forty different governing coalitions in its first fifty years after the end of World War II. Third, the charge of exclusion of new factions and ideas by the two parties misses the fact that the two American parties are very large and diverse. In other nations, political conflict is played out between multiple parties. In America, much of that conflict occurs within the parties, especially during the nomination process. Fourth, America's enduring two-party system is a product of its political culture and historical development. The idea that a multi-party system could simply be transplanted onto the American political landscape is a leap of faith little supported by actual experience.

STUDENT DEBATE

Are Three Parties Better than Two?

Yes

In today's political culture, many Americans may forget this country is not a two-party system. Americans almost always vote either Democrat or Republican, ignoring the diverse selection of parties available. Instead of only looking at the two largest parties, voters should make an effort to examine the full spectrum of parties, and keep an open mind to make the most informed choice.

Throughout our history, there have been many powerful third parties. The Republicans have only been around since the Civil War era, coming into existence as a fairly minor political coalition before taking the presidency under Lincoln. Theodore Roosevelt, in addition to running as a Republican, also started a third party, known as the Bull Moose Party in honor of its founder. In recent times, the most prominent third party has been the Reform Party. Originally created by billionaire Ross Perot after his independent run in 1992—which captured almost 20 million votes—the Reform Party leadership has since been overtaken by Minnesota Gov. Jesse Ventura and his allies.

There has been something of a backlash against the two-party system in recent years from a variety of people. Warren Beatty, who in addition to acting has also been involved in many major political campaigns, accused the two parties of abandoning their traditional right/left views by moving too close to the center. Pat Buchanan, a strong contender for the Reform Party's next presidential bid, recently attacked the two major parties as being "two wings on the same bird of prey." If the two parties seem too centrist, there are many third party alternatives available that more closely follow traditional conservative or liberal views.

There are more than fifty parties in the United States, with platforms ranging from environmentalism to manifest destiny, from fascism to socialism. Many of these parties have yet to actually get a candidate on a ballot, and instead serve as vessels for issues that are generally dismissed by the major parties as being too radical or extreme. For information about most of the nation's current parties, take a look at Politics1 on the World Wide Web, located at http://www.politics1.com/parties.htm. This site contains a comprehensive list of parties, with links to their home pages and related resources.

Political diversity is vital to our nation's survival. It brings fresh ideas and people to what would otherwise be a stagnant field. Two parties alone cannot accurately represent the views of every American. At best, they can only hope to gather a large number of loosely related voters under their banner. With third party alternatives available, Americans need not settle for a broad view. Instead, they can almost always find a party they more closely identify with.

Voting for a third party may seem futile; as things stand, there is very little chance of most third parties winning major offices. Voters must not adopt this attitude. If a party represents your views, regardless of whether it is a large or small faction, then make yourself heard by voting for it. Even if your chosen party does not win, the larger ones will take notice, and may even adopt some of your party's planks if they decide that enough voters are in support of them. Democracy as we know it can only work if voters take the time to examine their options and make informed choices based on their findings.

SOURCE: Staff Editorial, *Michigan Daily* (University of Michigan), October 29, 1999.

No American observers of the recent German elections might be puzzled that the process of building a government is not complete. In the United States the governing parties are firmly determined on Election Day, the victor being the political party that has won the presidency or a majority in the House or Senate. This is not the case in most democracies. The recent elections in Germany have instructively provided an example of the pitfalls of a multi-party system. The multi-party system is more fractious and unstable, failing to measure up when compared to a two-party system.

One major benefit provided by the two-party system is a stable government. The reactions toward President Clinton's troubles demonstrate its inherent strength. Imagine if the United States had three strong political parties and that a coalition of Democrats and the Mysterious Third Party held the majority in the Congress. As news of the Lewinsky scandal spreads, if the Mysterious Third Party decided to back out of the coalition, the country faces a situation in which selecting the Speaker of the House and the Senate Majority Leader becomes impossible until a new coalition is formed.

It is in exactly this sort of situation that multi-party European systems fail. It does not take a large issue to bring the government grinding to a halt. Petty fighting and minor slights have disabled numerous European countries in this fashion. Indeed, the European country with the most stable government, the United Kingdom, also operates within an essentially two-party system like the United States.

Another example of the problems a third-party candidate can cause is right here in Minnesota. Jesse Ventura has made the Reform Party an important part of the 1998 gubernatorial election on the strength of his charisma, name recognition, and populism. The Democratic-Farmer-Labor candidate, Hubert H. "Skip" Humphrey III has paid special attention to ensuring that Ventura is included in all debates. Voters who favor Ventura are more likely to come from Norm Coleman's Republican camp. The excitement in the Humphrey camp about providing fairness for Ventura seems to come primarily from the reduction in Coleman's voter base. Perhaps the Humphrey camp would not be as eager to include the Reform Party candidate if he were campaigning for the protection of the environment and support of labor unions. As it stands, Ventura, besides relying on his outsider image, is making inroads on traditionally Republican issued such as crime fighting and decreasing the size of government. The DFL's abuse of Ventura's candidacy could not occur in a two-party system. Moreover, should Humphrey achieve a plurality, he might be the next governor even though a majority of voters voted for more conservative candidates.

Carefully consider the consequences that a major third party would have on the American political landscape. Do we really want a system in which governing majorities sit precariously atop fragile coalitions and the election process is distorted? This hardly seems a fair trade for excessive diversity among candidates.

SOURCE: Staff Editorial, *Minnesota Daily* (University of Minnesota), October 6, 1998.

Figure 10.3 HOW AMERICAN PARTIES ARE ORGANIZED

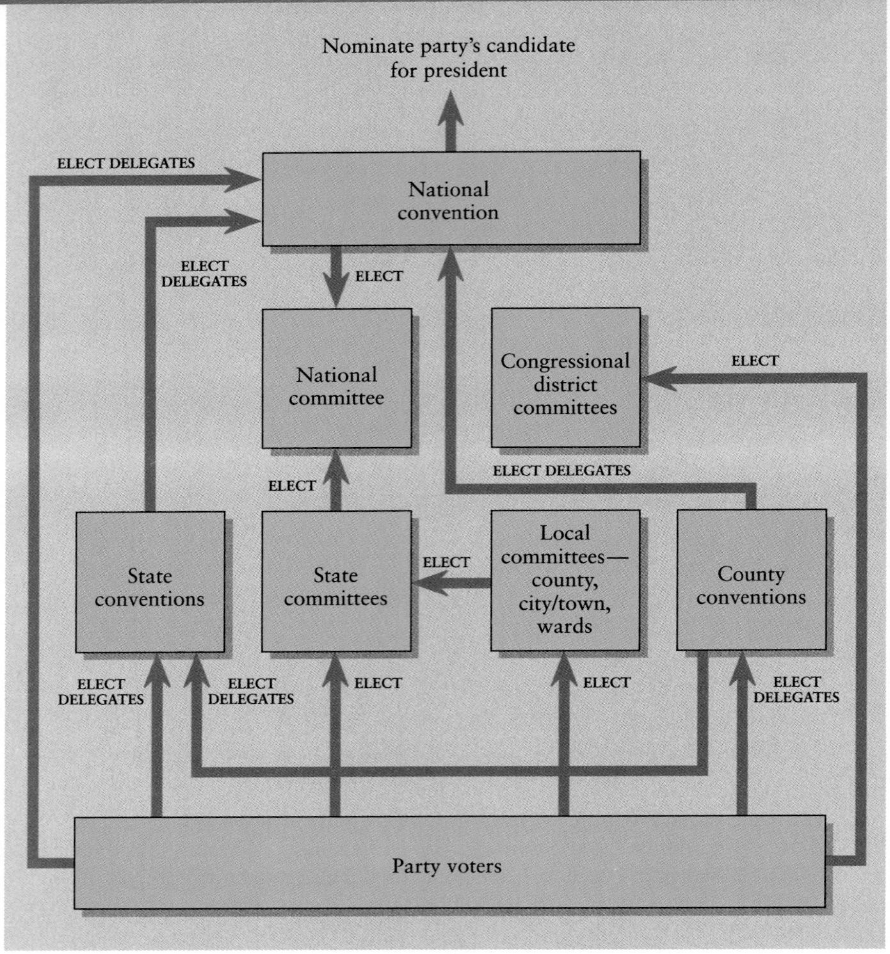

generally support liberal ideas and candidates. The rules also called for the use of proportional representation—a voting system liberals thought would give them an advantage by allowing the election of more women and minority delegates. (Although Republican rules do not require proportional representation, some state legislatures have moved to compel both parties to use this system in their presidential primaries.)

platform
a party document, written at a national convention, that contains party philosophy, principles, and positions on issues

The convention also approves the party **platform.** Platforms are often dismissed as documents filled with platitudes that are seldom read by voters. To some extent this criticism is well founded. Not one voter in a thousand so much as glances at the party platform, and even the news media pay little attention to the documents. Furthermore, the parties' presidential candidates make little use of the platforms in their campaigns; usually they prefer to develop and promote their own themes. Nonetheless, the platform can be an important document. The platform should be understood as a contract in which the various party factions attending the convention state their terms for supporting the ticket. For one faction, welfare reform may be a key issue. For another faction, tax reduction may be more important. For a third, the critical issue might be deficit reduction. When one of these "planks" is included in the platform, its promoters are asserting that this is what they want in exchange for their support for the ticket, while other party factions are agreeing that the position seems reasonable and appropriate. Thus, party platforms should be seen more as internal party documents than as public pledges.

NATIONAL COMMITTEE

Between conventions, each national political party is technically headed by its national committee. For the Democrats and Republicans, these are called the Democratic National Committee (DNC) and the Republican National Committee (RNC), respectively. These national committees raise campaign funds, head off factional disputes within the party, and endeavor to enhance the party's media image. The actual work of each national committee is overseen by its chairperson. Other committee members are generally major party contributors or fund-raisers and serve in a largely ceremonial capacity. In 1997, Senate hearings on campaign financing pointed to the importance of the national committees as fund-raising agencies. The DNC and RNC had each raised tens of millions of dollars for the 1996 national election campaigns.

For whichever party controls the White House, the party's national committee chair is appointed by the president. Typically, this means that that party's national committee becomes little more than an adjunct to the White House staff. For a first-term president, the committee devotes the bulk of its energy to the re-election campaign. The national committee chair of the party not in control of the White House is selected by the committee itself and usually takes a broader view of the party's needs, raising money and performing other activities on behalf of the party's members in Congress and in the state legislatures.

CONGRESSIONAL CAMPAIGN COMMITTEES

Each party also forms House and Senate campaign committees to raise funds for House and Senate election campaigns. Their efforts may or may not be coordinated with the activities of the national committees. For the party that controls the White House, the national committee and the congressional campaign committees are often rivals, since both groups are seeking donations from the same people but for different candidates: the national committee seeks funds for the presidential race while the congressional campaign committees approach the same contributors for support for the congressional contests. In recent years, the Republican Party has attempted to coordinate the fund-raising activities of all its committees. Republicans have sought to give the GOP's national institutions the capacity to invest funds in those close congressional, state, and local races where they can do the most good. The Democrats have been slower to coordinate their various committee activities, and this may have placed them at a disadvantage in recent congressional and local races.

Mayor Richard J. Daley of Chicago, the last of the big-city bosses, controlled an impressive political machine.

STATE AND LOCAL PARTY ORGANIZATIONS

Each of the two major parties has a central committee in each state. The parties traditionally also have county committees and, in some instances, state senate district committees, judicial district committees, and in the case of larger cities, citywide party committees and local assembly district "ward" committees as well. Congressional districts also may have party committees.

Some cities also have precinct committees. Precincts are not districts from which any representative is elected but instead are legally defined subdivisions of wards that are used to register voters and set up ballot boxes or voting machines. A precinct is typically composed of three hundred to six hundred voters. Well-organized political parties—especially the famous old machines of New York, Chicago, and Boston—provided for "precinct captains" and a fairly tight group of party members around them. Precinct captains were usually members of long standing in neighborhood party clubhouses, which were important social centers as well as places for distributing favors to constituents.[10]

machines
strong party organizations in late-nineteenth- and early-twentieth-century American cities. These machines were led by "bosses" who controlled party nominations and patronage

patronage
the resources available to higher officials, usually opportunities to make partisan appointments to offices and to confer grants, licenses, or special favors to supporters

In the nineteenth and early twentieth centuries, many cities and counties and even a few states upon occasion have had such well-organized parties that they were called **machines** and their leaders were called "bosses." Some of the great reform movements in American history were motivated by the excessive powers and abuses of these machines and their bosses. But few, if any, machines are left today. Traditional party machines depended heavily upon **patronage,** their power to control government jobs. With thousands of jobs to dispense, party bosses were able to recruit armies of political workers who, in turn, mobilized millions of voters. Today, because of civil service reform, party leaders no longer control many positions. Nevertheless, state and local party organizations are very active in recruiting candidates, conducting voter registration drives, and providing financial assistance to candidates. In many respects, federal election law has given state and local party organizations new life. Under current law, state and local party organizations can spend unlimited amounts of money on "party-building" activities such as voter registration and get-out-the-vote drives (see Chapter 11). As a result, the national party organizations, which have enormous fund-raising abilities but are limited by law in how much they can spend on candidates, each year transfer millions of dollars to the state and local organizations. The state and local parties, in turn, spend these funds, sometimes called **"soft money,"** to promote the candidacies of national, as well as state and local, candidates. In this process, as local organizations have become linked financially to the national parties, American political parties have become somewhat more integrated and nationalized than ever before. At the same time, the state and local party organizations have come to control large financial resources and play important roles in elections despite the collapse of the old patronage machines.[11]

soft money
money contributed directly to political parties for voter registration and organization

Parties and the Electorate

▶ What ties do people have to political parties?

Party organizations are more than just organizations; they are made up of millions of rank-and-file members. Individual voters tend to develop **party identification** with one of the political parties. Although it is a psychological tie, party identification also has a rational component. Voters generally form attachments to parties that reflect their views and interests. Once those attachments are formed, however, they are likely to persist and even to be handed down to children, unless some very strong factors convince individuals that their party is no longer an appropriate object for their affections. In some sense, party identification is similar to brand loyalty in the marketplace:

party identification
an individual voter's psychological ties to one party or another

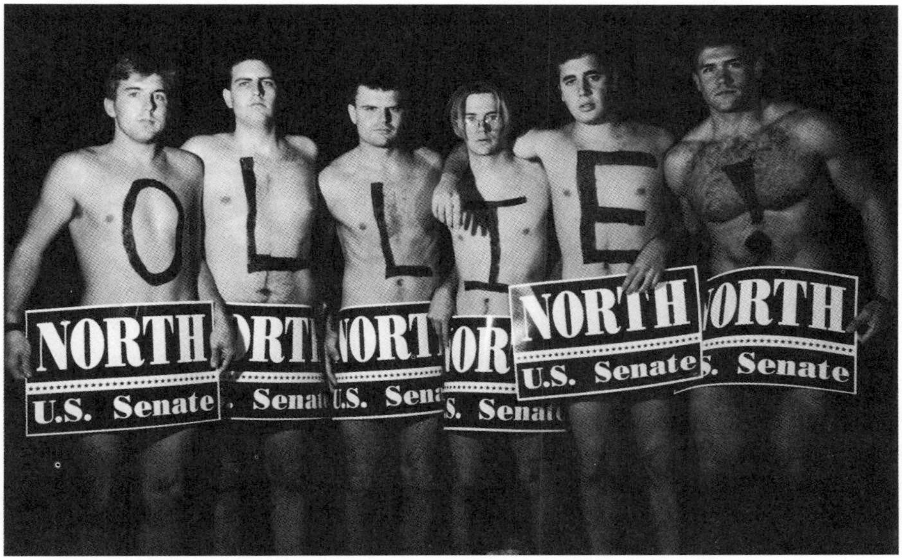

These James Madison University students were activists for Oliver North's candidacy for the U.S. Senate in 1994.

Figure 10.4 AMERICANS' PARTY IDENTIFICATION, 1952–1998

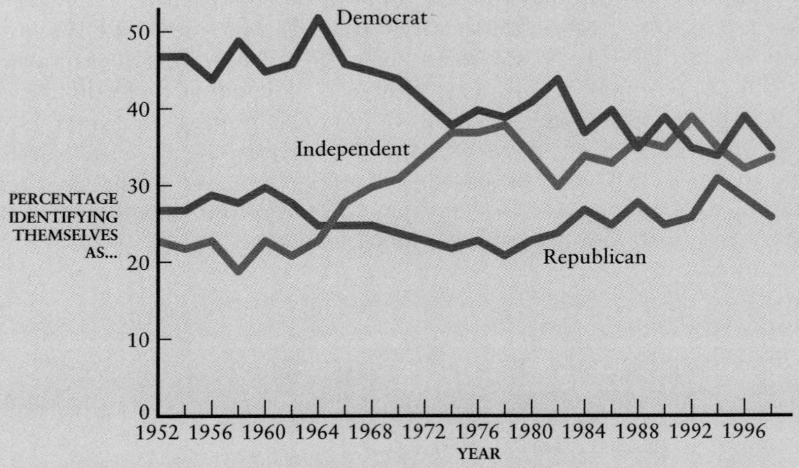

SOURCE: Harold W. Stanley and Richard G. Niemi, *Vital Statistics on American Politics, 1999–2000* (Washington, DC: Congressional Quarterly Press, 2000) p. 113.

consumers choose a brand of automobile for its appearance or mechanical characteristics and stick with it out of loyalty, habit, and unwillingness to constantly reexamine their choices, but they may eventually change if the old brand no longer serves their interests.

Although the strength of partisan ties in the United States has declined in recent years, most Americans continue to identify with either the Republican Party or the Democratic Party (see Figure 10.4). Party identification gives citizens a stake in election outcomes that goes beyond the particular race at hand. This is why strong party identifiers are more likely than other Americans to go to the polls and, of course, are more likely than others to support the party with which they identify. **Party activists** are drawn from the ranks of the strong identifiers. Activists are those who not only vote but also contribute their time, energy, and effort to party affairs. Activists ring doorbells, stuff envelopes, attend meetings, and contribute money to the party cause. No party could succeed without the thousands of volunteers who undertake the mundane tasks needed to keep the organization going.

party activists
partisans who contribute time, energy, and effort to support their party and its candidates

GROUP AFFILIATIONS

The Democratic and Republican parties are America's only national parties. They are the only political organizations that draw support from most regions of the country and from Americans of every racial, economic, religious, and ethnic group. The two parties do not draw equal support from members of every social stratum, however. When we refer to the Democratic or Republican "coalition," we mean the groups that generally support one or the other party. In the United States today, a variety of group characteristics are associated with party identification. These include race and ethnicity, gender, religion, class, ideology, and region.

Race and Ethnicity Since the 1930s and Franklin Roosevelt's New Deal, African Americans have been overwhelmingly Democratic in their party identification. More than 90 percent of African Americans describe themselves as Democrats and support Democratic candidates in national, state, and local elections. Approximately 25 percent of the Democratic Party's support in presidential races comes from African American voters.

Latino voters do not form a monolithic bloc, by contrast. Cuban Americans are generally Republican in their party affiliations, whereas Mexican Americans favor the Democrats by a small margin. Other Latino voters, including those from Puerto Rico, are overwhelmingly Democratic. Asian Americans tend to be divided as well, but along class lines. The Asian American community's influential business and professional stratum identifies with the Republicans, but less-affluent Asian Americans tend to support the Democrats.

Gender Women are somewhat more likely to support Democrats, and men somewhat more likely to support Republicans, in surveys of party affiliation. This difference is known as the **gender gap.** In the 1992 presidential election, women gave Bill Clinton 47 percent of their votes, while only 41 percent of the men who voted supported Clinton. In 1996, the gender gap was even more pronounced: women voted for Clinton 54 percent of the time, while only 43 percent of voting men did so.

gender gap
a distinctive pattern of voting behavior reflecting the differences in views between men and women

Religion Jews are among the Democratic Party's most loyal constituent groups and have been since the New Deal. Nearly 90 percent of all Jewish Americans describe themselves as Democrats. Catholics were also once a

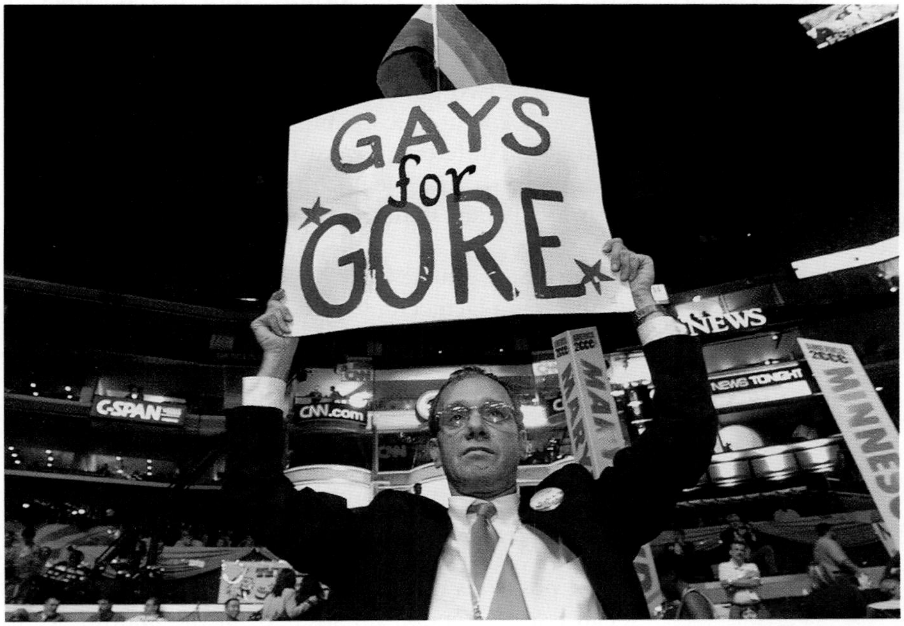

Sexual orientation can play a role in party affiliation. According to exit polls taken during the 2000 election, 70 percent of those identifying themselves as gay or lesbian voted for Al Gore; of those who did not identify themselves as gay or lesbian, 48 percent voted for Gore.

Students and Politics

Monica Daniels, 20, isn't going to vote in the March 7 Maryland primaries, part of the Super Tuesday lineup that may decide each party's presidential pick. But if the Baltimore legal assistant did vote, she might have cast her ballot for Republican George W. Bush.

"I like him," Daniels said. "I don't know why. Maybe because he's (President) Bush's son."

As Daniels attempted to explain her attraction to Bush as a candidate, her friend Keisha Eley, 19, erupted in laughter.

"You crazy, girl!" exclaimed Eley, a student at the Community College of Baltimore County. "He went to that Bob Jones college, talked about Catholics . . . I'm not Catholic but that ain't right. I wish (President) Clinton could run again."

Both young women are African American, and a generation ago, it might have been unthinkable for an African American to consider voting for a Republican candidate. And while young African Americans aren't jumping in large numbers to the GOP, studies show they are more willing than their parents and grandparents to stray from the Democratic Party.

About two hours away from Baltimore at the University of Maryland–Eastern Shore, a historically black college, a similar conversation occurs between a group of young African Americans in Waters Dining Hall, the main eating spot on campus.

"I like the Bush family," said Lockenvar Simpson, a twenty-year-old sophomore. Simpson, who described himself as an independent, said he probably would vote for Bush in Tuesday's primary.

"Are you sure about that?" asked senior Eric Brown, 22, who plans to vote for Vice President Al Gore. "If you let Republicans in, it will break down everything we've gained. We'll go back to the George Bush/Ronald Reagan era."

"What's wrong with the George Bush/Reagan era?" Simpson shot back.

"I don't like Reagan and Bush. I'm a Democrat," Brown answered.

Debates like the ones in Baltimore and the Eastern Shore illustrate the changing nature of African American voting patterns. David Bositis, a senior political analyst for the Joint Center for Political and Economic Studies, said various studies of African American political attitudes show that young blacks are less wedded to the Democratic Party than past generations.

SOURCE: Shannon Shelton, "Some Young African Americans Drawn to Republicans," Medill News Service, March 5, 2000.

strongly pro-Democratic group but have been shifting toward the Republican Party since the 1970s, when the GOP began to focus on abortion and other social issues deemed to be important to Catholics. Protestants are more likely to identify with the Republicans than with the Democrats. Protestant fundamentalists, in particular, have been drawn to the GOP's conservative stands on social issues, such as school prayer and abortion.

Class Upper-income Americans are considerably more likely to affiliate with the Republicans, whereas lower-income Americans are far more likely to identify with the Democrats. This divide is reflected by the differences between the two parties on economic issues. In general, the Republicans support cutting taxes and social spending—positions that reflect the interests of the wealthy. The Democrats, however, favor increasing social spending, even if this requires increasing taxes—a position consistent with the interests of less-affluent Americans. One important exception to this principle is that relatively affluent individuals who work in the public sector or such related institutions as foundations and universities also tend to affiliate with the Democrats. Such individuals are likely to appreciate the Democratic Party's support for an expanded governmental role and high levels of public spending.

Ideology Ideology and party identification are very closely linked. Most individuals who describe themselves as conservatives identify with the Republican Party, whereas most who call themselves liberals support the Democrats. This division has increased in recent years as the two parties have taken very different positions on social and economic issues. Before the 1970s, when party differences were more blurred, it was not uncommon to find Democratic conservatives and Republican liberals. Both these species are rare today.

Region Between the Civil War and the 1960s, the "Solid South" was a Democratic bastion. Today, the South is becoming solidly Republican, as is much of the West and Southwest. The area of greatest Democratic Party strength is the Northeast. The Midwest is a battleground, more or less evenly divided between the two parties.

The explanations for these regional variations are complex. Southern Republicanism has come about because conservative white southerners identify the Democratic Party with the civil rights movement and with liberal positions on abortion, school prayer, and other social issues. Republican strength in the South and in the West is also related to the weakness of organized labor in these regions, as well as to the dependence of the two regions upon military programs supported by the Republicans. Democratic strength in the Northeast is a function of the continuing influence of organized labor in the large cities of this region, as well as of the region's large population of minority and elderly voters, who benefit from Democratic social programs.

Age Age is another factor associated with partisanship. At the present time, individuals younger than fifty or older than sixty-five are fairly evenly divided between Democrats and Republicans, while those between the ages of fifty and sixty-four are much more likely to be Democrats. There is nothing about a particular numerical age that leads to a particular party loyalty. Instead, individuals from the same age cohort are likely to have experienced a similar set of events during the period when their party loyalties were formed. Thus, Americans between the ages of fifty and sixty-four came of political age during the cold-war, Vietnam, and civil-rights eras. Apparently among voters whose initial perceptions of politics were shaped during this period, more responded favorably to the role played by the Democrats than to the actions of the Republicans. Interestingly, among the youngest group of Americans, a group that came of age during an era of political scandals that tainted both parties, the majority describe themselves as Independents.

Figure 10.5 on the next page indicates the relationship between party identification and a number of social criteria. Race, religion, and income seem to have the greatest influence on Americans' party affiliations. None of these social characteristics are inevitably linked to partisan identification, however. There are black Republicans, southern white Democrats, Jewish Republicans, and even an occasional conservative Democrat. The general party identifications just discussed are broad tendencies that both reflect and reinforce the issue and policy positions the two parties take in the national and local political arenas.

Parties and Elections

▶ What are the important electoral functions of parties?

Parties play an important role in the electoral process. They provide the candidates for office, get out the vote, and facilitate mass electoral choice.

RECRUITING CANDIDATES

One of the most important but least noticed party activities is the recruitment of candidates for local, state, and national office. Each election year, candidates must be found for thousands of state and local offices as well as congressional seats. Where they do not have an incumbent running for re-election, party leaders attempt to identify strong candidates and to interest them in entering the campaign.

Figure 10.5 PARTY IDENTIFICATION BY SOCIAL GROUPS, 1999

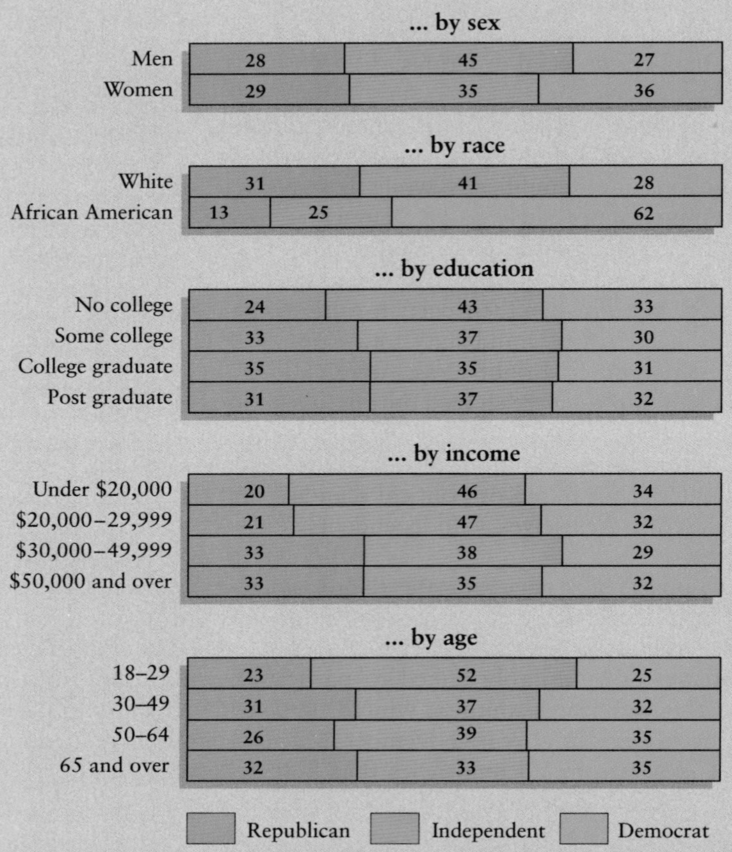

SOURCE: Harold W. Stanley and Richard G. Niemi, *Vital Statistics on American Politics, 1999–2000* (Washington, DC: Congressional Quarterly Press, 2000), p. 115.

An ideal candidate will have an unblemished record and the capacity to raise enough money to mount a serious campaign. Party leaders are usually not willing to provide financial backing to candidates who are unable to raise substantial funds on their own. For a House seat this can mean several hundred thousand dollars; for a Senate seat a serious candidate must be able to raise several million dollars. Often, party leaders have difficulty finding attractive candidates and persuading them to run. In 1998, for example, Democratic leaders in Kansas and Washington reported difficulties in recruiting congressional candidates. A number of potential candidates reportedly were reluctant to leave their homes and families for the hectic life of a member of Congress. GOP leaders in Washington and Massachusetts have had similar problems finding candidates to oppose popular Democratic incumbents.[12] Candidate recruitment has become particularly difficult in an era when political campaigns often involve mudslinging and candidates must assume that their personal lives will be intensely scrutinized in the press.[13]

NOMINATIONS

Article I, Section 4, of the Constitution makes only a few provisions for elections. It delegates to the states the power to set the "times, places, and manner" of holding elections, even for U.S. senators and representatives. It does, however, reserve to Congress the power to make such laws if it chooses to do so. The Constitution has been amended from time to time to expand the right to participate in elections. Congress has also occasionally passed laws about elections, congressional districting, and campaign practices. But the Constitution and the laws are almost completely silent on nominations, setting only citizenship and age requirements for candidates. The president must be at least thirty-five years of age, a natural-born citizen, and a resident of the United States for fourteen years. A senator must be at least thirty, a U.S. citizen for at least nine years, and a resident of the state he or she represents. A member of the House must be at least twenty-five, a U.S. citizen for seven years, and a resident of the state he or she represents.

Nomination is the process by which a party selects a single candidate to run for each elective office. The nominating process can precede the election by many months, as it does when the many candidates for the presidency are eliminated from consideration through a grueling series of debates and state primaries until there is only one survivor in each party—the party's nominee.

nomination
the process through which political parties select their candidates for election to public office

Nomination is the parties' most serious and difficult business. When more than one person aspires to an office, the choice can divide friends and associates. In comparison to such an internal dispute, the electoral campaign against the opposition is almost fun, because there the fight is against the declared adversaries.

GETTING OUT THE VOTE

The actual election period begins immediately after the nominations. Historically, this has been a time of glory for the political parties, whose popular base of support is fully displayed. All the paraphernalia of party committees and all the committee members are activated into local party work forces

The first step in the electoral process involves voter registration. This aspect of the process takes place all year round. There was a time when party workers were responsible for virtually all of this kind of electoral activity, but they have been supplemented (and in many states virtually displaced) by civic groups such as the League of Women Voters, unions, and chambers of commerce.

Those who have registered have to decide on election day whether to go to the polling place, stand in line, and actually vote for the various candidates and referenda on the ballot. Political parties, candidates, and campaigning can make a big difference in convincing the voters to vote.

FACILITATING VOTER CHOICE

On any general election ballot, there are likely to be only two or three candidacies where the nature of the office and the characteristics and positions of the

Parties are responsible for nominating candidates to run for office. Here, the 2000 Republican presidential hopefuls get ready for a televised debate.

candidates are well known to voters. But what about the choices for judges, the state comptroller, the state attorney general, and many other elective positions? And what about referenda? This method of making policy choices is being used more and more as a means of direct democracy. A referendum may ask: Should there be a new bond issue for financing the local schools? Should there be a constitutional amendment to increase the number of county judges? In 1996, Californians approved Proposition 201, a referendum that called for an end to most statewide affirmative action programs, including those employed for college admission. Another famous proposition on the 1978 California ballot was a referendum to reduce local property taxes. It started a taxpayer revolt that spread to many other states. By the time it had spread, most voters knew where they stood on the issue. But the typical referendum question is one on which few voters have clear and knowledgeable positions. Parties and campaigns help most by giving information when voters must choose among obscure candidates and vote on unclear referenda.

Parties and Government

▶ How do the differences between Democrats and Republicans affect Congress, the president, and the policy making process?

When the dust of the campaign has settled, does it matter which party has won? It can.

PARTIES AND POLICY

One of the most familiar observations about American politics is that the two major parties try to be all things to all people and are therefore indistinguishable from each other. Data and experience give some support to this observation. Parties in the United States are not programmatic or ideological, as they have sometimes been in Britain or other parts of Europe. But this does not mean there are no differences between them. Since the 1980s, important differences have emerged between the positions of Democratic and Republican party leaders on a number of key issues, and these differences are still apparent today. For example, the national leadership of the Republican Party supports maintaining high levels of military spending, cuts in social programs, tax relief for middle- and upper-income voters, tax incentives to businesses, and the "social agenda" backed by members of conservative religious denominations. The national Democratic leadership, on the other hand, supports expanded social welfare spending, cuts in military spending, increased regulation of business, and a variety of consumer and environmental programs.

These differences reflect differences in philosophy and differences in the core constituencies to which the parties seek to appeal. The Democratic Party at the national level seeks to unite organized labor, the poor, members of racial minorities, and liberal upper-middle-class professionals. The Republicans, by contrast, appeal to business, upper-middle- and upper-class groups in the private sector, and social conservatives. Often, party leaders will seek to develop issues they hope will add new groups to their party's constituent base. During the 1980s, for example, under the leadership of Ronald Reagan, the Republicans devised a series of "social issues," including support for school prayer, opposition to abortion, and opposition to affirmative action, designed to cultivate the support of white southerners. This effort was extremely successful in increasing Republican strength in the once solidly Democratic South. In the 1990s, under the leadership of Bill Clinton, who called himself a "new Democrat," the Democratic Party sought to develop new social programs designed to solidify the party's base among working-class and poor voters, and new, somewhat more conservative economic programs aimed at attracting the votes of middle- and upper-middle-class voters.

As these examples suggest, parties do not always support policies just because they are already favored by their constituents. Instead, party leaders can play the role of **policy entrepreneurs,** seeking ideas and programs that will expand their party's base of support while eroding that of the opposition. It is one of the essential characteristics of party politics in America that a party's programs and policies often lead, rather than follow, public opinion. Like their counterparts in the business world, party leaders seek to identify and develop "products" (programs and policies) that will appeal to the public. The public, of course, has the ultimate voice. With its votes it decides whether or not to "buy" new policy offerings.

policy entrepreneur
an individual who identifies a problem as a political issue and brings a policy proposal into the political agenda

Thus, for example, in 1999, Democratic presidential hopefuls Al Gore and Bill Bradley both proposed new programs in the realms of health care, education, and social services, which they hoped would expand their own political bases as well as increase support for the Democratic Party. On the Republican side, Senator John McCain championed the issue of campaign finance reform.

PARTIES IN CONGRESS

The ultimate test of the party system is its relationship to and influence on the institutions of government. Congress, in particular, depends more on the party

majority party

the party that holds the majority of legislative seats in either the House or the Senate

minority party

the party that holds a minority of legislative seats in either the House or the Senate

system than is generally recognized. For one thing, the speakership of the House is essentially a party office. All the members of the House take part in the election of the Speaker. But the actual selection is made by the **majority party,** that is, the party that holds a majority of seats in the House. (The other party is known as the **minority party.**) When the majority party caucus presents a nominee to the entire House, its choice is then invariably ratified in a straight vote along party lines.

The committee system of both houses of Congress is also a product of the two-party system. Although the rules organizing committees and the rules defining the jurisdiction of each are adopted like ordinary legislation by the whole membership, all other features of the committees are shaped by parties. For example, each party is assigned a quota of members for each committee, depending upon the percentage of total seats held by the party. On the rare occasions when an independent or third-party candidate is elected, the leaders of the two parties must agree against whose quota this member's committee assignments will count. Presumably the member will not be able to serve on any committee until the question of quota is settled.

As we shall see in Chapter 13, the assignment of individual members to committees is a party decision. Each party has a "committee on committees" to make such decisions. Permission to transfer to another committee is also a party decision. Moreover, advancement up the committee ladder toward the chair is a party decision. Since the late nineteenth century, most advancements have been automatic—based upon the length of continual service on the committee. This seniority system has existed only because of the support of the two parties, however, and either party can depart from it by a simple vote. During the 1970s, both parties reinstituted the practice of reviewing each chair—voting anew every two years on whether each committee's chair would continue to be held by the same person. In their 1994 campaign document, the "Contract with America," House Republican candidates pledged to limit committee and subcommittee chairs to three two-year terms if the GOP won control of Congress. For years, Republicans had argued that entrenched Democratic committee chairs had become powerful, arrogant, and indifferent to the popular will. When Republicans took control of Congress in 1994, they reaffirmed their pledge to limit the terms of committee and subcommittee chairs. As they approached the 2000 congressional elections, however, some GOP leaders now regretted the commitment they had made six years earlier. Powerful Republican committee chairs were not very enthusiastic about the idea of surrendering their positions if the GOP maintained control of the House. Some Republican committee chairs hoped to trade positions with one another and begin new stints in charge of new panels. Younger members who had hoped to benefit from the three-term rule by claiming the vacated chairs were prepared to fight for what they now regarded as their due. Thus, a pledge made in 1994 when the GOP was out of power seemed to portend sharp conflicts among Republican members if the GOP retained power in 2000.

The continuing importance of parties in Congress became especially evident after the Republicans won control of Congress in 1994. During the first few months of the 104th Congress, the Republican leadership was able to maintain nearly unanimous support among party members on vote after vote as it sought to implement the GOP's legislative agenda. Between 1995 and 1999, however, splits within the party began to surface over issues such as welfare reform and balancing the budget. This legislative struggle will be discussed further in Chapter 13.

PRESIDENT AND PARTY

As we saw earlier, the party that wins the White House is always led, in title anyway, by the president. The president normally depends upon fellow party members in Congress to support legislative initiatives. At the same time, members of the party in Congress hope that the president's programs and personal prestige will help them raise campaign funds and secure re-election. During his two terms in office, President Bill Clinton had a mixed record as party leader. In the realm of trade policy, Clinton sometimes found more support among Republicans than among Democrats. In addition, although Clinton proved to be an extremely successful fund-raiser, congressional Democrats often complained that he failed to share his largesse with them. At the same time, however, a number of Clinton's policy initiatives seemed calculated to strengthen the Democratic Party as a whole. Clinton's early health care initiative would have linked millions of voters to the Democrats for years to come, much as FDR's Social Security program had done in a previous era. But by the middle of Clinton's second term, the president's acknowledgement of his sexual affair with a White House intern threatened his position as party leader. Initially, Democratic candidates nationwide feared that the scandal would undermine their own chances for election, and many moved to distance themselves from the president. The Democrats' surprisingly good showing in the 1998 elections, however, strengthened Clinton's position and gave him another chance to shape the Democratic agenda.

Between the 1998 and 2000 elections, however, the president's initiatives on Social Security and nuclear disarmament failed to make much headway in a Republican-controlled Congress. The GOP was not prepared to give Clinton anything for which Democrats could claim credit in the 2000 elections. Lacking strong congressional leadership, however, the GOP did agree to many of Clinton's budgetary proposals in 1999 and dropped its own plan for large-scale cuts in federal taxes. Clinton's popular approval rating fell slightly after 1998 as some Americans apparently decided they had had enough of Bill Clinton. Some pundits called this "Clinton fatigue." In his 2000 presidential bid, Vice President Al Gore took great pains to distance himself from his old friend and boss. In an October 1999 debate with Bill Bradley, Gore said he had felt "anger and disappointment" toward President Clinton after the previous year's revelations of Clinton's sexual misconduct.[14]

Parties and Democracy

▶ Do parties help or hinder democracy?

Democracy and political parties arose together in the modern world. Without democracy, a system of competing political parties never could have emerged.

Politics on the Web

Political party organizations were among the earliest users of the Internet. Parties recognized that Internet Web sites were an easy, inexpensive way to establish a public presence on an emerging medium, promote ideological and policy positions, and perhaps even recruit members. National party sites have become forums where Democrats and Republicans can continue policy debates. Although obviously partisan, these sites can provide a fascinating unmediated look at the official party stance on many current issues.

The Internet also provides a forum for nontraditional political parties. Anyone with a modem and a text editor can set up a Web site. Obscure entities such as the New Party, the Patriot Party, and the Pansexual Party coexist with the Communists, the Libertarians, and Ross Perot's We the People Party. The Internet may help existing third parties raise money, advertise their positions, and gain recruits; it may also encourage the formation of new political parties.

www.wwnorton.com/wtp3e

At the same time, without a system of competing political parties, democracy never could have flourished. Without a strong opposition, rulers never would have surrendered power, and without well-organized parties, ordinary people never could have acquired or used the right to vote. It is because of this strong historical association between democracy and political parties that the current weakness of American political parties is a matter of concern.

Healthy political parties are extremely important for maintaining political equality, democracy, and liberty in America. First, strong parties are generally an essential ingredient for effective electoral competition by groups lacking substantial economic or institutional resources. Party building has typically been the strategy pursued by groups that must organize the collective energies of large numbers of individuals to counter their opponents' superior material means or institutional standing. Historically, disciplined and coherent party organizations were generally developed first by groups representing the political aspirations of the working classes. Parties, French political scientist Maurice Duverger notes, "are always more developed on the Left than on the Right because they are always more necessary on the Left than on the Right."[15] In the United States, the first mass party was built by the Jeffersonians as a counterweight to the superior social, institutional, and economic resources that could be deployed by the incumbent Federalists. In a subsequent period of American history, the efforts of the Jacksonians to construct a coherent mass party organization were impelled by a similar set of circumstances. Only by organizing the power of numbers could the Jacksonian coalition hope to compete successfully against the superior resources that could be mobilized by its adversaries.

In the United States, the political success of party organizations forced their opponents to copy them in order to meet the challenge. It was, as Duverger points out, "contagion from the Left" that led politicians of the Center and Right to attempt to build strong party organizations.[16] These efforts were sometimes successful. In the United States during the 1830s, the Whig Party, which was led by northeastern business interests, carefully copied the effective organizational techniques devised by the Jacksonians. The Whigs won control of the national government in 1840. But even when groups nearer the top of the social scale responded in kind to organizational efforts by their inferiors, the net effect nonetheless was to give lower-class groups an opportunity to compete on a more equal footing. In the absence of coherent mass organization, middle- and upper-class factions almost inevitably have a substantial competitive edge over their lower-class rivals. Even when both sides organize, the net effect is still to erode the relative advantage of the well-off.

Second, political parties are bulwarks of liberty. The Constitution certainly provides for freedom of speech, freedom of assembly, and freedom of the press. Maintaining these liberties, though, requires more than parchment guarantees. Of course, as long as freedom is not seriously threatened, abstract guarantees suffice to protect it. If, however, those in power actually threaten citizens' liberties, the preservation of freedom may come to depend upon the presence of a coherent and well-organized opposition. As we saw earlier in this chapter, in the first years of the Republic, it was not the Constitution or the courts that preserved free speech in the face of Federalist efforts to silence the government's critics; it was the vigorous action of the Jeffersonian-Republican opposition that saved liberty. To this day, the presence of an opposition party serves as a fundamentally important check on attempts by those in power to skirt the law and infringe upon citizens' liberties. For example, twenty-five years ago, although it was the news media that revealed President Richard Nixon's abuses of power, the concerted efforts of Nixon's Democratic opponents in Congress were required finally to drive the president from office.

Third, parties promote voter turnout. Party competition has long been known to be a key factor in stimulating voting. As political scientists Stanley Kelley, Richard Ayres, and William Bowen note, competition gives citizens an incentive to vote and politicians an incentive to get them to vote.[17] The origins of the American national electorate can be traced to the competitive organizing activities of the Jeffersonian Republicans and the Federalists. According to historian David Fischer,

> During the 1790s the Jeffersonians revolutionized electioneering. . . . Their opponents complained bitterly of endless "dinings," "drinkings," and celebrations; of handbills "industriously posted along every road"; of convoys of vehicles which brought voters to the polls by the carload; of candidates "in perpetual motion."[18]

The Federalists, although initially reluctant, soon learned the techniques of mobilizing voters: "mass meetings, barbecues, stump-speaking, festivals of many kinds, processions and parades, runners and riders, door-to-door canvassing, the distribution of tickets and ballots, . . . free transportation to the polls, outright bribery and corruption of other kinds."[19]

The result of this competition for votes was described by historian Henry Jones Ford in his classic *Rise and Growth of American Politics*.[20] Ford examined the popular clamor against John Adams and Federalist policies in the 1790s that made government a "weak, shakey affair" and appeared to contemporary observers to mark the beginnings of a popular insurrection against the government.[21] Attempts by the Federalists initially to suppress mass discontent, Ford observed, might have "caused an explosion of force which would have blown up the government."[22] What intervened to prevent rebellion was Jefferson's "great unconscious achievement," the creation of an opposition party that served to "open constitutional channels of political agitation."[23] The creation of the Jeffersonian Republican Party diverted opposition to the administration into electoral channels. Party competition gave citizens a sense that their votes were valuable and that it was thus not necessary to take to the streets to have an impact upon political affairs. Whether or not Ford was correct in crediting party competition with an ability to curb civil unrest, it is clear that competition between the parties promoted voting.

Finally, political parties make democratic government possible. We often do not appreciate that democratic government is a contradiction in terms. Government implies policies, programs, and decisive action. Democracy, on the other hand, implies an opportunity for all citizens to participate fully in the governmental process. The contradiction is that full participation by everyone is often inconsistent with getting anything done. At what point should participation stop and governance begin? How can we make certain that popular participation will result in a government capable of making decisions and developing needed policies? The problem of democratic government is especially acute in the United States because of the system of separated powers bequeathed to us by the Constitution's framers. Our system of separated powers means that it is very difficult to link popular participation and effective decision making.

Often, after the citizens have spoken and the dust has settled, no single set of political forces has been able to win control of enough of the scattered levers of power to actually do anything. Instead of government, we have a continual political struggle.

Strong political parties are a partial antidote to the inherent contradiction between participation and government. Strong parties can both encourage popular involvement and convert participation into effective government. More than fifty years ago, a committee of the academic American Political Science Association (APSA) called for the development of a more "responsible" party government. By **responsible party government,** the committee meant political parties that mobilized voters and were sufficiently well organized to develop and implement coherent programs and policies after the election. Strong parties can link democratic participation and government.

responsible party government
a set of principles that idealizes a strong role for parties in defining their stance on issues, mobilizing voters, and fulfilling their campaign promises once in office

Although they are significant factors in politics and government, American political parties today are not as strong as the "responsible parties" advocated by the APSA. Many politicians are able to raise funds, attract volunteers and win office without much help from local party organizations. Once in office, these politicians have no particular reason to submit to party discipline; instead they steer independent courses. They are often supported by voters who see independence as a virtue and party discipline as "boss rule." Sometimes analysts refer to this pattern as a "candidate-centered" politics to distinguish it from a political process in which parties are the dominant forces. The problem with a candidate-centered politics is that it tends to be associated with low turnout, high levels of special-interest influence, and a lack of effective decision making. In short, many of the problems that have plagued American politics in recent years can be traced directly to the independence of American voters and politicians and the candidate-centered nature of American national politics.

The health of America's parties should be a source of concern to all citizens who value liberty, equality, and democracy. Can political parties be strengthened? The answer is, in principle, yes. For example, political parties could be strengthened if the rules governing campaign finance were revised to make candidates more dependent financially upon state and local party organizations rather than on personal resources or private contributors. Such a reform, to be sure, would require more strict regulation of party fund-raising practices to prevent the types of "soft money" abuses you will read about in Chapter 11. The potential benefit, however, of a greater party role in political finance could be substantial. If parties controlled the bulk of the campaign funds, they would become more coherent and disciplined, and might come to resemble the responsible parties envisioned by the APSA. Political parties have been such important features of American democratic politics that we need to think long and hard about how to preserve and strengthen them.

The Citizen's Role

American political parties are very open to citizen involvement. Students who attend local party meetings and volunteer to assist with communication and fund-raising efforts are usually welcome. In the nineteenth century, the national parties could rely upon the efforts of tens of thousands of patronage employees who were obligated to engage in political work. Today, the parties rely upon volunteers and enthusiasts. (For addresses and telephone numbers, check your local phone directory or check the World Wide Web for the addresses of the state and national party organizations.)

STUDENTS AND POLITICS

For some students, such volunteer work is the first step in a political career. For example, Cruz Bustamante, who in 1997 became the first Latino elected to be Speaker of the California state assembly, began his political career as a volunteer worker for local Democratic politicians in the Fresno, California, area. Interested in such issues as immigration, health care, and the status of farm workers, Bustamante saw politics as the best vehicle for doing something about these issues. In 1973, at the age of nineteen, he went to Washington as a congressional intern. He was not paid for his internship and needed support from his parents and five brothers and sisters who worked in the fields as agricultural laborers. After returning to California, Bustamante worked as a staff assistant to several Democratic legislators, and was elected to the legislature in 1993. In 1997, Bustamante replaced Assembly Speaker Willie Brown, who was unable to seek re-election because of the state's new term-limits law.[24]

Much of the work undertaken by party organizations at the local level is quite mundane. Thousands of envelopes are filled and sealed. A seemingly infinite number of postage stamps are licked. Many meetings are held. Politics at the "grass roots" is not very glamorous. However, if politics were only glamorous it could not be democratic. Grassroots party activity helps to ensure that the more glamorous world of Washington remains tied and responsive to Bozeman, Long Beach, Raleigh, and Utica. State and even national party leaders pay close attention to the views of local party organizations and activists. They depend upon these local organizations for ideas, for campaign workers, and often, for candidates. Many prominent politicians, including President Clinton, were themselves once young volunteers in a local party organization.

GET INVOLVED: Becoming a Party Activist

The American founders were suspicious of political parties. They saw parties as selfish factions that masqueraded under the banner of the public good. Nevertheless, political parties quickly developed into enduring institutions in which like-minded people organized themselves, built networks of influence, solicited public support, and put forth candidates for political office. The United States has had many political parties but, most of the time, two major parties have dominated the competition.

Today, the major parties are composed of a national organization and many state and local organizations. The parties conduct a broad range of activities. They sponsor speakers to influence people's ideas, conduct voter registration drives, solicit money to support campaign activities, and seek citizens' votes. Their busiest season is the time just prior to an election, especially a presidential election. That is when party candidates need a lot of people's time, energy, and money to run for office at local, regional, state, and national levels of government.

How do you become a party activist? First, decide which political party best represents your own values and visions. Most Americans who identify with a particular political party choose the Democratic Party or the Republican Party. If you think these parties are too close together on important issues, or if you are not particularly enamored of party politics "as usual," you may want to consider the Reform Party, the Green Party, the Natural Law Party, the Peace and Freedom Party, or other parties soliciting members and support. Determine which political party best captures your sympathies and passions.

Next, see if your campus has a student organization that is affiliated with the party that interests you. Many campuses have student chapters of the Democratic and Republican parties as well as some of the smaller parties. These campus chapters are likely to be linked to other campus chapters as well as to the local and state offices of the parties. These affiliates are always looking for new members with interest, enthusiasm, and commitment.

Alternatively, your school or political science department may have an internship program or an intern coordinating office. Local branches of political parties regularly work with internship offices to attract young people to their parties as well as to get energetic volunteers to perform innumerable labor-intensive tasks such as stuffing envelopes, manning phone banks, and knocking on doors. The advantages of taking this route to party activism are (1) program contacts should make it relatively easy for you to connect with the party of your choice and (2) you may be able to receive academic credit for your party involvement.

Still another option is to contact the party of your choice directly. If you want to work with one of the two major parties, consider doing the following.

- If you are a Democrat, contact the Democratic National Committee (DNC). The DNC can be reached by mail at 430 S. Capitol St., S.E., Washington, DC 20003. Or you can call the DNC at 202-863-8000. The DNC also has a Web site at http://www.democrats.org that contains general information about the Democratic Party plus links to available jobs and internships. Equally important, the Web site also directs you to contact information for all of the state Democratic Party organizations. In turn, the individual state Web pages have details on local opportunities for membership and participation.
- If you prefer the Republican Party, contact the Republican National Committee (RNC). The RNC can be reached by mail at 310 First Street, S.E., Washington, DC 20003, and by telephone at 202-863-8500. The RNC also has a Web site at http://www.rnc.org that contains general information about the Republican Party, its various activities, and job opportunities. It also has links to the individual state party offices, with each state Web site providing additional information on local contacts and involvement in party activities.

If your sympathies are not with the two major political parties, contact the party of your choice by inserting its name in a search engine (such as http://www.google.com), which should direct you to its Web site. Becoming an activist in one of the smaller parties means that you will be able to participate in a cause that deeply concerns you, even though the likelihood of your party's candidates winning public office is quite small.

Summary

Political parties seek to control government by controlling its personnel. Elections are one means to this end. Thus, parties take shape from the electoral process.

The two-party system dominates U.S. politics. During the course of American history, the government has generally been dominated by one or the other party for long periods of time. This is generally followed by a period of realignment during which new groups attempt to seize power and the previously dominant party may be displaced by its rival. There have been five electoral realignments in American political history.

Third parties are short-lived for several reasons. They have limited electoral support, the tradition of the two-party system is strong, and a major party often adopts the platform of a third party. Single-member districts with two competing parties also discourage third parties.

Party organizations exist at every level of American government. The national party organizations are generally less important than the state and local party units. Each party's national committee and congressional campaign committees help to recruit candidates and raise money. The national conventions have, for the most part, lost their nominating functions, but still play an important role in determining party rules and party platforms.

Parties influence voting through the ties of party identification, particularly the strong ties formed with party activists. A variety of group characteristics can influence party identification, including race and ethnicity, gender, religion, class, ideology, and region.

Nominating and electing are the basic functions of parties. Parties are critical for getting out the vote, recruiting candidates, facilitating popular choice, and organizing the government. Strong parties are essential to the continuing vitality of American democracy.

FOR FURTHER READING

Aldrich, John H. *Why Parties? The Origin and Transformation of Political Parties in America.* Chicago: University of Chicago Press, 1995.

Andersen, Kristi. *After Suffrage: Women in Partisan and Electoral Politics before the New Deal.* Chicago: University of Chicago Press, 1996.

Carmines, Edward G., and James A. Stimson. *Issue Evolution: Race and the Transformation of American Politics.* Princeton, NJ: Princeton University Press, 1989.

Edsall, Thomas Byrne, and Mary D. Edsall. *Chain Reaction: The Impact of Race, Rights, and Taxes on American Politics.* New York: Norton, 1993.

Gerring, John. *Party Ideologies in America.* New York: Cambridge University Press, 1998.

Gilmour, John B. *Strategic Disagreement: Stalemate in American Politics.* Pittsburgh, PA: University of Pittsburgh Press, 1995.

Green, John C., and Daniel M. Shea, eds. *The State of the Parties: The Changing Role of Contemporary Parties.* 2d ed. Lanham, MD: Rowman and Littlefield, 1996.

Lawson, Kay, and Peter Merkl. *When Parties Fail: Emerging Alternative Organizations.* Princeton, NJ: Princeton University Press, 1988.

Milkis, Sidney. *The President and the Parties: The Transformation of the American Party System since the New Deal.* New York: Oxford University Press, 1993.

Shefter, Martin. *Political Parties and the State: The American Historical Experience.* Princeton, NJ: Princeton University Press, 1994.

STUDY OUTLINE

1. In modern history, political parties have been the chief points of contact between governments and groups and forces in society. By organizing political parties, social forces attempt to gain some control over government policies and personnel.

What Are Political Parties?

1. Political parties as they are known today developed along with the expansion of suffrage, and actually took their shape from the electoral process.
2. Political parties, as coalitions of those with similar interests, are also important in making policy.

The Two-Party System in America

1. Historically, parties originate through either internal or external mobilization by those seeking to win governmental power.
2. The Democratic Party originated through a process of internal mobilization, as the Jeffersonian Party splintered into four factions in 1824, and Andrew Jackson emerged as the leader of one of these four groups.
3. The Republican Party grew through a process of external mobilization as antislavery groups formed a new party to oppose the 1854 Kansas-Nebraska Act.
4. The United States has experienced five realigning eras, which occur when the established political elite weakens sufficiently to permit the creation of new coalitions of forces capable of capturing and holding the reins of government.
5. American third parties have always represented social and economic protests ignored by the other parties.

Party Organization

1. Party organizations exist at virtually every level of American government—usually taking the form of committees made up of active party members.
2. Although national party conventions no longer have the power to nominate presidential candidates, they are still important in determining the party's rules and platform.
3. The national committee and the congressional campaign committees play important roles in recruiting candidates and raising money.

Parties and the Electorate

1. Individuals tend to form psychological ties with parties, called "party identification." This identification often follows demographic, ideological, and regional lines.

Parties and Elections

1. Parties are important in the electoral process for recruiting and nominating candidates for office.
2. Though not as important today as in the past, parties also can make a big difference in convincing voters to vote.
3. Parties also help voters choose among candidates.

Parties and Government

1. The differences between the two parties reflects a general difference in philosophy but also an attempt to appeal to core constituencies. These differences are often reflected in the policy agenda that party leaders adopt.
2. Political parties help to organize Congress. Congressional leadership and the committee system are both products of the two-party system.
3. The president serves as an informal party head by seeking support from congressional members of the party and by supporting their bids for re-election.

Parties and Democracy

1. Democracy depends on strong parties, which promote electoral competition and voter turnout and enable governance through their organizations in Congress.
2. The ties that parties have to the electorate are historically weak; the resulting "candidate-centered" politics has some negative consequences, including lower voter turnout, increased influence of interest groups, and a lack of effective decision making by elected leaders.
3. Parties could be strengthened through effective campaign finance reform.

PRACTICE QUIZ

1. A political party is different from an interest group in that a political party
   a) seeks to control the entire government by electing its members to office and thereby controlling the government's personnel.
   b) seeks to control only limited, very specific, functions of government.
   c) is entirely nonprofit.
   d) has a much smaller membership.

2. The periodic episodes in American history in which an "old" dominant political party is replaced by a "new" dominant political party are called
   a) constitutional revolutions.
   b) party turnovers.
   c) presidential elections.
   d) electoral realignments.

3. Through which mechanism did Boss Tweed and other party leaders in the late nineteenth and early twentieth centuries maintain their control?
   a) civil service reform
   b) soft money contributions
   c) machine politics
   d) electoral reform

4. On what level are U.S. political parties organized?
   a) national
   b) state
   c) county
   d) all of the above

5. Contemporary national party conventions are important because they
   a) determine the party's presidential candidate.
   b) determine the party's rules and platform.
   c) both a and b are correct.
   d) neither a nor b is correct.

6. Which party was founded as a political expression of the antislavery movement?
   a) American Independent
   b) Prohibition
   c) Republican
   d) Democratic

7. Historically, when do realignments occur?
   a) typically, every twenty years
   b) whenever a minority party takes over Congress
   c) when large numbers of voters permanently shift their support from one party to another
   d) in odd-numbered years

8. Parties today are most important in the electoral process in
   a) recruiting and nominating candidates for office.
   b) financing all of the campaign's spending.
   c) providing millions of volunteers to mobilize voters.
   d) creating a responsible party government.

9. What role do parties play in Congress?
   a) They select leaders, e.g., Speaker of the House.
   b) They assign members to committees.
   c) Both a and b are correct.
   d) Parties play no role in Congress.

10. Parties are important to democracy because they
   a) encourage electoral competition.
   b) promote voter turnout.
   c) make governance possible by organizing elected leaders into governing coalitions.
   d) all of the above.

CRITICAL THINKING QUESTIONS

1. Describe the factors that have contributed to the overall weakening of political parties in America. How are parties weaker? How do they remain important? What are the advantages of a political system with weak political parties? What are the disadvantages?

2. Historically, third parties have developed in American history when certain issues or constituencies have been ignored by the existing parties. Considering the similarities and differences between the Democratic and Republican parties, where might a budding third party find a constituency? What issues might it adopt? Finally, what structural and ideological obstacles might that third party face?

KEY TERMS

caucus (political) (p. 362)
divided government (p. 356)
electoral realignment (p. 356)
gender gap (p. 371)
machines (p. 368)
majority party (p. 378)
minority party (p. 378)
multiple-member district (p. 360)
national convention (p. 362)
nomination (p. 375)
party activists (p. 370)
party identification (p. 369)
party organization (p. 362)
patronage (p. 368)
platform (p. 366)
plurality system (p. 360)
policy entrepreneur (p. 377)
political parties (p. 349)
proportional representation (p. 360)
responsible party government (p. 382)
single-member district (p. 360)
soft money (p. 369)
third parties (p. 359)
two-party system (p. 350)

11 Campaigns

★ **The Role of Elections in a Democracy**

What functions do elections serve in the political process?

★ **Elections in America**

What different types of elections are held in the United States? What rules determine who wins elections?

How does the government determine the boundaries of electoral districts? How is the ballot determined?

★ **Election Campaigns**

What are the steps in a successful election campaign?

★ **Presidential Elections**

How is the president elected?

What factors have the greatest impact on a general election campaign?

★ **Money and Politics**

How do candidates raise and spend campaign funds? How does the government regulate campaign spending?

How does money affect how certain social groups achieve electoral success?

★ **How Voters Decide**

What are the primary influences on voters' decisions?

and Elections

STUDENTS AND POLITICS

IN the American tradition, elections are closely linked to questions of residence. Unlike Britain and a number of other nations, we require candidates for office to live in the jurisdictions they represent. In 2000, Hillary Rodham Clinton moved her official residence to the village of Chappaqua, New York, to qualify to run for the senate seat from New York that had been held by Daniel Patrick Moynihan, an influential Democrat who decided not to seek re-election. Even so, many Republicans accused the First Lady of being a "carpetbagger" who was not really familiar with the needs of the people of New York.

Not only does America require political candidates to live in the jurisdiction they represent, but U.S. election laws specify that citizens must actually reside in the jurisdiction where they wish to register to vote. Until a series of Supreme Court decisions in the 1960s and 1970s banned the practice, many state and local governments stipulated long terms of residence—often a year or more—before a newcomer was allowed to register. Today, residence requirements are typically fifteen days—just long enough for the local election board to complete the paperwork needed to add a new voter to the rolls.

College students often face a unique residence issue when they seek to register and vote. Often, students would like to vote where they attend college. Most American elections are held in November, during the school year, so voting at their parents' place of residence may require students to engage in the cumbersome process of casting absentee ballots. Moreover, as we have seen, students are often affected by a variety of local ordinances and policies, ranging from rules governing noisy parties through regulations managing the relationships between tenants and landlords, that give them a serious stake in the politics and policies of the municipalities in which their school is located.

While students may wish to vote where they attend school, the permanent residents and elected officials of these regions typically do not relish the idea of thousands of college students registering in their county. The area's permanent residents often view college students as transient outsiders lacking a long-term stake in the community. Public officials may simply see student voters as a threat to their own positions. For these reasons, many municipalities have sought to bar students from registering. Typically, however, the courts have ruled such local prohibitions to be unconstitutional. For example, District of Columbia courts recently struck down an effort by the city's government to prevent students from voting in Advisory Neighborhood Commission elections. As a result, student voters helped to elect two George Washington University students to the Commission governing the Foggy Bottom area of Washington, D.C., in which the university is located.[1]

Recently, opponents of student voting in Michigan sought to circumvent such court bans on restrictive local ordinances by introducing statewide legislation that would require all Michigan students to list the same address on their voter registration cards and driver's licenses. This legislation would effectively compel most students to vote at home rather than at school. The author of the legislation, State Senator Mike Rogers, R-Brighton, was running for Congress from the 8th Congressional District, home of Michigan State University. Rogers apparently believed that his candidacy would be hurt if MSU students were permitted to vote at school.

One MSU student quoted in the local papers felt the Rogers bill would further diminish voter turnout among college students. "I really don't think students who live in Detroit would drive an hour and a half to vote and then drive an hour and a half back for classes," she said. "They just won't vote."[2] An East Lansing resident, on the other hand, said college students were not really members of the community and were too easily "riled up" by their professors to be allowed to vote locally.[3] This controversy demonstrates the importance of the rules governing electoral participation and the stake students have in understanding and working to shape those rules.

- ***In this chapter, we shall examine the place of elections in American political life. We will first examine some of the formal aspects of electoral participation in the United States.*** These include types of elections, the ways that election winners are determined, electoral districts, the ballot, and the electoral college. As we shall see, all of these factors affect the type and level of influence that citizens have through the electoral process.
- ***In the next two sections, we will see how election campaigns are conducted in the United States.*** The campaign for any political office consists of a number of steps. Election campaigns are also becoming increasingly expensive to wage.
- ***We then turn to the broader issue of money and elections.*** Raising campaign funds is now a crucial factor for winning. Although attempts to reform campaign finance have been made, the money keeps pouring in. As we will see, this development has important consequences for democracy.
- ***Next, we assess the various factors that influence voters' decisions.*** Despite the growing importance of money to elections, it is still voters who decide the outcomes.

The Role of Elections in a Democracy

▶ What functions do elections serve in the political process?

Over the past two centuries, elections have come to play a significant role in the political processes of most nations. The forms that elections take and the purposes they serve, however, vary greatly from nation to nation. The most important difference among national electoral systems is that some provide the opportunity for opposition while others do not. Democratic electoral systems, such as those that have evolved in the United States and western Europe, allow opposing forces to compete against and even to replace current officeholders. Authoritarian electoral systems, by contrast, do not allow the defeat of those in power. In the authoritarian context, elections are used primarily to mobilize popular enthusiasm for the government, to provide an outlet for popular discontent, and to persuade foreigners that the regime is legitimate—i.e., that it has the support of the people. In the former Soviet Union, for example, citizens were required to vote even though no opposition to Communist Party candidates was allowed.

In democracies, elections can also serve as institutions of legitimation and as safety valves for social discontent. But beyond these functions, democratic elections facilitate popular influence, promote leadership accountability, and offer groups in society a measure of protection from the abuse of governmental power. Citizens exercise influence through elections by determining who should control the government. The chance to decide who will govern serves as an opportunity for ordinary citizens to make choices about the policies, programs, and directions of government action. In the United States, for example, recent Democratic and Republican candidates have differed significantly on issues of taxing, social spending, and governmental regulation. As American voters have chosen between the two parties' candidates, they have also made choices about these issues.

Elections promote leadership accountability because the threat of defeat at the polls exerts pressure on those in power to conduct themselves in a responsible manner and to take account of popular interests and wishes when they make their decisions. As James Madison observed in the Federalist Papers, elected leaders are "compelled to anticipate the moment when their power is to cease, when their exercise of it is to be reviewed, and when they must descend to the level from which they were raised, there forever to remain unless a faithful discharge of their trust shall have established their title to a renewal of it."[4] It is because of this need to anticipate the dissatisfaction of their constituents that elected officials constantly monitor public opinion polls as they decide what positions to take on policy issues.

Furthermore, the right to vote, or **suffrage,** can serve as an important source of protection for groups in American society. The passage of the 1965 Voting Rights Act, for example, enfranchised millions of African Americans in the South, paving the way for the election of thousands of new black public officials at the local, state, and national levels and ensuring that white politicians could no longer ignore the views and needs of African Americans. The Voting Rights Act was one of the chief spurs for the elimination of many overt forms of racial discrimination as well as for the diminution of racist rhetoric in American public life.

suffrage
the right to vote; also called franchise

Finally, while elections allow citizens a chance to participate in politics, they also allow the government a chance to exert a good deal of control over when, where, how, and which of its citizens will participate. Electoral processes are governed by a variety of rules and procedures that allow those in power a significant opportunity to regulate the character—and perhaps also the consequences—of mass political participation.

Elections in America

- What different types of elections are held in the United States? What rules determine who wins elections?
- How does the government determine the boundaries of electoral districts? How is the ballot determined?

midterm elections
congressional elections that do not coincide with a presidential election; also called off-year elections

In the United States, elections are held at regular intervals. National presidential elections take place every four years, on the first Tuesday in November; congressional elections are held every two years on the same Tuesday. (Congressional elections that do not coincide with a presidential election are sometimes called **midterm elections.**) Elections for state and local office also often coincide with national elections. Some states and municipalities, however, prefer to schedule their local elections for times that do not coincide with national contests to ensure that local results will not be affected by national trends.

In the American federal system, the responsibility for organizing elections rests largely with state and local governments. State laws specify how elections are to be administered, determine the boundaries of electoral districts, and specify candidate and voter qualifications. Elections are administered by state, county, and municipal election boards that are responsible for establishing and staffing polling places and verifying the eligibility of individuals who come to vote.

TYPES OF ELECTIONS

primary elections
elections used to select a party's candidate for the general election

closed primary
a primary election in which voters can participate in the nomination of candidates, but only of the party in which they are enrolled for a period of time prior to primary day

open primary
a primary election in which the voter can wait until the day of the primary to choose which party to enroll in to select candidates for the general election

Three types of elections are held in the United States: primary elections, general elections, and runoff elections. Americans occasionally also participate in a fourth voting process, the referendum, but the referendum is not actually an election.

Primary elections are used to select each party's candidates for the general election. In the case of local and statewide offices, the winners of primary elections face one another as their parties' nominees in the general election. At the presidential level, however, primary elections are indirect; they are used to select state delegates to the national nominating conventions, at which the major party presidential candidates are chosen. America is one of the only nations in the world to use primary elections. In most countries, nominations are controlled by party officials, as they once were in the United States. The primary system was introduced at the turn of the century by Progressive reformers who hoped to weaken the power of party leaders by taking candidate nominations out of their hands.

Under the laws of some states, only registered members of a political party may vote in a primary election to select that party's candidates. This is called a **closed primary.** Other states allow all registered voters to decide on the day of the primary in which party's primary they will participate. This is called an **open primary.**

The primary is followed by the general election—the decisive electoral contest. The winner of the general election is elected to office for a specified term.

In some states, however, mainly in the southeast, if no candidate wins an absolute majority in the primary, a runoff election is held before the general election. This situation is most likely to arise if there are more than two candidates, none of whom receives a majority of the votes cast. A runoff election is held between the two candidates who received the largest number of votes.

Some states also provide for referendum voting. The **referendum** process allows citizens to vote directly on proposed laws or other governmental actions. In recent years, voters in several states have voted to set limits on tax rates, to block state and local spending proposals, and to prohibit social services for illegal immigrants. Although it involves voting, a referendum is not an election. The election is an institution of representative government. Through an election, voters choose officials to act for them. The referendum, by contrast, is an institution of direct democracy; it allows voters to govern directly without intervention by government officials. The validity of referenda results, however, are subject to judicial action. If a court finds that a referendum outcome violates the state or national constitution, it can overturn the result. This happened in the case of a 1995 California referendum curtailing social services to illegal aliens.[5]

referendum
the practice of referring a measure proposed or passed by a legislature to the vote of the electorate for approval or rejection

THE CRITERIA FOR WINNING

In some countries, to win a seat in the parliament or other governing body, a candidate must receive an absolute majority (50% + 1) of all the votes cast in the relevant district. This type of electoral system is called a **majority system** and, in the United States, is used in primary elections by some southern states. Majority systems usually include a provision for a runoff election between the two top candidates, because if the initial race draws several candidates, there is little chance that any one will receive a majority.

majority system
a type of electoral system in which, to win a seat in the parliament or other representative body, a candidate must receive a majority of all the votes cast in the relevant district

In other nations, candidates for office need not win an absolute majority of the votes cast to win an election. Instead, victory is awarded to the candidate who receives the most votes, regardless of the actual percentage this represents. A candidate receiving 50 percent, 30 percent, or 20 percent of the vote can win if no other candidate received more votes. This type of electoral system is called a **plurality system** and is used in virtually all general elections in the United States.

plurality system
a type of electoral system in which, to win a seat in the parliament or other representative body, a candidate need only receive the most votes in the election, not necessarily a majority of votes cast

Most European nations employ a third type of electoral system, called **proportional representation.** Under proportional rules, competing political parties are awarded legislative seats in rough proportion to the percentage of the popular votes cast that each party won. A party that wins 30 percent of the vote will receive roughly 30 percent of the seats in the parliament or other representative body. In the United States, proportional representation is used by many states in presidential primary elections.

In general, proportional representation works to the advantage of smaller or weaker groups in society, whereas plurality and majority rules tend to help larger and more powerful forces. Proportional representation benefits smaller or weaker groups because it usually allows a party to win legislative seats with fewer votes than would be required under a majority or plurality system. In Europe, for example, a party that wins 10 percent of the national vote might win 10 percent of the parliamentary seats. In the United States, by contrast, a

proportional representation
a multiple-member district system that allows each political party representation in proportion to its percentage of the total vote

AMERICAN DEMOCRACY IN COMPARATIVE PERSPECTIVE

Electoral Systems

Because elections are the central institutional means for converting preferences into political power in free societies, students of comparative politics have focused upon the *efficiency* of elections. In other words, do the proportion of votes cast for a party's candidates match the actual number of seats awarded to that party in the national legislature?

The matter of efficiency is directly connected to the type of electoral method used. The American and British systems of elections are relatively simple and straightforward. Both countries' national elections employ a method known as "first-past-the-post," which assigns electoral victory to one political candidate per electoral district, based on a simple plurality principle. It is part of a broad family of election methods known as *single-member plurality/majority.* Among the world's 117 electoral democracies as of 1999, 42 (36 percent) rely on the single-member plurality/majority electoral method, as do approximately one in four of the world's most industrially developed democracies.

There are two basic advantages to this method. First, it affords a closer and more accountable relationship between a district and its elected representative to the national legislature. Second, the legislator knows she has the electoral support of at least a plurality of votes within the district. This offers more refined and loyal commitment of the representative to the district's interests (rather than a commitment solely to the national political party).

The disadvantage of the "first-past-the-post" system is its highly "inefficient," and disproportional nature. It "wastes" votes. How? Within any district, a party may win a plurality of votes and thereby win the district's single seat yet never come close to receiving a majority of votes cast in the district. When one adds up the total votes cast for a party across *all* the electoral districts in a country, one frequently finds the party receiving a larger proportion of seats in the legislature than the aggregate vote across the districts. For instance, in Britain following the May 1997 general elections to the House of Commons, nearly two in three of the 659 seats in the chamber were awarded to the Labour Party based on the outcome of elections, yet Labour received only 43 percent of the total vote cast.

In contrast to first-past-the-post is the *proportional representation* system of voting. This method is used in Japan, Hungary, Italy, Germany, Bolivia, New Zealand, and Sweden.

The advantage of multi-member proportional representation is its efficiency and minimal degree of disproportional distribution. With more than one representative per district, seats to the national legislature are not allocated for a district based on a plurality or majority of votes. Rather, each party is awarded a number of seats according to the proportion of votes received by the party in the district. Votes are more closely matched with subsequent seat allocations, thus minimizing the degree to which a democracy must violate principles of "one-person-one-vote." For instance, in Sweden's 1998 general elections, the difference between the proportion of votes received by the Social Democrats (36.4 percent) and the actual seats allocated to the party in the *Rikstag* (37.5 percent) was only 1.1 percent. But multi-member proportional representation systems bear a cost for some countries. If single-member plurality/majority systems tend to distort the representative process by disproportionately distributing seats relative to votes, proportional representation tends to complicate the process by giving political life to several relatively equal sized political parties, ensuring that often no party in the election has a strong plurality of votes, let alone majority of seats within the legislature. This compounds the difficulty of political compromise, policy cohesion, and the stability of government even within the most industrially advanced and developed democracies. For example, Italy has had fifty-eight different governments formed since 1946, a direct result of an electoral method that fragments the party system. Indeed, both Italy and Japan have chosen to move toward a mixed-member system in recent years, combining both single-member plurality/majority systems and proportional representation in order to minimize party system fragmentation, stabilize government, and enhance the public's confidence in and respect for the political system.

SOURCES: Arend Lijphart, *Patterns of Democracy: Government Forms and Performance in Thirty-Six Countries.* (New Haven: Yale University Press, 1999); *Electoral Reform Society,* on the Internet at http://www.electoral-reform.org.uk/; *The Center for Voting and Democracy,* on the Internet at http://www.igc.org/cvd/.

party that wins 10 percent of the vote would probably win no seats in Congress. Because they give small parties little chance of success, plurality and majority systems tend to reduce the number of competitive political parties. Proportional representation, on the other hand, tends to increase the number of parties. It is in part because of its use of plurality elections that the United States has usually had only two significant political parties, while with proportional representation, many European countries have developed multiparty systems.

ELECTORAL DISTRICTS

The boundaries for congressional and state legislative districts in the United States are redrawn by the states every ten years in response to population changes determined by the decennial census. The character of district boundaries is influenced by several factors. Some of the most important influences have been federal court decisions. In the 1963 case of *Gray v. Sanders,* and in the 1964 cases of *Wesberry v. Sanders* and *Reynolds v. Sims,* the Supreme Court held that legislative districts within a state must include roughly equal populations, so as to accord with the principle of "one person, one vote."[6] During the 1980s, the Supreme Court also declared that legislative districts should, insofar as possible, be contiguous, compact, and consistent with existing political subdivisions.[7]

gerrymandering
apportionment of voters in districts in such a way as to give unfair advantage to one racial or ethnic group or political party

Despite judicial intervention, state legislators routinely seek to influence electoral outcomes by manipulating the organization of electoral districts. This strategy is called **gerrymandering,** in honor of a nineteenth-century Massachusetts governor, Elbridge Gerry, who was alleged to have designed a

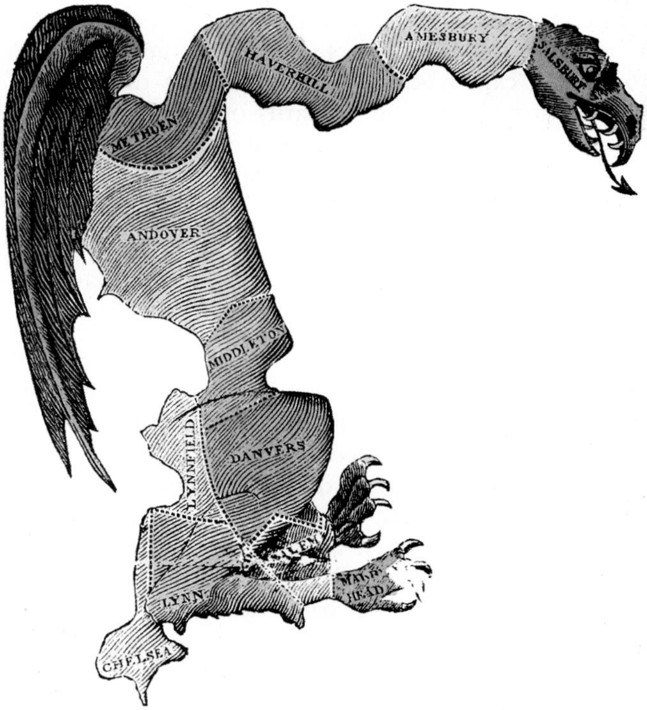

A cartoon of the original gerrymandered district in Massachusetts.

Figure 11.1 ELECTORAL GERRYMANDERING

North Carolina's 12th Congressional District and Georgia's 11th Congressional District were drawn in unusual shapes in an attempt to create minority election districts and encourage the election of minority representatives to Congress. Both these districts have been ruled unconstitutional by the U.S. Supreme Court.

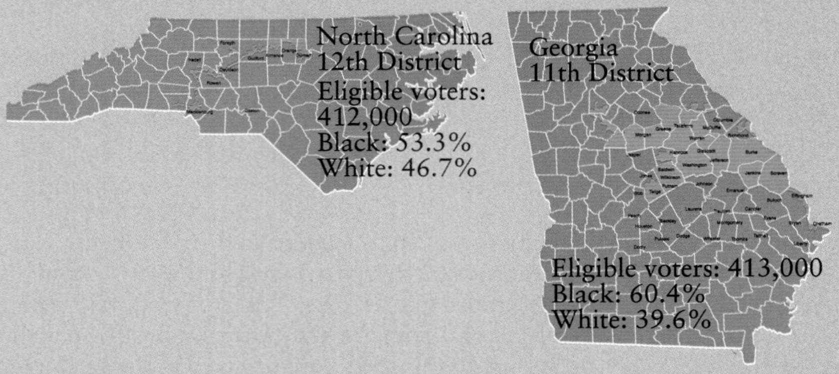

SOURCE: David Van Biema, "Snakes or Ladders?" *Time*, July 12, 1993, pp. 30–31. Reprinted with permission.

district in the shape of a salamander to promote his party's interests. The principle of gerrymandering is simple: different distributions of voters among districts can produce different electoral results. For example, by dispersing the members of a particular group across two or more districts, state legislators can dilute their voting power and prevent them from electing a representative in any district. Alternatively, by concentrating the members of a group or the adherents of the opposing party in as few districts as possible, state legislators can try to ensure that their opponents will elect as few representatives as possible. In recent years, the federal government has supported what is sometimes called **benign gerrymandering** through the creation of congressional districts made up primarily of minority group members. This practice was intended to increase the number of African Americans elected to public office (see Figure 11.1). The Supreme Court has viewed this effort as constitutionally dubious, however. Beginning with the 1993 case of *Shaw v. Reno,* the Court has undermined efforts to create such **minority districts.**[8]

benign gerrymandering
attempts to draw district boundaries so as to create districts made up primarily of disadvantaged or underrepresented minorities

minority district
a gerrymandered voting district that improves the chances of minority candidates by making selected minority groups the majority within the district

THE BALLOT

Prior to the 1890s, voters cast ballots according to political parties. Each party printed its own ballots, listed only its own candidates for each office, and employed party workers to distribute its ballots at the polls. Because only one party's candidates appeared on any ballot, it was very difficult for a voter to cast anything other than a straight party vote.

The advent of a new, neutral ballot represented a significant change in electoral procedure. The new ballot was prepared and administered by the state rather than the parties. Each ballot was identical and included the names of all candidates for office. This ballot reform made it possible for voters to make their choices on the basis of the individual rather than the collective merits of a party's candidates. Because all candidates for the same office now appeared on the same ballot, voters were no longer forced to choose a straight party ticket. This gave rise to the phenomenon of split-ticket voting in American elections.

If a voter supports candidates from more than one party in the same election, he or she is said to be casting a **split-ticket vote.** Voters who support only one party's candidates are casting a **straight-ticket vote.** Straight-ticket voting occurs most often when a voter casts a ballot for a party's presidential candidate and then "automatically" votes for the rest of that party's candidates. The result of this voting pattern is known as the **coattail effect.**

split-ticket voting
the practice of casting ballots for the candidates of at least two different political parties in the same election

straight-ticket voting
the practice of casting ballots for candidates of only one party

coattail effect
the result of voters casting their ballot for president or governor and "automatically" voting for the remainder of the party's ticket

Prior to the reform of the ballot, it was not uncommon for an entire incumbent administration to be swept from office and replaced by an entirely new set of officials. In the absence of a real possibility of split-ticket voting, any desire on the part of the electorate for change could be expressed only as a vote against all candidates of the party in power. Because of this, there always existed the possibility, particularly at the state and local levels, that an insurgent slate committed to policy change could be swept into power. The party ballot thus increased the potential impact of elections upon the government's composition. Although this potential may not always have been realized, the party ballot at least increased the chance that electoral decisions could lead to policy changes. By contrast, because it permitted choice on the basis of candidates' individual appeals, ticket splitting led to increasingly divided partisan control of government.

THE ELECTORAL COLLEGE

In the early history of popular voting, nations often made use of indirect elections. In these elections, voters would choose the members of an intermediate body. These members would, in turn, select public officials. The assumption underlying such processes was that ordinary citizens were not really qualified to choose their leaders and could not be trusted to do so directly. The last vestige of this procedure in America is the **electoral college,** the group of electors who formally select the president and vice president of the United States.

electoral college
the presidential electors from each state who meet after the popular election to cast ballots for president and vice president

When Americans go to the polls on election day, they are technically not voting directly for presidential candidates. Instead, voters within each state are choosing among slates of electors selected by each state's party and pledged, if elected, to support that party's presidential candidate. In each state (except Maine and Nebraska), the slate that wins casts all the state's electoral votes for its party's candidate.[9] Each state is entitled to a number of electoral votes equal to the number of the state's senators and representatives combined, for a total of 538 electoral votes for the fifty states. Occasionally, an elector will break his or her pledge and vote for the other party's candidate. For example, in 1976, when the Republicans carried the state of Washington, one Republican elector from that state refused to vote for Gerald Ford, the Republican presidential nominee. Many states have now enacted statutes formally binding electors to their pledges, but some constitutional authorities doubt whether such statutes are enforceable.

In each state, the electors whose slate has won proceed to the state's capital on the Monday following the second Wednesday in December and formally cast their ballots. These are sent to Washington, tallied by the Congress in January, and the name of the winner is formally announced. If no candidate receives a majority of all electoral votes, the names of the top three candidates would be submitted to the House, where each state would be able to cast one vote. Whether a state's vote would be decided by a majority, plurality, or some other fraction of the state's delegates would be determined under rules established by the House.

In 1800 and 1824, the electoral college failed to produce a majority for any candidate. In the election of 1800, Thomas Jefferson, the Jeffersonian Republican Party's presidential candidate, and Aaron Burr, that party's vice presidential candidate, received an equal number of votes in the electoral college, throwing the election into the House of Representatives. (The Constitution at that time made no distinction between presidential and vice presidential candidates, specifying only that the individual receiving a majority of electoral votes would be named president.) Some members of the Federalist Party in Congress suggested that they should seize the opportunity to damage the Republican cause by supporting Burr and denying Jefferson the presidency. Federalist leader Alexander Hamilton put a stop to this mischievous notion, however, and made certain that his party supported Jefferson. Hamilton's actions enraged Burr and helped lead to the infamous duel between the two men, in which Hamilton was killed. The Twelfth Amendment, ratified in 1804, was designed to prevent a repetition of such an inconclusive election by providing for separate electoral college votes for president and vice president.

In the 1824 election, four candidates—John Quincy Adams, Andrew Jackson, Henry Clay, and William H. Crawford—divided the electoral vote; no one of them received a majority. The House of Representatives eventually chose Adams over the others, even though Jackson had won more electoral and popular votes. After 1824, the two major political parties had begun to dominate presidential politics to such an extent that by December of each election year, only two candidates remained for the electors to choose between, thus ensuring that one would receive a majority. This freed the parties and the candidates from having to plan their campaigns to culminate in Congress, and Congress very quickly ceased to dominate the presidential selection process.

On all but three occasions since 1824, the electoral vote has simply ratified the nationwide popular vote. Since electoral votes are won on a state-by-state basis, it is mathematically possible for a candidate who receives a nationwide popular plurality to fail to carry states whose electoral votes would add up to a majority. Thus, in 1876, Rutherford B. Hayes was the winner in the electoral college despite receiving fewer popular votes than his rival, Samuel Tilden. In 1888, Grover Cleveland received more popular votes than Benjamin Harrison, but received fewer electoral votes. And in 2000, Al Gore outpolled his opponent, George W. Bush, but narrowly lost the electoral college by a mere four electoral votes.

The outcome of the 2000 contest, in which the electoral college produced a result that was inconsistent with the popular vote, led to many calls for the abolition of this institution and the introduction of some form of direct popular election of the president. Within days of the election, several members of Congress promised to introduce a constitutional amendment that would bring an end to the electoral college, which one congressman called an "anachronism." Efforts to introduce such a reform, however, will likely be blocked by political forces that believe they benefit from the present system. For example, minority groups that are influential in large urban states with many electoral votes feel that their voting strength would be diminished in a direct, nationwide, popular election. At the same time, some Republicans believe that their party's usual presidential strength in the South and in parts of the Midwest and West gives them a distinct advantage in the electoral college. Some Democrats and Republicans also fear that the direct popular election of the president would give third parties more influence over the outcome. Thus, while political pressure will be great to abolish the current system, efforts toward that end will likely face the same fate as the over-700 previous attempts to reform it.

Election Campaigns

▶ What are the steps in a successful election campaign?

A **campaign** is an effort by political candidates and their supporters to win the backing of donors, political activists, and voters in their quest for political office. Campaigns precede every primary and general election. Because of the complexity of the campaign process, and because of the amount of money that candidates must raise, presidential campaigns usually begin almost two years before the November presidential elections. The campaign for any office consists of a number of steps. Candidates must first organize groups of supporters who will help them raise funds and bring their name to the attention of the media and potential donors. This step is relatively easy for a candidate currently in the office. The current officeholder is called an **incumbent.** Incumbents usually are already well known and have little difficulty attracting supporters and contributors, unless of course they have been subject to damaging publicity while in office.

campaign
an effort by political candidates and their staffs to win the backing of donors, political activists, and voters in the quest for political office

incumbent
a candidate running for a position that he or she already holds

ADVISERS

The next step in a typical campaign involves recruiting advisers and creating a formal campaign organization (see Figure 11.2 on the next page). Most candidates, especially for national or statewide office, will need a campaign manager, a media consultant, a pollster, a financial adviser, and a press spokesperson, as well as a staff director to coordinate the activities of volunteer and paid workers. For a local campaign, candidates generally need hundreds of workers. State-level campaigns call for thousands of workers, and presidential campaigns require tens of thousands of workers nationwide.

Professional campaign workers, including the managers, consultants, and pollsters required in a modern campaign, prefer to work for candidates who seem to have a reasonable chance of winning. For individuals like James Carville, who helped manage Bill Clinton's 1992 campaign; Dick Morris, credited as the mastermind behind Clinton's 1996 victory; or Republican strategists Roger Ailes and Bob Teeter, politics is a profession, and repeated associations with winning campaigns are the route to professional success. Candidates seen as having little chance of winning often have difficulty hiring the most experienced professional consultants. Professional political consultants have taken the place of the old-time party bosses who once controlled political campaigns. Most consultants who direct campaigns specialize in politics, although some are drawn from the ranks of corporate advertising and may

Figure 11.2 THE TYPICAL ORGANIZATION OF A NATIONAL POLITICAL CAMPAIGN

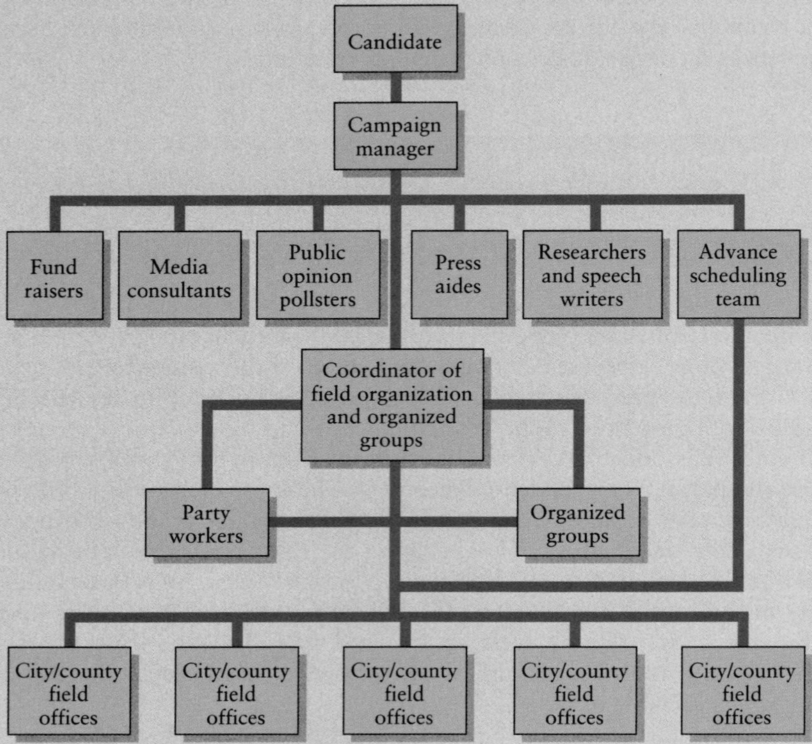

SOURCE: L. Sandy Maisel, *Parties and Elections in America,* 2nd ed. (New York: McGraw-Hill, 1993), p. 190. Copyright © 1993, McGraw-Hill. Used with permission.

work with commercial clients in addition to politicians. Campaign consultants conduct public opinion polls, produce television commercials, organize direct-mail campaigns, and develop the issues and advertising messages the candidate will use to mobilize support.

Together with their advisers, candidates must begin serious fund-raising efforts at an early stage in the campaign. To have a reasonable chance of winning a seat in the House of Representatives, a candidate may need to raise more than $500,000. To win a Senate seat, a candidate may need ten times that much. Candidates generally begin raising funds long before they face an election. For example, a year prior to the 1998 congressional elections, New York's Republican senator, Alfonse D'Amato, had already raised $9.7 million, nearly as much as he spent in his successful 1992 campaign. Throughout 1996 and 1997, D'Amato had raised money from the banking, insurance, real estate, and construction businesses that come under the jurisdiction of the Senate Banking, Housing, and Urban Affairs Committee, which he chaired. A professional staff of fund-raisers, headed by long-term D'Amato consultant Arthur Finkelstein, labored full-time on the senator's behalf. For his efforts, Finkelstein earned nearly $100,000 during the second half of 1996 alone. In many states, an incumbent able to raise as much money as D'Amato might be able to frighten away most potential challengers. In New York, however, Democratic candidates can count on the support of some of the party's wealthiest contributors; Democratic senatorial candidate and congressman Charles Schumer of Brooklyn was able to raise almost as much money as D'Amato. Schumer eventually won the election. Though partially supported by public funding, presidential candidates must raise huge amounts of money. For example, by December 1999, almost a year before the November 2000 national elections, Republican hopeful George W. Bush had already raised some $63 million to support his bid for office. We will look in more detail at political campaign fund-raising later in the chapter.

POLLING

Another important element of a campaign is public-opinion polling. To be competitive, a candidate must collect voting and poll data to assess the electorate's needs, hopes, fears, and past behavior. Polls are conducted throughout most political campaigns. Surveys of voter opinion provide the basic information that candidates and their staffs use to craft campaign strategies—i.e., to select issues, to assess their own strengths and weaknesses as well as those of the opposition, to check voter response to the campaign, and to measure the degree to which various constituent groups may be responsive to campaign appeals. The themes, issues, and messages that candidates present during a campaign are generally based upon polls and smaller face-to-face sessions with voters, called "focus groups." In the 1992 presidential campaign, Bill Clinton's emphasis on the economy, exemplified by the campaign staff's slogan "It's the economy, stupid," was based on the view that the economy was the chief concern among American voters. In preparation for the 1996 campaign, Clinton adopted a strategy of "triangulation" based upon consultant Richard Morris's interpretation of poll data. Morris advised Clinton that he would win the most votes by positioning himself between liberal Democrats and conservative Republicans, in a sense forming the apex of a triangle.[10] During the 2000 presidential race, Democratic candidate Al Gore based his decision to "distance" himself from President Clinton on poll data suggesting that the public had become weary of Clinton after years of crises and scandals, developing what some called "Clinton fatigue." First Lady Hillary Rodham Clinton, campaigning for a New York Senate seat, seemed to follow similar advice when she criticized

Students and Politics

Despite sniffling from the cold and running his hands through his frozen hair, Nick Watt still had a smile on his face Saturday.

Watt was one of a handful of students who campaigned door-to-door this weekend for Chub Conner, a Democrat running for state representative in the 104th District. The students, working as campaign volunteers, trudged through the snow and cold to knock on doors and hand out literature to voters.

"We had a bit of a sympathy factor going for us," said Jon Leahy, a member of Conner's campaign staff. "People see how hard we work and tend to feel sorry for us when it's raining or snowing."

Members of the College Democrats who came to support Conner were divided into teams and targeted various precincts to inform voters of Conner's campaign.

"Some people may think we're crazy for going out into the snow like this, but I don't mind," said Watt, a junior political science major . . . who has volunteered his time in Conner's campaign and Urbana Mayor Tod Satterthwaite's campaign for the 103rd District seat. "Volunteering has been a great experience. You get to persuade people to see what you see about the candidate."

Candidates running for state offices are not the only ones who are busy preparing for the upcoming elections. Many of them are working with student volunteers or interns who devote their time to the campaigns.

"I think my interns and volunteers are extremely valuable," Conner said. "I think it's great that students are willing to participate because it shows my campaign and issues are things they personally believe in."

Candidates, campaign managers, and students agree that volunteering and interning in campaigns are valuable experiences.

"I don't think campaigns could be successful without the help of volunteers," said Brad Carlson, campaign manager for Bill Brady, another 15th Congressional District candidate.

"You get firsthand experience and get to meet the candidates and voters," said Eric Pratt, a junior political science major. . . . "You learn more from these experiences than any poli-sci class, plus it's more fun.'

SOURCE: Robin Leephaibul, "Student Volunteers Integral in Campaigns," *Daily Illini* (University of Illinois), February 1, 2000.

several of her husband's policy positions. In recent years, pollsters have become central figures in most national campaigns and some have continued as advisers to their clients after they win the election.

THE PRIMARIES

For many candidates, the next step in a campaign is the primary election. In the case of all offices but the presidency, state and local primary elections determine which candidates will receive the major parties' official nominations. Of course, candidates can run for office without the Democratic or Republican nomination. In most states, however, independent and third-party candidates must obtain many thousands of petition signatures to qualify for the general election ballot. This requirement alone discourages most independent and third-party bids. More important, most Americans are reluctant to vote for candidates other than those nominated by the two major parties. Thus most of the time, a major party nomination is a necessary condition for electoral success. Some popular incumbents coast to victory without having to face a serious challenge. In most major races, however, candidates can expect to compete in a primary election.

There are essentially two types of primary contests: the personality clash and the ideological, or factional, struggle. In the first category are primaries that simply represent competing efforts by ambitious individuals to secure election to office. In 2000, for example, the major Democratic presidential aspirants, Al Gore (the eventual Democratic nominee) and Bill Bradley, were both moderate liberals who agreed on the broad outlines of most issues and policies. Whichever candidate they preferred, few Democratic loyalists considered refusing to support the other should he win the primary. Similarly, the major Republican presidential aspirants, George W. Bush (who ultimately received the Republican nomination) and John McCain, presented themselves as fiscally conservative and "pro-family" in their social views. Most Republican loyalists were willing to support a presidential bid by either individual. This type of primary can be very healthy for a political party because it can enhance interest in the campaign and can produce a nominee with the ability to win the general election.

The second type of primary—the ideological struggle—can have different consequences. Ideological struggles usually occur when one wing of a party decides that an incumbent is too willing to compromise or too moderate in his or her political views. For example, in 1992, President George Bush was challenged for the Republican presidential nomination by conservative columnist Pat Buchanan. Buchanan charged Bush with being too willing to compromise conservative principles. Such ideological challenges not only reveal rifts within a party coalition, but the friction and resentment they cause can undermine a party's general election chances. Through his ideological crusade, Buchanan damaged President Bush's re-election chances in 1992. In 2000, hoping to do even more damage, Buchanan abandoned the GOP to seek the Reform Party nomination. However, Buchanan's quixotic behavior, including publication of a book that appeared to praise Adolf Hitler and a bizarre alliance with a left-wing fringe group in New York, seemed to reduce his appeal to the electorate.

Ideological struggles can also produce candidates who are too liberal or too conservative to win the general election. Primary electorates are much

Caucus chairperson Charles Richardson gathers ballots from Republican Party members in Runnells, Iowa, during the 1996 caucus.

smaller and tend to be ideologically more extreme than the general electorate: Democratic primary voters are somewhat more liberal than the general electorate, and Republican primary voters are typically more conservative than the general electorate. Thus, the winner of an intraparty ideological struggle may prove too extreme for the general election. In 1994, for example, archconservative Oliver North won the Virginia Republican senatorial primary over a moderate opponent, but was drubbed in the general election. Many moderate Republicans, including Virginia's other senator, John Warner, refused to support North.

Presidential Elections

- How is the president elected?
- What factors have the greatest impact on a general election campaign?

Although they also involve primary elections, the major party presidential nominations follow a pattern that is quite different from the nominating process employed for other political offices. In some years, particularly when an incumbent president is running for re-election, one party's nomination may not be contested. If, however, the Democratic or Republican presidential nomination is contested, candidates typically compete in primaries or presidential nominating caucuses in all fifty states, attempting to capture national convention delegates. Most states use primary elections to choose the delegates for national conventions. A few states use the **caucus**, a nominating process that begins with precinct-level meetings throughout the state. Some caucuses, called **open caucuses**, are open to anyone wishing to attend. Other states use

caucus (political)
a normally closed meeting of a political or legislative group to select candidates, plan strategy, or make decisions regarding legislative matters

open caucus
a presidential nominating caucus open to anyone who wishes to attend

closed caucus
a presidential nominating caucus open only to registered party members

closed caucuses, open only to registered party members. Citizens attending the caucuses typically elect delegates to statewide conventions at which delegates to the national party conventions are chosen.

The primaries and caucuses usually begin in February of a presidential election year and end in June (see Figure 11.3). The early ones are most important because they can help front-running candidates secure media attention and financial support. Gradually, the primary and caucus process has become "front loaded," with states vying with one another to increase their political influence by holding their nominating processes first. Traditionally, the New Hampshire primary and the Iowa caucuses are considered the most important of the early events, and candidates spend months courting voter support in these two states. A candidate who performs well in Iowa and New Hampshire will usually be able to secure support and better media coverage for subsequent races. A candidate who fares badly in these two states may be written off as a loser.

winner-take-all system
a system in which all of a state's presidential nominating delegates are awarded to the candidate who wins the most votes, while runners-up receive no delegates

As noted in Chapter 10, the Democratic Party requires that state presidential primaries allocate delegates on the basis of proportional representation; Democratic candidates win delegates in rough proportion to their percentage of the primary vote. The Republican Party does not require proportional representation, but most states have now written proportional representation requirements into their election laws. A few states use the **winner-take-all system,** by which the candidate with the most votes wins all the party's delegates in that state.

When the primaries and caucuses are concluded, it is usually clear which candidates have won their parties' nominations. For example, in 2000, George W. Bush arrived at the GOP national convention with the party nomination in hand; similarly, Al Gore was the Democratic winner long before the party faithful assembled in Los Angeles.

THE CONVENTION

platform
a party document, written at a national convention, that contains party philosophy, principles, and positions on issues

The one major step that remains before a nomination is actually awarded is the national party convention. The Democratic and Republican national party conventions occur every four years to formally certify each party's presidential and vice presidential nominees. In addition, the conventions draft a statement of party principles, called a **platform**, and determine the rules that will govern party activities for the next four years.

The History of Political Conventions For more than fifty years after America's founding, presidential nominations were controlled by each party's congressional caucus—all the party's members in the House and the Senate. Critics referred to this process as the "King Caucus" and charged that it did not take proper account of the views of party members throughout the nation. In 1824, the King Caucus method came under severe attack when the Democratic Party caucus failed to nominate Andrew Jackson, the candidate with the greatest support among both party members and activists outside the Capitol. In the 1830s, the party convention was devised as a way of allowing party leaders and activists throughout the nation an opportunity to participate in selecting presidential candidates. The first party convention was held by the

THE 2000 PRESIDENTIAL ELECTION SEASON

Figure 11.3

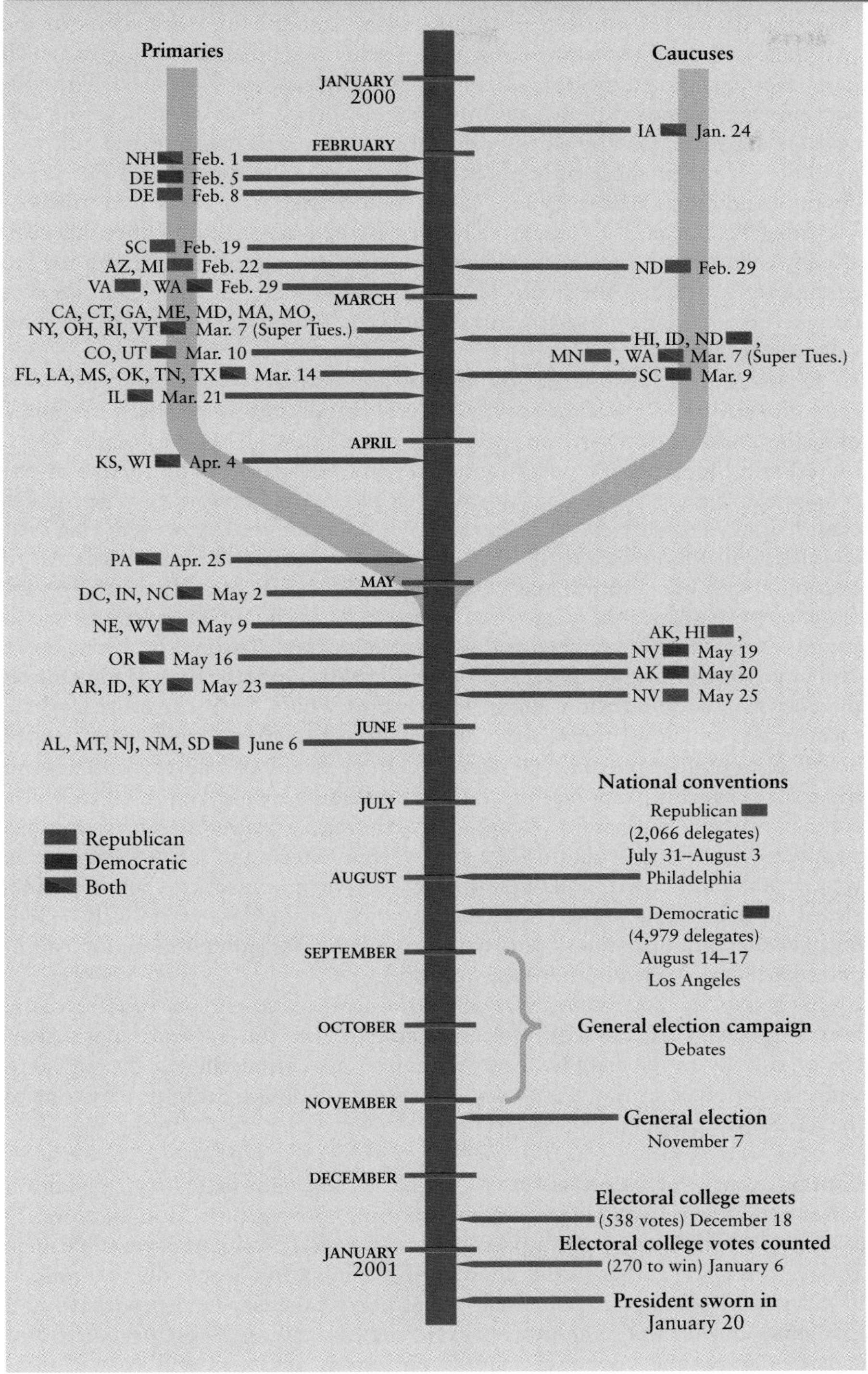

Anti-Masonic Party in 1831. The Democratic Party held its first convention in 1832, when Andrew Jackson was nominated for a second term.

As it developed during the course of the next century, the convention became the decisive institution in the presidential nominating processes of the two major parties. The convention was a genuine deliberative body in which party factions argued, negotiated, and eventually reached a decision. The convention was composed of delegations from each state. The size of a state's delegation depended on the state's population, and each delegate was allowed one vote for the purpose of nominating the party's presidential and vice presidential candidates. Before 1936, victory required the support of two-thirds of the delegates. Until 1968, state delegations voted according to the **unit rule**, which meant that all the members of the state delegation would vote for the candidate favored by the majority of the state's delegates. This practice was designed to maximize a state's influence in the nominating process. The unit rule was abolished in 1968.

unit rule
the convention voting system under which a state delegation casts all of its votes for the candidate supported by the majority of the state's delegates

Between the 1830s and World War II, national convention delegates were generally selected by a state's party leaders. Usually the delegates were public officials, political activists, and party notables from all regions of the state, representing most major party factions. Some delegates would arrive at the convention having pledged in advance to give their support to a particular presidential candidate. Most delegates were uncommitted, however. This fact, coupled with the unit rule, allowed state party leaders (i.e., the delegates) to negotiate with one another and with presidential candidates for their support. State party leaders might agree to support a candidate in exchange for a promise to name them or their followers to important national positions, or in exchange for promises of federal programs and projects for their state. During the course of a convention, alliances of states would form, dissolve, and re-form in the course of tense negotiations. Typically, many votes were needed before the nomination could be decided. Often, deadlocks developed between the most powerful party factions, and state leaders would be forced to find a compromise, or "dark-horse," candidate. Among the more famous dark-horse nominees were James Polk in 1844 and Warren Harding in 1920. Although he was virtually unknown, Polk won the Democratic nomination when it became clear that none of the more established candidates could win. Similarly, Harding, another political unknown, won his nomination after the major candidates had fought one another to a standstill.

In its day, the convention was seen as a democratic reform. In later years, however, new generations of reformers came to view the convention as a symbol of rule by party leaders. The convention also strengthened the independence and power of the presidency, by taking the nominating process out of the hands of Congress.

Contemporary Party Conventions Whereas the traditional party convention was a deliberative assembly, the contemporary convention acts more to ratify than to determine the party's presidential and vice presidential nominations. Today, as we saw earlier in this chapter, the nomination is actually determined in a series of primary elections and local party caucuses held in virtually all fifty states during several months prior to the convention. These primaries and caucuses determine how each state's convention delegates will vote. Candidates now arrive at the convention knowing who has enough delegate support in hand to assure a victory in the first round of balloting. State party leaders no longer serve as power brokers, and the party's presidential and vice presidential choices are made relatively quickly.

Even though the party convention no longer controls presidential nominations, it still has a number of important tasks. The first of these is the adoption of party rules concerning such matters as convention delegate selection and future presidential primary elections. In 1972, for example, the Democratic convention accepted rules requiring convention delegates to be broadly representative of the party's membership in terms of race and gender. After those rules were passed, the convention refused to seat several state delegations that were deemed not to meet this standard.

Another important task for the convention is the drafting of a party platform—a statement of principles and pledges around which the delegates can unite. Although the two major parties' platforms tend to contain many similar principles and platitudes, differences between the two platforms can be significant. In recent years, for example, the Republican platform has advocated tax cuts and taken strong positions on such social issues as affirmative action and abortion. The Democratic platforms, on the other hand, have focused on the importance of maintaining welfare and regulatory programs. A close reading of both parties' platforms can reveal some of the ideological differences between the parties.

Convention Delegates Today, convention **delegates** are generally political activists with strong positions on social and political issues. Generally, Republican delegates tend to be more conservative than Republican voters as a whole, whereas Democratic delegates tend to be more liberal than the majority of Democratic voters. In states such as Michigan and Iowa, local party caucuses choose many of the delegates who will actually attend the national convention. In most of the remaining states, primary elections determine how a state's delegation will vote, but the actual delegates are selected by state party officials.

delegates
political activists selected to vote at a party's national convention

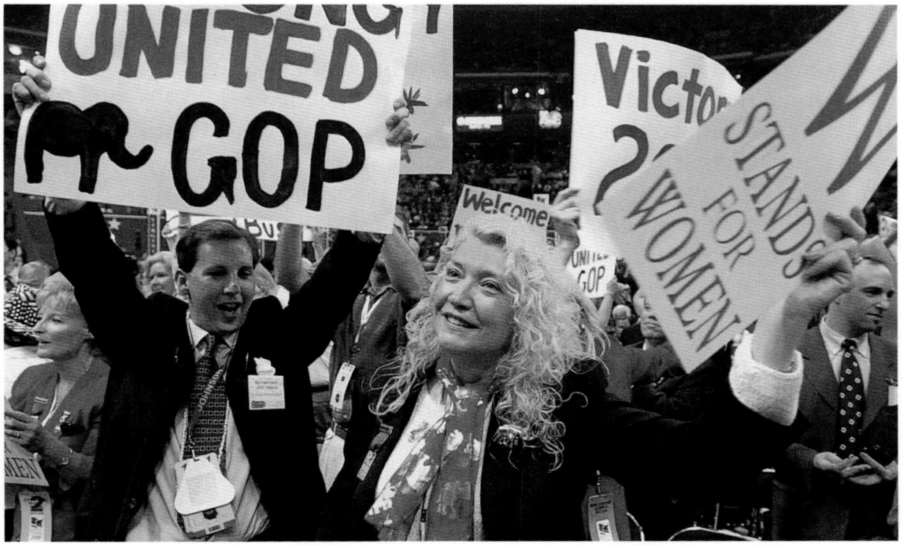

The 2000 Republican National Convention attempted to portray a more inclusive image of the party by showcasing a number of female and African American delegates and speakers.

Delegate votes won in primary elections are apportioned to candidates on the basis of proportional representation. Thus a candidate who received 30 percent of the vote in the California Democratic primary would receive roughly 30 percent of the state's delegate votes at the party's national convention.

As was mentioned earlier, the Democratic Party requires that a state's convention delegation be representative of that state's Democratic electorate in terms of race, gender, and age. Republican delegates, by contrast, are more likely to be male and white. The Democrats also reserve slots for elected Democratic Party officials, called **superdelegates.** All the Democratic governors and about 80 percent of the party's members of Congress now attend the national convention as delegates.

superdelegate
a convention delegate position, in Democratic conventions, reserved for party officials

Convention Procedure Each party convention lasts several days. The convention usually begins with the selection of party committees, including the credentials, rules, and platform committees, and the election of a temporary convention chairperson. This individual normally delivers a keynote address highlighting the party's appeals and concerns. After all the delegates have been seated by the credentials committee, a permanent chair is elected. This person presides over the presidential and vice presidential nominations, the adoption of a party platform, and any votes on rules that are proposed by the rules committee.

Although the actual presidential nomination is effectively decided before the convention, the names of a number of candidates are generally put in nomination and speeches made on their behalf at the convention. To be nominated is considered an honor, and ambitious politicians are eager for the media attention, however brief, that such a nomination brings.

All the nominating speeches, as well as speeches by party notables, are carefully scrutinized by the mass media, which report and analyze the major events of the convention. In the 1950s and 1960s, the television networks provided "gavel-to-gavel" coverage of the Democratic and Republican national conventions. Today, however, the major television networks carry convention highlights only. Because the parties are eager to receive as much media coverage as possible, they schedule convention events in order to reach large television audiences. The parties typically try to present the actual presidential nomination and the nominee's acceptance speech during prime viewing time, normally between 8:00 and 11:00 P.M. on a weeknight. In 1996, the major networks proclaimed that both national conventions were essentially too boring to merit detailed coverage. One important news program, ABC's *Nightline,* halted its coverage of the Republican convention earlier than had been scheduled after the program's anchor, Ted Koppel, decided that the GOP convention was little more than a staged media event.

After the nominating speeches are concluded, the voting begins. The names of the states are called alphabetically and the state delegation's vote reported by its chairperson. During this process, noisy and colorful demonstrations are staged in support of the nominees. When the nomination is formally decided, a lengthy demonstration ensues, with bands and colorful balloons celebrating the conclusion of the process. The party's vice presidential candidate is usually nominated the next day. This individual is almost always selected by the presidential nominee, and the choice is merely ratified by the convention. In 2000,

George W. Bush selected Dick Cheney, who had previously served as his father's secretary of defense, while Al Gore designated Connecticut senator Joe Lieberman as his running mate. Lieberman thus became the first Jewish political candidate in U.S. history to appear on a national ticket.

Once the nominations have been settled and most other party business has been resolved, the presidential and vice presidential nominees deliver acceptance speeches. These speeches are opportunities for the nominees to begin their formal campaigns on a positive note, and they are usually meticulously crafted to make as much of an impression on the electorate as possible.

The conventions of the two major parties are carefully scripted media events. Minor parties also hold conventions; however, these may become disorganized and even raucous. In 2000, for example, the Reform Party convention deteriorated into a pushing and shoving contest between supporters and opponents of controversial columnist Pat Buchanan. Buchanan's opponents claimed that he was attempting to "hijack" the party as a vehicle for airing his idiosyncratic cultural and social views—and to seize possession of more than $12 million in federal campaign funds to which the party was entitled. These anti-Buchanan forces eventually bolted the convention and held their own conclave, with each side vowing to litigate for control of the party and its funds.

THE GENERAL ELECTION CAMPAIGN AND HIGH-TECH POLITICS

For those candidates lucky enough to survive the nominating process, the last hurdle is the general election. There are essentially two types of general election in the United States today. The first type is the organizationally driven, labor-intensive election. In general, local elections and many congressional races fall into this category. Candidates campaign in such elections by recruiting large numbers of volunteer workers to hand out leaflets and organize rallies. The candidates make appearances at receptions, community group meetings, and local events, and even in shopping malls and on busy street corners. Generally, local and congressional campaigns depend less upon issues and policy proposals and more upon hard work designed to make the candidate more visible than his or her opponent. Statewide campaigns, some congressional races, and, of course, the national presidential election fall into the second category: the media-driven, capital-intensive electoral campaign.

In the nineteenth and early twentieth centuries, political campaigns were waged by the parties' enormous armies of patronage workers. Throughout the year, party workers cultivated the support of voters by helping them with legal problems, helping them find jobs, and serving as liaisons with local, state, and federal agencies. On election day throughout the nation hundreds of thousands of party workers marched from house to house reminding their supporters to vote, helping the aged and infirm to reach the polls, and calling in the favors they had accrued during the year. Campaigns resembled the maneuvers of huge infantries vying for victory. Historians have, in fact, referred to this traditional style of party campaigning as "militarist."

Contemporary political campaigns rely less on infantries and more on "air power." That is, rather than deploy huge armies of workers, contemporary campaigns make use of a number of communications techniques to reach voters and bid for their support. Six techniques are especially important.

Polling Surveys of voter opinion provide the information that candidates and their staffs use to craft campaign strategies. Candidates employ polls to select issues, to assess their own strengths and weaknesses (as well as those of the opposition), to check voter response to the campaign, and to determine the degree to which various constituent groups are susceptible to campaign appeals. Virtually all contemporary campaigns for national and statewide office as well as many local campaigns make extensive use of opinion polling. As we saw in Chapter 7, President Clinton made extensive use of polling data both during and after the 1996 presidential election to shape his rhetoric and guide his policy initiatives.

The Broadcast Media Extensive use of the broadcast media, television in particular, has become the hallmark of the modern political campaign. Generally, media campaigns attempt to follow the guidelines indicated by a candidate's polls, emphasizing issues and personal characteristics that appear important in the poll data. The broadcast media are now so central to modern campaigns that most candidates' activities are tied to their media strategies.[11] Candidate activities are designed expressly to stimulate television news coverage. For instance, members of Congress running for re-election or for president almost always sponsor committee or subcommittee hearings to generate publicity.

Extensive use of radio and television has become the hallmark of the modern statewide or national political campaign. One commonly used broadcast technique is the fifteen-, thirty-, or sixty-second television **spot advertisement,** which permits a candidate's message to be delivered to a target audience before uninterested or hostile viewers can tune it out. Examples of effective spot ads include George Bush's 1988 "Willie Horton" ad, which implied that Bush's opponent, Michael Dukakis, coddled criminals, and Lyndon Johnson's 1964 "daisy girl" ad, which suggested that his opponent, Barry Goldwater, would lead the United States into nuclear war. Television spot ads are used to establish candidate name recognition, to create a favorable image of the candidate and a negative image of the opponent, to link the candidate with desirable groups in the community, and to communicate the candidate's stands on selected issues. Media campaigns generally follow the trail outlined by a candidate's polls, emphasizing issues and personal characteristics that appear important in the poll data.

spot advertisement
a fifteen-, thirty-, or sixty-second television campaign commercial that permits a candidate's message to be delivered to a target audience

The 1992 presidential campaign introduced three new media techniques: the talk show interview, the "electronic town hall meeting," and the "infomercial." Candidates used television and radio interview programs to reach the large audiences drawn to this newly popular entertainment program format. Some of these programs allow audience members to telephone the show with questions, which gives candidates a chance to demonstrate that they are interested in the views of ordinary people. The **town meeting** format allows candidates the opportunity to appear in an auditoriumlike setting and interact with ordinary citizens, thus underlining the candidates' concern with the views and needs of the voters. Moreover, both the talk show appearance and the town meeting allow candidates to deliver their messages to millions of Americans without the input of journalists or commentators who might criticize or question the candidates' assertions.

town meeting
a media format in which candidates meet with ordinary citizens. Allows candidates to deliver messages without the presence of journalists or commentators

The **infomercial** is a lengthy presentation, often lasting thirty minutes. Although infomercials are designed to have the appearance of news programs,

infomercial
a lengthy campaign advertisement on television

they are actually presentations of a candidate's views. Independent candidate Ross Perot made frequent use of infomercials during the 1992 campaign.

Another use of the broadcast media in contemporary campaigns is the televised candidate debate. Televised presidential debates began with the famous 1960 Kennedy-Nixon clash. Today, both presidential and vice presidential candidates hold debates, as do candidates for statewide and even local offices. Debates allow candidates to reach voters who have not fully made up their minds about the election. Moreover, debates can increase the visibility of lesser-known candidates. In 1960, John F. Kennedy's strong performance in the presidential debate was a major factor in bringing about his victory over the much-better-known Richard Nixon.

The "daisy girl" from Lyndon Johnson's now-famous 1964 campaign commercial. As the little girl picked petals, she counted, "1–2–3. . . ." At the same time, the voice of an announcer ominously counted "10–9–8. . . ." When the announcer reached 0, a blinding nuclear explosion was shown, with President Lyndon Johnson saying, "These are the stakes: To make a world in which all of God's children can live or go into the dark. We must either love each other or we must die."

Phone Banks Through the broadcast media, candidates communicate with voters en masse and impersonally. Phone banks, on the other hand, allow campaign workers to make personal contact with hundreds of thousands of voters. Personal contacts of this sort are thought to be extremely effective. Again, polling data serve to identify the groups that will be targeted for phone calls. Computers select phone numbers from areas in which members of these groups are concentrated. Staffs of paid or volunteer callers, using computer-assisted dialing systems and prepared scripts, then place calls to deliver the candidate's message. The targeted groups are generally those identified by polls as either uncommitted or weakly committed, as well as strong supporters of the candidate who are contacted simply to encourage them to vote.

Direct Mail Direct mail serves both as a vehicle for communicating with voters and as a mechanism for raising funds. The first step in a direct-mail campaign is the purchase or rental of a computerized mailing list of voters deemed to have some particular perspective or social characteristic. Often sets of magazine subscription lists or lists of donors to various causes are employed. For example, a candidate interested in reaching conservative voters might rent subscription lists from the *National Review, Human Events,* or *Conservative Digest;* a candidate interested in appealing to liberals might rent subscription lists from the *New York Review of Books* or *The New Republic.* Considerable fine-tuning is possible. After obtaining the appropriate mailing lists, candidates usually send pamphlets, letters, and brochures describing themselves and their views to voters believed to be sympathetic. Different types of mail appeals are made to different electoral subgroups. Often the letters sent to voters are personalized. The recipient is addressed by name in the text and the letter appears actually to have been signed by the candidate. Of course, these "personal" letters are written and even signed by a computer.

In addition to its use as a political advertising medium, direct mail has also become an important source of campaign funds. Computerized mailing lists permit campaign strategists to pinpoint individuals whose interests, background, and activities suggest that they may be potential donors to the campaign. Letters of solicitation are sent to these potential donors. Some of the money raised is then used to purchase additional mailing lists. Direct-mail solicitation can be enormously effective.[12]

Professional Public Relations Modern campaigns and the complex technology upon which they rely are typically directed by professional public relations consultants. Virtually all serious contenders for national and statewide office retain the services of professional campaign consultants. Increasingly, candidates for local office, too, have come to rely upon professional campaign managers. Consultants offer candidates the expertise necessary to conduct accurate opinion polls, produce television commercials, organize direct-mail campaigns, and make use of sophisticated computer analyses.

The number of technologically oriented campaigns increased greatly after 1971. The Federal Election Campaign Act of 1971 prompted the creation of large numbers of political action committees (PACs) by a host of corporate and ideological groups. This development increased the availability of funds to political candidates—conservative candidates in particular—which meant in turn that the new technology could be used more extensively. Initially, the new techniques were employed mainly by individual candidates who often made little or no effort to coordinate their campaigns with those of other political aspirants sharing the same party label. For this reason, campaigns employing new technology sometimes came to be called "candidate-centered" efforts, as distinguished from the traditional party-coordinated campaign. Nothing about the new technology, however, precluded its use by political party leaders seeking to coordinate a number of campaigns. In recent years, party leaders—Republicans in particular—have learned to make good use of modern campaign technology. The difference between the old and new political methods is not that the latter are inherently candidate-centered while the former are strictly a party tool; it is a matter of the types of political resources upon which each method depends.

The Internet Still another new media technique was introduced in the 1996 presidential campaign. This was the use of the Internet as a political medium. The major candidates and many minor candidates created Web pages that provided biographical data, information about the candidates' positions on various issues, and even photographs of the candidates and their family members. The Web pages also provided voters with information about how to become involved in the candidates' campaign efforts. As discussed in Chapter 8, candidate Web sites are most likely to be visited by individuals who already agree with the candidate's views and hence are not likely to change many votes. Nevertheless, these sites may help reinforce the commitments of loyalists and can encourage the faithful to work on behalf of their candidate.

Students and Politics

Like other young presidential campaign volunteers, Joe Burns, 21, spent much of January stumping for his candidate, Republican businessman Steve Forbes. But while other trudged through blizzards in Iowa and New Hampshire, Burns sat in the warmth of his Syracuse University fraternity house.

An "ePrecinct" leader for the Forbes campaign, Burns spent his time e-mailing potential Forbes supporters, urging them to vote for Forbes in the caucuses or primaries.

"It's certainly different than traditional campaigning activities," Burns said. "It's easier to send out an e-mail than to drive to New Hampshire for a weekend and knock on doors in freezing weather."

The ePrecinct leaders add a personal touch that mass mailings can't, Burns said: "The voters know it's coming from a genuine Forbes supporter instead of a printing press."

Personalization is an important aspect of Sen. John McCain's on-line strategy as well. Young people interested in getting involved in the McCain campaign will find a Web site that devotes a page to each youth organizaion in each state.

"This is how we're making the Internet local to everybody," said Max Fose, Internet manager for the McCain campaign.

The pages vary widely. The Texas page simply lists contact information; Georgia, on the other hand, features waving flags, photos, links, upcoming events, and an inspirational letter from twenty-one-year-old Zach Procter, a student at Georgia Tech who serves as McCain's regional coordinator.

Excited over his candidate's victory in the Republican primary in New Hampshire, Procter planned to update the site "as soon as my roommate gets back from class," he said.

Procter said that he has signed up forty-six people across the state through his site. He has used it to organize everything from class e-mailings to a weekend trip to South Carolina. He's currently planning an electronic flyer campaign, in which he'll post a McCain poster on the site and encourage other McCain volunteers to download it, print it out, and put it up in their neighborhoods—saving on printing and distribution costs.

SOURCE: Andy Sullivan, "Virtual Campaigning Attracts Generation Y," Medill News Service, February 2, 1999.

FROM LABOR-INTENSIVE TO CAPITAL-INTENSIVE POLITICS

The displacement of organizational methods by the new political technology is, in essence, a shift from labor-intensive to capital-intensive competitive electoral practices. Campaign tasks that were once performed by masses of party workers with some cash now require fewer personnel but a great deal more money, for the new political style depends on polls, computers, and other electronic paraphernalia. Of course, even when workers and organization were the key electoral tools, money had considerable political significance. Nevertheless, during the nineteenth century, national political campaigns in the United States employed millions of people. Indeed, as many as 2.5 million individuals did political work during the 1880s.[13] The direct cost of campaigns, therefore, was relatively low. For example, in 1860, Abraham Lincoln spent only $100,000—which was approximately twice the amount spent by his chief opponent, Stephen Douglas.

Modern campaigns depend heavily on money. Each element of the new political technology is enormously expensive. A sixty-second spot announcement on prime-time network television costs hundreds of thousands of dollars each time it is aired. Opinion surveys can be quite expensive; polling costs in a statewide race can easily reach or exceed the six-figure mark. Campaign consultants can charge substantial fees. A direct-mail campaign can eventually become an important source of funds but is very expensive to initiate. The inauguration of a serious national direct-mail effort requires at least $1 million in "front-end cash" to pay for mailing lists, brochures, letters, envelopes, and postage.[14] Although the cost of televised debates is covered by the sponsoring organizations and the television stations and is therefore free to the candidates, even debate preparation requires substantial staff work, research, and, of course, money. It is the expense of the new technology that accounts for the enormous cost of recent American national elections.

Certainly "people power" is not irrelevant to modern political campaigns. Candidates continue to utilize the political services of tens of thousands of volunteer workers. Nevertheless, in the contemporary era, even the recruitment of campaign workers has become a matter of electronic technology. Employing a technique called "instant organization," paid telephone callers use phone banks to contact individuals in areas targeted by a computer (which they do when contacting potential voters, as we discussed before). Volunteer workers are recruited from among these individuals. A number of campaigns—Richard Nixon's 1968 presidential campaign was the first—have successfully used this technique.

The displacement of organizational methods by the new political technology has the most far-reaching implications for the balance of power among contending political groups. Labor-intensive organizational tactics allowed parties whose chief support came from groups nearer the bottom of the social scale to use the numerical superiority of their forces as a partial counterweight to the institutional and economic resources more readily available to the opposition. The capital-intensive technological format, by contrast, has given a major boost to the political fortunes of those forces whose sympathizers are better able to furnish the large sums now needed to compete effectively.[15] Indeed, the new technology permits financial resources to be more effectively harnessed and exploited than was ever before possible.

Dominated by the new technology, electoral politics has become a contest

Politics on the Web

In the end, Senator John McCain's bid for the presidency in 2000 was little more than an attention-grabber. But his legacy included an unprecedented success in using the Internet to raise funds, which briefly brought the medium to the forefront of American politics.

While it remains only one tool for candidates, campaigners believe that the Internet is indeed changing the political landscape, but in ways that are still uncertain. In 1998, over 63 percent of all campaigns had a Web site. Such sites are mainly used to raise money and recruit volunteers, but they can also function as important public-relations tools, because it is the *campaign*—and not the media, for example—that controls the information they broadcast.

How can the Internet improve upon a traditional campaign? Is the interactivity of the Web relevant to a campaign? Who visits campaign Web sites and why? The answers to these questions will become more clear over the next few election cycles.

www.wwnorton.com/wtp3e

in which the wealthy and powerful have a decided advantage. Furthermore, both political parties are compelled to rely heavily on the support of well-funded special interests—a situation that has become clear in the fund-raising scandals that have plagued both parties in recent years. We shall return to this topic later in this chapter.

The 2000 Elections

During periods of economic prosperity, Americans generally return the party in power to office. The 2000 national elections were held during a period of peace and one of the greatest periods of economic prosperity America has ever known. To further enhance the Democrats' prospects, Democratic partisans continued to outnumber Republican identifiers in the national electorate. Thus, all things considered, it seemed more than likely that Vice President Al Gore and his running mate, Connecticut senator Joe Lieberman, would lead the Democratic Party to victory against an inexperienced and little-known Republican presidential nominee—Texas governor George W. Bush. Bush is, of course, the eldest son of former president George Bush, who had been driven from office by Bill Clinton and Al Gore in 1992. Indeed, most academic models of election outcomes predicted an easy Democratic victory, with some even forecasting a Gore landslide.

Nevertheless, when the results of the vote finally became known, George W. Bush and his running mate, former defense secretary Dick Cheney, appeared to have eked out the narrowest of electoral college victories—271 to 267—over Gore and Lieberman (see Figure 11.4). Indeed, in terms of popular vote totals, the Gore/Lieberman ticket actually outpolled the Republicans by slightly more than 300,000 votes, or about three-tenths of one percent of the approximately 103 million votes cast across the nation.

Election night produced unusual drama and confusion when it became clear that the election's outcome would hinge on voting results in Florida, a state with twenty-five electoral votes. Initially, the television networks declared Gore the winner in Florida on the basis of exit poll results. This projection seemed to indicate that Gore would likely win the presidency. Later that night, however, as votes were counted, it became clear that the exit polls were incorrect and that the Florida results were much in doubt. In the early hours of the next morning, all of the votes were tallied and Bush seemed to have won by fewer than 2,000 votes, out of nearly six million cast across the state. Vice President Gore called Governor Bush and conceded defeat.

Within an hour, however, Gore was on the phone to Bush again—this time to withdraw his concession. Under Florida law, the narrowness of Bush's victory—less than one-tenth of one percent—triggered an automatic recount. Moreover, reports of election irregularities had begun to surface. For example, nearly 20,000 votes in Palm Beach County had been invalidated because voters, apparently confused by the ballot, had indicated more than one presidential choice. Given the closeness of the race and the various uncertainties, Democrats decided to await the results of a statewide recount of the vote.

DISTRIBUTION OF ELECTORAL VOTES IN THE 2000 ELECTION

Figure 11.4

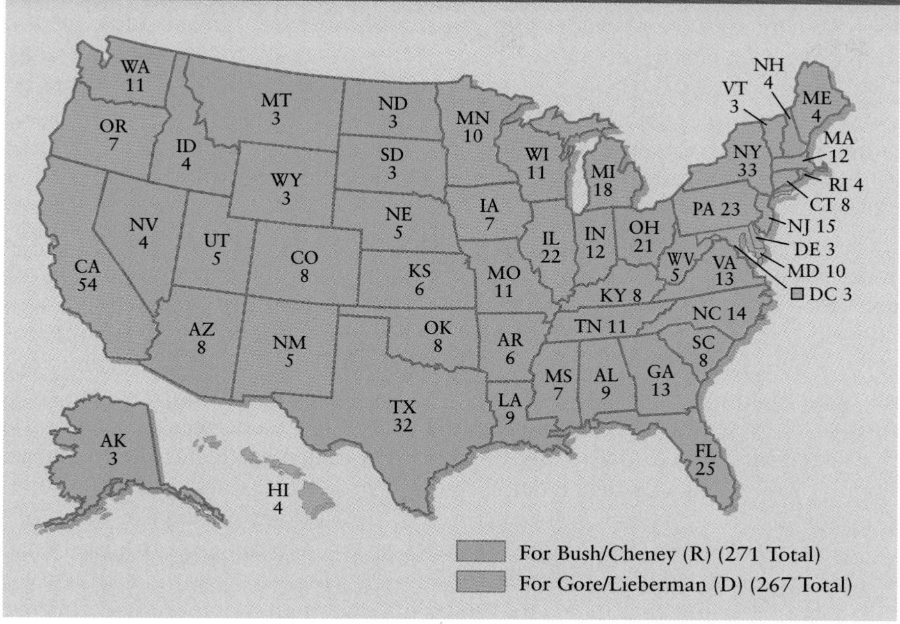

While the recount and the counting of overseas absentee ballots narrowed Bush's margin of victory to a mere 980 votes, it did not change the result. In the meantime, Democrats filed a series of court challenges to the outcome, calling for a hand recount in at least three counties, Miami-Dade, Broward, and Palm Beach. Although Katherine Harris, Florida's top election official, announced that she would not accept the results of these hand recounts, Florida's supreme court ruled that the recounts must be included in the state's official election results. Under disputed circumstances, Miami-Dade County decided not to recount and Palm Beach County missed the deadline for recounted ballots. Gore gained several hundred votes in Broward County but not enough to change the results. These events led to further lawsuits in the Florida courts, the U.S. Court of Appeals, and the U.S. Supreme Court, as Gore refused to concede defeat until all possible legal appeals had been made. Florida's supreme court gave Gore a last-minute reprieve by ordering the manual recounting of approximately 43,000 ballots statewide. Bush appealed this hand recount to the U.S. Supreme Court. By a narrow 5-4 margin, the Court blocked the further counting of Florida's disputed votes, effectively handing the presidency to Bush after a thirty-five-day struggle.

In Senate and House races, voting was also extremely close. Democrats gained some ground in both congressional chambers, but not enough to deprive the GOP of its control of either. Republicans held a narrow six-seat advantage in the House. The Senate was evenly divided 50-50, but with Vice

President Dick Cheney casting any tie-breaking votes, the GOP held a slight advantage. Against all odds, Republicans appeared to have carried the day. Given an extremely buoyant economy, a nation at peace, and an edge in partisan attachments, how could the Democrats have lost? How could the race even have been close?

One key reason Al Gore and the Democrats were unable to capitalize on what seeemed to be an ideal set of conditions was the tenor of Gore's national campaign. Early in the 2000 campaign, Gore made the fateful decision to distance himself from the person and political strategy of his boss, President Bill Clinton. Gore said repeatedly to interviewers, "I am my own man." Journalists correctly interpreted this declaration to mean that Gore wanted to distance himself from the scandals of the Clinton administration. Indeed, he sought to present a picture of moral rectitude and respect for family and religion, that would prevent Republicans from linking him to the moral laxity associated with Bill Clinton. Gore made much of the strength of his marriage and religious beliefs. He refused to allow Clinton to participate in his campaign. He selected as his running mate Senator Joe Lieberman, not only the first Jew nominated for national office by either major party, but a man known for his strong religious beliefs and attention to moral values. Lieberman had been one of the first Democrats to criticize Bill Clinton's conduct in the Monica Lewinsky scandal. Gore thus used Lieberman's nomination to distinguish himself from Clinton on a moral level.

Gore's assertion that he wanted to be his own man, however, had another component that many journalists overlooked. Gore sought not only to distinguish himself from Clinton's morals; he also distanced himself from his politics. In 1992 and 1996, Clinton had adopted centrist positions on most domestic and foreign policy issues. In the 1992 election, the Arkansas governor aimed to present himself as a "new Democrat," i.e., one who differed sharply from the liberalism of George McGovern and Walter Mondale, which had brought the party defeat in 1972 and 1984. He adopted moderate positions on economic policy and even seemed to question the Democratic Party's stance on civil rights. He talked about middle-class concerns like crime, welfare reform, and fiscal restraint. His strategy of moderation helped bring victory in 1992 and again in 1996. In the latter year's race, Clinton pursued a strategy of "triangulation," developed by his adviser, Dick Morris. This strategy called for the incumbent president to position himself midway between the liberalism of congressional Democrats and the conservatism of congressional Republicans. According to Morris, holding the center was the key to victory in the national election, and the strategy succeeded.

In choosing to be his own man, Gore abandoned Clinton's strategy. From his perspective, the problem with moderation and triangulation was that they failed to energize core Democratic constituencies, including liberal public interest groups, organized labor, and African Americans. Liberal groups had been furious with Clinton over his positions on welfare reform and education. Organized labor viewed Clinton as insufficiently committed to its cause; indeed, some unions considered backing Green Party candidate Ralph Nader and his message of opposition to global capitalism. African Americans felt a real rapport with Clinton and supported him as an individual, but expected more vigorous efforts from his successor with regard to civil rights causes.

Confronting a restive Democratic base, Gore chose to depart from "Clintonism" and move slightly to the left. He attacked drug companies for charging too much. He promised African Americans stronger support for affirmative action. He pledged to expand Social Security and Medicare coverage for the elderly. He courted organized labor by promising to raise the minimum wage and appealed to the powerful teachers' unions by opposing school choice and voucher programs. Most importantly, Gore rejected the notion of using the projected government revenue surplus to cut federal income taxes. Thus, he promised tax cuts to selected Democratic constituencies but argued that an across-the-board cut would benefit only the wealthiest one-percent of Americans, at the expense of everyone else. In short, Gore became his own man by abandoning triangulation in favor of a more traditional Democratic populism.

Gore's repositioning became clearly evident to the public during the first presidential debate. Bush presented himself as a centrist who would "bring the country together." He eschewed appeals based on race, class, or gender. He promised a tax cut for all Americans and embraced such middle-class issues as education reform. Gore, on the other hand, pursued the rhetoric of Democratic populism. His mantra throughout the debate was that Bush would give a tax cut to the wealthiest one-percent while ignoring poorer Americans. Rather than wrap himself in the Clinton mantle of moderation—and unprecedented prosperity—Gore chose to appeal to the Democratic base with a message of populism and a hint of class warfare. Soon after the first debate, Gore's standing in the polls dropped while Bush's rose. By demanding to be his own man and distancing himself from Clinton, Gore made it difficult for himself to claim credit for the prosperity of the Clinton era.

In the closing days of the campaign, Gore abandoned his populist theme and focused instead on his opponent's qualifications for the presidency—Bush was said to be inexperienced and to lack the intelligence needed for the office; also, an old drunk-driving conviction surfaced to cast doubt on his character. This change of campaign tactics helped Gore to close the gap in the final week of the campaign. On Election Day, Gore actually outpolled Bush by a relatively small margin, leading to the first instance since 1888 of the popular-vote winner losing in the electoral college. Against the backdrop of peace and unprecedented prosperity, though, the election should not even have been close. Forced to suffer the indignity of being excluded from the campaign, Bill Clinton must have secretly savored Al Gore's fumbling efforts to be his own man.

When the 2000 election finally ended, one important question remained: Could the nation be governed effectively? The House and Senate were almost evenly divided. The presidency was decided by a few hundred votes and a creaky institution last noticed in 1888. These results seemed tailor-made for a divided government and a divided nation. Consequently, the job of the next president and next Congress promised to be more difficult than at any other time in the nation's recent history.

Money and Politics

- How do candidates raise and spend campaign funds? How does the government regulate campaign spending?
- How does money affect how certain social groups achieve electoral success?

Modern national political campaigns are fueled by enormous amounts of money. In a national race, millions of dollars are spent on media time, as well as on public opinion polls and media consultants. In 2000, political candidates and independent groups spent a total of more than $3.0 billion on election campaigns. The average winning candidate in a campaign for a seat in the House of Representatives spent more than $500,000; the average winner in a senatorial campaign spent $4.5 million.[16] The 2000 Democratic and Republican presidential candidates received a total of $150 million in public funds to run their campaigns.[17] Each presidential candidate was also helped by tens of millions of dollars in so-called independent expenditures on the part of corporate and ideological "political action committees." As long as such political expenditures are not formally coordinated with a candidate's campaign, they are considered to be constitutionally protected free speech and are not subject to legal limitation or even reporting requirements. Likewise, independent **soft money** spending by political parties is also considered to be an expression of free speech.[18]

soft money
money contributed directly to political parties for voter registration and organization

SOURCES OF CAMPAIGN FUNDS

Federal Election Commission data suggest that approximately one-fourth of the private funds spent on political campaigns in the United States is raised through small, direct-mail contributions; about one-fourth is provided by large, individual gifts; and another fourth comes from contributions from PACs. The remaining fourth is drawn from the political parties and from candidates' personal or family resources.[19] Another source of campaign funds, which are not required to be reported to the Federal Election Commission, are independent expenditures by interest groups and parties.

Individual Donors Direct mail serves both as a vehicle for communicating with voters and as a mechanism for raising funds. Direct-mail fund-raising efforts begin with the purchase or rental of computerized mailing lists of voters deemed likely to support the candidate because of their partisan ties, interests, or ideology. Candidates send out pamphlets, letters, and brochures describing their views and appealing for funds. Tens of millions of dollars are raised by national, state, and local candidates through direct mail each year, usually in $25 and $50 contributions, although in 2000, Bush and Gore collected about three-quarters of their donor contributions from individuals giving the $1,000 maximum amount.[20]

political action committee (PAC)
a private group that raises and distributes funds for use in election campaigns

Political Action Committees Political action committees (PACs) are organizations established by corporations, labor unions, or interest groups to channel the contributions of their members into political campaigns. Under the terms of the 1971 Federal Elections Campaign Act, which governs campaign

FEDERAL CAMPAIGN FINANCE REGULATION

Box 11.1

Campaign Contributions

No individual may contribute more than $1,000 to any one candidate in any single election. Individuals may contribute as much as $20,000 to a national party committee and up to $5,000 to a political action committee. Full disclosure is required by candidates of all contributions over $100. Candidates may not accept cash contributions over $100.

Political Action Committees

Any corporation, labor union, trade association, or other organization may establish a political action committee (PAC). PACs must contribute to the campaigns of at least five different candidates and may contribute as much as $5,000 per candidate in any given election.

Presidential Elections

Candidates in presidential primaries may receive federal matching funds if they raise at least $5,000 in each of twenty states. The money raised must come in contributions of $250 or less. The amount raised by candidates in this way is matched by the federal government, dollar for dollar, up to a limit of $5 million. In the general election, major-party candidates' campaigns are fully funded by the federal government. Candidates may spend no money beyond their federal funding. Independent groups may spend money on behalf of a candidate so long as their efforts are not directly tied to the official campaign. Minor-party candidates may get partial federal funding.

Federal Election Commission (FEC)

The six-member FEC supervises federal elections, collects and publicizes campaign finance records, and investigates violations of federal campaign finance law.

finance in the United States, PACs are permitted to make larger contributions to any given candidate than individuals are allowed to make (see Box 11.1). Individuals may donate a maximum of $1,000 to any single candidate, but a PAC may donate as much as $5,000 to each candidate. Moreover, allied or related PACs often coordinate their campaign contributions, greatly increasing the amount of money a candidate actually receives from the same interest group. As a result, PACs have become central to campaign finance in the United States. Many critics assert that PACs corrupt the political process by allowing corporations and other interests to influence politicians with large contributions. It is by no means clear, however, that PACs corrupt the political process any more than large, individual contributions.

In recent years, candidates have learned to use several loopholes in the law governing PACs. For example, until a potential presidential candidate has actually declared his or her candidacy, expenditures by their political action committees generally do not count toward their presidential spending limits. A number of 2000 presidential hopefuls, including Dan Quayle, Jack Kemp, and John Kasich, began early to raise funds that were not subject to the nominal federal limits. In addition, candidates have discovered that federal regulations govern federal PACs, but not state PACs. Before 2000, a number of national candidates established state PACs, which then proceeded to engage in political activities at the national level. For example, Republican presidential hopeful

Lamar Alexander established a national PAC and a Tennessee PAC in preparation for the 2000 presidential race. While his national PAC was subject to federal rules, Alexander's Tennessee PAC accepted unlimited contributions. Nothing prevented the Tennessee PAC from engaging in nationally helpful activities such as polling in Iowa or sponsoring a lobster-fest in New Hampshire.

The Candidates On the basis of the Supreme Court's 1976 decision in *Buckley v. Valeo,* the right of individuals to spend their *own* money to campaign for office is a constitutionally protected matter of free speech and is not subject to limitation. Thus, extremely wealthy candidates often contribute millions of dollars to their own campaigns. Jon Corzine, for example, spent approximately $60 million of his own funds in a successful New Jersey Senate bid in 2000.

issue advocacy
independent spending by individuals or interest groups on a campaign issue but not directly tied to a particular candidate

Independent Spending As was noted above, "independent" spending is also free from regulation; private groups, political parties, and wealthy individuals, engaging in what is called **issue advocacy,** may spend as much as they wish to help elect one candidate or defeat another, as long as these expenditures are not coordinated with any political campaign. Many business and ideological groups engage in such activities. Some estimates suggest that groups and individuals spent as much as $150 million on issue advocacy—generally through television advertising—during the 1996 elections.[21] Issue advocacy and independent expenditures increased even more during the 2000 election cycle, to an estimated $400 million or more. The National Rifle Association, for example, spent $3 million dollars reminding voters of the importance of the right to bear arms, while the National Abortion and Reproductive Rights League spent nearly $5 million to express its support for Al Gore.

Some groups are careful not to mention particular candidates in their issues ads to avoid any suggestion that they might merely be fronts for a candidate's campaign committee. Most issues ads, however, are attacks on the opposing candidate's record or character. Organized labor spent more than $35 million in 1996 to attack a number of Republican candidates for the

Bill and Hillary Clinton thanked rock musician Lenny Kravitz and country singer LeAnn Rimes for performing at a Democratic National Committee fund-raiser that brought in over $26 million. In his last year as president, Bill Clinton attended numerous fund-raisers that brought in millions of dollars in soft money for the Democratic Party.

POLICY DEBATE

Campaign Finance Reform and Soft Money

Americans have long favored campaign finance reform, but the 1996 elections intensified cries for reform as never before. Chief among critics' complaints was the proliferation of "soft money"—money raised and spent by political parties. Unlike "hard money"—funds raised and spent directly on behalf of a candidate, subject to federal spending limits and other regulations spelled out in the Federal Election Campaign Act—soft money falls outside of federal regulations, as long as the funds are raised and spent by political parties or independent groups that have no formal affiliation with a candidate's campaign. Such spending is unregulated and subject only to limited disclosure. Although soft money made up a small percentage of all campaign spending up until 1992, it exploded in 1996. Aside from alarm over the sheer amount of money involved, some of the money apparently came from abroad, inviting charges that foreign governments were trying to shape American elections for their own benefit. Yet not all agree that the campaign finance system needs an overhaul.

Supporters of campaign finance reform argue that democratic values are subverted when a few wealthy, special interests dominate the campaign process. It is all but inevitable that candidates for office, as well as incumbents, will feel an obligation to those who expend thousands or millions of dollars on their behalf. More importantly, current campaign spending patterns overwhelmingly favor incumbents, making it even more difficult for challengers to vie for office. In 2000, incumbent senators spent on average about $3.6 million, whereas their challengers spent an average of $2.2 million; incumbents seeking re-election to the House of Representatives outspent their challengers by an average ratio of 2.3 to 1.

The particular evil posed by soft money is that it represents a throwback to an earlier time when campaign spending was unregulated. The current system of regulated hard money spending and unregulated soft money spending invites an intolerable situation: the buying and selling of American elections to the highest bidder. Ideas for reform are abundant. The only question is whether political leaders have the will to follow strong public support for real reform.

Opponents of campaign finance reform argue that most people misunderstand how and why campaigns operate as they do. Reform opponents point out that every attempt at campaign finance reform has been nothing short of disastrous. The last wave of reform laws, enacted in the 1970s, produced the current system, including the explosion of soft money spending. As several court decisions have suggested, tight limits on campaign spending may violate First Amendment rights and have a chilling effect on local political activities. To those who argue that too much is spent on campaigns, critics argue that, if anything, too little is spent on campaigns. In 1994, for example, Americans spent more than twice as much money on potato chips than they spent on all congressional elections. The momentous decision concerning who shall govern the country is surely more important than the level of money currently being spent. Moreover, research has demonstrated that voters are better informed in elections where more money is spent.

Contrary to popular impression, there is no simple connection between money spent and success at the polls. While money is obviously important, incumbents receive more money simply because it is well understood that incumbents are more likely to win. After all, they are more well known than their challengers, have more experience, and are knowledgeable about their jobs and how to keep them. Further, the idea that big money runs elections more than in the past is, good or bad, not new. Because of our relatively open democratic system, the vast majority of campaign money in the last century has always come from large corporations and the wealthy. Indeed, the 10 percent of citizens who give money to campaigns represents an increase in the percentage of Americans who gave in earlier times.

SOURCE: Bradley A. Smith, "Campaign Finance Regulation: Faulty Assumptions and Undemocratic Consequences," Cato Institute Policy Analysis 238, Washington, DC, September 13, 1995.

STUDENT DEBATE

Is Campaign Finance Reform Necessary?

Yes

Last week the Senate was once again given the opportunity to remove part of the stigma of cynicism associated with politics in this country. Unfortunately for the American people, the interests of wealthy political contributors overcame the interests of democracy as a few key Republican senators thwarted a vote on campaign finance reform.

***

The bill introduced by Sens. John McCain (R-Ariz.) and Russell P. Feingold (D-Wisc.) would have ended the unregulated "soft money" donations to political parties. Currently, the law places strict limits on the amount of money that can be donated to an individual's political campaign, but none on the amount that can be donated to political parties in general.

Most Democrats and a few GOP legislators have rightly complained that these contributions corrupt the legislative process. However, a majority of Republicans, led by majority leader Trent Lott (R-Miss.) and Sen. Mitch McConnell (R-Ky.), vehemently fought the legislation, stating the bill was a violation of free speech and an unwarranted governmental intrusion into campaigns. But in reality, these are euphemisms for their fear that reform might be a threat to their fund-raising advantage.

***

The main problem with the system now is that politicians become beholden to wealthy donors. With the obscenely high costs of running for office, politicians and wannabe politicians are forced to court special interests and other contributors for donations. This puts even the most incorruptible politician in an awkward position, and for those politicians with lesser morals, it puts the entire populace in a precarious position. With strict limits on donations, politicians would not owe anything to anyone but their constituents, helping ensure that legislation is passed for the right reasons.

Additionally, reform legislation would lower the amount of money needed to run in a campaign. This would have several effects.

For one, the focus would shift away from the size of the candidate's bank account, as is the case with the current presidential election. With less attention on finances, more attention can be spent on issues.

Second, by helping to equalize the playing field, campaign finance reform would ensure that money does not necessarily equal elect-ability.

Third, without costly campaigns a greater number of people, and certainly a more diverse group of people, would have the ability to run for office.

Furthermore, reform would vastly reduce the amount of time, energy, and resources now used for fundraising, leaving politicians with greater ability to perform their elected duties.

Yet some opponents of reform decry that while all of this might be true, they cannot in good conscience support reform because it is a violation of free speech. This reasoning, however, is extremely flawed. Currently, campaign contributions are regulated, and no court has ever overturned reform laws on the basis that they are a violation of free speech. All the proposed legislation does is eliminate the loopholes that have made past legislation virtually ineffective.

***

Fortunately, there is hope that campaign finance reform might have a better chance of success in the future. The bill has been passed in the House, and in the Senate, reform proponents have picked up three more votes than they had last year.

Campaign fiance reform legislation is the only way to ensure that wealth does not equal unfair political advantage and domination. If we don't want our democratic ideals to be held hostage to special interests, we must keep this issue in the forefront of our minds and choose candidates accordingly in the next elections.

SOURCE: Elaine Albenda, "A Voice for Campaign Finance Reform," *The Diamondback* (University of Maryland), November 3, 1999.

No

Though the term is used as if referring to the bogeyman, soft money is constitutionally protected speech. In 1976's *Buckley v. Valeo*, the Supreme Court found that in politics, money is speech. The Court noted that the communication of political messages requires the expenditure of money, and held that limiting spending and donations in federal elections was a direct burden restricting core constitutional conduct. In other words, when individuals and corporations give money to political parties, they are exercising their fundamental rights as American citizens. Banning soft money is a violation of those rights.

Banning soft money will do more harm than good to the extent that it will damage political parties. Soft money is the lifeblood of the parties, and as such is the energy behind American politics. As Clinton Rossiter said in "Parties and Politics in America," "there is no America without democracy, no democracy without politics, and no politics without parties." Political parties are unique entities that play a very specific role in American politics.

Parties promote agreement between interest groups. Above all, they want to win elections, and therefore parties work to compromise difference for the common cause. Parties also promote discussion of major issues. By creating a platform like the "Contract with America," a party frames the choices facing the electorate and helps voters make informed decisions. Parties foster effective government. The separation of powers often creates gridlock between the branches and the federalist system creates a division between the state and national government. Parties act as a unifying force that cuts through the divisions.

Parties provide responsibility and accountability. By establishing a platform and agenda, voters know who to blame or praise for the results of government action. Finally, parties promote political participation. They enroll voters and give citizens a way to join with others in political action.

Doing away with soft money, though catchy in name and appealing in polling data, would severely constrict the parties' abilities to perform these key functions. Though politicians like McCain claim that it will reduce the power of special interests and the potential corruption and influence-peddling that their money brings, it is hard to see how. Under current law, soft money cannot be used for any specific candidate, and parties are limited in how much money they can spend in coordinated efforts with their candidate. Soft money therefore does not pose the ominous threat to officeholder's virute that McCain believes. Doing away with soft money is just such a threat.

As a source of funds, parties probably constitute the cleanest money in politics. They raise money from individuals and orgainzed interests. Their mix of sources is more diverse than that of any major organization. As a result, parties are actually relatively free from special-interest influence. A candidate's integrity is seldom threatened in accepting party funds. As Larry J. Sabato, government and foreign affairs professor, pointed out in his book *The Party's Just Begun*: "The less party money there is available, the more candidates will have to rely on PAC money; the more resources the parties can share with their nominees, the less officeholders will be indebted to special interest groups."

The assault on soft money is an assault on political parties. Though motivated by good intentions, the result will be the erosion of First Amendment freedoms and the ability of political parties to do their important work. As the Committee for Party Renewal said in *amicus* brief before the Supreme Court, "Political parties are the most comprehensive and potentially most effective form of political association through which ordinary Americans can influence the direction of government. We should prize them as the cornerstones of representative democracy and work to assure their vitality." Opposing McCain-Feingold would be a good start.

SOURCE: Sam Waxman, "Proposed Soft Money Caps Limit Party Power," *Cavalier Daily* (University of Virginia), October 7, 1999.

House of Representatives. Business groups launched their own multimillion-dollar issues campaign to defend the GOP House members targeted by labor.[22] In 2000, liberal groups ran ads bashing Bush's record on capital punishment, tax reform, and Social Security. Conservative groups attacked Gore's views on gun ownership, abortion, and environmental regulation.

Parties and Soft Money State and local party organizations use soft money for get-out-the-vote drives and voter education and registration efforts. These are the party-building activities for which soft-money contributions are nominally made. Most soft-money dollars, however, are spent to assist candidates' re-election efforts in the form of issue advocacy, campaigns on behalf of a particular candidate thinly disguised as mere advocacy of particular issues. For example, in 1996, issue advocacy commercials sponsored by state Democratic Party organizations looked just like commercials for Clinton. The issue commercials praised the president's stand on major issues and criticized the GOP's positions. The only difference was that the issue ads did not specifically call for the re-election of President Clinton. In 2000, the Democratic Party raised and spent $371 million in support of its national, state, and local candidates. For its part, the GOP was able to raise more than $525 million. According to the Federal Election Commission, sources of Democratic funds included lawyers and lobbyists; the finance, insurance, and real estate industries; and organized labor. The GOP benefited from contributions by agribusiness, banks and financial interests, transportation concerns, healthcare corporations, and small business. Critics contend that soft money is less a vehicle for building parties than it is a mechanism for circumventing federal election laws.

In some instances, large donors to the Democratic and Republican parties do not want to be publicly identified. To accommodate these "stealth donors," both parties have created sham nonprofit groups to serve as the nominal recipients of the gifts. For example, the Democratic Party established an organization called "Vote Now '96," which ostensibly worked to increase voter turnout. This organization received several million dollars in donations that were used on behalf of the Clinton/Gore re-election effort. For their part, Republicans created two nonprofit groups that took in more than $3 million.[23]

In these instances, issues campaigns seem to violate federal election law by actually being coordinated with candidate or party committees. Democrats, for example, have charged that a 1996 issues campaign nominally run by Americans for Tax Reform, a conservative nonprofit group, was actually controlled by the Republican National Committee. Americans for Tax Reform spent roughly $4 million in 1996 on an issues campaign supporting Republican candidates in 150 House districts. The campaign was directed by a former RNC official. The RNC admits that it donated $4.6 million to the group, but denies any further involvement with the antitax group's efforts.[24]

Public Funding The Federal Elections Campaign Act also provides for public funding of presidential campaigns. As they seek a major party presidential nomination, candidates become eligible for public funds by raising at least $5,000 in individual contributions of $250 or less in each of twenty states. Candidates who reach this threshold may apply for federal funds to match, on a dollar-for-dollar basis, all individual contributions of $250 or less they receive. The funds are drawn from the Presidential Election Campaign Fund. Taxpayers can contribute $1 to this fund, at no additional cost to themselves, by checking a box on the first page of their federal income tax returns. Major party presidential candidates receive a lump sum (currently nearly $75 million) during the summer prior to the general election. They must meet all their general expenses from this money. Third-party candidates are eligible for public funding only if they received at least 5 percent of the vote in the previous presidential race. This stipulation effectively blocks preelection funding for third-party or independent candidates, although a third party that wins more than 5 percent of the vote can receive public funding after the election. In 1980, John Anderson convinced banks to loan him money for an independent candidacy on the strength of poll data showing that he would receive more than 5 percent of the vote and thus would obtain public funds with which to repay the loans. Under current law, no candidate is required to accept public funding for either the nominating races or general presidential election. Candidates who do not accept public funding are not affected by any expenditure limits. Thus, in 1992 Ross Perot financed his own presidential bid and was not bound by the $55 million limit to which the Democratic and Republican candidates were held that year. Perot accepted public funding in 1996. In 2000, George W. Bush refused public funding and raised enough money to finance his own primary campaign. Bush did accept public funding for the general election, though.

CAMPAIGN FINANCE REFORM

The United States is one of the few advanced industrial nations that permit individual candidates to accept large private contributions from individual or corporate donors. Most mandate either public funding of campaigns or, as in the case of Britain, require that large private donations be made to political parties rather than to individual candidates. The logic of such a requirement is that a contribution that might seem very large to an individual candidate would weigh much less heavily if made to a national party. Thus, the chance that a donor could buy influence would be reduced.

Over the past several years, a number of pieces of legislation have proposed similar restrictions on the private funding of campaigns. Political reform has been blocked, however, because the two major parties disagree over the form it should take. The Republicans have developed a very efficient direct-mail apparatus and would be willing to place limits on the role of PACs. The Democrats, by contrast, depend more heavily on PACs and fear that limiting their role would hurt the party's electoral chances.

In the aftermath of the 1996 national elections, the role of soft money came under intense scrutiny. Both political parties raised and spent tens of millions of dollars in soft money to help their presidential candidates, congressional candidates, and candidates for state and local offices. Senators John McCain and Russell Feingold repeatedly initiated an effort to pass legislation to restrict both soft-money contributions and issues advocacy. A combination of partisan and constitutional concerns, however, repeatedly doomed the McCain-Feingold initiative to defeat.

It is unclear whether campaign finance reform efforts will continue after the 2000 elections and, if so, what form they will take. A task force on campaign reform comprised of fourteen political scientists made the following recommendations:

1. Partial public funding should be offered to congressional candidates.
2. Contribution limits should be modestly increased and subsequently adjusted for inflation.
3. Reasonable limits should be imposed on soft money contributions and on total soft money spending by the parties.
4. Full disclosure of the sponsorship of all campaign-related issue advocacy should be required.
5. The administrative capacity and resources of the Federal Election Commission should be significantly increased.
6. Free air time providing direct access for candidates to communicate with citizens should be made available, either voluntarily by broadcasters or through specific mandates by Congress.

If campaign finance reform were to occur sometime after 2000, it would likely take the form of one or more of these recommendations.

IMPLICATIONS FOR DEMOCRACY

Ellen Malcolm, president of EMILY's List, at a fund-raising event for the group.

The important role played by private funds in American politics affects the balance of power among contending social groups. Politicians need large amounts of money to campaign successfully for major offices. This fact inevitably ties their interests to the interests of the groups and forces that can provide this money. In a nation as large and diverse as the United States, to be sure, campaign contributors represent many different groups and often represent clashing interests. Business groups, labor groups, environmental groups, and pro-choice and right-to-life forces all contribute millions of dollars to political campaigns. Through such PACs as EMILY's List, women's groups contribute millions of dollars to women running for political office. One set of trade associations may contribute millions to win politicians' support for telecommunications reform, while another set may contribute just as much to block the same reform efforts. Insurance companies may contribute millions of dollars to Democrats to win their support for changes in the health care system, while physicians may contribute equal amounts to prevent the same changes from becoming law.

Despite this diversity of contributors, however, not all interests play a role in financing political campaigns. Only those interests that have a good deal of money to spend can make their interests known in this way. These interests are not monolithic, but they do not completely reflect the diversity of American society. The poor, the destitute, and the downtrodden also live in America and have an interest in the outcome of political campaigns. Who is to speak for them?

THE ELECTORAL PROCESS AND AMERICAN POLITICAL VALUES

As we have seen throughout this book, Americans' most fundamental values often clash leaving us perplexed as to the best way to proceed. In the realm of electoral politics, the question of campaign finance produces such a clash of values. On the one hand, most Americans are wary of the high cost of campaigns and the apparently sinister role of campaign contributions in the political process. Through their contributions, wealthy individuals and well-heeled interest groups seek to influence election outcomes, the behavior of elected officials and, through so-called issue advertising, even the tenor of the political debate. Calls for campaign finance reform are widely heard and one 2000 presidential candidate, John McCain, made campaign finance reform his signature issue.

The problem, however, is that while reform of spending practices might appear to advance the goal of political equality, it might do so at the expense of liberty. If the government writes rules regulating campaign finance is there not a good chance that those currently in power will twist the rules to serve their own interests? Don't we want to encourage vigorous and lively political debate—even though it may be expensive? Should not any group of citizens be free to promote its political ideas at its own expense? These are questions worth pondering and, as we often see in political life, dilemmas with no quick and easy solution.

How Voters Decide

▶ What are the primary influences on voters' decisions?

Whatever the capacity of those with the money and power to influence the electoral process, it is the millions of individual decisions on election day that ultimately determine electoral outcomes. Sooner or later the choices of voters weigh more heavily than the schemes of campaign advisers or the leverage of interest groups.

Three types of factors influence voters' decisions at the polls: partisan loyalty, issue and policy concerns, and candidate characteristics.

PARTISAN LOYALTY

Many studies have shown that most Americans identify more or less strongly with one or the other of the two major political parties. Partisan loyalty was considerably stronger during the 1940s and 1950s than it is today. But even now most voters feel a certain sense of identification or kinship with the Democratic or Republican party. This sense of identification is often handed down from parents to children and is reinforced by social and cultural ties. Partisan identification predisposes voters in favor of their party's candidates and against those of the opposing party (see Figure 11.5 on the next page). At the level of the presidential contest, issues and candidate personalities may become very important, although even here many Americans supported George W. Bush or Al Gore in the 2000 race only because of partisan loyalty. But partisanship is more likely to assert itself in the less-visible races, where issues and the candidates are not as well known. State legislative races, for example, are often decided by voters' party ties. Once formed, voters' partisan loyalties seldom change. Voters tend to keep their party affiliations unless some crisis causes them to reexamine the bases of their loyalties and to conclude that they have not given their support to the appropriate party. During these relatively infrequent periods of electoral change, millions of voters can change their

Figure 11.5 THE EFFECT OF PARTY IDENTIFICATION ON THE VOTE, 2000

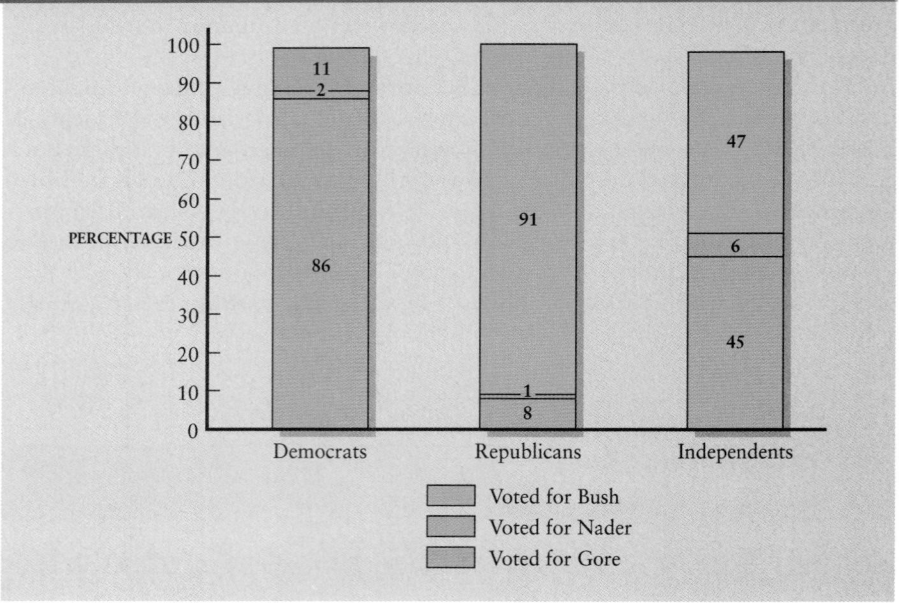

party ties. For example, at the beginning of the New Deal era, between 1932 and 1936, millions of former Republicans transferred their allegiance to Franklin Roosevelt and the Democrats.

ISSUES

Issues and policy preferences are a second factor influencing voters' choices at the polls. Voters may cast their ballots for the candidate whose position on economic issues they believe to be closest to their own. Similarly, they may select the candidate who has what they believe to be the best record on foreign policy. Issues are more important in some races than others. If candidates actually "take issue" with one another, that is, articulate and publicize very different positions on important public questions, then voters are more likely to be able to identify and act on whatever policy preferences they may have.

prospective voting
voting based on the imagined future performance of a candidate.

retrospective voting
voting based on the past performance of a candidate.

The ability of voters to make choices on the basis of issue or policy preferences is diminished, however, if competing candidates do not differ substantially or do not focus their campaigns on policy matters. Very often, candidates deliberately take the safe course and emphasize topics that will not be offensive to any voters. Thus, candidates often trumpet their opposition to corruption, crime, and inflation. Presumably, few voters favor these things. Although it may be perfectly reasonable for candidates to take the safe course and remain as inoffensive as possible, this candidate strategy makes it extremely difficult for voters to make their issue or policy preferences the basis for their choices at the polls.

Voters' issue choices usually involve a mix of their judgments about the past behavior of competing parties and candidates and their hopes and fears about candidates' future behavior. Political scientists call choices that focus on future behavior **prospective voting,** while those based on past performance are called **retrospective voting.** To some extent, whether prospective or retrospective evaluation is more important in a particular election depends on the strategies of competing candidates. Candidates always endeavor to define the issues of an election in terms that will serve their interests. Incumbents running during a period of prosperity will seek to take credit for the economy's happy state and define the election as revolving around their record of success. This strategy encourages voters to make retrospective judgments. By contrast, an insurgent running during a period of economic uncertainty will tell voters it is time for a change and ask them to make prospective judgments. Thus, Bill Clinton focused on change in 1992 and prosperity in 1996, and through well-crafted media campaigns was able to define voters' agenda of choices.

In 2000, the key issues at the presidential level were taxes, Social Security reform, healthcare, and education. Bush promised an across-the-board tax cut while Gore asserted that such a move would benefit wealthy Americans, at the expense of the middle class. Both candidates proposed plans to strengthen the Social Security system, with Bush advocating partial privatization of the system; Gore, on the other hand, promised to more adequately fund the current system. In the realm of healthcare, both candidates promised prescription drug plans for seniors. Associated Press exit polls conducted on Election Day indicated that Bush voters saw taxes as the central issue of the campaign, while Gore voters focused on prescription drugs and Social Security.

CANDIDATE CHARACTERISTICS

Candidates' personal attributes always influence voters' decisions. Some analysts claim that voters prefer tall candidates to short ones, candidates with shorter names to candidates with longer names, and candidates with lighter hair to candidates with darker hair. Perhaps these rather frivolous criteria do play some role. But the more important candidate characteristics that affect voters' choices are race, ethnicity, religion, gender, geography, and social background. In general, voters prefer candidates who are closer to themselves in terms of these categories; voters presume that such candidates are likely to have views and perspectives close to their own. Moreover, they may be proud to see someone of their ethnic, religious, or geographic background in a position of leadership. This is why, for many years,

Students and Politics

University of Southern California students majoring in the social sciences and communication have the opportunity to research the backgrounds of political candidates.

Project Vote Smart, an organization geared toward promoting voter education and awareness, is recruiting university students as interns as part of this effort.

"College students are great for this kind of work," said Aili Langseth, intern coordinator for the project. "They really have a strong drive and enthusiasm for finding out the most about a candidate."

Project Vote Smart started as a research project to determine whether voters provided with unbiased information about candidates would use it before going to the polls.

In the beginning, the program existed in only two states, but Langseth said the project then "took off like wildfire."

Unexpectedly, the night before the 1988 election, the group received tens of thousands of calls from voters asking for more information about candidates and the organization itself. It was obvious that the program would have to expand nationally to meet the demands of voters, Langseth said.

* * *

In order to remain bipartisan, the program enlisted the help of university interns for collecting information in several research categories. These include the candidate's political background, contact information, past experience, previous voting record, sources of campaign finance, performance evalutions from eighty liberal and conservative interest groups, and responses to a questionnaire on a wide variety of issues.

Project Vote Smart collects information on 13,000 candidates in presidential, congressional, gubernatorial, and state legislature elections.

"What students have been doing here is taking an active role in the political process by providing voters with the tools necessary to make an educated decision," Langseth said. "Their presence is invaluable."

SOURCE: Kenneth Fuller, "U. Southern California Students to Help Voters Make 'Smart' Decisions," *Daily Trojan* (University of Southern California), November 22, 1999.

politicians sought to "balance the ticket," making certain that their party's ticket included members of as many important groups as possible.

Just as candidates' personal characteristics may attract some voters, they may repel others. Many voters are prejudiced against candidates of certain ethnic, racial, or religious groups. And for many years voters were reluctant to support the candidacies of women, although this appears to be changing.

Voters also pay attention to candidates' personality characteristics, such as "decisiveness," "honesty," and "vigor." In recent years, integrity has become a key election issue. During the 1992 campaign, George Bush accused Bill Clinton of seeking to mislead voters about his anti–Vietnam War activities and his efforts to avoid the draft during the 1960s. This, Bush said, revealed that Clinton lacked the integrity required of a president. Clinton, in turn, accused Bush of resorting to mudslinging because of his poor standing in the polls—an indication of Bush's own character deficiencies. In the 2000 presidential race, Al Gore chose Joe Lieberman as his running mate in part because Lieberman had been sharply critical of Bill Clinton's moral lapses. The senator's presence on the Democratic ticket thus helped to defuse the GOP's efforts to link Gore to Clinton's questionable character. As the race progressed, Gore sought to portray Bush as lacking the intelligence and experience needed for the presidency. This effort met with some success, as a number of talk-show hosts began to caricature Bush as a simpleton who knew little about domestic or foreign policy. Exit polls indicated that many voters also had concerns about Bush's intelligence. For his part, Bush sought to portray Gore as dishonest and duplicitous—a man who would say anything to get elected. This effort, too, led to talk-show caricatures and raised concerns among voters. Ultimately, according to Associated Press exit polls, Bush won the votes of those who said they were concerned about "honesty," while Gore received the support of individuals who felt "experience" was an important presidential attribute.

The Citizen's Role

STUDENTS AND POLITICS

College students can be extremely effective campaigners. For example, Jonathan Sweeney, an Arizona State University student from Boston, Massachusetts, worked as a student campaigner for the Clinton-Gore ticket in 1992. Sweeney was credited with helping to register more than 5,000 new Democratic voters in the Tempe, Arizona, area. He received an invitation to the Clinton inaugural ball in Washington for his efforts.[25]

Sometimes students do even more than work in campaigns: sometimes they run for, and win, public office. Paul Soglin, the former mayor of Madison, Wisconsin, was a University of Wisconsin undergraduate when he began running for office. Similarly, Cornell University student David Lytell was for several years an important Ithaca, New York, alderman. After Lytell left Cornell, he went to work as a White House staffer, where he helped to design the White House Web page.

As these examples suggest, significant opportunities exist for citizen involvement in American electoral politics. The contemporary political process may be quasidemocratic, but it need not remain so.

Campaigning on Campus

The most visible aspect of American politics may be election campaigns. Candidates do their best to get the names, images, ideas, and sound bytes disseminated among potential donors and voters. They seek television and radio talk show appearances and they buy television time and radio advertisements. They hold fund-raising dinners. They often participate in mass mailings and telephone calling to targeted publics. They engineer media events to get print coverage. Generally, they seek to inundate the public with positive messages about themselves and negative messages about their opponents. Campaigning in a democracy is a high-visibility affair.

At any given moment, someone in America is considering, setting up, or actually running a campaign for elected office at the local, state, or national level. You can certainly get involved in a political campaign but your participation is likely to be highly restricted and guided. That is because today's political campaigns are increasingly orchestrated and conducted by professional political consultants who, along with the candidate, make the key decisions and then tell the amateurs what to do.

Your amateur status notwithstanding, you can participate in orchestrating and conducting a political campaign for elected office if you focus your sights on your own student government. In this area, all contenders are amateurs. Is a classmate, colleague, or friend running for the student senate or the student programming board? She will need strategists to figure out how best to get the attention and support of likely voters. She will need managers to recruit volunteers and coordinate their activities. Campaigning is hard work; it can be tiring; but it also can be exhilarating. Here are some practical suggestions for thinking through your campaign strategy.

- Gauge the preferences of the student body. Ask students what changes they think are needed or desirable. See if the concerns of residential students differ from those of commuter students or those involved in sororities and fraternities or students of particular racial, national, or religious identities. Know your electorate.
- Determine which students are most likely to vote. Student apathy on most campuses means that relatively few students will turn out for elections. Nonetheless, think strategically. What issues are likely to rouse students from apathy to action? Do students who are affiliated with particular groups have higher turnout rates than the general student population? How do you direct your appeal to likely voters?
- Develop a plan for getting your candidate known. Posters, signs, and flyers are common ways to get her name out in public. Now, can you get coverage in the student newspaper or on the student radio station? Can you create a catchy slogan that is likely to stick in people's minds? In an electoral campaign, gaining name recognition is half the battle.
- Figure out how to communicate your candidate's stand on key issues. Consider sponsoring or participating in candidate debates or forums, scheduling visits to student organizations and dormitories, forging alliances with student interest organizations likely to support your

candidate's views, or having her spend time talking to students in a central area of campus.

- As the election approaches, devote your energy to getting out the vote among those students most likely to support your candidate. Call the leaders of allied groups and urge them to get their members to vote. Hang "get out the vote" brochures on dormitory door handles. Place posters in strategic places. On the day of the election, remind students to vote (and suggest that they vote for your wonderful candidate).
- Finally, the best strategy is useless unless you have the organization and volunteers to survey student preferences and voting patterns, gain name recognition, set up debates, visits, and alliances, and get out the vote. Accordingly, work out a strategy for recruiting, coordinating, and deploying a cadre of volunteers.

Once you get past some of the frustrations of campaigning and share in its joys, you may decide to run for student office yourself. Perhaps you can make a positive difference on your campus. Which position should you seek? Should you go after a low-profile position with limited autonomy and responsibility? Or should you run for student body president? Talk to people already involved in student government. Find out the options and the responsibilities each position entails. Then consider the time and energy involved in running for office and the likely workload if you are elected to office. If you still have an interest and think you can handle the workload, go for it.

Summary

At the time of America's founding, the right to vote was generally limited to white males over the age of twenty-one. Many states also limited voting rights to those who owned property. Over the years, voting rights were expanded to give all adult Americans the right to participate in elections. Despite this, only about half of all American citizens over the age of eighteen actually vote in presidential elections. Turnout is limited by America's voter registration requirements and the absence of a strong party system to "get out the vote."

Three types of elections are held in the United States: general elections, primary elections, and runoff elections. In most contests, the candidate winning a plurality of the vote is the victor. In some contests, however, victory requires a majority of the votes cast, while others rely on proportional representation. State legislatures draw the boundaries of electoral districts. Often, political forces use a redistricting technique called gerrymandering to attempt to gain political advantage. Presidential elections are different from other American electoral contests. The president is elected indirectly through the electoral college.

Election campaigns are directed by candidates and their advisers. Candidates must secure endorsements, construct an organization, and raise money for both the primary and the general elections. Funds are raised from individuals and from political action committees. Presidential candidates must campaign in a series of statewide primaries and caucuses that lead up to the national party conventions, where the formal Democratic and Republican nominations take place. In addition to candidates' efforts, election outcomes are decided by partisan loyalty, voter response to issues, and voter response to candidates' personalities and qualifications.

The fact that many Americans do not vote gives the American political process a quasidemocratic character. Nonvoters tend to be drawn from low-income, low-education, and minority groups. Neither political party has shown much interest in vigorously promoting voter participation.

FOR FURTHER READING

Black, Earl, and Merle Black. *The Vital South: How Presidents Are Elected.* Cambridge, MA: Harvard University Press, 1992.

Carmines, Edward G., and James Stimson. *Issue Evolution: The Racial Transformation of American Politics.* Princeton, NJ: Princeton University Press, 1988.

Fowler, Linda, and Robert D. McClure. *Political Ambition: Who Decides to Run for Congress.* New Haven, CT: Yale University Press, 1989.

Ginsberg, Benjamin, and Martin Shefter. *Politics by Other Means: Institutional Conflict and the Declining Significance of Elections in America.* New York: Norton, 1999.

Sorauf, Frank. *Inside Campaign Finance: Myths and Realities.* New Haven, CT: Yale University Press, 1992.

Tate, Katherine. *From Protest to Politics: The New Black Voters in American Elections.* Cambridge, MA: Harvard University Press, 1994.

Wilcox, Clyde. *God's Warriors: The Christian Right in Twentieth-Century America.* Baltimore: Johns Hopkins University Press, 1991.

Witt, Linda, Karen Paget, and Glenna Matthews. *Running as a Woman: Gender and Power in American Politics.* New York: Free Press, 1994.

STUDY OUTLINE

The Role of Elections in a Democracy

1. In democratic systems, elections can be used to replace current officeholders as well as to serve as institutions of legitimation.
2. Elections also help to promote government accountability and serve as a source of protection for groups in society.

Elections in America

1. In the American federal system, the responsibility for organizing elections rests largely with state and local governments.
2. State legislators routinely seek to influence electoral outcomes by manipulating the organization of electoral districts.
3. Prior to the 1890s, voters cast ballots according to political parties. The advent of the neutral ballot allowed voters to choose individual candidates rather than a political party as a whole.
4. Americans do not vote directly for presidential candidates. Rather, they choose electors who are pledged to support a party's presidential candidate.

Election Campaigns

1. The first step in campaigning involves the organization of supporters to help the candidate raise funds and create public name recognition.
2. The next steps of campaigning involve hiring experts—campaign managers, media consultants, pollsters, etc.—to aid in developing issues and a message and communicating them to the public.
3. Because most of the time a major party nomination is necessary for electoral success, candidates must seek a party's nomination in primary elections.

Presidential Elections

1. Presidential candidates secure a party's nomination by running in state party primaries and caucuses.
2. Nominations of presidential candidates were first made in caucuses of a party's members of Congress. This system was replaced, in the 1830s, by nominating conventions, which were designed to be a more democratic, deliberative method of nominating candidates.
3. Contemporary conventions merely ratify a party's presidential and vice presidential nominations, although conventions still draft the party platform and adopt rules governing the party and its future conventions.
4. In recent years, the role of the parties during the general campaign has been transformed by the introduction of high-tech campaign techniques, including polls, using the broadcast media, phone banks, direct mail, and professional public relations.
5. In capital-intensive campaigns, the main technique is to use the broadcast media to present the electorate with themes and issues that will induce them to support one candidate over another.

Money and Politics

1. Campaign funds in the United States are provided by small, direct-mail contributions, large gifts, PACs, political parties, candidates' personal resources, and public funding. In 1996, some candidates also benefited from issues advocacy.
2. Campaign finance is regulated by the Federal Elections Campaign Act of 1971. Following the 1996 elections, the role of soft money was scrutinized. The McCain-Feingold bill, a bipartisan attempt to restrict soft money contributions and issues advocacy, failed in consecutive years to gain support in Congress.
3. The role played by private money in American politics affects the relative power of social groups. As a result, less affluent groups have considerably less power in the political system.

How Voters Decide

1. Three factors influence voters' decisions at the polls: partisan loyalty, issues, and candidate characteristics.
2. Partisan loyalty predisposes voters in favor of their party's candidates and against those of the opposing party.
3. The impact of issues and policy preferences on electoral choice is diminished if competing candidates do not differ substantially or do not focus their campaigns on policy matters.
4. Candidates' attributes and personality characteristics always influence voters' decisions.
5. The salience of these three bases of electoral choice varies from contest to contest and from voter to voter.

PRACTICE QUIZ

1. What is the most important difference between democratic and authoritarian electoral systems?
   a) The latter do not allow the defeat of those in power.
   b) There are no elections in authoritarian systems.
   c) Democratic systems use elections as a safety valve for social discontent.
   d) Authoritarian elections are not organized by party.
2. The neutral ballot made it possible for voters to
   a) vote the party line.
   b) split-ticket vote.
   c) send clear mandates for policy change.
   d) both a and b
3. What is the difference between an open and a closed primary?
   a) You must pay a poll tax to vote in a closed primary.
   b) Open primaries allow voters to split the ticket.
   c) In closed primaries, only registered members of a political party may vote to select that party's candidates.
   d) They are fundamentally the same thing.
4. What are the potential consequences of ideological struggles in primary contests?
   a) General election chances may be undermined.
   b) Party extremists may win the nomination.
   c) Typical party supporters may refuse to support the party's nominee.
   d) all of the above
5. What is the most fundamental change in national conventions in the twentieth century?
   a) They no longer nominate presidential candidates.
   b) Now party platforms are written at the convention.
   c) The participation of electoral officials in conventions has continued to decline.
   d) none of the above
6. Which of the following is not an example of a media technique introduced in the 1992 presidential campaign?
   a) the spot advertisement
   b) the town meeting
   c) the infomercial
   d) a, b, and c were all introduced in 1992.

7. In *Buckley v. Valeo,* the Supreme Court ruled that
   a) PAC donations to campaigns are constitutionally protected.
   b) The right of individuals to spend their own money to campaign is constitutionally protected.
   c) The political system is corrupt.
   d) The Federal Elections Campaign Act is unconstitutional.
8. Partisan loyalty
   a) is often handed down from parents to children.
   b) changes frequently.
   c) has little impact on electoral choice.
   d) is mandated in states with closed primaries.
9. Which of the following is *not* a factor that influences voters' decisions?
   a) partisanship
   b) issues
   c) candidate characteristics
   d) the electoral system used to determine the winner
10. If a state has ten members in the U.S. House of Representatives, how many electoral votes does that state have?
    a) two
    b) ten
    c) twelve
    d) can't tell from this information

CRITICAL THINKING QUESTIONS

1. Should race be taken into account when congressional districts are redrawn after each census? If twenty percent of a state is African American, should twenty percent of the districts have an African American majority?

2. What are the sources of campaign money in American politics? Why do candidates for public office need to raise so much money? How has the government sought to balance the competing ideals of free expression and equal representation in regard to campaign financing? Is this yet another example of a conflict between liberty and democracy?

KEY TERMS

benign gerrymandering (p. 396)
campaign (p. 399)
caucus (political) (p. 403)
closed caucus (p. 404)
closed primary (p. 392)
coattail effect (p. 397)
delegates (p. 407)
electoral college (p. 397)
gerrymandering (p. 395)
incumbent (p. 399)
infomercial (p. 410)
issue advocacy (p. 420)
majority system (p. 393)
midterm elections (p. 392)
minority district (p. 396)
open caucus (p. 403)
open primary (p. 392)
platform (p. 404)
plurality system (p. 393)
political action committee (PAC) (p. 418)
primary elections (p. 392)
proportional representation (p. 393)
prospective voting (p. 428)
referendum (p. 393)
retrospective voting (p. 428)
soft money (p. 418)
split-ticket voting (p. 397)
spot advertisement (p. 410)
straight-ticket voting (p. 397)
suffrage (p. 391)
superdelegate (p. 408)
town meeting (p. 410)
unit rule (p. 406)
winner-take-all system (p. 404)

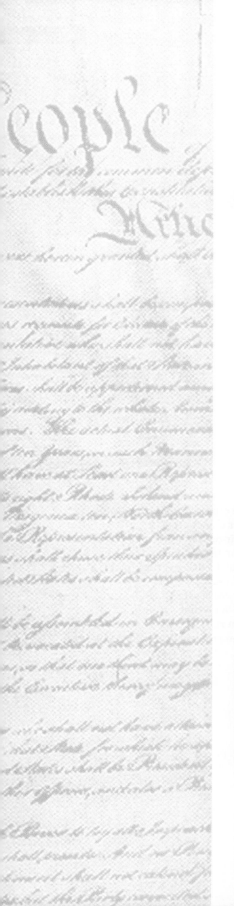

12 Groups and

★ **The Character of Interest Groups**

Why do interest groups form?
What interests are represented by these groups?
What are the organizational components of interest groups?
What are the benefits of interest-group membership?
What are the characteristics of interest-group members?

★ **The Proliferation of Groups**

Why has the number of interest groups grown in recent years?
What is the "New Politics" movement?

★ **Strategies: The Quest for Political Power**

What are some of the strategies interest groups use to gain influence?
What are the purposes of these strategies?

★ **Groups and Interests: The Dilemma**

What are the problems involved in curbing the influence of interest groups?

Interests

STUDENTS AND POLITICS

WHAT do college students and Kathie Lee Gifford have in common? Sweatshops. Not the sweatshops of athletic clubs and treadmills but of workers in factories making Nike, Gap, and other designer products. Early in the 1990s, human rights groups and a few labor groups began to complain about the barbarous conditions in factories not only in third world countries but in our own, where immigrants were found to be working as virtual slaves sewing garments for national retailers. The human rights efforts made no headway in getting public attention until April 1996, when Kathie Lee Gifford went on her popular morning TV show and tearfully acknowledged that the Kathie Lee line of clothing was being made by children in inhumane Honduran sweatshops.

In the fall of 1997, a group of Duke University students calling themselves Students Against Sweatshops persuaded the Duke administration to require all manufacturers of Duke identification apparel to pledge not to use sweatshop labor. The administration produced a "code of conduct" in 1998 that bars licensees from using child labor, paying sub-minimum wages, providing unsafe working conditions, and denying workers the right to organize. Word passed quickly to other campuses where sit-ins, "knit-ins," and mock fashion shows were used to dramatize the situation. By the summer of 1998, a national organization was founded—United Students Against Sweatshops (USAS)—that became a coordinating as well as a recruiting and information exchange center, with a Web site and an on-line mailing list, involving over one hundred campuses nationwide. Even during sit-ins, student activists at one site were bringing their laptops and cell phones in order to stay in touch with other campuses. One 1999 report said that "the anti-sweatshop movement is the largest wave of student activism to hit campuses since students rallied to free Nelson Mandela by calling for a halt to university investments in South Africa more than a decade ago."[1] In response to this activism, the White House created a monitoring arm, the Fair Labor Association (FLA), and invited universities to join, although they were given only one place on FLA's fourteen-member board. The sticking point immediately became the student demand that human rights groups, rather than U.S. industry and large trade unions, do the monitoring. In fact, many campus groups have persuaded their universities to hold out against joining FLA until it adopts stronger standards with more teeth.

As the new century was beginning, there was little sign that FLA-affiliated industries, let alone other industries, were doing anything significant to abide by any common standards. "In fact," say the investigative reporters, "no company has made a commitment to pay a living wage."[2]

Students and Politics

The oldest national student advocacy group, the United States Student Association (USSA), uses its grassroots support to maintain a paid staff of recent college graduates in Washington, including a full-time lobbyist. The USSA fights for issues such as minimizing student fare increases on public transportation and maintaining affirmative action in higher education. Though many believe that the USSA's liberal positions are not representative of the full range of students' opinions, the organization continues to have a large support base and has helped win several legislative victories in Congress on matters of affirmative action and student financial aid, including increasing Pell grants and blocking legislation that would have prohibited consideration of gender, race, or national origin in admissions at universities that receive federal funds. The organization has gained a strong trust from its membership, due to its obvious influence on powerful members of both parties, including Senator Barbara Boxer of California, who has called the USSA "an effective and forceful voice for students on Capitol Hill."

Although the student movement has "had only minimal impact on the daily life of sweatshop workers," the campus groups have "succeeded in raising awareness . . . , [have] contributed to industry acceptance [of external] labor standards . . . and [have] given thousands of students experience in the nuts and bolts of social activism. . . ."[3] And the fight is not yet over or lost.

USAS is an impressive effort, not only because it is student-driven but because organizers and activists are few in number and are spread across a very large continent. And it may not last; it may go the way of other student political groups. For example, the National Association of Students in Higher Education (NASHE), organized in 1995 to defend student aid programs from severe cuts as part of Republican efforts to balance the federal budget, was not long-lived. Rallies were held on a number of campuses and letters and calls bombarded members of Congress. Four years later, NASHE was little more than a shell. But the effort was not in vain. On January 20, 2000, President Clinton proposed a $31 billion package of tax breaks and financial aid for college attendance. It would include tax credits to ease the cost of tuition and fees, re-enrollment incentives, minority student assistance, and significant increases in Pell grants to students from low-income families. NASHE got no mention in the footnotes of President Clinton's address, but surely the NASHE activists deserve some credit and satisfaction for the outcome. Most of them have graduated and have gone on to other pursuits—which is another factor making student political activism so difficult to sustain. But the experiences they all had will almost certainly be repeated time after time in community, group, and political party participation throughout their lives. Civic and political participation is never an end in itself, but it can be an awfully good beginning.

There is nothing about college student experience in politics that is unique, except the brief, temporary status of being a college student. Americans organize in groups and have always organized in groups. This propensity to organize so impressed America's greatest foreign observer, Alexis de Tocqueville, that in the 1830s he singled out "voluntary association" as the genius of American democracy. Tocqueville observed that Americans were not particularly civic-minded most of the time, as they happily went their individual ways seeking their fortunes as opportunity and imagination drove them. But, not unlike the Minutemen of the Revolution, when a threat to their community or their own way of life was perceived, Tocqueville noted that Americans mobilized into "voluntary associations" for as long as it was necessary to put things right.[4]

As long as freedom exists, groups will organize and attempt to exert their influence over the political process. And groups will form wherever power exists. It should therefore be no surprise that the most impressive growth in the number and scale of interest groups has been at the national level since the 1930s. But even as the growth of the national government leveled off in the 1970s and

1980s, and actually declined in the late 1980s and 1990s, the spread of interest groups continued. It is no longer just the expansion of the national government that spawns interest groups, but the *existence* of that government with all the power it possesses. As long as there is a powerful government in the United States, there will be a large network of interest groups around it.

The framers of the American Constitution feared the power that could be wielded by organized interests. Yet they believed that interest groups thrived because of liberty—the freedom that all Americans enjoyed to organize and express their views. If the government were given the power to regulate or in any way to forbid efforts by organized interests to interfere in the political process, the government would in effect have the power to suppress liberty. The solution to this dilemma was presented by James Madison:

> Take in a greater variety of parties and interest [and] you make it less probable that a majority of the whole will have a common motive to invade the rights of other citizens. . . . [Hence the advantage] enjoyed by a large over a small republic.[5]

According to the Madisonian theory, a good constitution encourages multitudes of interests so that no single interest, which he called a "faction," can ever tyrannize the others. The basic assumption is that competition among interests will produce balance, with all the interests regulating each other.[6] Today, this Madisonian principle of regulation is called **pluralism.** According to pluralist theory, all interests are and should be free to compete for influence in the United States. Moreover, according to a pluralist doctrine, the outcome of this competition is compromise and moderation, since no group is likely to be able to achieve any of its goals without accommodating itself to some of the views of its many competitors.[7]

pluralism
the theory that all interests are and should be free to compete for influence in the government. The outcome of this competition is compromise and moderation

Tens of thousands of organized groups have formed in the United States, ranging from civic associations to huge nationwide groups like the National Rifle Association (NRA), whose chief cause is opposition to restrictions on gun ownership, or Common Cause, a public-interest group that advocates a variety of liberal political reforms. Despite the array of interest groups in American politics, however, we can be sure neither that all interests are represented equally nor that the results of this group competition are consistent

The NRA attempted to deflect some liberal criticism by starting a publicity campaign for gun safety, symbolized by mascot Eddie the Eagle.

with the common good. One criticism of interest-group pluralism is its class bias in favor of those with greater financial resources. As one critic put it, "The flaw in the pluralist heaven is that the heavenly chorus sings with a strong upper-class accent."[8] Another assumption of pluralism is that all groups have equal access to the political process and that achieving an outcome favorable to a particular group depends only upon that group's strength and resources, not upon biases inherent in the political system. But, as we shall see, group politics is a political format that has worked and continues to work more to the advantage of some types of interests than others.

- ***In this chapter, we will examine some of the antecedents and consequences of interest-group politics in the United States. We will first seek to understand the character of interest groups.*** We will look at types of interests, the organizational components of groups, and the characteristics of members. We will also examine the important question of why people join interest groups.
- ***Second, we will assess the growth of interest-group activity in recent American political history.*** The number of interest groups has proliferated in recent years and we will examine the reasons why.
- ***Third, we will review and evaluate the strategies that competing groups use in their struggles for influence.*** The quest for political influence takes many forms.
- ***We conclude by evaluating some of the potential problems in trying to reduce the influence of interest groups in the political process.*** Interest-group politics is biased in favor of the most wealthy and powerful, but attempts to limit this influence are limits on liberty itself.

The Character of Interest Groups

- Why do interest groups form?
- What interests are represented by these groups?
- What are the organizational components of interest groups?
- What are the benefits of interest-group membership?
- What are the characteristics of interest-group members?

interest group
a voluntary membership association that pursues a common cause through political participation

An **interest group** is a voluntary membership association organized to pursue a common interest (or interests), through political participation, toward the ultimate goal of getting favorable public policy decisions from government. Individuals form groups in order to increase the chance that their views will be heard and their interests treated favorably by the government. Interest groups are organized to influence governmental decisions.

Interest groups are sometimes referred to as "lobbies," but that is somewhat misleading; "lobbying" refers to just one strategy interest groups employ to influence policy makers (as we will see later in this chapter). Interest groups are also sometimes confused with political action committees, which are actually groups that focus on influencing elections rather than trying to influence the elected. One final distinction that we should make is that interest groups are also different from political parties: Interest groups tend to concern themselves with the *policies* of government; parties tend to concern themselves with the *personnel* of government.

There are an enormous number of interest groups in the United States, and millions of Americans are members of one or more groups, at least to the extent of paying dues or attending an occasional meeting. By representing the interests of such large numbers of people and encouraging political participation, organized groups can and do enhance American democracy. Organized groups educate their members about issues that affect them. Groups lobby members of Congress and the executive, engage in litigation, and generally represent their members' interests in the political arena. Groups mobilize their members for elections and grassroots lobbying efforts, thus encouraging participation. Interest groups also monitor government programs to make certain that their members are not adversely affected. In all these ways, organized interests can be said to promote democratic politics. But because not all interests are represented equally, interest-group politics works to the advantage of some and the disadvantage of others.

WHAT INTERESTS ARE REPRESENTED?

Business and Agricultural Groups Interest groups come in as many shapes and sizes as the interests they represent. When most people think about interest groups, they immediately think of groups with a direct economic interest in governmental actions. These groups are generally supported by groups of producers or manufacturers in a particular economic sector. Examples of this type of group include the National Petroleum Refiners Association and the American Farm Bureau Federation. At the same time that broadly representative groups such as these are active in Washington, specific companies, such as Shell Oil, IBM, and General Motors, may be active on certain issues that are of particular concern to them.

President Bill Clinton greets members of the American Federation of State, County, and Municipal Employees.

Labor Groups Labor organizations are equally active lobbyists. The AFL-CIO, the United Mine Workers, and the Teamsters are all groups that lobby on behalf of organized labor. In recent years, groups have arisen to further the interests of public employees, the most significant among these being the American Federation of State, County, and Municipal Employees.

Professional Associations Professional lobbies like the American Bar Association and the American Medical Association have been particularly successful in furthering their members' interests in state and federal legislatures. Financial institutions, represented by organizations such as the American Bankers Association and the National Savings & Loan League, although often less visible than other lobbies, also play an important role in shaping legislative policy.

Public Interest Groups Recent years have witnessed the growth of a powerful "public interest" lobby, purporting to represent interests whose concerns are not addressed by traditional lobbies. These groups have been most visible in the consumer protection and environmental policy areas, although public interest groups cover a broad range of issues. The National Resources Defense

Council, the Sierra Club, the Union of Concerned Scientists, and Common Cause are all examples of public interest groups.

Ideological Groups Closely related to and overlapping public interest groups are ideological groups, organized in support of a particular political or philosophical perspective. People for the American Way, for example, promotes liberal values, whereas the Christian Coalition focuses on conservative social goals and the National Taxpayers Union campaigns to reduce the size of the federal government.

Public-Sector Groups The perceived need for representation on Capitol Hill has generated a public-sector lobby in the past several years, including the National League of Cities and the "research" lobby. The latter group comprises think tanks and universities that have an interest in obtaining government funds for research and support, and it includes such institutions as Harvard University, the Brookings Institution, and the American Enterprise Institute. Indeed, universities have expanded their lobbying efforts even as they have reduced faculty positions and course offerings.[9]

ORGANIZATIONAL COMPONENTS

Although there are many interest groups, most share certain key organizational components. These include leadership, money, an agency or office, and members.

First, every group must have a leadership and decision-making structure. For some groups, this structure is very simple. For others, it can be quite elaborate and involve hundreds of local chapters that are melded into a national apparatus. Interest-group leadership is, in some respects, analogous to business leadership. Many interest groups are initially organized by political entrepreneurs with a strong commitment to a particular set of goals. Such entrepreneurs see the formation of a group as a means both for achieving those goals and for enhancing their own influence in the political process. Just as is true in the business world, however, successful groups often become bureaucratized; the initial entrepreneurial leadership is replaced by a paid professional staff. In the 1960s, for example, Ralph Nader led a loosely organized band of consumer advocates ("Nader's Raiders") in a crusade for product safety that resulted in the enactment of a number of pieces of legislation and numerous regulations, such as the requirement that all new cars be equipped with air bags. Today, Nader remains active in the consumer movement, and his ragtag band of raiders has been transformed into a well-organized and well-financed phalanx of interlocked groups, including Public Citizen, the Center for the Study of Responsive Law, and the Center for Science in the Public Interest. All of these groups are now led by professional staffs, which proved capable of staying alive and vigorous even as Nader moved on to become the nominee of the Green Party for president of the United States in the 2000 election.

Consumer activist Ralph Nader, shown here at a demonstration in support of mandatory air bags in cars, founded a network of consumer advocacy groups.

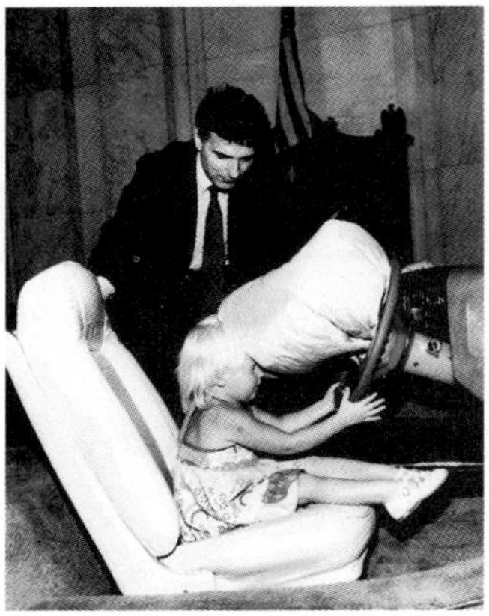

Second, every interest group must build a financial structure capable of sustaining an organization and funding the group's activities. Most interest groups rely on membership dues and voluntary contributions from sympathizers. Many also sell some ancillary services to members, such as insurance and vacation tours. Third, most groups establish an agency that actually carries

Members and supporters of the National Organization for Women regularly participate in rallies organized by the group. This rally was held on the Mall in Washington in 1995.

out the group's tasks. This may be a research organization, a public relations office, or a lobbying office in Washington or a state capital.

Finally, all interest groups must attract and keep members. Somehow, groups must persuade individuals to invest the money, time, energy, or effort required to take part in the group's activities. Members play a larger role in some groups than in others. In **membership associations,** group members actually serve on committees and engage in projects. In the case of labor unions, members may march on picket lines, and in the case of political or ideological groups, members may participate in demonstrations and protests. In another set of groups, **"staff organizations,"** a professional staff conducts most of the group's activities; members are called upon only to pay dues and make other contributions. Among the well-known public interest groups, some, such as the National Organization for Women (NOW), are membership groups, whereas others, such as Defenders of Wildlife and the Children's Defense Fund, are staff organizations.

membership association
an organized group in which members actually play a substantial role, sitting on commitees and engaging in group projects

staff organization
a type of membership group in which a professional staff conducts most of the group's activities

The "Free Rider" Problem Whether they need individuals to volunteer or merely to write checks, both types of groups need to recruit and retain members. Yet many groups find this task difficult, even when it comes to recruiting members who agree strongly with the group's goals. Why? As economist Mancur Olson explains, the benefits of a group's success are often broadly available and cannot be denied to nonmembers.[10] Such benefits can be called **collective goods.** This term is usually associated with certain government benefits, but it can also be applied to beneficial outcomes of interest-group activity. Following Olson's own example, suppose a number of private property owners live near a mosquito-infested swamp. Each owner wants this swamp cleared. But if one or a few of the owners were to clear the swamp alone, their

collective goods
benefits, sought by groups, that are broadly available and cannot be denied to nonmembers

free riders
those who enjoy the benefits of collective goods but did not participate in acquiring them

actions would benefit all the other owners as well, without any effort on the part of those other owners. Each of the inactive owners would be a **free rider** on the efforts of the ones who cleared the swamp. Thus, there is a disincentive for any of the owners to undertake the job alone.

Since the number of concerned owners is small in this particular case, they might eventually be able to organize themselves to share the costs as well as enjoy the benefits of clearing the swamp. But suppose the numbers of interested people are increased. Suppose the common concern is not the neighborhood swamp but polluted air or groundwater involving thousands of residents in a region, or in fact millions of residents in a whole nation. National defense is the most obvious collective good whose benefits are shared by every resident, regardless of the taxes they pay or the support they provide. As the number of involved persons increases, or as the size of the group increases, the free rider phenomenon becomes more of a problem. Individuals do not have much incentive to become active members and supporters of a group that is already working more or less on their behalf. The group would no doubt be more influential if all concerned individuals were active members—if there were no free riders. But groups will not reduce their efforts just because free riders get the same benefits as dues-paying activists. In fact, groups may try even harder precisely because there are free riders, with the hope that the free riders will be encouraged to join in.

Why Join? Despite the free rider problem, interest groups offer numerous incentives to join. Most importantly, they make various "selective benefits" available only to group members. These benefits can be information-related, material, solidary, or purposive. Table 12.1 gives some examples of the range of benefits in each of these categories.

informational benefits
special newsletters, periodicals, training programs, conferences, and other information provided to members of groups to entice others to join

Informational benefits are the most widespread and important category of selective benefits offered to group members. Information is provided through conferences, training programs, and newsletters and other periodicals sent automatically to those who have paid membership dues.

material benefits
special goods, services, or money provided to members of groups to entice others to join

Material benefits include anything that can be measured monetarily, such as special services, goods, and even money. A broad range of material benefits can be offered by groups to attract members. These benefits often include discount purchasing, shared advertising, and, perhaps most valuable of all, health and retirement insurance.

solidary benefits
selective benefits of group membership that emphasize friendship, networking, and consciousness-raising

Another option identified on Table 12.1 is that of **solidary benefits.** The most notable of this class of benefits are the friendship and "networking" opportunities that membership provides. Another benefit that has become extremely important to many of the newer nonprofit and citizen groups is what has come to be called "consciousness-raising." One example of this can be seen in the claims of many women's organizations that active participation conveys to each member of the organization an enhanced sense of her own value and a stronger ability to advance individual as well as collective civil rights. A similar solidary or psychological benefit has been the mainstay of the appeal of group membership to discouraged and disillusioned African Americans since their emergence as a constitutionally free and equal people.

purposive benefits
selective benfits of group membership that emphasize the purpose and accomplishments of the group

A fourth type of benefit involves the appeal of the purpose of an interest group. The benefits of religious interest groups provide us with the best examples of such **purposive benefits.** The Christian Right is a powerful movement

SELECTIVE BENEFITS OF INTEREST GROUP MEMBERSHIP — Table 12.1

Category	Benefits
Informational benefits	Conferences
	Professional contacts
	Training programs
	Publications
	Coordination among organizations
	Research
	Legal help
	Professional codes
	Collective bargaining
Material benefits	Travel packages
	Insurance
	Discounts on consumer goods
Solidary benefits	Friendship
	Networking opportunities
Purposive benefits	Advocacy
	Representation before government
	Participation in public affairs

SOURCE: Adapted from Jack Walker, Jr., *Mobilizing Interest Groups in America: Patrons, Professions, and Social Movements* (Ann Arbor: University of Michigan Press, 1991), p. 86.

made up of a number of interest groups that offer virtually no material benefits to their members. The growth and success of these groups depends upon the religious identifications and affirmations of their members. Many such religiously based interest groups have arisen, especially at state and local levels, throughout American history. For example, both the abolition and the prohibition movements were driven by religious interest groups whose main attractions were nonmaterial benefits.

Ideology itself, or the sharing of a commonly developed ideology, is another important nonmaterial benefit. Many of the most successful interest groups of the past twenty years have been citizen groups or public interest groups, whose members are brought together largely around shared ideological goals, including government reform, election and campaign reform, civil rights, economic equality, "family values," or even opposition to government itself.

The AARP and the Benefits of Membership One group that has been extremely successful in recruiting members and mobilizing them for political action is the American Association of Retired Persons (AARP). The AARP was founded in 1958 as a result of the efforts of a retired California high school principal, Ethel Percy Andrus, to find affordable health insurance for herself and for the thousands of members of the National Retired Teachers Association (NRTA). In 1955 she found an insurer who was willing to give NRTA members a low, group rate. In 1958, partly at the urging of the insurer (who found that insuring the elderly was quite profitable), Andrus founded the AARP. For the insurer it provided an expanded market; for Andrus it was a

A subscription to *Modern Maturity* is one of the selective benefits of membership in the AARP.

way to serve the ever-growing elderly population, whose problems and needs were expanding along with their numbers and their life expectancy.

Today, the AARP is a large and powerful organization with an annual income of $540 million. In addition, the organization receives $90 million in federal grants. Its national headquarters in Washington, D.C., staffed by 1,750 full-time employees, is so large that it has its own zip code. Its monthly periodical, *Modern Maturity*, has a circulation larger than the combined circulations of *Time*, *Newsweek*, and *US News & World Report*.[11]

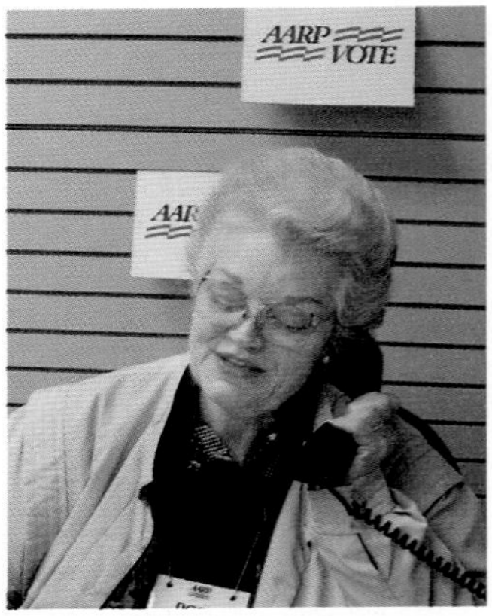

The political power of a group as large and well organized as the AARP is tremendous. AARP members use a "telephone tree" to mobilize and protest whenever programs benefiting the elderly are threatened.

How did this large organization overcome the free rider problem and recruit thirty-three million older people as members? First, no other organization on earth has ever provided more successfully the selective benefits necessary to overcome the free rider problem. It helps that the AARP began as an organization to provide affordable health insurance for aging members rather than as an organization to influence public policy. But that fact only strengthens the argument that members need short-term individual benefits if they are to invest effort in a longer-term and less concrete set of benefits. As the AARP evolved into a political interest group, its leadership also added more selective benefits for individual members. They provided guidance against consumer fraud, offered low-interest credit cards, evaluated and endorsed products that were deemed of best value to members, and provided auto insurance and a discounted mail-order pharmacy.

In a group as large as the AARP, members are bound to disagree on particular subjects, often creating serious factional disputes. But the resources of the AARP are so extensive that its leadership has been able to mobilize itself for each issue of importance to the group. One of its most successful methods of mobilization for political action is the "telephone tree," with which AARP leaders can quickly mobilize thousands of members for and against proposals that affect Social Security, Medicare, and other questions of security for the aging. A "telephone tree" in each state enables the state AARP chair to phone all of the AARP district directors, who then can phone the presidents of the dozens of local chapters, who can call their local officers and individual members. Within twenty-four hours, thousands of individual AARP members can be contacting local, state, and national officials to express their opposition to proposed legislation. It is no wonder that the AARP is respected and feared throughout Washington, D.C.

THE CHARACTERISTICS OF MEMBERS

Membership in interest groups is not randomly distributed in the population. People with higher incomes, higher levels of education, and management or professional occupations are much more likely to become members of groups than those who occupy the lower rungs on the socioeconomic ladder (see Figure 12.1).[12] Well-educated, upper-income business and professional people are more likely to have the time and the money and to have acquired through the educational process the concerns and skills needed to play a role in a group or association. Moreover, for business and professional people, group membership may provide personal contacts and access to information that can help advance their careers. At the same time, of course, corporate entities—businesses and the like—usually have ample resources to form or participate in groups that seek to advance their causes.

INTEREST GROUP MEMBERSHIP BY INCOME LEVEL

Figure 12.1

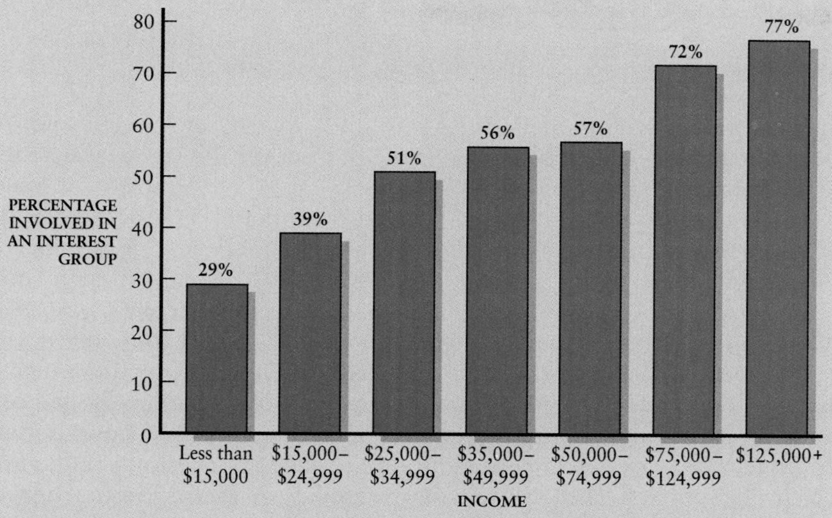

SOURCE: Kay Lehman Scholzman, "Voluntary Organizations in Politics: Who Gets Involved?" in *Representing Interests and Interest Group Representation,* ed. William Crotty, Mildred A. Schwartz, and John C. Green (Lanham, MD: University Press of America, 1994), p. 76.

The percentage of Americans who report that they are involved in an organization that takes a stand on political issues increases with income level.

The result is that interest-group politics in the United States tends to have a very pronounced upper-class bias. Certainly, there are many interest groups and political associations that have a working-class or lower-class membership—labor organizations or welfare-rights organizations, for example—but the great majority of interest groups and their members are drawn from the middle and upper-middle classes. In general, the "interests" served by interest groups are the interests of society's "haves." Even when interest groups take opposing positions on issues and policies, the conflicting positions they espouse usually reflect divisions among upper-income strata rather than conflicts between the upper and lower classes.

In general, to obtain adequate political representation, forces from the bottom rungs of the socioeconomic ladder must be organized on the massive scale associated with political parties. Parties can organize and mobilize the collective energies of large numbers of people who, as individuals, may have very limited resources. Interest groups, on the other hand, generally organize smaller numbers of the better-to-do. Thus, the relative importance of political parties and interest groups in American politics has far-ranging implications for the distribution of political power in the United States. As we saw in Chapter 10, political parties have declined in influence in recent years. Interest groups, on the other hand, as we shall see in the next section, have become much more numerous, more active, and more influential in American politics.

The Proliferation of Groups

- Why has the number of interest groups grown in recent years?
- What is the "New Politics" movement?

If interest groups and our concerns about them were a new phenomenon, we would not have begun this chapter with Madison in the eighteenth century and de Tocqueville in the nineteeth. As long as there is government, as long as government makes policies that add value or impose costs, and as long as there is liberty to organize, interest groups will abound; and if government expands so will interest groups. There was, for example, a spurt of growth in the national government during the 1880s and 1890s, arising largely from the first government efforts at economic intervention to fight large monopolies and to regulate some aspects of interstate commerce. In the latter decade, a parallel spurt of growth occurred in national interest groups, including the imposing National Association of Manufacturers (NAM) and numerous other trade associations. Many groups organized around specific agricultural commodities, as well. This period also marked the beginning of the expansion of trade unions as interest groups. Later, in the 1930s, interest groups with headquarters and representation in Washington began to grow significantly, concurrent with that decade's historic and sustained expansion within the national government (see Chapter 4).

Over the past thirty years, there has been an even greater increase both in the number of interest groups seeking to play a role in the American political process and in the extent of their opportunity to influence that process. This explosion of interest-group activity has two basic origins—first, the expansion of the role of government during this period; and second, the coming of age of a new and dynamic set of political forces in the United States—a set of forces that have relied heavily on "public interest" groups to advance their causes.

THE EXPANSION OF GOVERNMENT

Modern governments' extensive economic and social programs have powerful politicizing effects, often sparking the organization of new groups and interests. The activities of organized groups are usually viewed in terms of their effects upon governmental action. But interest-group activity is often as much a consequence as an antecedent of governmental programs. Even when national policies are initially responses to the appeals of pressure groups, government involvement in any area can be a powerful stimulus for political organization and action by those whose interests are affected. For example, during the 1970s, expanded federal regulation of the automobile, oil, gas, education, and health care industries impelled each of these interests to increase substantially its efforts to influence the government's behavior. These efforts, in turn, spurred the organization of other groups to augment or counter the activities of the first.[13] Similarly, federal social programs have occasionally sparked political organization and action on the part of clientele groups seeking to influence the distribution of benefits and, in turn, the organization of groups opposed to the programs or their cost. For example, federal programs and court decisions in such areas as abortion and school prayer were the stimuli for political action and organization by fundamentalist religious groups. Thus, the expansion of government in recent decades has also stimulated increased group activity and organization.

One contemporary example of a proposed government program that sparked intensive organization and political action by affected interests is the case of regulating the tobacco industry. In 1997, an enormous lobbying battle broke out in Washington, D.C., over a proposed agreement regarding the liability of tobacco companies for tobacco-related illnesses. This agreement, reached between tobacco companies, state governments, trial lawyers (representing individuals and groups suing tobacco companies), and antismoking groups, called for the tobacco industry to pay the states and the trial lawyers nearly $400 billion over the next twenty-five years. In exchange the industry would receive protection from much of the litigation with which it is currently plagued. The settlement as negotiated would have required congressional and presidential approval.

After the settlement was proposed in June 1997, both the White House and some members of Congress began raising objections. Because of the enormous amounts of money involved, all the interested parties began intensive lobbying efforts aimed at both Congress and the executive branch. The tobacco industry retained nearly thirty lobbying firms at an initial cost of nearly $10 million to press its claims. During the first six months of 1997, the tobacco industry also contributed more than $2.5 million to political parties and candidates whom the industry thought could be helpful to its cause. One Washington lobbying firm, Verner, Liipfert, Bernhard, McPherson, and Hand, alone received nearly $5 million in fees from the four leading cigarette makers. The firm assigned a number of well-connected lobbyists, including former Texas governor Ann Richards, to press its clients' cause. Verner, Liipfert also hired pollsters, public relations firms, and economists to convince the public and the Washington establishment that the tobacco settlement made good sense.[14] Eventually a compromise settlement was reached between the tobacco companies and the state governments.

THE NEW POLITICS MOVEMENT AND PUBLIC INTEREST GROUPS

The second factor accounting for the explosion of interest-group activity in recent years has been the emergence of a new set of forces in American politics that can collectively be called the "New Politics" movement.

The **New Politics movement** is made up of upper-middle-class professionals and intellectuals for whom the civil rights and antiwar movements were formative experiences, just as the Great Depression and World War II had been for their parents. The crusade against racial discrimination and the Vietnam War led these young men and women to see themselves as a political force in opposition to the public policies and politicians associated with the nation's postwar regime. In more recent years, the forces of New Politics have focused their attention on such issues as environmental protection, women's rights, and nuclear disarmament.

New Politics movement
a political movement that began in the 1960s and 1970s, made up of professionals and intellectuals for whom the civil rights and antiwar movements were formative experiences. The New Politics movement strengthened public interest groups

Members of the New Politics movement constructed or strengthened public interest groups such as Common Cause, the Sierra Club, the Environmental Defense Fund, Physicians for Social Responsibility, the National Organization for Women, and the various organizations formed by consumer activist Ralph Nader. Through these groups, New Politics forces were able to influence the media, Congress, and even the judiciary and enjoyed a remarkable degree of success during the late 1960s and early 1970s in securing the enactment of policies they favored. New Politics activists also played a major role in securing the enactment of environmental, consumer, and occupational health and safety legislation.

public interest groups groups that claim they serve the general good rather than their own particular interest

New Politics groups sought to distinguish themselves from other interest groups—business groups, in particular—by styling themselves as **public interest groups,** terminology which suggests that they served the general good rather than their own selfish interest. These groups' claims to represent *only* the public interest should be viewed with caution, however. Quite often, goals that are said to be in the general or public interest are also or indeed primarily in the particular interest of those who espouse them. It is not uncommon to find decidedly private interests seeking to hide behind the term "public interest."

One important liberal public interest group, Citizen Action, which claims a nationwide membership of more than two million, was forced to close its national offices and dismiss its twenty national staff members after federal prosecutors charged that the group had been involved in an illegal financial arrangement with the Teamsters Union. According to court papers filed in 1997, Citizens Action accepted contributions from the union and then made contributions to the 1996 re-election campaign of Teamsters president Ron Carey. In effect, Citizen Action served as a conduit for the illegal transfer of Teamsters funds into Carey's campaign. Before its demise, Citizen Action specialized in "issue campaigns" aimed at exposing lies and hypocrisy on the part of conservative politicians. While Citizen Action was foundering, a federal grand jury was looking into the fund-raising relationships between the Republican National Committee (RNC) and several Republican public interest groups, as part of an investigation of allegations that the RNC used these groups as conduits for political contributions from foreign business interests.[15]

These examples of the involvement of "public-interest" groups in what amounts to money laundering suggest that the term *public interest* should be used cautiously. Claims that a group and its programs serve only some abstract public interest should be treated with a healthy measure of skepticism.

Many groups regularly demonstrate at the U.S. Capitol building. Members of Greenpeace, an environmental group, are shown here protesting against proposed environmental deregulation.

Strategies: The Quest for Political Power

- What are some of the strategies interest groups use to gain influence?
- What are the purposes of these strategies?

As we have seen, people form interest groups in order to improve the probability that they and their interests will be heard and treated favorably by the government. The quest for political influence or power takes many forms, but among the most frequently used strategies are lobbying, establishing access to key decision makers, using the courts, going public, and using electoral politics. These "tactics of influence" do not exhaust all the possibilities, but they

HOW INTEREST GROUPS INFLUENCE CONGRESS

Figure 12.2

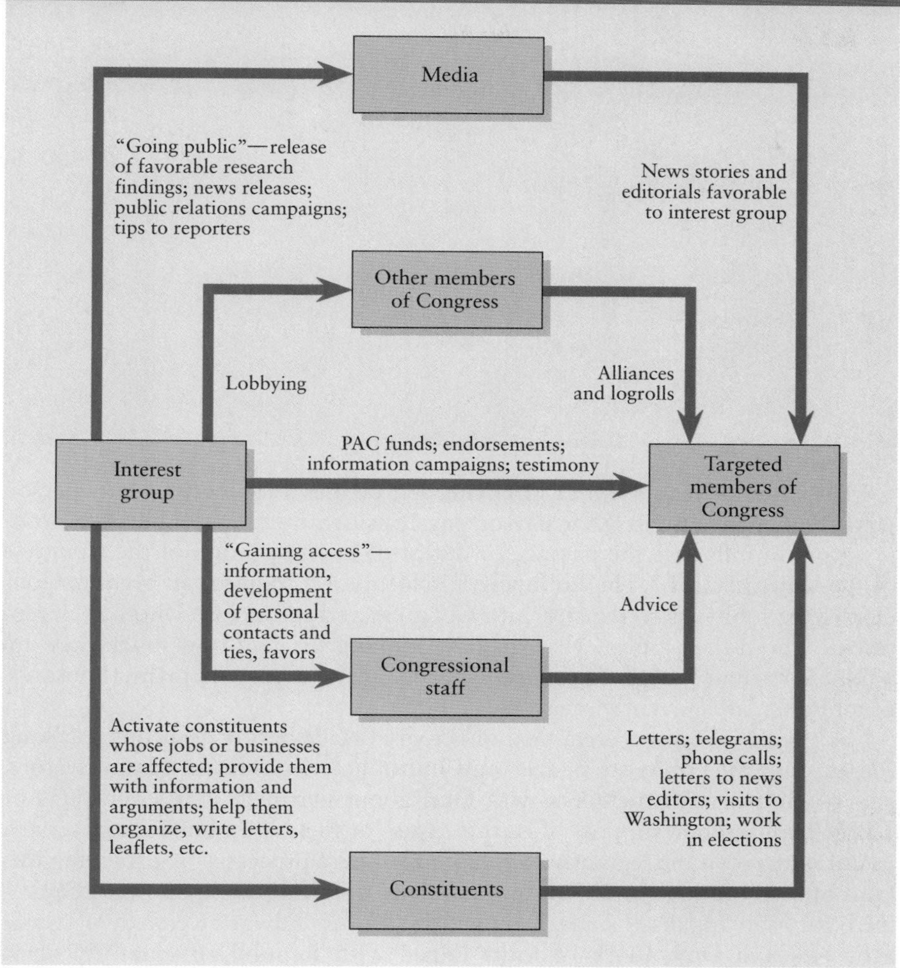

paint a broad picture of groups competing for power through the maximum utilization of their resources (see Figure 12.2).

LOBBYING

Lobbying is an attempt by an individual or a group to influence the passage of legislation by exerting direct pressure on members of the legislature. The person doing the lobbying is called a lobbyist. The First Amendment to the Constitution provides for the right to "petition the Government for a redress of grievances." But as early as the 1870s, "lobbying" became the common term for petitioning—and it is not an inaccurate one. Petitioning cannot take place on the floor of the House or Senate. Therefore, petitioners must confront members of Congress in the lobbies of the legislative chamber; this activity gave rise to the term "lobbying."

lobbying
a strategy by which organized interests seek to influence the passage of legislation by exerting direct pressure on members of the legislature

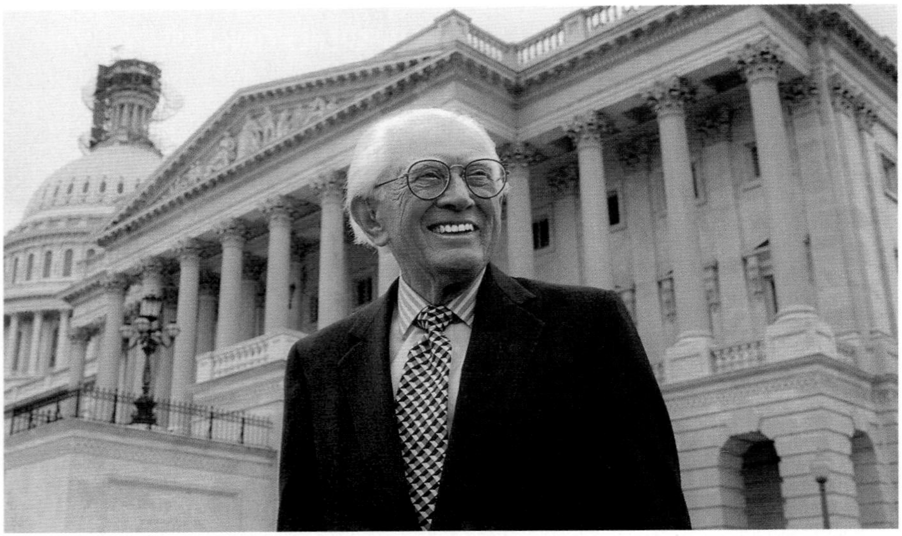

According to the Center for Responsive Politics, 144 former members of Congress have stayed in Washington as registered lobbyists. Howard Metzenbaum, pictured here in front of the Capitol building, is a former senator from Ohio now working as a lobbyist for the Consumer Federation of America.

The Federal Regulation of Lobbying Act defines a lobbyist as "any person who shall engage himself for pay or any consideration for the purpose of attempting to influence the passage or defeat of any legislation of the Congress of the United States." The Lobbying Disclosure Act requires all organizations employing lobbyists to register with Congress and to disclose whom they represent, whom they lobby, what they are looking for, and how much they are paid. More than 7,000 organizations, collectively employing many thousands of lobbyists, are currently registered.

Lobbying involves a great deal of activity on the part of someone speaking for an interest. Lobbyists badger and buttonhole legislators, administrators, and committee staff members with facts about pertinent issues and facts or claims about public support of certain issues or facts.[16] Lobbyists can serve a useful purpose in the legislative and administrative processes by providing this kind of information. In 1978, during debate on a bill to expand the requirement for lobbying disclosures, Democratic senators Edward Kennedy of Massachusetts and Dick Clark of Iowa joined with Republican senator Robert Stafford of Vermont to issue the following statement: "Government without lobbying could not function. The flow of information to Congress and to every federal agency is a vital part of our democratic system."[17] But they also added that there is a darker side to lobbying—one that requires regulation.

Types of Lobbyists The business of lobbying is uneven and unstable. Some groups send their own loyal members to Washington to lobby for them. These representatives usually possess a lot of knowledge about a particular issue and the group's position on it, but they have little knowledge about or experience in Washington or national politics. They tend not to remain in Washington beyond the campaign for their issue.

Other groups select lobbyists with a considerable amount of Washington experience. Many retired or defeated members of Congress join or form Washington law firms and spend all their time lobbying. An even larger number of former government officials and congressional staff members remain in Washington in order to make a living from their expertise and their connections.

(Laws that limit the freedom of former government employees to take jobs in directly related private companies do not apply to former employees of congressional committees.) The senior partnerships of Washington's top law firms are heavily populated with these former officials and staffers, and they practice law before the very commissions and committees on which they once served. There's an old saying about members of Congress—"they never go back to Pocatello"—and it is as true today as when it was coined. During the battle over the 1996 federal budget, for example, medical specialists seeking favorable treatment under Medicare reimbursement rules retained a lobbying team that included former Minnesota Republican congressman Vin Weber, former New York Democratic congressman Tom Downey, and former Clinton chief legislative aide Patrick Griffin. Former Senate Finance Commitee chair Robert Packwood was retained by lumber mills and other small businesses to secure a cut in the estate tax. Similarly, in a fight between major airlines and regional carriers over airline taxes, the major airlines hired former transportation secretary James Burnley, former deputy Federal Aviation Administration administrator Linda Daschle (whose husband, Tom, is the Senate minority leader), former Reagan chief of staff Ken Duberstein, and former RNC chair Haley Barbour. The regional carriers retained former members of Congress Tom Downey and Rod Chandler, as well as a former top Senate Finance Committee staff member, Joseph O'Neil. In this battle of the titans, the major airlines ultimately prevailed.[18]

The Lobbying Industry The lobbying industry in Washington is growing. New groups are moving in all the time, relocating from Los Angeles, Chicago, and other major cities. Local observers estimate that the actual number of people engaged in significant lobbying (part-time or full-time) is close to seventeen thousand. In addition to the various unions, commodity groups, and trade associations, many important business corporations keep their own representatives in Washington.

Many groups—even those with reputations for being powerful—are constantly forming and reforming lobby coalitions in order to improve their effectiveness with Congress and with government agencies. The AFL and the CIO, for example, merged in 1955, largely for political advantage, despite many economic disagreements between them. In the 1970s, the venerable National Association of Manufacturers tried vainly to work out a merger with the Chamber of Commerce of the United States. During that same period, more than two hundred top executives of some of America's leading business corporations—including AT&T, Boeing, Du Pont, General Motors, Mobil Oil, and General Electric—joined in Washington to form a business roundtable, hoping to coordinate their lobbying efforts on certain issues. In subsequent years, the roundtable worked effectively to promote business interests on issues such as labor law reform, tax policy, and consumer protection.

In 1993, President Clinton proposed that companies employing lobbyists be prohibited from deducting lobbying costs as business expenses from their federal taxes. This would, in effect, make it more difficult and costly for firms to employ lobbyists on behalf of their concerns. Not surprisingly, this proposal was bitterly resented by the lobbying industry, which saw it as a mortal threat to its own business interests. How did lobbying firms respond? By lobbying, of course. The American League of Lobbyists, a trade group representing the lobbying industry, quickly mobilized its members to conduct a vigorous campaign to defeat the proposal. One worried Washington lobbyist, however, observed, "This seems so self-serving, you wonder who is going to listen to us anyway."[19]

Clinton's proposal would have potentially reduced the influence of business groups in the policy process. This would, of course, work to the advantage of liberal public interest groups linked to the Democratic Party. For this reason, a variety of business groups joined forces with the lobbying industry to oppose the administration's efforts. In 1994, Congress first passed and then rejected legislation requiring disclosure of lobbying activities and prohibiting lobbyists from giving gifts worth more than twenty dollars to members.[20] Such lobbying-reform legislation could force interest groups to rely more heavily upon other "tactics of influence."

GAINING ACCESS

access
the actual involvement of interest groups in the decision-making process

Lobbying is an effort by outsiders to exert influence on Congress or government agencies by providing them with information about issues, support, and even threats of retaliation. **Access** is actual involvement in the decision-making process. It may be the outcome of long years of lobbying, but it should not be confused with lobbying. If lobbying has to do with "influence on" a government, access has to do with "influence within" it. Many interest groups resort to lobbying because they have insufficient access or insufficient time to develop it. Access is usually a result of time and effort spent cultivating a position within the inner councils of government. This method of gaining access often requires the sacrifice of short-run influence.

iron triangle
the stable, cooperative relationship that often develops between a congressional committee, an administrative agency, and one or more supportive interest groups

Figure 12.3 illustrates one of the most important access patterns in recent American political history: that of the defense industry. Each such pattern, or **iron triangle,** is almost literally a triangular shape, with one point in an executive branch program, another point in a Senate or House legislative committee or subcommittee, and a third point in some highly stable and well-organized interest group. The points in the triangular relationship are mutually supporting; they count as access only if they last over a long period of time. For example, access to a legislative committee or subcommittee requires that at least one member of it support the interest group in question. This member also must have built up considerable seniority in Congress. An interest cannot feel comfortable about its access to Congress until it has one or more of its "own" people with ten or more years of continuous service on the relevant committee or subcommittee.

issue network
a loose network of elected leaders, public officials, activists, and interest groups drawn together by a specific policy issue

A number of important policy domains, such as the environmental and welfare arenas, are controlled, not by highly structured and unified iron triangles, but by rival **issue networks.** These networks consist of like-minded politicians, consultants, public officials, political activists, and interest groups who have some concern with the issue in question. Activists and interest groups recognized as being involved in the area are sometimes called "stakeholders," and are customarily invited to testify before congressional committees or give their views to government agencies considering action in their domain.

Gaining Access to the Bureaucracy A bureaucratic agency is the third point in the iron triangle, and thus access to it is essential to the success of an interest group. Working to gain influence in an executive agency is what we call "corri-

THE IRON TRIANGLE IN THE DEFENSE SECTOR

Figure 12.3

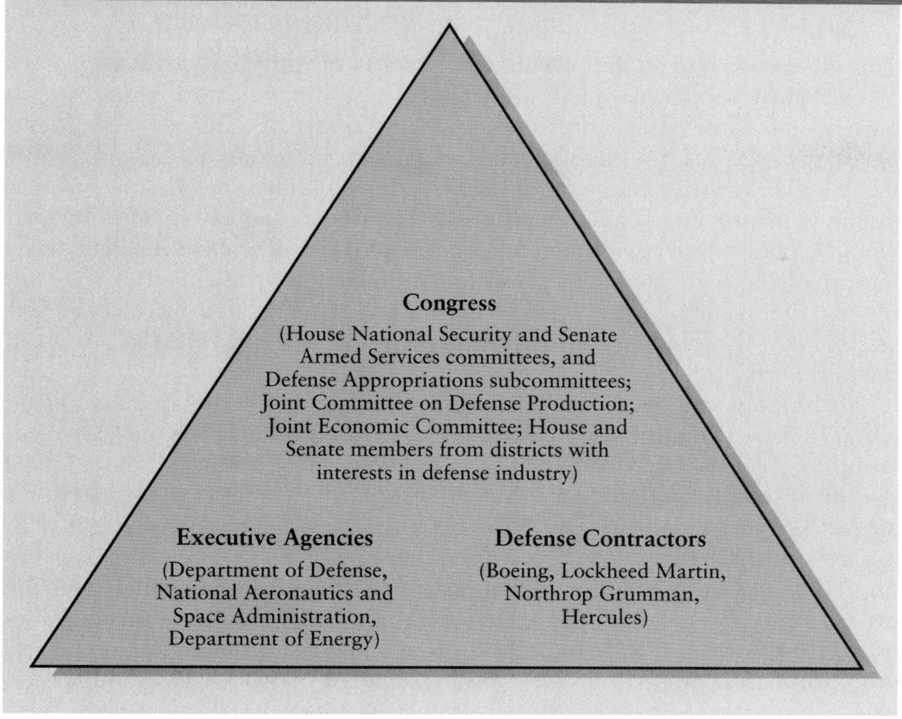

Defense contractors are powerful actors in shaping defense policy; they act in concert with defense committees and subcommittees in Congress and executive agencies concerned with defense.

doring"—the equivalent of lobbying in the executive branch. Even when an interest group is very successful at getting its bill passed by Congress and signed by the president, the prospect of full and faithful implementation of that law is not guaranteed. Often, a group and its allies do not pack up and go home as soon as the president turns their lobbied-for new law over to the appropriate agency. Agencies, too, can fall under the influence of or be **captured** by an interest group or a coalition of well-organized groups.[21] Granted, agencies are not passive and can do a good bit of capturing themselves. The point is that those groups that ignore the role of the agency in implementing legislation are simply not going to have any role in the outcome of agency decisions.

capture
an interest's acquisiton of substantial influence over the government agency charged with regulating its activities

One lawyer for an important public interest group gave an unusually frank assessment of the need of an interest group to persist in its efforts to influence the agency: "You can't be successful at a regulatory agency unless you have the financial resources to sue their asses off."[22] That may be a self-serving overstatement, but it should not be discounted. One of the most thorough studies of interest-group activity reported that an average of 40 percent of all of the group representatives surveyed "regularly contacted" both legislative *and* executive branch organizations; while only 13 percent and 16 percent, respectively, regularly contacted only the legislature or only the executive branch.[23] Of course, few of these contacts with agencies actually involve the threat to sue. But that possibility is not something an agency can take lightly; some groups do use the lawsuit—a most formal technique of influence—to stop an agency from taking an action. Some use lawsuits to gain a more favorable interpretation of a rule. And some—most particularly women's groups, certain other civil rights groups, and a number of environmental groups—use lawsuits

A Food and Drug Administration advisory committee hearing to debate the use of RU-486, popularly known as "the abortion pill."

to get an agency to act more vigorously, as we shall see in the next section. This last category is an important aspect of the New Politics movement.

A slightly less formal method of influence occurs when an interest group participates in the regular decision-making processes of an agency. For example, many agencies hold public hearings prior to taking an action—especially if the action involves taking over property for building a road or some other public work, or intervening against a company's or community's action that would violate some environmental protection law.[24] But unfortunately, hearings involving high-stakes local decisions to be made by a federal or state administrative agency can end up in heated and often stalemated and inconclusive sessions involving individuals and interest groups pleading "NIMBY"—not in my backyard.

So broad is the discretion granted to agencies by Congress, and so eager are agencies to gain the support and cooperation of the people they are regulating or serving, that virtually all agencies join in the trumpet call to kindle the spirit of participation. Some even refer to participation in agency decisions as "participatory democracy." Moreover, the broad discretion delegated to agencies in the laws passed by Congress gives all activist interest groups the unprecedented hope that the efforts made on behalf of their members will pay off where it counts—in implementation. These conditions have produced an explosive growth not only of interest groups in general but of public interest groups in particular.

USING THE COURTS (LITIGATION)

Interest groups sometimes turn to litigation when they lack access or when they are dissatisfied with government in general or with a specific government program and feel they have insufficient influence to change the situation. Interest groups can use the courts to affect public policy in at least three ways: (1) by bringing suit directly on behalf of the group itself, (2) by financing suits brought by individuals, or (3) by filing a companion brief as *"amicus curiae"* (literally "friend of the court") to an existing court case (see Chapter 16 for a discussion of *amicus curiae* briefs).

One way in which lobbying firms gain access is to hire former members of Congress. Former Republican Senate Finance Committee Chair Bob Packwood, shown here meeting with Bob Dole, opened his own lobbying firm after resigning from the Senate.

Among the most significant modern illustrations of the use of the courts as a strategy for political influence are those that accompanied the "sexual revolution" of the 1960s and the emergence of the movement for women's rights.

The 1973 Supreme Court case of *Roe v. Wade,* which took away a state's power to ban abortions, sparked a controversy that brought conservatives to the fore on a national level.[25] These conservative groups made extensive use of the courts to whittle away the scope of the privacy doctrine. They obtained rulings, for example, that prohibit the use of federal funds to pay for voluntary abortions. And in 1989, right-to-life groups were able to use a strategy of litigation that significantly undermined the *Roe v. Wade* decision, namely in the case of *Webster v. Reproductive Health Services* (see Chapter 5), which restored the right of states to place restrictions on abortion.[26] The *Webster* case brought more than three hundred interest groups on both sides of the abortion issue to the Supreme Court's door.

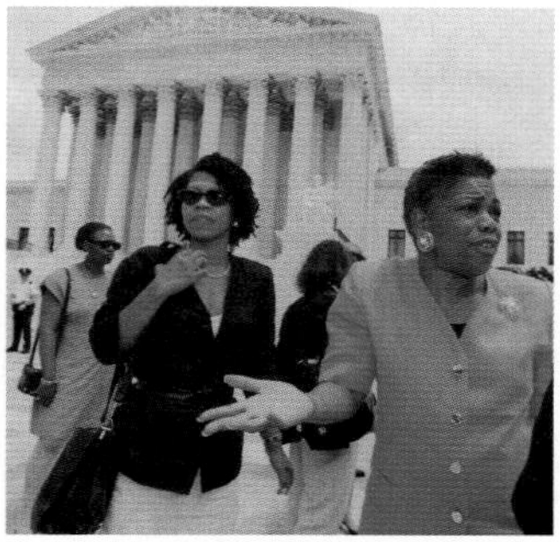

Elaine Jones (right), director of the NAACP Legal Defense Fund, spoke with reporters outside the Supreme Court after the Court struck down redistricting plans in Texas and North Carolina.

Another extremely significant set of contemporary illustrations of the use of the courts as a strategy for political influence are those found in the history of the NAACP. The most important of these court cases was, of course, *Brown v. Board of Education of Topeka, Kansas,* in which the U.S. Supreme Court held that legal segregation of the schools was unconstitutional.[27]

Business groups are also frequent users of the courts because of the number of government programs applied to them. Litigation involving large businesses is most mountainous in such areas as taxation, antitrust, interstate transportation, patents, and product quality and standardization. Often a business is brought to litigation against its will by virtue of initiatives taken against it by other businesses or by government agencies. But many individual businesses bring suit themselves in order to influence government policy. Major corporations and their trade associations pay tremendous amounts of money each year in fees to the most prestigious Washington law firms. Some of this money is expended in gaining access. A great proportion of it, however, is used to keep the best and most experienced lawyers prepared to represent the corporations in court or before administrative agencies when necessary.

New Politics forces made significant use of the courts during the 1970s and 1980s, and judicial decisions were instrumental in advancing their goals. Facilitated by changes in the rules governing access to the courts ("standing" is discussed in Chapter 16), the New Politics agenda was clearly visible in court decisions handed down in several key policy areas. In the environmental policy area, New Politics groups were able to force federal agencies to pay attention to environmental issues, even when the agency was not directly involved in activities related to environmental quality. For example, the Federal Trade Commission (FTC) became very responsive to the demands of New Politics activists during the 1970s and 1980s. The FTC stepped up its activities considerably, litigating a series of claims arising under regulations prohibiting deceptive advertising in cases ranging from false claims for over-the-counter drugs to inflated claims about the nutritional value of children's cereal.

And while feminists and equal rights activists enjoyed enormous success in litigating discrimination claims under Title VII of the Civil Rights Act of 1964, anti–nuclear power activists succeeded in virtually shutting down the nuclear power industry. Despite significant defeats, challenges to power plant siting and licensing regulations were instrumental in discouraging energy companies from pursuing nuclear projects over the long term.[28]

GOING PUBLIC

going public
a stratey that attempts to mobilize the widest and most favorabe climate of public opinion

Going public is a strategy that attempts to mobilize the widest and most favorable climate of opinion. Many groups consider it imperative to maintain this climate at all times, even when they have no issue to fight about. An increased use of this kind of strategy is usually associated with modern advertising. As early as the 1930s, political analysts were distinguishing between the "old lobby" of direct group representation before Congress and the "new lobby" of public relations professionals addressing the public at large to reach Congress.[29]

institutional advertising
advertising designed to create a positive image of an organization

Institutional Advertising One of the best known ways of going public is the use of **institutional advertising.** A casual scanning of important mass circulation magazines and newspapers will provide numerous examples of expensive and well designed ads by the major oil companies, automobile and steel companies, other large corporations, and trade associations. The ads show how much these organizations are doing for the country, for the protection of the environment, or for the defense of the American way of life. Their purpose is to create and maintain a strongly positive association between the organization and the community at large, in the hope that these favorable feelings can be drawn on as needed for specific political campaigns later on.

Social Movements Many groups resort to going public because they lack the resources, the contacts, or the experience to use other political strategies. The sponsorship of boycotts, sit-ins, mass rallies, and marches by Martin Luther King's Southern Christian Leadership Conference (SCLC) and related organizations in the 1950s and 1960s is one of the most significant and successful cases of going public to create a more favorable climate of opinion by calling attention to abuses. The success of these events inspired similar efforts on the part of women. Organizations such as the National Organization for Women (NOW) used public strategies in their drive for legislation and in their efforts to gain ratification of the Equal Rights Amendment. In 1993, gay rights groups organized a mass rally as part of their effort to eliminate restrictions on military service and other forms of discrimination based on individuals' sexual preferences. Gay rights leaders met with President Clinton in mid-April 1993 and were assured of his support for a demonstration in Washington to be held at the end of the month.[30] Although President Clinton had campaigned actively for gay and lesbian support during the election, he did not attend the march for fear of offending religious conservatives.

grassroots mobilization
campaign in which a group mobilizes its membership to contact government officials in support of the group's position

Grassroots Mobilization Another form of going public is **grassroots mobilization.** In such a campaign, a lobby group mobilizes its members and their families throughout the country to write to their elected representatives in support of the group's position. For example, in 1993, lobbyists for the Nissan Motor Company sought to organize a "grassroots" effort to prevent President Clinton from raising tariffs on imported minivans, including Nissan's Pathfinder model. Nissan's twelve hundred dealers across the nation, as well as those dealers' employees and family members, were urged to dial a toll-free number that would automatically generate a prepared mailgram opposing the tariff to be sent to the president and each dealer's senators. The mailgram warned that the proposed tariff increase would hurt middle-class auto purchasers and small businesses, such as the dealerships.[31]

Among the most effective users of the grassroots effort in contemporary American politics is the religious Right. Networks of evangelical churches have the capacity to generate hundreds of thousands of letters and phone calls to Congress and the White House. For example, the religious Right was outraged when President Clinton announced soon after taking office that he planned to end the military's ban on gay and lesbian soldiers. The Reverend Jerry Falwell, an evangelical leader, called upon viewers of his television program to dial a telephone number that would add their names to a petition urging Clinton to retain the ban on gays in the military. Within a few hours, 24,000 people had called to support the petition.[32]

Grassroots campaigns have been so effective throughout the last few years that a number of Washington consulting firms have begun to specialize in this area. One example is Bonner and Associates, which was reportedly paid $3 million by a single trade association to generate a grassroots effort to defeat one bill on the Senate floor.[33] The annual tab for grassroots lobbying has been estimated at $1 billion, and the following case study illustrates why: The recent eight-year battle over the deregulation of electric power generation, transmission, and distribution—the nation's last regulated monopoly and our eighth-biggest industry—seemed to be finally coming to a head. Then it flopped. But not until "the K Street crowd" had spent $50 million (over 1997, 1998, and 1999) on direct lobbying and another large but undetermined amount on grassroots appeals.[34,35] For example, between 1997 and 1999, the American Public Power Association, which represents municipal power utilities, spent $3.2 million on direct lobbying and $180,000 on grassroots campaigning. The Edison Electric Institute, the principal trade association of the private, investor-owned power companies, spent $41.2 million on direct lobbying and $1.5 million on grassroots campaigning. Five other major interest groups and trade associations, representing different slices of interest in electric power, spent varying amounts, some of which they were unwilling to report.[36]

Grassroots lobbying has become more prevalent in Washington over the last couple of decades because the adoption of congressional rules limiting gifts to members has made traditional lobbying more difficult. This circumstance makes all the more compelling the question

Students and Politics

With the symbols of the federal government at their backs, college students from around the country urged Congressional leaders to listen to their voices Tuesday.

Cheers of "We gotta beat back education attack" and "We are students fighting for justice and an education" filled the Capitol area, catching the attention of local tourists.

Over 350 students from 22 states rallied on Capitol Hill, urging politicians to put student concerns on their agenda. Meetings with individual representatives followed the rally.

"Our youth community is reflective of our nation's future," said Kendra Fox-Davis, president of the United States Student Association, a student rights lobbying group that organized the rally. "Young people today are struggling, and today is our opportunity to take that message to Capitol Hill."

The USSA said higher education reform is top on their agenda.

"It seems we are dealing with a conscious choice by politicians and candidates to keep youth disenfranchised from politics and government," said Ali Fischer, USSA vice president. "Politicians make an active choice not to engage youth because they fear the fundamental change that youth require in exchange for our active participation."

Haley Carlson, a student at the University of Wisconsin at Stout, said she took a twenty-hour car ride to get to Washington because she feels there are "a lot of student issues that aren't getting taken care of."

Carlson said that she has encountered problems with financial aid, an issue that is very important to students. She said she is not the only person with that problem.

"Education is a right, not a privilege," said Fox-Davis. USAA members urged their representatives to increase federal money for financial aid.

Another concern of the students is safety, specifically the 1999 Violence Against Women Act now in committee and hate crimes legislation that was proposed in the wake of the death of Matthew Shepard, a gay college student at the University of Wyoming. Students also expressed interest in affirmative action and racial profiling issues being discussed in several states.

SOURCE: Sarah Lechner, "Student Advocacy Group Lobbies Capitol Hill," U-WIRE D.C. Bureau, March 14, 2000.

of whether grassroots campaigning has reached an intolerable extreme. One case in particular may have tipped it over: In 1992, ten giant companies in the financial services, manufacturing, and technology industries began a grassroots campaign and spent untold millions of dollars over the next three years to influence a congressional decision that would limit their investors' ability to sue them for fraud. Retaining an expensive consulting firm, these corporations paid for the use of specialized computer software to persuade Congress that there was "an outpouring of popular support for the proposal." Thousands of letters from individuals flooded Capitol Hill. Many of those letters were written and sent by people who sincerely believed that investor lawsuits are often frivolous and should be curtailed. But much of the mail was phony, generated by the Washington-based campaign consultants; the letters came from people who had no strong feelings or even no opinion at all about the issue. More and more people, including leading members of Congress, are becoming quite skeptical of such methods, charging that these are not genuine grassroots campaigns but instead represent "Astroturf lobbying" (a play on the name of an artificial grass used on many sports fields). Such Astroturf campaigns have increased in frequency in recent years as members of Congress have grown more and more skeptical of Washington lobbyists and far more concerned about demonstrations of support for a particular issue by their constituents. But after the firms mentioned above spent millions of dollars and generated thousands of letters to members of Congress, they came to the somber conclusion that "it's more effective to have 100 letters from your district where constituents took the time to write and understand the issue," because "Congress is sophisticated enough to know the difference."[37]

Students and Politics

In 1996, in response to predictions of an unfunded Social Security system within twenty-five years, American University student Mike Panetta founded X-PAC, a political action committee that promotes and publicizes the interests and views of Generation X-ers on Social Security reform. By working only ten hours a week on the X-PAC web page and a few publicity projects, Panetta has generated considerable support for his organization and greater interest among his generation in the issue, especially since merging with College of William and Mary student Christian Klein's PAC 20/20, which has solicited money for pro–Social Security reform candidates and held events such as the Easter fund-raiser at William and Mary. Klein and Panetta admit to fearing that the Social Security system will lose large amounts of money once the baby boomer generation retires: PAC 20/20 was named not as a reference to perfect vision on the issue, but for the year that the government program will go bankrupt. "Anyone can start an interest group or a PAC," says Panetta. "Just stick to your guns and keep your eye on the target. Some people will try to bring you down, but with a little homework and a good idea, you can be a player and make a difference."

SOURCE: Mike Panetta, interview with author, January 8, 1998.

USING ELECTORAL POLITICS

Many interest groups decide that it is far more effective to elect the right legislators than to try to influence the incumbents through lobbying or through a changed or mobilized mass opinion. Interest groups can influence elections by two means: financial support funded through political action committees, and campaign activism.

Political Action Committees By far the most common electoral strategy employed by interest groups is that of giving financial support to the parties or to particular candidates. But such support can easily cross the threshold into outright bribery. Therefore, Congress has occasionally made an effort to regulate this strategy. Congress's most recent effort was the Federal Election Campaign Act of 1971 (amended in 1974). This act limits campaign contributions and requires that each candidate or campaign committee itemize the full name and address, occupation, and principal business of each person who contributes more than $100. These provisions have been effective up to a point, considering the rather large number of embarrassments, indictments, resignations, and criminal convictions in the aftermath of the Watergate scandal.

The Watergate scandal was triggered by the illegal entry of Republican workers into the office of the Democratic National Committee in the Watergate apartment building. But an investigation quickly revealed numerous violations of campaign finance laws, involving millions of dollars in unregistered cash from corporate executives to President Nixon's re-election committee. Many of these revelations were made by the famous Ervin Committee, whose official name and jurisdiction was the Senate Select Committee to Investigate the 1972 Presidential Campaign Activities.

Reaction to Watergate produced further legislation on campaign finance in 1974 and 1976, but the effect has been to restrict individual rather than interest-group campaign activity. Individuals may now contribute no more than $1,000 to any candidate for federal office in any primary or general election. A **political action committee (PAC)**, however, can contribute $5,000, provided it contributes to at least five different federal candidates each year. Beyond this, the laws permit corporations, unions, and other interest groups to form PACs and to pay the costs of soliciting funds from private citizens for the PACs. In other words, PACs are interest groups that choose to operate in the electoral arena, in addition to whatever they do within the interest-group system. The option to form a PAC was made available by law only in the early-1970s. Until then, it was difficult—if not downright illegal—for corporations, including unions, to get directly involved in elections by supporting parties and candidates.

political action committee (PAC)
a private group that raises and distributes funds for use in election campaigns

Electoral spending by interest groups has been increasing steadily despite the flurry of reform following Watergate. Table 12.2 presents a dramatic picture of the growth of PACs as the source of campaign contributions. The dollar amounts for each year reveal the growth in electoral spending. The number of PACs has also increased significantly—from 480 in 1972 to more than

PAC SPENDING, 1977–98 — Table 12.2

Years	Contributions
1977–78 (est.)	$ 77,800,000
1979–80	131,153,384
1981–82	190,173,539
1983–84	266,822,476
1985–86	339,954,416
1987–88	364,201,275
1989–90	357,648,557
1991–92	394,785,896
1993–94	388,102,643
1995–96	429,887,819
1997–98	470,830,847

SOURCE: Federal Election Commission.

Figure 12.4 GROWTH OF POLITICAL ACTION COMMITTEES, 1977–98

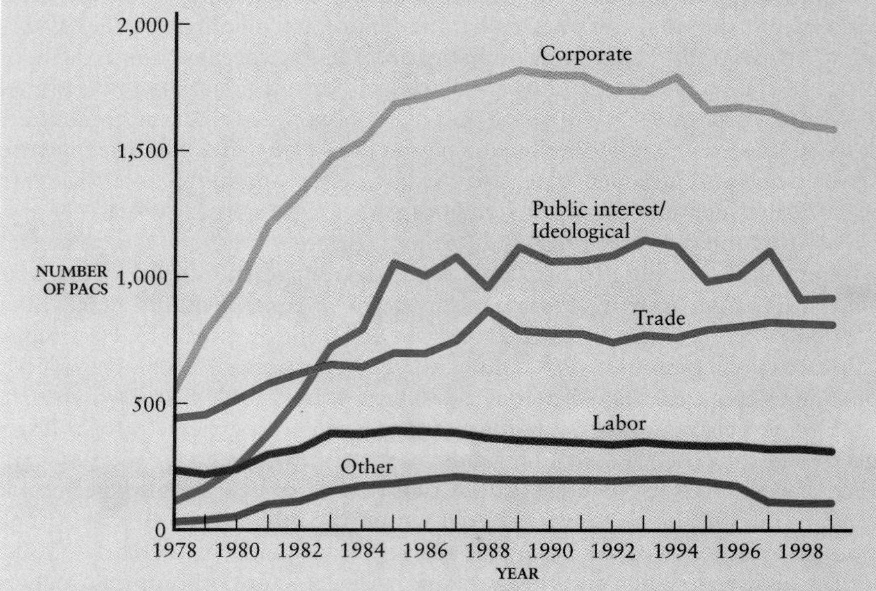

SOURCE: Federal Election Commission.

4,500 in 1999 (see Figure 12.4). Although the reform legislation of the early and mid-1970s attempted to reduce the influence that special interests have over elections, the effect has been almost the exact opposite. Opportunities for legally influencing campaigns are now widespread. And while PACs represent only one source of spending on campaigns and elections, they are a major cause behind the dramatic increases in the costs of recent elections. The total extent of spending on national elections for 2000 will not be known until virtually the end of 2001, but it is estimated to be more than double that of 1996, or over $3 billion.

PACs and campaign contributions provide organized interests with such a useful tool for gaining access to the political process that interests of all political stripes are now willing to suspend their conflicts and rally to the defense of PACs when they come under attack. This support has helped to make the present campaign funding system highly resistant to reform. As we saw in Chapter 11, in May 1996, the Senate considered a bipartisan campaign finance bill sponsored by Senators John McCain, Russell Feingold, and Fred Thompson, which would have abolished PACs. The bill was staunchly opposed by a coalition of business groups, labor unions, liberal groups like EMILY's List, and conservative groups like Americans for Tax Reform. Though these groups disagree on many substantive matters, they agreed on the principle that abolition of PACs would "diminish the ability of average citizens to join together to have their voices heard." A less positive interpretation was offered by Common Cause president Ann McBride, a proponent of abolishing PACs, who

Senators John McCain, left, and Russell Feingold, right, led a bipartisan effort to pass a campaign-finance reform bill in the 105th Congress.

characterized the pro-PAC alliance as an example of "labor and business coming together and agreeing on the one thing that they can agree on, which is maintaining the status quo and their ability to use money to buy outcomes on Capitol Hill."[38]

Given the enormous costs of television commercials, polls, computers, and other elements of the new political technology (see Chapter 11), most politicians are eager to receive PAC contributions and are at least willing to give a friendly hearing to the needs and interests of contributors. It is probably not the case that most politicians simply sell their services to the interests that fund their campaigns. But there is considerable evidence to support the contention that interest groups' campaign contributions do influence the overall pattern of political behavior in Congress and in the state legislatures.

During the 1996 national election campaign, for example, thousands of special interest groups donated more than $1.5 billion to political parties and candidates at the national, state, and local levels. Business groups raised $242 million, mainly for Republicans, while organized labor donated $35 million to Democratic candidates and spent another $35 million directly to campaign for Democrats.[39] In response to charges that both Dole and President Clinton were allowing major campaign contributors—including foreign firms—too much influence in the political process, Republican presidential candidate Bob Dole called for new campaign spending rules that would abolish large private contributions and prohibit noncitizens from contributing money to American political candidates.[40] Democrats immediately questioned Dole's sincerity, noting that the former Senate majority leader had personally raised some $100 million in campaign funds during the course of his long political career. While the two parties traded charges, Democratic fund-raiser John Huang was being

John Huang, shown here with President Clinton, was accused in 1998 of soliciting illegal foreign donations to the Democratic National Committee.

forced to resign from the Democratic National Committee campaign staff amid allegations that he funneled millions of dollars in contributions from a wealthy Indonesian family into Democratic campaign coffers.[41] In late 1999, a House Government Reform Committee investigation into White House fund-raising practices failed to uncover any wrongdoing.

PACs provide more than just the financial support that individual candidates receive. Under present federal law, there is no restriction on the amount that individuals and interests can contribute directly to the parties for voter registration, grassroots organizing, and other party activities not directly linked to a particular candidate's campaign. Such contributions, called **soft money,** allow individuals and interest groups to circumvent restrictions on campaign contributions. Critics argue that soft money contributions allow wealthy donors to have unfair influence in the political process. Perhaps this potential does exist. However, soft money also provides the national and state parties with the means to engage in voter registration and turnout drives. In 1996, the Supreme Court ruled in the case of *Colorado Republican Party v. Federal Election Commission* that the government could not restrict political parties' use of soft money.[42] In 1997, legislation designed to circumvent the Court's ruling and reduce the role of soft money was introduced by Senators McCain and Feingold, but was blocked by a Senate filibuster.

soft money
money contributed directly to political parties for voter registration and organization

Often, the campaign spending of activist groups is carefully kept separate from party and candidate organizations in order to avoid the restrictions of federal campaign finance laws. So long as a group's campaign expenditures are not coordinated with those of a candidate's own campaign, the group is free to spend as much money as it wishes. Such expenditures are viewed as "issues advocacy" and are protected by the First Amendment and thus not subject to statutory limitation.[43]

During the 2000 election campaign, another source of PAC money surfaced—the "stealth PAC," so-called because it "flew under the radar" of the Federal Election Commission's requirement that an independent expenditure by an individual or PAC be publicly disclosed. In that year's primaries, stealth PACs engaged in issues advocacy. However, because no reporting requirements were in place, no one knew exactly how much money they were spending, how many of them existed, where their money came from, or which candidates they supported. Nevertheless, the media and "watchdog" public-interest groups were able to bring some details about them to the public's attention. For example, it was discovered that two prominent fundraisers for George W. Bush's presidential campaign spent $2.5 million on a series of "Republicans for Clean Air" ads that were critical of Senator John McCain, Bush's most formidable opponent in the Republican primaries. Later in 2000, campaign finance reformers in Congress won a small victory when they passed legislation that requires stealth PACs to fully disclose the names of their contributors and to detail where their money is spent. In support of this legislation, Maine senator Olympia Snowe said, "This is a good opportunity to bring sunshine to the political process." Still, other reformers wondered whether such a small success could translate into momentum for more substantive reforms.

Campaign Activism Financial support is not the only way that organized groups seek influence through electoral politics. Sometimes, activism can be

POLICY DEBATE

Is the National Rifle Association Too Powerful?

Few interest groups in American politics are more powerful, or more feared, than the National Rifle Association (NRA). Formed in 1871 to improve marksmanship skills, this formerly nonpolitical group became politically active in the 1960s when the government moved to enact stronger gun laws. In the 1970s, the NRA began devoting more resources to political battles and less to traditional hunting and sporting activities. Today, the NRA exercises great influence in Congress. In the summer of 1999, for example, it almost single-handedly halted a series of widely popular gun laws advanced in Congress in the wake of the April mass shooting at Columbine High School. The NRA's many successes in blocking popular gun control measures have prompted critics to charge that the NRA is simply too powerful and that it throttles the democratic process.

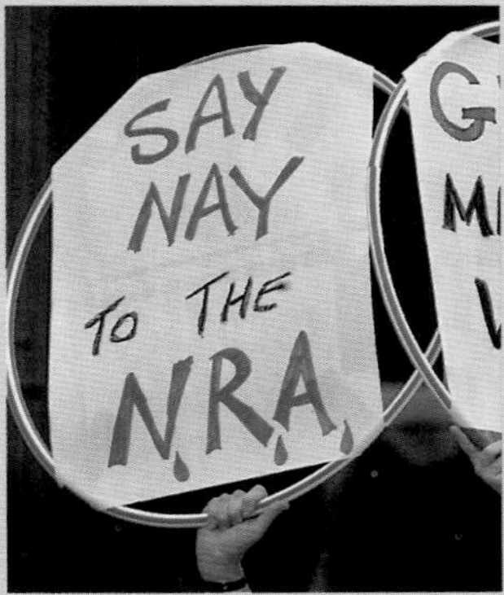

Critics note first that public opinion polls have consistently supported stronger gun measures for decades, so that when the NRA opposes such proposals as mandatory trigger locks or stronger regulation of sales at gun shows, it is thwarting commonsense measures that are the clear will of the majority. Second, the NRA employs scare tactics to whip up its supporters and silence its critics. In its literature, the NRA refers to gun control supporters by such terms as "gun grabbers" and "the criminal's best friend." The federal agency charged with enforcing gun laws, the Bureau of Alcohol, Tobacco, and Firearms (ATF), has been compared to Nazi storm troopers in NRA publications. Such overheated rhetoric is used to demonize NRA "enemies" and to mobilize the organization's three million members. Third, critics charge that the NRA's heavy political spending buys votes and harasses critics. Consistently one of the biggest-spending interest groups, the NRA's political action committee (PAC) spends tens of millions of dollars each year to influence legislation, rally supporters, and discredit opponents. After a successful political effort in Congress, *The Washington Post* wrote that the NRA "has done a bang-up job of buying support in Congress." Fourth, the NRA has been accused of being too extremist. In recent years, the organization has lost support from members who feel the group has gone too far. For example, former NRA president Richard Riley said that "there could be a lot of members who resign because the NRA has been embarrassed by some of the people running it now."

NRA supporters agree that it has logged many successes but argue that most criticisms simply reflect the frustration of opponents who wish they could be as effective as the NRA. First, the NRA is a legal organization that engages in the interest group process in the same way as hundreds of other interest groups, and while its successes may not always reflect popular preferences, the NRA's job is to advance the interests of its members. And if it gives ground on limited gun controls, it may ultimately lead to gun take-aways. Much of the NRA's success lies in the fact that its members care more about the issue than gun control supporters do, such that they will write letters, contribute money, attend meetings, and otherwise invest personal efforts when their opponents do not. If gun control supporters worked harder, they might have more success. (In fact, up until the 1980s, there was no effective gun control group to oppose the NRA.) Second, unlike many groups that rely on wealthy, elitist donors and supporters, the real muscle of the NRA is its grassroots support—average gun owners all across America who take a personal interest in gun issues. Third, much research has demonstrated that groups like the NRA do not "buy" votes in Congress; rather, they spend their money to reward their supporters and to try to defeat opponents. Related to this is the "myth" of NRA invincibility. Studies of those who win and lose seats in Congress show that the NRA rarely succeeds by itself in defeating incumbents it opposes, and NRA supporters have lost often enough to demonstrate that the organization is less than invincible.

STUDENT DEBATE

Is the National Rifle Association Too Influential?

Yes

Guns kill people. Guns kill animals. Guns are for killing. There is no getting around that fact. Every year in this country, people are murdered with guns. Rifles, pistols, revolvers, semi-automatic weapons. All these types of guns are involved in murders, suicides, robberies, hunting, and even accidental shootings. Children are killed by guns, the elderly are killed by guns, the middle aged and even the youthful are killed by guns. Rich or poor, when a person is shot with a gun, it is dangerous and possibly deadly.

In 1994 alone there were 38,505 fire-arm related deaths. This number includes homicides, suicides, and unintentional deaths. The Centers for Disease Control also estimates that for every gun-related fatality, there are at least three gun-related non-fatal injuries. Eighty percent of these gun related injuries are treated with money provided by the taxpayers of America. Guns kill more people under the age of twenty-four than even motor vehicles. Persons who live in homes with guns have a suicide rate 5 times greater than people who do not. Clearly firearms are dangerous and deadly. The United States has the proud distinction of being the richest industrialized nation with the highest rate of gun-related fatalities. Go USA!

I personally do not care to own or ever handle a gun. There are many people who feel as I do, but there is a stronger element of the American culture who embrace their right to own firearms and will continue to fight tirelessly to protect that right.

Americans who want to protect their gun ownership rights have a stronger voice in Congress. The NRA is undeniably one of the most prominent and successful conservative lobbyists in Washington today. In a town where money speaks volumes, the NRA can afford to keep talking. In the 1997–98 election cycle alone, the NRA and other gun ownership advocates contributed 1.8 million dollars to congressional campaigns.

Compare that figure to the amount gun control advocates contributed in the same year—only 150,364 dollars—and you can see how gun owners and their supporters seem to have the political upper hand in Washington.

This majority in Washington will resist any tighter restrictions on gun ownership. While I do not agree with them in principle, I see their point. The violence in this nation will not be helped by some hard-to-enforce, mandatory waiting period. The violence this nation experiences runs too deeply to be stopped at this late stage by restrictions. Gun violence will only change when this society decides to limit their use of firearms.

There will always be that element of American society that wants to hold onto their guns. They will say that it's their right to shoot cans for sport, or hunt, or to start another Revolutionary War. That will be their choice. However, if the majority of American people are willing to change their opinions of gun ownership after years of tradition, then maybe we might build a nation of responsible, nonviolent people. It has to start with this generation.

Each of us must make our personal choice about guns. We must not buy guns or embrace violence. We must teach our children how to resolve conflicts peacefully. We must stop glorifying gun violence in our forms of entertainment. We must change our romanticizing of America's gun-rich past and look to a gun-sensible future. Even if we were to pass the tightest restrictions on guns possible, they would do nothing to stop the violence in America. If we want a peaceful future, we as a nation must first choose to live without guns, not be forced unwillingly to do so by legislation. I am not old enough to remember prohibition, but I think we are all aware of how fiercely people resist well-intentioned legislation when they are not behind it themselves.

SOURCE: Lora J. Machel, "Cold Truth about Guns," *Arizona Daily Wildcat* (University of Arizona), August 27, 1999.

No

Apathy is everywhere these days. It flourishes among millions of Americans who sit back and let vocal minorities decide their fate.

***

We seem to be a nation of followers rather than leaders. Why are people so afraid and reluctant to stand up for what they believe?

***

Quite frankly, there are many people who just don't give a damn. Lacking strong convictions about anything, they simply tune out. They rarely follow the news and avoid controversy like the plague.

***

Then there are the go-with-the-flow types who hesitate to rock the boat. This group often holds deep political and social beliefs, yet seldom voices them. Being stigmatized or stereotyped by friends and relatives is a constant fear. Bumper stickers, letters to the editor, and campaign signs are practically out of the question.

I guess that leaves people like me, who have gotten past the point of caring what other people think. We are the ones who not only strongly believe in something, but make the grassroots effort to defend it. In my case, I am an ardent supporter of individual rights and personal freedom. Out of this stemmed my outrage when I realized that insincere, left-leaning, anti-American politicians were trying to trample on my Second Amendment rights with their gun grabbing schemes.

What made me furious was their arrogant insinuation that peaceful gun owners like myself should be demonized and punished for firearms misuse by criminals.

Instead of locking up armed felons or promoting gun safety education, they try to disarm me when I have done nothing wrong.

As a result of this egregious threat to my freedom, I decided to take action several years ago and joined the fight. I wasn't going to sit idly while a gang of smug, phony ambulance chasers systematically chipped away at my liberties.

Today, I am a proud member of the National Rifle Association in addition to three other pro-gun organizations. I have no qualms about writing letters to the editors at various newspapers, calling legislators, contributing money, and letting people know how I feel. The really unfortunate reality is that apathetic people are too embarrassed or unmotivated to get involved, so they get a free ride on the backs of others like me.

For instance, there are an estimated 70–80 million gun owners in the United States, yet only three million are NRA members. Where are all these people when we need them?

Perhaps they're sitting on the sidelines in the "don't rock the boat" category, afraid of what the liberal elite might think if they stand up for their rights by supporting such a conservative organization. Perhaps they're like my brother, who generally agrees with my beliefs yet teases me for taking an active role. Maybe they're just too good to join the rest of the troops, reluctant to get their hands dirty and too lazy to pull their weight.

Although the NRA is already the fourth most powerful lobbying group in the country, according to "Fortune," it is not nearly as influential as it should be.

If even a tenth of gun owners bothered to do their share, we could stop the anti-gunners cold. The same holds true for many other worthy organizations that suffer from the public's unwillingness to contribute.

It's rather sad to think of all the good people and causes that routinely lack the support they deserve because of indifferent silence from the masses.

If society could shed its apathetic attitude, the world would be a much more productive and representative place.

SOURCE: Reid Lusk, "Apathetic Attitude Hinders Worthy Causes," *Rocky Mountain Collegian* (Colorado State University), March 18, 1999.

even more important than campaign contributions. Campaign activism on the part of conservative groups played a very important role in bringing about the Republican capture of both houses of Congress in the 1994 congressional elections. For example, Christian Coalition activists played a role in many races, including ones in which Republican candidates were not overly identified with the religious Right. One postelection study suggested that more than 60 percent of the more than 600 candidates supported by the Christian Right were successful in state, local, and congressional races in 1994.[44] The efforts of conservative Republican activists to bring voters to the polls is one major reason that turnout among Republicans exceeded Democratic turnout in a midterm election for the first time since 1970. This increased turnout was especially marked in the South, where the Christian Coalition was most active. In many Congressional districts, Christian Coalition efforts on behalf of the Republicans were augmented by grassroots campaigns launched by the NRA and the National Federation of Independent Business (NFIB). The NRA had been outraged by Democratic support for gun control legislation, while the NFIB had been energized by its campaign against employer mandates in the failed Clinton health care reform initiative. Both groups are well organized at the local level and were able to mobilize their members across the country to participate in congressional races.

In 1996, by contrast, it was the Democrats who benefited from campaign activism. Organized labor made a major effort to mobilize its members for the campaign. Conservative activists, on the other hand, were not enthusiastic about GOP presidential candidate Bob Dole or his running mate Jack Kemp and failed to mobilize their forces for a maximum campaign effort. Dole belat-

In 2000, Democratic presidential candidate Al Gore won the endorsements of all the major trade unions and worked closely with their leaders to make certain that union members—an important Democratic constituency—went to the polls. In Michigan, for example, the United Auto Workers (UAW) negotiated a contract provision which gave its members the day off (with pay) on Election Day, to permit them to vote.

AMERICAN DEMOCRACY IN COMPARATIVE PERSPECTIVE

Interest Group Corporatism

To those who compare and contrast different political systems around the world, the United States is a classic pluralist democracy. As with all types of electoral democracies, forging a policy agenda in the United States relies on the nature of the relationship between government and the general public. This relationship, however, is largely mediated by a diverse array of competitive, decentralized, and uncoordinated social, political, economic, and cultural groups, and is known as *interest group pluralism*. This pattern stands in contrast to its principal alternative, *interest group corporatism*, a pattern of interaction between interest groups (such as labor unions and business federations) and government in which interest groups are hierarchically organized; the actions of similar groups (e.g., local labor unions) across the country are closely coordinated by central and national leadership; and nationally organized "peak organizations" ensure the coordination and compliance of all affiliated groups and monopolize both the strategy and practice of negotiating directly with government, as well as implementing the outcomes of these negotiations.

Interest group pluralism is a characteristic commonly, though not exclusively, found in *consensual democracies* (see Chapter 2). The vast diversity and decentralized and competitive nature of interest groups in this type of electoral democracy allow multiple entrance points into the political arena for organized and active citizens, increasing the likelihood that government must consider a broader but often uncoordinated front of interests when formulating public policy. Consistent with the logic of consensual democracy, interest group pluralism expands the inclusiveness of the political system. That is, the institutions of governance in society are more exposed to multiple and largely uncoordinated pressures from groups.

Interest group corporatism, on the other hand, is a classic feature of majoritarian democracy. The peak organizations and centrally organized nature of interest groups tend to reduce the abundant diversity of interest, funneling and screening public demands through a more restricted array of "gates" into the political arena. This allows for a more regularized and predictable flow of information and demands upon government. As the name implies, majoritarian democracies ideally prefer a design to political institutions (e.g., constitutions, legislatures, executives, courts), which tends to reward political winners with temporary disproportionate power and influence over policy. Thus, political winners enjoy most of the rewards of victory (political appointments, etc.) and share very little with the losers, who are left to await the next round of competition.

Germany is a classic interest group corporatist democracy. Its labor unions are centrally coordinated through peak organizations. The Federation of German Labor (DGB) coordinates various labor unions, while large businesses are organized through the Federal Association of German Employers (BDA), and industrial concerns are organized through the Federation of German Industry (BDI). The BDA consists of sixty-four employer associations that represent nearly all large and medium employers in Germany, and the BDI organizes thirty-nine separate major industries. The DGB claims to represent 85 percent of the approximately ten million unionized workers in the German workforce (31 percent of German workers were unionized as of 1995). Germany's codetermination laws *(Mitbestimmung)* require all unions to be represented on the boards of large corporations. These peak business and union associations are closely aligned with the major political parties of Germany (the DGB with the left-of-center Social Democrats, and the BDA and BDI with the right-of-center Christian Democratic Union), although as in all corporatist democracies, these players maintain close working relationships with all major political parties in order to ensure continuity in policy despite shifting electoral fortunes of the political parties.

These organizations are professionally staffed and hierarchically organized within the German federal system. The corporatist logic of Germany requires the DGB to be an active player in the negotiations between government, business, and labor over wages and pension schemes, as well as an active participant in shaping federal policy in both the bureaucracy and the various committees of the national legislature.

As with any feature of democracy, no country is a perfect reflection of either interest group pluralism or interest group corporatism. Germany's strong federal system and constitution, as well as its complicated electoral system, all reflect features of consensual democracy. Yet, it blends these features with interest group corporatism, a feature more common among majoritarian democracies.

SOURCES: Arend Lijphart, *Patterns of Democracy: Government Forms and Performance in Thirty-Six Countries* (New Haven: Yale University Press, 1999); Kathleen Thelen, *Union in Parts: Labor Politics in Postwar Germany* (Ithaca: Cornell University Press, 1991).

Box 12.1

INTEREST GROUP STRATEGIES

Lobbying

Influencing the passage or defeat of legislation

Two types of lobbyists:

Amateur—loyal members of a group seeking passage of legislation that is currently under scrutiny

Paid—often lawyers, professionals, or former government officials without a personal interest in the legislation who are not full-time lobbyists

Access

Development of close ties to decision-makers on Capitol Hill or in the executive branch

Litigation

Taking action through the courts, usually in one of three ways:

Filing suit against a specific government agency or program

Financing suits brought against the government by individuals

Filing companion briefs as *amicus curiae* (friend of the court) to existing court cases

Going Public

Especially via advertising; also through boycotts, strikes, rallies, marches, and sit-ins, generating positive news coverage

Partisan Politics

Giving financial support to a particular party or candidate

Congress passed the Federal Election Campaign Act of 1971 to try to regulate this practice by limiting the amount of funding interest groups can contribute to campaigns

edly recognized his need for the support of these activists, but was never able to energize them in sufficient numbers to affect the outcome of the election.[45]

One remarkable fact about the political activity of interest groups is how infrequently major interest groups have tried to form their own party. The fact that they have rarely done so is to a large extent attributable to the strength of the two-party tradition in the United States. But there is also a significant negative influence: the barriers erected by state laws regarding the formation of new political parties. As a consequence, significant interests such as "the working class," women, and African Americans have not been able to find clear expression in the electoral process. Their interests are always being adulterated by other interests within their chosen party. Yet this situation has a positive side: the two-party system has—unintentionally—softened social demarcations by cutting across classes, races, and other fundamental interests that deeply divide people. These interests are adulterated and softened, subduing what might otherwise become the kind of class conflict that we see so often in European history, where class, race, and ethnic interests have become radicalized when they are not forced to reconcile themselves with other interests in a broad political party.[46]

Groups and Interests: The Dilemma

▶ What are the problems involved in curbing the influence of interest groups?

James Madison wrote that "liberty is to faction as air is to fire."[47] By this he meant that the organization and proliferation of interests was inevitable in a free society. To seek to place limits on the organization of interests, in Madison's view, would be to limit liberty itself. Madison believed that interests should be permitted to regulate themselves by competing with one another. So long as competition among different interests was free, open, and vigorous—that is, so long as pluralism thrives—there would be some balance of power among them and no one interest would be able to dominate the political or governmental process.

There is considerable competition among organized groups in the United States. As we saw, tobacco interests, consumer groups, and trial lawyers fought each other to a standstill in 1998. Similarly, prochoice and antiabortion forces continue to be locked in a bitter struggle. Nevertheless, interest-group politics is not as free of bias as Madisonian theory might suggest. Although the weak and poor do occasionally become organized to assert their rights, interest-group politics is generally a form of political competition in which the wealthy and powerful are best able to engage. In the realm of group politics, liberty seems inconsistent with equality.

Moreover, although groups sometimes organize to promote broad public concerns, interest groups more often represent relatively narrow, selfish interests. Small, self-interested groups can be organized much more easily than large and more diffuse collectives. For one thing, the members of a relatively small group—say, bankers or hunting enthusiasts—are usually able to recognize their shared interests and the need to pursue them in the political arena. Members of large and more diffuse groups—say, consumers or potential victims of firearms—often find it difficult to recognize their shared interests or the need to engage in collective action to achieve them.[48] This is why causes presented as public interests by their proponents often turn out, upon examination, to be private interests wrapped in a public mantle. Thus, group politics often appears to be inconsistent with democracy.

To make matters still more complicated, group politics seems to go hand-in-hand with government. As we saw earlier, government programs often lead to a proliferation of interest groups as competing forces mobilize to support, oppose, or take advantage of the government's actions. Often, the government explicitly encourages the formation of interest groups. From the perspective of a government agency, nothing is more useful than a well-organized constituency for its programs. Agencies such as the Department of Veterans Affairs, the Social Security Administration, and the Department of Agriculture devote a great deal of energy to the organization and mobilization of groups of "stakeholders" to support the agencies and their efforts. This strategy, a variant of what is sometimes called "interest-group liberalism," can be very effec-

Politics on the Web

The Internet provides interest groups with an inexpensive means to recruit new members and reach their current membership. In addition to keeping members continuously informed of a group's actions and relevant policy decisions, a website can help build the kind of "grassroots" lobbying so important to modern interest-group strategies. For example, on the Greenpeace Web site one can find information on the group's activities, the progress of environmental legislation, the group's mission statement, and a history of the organization. The National Rifle Association maintains an active Web site, monitoring current legislation, recommending books and articles, and publicizing local courses in safe gun usage. Not surprisingly, these sites also give interest groups the opportunity to recruit new members. With all of the money that they save on mail and recruitment costs, groups have more money to directly influence the decisions of policy makers. And money is what interest-group politics in the United States is all about.

www.wwnorton.com/wtp3e

tive. One reason that the Social Security program is considered politically invulnerable despite its fiscal shortcomings is that it is so strongly supported by a powerful group—the AARP. Significantly, the Social Security Administration played an important early role in the formation of the AARP, precisely because agency executives realized that this group could become a useful ally.

The responsiveness of government agencies to interest groups is a challenge to democracy. Groups seem to have a greater impact than voters upon the government's policies and programs. Yet, before we decide that we should do away with interest groups, we should think carefully: if there were no organized interests, would the government pay more attention to ordinary voters, or would the government simply pay no attention to anyone? In his great work *Democracy in America,* Alexis de Tocqueville argued that the proliferation of groups promoted democracy by encouraging governmental responsiveness. Does group politics foster democracy or impede democracy? It does both.

Thus, we have dilemmas for which there is no ideal answer. To regulate interest-group politics is, as Madison warned, to limit freedom and to expand governmental power. Not to regulate interest-group politics, on the other hand, may be to ignore equality and democracy. Those who believe that there are simple solutions to the issues of political life would do well to ponder this problem.

The Citizen's Role

The dilemmas posed by group politics raise questions for citizens, as well. If you can't beat them, should you join them?

Like political parties, interest groups are always looking for volunteers and members. Given the enormous number of groups in America today, every student should be able to find several whose causes seem worthwhile. One useful way to become involved in the world of group politics is to secure an internship in Washington with the national office of a public interest group. Washington is the home of groups from every part of the political spectrum, espousing every known cause from the defense of wildlife through the defense of upper-middle-class taxpayers. National, state, and local groups employ tens of thousands of college students every year. Student interns can become important staff members of a public interest group. Student interns research, attend congressional or state legislative hearings, communicate with citizens, and even help develop strategies. Working for an interest group can be one of the most effective ways of participating in politics.

STUDENTS AND POLITICS

While Steve Ma was growing up in suburban New Jersey, he didn't realize that his home state ranked last in the nation in industry compliance with clean water legislation. The extent of the problem and his ability to act became clear, however, when in high school he happened upon a protest over the Exxon *Valdez* oil spill. Concerned that government was taking inadequate action both in environmental legislation and in promoting citizen awareness, Ma began to search for a venue to make his voice heard. He found the place in the Student Public Interest Research Group (PIRG) of New Jersey at Rutgers University.

PIRGs exist in numerous states to promote various consumer rights, including minimizing student tuition increases, protecting the environment, and fighting homelessness. One of Ma's first activities with PIRG was to publish a guide to the goods and services available in New Brunswick, N.J., including critiques of landlords and apartment buildings, restaurant recommendations, and ratings of bookstores that paid for returned textbooks. As the year progressed, he worked on larger projects: he and his chapter worked with local businesses to find cost-effective ways to reduce pollution emissions, saving both the environment and the money necessary to clean contaminated areas. He also worked as an intern at New Jersey PIRG, researching and helping to write a report on the failed implementation of the New Jersey Motor Voter Bill, which required the state's Department of Motor Vehicles to distribute voter registration information to customers.

Over the next year, New Jersey PIRG lobbied heavily for the Clean Water Enforcement Act, a bill that would make New Jersey's clean water laws the most stringent in the nation. "We did so much against millions of dollars of industry lobbying," says Ma. "I actually lobbied the governor himself."[49] The bill passed by a close vote. Since then, New Jersey's compliance with water regulations has increased from last in the nation to fifteenth.

New Jersey PIRG next worked to pass a federal bill that would give redemption value to all recycled cans and bottles. As part of the campaign, Ma led an effort to collect aluminum cans, clean them, and mail them to the White House with stickers stating an individual's support for the bill. "I was literally climbing in dumpsters," he says, "retrieving cans and bottles people had thrown away."[50] PIRG ultimately failed in its efforts to pass the bill, but did create enough publicity for a hearing on the matter in a congressional committee.

After graduating with a B.S. in human ecology, Ma enrolled at Indiana University for his masters in public affairs. As part of his graduate work, he helped to organize a new PIRG in Indiana. After earning his degree, he began work as a full-time grassroots organizer at the California PIRG in Sacramento. "There is really an opportunity at the state level to create the issue," says Ma. "It sounds clichéd, but states are the laboratories of democracy. We were really effective; we had our heads on straight, an eye on the future, and an incredible ability to organize. Classrooms are good, but good internships in which you can do things like lobby the governor and organize meetings are invaluable."[51]

But what about the Madisonian dilemma? Should you become involved in group politics? Would you be contributing to the solution or exacerbating the problem?

GET INVOLVED Fighting the Good Fight

You may have strong views about one or more issues that candidates running for office ignore, downplay, or oppose. How do you get the candidates to consider your views seriously and thoughtfully? Perhaps it is between elections. How do you get your ideas on politicians' agendas or bureaucrats' platters when public officials are likely to be overwhelmed with other matters? A common answer in American politics is "Join an interest group."

People with similar views on a specific issue (for example, a particular piece of gun control legislation) or general issue areas (for example, the protection of civil liberties) often mobilize, organize, and aggregate their resources in the hope of influencing candidates, politicians, and bureaucrats. Large groups with millions of members have so much potential clout on election day that they usually can get both attention and sympathy from lawmakers. Small groups with considerable wealth for funding political campaigns are also hard to ignore. All of these groups try to communicate their interests in ways that shape American politics.

Inventory your interests. Which issue or issues rouse your passions? What injustices do you consider intolerable? Who is not being properly represented in public life? Which class discussions have you found most provocative? What issues do you discuss with friends late into the night? What have you studied or written about that moves you? Ask yourself which issue or issue area is compelling to the point that you want to get involved in it.

For any interest that you find compelling, there are likely to be many other people who share that interest. Furthermore, there are likely to be some people who have organized a group or association aimed at promoting that interest. Consider seeking out interest groups that are already organized and active in the area that concerns you. How can you begin your search?

It is often easiest to begin on your own campus. Ask students, faculty, and staff if they know of any campus groups working on gun control, human rights, legalization of marijuana, or whatever your particular interest is. See if your college publishes a directory of student organizations. Make a point of reading posted flyers and notifications of coming events in the campus newspaper. Observe who sets up card tables or sponsors marches to pursue their causes on campus.

Do not be discouraged if your campus search is unsuccessful. Interest groups abound in communities, at the regional and state level, and nationwide. Talk to your family and neighbors, particularly those who are politically savvy and involved. Try the local telephone book. It may have a section on community groups. Experiment with a search engine on the Internet. Persevere. Know that while you are looking for an interest group that fits your priorities, there are likely to be several appropriate interest groups hoping to make contact with people just like you.

Once you identify the appropriate interest group, make contact, ask questions, and discuss how you can contribute to the group's efforts. Interest groups generally carry out multiple functions. They try to enhance public awareness, raise money, build coalitions, find sympathetic candidates, and influence how public officials think and act. Are you a people-person? Do you want to do outreach to the public? Are you willing to help organize a fund-raising event? Would you be good at researching various candidates' positions on key issues? Can you imagine yourself making an appointment with a politician and making a pitch to him or her?

Be aware that the interest group may want to channel your energies into limited activities that are less exciting or challenging than you prefer. New people to a group usually have to pay their dues by doing some dull, routine work.

Nonetheless, remember two things. First, you will only be a new person for a short while. Second, interest groups need to keep volunteers happy or they will lose them; that means that you probably have a good chance of working your way into a more engaging activity within the group.

As a college student working with a local or national interest group, you may have the opportunity to build a campus chapter of the interest group from the ground up. For example, if you are involved with Amnesty International (an organization that monitors human rights abuses) or Mothers Against Drunk Driving (a group that supports efforts to prevent and punish people who drink and drive), you may ask about the possibility of starting a campus affiliate. If the larger interest group approves, it will likely provide some assistance. However, you will still find yourself with considerable responsibility for doing campus recruitment, publicity, event planning, and fund-raising, as well as coordination with other campus chapters and the larger group.

Of course, you cannot and should not do everything yourself. You will need to achieve sufficient visibility to attract members. Are your friends interested? Can you make announcements in class? Should you plaster flyers around campus? Can you afford to run an advertisement in the school paper? Once you attract a core membership, you will need to consider the best way for your group to pursue its main interest and how labor should be divided among members. In effect, your campus interest group will face the same challenges that every interest group faces as it competes for influence in American politics.

Is fighting the good fight worth your time and energy? That is something that you must decide for yourself. Still, consider that an interest group's struggle for political influence can be fulfilling in itself; that small gains can have a large impact on people's lives; and that even today's failures may be the basis for tomorrow's victories.

Summary

Interest groups are pervasive in America. James Madison predicted that special interest groups would proliferate in a free society, but that competition among them would lead to moderation and compromise. Today, this theory is called pluralism. Individuals join or form groups to enhance their influence. To succeed, groups need leadership, a financial base, and active members. Recruiting new members can be difficult because of the "free rider" problem. Interest groups overcome this problem by offering selective benefits to members only. These include information, material benefits, solidary benefits, or purposive benefits.

The number of interest groups in America has increased because of the expansion of the government into new areas. This increase has included not only economic interests, but also "public interest" groups whose members do not seek economic gain. Both economic and public interest groups seek influence through a variety of techniques.

Lobbying is the act of petitioning legislators. Lobbyists—individuals who receive some form of compensation for lobbying—are required to register with the House and Senate. In spite of an undeserved reputation for corruption, lobbyists serve a useful function, providing members of Congress with a vital flow of information.

Access is participation in government. Groups with access have less need for lobbying. Most groups build up access over time through great effort. They work years to get their members into positions of influence on congressional committees. Means of gaining access include corridoring in the bureaucracy, grassroots approaches, and influence peddling.

Litigation sometimes serves interest groups when other strategies fail. Groups may bring suit on their own behalf, finance suits brought by individuals, or file *amicus curiae* briefs.

Going public is an effort to mobilize the widest and most favorable climate of opinion. Advertising is a common technique in this strategy. Other techniques are boycotts, strikes, rallies, and marches.

Groups engage in electoral politics either by embracing one of the major parties, usually through financial support, or through a nonpartisan strategy. Interest groups' campaign contributions now seem to be flowing into the coffers of candidates at a faster rate than ever before.

FOR FURTHER READING

Cigler, Allan J., and Burdett A. Loomis, eds. *Interest Group Politics*. Washington, DC: Congressional Quarterly Press, 1983.

Clawson, Dan, Alan Neustadtl, and Denise Scott. *Money Talks: Corporate PACs and Political Influence*. New York: Basic Books, 1992.

Costain, Anne. *Inviting Women's Rebellion: A Political Process Interpretation of the Women's Movement*. Baltimore, MD: Johns Hopkins University Press, 1992.

Day, Christine. *What Older Americans Think: Interest Groups and Aging Policy*. Princeton, NJ: Princeton University Press, 1990.

Goldfield, Michael. *The Decline of Organized Labor in the United States*. Chicago: University of Chicago Press, 1987.

Hansen, John Mark. *Gaining Access: Congress and the Farm Lobby, 1919–1981*. Chicago: University of Chicago Press, 1991.

Heinz, John P., Edward O. Laumann, Robert L. Nelson, and Robert H. Salisbury. *The Hollow Core: Private Interests in National Policy Making*. Cambridge, MA: Harvard University Press, 1993.

Lowi, Theodore J. *The End of Liberalism*. New York: Norton, 1979.

Moe, Terry M. *The Organization of Interests*. Chicago: University of Chicago Press, 1980.

Olson, Mancur, Jr. *The Logic of Collective Action: Public Goods and the Theory of Groups*. Cambridge, MA: Harvard University Press, 1971.

Olzak, Susan. *The Dynamics of Ethnic Competition and Conflict*. Stanford, CA: Stanford University Press, 1992.

Petracca, Mark, ed. *The Politics of Interests: Interest Groups Transformed*. Boulder, CO: Westview, 1992.

Pope, Jacqueline. *Biting the Hand that Feeds Them: Women on Welfare at the Grass Roots Level*. New York: Praeger, 1989.

Sanders, Elizabeth. *Roots of Reform: Farmers, Workers, and the American State, 1877–1917*. Chicago: University of Chicago Press, 1999.

Schlozman, Kay Lehman, and John T. Tierney. *Organized Interests and American Democracy*. New York: Harper & Row, 1986.

Staggenborg, Suzanne. *The Pro-Choice Movement: Organization and Activism in the Abortion Conflict*. New York: Oxford University Press, 1991.

Truman, David. *The Governmental Process: Political Interests and Public Opinion*. New York: Knopf, 1951.

Vogel, David. *Fluctuating Fortunes*. New York: Basic Books, 1989.

STUDY OUTLINE

The Character of Interest Groups

1. An enormous number of diverse interest groups exists in the United States.
2. Most interest groups share key organizational components, such as mechanisms for member recruitment, financial and decision-making processes, and agencies that actually carry out group goals.
3. Interest-group politics in the United States tends to have a pronounced upper-class bias because of the characteristics of interest-group members.
4. Because of natural disincentives to join interest groups, groups offer material, solidary, and purposive benefits to entice people to join.

The Proliferation of Groups

1. The modern expansion of governmental economic and social programs has contributed to the enormous increase in the number of groups seeking to influence the American political system.
2. The second factor accounting for the explosion of interest-group activity in recent years was the emergence of a new set of forces in American politics: the New Politics movement.

Strategies: The Quest for Political Power

1. Lobbying is an effort by outsiders to influence Congress or government agencies by providing them with information about issues, giving them support, and even threatening them with retaliation.
2. Access is actual involvement and influence in the decision-making process.
3. Interest groups often turn to litigation when they lack access or feel they have insufficient influence over the formulation and implementation of public policy.
4. Going public is a strategy that attempts to mobilize the widest and most favorable climate of opinion.
5. Many groups use a nonpartisan strategy in electoral politics to avoid giving up access to one party by embracing the other.

Groups and Interests: The Dilemma

1. The organization of private interests into groups to advance their own views is a necessary and intrinsic element of the liberty of citizens to pursue their private lives, and to express their views, individually and collectively.
2. The organization of private interests into groups is biased in favor of the wealthy and the powerful, who have superior knowledge, opportunity, and resources with which to organize.

PRACTICE QUIZ

1. The theory that competition among organized interests will produce balance with all the interests regulating one another is
   a) pluralism.
   b) elite power politics.
   c) democracy.
   d) socialism.
2. To overcome the free rider problem, groups
   a) provide general benefits.
   b) litigate.
   c) go public.
   d) provide selective benefits.
3. Politically organized religious groups often make use of
   a) material benefits.
   b) solidary benefits.
   c) purposive benefits.
   d) none of the above.
4. Which of the following best describes the reputation of the AARP in the Washington community?
   a) It is respected and feared.
   b) It is supported and well liked by all political forces.
   c) It is believed to be ineffective.
   d) It wins the political battles it fights.
5. Which types of interest groups are most often associated with the New Politics movement?
   a) public interest groups
   b) professional associations
   c) government groups
   d) labor groups
6. Access politics, exemplified by defense contractors acting in concert with congressional committees and executive agencies, is an example of
   a) campaign activism.
   b) public interest politics.

c) an iron triangle.
d) the role of conservative interest groups.

7. "Corridoring" refers to
a) lobbying the corridors of Congress.
b) a litigation technique.
c) lobbying the president and the White House staff.
d) lobbying an executive agency.

8. In which of the following ways do interest groups use the courts to affect public policy?
a) filing *amicus* briefs
b) bringing lawsuits
c) financing those bringing suit
d) all of the above

9. According to this text, what is the limit a PAC can contribute to a primary or general election campaign?
a) $1,000
b) $5,000
c) $10,000
d) $50,000

10. Which of the following is not an activity in which interest groups frequently engage?
a) starting their own political party
b) litigation
c) lobbying
d) contributing to campaigns

CRITICAL THINKING QUESTIONS

1. A dilemma is presented by the values of liberty and equality in regard to interest-group activity. On the one hand, individuals should have the liberty to organize themselves politically in order to express their views. On the other hand, there is a strong class bias in the politics of organized interests. How has the U.S. government sought to regulate group activity in order to balance these competing values? What else might government do to make group politics less biased? What are the potential consequences—both good and bad—of the actions you suggest?
2. Describe the different techniques of influence used by organized interests. When is one technique preferable to another? With the rise of the New Politics movement, different techniques are now used more frequently. Which ones? Why, do you think, are these techniques so well suited to New Politics?

KEY TERMS

access (p. 454)
capture (p. 455)
collective goods (p. 443)
free riders (p. 444)
going public (p. 458)
grassroots mobilization (p. 458)
informational benefits (p. 444)
institutional advertising (p. 458)
interest group (p. 440)
iron triangle (p. 454)
issue network (p. 454)
lobbying (p. 451)
material benefits (p. 444)
membership association (p. 443)
New Politics movement (p. 449)
pluralism (p. 439)
political action committee (PAC) (p. 461)
public interest groups (p. 450)
purposive benefits (p. 444)
soft money (p. 464)
solidary benefits (p. 444)
staff organization (p. 443)

PART IV

Institutions

13 Congress

★ **Congress: Representing the American People**

How does Congress represent the United States as a whole? In what ways is it not representative?

In what specific ways do members of Congress act as agents for their constituencies?

In what ways does the electoral system determine who is elected to Congress?

★ **The Organization of Congress**

What are the basic building blocks of congressional organization? What is the role of each in forming legislation?

★ **Rules of Lawmaking: How a Bill Becomes a Law**

How do the rules of congressional procedure influence the fate of legislation as well as determine the distribution of power in Congress?

★ **How Congress Decides**

What sorts of influences inside and outside of government determine how members of Congress vote on legislation? How do these influences vary according to the type of issue?

★ **Beyond Legislation: Other Congressional Powers**

Besides the power to pass legislation, what other powers allow Congress to influence the process of government?

★ **Congress and Democracy**

How do the institutional features of Congress affect meaningful representation?

What can Congress and citizens do to bring Congress closer to the American people?

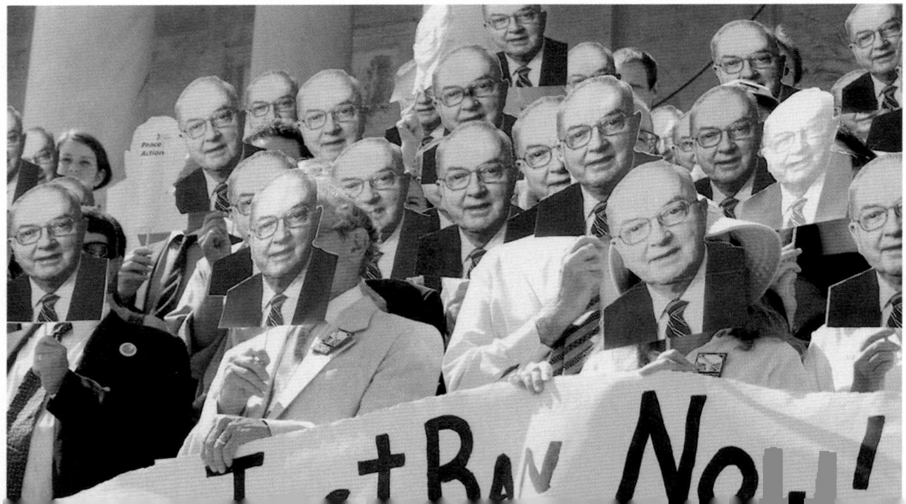

STUDENTS AND POLITICS

If you want to find out what your congressional representative or senator has been doing lately, there are many ways to do so. You can watch your mailbox—most congressional offices send newsletters to constituents to report the office's activities. You can find your representative's home page on the World Wide Web. To get a sense of what is happening in Congress you can tune your television to C-SPAN; chances are that some congressional debate or committee hearing will be in progress. If you want to make your views known to your congressional representative, that is also pretty easy. You can send a postcard or a letter—the address of your representative can usually be found in the blue pages of your local telephone book. You can also call or fax his or her Washington office. The number isn't hard to get; consult your local phone book or call Washington, D.C., directory information.

Many citizens have kept up with new technologies, weaving them into their efforts to influence Congress. Small groups with limited funding now find it easier to contact potential supporters and make their voices heard on Capitol Hill. Groups representing young people and students, such as the National Association of Twentysomethings and the Generation X Coalition, rely on the Internet to publicize their views and to attract support for their lobbying efforts in Congress. Groups also continue to use more old-fashioned methods—such as face-to-face contact—to influence Congress. The United States Student Association, a fifty-year-old organization, sponsors an annual national student lobby day, in which students come to Washington to learn about the legislative process and to lobby their state congressional delegations about issues that concern them, such as educational loans and grants.[1]

Despite these many different ways people can learn about Congress and contact their representatives and senators, citizens regularly complain that Congress is "out of touch." In one poll, only 12 percent of Americans said they believed that congressional representatives "pay a good deal of attention to the people who elect them when deciding what to do in Congress." Eighty percent felt that members of Congress lost touch with their constituents soon after being elected.[2] Many Americans believe there is something about politics in Washington that is corrupting. One voter described what happens to members of Congress in this way: "You find so many good people going in and the next thing you know they're corrupted."[3] Congress seems to be the least trusted of America's national institutions.

What is puzzling is that these feelings of distrust and alienation from Congress have grown stronger precisely as access to Congress and its members has increased. Most of the proceedings of Congress have been open to the public since the passage of numerous "sunshine reforms" in the 1970s; today

Congress conducts very few secret hearings. Public opinion polls taken before Congress became more accessible and open showed higher levels of trust and a greater belief that citizens could influence their representatives' decisions. Why has trust in Congress dropped rather than increased as new forms of access and increased openness have been put into place?

One answer to this puzzle is the growing professionalization of Congress as an institution. Professionalization means that Congress has grown more complex as an institution, with more powerful committees, longer terms for members, larger staffs, and higher salaries.[4] In many ways, professionalization makes Congress more capable of reaching informed decisions and makes it easier for members of Congress to serve their constituents. But professionalization also has a downside. It enhances the independence of individual congressional members, often making it harder for the institution as a whole to reach decisions. Moreover, as Congress has professionalized, narrowly focused, well-funded professional interest groups have formed to influence Congress. The growth and sophistication of these groups has made many ordinary citizens feel shut out, canceling out the positive side of the new openness and professionalization of Congress in the public mind. The public feeling of distance from Congress is compounded by the decline of political parties among the electorate. A crucial link that once connected Congress with voters has been severed.

In this chapter we will try to understand the relationship between Congress and the American people. Congress is central to American democracy because it serves as the voice of the people and because it controls a formidable battery of powers that it uses to shape policies.

- ***To understand the pivotal role that Congress plays in American democracy, we will first examine the concept of representation.*** We will look closely at what it means to say that Congress represents the people. We will also look at how members of Congress act on behalf of their constituents and how the electoral process affects the relationship between Congress and the people.
- ***Next, we will discuss the legislative process.*** We will study the building blocks of congressional organization, including political parties, the committee system, congressional staff, and caucuses. We then turn to the rules of congressional procedure, through which laws are formulated.
- ***We then look at congressional decision making, examining the influences on the legislation that Congress produces.*** The complex legislative process is subject to a variety of influences from inside and outside government, including constituencies, interest groups, and party leaders.
- ***We next turn to other powers that allow Congress to influence the process of government.*** In addition to the power to make law, Congress has an array of instruments to use in its relationship with the president and the executive branch.
- ***We conclude by taking a closer look at Congress and democracy.*** In assessing whether Congress fulfills democratic principles, we raise the question "why do ordinary people feel so distant from Congress and how can they exercise more influence over Congress?"

Perspectives on Politics

OPINIONS OF INSTITUTIONS, GROUPS, AND THE MEDIA

Percentage of eighteen- to twenty-nine-year-olds reporting, "I have a favorable overall opinion of . . ."

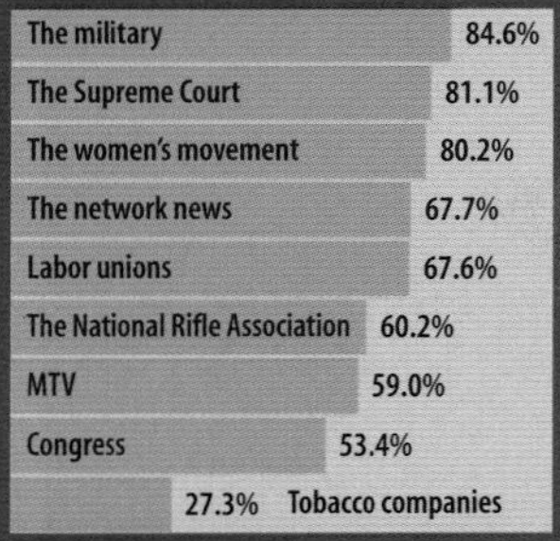

SOURCE: 1994 Times-Mirror poll, reported in Susan A. MacManus, *Young v. Old: Generational Combat in the 21st Century* (Boulder, CO: Westview, 1996), p. 234.

Congress: Representing the American People

- How does Congress represent the United States as a whole? In what ways is it not representative?
- In what specific ways do members of Congress act as agents for their constituencies?
- In what ways does the electoral system determine who is elected to Congress?

Congress is the most important representative insitution in American government. Each member's primary rsponsibility is to the district, to his or her **constituency,** not to the congressional leadership, a party, or even Congress itself. Yet the task of representation is not a simple one. Views about what constitutes fair and effective representation differ and constituents can make very different kinds of demands on their representatives. Members of Congress must consider these diverse views and demands as they represent their districts.

constituency
the district comprising the area from which an official is elected

HOUSE AND SENATE: DIFFERENCES IN REPRESENTATION

The framers of the Constitution provided for a **bicameral** legislature—that is, a legislative body consisting of two chambers. As we saw in Chapter 3, the framers intended each of these chambers, the House of Representatives and the Senate, to serve a different constituency. Members of the Senate, appointed by state legislatures for six-year terms, were to represent the elite members of society and to be more attuned to the interests of property than of population. Today, members of the House and Senate are elected directly by the people. The 435 members of the House are elected from districts apportioned according to population; the 100 members of the Senate are elected by state, with two senators from each. Senators continue to have much longer terms in office and usually represent much larger and more diverse constituencies than do their counterparts in the House (see Table 13.1).

bicameral
having a legislative assembly composed of two chambers or houses; opposite of unicameral

DIFFERENCES BETWEEN THE HOUSE AND THE SENATE — Table 13.1

	House	Senate
Minimum age of member	25 years	30 years
U.S. citizenship	at least 7 years	at least 9 years
Length of term	2 years	6 years
Number per state	Depends on population: 1 per 30,000 in 1789; now 1 per 550,000	2 per state
Constituency	Tends to be local	Both local and national

The House and Senate play different roles in the legislative process. In essence, the Senate is the more deliberative of the two bodies—the forum in which any and all ideas can receive a thorough public airing. The House is the more centralized and organized of the two bodies—better equipped to play a routine role in the governmental process. In part, this difference stems from the different rules governing the two bodies. These rules give House leaders more control over the legislative process and provide for House members to specialize in certain legislative areas. The rules of the much-smaller Senate give its leadership relatively little power and discourage specialization.

Both formal and informal factors contribute to differences between the two chambers of Congress. Differences in the length of terms and requirements for holding office specified by the Constitution in turn generate differences in how members of each body develop their constituencies and exercise their powers of office. The result is that members of the House most effectively and frequently serve as the agents of well-organized local interests with specific legislative agendas—for instance, used-car dealers seeking relief from regulation, labor unions seeking more favorable legislation, or farmers looking for higher subsidies. The small size and relative homogeneity of their constituencies and the frequency with which they must seek re-election make House members more attuned to the legislative needs of local interest groups.

Senators, on the other hand, serve larger and more heterogeneous constituencies. As a result, they are somewhat better able than members of the House to serve as the agents for groups and interests organized on a statewide or national basis. Moreover, with longer terms in office, senators have the luxury of considering "new ideas" or seeking to bring together new coalitions of interests, rather than simply serving existing ones.

SOCIOLOGICAL VS. AGENCY REPRESENTATION

We have become so accustomed to the idea of representative government that we tend to forget what a peculiar concept representation really is. A representative claims to act or speak for some other person or group. But how can one person be trusted to speak for another? How do we know that those who call themselves our representatives are actually speaking on our behalf, rather than simply pursuing their own interests?

There are two circumstances under which one person reasonably might be trusted to speak for another. The first of these occurs if the two individuals are so similar in background, character, interests, and perspectives that anything said by one would very likely reflect the views of the other as well. This principle is at the heart of what is sometimes called **sociological representation**—the sort of representation that takes place when representatives have the same racial, ethnic, religious, or educational backgrounds as their constituents. The assumption is that sociological similarity helps to promote good representation; thus, the composition of a properly constituted representative assembly should mirror the composition of society.

sociological representation
a type of representation in which representatives have the same racial, ethnic, religious, or educational backgrounds as their constituents. It is based on the principle that if two individuals are similar in background, character, interests, and perspectives, then one could correctly represent the other's views

The second circumstance under which one person might be trusted to speak for another occurs if the two are formally bound together so that the representative is in some way accountable to those he or she purports to represent. If representatives can somehow be punished or held to account for failing to speak properly for their constituents, then we know they have an incentive to provide good representation even if their own personal backgrounds, views, and interests differ from those they represent. This principle is called **agency representation**—the sort of representation that takes place when constituents have the power to hire and fire their representatives.

agency representation
the type of representation by which representatives are held accountable to their constituency if they fail to represent that constituency properly. This is the incentive for good representation when the personal backgrounds, views, and interests of the representative differ from those of his or her constituency

Both sociological and agency representation play a role in the relationship between members of Congress and their constituencies.

The Social Composition of the U.S. Congress The extent to which the U.S. Congress is representative of the American people in a sociological sense can be seen by examining the distribution of important social characteristics in the House and Senate today. It comes as no surprise that the religious affiliations of members of both the House and Senate are overwhelmingly Protestant—the distribution is very close to the proportion in the population at large—although the Protestant category is composed of more than fifteen denominations. Catholics are the second largest category of religious affiliation, and Jews a much smaller third category.[5] Religious affiliations directly affect congressional debate on a limited range of issues where different moral views are at stake, such as abortion.

Statistics on ethnic or national background are difficult to get and generally unreliable. Individual members of Congress may make a point of their ethnic backgrounds, but an actual count has not been done. Occasionally, an issue like support for Israel or for the Greek community in Cyprus may activate members of Congress along religious or ethnic lines. But these exceptions actually underscore the essentially symbolic nature of these social characteristics.

African Americans, women, Hispanic Americans, and Asian Americans have increased their congressional representation in the past two decades (see Figure 13.1 on the next page). In 2001, fifty-nine women served in the House (up from only twenty-nine in 1990). Thirteen women now serve in the Senate.

A few of the sixty-seven women who served in the 105th Congress. Shown here, from left to right, are Senators Susan Collins, Patty Murray, Olympia Snowe, Carol Mosely-Braun, Kay Bailey Hutchison, Barbara Mikulski, Dianne Feinstein, and Mary Landrieu.

Figure 13.1

WOMEN, AFRICAN AMERICANS, AND LATINOS IN THE U.S. CONGRESS, 1971–99

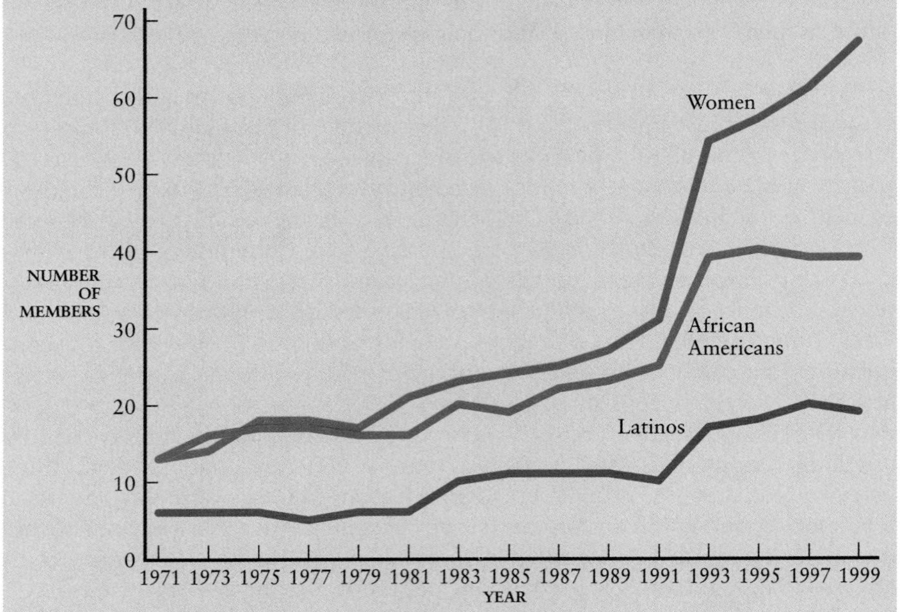

SOURCE: Harold W. Stanley and Richard G Niemi, eds., *Vital Statistics on American Politics 1999–2000,* (Washington, DC: AEI Press, 2000), p. 201.

However, the representation of women and minorities in Congress is still not comparable to their proportions in the general population. Since many important contemporary national issues do cut along racial and gender lines, a considerable amount of clamor for reform in the representative process is likely to continue until these groups are fully represented.

The occupational backgrounds of members of Congress have always been a matter of interest because so many issues cut along economic lines that are relevant to occupations and industries. The legal profession is the dominant career of most members of Congress prior to their election. Public service or politics is also a significant background. In addition, many members of Congress also have important ties to business and industry.[6] One composite portrait of a typical member of Congress has been that of "a middle-aged male lawyer whose father was of the professional or managerial class; a native-born 'white,' or—if he cannot avoid being an immigrant—a product of northwestern or central Europe or Canada, rather than of eastern or southern Europe, Latin America, Africa or Asia."[7] This is not a portrait of the U.S. population. Congress is not a sociological microcosm of American society, and it probably can never become one. One obvious reason is that the skills and resources needed to achieve political success in the United States are much more likely to be found among well-educated and relatively well-to-do Americans than among members of minority groups and the poor. Take money, for example. As we saw in Chapter 11, successful congressional candidates must be able to raise hundreds of thousands of dollars to finance their campaigns. Poor people from the inner city are much less likely to be able to convince corporate political action committees to provide them with these funds.

Is Congress still able to legislate fairly or to take account of a diversity of views and interests if it is not a sociologically representative assembly? The task is certainly much more difficult. Yet there is reason to believe it can. Representatives, as we shall see shortly, can serve as the agents of their constituents, even if they do not precisely mirror their sociological attributes. Yet, sociological representation is a matter of some importance, even if it is not an absolute prerequisite for fair legislation on the part of members of the House and Senate. At the least, the social composition of a representative assembly is important for symbolic purposes—to demonstrate to groups in the population that they are taken seriously by the government. Concern about the proportion of women, African Americans, and ethnic minorities in Congress and elsewhere in government would exist whether or not these social characteristics influenced the outcomes of laws and policies. It is rare to find a social group whose members do not feel shortchanged if someone like themselves is not a member of the assembly. Thus, the symbolic composition of Congress is ultimately important for the political stability of the United States. If Congress is not representative symbolically, then its own authority and indeed that of the entire government would be reduced.[8]

Representatives as Agents A good deal of evidence indicates that whether or not members of Congress share their constituents' sociological characteristics, they *do* work very hard to speak for their constituents' views and serve their constituents' interests in the governmental process. The idea of representative as agent is similar to the relationship of lawyer and client. True, the relationship between the member of Congress and as many as 550,000 "clients" in the district, or the senator and millions of "clients" in the state, is very different from that of the lawyer and client. But the criteria of performance are comparable. One expects at the very least that each representative will constantly be seeking to discover the interests of the constituency and will be speaking for those interests in Congress and in other centers of government.[9]

Members of Congress can reach out to their constituents by mailing thousands of newsletters free of charge.

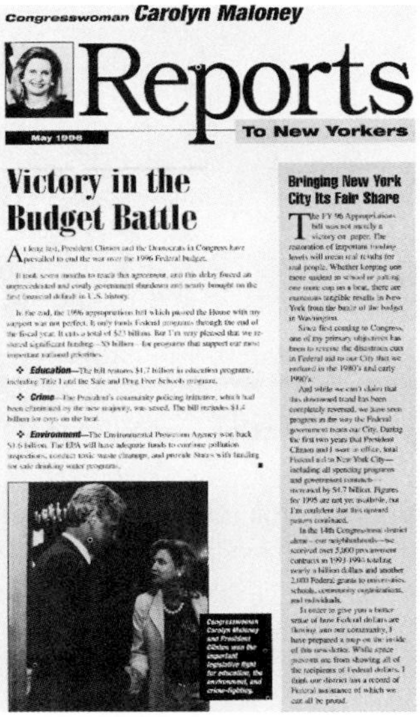

There is constant communication between constituents and congressional offices. For example, each year the House and Senate post offices handle nearly 100 million pieces of incoming mail, and in recent years, members of Congress have spent as much as $112 million annually to send out 458 million pieces of mail.[10]

The seriousness with which members of the House attempt to behave as representatives can be seen in the amount of time spent on behalf of their constituents. Well over a quarter of their time and nearly two-thirds of the time of their staff members is devoted to constituency service (called "case work"). This service is not merely a matter of writing and mailing letters. It includes talking to constituents, providing them with minor services, presenting special bills for them, and attempting to influence decisions by regulatory commissions on their behalf.[11]

Although no members of Congress are above constituency pressures (and they would not want to be), on many issues constituents do not have very strong views and representatives are free to act as they think best. Foreign policy issues often fall into this category. But in many districts there are two or three issues on which constituents have such pronounced opinions that representatives feel they have little freedom of choice. For example, representatives from districts that grow wheat, cotton, or tobacco probably will not want to exercise a great deal of independence on relevant agricultural legislation. In the oil-rich states (such as Oklahoma, Texas, and California), senators and members of the House are likely to be leading advocates of oil interests. For one thing, representatives are probably fearful of voting against their district interests; for another, the districts are unlikely to have elected representatives who would *want* to vote against them.

The influence of constituencies is so pervasive that both parties have strongly embraced the informal rule that nothing should be done to endanger the re-election chances of any member. Party leaders obey this rule fairly consistently by not asking any member to vote in a way that might conflict with a district interest.

THE ELECTORAL CONNECTION

The sociological composition of Congress and the activities of representatives once they are in office are very much influenced by electoral considerations. Three factors related to the U.S. electoral system affect who gets elected and what they do once in office. The first set of issues concerns who decides to run for office and which candidates have an edge over others. The second issue is that of incumbency advantage. Finally, the way congressional district lines are drawn can greatly affect the outcome of an election. Let us examine more closely the impact that these considerations have on representation.

Voters' choices are restricted from the start by who decides to run for office. In the past, decisions about who would run for a particular elected office were made by local party officials. A person who had a record of service to the party, or who was owed a favor, or whose "turn" had come up might be nominated by party leaders for an office. Today, few party organizations have the power to slate candidates in that way. Instead, the decision to run for Congress is a more personal choice. One of the most important factors determining who runs for office is a candidate's individual ambition.[12] A potential candidate may also assess whether he or she can attract enough money to mount a credible campaign. The ability to raise money depends on connections with other politicians, interest groups, and national party organizations. In the past, the difficulty of raising campaign funds posed a disadvantage to female candidates. Since the 1980s, however, a number of powerful **political action committees (PACs)** have emerged to recruit women and fund their campaigns. The largest of them, EMILY's List, has become one of the most powerful fund-raisers of all PACs. Recent research shows that money is no longer the barrier it once was to women running for office.[13]

political action committee (PAC)
a private group that raises and distributes funds for use in election campaigns

Features distinctive to each congressional district also affect the field of candidates. Among them are the range of other political opportunities that may lure potential candidates away. In addition, the way the congressional district overlaps with state legislative boundaries may affect a candidate's decision to run. A state-level representative or senator who is considering running for the U.S. Congress is more likely to assess her prospects favorably if her

THE POWER OF INCUMBENCY

Figure 13.2

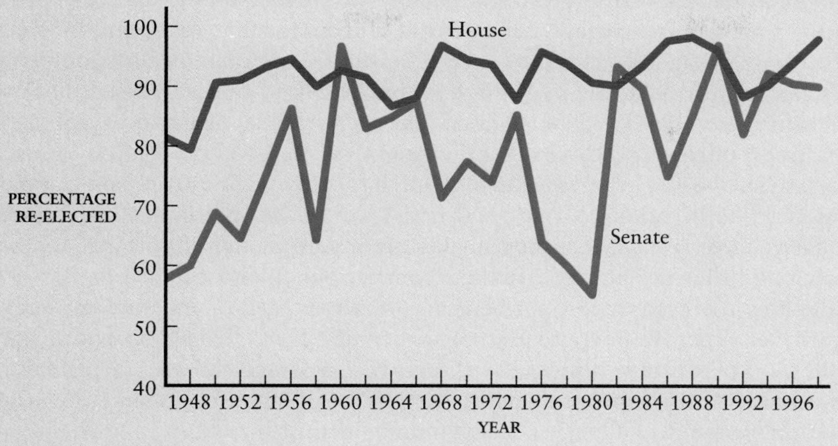

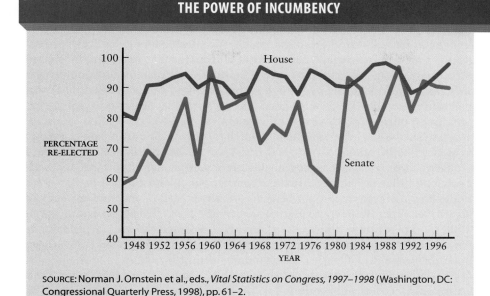

SOURCE: Norman J. Ornstein et al., eds., *Vital Statistics on Congress, 1997–1998* (Washington, DC: Congressional Quarterly Press, 1998), pp. 61–2.

Members of Congress who run for re-election have a very good chance of winning.

state district coincides with the congressional district (because the voters will already know her). And for any candidate, decisions about running must be made early, because once money has been committed to already-declared candidates, it is harder for new candidates to break into a race. Thus, the outcome of a November election is partially determined many months earlier, when decisions to run are finalized.

Incumbency plays a very important role in the American electoral system and in the kind of representation citizens get in Washington. Once in office, members of Congress possess an array of tools that they can use to stack the deck in favor of their re-election. The most important of these is constituency service: taking care of the problems and requests of individual voters. Through such services and through regular newsletter mailings, the incumbent seeks to establish a "personal" relationship with his or her constituents. The success of this strategy is evident in the high rates of re-election for congressional incumbents: as high as 98 percent for House members and 90 percent for members of the Senate in recent years (see Figure 13.2). It is also evident in what is called "sophomore surge"—the tendency for candidates to win a higher percentage of the vote when seeking future terms in office.

incumbency
holding a political office for which one is running

As in past elections, voters returned large numbers of congressional incumbents to office in 2000—specifically, 97.8 percent to the House and 82.7 percent to the Senate. There were several notable exceptions, however. Candidates who were associated with strong ideological positions were especially vulnerable. For example, some of the incumbents who lost their seats were closely connected to the controversial impeachment of Bill Clinton. Surely the most unusual contest involving the defeat of an incumbent was the race for the Senate in Missouri. There, Republican incumbent John Ashcroft lost the election to Missouri's Democratic governor, Mel Carnahan, who was killed in a plane crash less than one month before.

Incumbency can help a candidate by scaring off potential challengers. In many races, potential candidates may decide not to run because they fear that the incumbent simply has too much money or is too well liked or too well known. Potentially strong challengers may also decide that a district's partisan leanings are too unfavorable. The efforts of incumbents to raise funds to ward off potential challengers starts early. Kansas Democrat Dennis Moore, who was elected to the House in 1998, held his first fund-raiser for the 2000 campaign in December 1998—before he had even been sworn into office! Representative Thomas M. Davis III of Virginia decided to run for the House in 1994 when he saw that the incumbent had only $25,000 in her campaign warchest. As he noted, "If she had had $250,000 in the bank, I guarantee I wouldn't have run." Most incumbents are aware of the importance of fund-raising and they are able to use their connections to constituents and to other politicians to discourage opponents. The advantages of incumbents tend to grow over time. Democratic Wisconsin senator Herb Kohl first won office in 1988 by 4 percentage points; in his next race, the margin was 17 percent. As the 2000 election approached, his strength as an incumbent had discouraged potentially strong challengers from running against him.[14]

The advantage of incumbency thus tends to preserve the status quo in Congress. This fact has implications for the social composition of Congress. For example, incumbency advantage makes it harder for women to increase their numbers in Congress because most incumbents are men. Women who run for open seats (for which there are no incumbents) are just as likely to win as male candidates.[15] Supporters of **term limits** argue that such limits are the only way to get new faces into Congress. They believe that incumbency advantage and the tendency of many legislators to view politics as a career mean that very little turnover will occur in Congress unless limits are imposed on the number of terms a legislator can serve.

term limits
legally prescribed limits on the number of terms an elected official can serve

Yet the percentage of incumbents who are returned to Congress after each election also depends on how many members decide to run again. Because each year some members decide to retire, turnover in Congress is greater than the re-election rates of incumbents suggest. On average 10 percent of the House and Senate decide to retire each election. In some years, the number of retirements is higher, as in 1992, when 20 percent of House members decided to retire; thus, the 90 percent of incumbents who were re-elected that year were a subset of all the eligible incumbents (80 percent). Opponents of term limits argue that, over time, such retirements ensure that there is sufficient turnover in Congress despite the high rates at which incumbents are re-elected.

The final factor that affects who wins a seat in Congress is the way congressional districts are drawn. Every ten years, state legislatures must redraw congressional districts to reflect population changes. This is a highly political process: districts are shaped to create an advantage for the majority party in the state legislature, which controls the **redistricting** process. In this complex process, those charged with drawing districts use sophisticated computer technologies to come up with the most favorable district boundaries. Redistricting can create open seats and pit incumbents of the same party against one another, ensuring that one of them will lose. Redistricting can also give an advantage to one party by clustering voters with some ideological or sociological characteristics in a single district, or by separating those voters into two or more districts.

redistricting
the process of redrawing election districts and redistributing legislative representatives. This happens every ten years to reflect shifts in population or in response to legal challenges to existing districts

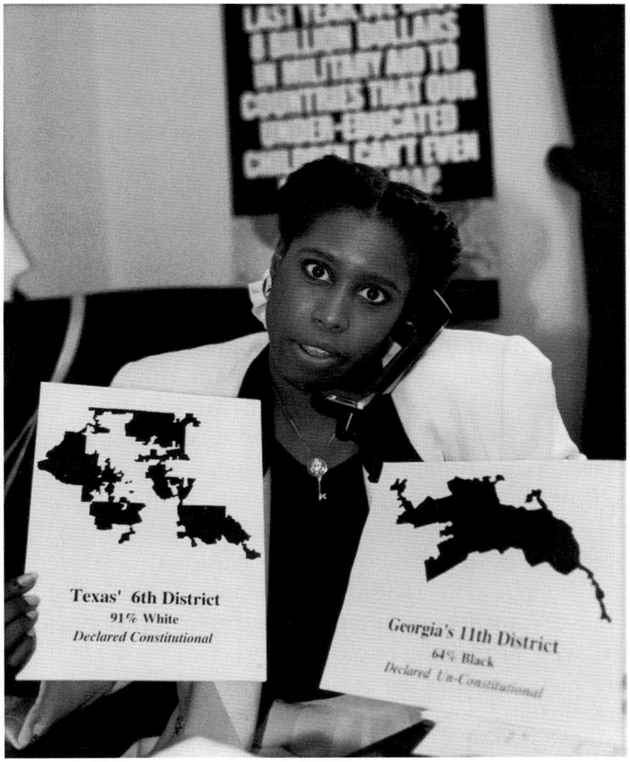

Representative Cynthia McKinney, a Democrat from Georgia, holds maps of her Congressional district (right) and the 6th District of Texas. In 1995, the Supreme Court held that McKinney's district, which was 64 percent African American, was unfairly based on race. No challenge was made to Texas's 6th District, which was predominantly white. McKinney handily won re-election in 1996 even though her district had been redrawn to include more white voters.

As we saw in Chapter 11, since the passage of the 1982 amendments to the 1964 Civil Rights Act, race has become a major—and controversial—consideration in drawing voting districts. These amendments, which encouraged the creation of districts in which members of racial minorities have decisive majorities, have greatly increased the number of minority representatives in Congress. After the 1991–92 redistricting, the number of predominantly minority districts doubled, rising from twenty-six to fifty-two. Among the most fervent supporters of the new minority districts were white Republicans, who used the opportunity to create more districts dominated by white Republican voters. These developments raise thorny questions about representation. Some analysts argue that the system may grant minorities greater sociological representation, but it has made it more difficult for minorities to win substantive policy goals. This was a common argument after the sweeping Republican victories in the 1994 congressional elections. Others dispute this argument, noting that the strong surge of Republican voters was more significant than any losses due to racial redistricting.[16]

In 1995, the Supreme Court limited racial redistricting in *Miller v. Johnson,* in which the Court stated that race could not be the predominant factor in creating electoral districts.[17] Yet concerns about redistricting and representation have not disappeared. The distinction between race being a "predominant" factor and its being one factor among many is very hazy. Because the drawing of district boundaries affects incumbents as well as the field of candidates who decide to run for office, it continues to be a key battleground on which political parties fight about the meaning of representation.

DIRECT PATRONAGE

As we saw in the preceding discussion, members of Congress often have an opportunity to provide direct benefits, or **patronage,** for their constituents. The most important of these opportunities for direct patronage is in legislation that has been described half-jokingly as the **pork barrel.** This type of legislation specifies a project to be funded or other authorizations, as well as the location of the project within a particular district. Many observers of Congress argue that pork-barrel bills are the only ones that some members are serious about moving toward actual passage, because they are seen as so important to members' re-election bids.

patronage
the resources available to higher officials, usually opportunities to make partisan appointments to offices and to confer grants, licenses, or special favors to supporters

pork barrel
appropriations made by legislative bodies for local projects that are often not needed but that are created so that local representatives can win re-election in their home districts

A common form of pork barreling is the "earmark," the practice through which members of Congress insert into otherwise pork-free bills language that provides special benefits for their own constituents. For example, the massive transportation bill enacted in 1998 contains billions of dollars in earmarks. One senator, Ted Kennedy (D-Mass.) claimed that he was able to obtain nearly $200 million in earmarks for his state. In addition to $100 million for highway construction in Boston, these included a myriad of small items such as $1.6 million for the Longfellow National Historic Site and $3.17 million for the Silvio Conte National Fish and Wildlife Refuge. The chairman of the House Transportation and Infrastructure Committee, Bud Schuster (R-Penn.), has won broad bipartisan support for expensive transportation acts by offering members special projects earmarked for their districts. He defends the practice as a routine part of the political process: "Angels in heaven don't decide where highway and transit systems are going to be built. It's a process."[18]

The building of dams is a classic example of pork-barrel spending.

A limited amount of other direct patronage also exists (see Figure 13.3). One important form of constituency service is intervention with federal administrative agencies on behalf of constituents. Members of the House and Senate and their staff members spend a great deal of time on the telephone and in administrative offices seeking to secure favorable treatment for constituents and supporters. Among the kind of services that members of Congress offer to constituents is assistance for senior citizens who are having Social Security or Medicare benefit eligibility problems. They may also assist constituents in finding federal grants for which they may be eligible to apply. As Representative Pete Stark (D-Calif.) puts it on his website, "We cannot make the decision for a federal agency on such matters, but we can make sure that you get a fair shake."[19] A small but related form of patronage is getting an appointment to one of the military academies for the child of a constituent. Traditionally, these appointments are allocated one to a district.

A different form of patronage is the **private bill**—a proposal to grant some kind of relief, special privilege, or exemption to the person named in the bill. The private bill is a type of legislation, but it is distinguished from a public bill, which is supposed to deal with general rules and categories of behavior, people, and institutions. As many as 75 percent of all private bills introduced (and one-third of the ones that pass) are concerned with providing relief for foreign nationals who cannot get permanent visas to the United States because the immigration quota for their country is filled or because of something unusual about their particular situation.[20]

private bill
a proposal in Congress to provide a specific person with some kind of relief, such as a special exemption from immigration quotas

Private legislation is a congressional privilege that is often abused, but it is impossible to imagine members of Congress giving it up completely. It is one

HOW MEMBERS OF CONGRESS REPRESENT THEIR DISTRICTS

Figure 13.3

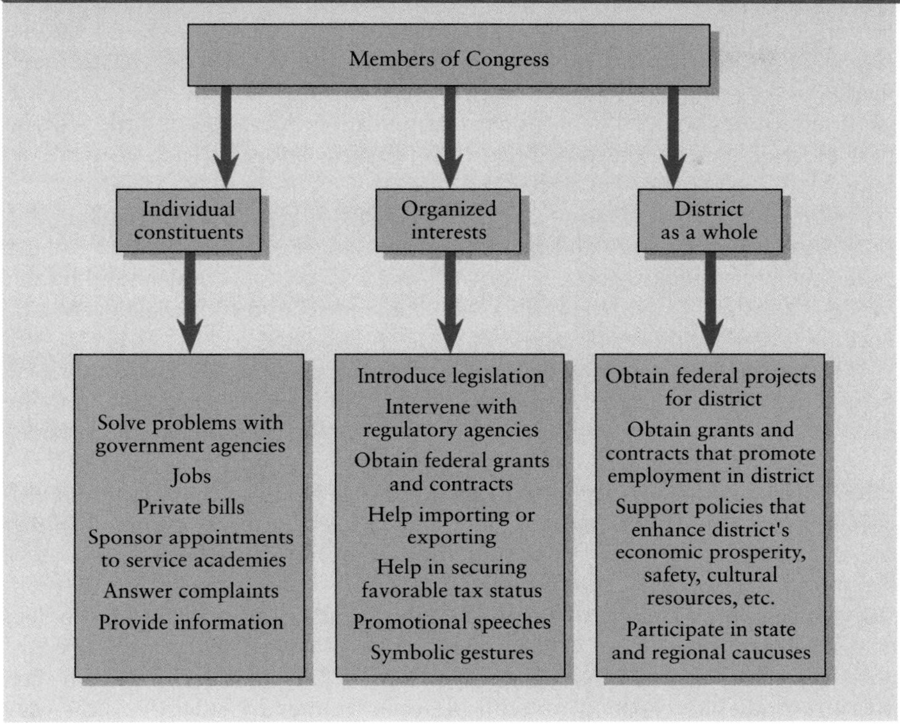

of the easiest, cheapest, and most effective forms of patronage available to each member. It can be defended as an indispensable part of the process by which members of Congress seek to fulfill their role as representatives. And obviously they like the privilege because it helps them win re-election.

The Organization of Congress

▶ What are the basic building blocks of congressional organization? What is the role of each in forming legislation?

The United States Congress is not only a representative assembly. It is also a legislative body. For Americans, representation and legislation go hand in hand. As we saw earlier, however, many parliamentary bodies are representative without the power to legislate. It is no small achievement that the U.S. Congress both represents *and* governs.

It is extraordinarily difficult for a large, representative assembly to formulate, enact, and implement laws. The internal complexities of conducting business within Congress—the legislative process—alone are daunting. In addition, there are many individuals and institutions that have the capacity to influence the legislative process. For example, legislation to raise the salaries of members of the House of Representatives received input from congressional leaders of both parties, special legislative task forces, the president, the national chairs of the two major parties, public interest lobbyists, the news media, and the mass public before it became law in 1989. Since successful legislation requires the confluence of so many distinct factors, it is little wonder that most of the thousands of bills considered by Congress each year are defeated long before they reach the president.

Before an idea or proposal can become a law, it must pass through a complex set of organizations and procedures in Congress. Collectively, these are called the policy-making process, or the legislative process. Understanding this process is central to understanding why some ideas and proposals eventually become law while most do not.

Over its more than two-hundred-year history, Congress has established procedures for creating a division of labor, setting an agenda, maintaining order through rules and procedures, and placing limits on debate and discussion. Still, congressional policy making often is an unwieldy process and the often torturous deliberation affects the kind of legislation that Congress ultimately produces. To win support for their ideas within this complex framework, sponsors of legislation must build compromises that accommodate a broad range of interests. As a consequence, it is far easier to pass bills that represent incremental change rather than comprehensive reform. In addition, legislation often resembles a Christmas tree—festooned with a variety of measures added on by individual congressional representatives. Although such measures may have little to do with the policy under consideration, they are needed to build majority support in Congress.

To exercise its power to make the law, Congress must first bring about something close to an organizational miracle. The building blocks of congressional organization include the political parties, the committee system, congressional staff, the caucuses, and the parliamentary rules of the House and Senate. Each of these factors plays a key role in the organization of Congress and in the process through which Congress formulates and enacts laws.

PARTY LEADERSHIP IN THE HOUSE AND THE SENATE

Every two years, at the beginning of a new Congress, the members of each party gather to elect their House leaders. This gathering is traditionally called the **conference** (House Democrats call theirs the **caucus**). The elected leader of the majority party is later proposed to the whole House and is automatically elected to the position of **Speaker of the House,** with voting along straight party lines. The House majority conference or caucus then also elects a **majority leader.** The minority party goes through the same process and selects the **minority leader.** Both parties also elect whips to line up party members on important votes and to relay voting information to the leaders.

Next in line of importance for each party after the Speaker and majority or minority leader is its Committee on Committees (called the Steering and Policy Committee by the Democrats), whose tasks are to assign new legislators to committees and to deal with the requests of incumbent members for transfers from one committee to another. Currently, the Speaker serves as chair of the

conference
a gathering of House Republicans every two years to elect their House leaders. Democrats call their gathering the caucus

caucus (political)
a normally closed meeting of a political or legislative group to select candidates, plan strategy, or make decisions regarding legislative matters

Speaker of the House
the chief presiding officer of the House of Representatives. The Speaker is elected at the beginning of every Congress on a straight party vote. The Speaker is the most important party and House leader, and can influence the legislative agenda, the fate of individual pieces of legislation, and members' positions within the House

majority leader
the elected leader of the majority party in the House of Representatives or in the Senate. In the House, the majority leader is subordinate in the party hierarchy to the Speaker of the House

minority leader
the elected leader of the minority party in the House or Senate

Republican Committee on Committees, while the minority leader chairs the Democratic Steering and Policy Committee. (The Republicans have a separate Policy Committee.) At one time, party leaders strictly controlled committee assignments, using them to enforce party discipline. Today, in principle, representatives receive the assignments they want. But assignments on the most important committees are often sought by several individuals, which gives the leadership an opportunity to cement alliances (and, perhaps, make enemies) as it resolves conflicting requests.

Generally, representatives seek assignments that will allow them to influence decisions of special importance to their districts. Representatives from farm districts, for example, may request seats on the Agriculture Committee.[21] Seats on powerful committees such as Ways and Means, which is responsible for tax legislation, and Appropriations are especially popular.

Within the Senate, the president pro tempore exercises primarily ceremonial leadership. Usually, the majority party designates a member with the greatest seniority to serve in this capacity. Real power is in the hands of the majority leader and minority leader, each elected by party conference. Together they control the Senate's calendar, or agenda for legislation. In addition, the senators from each party elect a whip. Each party also elects a Policy Committee, which advises the leadership on legislative priorities.

The structure of majority party leadership in the House and the Senate is shown below and on the next page in Figures 13.4 and 13.5.

In addition to these tasks of organization, congressional party leaders may also seek to establish a legislative agenda. Since the New Deal, presidents have

MAJORITY PARTY STRUCTURE IN THE HOUSE OF REPRESENTATIVES **Figure 13.4**

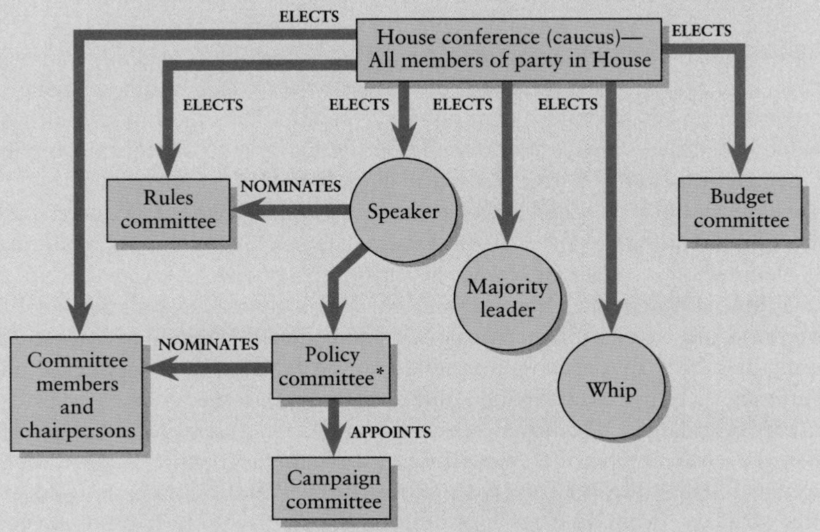

*Includes Speaker (chair), majority leader, chief and deputy whips, caucus chair, four members appointed by the Speaker, and twelve members elected by regional caucuses.

Figure 13.5 MAJORITY PARTY STRUCTURE IN THE SENATE

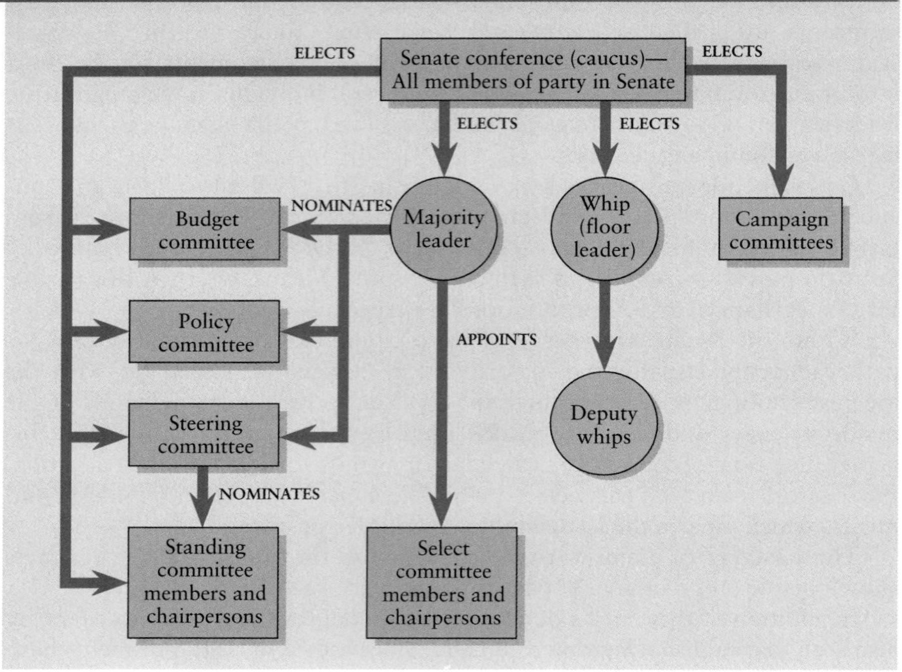

taken the lead in creating legislative agendas (this trend will be discussed in the next chapter). But in recent years congressional leaders, facing a White House controlled by the opposing party, have attempted to devise their own agendas. Democratic leaders of Congress sought to create a common Democratic perspective in 1981 when Ronald Reagan became president. The Republican Congress elected in 1994 expanded on this idea, calling its agenda the "Contract with America." In both cases, the majority party leadership has sought to create a consensus among its congressional members around an overall vision to guide legislative activity and to make individual pieces of legislation part of a bigger picture that is distinct from the agenda of the president.

Congressional party leaders have used various strategies to construct such agendas and build consensus around them. Democratic leaders staged an annual Democratic Issues Conference to bring party members together to consider a common agenda. Ongoing task forces produced issue handbooks that highlighted the party's distinctive policy perspectives. These activities did not commit members to particular policies, but instead served to educate members, giving them a shared background on important issues.[22] But these efforts fell short of creating a common agenda. Committee and subcommittee chairs followed their own priorities, not those of the party leadership.

When Bill Clinton was elected president in 1992, Republicans followed a similar strategy, using an annual issues conference to promote a common Republican agenda in Congress. But the Contract with America went further in seeking party unity on policy. With much public fanfare Republican candidates signed the contract, promising to promote its objectives once they were elected. This device no doubt served to promote the unusual coherence and loyalty to the leadership agenda displayed by House Republicans in 1995.

THE COMMITTEE SYSTEM: THE CORE OF CONGRESS

The committee system is central to the operation of Congress. At each stage of the legislative process, Congress relies on committees and subcommittees to do the hard work of sorting through alternatives and writing legislation. There are several different kinds of congressional committees; these include standing committees, select committees, joint committees, and conference committees.

Standing committees are the most important arenas of congressional policy making. These committees continue in existence from congress to congress; they have the power to propose and write legislation. The jurisdiction of each standing committee covers a particular subject matter, which in most cases parallels the major departments or agencies in the executive branch (see Table 13.2). Among the most important standing committees are those in charge of finances. The House Ways and Means Committee and the Senate Finance Committee are powerful because of their jurisdiction over taxes, trade, and expensive entitlement programs such as Social Security and Medicare. The Senate and House Appropriations committees also play important ongoing roles because they decide how much funding various programs will actually receive; they also determine exactly how the money will be spent. A seat on an

standing committee
a permanent committee with the power to propose and write legislation that covers a particular subject, such as finance or appropriations

PERMANENT COMMITTEES OF CONGRESS — Table 13.2

House committees	
Agriculture	National Security
Appropriations	Resources
Banking and Financial Services	Rules
Budget	Science
Commerce	Select Intelligence
Education and the Workforce	Small Business
Government Reform and Oversight	Standards of Official Conduct
House Oversight	Transportation and Infrastructure
International Relations	Veterans' Affairs
Judiciary	Ways and Means

Senate committees	
Agriculture, Nutrition, and Forestry	Finance
Appropriations	Foreign Relations
Armed Services	Governmental Affairs
Banking, Housing, and Urban Affairs	Judiciary
Budget	Labor and Human Resources
Commerce, Science, and Transportation	Rules and Administration
Energy and Natural Resources	Select Intelligence
Environment and Public Works	Small Business
	Veterans' Affairs

Select committees are sometimes convened to investigate government abuses. Former national security adviser Robert C. McFarlane testified before a joint House-Senate Select Committee about his role in the Iran-Contra affair.

select committee
a (usually) temporary legislative committee set up to highlight or investigate a particular issue or address an issue not within the jurisdiction of existing committees

joint committee
a legislative committee formed of members of both the House and the Senate

conference committee
a joint committee created to work out a compromise on House and Senate versions of a piece of legislation

seniority
priority or status ranking given to an individual on the basis of length of continuous service on a committee in Congress

appropriations committee allows a member the opportunity to direct funds to a favored program—perhaps one in his or her home district.

Except for the House Rules Committee, all standing committees receive proposals for legislation and process them into official bills. The House Rules Committee decides the order in which bills come up for a vote on the House floor and determines the specific rules that govern the length of debate and opportunity for amendments. The Senate, which has less formal organization and fewer rules, does not have a rules committee.

Select committees are usually not permanent and usually do not have the power to report legislation. (The House and Senate Select Intelligence committees are permanent, however, and do have the power to report legislation.) These committees may hold hearings and serve as focal points for the issues they are charged with considering. Congressional leaders form select committees when they want to take up issues that fall between the jurisdictions of existing committees, to highlight an issue, or to investigate a particular problem. Examples of select committees investigating political scandals include the Senate Watergate Committee of 1973, the committees set up in 1987 to investigate the Iran-Contra affair, and the Whitewater Committee of 1995–96. Select committees set up to highlight ongoing issues have included the House Select Committee on Hunger, established in 1984, and the House Select Narcotics Committee. A few select committees have remained in existence for many years, such as the select committees on aging; hunger; children, youth, and families; and narcotics abuse and control. In 1995, however, congressional Republicans abolished most of these select committees, both to streamline operations and to remove a forum used primarily by Democratic representatives and their allies.

Joint committees involve members from both the Senate and the House. There are four such committees: economic, taxation, library, and printing. These joint committees are permanent, but they do not have the power to report legislation. The Joint Economic Committee and the Joint Taxation Committee have often played important roles in collecting information and holding hearings on economic and financial issues.

Finally, **conference committees** are temporary committees whose members are appointed by the Speaker of the House and the presiding officer of the Senate. These committees are charged with reaching a compromise on legislation once it has been passed by the House and the Senate. Conference committees play an extremely important role in determining what laws are actually passed, because they must reconcile any differences in the legislation passed by the House and Senate.

Assignments to standing committees are made by a "committee on committees" appointed by the leadership of each party in each chamber of Congress. For the most part, these committees try to accommodate the requests of individual members for assignments. The decision about which committee seats to pursue is the most important choice an incoming member of Congress faces. Members are guided by different considerations in requesting committee assignments, but most prominent are serving constituent interests, making good public policy, and winning more influence in Congress.[23]

Within each committee, hierarchy is based on seniority. **Seniority** is determined by years of continuous service on a particular committee, not years of service in the House or Senate. In general, each committee is chaired by the most senior member of the majority party. But the principle of seniority is not absolute. Both Democrats and Republicans have violated it on occasion. At the start of the 104th Congress in 1995, House Republicans violated the principle of seniority in the selection of a number of key committee chairs, for example.

Over the years, Congress has reformed its organizational structure and operating procedures. Most changes have been made to improve efficiency, but some reforms have also represented a response to political considerations. In the 1970s, for example, a series of reforms substantially altered the organization of power in Congress. Among the most important changes put into place at that time were an increase in the number of subcommittees; greater autonomy for subcommittee chairs; the opening of most committee deliberations to the public; and a system of multiple referral of bills, which allowed several committees to consider one bill at the same time. One of the driving impulses behind these reforms was an effort to reduce the power of committee chairs. In the past, committee chairs exercised considerable power; they determined hearing schedules, selected subcommittee members, and appointed committee staff. Some chairs used their power to block consideration of bills they opposed. Because of the seniority system, many of the key committees were chaired by southern Democrats who stymied liberal legislation throughout the 1960s and early 1970s. By enhancing subcommittee power and allowing more members to chair subcommittees and appoint subcommittee staff, the reforms undercut the power of committee chairs.

Yet the reforms of the 1970s created new problems for Congress. As a consequence of the reforms, power has become more fragmented, making it harder to reach agreement on legislation. With power dissipated over a large number of committees and subcommittees, members spend more time in unproductive "turf battles." In addition, as committees expanded in size, members found they had so many committee responsibilities that they had to run from meeting to meeting. Thus their ability to specialize in a particular policy area has diminished as their responsibilities have increased.[24] The Republican leadership of the 104th Congress (1995–96) sought to reverse the fragmentation of congressional power and concentrate more authority in the party leadership. Toward this end they reduced the number of subcommittees and limited the time committee chairs could serve to three terms. Although congressional leaders since then claim to have restored more power to committees, committees have not regained the central role they once held in policy making. Sharp partisan divisions among members of Congress and divisions among Republicans have made it difficult for committees to deliberate and bring bipartisan expertise to bear on policy making as in the past. With committees less able to engage in effective decision making and often unable to act, it has become more common in recent years for party-driven legislation to go directly to the floor, bypassing committees.[25]

THE STAFF SYSTEM: STAFFERS AND AGENCIES

A congressional institution second in importance only to the committee system is the staff system. Every member of Congress employs many staff members, whose tasks include handling constituency requests and, to a large and growing extent, dealing with legislative details and the activities of administrative agencies. Increasingly, staffers bear the primary responsibility for formulating and drafting proposals, organizing hearings, dealing with administrative agencies, and negotiating with lobbyists. Indeed, legislators typically deal with one another through staff, rather than through direct, personal contact. Representatives and senators together employ nearly eleven thousand staffers in their Washington and home offices. Today, staffers even develop policy ideas, draft legislation, and in some instances, have a good deal of influence over the legislative process.

In addition to the personal staffs of individual senators and representatives, Congress also employs roughly two thousand committee staffers. These individuals make up the permanent staff, who stay attached to every House and Senate committee regardless of turnover in Congress and who are responsible for organizing and administering the committee's work, including research, scheduling, organizing hearings, and drafting legislation. Committee staffers can come to play key roles in the legislative process. One example of the importance of committee staffers is the success of the House Transportation and Infrastructure Committee. In a period when many committees have become less able to deliberate or have been unable to get their expenditures approved in the budget process, the Transportation Committee has been notably successful in passing very expensive legislation. One key to the committee's success is its staff. As is common for committee staff, most of the transportation committee senior staff are trained as lawyers. The committee's chief of staff has been a committee aide for over twenty-four years and has vast knowledge of the legislative process and transportation policy in particular. The combination of legal, political, and budgetary expertise that staffers accumulate is critical to the success of the large and complex bills considered in the Transportation Committee.[26]

As Figure 13.6 shows, the number of congressional staff members grew rapidly during the 1960s and 1970s, leveled off in the 1980s, and decreased dramatically in 1995. This sudden drop fulfilled the Republican congressional candidates' campaign promise to reduce the size of committee staffs.

staff agency
a legislative support agency responsible for policy analysis

Not only does Congress employ personal and committee staff, but it has also established **staff agencies** designed to provide the legislative branch with resources and expertise independent of the executive branch. These agencies enhance Congress's capacity to oversee administrative agencies and to evaluate presidential programs and proposals. They include the Congressional Research Service, which performs research for legislators who wish to know the facts and competing arguments relevant to policy proposals or other legislative business; the General Accounting Office, through which Congress can investigate the financial and administrative affairs of any government agency or program; and the Congressional Budget Office, which assesses the economic

Students and Politics

Alisa Wrase, a student at Florida Atlantic University, interning in the office of Senator Bob Graham (D-Fl.): "While I have have had an interest in politics for a few years, I never thought that I could have a voice or act in a way that could affect decision making. By taking this internship, I have realized that it is not only our elected officials who have the say in the decisions, but also the staff that keeps these officials updated and ready for new issues. . . . I have been able to help write a floor speech, research various topics of interest to the senator and myself, and help constituents with any problems or concerns of their own.

"Through my two months of legislative exposure, I have been able to see and do more than I ever thought possible. My supervisors have expected me to conduct meetings, update and edit constituent letters, and research issues that the senator has requested information about. Besides these tasks, I have been able to give the senator information about a bill that he chose, upon my recommendation, to cosponsor. With my research and interest, I was able to have the senator be the original Democratic cosponsor of the Internet Gambling Prohibition Act of 1997, introduced to the Senate on Wednesday, March 19th. This bill is especially exciting because of its bipartisan effort to correct a source of addiction without taking any power away from the states. Without my memos and work on the bill, the senator would probably never have even known that this bill was going to be introduced, much less cosponsor it and put in a floor statement for the *Congressional Record*."

SOURCE: The Washington Center for Internships and Academic Seminars, in agreement with W. W. Norton.

THE GROWTH OF CONGRESSIONAL STAFFS, 1930–99

Figure 13.6

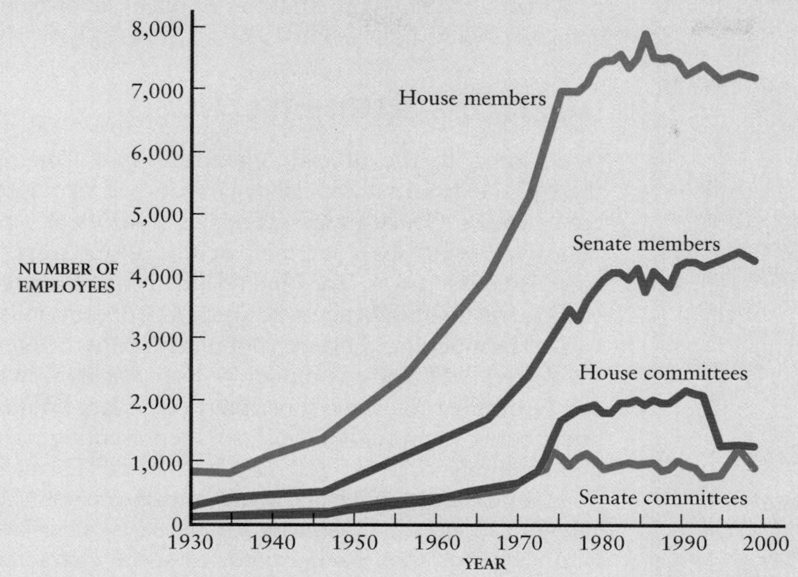

SOURCE: Norman J. Ornstein et al., eds., *Vital Statistics on Congress, 1999–2000* (Washington, DC: AEI Press, 2000), p. 129.

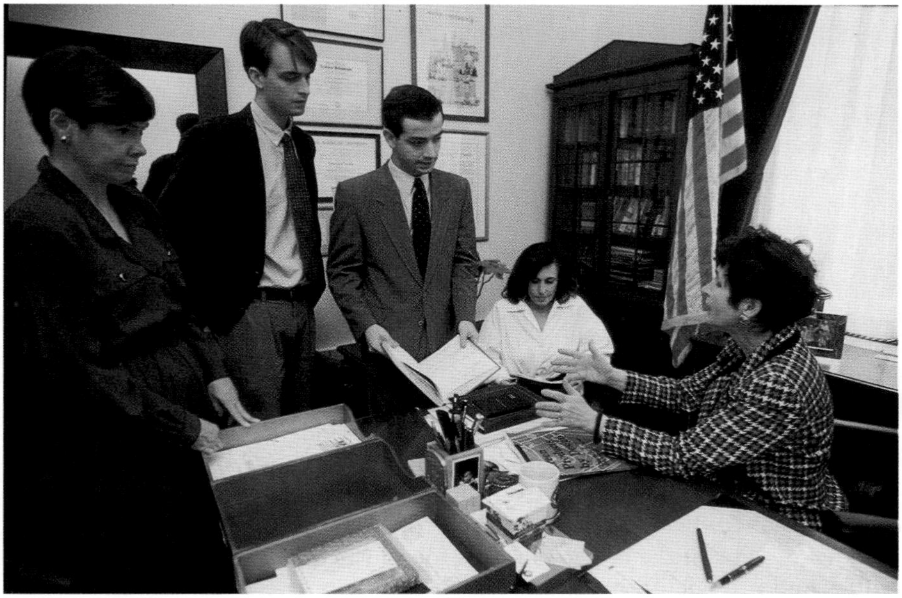

Representative Connie Morella meets with staff in her Capitol Hill office. Staffers typically perform routine office work and deal with requests from constituents, but some also help in developing new policy initiatives and drafting legislation.

implications and likely costs of proposed federal programs, such as health care reform proposals. A fourth agency, the Office of Technology Assessment, which provided Congress with analyses of scientific or technical issues, was abolished in 1995.

INFORMAL ORGANIZATION: THE CAUCUSES

In addition to the official organization of Congress, there also exists an unofficial organizational structure—the caucuses. **Caucuses** are groups of senators or representatives who share certain opinions, interests, or social characteristics. They include ideological caucuses such as the liberal Democratic Study Group, the conservative Democratic Forum (popularly known as the "boll weevils"), and the moderate Republican Wednesday Group. At the same time, there are a large number of caucuses composed of legislators representing particular economic or policy interests, such as the Travel and Tourism Caucus, the Steel Caucus, the Mushroom Caucus, and Concerned Senators for the Arts. Legislators who share common backgrounds or social characteristics have organized caucuses such as the Congressional Black Caucus, the Congressional Caucus for Women's Issues, and the Hispanic Caucus. All these caucuses seek to advance the interests of the groups they represent by promoting legislation, encouraging Congress to hold hearings, and pressing administrative agencies for favorable treatment. The Congressional Black Caucus, for example, which in 1996 included forty representatives and one senator, has played an active role in Congress since 1970.

Before 1995, many of the largest and most effective caucuses were registered as Legislative Service Organizations (LSOs). LSOs were allotted office space in congressional buildings and congressional members were allowed to transfer some of their own budgets to the LSO. Several of the most effective LSOs, including the Black Caucus, the Hispanic Caucus, and the Women's Caucus, were closely tied to the Democratic Party. One LSO, the Democratic Study Group (DSG), once employed eighteen full-time analysts to help congressional Democrats evaluate proposed and pending legislation. In 1995, the Republican leadership of the 104th Congress took away the budgets, staffs, and offices of all LSOs, in part because of these LSOs' links to the Democrats.[27] But most caucuses continued their activities, and new ones were created after this change. Of course, some of the larger caucuses found it harder to coordinate their activities and provide information to their members after they lost their status as LSOs, but caucuses continue to be an important part of congressional organization.[28]

Students and Politics

Scott Hibbard studied political science at the University of Colorado and become increasingly interested in international affairs during a junior year abroad in England. After graduation, Scott worked in a factory for several months to finance a job search in Washington. Two months after arriving, he accepted a job as a mail clerk for Democratic senator Dale Bumpers (D-Ariz.). Within a year, he was working on the legislative staff and eventually moved on to the senator's committee staff, where he worked on international trade issues and domestic economic policies. "I felt extremely fortunate to have landed a job with a man whom I truly respected. Also, being in the Senate was great. My friends and I talked politics incessantly as we watched major issues unfold before our eyes. We really felt that we were a part of the national debate."

Scott later took a job in the House of Representatives, where he became more directly involved in the legislative process. Working as a legislative aide to Representative Tom McMillen (D-Md.), a member of the House Energy and Commerce Committee, he helped get amendments attached to major pieces of legislation affecting the telecommunications and banking industries. He worked closely with constituents and fellow staffers on a wide range of issues, followed major trade and budget debates, and represented the congressman in a number of forums. He wrote speeches and correspondence and worked on a variety of legislative projects. When Congressman McMillen lost his bid for re-election, Scott left Capitol Hill and went to work for an independent government agency, the U.S. Institute of Peace. "Working for Tom was both a great experience and a great education. It was particularly interesting to see the legislative process from a different perspective. The House and Senate are very different bodies, with very different styles. While the Senate may be the 'world's greatest deliberative body,' any House member will be quick to remind you that they are part of 'the People's House.'"

SOURCE: Scott Hibbard, interview with author, November 7, 1999.

caucus (congressional)

an association of members of Congress based on party, interest, or social group, such as gender or race

The Black Caucus, gathered here to publicize its position on a sexual harassment case, has been a powerful force in American politics since 1970.

Rules of Lawmaking: How a Bill Becomes a Law

▶ How do the rules of congressional procedure influence the fate of legislation as well as determine the distribution of power in Congress?

The institutional structure of Congress is a key factor in shaping the legislative process. A second and equally important set of factors is the rules of congressional procedure. These rules govern everything from the introduction of a **bill** through its submission to the president for signing (see Figure 13.7 on the next page). Not only do these regulations influence the fate of every bill, they also help to determine the distribution of power in the Congress.

bill
a proposed law that has been sponsored by a member of Congress and submitted to the clerk of the House or Senate

COMMITTEE DELIBERATION

Even if a member of Congress, the White House, or a federal agency has spent months developing and drafting a piece of legislation, it does not become a bill until it is submitted officially by a senator or representative to the clerk of the House or Senate and referred to the appropriate committee for deliberation. No floor action on any bill can take place until the committee with jurisdiction over it has taken all the time it needs to deliberate. During the course of its deliberations, the committee typically refers the bill to one of its subcommittees, which may hold hearings, listen to expert testimony, and amend the proposed legislation before referring it to the full committee for consideration. The full committee may accept the recommendation of the subcommittee or hold its own hearings and prepare its own amendments. Or, even more frequently, the committee and subcommittee may do little or nothing with a bill that has been

Figure 13.7 HOW A BILL BECOMES A LAW

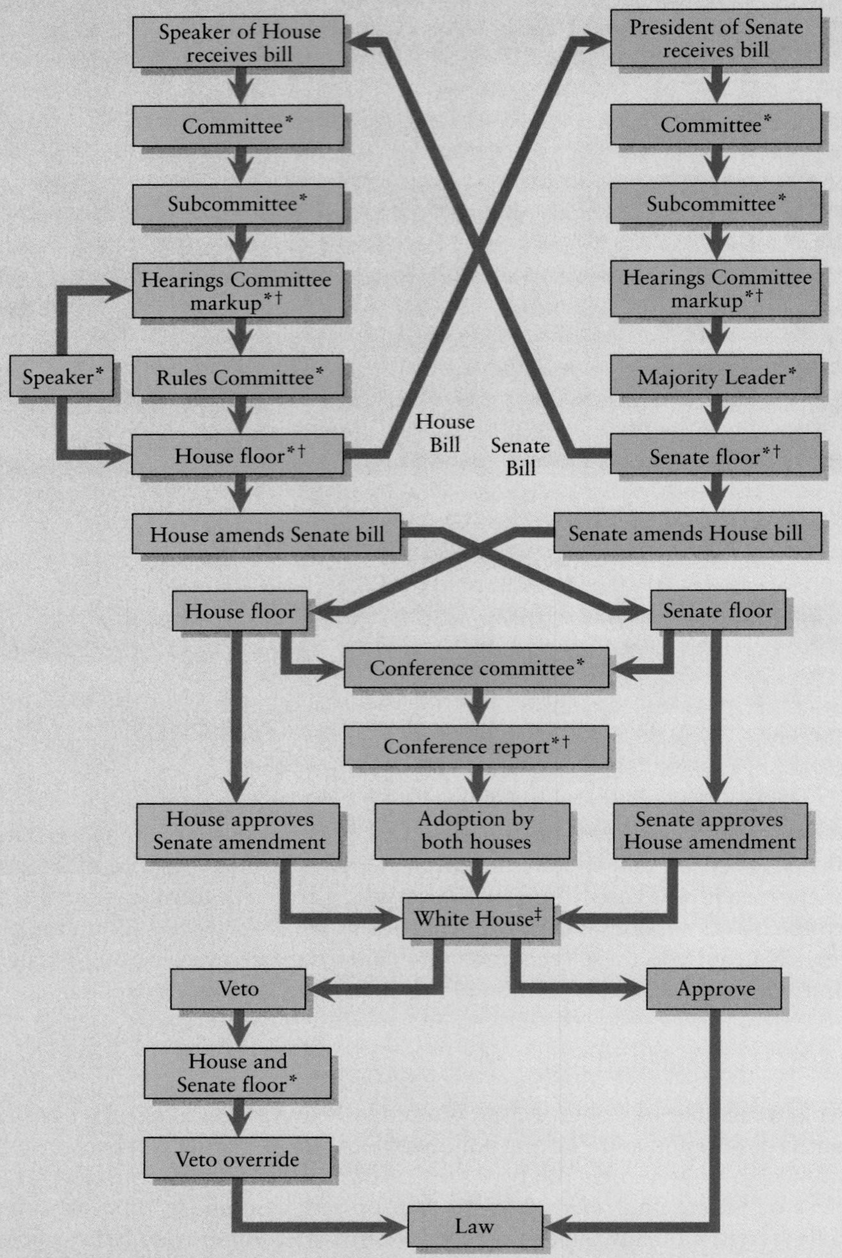

*Points at which a bill can be amended.
†Points at which a bill can die.
‡If the president neither signs nor vetoes a bill within ten days, it automatically becomes law.

submitted to them. Many bills are simply allowed to "die in committee" with little or no serious consideration given to them. Often, members of Congress introduce legislation that they neither expect nor desire to see enacted into law, merely to please a constituency group. These bills die a quick and painless death. Other pieces of legislation have ardent supporters and die in committee only after a long battle. But, in either case, most bills are never reported out of the committees to which they are assigned. In a typical congressional session, 95 percent of the roughly eight thousand bills introduced die in committee—an indication of the power of the congressional committee system.

The relative handful of bills that are reported out of committee must, in the House, pass one additional hurdle within the committee system—the Rules Committee. This powerful committee determines the rules that will govern action on the bill on the House floor. In particular, the Rules Committee allots the time for debate and decides to what extent amendments to the bill can be proposed from the floor. A bill's supporters generally prefer a **closed rule,** which puts severe limits on floor debate and amendments. Opponents of a bill usually prefer an **open rule,** which permits potentially damaging floor debate and makes it easier to add amendments that may cripple the bill or weaken its chances for passage. Thus, the outcome of the Rules Committee's deliberations can be extremely important and the committee's hearings can be an occasion for sharp conflict.

closed rule
a provision by the House Rules Committee limiting or prohibiting the introduction of amendments during debate

open rule
a provision by the House Rules Committee that permits floor debate and the addition of new amendments to a bill

DEBATE

Party control of the agenda is reinforced by the rule giving the Speaker of the House and the president of the Senate the power of recognition during debate on a bill. Usually the chair knows the purpose for which a member intends to speak well in advance of the occasion. Spontaneous efforts to gain recognition are often foiled. For example, the Speaker may ask, "For what purpose does the member rise?" before deciding whether to grant recognition.

In the House, virtually all of the time allotted by the Rules Committee for debate on a given bill is controlled by the bill's sponsor and by its leading opponent. In almost every case, these two people are the committee chair and the ranking minority member of the committee that processed the bill—or those they designate. These two participants are, by rule and tradition, granted the power to allocate most of the debate time in small amounts to members who are seeking to speak for or against the measure. Preference in the allocation of time goes to the members of the committee whose jurisdiction covers the bill.

In the Senate, the leadership has much less control over floor debate. Indeed, the Senate is unique among the world's legislative bodies for its commitment to unlimited debate. Once given the floor, a senator may speak as long as he or she wishes. On a number of memorable occasions, senators have used this right to prevent action on legislation that they opposed. Through this tactic, called the **filibuster,** small minorities or even one individual in the Senate can force the majority to give in. During the 1950s and 1960s, for example, opponents of civil rights legislation often sought to block its passage by staging a filibuster. The votes of three-fifths of the Senate, or sixty votes, are needed to end a filibuster. This procedure is called **cloture.**

filibuster
a tactic used by members of the Senate to prevent action on legislation they oppose by continuously holding the floor and speaking until the majority backs down. Once given the floor, senators have unlimited time to speak, and it requires a vote of three-fifths of the Senate to end a filibuster

cloture
a rule allowing a majority of two-thirds or three-fifths of the members in a legislative body to set a time limit on debate over a given bill

Whereas the filibuster was once an extraordinary tactic used only on rare occasions, in recent years it has been used increasingly often. In 1994, the filibuster was used by Republicans and some Democrats to defeat legislation that would have prohibited employers from permanently replacing striking workers. Later, Republicans threatened to filibuster health care reform legislation. Some Democrats argued that Senate Republicans had begun to use the filibuster as a routine instrument of legislative obstructionism to make up for their minority status in Congress, and proposed rule changes that would make filibustering more difficult. One of the most senior Democrats in the Senate, however, former majority leader Robert Byrd of West Virginia, warned against limiting the filibuster, saying, "The minority can be right, and on many occasions in this country's history, the minority was right."[29] After the GOP won control of the Senate in 1994, many Democrats began to agree with Senator Byrd. They used the filibuster to block Republican initiatives on environmental and social policy. A Democratic-led filibuster in 1996, for example, halted Republican efforts to open up large areas of protected federal land in Utah for development.

Senator Strom Thurmond of South Carolina leaving the Senate chamber after delivering a twenty-four-hour, nineteen-minute filibuster against a civil rights bill in 1957.

Although it is the best known, the filibuster is not the only technique used to block Senate debate. Under Senate rules, members have a virtually unlimited ability to propose amendments to a pending bill. Each amendment must be voted on before the bill can come to a final vote. The introduction of new amendments can be stopped only by unanimous consent. This, in effect, can permit a determined minority to filibuster-by-amendment, indefinitely delaying the passage of a bill. This tactic was briefly used by Republicans in 1994 to delay the administration's health care initiative. Senators can also place "holds," or stalling devices, on bills to delay debate. Senators place holds on bills when they fear that openly opposing them will be unpopular. Because holds are kept secret, the senators placing the holds do not have to take public responsibility for their actions. Such holds blocked bipartisan efforts to enact popular health insurance reforms for much of 1996. In 1997, opponents of this practice introduced an amendment that would have required publicizing the identity of the senator putting a bill on hold. But when the Senate voted on the measure, the proposal to end the practice of anonymous holds had "mysteriously disappeared."[30] Although no one took credit for killing the measure, it was evident that the majority of senators wanted to maintain the practice.

Once a bill is debated on the floor of the House and the Senate, the leaders schedule it for a vote on the floor of each chamber. By this time, congressional leaders know what the vote will be; leaders do not bring legislation to the floor unless they are fairly certain it is going to pass. As a consequence, it is unusual for the leadership to lose a bill on the floor. On rare occasions, the last moments of the floor vote can be very dramatic, as each party's leadership puts its whip organization into action to make sure that wavering members vote with the party.

CONFERENCE COMMITTEE: RECONCILING HOUSE AND SENATE VERSIONS OF LEGISLATION

Getting a bill out of committee and through one of the houses of Congress is no guarantee that a bill will be enacted into law. Frequently, bills that began with similar provisions in both chambers emerge with little resemblance to each other. Alternatively, a bill may be passed by one chamber but undergo substantial revision in the other chamber. In such cases, a conference commit-

This conference committee is meeting to reconcile the differences between House and Senate versions of a budget bill.

tee composed of the senior members of the committees or subcommittees that initiated the bills may be required to iron out differences between the two pieces of legislation. Sometimes members or leaders will let objectionable provisions pass on the floor with the idea that they will get the change they want in conference. Usually, conference committees meet behind closed doors. Agreement requires a majority of each of the two delegations. Legislation that emerges successfully from a conference committee is more often a compromise than a clear victory of one set of forces over another.

When a bill comes out of conference, it faces one more hurdle. Before a bill can be sent to the president for signing, the House-Senate conference committee's version of the bill must be approved on the floor of each chamber. Usually such approval is given quickly. Occasionally, however, a bill's opponents use this round of approval as one last opportunity to defeat a piece of legislation.

PRESIDENTIAL ACTION

Once adopted by the House and Senate, a bill goes to the president, who may choose to sign the bill into law or **veto** it. The veto is the president's constitutional power to reject a piece of legislation. To veto a bill, the president returns it unsigned within ten days to the house of Congress in which it originated. If Congress adjourns during the ten-day period, and the president has taken no action, the bill is also considered to be vetoed. This latter method is known as the **pocket veto.** The possibility of a presidential veto affects how willing members of Congress are to push for different pieces of legislation at different times. If they think a proposal is likely to be vetoed they might shelve it for a later time.

A presidential veto may be overridden by a two-thirds vote in both the House and Senate. A veto override says much about the support that a president can expect from Congress, and it can deliver a stinging blow to the executive

veto
the president's constitutional power to turn down acts of Congress. A presidential veto may be overriden by a two-thirds vote of each house of Congress

pocket veto
a presidential veto that is automatically triggered if the president does not act on a given piece of legislation passed during the final ten days of a legislative session

branch. Presidents will often back down from a veto threat if they believe that Congress will override the veto. In 1999 President Clinton threatened to veto a major defense spending bill, which be believed was filled with unnecessary special interest spending. He ultimately signed the measure, however, when it became evident that enough Democrats would join Republicans to override his veto. Between 1995, when Republicans took over Congress, and 1999 Clinton used his veto power thirty times, effectively blocking much of the Republican agenda. Due to the close partisan balance in Congress and the sharp division between Republicans and Democrats, there was only one successful override of Clinton's vetoes.

How Congress Decides

▶ What sorts of influences inside and outside of government determine how members of Congress vote on legislation? How do these influences vary according to the type of issue?

Representative John Conyers meets with constituents in his Capitol Hill office.

What determines the kinds of legislation that Congress ultimately produces? According to the most simple theories of representation, members of Congress would respond to the views of their constituents. In fact, the process of creating a legislative agenda, drawing up a list of possible measures, and deciding among them is a very complex process, in which a variety of influences from inside and outside government play important roles. External influences include a legislator's constituency and various interest groups. Influences from inside government include party leadership, congressional colleagues, and the president. Let us examine each of these influences individually and then consider how they interact to produce congressional policy decisions.

CONSTITUENCY

Because members of Congress, for the most part, want to be re-elected, we would expect the views of their constituents to be a primary influence on the decisions that legislators make. Yet constituency influence is not so straightforward. In fact, most constituents do not even know what policies their representatives support. The number of citizens who *do* pay attention to such matters—the attentive public—is usually very small. Nonetheless, members of Congress spend a lot of time worrying about what their constituents think, because these representatives realize that the choices they make may be scrutinized in a future election and used as ammunition by an opposing candidate. Because of this possibility, members of Congress try to anticipate their constituents' policy views.[31] Legislators are more likely to act in accordance with those views if they think that voters will take them into account during elections. In October 1998, for example, thirty-one House Democrats broke party ranks and voted in favor of an impeachment inquiry against President Clinton because they believed a "no" vote could cost them reelection that November. In this way, constituents may affect congressional policy choices even when there is little direct evidence of their influence.

INTEREST GROUPS

Interest groups are another important external influence on the policies that Congress produces. When members of Congress are making voting decisions, those interest groups that have some connection to constituents in particular members' districts are most likely to be influential. For this reason, interest groups with the ability to mobilize followers in many congressional districts may be especially influential in Congress. In recent years, Washington-based interest groups with little grassroots strength have recognized the importance of locally generated activity. They have, accordingly, sought to simulate grassroots pressure, using a strategy that has been nicknamed "Astroturf lobbying." Such campaigns encourage constituents to sign form letters or postcards, which are then sent to congressional representatives. Sophisticated "grassroots" campaigns set up toll-free telephone numbers for a system in which simply reporting your name and address to the listening computer will generate a letter to your congressional representative. One Senate office estimated that such organized campaigns to demonstrate "grassroots" support account for two-thirds of the mail the office received. As such campaigns increase, however, they may become less influential, because members of Congress are aware of how rare actual constituent interest actually is.[32]

Students and Politics

Andy Pederson, a student at the University of Wisconsin at Milwaukee, interning at the Children's Rights Council:

"I have participated in the legislative process through lobbying and advocating issues before Congress. Congress has increasingly begun to deal with issues regarding family structure and child support. In advocating an issue, we obtain and evaluate legislation and then inform staff members and legislators on new ideas or proposals to reform existing ideas. Providing information, statistics, and knowledge to congressional staffs is invaluable in the legislative process.

"Another way of advocating an issue is through grassroots mobilization. This is primarily achieved through keeping the members of the Children's Rights Council informed through newsletters and mailings that keep them up to date on pending legislation. Individuals also call the Council seeking help on specific issues or situations, and we are able to offer them resources. Most often, people want to become involved; they just don't know how to or what is at stake.

"The political process can be long and tiresome. Results are rarely seen immediately. But through this internship I have learned that individual citizens can make a difference if they participate in the process."

SOURCE: The Washington Center for Internships and Academic Seminars, in agreement with W. W. Norton.

Interest groups also have substantial influence in setting the legislative agenda and in helping to craft specific language in legislation. Today, sophisticated lobbyists win influence by providing information about policies to busy members of Congress. As one lobbyist noted, "You can't get access without knowledge. . . . I can go in to see [former Energy and Commerce Committee chair] John Dingell, but if I have nothing to offer or nothing to say, he's not going to want to see me."[33] In recent years, interest groups have also begun to build broader coalitions and comprehensive campaigns around particular policy issues. These coalitions do not rise from the grass roots, but instead are put together by Washington lobbyists who launch comprehensive lobbying campaigns that combine simulated grassroots activity with information and campaign funding for members of Congress. In 1995, the Republican congressional leadership worked so closely with lobbyists that critics charged that the boundaries between lobbyists and legislators had been erased, and that lobbyists had become "adjunct staff to the Republican leadership."[34]

PARTY DISCIPLINE

In both the House and Senate, party leaders have a good deal of influence over the behavior of their party members. This influence, sometimes called "party discipline," was once so powerful that it dominated the lawmaking process. At the turn of the century, party leaders could often command the allegiance of more than 90 percent of their members. A vote on which 50 percent or more of the members of one party take one position while at least 50 percent of the members of the other party take the opposing position is called a **party vote.** At the beginning of the twentieth century, nearly half of all **roll-call votes** in the House of Representatives were party votes. Today, this type of party-line voting is rare in Congress. It is, however, fairly common to find at least a majority of the Democrats opposing a majority of the Republicans on any given issue.

party vote
a roll-call vote in the House or Senate in which at least 50 percent of the members of one party take a particular position and are opposed by at least 50 percent of the members of the other party. Party votes are rare today, although they were fairly common in the nineteenth century

roll-call vote
a vote in which each legislator's yes or no vote is recorded as the clerk calls the names of the members alphabetically

Typically, party unity is greater in the House than in the Senate. House rules grant greater procedural control of business to the majority party leaders, which gives them more influence over House members. In the Senate, however, the leadership has few sanctions over its members. Senate minority leader Tom Daschle once observed that a Senate leader seeking to influence other senators has as incentives "a bushel full of carrots and a few twigs."[35]

Party unity has been on the rise in the last decade because the divisions between the parties have deepened on many high profile issues such as abortion, affirmative action, the minimum wage, and school vouchers (see Figure 13.8). Party unity scores rise when congressional leaders try to put a partisan stamp on legislation. For example, in 1995, then-Speaker Newt Gingrich sought to enact a Republican Contract with America that few Democrats supported.

Figure 13.8 PARTY UNITY SCORES BY CHAMBER

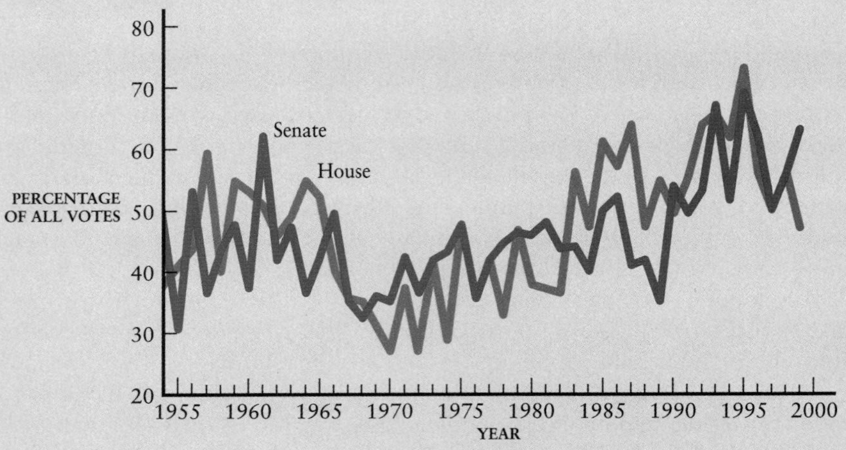

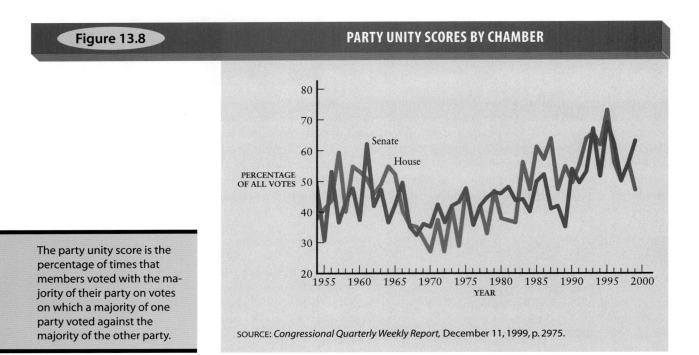

The party unity score is the percentage of times that members voted with the majority of their party on votes on which a majority of one party voted against the majority of the other party.

SOURCE: *Congressional Quarterly Weekly Report,* December 11, 1999, p. 2975.

The result was more party unity in the House than in any year since 1954. In 1998, party unity scores rose as bitter divisions between Democrats and Republicans over impeachment reduced either party's willingness to compromise on legislation.

To some extent, party unity is based on ideology and background. Republican members of Congress are more likely than Democrats to be drawn from rural or suburban areas. Democrats are likely to be more liberal on economic and social questions than their Republican colleagues. These differences certainly help to explain roll-call divisions between the two parties. Ideology and background, however, are only part of the explanation of party unity. The other part has to do with party organization and leadership. Although party organization has weakened since the turn of the century, today's party leaders still have some resources at their disposal: (1) committee assignments, (2) access to the floor, (3) the whip system, (4) logrolling, and (5) the presidency. These resources are regularly used and are often effective in securing the support of party members.

Leadership PACs Leaders have increased their influence over members in recent years with aggressive use of leadership political action committees. Leadership PACs are organizations that members of Congress use to raise funds that they then distribute to other members of their party running for election. Republican congressional leaders pioneered the aggressive use of leadership PACS to win their congressional majority in 1995, and the practice has spread widely since that time. For example, House Speaker J. Dennis Hastert established a leadership PAC called Keep Our Majority PAC in preparation for the 2000 election. The influential House Whip Tom DeLay (R-Tex.) has been especially aggressive in raising funds with his PAC, Americans for a Republican Majority (ARMPAC). By 1999, there were close to one hundred such PACS, with leaders, as well as members aspiring to leadership positions, setting up their own organizations. Republicans have been in the forefront of the movement to create leadership PACs. Money from these PACs can be directed to the most vulnerable candidates or to candidates who are having trouble raising money. As such, it enhances the power of the party and creates a bond between the leaders and the members who receive their help.[36]

Committee Assignments Leaders can create debts among members by helping them get favorable committee assignments. These assignments are made early in the congressional careers of most members and cannot be taken from them if they later balk at party discipline. Nevertheless, if the leadership goes out of its way to get the right assignment for a member, this effort is likely to create a bond of obligation that can be called upon without any other payments or favors. This is one reason the Republican leadership gave freshmen favorable assignments when the Republicans took over Congress in 1995.

Access to the Floor The most important everyday resource available to the parties is control over access to the floor. With thousands of bills awaiting passage and most members clamoring for access in order to influence a bill or to publicize themselves, floor time is precious. In the Senate, the leadership allows ranking committee members to influence the allocation of floor time—who will speak for how long; in the House, the Speaker, as head of the

PARTY DISCIPLINE

Party discipline is maintained through a number of sources:

Committee assignments: by giving favorable committee assignments to members, party leaders create a sense of debt.

Access to the floor: ranking committee members in the Senate, and the Speaker of the House, control the allocation of floor time, so House and Senate members want to stay on good terms with these party leaders in order that their bills get time on the floor.

Whip system: party leaders use whips to track how many votes they have for a given piece of legislation; if the vote is close, they can try to influence members to switch sides.

Logrolling: members who may have nothing in common can agree to support one another's legislation because each needs the other's vote.

Presidency: the president's legislative proposals are often the most important part of Congress's agenda. Party leaders use the president's support to rally members.

majority party (in consultation with the minority leader), allocates large blocks of floor time. Thus, floor time is allocated in both houses of Congress by the majority and minority leaders. More importantly, the Speaker of the House and the majority leader in the Senate possess the power of recognition. Although this power may not appear to be substantial, it is a formidable authority and can be used to stymie a piece of legislation completely or to frustrate a member's attempts to speak on a particular issue. Because the power is significant, members of Congress usually attempt to stay on good terms with the Speaker and the majority leader in order to ensure that they will continue to be recognized.

Some House members, Republicans in particular, have also taken advantage of "special orders," under which members can address the floor after the close of business. These addresses are typically made to an empty chamber, but are usually carried live by C-SPAN, a cable television channel. As the 106th Congress ended, Speaker Dennis Hastert addressed an empty House chamber to proclaim that the Congress had "made great progress in preparing America for the next century."[37] Knowing that the press would highlight the meager accomplishments of the conflict-ridden post-impeachment Congress, Hastert was ensured that his own more positive assessment would directly reach television audiences.

whip system
a communications network in each house of Congress; whips take polls of the membership in order to learn their intentions on specific legislative issues and to assist the majority and minority leaders in various tasks

The Whip System Some influence accrues to party leaders through the **whip system,** which is primarily a communications network. Between twelve and twenty assistant and regional whips are selected to operate at the direction of the majority or minority leader and the whip. They take polls of all the members in order to learn their intentions on specific bills. This enables the leaders to know if they have enough support to allow a vote as well as whether the vote is so close that they need to put pressure on a few undecided members. Leaders also use the whip system to convey their wishes and plans to the members, but only in very close votes do they actually exert pressure on a member. In those instances, the Speaker or a lieutenant will go to a few party members who have indicated they will switch if their vote is essential. The whip system helps the leaders limit pressuring members to a few times per session.

The whip system helps maintain party unity in both houses of Congress, but it is particularly critical in the House of Representatives because of the large number of legislators whose positions and votes must be accounted for. The majority and minority whips and their assistants must be adept at inducing compromise among legislators who hold widely differing viewpoints. The whips' personal styles and their perception of their function significantly affect the development of legislative coalitions and influence the compromises that emerge.

logrolling
a legislative practice wherein agreements are made between legislators in voting for or against a bill. Unlike bargaining, logrolling parties have nothing in common but their desire to exchange support

Logrolling An agreement between two or more members of Congress who have nothing in common except the need for support is called **logrolling.** The agreement states, in effect, "You support me on bill X and I'll support you on another bill of your choice." Since party leaders are the center of the communications networks in the two chambers, they can help members create large logrolling coalitions. Hundreds of logrolling deals are made each year, and although there are no official record-keeping books, it would be a poor party

POLICY DEBATE

Tax Cuts vs. Social Welfare Spending

Since the start of the 1980s, a more conservative national mood has supported reductions in the size and cost of the federal government. While most citizens continue to favor most government spending programs, from Social Security to national defense, a new generation of conservative leaders has championed the popular cause of lower taxes and smaller government. As the federal budget began to show a surplus in the late 1990s, these Republicans argued for a large tax cut that would return much of the surplus to taxpayers. Acknowledging that few citizens enjoy paying taxes, critics of tax-cut enthusiasts have argued that the real agenda behind the tax-cut chant is a backdoor effort to cut popular and necessary government programs that conservatives have failed to cut through the regular political process. These critics, mainly Democrats, argue that the budget surplus should be used to address long-neglected social needs with improved government programs.

Supporters of reduced taxes and smaller government point out that the government itself has grown out of control. For instance, from 1789 to 1980, the total accumulated federal debt stood at $1 trillion. Between 1980 and 1992, however, the total federal debt ballooned to over $4 trillion, a clear indication that government spending has spiraled out of control. At the same time, public opinion polls show that Americans have less and less trust in their government to spend tax dollars wisely or well. A family that spends irresponsibly and beyond its means must learn to tighten its belt, spend less, and aim to balance its checkbook. The government, most citizens agree, must do the same. By reducing taxes, the government can turn over to citizens more control over their own spending and wealth. As it is, the average family spends more on taxes than on food, shelter, and clothing combined. Two wage earners have become necessary for most families to make ends meet. By cutting taxes, citizens can direct more of their own resources toward home purchases, saving for college, or other family priorities. Such an approach is an economical substitute for large, inefficient government programs designed to serve the same purposes. In short, citizens have made their preferences for the end of big government clear. Tax relief provides the avenue to achieve that end.

Opponents of big tax cuts argue that the conservative agenda offers a false promise—that citizens can continue to have the programs and services they favor while also getting big tax cuts. The ballooning deficits of the 1980s did indeed sound an alarm, but the crisis was not big government out of control. Rather, it was conservatives who cynically cut taxes and actually increased spending in areas like national defense, knowing that large deficits would be the result. Rather than take the blame, conservatives pointed their fingers at social welfare and other domestic spending programs. Large and expensive government programs like Social Security, Medicare, Medicaid, and national defense remained mostly untouched. Instead, public anger was directed at programs like Aid to Families with Dependent Children (AFDC), child nutrition programs, education, and environmental programs, which constitute less than 10 percent of the federal budget. Opponents of tax cuts argue that the budget surplus would be far better spent by restoring spending on these social programs and by creating new spending programs in areas where there is strong public support, such as health care.

For all the criticism of tax rates, Americans pay a smaller proportion of income in taxes than citizens of most other Western nations. Surveys consistently show that, despite general cynicism about government—a cynicism fed in part by the drumbeat of tax-cut advocates—most Americans support reasonable domestic welfare and related expenditures. For better and worse, taxes are the price we pay to have our government and our society.

STUDENT DEBATE

Should Congress Cut Taxes?

Yes

[What are] the relative merits of tax cuts and debt reduction[?] Let's see if we can shed some light on the question.

I should begin by saying that paying off the debt sounds to me like a great idea. There's no conflict between debt reduction and tax cuts, because debt reduction is a tax cut. The federal debt is owed by the federal government and, since the government has no resources of its own, this means it is owed by the American people. So when the government pays down the debt, it means that I owe less than I did last year, and the effect is that I have more money. This is the definition of a tax cut. The other side of the same coin is that eliminating the debt will mean lower interest rates, and this will spark entrepreneurship, job creation, and economic growth, exactly as an income tax cut would.

So, that's that: The way to go is to invest the entire surplus in paying down the debt, right? Wrong. The problem is that large-scale debt reduction is just not going to happen. I find myself in complete agreement with Alan Greenspan, the Chairman of the Federal Reserve, who said in congressional testimony: "If I became concerned that the surplus is going to be employed for increased spending programs, (then) I would be strongly in favor of tax cuts now." Well, I am concerned, based on the facts that: a) many congressmen have proposed new spending, and b) even more of them have already voted for it. Even conservative Republicans are quietly nickel-and-diming the surplus down to zero as you read this.

Therefore, I've got no choice but to support the Republican tax plan. This, by the way, would lower everyone's income tax by one percentage point (basically, however much money you make, you would get to keep an extra one percent of it), lower capital gains taxes, repeal the death tax, expand IRA's and jimmy with a million other things in the tax code. Half of this stuff is meaningless to me, but I still like the sound of it because I'm for anything that will get this money out of the Congress' clutches.

I've heard frustrated comments from pundits who object to congressmen calling Congress irresponsible. Aren't they, the argument goes, talking about themselves? The government seems to be saying, "stop me before I spend again." But it's not as if Congress were one person. As I see it, the math probably works out like this: about 40 percent of congressmen are committed to spending, because it's the most efficient way for them to score political points in their districts; about 40 percent want to give away goodies of some kind, but don't care if it's as a tax cut or spending increase; and the other 20 percent are committed fiscal conservatives, who are serious about seeing tax cuts or deficit reduction. There's a constituency here for spending, and one for tax cuts, but none for serious deficit reduction. So, if the 20 percent fiscal conservatives can take the initiative and ally with the 40 percent "either-way" faction, they will have a majority in favor of tax cuts. But, if they fail to pass tax cuts, and the surplus money sits around the Capitol, there will be an enormous, 80 percent-or-so majority in favor of a spending spree. What the fiscal conservatives are really saying is more like, "stop the other 80 percent of us before they spend again," which is very sensible.

What's the upshot? The Republican tax plan isn't perfect, but it's probably safer than futile attempts at debt reduction. It's certainly a lot better than the president's budget, which would save less and spend more. Since Congress is irresponsible, the sensible course is to give a good-sized tax cut back to the taxpayers and maintain a small surplus. As long as the economy is healthy, the debt problem will take care of itself. More serious is the seemingly unstoppable drift toward accumulation of money and power in Washington, D.C. Tax money is the fuel for this trend, and nothing could be more irresponsible than throwing the full budget surplus into that furnace.

SOURCE: Nathaniel Krause, "Mo' Money, Mo' Problems: Don't Keep the Surplus," *Daily Illini* (University of Illinois), August 30, 1999.

No

On Monday, it was announced by President Clinton that the federal budget surplus for the current year had exceeded projections and totaled $115 billion. The issue facing everyone is what to do with the newly found money.

The surplus, which is the largest in our nation's history and the first back-to-back surplus since 1957, can be used to fund a host of federal programs or it can be given back in a tax cut.

Right now, the smart money is not on the tax cut, which Clinton vetoed last week. The bill sponsored by House Republicans planned $792 billion in reduced taxes over a 10-year period.

As an average, that works out to almost $80 billion a year, which I hate to say is dangerously close to the amount of the budget surplus.

If tax revenues were to fall or the economy to falter, we would be faced with the issue of either cutting services or swallowing another painful tax increase.

The last time we had a tax increase, many Americans paid out more because their financial planning had not anticipated the changes in the tax code.

Since people are comfortable with the current tax situation, despite their griping on April 15, we should not rock the boat with a new roller coaster of tax plans.

Besides, neither party has studied the repercussions of the proposed tax cut, and I am leery of meddling with what works.

Also, history does not support a tax cut. The last tax cut we received was under Reagan, and after that, the federal budget deficit ballooned so much that it required two tax increases, one under Bush and the other under Clinton.

Rather than be short-sighted and push a tax cut that could risk the financial health of the nation, the money should be used to shore up social programs that soon will find themselves overburdened.

With a large percentage of the population aging, attention should be paid to Social Security and Medicare.

Both programs are in need of an overhaul and additional funding, and the current budget surplus is the means with which to do it.

As it is, the health care system of this nation is woefully underfunded and the coverage for some segments of the population grossly inadequate. Currently, there are 44 million people in this nation who are uninsured. This represents one-sixth of the total population.

***

Over the summer, I worked at the Des Moines county hospital and saw firsthand the state of our nation's health care system.

Even though coverage was never denied to anyone seeking attention, because the recipients were uninsured, the hospital had to write off most coverage as a fiscal loss.

We were reimbursed by both federal and local programs, but as a percentage of funding, the local government paid the larger chunk. Despite both sources of income, the hospital still operated at a net loss.

That is why I can honestly say that any plan to increase insurance health care coverage is a good idea, especially since it will reduce the burden paid directly by taxpayers.

SOURCE: Aaron Woell, "Budget Surplus Tax Cut Can Do Little to Aid Americans," *Iowa State Daily* (Iowa State University), September 29, 1999.

leader whose whips did not know who owed what to whom. In some instances, logrolling produces strange alliances. A most unlikely alliance emerged in Congress in October 1991, which one commentator dubbed "the corn for porn plot."[38] The alliance joined Senate supporters of the National Endowment for the Arts (NEA) with senators seeking limits on the cost of grazing rights on federal lands. The NEA, which provides federal funding to the arts, had been under fire from conservative senator Jessie Helms (R-N.C.) for funding some controversial artists whose work Helms believed to be indecent. In an effort to prevent federal support for such works, Helms attached a provision to NEA's funding that would have prohibited the agency from awarding grants to any work that in a "patently offensive way" depicted "sexual or excretory activities or organs." Supporters of the NEA condemned such restrictions as a violation of free speech and pointed out that many famous works of art could not have been funded under such restrictions. When it appeared that the amendment would pass, NEA supporters offered Western senators a deal. In exchange for voting down the Helms amendment, they would eliminate a planned hike in grazing fees. Republican senators from sixteen Western states switched their votes and defeated the Helms amendment. Although Helms called his defeat the product of "backroom deals and parliamentary flimflam," his amendment was simply the victim of the time-honored congressional practice of logrolling.[39]

The Presidency Of all the influences that maintain the clarity of party lines in Congress, the influence of the presidency is probably the most important. Indeed, the office is a touchstone of party discipline in Congress. Since the late 1940s, under President Harry Truman, presidents each year have identified a number of bills to be considered part of their administration's program. By the mid-1950s, both parties in Congress began to look to the president for these proposals, which became the most significant part of Congress's agenda. The president's support is a criterion for party loyalty, and party leaders are able to use it to rally some members.

WEIGHING DIVERSE INFLUENCES

Clearly, many different factors affect congressional decisions. But at various points in the decision-making process, some factors are likely to be more influential than others. For example, interest groups may be more effective at the committee stage, when their expertise is especially valued and their visibility is less obvious. Because committees play a key role in deciding what legislation actually reaches the floor of the House or Senate, interest groups can often put a halt to bills they dislike, or they can ensure that the options that do reach the floor are those that the group's members support.

Once legislation reaches the floor and members of Congress are deciding among alternatives, constituent opinion will become more important. Legislators are also influenced very much by other legislators: many of their assessments about the substance and politics of legislation come from fellow members of Congress.

The influence of the external and internal forces described in the preceding section also varies according to the kind of issue being considered. On policies of great importance to powerful interest groups—farm subsidies, for exam-

Politics on the Web

The Internet has altered the relationship between members of Congress and the public. For citizens, the Internet allows more access to information about politics and about specific members of Congress—how they voted on every bill, speeches they have made, and even from whom they have received campaign contributions. In addition, Internet e-mail allows citizens to contact their members of Congress with little effort and cost. Of course, there is a downside to such enhanced participation: our representatives could easily be inundated with constituent messages, increasing their already tremendous workload.

For members of Congress, the Internet provides a practically free way to advertise their positions on key issues, which in reelection campaigns could save a lot of money. This, in turn, could undercut the impact of special interests, PACs, wealthy supporters, and the "conventional" media. Thus the Internet could give poorly financed challengers a more equal voice in a campaign.

www.wwnorton.com/wtp3e

ple—those groups are likely to have considerable influence. On other issues, members of Congress may be less attentive to narrow interest groups and more willing to consider what they see as the general interest.

Finally, the mix of influences varies according to the historical moment. The 1994 electoral victory of Republicans allowed their party to control both houses of Congress for the first time in forty years. That fact, combined with an unusually assertive Republican leadership, meant that party leaders became especially important in decision making. The willingness of moderate Republicans to support measures they had once opposed indicated the unusual importance of party leadership in this period. As House minority leader Richard Gephardt put it, "When you've been in the desert 40 years, your instinct is to help Moses."[40]

Beyond Legislation: Other Congressional Powers

▶ Besides the power to pass legislation, what other powers allow Congress to influence the process of government?

In addition to the power to make the law, Congress has at its disposal an array of other instruments through which to influence the process of government. The Constitution gives the Senate the power to approve treaties and appointments. And Congress has a number of other powers through which it can share with the other branches the capacity to administer the laws.

OVERSIGHT

oversight
the effort by Congress, through hearings, investigations, and other techniques, to exercise control over the activities of executive agencies

appropriations
the amounts of money approved by Congress in statutes (bills) that each unit or agency of government can spend

Oversight, as applied to Congress, refers not to something neglected, but to the effort to oversee or to supervise how legislation is carried out by the executive branch. Oversight is carried out by committees or subcommittees of the Senate or the House, which conduct hearings and investigations in order to analyze and evaluate bureaucratic agencies and the effectiveness of their programs. Their purpose may be to locate inefficiencies or abuses of power, to explore the relationship between what an agency does and what a law intended, or to change or abolish a program. Most programs and agencies are subject to some oversight every year during the course of hearings on **appropriations,** that is, the funding of agencies and government programs.

Committees or subcommittees have the power to subpoena witnesses, take oaths, cross-examine, compel testimony, and bring criminal charges for contempt (refusing to cooperate) and perjury (lying). Hearings and investigations are similar in many ways, but they differ on one fundamental point. A hearing is usually held on a specific bill, and the questions asked are usually intended to build a record with regard to that bill. In an investigation, the committee or subcommittee does not begin with a particular bill, but examines a broad area or problem and then concludes its investigation with one or more proposed bills. One example of an investigation is the congressional inquiry into the Reagan administration's shipment of arms to the government of Iran.

ADVICE AND CONSENT: SPECIAL SENATE POWERS

The Constitution has given the Senate a special power, one that is not based on lawmaking. The president has the power to make treaties and to appoint top executive officers, ambassadors, and federal judges—but only "with the Advice and Consent of the Senate" (Article II, Section 2). For treaties, two-thirds of those present must concur; for appointments, a simple majority is required.

The power to approve or reject presidential requests also involves the power to set conditions. The Senate only occasionally exercises its power to reject treaties and appointments, and usually that is when opposite parties control the Senate and the White House. During the final two years of President Reagan's term, for example, Senate Democrats rejected Judge Robert Bork's Supreme Court nomination and gave clear indications that they would reject a second Reagan nominee, Judge Douglas Ginsburg, who withdrew his nomination before the Senate could act. These instances, however, actually underscore the restraint with which the Senate usually uses its power to reject presidential requests. For example, only nine judicial nominees have been rejected by the Senate during the past century, whereas hundreds have been approved.

executive agreement
an agreement, made between the president and another country, that has the force of a treaty but does not require the Senate's "advice and consent"

Most presidents make every effort to take potential Senate opposition into account in treaty negotiations and will frequently resort to **executive agreements** with foreign powers instead of treaties. The Supreme Court has held that such agreements are equivalent to treaties, but they do not need Senate approval.[41] In the past, presidents sometimes concluded secret agreements without informing Congress of the agreements' contents, or even their existence. For example, American involvement in the Vietnam War grew in part out of a series of secret arrangements made between American presidents and the South Vietnamese during the 1950s and 1960s. Congress did not even learn of the existence of these agreements until 1969. In 1972, Congress passed the Case Act, which requires that the president inform Congress of any executive agreement within sixty days of its having been reached. This provides Congress with the opportunity to cancel agreements that it opposes. In addition, Congress can limit the president's ability to conduct foreign policy through executive agreement by refusing to appropriate the funds needed to implement an agreement. In this way, for example, executive agreements to provide American economic or military assistance to foreign governments can be modified or even canceled by Congress.

IMPEACHMENT

impeachment
the formal charge by the House of Representatives that a government official has committed "Treason, Bribery, or other high Crimes and Misdemeanors."

The Constitution also grants Congress the power of **impeachment** over the president, vice president, and other executive officials. Impeachment means to charge a government official (president or otherwise) with "Treason, Bribery, or other high Crimes and Misdemeanors" and bring them before Congress to determine their guilt. Impeachment is thus like a criminal indictment in which the House of Representatives acts like a grand jury, voting (by simple majority) on whether the accused ought to be impeached. If a majority of the House votes to impeach, the impeachment trial moves to the Senate, which acts like a trial jury by voting whether to convict and forcibly remove the person from office (this vote requires a two-thirds majority of the Senate).

Controversy over Congress's impeachment power has arisen over the grounds for impeachment, especially the meaning of "high Crimes and Misdemeanors." A strict reading of the Constitution suggests that the only impeachable offense is an actual crime. But a more commonly agreed upon definition is that "an impeachable offense is whatever the majority of the House of Representatives considers it to be at a given moment in history."[42] In other words, impeachment, especially impeachment of a president, is a political decision.

The political nature of impeachment was very clear in the two instances of impeachment that have occurred in American history. In the first, in 1867, President Andrew Johnson, a southern Democrat who had battled a congressional Republican majority over Reconstruction, was impeached by the House but saved from conviction by one vote in the Senate. In 1998, the House impeached President Bill Clinton on two counts, for lying under oath and obstructing justice, in the investigation into his sexual affair with White House intern Monica Lewinsky. The vote was highly partisan, with only five Democrats voting for impeachment on each charge. In the Senate, where a two-thirds majority was needed to convict the president, only forty-five Senators voted to convict on the first count of lying and fifty voted to convict on the second charge of obstructing justice. As in the House, the vote for impeachment was highly partisan with all Democrats and only five Republicans supporting the president's ultimate acquittal.

The impeachment power is a considerable one; its very existence in the hands of Congress is a highly effective safeguard against the executive tyranny so greatly feared by the framers of the Constitution.

Congress and Democracy

- How do the institutional featues of Congress affect meaningful representation?
- What can Congress and citizens do to bring Congress closer to the American people?

Much of this chapter has described the major institutional components of Congress and has shown how they work as Congress makes policy. But what do these institutional features mean for how Congress represents the American public? If the chief complaint of many Americans is that Congress is out of touch with ordinary people, what can Congress do—and what can citizens do—to bring Congress closer to the people?

As we noted at the beginning of this chapter, Congress instituted a number of reforms in the 1970s to make itself looser and more accessible. These reforms sought to respond to public views that Congress had become a stodgy institution ruled by a powerful elite that made decisions in private. We have seen that these reforms increased the number of subcommittees, prohibited

AMERICAN DEMOCRACY IN COMPARATIVE PERSPECTIVE

Legislative "Bicameralism"

Legislative bodies among electoral democracies are of two basic types: bicameral (consisting of two separately elected chambers of representatives) and unicameral (one chamber of representatives). Approximately one in three countries in the world have, like the United States, bicameral legislatures; two of three prefer unicameral legislatures. Bicameral legislatures are most common in large countries—especially among the advanced industrial electoral democracies of Europe, North America, and Asia—where political interests among the public are exposed to degrees of sharp regional diversity.

Americans may be excused for assuming that the legislative process ought to be a tussle between two powerful and roughly equally balanced chambers of representatives. Each chamber—the Senate and the House—has various checks and balances on the other, both can veto the other chamber, both must ordinarily come to agreement and iron out their differences before legislation can become law, and both actively serve to shape the national political agenda through their legislative activities. However, this is not the case among most bicameral legislatures within the family of advanced industrial electoral democracies. Indeed, according to the classification system devised by Arend Lijphart, only three other countries within the group of democracies have "strong" national bicameral legislatures where both chambers have such power. These are Germany, Switzerland, and Australia.

What distinguishes the legislative process in these four democracies from the process in other countries within the family of advanced industrial democracies that practice bicameralism? First, strong bicameral legislatures are characterized by *political symmetry* between the two chambers of the national legislature. Symmetry implies that both chambers enjoy roughly equal constitutional powers over legislative issues, including the power to formally veto and check the power of the other chamber, and importantly, symmetrical balance assumes that both chambers have a claim to legitimate electoral support. Namely, both the upper and lower chambers are directly elected by the public. All lower chambers in the national legislatures among advanced industrial democracies are directly elected, through a variety of means. However, such is not the case for most upper chambers among this set of democracies. Many of the upper chambers have portions, or sometimes entire bodies of representatives, that are appointed by the formal sovereign to sit within the chamber, thus bypassing the electoral contest. Others are indirectly elected by special electoral bodies, which may be held accountable by the electorate, but without having their decisions sanctioned by the electorate.

The second feature of strong bicameral legislatures is the *congruence* between the two chambers. Congruence refers to the manner of selecting the membership to the upper and lower chambers in a bicameral system. Congruence is present when the two chambers are selected by electoral formulas that are basically similar and that do not allow any degree of overrepresentation among their constituent parts. For instance, the United States overrepresents small states in the U.S. Senate: Rhode Island (with roughly one million people) receives as many senators as California (with roughly twenty-nine million people). When the number of representatives of a specified constituency does not vary by population, as in the case of the U.S. Senate, overrepresentation of the smallest states is maximized. However, when representation varies by population, the upper chamber achieves no such overrepresentation. This is the case, for instance, in Belgium. Overrepresentation ensures that the constituency base for the upper chamber of the national legislature differs from the lower chamber. As such, it allows the upper chamber to exercise distinctive power vis-à-vis the lower chamber of the national legislature, which accordingly enhances the degree of bicameralism within the national legislative system. When congruence is low (when there are different methods of selection or electoral algorithms for the respective chambers) and symmetry is high, the legislative process within a country is strongly bicameral. When congruence is high (similar methods and rules of selection/election) and symmetry is low (when the lower chambers dominates the legislative process) the degree of bicameralism is very weak.

SOURCE: Arend Lijphart, *Patterns of Democracy: Government Forms and Performance in Thirty-Six Countries* (New Haven: Yale University Press, 1999).

most secret hearings, and increased the staff support for Congress. These reforms spread power more evenly throughout the institution and opened new avenues for the public to contact and influence Congress.

But the opening of Congress seemed only to spark more discontent. In fact the congressional reforms enacted in the 1970s actually made Congress less effective and, ironically, more permeable to special interests. The fragmentation of power in Congress has made it harder for members to reach decisions. "Turf battles"—struggles over who should take charge of what—often take more congressional energy than deliberations over policy. The decentralization of power in Congress has made each member more of an independent operator. Members are now less willing to compromise and more eager to take positions that benefit them individually, even if they undermine possibilities for enacting policy. These circumstances have created a Congress that sometimes seems to spend endless hours in increasingly negative debates that do not produce results. The public, therefore, has come to view Congress as a group of privileged elites concerned only about their own prerogatives. The word "gridlock" seems to sum up the state of congressional decision making.

Ironically, the measures that sought to ensure more public access to Congress have increased the access of interest groups. Open committee meetings have made it possible for sophisticated interest groups to monitor and influence every aspect of developing legislation. The narrow perspective put forth by an interest group makes it difficult for members of Congress to keep their eyes on the big picture of what it wants to achieve. Hundreds of amendments can undermine the overall thrust of legislation. Open meetings also deprive members of Congress of the political "cover" often necessary to make compromises. Worried that particular actions could be used against them in a future election, members of Congress have become very risk-averse. In this sense, too much accountability can paralyze the institution.

The very strong role of the Republican congressional leadership elected in 1995 only temporarily quieted complaints about congressional gridlock. Doubts about congressional effectiveness and representativeness remain. The reforms of the 1970s, intended to distribute power more equally inside Congress in order to provide more equal representation to all constituents, instead made it more difficult for members to build coalitions and for legislators to become experts in particular policy areas. The unanticipated, negative consequences of these reforms have highlighted the trade-off between representation and effectiveness in Congress.[43] Americans are becoming increasingly aware that greater individual access to Congress and more symbolic representation do not add up to more power. The results have increased public cynicism and apathy. Rebuilding public faith in Congress may require yet another round of institutional reform, as well as efforts to organize and mobilize broad social interests to achieve meaningful representation.

But what does "meaningful representation" entail? A member of Congress can interpret his job as representative in two different ways: as a delegate or as a trustee. As a **delegate,** a member of Congress acts on the express preferences of his constituents; as a **trustee,** the member is more loosely tied to constituents and makes the decisions he thinks best. The delegate role appears to be the most democratic because it forces the representative to heed the desires of his constituents. But this requires the representative to be in constant touch with constituents; it also requires constituents to follow each policy issue very

delegate
the role of a representative who votes according to the preferences of his or her constituency

trustee
the role of a representative who votes based on what he or she thinks is best for his or her constituency

closely. The problem with this form of representation is that most people do not follow every issue so carefully; instead they focus only on extremely important issues or issues of particular interest to them. Many people are too busy to get the information necessary to make informed judgments even on issues they care about. Thus, adhering to the delegate form of representation risks that the voices of only a few active and informed constituents get heard. Although it seems more democratic at first glance, the delegate form of representation may actually open Congress up even more to the influence of the voices of special interests.

If a congressional member acts as a trustee, on the other hand, there is a danger that she will not pay sufficient attention to the wishes of constituents. In this scenario, the only way the public can exercise influence is by voting every two years for representatives or every six years for senators. Yet, most members of Congress take this electoral check very seriously. They try to anticipate the wishes of their constituents even when they don't know exactly what those interests are, because they know that unpopular decisions can be used against them in the coming election.

The public understands the trade-offs entailed in these different forms of representation and is, in fact, divided on how members of Congress should represent it. In a recent poll 69 percent of respondents agreed that when a congressional representative votes, the views of the district should be the most important; only 25 percent believed that the representative's own principles and judgment should prevail. Yet the public also recognizes that representatives are often better informed about issues than the public. On a different survey, 65 percent of respondents agreed that in making a decision members of Congress should ask themselves how the majority of the public would think if they were well informed on all sides of the issue; only 29 percent said the representative should be guided instead by what the majority actually thinks.[44]

What the public dislikes most about Congress stems from suspicions that Congress acts as neither a trustee nor a delegate of the broad public interest, but instead is swayed by narrow special interests with lots of money.[45] Indeed, there is plenty of reason for the public to worry about the power of such groups: lobbying groups have continually adjusted their tactics to increase their ability to influence Congress. As reporter Jeffrey H. Birnbaum notes, lobbyists no longer fit the old caricature of "fat, cigar-smoking men who [shoved] hundred-dollar bills into the pockets of lawmakers."[46] Their tactics have grown much more sophisticated. Interest groups have used "Astroturf" lobbying to simulate a surge of grassroots interest on the part of constituents. More recently, as Congress has come to discount such influence as not really representing its constituents, lobbyists have changed tactics: they now concentrate on "grasstops" organizing, in which they mobilize important friends or associates of the representative or senator to present information favorable to the interest group's perspective. This new strategy is more subtle and may be more effective because it relies on a previous relationship of trust.

Moreover, many of the new technologies that make Congress more open have been used most effectively by special-interest groups. One professional consulting organization has created a subsidiary called NetRoots, which creates Web sites for lobbying campaigns, helping interest groups mimic grassroots influence through the Internet. A Web site for companies that oppose President Clinton's stands on global warming, for example, provides different,

Perspectives on Politics

INTEREST-GROUP INFLUENCE IN CONGRESS

Responses of Americans to the statement, "Congress is too heavily influenced by interest groups when making decisions."

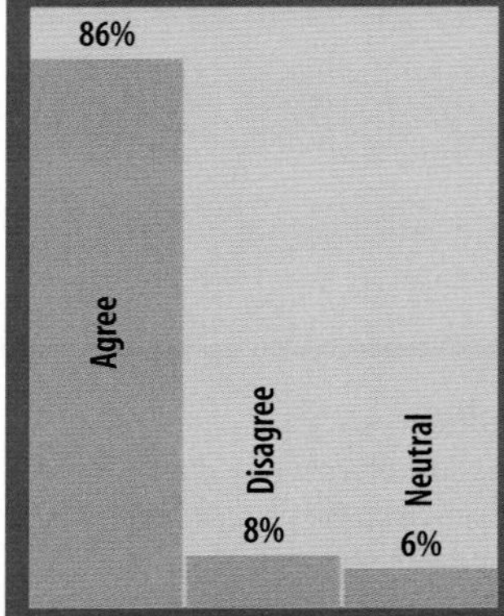

SOURCE: John R. Hibbing and Elizabeth Theiss-Morse, *Congress as Public Enemy: Public Attitudes toward American Political Institutions* (New York: Cambridge University Press, 1995), p. 64.

predrafted e-mails that sound as though they were written by senior citizens, small businesses, or other concerned individuals. These letters "can be launched directly to congressional representatives with the click of a mouse."[47]

The Citizen's Role

Are ordinary citizens powerless in the face of such activity by special-interest groups? The changing tactics of interest-group politics suggest that citizens, when they are organized and active, can greatly influence representatives. After all, what the most sophisticated interest groups are doing today is trying to convince members of Congress that there is genuine widespread grassroots support for their cause. This reflects the belief—rooted in long experience—that what really sways representatives most is evidence that their constituents care about particular issues. To influence all of Congress, it is particularly important to build grassroots organization that is geographically broad. If members of Congress from many parts of the country are getting the same message from their constituents, there is a greater chance of successfully influencing policy.

The experience of some groups that have organized such broad-based grassroots activity indicates that ordinary citizens can affect what Congress does. In recent years, significant grassroots activism has emerged to influence government spending for research on diseases. The striking success of AIDS activists in dramatically increasing funding for AIDS research has inspired other groups to try similar strategies. One example is the National Breast Cancer Coalition, which represents 350 separate organizations around the country. Its aim has been to increase expenditures for federally sponsored research on breast cancer. When the coalition formed in 1991, the federal government spent $90 million a year on breast cancer research; by 1997 that amount had increased to $509 million.[48] Building on its grassroots strength and borrowing tactics from highly successful AIDS activists, the coalition sent six hundred thousand letters to Congress and to the White House in its first year alone. Initially told that the National Cancer Institute's priorities could not be changed so easily, they turned to the Defense Department, which had already spent some funds for breast cancer research. Today, the Defense Department is the second largest funder of breast cancer research, and citizens can monitor and affect its agenda through an independent panel overseeing the program. Both the increased expenditures and the ongoing public influence over the research agenda were a direct result of the grassroots activity of these local groups organized into a national coalition.

Organizing such grassroots groups takes time, expertise, and some resources. But the example of such groups as the Breast Cancer Coalition and AIDS activists indicate that, when organized, ordinary citizens can be effective. It is important for individuals who feel that Congress is out of touch to recognize that the path of influence may require considerable effort, but that it is available. In addition, ordinary citizens who may not want to participate so actively need to remember that they can influence their congressional representatives indirectly by voting. One of the first breaks in the unity of congressional Republicans in 1995 came from a moderate Republican from New York who knew that the voters in her district would not support the loosening of environmental regulations proposed by the Republican leadership. Her decision to break with her Republican colleagues indicates the power of the electoral threat in making representatives attentive to the views of their constituents.

GET INVOLVED: Making Contact with Congress

The U.S. Congress can seem like a complex, distant institution because it has so many members, so many committees and subcommittees, so many hearings, investigations, and debates, and so much of this activity takes place in what is for most Americans the nation's faraway capital. One way for you to make Congress more approachable and accessible is to make contact with its nearest embodiment, your congressional representative's local field office.

All U.S. senators and representatives have offices in Washington, D.C. But they also have one or more local field offices in their home districts. These field offices are generally run by deputies who have the job of keeping their bosses visible among voters and donors as well as keeping them informed about local events, issues, and electoral concerns. While members of Congress do not spend much time in their field offices when Congress is in session, they regularly return to them for special occasions and during congressional recesses.

Making contact with a member's local field office is fairly simple. Most telephone directories have a section near the beginning that lists government offices. Your local directory is likely to name your U.S. senators and representative, as well as provide addresses and phone numbers for their nearest field offices. Alternatively, call your local city hall and request contact information for your representatives' field offices.

Once you have the telephone number, call the field office directly and ask to speak with the appropriate person regarding internships, volunteer opportunities, and part-time positions. Try to make a good impression over the telephone. Speak clearly. State your point briefly and precisely. Be prepared to answer questions about your background, education, community service experience, interests, and goals. If all goes well, you may be asked to come in for an interview.

For the interview, dress professionally, bring a résumé that covers your education, extracurricular activities, and community service experiences, and be on time. Furthermore, research your member of Congress. What are his or her positions on key issues? Do you agree with them? There is a good chance that you will be asked a question such as, "What is it about Congressperson X that motivates you to want to work for him?" Prepare an answer for that type of question.

If you are offered an entry-level position in the field office, the kind of work that you will do is likely to depend on what the office needs at any one moment and on how much initiative you are willing to show over time. The most common type of field office job is administrative aide. Field offices virtu-

Perspectives on Politics

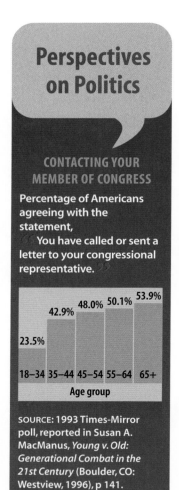

CONTACTING YOUR MEMBER OF CONGRESS

Percentage of Americans agreeing with the statement, "You have called or sent a letter to your congressional representative."

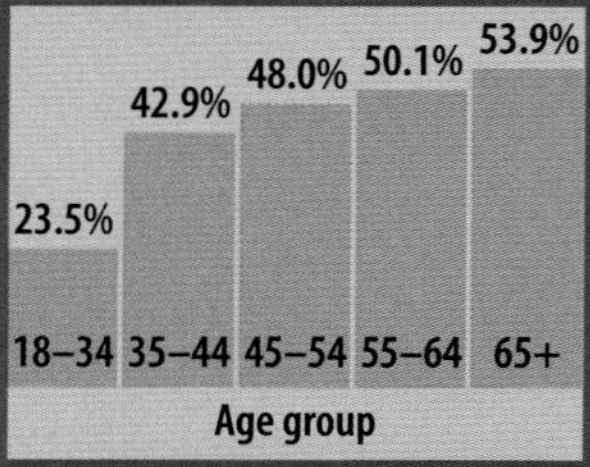

SOURCE: 1993 Times-Mirror poll, reported in Susan A. MacManus, *Young v. Old: Generational Combat in the 21st Century* (Boulder, CO: Westview, 1996), p 141.

ally always need energetic people who are willing to respond to innumerable constituent requests (and complaints), call constituents about key issues, help to organize local appearances and events, and work on the member's next election campaign.

Field offices also need people to engage in mundane tasks such as copying documents, sorting mail, and routing phone calls. This is not very exciting work, but keep three things in mind. One is that even "busy work" contributes to the overall effort of your representative to serve her constituents. Second, spending time in the field office will expose you to key issues and to Congress–constituent relations. In time, you are likely to become acquainted with your member of Congress and other notable people who stop by the office. Third, even aides who do busy work can develop reputations for being bright, enthusiastic, committed, and responsible. Such a reputation is an important asset. It positions you to take on more challenging work when new opportunities arise. It also gives you credibility if you wish to initiate projects.

There should be ample opportunity for you to suggest projects that will benefit your representative and your community. You might offer to organize an event at your college. You might arrange to have him speak in one of your classes. Perhaps you can become a liaison between your field office and the campus chapter of your representative's political party. Maybe you could promote an event designed to attract high school and college students from different parts of the region. If you are willing to show initiative, you will often be rewarded with potentially challenging ways to contribute as well as with your coworkers' and boss's gratitude.

Finally, if you can swing it, imagine how much fun it would be to take a trip to Washington, D.C., as in "insider." You might visit your member of Congress's Capitol Hill office, meet folks you've probably spoken with on the phone but never seen in person, get tickets to attend sessions of the U.S. Senate or House of Representatives, and maybe even finagle your way into a D.C. reception as a member of your congressperson's staff.

Summary

The U.S. Congress plays a vital role in American democracy. It is both the key national representative body and the focal point for decision making in Washington, D.C. Throughout American history, Congress has sought to combine representation and power as it made policy. In recent years, however, many Americans have become disillusioned with the ability of Congress to represent fairly and to exercise power responsibly.

Both sociological and agency representation play a role in the relationship between members of Congress and their constituencies. However, Congress is not fully representative because it is not a sociological microcosm of the United States. Members of Congress do seek to act as agents for their constituents by representing the views and interests of those constituents in the governmental process.

The activities of members of Congress are strongly influenced by electoral considerations. Who gets elected to Congress is influenced by who runs for office, the power of incumbency, and the way congressional districts are drawn. In order to assist their chances of re-election, members of Congress provide services and patronage to their constituents.

In order to make policy, Congress depends on a complex internal organization. Six basic dimensions of Congress affect the legislative process: (1) the parties, (2) the committees, (3) the staff, (4) the caucuses, (5) the rules, and (6) the presidency.

Since the Constitution provides only for a presiding officer in each house, some method had to be devised for conducting business. Parties quickly assumed the responsibility for this. In the House, the majority party elects a leader every two years. This individual becomes Speaker. In addition, a majority leader and a minority leader (from the minority party) and party whips are elected. Each party has a committee whose job it is to make committee assignments. Party structure in the Senate is similar, except that the vice president of the United States is the Senate president.

The committee system surpasses the party system in its importance in Congress. In the early nineteenth century, standing committees became a fundamental aspect of Congress. They have, for the most part, evolved to correspond to executive branch departments or programs and thus reflect and maintain the separation of powers.

Congress also establishes rules of procedure to guide policy making. The Senate has a tradition of unlimited debate, on which the various cloture rules it has passed have had little effect. Filibusters still occur. The rules of the House, on the other hand, restrict talk and support committees; deliberation is recognized as committee business. The House Rules Committee has the power to control debate and floor amendments. The rules prescribe the formal procedure through which bills become law. Generally, the parties control scheduling and agenda, but the committees determine action on the floor. Committees, seniority, and rules all limit the ability of members to represent their constituents. Yet, these factors enable Congress to maintain its role as a major participant in government.

Many different factors affect how Congress ultimately decides on legislation. Among the most important influences are constituency preferences, interest group pressures, and party discipline. Typically party discipline is stronger in the House than in the Senate. Parties have several means of maintaining discipline: (1) favorable committee assignments create obligations; (2) floor time in the debate on one bill can be allocated in exchange for a specific vote on another; (3) the whip system allows party leaders to assess support for a bill and convey their wishes to members; (4) party leaders can help members create large logrolling coalitions; and (5) the president can champion certain pieces of legislation and thereby muster support along party lines. In most cases, party leaders accept constituency obligations as a valid reason for voting against the party position.

In addition to the power to make law, Congress possesses other formidable powers in its relationship with the executive branch. Among these are oversight, advice and consent on treaties and appointments, and the power to impeach executive officials. In spite of its array of powers, Congress is often accused of being ineffective and out of touch with the American people. At the heart of these criticisms lies the debate over whether members of Congress should act more as delegates or as trustees. An even more important concern facing Congress is whether it has become beholden to special interests and has, in effect, shut ordinary citizens out of the political process.

FOR FURTHER READING

Burrell, Barbara C., *A Woman's Place Is in the House: Campaigning for Congress in the Feminist Era.* Ann Arbor: University of Michigan Press, 1994.

Cook, Elizabeth Adell, Sue Thomas, and Clyde Wilcox, eds. *The Year of the Woman: Myth and Reality.* Boulder, CO: Westview, 1994.

Davidson, Roger H., ed. *The Postreform Congress.* New York: St. Martin's, 1991.

Dodd, Lawrence, and Bruce I. Oppenheimer, eds. *Congress Reconsidered.* 5th ed. Washington, DC: Congressional Quarterly Press, 1993.

Fenno, Richard F. *Congressmen in Committees.* Boston: Little, Brown, 1973.

Fenno, Richard F. *Homestyle: House Members in Their Districts.* Boston: Little, Brown, 1978.

Fiorina, Morris. *Congress: Keystone of the Washington Establishment.* 2nd ed. New Haven, CT: Yale University Press, 1989.

Fowler, Linda, and Robert McClure. *Political Ambition: Who Decides to Run for Congress?* New Haven, CT: Yale University Press, 1989.

Light, Paul. *Forging Legislation.* New York: Norton, 1991.

Mayhew, David R. *Congress: The Electoral Connection.* New Haven, CT: Yale University Press, 1974.

Sinclair, Barbara. *The Transformation of the U.S. Senate.* Baltimore: Johns Hopkins University Press, 1989.

Smith, Steven S., and Christopher Deering. *Committees in Congress.* 2nd ed. Washington, DC: Congressional Quarterly Press, 1990.

Thomas, Sue. *How Women Legislate.* New York: Oxford University Press, 1994.

STUDY OUTLINE

Congress: Representing the American People

1. The House and Senate play different roles in the legislative process. The Senate is more deliberative, whereas the House is characterized by greater centralization and organization.
2. House members are more attuned to localized narrow interests in society, whereas senators are more able than House members to represent statewide or national interests.
3. In recent years, the House has exhibited more partisanship and ideological division than the Senate.
4. Congress is not fully representative because it is not a sociological microcosm of American society.
5. Members of Congress frequently communicate with constituents and devote a great deal of staff time to constituency service.
6. Electoral motivations have a strong impact on both sociological and agency representation in Congress.
7. Incumbency affords members of Congress resources such as constituency service and mailing to help secure re-election.
8. In recent years, turnover rates in Congress have increased, although this is due more to incumbent retirement than to the defeat of incumbents in elections.
9. Members of Congress can supply benefits to constituents by passing pork-barrel legislation. Pork-barrel votes are exchanged by members of Congress for votes on other issues.

The Organization of Congress

1. At the beginning of each Congress, Democrats and Republicans gather to select their leaders. The leader of the majority party in the House of Representatives is elected Speaker of the House by a strict party-line vote.
2. In the Senate, the president pro tempore serves as the presiding officer, although the majority and minority leaders control the calendar and agenda of the Senate.
3. The committee system provides Congress with a second organizational structure that is more a division of labor than the party-based hierarchies of power.
4. With specific jurisdiction over certain policy areas and the task of processing proposals of legislation into bills for floor consideration, standing committees are the most important arenas of congressional policy making.
5. Power within committees is based on seniority, although the seniority principle is not absolute.
6. In the 1970s, reforms fragmented power in Congress—the committee system, specifically—by increasing both

the number of subcommittees and the autonomy of subcommittee chairpersons.

7. Each member of Congress has a personal staff that deals with constituency requests and, increasingly, with the details of legislative and administrative oversight.
8. Groups of senators or representatives who share certain opinions, interests, or social characteristics form informal organizations called caucuses.

Rules of Lawmaking: How a Bill Becomes a Law

1. Committee deliberation is necessary before floor action on any bill.
2. Many bills receive little or no committee or subcommittee action; they are allowed to "die in committee."
3. Bills reported out of committee in the House must go through the House Rules Committee before they can be debated on the floor. The Rules Committee allots the time for floor debate on a bill and the conditions under which a bill may (or may not) be amended.
4. In the Senate, rules of debate are much less rigid. In fact, senators may delay Senate action on legislation by refusing to yield the floor; this is known as a filibuster.
5. Conference committees are often required to reconcile House and Senate versions of bills that began with similar provisions but emerged with significant differences.
6. After being adopted by the House and the Senate, a bill is sent to the president, who may choose to sign the bill or veto it. Congress can override a president's veto by a two-thirds vote in both the House and the Senate.

How Congress Decides

1. Creating a legislative agenda, drawing up a list of possible measures, and deciding among them is a complex process in which a variety of influences from inside and outside government play important roles.
2. Interest groups can influence congressional decision making by mobilizing followers in congressional districts, setting the agenda, or writing legislative language.
3. Party discipline is still an important factor in congressional voting, despite its decline throughout the twentieth century.
4. Party unity is typically greater in the House than in the Senate. Party unity on roll-call votes has increased in recent sessions of Congress.
5. Party unity is a result of a combination of the ideology and background of individual members and the resources party leaders have at their disposal.
6. The influence of the presidency is probably the most important of all the resources that maintain party discipline in Congress.

Beyond Legislation: Other Congressional Powers

1. Congress has increasingly relied on legislative oversight of administrators.
2. The Senate also has the power of approving or rejecting presidential treaties and appointments.
3. Congress has the power to impeach executive officials.

Congress and Democracy

1. Congressional reforms of the 1970s fragmented power in Congress and made it more open to special interests.
2. What the public dislikes most about Congress stems from suspicions that Congress does not act as a trustee or as a delegate of any broad interest but that it is swayed by narrow special interests with money.

PRACTICE QUIZ

1. Members of Congress can work as agents of their constituents by
   a) providing direct patronage.
   b) taking part in a party vote.
   c) joining a caucus.
   d) supporting term limits.
2. Why has public approval of Congress as an institution declined since the 1970s?
   a) Constituents don't like their own representatives in Congress.
   b) Congress has become increasingly inaccessible to the public since the 1970s.
   c) Citizens can now see members of Congress on television every night.
   d) Congress has increasingly opened itself up to the control of special interests.
3. Because they have larger and more heterogeneous constituencies, senators
   a) are more attuned to the needs of localized interest groups.
   b) care more about re-election than House members.
   c) can better represent the national interest.
   d) face less competition in elections than House members.
4. Sociological representation is important in understanding the U.S. Congress because
   a) members often vote based on their religion.
   b) Congress is a microcosm of American society.

c) the symbolic composition of Congress is important for the political stability of the United States.
d) there is a distinct "congressional sociology."

5. What type of representation is described when constituents have the power to hire and fire their representative?
   a) agency representation
   b) sociological representation
   c) democratic representation
   d) trustee representation

6. Incumbency is an important factor in deciding who is elected to Congress because
   a) incumbents have tools they can use to help ensure re-election.
   b) potentially strong challengers may be dissuaded from running because of the strength of the incumbent.
   c) Both a and b are true.
   d) Neither a nor b is true.

7. Some have argued that the creation of minority congressional districts has
   a) lessened the sociological representation of minorities in Congress.
   b) made it more difficult for minorities to win substantive policy goals.
   c) been a result of the media's impact on state legislative politics.
   d) lessened the problem of "pork barrel" politics.

8. Which of the following is *not* an important influence on how members of Congress vote on legislation?
   a) the media
   b) constituency
   c) interest groups
   d) party leaders

9. Which of the following types of committees does *not* include members of both the House and the Senate?
   a) standing committee
   b) joint committee
   c) conference committee
   d) No committees include both House members and senators.

10. An agreement between members of Congress to trade support for each other's bill is known as
    a) oversight.
    b) filibuster.
    c) logrolling
    d) patronage.

CRITICAL THINKING QUESTIONS

1. Two of Congress's chief responsibilities are representation and lawmaking. Describe the ways in which these two responsibilities might conflict with one another. How do these responsibilities support and reinforce one another? What would Congress be like if its sole function were representative? What would it be like if it were solely legislative?

2. Describe the process by which a bill becomes a law. At the various stages of this process, assess who—both within government and outside of government—makes and influences decisions. Are there stages at which the process is more democratic than it is at others? Are there stages at which the people have less influence? In your judgment, is the overall process democratic?

KEY TERMS

agency representation (p. 485)
appropriations (p. 517)
bicameral (p. 483)
bill (p. 503)
caucus (congressional) (p. 502)
caucus (political) (p. 494)
closed rule (p. 505)
cloture (p. 505)
conference (p. 494)
conference committee (p. 498)
constituency (p. 483)
delegate (p. 521)
executive agreement (p. 518)
filibuster (p. 505)
impeachment (p. 518)
incumbency (p. 489)
joint committee (p. 498)
logrolling (p. 512)
majority leader (p. 494)
minority leader (p. 494)
open rule (p. 505)
oversight (p. 517)
party vote (p. 510)
patronage (p. 492)
pocket veto (p. 507)
political action committee (PAC) (p. 488)
pork barrel (p. 492)
private bill (p. 492)
redistricting (p. 490)
roll-call vote (p. 510)
select committee (p. 498)
seniority (p. 498)
sociological representation (p. 484)
Speaker of the House (p. 494)
staff agency (p. 500)
standing committee (p. 497)
term limits (p. 490)
trustee (p. 521)
veto (p. 507)
whip system (p. 512)

14 The Presidency

★ **The Constitutional Basis of the Presidency**

What were the conflicting views over presidential power of the framers of the Constitution?

What factors led to the growth of a more powerful presidency?

★ **The Constitutional Powers of the Presidency**

What powers does the Constitution provide to the president as head of state? Have presidents used these powers to make the presidency too powerful or even imperial?

What powers does the Constitution provide to the president as head of government?

★ **Institutional Resources of Presidential Power**

What institutional resources does the president use to manage the executive branch?

Which of these resources have presidents increasingly relied on?

★ **Political Resources of Presidential Power**

What political resources can the president draw on in exercising the powers of the presidency? Which of these resources is a potential liability? Why?

★ **The Presidency and Democracy**

How did the presidency develop into a truly democratic institution?

How did the development of a mass presidential constituency contribute to the rise of presidential government?

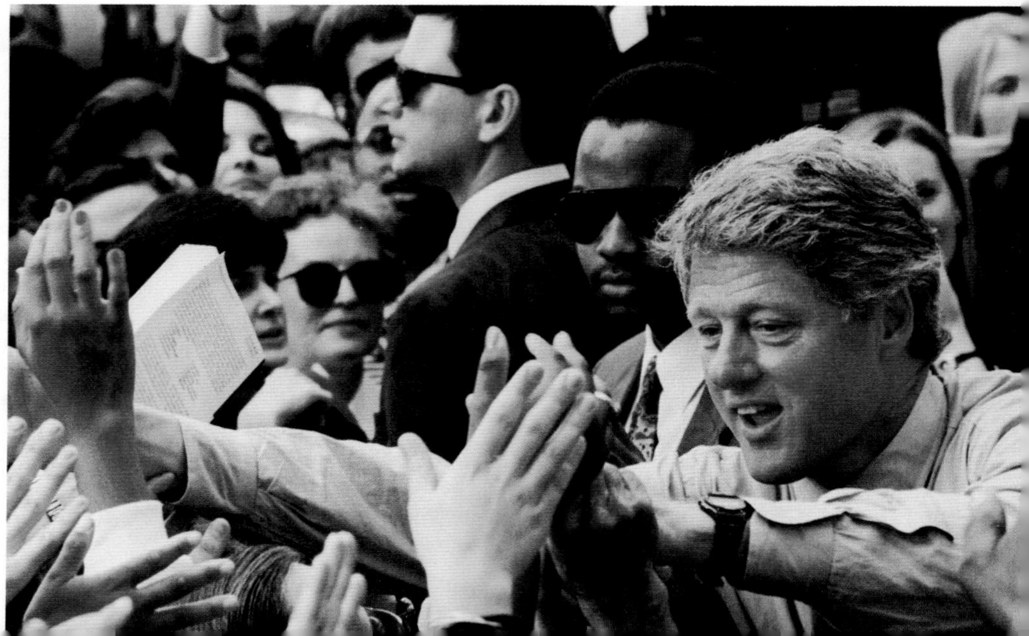

STUDENTS AND POLITICS

IN late November 1999, the front pages of student newspapers all over America were carrying accounts of the "Battle in Seattle" over international trade negotiations as representatives of 135 nations were assembling in Seattle, Washington, for the opening of the World Trade Organization (WTO) meeting. It was an arrestingly unusual campus front-page story, this report on the ceremonial speeches preceding a formal gathering to discuss issues as dry as rules about lowering trade barriers, cutting or raising tariffs, eliminating trade sanctions, and fighting over embargoes against allegedly unhealthy meats or seeds. But to the surprise of almost everyone, several hundred students joined several thousand trade union members in the streets of Seattle, chained together around the convention hall to interfere with the opening ceremonies of the WTO meeting. As *The New York Times* put it, "Tuesday's street scene in Seattle—the chanting demonstrators, the tear gas, the National Guard—seemed a flashback to the 1960s."[1] Others chimed in to point out the irony of students in Nike sneakers protesting Nike's (and other corporations') low-wage and anti-environmental policies.

With teargas still lingering in the air and the lungs of a number of students, the WTO sessions began. But the effect of the demonstrations was not to be denied; the messages were indeed heard. Cutting through the denunciatory language of some of the WTO representatives—largely indignant about the need to postpone the opening ceremonies for twenty-four hours—was the voice of President Bill Clinton. The demonstrations had in fact altered his agenda. President Clinton had called the WTO meeting and had brought it to Seattle in order to advance the cause of free trade as a major, perhaps his most important, legacy. But in his opening address, his first words amounted to an appeal to the ministers of the 135 member countries to listen to the demonstrators. While denouncing those who had engaged in any violence, Clinton asserted, to the surprise and dismay of many in the audience, that "what they are telling us in the streets is that this is an issue we've been silent on, and we won't be silent anymore." He then proceeded to announce two initiatives to help the poorest nations, mostly African, whose people were most likely to be victimized by unconstrained globalization, including a proposal to eliminate all tariffs on goods exported by the poorest nations. But the details were few, mainly because the proposals had been hastily put together to display responsiveness to the demonstrations.[2]

In his penultimate address the following evening, President Clinton stressed mainly what most delegates had come to hear, that trade expansion was working and that every effort should be made to reduce all types of trade barriers. But he added that WTO processes nevertheless should be open not only to public exposure but to public participation and that some of the trade expansion rate would have to be sacrificed to pay heed to world worker rights and world environmental conditions. These were precisely the issues that had brought the students and the workers to Seattle, in a most unusual (for America) alliance.

A great deal of criticism was directed against President Clinton and all of his recent predecessors for being too responsive to public opinion polls. The Seattle experience reminds us that no president would be foolish enough to keep his eye on the polling data without keeping his ear to the ground. But the events in Seattle show that effective participation by citizens does not necessarily require a presence in Washington, D.C., a full-page ad in *The New York Times*, an organized interest group with trained lobbyists, or an hour on *Larry King Live*.

The good news is that the president is responsive to all forms of public opinion, including student demonstrations. The bad news is that the president is also vulnerable to all forms of public opinion. As we learned in the crisis over President Clinton's affair with Monica Lewinsky, Americans make a very fundamental distinction between the president and the presidency. President Clinton's personal approval ratings were low and continued to drop throughout the crisis. When asked if Clinton should be removed from office if he lied under oath about the affair, 55 percent of respondents said yes. When asked if he should be removed from office if he had encouraged Lewinsky to lie while under oath, 63 percent said yes. But when asked whether they approved or disapproved of the way President Clinton was handling his job, these approval ratings moved *upward* during the crisis, reaching a whopping 68 percent, the highest approval rating Clinton received in eight years in office.[3]

This vulnerability of the president to virtually all sources of public expression, coupled with the steadfast support of the institution, points to the dual nature of the presidency. Despite public disapproval of President Clinton's personal conduct, his power as occupant of that institution was not seriously impaired. The same can be said about Seattle. Despite the clamor in the streets, and despite President Clinton's vulnerability to it, and even despite his obvious and direct responsiveness to those demands, his role as president of the world's most powerful nation was felt among all the representatives at the WTO meeting. They, as well as virtually all Americans, looked to the president as the embodiment of the American polity, especially in foreign affairs. It is the office that wields the great power, not necessarily the person.

This duality does not mean that the institution of the presidency is more monarchy than democracy. Seattle, once again, is one small but telling indication that the American presidency is the most democratized executive power and the American president the most democratized leader in any known democracy in any epoch. The presidential selection process—from the announcement of candidacies, to the nomination of candidates, to election of one of them as president—is the most open, participatory, and democratic of all elective offices around the world. Access to the president by the media is more extensive in the United States than anywhere else in the world. And, as we have seen, Americans, from students to the elderly, have more direct access to the president than do citizens of any other democracy.

Of course, we cannot and should not sentimentalize Seattle, nor should we jump to dramatic conclusions about the political influence of each and every American citizen. Access to the president is not equal, as we saw during the

1996 presidential campaign when President Clinton sponsored White House "coffees" where, for a donation of ten thousand dollars or more to his campaign, one could meet with the president for a short time and express one's political concerns. Larger donors to Clinton's re-election campaign were also given the privilege of spending the night in the Lincoln Bedroom at the White House. These opportunities are not available to everyone. But given the proper forum, the average citizen can exercise some influence. The role of the citizen is to recognize one's capability and act on it when necessary.

Our task is to explain how the presidency gained so much power and why this power leaves the president so vulnerable to the popular will. Why did the presidency not only become stronger but also displace Congress as the center, in a new system that we call presidential government? Why did that strong presidency become the center of a new, mass popular democracy with a single, national constituency? And why, as the power of the presidency has increased, have popular expectations of and popular influences on presidential performance increased at an even faster rate?

- ***Our focus in the first three parts of this chapter is to explore the resources of presidential power, which we will divide into three categories: constitutional, institutional, and political.*** The Constitution provides an array of powers to the president as head of state and as head of government. Although we give these two categories separate treatment, the presidency can be understood only as a combination of the two.
- ***We turn next to the institutional resources that presidents use as tools of management.*** Without these resources, such as the Cabinet, presidents would be unable to use the powers provided by the Constitution.
- ***We will then examine the political resources of presidential power.*** Presidents rely on their party, interest groups, the media, and public opinion in order to build support for their programs and persuade Congress to cooperate. These resources offer great strength to the president but, as we will see, can also be a great liability.
- ***We conclude by assessing the presidency as an institution of democracy.*** The presidency has developed into a democratic institution with a mass constituency so great that we now have a "presidential government." We will explain how this development occurred.

The Constitutional Basis of the Presidency

- What were the conflicting views over presidential power of the framers of the Constitution?
- What factors led to the growth of a more powerful presidency?

THE FRAMERS' VIEW

The dual nature of the presidency has been the source of fundamental dispute since John Adams succeeded General Washington in 1797, and since scholars turned their attention to puzzling out the intent of the framers. The framers, wanting "energy in the executive," provided for a single-headed office. But with no explicit powers independent of Congress, the president is constitutionally little more than a chief clerk, whose main objective is to see that the laws, as enacted by Congress, are "faithfully executed." The president would have to provide that energy and leadership by asserting powers beyond the Constitution itself and inherent in the Office of Chief Executive.

expressed powers
specific powers granted to Congress under Article I, Section 8, of the Constitution

Article II of the Constitution, which establishes the presidency and defines a small number of **expressed powers** of the office, is the basis for the dual nature of the presidency. Although Article II has been called "the most loosely drawn chapter of the Constitution,"[4] the framers were neither indecisive nor confused. They held profoundly conflicting views of the executive branch, and Article II was probably the best compromise they could make. The formulation the framers agreed upon is magnificent in its ambiguity: "The executive Power shall be vested in a President of the United States of America" (Article II, Section 1, first sentence). The meaning of "executive power," however, is not defined except indirectly in the very last sentence of Section 3, which provides that the president "shall take Care that the Laws be faithfully executed."

delegated powers
constitutional powers that are assigned to one governmental agency but that are exercised by another agency with the express permission of the first

One very important conclusion can be drawn from these two provisions: The office of the president was to be primarily an office of **delegated powers.** Since, as we have already seen, all of the powers of the national government are defined as powers of Congress and are incorporated into Article I, Section 8, then the "executive power" of Article II, Section 3, must be understood to be defined as the power to execute faithfully the laws *as they are adopted by Congress*. This does not doom the presidency to weakness. Presumably, Congress can pass laws delegating almost any of its powers to the president. But presidents are not free to discover sources of executive power completely independent of the laws as passed by Congress. In 1890, the Supreme Court did hold that the president could be bold and expansive in the inferences drawn from the Constitution as to "the rights, duties and obligations" of the presidency, but the **inherent powers** of the president would have to be inferred from the Constitution, not from some independent or absolute idea of executive power.[5]

inherent powers
powers claimed by a president that are not expressed in the Constitution, but are inferred from it

CONGRESSIONAL DELEGATION OF POWER

The most important constitutional effect of Congress's actions during the New Deal was the enhancement of presidential power. Most major acts of Congress in this period involved significant exercises of control over the economy. But few programs specified the actual controls to be used. Instead, Congress authorized the president, or, in some cases, a new agency—to determine what the controls would be. Some of the new agencies were independent commissions responsible to Congress. But most of the new agencies and programs of the New Deal were placed in the executive branch directly under presidential authority.

Technically, this form of congressional act is called the "delegation of power." In theory, the delegation of power works as follows: (1) Congress recognizes a problem; (2) Congress acknowledges that it has neither the time nor the expertise to deal with the problem; and (3) Congress therefore sets the basic policies and then delegates to an agency the power to "fill in the details." But in practice, Congress was delegating not merely the power to "fill in the details," but actual and real policy-making powers, that is, real legislative powers, to the executive branch. During the 1930s, the growth of the national government through acts delegating legislative power tilted the American national structure away from a Congress-centered government toward a president-centered government.[6]

However, although it would be difficult to underestimate the importance of congressional delegation of power to the president as the major contributor to the rise of president-centered government, there is still another factor that is immense in its importance. This is the process of presidential selection that was first laid out in the Constitution but then elaborated upon by informal developments as well as formal changes of party rules and legislation. We turn to that phenomenon in the next section.

PRESIDENTIAL SELECTION

Immediately following the first sentence of Section 1, Article II of the constitution defines the manner in which the president is to be chosen. This is a very odd sequence, but it does say something about the struggle the delegates were having over how to provide great power of action or energy to the executive and at the same time to balance that power with limitations. The struggle was between those delegates who wanted the president to be selected by, and thus responsible to, Congress and those delegates who preferred that the president be elected directly by the people. Direct popular election would create a more independent and more powerful presidency. With the adoption of a scheme of indirect election through an electoral college in which the electors would be selected by the state legislatures (and close elections would be resolved in the House of Representatives), the framers hoped to achieve a "republican" solution: a strong president responsible to state and national legislators rather than directly to the electorate. This indirect method of electing the president probably did dampen the power of most presidents in the nineteenth century.

The presidency was strengthened somewhat in the 1830s with the introduction of the national convention system of nominating presidential candidates. Until then, presidential candidates had been nominated by their party's congressional delegates. This was the **caucus** system of nominating candidates, and it was derisively called "King Caucus" because any candidate for president had to be beholden to the party's leaders in Congress in order to get the party's nomination and the support of the party's congressional delegation in the presidential election. The national nominating convention arose outside Congress in order to provide some representation for a party's voters who lived in districts where they weren't numerous enough to elect a member of Congress. The political party in each state made its own provisions for selecting delegates to attend the presidential nominating convention, and in virtually all states the selection was dominated by the party leaders (called "bosses" by the opposition party). Only in recent decades have state laws intervened to regularize the selection process and to provide (in all but a few instances) for open election of delegates. The convention system quickly became the most popular method of nominating candidates for all elective offices and remained

caucus (political)
a normally closed meeting of a political or legislative group to select candidates, plan strategy, or make decisions regarding legislative matters

so until well into the twentieth century, when it succumbed to the criticism that it was a nondemocratic method dominated by a few leaders in a "smoke-filled room." But in the nineteenth century, it was seen as a victory for democracy against the congressional elite. And the national convention gave the presidency a base of power independent of Congress.

This additional independence did not immediately transform the presidency into the office we recognize today, but the national convention did begin to open the presidency to larger social forces and newly organized interests in society. In other words, it gave the presidency a mass popular base that would eventually support and demand increased presidential power. Improvements in telephone, telegraph, and other forms of mass communication allowed individuals to share their complaints and allowed national leaders—especially presidents and presidential candidates—to reach out directly to people to ally themselves with, and even sometimes to create, popular groups and forces. Eventually, though more slowly, the presidential selection process began to be further democratized, with the adoption of primary elections through which millions of ordinary citizens were given an opportunity to take part in the presidential nominating process by popular selection of convention delegates.

But despite political and social conditions favoring the enhancement of the presidency, the development of presidential government as we know it today did not mature until the middle of the twentieth century. For a long period, even as the national government began to grow, Congress was careful to keep tight reins on the president's power. The real turning point in the history of American national government came during the administration of Franklin Delano Roosevelt. Since FDR, the tug of war seems to have been won for the chief executive presidency, because after FDR, as we shall see, every president was strong whether he was committed to the strong presidency or not.

Even though the presidency is an office of delegated powers, for a century and a half after the Founding, many feared that the president's power could become dictatorial. This political cartoon criticized President Andrew Jackson's use of the veto power.

BORN TO COMMAND.
OF VETO MEMORY.
HAD I BEEN CONSULTED.
KING ANDREW THE FIRST.
F.9318 CARTOON BRANDING ANDREW JACKSON AS A DICTATOR.

The Constitutional Powers of the Presidency

- What powers does the Constitution provide to the president as head of state? Have presidents used these powers to make the presidency too powerful or even imperial?
- What powers does the Constitution provide to the president as head of government?

The heart of presidential power as defined by the Constitution is found in Article II, Sections 2 and 3, where the several clauses define the presidency in two dimensions: the president as head of state and the president as head of government. Although these will be given separate treatment here, the presidency can be understood only by the combination of the two.

THE PRESIDENT AS HEAD OF STATE: SOME IMPERIAL QUALITIES

The constitutional position of the president as head of state is defined by three constitutional provisions, which are the source of some of the most important powers on which presidents can draw. The areas can be classified as follows:

1. *Military.* Article II, Section 2, provides for the power as "Commander in Chief of the Army and Navy of the United States, and of the Militia of the several States, when called in to the actual Service of the United States."
2. *Judicial.* Article II, Section 2, also provides the power to "grant Reprieves and Pardons for Offences against the United States, except in Cases of Impeachment."
3. *Diplomatic.* Article II, Section 2, also provides the power "by and with the Advice and Consent of the Senate to make Treaties." Article II, Section 3, provides the power to "receive Ambassadors and other public Ministers."

Military First, the position of **commander in chief** makes the president the highest military authority in the United States, with control of the entire defense establishment. No American president, however, would dare put on a military uniform for a state function—not even a former general like Eisenhower—even though the president is the highest military officer in war and in peace. The president is also head of the secret intelligence network, which includes not only the Central Intelligence Agency (CIA) but also the National Security Council (NSC), the National Security Agency (NSA), the Federal Bureau of Investigation (FBI), and a host of less well known but very powerful international and domestic security agencies. But these impressive powers must be read in the context of Article I, wherein seven of the eighteen clauses of Section 8 provide particular military and foreign policy powers to Congress, including the power to declare wars for which presidents are responsible. Presidents have tried to evade this at their peril. In full awareness of the woe visited upon President Lyndon Johnson for evading and misleading Congress at the outset of the Vietnam War, President George Bush sought explicit congressional authorization for the Gulf War in January 1991.

commander in chief
the power of the president as commander of the national military and the state national guard units (when called into service)

Judicial The presidential power to grant reprieves, pardons, and amnesties involves the power of life and death over all individuals who may be a threat to the security of the United States. Presidents may use this power on behalf of a particular individual, as did Gerald Ford when he pardoned Richard Nixon in 1974 "for all offenses against the United States which he . . . has committed or may have committed." Or they may use it on a large scale, as did President Andrew Johnson in 1868, when he gave full amnesty to all southerners who had participated in the "Late Rebellion," and President Carter in 1977, when he declared an amnesty for all the draft evaders of the Vietnam War. This power of life and death over others helped elevate the president to the level of earlier conquerors and kings by establishing him as the person before whom supplicants might come to make their pleas for mercy.

Diplomatic The ultimate status of the president as head of state is the power to make treaties for the United States (with the advice and consent of the Senate). And when President Washington received Edmond Genêt ("Citizen Genêt") as the formal emissary of the revolutionary government of France in 1793 and had his cabinet officers and Congress back his decision, he established a greatly expanded interpretation of the power to "receive Ambassadors and other public Ministers," extending it to the power to "recognize" other countries. That power gives the president the almost unconditional authority to review the claims of any new ruling groups to determine if they indeed control the territory and population of their country, so that they can commit it to treaties and other agreements.

The Imperial Presidency? Have presidents used these three constitutional powers—military, judicial, and diplomatic—to make the presidency too powerful, indeed "imperial?"[7] Debate over the answer to this question is no better illustrated or dramatized than by the presidential practice of using executive agreements instead of treaties to establish relations with other countries.[8] An **executive agreement** is exactly like a treaty because it is a contract between two countries, but an executive agreement does not require a two-thirds vote of approval by the Senate. Ordinarily, executive agreements are used to carry out commitments already made in treaties, or to arrange for matters well below the level of policy. But when presidents have found it expedient to use an executive agreement in place of a treaty, Congress has gone along. This verges on an imperial power.

executive agreement
an agreement, made between the president and another country, that has the force of a treaty but does not require the Senate's "advice and consent"

Many recent presidents have even gone beyond formal executive agreements to engage in what amounts to unilateral action. They may seek formal congressional authorization, as in 1964 when President Lyndon Johnson convinced Congress to adopt the Gulf of Tonkin Resolution authorizing him to expand the American military presence in Vietnam. Johnson interpreted the resolution as a delegation of discretion to use any and all national resources according to his own judgment. Others may not even bother with the authorization but merely assume it, as President Nixon did when he claimed to need no congressional authorization to continue or to expand the Vietnam War.

War Powers Resolution
a resolution of Congress that the president can send troops into action abroad only by authorization of Congress, or if American troops are already under attack or serious threat

These presidential claims and actions led to a congressional reaction, however. In 1973, Congress passed the **War Powers Resolution** over President Nixon's veto. This resolution asserted that the president could send American

The Gulf of Tonkin resolution gave President Lyndon B. Johnson congressional authorization to expand the U.S. military presence in Vietnam; however, Johnson (shown here greeting American troops in Vietnam) interpreted the resolution as justification to involve any and all of the nation's resources in war.

troops into action abroad only in the event of a declaration of war or other statutory authorization by Congress, or if American troops were attacked or directly endangered. This was an obvious effort to revive the principle that the presidency is an office of delegated powers—that is, powers granted by Congress—and that there is no blanket prerogative.

Nevertheless, this resolution has not prevented presidents from using force when they have deemed it necessary. For example, although President Clinton appeared at first to be reluctant to take bold international initiatives, he did not hesitate to use direct action when events seemed to threaten his own position or his view of the national interest. Clinton's series of unilateral actions in Bosnia dramatically tested his independence from Congress. First, Clinton unilaterally approved the use of American planes to bomb Serbian strategic positions in the late summer of 1995 (which pressured the Serbs to participate in peace negotiations with Croats and Bosnian Muslims). Second, to make the peace negotiations succeed, Clinton unilaterally pledged the American military to monitor the implementation of the agreement, including committing twenty thousand U.S. troops to monitor the agreement on the ground. With U.S. forces already in Bosnia, all Congress could do was pass a resolution in December 1995, after a long debate, to authorize financial support for the troops but also to disapprove of Clinton's actions and to demand further reporting to Congress in the future.

THE DOMESTIC PRESIDENCY: THE PRESIDENT AS HEAD OF GOVERNMENT

The constitutional basis of the domestic presidency also has three parts. And here again, although real power grows out of the combination of the parts, the analysis is greatly aided by examining the parts separately:

1. *Executive.* The "executive power" is vested in the president by Article II, Section 1, to see that all the laws are faithfully executed (Section 3), and to appoint, remove, and supervise all executive officers and to appoint all federal judges (Section 2).
2. *Military.* This power is derived from Article IV, Section 4, which stipulates that the president has the power to protect every state "against Invasion; and . . . against domestic Violence."
3. *Legislative.* The president is given the power under various provisions to participate effectively and authoritatively in the legislative process.

Executive Power The most important basis of the president's power as chief executive is to be found in Article II, Section 3, which stipulates that the president must see that all the laws are faithfully executed, and Section 2, which provides that the president will appoint, remove, and supervise all executive officers, and appoint all federal judges. The power to appoint the principal executive officers and to require each of them to report to the president on subjects relating to the duties of their departments makes the president the true chief executive officer (CEO) of the nation. In this manner, the Constitution focuses executive power and legal responsibility upon the president. The famous sign on President Truman's desk, "The buck stops here," was not merely an assertion of Truman's personal sense of responsibility but was in fact recognition by him of the legal and constitutional responsibility of the president. The president is subject to some limitations, because the appointment of all such officers, including ambassadors, ministers, and federal judges, is subject to a majority approval by the Senate. But these appointments are at the discretion of the president, and the loyalty and the responsibility of each appointment are presumed to be directed toward the president.

Military Sources of Domestic Presidential Power Although Article IV, Section 4, provides that the "United States shall [protect] every State . . . against Invasion . . . and . . . domestic Violence," Congress has made this an explicit presidential power through statutes directing the president as commander in chief to discharge these obligations.[9] The Constitution restrains the president's use of domestic force by providing that a state legislature (or governor when the legislature is not in session) must request federal troops before the president can send them into the state to provide public order. Yet this proviso is not absolute. First, presidents are not obligated to deploy national troops merely because the state legislature or governor makes such a request. And more important, the president may deploy troops in a state or city without a specific request from the state legislature or governor if the president considers it necessary in order to maintain an essential national service during an emergency, in order to enforce a federal judicial order, or in order to protect federally guaranteed civil rights.

One historic example of the unilateral use of presidential emergency power to protect the states against domestic disorder, even when the states don't request it, was the decision by President Dwight Eisenhower in 1957 to send troops into Little Rock, Arkansas, literally against the wishes of the state of Arkansas, to enforce court orders to integrate Little Rock's Central High School. The governor of Arkansas, Orval Faubus, had actually posted the Arkansas National Guard at the entrance of Central High School to prevent

In 1957, Arkansas governor Orval Faubus ignored a federal court order and used the state's National Guard to prevent nine black students from attending Little Rock's Central High School. President Dwight Eisenhower was forced to send a thousand soldiers to protect the black students. The troops stayed for the entire school year.

the court-ordered admission of nine black students. After an effort to negotiate with Governor Faubus failed, President Eisenhower reluctantly sent a thousand paratroopers to Little Rock, who stood watch while the black students took their places in the all-white classrooms. This case makes quite clear that the president does not have to wait for a request by a state legislature or governor before acting as a domestic commander in chief.[10]

However, in most instances of domestic disorder—whether from human or from natural causes—presidents tend to exercise unilateral power by declaring a "state of emergency," thereby making available federal grants, insurance, and direct assistance. In 1992, in the aftermath of the devastating riots in Los Angeles and the hurricanes in Florida, American troops were very much in evidence, sent in by the president, but in the role more of Good Samaritans than of military police.

The President's Legislative Power The president plays a role not only in the administration of government but also in the legislative process. Two constitutional provisions are the primary sources of the president's power in the legislative arena. The first of these is the provision in Article II, Section 3, providing that the president "shall from time to time give to the Congress Information of the State of the Union, and recommend to their Consideration such Measures as he shall judge necessary and expedient." The second of the president's legislative powers is of course the veto power assigned by Article I, Section 7.[11]

Delivering a "State of the Union" address does not at first appear to be of any great import. It is a mere obligation on the part of the president to make recommendations for Congress's consideration. But as political and social conditions began to favor an increasingly prominent role for presidents, each president, especially since Franklin Delano Roosevelt, began to rely on this provision to become the primary initiator of proposals for legislative action in Congress and the principal source for public awareness of national issues, as well as the most important single individual participant in legislative decisions. Few today doubt that the president and the executive branch together are the primary source for many important congressional actions.[12]

The **veto** is the president's constitutional power to turn down acts of Congress (see Figure 14.1 on the next page). It alone makes the president the most important single legislative leader.[13] No bill vetoed by the president can become law unless both the House and Senate override the veto by a two-thirds vote. In the case of a **pocket veto,** Congress does not even have the option of overriding the veto, but must reintroduce the bill in the next session. A pocket veto can occur when the president is presented with a bill during the last ten days of a legislative session. Usually, if a president does not sign a bill within ten days, it automatically becomes law. But this is true only while Congress is in session. If a president chooses not to sign a bill presented within the last ten days that Congress is in session, then the ten-day limit does not expire until Congress is out of session, and instead of becoming law, the bill is vetoed. In 1996 a new power was added to the president's lineup—the **line-item veto**—giving the president power to strike specific spending items from appropriations bills passed by Congress, unless reenacted by a two-thirds vote of both House and Senate. In 1997, President Clinton used this power eleven times to strike eighty-two items from the federal budget. But in 1998 the Supreme

THE ROLES OF THE PRESIDENT

- Chief of State (president acting on behalf of all Americans)
- Commander in Chief (president in charge of military)
- Chief Jurist (president's judicial responsibilities)
- Chief Diplomat (president managing our relations with other nations)
- Chief Executive (president as "boss" of executive branch)
- Chief Legislator (president's legislative powers)
- Chief Politician (president's party leadership)

veto
the president's constitutional power to turn down acts of Congress. A presidential veto may be overridden by a two-thirds vote of each house of Congress

pocket veto
a presidential veto that is automatically triggered if the president does not act on a given piece of legislation passed during the final ten days of a legislative session

line-item veto
the power of the executive to veto specific provisions (lines) of a bill passed by the legislature

Figure 14.1 THE VETO PROCESS

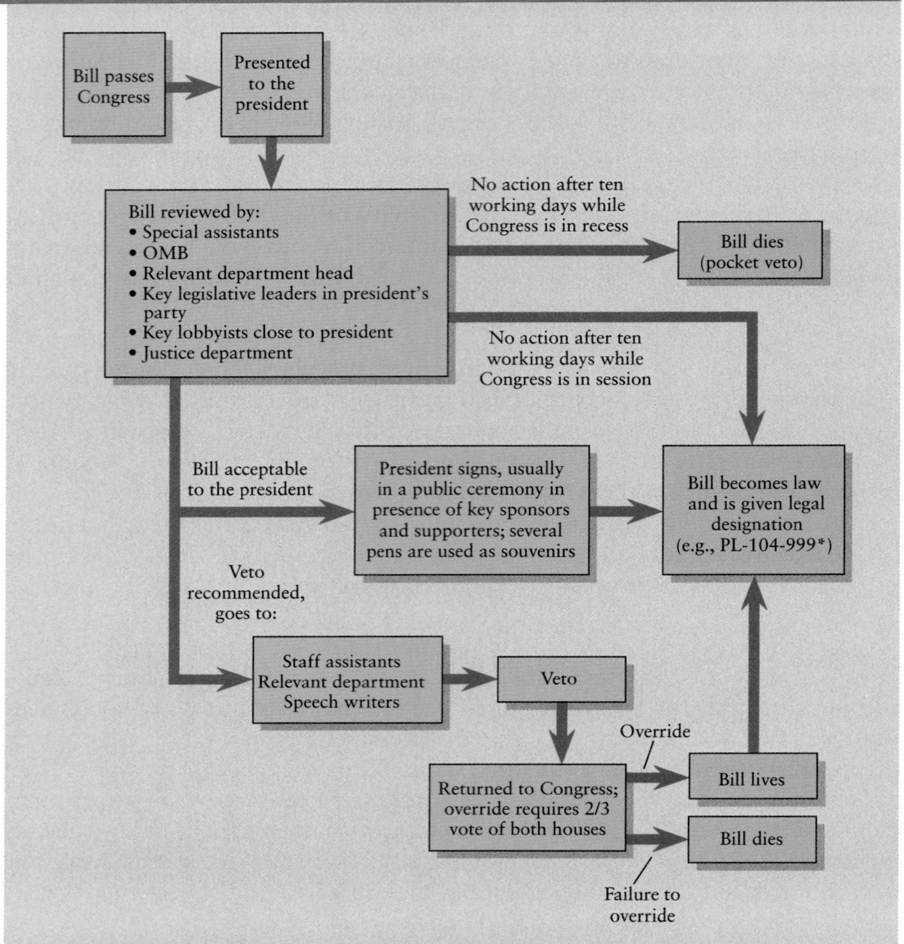

*PL = public law; 104 = number of Congress (104th was 1995–96); 999 = number of the law.

Court ruled that the Constitution does not authorize the line-item veto. Only a constitutional amendment would restore this power to the president.

Use of the veto varies according to the political situation that each president confronts. During Bill Clinton's first two years in office, when Democrats controlled both houses of Congress, he vetoed no bills. Following the congressional elections of 1994, however, Clinton confronted a Republican-controlled Congress with a definite agenda, and he began to use his veto power more vigorously.

legislative initiative
the president's inherent power to bring a legislative agenda before Congress

Clinton also recaptured some of his leadership by finding the path of legislative initiative that he had lost with the Republican takeover of the House and Senate after the 1994 congressional elections. Although not explicitly stated, the Constitution provides the president with the power of **legislative initiative.** To "initiate" means to originate, and in government that can mean power. The framers of the Constitution clearly saw legislative initiative as one of the keys to executive power. Initiative obviously implies the ability to formulate proposals for important policies, and the president, as an individual with a great deal of staff assistance, is able to initiate decisive action more frequently than Congress, with its large assemblies that have to deliberate and debate before taking action. With some important exceptions, Congress banks on the president to set the agenda of public policy. And quite clearly, there is power in initiative; there is power in being able to set the terms of discourse in the making of public policy.

During Clinton's time in office, the terms of discourse were largely set by the president, and he tended to get the credit even on many of the occasions where the groundwork had been done by the Republicans. Important crime legislation, drug-control legislation, gun-control legislation, and the all-important welfare reform laws of 1996 were all presidential initiatives, even though the two most important of these—crime and welfare—contain many features first advanced by the Republicans in Congress. The same seems to have been true of budget and fiscal matters. For example, it was Clinton, not the tax-cutting Republicans, who established the principle that the Social Security surplus should not be any longer drawn upon to pay for other programs or for tax cuts.

Regarding areas of foreign policy, it was also largely Clinton who set the agenda. Let's look at what happened in 1999. First of all, it was Clinton who led a multilateral effort to save Kosovo from the aggressive advances made by Serbia. Clinton also resumed negotiations with the Russians and maintained multilateral discussion on arms control. Clinton managed to maintain discussion of America's $1 billion delinquency in U.N. dues until Congress finally included authorization for those payments in the budget. His frequent travels abroad—making him the most-traveled president in history—kept him on the front page and in the lead lines of television coverage on a daily basis. He seemed almost to be in several places at the same time, given his critical role in the movements toward peace between Israel and the Palestinians and between the antagonistic Protestant and Catholic factions in Northern Ireland. Even amid the bombast of the World Trade Organization meeting in Seattle, Clinton was the center of attention.

The president's initiative does not end with policy making involving Congress and the making of laws in the ordinary sense of the term. The president has still another legislative role (in all but name) within the executive branch. This is designated as the power to issue **executive orders.** The executive order is first and foremost simply a normal tool of management, a power possessed by virtually any CEO to make "company policy"—rules setting procedures, etiquette, chains of command, functional responsibilities, etc. But evolving out of this normal management practice is a recognized presidential power to promulgate rules that have the effect and the formal status of legislation. Most of the executive orders of the president provide for the reorganization of structures and procedures or otherwise direct the affairs of the executive branch—either to be applied across the board to all agencies or applied in some important respect to a single agency or department. One of the most important examples is Executive Order No. 8248, September 8, 1939, establishing the divisions of the Executive Office of the President. Another one of equal importance is President Nixon's executive order establishing the Environmental

executive order
a rule or regulation issued by the president that has the effect and formal status of legislation

Protection Agency in 1970–71, which included establishment of the Environmental Impact Statement. President Reagan's Executive Order No. 12291 of 1981 was responsible for a regulatory reform process that was responsible for more genuine deregulation in the past twenty years than was accomplished by any acts of congressional legislation. (For more on this executive order, see Chapter 17.) President Clinton's most important policy toward gays and gay rights in the military took the form of an executive order referred to as "Don't ask, don't tell."

In sum, President Clinton's ability to regain the policy initiative after the Republican triumph in Congress in 1994 and to keep the policy initiative during and after his impeachment crisis confirms the proposition that the presidency and presidential power includes legislative leadership. This legislative or policy leadership role of the presidency is an institutionalized feature of the office that exists independent of the occupant of the office. That is to say, anyone duly elected president would possess these powers regardless of his or her individual energy or leadership characteristics.[14]

Institutional Resources of Presidential Power

- What institutional resources does the president use to manage the executive branch?
- Which of these resources have presidents increasingly relied on?

Constitutional sources of power are not the only resources available to the president. Presidents possess a variety of other formal and informal resources that have important implications for their ability to govern (see Figure 14.2 on page 546). Without these other resources, presidents would lack the ability—the tools of management and public mobilization—to make much use of the power and responsibility given to them by Congress. Let us first consider the president's formal institutional resources and then, in the section following, turn to the more informal political resources that affect a president's capacity to govern, in particular the president's base of popular support.

PATRONAGE AS A TOOL OF MANAGEMENT

patronage
the resources available to higher officials, usually opportunities to make partisan appointments to offices and to confer grants, licenses, or special favors to supporters

The first tool of management available to most presidents is a form of **patronage**—the choice of high-level political appointees. These appointments allow the president to fill top management positions with individuals who will attempt to carry out the president's agenda. But the president must appoint individuals who have experience and interest in the programs that they are to administer and who share the president's goals with respect to these programs. At the same time, presidents use the appointment process to build links to powerful political and economic constituencies by giving representation to important state political party organizations, the business community, organized labor, the scientific and university communities, organized agriculture, and certain large and well-organized religious groups.

THE CABINET

In the American system of government, the **Cabinet** is the traditional but informal designation for the heads of all the major federal government departments. The Cabinet has no constitutional status. Unlike in England and many other parliamentary countries, where the cabinet *is* the government, the American Cabinet is not a collective body. It meets but makes no decisions as a group. Each appointment must be approved by the Senate, but Cabinet members are not responsible to the Senate or to Congress at large. Cabinet appointments help build party and popular support, but the Cabinet is not a party organ. The Cabinet is made up of directors, but is not a true board of directors.

Aware of this fact, the president tends to develop a burning impatience with and a mild distrust of Cabinet members; to make the Cabinet a rubber stamp for actions already decided on; and to demand results, or the appearance of results, more immediately and more frequently than most department heads can provide. Since Cabinet appointees generally have not shared political careers with the president or with each other, and since they may meet literally for the first time after their selection, the formation of an effective governing group out of this motley collection of appointments is unlikely. Although President Clinton's insistence on a Cabinet diverse enough to resemble American society could be considered an act of political wisdom, it virtually guaranteed that few of his appointees had ever spent much time working together or even knew the policy positions or beliefs of the other appointees.[15]

Some presidents have relied more heavily on an "inner Cabinet," the **National Security Council (NSC)**. The NSC, established by law in 1947, is composed of the president, the vice president, the secretaries of state, defense, and the treasury, the attorney general, and other officials invited by the president. It has its own staff of foreign-policy specialists run by the special assistant to the president for national security affairs. For these highest appointments, presidents turn to people from outside Washington, usually longtime associates. A counterpart, the Domestic Council, was created by law in 1970, but no specific members were designated for it. President Clinton hit upon his own version of the Domestic Council, called the National Economic Council, which shares competing functions with the Council of Economic Advisers.

Presidents have obviously been uneven and unpredictable in their reliance on the NSC and other subcabinet bodies, because executive management is inherently a personal matter. Despite all the personal variations, however, one generalization can be made: Presidents have increasingly preferred the White House staff instead of the cabinet as their means of managing the gigantic executive branch.

THE WHITE HOUSE STAFF

The **White House staff** is composed mainly of analysts and advisers.[16] Although many of the top White House staff members are given the title "special assistant" for a particular task or sector, the types of judgments they are expected to make and the kinds of advice they are supposed to give are a good deal broader and more generally political than those coming from the Executive Office of the President or from the cabinet departments. The members of

THE CABINET DEPARTMENTS

Department	Year created
State	1789
Treasury	1789
Defense*	1947
Justice	1789
Interior†	1849
Agriculture	1889
Commerce	1913
Labor	1913
Health and Human Services††	1953
Housing and Urban Development	1965
Transportation	1966
Energy	1977
Education	1979
Veterans Affairs	1989

*Formerly the War and Navy Departments, created in 1789 and 1798, respectively.
†Created in 1862; made part of Cabinet in 1889.
††Formerly Health, Education, and Welfare; reorganized in 1979 (when separate Department of Education was created).

Cabinet
the secretaries, or chief administrators, of the major departments of the federal government. Cabinet secretaries are appointed by the president with the consent of the Senate

National Security Council (NSC)
a presidential foreign policy advisory council composed of the president; the vice president; the secretaries of state, defense, and the treasury; the attorney general; and other officials invited by the president

White House staff
analysts and advisers to the president, often given the title "special assistant"

Figure 14.2 THE INSTITUTIONAL PRESIDENCY

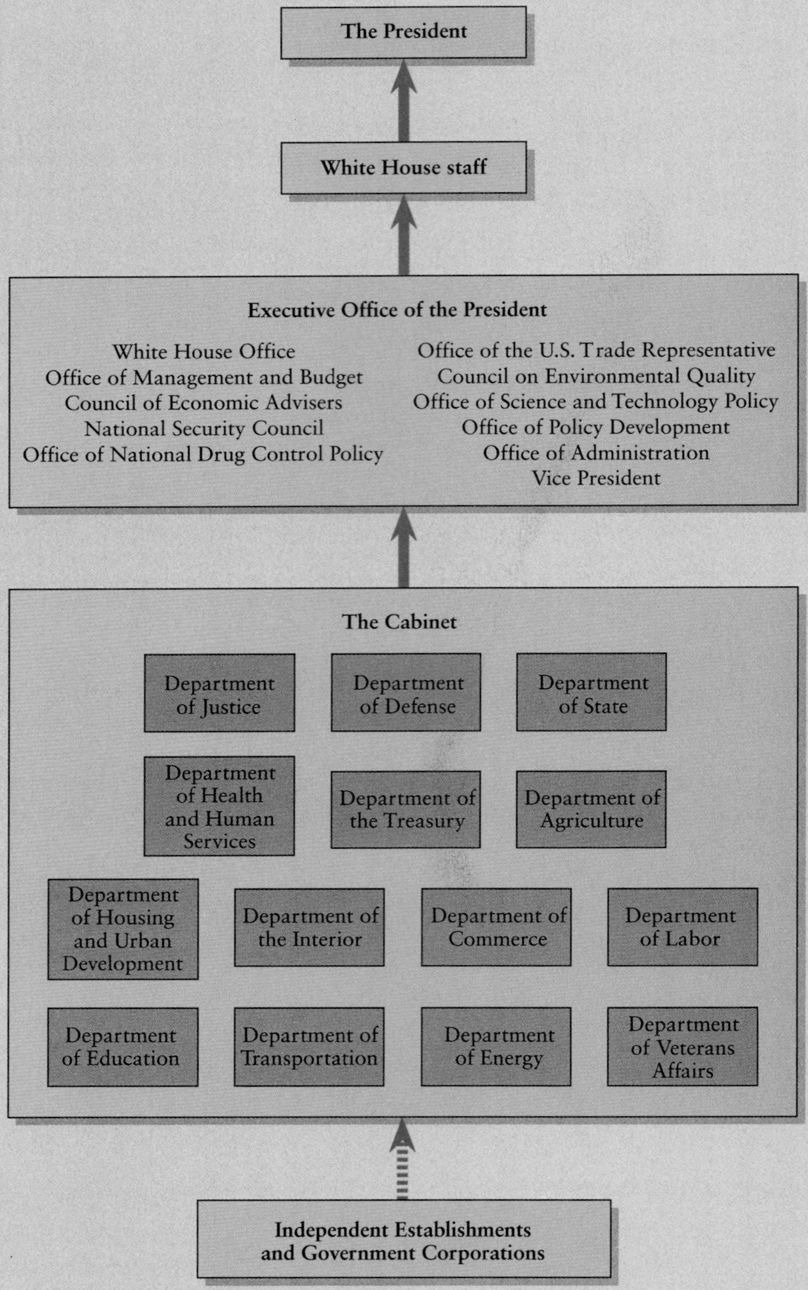

SOURCE: Office of the Federal Register, National Archives and Records Administration, *The United States Government Manual, 1995–96* (Washington, DC: Government Printing Office, 1995), p. 22.

THE EXPANDING (AND SHRINKING) WHITE HOUSE STAFF, 1937–98

Figure 14.3

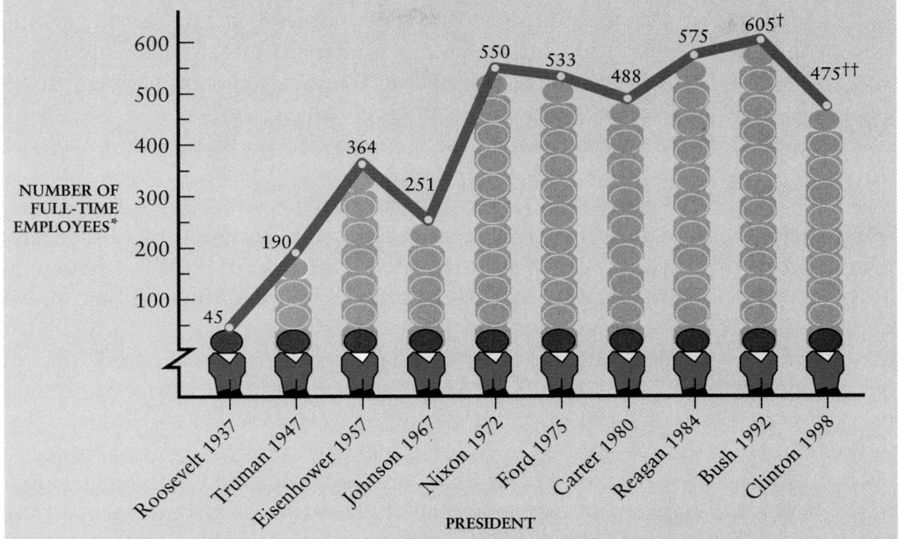

*These figures do not include the employees temporarily detailed to the White House from outside agencies (about 50–75 in 1992 and 1996).
†The vice president employs more than 20 people, and there are at least 100 people on the staff of the National Security Council. These people work in the White House and the Executive Office buildings, but are not included in these totals.
††These figures include the staffs of the Office of the President and the Executive Residence.
SOURCES: 1937–84: Thomas E. Cronin, "The Swelling of the Presidency: Can Anyone Reverse the Tide?" in *American Government: Readings and Cases,* 8th ed., ed. Peter Woll (Boston: Little, Brown, 1984), p. 347; 1992 and 1998: provided by the Office of Management and Budget and the White House.

the White House staff also tend to be more closely associated with the president than other presidentially appointed officials.

From an informal group of fewer than a dozen people (popularly called the **Kitchen Cabinet**), and no more than four dozen at the height of the domestic Roosevelt presidency in 1937, the White House staff has grown substantially with each successive president (see Figure 14.3).[17] Richard Nixon employed 550 people in 1972. President Carter, who found so many of the requirements of presidential power distasteful, and who publicly vowed to keep his staff small and decentralized, built an even larger and more centralized staff. President Clinton reduced the White House staff by 20 percent, but a large White House staff is still essential.

Kitchen Cabinet
an informal group of advisers to whom the president turns for counsel and guidance. Members of the official Cabinet may or may not also be members of the Kitchen Cabinet

The biggest variation among presidential management practices lies not in the size of the White House staff but in its organization. President Reagan went to the extreme in delegating important management powers to his chief of staff, and he elevated his budget director to an unprecedented level of power in *policy* making rather than merely *budget* making. President Bush centralized his staff even more under chief of staff John Sununu. At the same time, Bush continued to deal directly with his Cabinet heads, the press, and key members of Congress. President Clinton showed a definite preference for competition among equals in his cabinet and among senior White House officials, obviously liking competition and conflict among staff members, for which FDR's staff was also famous. But the troubles Clinton had in turning this conflict and competition into coherent policies and well-articulated messages suggests that he might have done better to emulate his immediate predecessors in their preference for hierarchy and centralization.[18]

THE EXECUTIVE OFFICE OF THE PRESIDENT

Executive Office of the President (EOP)
the permanent agencies that perform defined management tasks for the president. Created in 1939, the EOP includes the Office of Management and Budget, the Council of Economic Advisers, the National Security Council, and other agencies

The development of the White House staff can be appreciated only in its relation to the still-larger **Executive Office of the President (EOP).** Created in 1939, the EOP is a major part of what is often called the "institutional presidency"—the permanent agencies that perform defined management tasks for the president. The most important and the largest EOP agency is the Office of Management and Budget (OMB). Its roles in preparing the national budget, designing the president's program, reporting on agency activities, and overseeing regulatory proposals make OMB personnel part of virtually every conceivable presidential responsibility. The status and power of the OMB have grown in importance with each successive president. The process of budgeting at one time was a "bottom-up" procedure, with expenditure and program requests passing from the lowest bureaus through the departments to "clearance" in OMB and hence to Congress, where each agency could be called in to reveal what its "original request" had been before OMB revised it. Now the budgeting process is a "top-down"; OMB sets the terms of discourse for agencies as well as for Congress. The director of OMB is now one of the most powerful officials in Washington.

The staff of the Council of Economic Advisers (CEA) constantly analyzes the economy and economic trends and attempts to give the president the ability to anticipate events rather than to wait and react to events. The Council on Environmental Quality was designed to do the same for environmental issues as the CEA does for economic issues. The National Security Council (NSC) is composed of designated cabinet officials who meet regularly with the president to give advice on the large national security picture. The staff of the NSC assimilates and analyzes data from all intelligence-gathering agencies (CIA, etc.). Other EOP agencies perform more specialized tasks.

Somewhere between fifteen hundred and two thousand highly specialized people work for EOP agencies.[19] The importance of each agency in the EOP varies according to the personal orientation of each president. For example, the NSC staff was of immense importance under President Nixon, especially because it served essentially as the personal staff of presidential assistant Henry Kissinger. But it was of less importance to President Bush, who looked outside the EOP altogether for military policy matters, much more to the Joint Chiefs of Staff and its chair, General Colin Powell.

Perspectives on Politics

GENERATIONAL DIVIDES

"What should the government do with the 1998 budget surplus?"

	Age group			
	18–29	30–49	50–64	65+
Tax cut	13%	13%	9%	6%
Pay off national debt	14	22	27	27
Social spending	57	34	17	15
Fix Social Security	15	31	45	46
Don't know/no answer	1	*	2	6

SOURCE: The Pew Research Center, http://www.people-press.org/jan98rpt.htm.

THE VICE PRESIDENCY

The vice presidency is a constitutional anomaly even though the office was created along with the presidency by the Constitution. The vice president exists for two purposes only: to succeed the president in case of death, resignation, or incapacitation and to preside over the Senate, casting a tie-breaking vote when necessary.[20]

The main value of the vice presidency as a political resource for the president is electoral. Traditionally, a presidential candidate's most important rule for the choice of a running mate is that he or she bring the support of at least one state (preferably a large one) not otherwise likely to support the ticket. Another rule holds that the vice presidential nominee should provide some regional balance and, wherever possible, some balance among various ideological or ethnic subsections of the party. It is very doubtful that John Kennedy would have won in 1960 without his vice presidential candidate, Lyndon Johnson, and the contribution Johnson made to winning in Texas. George W. Bush's choice of Dick Cheney in 2000 was completely devoid of direct electoral value, since Cheney came from one of our least populous states (Wyoming, which casts only three electoral votes). But given Cheney's stalwart right-wing record both in Congress and as President Bush's secretary of defense, coupled with his even more prominently right-wing wife, Lynne Cheney, his inclusion on the Republican ticket was clearly an effort to consolidate the support of the restive right wing of his party. Al Gore's choice of Joe Lieberman was also remote from electoral consideration. Lieberman's home state, Connecticut, contributes only eight electoral votes and was already certain to go Democratic. And as the first Jewish vice presidential nominee, Lieberman could add only marginally to the national Democratic vote because 80 percent of the Jewish vote was already Democratic. However, as a devoutly religious man and the first and only Democrat in the Senate to denounce President Clinton's behavior in the Lewinsky affair—and as a conservative Democrat—Lieberman's presence was a message to the nation that Gore was not a "Clinton clone" and was solidly mainstream in all the policy initiatives he had promised to take as president.

Presidents have constantly promised to give their vice presidents more responsibility, but they almost always break their promises, indicating that they are unable to utilize the vice presidency as a management or political resource after the election. No one can explain exactly why. Perhaps it is just too much trouble to share responsibility. Perhaps the president as head of state feels unable to share any part of that status. Perhaps, like many adult Americans who do not draw up their wills, presidents may simply dread contemplating their

Students and Politics

Cal Poly political science junior Eddie Drake's fall quarter internship was by no means the stereotypical college internship. He made no coffee, and he only visited the copy machine every other week. Oh, he also got to hang out with the president of the United States and help write policy for the vice president.

Last March, Drake competed with over 3,000 students for 80 spots in a scholastic internship program at the White House. After conducting background checks on him and his family, reviewing his thirty-page application and reading clippings of his past *Mustang Daily* columns "Ed-Words," he received a letter of acceptance from the White House in July.

Drake was assigned to Al Gore's Office for Electronic Commerce, a working group headed by the vice president. Drake's department dealt with issues concerning the Internet and whether there should be policies for it, such as paying a user tax, international trade tariffs or increased governmental restrictions.

"Our main goal was to craft and shape the administration's policy so that it will be beneficial to all people in the United States, especially to business," Drake said.

Most of the time Drake was doing research and writing letter drafts for congressmen and the president, communicating where he thought the e-commerce policies stood.

While Drake was a moderate Democrat when he arrived at the White House, he left as a full Democrat.

"You learn to accept everyone and everything you see. The Democratic ideology is that you're always welcome in the party—it's not for members only, it's for the little guy and for the average person who wants to get ahead," Drake said.

Drake plans to return to the same White House position this summer, hopefully as a paid employee. After college, he hopes that some of the connections he made will help get his foot into the door of politics.

"I don't know much about anything but politics. When I was working as part of a team out there, it was so incredibly fulfilling," Drake said.

SOURCE: Kelly Hendricks, "Cal Poly Junior Interns at White House," *Mustang Daily* (California Poly State University), January 19, 2000.

During his term as vice president, Al Gore promoted his plan to "reinvent" government on David Letterman's television show, where he railed against the government's procurement requirements, which even specified the number of pieces into which a government ashtray may shatter.

own death. But management style is certainly a factor. George Bush, as vice president, was "kept within the loop" of decision making because President Reagan delegated so much power. A copy of virtually everything made for Reagan was made for Bush, especially during the first term, when Bush's close friend James Baker was chief of staff. President Bush did not take such pains to keep Dan Quayle "in the loop," but President Clinton relied greatly on his vice president, Al Gore, and Gore emerged as one of the most trusted and effective figures in the Clinton White House.

Vice President Gore's enhanced status was signaled early on, when President Clinton kept him visibly present at all public appearances during the transition and during the vital public and private efforts to present and campaign for the president's program early in 1993. He remained one of the most consistently praised members of the administration. Gore's most important task was to oversee the National Performance Review (NPR), an ambitious program to "reinvent" the way the federal government conducts its affairs. The NPR was initially dismissed as show rather than substance, but even the administration's toughest critics admitted that Gore led the drive to streamline the federal government with energy and effectiveness.

THE FIRST LADY

The president serves as both chief executive and chief of state—the equivalent of Great Britain's prime minister and king rolled into one, simultaneously leading the government and serving as a symbol of the nation at official ceremonies and functions. For their part, most first ladies (all presidents so far have been men) limit their activities to the ceremonial portion of the presidency. First ladies greet foreign dignitaries, visit other countries, attend important national ceremonies, and otherwise act as America's "queen" when the president is called upon to serve in a kingly capacity.

Because the first lady is generally associated exclusively with the head of state aspect of America's presidency, she is usually not subject to the same sort of media scrutiny or partisan attack as that aimed at the president. The first lady is generally a symbol of the nation rather than of a partisan perspective or policy position. It is generally deemed inappropriate to attack her, much as it would be considered unseemly to launch an attack on the Statue of Liberty or the Washington Monument. Thus, even during the heat of the Watergate affair, no newspaper or politician attacked President Richard Nixon's wife, Pat.

Some first ladies have not resigned themselves to purely symbolic roles in the administration, however. Hillary Rodham Clinton initially played an important political and policy role in her husband's administration. During the 1992 campaign, Bill Clinton often intimated that she would be active in the policy realm by joking that the voters would get "two for the price of one" if they cast their ballots for him. After the election, Hillary took a leading role in a number of policy areas, most notably in crafting the health care reform proposals that were expected to be the centerpiece of Bill Clinton's first term.

At first, Hillary Clinton was an effective political operative precisely because the media and opposing politicians were reluctant to attack a first lady. In due course, however, she came to be seen less as a national symbol and more as a politician, and she, too, became vulnerable to the intensive media scrutiny and partisan attack that is the norm in American politics today. Opponents accused her of profiting from shady commodities trades, planning the firing of members of the White House travel office to make room for presidential cronies, and, of course, involvement in the Whitewater affair, a set of shady Arkansas real estate deals to which the president's foes sought to connect him. By 1995, Hillary Clinton was forced to withdraw to the more traditional role of a first lady, but that turned out to be only temporary. She lit a firestorm in 1999 by letting it be known that she planned to run for the U. S. Senate from New York, a state that she and President Clinton made their home only in 2000. Her eventual election to that office clearly sets her apart from all previous first ladies.

Former First Lady Hillary Rodham Clinton played a prominent role in President Clinton's 1993 health care reform plan.

Political Resources of Presidential Power

▶ What political resources can the president draw on in exercising the powers of the presidency? Which of these resources is a potential liability? Why?

All presidents come to office with great strength. The Constitution and the institutional resources of presidential power that they accrue ensure this. Yet as Richard Neustadt argued in his book *Presidential Power,* a president's formal institutional resources of power are not the most important ones. Other political institutions, such as Congress, also possess formidable powers. As Neustadt put it, "presidential power is the power to persuade."[21] But presidents have varied in their ability to "persuade" and thus vary in their real power. Their capacity to exercise that power and govern effectively is affected by a number of political resources that presidents have grown to rely on, foremost among them the American people. These resources are a source of great strength but also, as we'll see, a potential source of weakness.

ELECTIONS AS A RESOURCE

mandate
a claim by a victorious candidate that the electorate has given him or her special authority to carry out promises made during the campaign

Any ordinary citizen, legitimately placed in office, would be a very powerful president. Yet there is no denying that a decisive presidential election translates into a more effective presidency. Some presidents claim that a landslide election gives them a **mandate,** by which they mean that the electorate approved the programs offered in the campaign and that Congress ought therefore to go along. And Congress is not unmoved by such an appeal. The electoral landslides of 1964 and 1980 gave Presidents Johnson and Reagan real strength during their "honeymoon" years. In contrast, the close elections of Kennedy in 1960, Nixon in 1968, and Carter in 1976 seriously hampered those presidents' effectiveness. Although Bush was elected decisively in 1988, he had no legislative commitments that would have profited from any claim to an electoral mandate.

President Clinton, an action-oriented president, was nevertheless seriously hampered by having been elected in 1992 by a minority of the popular vote, a mere 43 percent. Clinton was re-elected in 1996 with 49 percent of the vote, a larger percentage of the electorate, but still a minority. His appeals to bipartisanship in 1997 reflected his lack of a mandate from the electorate.

The outcome of the 2000 presidential election indicated a popular-vote deadlock of 48 percent to 48 percent, reflecting a difference of a mere 200,000 votes out of approximately 101 million cast. Given the closeness of the election—as well as the close partisan balance in Congress—it mattered little who won, since any president possessing such a narrow margin of victory would have little claim to mandate. In this context, the United States can look forward to a long siege of stalemate between the president and Congress until, at the earliest, the 2002 congressional elections and perhaps beyond, i.e., if those elections do not produce a significant shift in the number of House and Senate seats held by the president's party.

PARTY AS A PRESIDENTIAL RESOURCE

Although on the decline, the president's party is far from insignificant as a political resource (see also Chapter 10). Figure 14.4 dramatically demonstrates the point with a forty-four-year history of the presidential "batting average" in Congress—the percentage of winning roll-call votes in Congress on bills publicly supported by the president. Bill Clinton, in his first two years in office, enjoyed high averages of legislative success—86 percent in both 1993 and 1994—but that figure dropped dramatically to 35 percent in 1995 following the Republican takeover of Congress in the 1994 elections.

The relatively low batting averages for Republican presidents such as Nixon, Ford, Reagan, and Bush are clearly attributable to the political party as a presidential resource. Democrats support Democratic presidents and Republicans support Republican presidents. Prior to 1995, during the years included in Figure 14.4, Democrats held the majority in the House of Representatives for all but the 1952–54 Congress and in the Senate except for the 1952–54 and 1980–86 Congresses; it is thus to be expected that the averages for Democratic presidents would be higher than they would be for Republican presidents. As Figure 14.4 shows clearly, the political party is the key factor.

THE BATTING AVERAGE; PRESIDENTIAL SUCCESS ON CONGRESSIONAL VOTES, 1953–99

Figure 14.4

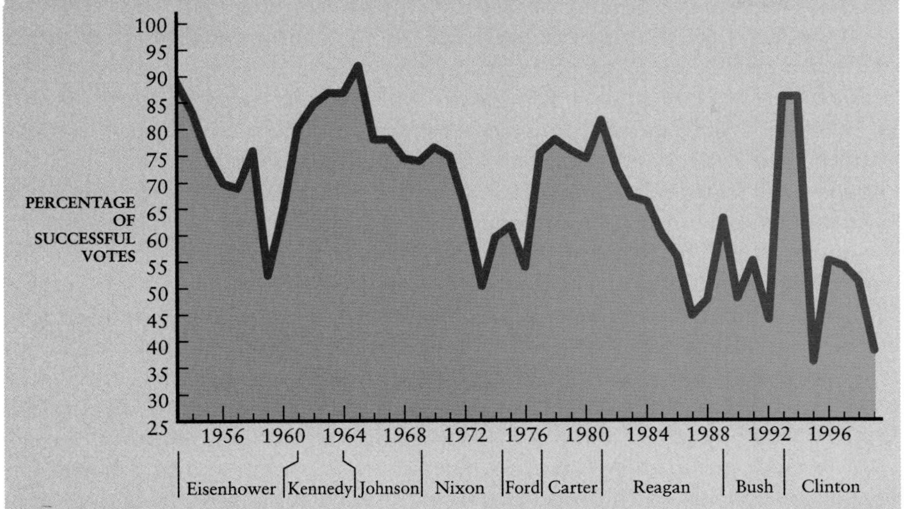

SOURCE: *Congressional Quarterly Weekly Report,* December 11, 1999, p. 2972.

The presidential "batting average" is the percentage of votes on which the president took a position and that position was successful.

At the same time, party has its limitations as a resource. The more unified the president's party is behind legislative requests from the White House, the more unified the opposition party is also likely to be. Unless the president's party majority is very large, appeals must also be made to the opposition to make up for the inevitable defectors within the ranks of the president's own party. Consequently, the president often poses as being above partisanship in order to win "bipartisan" support in Congress. But in pursuing a bipartisan strategy, a president cannot concentrate solely on building the party loyalty and party discipline that would maximize the value of the party's support in Congress. This is a dilemma for all presidents, particularly those faced with an opposition-controlled Congress.

GROUPS AS A PRESIDENTIAL RESOURCE

In the twentieth century, the classic case of groups as a resource for the presidency was the Roosevelt or **New Deal coalition.**[22] The New Deal coalition was composed of an inconsistent, indeed contradictory, set of interests. Some of these interests were not organized interest groups, but were regional interests, such as southern whites, or residents of large cities in the industrial Northeast and Midwest, or blacks who later succeeded in organizing as an interest group. In addition to these sectional interests that were drawn to the New Deal, the coalition included several large, self-consciously organized interest groups. The most important in the New Deal coalition were organized

New Deal coalition
the coalition of northern urban liberals, southern white conservatives, organized labor, and blacks that dominated national politics until the 1960s

labor, agriculture, and the financial community.[23] All of the parts were held together by a judicious use of patronage—not merely patronage in jobs but patronage in policies. Many of the groups were permitted virtually to write their own legislation. In exchange, the groups supported President Roosevelt and his successors in their battles with opposing coalitions.

Republican presidents have had their group coalition base also. The most important segments of organized business have tended to support Republican presidents. They have most often been joined by upper-income groups, as well as by some ethnic groups. In recent years, Republican presidents have expanded their interest coalition base. President Reagan, for example, won the support of traditionally Democratic southern white and northern blue-collar voters. This expanded base of support served him well in his struggles with Congress. When the Reagan/Republican coalition began to loosen toward the end of the Bush administration, the astute Bill Clinton was quick to sense it. His 1992 campaign succeeded in part because he brought back together many of the original interests that had made up the New Deal coalition. But he attempted to go even beyond those interests by holding an unprecedented "economic summit" in Little Rock, Arkansas, less than a month after his election. It was a very public meeting of some three hundred bankers, corporate executives, interest-group representatives, prominent economists, and a sprinkling of average citizens—with Clinton himself presiding for almost the entire forty-eight hours of speech-making and serious discussion. It was indeed an extraordinary effort to expand the president's coalition base.

In 2000, Al Gore's campaign strategy was to mobilize the mass base of the Democratic Party with a populist appeal to working families, African Americans, the poor, and the elderly. He was able to win the endorsement of all the major trade unions, despite some of their misgivings about his views on international trade. In a sense, Gore sought to return to the class politics of the New Deal coalition, but without the support of southern whites.

In contrast, George W. Bush attempted to rebuild the GOP base that had been shattered during the 1998 fall of former house speaker Newt Gingrich. In July 1999, at a meeting of Republican governors in St. Louis, twenty-three of twenty-nine governors, along with nineteen Republican senators and 136 Republican House members, endorsed Bush for president. They did so because Bush appeared to them to be the only Republican candidate who could pull the party together and win the presidency. Consequently, Bush's strategy was not to challenge Gore head-on, but instead, to consolidate the GOP base. To do so, Bush promised a massive tax cut to appeal to upper-income groups and espoused family values to appeal to rural and small-town conservatives.

The interest bases of the two parties have remained largely unchanged since 1980, when the GOP completed its absorption of most white southerners and religious conservatives. But whether these coalitions will last remains to be seen.

PRESIDENTIAL USE OF THE MEDIA

While the media have grown increasingly important during presidential campaigns (see Chapter 11), their importance is even greater during a president's term in office. Modern presidents have sought a more direct relationship with the public and have used the media to achieve this end. Modern presidents

Politics on the Web

The Clinton administration used the Internet aggressively to advance its political agenda. Most of the White House Web site is devoted to political information, such as news releases, government statistics, and the president's current activities (although it did include a page devoted to Socks the Cat!). The site also includes an archive where one can find speeches, search White House documents, and view photos. Finally, the site provides citizen's resources—how to contact federal agencies, find out about veterans and Social Security benefits, and other "casework" information.

E-mail access was another change instituted by the Clinton White House. Although it is unlikely that the president sits by the computer and answers all or any of his own e-mail, this ability to contact our highest public official with a few clicks of a mouse can have beneficial results. Just the ability to express an opinion and interact with governmental officials might increase the public's faith and trust in governmental institutions.

www.wwnorton.com/wtp3e

have learned that they can use their relationship with the media to mobilize popular support for their programs and to attempt to force Congress to follow their lead.

In the media, reporting on what is new sells newspapers. The president has at hand the thousands of policy proposals that come up to the White House through the administrative agencies; these can be fed to the media as newsworthy initiatives. Consequently, virtually all newspapers and television networks habitually look to the White House as the chief source of news about public policy. They tend to assign one of their most skillful reporters to the White House "beat." And since news is money, they need the president as much as the president needs them in order to meet their mutual need to make news. Members of Congress, especially senators, are also key sources of news, but the White House has more control over what and when, which is what political initiative is all about.

Different presidents use the media in quite different ways. One of the first presidents to use the media was Theodore Roosevelt, who referred to the presidency as a "bully pulpit" because its visibility allowed him to preach to the nation and bring popular pressure to bear against his opponents in Congress. But the first president to try to reach the public directly through the media was Franklin Roosevelt. During the 1930s, FDR used radio broadcasts known as "fireside chats," press conferences, speeches, and movie newsreels to rally support for his New Deal programs and, later, to build popular support for American rearmament in the face of the growing danger in Europe and the Far East. FDR also cultivated strong relationships with national news correspondents to ensure favorable publicity for his programs. FDR's efforts to reach out to the

During the 1992 presidential campaign, Bill Clinton appeared on MTV to court the votes of young Americans. Clinton answered questions about his vision for America but also about his personal life, including whether he would inhale if he smoked marijuana and what type of underwear he wears (boxers).

American people and mobilize their support were among the factors that made him one of the strongest presidents in American history. His appeals to the American people allowed FDR to "reach over the heads" of congressional opponents and force them to follow his lead because their constituents demanded it.

A president's personality also affects how the press conference is used. Since 1961, the presidential press conference has been a distinctive institution, available whenever the president wants to dominate the news. Between 300 and 400 certified reporters attend and file their accounts within minutes of the concluding words, "Thank you, Mr. President." But despite the importance of the press conference, its value to each president has varied. President Clinton tended to combine high profile elaborate press conferences and prime-time broadcasts with the more personal one-on-one approach with reporters. President Clinton also appeared on informal and basically nonpolitical talk shows, such as those of Larry King and Oprah Winfrey. Such an informal approach has its risks, however: President Clinton was widely perceived as lacking the gravity a president is expected to possess. It is hard to argue with this conclusion when one considers that he was the first president to have answered a question (on MTV) about what kind of underwear he wears.

Of course, in addition to the presidential press conference there are other routes from the White House to news prominence.[24] For example, President Nixon preferred direct television addresses, and President Carter tried to make initiatives more homey with a television adaptation of President Roosevelt's "fireside chats." President Reagan made unusually good use of prime-time television addresses and also instituted more informal but regular Saturday afternoon radio broadcasts, a tradition that President Clinton continued.

PUBLIC OPINION

Most Americans feel that presidents should follow public opinion. Interestingly, however, many of the most successful presidents have been public opinion leaders rather than followers.

In 1963, President John Kennedy signed a nuclear test ban treaty with the Soviet Union, even though public opinion polls seemed to show that most Americans thought the treaty was a bad idea. Kennedy believed that the treaty served the national interest and that most Americans did not know enough about the issue at stake to have fixed views on the topic. He assured his nervous advisers that, since most Americans lacked strong views on the topic, they would assume that the president's actions were correct. Kennedy was right: after he signed the treaty, polls showed that most Americans supported his decision.

President George Bush used the same logic during the Persian Gulf crisis that followed the Iraqi invasion of Kuwait. At the time, opinion was divided both within Congress and among the broader public. Congressional leaders tried to constrain the president's ability to use forces in combat, urging him instead to rely on diplomacy and economic sanctions to compel Iraq's withdrawal. Congressional criticism, especially televised Senate hearings, helped erode Bush's popular standing and almost undermined his power to act. In January 1991, however, Bush sought and narrowly received congressional approval to use force against Iraq. The overwhelming success of the American military effort produced a surge of popular support for Bush; his approval rating rose to over 90 percent.

Presidents who devote too much of their time to the vicissitudes of public opinion polls often discover that they are several steps behind shifts in opinion, for polls tell politicians what the public wanted yesterday, not what it will think tomorrow. This was certainly President Clinton's experience in 1993–94 with the issue of health care reform. Administration polls continually showed public support for the president's policy initiatives—until opponents of his efforts began getting their own message through. Using several highly effective media campaigns, Clinton's opponents convinced millions of Americans that the president's program was too complex and that it would reduce access to health care. The president was left promoting an unpopular program.

Bill Clinton relied heavily on public opinion in formulating and presenting many of his administration's programs. Several members of his staff were hired specifically to shape and influence public opinion. For example, Dick Morris had a reputation as an uncanny diviner of the polls. One of the most fateful reliances on public opinion in the history of modern polling was its role in Clinton's decision following the exposure of Monica Lewinsky's taped admission of their affair in January 1998. When confronted with data demonstrating that public opinion was intensely negative on sexual misconduct, Clinton decided to "tough it out" and to try to win by denial of "any sexual relationship with that woman . . . ." By the time Clinton could no longer deny the affair, after eight months of mounting testimony against him, in August 1998, public opinion had actually turned in his favor.

Politicians are generally better off if they try to do what they believe is best and then hope that the public will come to agree with them. Most politicians, however, are afraid to use such a simple approach.

MASS POPULARITY AS A RESOURCE (AND A LIABILITY)

In addition to utilizing the media and public opinion polls, recent presidents, particularly Bill Clinton, have reached out directly to the American public to gain its approval. President Clinton's enormously high public profile, as is indicated by the number of public appearances he made (see Figure 14.5 on the next page), is only the most recent dramatic expression of the presidency as a **"permanent campaign"** for re-election. A study by political scientist Charles O. Jones shows that President Clinton engaged in campaignlike activity throughout his presidency and was the most-traveled American president in history. In his first twenty months in office, he made 203 appearances outside of Washington, compared with 178 for George Bush and 58 for Ronald Reagan. Clinton's tendency to go around rather than through party organizations is reflected in the fact that while Presidents Bush and Reagan devoted about 25 percent of their appearances to party functions, Clinton's comparable figure was only 8 percent.[25] Throughout the controversy over campaign-finance abuses during 1997, President Clinton attended numerous fund-raising events to raise enough money to pay off the $30 million or more of debt from the 1996 presidential campaign. In fact, during the most intense moments of the Monica Lewinsky scandal of early 1998, Clinton continued his fund-raising,

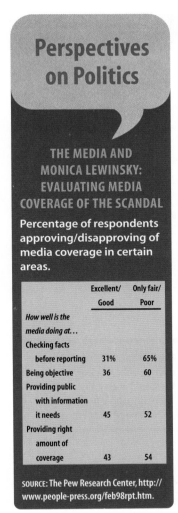

Perspectives on Politics

THE MEDIA AND MONICA LEWINSKY: EVALUATING MEDIA COVERAGE OF THE SCANDAL

Percentage of respondents approving/disapproving of media coverage in certain areas.

	Excellent/ Good	Only fair/ Poor
How well is the media doing at...		
Checking facts before reporting	31%	65%
Being objective	36	60
Providing public with information it needs	45	52
Providing right amount of coverage	43	54

SOURCE: The Pew Research Center, http://www.people-press.org/feb98rpt.htm.

permanent campaign
description of presidential politics in which all presidential actions are taken with re-election in mind

Figure 14.5 PUBLIC APPEARANCES BY PRESIDENTS, 1929–95

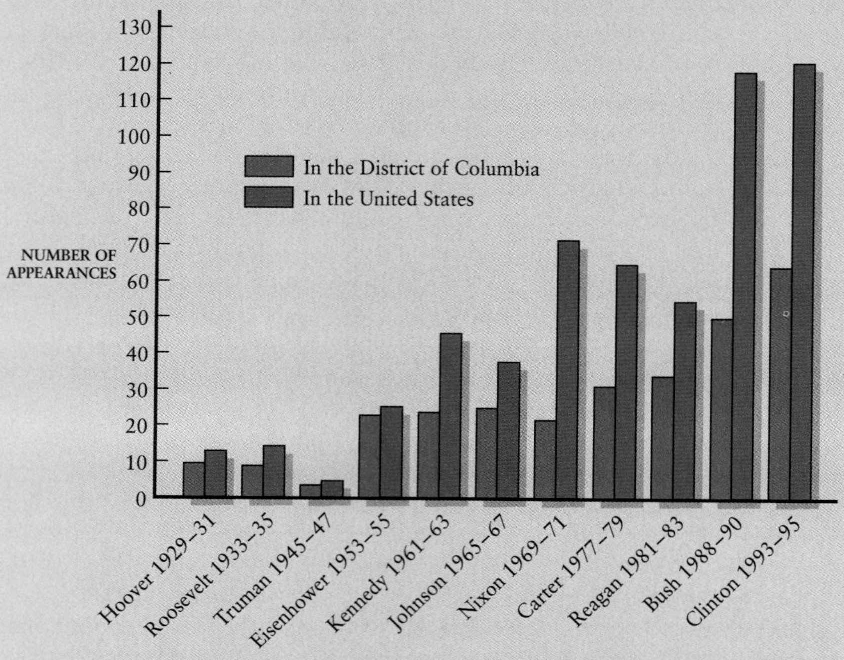

SOURCE: Samuel Kernell, *Going Public*, 3rd ed. (Washington DC: Congressional Quarterly Press, 1998), p. 118.

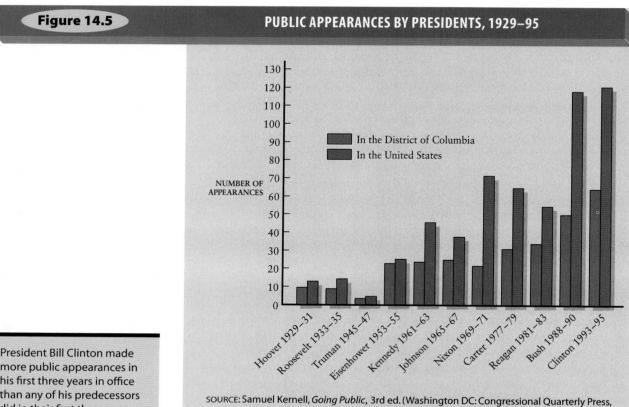

President Bill Clinton made more public appearances in his first three years in office than any of his predecessors did in their first three years.

and the Democratic National Committee had to add staff to answer all the telephone calls and mail that were responding positively to President Clinton's appeals. This is the essence of the permanent campaign.

Even with the help of all other institutional and political resources, successful presidents have to be able to mobilize mass opinion in their favor in order to keep Congress in line. But as we shall see, each president tends to *use up* mass resources. Virtually everyone is aware that presidents are constantly making appeals to the public over the heads of Congress and the Washington community. But again we have to say, our public is not made up of fools. The American people react to presidential actions rather than mere speeches or other image-making devices.

The public's sensitivity to presidential actions can be seen in the tendency of all presidents to lose popular support. Despite the twists and turns shown on Figure 14.6, the percentage of positive responses to "Do you approve of the way the president is handling his job?" starts out at a level significantly higher than the percentage of votes the president got in the previous national election and then declines over the next four years. Though the shape of the line differs, the destination is the same.

This general downward tendency is to be expected if American voters are rational, inasmuch as almost any action taken by the president can be divisive,

PRESIDENTIAL PERFORMANCE RATINGS FROM KENNEDY TO CLINTON

Figure 14.6

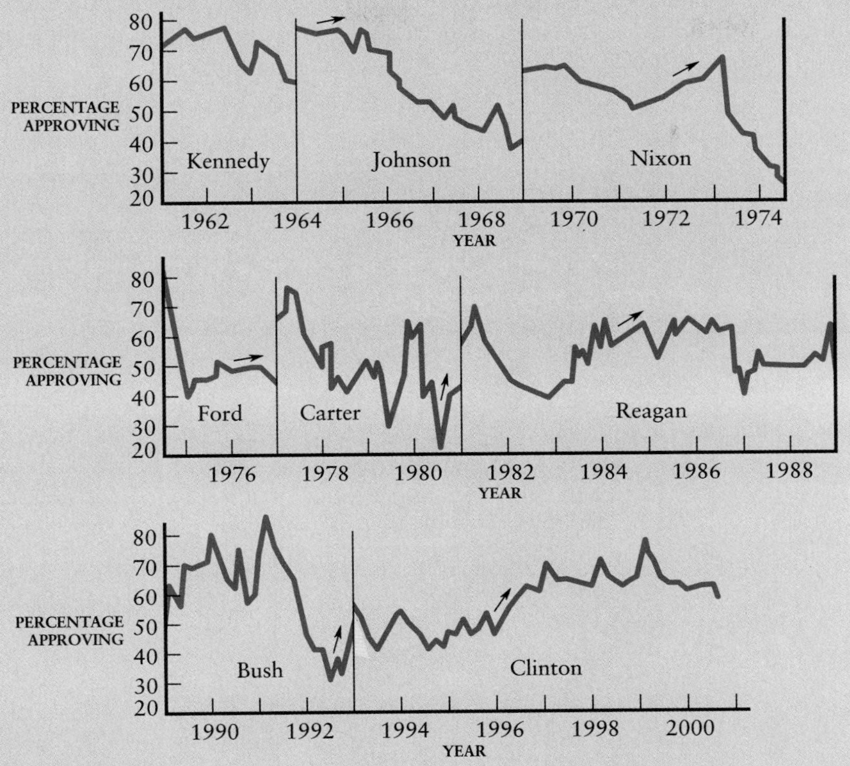

Note: Arrows indicate preelection upswings.
SOURCES: Courtesy of the Gallup Organization and Louis Harris & Associates.

In presidential performance rating polls, respondents are asked, "Do you approve of the way the president is handling his job?" This graph shows the percentage of positive responses.

with some voters approving and other voters disapproving. Public disapproval of specific actions has a cumulative effect on the president's overall performance rating. Thus all presidents are faced with the problem of boosting their approval ratings. And the public generally reacts favorably to presidential actions in foreign policy or, more precisely, to international events associated with the president. Analysts call this the **rallying effect.** Nevertheless the rallying effect turns out to be only a momentary reversal of the more general tendency of presidents to lose popular support.

rallying effect
the generally favorable reaction of the public to presidential actions taken in foreign policy, or more precisely, to decisions made during international crises

Looking again at Figure 14.6, the one notable exception to this general downward trend of presidential approval was during Clinton's second term (1997–2001). As expected, Clinton's approval rating surged before and after his re-election and then dropped over the course of 1997. But Clinton experienced two important upward blips, one early in 1998 and the other early in 1999, that were both related to the impeachment controversy, not to an international crisis. In both cases, Americans were disapproving of Clinton's behavior but they rallied behind the presidency as an institution. This rallying effect may well be what kept Clinton in office, and he was able to serve effectively during his last few years as president. Public support of the presidency is consistently high, and the public rallies around it when it is endangered by war or scandal. But that very support can work against the president, and Clinton will probably follow most of his predecessors by leaving office as a disappointment—while the presidency itself remains stronger than ever.

The Presidency and Democracy

▶ Did the development of a mass presidential constituency make the institution more democratic? More powerful?

Most of the real power of the modern presidency comes from powers granted by the Constitution and the laws made by Congress delegating powers to the president.[26] Thus, any person properly elected and sworn in as president will possess almost all of the power held by the strongest of presidents in American history. Even a "lame duck" president (a sitting president who loses the election in November, but who does not leave office until January) still possesses all of the power of the office. For example, during the weeks after his electoral defeat in 1992, President Bush committed troops to Somalia and conducted a series of air strikes against Iraq.

The presidency has become a genuinely democratic institution, and its mass popular base is respected by Congress and by all of the social forces and organized interests that seek to influence the national government. But we must recognize an extremely important fact about the presidency: the popular base of the presidency is important less because it gives the president power, and more because it gives the president *consent to use* all of the power already vested in the presidency by the Constitution and by Congress. The other formal and informal resources lodged in the presidency—the resources we have studied throughout this chapter—are just that: resources. But resources are not power; they must be converted into power. Democratization, more than the Constitution and laws, was responsible for the enormous expansion of real presidential power in the twentieth century. The formal resources of the presidency have remained about the same for two hundred years. Democratization combined with these formal powers to give us presidential government.

A PRESIDENTIAL CONSTITUENCY: CITIZENS AND THE PRESIDENT

In the United States, as a general rule, democratization follows power. As already observed, many larger social forces were gathering around the presidency and looking to the presidency even before the New Deal and the rise of presidential government. But these social forces did not begin to come together as a discernible constituency or a presidential support structure until the New Deal. Relations between the presidency and this larger constituency did not

POLICY DEBATE

Should Bill Clinton Have Been Impeached?

The Monica Lewinsky scandal that unfolded in 1998 and 1999 nearly ended the presidency of Bill Clinton. Republican anger at what his opponents charged was perjury and obstruction of justice concerning his sexual relationship with the White House intern precipitated the first impeachment trial of a president since that of President Andrew Johnson in 1868. While Clinton was acquitted by the Senate and was able to complete his presidency, Clinton's sexual dalliance with Lewinsky prompted many to ask whether his moral lapse compromised his presidency. Since presidents are viewed by many as not only political leaders, but cultural and moral leaders, can a president who commits adultery effectively lead the nation?

Critics of Clinton, as well as many analysts and commentators, argued that the president's responsibility to the nation extends far beyond just policy leadership. As political scientist Clinton Rossiter once noted, Americans see the president as "a moral spokesman for us all." Since the country's founding, Americans have looked to presidents for moral leadership, especially in times of turmoil and crisis. The nation's first president, George Washington, was more than simply a politician. He was widely admired for his personal qualities, including bravery and honesty. Abraham Lincoln embodied high moral principle in opposing slavery and leading the country through its greatest crisis. Franklin D. Roosevelt provided optimism, confidence, and hope to the country when it was gripped by the Great Depression in the 1930s. Roosevelt's importance as a moral force guiding the nation underscores the fact that citizens look to presidents as a source of hope and inspiration. From the presidential faces carved into the side of Mount Rushmore to presidential portraits posted in classrooms across America, presidents are role models who inspire the nation. Not only are they judged on their moral probity, but presidents find that their ability to serve as moral leaders is a key component to successful governance. Even though Clinton was not turned out of office, critics argue, he should have resigned because he failed to adhere to the high moral standard that is integral to the presidency.

On the other hand, some analysts point to the Clinton example to draw the opposite conclusion—that presidents are morally fallible, like the citizens they govern, and that presidents are elected to govern effectively. This distinction was made clear by the Clinton case. While a majority of Americans disapproved of Clinton's sexual indiscretion, a majority also felt that he should stay in office, as his private moral behavior was not related to, and did not affect, his continued service as president. Historians also point out that our most venerated presidents also committed personal indiscretions. For example, Thomas Jefferson was accused during his presidency of fathering illegitimate children with one of his slaves. Jefferson never commented on the accusations during his life, but recent DNA testing has concluded that in fact Jefferson did have at least one child with his slave Sally Hemmings. President Grover Cleveland admitted to fathering an illegitimate child. Franklin Roosevelt carried on a long-term extramarital affair with a woman who was even with him the day he died. John F. Kennedy, one of America's most admired modern presidents, had numerous extramarital affairs. These presidential indiscretions, though improper, did not prevent these presidents from doing their jobs. Less admired presidents, such as Warren Harding, were also guilty of sexual indiscretions. The point, according to some analysts, is that there seems to be no connection between a president's personal indiscretions and the ability to govern successfully, as long as the two remain separated. Beyond this, recent public opinion polling seems to show that it is not especially concerned about "moral leadership." As political scientist John Zaller concluded in his study of the Clinton-Lewinsky matter, "the public is, within broad limits, functionally indifferent to presidential character."

STUDENT DEBATE

Should Clinton Have Been Impeached?

Yes

"Every time the president talks about trust, it makes chills run up and down my spine. The very idea that the word 'trust' could ever come out of his mouth after what he has done to this country and the way he has trampled on the truth is a travesty of the American political system . . . There's just no such thing as truth when it comes to him."—Bill Clinton, speaking about then President Bush in the 1992 campaign.

Now, six-and-a-half years later, we know that these words are more applicable to the man who issued them. During the president's 1996 campaign, fellow Democrat Bob Kerrey observed that Bill Clinton "is an unusually good liar. Unusually good." However, despite his inability to humble himself enough even to be minimally honest or to obey the law, President Clinton will likely survive his impeachment trial.

The defenses of the president have come in all shapes and sizes over the past year. "It's only about sex." "The economy is the best it's ever been." There is a "vast right-wing conspiracy transfixed with the political destruction of Bill Clinton." "Ken Starr is a sex-obsessed person who's out to get the president." This is about "a civil case, which has been thrown out of court." And "Judge not, lest ye be judged."

What all of these arguments amount to is, in the words of William Bennett, "The Death of Outrage." Even if the president did nothing, which is absolutely not the case, engaging in these defenses of Bill Clinton lowers the moral and intellectual standards of behavior and leadership in the United States. If it continues, our country will surely live to regret it. When an issue forces public debate and challenges American ideals in the future, there will be no high ground with compelling moral power to which we can turn. We are defining down accountability, responsibility, and the sanctity of public office. If the defenses of Bill Clinton are not challenged, we not only become complicit in the president's lies, but also in his personal destruction of others.

Jim McDougal, one time Whitewater business partner with the Clintons, has said "the Clintons are sort of like tornadoes moving through people's lives." The tornadoes have accounted for ruining the lives or reputations of Billy Dale and the White House Travel Office staff, the Arkansas State Troopers, Bernard Nussbaum, Susan McDougal, Gennifer Flowers, Paula Jones, Monica Lewinsky, Sidney Blumenthal, Betty Currie, Webster Hubbell, Donna Shalala, Harold Ickes, Kent Masterson Brown, Vince Foster, the Secret Service, Jim Guy Tucker, Bruce Babbitt, Patricia and Glenn Mendoza, and Robert Rubin, to list a few. All of these people are victims of our president's dysfunctional personality which allows him to lie without shame or remorse. Mr. Clinton cannot follow his conscience because he has none. He says and does whatever the moment requires, projecting as much patented sincerity on one side of the issue today as he did on the other side of the issue yesterday.

If we fail to pass negative judgment on a man with as little selflessness as Bill Clinton in the office that he holds, we only aid him in eroding the institutions and the principles on which our country was founded. Those who cite, in defense of Bill Clinton, the Biblical passage where Jesus says "if any of you is without sin, let him be the first to throw a stone at her" forget that Jesus instructs the adulterous woman to "go now and leave your life of sin." Mr. Clinton, though, is no different now than he was the day he lied in court.

In his State of the Union address, this president, who once told us "the era of big government is over," proceeded to spend every penny of the budget surplus produced by the largest tax revenue since World War II. Of course, Mr. Clinton made it sound like Christmas to the uninformed viewer. He threw in a few tax credits for the lower class, encouraging them to be unmotivated to work their way up in the world. For them, that would mean entering another tax bracket where tax credits don't exist, and marginal rates aren't so friendly. It was Bill Clinton in true form—charming his way out of another contradiction like no ordinary liar could.

But then again, Bill Clinton "is an unusually good liar. Unusually good."

SOURCE: Calvin Thigpen, "Failure to Impeach Clinton Suggests 'Lying Is Okay'," *Daily Mississippian* (University of Mississippi), February 9, 1999.

No

Bill Clinton is fond of deflecting blame for the Monica Lewinsky scandal away from himself and onto special prosecutor Kenneth Starr. The country would be better served if he admitted that the whole affair is his fault, and no one else's.

Starr deserves, without a doubt, much criticism. His office illegally leaked confidential information to the press and badgered and intimidated potential witnesses.

The media, also, deserves criticism for its handling of Lewinskygate. They have reported the developments in the case with all the professionalism and restraint of supermarket tabloids. Their shameless exploitation of the scandal in order to boost sales and ratings has done severe damage to the American people's already limited respect for their profession.

But despite Starr's ethical misconduct and the media's sensationalistic reporting, Bill Clinton is ultimately responsible for the entire scandal. It was his actions, not the exposure of those actions, which produced the current turmoil. Clinton needs to face the fact that he has done terrible harm to the office he holds and the country he was elected to serve.

All that having been said, Clinton should not resign, and more importantly does not deserve to be impeached. The evidence simply does not warrant either action. From a legal standpoint, Clinton committed no crimes worthy of impeachment. There is no evidence that he obstructed justice, and although he clearly misled prosecutors during testimony for the Paula Jones lawsuit, he did not technically perjure himself.

Another argument for impeachment is that Clinton deserves official censure because of the severity of his moral transgressions. To my mind, this argument has even more flaws than the case for impeachment due to legal transgressions. At its heart lies the assumption that the president should be a person who acts ethically and morally in all facets of his life. Many a talk radio host and TV pundit claimed that by cheating on his wife, Clinton has shown himself to be morally unfit to lead the country.

But lapses in ethical judgment are not always indicative of complete moral corruption. Obviously, Clinton's relationship with Lewinsky was, in his words, "wrong." But there is little evidence to suggest that Clinton has no values whatsoever. Quite the contrary, his political record shows that he possesses something of a moral compass. He fought the good fight for health care, launched a badly needed campaign on race relations, and has supported women's rights and education throughout his presidency.

Of course, Clinton's most grievous act was lying to the American people. Granted, that is a serious offense, but in this case it does not warrant impeachment. First and foremost, Clinton lied in order to cover up a personal affair. He did not lie in order to start a war, as Lyndon Johnson did regarding the Gulf of Tonkin, nor to cover up serious crimes and abuses of power, as Richard Nixon did during Watergate.

Clinton lied to hide his private mistakes from a ravenous media and blood-thirsty Republicans. It would have taken considerable courage, more courage than most people have, to confess to the affair when the press discovered it. For Congress to impeach Clinton for having only a typical amount of integrity would be unjustifiably harsh.

Finally, if Congress impeaches Clinton, they will severely damage the balance of power among the branches of government. Up to this point, Congress has only initiated impeachment proceedings in the most dire of circumstances. Lies told in order to hide personal misconduct do not constitute dire circumstances. Impeaching Clinton for such trivial misdoings would set a precedent of impeachment for minor misdeeds and seriously compromise the executive branch of government. If Clinton is impeached, then the government as we have known it in the twentieth century will be radically changed.

The most compelling argument against impeachment has nothing to do with the particulars of Clinton's case, however.

Impeachment would needlessly further a scandal that has already taken a terrible toll on the country. If members of Congress wish to do what is best for America, they will read Kenneth Starr's final report, nod solemnly, and then turn to issues that actually affect the American people, such as campaign finance reform and Social Security reform.

SOURCE: Josh M. Feldman, "President's Wrongdoings Do Not Warrant Impeachment," *Columbia Daily Spectator* (Columbia University), September 9, 1998.

President Clinton is shown here meeting with important donors to the Democratic Party. Many criticize the need for financial backing as creating too great an opportunity for wealthy interests to influence presidential decisions.

become institutionalized until even later. Institutionalized relations bring close and constant communication with party, interest groups, polls, the media, and the other segments of political society that we have discussed in this and other chapters. This presidential constituency varies between Democratic and Republican administrations; it is more working-class, elderly, urban, ethnic, and intellectual during Democratic administrations and more rural, suburban, middle- and professional-class, wealthy, and "higher" in ethnic status during Republican administrations. In either case, however, it is a popular and democratized constituency. In sum, presidential power is democratized power, and democratization has made the presidency far more powerful. Yet we must not forget the duality of the presidency discussed at the beginning of this chapter: the presidency may be more powerful, but it is also more vulnerable. The dark side of presidential vulnerability is weakness, indecision, deceit, and fear of governing. The bright side of presidential vulnerability is energy, openness, vigor, and, above all, accountability to the people. Would we have it any other way? The epoch of presidential government continues today, and it is a people's epoch, for better or for worse.

GET INVOLVED: Working in the White House

Johanna Atienza was a twenty-year-old junior majoring in political science at a West Coast university when she learned from other students that her school had a Washington, D.C., internship program. She was immediately interested: "What better way is there to learn about politics than from the inside?" She also felt that a semester in the nation's capital would help her to understand if the people who worked in the federal government really cared about the average citizen.

A speaker at the information session she attended spelled out the options for internships in Washington, D.C. Some were in government. Others were with

AMERICAN DEMOCRACY IN COMPARATIVE PERSPECTIVE

Parliamentary and Presidential Executives

Among democracies of the world, one finds two basic forms of executive leadership, the *parliamentary (cabinet) executive* and the *presidential executive.* A presidential executive is distinguished by a single person who is popularly elected by the public. This executive's term of office is fixed and is independent of the national legislature (neither the president nor the assembly can terminate the tenure of the other), and the president selects and manages a cabinet that attends to the affairs of government. At the core of a presidential system is the person of the president; personality and leadership qualities are essential features that extend and complement the formal constitutional powers of the president.

By contrast, a parliamentary executive relies on the assembly or national legislature for its ultimate legitimacy. Political parties are at the center of parliamentary executives. In a classic parliamentary executive, following national elections, key leaders of political parties from the lower chamber of the national legislature negotiate to select a coalition of parties that will subsequently appoint individual ministers to comprise the executive cabinet. Members of the cabinet remain legislators and have no independence from the tenure of the assembly. The executive cabinet is chaired by a *prime minister* who assumes the role of being the "first among equals" among her fellow ministers. The actual decisions of government remain largely collegial, forged from negotiation and discussion among the various ministers within the cabinet. The tenure of the cabinet and the prime minister can be terminated by the assembly, but the tenure of the national legislature cannot be terminated by the cabinet or the prime minister. Finally, neither the prime minister nor the other members of the executive cabinet are elected by the public—they are invested by the national legislature.

Of today's world democracies, less than a third practice the presidential form of executive leadership. Classic presidential executives are most common in North and South America, though versions of this model of executive leadership can be found around the world. Besides the United States, democracies that rely on the presidential system include Costa Rica, Bolivia, Venezuela, South Korea, Poland, Romania, Bulgaria, and Colombia. The most common means of executive leadership is some form of parliamentary executive. Most of the European democracies are parliamentary. However, there are few systems that perfectly match the ideal model of a presidential or parliamentary executive. For instance, the United States does not have a popularly elected president, and, in Great Britian, the prime minister is far more powerful relative to the cabinet than is the typical case of prime ministers in parliamentary democracies on the European continent. Furthermore, the British prime minister can effectively dissolve the assembly (the House of Commons) by simply calling for new elections (subject to the approval of the monarch).

Among the approximately thirty-two electoral democracies where presidents are directly or indirectly elected by the public as of the late 1990s, the powers of the American president with respect to legislation (such as initiating legislation, vetoing legislation and having those vetoes overridden by the legislature, initiating annual budget bills, and ruling by decree in emergencies) are no more than "average"; basically, the president shares power with an independent legislature (thus the concept of separate powers). The legislative powers of the Brazilian, Chilean, Colombian, Ecuadorian, Mexican, Panamanian, Paraguayan, and Uruguayan presidents are all notably greater than that of the American president. The Brazilian president, for instance, may declare an "urgent" situation and rule by decree and enjoys many more technical advantages when it comes to surviving the threats of veto overrides of legislation.

Students of comparative government cite specific advantages to the presidential type of executive. Specifically, these are accountability (one person is easier to blame and reward than a collegial body), electoral identifiableness (it is easier for the electorate to identify with the candidate of the present, rather than a collective that is selected by the political party, as in cabinet governments), mutual checks (the president stands largely apart from the legislature, fostering more active checks and balances to power), and enhanced political arbitration (because the president stands apart from direct connection to partisan political negotiations and can serve to reconcile intractable issues between political parties). These same strengths attributed to the presidential executive highlight the weaknesses of the parliamentary executive: weaker accountability, weaker identification with the electorate, concentrated powers of the executive and legislature that are not checked and balanced, and the absence of a clear separate arbitrator to political intransigence. However, for a number of students of government, these very weaknesses of the parliamentary system of government enhance its democratic quality—collegiality and collective decision making tied to the legislative body make arrogant and imbalanced executive power less likely to distort the democratic process.

the media, interest groups, and other private organizations involved in politics. Johanna's ears perked up when she learned that the White House had an intern program. The speaker suggested that she call the White House directly.

That first phone call was the beginning of her trip into what sometimes seemed like a fantasyland. After speaking directly to the White House director of the internship program, who answered her questions, Johanna received an application that asked for basic information, such as her name, address, telephone numbers, and so forth; two essays, one on why she wanted to be a White House intern and the other describing a formative experience in her life; a writing sample of approximately 500 words; and two letters of recommendation. Johanna filled out the form, devoted considerable thought and effort to the essays, and submitted the first page of a paper she had written for one of her classes as her writing sample.

Between Thanksgiving and Christmas, she received a large envelope with a return address that read, "The White House—Washington." Johanna's immediate reaction: "I was screaming!" She had been accepted into the program. Still, she needed to pass one more test. She had to fill out a form (for the FBI) that asked such questions as "Do you advocate the overthrow of the U.S. Government?" and "Have you taken illegal drugs?" The form also asked her to detail her addresses for the past seven or eight years. Johanna submitted the form. She assumed that she passed the FBI security test because she never heard anything more about it.

Several weeks later, she moved to the nation's capital. Her assignment was to work with the people who scheduled travel for the President and the First Lady. Over the next three months, Johanna met and worked with some of the top officials in the White House. She also had the opportunity to meet President Bill Clinton and Hillary Clinton. While it was exciting to wander around the maze of offices in the White House, Johanna reports, she was often so busy that she had little time to realize that she was indeed wandering through White House corridors.

What did Johanna learn from her three-month participation in the day-to-day life of White House politics that she was unlikely to learn in a classroom? First, she was struck by the incredible complexity of the presidency and Washington politics. Procedures are detailed and time-consuming. Things moved remarkably slowly, if at all. Second, however, she gained tremendous respect for the people who work in the White House. In general, the staff believed that "you can do some good, you really can." They were dedicated people who worked long hours, often for little money. Even the older aides worked long hours and devoted themselves to public service.

Johanna went to the White House asking herself whether the staff and politicians in Washington, D.C., really care about the people back home. She returned to the West Coast with a strong sense that the people who work in the White House for the President of the United States do indeed strive to make life a little better for the rest of us.

Should other students apply for the White House intern program—even though the application process takes time and effort? Johanna answers without hesitation, "Definitely." See if your school has a Washington, D.C., program. If not, call the White House directly and ask for the intern office. At this time next year, you could be one of the bright young people wandering their way through the West Wing.

Summary

The foundations for presidential government were laid in the Constitution, which provides for a unitary executive who is head of state as well as head of government. The first section of this chapter reviewed the powers of each: the head of state with its military, judicial, and diplomatic powers; the head of government with its executive, military, and legislative powers.

The second and third sections of this chapter focused on the president's institutional and political resources. The Cabinet, the other top appointments, the White House staff, and the Executive Office of the President are some of the impressive institutional resources of presidential power. The president's political party, the supportive group coalitions, and access to the media and, through that, access to the millions of Americans who make up the general public are formidable political resources that can be used to bolster a president's power. But these resources are not cost- or risk-free. A direct relationship with the mass public is the president's most potent modern resource, but it is also the most problematic.

The final section of this chapter traced the rise of modern presidential government after the much longer period of congressional dominance. There is no mystery in the shift to government centered on the presidency. Congress built the modern presidency by delegating to it not only the power to implement the vast new programs of the 1930s but also by delegating its own legislative power to make the policies themselves. Presidential government is now an established fact of American politics.

FOR FURTHER READING

Barber, James David. *The Presidential Character.* Englewood Cliffs, NJ: Prentice-Hall, 1985.

Drew, Elizabeth. *On the Edge: The Clinton Presidency.* New York: Simon & Schuster, 1994.

Hart, John. *The Presidential Branch: From Washington to Clinton.* Chatham, NJ: Chatham House, 1995.

Hinckley, Barbara, and Paul Brace. *Follow the Leader: Opinion Polls and Modern Presidents.* New York: Basic Books, 1992.

Kernell, Samuel. *Going Public: New Strategies of Presidential Leadership.* Washington, DC: Congressional Quarterly Press, 1986.

Lowi, Theodore J. *The Personal President: Power Invested, Promise Unfulfilled.* Ithaca, NY: Cornell University Press, 1985.

Milkis, Sidney M. *The President and the Parties: The Transformation of the American Party System since the New Deal.* New York: Oxford University Press, 1993.

Nelson, Michael, ed. *The Presidency and the Political System.* 4th ed. Washington, DC: Congressional Quarterly Press, 1994.

Neustadt, Richard E. *Presidential Power: The Politics of Leadership from Roosevelt to Reagan.* Rev. ed. New York: Free Press, 1990.

Pfiffner, James P. *The Modern Presidency.* New York: St. Martin's, 1994.

Skowronek, Stephen. *The Politics Presidents Make: Presidential Leadership from John Adams to George Bush.* Cambridge, MA: Harvard University Press, 1993.

Spitzer, Robert. *The Presidential Veto: Touchstone of the American Presidency.* Albany, NY: SUNY Press, 1988.

Tulis, Jeffrey. *The Rhetorical Presidency.* Princeton, NJ: Princeton University Press, 1987.

Watson, Richard A., and Norman Thomas. *The Politics of the Presidency.* Washington, DC: Congressional Quarterly Press, 1988.

STUDY OUTLINE

The Constitutional Powers of the Presidency

1. The president as head of state is defined by three constitutional provisions—military, judicial, and diplomatic—that are the source of some of the most important powers on which the president can draw.
2. The position of commander in chief makes the president the highest military authority in the United States, with control of the entire military establishment.
3. The presidential power to grant reprieves, pardons, and amnesties allows the president to choose freedom or confinement, and even life or death for all individuals who have violated, or are suspected of having violated, federal laws, including people who directly threaten the security of the United States.
4. The power to receive representatives of foreign countries allows the president almost unconditional authority to determine whether a new ruling group can indeed commit its country to treaties and other agreements.
5. The president's role as head of government rests on a constitutional foundation consisting of three principal sources: executive power, domestic military authority, and legislative power.
6. The Constitution delegated to the president, as commander in chief, the obligation to protect every state against invasion and domestic violence.
7. The president's legislative power consists of the obligation to make recommendations for consideration by Congress and the ability to veto legislation.

Institutional Resources of Presidential Power

1. Presidents have at their disposal a variety of institutional resources—such as the power to fill high-level political positions—that directly affect a president's ability to govern.
2. Presidents increasingly have preferred the White House staff to the Cabinet as a tool for managing the gigantic executive branch.
3. The White House staff, which is composed primarily of analysts and advisers, has grown from an informal group of fewer than a dozen people to a new presidential bureaucracy.
4. The Executive Office of the President, often called the institutional presidency, is larger than the White House staff, and comprises the president's permanent management agencies.

Political Resources of Presidential Power

1. The president also has political resources on which to draw in exercising the powers of office.
2. Presidents often use their electoral victories to increase their power by claiming the election was a mandate for a certain course of action.
3. Although its traditional influence is on the decline, the president's party is still significant as a means of achieving legislative success.
4. Interest groups and coalitions supportive of the president's agenda are also a dependable resource for presidential government.
5. Over the past half-century, the American executive branch has harnessed mass popularity successfully as a political resource.

The Presidency and Democracy

1. The democratization of the presidency through the growth of a mass popular base has made the institution more powerful.

PRACTICE QUIZ

1. Which article of the Constitution established the presidency?
   a) Article I
   b) Article II
   c) Article III
   d) none of the above
2. Which of the following does not represent a classification of a constitutional provision designating the president as head of state?
   a) legislative
   b) military
   c) judicial
   d) diplomatic
3. Which of the following does not require the advice and consent of the Senate?
   a) an executive agreement
   b) a treaty
   c) Supreme Court nominations
   d) All of the above require the advice and consent of the Senate.

4. Which of the following terms has been used to describe the presidency as it has used constitutional and other powers to make itself more powerful?
   a) "the delegated presidency"
   b) "the imperial presidency"
   c) "the personal presidency"
   d) "the preemptive presidency"

5. By what process can Congress reject a presidential veto?
   a) veto override
   b) pocket veto
   c) executive delegation
   d) impeachment

6. Which of the following describes the presidential foreign policy advisory council composed of the president; the vice president; the secretaries of state, defense, and the treasury; the attorney general; and others?
   a) the "Inner Cabinet"
   b) the National Security Council
   c) both a and b
   d) neither a nor b

7. The Office of Management and Budget is part of
   a) the Executive Office of the President.
   b) the White House staff.
   c) the Kitchen Cabinet.
   d) both a and b.

8. In what book did Woodrow Wilson describe American government in 1885?
   a) *A Separated System*
   b) *Checks and Balances*
   c) *Presidential Government*
   d) *Congressional Government*

9. Which twentieth-century presidency transformed the American system of government from a Congress-centered to a president-centered system?
   a) Woodrow Wilson's
   b) Franklin Roosevelt's
   c) Richard Nixon's
   d) Jimmy Carter's

10. How many people work for agencies within the Executive Office of the President?
   a) 25 to 50
   b) 700 to 1,000
   c) 1,500 to 2,000
   d) 4,500 to 5,000

CRITICAL THINKING QUESTIONS

1. At times, the Congress has been the dominant branch of government. At other times, the presidency has predominated. Describe the changes in the relationship between the presidency and the Congress throughout American history. What factors contributed to the dominance of Congress? What factors contributed to the resurgence of the presidency? Which branch of government dominates now? Why do you think so?

2. Presidents have constitutional, institutional, and political sources of power. Which of the three do you think most accounts for the powers of the presidency? Is it, in fact, possible to discern among these the true source of presidential power? Select a president and discuss the ways in which that particular president used each source of power to succeed in the presidency.

KEY TERMS

Cabinet (p. 545)
caucus (political) (p. 535)
commander in chief (p. 537)
delegated powers (p. 534)
executive agreement (p. 538)
Executive Office of the President (EOP) (p. 548)
executive order (p. 543)
expressed powers (p. 534)
inherent powers (p. 534)
Kitchen Cabinet (p. 547)
legislative initiative (p. 542)
line-item veto (p. 541)
mandate (p. 552)
National Security Council (NSC) (p. 545)
New Deal coalition (p. 553)
patronage (p. 544)
permanent campaign (p. 557)
pocket veto (p. 541)
rallying effect (p. 559)
veto (p. 541)
War Powers Resolution (p. 538)
White House staff (p. 545)

15 Bureaucracy in

★ **Bureaucracy and Bureaucrats**

Why do bureaucracies exist? Why are they needed?
Has the federal bureaucracy grown too large?
What roles do government bureaucrats perform? What types of access do citizens have to the bureaucracy?

★ **The Organization of the Executive Branch**

What are the agencies that make up the executive branch?
How can one classify these agencies according to their missions?

★ **Can Bureaucracy Be Reinvented?**

Can government be made more responsive and efficient? Why or why not?

★ **Can the Bureaucracy Be Reduced?**

What methods have been used to reduce the size and the role of the federal bureaucracy?
How effective can efforts to reduce the bureaucracy be?

★ **Can Bureaucracy Be Controlled?**

How can bureaucracy and democracy coexist? What popular controls over the bureaucracy exist?
How do the president and Congress manage and oversee the bureaucracy?
What is the most effective means to guarantee a responsible bureaucracy?

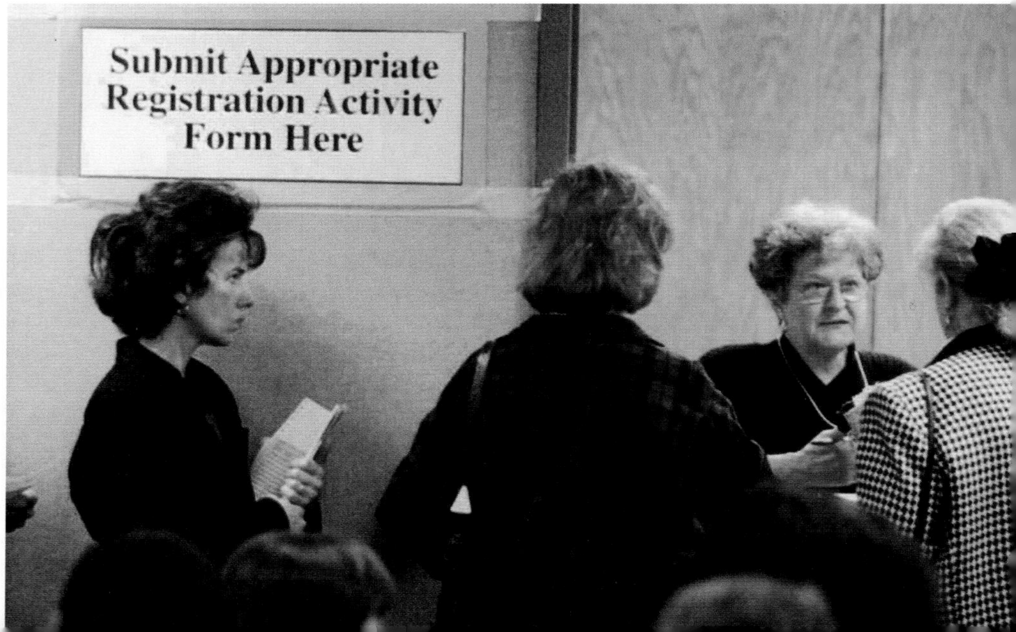

a Democracy

STUDENTS AND POLITICS

THE "real world" that college students are told they are preparing for is largely a world of work—of earning a living by collaborating in the production of goods and services for which other people are willing to pay. For most students, college is an opportunity to improve their employment prospects. And with the exception of a few who will own and operate small businesses or independent medical or law practices or who will be self-supporting artists or musicians, most college graduates will go from a bachelor's, graduate, or professional degree directly to salaried employment in a private company or a public organization of a hundred or more employees. In other words, most college graduates will work for somebody else. The source of income for most will be a salary, which will come from an employer who makes the job possible.

That job will typically consist of a set of responsibilities and tasks defined by the employer to meet the needs of the organization. Specific assignments come from the employee's immediate superior. Often a new employee's real work begins after weeks or months of on-the-job training. This is true even for many who have advanced degrees or significant experience, because the organization—whether a private company or a government agency—will need to accustom the new employee to the special way the organization operates. To gain maximum efficiency, the employer provides a salary sufficient to get each employee to contribute precisely to the mission of the organization—whether the output of the organization is computers, television programs, welfare services, or environmental regulations. The organization has a mission defined by its output, and all of the jobs within that organization serve that mission.

In the course of a career, the average person will make several job changes. But with the exception of the few who will have enough capital to form a private practice or establish an independently owned company, the job changes will be from one position to another—one with more responsibility and higher pay—within one relatively large organization or from one large organization to another. For most people this will be the very definition of a career—moving upward, step by step, to higher levels of responsibility in return for higher salary and more privileges. Success in one's career is typically defined by the size of one's salary and other benefits, by titles that convey the level of responsibility one holds, and by certain additional titles and prizes that convey recognition for meritorious contributions.

Turn now to Table 15.1 on the next page, which identifies the basic characteristics of bureaucracy. These characteristics are found in virtually *all* organizations, whether public or private, military or religious, for profit or nonprofit, producers of goods or providers of services. Most organizations are bureaucracies, and most of their employees are bureaucrats.

Table 15.1 THE SIX PRIMARY CHARACTERISTICS OF BUREAUCRACY

Characteristic	Explanation
Division of labor	Workers are specialized. Each worker develops a skill in a particular job and performs the job routinely and repetitively, thereby increasing productivity.
Allocation of functions	Each task is assigned. No one makes a whole product; each worker depends on the output of other workers.
Allocation of responsibility	Each task becomes a personal responsibility—a contractual obligation. No task can be changed without permission.
Supervision	Some workers are assigned the special task of watching over other workers rather than contributing directly to the creation of the product. Each supervisor watches over a few workers (a situation known as "span of control"), and communications between workers or between levels move in a prescribed fashion (known as "chain of command").
Purchase of full-time employment	The organization controls all the time the worker is on the job, so each worker can be assigned and held to a task. Some part-time and contracted work is tolerated, but it is held to a minimum.
Identification of career within the organization	Workers come to identify with the organization as a way of life. Seniority, pension rights, and promotions are geared to this relationship.

But if bureaucracy is so common in the workplace, why have "bureaucracy" and "bureaucrat" become such negative words? Why has "bureaucracy" come to mean only government, when in fact it is a universal phenomenon? Why do we call government activity we don't like "bureaucracy" and government activity we approve of "administration"? Why do we reserve the term "bureaucrat" for people whose work we don't like when as a matter of fact most of us are or will be bureaucrats ourselves?

- ***We begin this chapter by clarifying what we mean by "bureaucracy."*** Before we can understand the nature and character of the executive branch of the U.S. government, we must first examine why bureaucracy is necessary. From there, we then turn to the size, role, functions, and characteristics of the federal bureaucracy and bureaucrats.
- ***We next examine the organization of the executive branch as a whole, looking at the Cabinet departments, agencies, and bureaus that make up its operating parts.*** Since the executive branch is vast and there are far too many agencies for us to identify here, we will instead evaluate the different broad purposes that federal agencies serve.

- ***We next turn to ways in which the size and role of the federal bureaucracy can be reduced.*** Although efforts to downsize government have been popular in recent years, we question whether these attempts are effective or even address the most pressing problem regarding the control of the federal bureaucracy.
- ***We conclude this chapter by asking whether bureaucracy and democracy are contradictory.*** The bureaucracy is intended to be accountable to the president and Congress and through them to the American people. We will examine the ways in which the president and Congress have tried to manage the bureaucracy and hold it accountable and whether these management techniques have been effective. We conclude by reviewing the role of the average citizen in holding bureaucracy accountable.

Bureaucracy and Bureaucrats

- Why do bureaucracies exist? Why are they needed?
- Has the federal bureaucracy grown too large?
- What roles do government bureaucrats perform? What types of access do citizens have to the bureaucracy?

Bureaucracy is nothing more nor less than a form of organization, as defined by the attributes in Table 15.1. To gain some objectivity, and to appreciate the universality of bureaucracy, let us take the word and break it into its two main parts—*bureau* and *cracy. Bureau,* a French word, can mean either "office" or "desk." *Cracy* is the Greek word for "rule" or "form of rule." For example, "democracy" means rule by the people *(demos),* a form of government in which the people prevail. "Theocracy" refers to rule by clergy or churches. "Gerontocracy" would describe a system ruled by the elders of the community. Putting *bureau* and *cracy* back together produces a very interesting definition: **Bureaucracy** is a form of rule by offices and desks. Each member of an organization has an office, meaning a place as well as a set of responsibilities. That is, each "office" comprises a set of tasks that are specialized to the needs of the organization, and the person holding that office (or position) performs those specialized tasks. Specialization and repetition are essential to the efficiency of any organization. Therefore, when an organization is inefficient, it is almost certainly because it is not bureaucratized enough!

bureaucracy
the complex structure of offices, tasks, rules, and principles of organization that are employed by all large-scale institutions to coordinate effectively the work of their personnel

Americans depend on government bureaucracies to accomplish the most spectacular achievements and the most mundane. Yet, they often do not realize that public bureaucracies are essential for providing the services they use everyday and rely on in emergencies. On a typical day, a college student might check the weather forecast, drive on an interstate highway, mail the rent check, drink from a public water fountain, check the calories on the side of a yogurt container, attend a class, log on to the Internet, and meet a relative at the airport. Each of these activities is possible because of the work of

Government bureaucracy performs many important tasks. For example, government bureaucrats in the Federal Emergency Management Agency (left) coordinate relief efforts to areas devastated by natural disasters. These soldiers (right), for instance, were sent to Florida to work in areas damaged by a hurricane.

a government bureaucracy: the U.S. Weather Service, the U.S. Department of Transportation, the U.S. Postal Service, the Environmental Protection Agency, the Food and Drug Administration, the student loan programs of the U.S. Department of Education, the Advanced Research Projects Agency (which developed the Internet in the 1960s), and the Federal Aviation Administration. Without the ongoing work of these agencies, many of these common activities would be impossible, unreliable, or more expensive.

In emergencies, government bureaucracies are often the main source of organizational expertise that can address urgent needs. The Federal Emergency Management Agency (FEMA) has long experience in providing assistance after national disasters such as hurricanes, floods, and earthquakes. FEMA's services range from cleanup to emergency housing to loans for reconstruction. Government bureaucracies also provide protection from less visible but equally deadly dangers. The federal Centers for Disease Control (CDC) tracks disease outbreaks around the country, often uncovering patterns of illness that would otherwise be missed. For example, the CDC conducted studies showing that freshmen dormitory residents were at a higher risk for infection with the deadly meningitis bacteria and recommended vaccination.

These routine and exceptional tasks require the organization, specialization, and expertise found in bureaucracies. To provide these services, government bureaucracies employ specialists such as meteorologists, doctors, and scientists. To do their job effectively, these specialists require resources and tools (ranging from paper to blood samples); they have to coordinate their work with others (for example, the traffic engineers must communicate with construction engineers); and there must be effective outreach to the public (for example, private doctors must be made aware of health warnings). Bureaucracy provides a way to coordinate the many different parts that must work together in order to provide good services.

THE SIZE OF THE FEDERAL SERVICE

In his State of the Union address in 1996, President Bill Clinton declared that "the era of big government is over." With his re-election campaign looming, Clinton was capitalizing on popular sentiment that the federal government had grown too large. Despite fears of bureaucratic growth getting out of hand, however, the federal service has hardly grown at all during the past twenty-five years; it reached its peak postwar level in 1968 with 3.0 million civilian employees plus an additional 3.6 million military personnel (a figure swollen by Vietnam). The number of civilian federal employees has since fallen to approximately 2.7 million in 1998; the number of military personnel totals only 1.4 million.[1]

The growth of the federal service is even less imposing when placed in the context of the total workforce and when compared to the size of state and local public employment. Figure 15.1 indicates that, since 1950, the ratio of federal employment to the total workforce has been steady, and in fact has *declined* slightly in the past thirty years. In 1950, there were 4.3 million state and

EMPLOYEES IN THE FEDERAL SERVICE AND IN THE NATIONAL WORKFORCE, 1946–99

Figure 15.1

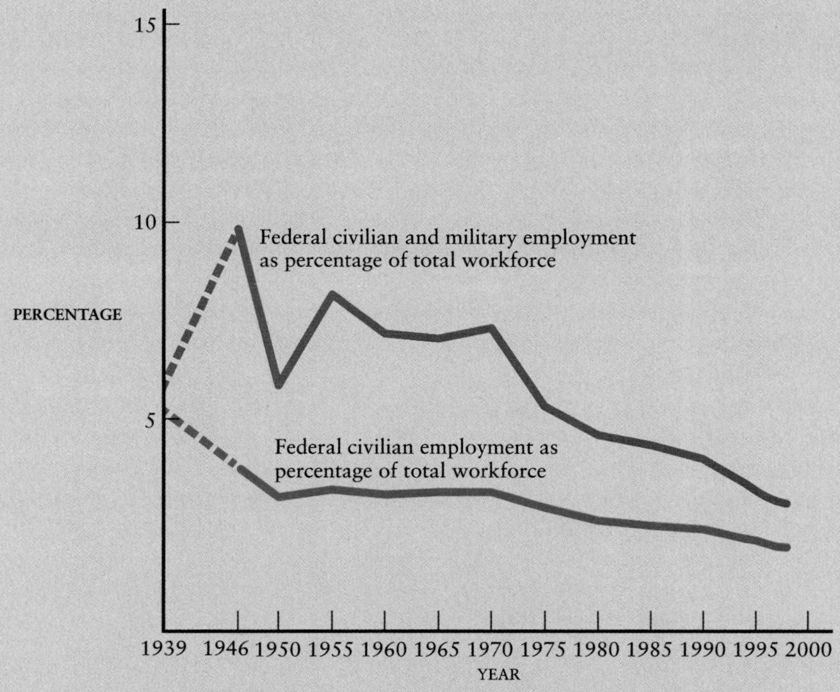

SOURCES: Office of Management and Budget, *Budget of the United States Government, FY, 2000, Historical Tables* (Washington, DC: Government Printing Office, 2000), p. 280, and U.S. Department of Labor, Bureau of Labor Statistics, *Employment and Earnings* (monthly).

local civil service employees (about 6.5 percent of the country's workforce). In 1998, there were almost 16.0 million (nearly 12 percent of the workforce). Federal employment, in contrast, exceeded 5 percent of the workforce only during World War II (not shown), and almost all of that momentary growth was military. After the demobilization, which continued until 1950 (as shown in Figure 15.1), the federal service has tended to grow at a rate that keeps pace with the economy and society. That is demonstrated by the lower line on Figure 15.1, which shows a constant relation between federal civilian employment and the size of the U.S. workforce. Variations in federal employment since 1946 have been in the military and are directly related to war and the cold war (as shown by the top line on Figure 15.1).

Another useful comparison is to be found in Figure 15.2. Although the dollar increase in federal spending shown by the bars looks impressive, the trend line indicating the relation of federal spending to the Gross Domestic Product (GDP) shows that in 1998, this percentage was barely higher than in 1960.

In sum, the national government is indeed "very large," but it has not been growing any faster than the economy or the society. The same is roughly true of the growth pattern of state and local public personnel. Bureaucracy keeps pace with society, despite people's seeming dislike for it, because the control towers, the prisons, the Social Security system, and other essential elements cannot be operated without bureaucracy. The United States certainly could not

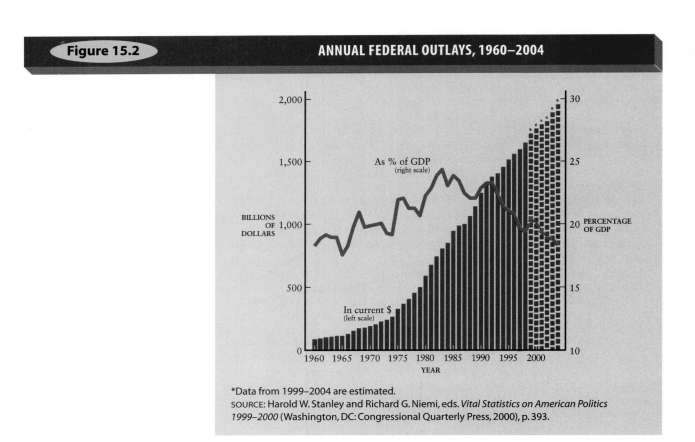

Figure 15.2 ANNUAL FEDERAL OUTLAYS, 1960–2004

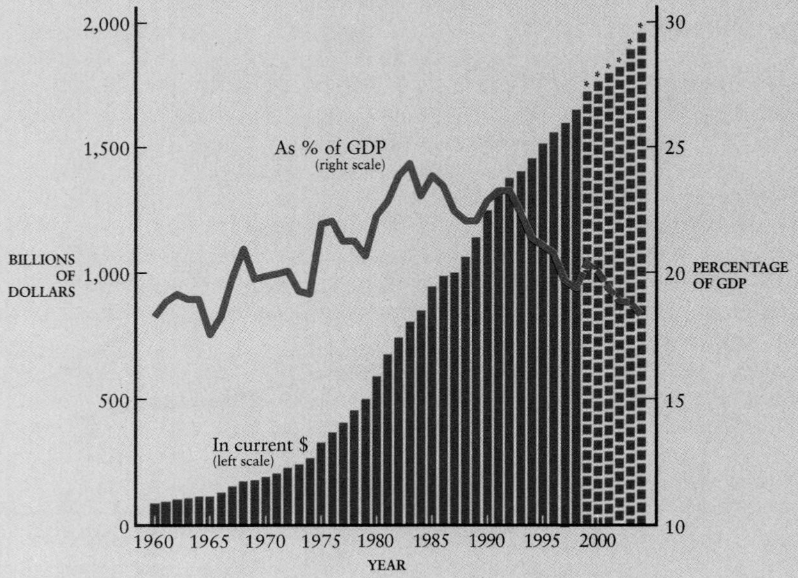

*Data from 1999–2004 are estimated.

SOURCE: Harold W. Stanley and Richard G. Niemi, eds. *Vital Statistics on American Politics 1999–2000* (Washington, DC: Congressional Quarterly Press, 2000), p. 393.

have conducted a successful war in the Persian Gulf without a gigantic military bureaucracy.

Although the federal executive branch is large and complex, everything about it is commonplace. Bureaucracies are commonplace because they touch so many aspects of daily life. Government bureaucracies implement the decisions made by the political process. Bureaucracies are full of routine because that assures the regular delivery of services and ensures that each agency fulfills its mandate. Public bureaucracies are powerful because legislatures and chief executives, and indeed the people, delegate to them vast power to make sure a particular job is done—enabling citizens to be more free to pursue their private ends. Citizens appreciate this fact even when they profess to be anti–big government. For example, when Housing and Urban Development (HUD) Secretary Andrew Cuomo announced plans in June 1997 to eliminate twenty-two federal employees in its Oklahoma City branch, Republican member of Congress Frank Lucas raised a loud public protest on behalf of his Oklahoma City constituents. His claim was that twenty-one of the twenty-two were survivors of the Alfred P. Murrah Federal Building bombing and that "some anonymous bureaucrat in Washington" was responsible (somehow markedly different from the "bureaucrats" in Oklahoma City he was defending). Yet the same vociferous representatives will argue that bureaucracies are a threat to freedom, because their size, their momentum, and the interests of the civil servants themselves in keeping their jobs impel bureaucracies and bureaucrats to resist any change of direction.

Perspectives on Politics

Percentage of respondents reporting a favorable impression of certain federal departments and agencies.

Postal Service	89%
Park Service	85%
Centers for Disease Control	79%
Defense	76%
FDA	75%
NASA	73%
Federal Aviation Administration	70%
EPA	69%
Agriculture	68%
FBI	67%
SSA	62%
Education	61%
Veterans Administration	59%
Commerce	58%
Justice	56%
FTC	53%
HUD	51%
CIA	51%
IRS	38%

SOURCE: The Pew Research Center (1997–98), http://www.people-press.org/trusttab.htm.

BUREAUCRATS

"Government by offices and desks" conveys to most people a picture of hundreds of office workers shuffling millions of pieces of paper. There is a lot of truth in that image, but we have to look more closely at what papers are being shuffled and why. More than seventy years ago, an astute observer defined bureaucracy as "continuous routine business."[2] As we saw at the beginning of this chapter, almost any organization succeeds by reducing its work to routines, with each routine being given to a different specialist. But specialization separates people from each other; one worker's output becomes another worker's input. The timing of such relationships is essential, and this requires that these workers stay in communication with each other. Communication is the key. In fact, bureaucracy was the first information network. Routine came first; voluminous routine came as bureaucracies grew and specialized.

What Do Bureaucrats Do? Bureaucrats, whether in public or in private organizations, communicate with each other in order to coordinate all the specializations within their organization. This coordination is necessary in order to carry out the primary task of bureaucracy, which is **implementation**, that is, implementing the objectives of the organization as laid down by its board of directors (if a private company) or by law (if a public agency). In government, the "bosses" are ultimately the legislature and the elected chief executive.

implementation
the efforts of departments and agencies to translate laws into specific bureaucratic routines

When the bosses—Congress, in particular, when it is making the law—are clear in their instructions to bureaucrats, implementation is a fairly straightforward process. Bureaucrats translate the law into specific routines for each of the employees of an agency. But what happens to routine administrative implementation when there are several bosses who disagree as to what the instructions ought to be? This requires yet another job for bureaucrats: interpretation. Interpretation is a form of implementation, in that the bureaucrats still have to carry out what they believe to be the intentions of their superiors. But when bureaucrats have to interpret a law before implementing it, they are in effect engaging in *lawmaking*. Congress often deliberately delegates to an administrative agency the responsibility of lawmaking. Members of Congress often conclude that some area of industry needs regulating or some area of the environment needs protection, but they are unwilling or unable to specify just how that should be done. In such situations, Congress delegates to the appropriate agency a broad authority within which the bureaucrats have to make law, through the procedures of **rulemaking** and **administrative adjudication.**

rulemaking
a quasi-legislative administrative process that produces regulations by government agencies

administrative adjudication
applying rules and precedents to specific cases to settle disputes with regulated parties

Rulemaking is exactly the same as legislation; in fact it is often referred to as "quasi-legislation." The rules issued by government agencies provide more detailed and specific indications of what the policy actually will mean. For example, the Occupational Health and Safety Administration is charged with ensuring that our workplaces are safe. OSHA has regulated the use of chemicals and other well-known health hazards. In recent years, the widespread use of computers in the workplace has been associated with a growing number of cases of repetitive stress injury, which hurts the hands, arms, and neck. To repond to this new threat to workplace health, OSHA issued a new set of ergonomic rules in November 1999 that tell employers what they must do to prevent and address such injuries among their workers. Such rules only take force after a period of public comment. Reaction from the people or businesses that will be subject to the rules may cause an agency to modify the rules they first issue. The rules about ergonomic safety in the workplace, for example, are sure to be contested by many businesses, which view them as too costly. The rulemaking process is thus a highly political one. Once rules are approved, they are published in the *Federal Register* and have the force of law.

Administrative adjudication is very similar to what the judiciary ordinarily does: applying rules and precedents to specific cases in order to settle disputes. In administrative adjudication, the agency charges the person or business suspected of violating the law. The ruling in an adjudication dispute applies only to the specific case being considered. Many regulatory agencies use administrative adjudication to make decisions about specific products or practices. For example, in December 1999, the Consumer Product Safety Commission held hearings on the safety of bleachers, sparked by concern over the death of children after falls from bleachers. It will issue guidelines about bleacher construction designed to prevent falls. These guidelines have the force of law. Likewise, product recalls are often the result of adjudication.

A good case study of the role agencies can play is the story of how ordinary federal bureaucrats created the Internet. Yes, it's true: what became the Internet was developed largely by the U.S. Department of Defense, and defense considerations still shape the basic structure of the Internet. In 1957, immediately following the profound American embarrassment over the Soviet Union's launching of *Sputnik,* Congress authorized the establishment of the Advanced Research Projects Agency (ARPA) to develop, among other things, a means of maintaining communications in the event the existing telecommunications network (the telephone system) was disabled by a strategic attack. Since the telephone network was highly centralized and therefore could have been completely disabled by a single attack, ARPA developed a decentralized, highly redundant network. Redundancy in this case improved the probability of functioning after an attack. The full design, called by the pet name of Arpanet, took almost a decade to create. By 1971, around twenty universities were connected to the Arpanet. The forerunner to the Internet was born.[3]

Government bureaucrats do essentially the same things that bureaucrats in large private organizations do, and neither type deserves the disrespect embodied in the term "bureaucrat." But because of the authoritative, coercive nature of government, far more constraints are imposed on public bureaucrats than on private bureaucrats, even when their jobs are the same. During the 1970s and 1980s, the length of time required to develop an administrative rule from a proposal to actual publication in the *Federal Register* (when it takes on full legal status) grew from an average of 15 months to an average of 35 to 40 months. Inefficiency? No. Most of the increased time is attributable to new procedures requiring more public notice, more public hearings, more hearings held out in the field rather than in Washington, more cost-benefit analysis, and stronger legal obligations to prepare "environmental impact statements" demonstrating that the proposed rule or agency action will not have an unacceptably large negative impact on the human or physical environment.[4] Thus, a great deal of what is popularly paraded as the lower efficiency of public agencies can be attributed to the political, judicial, legal, and public-opinion restraints and extraordinarily high expectations imposed on public bureaucrats.

We will have more to say at the end of this chapter about bureaucratic accountability and the potential role of citizens in it. Suffice it to say here that if a private company such as Microsoft were required to open up all its decision processes and management practices to full view by the media, their competitors, and all interested citizens, Microsoft—despite its profit motive and the pressure of competition—would be far less efficient, perhaps no more efficient than public bureaucracies.

Buried in red tape? This Food and Drug Administration reviewer now works on a laptop computer. The FDA is striving to computerize its operations and reduce agency review time.

The Merit System: How to Become a Bureaucrat In return for all these inconveniences, public bureaucrats are rewarded in part with greater job security than employees of most private organizations enjoy. More than a century ago, the federal government attempted to imitate business by passing the Civil Service Act of 1883, which was followed by almost universal adoption of equivalent laws in state and local governments. These laws required that appointees to public office be qualified for the job to which they are appointed. This policy came to be called the **merit system;** its ideal was not merely to put an end to political appointments under the "spoils system" but also to require adequate preparation for every job by holding competitive examinations through which the very best candidates were to be hired. At the higher levels of government agencies, including such posts as cabinet secretaries and assistant secretaries, many jobs are filled with political appointees, not part of the merit system.

merit system
a product of civil service reform, in which appointees to positions in public bureaucracies must objectively be deemed qualified for the position

As a further safeguard against political interference (and to compensate for the lower-than-average pay given to public employees), merit system employees—genuine civil servants—were given a form of tenure: legal protection against being fired without a show of cause. Reasonable people may disagree about the value of job tenure and how far it should extend in the civil service, but the justifiable objective of tenure—cleansing bureaucracy of political interference while upgrading performance—cannot be disputed.

The Organization of the Executive Branch

- What are the agencies that make up the executive branch?
- How can one classify these agencies according to their missions?

department
the largest subunit of the executive branch. The secretaries of the fourteen departments form the Cabinet

independent agency
an agency that is not part of a Cabinet department

government corporation
a government agency that performs a service normally provided by the private sector

Cabinet departments, agencies, and bureaus are the operating parts of the bureaucratic whole. Figure 15.3 is an organizational chart of one of the largest and most important of the fourteen **departments,** the Department of Agriculture. At the top is the head of the department, who in the United States is called the "secretary" of the department.[5] Below the secretary and the deputy secretary is a second tier of "undersecretaries" who have management responsibilities for one or more operating agencies, shown in the smaller print directly below each undersecretary. Those operating agencies are the third tier of the department, yet they are the highest level of responsibility for the actual programs around which the entire department is organized. This third tier is generally called the "bureau level." Each bureau-level agency is usually operating under a statute, adopted by Congress, that set up the agency and gave it its authority and jurisdiction. The names of these bureau-level agencies are often quite well known to the public—the Forest Service and the Agricultural Research Service, for example. These are the so-called line agencies, or agencies that deal directly with the public. Sometimes these agencies are officially called "bureaus," as in the Federal Bureau of Investigation (FBI), which is a part of the third tier of the Department of Justice. But "bureau" is also the conventional term for this level of administrative agency, even though many agencies or their supporters have preferred over the years to adopt a more palatable designation, such as "service" or "administration." Each bureau is, of course, subdivided into still other units, known as divisions, offices, or units—all are parts of the bureaucratic hierarchy.

Not all government agencies are part of Cabinet departments. Some **independent agencies** are set up by Congress outside the departmental structure altogether, even though the president appoints and directs the heads of these agencies. Independent agencies usually have broad powers to provide public services that are either too expensive or too important to be left to private initiatives. Some examples of independent agencies are the National Aeronautics and Space Administration (NASA), the Central Intelligence Agency (CIA), and the Environmental Protection Agency (EPA). **Government corporations** are a third type of government agency, but are more like private businesses performing and charging for a market service, such as delivering the mail (the United States Postal Service) or transporting railroad passengers (Amtrak).

Yet a fourth type of agency is the independent regulatory commission, given broad discretion to make rules. The first regulatory agencies established by Congress, beginning with the Interstate Commerce Commission in 1888, were set up as independent regulatory commissions because Congress recognized that regulatory agencies are "minilegislatures," whose rules are exactly the same as legislation but require the kind of expertise and full-time attention that is beyond the capacity of Congress. Until the 1960s, most of the regulatory agencies that were set up by Congress, such as the Federal Trade

Figure 15.3

ORGANIZATIONAL CHART OF THE DEPARTMENT OF AGRICULTURE, 1998

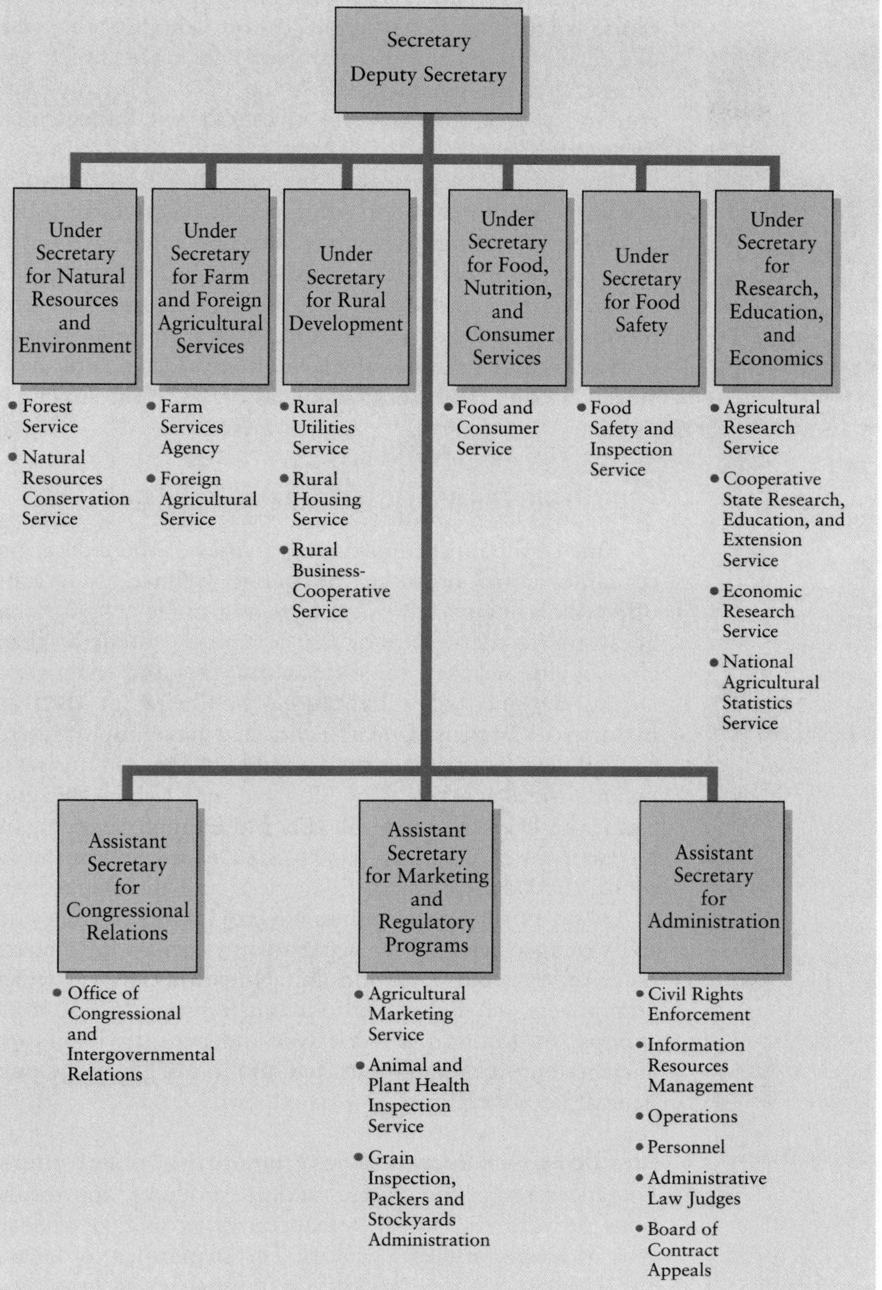

SOURCE: U.S. Department of Agriculture World Wide Web home page, http://www.usda.gov/agencies/agchart.htm (accessed 5/11/98).

Commission (1914) and the Federal Communications Commission (1934), were independent regulatory commissions. But beginning in the late 1960s and the early 1970s, all new regulatory programs, with two or three exceptions (such as the Federal Election Commission), were placed within existing departments and made directly responsible to the president. Since the 1970s, no major new regulatory programs have been established, independent or otherwise.

The different agencies of the executive branch can be classified into three main groups by the services that they provide to the American public. The first category of agencies provide services and products that seek to promote the public welfare. The second group of agencies work to promote national security. The third group provides services that help to maintain a strong economy. Let us look more closely at what each set of agencies offers to the American public.

Student Perspectives

In the wake of any failure by the federal government, it is typical to ask ourselves "are tax dollars being allocated effectively?" This question probably faces the National Aeronautics and Space Administration more than any other federal agency.

In September, the $125 million Mars Climate Orbiter disappeared because of a failure to convert from English to metric measurement units to calculate how the orbiter should have entered the Martian atmosphere. Currently, the Hubble Space Telescope is temporarily inoperable due to a broken gyroscope. Yet another failure seems to have occurred last weekend, when the $165 million Mars Polar Lander ceased communicating with Earth. These disappointments and others have given substantial bite to arguments in favor of reallocating NASA's funds or entrusting space exploration to the private sector.

But even a cursory overview of NASA's past achievements ought to sway most people away from NASA's critics. Few people realize the importance of satellites in all types of communications mediums—many of which were put into orbit by NASA. The Viking missions to Mars in the 1970s as well as the Pathfinder mission in 1996 both significantly increased our knowledge of the red planet. The 1969 Apollo 11 landing on the moon is yet another obvious example and the data continually being collected by the Hubble Space Telescope has proved invaluable to learning about the universe.

The purpose of government is to provide services the private sector could not or won't provide. While the private sector will likely play a role in space exploration in the near future, there will always be a role for government agencies like NASA. Despite its occasional failures, the services NASA offers are still invaluable. We cannot afford to place a dollar value on knowledge.

SOURCE: Staff Editorial, "Successful or Not, NASA Must Be Supported," *Michigan Daily* (University of Michigan), December 8, 1999.

PROMOTING THE PUBLIC WELFARE

One of the most important activities of the federal bureaucracy is to promote the public welfare. Americans often think of government welfare as a single program that goes only to the very poor but a number of federal agencies provide services, build infrastructure, and enact regulations designed to enhance the well-being of the vast majority of citizens. Departments that have important responsibilities for promoting the public welfare in this sense include the Department of Housing and Urban Development, the Department of Health and Human Services, the Department of Veterans Affairs, the Department of the Interior, the Department of Education, and the Department of Labor. Ensuring the public welfare is also the main activity of agencies in other departments, such as the Department of Agriculture's Food and Nutrition Service, which administers the federal school lunch program and food stamps. In addition, a variety of independent regulatory agencies enforce regulations that aim to safeguard the public health and welfare.

How Do Federal Bureaucracies Promote the Public Welfare?

To get a sense of the diverse services, products, and regulations provided by public bureaucracies let us take a closer look at several of these agencies. The Department of Health and Human Services (HHS) administers the program that comes closest to the popular understanding of welfare—Temporary Assistance to Needy Families (TANF). Yet this program is one of the smallest activities of the department. HHS also oversees the National Institutes of Health, which is responsible for cutting-edge biomedical research. The National Institutes of Health (NIH) occupies a large campus-like setting with seventy-five buildings outside of Washington, D.C. In their own labs and in the grants they provide to outside researchers, the NIH's central aim is to advance knowledge about health and diseases. Five of the scientists working in NIH labs have been awarded Nobel prizes for their research. The NIH is one of the leaders in experimenting with gene therapy, which is expected to open new possibilities for curing diseases in the future. HHS is also responsible for the two major health programs provided by the federal government: Medicaid, which provides health care for low-income families and for many elderly and disabled people in nursing homes, and Medicare, which is the health insurance available to all elderly people in the United States. The Administration on Aging is another agency under HHS; it provides services to the elderly such as "meals on wheels," which is designed to help keep the elderly independent.

A different notion of the public welfare, but one highly valued by most Americans, is provided by the National Park Service, which is under the Department of the Interior. First created in 1916, the National Park Service is responsible for the care and upkeep of national parks and historic sites. The Park Service also preserves historic sites, including Civil War battlegrounds such as Gettysburg, where President Lincoln made his famous address. Over 280 million people visit national parks each year. The Department of the Interior also houses the U.S. Fish and Wildlife Service, which is one of the oldest public conservation agencies in the world. The Fish and Wildlife Service seeks to protect wildlife habitats and since 1973 has also been charged with administering the Endangered Species Act. Since the nineteenth century, Americans have seen protection of the natural environment as an important public goal and have looked to federal agencies to implement laws and administer programs that preserve natural areas and keep them open to the public.

The United States has no "Department of Regulation" but has many **regulatory agencies.** Some of these are bureaus within departments, such as the

regulatory agencies
departments, bureaus, or independent agencies whose primary mission is to impose limits, restrictions, or other obligations on the conduct of individuals or companies in the private sector

Regulatory agencies have a strong presence in the lives of all Americans. For instance, the foods we eat are subject to myriad regulations from federal, state, and local agencies.

Food and Drug Administration (FDA) within the Department of Health and Human Services, the Occupational Safety and Health Administration (OSHA) in the Department of Labor, and the Animal and Plant Health Inspection Service in the Department of Agriculture. As we saw earlier, other regulatory agencies are independent regulatory commissions, such as the Federal Communications Commission (FCC) and the Environmental Protection Agency (EPA). But whether departmental or independent, an agency or commission is regulatory if Congress delegates to it relatively broad powers over a sector of the economy or a type of commercial activity and authorizes it to make rules restricting the conduct of people and businesses within that jurisdiction. Rules made by regulatory agencies have the force and effect of law.

The activities of these agencies seek to promote the welfare of all Americans, often working behind the scenes. The FDA, for example, works to protect public health by setting standards for food processing and inspecting plants to ensure that those standards are met. The EPA sets standards to limit polluting emissions from automobiles. The regulations required automobile manufacturers to change the way they designed cars and the result has been cleaner air in many metropolitan areas.

Bureaucracies, Clienteles, and the Public Some of the public agencies that provide services that enhance well-being are tied to a specific group or segment of American society that is often thought of as the main clientele of that agency. For example, the Department of Agriculture was established in 1862 to promote the interests of farmers. The departments of Commerce and Labor were founded in 1903 as a single department "to foster, promote and develop the foreign and domestic commerce, the mining, the manufacturing, the shipping, and fishing industries, and the transportation facilities of the United States."[6] They remained one department until 1913, when Congress separated them into two. Likewise, the Department of Veterans Affairs has strong links to veterans' organizations, such as the American Legion and the Veterans of Foreign Wars. The Department of Labor has a close relationship with organized labor. The Department of Education relies on teachers' organizations for support. Figure 15.4 is a representation of this type of politics. This configuration is known as an **iron triangle,** a pattern of stable relationships between an agency in the executive branch, a congressional committee or subcommittee, and one or more organized groups of agency clientele. (Iron triangles were discussed in detail in Chapter 12.)

iron triangle
the stable, cooperative relationships that often develop between a congressional committee, an administrative agency, and one or more supportive interest groups. Not all of these relationships are triangular, but the iron triangle is the most typical

These relationships with particular clienteles are often important in preserving agencies from political attack. During his 1980 campaign, Ronald Reagan promised to dismantle the Department of Education as part of his commitment to get government "off people's backs." After his election, President Reagan even appointed a secretary of the department who was publicly committed to eliminating it. Yet, by the end of his administration, the Department of Education was still standing and barely touched. In 1995, the Republican Congress vowed to eliminate the Department of Education, along with two other departments, but it, too, failed. The educational constituency of the department mobilized to save it each time.

Such clientele groups generally have more influence over federal agencies than do people who are not part of the clientele group. But the ability of clientele groups to get their way is not automatic, as agencies have to balance limited resources, competing interests, and political pressures. For example, the Department of Veterans Affairs long resisted the efforts of Vietnam veterans to be compensated for exposure to Agent Orange, a chemical defoliant used extensively during the Vietnam War. Veterans charged that exposure to Agent Orange had left them with a variety of diseases ranging from cancer to severe birth defects in their children. Only after decades of lobbying, law suits, and federally-sponsored studies did the Department of Veterans Affairs provide assistance to affected veterans.

Moreover, federal agencies increasingly seek public support outside their direct clients for their activities. In some cases, key clientele groups will work to build more widespread support for agency activities. For example, the AFL-CIO, which represents organized labor, built a broad coalition of student organizations, church groups, consumer groups, and civil rights activists

IRON TRIANGLES

Figure 15.4

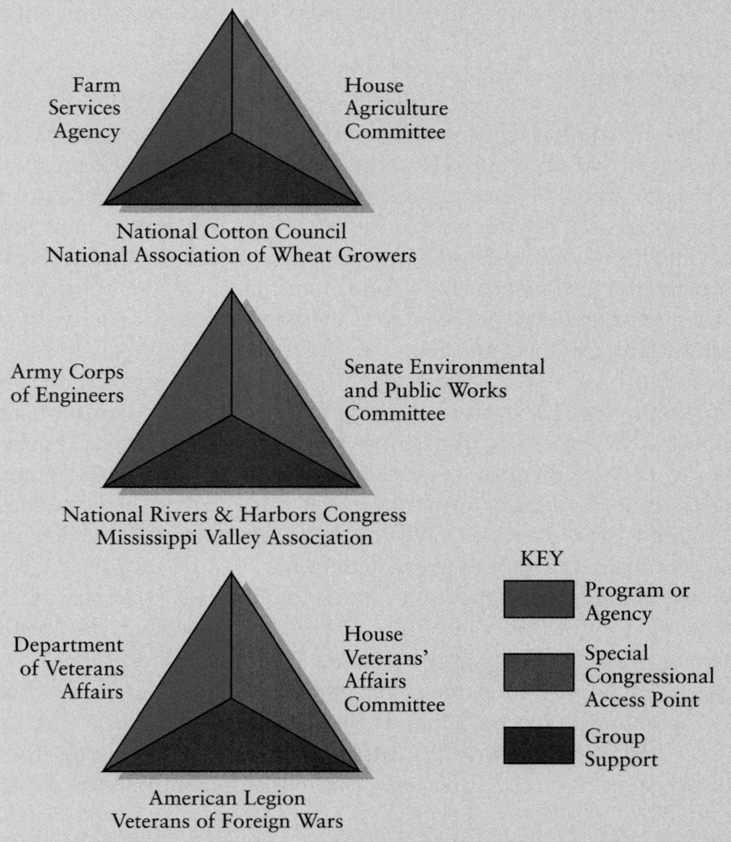

SOURCE: Adapted from U.S. House of Representatives, *Report of the Subcommittee for Special Investigations of the Committee on Armed Services,* 86th Cong., 1st sess. (Washington, DC: Government Printing Office, 1960), p. 7. Reprinted from Theodore J. Lowi, *Incomplete Conquest: Governing America,* 2nd ed. (New York: Holt, Rinehart and Winston, 1981), p. 139.

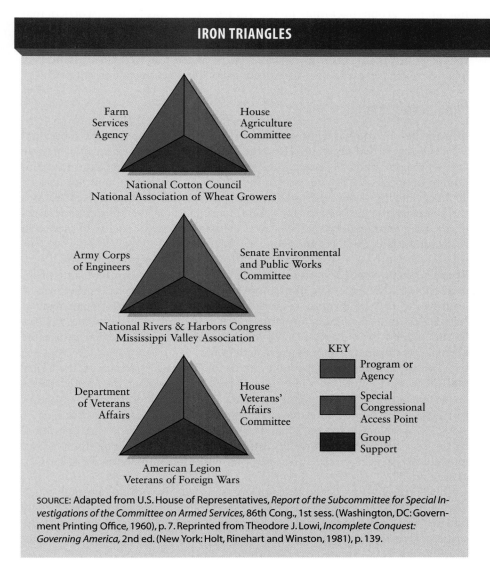

opposed to sweatshops in the United States. These groups helped to support the Department of Labor's campaign to uncover and eliminate such manufacturing practices in the United States. Agency failure to consider public opinion can result in embarrassing incidents, which bureaucrats prefer to avoid. In 1981, the Department of Agriculture's Food and Nutrition Service, which administers the federal school lunch program, had to retract its cost-cutting decision to classify ketchup as a vegetable after a public outcry that the agency was harming children.

Attentiveness to the public often means making the public aware of services and improving the way services are delivered. The Social Security Administration is an independent agency that administers old-age and disability insurance, the federal government's most important and expensive welfare program. Old-age insurance, or Social Security, is supported by the American Association of Retired Persons (AARP), generally considered the most powerful interest group operating in the United States today. But, worried that younger workers are losing confidence in Social Security, the agency has recently begun to issue annual statements to each worker, outlining the benefits that they can count on from Social Security when they retire and indicating what benefits are available if they become disabled before retirement.

PROVIDING NATIONAL SECURITY

One of the remarkable features of American federalism is that the most vital agencies for providing security for the American people are located in state and local governments—namely the police. But some agencies vital to maintaining national security do exist in the national government, and they can be grouped into two categories: (1) agencies for control of conduct defined as a threat to internal national security and (2) agencies for defending American security from external threats. The departments of greatest concern in these two areas are Justice, Defense, and State.

Agencies for Internal Security As long as the country is not in a state of insurrection, most of the task of maintaining national security takes the form of legal work, and the primary responsibility for that lies in the Department of Justice. It is indeed a luxury, and rare in the world, when national security can be maintained by routines of civil law with an army of lawyers, instead of martial law imposed by a real army with guns.

The largest and most important unit of the Justice Department is the Criminal Division. Lawyers in the Criminal Division represent the United States government when it is the plaintiff enforcing the federal criminal laws, except for those cases (about 25 percent) specifically assigned to other divisions or agencies. Criminal litigation is handled by U.S. attorneys, who are appointed by the president. There is one U.S. attorney in each of the ninety-four federal judicial districts; he or she supervises the work of a number of assistant U.S. attorneys.

The Civil Division of the Justice Department deals with litigation in which the United States is the defendant being sued for injury and damages allegedly inflicted by a government official. The missions of the other divisions of the Justice Department—Antitrust, Civil Rights, Environment and Natural Resources, and Tax—are described by their names.

The best-known bureau of the Justice Department is the Federal Bureau of Investigation (FBI). The FBI handles no litigation but instead serves as the principal information-gathering agency for the department and for the president. Established in 1908, the FBI expanded and advanced in stature during the 1920s and 1930s under the direction of J. Edgar Hoover.

J. Edgar Hoover built the FBI into one of the most famous and most feared government agencies in American history.

Despite its professionalism and its fierce pride in its autonomy, the FBI has not been unresponsive to the partisan commitments of Democratic and Republican administrations. Although the FBI has always achieved its best publicity from the spectacular apprehension of famous criminals, such as John Dillinger, George "Machine Gun" Kelly, and Bonnie and Clyde,[7] it has followed the president's direction in focusing on particular crime problems. Thus it has infiltrated Nazi and Mafia organizations; it operates the vast loyalty and security investigation programs covering all federal employees since the Truman presidency; it monitored and infiltrated the Ku Klux Klan and the civil rights movement in the 1950s and 1960s; and it has infiltrated radical political groups and extreme religious cults and survivalist militias in the 1980s and 1990s.

Agencies for External National Security Two departments occupy center stage in maintaining external national security: the departments of State and Defense.

Although diplomacy is generally considered the primary task of the State Department, diplomatic missions are only one of its organizational dimensions. As of 1996, the State Department comprised nineteen bureau-level units, each under the direction of an assistant secretary. Six of these are geographic or regional bureaus concerned with all problems within a defined region of the world; nine are "functional" bureaus, handling such things as economic and business affairs, intelligence and research, and international organizations. Four are bureaus of internal affairs, which handle such areas as security, finance and management, and legal issues.

These bureaus support the responsibilities of the elite of foreign affairs, the foreign service officers (FSOs), who staff U.S. embassies around the world and who hold almost all of the most powerful positions in the department below the rank of ambassador.[8] The ambassadorial positions, especially the plum positions in the major capitals of the world, are filled by presidential appointees, many of whom get their positions by having been important donors to the victorious political campaign.

Despite the importance of the State Department in foreign affairs, fewer than 20 percent of all U.S. government employees working abroad are directly under its authority. By far the largest number of career government professionals working abroad are under the authority of the Defense Department.

The creation of the Department of Defense by legislation between 1947 and 1949 was an effort to unify the two historic military departments, the War Department and the Navy Department, and to integrate them with a new department, the Air Force. Real unification, however, did not occur. The Defense Department simply added more pluralism to an already pluralistic national security establishment.

The American military, following worldwide military tradition, is organized according to a "chain of command"—a tight hierarchy of clear responsibility and rank, made clearer by uniforms, special insignia, and detailed organizational charts and rules of order and etiquette. The "line agencies" in the Department of Defense are the military commands, distributed geographically by divisions and fleets to deal with current or potential enemies. The "staff agencies," such as logistics, intelligence, personnel, research and development, quartermaster, and engineering, exist to serve the "line agencies." At the top of the military chain of command are chiefs of staff (called chief of naval operations in the Navy, and commandant in the Marines). These chiefs of staff also constitute the membership of the Joint Chiefs of Staff—the center of military policy and management.

National Security and Democracy Of all the agencies in the federal bureaucracy, those charged with providing national security most often come into tension with the norms and expectations of American democracy. Two issues in particular arise as these agencies work to ensure the national security: (1) the trade-offs between respecting the personal rights of individuals versus protecting the general public and (2) the need for secrecy in matters of national security versus the public's right to know what the government is doing. Standards about what is an acceptable trade-off in each area vary depending on whether the country is at war or peace. The nature of the threat facing national security also affects judgments about the appropriate trade-offs. Needless to say, Americans often disagree about such threats and therefore take different views about what activities the government should be able to pursue to defend our national security.

When national security is at stake, federal agencies have taken actions that are normally considered incompatible with individual rights. For example, in World War II, thousands of American citizens of Japanese descent were interned for national security reasons. Although the Supreme Court declared this action justified, the federal government has since acknowledged that it constituted unjustified discrimination and has offered reparations to those who were interned. In the 1960s, FBI director J. Edgar Hoover authorized extensive wiretaps on civil rights leader Martin Luther King, Jr., which most people today regard as an illegal invasion of his personal privacy. Many violations of individual privacy or personal rights were justified by the cold war. Today, questions about domestic terrorism raise similar issues about what the government should and should not do to protect lives and property.

Protecting the national security often requires the government to conduct its activities in secret. Yet, as Americans have come to expect a more open government in the past three decades, many critics believe that federal agencies charged with national security keep too many secrets from the American public. In the words of one critic "the United States Government must rest, in the words of the Declaration of Independence, on 'the consent of the governed.' And there can be no meaningful consent where those who are governed do not know to what they are consenting."[9] The effort to make more information related to national security more available to the public began in 1966 with the passage of the Freedom of Information Act. Strengthened in 1974 after Watergate, the act allows any person to request classified information from any federal agency. It is estimated that the federal government spends $80 million a year responding to 600,000 requests for information.[10]

The information obtained from the Freedom of Information Act often reveals unflattering or unsuccessful aspects of national security activities. One private organization, the National Security Archive, makes extensive use of the

Freedom of Information Act to obtain information about the activities of national security agencies. These include documents about a wide range of activities such as American involvement in the Cuban Bay of Pigs invasion in 1961 and human rights abuses in Latin America and the Caribbean in the past three decades. Such documents are often kept secret not because they threaten national security but rather because they are embarrassing or show that federal agencies violated accepted norms of human rights. The National Security Archive has published many of these documents and maintains an archive in Washington, D.C., that is open to the public.

Despite these procedures to promote openness, many critics charge that the government still keeps too many secrets. Material obtained under the Freedom of Information Act often arrives years after the initial request with much of the information still blacked out for security reasons. In 1995 Senator Daniel Patrick Moynihan led a commission on government secrecy that evaluated the secrecy practices of the federal government. The commission declared that, with the end of the cold war, "the culture of secrecy" maintained by national security agencies was not necessary and in fact impedes our security by hiding information.[11] The commission recommended much stricter standards for classifying information as secret in the first place. It proposed a national declassification center to make documents available much more quickly and at less cost than the case-by-case decision making under the Freedom of Information Act.

There are no easy answers to the questions about how the needs for national security should be reconciled with the values of a democratic society. It is clear, however, that in the post–cold war era, many practices once taken for granted are likely to be challenged.

MAINTAINING A STRONG ECONOMY

In our capitalist economic system the government does not directly run the economy. Yet many federal government activities are critical to maintaining a strong economy. Foremost among these are the agencies that are responsible for fiscal and monetary policy. Other agencies, such as the Internal Revenue Service (IRS), transform private resources into use for public purposes. Tax policy may also strengthen the economy through decisions about who to tax, how much, and when. Finally, the federal government, through such agencies as the Department of Transportation, the Commerce Department, and the Energy Department may directly provide services or goods that bolster the economy.

Fiscal and Monetary Agencies The best term for government activity affecting or relating to money is **fiscal policy.** The *fisc* was the Roman imperial treasury; "fiscal" can refer to anything and everything having to do with public finance. However, we in the United States choose to make a further distinction, reserving "fiscal" for taxing and spending policies and using "monetary" for policies having to do with banks, credit, and currency. Yet a third term, "welfare," deserves to be treated as an equal member of this redistributive category.[12]

fiscal policy
the use of taxing, monetary, and spending powers to manipulate the economy

The administration of fiscal policy occurs primarily in the Treasury Department. In addition to collecting income, corporate, and other taxes, the Treasury is also responsible for managing the enormous national debt—$3.72 trillion in 1998. (The national debt was a mere $710 billion in 1980.)[13] Debt is not simply something the country owes; it is something a country has to manage and administer. The debt is also a fiscal instrument in the hands of the federal government that can be used—through manipulation of interest rates and through the buying and selling of government bonds—to slow down or to speed up the activity of the entire national economy, as well as to defend the value of the dollar in international trade.

The Treasury Department is also responsible for printing the U.S. currency, but currency represents only a tiny proportion of the entire money economy. Most of the trillions of dollars used in the transactions of the private and public sectors of the U.S. economy exist in computerized accounts, not in currency.

Federal Reserve System
a system of twelve Federal Reserve Banks that facilitates exchanges of cash, checks, and credit; regulates member banks; and uses monetary policies to fight inflation and deflation

Another important fiscal agency (although for technical reasons it is called an agency of monetary policy) is the **Federal Reserve System,** which is headed by the Federal Reserve Board. The Federal Reserve System (called simply the Fed) has authority over the interest rates and lending activities of the nation's most important banks. Congress established the Fed in 1913 as a clearinghouse responsible for adjusting the supply of money and credit to the needs of commerce and industry in different regions of the country. The Fed is also responsible for ensuring that banks do not overextend themselves, a policy that guards against a chain of bank failures during a sudden economic scare, such as occurred in 1929. The Federal Reserve Board directs the operations of the twelve district Federal Reserve Banks, which are essentially "bankers' banks," serving the monetary needs of the hundreds of member banks in the national banking system.[14] The Fed has become one of the most important actors in economic policy through its power to raise and lower interest rates. Leading financial actors in the banking industry and in the stock market anxiously anticipate quarterly meetings of the Federal Reserve Board, in which decisions about interest rates are made.

revenue agencies
agencies responsible for collecting taxes. Examples include the Internal Revenue Service for income taxes, the U.S. Customs Service for tariffs and other taxes on imported goods, and the Bureau of Alcohol, Tobacco, and Firearms for collection of taxes on the sales of those particular products

Revenue Agencies One of the first actions of Congress under President George Washington was to create the Department of the Treasury, and probably its oldest function is the collection of taxes on imports, called tariffs. Now housed in the United States Customs Service, federal customs agents are located at every U.S. seaport and international airport to oversee the collection of tariffs. But far and away the most important of the **revenue agencies** is the Internal Revenue Service (IRS). The Customs Service and the IRS are two of at least twelve bureaus within the Treasury Department.

The IRS is not unresponsive to political influences, especially given the fact that is must maintain cooperative relationships with the two oldest and most important congressional committees, the House Ways and Means Committee and the Senate Finance Committee. Nonetheless, as one expert put it, "probably no organization in the country, public or private, creates as much clientele *dis*favor as the Internal Revenue Service. The very nature of its work brings it into an adversary relationship with vast numbers of Americans every year."[15] Yet few scandals have soiled its record. Complaints against the IRS have cascaded during the past few years, particularly since 1996 presidential candidate Steve Forbes staged his entire campaign on the need to abolish the IRS and the income tax itself. But aside from the principle of the income tax, all the other complaints against the IRS are against its needless complexity, its lack of sensitivity and responsiveness to individual taxpayers, and its overall lack of efficiency. As one of its critics put it, "Imagine a company that's owed $216

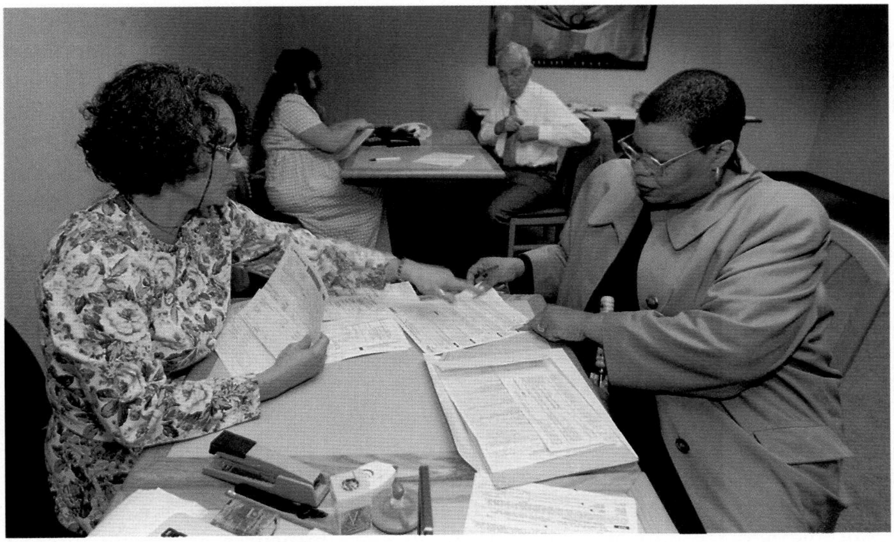

A revenue specialist instructs a taxpayer on her income taxes as part of a free service offered by the Internal Revenue Service (IRS). Despite such services and other attempts to improve its image, the IRS remains the most despised government agency.

billion plus interest, a company with a 22-percent error rate. A company that spent $4 billion to update a computer system—with little success. It all describes the Internal Revenue Service.[16]

Such complaints led Congress to pass the IRS Restructuring and Reform Act of 1998, which instituted a number of new protections for taxpayers. The new laws aim to make IRS agents more "customer-friendly" and limit the agency's ability to collect money owed through liens on individual income or wages. Moreover, the new law mandates the firing of IRS employees who harass taxpayers or violate their rights. While many applaud the new law, there is also mounting concern that it has made tax agents too timid and that revenue collection is declining as a consequence of the law.[17]

The politics of the IRS is most interesting, because, although thousands upon thousands of individual corporations and wealthy individuals have a strong and active interest in American tax policy, key taxation decisions are set by agreements between the president, the Treasury Department, and the leading members of the two tax committees in Congress. External influence is not spread throughout the fifty states, but instead is much more centralized in the majority political party, a few key figures in Congress, and a handful of professional lobbyists. Suspicions of unfair exemptions and favoritism are widespread, and they do exist, but these exemptions come largely from Congress, *not* from the IRS itself.

Economic Development Agencies Federal agencies also conduct programs designed to strengthen particular segments of the economy or to provide specific services aimed to strengthen the entire economy. Created in 1889, the Department of Agriculture is the fourth oldest cabinet department. Its initial mission, to strengthen American agriculture through research and assist farmers by providing information about effective farming practices, reflected the enormous importance of agriculture in the American economy. Through its Agricultural Extension Service, the Department of Agriculture established an important presence in rural areas throughout the country. It also built strong support for its activities among the nation's farmers and at the many land grant colleges, where agricultural research has been conducted for over one hundred years.

At first glance, the Department of Transportation, which oversees the nation's highway and air traffic systems, may seem to have little to do with economic development. But effective transportation is the backbone of a strong economy. The interstate highway system, for example, is widely acknowledged as a key factor in promoting economic growth in the decades after World War II. The Departments of Commerce and Energy also oversee programs designed to ensure a strong economy. The Small Business Administration in the Department of Commerce provides loans and technical assistance to small businesses across the country.

In recent decades dissatisfaction with government has led to calls to keep government out of the economy. Yet if the federal government were to disappear, chances are high that the economy would fall into chaos. There is widespread agreement that the federal government should set the basic rules for economic activity and intervene—through such measures as setting interest rates—to keep the economy strong. Some analysts argue that the government role should go beyond such rule setting to include more active measures such as investment in infrastructure. These advocates of government action point to the economic benefits of government investments in the interstate highway system and the government research in the 1960s that led to the creation of the Internet.

Can Bureaucracy Be Reinvented?

▶ Can government be made more responsive and efficient? Why or why not?

When citizens complain that government is too bureaucratic, what they often mean is that government bureaucracies seem inefficient and waste money. The poster child for such bureaucratic inefficiency in the late 1980s was the Department of Defense, which was revealed to have spent $640 apiece for toilet seats and $435 apiece for hammers.[18] Many citizens also had personal experience with the federal government: a mountain of forms to fill out, lengthy waits, and unsympathetic service. Why can't government do better? many citizens asked. The application of new technologies and innovative management strategies in the private sector during the 1980s made government agencies look even more lumbering and inefficient by comparison. People were coming to expect faster service and more customer-friendly interactions in the private sector. But how can public sector bureaucracies change their ways when they are not subject to tests of efficiency and cost-effectiveness that often prompt innovation in the private sector?

In 1993, President Clinton launched the National Performance Review (NPR)—a part of his promise to "reinvent government"—to make the federal bureaucracy more efficient, accountable, and effective. Vice President Al Gore

POLICY DEBATE

Reinventing Government: The National Performance Review

With the growth of the modern federal bureaucracy came the escalation of reformist cries. In the 1930s, a report by a committee charged with evaluating the growth of the national government called for a larger and more diversified bureaucracy to aid the president. But by the 1980s, reformers were calling for a smaller, less expensive bureaucracy with reduced powers that was also more compatible with democratic values of accountability. The Clinton administration, too, embraced the call for smaller government. In its National Performance Review (NPR), headed by Vice President Al Gore, a wide variety of recommendations were offered to make government work better at lower cost. The initial report, presented in September 1993, made 384 recommendations, incorporating 1,250 specific actions designed to save over $100 billion over five years. In the next two years, many of the report's recommendations were implemented by presidential directive, congressional enactment, and agency agreement.

Supporters of the effort have applauded the downsizing project. While smaller and less expensive government has been its primary goal, the NPR has also sought to encourage initiative within agencies and make them more responsive to citizens and others they serve. For example, the Food and Drug Administration (FDA) had been criticized for taking too long to approve new drugs and therapies for such illnesses as cancer and AIDS. Under NPR guidelines, the FDA announced in 1996 that it would accelerate the approval process for new cancer therapies. It also agreed to make promising but not yet fully approved cancer therapies available to patients lacking other treatment possibilities. And it pledged to be more responsive to the perspectives of cancer patients and others affected by FDA rulings.

By the end of 1995, agencies had implemented about 400 specific recommendations, producing $58 billion in savings. An additional $28 billion in annual reductions were also announced, as well as the elimination of 16,000 pages of regulations. Efforts to democratize the enforcement of regulations were also announced, designed to improve relations between regulatory agencies and those being regulated. As part of the NPR effort, President Clinton's 1997 budget proposed a 22 percent, six-year reduction in the overall size of domestic agencies. Congress proposed an even greater reduction. Efforts to reduce the size of the bureaucracy, while making it more efficient and responsive, will continue because of bipartisan agreement and public support.

Critics of the NPR point out its goals have more to do with politics than good policy. The image of a Washington-centered bureaucracy dominated by career civil servants contradicts the facts: 90 percent of all federal employees work outside of the Washington, D.C., area; the only part of the bureaucracy that has grown in size in the last thirty years is the number of political appointees; the federal civilian workforce of 2.1 million employees is actually smaller than it was in 1960, despite the fact that the government does more today; and major domestic social programs are carried out by state and local governments or private contractors, not by federal employees.

Given these facts, the main reason for the NPR, according to critics, has been political—to appeal to voters who supported Ross Perot's 1992 and 1996 presidential campaigns, which criticized government waste. The underlying concept of the NPR, to develop a bureaucracy that costs less but also works better, is contradictory. Government workers have pointed out that they have suffered from more than a decade of budget cuts, and that further cuts would simply result in doing less with less. Although the NPR did produce some initial savings, most of the proposed savings were difficult to implement, much less measure. For example, some early savings were reported by the administration to be $6 billion. But a review by the Congressional Budget Office reported that these savings were actually only $2.5 billion.

In sum, the NPR, according to critics, is just one more politically inspired pseudo-reform that will pass into history when a new presidential administration takes over.

STUDENT DEBATE

Does Privatization of Government Work?

Yes Private prisons are a growing sector of the U.S. economy. With incarceration rates on the rise in this country, corporations such as the Correction Corporation of America (CCA) stand to profit from all the criminals being put behind bars. These companies are state-contracted, and they privately own and operate some of the facilities housing America's felons.

Many question the government's decision to dole out its authority and responsibility to house those guilty of serious crimes to private companies trying to make a profit.

This question is especially relevant to Texans, because Texas houses the most criminals in private prisons of all the states, at around 30,000.

The benefits of prison privatization far outweigh any of its supposed disadvantages.

Opponents claim private prisons do not have the same level of security that public prisons have and that prisoners are more likely to escape, citing an incident at a CCA-run prison where six inmates were able to cut a hole in a fence and escape.

***

Just because there was an escape at a prison does not mean the people there do not care about security. Private prisons want to make a profit, and it would be very self-destructive for them not to care about security, because if they did not they obviously would not be allowed to operate for long. Caring about both profits and security does not create a conflict of interest.

In a recent *Washington Post* article, U.S. Representative Ted Strickland stated private prisons have "potentially corrupting effects on public policy."

He further said prison corporations like the CCA could become powerful lobbyists in Congress for long-term and mandatory sentencing in order to maximize profits.

But this complaint is unfounded. Most people would like nothing more than to see violent criminals go to jail for longer periods of time. In the last two decades, the incarceration rate in the United States has tripled, and the violent crime rate has fallen. Most people would like this trend to continue.

Strickland also suggests that since private prisons control good conduct reports, they may have the tendency to give bad reports in order to keep the prisoners in jail as long as possible, again, to maximize profits. Someone who is in for a fifty-year sentence may actually serve the full time.

Stating that prisoners may actually go full-term in private prisons cannot possibly be used as an argument against their existence.

***

The main argument in favor of private prisons centers around money. The corrections corporations bid on prospects for the facilities, and the state government has the final say on when, where, and by whom these are built. Obviously, the corporation with the lowest bid would win.

This can be much cheaper than building a public prison. If a single prison can be built for less, then more prisons can be built for the same amount of money.

Also, in most private prisons the cost per prisoner is lower, which creates lower maintenance costs.

***

Private prisons are a good way to save taxpayers money and will help keep dangerous people away from the public.

In a time when the U.S. prison population exceeds 1 million people, the bottom line must be considered. Private prisons will help to ease overcrowding, help keep violent offenders off the streets for longer, and they will be able to do it for less money.

The benefits are obvious, and the corrections industry should be allowed to grow and ease the public prison system's back-breaking load.

SOURCE: Jeff Becker, "Benefits of Prison Privatization Outweigh Alleged Disadvantages," *The Battalion* (Texas A & M University), June 22, 1999.

No

People across the political spectrum praise privatization as a way to reinvent government by cutting costs to save programs. In some cases, this works. City garbage collection contracts, public works construction contracts and military and medical government research contracts have yielded positive results.

Now the nation is going one step further. Private prisons now house our convicts, and many corporations, including Lockheed, are making bids for contracts to take over federal agencies, such as Medicaid, welfare, and other entitlement programs. These are not garbage-collection contracts. These agencies directly impact the security of millions of Americans.

In the past year, at least eight states have voided prison contracts because the contractors go over budget and have to request federal loans and corporate welfare to save the project. This ends up costing the government more than if the agency had never been privatized. Other states, including Oklahoma, are voiding contracts because of prisoner abuse.

Even worse, these contractors are allowed to give money to the officials responsible for making the unfair sentencing laws that keep the prisons booming. This type of corruption is especially threatening since sentencing laws vary from state to state and smaller public officials are often easier to corrupt.

Privatization is racking up failures, from Florida's pathetic deadbeat dad tracking agencies to Mississippi's disastrous welfare distribution and job placement programs. California and Connecticut have terminated contracts for child support collection and child welfare services after making the mistake of giving over an entire state agency to a cold, for-profit entity.

The list of potential problems is endless. First, civil service jobs pay more than corporate jobs providing the same services. Yet the corporations still fail to spend less than the government, and they rely on government aid to stay afloat. It's also hazardous to lower the pay of people handling sensitive and private information. These people become more prone to corruption.

Also, instead of having agencies run by government-appointed officials, we have private organizations that can run virtually unchecked by the voters. This reduces public control over its own tax money. Furthermore, it puts the lawmakers in a position to be unduly influenced. While a government agency cannot donate money to public officials, a private agency can.

Not all privatization is bad. Industries such as technology and medical research, where competition is necessary to promote development, definitely need to be partially privatized.

But privatizing welfare and prisons is a high-stakes gamble, especially when those agencies are funded by loosely-regulated state block grants, which allow unused grant money to be diverted to other projects such as "rainy-day accounts" by politicians hoping to further their own agendas.

Normally, cutting costs is a good thing. But when program effectiveness and public well-being is sacrificed, bureaucratic pork spending doesn't look so bad after all.

SOURCE: Staff Editorial, "Government Agencies Should Remain Public," *The Oklahoma Daily* (University of Oklahoma), March 24, 1998.

took charge of the new effort. The inspiration for the reinvention campaign came from new ideas and practices in private management. Among these are the notion that the typical bureaucratic emphasis on detailed rules and narrow responsibilities for each member of the bureaucracy needs to be replaced with a much more flexible system of organization. New organizations are "mission-driven" rather than "rule-driven." This means that these organizations place more emphasis on achieving their goals by a variety of means that work rather than following a strict set of rules. This approach allows organizations to accomplish work more quickly and at lower costs but it also permits them to be more responsive to the particular needs of their customers.

The National Performance Review has sought to prod federal agencies into adopting similar practices. Clinton promised that the result would be a government that would "work better and cost less." Virtually all observers agree that the NPR has made substantial progress. Its original goal was to save more than $100 billion over five years, in large part by cutting the federal workforce by 12 percent (more than 270,000 jobs) by the end of 1999. Actually, by the end of 1999, $136 billion in saving were already assured through legislative or administrative action, and the federal workforce had been cut by 377,000.[19]

The NPR has also focused on cutting red tape, streamlining procurement (how the government purchases goods and services), improving the coordination of federal management, and simplifying federal rules. For instance, the OMB abolished the notorious ten-thousand-page Federal Personnel Manual and the Standard Form 171, the government's lengthy job application form. Another example is even more revealing of the nature of the NPR's work: the Defense Department's method for reimbursing its employees' travel expenses used to take seventeen steps and two months; an employee-designed reform encouraged by the NPR streamlined this to a four-step, computer-based procedure taking less than fifteen minutes, with an anticipated savings of $1 billion over five years.

Federal agencies were also instructed to develop customer service plans, which made responsiveness to citizens—now called customers—a central priority. Many agencies responded by such measures as improving the response time in their toll-free numbers. The Social Security Adminstration, for example, retrained employees, overhauled its telephone technology, and altered work schedules so that customer calls to the SSA would be answered within five minutes.[20] The National Performance Review has clearly led to improved service and greater efficiency in some government agencies. In others, such as the IRS, little progress has been made as the agency encountered problems that ranged from difficulties with a new computer system to confusion within the organization about the expectations associated with reform efforts.

Can government bureaucracy be reinvented? The answer from the reinvention experience is "yes, but." Certainly government bureaucracies can make more effective use of technology; they can grant frontline employees more power to respond to citizen requests and train employees to be more accommodating and helpful. Likewise government procurement can be (and has been) overhauled; there is no excuse for $435 hammers. But reform of public bureaucracies presents special challenges. Government bureaucracies are not just like the private sector organizations that the reinvention effort seeks to emulate.[21] In the first place, politics often places limits on the actions of government agencies in a way that has no parallel in the private sector. Political objectives led Clinton to promise a government that "cost less and worked better." The need to show immediate cost savings hampered reform efforts in a variety of ways. Employees fearful of losing their jobs are rarely enthusiastic partners in reform. Similarly, as we have seen, congressional dissatisfaction with the IRS led to new legislation in 1998 that may make the IRS more customer-friendly but less effective in collecting revenue. Second, the relationship between citizens and the bureaucracy differs in important ways from the relationship between businesses and their customers. As Don Kettl points out in his review of the NPR, government agencies often have multiple customers and the essence of government is to balance competing demands: "Should the Forest Service serve lumber companies in the federal forests by maximizing logging? Or should it serve environmentalists by preserving old-growth forests?"[22] Defining just who is the customer is not always easy—nor should it be. Moreover, thinking of citizens as customers can be misleading. Taxpayers, for example, cannot *choose* whether to do business with the IRS; they are often unwilling and unenthusiastic "customers." Finally, federal bureaucracies are much more likely to rely on nonprofits, state and local governments, and on citizen compliance to achieve their objectives than are private companies. This means that government agencies must pay much more attention to coordination and cooperation with other organizations in order to achieve their objectives.

These features of public bureaucracies do not mean that reform is impossible. They do mean that it is likely to be more complex than in the private sector. Reforming government bureaucracies is not simply a matter of management technique, it is also a political matter.

Can the Bureaucracy Be Reduced?

- What methods have been used to reduce the size and the role of the federal bureaucracy?
- How effective can efforts to reduce the bureaucracy be?

Some Americans would argue that bureaucracy is always too big and that it always should be reduced. In the 1990s Americans seemed particularly enthusiastic about reducing (or to use the popular contemporary word, "downsizing") the federal bureaucracy. This downsizing could be achieved in at least three ways: termination, devolution, or privatization.

TERMINATION

The only *certain* way to reduce the size of the bureaucracy is to eliminate programs. Variations in the levels of federal personnel and expenditures (as was shown in Figures 15.1 and 15.2) demonstrate the futility of trying to make permanent cuts in existing agencies. Furthermore, most agencies have a supportive constituency that will fight to reinstate any cuts that are made. Termination is the only way to ensure an agency's reduction and it is a rare

The process of closing military bases has been difficult. Members of Congress used to try to overturn decisions to close bases in their districts. Because that is no longer possible, members of Congress such as Senator Dianne Feinstein of California have sought to convert military bases for other government purposes. Critics say this isn't reducing bureaucracy, just shifting it around.

occurrence, even with the Reagan and Bush administrations, both of which proclaimed a strong commitment to the reduction of the national government. In fact, not a single national government agency or program was terminated during the twelve years of Reagan and Bush.

The Republican-led 104th Congress (1995–96) was even more committed to the termination of programs. Newt Gingrich, Speaker of the House, took Congress by storm with his promises of a virtual revolution in government. But when the dust had settled at the end of the first session of the first Gingrich-led Congress, no significant progress had been made toward downsizing through termination of agencies and programs.[23] This lack of success is a reflection of Americans' love/hate relationship with the national government. As antagonistic as Americans may be toward bureaucracy in general, they grow attached to the services being rendered and protections being offered by particular bureaucratic agencies; that is, they fiercely defend their favorite agencies while perceiving no inconsistency between that defense and their antagonistic attitude toward the bureaucracy in general. A good case in point is the agonizing problem of closing military bases in the wake of the end of the cold war with the former Soviet Union, when the United States no longer needs so many bases. Since every base is in some congressional member's district, it proved impossible for Congress to decide to close any of them. Consequently, between 1988 and 1990, Congress established a Defense Base Closure and Realignment Commission to decide on base closings, taking the matter out of Congress's hands altogether.[24] And even so, the process has been slow and agonizing.

Elected leaders have come to rely on a more incremental approach to downsizing the bureaucracy. Much has been done by budgetary means, reducing the budgets of all agencies across the board by small percentages, and cutting some less-supported agencies by larger amounts. Yet these changes are still incremental, leaving the existence of agencies unaddressed.

An additional approach has been taken to thwart the highly unpopular regulatory agencies, which are so small (relatively) that cutting their budgets contributes virtually nothing to reducing the deficit. This approach is called **deregulation,** simply defined as a reduction in the number of rules promulgated by regulatory agencies. President Reagan used this strategy successfully and was very proud of it. Presidents Bush and Clinton have proudly followed Reagan's lead. But deregulation by rule reduction is still incremental and has certainly not satisfied the hunger of the American public in general and Washington representatives in particular for a genuine reduction of bureaucracy.

deregulation
a policy of reducing or eliminating regulatory restraints on the conduct of individuals or private institutions

DEVOLUTION

The next best approach to genuine reduction of the size of the bureaucracy is **devolution**—downsizing the federal bureaucracy by delegating the implementation of programs to state and local governments. In some instances this may amount to genuine termination of certain programs, because some states will choose not to have the program at all, if the federal laws provide that much discretion to the states. In fact, many politicians favor devolution precisely because they see it as a politically safer way to terminate programs. But the problem that arises with devolution is that programs that were once uniform across the country (because they were the national government's responsibility) can become highly variable, with some states providing benefits not available in other states. To a point, variation can be considered one of the virtues of federalism. But there are dangers inherent in large variations and inequalities in the provision of services and benefits in a democracy. For example, since the Food and Drug Administration (FDA) has been under attack in recent years, could the problem be solved by devolving its regulatory tasks to the states? Would people care if drugs would require "caution" labels in some states and not in others? Would Americans want each state to set its own air and water pollution control policies without regard to the fact that pollution flows across state boundaries? Devolution, as attractive as it may be, is not an approach that can be applied across the board without analyzing carefully the nature of the program and of the problems it is designed to solve. Even the capacity of states to handle "devolved" programs will vary. According to the Washington research organization the Brookings Institution, the level of state and local government employment varies from state to state—from a low of 400 per 10,000 residents in some states to a high of 700 per 10,000 in others. "Such administrative diversity is bound to mediate the course and consequences of any substantial devolution of federal responsibility; no one-size-fits-all devolution [from federal to state and local government] can work."[25]

devolution
a policy to remove a program from one level of government by delegating it or passing it down to a lower level of government, such as from the national government to the state and local governments

PRIVATIZATION

Privatization seems like a synonym for termination, but that is true only at the extreme. Most of what is called "privatization" is not termination at all but the provision of government goods and services by private contractors under direct government supervision. Except for top-secret strategic materials, virtually all of the production of military hardware, from boats to bullets, is done on a privatized basis by private contractors. Billions of dollars of research services are bought under contract by governments; these private contractors are universities as well as ordinary industrial corporations and private "think tanks." **Privatization** simply means that a formerly public activity is picked up under contract by a private company or companies. But such programs are still very much government programs; they are paid for by government and supervised by government. Privatization downsizes the government only in that the workers providing the service are no longer counted as part of the government bureaucracy.

privatization
removing all or part of a program from the public sector to the private sector

None of this analysis and criticism is intended to discourage efforts to downsize the government bureaucracies. But in the process of trying to downsize the government, two fundamental points ought to be kept clearly in mind. First, the federal bureaucracy is here to stay, and even if so-called revolutionary campaigns to downsize the government are completely successful, they will not reduce the federal bureaucracy by very much. Second, government must therefore concentrate on a much older but now much more pressing problem: how to make the bureaucracy that exists more compatible with the democracy the American people desire.

Can Bureaucracy Be Controlled?

- How can bureaucracy and democracy coexist? What popular controls over the bureaucracy exist?
- How do the president and Congress manage and oversee the bureaucracy?
- What is the most effective means to guarantee a responsible bureaucracy?

The title of this chapter, "Bureaucracy in a Democracy," is intended to convey the sense that the two are contradictory.[26] Americans cannot live with bureaucracy, but they also cannot live without it. The task is neither to retreat from bureaucracy nor to attack it, but to take advantage of its strengths while making it more accountable to the demands of democratic politics and representative government. This task will be the focus of the remainder of this chapter.

Two hundred years, millions of employees, and trillions of dollars after the Founding, we must return to James Madison's observation, "You must first enable the government to control the governed; and in the next place oblige it to control itself."[27] Today the problem is the same, only now the process has a name: administrative accountability. Accountability implies that there is some higher authority by which the actions of the bureaucracy will be guided and judged. The highest authority in a democracy is *demos*—the people—and the guidance for bureaucratic action is the popular will. But that ideal of accountability must be translated into practical terms by the president and Congress.

THE PRESIDENT AS CHIEF EXECUTIVE

In 1937, President Franklin Roosevelt's Committee on Administrative Management gave official sanction to an idea that had been growing increasingly

AMERICAN DEMOCRACY IN COMPARATIVE PERSPECTIVE

Bureaucracy, Public Trust, and Corruption

Bureaucracies are to governments as wheels are to automobiles. To validate the purchase, the car must get you to where you want to go. So with government. To legitimize the expense and the restrictions that come with government and public authority, the public must see that the policies they value are effectively implemented and managed within their society. Executives, legislatures, and judges may fashion those polices in order to keep the concentration of power in check, but bureaucracies nevertheless serve as the agents of the government and deliver the product of policy day in and day out to government's principal client—the public. Essential to the success of bureaucracies is the public trust afforded civil servants.

Cultural traditions have shaped the bureaucracies of different countries. In the United States (as well as, for example, New Zealand), a weak central state tradition has led to what students of comparative bureaucracy call a *departmental* system of administration in national government. In such a system, candidates are recruited for special departmental duties, and these civil servants do not generally move between departments. This system stands in contrast with a *unified* system of bureaucracy. Candidates in this system are recruited into the "culture" of administration not into a specific department or agency. Bureaucrats are often seen as "generalists" in unified systems.

Some countries exhibit far more of the "generalist" administrative culture than others. For instance, the tradition of deference to authority allied with a strong sense of pragmatism within the British culture acts to place a heavy preference for the amateur bureaucrat serving the more senior minister in the British cabinet. Key cabinet ministries, such as Treasury, Foreign, and Defense, are at the core of policy making and agenda setting within Britain. The ministries rely on bureaucrats for the expertise and energy to execute the various technical and administrative duties associated with the agencies. General skills, a broad but rich university education, and judgment honed by years of experience are generally valued over specialized expertise, thus allowing the senior civil servants—the *mandarins*—and their cabinet ministers to serve as the principal sources of authority and direction of policy.

In contrast, other unified systems of bureaucracy, such as those in France, Japan, and Germany, rely heavily on technical experts—trained in areas of administrative specialization and vetted through careful systems of technical and specialized exams—who assume positions where their specialized talents will heavily influence the implementation and eventual shaping of policy. The most elite group of civil servants in France are the *Corps*—those who have graduated from the elite national schools of administration. Nothing in Britain or the United States matches the special role of the *Corps* in fashioning and manipulating policy.

Arguably, the most dangerous threat to the legitimacy and effectiveness of the bureaucracy is not the quality of the recruited candidate or the particular organizational logic of bureaucracy. Rather, it is the *perception of trust* held by the public. There is ample evidence that the citizens of major democracies are not only distrustful of their bureaucracies, but they may well in fact perceive high degrees of corruption within the broader public sector overall.

Among public servants, bribe-taking and misuse of public funds (e.g., illegal receipt of campaign contributions) are the most common forms of corruption. Recent scandals in the United States, Britain, France, Germany, Italy, Japan, and Spain feed the perception of corruption in public service and undermine the claim of the integrity of civil servants. Indeed, corruption—to the extent it exists among the bureaucracy of a society—has three general consequences, each with high costs for society.

First, it weakens the public trust, thereby weakening the capacity of government to mobilize public support for reform and policy compliance. Second, it raises the costs of public service. Knowing you will have to pay more (in the form of bribes) for public contracts ratchets the costs of public services, which are passed on to the taxpayer. Third, public corruption serves to discourage foreign investment by both public and private actors. Recent policy recommendations from the Organization for Economic Cooperation and Development (OECD) and the World Bank draw attention to the perceptions and cost of public corruption in the democracies of the world.

SOURCES: Rod Hague, Martin Harrop, and Shaun Breslin, *Political Science: A Comparative Introduction,* 2nd ed. (Worth, 1998); David Martin Roodman, "Government Corruption Widespread," in Lester Brown, Michael Renner, and Brian Halweil, *Vital Signs 1999: The Environmental Trends That Are Shaping Our Future,* (World Watch Institute, 1999); and David Kaufman, "Corruption: The Facts," *Foreign Policy* 107, (Summer 1997), pp. 114–31.

urgent: "The president needs help." The national government had grown rapidly during the preceding twenty-five years, but the structures and procedures necessary to manage the burgeoning executive branch had not yet been established. The response to the call for "help" for the president initially took the form of three management policies: (1) All communications and decisions that related to executive policy decisions must pass through the White House; (2) In order to cope with such a flow, the White House must have adequate staffs of specialists in research, analysis, legislative and legal writing, and public affairs; and (3) The White House must have additional staff to follow through on presidential decisions—to ensure that those decisions are made, communicated to Congress, and carried out by the appropriate agency.

Making the Managerial Presidency Establishing a management capacity for the presidency began in earnest with FDR, but it did not stop there.[28] The story of the modern presidency can be told largely as a series of responses to the plea for managerial help. Indeed, each expansion of the national government into new policies and programs in the twentieth century was accompanied by a parallel expansion of the president's management authority. This pattern began even before FDR's presidency, with the policy innovations of President Woodrow Wilson between 1913 and 1920. Congress responded to Wilson's policies with the 1921 Budget and Accounting Act, which turned over the prime legislative power of budgeting to the White House. Each successive president has continued this pattern, creating what we now know as the "managerial presidency."

Presidents John Kennedy and Lyndon Johnson were committed both to government expansion and to management expansion, in the spirit of their party's hero, FDR. President Nixon also strengthened and enlarged the managerial presidency, but for somewhat different reasons. He sought the strongest possible managerial hand because he had to assume that the overwhelming majority of federal employees had sympathies with the Democratic Party, which had controlled the White House and had sponsored governmental growth for twenty-eight of the previous thirty-six years.[29]

President Jimmy Carter was probably more preoccupied with administrative reform and reorganization than any other president in this century. His reorganization of the civil service will long be recognized as one of the most significant contributions of his presidency. The Civil Service Reform Act of 1978 was the first major revamping of the federal civil service since its creation in 1883. The 1978 act abolished the century-old Civil Service Commission (CSC) and replaced it with three agencies, each designed to handle one of the CSC's functions on the theory that the competing demands of these functions had given the CSC an "identity crisis." The Merit Systems Protection Board (MSPB) was created to defend competitive merit recruitment and promotion from political encroachment. A separate Federal Labor Relations Authority (FLRA) was set up to administer collective bargaining and individual personnel grievances. The third new agency, the Office of Personnel Management (OPM), was created to manage recruiting, testing, training, and the retirement system. The Senior Executive Service was also created at this time to recognize and foster "public management" as a profession and to facilitate the movement of top, "supergrade" career officials across agencies and departments.[30]

Carter also tried to impose a stringent budgetary process on all executive agencies. Called "zero-base budgeting," it was a method of budgeting from the bottom up, wherein each agency was required to rejustify its entire mission rather than merely its next year's increase. Zero-base budgeting did not succeed, but the effort was not lost on President Reagan. Although Reagan gave the impression of being a laid-back president, he actually centralized management to an unprecedented degree. From Carter's "bottom-up" approach, Reagan went to a "top-down" approach, whereby the initial budgetary decisions would be made in the White House and the agencies would be required to fit within those decisions. This process converted the Office of Management and Budget (OMB) into an agency of policy determination and presidential management.[31] President Bush took Reagan's centralization strategy even further in using the White House staff instead of Cabinet secretaries for managing the executive branch.[32]

President Clinton was often criticized for the way he managed his administration. His easygoing approach to administration led critics to liken his management style to college "bull sessions" complete with pizza and "all-nighters." Intense criticism of a chaotic White House prompted the President to adopt a more disciplined approach with a stronger chief of staff in his second term. Yet, as we have seen, Clinton also inaugurated one of the most systematic efforts "to change the way government does business" in his National Performance Review. Heavily influenced by the theories of management consultants who prized decentralization, customer responsiveness and employee initiative, Clinton sought to infuse these new practices into government.[33]

The Problem of Management Control by the White House Staff The Cabinet's inability to perform as a board of directors (see Chapter 14), and the inability of any other agency to perform that function have left a management vacuum in the U.S. government. OMB has met part of the need, and indeed the management power of the director of OMB seems to increase with each new president. But the need for executive management control goes far beyond what even the boldest of OMB directors can achieve. The White House staff has filled this vacuum to a certain extent precisely because, in the past thirty years, the "special assistants to the president" have been given relatively specialized jurisdictions over one or more departments or strategic issues. These staffers have additional power and credibility beyond their access to the president because they also have access to confidential information. Since information is the most important bureaucratic resource, White House staff members gain management power by having access to the CIA for international intelligence and the FBI and Treasury for knowledge about the personal life of every government official (since each government employee has to go through a rigorous FBI security clearance procedure prior to being appointed and promoted).

Responsible bureaucracy, however, is not going to come simply from more presidential power, more administrative staff, and more management control. All this was inadequate to the task of keeping the National Security Council staff from seizing the initiative to run its own policies toward Iran and Nicaragua for at least two years (1985–86) after Congress had explicitly restricted activities toward Nicaragua and the president had forbidden negotiations with Iran. The Tower Commission, appointed to investigate the Iran-Contra affair, concluded that although there was nothing fundamentally

In 1987, Oliver North, an aide to President Reagan's National Security Council, testified before a joint congressional committee investigating the Iran-Contra affair. Such congressional investigations are a classic example of oversight.

wrong with the institutions involved in foreign-policy making—the Department of State, the Department of Defense, the White House, and Congress—there had been a "flawed process," "a failure of responsibility," and a thinness of the president's personal engagement in the issues. The Tower Commission found that "at no time did [President Reagan] insist upon accountability and performance review."[34]

No particular management style is guaranteed to work. Each White House management innovation, from one president to the next, shows only the inadequacy of the approaches of previous presidents. And as the White House and the Executive Office of the President grow, the management bureaucracy itself becomes a management problem. Something more and different is obviously needed.

CONGRESS AND RESPONSIBLE BUREAUCRACY

Congress is constitutionally essential to responsible bureaucracy because ultimately the key to bureaucratic responsibility is legislation. When a law is passed and its intent is clear, the accountability for implementation of that law is also clear. Then the president knows what to "faithfully execute," and the responsible agency understands what is expected of it. But when Congress enacts vague legislation, agencies must resort to their own interpretations. The president and the federal courts often step in to tell agencies what the legislation intended. And so do the most intensely interested groups. Yet when everybody, from president to courts to interest groups, gets involved in the actual interpretation of legislative intent, to whom and to what is the agency accountable? Even when the agency wants to behave responsibly, how shall accountability be accomplished?

oversight
the effort by Congress, through hearings, investigations, and other techniques, to exercise control over the activities of executive agencies

Congress's answer is **oversight.** The more power Congress has delegated to the executive, the more it has sought to reinvolve itself in directing the interpretation of laws through committee and subcommittee oversight of each agency. The standing committee system in Congress is well suited for oversight, inasmuch as most of the congressional committees and subcommittees have jurisdictions roughly parallel to one or more departments and agencies, and members of Congress who sit on these committees can develop expertise equal to that of the bureaucrats. Appropriations committees as well as authorization committees have oversight powers—as do their respective subcommittees. In addition to these, the Government Reform and Oversight Committee in the House and the Governmental Affairs Committee in the Senate have oversight powers not limited by departmental jurisdiction.

The best indication of Congress's oversight efforts is the use of public hearings, before which bureaucrats and other witnesses are summoned to discuss and defend agency budgets and past decisions. The data drawn from systematic studies of congressional committee and subcommittee hearings and meetings show quite dramatically that Congress has tried through oversight to keep pace with the expansion of the executive branch. Between 1950 and 1980, for example, the annual number of committee and subcommittee meetings in the House of Representatives rose steadily from 3,210 to 7,022; in the Senate, the number of such meetings rose from 2,607 to 4,265 (in 1975–76). Beginning in 1980 in the House and 1978 in the Senate, the number of committee and subcommittee hearings and meetings slowly began to decline, reaching 4,222 in the House and 2,597 in the Senate by the mid-1980s. This pattern of rise and decline in committee and subcommittee oversight activity strongly suggests that congressional vigilance toward the executive branch is responsive more to long-term growth in government than to yearly activity or to partisan considerations.[35] This is one of the best and most reassuring indications that Congress is committed to keeping the bureaucracy accountable. New questions about the ability of Congress to exercise oversight arose when the Republicans took over Congress in 1995. Reductions in committee staffing and an emphasis on using investigative oversight to uncover scandal meant much less time spent on programmatic oversight. Moreover, congressional Republicans complained that they could not get sufficient information about programs from the White House to conduct effective oversight. Congressional records show that in 1991–92, when Democrats controlled the House, they issued reports on fifty-five federal programs, while in 1997–98, the Republican Congress issued only fourteen.[36]

Although congressional oversight is potent because of Congress's power to make, and therefore to change, the law, often the most effective and influential lever over bureaucratic accountability is "the power of the purse"—the ability of the House and Senate committees and subcommittees on appropriations to look at agency performance through the microscope of the annual appropriations process (see Chapter 13). This annual process makes bureaucrats attentive to Congress because they know that Congress has a chance each year to reduce their funding.[37] A more recent evaluation of the budget and appropriations process by the NPR expresses one serious concern about oversight through appropriation: pressure to cut appropriations "has put a premium on preserving particular programs, projects, and activities from Executive Branch as well as congressional action."[38] This may be another explanation for why there may be some downsizing but almost no terminations of federal agencies.

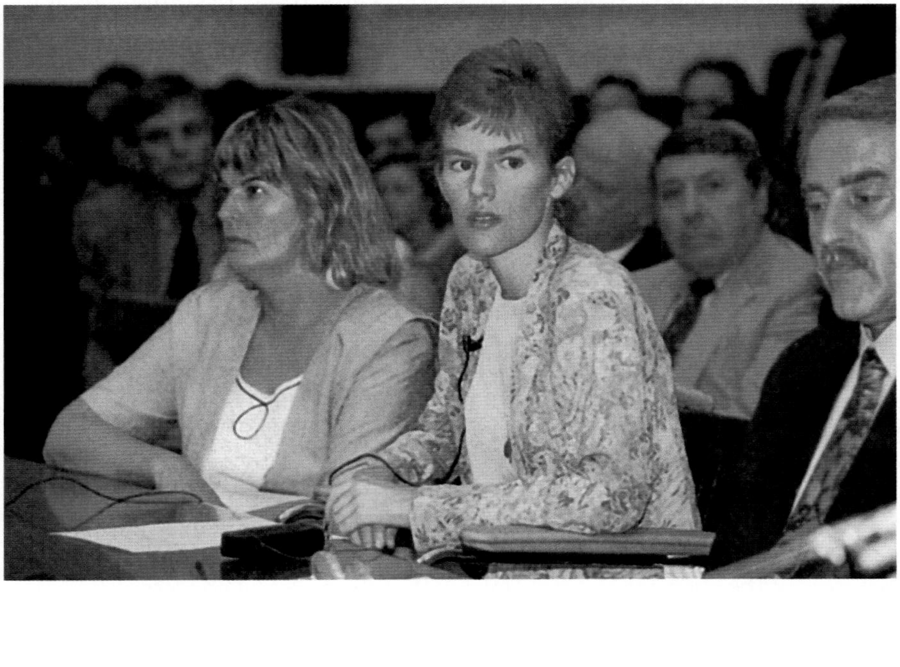

In a public hearing before a House subcommittee, Kimberly Bergalis, who contracted AIDS from her dentist and later died from the disease, urged the subcommittee to enact legislation to make AIDS testing mandatory for health care workers.

Politics on the Web

Can the Internet assist in efforts to "reinvent" government? In the long run it could, by helping to streamline agencies, publicize decisions, and improve communication. More importantly, the Internet can make a tremendous difference in the public's trust in government. In recent years federal agencies have used the Internet to help dispel negative public perceptions. For example, the Internal Revenue Service has made all tax forms available on the Web; now you can submit your taxes electronically, increasing accuracy and speeding refunds. Detailed data from the Census Bureau, campaign spending reports, and national and world economic statistics are also easily accessible on the Web. Even the Central Intelligence Agency, long suspicious of publicity, has developed a popular "kid secret zone" on its Web site. The hope is that these and similar efforts will counter the hostility and distrust that Americans have shown toward government, particularly the bureaucracy.

www.wwnorton.com/wtp3e

Oversight can also be carried out by individual members of Congress. Such inquiries addressed to bureaucrats are considered standard congressional "case work" and can turn up significant questions of public responsibility even when the motivation is only to meet the demand of an individual constituent. Oversight also takes place through communications between congressional staff and agency staff. The number of congressional staff has been enlarged tremendously since the Legislative Reorganization Act of 1946, and the legislative staff, especially the staff of the committees, is just as professionalized and specialized as the staff of executive agencies. In addition, Congress has created for itself three large agencies whose obligations are to engage in constant research on problems taking place in or confronted by the executive branch. These are the General Accounting Office (GAO), the Congressional Research Service (CRS), and the Congressional Budget Office (CBO). Each of these agencies is designed to give Congress information independent of the information it can get directly from the executive branch through hearings and other communications.[39] Another source of information for oversight is direct from citizens through the Freedom of Information Act (FOIA), which we have seen gives ordinary citizens the right of access to agency files and agency data to determine whether derogatory information exists in the file about the citizens themselves and to learn about what the agency is doing in general. Nevertheless, the information gained by citizens through FOIA can be effective only through the institutionalized channels of congressional committees and, on a few occasions, through public-interest litigation in the federal courts.

Citizens and Bureaucracy

Whether it has to do with taxes and the IRS, or passports and the State Department, or the motor vehicles agency or absentee voting or traffic cops at the state and local levels, citizens have more tools available to them than they may think. Public access to the workings of bureaucracies has been vastly facilitated in the past thirty years, in large part due to FOIA, which was enacted in 1966. Under FOIA, ordinary citizens can request documents from any government agency; even CIA and FBI files are available under certain conditions. It takes a lot of time and effort to get such files, but it can be done. The news media can (and do) also use FOIA, which is why newspapers and their reporters have so much more access to public bureaucracies than they ever had before. The public in general and interested citizens in particular gain from this access. Moreover, although general newspapers have limited space and resources for reporting on all agencies, specialized newspapers are actively involved in investigating and reporting on agency activities. This textbook regularly cites the *Congressional Quarterly,* which reports regularly on the activities of the legislative branch but which often has good materials on agencies in the executive branch, as well. The *National Journal* also reports extensively on government agencies. Innumerable trade magazines, whose subscribers are largely the companies and individuals whose livings are earned in a particular trade or sector of the economy, perform superbly as critics and exposers of the agencies and decisions within their area of concern.

The activities of important "think tanks" (independently financed policy-research organizations in Washington, D.C., and elsewhere around the country) revolve around the formation and implementation of public policy. The Brookings Institution, for example, has been studying government policies and agencies for more than six decades, and, although considered more favorably disposed toward Democratic administrations, it is widely respected in all quarters. The same might be said of the best-known conservative-leaning think thank, the American Enterprise Institute, which has been a particularly important source of analysis and criticism of policies and agencies for the past twenty years.

Many of these information sources are already on the Internet. The same is true for a wide variety of government-provided publications of information on agencies and policies. Fortunately, virtually every college and university in the United States provides access to the Internet.

Such access to information can help make bureaucracies more responsive to citizens' demands. In the first place, bureaucrats who know that their actions will be open to public scrutiny are more likely to take public wishes into account in their daily work. Second, when questionable bureaucratic practices are uncovered, citizens, through their congressional representatives, can work to change the laws and procedures that bureaucracies follow. The 1998 reform of the IRS, which, among other things, shifted the burden of proof from citizens to the government when there is a dispute, provides an example of this process. Finally, citizen dissatisfaction with bureaucracy can push politicians to institute reforms. When Clinton came to office, he wanted to take a more active governing approach than his Republican predecessors but realized that public distrust of government stood in the way. His effort to reinvent government, making bureaucracies more "customer-friendly," was a direct response to widespread public dissatisfaction.

Michael Ravnitsky with some of the 900 FBI files he has requested under the Freedom of Information Act.

The bad news is that, although citizen influence on bureaucracy is definitely possible, it can be expensive—in time and money. This gives it an upper-middle-class bias. The poor and uneducated lack virtually all the resources necessary to use the channels and opportunities available. But this class bias exists in all endeavors and walks of life; it is not particularly worse in the realm of bureaucracy. In fact, in many respects, now that political parties play less of a role in running the government, interaction with federal, state, and local agencies may be less daunting and discouraging than trying to influence legislatures.

Getting Inside the Bureaucracy

Cabinet departments, agencies, and bureaus constitute a vast network of offices, functions, and people who do the day-to-day business of the federal government. They execute laws, maintain national security, collect revenues, regulate public affairs, and promote the welfare of the poeple. Many more bureaucra cies exist to carry out the business of state, regional, and local governments across the nation. One way to get involved in politics is to take a temporary job inside of a government office. Perhaps you would like to spend a semester or summer working in the U.S. Attorney's Office or the Environmental Protection Agency or the Smithsonian Institution.

You may be eligible to participate in an internship program that places students in government bureaus and provides course credit for successfully completing internships. The advantage of working through an established internship program is that it may help place you in an appropriate agency, offer low-cost housing if you need to move to Washington, D.C., or to a state capital, and provide you with the supervision necessary for getting college credit. Check with your political science department or public administration department to see if your school offers an internship program.

If not, you still have many options. If you want to find an internship in the federal bureaucracy, here are several approaches to take:

- Consult the American Political Science Association by phone (202-483-2512), e-mail (apsa@apsanet.org), or on the Internet (http://www.apsanet.org) to find out about internship opportunities in Washington, D.C.
- Contact George Washington University, which has a Washington, D.C., internship program for students from other schools.
- Call the local field office of your U.S. congressional representative or U.S. senator and ask if they can help you to locate an internship in Washington, D.C.
- Ask your college librarian to help you access published guides to internship opportunities in the nation's capital.
- If you know which particular agency interests you, go to the agency's Web site or call its general information number to inquire about internship opportunites for college students.

With a little initiative and perseverance, there is a good chance that you can find openings throughout the federal bureaucracy.

Once you locate an appropriate internship opportunity, you will probably have to fill out an application form and solicit letters of recommendation. Fill out the application form clearly and neatly. Assume that the form's appearance will be taken as a reflection of your own commitment to the internship. If the application requires an essay about yourself or your experiences, remember two things. First, the essay is likely to be the best evidence of your intelligence and writing ability; therefore, craft an essay that you believe represents you well. Second, be honest about yourself (it is usually easy to spot a contrived essay). It may be that your honesty and integrity will neutralize a lack of experience or mediocre grades.

Solicit letters of recommendation from teachers who (1) have given you relatively good grades, (2) can speak to your classroom performance and qualifications for the internship, and (3) know you well enough to write an individualized letter about you. Do not be shy about asking for recommendation letters but do so several weeks in advance of any deadlines. When teachers agree to write letters, provide them with an updated résumé listing your academic, extracurricular, and community-service accomplishments, the appropriate form (if there is one), and a stamped, addressed envelope for each recommendation. Also, let them know when the deadline is. Later, it is appropriate to write them a thank you note and let them know the outcome of your application.

Once you have secured your internship (and housing, if necessary), be professional in appearance, demeanor, and language. If you find yourself doing busy work (stuffing envelopes, Xeroxing reams of documents, etc.), don't complain. Instead, learn what needs to be done in your part of the agency and let your supervisor know that you are willing to volunteer to undertake a useful project or help someone out on an ongoing project. Gain a reputation for working smart and working hard and remain alert for opportunities. There is a good chance you can work yourself into a fascinating internship experience in virtually any government agency.

When your internship is over, be sure to thank people in the agency for having had the opportunity to work with them and learn from them. Leave your internship with grace and good feelings; it may be that you will want to call on your former supervisor or coworkers in the future. The first lesson in "networking" is to assume that today's acquaintances are tomorrow's contacts. That is why it is not unusual for a short-term internship in a government agency to turn into a full-time career in the bureaucracy.

Summary

Bureaucracy is a universal form of organization, found in businesses, churches, foundations, and universities, as well as in the public sphere. All essential government services and regulations are carried out by bureaucracies—specifically, by administrative agencies. Bureaucrats are appointed to their offices based on the "merit system."

The agencies of the executive branch can be grouped according to the services that they provide: (1) promoting the public welfare, (2) promoting national security, and (3) maintaining a strong economy. All of these agencies are alike in that they are all bureaucratic. These agencies differ in the way they are organized, in the way they participate in the political process, and in their levels of responsiveness to political authority. In recent years, attempts have been made to "downsize" the bureaucracy by termination, devolution, and privatization. Although these efforts are popular with the American people, they cannot reduce the size of the bureaucracy by much.

The executive and the legislative branches do the toughest job any government is called on to do: making the bureaucracy accountable to the people. Democratizing bureaucracy is the unending task of politics in a democracy.

FOR FURTHER READING

Arnold, Peri E. *Making the Managerial Presidency: Comprehensive Organization Planning*. Princeton: Princeton University Press, 1986.

Fesler, James W., and Donald F. Kettl. *The Politics of the Administrative Process*. Chatham, NJ: Chatham House, 1991.

Skowronek, Stephen. *Building a New American State: The Expansion of National Administrative Capacities, 1877–1920*. New York: Cambridge University Press, 1982.

Wildavsky, Aaron. *The New Politics of the Budget Process*. 2nd ed. New York: HarperCollins, 1992.

Wilson, James Q. *Bureaucracy: What Government Agencies Do and Why They Do It*. New York: Basic Books, 1989.

Wood, Dan B. *Bureaucratic Dynamics: The Role of Bureaucracy in a Democracy.* Boulder, CO: Westview, 1994.

STUDY OUTLINE

Bureaucracy and Bureaucrats

1. Bureaucracy is simply a form of organization. Specialization and repetition are essential to the efficiency of any organization.
2. Despite fears of bureaucratic growth, the federal service has grown little during the past twenty-five years. The national government is large, but the federal service has not been growing any faster than the economy or the society.
3. The primary task of bureaucracy is to implement the laws passed by Congress.
4. Because statutes and executive orders often provide only vague instructions, one important job of the bureaucrat is to interpret the intentions of Congress and the president prior to implementation of orders.
5. The lower efficiency of public agencies can be attributed to the added constraints put on them, as compared to those put on private agencies.
6. Through civil service reform, national and state governments have attempted to reduce political interference in public bureaucracies by granting certain public bureaucrats legal protection from being fired without a show of cause.

The Organization of the Executive Branch

1. Cabinet departments, agencies, and bureaus are the operating parts of the bureaucracy. Not all government agencies are part of Cabinet departments. Independent agencies, government corporations, and independent regulatory commissions also are part of the executive branch.
2. The different agencies of the executive branch can be classified into three main groups by the services that they provide to the American public. The first category of agencies provides services and products that seek to promote the public welfare. Some of these agencies are particularly tied to a specific group or segment of American society that is often thought of as the main clientele of that agency.
3. The second category of agencies work to promote national security from internal and external threat.
4. The third group of agencies provides services that help to maintain a strong economy. Foremost among these are the agencies that are responsible for fiscal and monetary policy. In addition, the federal government may directly provide services or goods that bolster the economy.

Can Bureaucracy Be Reinvented?

1. The National Performance Review is an effort to make the bureaucracy more efficient, accountable, and effective.
2. While government bureaucracies can be made more responsive and efficient, reform is not simply a matter of management techniques but also a political matter.

Can the Bureaucracy Be Reduced?

1. The bureaucracy can be reduced in three ways: termination, devolution, and privatization.

Can Bureaucracy Be Controlled?

1. Each expansion of the national government in the twentieth century was accompanied by a parallel expansion of presidential management authority, but the expansion of presidential power cannot guarantee responsible bureaucracy.
2. Although Congress attempts to control the bureaucracy through oversight, a more effective way to ensure accountability may be to clarify legislative intent.

PRACTICE QUIZ

1. Which of the following best describes the growth of the federal service in the past twenty-five years?
   a) rampant, exponential growth
   b) little growth at all
   c) decrease in the total number of federal employees.
   d) vast, compared to the growth of the economy and the society

2. What task must bureaucrats perform if Congress charges them with enforcing a law through explicit directions?
   a) implementation
   b) interpretation
   c) lawmaking
   d) quasi-judicial decision making

3. Which of the following was *not* a component of the Civil Service Act of 1883?
   a) the merit system
   b) a type of tenure system
   c) a spoils system
   d) All of the above were associated with the Civil Service Act of 1883.

4. Which of the following is a way in which the bureaucracy might be reduced?
   a) devolution
   b) termination
   c) privatization
   d) all of the above
5. Which of the following is *not* an example of a clientele agency?
   a) Department of Justice
   b) Department of Commerce
   c) Department of Agriculture
   d) Department of Housing and Urban Development
6. The concept of oversight refers to the effort made by
   a) Congress to make executive agencies accountable for their actions.
   b) the president to make Congress accountable for its actions.
   c) the courts to make executive agencies responsible for their actions.
   d) the states to make the executive branch accountable for its actions.
7. Which president instituted the bureaucratic reform of the National Performance Review?
   a) Richard Nixon
   b) Lyndon Johnson
   c) Jimmy Carter
   d) Bill Clinton
8. Which of the following are *not* part of the executive branch?
   a) cabinet departments
   b) government corporations
   c) independent regulatory commissions
   d) All of the above are parts of the executive branch.

CRITICAL THINKING QUESTIONS

1. Often the efficiency of public bureaucracies is judged in terms of the efficiency of private business and other organizations. In many instances, government has been expected to do things that businesses in the marketplace have chosen not to do or have found unprofitable. Might the tasks that government is asked to perform be more prone to inefficiency? Think about the ways in which business might be able to perform some tasks that government currently performs. Would business necessarily perform these tasks more efficiently? Should efficiency be the only priority in the public enterprise?
2. Describe the ways in which the public controls its bureaucracy. How much and what kind of control should the public exercise? Through elected officials—i.e., the president and the Congress—the public can achieve some control over the bureaucracy. What are the relative advantages and disadvantages of presidential and congressional control of the bureaucracy?

KEY TERMS

administrative adjudication (p. 578)
bureaucracy (p. 573)
department (p. 580)
deregulation (p. 599)
devolution (p. 599)
Federal Reserve System (p. 590)
fiscal policy (p. 589)
government corporation (p. 580)
implementation (p. 577)
independent agency (p. 580)
iron triangle (p. 584)
merit system (p. 579)
oversight (p. 604)
privatization (p. 600)
regulatory agencies (p. 583)
revenue agencies (p. 590)
rulemaking (p. 578)

16 The Federal

★ **The Legal System**

Within what broad categories of law do cases arise?

How is the U.S. court system structured?

★ **Federal Jurisdiction**

What is the importance of the federal court system?

What factors play a role in the appointment of federal judges?

What shapes the flow of cases through the Supreme Court?

★ **The Power of the Supreme Court: Judicial Review**

What is the basis for the Supreme Court's power of judicial review?

How does the power of judicial review make the Supreme Court a lawmaking body?

How does a case reach the Supreme Court? Once accepted, how does a case proceed?

What factors influence the judicial philosophy of the Supreme Court?

★ **Judicial Power and Politics**

How has the power of the federal courts been limited throughout much of American history?

How have the role and power of the federal courts been transformed over the last fifty years?

How has the increase in the Supreme Court's power changed its role in the political process?

Courts

STUDENTS AND POLITICS

In the year 2000, there were two million prisoners in the jails and penitentaries of the United States. But hundreds, perhaps thousands, of prisoners are serving sentences for crimes they did not commit. The Bill of Rights is filled with safeguards against conviction of the innocent, but for those who have no means to defend themselves or to give voice to miscarriages of justice, those safeguards are, in the words of *Federalist* #48, "mere demarcation on parchment. . . ."

Yet, the voice against injustice does not always spring from the pocket of the wealthy. Courts can be responsive to quite unpowerful and unwealthy voices. One example is David Protess's journalism class at Northwestern's Medill School of Journalism. For several years, students in Professor Protess's class have examined death row cases in an exercise known as getting at the truth. The students' grades do not depend on their conclusions, but on their investigative techniques. If students doubt the guilt of an inmate, they must reevaluate the crime by exploring the trial records, locating witnesses, and attempting to re-interview them. Their primary incentive and their only guide is the statistic they learn during their first class meeting: nationwide, for every seven executions carried out since the death penalty was reinstituted in 1976, one death-row prisoner has been found innocent and set free.[1] They look for cases in which no directly incriminating evidence—such as blood or semen—was presented at trial, no credible eyewitnesses testified, and there was no reliable confession and no other "viable suspect." The students get together, review the record thoroughly, identify witnesses and practice interviewing them, and also prepare for interviewing the inmate himself or herself. In interviewing witnesses or the inmate, they learn how to play "good cop" to the "bad cop" usually played by the professor or by the private detective who assists the class.

Such intense yet simple and brief preparation has produced impressive results. In 1996, Professor Protess and his students reviewed and helped clear four men imprisoned for eighteen years for a double murder they did not commit. In 1999 the four freed men agreed to a $36 million settlement in a civil suit against Cook County (Chicago).[2]

As this case was being settled, another was coming to a head. Meanwhile, the Northwestern students were being dubbed in the press as the "Last Chance Club," as they mounted what a London newspaper called "the biggest challenge to capital punishment for almost a quarter of a century."[3] Anthony Porter, erstwhile gang member and small-time criminal had been sentenced to death in 1982 for the drug-related murder of two teenagers in Chicago. In 1997, after fifteen years on death row, the "Last Chance Club," with the help of Protess's private investigator, located the estranged wife of Alstory Simon, who told the students that she had been with Simon at the time of the encounter and that it was Simon, not Porter, who had shot the two teenagers over sales and payments of drugs. A videotaped confession by Simon led the Cook County Criminal County Judge to reopen the Porter case in order to examine the new evidence. And on February 5, 1999, Porter was released on a $10,000 recognizance bond (requiring no money for bail) pending study by prosecutors of the Simon confession. Outstanding charges against Porter for armed robbery were still valid but he was free of the death sentence and would probably be allowed eventually to count the eighteen years of time served on death row as sufficient to satisfy the other conviction.

On January 31, 2000, Illinois governor George H. Ryan, a conservative Republican, announced that although he still espoused the death penalty for crimes that shock sensibility, "How do you prevent another Anthony Porter—another innocent man or woman from paying the ultimate penalty for a crime he or she did not commit?"[4] He went on to declare that he would not approve any more executions "until I can be sure that everyone sentenced to death in Illinois is truly guilty. . . ."

The shock waves of the Porter case also reached Washington. Senator Patrick Leahy, a Vermont Democrat, speaking of Anthony Porter, asked "Was he cleared by the State? No. He was cleared by a class of undergraduate journalism students at Northwestern University, who took on his case as a class project. That got him out." Senator Leahy announced he was sponsoring national legislation to provide additional protection against such wrongful convictions.[5] Presidential candidate George W. Bush was hit with questions on the death penalty during his intense campaigning in the South Carolina primary and was forced to respond that he was "confident that every person that has been put to death in Texas under my watch has been guilty of the crime charged." But that did not put an end to those questions about Texas or to the spreading consensus among top journalists that "there is an epidemic of police and prosecutorial misconduct and . . . the scandals in Los Angeles and Illinois are festering sores. . . ."[6] The small spark in Illinois may very well have started a prairie fire.

Every year nearly twenty-five million cases are tried in American courts and one American in every nine is directly involved in litigation. Cases can arise from disputes between citizens, from efforts by government agencies to punish wrongdoing, or from citizens' efforts to prove that a right provided them by law has been infringed upon as a result of government action—or inaction. Many critics of the U.S. legal system assert that Americans have become much too litigious (ready to use the courts for all purposes), and perhaps that is

Students and Politics

Clashes between university administrations and students with strong religious views have become more pronounced since the 1995 *Rosenberger v. University of Virginia* decision. In a 1997 suit filed in U.S. District Court in Connecticut, four students at Yale University sued the school over the requirement that all students live on campus during their freshman and sophomore years. The plaintiffs, dubbed the "Yale Four," claimed that such a requirement discriminates against their religion, Orthodox Judaism, which requires modesty in interactions with the opposite sex. (Yale dormitories frequently have coed floors and bathrooms.) The administration held that living on campus and exposure to students of different backgrounds and beliefs is integral to the learning experience at Yale. "We believe the undergraduate experience is more than just the classroom," says Richard Levin, Yale's president. "And we believe these aren't just dormitories, but communities. . . . These students want the education, but they don't want the encounter." But Batsheva Greer, one of the plaintiffs, could not reconcile religion and university policy. "It's not like I was debating the issue," she said of her decision to join the lawsuit. "It was definite in my mind. There was just no question that I would be sacrificing my religious upbringing to live on campus. . . . We're not out to change the university. We're just trying to live in accordance with Judaism."

SOURCE: Samuel G. Freedman, "Yeshivish at Yale," *The New York Times* Magazine section, May 24, 1998, p. 23.

true. But the heavy use that Americans make of the courts is also an indication of the extent of conflict in American society. And given the existence of social conflict, it is far better that Americans seek to settle their differences through the courts rather than by fighting or feuding.

The framers of the American Constitution called the Supreme Court the "least dangerous branch" of American government. Today, it is not unusual to hear friends *and* foes of the Court refer to it as the "imperial judiciary."[7] Before we can understand this transformation and its consequences, however, we must look in some detail at America's judicial process.

- ***In this chapter we will first examine the legal system, including the types of cases that the federal courts consider and the types of law with which they deal.***
- ***Second, we will assess the organization and structure of the federal court system as well as the flow of cases through the courts.***
- ***Third, we will consider judicial review and how it makes the Supreme Court a "lawmaking body."*** We will also analyze the procedures of and influences on the Supreme Court.
- ***Finally, we will consider the role and power of the federal courts in the American political process, looking in particular at the growth of judicial power in the United States.*** We conclude by looking at how this changing role affects liberty and democracy.

Some critics contend that American society has become too litigious, citing an increase in the number of "frivolous lawsuits" filed each year, such as the one filed by this homeless man against the Morristown Public Library, which had ejected him for offensive personal hygiene.

The Legal System

- Within what broad categories of law do cases arise?
- How is the U.S. court system structured?

Originally, a "court" was the place where a sovereign ruled—where the king and his entourage governed. Settling disputes between citizens was part of governing. According to the Bible, King Solomon had to settle the dispute between two women over which of them was the mother of the child both claimed. Judging is the settling of disputes, a function that was slowly separated from the king and the king's court and made into a separate institution of government. Courts have taken over from kings the power to settle controversies by hearing the facts on both sides and deciding which side possesses the greater merit. But since judges are not kings, they must have a basis for their authority. That basis in the United States is the Constitution and the law. Courts decide cases by hearing the facts on both sides of a dispute and applying the relevant law or principle to the facts. This is all the more sensitive a matter because courts have been given the authority to settle disputes not only between citizens but between citizens and the government itself, where the courts are obliged to maintain the same neutrality and impartiality as they do between disputes involving two citizens. This is the essence of the "rule of law," that "the state" and its officials must be judged by the same laws as the citizenry. But since judges must apply the law as well as being subject to it,

criminal law

the branch of law that deals with disputes or actions involving criminal penalties (as opposed to civil law); it regulates the conduct of individuals, defines crimes, and provides punishment for criminal acts

plaintiff

the individual or organization who brings a complaint in court

defendant

the one against whom a complaint is brought in a criminal or civil case

civil law

a system of jurisprudence, including private law and governmental actions, to settle disputes that do not involve criminal penalties

precedents

prior cases whose principles are used by judges as the bases for their decisions in present cases

stare decisis

literally, "let the decision stand." The doctrine that a previous decision by a court applies as a precedent in similar cases until that decision is overruled

public law

cases in private law, civil law, or criminal law in which one party to the dispute argues that a license is unfair, a law is inequitable or unconstitutional, or an agency has acted unfairly, violated a procedure, or gone beyond its jurisdiction

they must conduct themselves as closely as possible by the principle that they are not making personal judgments but are almost mechanistically applying the Constitution and the laws to the facts. There are obviously elements of myth as well as truth in this principle. But the American judicial system, from bottom to top, must have been doing something right because, compared to the other branches, it has been amazingly free of institutional crises during its history.

CASES AND THE LAW

Court cases in the United States proceed under three broad categories of law: criminal law, civil law, and public law.

Cases of **criminal law** are those in which the government charges an individual with violating a statute that has been enacted to protect the public health, safety, morals, or welfare. In criminal cases, the government is always the **plaintiff** (the party that brings charges) and alleges that a criminal violation has been committed by a named **defendant.** Most criminal cases arise in state and municipal courts and involve matters ranging from traffic offenses through robbery and murder. Another large and growing body of federal criminal law deals with such matters as tax evasion, mail fraud, and the sale of narcotics. Defendants found guilty of criminal violations may be fined or sent to prison.

Cases of **civil law** involve disputes among individuals or between individuals and the government where no criminal violation is charged. Unlike criminal cases, the losers in civil cases cannot be fined or sent to prison, although they may be required to pay monetary damages for their actions. In a civil case, the one who brings a complaint is the plaintiff and the one against whom the complaint is brought is the defendant. The two most common types of civil cases involve contracts and torts. In a typical contract case, an individual or corporation charges that it has suffered because of another's violation of a specific agreement between the two. For example, the Smith Manufacturing Corporation may charge that Jones Distributors failed to honor an agreement to deliver raw materials at a specified time, causing Smith to lose business. Smith asks the court to order Jones to compensate it for the damage allegedly suffered. In a typical tort case, one individual charges that he or she has been injured by another's negligence or malfeasance. Medical malpractice suits are one example of tort cases.

In deciding civil cases, courts apply statutes (laws) and legal **precedent** (prior decisions). State and federal statutes, for example, often govern the conditions under which contracts are and are not legally binding. Jones Distributors might argue that it was not obliged to fulfill its contract with the Smith Corporation because actions by Smith, such as the failure to make promised payments, constituted fraud under state law. Attorneys for a physician being sued for malpractice, on the other hand, may search for prior instances in which courts ruled that actions similar to those of their client did not constitute negligence. Such precedents are applied under the doctrine of ***stare decisis,*** a Latin phrase meaning "let the decision stand."

A case becomes a matter of the third category, **public law,** when a plaintiff or defendant in a civil or criminal case seeks to show that their case involves the powers of government or rights of citizens as defined under the Constitution or by statute. One major form of public law is constitutional law, under which a court will examine the government's actions to see if they conform to the Constitution as it has been interpreted by the judiciary. Thus, what began as an ordinary criminal case may enter the realm of public law if a defendant claims that his or her constitutional rights were violated by the police. Another important arena of public law is administrative law, which involves disputes over the jurisdiction, procedures, or authority of administrative agencies. Under this type of law, civil litigation between an individual and the government may become a matter of public law if the individual asserts that the government is violating a statute or abusing its power under the Constitution. For example, landowners have asserted that federal and state restrictions on land use constitute violations of the Fifth Amendment's restrictions on the government's ability to confiscate private property. Recently, the Supreme Court has been very sympathetic to such claims, which effectively transform an ordinary civil dispute into a major issue of public law.

Most of the important Supreme Court cases we will examine in this chapter involve judgments concerning the constitutional or statutory basis of the actions of government agencies. As we shall see, it is in this arena of public law that the Supreme Court's decisions can have significant consequences for American politics and society.

TYPES OF COURTS

In the United States, systems of courts have been established both by the federal government and by the governments of the individual states. Both systems have several levels, as shown in Figure 16.1. More than 99 percent of all court

THE U.S. COURT SYSTEM — Figure 16.1

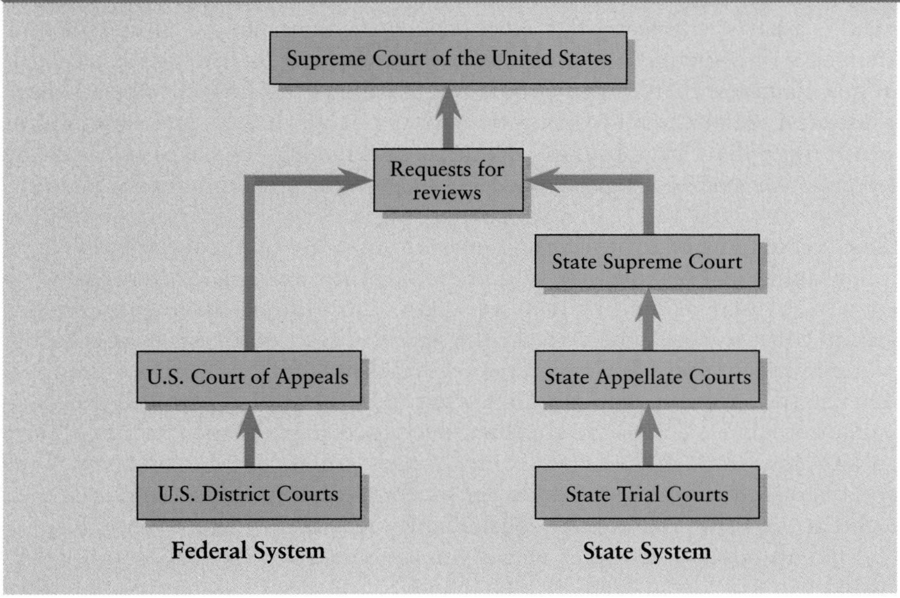

The state and federal court systems parallel each other until they reach the Supreme Court.

cases in the United States are heard in state courts. The overwhelming majority of criminal cases, for example, involve violations of state laws prohibiting such actions as murder, robbery, fraud, theft, and assault. If such a case is brought to trial, it will be heard in a state **trial court,** in front of a judge and sometimes a jury, who will determine whether the defendant violated state law. If the defendant is convicted, he or she may appeal the conviction to a higher court, such as a state **appellate court,** and from there to a state's **supreme court.** Similarly, in civil cases, most litigation is brought in the courts established by the state in which the activity in question took place. For example, a patient bringing suit against a physician for malpractice would file the suit in the appropriate court in the state where the alleged malpractice occurred. The judge hearing the case would apply state law and state precedent to the matter at hand. (It should be noted that in both criminal and civil matters, most cases are settled before trial through negotiated agreements between the parties. In criminal cases these agreements are called **plea bargains.**)

trial court
the first court to hear a criminal or civil case

appellate court
a court that hears the appeals of trial court decisions

supreme court
the highest court in a particular state or in the United States. This court primarily serves an appellate function

Although each state has its own set of laws, these laws have much in common from state to state. Murder and robbery, obviously, are illegal in all states, although the range of possible punishments for those crimes varies from state to state. Some states, for example, provide for capital punishment (the death penalty) for murder and other serious offenses; other states do not. As we saw in Chapter 4, however, some acts that are criminal offenses in one state may be legal in another state. Prostitution, for example, is legal in some Nevada counties, although it is outlawed in all other states. Considerable similarity among the states is also found in the realm of civil law. In the case of contract law, most states have adopted the **Uniform Commercial Code** in order to reduce interstate differences. In areas such as family law, however, which covers such matters as divorce and child custody arrangements, state laws vary greatly.

plea bargains
negotiated agreements in criminal cases in which a defendant agrees to plead guilty in return for the state's agreement to reduce the severity of the criminal charge the defendant is facing

Uniform Commercial Code
code used in many states in the area of contract law to reduce interstate differences in judicial decisions

Cases are heard in the federal courts if they involve federal laws, treaties with other nations, or the U.S. Constitution; these areas are the official **jurisdiction** of the federal courts. In addition, any case in which the U.S. government is a party is heard in the federal courts. If, for example, an individual is charged with violating a federal criminal statute, such as evading the payment of income taxes, charges would be brought before a federal judge by a federal prosecutor. Civil cases involving the citizens of more than one state and in which more than fifty thousand dollars is at stake may be heard in either the federal or the state courts, usually depending on the preference of the plaintiff.

jurisdiction
the sphere of a court's power and authority

Federal courts serve another purpose in addition to trying cases within their jurisdiction: that of hearing appeals from state-level courts. Individuals found guilty of breaking a state criminal law, for example, can appeal their convictions to a federal court by raising a constitutional issue and asking a federal court to determine whether the state's actions were consistent with the requirements of the U.S. Constitution. An appellant might assert, for example, that the state court denied him or her the right to counsel, imposed excessive bail, or otherwise denied the appellant **due process.** Under such circumstances, an appellant can ask the federal court to overturn his or her conviction. Federal courts are not obligated to accept such appeals and will do so only if they feel that the issues raised have considerable merit and if the appellant has exhausted all possible remedies within the state courts. (This procedure is discussed in more detail later in this chapter.) The decisions of state supreme

due process of law
the right of every citizen against arbitrary action by national or state governments

courts may also be appealed to the U.S. Supreme Court if the state court's decision has conflicted with prior U.S. Supreme Court rulings or has raised some important question of federal law. Such appeals are accepted by the U.S. Supreme Court at its discretion.

Although the federal courts hear only a small fraction of all the civil and criminal cases decided each year in the United States, their decisions are extremely important. It is in the federal courts that the Constitution and federal laws that govern all Americans are interpreted and their meaning and significance established. Moreover, it is in the federal courts that the powers and limitations of the increasingly powerful national government are tested. Finally, through their power to review the decisions of the state courts, it is ultimately the federal courts that dominate the American judicial system.

Federal Jurisdiction

- What is the importance of the federal court system?
- What factors play a role in the appointment of federal judges?
- What shapes the flow of cases through the Supreme Court?

Of all the cases heard in the United States in 1996, federal district courts (the lowest federal level) received 272,661. Although this number is up substantially from the 87,000 cases heard in 1961, it still constitutes under 1 percent of the judiciary's business. The federal courts of appeal listened to 51,524 cases in 1996, and the U.S. Supreme Court reviewed 7,601 in its 1997–98 term. Only 80 cases were given full-dress Supreme Court review (the nine justices actually sitting *en banc*—in full court—and hearing the lawyers argue the case).[8]

THE LOWER FEDERAL COURTS

Most of the cases of original federal jurisdiction are handled by the federal district courts. Courts of **original jurisdiction** are the courts that are responsible for discovering the facts in a controversy and creating the record on which a judgment is based. Although the Constitution gives the Supreme Court original jurisdiction in several types of cases, such as those affecting ambassadors and those in which a state is one of the parties, most original jurisdiction goes to the lowest courts—the trial courts. (In courts that have appellate jurisdiction, judges receive cases after the factual record is established by the trial court. Ordinarily, new facts cannot be presented before appellate courts.)

original jurisdiction
the authority to initially consider a case. Distinguished from appellate jurisdiction, which is the authority to hear appeals from a lower court's decision

There are eighty-nine district courts in the fifty states, plus one in the District of Columbia and one in Puerto Rico, and three territorial courts. These courts are staffed by 610 federal district judges. District judges are assigned to district courts according to the workload; the busiest of these courts may have as many as twenty-eight judges. Only one judge is assigned to each case, except where statutes provide for three-judge courts to deal with special issues. The routines and procedures of the federal district courts are essentially the same as those of the lower state courts, except that federal procedural requirements tend to be stricter. States, for example, do not have to provide a grand jury, a twelve-member trial jury, or a unanimous jury verdict. Federal courts must provide all these things.

THE APPELLATE COURTS

Roughly 10 percent of all lower court and federal agency cases are accepted for review by the federal appeals courts and by the Supreme Court in its capacity as an appellate court. The country is divided into twelve judicial circuits, each of which has a U.S. Court of Appeals. Every state, the District of Columbia, and each of the territories is assigned to the circuit in the continental United States that is closest to it.

Except for cases selected for review by the Supreme Court, decisions made by the appeals courts are final. Because of this finality, certain safeguards have been built into the system. The most important is the provision of more than one judge for every appeals case. Each court of appeals has from six to twenty-eight permanent judgeships, depending on the workload of the circuit. Although normally three judges hear appealed cases, in some instances a larger number of judges sit together *en banc.*

Another safeguard is provided by the assignment of a Supreme Court justice as the circuit justice for each of the twelve circuits. Since the creation of the appeals court in 1891, the circuit justice's primary duty has been to review appeals arising in the circuit in order to expedite Supreme Court action. The most frequent and best-known action of circuit justices is that of reviewing requests for stays of execution when the full Court is unable to do so—primarily during the summer, when the Court is in recess.

THE SUPREME COURT

chief justice
justice on the Supreme Court who presides over the Court's public sessions

The Supreme Court is America's highest court. Article III of the Constitution vests "the judicial power of the United States" in the Supreme Court, and this court is supreme in fact as well as form. The Supreme Court is made up of a chief justice and eight associate justices. The **chief justice** presides over the Court's public sessions and conferences. In the Court's actual deliberations and decisions, however, the chief justice has no more authority than his colleagues. Each justice casts one vote. To some extent, the influence of the chief justice is a function of his or her own leadership ability. Some chief justices, such as the late Earl Warren, have been able to lead the court in a new direction. In other instances, forceful associate justices, such as the late Felix Frankfurter, are the dominant figures on the Court.

The Supreme Court building in Washington, D.C.

The Constitution does not specify the number of justices that should sit on the Supreme Court; Congress has the authority to change the Court's size. In the early nineteenth century, there were six Supreme Court justices; later there were seven. Congress set the number of justices at nine in 1869, and the Court has remained that size ever since. In 1937, President Franklin D. Roosevelt, infuriated by several Supreme Court decisions that struck down New Deal programs, asked Congress to enlarge the Court so that he could add a few sympathetic justices to the bench. Although Congress balked at Roosevelt's "court packing" plan, the Court gave in to FDR's pressure and began to take a more favorable view of his policy initiatives. The president, in turn, dropped

The members of the Supreme Court in 2000 (from left to right): Antonin Scalia, Ruth Bader Ginsburg, John Paul Stevens, David Souter, Chief Justice William Rehnquist, Clarence Thomas, Sandra Day O'Connor, Stephen Breyer, and Anthony Kennedy.

his efforts to enlarge the Court. The Court's surrender to FDR came to be known as "the switch in time that saved nine."

HOW JUDGES ARE APPOINTED

Federal judges are appointed by the president and are generally selected from among the more prominent or politically active members of the legal profession. Many federal judges previously served as state court judges or state or local prosecutors. In an informal nominating process, candidates for vacancies on the U.S. District Court are generally suggested to the president by a U.S. senator from the president's own party who represents the state in which the vacancy has occurred. Senators often see such a nomination as a way to reward important allies and contributors in their states. If the state has no senator from the president's party, the governor or members of the state's House delegation may make suggestions. In general, presidents endeavor to appoint judges who possess legal experience and good character and whose partisan and ideological views are similar to the president's own. During the presidencies of Ronald Reagan and George Bush, most federal judicial appointees were conservative Republicans. Bush established an advisory committee to screen judicial nominees in order to make certain that their legal and political philosophies were sufficiently conservative. Bill Clinton's appointees to the federal bench, on the other hand, tended to be liberal Democrats. Clinton also made a major effort to appoint women and African Americans to the federal courts. Nearly half of his nominees were drawn from these groups.

Once the president has formally nominated an individual, the nominee must be considered by the Senate Judiciary Committee and confirmed by a majority vote in the full Senate. Before the president makes a formal nomination, however, the senators from the candidate's own state must indicate that they support the nominee. This is an informal but seldom violated practice called **senatorial courtesy.** Because the Senate will rarely approve a nominee opposed by a senator from his or her own state, the president will usually not

senatorial courtesy
the practice whereby the president, before formally nominating a person for a federal judgeship, seeks the indication that senators from the candidate's own state support the nomination

bother to present such a nomination to the Senate. Through this arrangement, senators are able to exercise veto power over appointments to the federal bench in their own states. In recent years, the Senate Judiciary Committee has also sought to signal the president when it has had qualms about a judicial nomination. After the Republicans won control of the Senate in 1994, for example, Judiciary Committee chair Orrin Hatch of Utah let President Clinton know that he considered two of Clinton's nominees to be too liberal. The president withdrew the nominations.

Federal appeals court nominations follow much the same pattern. Since appeals court judges preside over jurisdictions that include several states, however, senators do not have as strong a role in proposing potential candidates. Instead, potential appeals court candidates are generally suggested to the president by the Justice Department or by important members of the administration. The senators from the nominee's own state are still consulted before the president will formally act.

If political factors play an important role in the selection of district and appellate court judges, they are decisive when it comes to Supreme Court appointments. Because the high court has so much influence over American law and politics, virtually all presidents have made an effort to select justices who share their own political philosophies. Presidents Ronald Reagan and George Bush, for example, appointed five justices whom they believed to have conservative perspectives: Justices Sandra Day O'Connor, Antonin Scalia, Anthony Kennedy, David Souter, and Clarence Thomas. Reagan also elevated William Rehnquist to the position of chief justice. Reagan and Bush sought appointees who believed in reducing government intervention in the economy and who supported the moral positions taken by the Republican Party in recent years, particularly opposition to abortion. However, not all the Reagan and Bush appointees have fulfilled their sponsors' expectations. Bush appointee David Souter, for example, has been attacked by conservatives as a turncoat for his decisions on school prayer and abortion rights. Nevertheless, through their appointments, Reagan and Bush were able to create a far more conservative Supreme Court. For his part, President Bill Clinton endeavored to appoint liberal justices. Clinton named Ruth Bader Ginsburg and Stephen Breyer to the Court, hoping to counteract the influence of the Reagan and Bush appointees. (Table 16.1 shows information about the current Supreme Court justices.)

In recent years, Supreme Court nominations have come to involve intense partisan struggle. Typically, after the president has named a nominee, interest groups opposed to the nomination have mobilized opposition in the media, the public, and the Senate. When President Bush proposed conservative judge Clarence Thomas for the Court, for example, liberal groups launched a campaign to discredit Thomas. After extensive research into his background, opponents of the nomination were able to produce evidence suggesting that Thomas had sexually harassed a former subordinate, Anita Hill. Thomas denied the charge. After contentious Senate Judiciary Committee hearings, highlighted by testimony from both Thomas and Hill, Thomas narrowly won confirmation.

Likewise, conservative interest groups carefully scrutinized Bill Clinton's liberal nominees, hoping to find information about them that would sabotage their appointments. During his two opportunities to name Supreme Court justices, Clinton was compelled to drop several potential appointees because of information unearthed by political opponents.

SUPREME COURT JUSTICES, 2000 (IN ORDER OF SENIORITY)

Table 16.1

Name	Year of birth	Prior experience	Appointed by	Year of appointment
William H. Rehnquist* *Chief Justice*	1924	Assistant attorney general	Nixon	1972
John Paul Stevens	1920	Federal judge	Ford	1975
Sandra Day O'Connor	1930	State judge	Reagan	1981
Antonin Scalia	1936	Law professor, federal judge	Reagan	1986
Anthony Kennedy	1936	Federal judge	Reagan	1988
David Souter	1939	Federal judge	Bush	1990
Clarence Thomas	1948	Federal judge	Bush	1991
Ruth Bader Ginsburg	1933	Federal judge	Clinton	1993
Stephen Breyer	1938	Federal judge	Clinton	1994

*Appointed chief justice by Reagan in 1986.

These struggles over judicial appointments indicate the growing intensity of partisan struggle in the United States today. They also indicate how much importance competing political forces attach to Supreme Court appointments. Because these contending forces see the outcome as critical, they are willing to engage in a fierce struggle when Supreme Court appointments are at stake.

In testimony before the Senate Judiciary Committee, Anita Hill alleged that Supreme Court nominee Clarence Thomas had sexually harassed her. Hill's testimony brought nationwide attention to the nomination hearings. The Senate subsequently approved Thomas by the narrowest ratification margin in history, 52 to 48.

The Power of the Supreme Court: Judicial Review

- What is the basis for the Supreme Court's power of judicial review?
- How does the power of judicial review make the Supreme Court a lawmaking body?
- How does a case reach the Supreme Court? Once accepted, how does a case proceed?
- What factors influence the judicial philosophy of the Supreme Court?

judicial review
the power of the courts to declare actions of the legislative and executive branches invalid or unconstitutional. The Supreme Court asserted this power in Marbury v. Madison

One of the most important powers of the Supreme Court is the power of **judicial review**—the authority and the obligation to review any lower court decision where a substantial issue of public law is involved. The disputes can be over the constitutionality of federal or state laws, over the propriety or constitutionality of the court procedures followed, or over whether public officers are exceeding their authority. The Supreme Court's power of judicial review has come to mean review not only of lower court decisions but also of state legislation and acts of Congress. For this reason, if for no other, the Supreme Court is more than a judicial agency—it is a major lawmaking body.

The Supreme Court's power of judicial review over lower court decisions has never been at issue. Nor has there been any serious quibble over the power of the federal courts to review administrative agencies in order to determine whether their actions and decisions are within the powers delegated to them by Congress. There has, however, been a great deal of controversy occasioned by the Supreme Court's efforts to review acts of Congress and the decisions of state courts and legislatures.

Chief Justice John Marshall established the Supreme Court's power to rule on the constitutionality of federal and state laws.

JUDICIAL REVIEW OF ACTS OF CONGRESS

Since the Constitution does not give the Supreme Court the power of judicial review over congressional enactments, the Court's exercise of it is something of a usurpation. It is not known whether the framers of the Constitution opposed judicial review, but "if they intended to provide for it in the Constitution, they did so in a most obscure fashion."[9] Disputes over the intentions of the framers were settled in 1803 in the case of *Marbury v. Madison*.[10] Although Congress and the president have often been at odds with the Court, its legal power to review acts of Congress has not been seriously questioned since 1803. One reason is that judicial power has been accepted as natural, if not intended. Another reason is that the Supreme Court has rarely reviewed the constitutionality of acts of Congress, especially in the past fifty years. When such acts do come up for review, the Court makes a self-conscious effort to give them an interpretation that will make them constitutional. In some instances, however, the Court reaches the conclusion that a congressional enactment directly violates the Constitution. For example, in 1998, the Court invalidated a statute through which Congress had given the president the authority to reject specific projects contained in spending bills. The Court ruled that this "line-item veto" power violated the constitutionally mandated separation of powers.[11]

AMERICAN DEMOCRACY IN COMPARATIVE PERSPECTIVE

Judicial Review

If there is one fact of the American constitutional tradition that stands as original, it is the concept of *judicial review.* It directly influenced constitutional development in Latin and South America during the revolutionary nineteenth century and, indirectly, contributed to a recasting of philosophical interpretations of separate powers and parliamentary authority throughout continental Europe in the years following World War I. It has also served, ironically, as the model by which former British colonies (members of the British Commonwealth) constructed their constitutions during the second half of the twentieth century. Judicial review, like all major concepts undergirding the democratic process, is not uniformly applied or practiced across the democracies of the world today. Indeed, the American tradition of a strong judicial review is shared by only a few other democracies.

Two different types of judicial review systems can be distinguished among most democracies of the contemporary world. The first is the *diffused* system of judicial review. In this system, all levels of courts and judges may act as a constitutional judge. The various levels of the courts may have different degrees of jurisdiction and their scope may not be equally broad, but the concept of judicial review is such that all judges specified within the constitutional system may rule on the constitutionality of legislative acts. This underscores the preeminence of constitutional law: As all law basically derives from the written constitution, and as all judges are viewed as principal agents for adjudicating law, all judges (within the system as specified by the constitution, such as the federal court system of the United States) may judge the constitutionality of legislation. The key restriction, however, is that the legislation must be examined within a specific context and can only be initiated through a specified process. The complaints and actions of parties must be directly affected by the legislation in question, and the decision rendered by the judges must have some direct and concrete application to the incident prompting the action of the court. Finally, in these systems of judicial review, if a judge finds the legislative act unconstitutional, the law is null and void at that point.

The second variety of judicial review found among democracies is the *concentrated* form. While similar to the diffused system, there are two major differences. First, unlike the diffused system, the concentrated system restricts judicial review to only one supreme court or a single organ of the state charged explicitly with the task of reviewing the constitutionality of legislation. How the single organ—the supreme court, tribunal, or council—can actually hear the case, that is, what initiates the process, varies among the democracies that employ this type of judicial review. Yet lower courts are greatly restricted in their role with regard to judicial review. The second difference reflects a fundamental difference in logic between the diffuse and concentrated systems of judicial review. In the diffused system, there is no presumption of the constitutionality of a law simply because it has not been challenged and evaluated by a responsible court. On the other hand, in concentrated systems of judicial review, legislative law is in fact assumed to be constitutional until such time as the single supreme court has said otherwise.

The rules of governing judicial review and the degree of judicial activism within a democracy remain largely independent. Judicial activism varies greatly among democracies, and there is no clear pattern between the type of judicial review system and the degree of judicial activism shown toward legislation.

SOURCES: Arend Lijphart, *Patterns of Democracy: Government Forms and Performance in Thirty-Six Countries* (New Haven: Yale University Press, 1999); Allan R. Brewer-Carías, *Judicial Review in Comparative Law* (New York: Cambridge University Press, 1989).

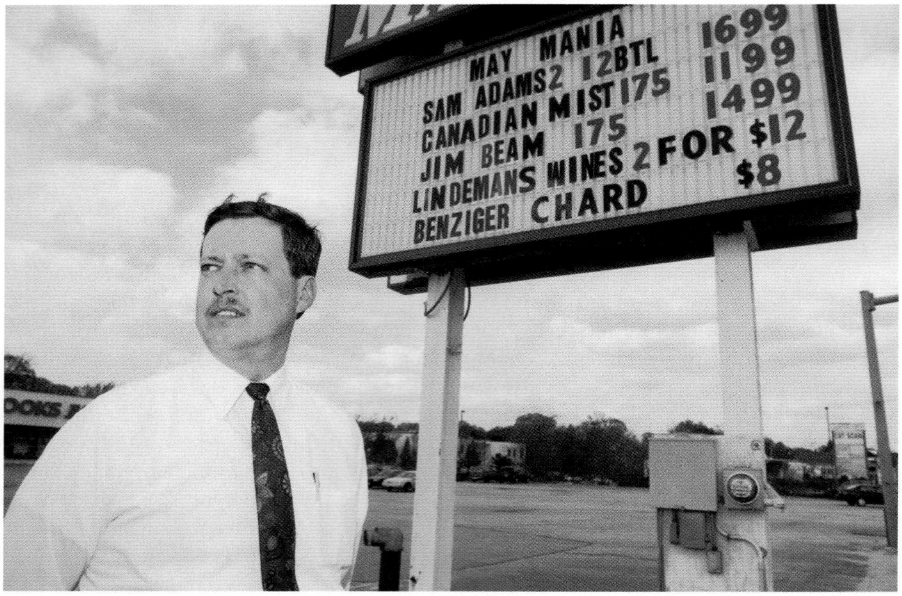

The Supreme Court has the power to overturn state laws. In 1996, the Supreme Court found unconstitutional a Rhode Island law that had prohibited the advertising of prices of alcoholic beverages. The Court claimed that the Rhode Island law had violated the First Amendment right of free speech.

JUDICIAL REVIEW OF STATE ACTIONS

supremacy clause
Article VI of the Constitution, which states that laws passed by the national government and all treaties are the supreme law of the land and superior to all laws adopted by any state or any subdivision

The power of the Supreme Court to review state legislation or other state action and to determine its constitutionality is neither granted by the Constitution nor inherent in the federal system. But the logic of the **supremacy clause** of Article VI of the Constitution, which declares it and laws made under its authority to be the supreme law of the land, is very strong. Furthermore, in the Judiciary Act of 1789, Congress conferred on the Supreme Court the power to reverse state constitutions and laws whenever they are clearly in conflict with the U.S. Constitution, federal laws, or treaties.[12] This power gives the Supreme Court appellate jurisdiction over all of the millions of cases handled by American courts each year.

The supremacy clause of the Constitution not only established the federal Constitution, statutes, and treaties as the "supreme law of the land," but also provided that "the Judges in every State shall be bound thereby, any Thing in the Constitution or Laws of the State to the Contrary notwithstanding." Under this authority, the Supreme Court has frequently overturned state constitutional provisions or statutes and state court decisions it deems to contravene rights or privileges guaranteed under the federal Constitution or federal statutes.

The civil rights area abounds with examples of state laws that were overturned because the statutes violated guarantees of due process and equal protection contained in the Fourteenth Amendment to the Constitution. For example, in the 1954 case of *Brown v. Board of Education,* the Court overturned statutes from Kansas, South Carolina, Virginia, and Delaware that either required or permitted segregated public schools, on the basis that such statutes denied black schoolchildren equal protection of the law. In 1967, in

Loving v. Virginia, the Court invalidated a Virginia statute prohibiting interracial marriages.[13]

State statutes in other subject matter areas are equally subject to challenge. In *Griswold v. Connecticut,* the Court invalidated a Connecticut statute prohibiting the general distribution of contraceptives to married couples on the basis that the statute violated the couples' rights to marital privacy.[14] In *Brandenburg v. Ohio,* the Court overturned an Ohio statute forbidding any person from urging criminal acts as a means of inducing political reform or from joining any association that advocated such activities on the grounds that the statute punished "mere advocacy" and therefore violated the free speech provisions of the Constitution.[15]

JUDICIAL REVIEW AND LAWMAKING

When courts of original jurisdiction apply existing statutes or past cases directly to citizens, the effect is the same as legislation. Lawyers study judicial decisions in order to discover underlying principles, and they advise their clients accordingly. Often the process is nothing more than reasoning by analogy: the facts in a particular case are so close to those in one or more previous cases that the same decision should be handed down. Such judge-made law is called common law.

The appellate courts, however, are in another realm. Their rulings can be considered laws, but they are laws governing the behavior only of the judiciary. They influence citizens' conduct only because, in the words of Justice Oliver Wendell Holmes, who served on the Supreme Court from 1900 to 1932, lawyers make "prophecies of what the courts will do in fact."[16]

The written opinion of an appellate court is about halfway between common law and statutory law. It is judge-made and draws heavily on the precedents of previous cases. But it tries to articulate the rule of law controlling the case in question and future cases like it. In this respect, it is like a statute. But it differs from a statute in that a statute addresses itself to the future conduct of citizens, whereas a written opinion addresses itself mainly to the willingness or ability of courts in the future to take cases and render favorable opinions. Decisions by appellate courts affect citizens by giving them a cause of action or by taking it away from them. That is, they open or close access to the courts.

A specific case may help clarify the distinction. Before the Second World War, one of the most insidious forms of racial discrimination was the "restrictive covenant," a clause in a contract whereby the purchasers of a house agreed that if they later decided to sell it, they would sell only to a Caucasian. When a test case finally reached the Supreme Court in 1948, the Court ruled unanimously that citizens had a right to discriminate with restrictive covenants in their sales contracts but that the courts could not enforce these contracts. Its argument was that enforcement would constitute violation of the Fourteenth Amendment provision that no state shall "deny to any person within its jurisdiction equal protection under the law."[17] The Court was thereby predicting what it would and would not do in future cases of this sort. Most states have now enacted statutes that forbid homeowners to place such covenants in sales contracts.

The 1963 case *Gideon v. Wainwright* extends the point. When the Supreme Court ordered a new trial for Clarence Earl Gideon because he had been denied the right to legal counsel,[18] it said to all trial judges and prosecutors that henceforth they would be wasting their time if they cut corners in trials of indigent defendants. It also invited thousands of prisoners to appeal their convictions. (See Chapter 5 for a further discussion of this case.)

Many areas of civil law have been constructed in the same way—by judicial messages to other judges, some of which are codified eventually into legislative enactments. An example of great concern to employees and employers is that of liability for injuries sustained at work. Courts have sided with employees so often that it has become virtually useless for employers to fight injury cases. It has become "the law" that employers are liable for such injuries, without regard to negligence. But the law in this instance is simply a series of messages to lawyers that they should advise their corporate clients not to appeal injury decisions. In recent years, the Supreme Court has also been developing law in the realm of sexual harassment in the workplace. In one 1998 case, for example, the Court ruled that an employer can be held responsible if one of its employees is sexually harassed by a supervisor, even if the company was unaware of the supervisor's specific behavior.[19]

The appellate courts cannot decide what types of behavior will henceforth be a crime. They cannot directly prevent the police from forcing confessions from suspects or intimidating witnesses. In other words, they cannot directly change the behavior of citizens or eliminate abuses of government power. What they can do, however, is make it easier for mistreated persons to gain redress.

In redressing wrongs, the appellate courts—and even the Supreme Court itself—often call for a radical change in legal principle. Changes in race relations, for example, would probably have taken a great deal longer if the Supreme Court had not rendered the 1954 decision *Brown v. Board of Education* that redefined the rights of African Americans.

Similarly, the Supreme Court interpreted the doctrine of the separation of church and state so as to alter significantly the practice of religion in public institutions. For example, in a 1962 case, *Engel v. Vitale,* the Court declared that a once widely observed ritual—the recitation of a prayer by students in a public school—was unconstitutional under the establishment clause of the First Amendment. Almost all the dramatic changes in the treatment of criminals and of persons accused of crimes have been made by the appellate courts, especially the Supreme Court. The Supreme Court brought about a veritable revolution in the criminal process with three cases over less than five years: *Gideon v. Wainwright,* in 1963, was just discussed. *Escobedo v. Illinois,* in 1964, gave suspects the right to remain silent and the right to have counsel present during questioning. But the *Escobedo* decision left confusions that allowed differing decisions to be made by lower courts. In *Miranda v. Arizona,* in 1966, the Supreme Court cleared up these confusions by setting forth what is known as the ***Miranda* rule:** arrested people have the right to remain silent, the right to be informed that anything they say can be held against them, and the right to counsel before and during police interrogation (see Chapter 5).[20] In 2000, the Supreme Court considered overruling *Miranda* in *Dickerson v. United States,* but it decided that the wide acceptance of Miranda rights in the legal culture is "adequate reason not to overrule" it.

***Miranda* rule**
the requirement, articulated by the Supreme Court in *Miranda v. Arizona,* that persons under arrest must be informed prior to police interrogation of their rights to remain silent and to have the benefit of legal counsel

One of the most significant changes brought about by the Supreme Court was the revolution in legislative representation unleashed by the 1962 case of *Baker v. Carr.*[21] In this landmark case, the Supreme Court held that it could no longer avoid reviewing complaints about the apportionment of seats in state legislatures. Following that decision, the federal courts went on to force reapportionment of all state, county, and local legislatures in the country.

HOW CASES REACH THE SUPREME COURT

Given the millions of disputes that arise every year, the job of the Supreme Court would be impossible if it were not able to control the flow of cases and its own caseload. Its original jurisdiction is only a minor problem. The original jurisdiction includes (1) cases between the United States and one of the fifty states, (2) cases between two or more states, (3) cases involving foreign ambassadors or other ministers, and (4) cases brought by one state against citizens of another state or against a foreign country. The most important of these cases are disputes between states over land, water, or old debts. Generally, the Supreme Court deals with these cases by appointing a "special master," usually a retired judge, to actually hear the case and present a report. The Supreme Court then allows the states involved in the dispute to present arguments for or against the master's opinion.[22]

Rules of Access Over the years, the courts have developed specific rules that govern which cases within their jurisdiction they will and will not hear. In order to have access to the courts, cases must meet certain criteria. These rules of access can be broken down into three major categories: case or controversy, standing, and mootness.

Article III of the Constitution and Supreme Court decisions define judicial power as extending only to "cases and controversies." This means that the case before a court must be an actual controversy, not a hypothetical one, with two truly adversarial parties. The courts have interpreted this language to mean that they do not have the power to render advisory opinions to legislatures or agencies about the constitutionality of proposed laws or regulations. Furthermore, even after a law is enacted, the courts will generally refuse to consider its constitutionality until it is actually applied.

Parties to a case must also have **standing,** that is, they must show that they have a substantial stake in the outcome of the case. The traditional requirement for standing has been to show injury to oneself; that injury can be personal, economic, or even aesthetic, for example. In order for a group or class of people to have standing (as in class action suits), each member must show specific injury. This means that a general interest in the environment, for instance, does not provide a group with sufficient basis for standing.

standing
the right of an individual or organization to initiate a court case

The Supreme Court also uses a third criterion in determining whether it will hear a case: that of **mootness.** In theory, this requirement disqualifies cases that are brought too late—after the relevant facts have changed or the problem has been resolved by other means. The criterion of mootness, however, is subject to the discretion of the courts, which have begun to relax the rules of mootness, particularly in cases where a situation that has been resolved is likely to come up again. In the abortion case *Roe v. Wade,* for example, the Supreme Court rejected the lower court's argument that because the pregnancy had already come to term, the case was moot. The Court agreed to hear the case because no pregnancy was likely to outlast the lengthy appeals process.

mootness
a criterion used by courts to screen cases that no longer require resolution.

Students and Politics

During this [1999–2000] school year every UW-Madison student will pay about $445 in segregated fees. Of that amount, $43.34 will go to fund a variety of student organizations and student government. It is the approximately $13 of those fees that goes to fund a multitude of student groups that UW alumnus Scott Southworth takes issue with.

"No student regardless of their political and ideological beliefs, should be forced to fund the political and ideological activities of any group," Southworth said.

As a UW law student in April 1996 Southworth filed a lawsuit challenging the way student organizations are funded in the University of Wisconsin System.

Southworth's arguments are based on the idea that every student has rights to free speech and free association and that those rights are abridged when any student is forced to support, through their student fees, a group they oppose.

"No matter how important you think your group is, no matter how important you think your message is people aren't required to pay for it," Southworth said.

The University of Wisconsin System has countered by arguing that student fees are necessary to create a campus forum for diverse viewpoints to be expressed.

* * *

[On March 22, 2000, the] U.S. Supreme Court unanimously decided . . . to maintain UW-Madison's mandatory student fees system after hearing the [*Southworth*] case. . . .

Southworth, the lead plaintiff, said he was disappointed in the Court's opinion but is not discouraged by this setback.

"This is not a definitive win for the university," he said. "This is a big battle and this is one phase in a long war. If it doesn't happen in my case, it will happen in another case."

Despite the decision, Southworth said he would continue to pursue the rights of students at public universities.

SOURCES: Beth A. Williams, "Southworth in D.C.," *Badger Herald* (University of Wisconsin-Madison), December 15, 1999; Alicia Hammond, "Southworth Decision Overturned," *Badger Herald* (University of Wisconsin-Madison), March 23, 2000.

Putting aside the formal criteria, the Supreme Court is most likely to accept cases that involve conflicting decisions by the federal circuit courts, cases that present important questions of civil rights or civil liberties, and cases in which the federal government is the appellant. Ultimately, however, the question of which cases to accept can come down to the preferences and priorities of the justices. If a group of justices believes that the Court should intervene in a particular area of policy or politics, they are likely to look for a case or cases that will serve as vehicles for judicial intervention. For many years, for example, the Court was not interested in considering challenges to affirmative action or other programs designed to provide particular benefits to minorities. In recent years, however, several of the Court's more conservative justices have been eager to push back the limits of affirmative action and racial preference, and have therefore accepted a number of cases that would allow them to do so. In 1995, the Court's decisions in *Adarand Constructors v. Pena*, *Missouri v. Jenkins*, and *Miller v. Johnson* placed new restrictions on federal affirmative action programs, school desegregation efforts, and attempts to increase minority representation in Congress through the creation of "minority districts" (see Chapter 11).[23]

Writs Decisions handed down by lower courts can reach the Supreme Court in one of two ways: through a *writ of certiorari*, or, in the case of convicted state prisoners, through a writ of *habeas corpus*. A writ is a court document conveying an order of some sort. In recent years, an effort has been made to give the Court more discretion regarding the cases it chooses to hear. Before 1988, the Supreme Court was obligated to review cases on what was called a writ of appeal. This has since been eliminated, and the Court now has virtually complete discretion over what cases it will hear.

Most cases reach the Supreme Court through the **writ of *certiorari***, which is granted whenever four of the nine justices agree to review a case. The Supreme Court was once so inundated with appeals that in 1925 Congress enacted laws giving it some control over its caseload with the power to issue writs of *certiorari*. Rule 10 of the Supreme Court's own rules of procedure defines *certiorari* as "not a matter of right, but of sound judicial discretion . . . granted only where there are special and important reasons therefor." The reasons provided for in Rule 10 are:

1. Where a state has made a decision that conflicts with previous Supreme Court decisions;

HOW CASES REACH THE SUPREME COURT

Figure 16.2

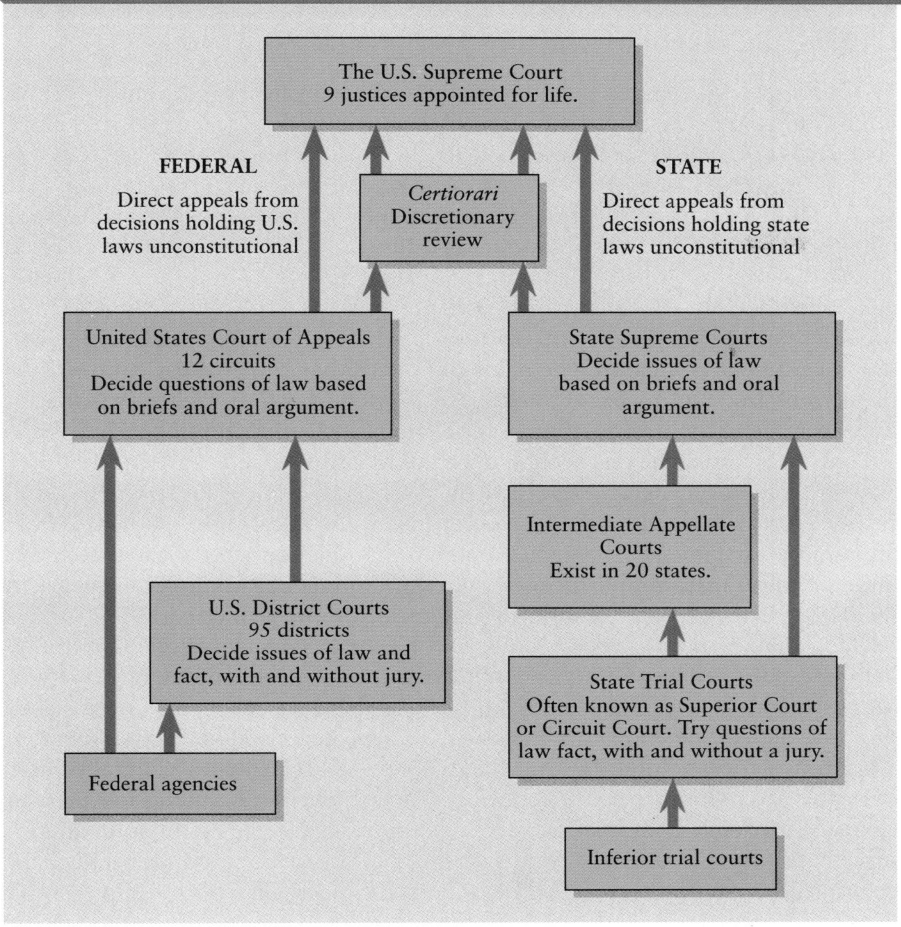
The U.S. Supreme Court
9 justices appointed for life.
FEDERAL
Direct appeals from decisions holding U.S. laws unconstitutional
Certiorari
Discretionary review
STATE
Direct appeals from decisions holding state laws unconstitutional
United States Court of Appeals
12 circuits
Decide questions of law based on briefs and oral argument.
State Supreme Courts
Decide issues of law based on briefs and oral argument.
Intermediate Appellate Courts
Exist in 20 states.
U.S. District Courts
95 districts
Decide issues of law and fact, with and without jury.
State Trial Courts
Often known as Superior Court or Circuit Court. Try questions of law fact, with and without a jury.
Federal agencies
Inferior trial courts

2. Where a state court has come up with an entirely new federal question;
3. Where one court of appeals has rendered a decision in conflict with another;
4. Where there are other inconsistent rulings between two or more courts or states;
5. Where a single court of appeals has sanctioned too great a departure by a lower court from normal judicial proceedings (a reason rarely given).

writ of *certiorari*
a decision of at least four of the nine Supreme Court justices to review a decision of a lower court; from the Latin "to make more certain"

The **writ of *habeas corpus*** is a fundamental safeguard of individual rights. Its historical purpose is to enable an accused person to challenge arbitrary detention and to force an open trial before a judge. But in 1867, Congress's distrust of southern courts led it to confer on federal courts the authority to issue writs of *habeas corpus* to prisoners already tried or being tried in state courts of proper jurisdiction where the constitutional rights of the prisoner were possibly being violated. This writ gives state prisoners a second channel toward Supreme Court review in case their direct appeal from the highest state court fails (see Figure 16.2). The writ of *habeas corpus* is discretionary; that is, the Court can decide which cases to review.

writ of *habeas corpus*
a court order that the individual in custody be brought into court and shown the cause for detention. *Habeas corpus* is guaranteed by the Constitution and can be suspended only in cases of rebellion or invasion

CONTROLLING THE FLOW OF CASES

In addition to the judges themselves, three other agencies or groups play an important role in shaping the flow of cases through the federal courts: the solicitor general, the Federal Bureau of Investigation, and federal law clerks.

solicitor general
the top government lawyer in all cases before the Supreme Court where the government is a party

The Solicitor General If any single person has greater influence than individual judges over the federal courts, it is the **solicitor general** of the United States. The solicitor general is the third-ranking official in the Justice Department (below the attorney general and the deputy attorney general) but is the top government lawyer in virtually all cases before the Supreme Court where the government is a party. The solicitor general has the greatest control over the flow of cases; his or her actions are not reviewed by any higher authority in the executive branch. More than half the Supreme Court's total workload consists of cases under the direct charge of the solicitor general.

The solicitor general exercises especially strong influence by screening cases before any agency of the federal government can appeal them to the Supreme Court; indeed, the justices rely on the solicitor general to "screen out undeserving litigation and furnish them with an agenda to government cases that deserve serious consideration."[24] Typically, more requests for appeals are rejected than are accepted by the solicitor general. Agency heads may lobby the president or otherwise try to circumvent the solicitor general, and a few of the independent agencies have a statutory right to make direct appeals, but these are almost inevitably doomed to ***per curiam*** rejection—rejection through a brief, unsigned opinion by the whole Court—if the solicitor general refuses to participate. Congress has given only a few agencies, including the Federal Communications Commission, the Federal Maritime Commission, and in some cases, the Department of Agriculture (even though it is not an independent agency), the right to appeal directly to the Supreme Court without going through the solicitor general.

per curiam
decision by an appellate court, without a written opinion, that refuses to review the decision of a lower court; amounts to a reaffirmation of the lower court's opinion

The solicitor general can enter a case even when the federal government is not a direct litigant by writing an ***amicus curiae*** ("friend of the court") brief. A "friend of the court" is not a direct party to a case but has a vital interest in its outcome. Thus, when the government has such an interest, the solicitor general can file as *amicus curiae,* or a federal court can invite such a brief because it wants an opinion in writing. The solicitor general also has the power to invite others to enter cases as *amici curiae.*

amicus curiae
literally, "friend of the court"; individuals or groups who are not parties to a lawsuit but who seek to assist the Supreme Court in reaching a decision by presenting additional briefs

In addition to exercising substantial control over the flow of cases, the solicitor general can shape the arguments used before the federal courts. Indeed, the Supreme Court tends to give special attention to the way the solicitor general characterizes the issues. The solicitor general is the person appearing most frequently before the Court and, theoretically at least, is the most disinterested. The credibility of the solicitor general is not hurt when several times each year he or she comes to the Court to withdraw a case with the admission that the government has made an error.

The solicitor general's sway over the flow of cases does not, however, entirely overshadow the influence of the other agencies and divisions in the Department of Justice. The solicitor general is counsel for the major divisions in the department, including the Antitrust, Tax, Civil Rights, and Criminal divisions. Their activities generate a great part of the solicitor general's agenda.

This is particularly true of the Criminal Division, whose cases are appealed every day. These cases are generated by initiatives taken by the United States attorneys and the district judges before whom they practice.

The FBI Another important influence on the flow of cases through the federal appellate judiciary comes from the Federal Bureau of Investigation (FBI), one of the bureaus of the Department of Justice. Its work provides data for numerous government cases against businesses, individual citizens, and state and local government officials. Its data are the most vital source of material for cases in the areas of national security and organized crime.

The FBI also has the important function of linking the Justice Department very closely to cases being brought by state and local government officials. Since the FBI has a long history of cooperation with state and local police forces, the solicitor general often joins (as *amicus curiae*) appeals involving state criminal cases.

Law Clerks Every federal judge employs law clerks to research legal issues and assist with the preparation of opinions. Each Supreme Court justice is assigned four clerks. The clerks are almost always honors graduates of the nation's most prestigious law schools. A clerkship with a Supreme Court justice is a great honor and generally indicates that the fortunate individual is likely to reach the very top of the legal profession. The work of the Supreme Court clerks is a closely guarded secret, but it is likely that some justices rely heavily upon their clerks for advice in writing opinions and in deciding whether an individual case ought to be heard by the Court. In a recent book, a former law clerk to retired justice Harry Blackmun charged that Supreme Court justices yielded "excessive power to immature, ideologically driven clerks, who in turn use that power to manipulate their bosses."[25]

Law clerks play an important role in the Supreme Court justices' decisions to accept cases, in researching the backgrounds of cases that are accepted, and in drafting opinions. Here, Chief Justice Rehnquist meets with his law clerks.

Lobbying for Access: Interests and the Court At the same time that the Court exercises discretion over which cases it will review, groups and forces in society often seek to persuade the justices to listen to their problems. Interest groups use several different strategies to get the Court's attention. Lawyers representing these groups try to choose the proper client and the proper case, so that the issues in question are most dramatically and appropriately portrayed. They also have to pick the right district or jurisdiction in which to bring the case. Sometimes they even have to wait for an appropriate political climate.

Group litigants have to plan carefully when to use and when to avoid publicity. They must also attempt to develop a proper record at the trial court level, one that includes some constitutional arguments and even, when possible, errors on the part of the trial court. One of the most effective litigation strategies used in getting cases accepted for review by the appellate courts is bringing the same type of suit in more than one circuit (i.e., developing a "pattern of cases"), in the hope that inconsistent treatment by two different courts will improve the chance of a Supreme Court review.

Congress will sometimes provide interest groups with legislation designed to facilitate their use of litigation. One important recent example is the 1990 Americans with Disabilities Act (ADA), enacted after intense lobbying by public interest and advocacy groups. The ADA, in conjunction with the 1991 Civil Rights Act, opens the way for disabled individuals to make effective use of the courts to press their interests.

The two most notable users of the pattern of cases strategy in recent years have been the National Association for the Advancement of Colored People (NAACP) and the American Civil Liberties Union (ACLU). For many years, the NAACP (and its Defense Fund—now a separate group) has worked through local chapters and with many individuals to encourage litigation on issues of racial discrimination and segregation. Sometimes it distributes petitions to be signed by parents and filed with local school boards and courts, deliberately sowing the seeds of future litigation. The NAACP and the ACLU often encourage private parties to bring suit and then join the suit as *amici curiae*.

One illustration of an interest group employing a carefully crafted litigation strategy to pursue its goals through the judiciary was the Texas-based effort to establish a right to free public school education for children of illegal aliens. The issue arose in 1977 when the Texas state legislature, responding to a sudden public backlash against illegal immigration from Mexico, enacted a law permitting school districts to charge undocumented children hefty tuition for the privilege of attending public school. A public-interest law organization, the Mexican-American Legal Defense Fund, prepared to challenge the law in court after determining that public opposition precluded any chance of persuading the legislature to change its own law.

Part of the defense fund's litigation strategy was to bring a lawsuit in the northern section of Texas, far from the Mexican border, where illegal immigration would be at a minimum. Thus, in Tyler, Texas, where the complaint was initially filed, the trial court found only sixty undocumented alien students in a school district composed of 16,000. This strategy effectively contradicted the state's argument that the Texas law was necessary to reduce the burdens on educational resources created by masses of incoming aliens. Another useful litigation tactic was to select plaintiffs who, although illegal

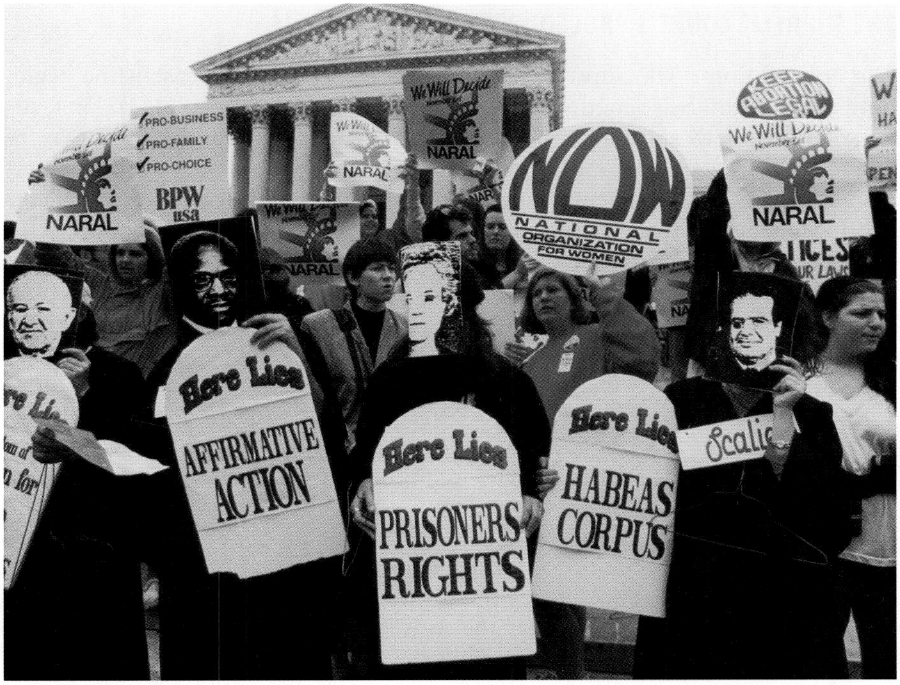

The Supreme Court is open to outside political influence. Interest groups lobby the Court formally by filing *amicus curiae* briefs, and informally through public opinion. In 1989, members of the National Organization for Women and the National Abortion Rights Action League gathered while the Court met to rule on *Webster v. Reproductive Health Services,* an important abortion rights case.

aliens, were nevertheless clearly planning to remain in Texas even without free public education for their children. Thus, all of the plaintiffs came from families that had already lived in Tyler for several years and included at least one child who was an American citizen by virtue of birth in the United States. By emphasizing the stability of such families, the defense fund argued convincingly that the Texas law would not motivate families to return to the poverty in Mexico from which they had fled, but would more likely result in the creation of a subclass of illiterate people who would add to the state's unemployment and crime rates. Five years after the lawsuit on behalf of the Tyler children began, the U.S. Supreme Court in the case of *Plyler v. Doe* held that the Texas law was unconstitutional under the equal protection clause of the Fourteenth Amendment.[26]

In many states, it is considered unethical and illegal for attorneys to engage in "fomenting and soliciting legal business in which they are not parties and have no pecuniary right or liability." The NAACP was sued by the state of Virginia in the late 1950s in an attempt to restrict or eliminate its efforts to influence the pattern of cases. The Supreme Court reviewed the case in 1963, recognized that the strategy was being utilized, and held that it was protected by the First and Fourteenth Amendments, just as other forms of speech and petition are protected.[27]

Thus, many pathbreaking cases are eventually granted *certiorari* because continued refusal to review one or more of them would amount to a rule of law just as much as if the courts had handed down a written opinion. In this sense, the flow of cases, especially the pattern of significant cases, influences the behavior of the appellate judiciary.

THE SUPREME COURT'S PROCEDURES

briefs
written documents in which attorneys explain, using case precedents, why the court should find in favor of their client

oral argument
stage in Supreme Court procedure in which attorneys for both sides appear before the Court to present their positions and answer questions posed by justices

The Preparation The Supreme Court's decision to accept a case is the beginning of what can be a lengthy and complex process (see Figure 16.3). First, the attorneys on both sides must prepare **briefs**—written documents that may be several hundred pages long in which the attorneys explain why the Court should rule in favor of their client. Briefs are filled with referrals to precedents specifically chosen to show that other courts have frequently ruled in the same way that the Supreme Court is being asked to rule. The attorneys for both sides muster the most compelling precedents they can in support of their arguments.

As the attorneys prepare their briefs, they often ask sympathetic interest groups for their help. Groups are asked to file *amicus curiae* briefs that support the claims of one or the other litigant. In a case involving separation of church and state, for example, liberal groups such as the ACLU and Citizens for the American Way are likely to be asked to file *amicus* briefs in support of strict separation, whereas conservative religious groups are likely to file *amicus* briefs advocating increased public support for religious ideas. Often, dozens of briefs will be filed on each side of a major case. *Amicus* filings are one of the primary methods used by interest groups to lobby the Court. By filing these briefs, groups indicate to the Court where their group stands and signal to the justices that they believe the case to be an important one.

Oral Argument The next stage of a case is **oral argument,** in which attorneys for both sides appear before the Court to present their positions and answer

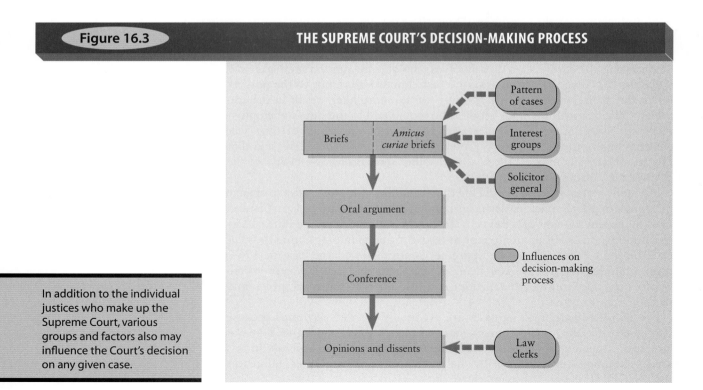

Figure 16.3 THE SUPREME COURT'S DECISION-MAKING PROCESS

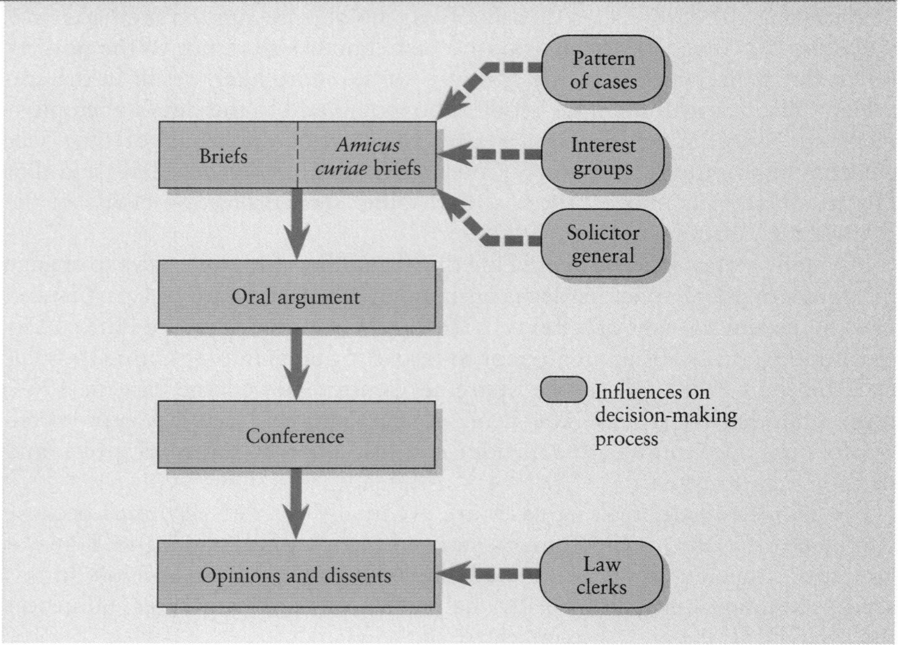

In addition to the individual justices who make up the Supreme Court, various groups and factors also may influence the Court's decision on any given case.

the justices' questions. Each attorney has only a half hour to present his or her case, and this time includes interruptions for questions. Certain members of the Court, such as Justice Antonin Scalia, are known to interrupt attorneys dozens of times. Others, such as Justice Clarence Thomas, seldom ask questions. For an attorney, the opportunity to argue a case before the Supreme Court is a singular honor and a mark of professional distinction. It can also be a harrowing experience, as justices interrupt a carefully prepared presentation. Nevertheless, oral argument can be very important to the outcome of a case. It allows justices to better understand the heart of the case and to raise questions that might not have been addressed in the opposing side's briefs. It is not uncommon for justices to go beyond the strictly legal issues and ask opposing counsel to discuss the implications of the case for the Court and the nation at large.

This 1935 photo is the only known photograph of the Supreme Court hearing oral arguments.

The Conference Following oral argument, the Court discusses the case in its Wednesday or Friday conference. The chief justice presides over the conference and speaks first; the other justices follow in order of seniority. The Court's conference is secret, and no outsiders are permitted to attend. The justices discuss the case and eventually reach a decision on the basis of a majority vote. If the Court is divided, a number of votes may be taken before a final decision is reached. As the case is discussed, justices may try to influence or change one another's opinions. At times, this may result in compromise decisions. On the current Court, for example, several justices, including Rehnquist, Scalia, and Thomas, are known to favor overturning the 1973 *Roe v. Wade* decision that prohibited the states from outlawing abortions. Other justices, including Souter, Breyer, and Ginsburg, are known to oppose such a course of action. This division has resulted in several compromise decisions, in which the Court has allowed some state restriction of abortion but has not permitted states to outlaw abortion altogether.

Opinion Writing After a decision has been reached, one of the members of the majority is assigned to write the **opinion**. This assignment is made by the chief justice, or by the most senior justice in the majority if the chief justice is on the losing side. The assignment of the opinion can make a significant difference to the interpretation of a decision. Every opinion of the Supreme Court sets a major precedent for future cases throughout the judicial system. Lawyers and judges in the lower courts will examine the opinion carefully to ascertain the Supreme Court's meaning. Differences in wording and emphasis can have important implications for future litigation. Once the majority opinion is drafted, it is circulated to the other justices. Some members of the majority may decide that they cannot accept all the language of the opinion and therefore write "concurring" opinions that support the decision but offer a somewhat different rationale or emphasis. In assigning an opinion, serious thought must be given to the impression the case will make on lawyers and on the public, as well as to the probability that one justice's opinion will be more widely accepted than another's.

opinion
the written explanation of the Supreme Court's decision in a particular case

One of the more dramatic instances of this tactical consideration occurred in 1944, when Chief Justice Harlan F. Stone chose Justice Felix Frankfurter to write the opinion in the "white primary" case *Smith v. Allwright*. The chief justice believed that this sensitive case, which overturned the southern practice of prohibiting black participation in nominating primaries, required the efforts of the most brilliant and scholarly jurist on the Court. But the day after Stone made the assignment, Justice Robert H. Jackson wrote a letter to Stone urging a change of assignment. In his letter, Jackson argued that Frankfurter, a foreign-born Jew from New England, would not win the South with his opinion, regardless of its brilliance. Stone accepted the advice and substituted Justice Stanley Reed, an American-born Protestant from Kentucky and a southern Democrat in good standing.[28]

dissenting opinion
a decision written by a justice in the minority in a particular case in which the justice wishes to express his or her reasoning in the case

Dissent Justices who disagree with the majority decision of the Court may choose to publicize the character of their disagreement in the form of a **dissenting opinion.** Dissents can be used to express irritation with an outcome or to signal to defeated political forces in the nation that their position is supported by at least some members of the Court. Ironically, the most dependable way an individual justice can exercise a direct and clear influence on the Court is to write a dissent. Because there is no need to please a majority, dissenting opinions can be more eloquent and less guarded than majority opinions. Some of the greatest writing in the history of the Court is found in the dissents of Oliver Wendell Holmes, Louis D. Brandeis, and William O. Douglas, the last of whom wrote thirty-five dissents in the Court's 1952–53 term alone. Although there is no great dissenter in the current Court, Justice John Paul Stevens stands out with sixteen dissents in the 1996–97 term and thirteen in the 1998–99 term; the next highest numbers of dissents written during those terms were nine and eight, respectively.

Dissent plays a special role in the work and impact of the Court because it amounts to an appeal to lawyers all over the country to keep bringing cases of the sort at issue. Therefore, an effective dissent influences the flow of cases through the Court as well as the arguments that will be used by lawyers in later cases. Even more important, dissent emphasizes the fact that, although the Court speaks with a single opinion, it is the opinion only of the majority—and one day the majority might go the other way.

Oliver Wendell Holmes, Jr., the "great dissenter."

EXPLAINING SUPREME COURT DECISIONS

The Supreme Court explains its decisions in terms of law and precedent. But although law and precedent do have an effect on the Court's deliberations and eventual decisions, it is the Supreme Court that decides what laws actually mean and what importance precedent will actually have. Throughout its history, the Court has shaped and reshaped the law. In the late nineteenth and early twentieth centuries, for example, the Supreme Court held that the Constitution, law, and precedent permitted racial segregation in the United States. Beginning in the late 1950s, however, the Court found that the Constitution prohibited segregation on the basis of race and indicated that the use of racial categories in legislation was always suspect. By the 1970s and 1980s, the Court once again held that the Constitution permitted the use of racial categories—when such categories were needed to help members of minority groups achieve full participation in American society. In the 1990s, the Court began to retreat from this position, too, indicating that governmental efforts to provide extra help to racial minorities could represent an unconstitutional infringement on the rights of the majority.

POLICY DEBATE

Abortion and the Right to Privacy

Although the word "privacy" does not appear in the Bill of Rights, the courts have agreed that such a fundamental right exists. They disagree, however, about exactly from where the protection arises and about how far it should be applied. Nowhere is this disagreement more protracted than for the issue of abortion.

Since its 1973 landmark ruling in *Roe v. Wade,* the Supreme Court has repeatedly found that the right to privacy protects the right of a woman to end a pregnancy via abortion, subject to some court-approved restrictions. Abortion opponents, of course, have rejected the premise of *Roe* that privacy protects an act they consider murder. For example, members of Congress who oppose abortion have succeeded in restricting federal Medicaid funding for abortions. Today's more conservative Supreme Court has allowed states to impose restrictions such as parental notification for minors and twenty-four-hour waiting periods for those seeking abortions.

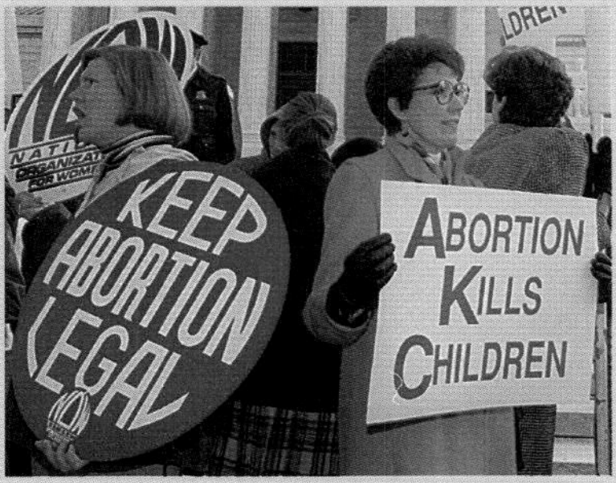

Supporters of privacy-based protection for abortion argue that, as a matter of law and tradition, a developing fetus cannot be accorded the same legal status as the woman carrying a fetus. If privacy means anything, it must extend to the right of a woman to decide, at least during the early months of pregnancy (when the vast majority of abortions are performed, and before the point of viability, when the fetus can live outside of the woman), whether or not to have an abortion. For the government to require women to carry most or all pregnancies to term represents extreme government intrusion into the innately personal decision over procreation. The principle of individual liberty must allow women to make such fundamental decisions themselves.

Further, the idea that all abortions are murder means that a fertilized egg does and should possess the same traits as a full-term baby, an idea that is rejected by medical science, most Americans, and many religions. For example, when a spontaneous abortion occurs early in a pregnancy, it is called a "miscarriage," for which funeral services are not held. A late-term spontaneous abortion, called a "stillbirth," evokes a different and more complex response, reflecting the evident difference in development. Abortion laws properly reflect these differences. Finally, the Constitution speaks to the issue by noting that citizenship, and therefore the rights stemming from it, begins at birth.

Opponents of abortion argue that the relative differences observed in fetal development do not obviate the fact that, by genetic makeup, even a fertilized egg is a person. The right to privacy does not and cannot provide an excuse for murder. The absence of birth does not, in and of itself, mean that a fetus is without rights. Even if the Constitution's framers had all agreed that the Bill of Rights protected the liberty associated with privacy, there is no reason to believe that they would have countenanced its extension to abortion. Furthermore, to say that such matters are purely a matter of personal choice is to turn a blind eye to the sort of evil that government has every right to regulate or prohibit. And while pregnancy is a developmental process for the fetus, it is precisely because there is no magic, agreed-upon point at which a fetus becomes a person that the fetus must be protected as a person at all stages.

Women who become pregnant, whether by accident or intent, assume a special obligation to the innocent life they carry. Although some who oppose abortions are willing to allow exceptions for cases of rape or incest, such cases account for only a tiny percentage of all abortions. Legal abortion is harmful in other respects. It demeans respect for life by allowing, even encouraging, abortion as a means of birth control. If later-term abortions are allowed because of, say, fetal defect, it is a short step to euthanasia (so-called mercy killing) of living persons. Above all, the right of a fetus to live must supersede the privacy rights, however defined, of pregnant women.

STUDENT DEBATE

Should Abortion Remain Legal?

Yes

The powers that be in Washington have once again made a very big decision regarding the freedom a woman has to make choices about her own reproductive system. But somehow, I don't think too many people will have noticed it by today.

For the second consecutive year, the U.S. House of Representatives has voted to ban the testing, development, and approval of abortion-inducing drugs such as RU-486, the controversial pill popular in Europe. The decision was won by a mere three votes—a victory, albeit a shaky one, for abortion foes.

Yet it appeared as a small blip on the radar screens of America, yielding only a sound bite on CNN.

The legislation was buried in an agricultural bill—most people didn't see the vote coming.

It isn't right for the U.S. government to try to hide such a monumental decision without making it more known to the public. What does agriculture have to do with a woman's body?

By quietly banning even further research into the possibilities abortion-inducing drugs may yield, the House has overstepped its boundaries. The U.S. Food and Drug Administration concluded in 1996 that RU-486 was safe and effective, but the House has obviously ignored such findings.

Abortion is a medical and scientific procedure and should be left to the experts to research and perform on the women who want safe, effective, and noninvasive abortions—what abortion-inducing drugs such as RU-486 seek to provide.

It is on that point the issue becomes a logical and scientific one. By voting down the proposal that would allow for more research into the possibilities for abortion pills, politicians are blurring the line between science and ethics, logic and their emotions, and the issue is too important to be tacked on to a bill many Americans didn't even know existed.

These representatives aren't doctors, let alone obstetricians or gynecologists. Most of them aren't even women. Yet it is the establishment, made up of wealthy, older, white men, who are so adamantly against a medical procedure that they themselves need never experience. For some reason, it threatens their comfort zone.

But they never have to face that kind of decision. They won't have to decide whether or not to have a child conceived in rape or a child who will be born only to grow up with severe physical problems.

While there are countless emotional questions a woman must face when she considers abortion, the vote of a government representative should reflect logical thinking, not personal morals.

For example, consider this: The overwhelming majority of public officeholders are men. Therefore, humans who aren't even capable of getting pregnant should not be dictating the physiological rights of those who can.

***

As long as the U.S. government tries to govern the female body while pretending to uphold democracy, it is important for Americans to continue the discussion of such important issues and to fight for what they believe, be they pro-choice or pro-life.

That's where the *Collegian*'s opinions page comes in. It's a forum for the Penn State and surrounding communities to keep talking about such issues as abortion, politics, university controversy, whatever is on their minds.

And I, for one, plan on making as much noise as I can. Isn't it your turn to take a stand?

SOURCE: Brooke Sample, "Government Needs to Consider Logic in Abortion," *Daily Collegian* (Pennsylvania State University), June 11, 1999.

No

A young baby girl rests peacefully in her mother's womb. Suddenly, sharp metal forceps enter and grab each of her limbs, twisting them and tearing them away from the rest of her body. Because the baby's skull has hardened to bone by this time, it must be crushed or compressed to facilitate removal.

An innocent baby boy is sleeping to the sound of his mother's heart when the amniotic fluid is removed and replaced with concentrated salt. The little boy breathes in, swallows the salt and is poisoned. The chemical also causes painful burning and deterioration of his skin. Within seventy-two hours he is dead, shriveled and burnt.

Although horrifying and graphic, these details are facts and soon College Station-Bryan will have an abortion clinic that performs them. Many pro-life activists have fought to prevent this addition to Planned Parenthood, but the fact remains that abortion is legal. Fighting the clinics might keep abortion out of the city, but it will not keep the woman from getting an abortion. It is time for those who believe in life to step forward and fight the law.

In a recent interview, a health representative at Planned Parenthood in Bryan said that a woman outside of a large city will simply drive to another in order to receive an abortion. As long as the law stands, the number of abortion providers will continue to grow in an effort to provide this service conveniently.

***

Out of the ten Planned Parenthood clinics in southeast Texas, only one performs abortions. Planned Parenthood primarily provides excellent women's healthcare at more affordable prices. This is a necessary service for many women who are unable to afford a private doctor. Some locations provide mammograms to help detect breast cancer early.

All locations provide counseling in sexual health education. Teenagers who find it difficult to talk to their parents about intimacy issues can find guidance and confidentiality here.

Unfortunately, Planned Parenthood also fights to keep abortion legal. According to their Web site, it advocates public policies that guarantee these rights and ensure access to such services. It is fighting to keep abortion legal and is clearly winning.

A lawyer does not appeal to the executioner to free his death-row client, but instead he appeals to the governor. In the same sense, pro-life activists should not fight the clinics and doctors that perform abortions, but should concentrate on the laws that enable them to carry out these services. Planned Parenthood abortion clinics would not exist without the legalization of abortion, so why not fight the law and kill the real problem.

Those fighting the law have evidence it is working. The Centers for Disease Control reported in 1997 that abortion rates have decreased every year since 1992. In the last twenty-five years, pro-life literature has been circulating. "Right to Know" legislation exists in many states to inform women of abortion risks, its realities, and the alternatives.

The uneducated are constantly claiming that abortion is only the removal of cells that may or may not form a child. The majority of abortions occur in the first seven to ten weeks when the child's face is recognizably human. It is sucked or torn from the womb and the baby's small heartbeat and already measurable brain waves cease to exist. No funeral is held for the child that no one wanted.

"Before I formed you in the womb I knew you, before you were born I set you apart." (Jeremiah 1:5) Life is sacred. Stop the clinics by changing the law.

SOURCE: Christina Barrows, "Pro-Life Should Work to Fight Abortion," *The Battalion* (Texas A&M University), February 2, 1999.

Although it is not the only relevant factor, the prime explanation for these movements is shifts in judicial philosophy. These shifts, in turn, result from changes in the Court's composition as justices retire and are replaced by new justices who, as we saw earlier, tend to share the philosophical outlook of the president who appointed them.

Activism and Restraint One element of judicial philosophy is the issue of activism versus restraint. Over the years, some justices have believed that courts should interpret the Constitution according to the stated intentions of its framers and defer to the views of Congress when interpreting federal statutes. The late justice Felix Frankfurter, for example, advocated judicial deference to legislative bodies and avoidance of the "political thicket," in which the Court would entangle itself by deciding questions that were essentially political rather than legal in character. Advocates of **judicial restraint** are sometimes called "strict constructionists," because they look strictly to the words of the Constitution in interpreting its meaning.

judicial restraint
judicial philosophy whose adherents refuse to go beyond the clear words of the Constitution in interpreting its meaning

The alternative to restraint is **judicial activism.** Activist judges such as the former chief justice Earl Warren and two of the leading members of his Court, Justices Hugo Black and William O. Douglas, believed that the Court should go beyond the words of the Constitution or a statute to consider the broader societal implications of its decisions. Activist judges sometimes strike out in new directions, promulgating new interpretations or inventing new legal and constitutional concepts when they believe these to be socially desirable. For example, Justice Harry Blackmun's decision in *Roe v. Wade* was based on a constitutional right to privacy that is not found in the words of the Constitution. Blackmun and the other members of the majority in the *Roe* case argued that the right to privacy was implied by other constitutional provisions. In this instance of judicial activism, the Court knew the result it wanted to achieve and was not afraid to make the law conform to the desired outcome.

judicial activism
judicial philosophy that posits that the Court should go beyond the words of the Constitution or a statute to consider the broader societal implications of its decisions

Harry Blackmun, author of the Supreme Court's decision in *Roe v. Wade.*

Political Ideology The second component of judicial philosophy is political ideology. The liberal or conservative attitudes of justices play an important role in their decisions.[31] Indeed, the philosophy of activism versus restraint is, to a large extent, a smokescreen for political ideology. For the most part, liberal judges have been activists, willing to use the law to achieve social and political change, whereas conservatives have been associated with judicial restraint. Interestingly, however, in recent years some conservative justices who have long called for restraint have actually become activists in seeking to undo some of the work of liberal jurists over the past three decades.

From the 1950s to the 1980s, the Supreme Court took an activist role in such areas as civil rights, civil liberties, abortion, voting rights, and police procedures. For example, the Supreme Court was more responsible than any other governmental institution for breaking down America's system of racial segregation. The Supreme Court virtually prohibited states from interfering with the right of a woman to seek an abortion and sharply curtailed state restrictions on voting rights. And it was the Supreme Court that placed restrictions on the behavior of local police and prosecutors in criminal cases. In a series of decisions between 1989 and 2000, however, the conservative justices appointed by Reagan and Bush were able to swing the Court to a more conservative position on civil rights, affirmative action, abortion rights, property rights, criminal procedure, voting rights, desegregation, and the power of the national government.

Yet the efforts by Reagan and Bush to reshape the federal judiciary were not fully successful. Often in American history, judges have surprised and disappointed the presidents who named them to the bench. Justice Souter, for example, has been far less conservative than President Bush and the Republicans who supported Souter's appointment thought he would be. Likewise, Justices O'Connor and Kennedy have disappointed conservatives by opposing limitations on abortion.

Nevertheless, with a combined total of twelve years in office, Reagan and Bush were also able to exercise a good deal of influence on the composition of the federal district and appellate courts. By the end of Bush's term, he and Reagan together had appointed nearly half of all federal judges. Thus, whatever impact Reagan and Bush ultimately have on the Supreme Court, their appointments will certainly influence the temperament and behavior of the district and circuit courts for years to come. One important example of the continuing legacy of Reagan and Bush came in November 1997, when the Court refused to hear a challenge to the constitutionality of California's Proposition 209 (see Chapter 6). This ballot measure, adopted by California's voters in 1996, abolished state programs of affirmative action in such realms as higher education and government hiring. By refusing to hear a challenge to the proposition, the Supreme Court, in effect, struck a blow at part of the civil rights legacy of the 1960s and 1970s. Critics charged that, coming on the heels of an earlier decision by the California Board of Regents to ban the use of race as a criterion for university admissions in California, the Court's refusal to listen to objections to Proposition 209 would inflame the state's already volatile racial climate.[29]

President Clinton promised to appoint more liberal jurists to the district and appellate courts, as well as to increase the number of women and minorities serving on the federal bench. During his first two years in office, Clinton held to this promise; more than 60 percent of his 128 judicial nominees were women or members of minority groups (see Figure 16.4 on the next page).[30] A large number of judicial vacancies remained unfilled, however, when the Republicans took control of Congress at the end of 1994. Soon after the election, Senator Orrin Hatch of Utah, the new chair of the Senate Judiciary Committee, which confirms judicial nominations, indicated his intention to oppose any nominee whom he deemed to be too liberal. This prompted the Clinton White House to withdraw some nominations and to search for district and appellate nominees who would be more acceptable to the Republicans.[31]

The political struggles of the 1980s and 1990s amply illustrate the importance of judicial ideology. Is abortion a fundamental right or a criminal activity? How much separation must there be between church and state? Does the use of the Voting Rights Act to increase minority representation constitute a violation of the rights of whites? The answers to these and many other questions cannot be found in the words of the Constitution. They must be located, instead, in the hearts of the judges who interpret that text.

Figure 16.4

THE DIVERSITY OF FEDERAL COURT APPOINTEES FROM REAGAN TO CLINTON

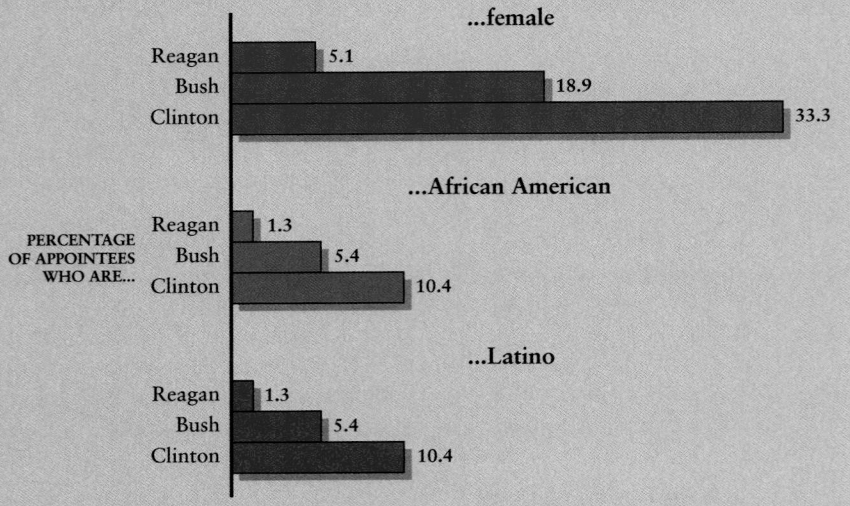

SOURCE: Harold W. Stanley and Richard G. Niemi, *Vital Statistics on American Politics, 1999–2000* (Washington, DC: Congressional Quarterly Press, 2000), pp. 276–277.

Judicial Power and Politics

- How has the power of the federal courts been limited throughout much of American history?
- How have the role and power of the federal courts been transformed over the last fifty years?
- How has the increase in the Supreme Court's power changed its role in the political process?

One of the most important institutional changes to occur in the United States during the past half-century has been the striking transformation of the role and power of the federal courts, and of the Supreme Court in particular. Understanding how this transformation came about is the key to understanding the contemporary role of the courts in America.

TRADITIONAL LIMITATIONS ON THE FEDERAL COURTS

For much of American history, the power of the federal courts was subject to five limitations.[32] First, courts were constrained by judicial rules of standing that limited access to the bench. Claimants who simply disagreed with governmental action or inaction could not obtain access. Access to the courts was limited to individuals who could show that they were particularly affected by the government's behavior in some area. This limitation on access to the courts diminished the judiciary's capacity to forge links with important political and social forces.

Second, courts were traditionally limited in the character of the relief they could provide. In general, courts acted only to offer relief or assistance to individuals and not to broad social classes, again inhibiting the formation of alliances between the courts and important social forces. Third, courts lacked enforcement powers of their own and were compelled to rely on executive or state agencies to ensure compliance with their edicts. If the executive or state agencies were unwilling to assist the courts, judicial enactments could go unheeded, as when President Andrew Jackson declined to enforce Chief Justice John Marshall's 1832 order to the state of Georgia to release two missionaries it had arrested on Cherokee lands. Marshall asserted that the state had no right to enter the Cherokee lands without their assent.[33] Jackson is reputed to have said, "John Marshall has made his decision, now let him enforce it."

Fourth, federal judges are, of course, appointed by the president (with the consent of the Senate). As a result, the president and Congress can shape the composition of the federal courts and ultimately, perhaps, the character of judicial decisions. Finally, Congress has the power to change both the size and jurisdiction of the Supreme Court and other federal courts. In many areas, federal courts obtain their jurisdiction not from the Constitution but from congressional statutes. On a number of occasions, Congress has threatened to take matters out of the Court's hands when it was unhappy with the Court's policies.[34] For example, in 1996 Congress enacted several pieces of legislation designed to curb the jurisdiction of the federal courts. One of these laws was the Prison Litigation Reform Act, which limits the ability of federal judges to issue "consent decrees" under which the judges could take control of state prison systems. Another jurisdictional curb was included in the Immigration Reform Act, which prohibited the federal courts from hearing class action suits against Immigration and Naturalization Service deportation orders. As to the size of the Court, on one memorable occasion, presidential and congressional threats to expand the size of the Supreme Court—Franklin Roosevelt's "court packing" plan—encouraged the justices to drop their opposition to New Deal programs.

As a result of these five limitations on judicial power, through much of their history the chief function of the federal courts was to provide judicial support for executive agencies and to legitimate acts of Congress by declaring them to be consistent with constitutional principles. Only on rare occasions have the federal courts actually dared to challenge Congress or the executive branch.[35]

TWO JUDICIAL REVOLUTIONS

Since the Second World War, however, the role of the federal judiciary has been strengthened and expanded. There have actually been two judicial revolutions in the United States since World War II. The first and most visible of these was the substantive revolution in judicial policy. As we saw earlier in this chapter and in Chapters 5 and 6, in policy areas, including school desegregation, legislative apportionment, and criminal procedure, as well as obscenity, abortion, and voting rights, the Supreme Court was at the forefront of a series of sweeping changes in the role of the U.S. government, and ultimately, in the character of American society.[36]

But at the same time that the courts were introducing important policy innovations, they were also bringing about a second, less visible revolution. During the 1960s and 1970s, the Supreme Court and other federal courts instituted a series of changes in judicial procedures that fundamentally expanded the power of the courts in the United States. First, the federal courts liberalized the concept of standing to permit almost any group that seeks to challenge the actions of an administrative agency to bring its case before the federal bench. In 1971, for example, the Supreme Court ruled that public interest groups could use the National Environmental Policy Act to challenge the actions of federal agencies by claiming that the agencies' activities might have adverse environmental consequences.[37]

Congress helped to make it even easier for groups dissatisfied with government policies to bring their cases to the courts by adopting Section 1,983 of the U.S. Code, which permits the practice of "fee shifting"—that is, allowing citizens who successfully bring a suit against a public official for violating their constitutional rights to collect their attorneys' fees and costs from the government. Thus, Section 1983 encourages individuals and groups to bring their problems to the courts rather than to Congress or the executive branch. These changes have given the courts a far greater role in the administrative process than ever before. Many federal judges are concerned that federal legislation in areas such as health care reform would create new rights and entitlements that would give rise to a deluge of court cases. "Any time you create a new right, you create a host of disputes and claims," warned Barbara Rothstein, chief judge of the federal district court in Seattle, Washington.[38]

class action suit

a legal action by which a group or class of individuals with common interests can file a suit on behalf of everyone who shares that interest

Second, the federal courts broadened the scope of relief to permit themselves to act on behalf of broad categories or classes of persons in "class action" cases, rather than just on behalf of individuals.[39] A **class action suit** is a procedural device that permits large numbers of persons with common interests to join together under a representative party to bring or defend a lawsuit. One example of a class action suit is the case of *In re Agent Orange Product Liability Litigation,* in which a federal judge in New York certified Vietnam War veterans as a class with standing to sue a manufacturer of herbicides for damages allegedly incurred from exposure to the defendant's product while in Vietnam.[40] The class potentially numbered in the tens of thousands.

Federal judge W. Arthur Garrity implemented the desegregation of the Boston public school system through a series of controversial court decisions.

Third, the federal courts began to employ so-called structural remedies, in effect retaining jurisdiction of cases until the court's mandate had actually been implemented to its satisfaction.[41] The best known of these instances was Federal judge W. Arthur Garrity's effort to operate the Boston school system from his bench in order to ensure its desegregation. Between 1974 and 1985, Judge Garrity issued fourteen decisions relating to different aspects of the Boston school desegregation plan that had been developed under his authority and put into effect under his supervision.[42] In another recent case, Federal judge Leonard B. Sand imposed fines that would have forced the city of Yonkers, New York, into bankruptcy if it had refused to accept his plan to build public housing in white neighborhoods. After several days of fines, the city gave in to the judge's ruling.

Through these three judicial mechanisms, the federal courts paved the way for an unprecedented expansion of national judicial power. In essence, liberalization of the rules of standing and expansion of the scope of judicial relief drew the federal courts into linkages with important social interests and classes, while the introduction of structural remedies enhanced the courts' ability to serve these constituencies. Thus, during the 1960s and 1970s, the power of the federal courts expanded in the same way the power of the executive expanded during the 1930s—through links with constituencies, such as civil rights, consumer, environmental, and feminist groups, that staunchly defended the Supreme Court in its battles with Congress, the executive, or other interest groups.

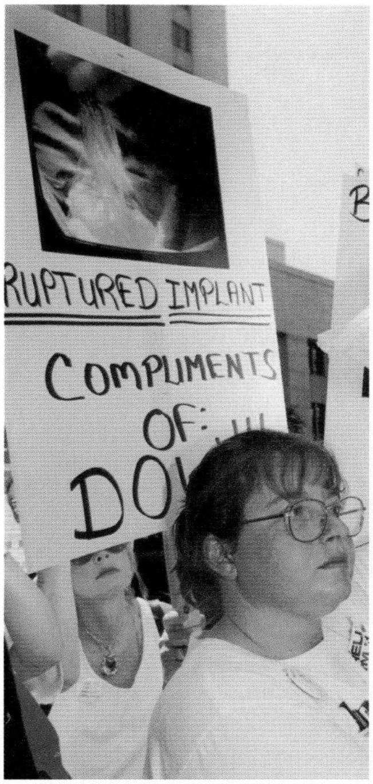

Outside the Los Angeles federal courthouse, women suffering the effects of defective silicone breast implants protested Dow Chemical's failure to pay the settlement of a class action suit. Federal courts have been the site of numerous class action suits in recent decades.

THE JUDICIARY: LIBERTY AND DEMOCRACY

In the original conception of the framers, the judiciary was to be the institution that would protect individual liberty from the government. As we saw in Chapter 3, the framers believed that in a democracy the great danger was what they termed "tyranny of the majority"—the possibility that a popular majority, "united or actuated by some common impulse or passion," would "trample on the rules of justice."[43] The framers hoped that the courts would protect liberty from the potential excesses of democracy. And for most of American history, this was precisely the role played by the federal courts. The courts' most important decisions were those that protected the freedoms—to speak, worship, publish, vote, and attend school—of groups and individuals whose political views, religious beliefs, or racial or ethnic backgrounds made them unpopular.

In recent years, however, the courts have been changing their role in the political process. Rather than serve simply as a bastion of individual liberty against the excessive power of the majority, the judiciary has tried to play an active role in helping groups and forces in American society bring about social and political change in the fight for equality. In a sense, the judiciary has entered the political process and has begun to behave more like the democratic institutions whose sometimes misdirected impulses toward tyranny the courts were supposed to keep in check. This change poses a basic dilemma for students of American government. If the courts have become simply one more part of the democratic political process, then who is left to protect the liberty of individuals?

The Citizen's Role

The framers of the Constitution deliberately designed the judiciary to be independent of the ebb and flow of public sentiment. For this reason, federal judges are appointed for life. In many states, judges are appointed or elected for long terms. Citizen participation in the judicial process is, by design, limited.

One area, however, in which tens of thousands of citizens participate in the judicial process every year is through jury service. Citizens serve on grand juries, which are the bodies that conduct inquiries and hand down indictments, and trial juries. Trial juries decide the guilt or innocence of defendants in criminal cases and determine which side will prevail in civil cases. Juries have enormous power. In most instances, their findings of facts are final, and in most instances a jury verdict of "innocent" in a criminal case is conclusive. Although juries are formally bound to administer the law as presented to them by the judge, juries often stray from the letter of the law, and there is little that can be done to stop them. Some "antigovernment" groups are fond of arguing that juries should determine what the law is regardless of the judge's instructions.

Another important source of citizen activity and potential influence on the judiciary is the opportunity to file *amicus curiae* briefs. Although *amicus curiae* is translated as "friend of the court," it is better understood to mean an "adjunct adversary" permitted to intervene on behalf of one side or the other in which an important issue, usually constitutional in nature, is involved.

The *amicus curiae* brief has been quite effectively employed by African Americans pursuing civil rights cases. This was of particular importance in the earliest cases, beginning with *Shelly v. Kraemer* in 1948 and culminating with *Brown v. Board of Education* in 1954.[44] The NAACP and related organizations continue to maintain an interest in this method of interest group activity along with their continued efforts to influence Congress. In the past two decades, these "outside" interest groups have been joined by a very important "inside" interest group as an *amicus curiae,* the Congressional Black Caucus (CBC). This is an important caucus in the U.S. Congress, made up of the African American members of Congress (mostly from the Democratic Party). Their primary mission, of course, is to advance the interests of African Americans and other minorities in civil rights legislation. But since there has been little new legislative activity, the CBC has found itself concentrating more on the courts in order to advance its agenda of implementing existing civil rights legislation. Since the passage of the 1982 amendments to the 1964 Civil Rights Act (see Chapter 11), race has become the most important consideration in drawing voting districts following each decennial census. Drawing the district so as to guarantee that some will elect blacks to send to Congress—a form of "benign gerrymandering" (see Chapter 11)—was at first approved but then came under considerable scrutiny in the federal court system. The Justice Department under presidents Reagan and Bush opposed such districts and took their opposition to the judiciary. Attorney General Reno defended the so-called majority-minority districts. Both sides went before the Supreme Court accompanied by *amicus curaie* briefs written and promoted by the CBC. Thus, what had been a purely congressional organization became an important interest group directly representing the African American community and other minorities in court.[45]

The *amicus curaie* device is used by groups other than civil rights interests. In fact, a large number of such efforts were made in abortion litigation. Demands for the reversal of *Roe v. Wade* and *Webster v. Reproductive Health Services* included a cast of thousands. Although the Supreme Court receives thousands of letters a day from citizens, the volume increased dramatically during the litigation over *Webster;* on one day in April, the Court's mailroom received 46,000 letters on both sides of the abortion issue. Groups on both sides came forward in greater numbers than ever, and seventy-eight *amicus* briefs were filed, representing the interests of thousands of individuals and

Politics on the Web

In the future, the Internet will greatly improve communications between the judiciary and the general public by dramatically increasing the speed and ease with which information is available. Already, the LEXIS on-line service has revolutionized legal research in this country, making statutes and opinions from hundreds of state and federal court cases available to subscribers in their homes or offices, as well as in law school and university libraries. Supreme Court decisions on important issues from abortion to civil rights to criminal justice will be available almost instantly to interested citizens. The courts have even begun posting audio content, such as oral arguments from the Supreme Court case *Clinton v. Jones.* In addition, the filing of court documents and *amicus curiae* briefs could become dramatically easier, as electronic submission makes the cumbersome rules of paper filing obsolete. The Internet shifts tremendous power—the power of information—to the legal consumer. Thus, the Internet has the potential to significantly streamline the conduct of judicial business in the United States.

www.wwnorton.com/wtp3e

over 400 organizations. This was the largest number of *amicus* briefs ever filed on a single case.[46]

Democracy is where you find it, not where it is officially provided by paternalistic rulers. That is the only way to understand and appreciate the potential role of citizens in the judicial process. As one Kansas State University philosophy major put it, after serving on a trial jury, "There are real people on juries, and, in the end, I feel juries do reach the correct verdicts, and justice does prevail."[47] No one can say precisely when justice has been done. But we can say that when the voice of the ordinary citizen is heard—and heeded—then we have moved much closer to the ideal of justice.

GET INVOLVED Serving Jury Duty

Many Americans shudder when they hear the words, "jury duty." They do not want to interrupt their family lives, schooling, or jobs with one or two weeks of jury service. They detest the prospect of waiting around for hours, if not days, to see if they will be impaneled on a jury. They may not want the responsibility of having to decide if someone should go to jail or pay out large sums of money. Accordingly, people are quite inventive in thinking up ways to get excused from serving on juries.

Nevertheless, millions of Americans do report for jury duty. Along with voting and military service, jury duty is one of the most direct and popular means for people to get involved in public life. It is also a crucial form of participation. The American Revolution contested British efforts to shut down American juries and the U.S. Constitution protected citizens' rights by having juries resolve serious conflicts. Jury service is a major pillar of liberty and democracy.

The two major court systems operating in the United States today rely on juries to render decision. The state court systm is the one most likely to tap you for jury service. The federal court system has similarities to the state system but it also has its own distinctive characteristics regarding jury duty.

Federal jurors are chosen at random. Generally, the federal courts use voter registration lists and driver's license lists as the pools from which they draw prospective jurors' names. If your name is drawn, you are sent a brief application to determine if you meet the legal qualifications to sit on a federal jury. You are required by law to fill out the application and return it by a specific date. You will be *disqualified* from federal jury service if your application reveals one of the following:

- You are not a citizen of the United States, eighteen years or older, who has resided for a period of one year within the judicial district;
- You are unable to read, write, and understand the English language with the degree of proficiency necessary to fill out the application form;
- You are unable to speak the English language;
- You are incapable by reason of mental or physical infirmity to render jury service; or

- You have felony charges pending against you or have been convicted of a felony and your civil rights have not been restored.

Furthermore, the following people are automatically exempted from federal jury service and cannot serve, even if they wish to do so:

- Members of the armed forces on active duty;
- Members of professional fire and police departments; and
- Public officers of federal, state, and local governments who are actively engaged in the performance of public duties.

Currently, if you are summoned for federal jury duty, you will be paid $40 per day for your jury service. If the dates that you are summoned conflict with your school schedule, you may request a temporary deferment—which the court has the discretion to grant or refuse.

You may be eligible to serve on two kinds of juries. One is a trial jury, which typically is comprised of six to twelve members (criminal juries usually have twelve members) plus alternates. Potential jurors may be questioned by attorneys for both sides as well as by the judge in a process called "voir dire." Some individuals may be excused from the jury because the attorneys and/or the judge think that they may have some sort of bias that could prejudice their evaluation of the evidence. Other jurors will be impaneled to hear the evidence and render a decision.

Impaneled jurors spend most of their time listening to evidence during the trial. When the presentation of evidence is completed, the judge instructs jurors on the law and then sends them to deliberate in private in order to reach a verdict, which, generally, must be unanimous. Trial jurors usually serve just a day or two; however, some jurors end up sitting for weeks and even months during long, drawn-out trials.

The other type of jury is a grand jury. A grand jury is a specialized institution with sixteen to twenty-three members. Grand jurors hear evidence from the U.S. Attorney (as well as Assistant U.S. Attorneys) who tries to show that there is a good reason to believe that a given suspect has committed a particular crime. If grand jurors are presuaded, an indictment is issued and the suspect is tried in front of a trial jury. Grand jurors may serve for up to eighteen months.

Serving jury duty usually entails some personal sacrifice; sometimes, it requires considerable sacrifice. Nonetheless, this is necessary if Americans are to preserve and protect liberty and democracy rather than entrust crucial public decisions to a few powerful individuals. Recognizing this, many Americans make the sacrifice without complaint while creative court administrators experiment with ways to make jury service less burdensome and more rewarding for citizens.

Summary

Millions of cases come to trial every year in the United States. The great majority—nearly 99 percent—are tried in state and local courts. The types of law are common law, civil law, criminal law, and public law.

Three kinds of cases fall under federal jurisdiction: (1) civil cases involving citizens from different states, (2) civil cases where a federal agency is seeking to enforce federal laws that provide for civil penalties, and (3) cases involving federal criminal statutes or where state criminal cases have been made issues of public law. Judicial power extends only to cases and controversies. Litigants must have standing to sue, and courts neither hand down opinions on hypothetical issues nor take the initiative.

The organization of the federal judiciary provides for original jurisdiction in the federal district courts, the U.S. Court of Claims, the U.S. Tax Court, the Customs Court, and some federal agencies.

Each district court is in one of the twelve appellate districts, called circuits, presided over by a court of appeals. Appellate courts admit no new evidence; their rulings are based solely on the records of the court proceedings or agency hearings that led to the original decision. Appeals court rulings are final unless the Supreme Court chooses to review them. The Supreme Court has some original jurisdiction, but its major job is to review lower court decisions involving substantial issues of public law.

Federal judges are appointed by the president, subject to confirmation by the Senate. Presidents generally attempt to select judges whose political philosophy is similar to their own. Over time, presidents have been able to exert a great deal of influence over the federal courts through their appointments.

There is no explicit constitutional authority for the Supreme Court to review acts of Congress. Nonetheless, the 1803 case of *Marbury v. Madison* established the Court's right to review congressional acts. The supremacy clause of Article VI and the Judiciary Act of 1789 give the Court the power to review state constitutions and laws.

Both appellate and Supreme Court decisions, including the decision not to review a case, make law. The impact of such law usually favors the status quo. Yet, many revolutionary changes in the law have come about through appellate court and Supreme Court rulings—in the criminal process, in apportionment, and in civil rights. Judge-made law is like a statute in that it articulates the law as it relates to future controversies. It differs from a statute in that it is intended to guide judges rather than the citizenry in general.

Most cases reach the Supreme Court through a writ of *certiorari* or a writ of *habeas corpus*. Once the Court has accepted a case, attorneys for both sides prepare briefs and seek *amicus curiae* briefs from sympathetic groups. Cases are presented to the Court in oral argument, are discussed by the justices during the Court's conference, and are decided by a majority vote of the justices. The Court's opinion is written by a member of the majority. Members of the minority may write dissenting opinions, while other members of the majority may write concurring opinions.

The influence of any individual member of the Supreme Court is limited. Writing the majority opinion for a case is an opportunity for a justice to influence the judiciary. But the need to frame an opinion in such a way as to develop majority support on the Court may limit such opportunities. Dissenting opinions can have more impact than the majority opinion; they stimulate a continued flow of cases around an issue. The solicitor general is the most important single influence outside the Court itself because he or she controls the flow of cases brought by the Justice Department and also shapes the argument in those cases. But the flow of cases is a force in itself, which the Department of Justice cannot entirely control. Social problems give rise to similar cases that ultimately must be adjudicated and appealed. Some interest groups try to develop such case patterns as a means of gaining power through the courts.

In recent years, the importance of the federal judiciary—the Supreme Court in particular—has increased substantially as the courts have developed new tools of judicial power and forged alliances with important forces in American society.

FOR FURTHER READING

Abraham, Henry. *The Judicial Process.* 6th ed. New York: Oxford University Press, 1993.

Bryner, Gary, and Dennis L. Thompson. *The Constitution and the Regulation of Society.* Provo, UT: Brigham Young University, 1988.

Davis, Sue. *Justice Rehnquist and the Constitution.* Princeton: Princeton University Press, 1989.

Graber, Mark A. *Transforming Free Speech: The Ambiguous Legacy of Civil Libertarianism.* Berkeley: University of California Press, 1991.

Kahn, Ronald. *The Supreme Court and Constitutional Theory,* 1953–1993. Lawrence: University Press of Kansas, 1994.

McCann, Michael W. *Rights at Work.* Chicago: University of Chicago Press, 1994.

Mezey, Susan G. *No Longer Disabled: The Federal Courts and the Politics of Social Security Disability.* New York: Greenwood, 1988.

O'Brien, David M. *Storm Center: The Supreme Court in American Politics.* 5th ed. New York: Norton, 2000.

Rosenberg, Gerald. *The Hollow Hope: Can Courts Bring about Social Change?* Chicago: University of Chicago Press, 1991.

Rubin, Eva. *Abortion, Politics and the Courts.* Westport, CT: Greenwood Press, 1982.

Silverstein, Mark. *Judicious Choices: The New Politics of Supreme Court Confirmations.* New York: Norton, 1994.

STUDY OUTLINE

The Legal System

1. Court cases in the United States proceed under three categories of law: criminal, civil, and public.
2. In the area of criminal law, either a state government or the federal government is the plaintiff who alleges that someone has committed a crime.
3. Civil cases are those between individuals or between individuals and the government in which no criminal violation is charged. In deciding these cases, courts apply statutes and legal precedent.
4. Public law involves questions of whether the government has the constitutional or statutory authority to take action.
5. By far, most cases are heard by state courts.
6. Cases are heard in federal courts if the U.S. government is a party in the case or the case involves federal statutes, treaties with other nations, or the U.S. Constitution.
7. Although the federal courts hear only a fraction of all the cases decided every year in the United States, federal court decisions are extremely important.

Federal Jurisdiction

1. The eighty-nine federal district courts are trial courts of original jurisdiction and their cases are, in form, indistinguishable from cases in the state trial courts.
2. The twelve U.S. courts of appeals review and render decisions in approximately 10 percent of all lower-court and agency cases.
3. Federal judges are appointed by the president and confirmed by a majority vote of the full Senate.
4. The Supreme Court is the highest court in the country and has the power and the obligation to review any lower court decision involving a substantial issue of public law, state legislation, or act of Congress.
5. The Constitution does not specify the number of justices that should sit on the Supreme Court, although since 1869 there have been nine—one chief justice and eight associate justices.
6. The solicitor general can influence the Court by screening cases before they reach the Supreme Court, submit-

ting *amicus* briefs, and shaping the arguments used before the Court.

The Power of the Supreme Court: Judicial Review

1. The Supreme Court's power to review acts of Congress, although accepted as natural and rarely challenged, is not specifically granted by the Constitution.
2. The Supreme Court's power to review state action or legislation derives from the Constitution's supremacy clause, although it is neither granted specifically by the Constitution nor inherent in the federal system.
3. Appeals of lower court decisions can reach the Supreme Court in one of two ways: through a writ of *certiorari,* or, in the case of convicted state prisoners, through a writ of *habeas corpus.*
4. Over the years, courts have developed specific rules that govern which cases within their jurisdiction they hear. These rules of access can be broken down into three categories: case or controversy, standing, and mootness.
5. Groups and forces in society attempt to influence justices' rulings on particular issues.
6. After filing written arguments, or briefs, attorneys present oral argument to the Supreme Court. After oral argument, the justices discuss the case and vote on a final decision.
7. The Supreme Court always explains its decisions in terms of law and precedent.
8. Despite the rule of precedent, the Court often reshapes law. Such changes in the interpretation of law can be explained, in part, by changes in the judicial philosophy of activism versus restraint and by changes in political ideology.

Judicial Power and Politics

1. For much of American history, the power of the federal courts was subject to five limitations: standing, the limited relief courts could provide, the lack of enforcement powers, political appointment, and the power of Congress to change the size and jurisdiction of federal courts.
2. The role of the federal judiciary has been strengthened since World War II by two judicial revolutions. The first revolution was a substantive revolution in several policy areas. The second revolution involved changes in judicial procedures that lessened traditional limitations on the courts.

PRACTICE QUIZ

1. Which of the following is a brief submitted to the Supreme Court by someone other than one of the parties in the case?
   a) *amicus curiae*
   b) *habeas corpus*
   c) solicitor general
   d) *ex post* brief
2. By what term is the practice of the courts to uphold precedent known?
   a) *certiorari*
   b) *stare decisis*
   c) rule of four
   d) senatorial courtesy
3. Which government official is responsible for arguing the federal government's position in cases before the Supreme Court?
   a) the vice president
   b) the attorney general
   c) the U.S. district attorney
   d) the solicitor general
4. Which of the following helps to explain the expanded power of the judiciary since World War II?
   a) changes in judicial procedure
   b) changes in judicial policy areas
   c) Neither a nor b is correct.
   d) Both a and b are correct.
5. What is the name for the body of law that involves disputes between private parties?
   a) civil law
   b) privacy law
   c) household law
   d) common law
6. Under what authority is the number of Supreme Court justices decided?
   a) the president
   b) the chief justice
   c) Congress
   d) the Constitution
7. Which of the following does not influence the flow of cases heard by the Supreme Court?
   a) the Supreme Court itself
   b) the solicitor general
   c) the attorney general
   d) the FBI

8. Which of the following cases involved the "right to privacy?"
   a) *Griswold v. Connecticut*
   b) *Brown v. Board of Education*
   c) *Schneckloth v. Bustamante*
   d) *Marbury v. Madison*

9. Which of the following Supreme Court cases from the 1960s involved the rights of criminal suspects?
   a) *Gideon v. Wainwright*
   b) *Miranda v. Arizona*
   c) *Escobedo v. Illinois*
   d) all of the above

10. Where do most trials in America take place?
    a) state and local courts
    b) appellate courts
    c) federal courts
    d) the Supreme Court

CRITICAL THINKING QUESTIONS

1. Judicial philosophies of activism and restraint are often confused with the political ideologies of liberalism and conservatism in the courts. What do you think the roots of this confusion are? To what extent is the common understanding correct? To what extent is it incorrect? Are there ways in which conservatives have been or could be activists in the courts? Are there ways in which liberals have exercised or could exercise judicial restraint?

2. In many ways, courts are expected to be apolitical institutions of government. In what ways are courts, judges, and justices shielded from politics and political pressure? In what ways are they vulnerable to political pressure? Are the courts an appropriate place for politics? What is the danger of having too much or too little political accountability in judicial decision making?

KEY TERMS

amicus curiae (p. 632)
appellate court (p. 618)
briefs (p. 636)
chief justice (p. 620)
civil law (p. 616)
class action suit (p. 646)
criminal law (p. 616)
defendant (p. 616)
dissenting opinion (p. 638)
due process of law (p. 618)
judicial activism (p. 642)
judicial restraint (p. 642)
judicial review (p. 624)
jurisdiction (p. 618)
***Miranda* rule** (p. 628)
mootness (p. 629)
opinion (p. 637)
oral argument (p. 636)
original jurisdiction (p. 619)
per curiam (p. 632)
plaintiff (p. 616)
plea bargains (p. 618)
precedents (p. 616)
public law (p. 616)
senatorial courtesy (p. 621)
solicitor general (p. 632)
standing (p. 629)
stare decisis (p. 616)
supremacy clause (p. 626)
supreme court (p. 618)
trial court (p. 618)
Uniform Commercial Code (p. 618)
writ of *certiorari* (p. 631)
writ of *habeas corpus* (p. 631)

PART V

Policy

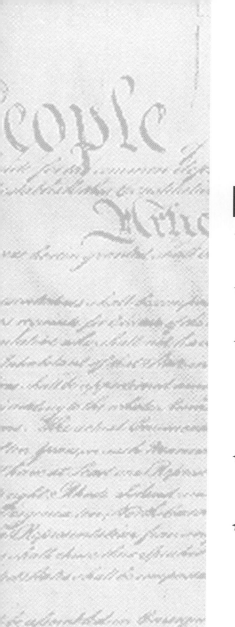

17 Government and

★ **Why Is Government Involved in the Economy?**

What are the basic principles behind government involvement in the economy? What basic economic roles does government serve?

★ **Should Government Be Involved in the Economy?**

What are the main arguments in the debate over the proper role of the government in the economy?

★ **What Are the Goals of Economic Policy?**

What are government leaders trying to achieve by passing specific economic policies?

How is the national government fundamental in promoting a strong and stable national economy, business development, and international trade?

How is the national government fundamental in regulating industrial relations and protecting the environment and consumers?

★ **What Are the Tools of Economic Policy?**

How can we classify the broad set of tools used by the government to accomplish its economic policy goals? More specifically, what are these tools called?

★ **The Politics of Economic Policy Making**

How do political leaders disagree about what the priorities of economic policy should be? What groups have the most influence on economic policy making? Does economic policy serve the public interest or special interests? How does the debate over economic policy reflect the broader debate over American political values?

the Economy

STUDENTS AND POLITICS

WE begin our discussion of public policy with economic policy because governments in America have always played a role in the economy. Unlike with most other countries, we must use "governments" in the plural when referring to the United States because of federalism, but that should not mask the importance of government itself and of the many public policies that have helped the American economy grow into the world's strongest, a fact that is ignored or unknown by many Americans. Despite the increasing hostility of some Americans toward government (especially the national government), we must reassert the fundamental fact that all Americans want government some of the time. A broad popular consensus in the United States has always supported government's (mostly state and local) providing a police force, a fire department, schools, roads, and public safety measures, among many other services. And even at the national level, some economic policies enjoy a broad supportive consensus.

One example of a broadly supported policy, at least among college students and their families, is federal aid for college tuition. The first such federal commitment was the G.I. bill, which provided college assistance to all who served in the armed forces during World War II. The G.I. bill was one of the largest and most popular public policies ever enacted in America. In recent years the government has moved in the direction of an equivalent for college assistance for any and all Americans, in recognition of the fact that a globalizing economy requires a lifetime of learning. The most recent step in that direction was made in August 1997, when Congress enacted and President Clinton signed into law the Taxpayer Relief Act (TRA), which included several provisions benefiting college students and their parents:

1. A "hope scholarship" tax credit of $1,500 for two years of college, beginning in 1998, for families whose gross annual incomes are less than $100,000;
2. A "lifetime learning" annual tax credit of $1,000 for any family whose gross income is below a certain ceiling;
3. "Educational savings accounts," created by exempting from tax penalties withdrawals from individual retirement accounts if the money is used for education;
4. Tax deductions for interest payments on educational loans during the first five years after graduation;
5. An increased maximum of $3,000 per year for Pell grants for high-need students;
6. Community service loan forgiveness, whereby student loan obligations will be reduced in return for low-paying jobs with certain charitable institutions; and

7. Tax relief for lifetime learning, allowing workers to exclude up to $5,250 of employer-provided education benefits from their income.

These provisions went through Congress without much controversy, probably because they were so welcome to thousands of parents and their appreciative children. From the standpoint of the parents, each of these provisions provides for a windfall—a free good: they will be able to keep a worthwhile chunk of money that otherwise they would have paid out in taxes. Nevertheless, each of these provisions is a policy, and the goal of each is to keep more kids in high school, encourage more students to pursue post–high school education, and to keep them pursuing educational goals during their entire working lifetimes. Moreover, each is coercive. Each attempts to get people to do something that they weren't going to do, or to get them to do more of something that they might not have chosen to do. For hard-pressed families living on $60,000–$70,000 per year (income ceilings vary from one provision to another) or less, these deductions against taxes for interest and tuition payments are very powerful incentives.

These are examples of public policies on which students are experts. You are aware of the necessity of higher education. You know your and your parents' limits and sacrifices. Virtually all of you are accumulating debt and are anticipating sharing the debt burden with your parents. All of you can calculate, at least roughly, the value to your parents of being able to reduce the total amount of debt they take on and to deduct interest payments on this debt from their income taxes. These policies are definitely in their interest, and yours.

Competition within a global marketplace has forced the American government to help maintain the United States' preeminent position in the world economy. Encouraging more Americans to attend or return to college is just one of many policies that the national government has adopted toward that goal. No one can predict exactly what demands will be placed on the government in the future, but whether it's a global economic crisis or a local crime wave, you can be certain that government will respond.

The point here and in the next two chapters is that governments have a purpose, and that purpose is the pursuit of goals that we call public policy. **Public policy** can be defined simply as an officially expressed purpose or goal backed by a sanction (a reward or a punishment). Public policy can be embodied in a law, a rule, a regulation, or an order.

public policy
a law, rule, statute, or edict that expresses the government's goals and provides for rewards and punishments to promote their attainment

The job of this chapter and the succeeding two chapters is to step beyond the politics and the institutions to look at the purposes of government—the public policies. This chapter will focus on policies toward the economy. Chapter 18 will cover social and welfare policies. Chapter 19 will concentrate on foreign policy and international affairs.

- ***In this chapter, we will first look at the reasons why government is involved in the economy.*** We will see that there are several basic economic roles that government serves, such as managing the economy, protecting the welfare and property of individuals, regulating competition, and providing public goods.
- ***Next, we will examine the most influential theories in the debate over the proper role of government in the economy.*** These theories include the laissez-faire, Keynesian, and monetarist approaches.

- ***We then turn to the goals of economic policy.*** These include promoting a strong and stable economy, encouraging business development, promoting international trade, regulating industrial relations, protecting the environment, and protecting consumers.
- ***We will then classify and review the tools of economic policy.*** Our discussion will focus on four major categories: monetary policies, fiscal policies, regulatory policies, and subsidies and contracting.
- ***The chapter then assesses the politics of economic policy making.*** We will look at the debate among political leaders over the priorities of economic policy and the role that interest groups play in that debate. We will also examine whether econoomic policies serve special interests or the public interest.
- ***We will conclude by looking at how citizens can evaluate how economic policies affect them.***

Why Is Government Involved in the Economy?

▶ What are the basic principles behind government involvement in the economy? What basic economic roles does government serve?

The belief in the separation of public and private spheres is central to our understanding of the American economy. Americans are raised to believe that at one time the economy was wholly unregulated and operated on its own in the private sphere. It is true that the capitalist economy is real and has a definite structure; but it is not a structure that is independent of the government. Capitalism is a political economy; that is, the government created the conditions for a market economy and facilitated people's efforts in that economy. Capitalism is inconceivable outside of the policies that have structured it.

At the most basic level, government makes it possible for markets to function efficiently by setting the rules for economic exchange and punishing those who violate the rules. Among the most important rules for the economy are those that define property rights, contracts, and standards for goods. This kind of government rule-making allows markets to expand by making it easier for people who do not know one another to engage in economic transactions. They no longer have to rely only on personal trust to do business. Likewise, government helps markets expand by creating money and standing behind its value. Money allows diverse goods to be traded and greatly simplifies economic transactions. The importance of government to basic market transactions is evident in periods when government authority is very weak. Governments that are on the losing side of wars, for example, are often so weak that they cannot enforce the basic rules needed for markets to function. In these settings, markets often break down, money loses its value, and economies contract as the basic conditions for doing business disappear.

Government involvement in the economy now extends far beyond these basic market-creating functions. As we shall see in this section, government has become involved in many aspects of the economy in order to promote the public well-being. Of course, there is often vigorous disagreement about the extent to which government should intervene in the economy to promote the public welfare. In addition, beliefs about which forms of government intervention in the economy are most necessary and most effective have changed over time. Nonetheless, when government seeks to influence the economy, it does so in order to make the economy better serve the needs of society.

MANAGING THE ECONOMY

Until 1929, most Americans believed that the government had little role to play in managing the economy. The world was guided by the theory that the economy, if left to its own devices, would produce full employment and maximum production. This traditional view of the relationship between government and the economy crumbled in 1929 before the stark reality of the Great Depression of 1929–1933. Some misfortune befell nearly everyone. Around 20 percent of the work force became unemployed, and few of these individuals had any monetary resources or the old family farm to fall back upon. Banks failed, wiping out the savings of millions who had been prudent enough or fortunate enough to have any. Thousands of businesses failed, throwing middle-class Americans onto the bread lines alongside unemployed laborers and dispossessed farmers. The Great Depression had finally proven to Americans that imperfections in the economic system could exist.

Demands grew for the federal government to act. In Congress, some Democrats proposed that the federal government finance public works to aid the economy and put people back to work. Other members introduced legislation to provide federal grants to the states to assist their relief efforts.

When President Franklin D. Roosevelt took office in 1933, he energetically threw the federal government into the business of fighting the Depression. He proposed a variety of temporary measures to provide federal relief and work programs. Most of the programs he proposed were to be financed by the federal government but administered by the states. In addition to these temporary measures, Roosevelt presided over the creation of several important federal programs designed to provide future economic security for Americans. Since that time, the government has been instrumental in ensuring that the economy will never again collapse as it did during the Depression.

The experience of the 1930s transformed public expectations about federal government involvement in the economy. Since that time, the public has held the government—and the president in particular—responsible for ensuring a healthy economy. Presidents who preside over periods of economic downturn are generally punished by the electorate. In 1992, economic recession and relatively high levels of unemployment greatly improved the challenger Bill Clinton's presidential prospects, even though he was not widely known when he started campaigning. Many other potential Democratic candidates who were more well-known had decided not to run because the incumbent, President George H. W. Bush, was so popular in the wake of the 1990 Gulf War. The sagging economy, however, quickly eroded Bush's popularity. Clinton's campaign took as its central theme the slogan, "It's the economy, stupid." This emphasis on the economy is widely credited as the strategy that got Clinton elected in 1992. The booming economy of the late 1990s also helped Clinton.

Even though he lost much personal popularity after the Monica Lewinsky scandal, Americans continued to give his administration very high approval ratings because the economy was so vibrant.

PROTECTING THE WELFARE AND PROPERTY OF INDIVIDUALS

One of the central reasons for government involvement in the economy is to protect the welfare and property of individuals and businesses. Because the threats to welfare and property change as the economy grows and new technologies emerge, government actions are constantly being updated and adapted to meet new conditions.

Maintenance of law and order is one of the most important ways that government can protect welfare and property. The federal government has also passed laws designed to protect individuals and businesses in economic transactions. Federal racketeering laws, for example, aim to end criminal efforts to control businesses through such illegal means as extortion and kickbacks. Federal laws also protect consumers from fraud and deceptive advertising. The old adage *caveat emptor*—let the buyer beware—may still be good advice but government laws have helped to curb deceitful business practices and provide recourse for consumers who believe that they have been cheated.

The government's job of protecting private property has become more difficult in today's technological environment. With growth of the computer industry and the vast sums of money that have been made from software, protection of "intellectual property" has become a growing area of law in the United States. The federal government has long sought to protect property through patent law and copyrights. But establishing ownership of ideas and guaranteeing that the owners of an idea reap the economic benefits have become more complex as new technologies make it easier to reproduce the work of others. These concerns do not stop at our nation's shores. The protection of intellectual property has been a key issue in American trade negotiations with China. The widespread pirating of videos, compact discs, and software in China and many other countries has cost the American owners of such intellectual property billions of dollars. The federal government has treated this effort to protect American property as a matter of utmost importance.

REGULATING COMPETITION

Beginning in the nineteenth century, as many sectors of the national economy flourished, certain companies began to exert monopolistic control over those sectors. Decreased competition threatened the efficiency of the market and the equitable distribution of its benefits. As a result, the national government stepped in to "level the playing field."

Another major reason why Congress began to adopt national business regulatory policies was that the regulated companies themselves felt burdened by the inconsistencies among the states. These companies often preferred a single, national regulatory authority, no matter how burdensome, because it would ensure consistency throughout the United States; the companies could thereby treat the nation as a single market.[1]

Political shifts and advances in technology make the regulation of competition a moving target. In 1913, when telephone service was becoming widely available, the federal government sanctioned AT&T's status as a publicly regulated monopoly. It believed that a single company—publicly regulated—could provide the best service in this industry. By the 1980s views about the necessity and effectiveness of such monopoly control had changed and the federal government moved to break up AT&T and open the field to new competitors. Creating competition in the telephone industry, it was hoped, would reduce prices and make the industry more responsive to consumers. And, indeed, although consumers have many complaints about telephone companies, prices dropped dramatically as competitors arose. Today, there is considerable concern about emerging monopolies in high technology. In 1999, when the federal government declared Microsoft Corporation a monopoly, it cited the negative impact of monopoly on future innovation as a reason to move against the software giant.

PROVIDING PUBLIC GOODS

public goods
goods that are provided by the government because they either are not supplied by the market or are not supplied in sufficient quantities

Government makes the market economy possible by providing **public goods.** This term refers to facilities the state provides, because no single participant can afford to provide those facilities itself. The provision of public goods may entail supplying the physical marketplace itself—like the commons in New England towns or the provision of an interstate highway system to stimulate the trucking industry. The provision of social goods is essential to market operation, and the manner in which the government provides those goods will affect the market's character.

In the United States, public goods related to transportation have been particularly important in promoting economic development. From the first canal systems that spread commerce into the interior of the country to the contemporary public role in supporting and regulating air transportation, government has created the conditions for reliable and efficient business activity. In some cases, government will supply a public good to stimulate the economy and then allow private companies to take over. The federal government brought electricity to rural areas in the 1930s to promote economic development, but over time the provision of electricity has been taken over by private companies. Government often supplies public goods that are too big or too risky for private actors to tackle. Major dams and hydroelectric projects are an example. By bringing water and energy to new areas, such public projects transformed the American West.

Should Government Be Involved in the Economy?

▶ What are the main arguments in the debate over the proper role of the government in the economy?

Not surprisingly, there are deep differences of opinion about whether, how much, and in what ways government should be involved in the economy. Ideas about the appropriate role for government have shifted in response to unanticipated or tenacious economic problems such as recession or inflation. Beliefs about the proper government role also vary depending on the criteria that are used to judge the success or failure of government actions in the economy. For example, many economists posit that there is a trade-off between economic efficiency and economic equality: to gain more equality, an economy has to sacrifice some efficiency. If this is so, it is a political choice whether economic efficiency is emphasized or equity is promoted as a public goal. Other economic analysts maintain that there is no such stark choice. They argue that, with the proper economic and social institutions, an economy can work toward equity and efficiency at the same time. Different theories about how the economy works envision quite distinct roles for government.

LAISSEZ-FAIRE

Ideas that envision only a minimal role for government in the economy are often called **laissez-faire capitalism** (literally, "let to make") approaches. Proponents of laissez-faire argue that the economy will flourish if the government leaves it alone. The argument for laissez-faire was first elaborated in the late 1700s by the great Scottish economist Adam Smith. Smith believed that most government involvement in the economy—such as the government-authorized monopolies that dominated trade in his day—depressed economic growth. Instead, he argued that competition among free enterprises would unleash economic energy, fostering growth and innovation. In his view, the self-seeking behavior of individuals, when subject to the discipline of market competition, would create products that consumers want at the best possible price. Smith praised "the invisible hand" of the market, by which he meant that millions of individual economic transactions together create a greater good—far better than could be created by the government. Smith believed that the government role should be restricted to national defense, establishing law and order (including the protection of private property), and provide basic public goods (such as roads) that facilitate commerce.

Laissez-faire ideas were especially influential in the years before the 1930s, when the prolonged worldwide economic depression opened the door to new thinking about the role of government. After that time advocates of laissez-faire lost influence, although the hands-off approach to economy continued to have articulate defenders. In the 1970s, University of Chicago economist Robert Lucas gave new force to laissez-faire ideas with his "rational expectations theory." Lucas argued that government intervention was bound to fail because people will anticipate government action and compensate for it. In this view, all of government's efforts would be undone as people adjust their actions.

Proponents of laissez-faire approaches are far more concerned about economic growth and efficiency than about economic inequality. They believe that government intervention to reduce inequality is misguided and often produces outcomes that leave everyone worse off. After decades of being marginal to public debate and policy, laissez-faire approaches gained new influence in the last two decades of the twentieth century.

Adam Smith's laissez-faire approach to capitalism dominated Western economic policy for much of the nineteenth and early-twentieth centuries. However, in the wake of a global depression in the 1930s, the hands-off role of the government, as articulated by Smith's doctrine, seemed an inadequate response to the economic issues of the time.

laissez-faire capitalism
an economic system in which the means of production and distribution are privately owned and operated for profit with minimal or no government interference

John Maynard Keynes's ideas offer an alternative to laissez-faire. Keynes argued for the necessity of government intervention in the economy, especially in times of economic downturn, when "the invisible hand" of the economy cannot reverse the downward spiral

KEYNESIANS

In the 1930s, the ideas of the British economist John Maynard Keynes laid the foundation for a revolution in thinking about the role of the government in the economy. With the industrialized world engulfed in economic depression, political leaders improvised as they sought to assist the armies of unemployed workers and destitute families that had no means to support themselves. Prevailing theories of laissez-faire offered little help. With their emphasis on balanced budgets and their faith in the working of the free market, such ideas saw little role for government even under such dire circumstances. Keynes's theories fundamentally challenged this hands-off approach.[2]

Keynes argued that industrialized economies experience periodic downturns in the business cycle. In these downturns, businesses lay workers off; workers in turn spend less, leading businesses to lay off yet more workers. By themselves economies cannot halt such self-reinforcing downward spirals. Government can, Keynes argued. By pumping money into the economy, government can stimulate demand and create a virtuous cycle of increased production and jobs that will pull the economy out of recession. In this view, mature economies can be expected to experience periods of insufficient demand; this government action will regularly be needed to regulate demand. Governments can do this in several ways. They can increase public spending through such measures as public works or public employment. Alternatively, governments can stimulate demand through temporary tax cuts. Tax cuts will allow workers to keep more of their earnings; their increased spending power will boost consumption and increase demand.

Keynesianism
economic theory, based on the ideas of British economist John Maynard Keynes, that argues that the government can stimulate the economy by increasing public spending or by cutting taxes

Keynesian ideas provided an ongoing role for government in the economy; they also linked the economic well-being of workers to the health of the economy as a whole. To stimulate the economy, **Keynesianism** called for putting money into the hands of the working people, who would be most likely to spend it. This theory made Keynesians especially attentive to issues of economic equity. The theory did not call for eliminating inequality but it did suggest that great imbalances in income could lead to insufficient demand and harm the economy as a whole. Keynesians also placed a heavy emphasis on reducing unemployment.

After World War II, Keynesian ideas guided economic policy making across the industrialized world. By the 1960s, Keynesians believed they could ensure ongoing prosperity by "fine-tuning" the economy: policy makers could stimulate demand with spending or tax cuts when recession loomed and then cut back on spending or increase taxes when inflation threatened. Republican president Richard Nixon reflected the strong consensus behind Keynesian ideas, when he remarked, "I am now a Keynesian."

Yet, by the time Keynesian ideas became the accepted wisdom, new economic conditions threatened their effectiveness. Many observers argued that increased international trade made Keynesian remedies less useful. Increased consumer spending power could "leak out" of the economy as workers bought goods manufactured abroad; in this case, their spending would not stimulate production at home. There is little consensus about how much increased international economic competition has weakened Keynesian tools. But in the past three decades, confidence that the government can fine-tune the economy has diminished and Keynesians lost the great influence they once had in economic policy.

MONETARISTS

Monetarists believe that the role of the government in managing the economy should be limited to regulating the supply of money. More active government management of the economy, monetarists argue, either has little effect or actually makes the economy worse. In contrast to Keynesians, monetarists do not believe that government can act quickly enough to fine-tune the economy. Instead, they maintain that government should promote economic stability by regulating the money supply. The most prominent monetarist in the United States, the economist Milton Friedman, recommended that the federal government let the growth in the money supply match the rate of economic growth. In this way, inflation could be kept low even as economic growth continued. This strict version of **monetarism** envisions a hands-off approach for the government; the theory calls for little exercise of discretion on the part of government officials. Instead, they must follow a simple rule about how much to increase the supply of money.

Monetarists are much more concerned about ensuring economic stability than with promoting equity. Their approach emphasizes the need to control inflation and devotes little attention to the problem of unemployment. Indeed they are often ready to accept higher levels of unemployment as the price for economic stability. Friedman, as the title of his most famous and popular book, *Free to Choose,* suggests, placed a premium on individual choice and individual liberty.[3] He believed that most government involvement in the economy restricted individual liberty and failed to produce any gains in individual economic welfare.

In the late 1970s, when high levels of inflation plagued the American economy, monetarists became especially influential in economic policy making. However, today it is impractical to implement a strict version of monetarism. Instead, economic policy makers have sought to manipulate interest rates to ensure a healthy and stable economy.

Monetarists such as Milton Friedman advocate a government-regulated money supply as a means to ensure economic stability. Monetarism is a hands-off approach in that it envisions an extremely limited role for government in the economy.

monetarism

economic theory that contends that the role of the government in the economy should be limited to regulating the supply of money

What Are the Goals of Economic Policy?

- What are government leaders trying to achieve by passing specific economic policies?
- How is the national government fundamental in promoting a strong and stable national economy, business development, and international trade?
- How is the national government fundamental in regulating industrial relations and protecting the environment and consumers?

The goals of economic policy often shift as a new administration takes power in Washington, but such shifts are usually a matter of emphasis. Political leaders realize that the public expects the government to achieve multiple goals in its economic policy. Public expectations about what government economic policy can and should do have expanded over the course of our nation's history. This growth in public expectations has made economic policy more complex as government strives to achieve multiple goals, some of which may conflict with one another.

Three major goals have guided government involvement in the economy since the early years of our nation's history: promoting a strong and stable economy, encouraging business development, and regulating international trade. Over time, the federal government has taken on greater responsibility for meeting each of these goals. The Great Depression of the 1930s marked a decisive turning point. As Washington created new agencies and new measures to monitor the nation's economic health, it transformed public expectations about the federal role in the economy. The federal government assumed primary responsibility for achieving established goals and it faced heightened expectations about its ability to reach those goals. In addition, the federal government took on one important new goal, to regulate industrial relations. By the 1970s, two additional goals for national economic policy had emerged: protecting the environment and protecting consumers.

PROMOTE A STRONG AND STABLE ECONOMY

A strong and stable economy is the basic goal of all economic policy. What makes reaching this goal so difficult is that the key elements of a strong economy—economic growth, full employment, and low inflation—often appear to conflict with one another. Economic policy must manage the trade-offs among these goals. This is a complicated task because there is much disagreement about whether pursuing one of these economic goals really does mean sacrificing the others. Moreover, the trade-offs among these goals appear to change over time. The expansion of the American economy in the latter half of the 1990s defied all previous expectations about the relationship between growth, employment, and inflation. The fast pace of economic growth, combined with low inflation and very high employment suggested that is was now possible to combine all three central goals of economic policy.[4] Yet policy makers remain alert to any indications that these favorable conditions may be eroding.

Economic Growth Since the 1930s, the federal government has carefully tracked national economic growth. Economic growth is measured in several different ways. The two most important measures are the Gross National Product (GNP), which is the market value of the goods and services produced in the economy, and the **Gross Domestic Product (GDP),** the same measure but excluding income from foreign investments. Since 1997, the American economy has grown at a rate of over 4 percent a year, a rate considered high by modern standards (see Figure 17.1).

Gross Domestic Product (GDP)
index of the total output of goods and services produced in the economy

The engine of American economic growth has shifted over the centuries. In the 1800s, our nation's rich endowment of natural resources was especially important in propelling growth. Manufacturing industries became the driving force of economic growth in the late nineteenth century as mass production made it possible to produce goods at a pace that was once unimaginable. In more recent times, the high technology boom has fostered unanticipated and vigorous economic growth that has made the United States the envy of the

CHANGES IN REAL GROSS DOMESTIC PRODUCT, 1960–1999

Figure 17.1

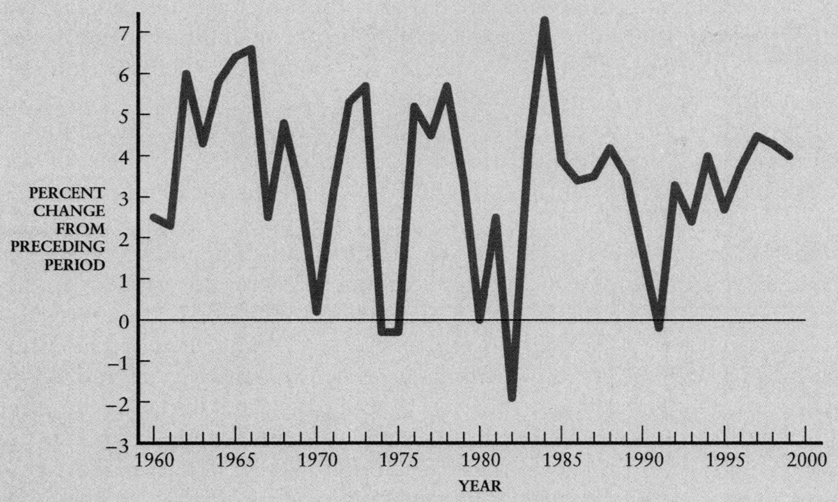

SOURCE: *Economic Report of the President 2000* (Washington, D.C.: Government Printing Office, 2000), p. 310.

world. Despite these very different economic engines, the basic prerequisites of growth are similar in each case: strong investment, technological innovation, and a productive workforce. Throughout the nation's history the federal government has adopted policies to promote each of these conditions needed to sustain economic growth.

The most fundamental way that government affects investment is by promoting business confidence. Businesses that fear political instability, unpredictable government action, or widespread disregard of the law are unlikely to invest. The effort to promote business confidence may lead presidents to take actions they would otherwise prefer to avoid. For example, when President Clinton took office, he hoped to increase spending on domestic social programs valued by his Democratic constituents. However, his economic advisers convinced him that deficit reduction was needed to gain the confidence of Wall Street and improve the investment climate.[5]

Businesses also need access to new sources of capital in order to grow. The federal government promotes reliable access to new investment through its regulation of financial markets. The most important federal agency in this regard is the Securities and Exchange Commission (SEC), created after the stock market crash of 1929. The SEC requires companies to disclose information about the stocks and bonds they are selling, inform buyers of the investment risks, and protect investors against fraud. In this way, the SEC helps to maintain investor confidence and a strong supply of capital for American business.

Public investment is another important source of growth in the American economy. Such investment may be expressly designed to promote growth in accordance with the Keynesian principles outlined earlier in this chapter. In the

1930s and again in the late 1970s, the federal government promoted public investment as a means to spark economic growth. Other kinds of public investment promote growth as a byproduct of other more central objectives. Historically, the most important area of growth propelling government spending has been in the military sector. The long rise in military spending after World War II, sometimes called "military Keynesianism," helped to stimulate the American economy for many decades.

The second important condition for economic growth is innovation. The federal government has sought to support innovation in a variety of ways. One of the most important is through the National Science Foundation. Created in 1950, the National Science Foundation supports basic research across a range of scientific fields. The aim is to advance fundamental knowledge that may be useful in many different applications.[6] Federal government sponsorship of health research began in the late 1800s. Today, the National Institutes of Health conduct basic and applied research in biomedicine. The Human Genome project—the effort to map the basic genetic structure of human life—was initiated by government researchers and only later taken up by private corporations. Research sponsored by the military has long been an important source of innovation for the American economy. Such key twentieth-century innovations as radar and nuclear power stemmed from military research. And as we saw in Chapter 15, military research also created the technology for the twenty-first century with ARPANET, the precursor of the Internet.

A third fundamental condition for economic growth is a sufficient and productive workforce. Federal immigration policy has played a key role in ensuring an adequate supply of labor throughout American history. In the late nineteenth century, the huge wave of immigrants from Europe supplied the labor for burgeoning industries across the United States. Immigration policy often also targets particular groups for admission to the United States based on the needs of employers. One example was the Bracero program launched in 1942. The Bracero program admitted Mexican agricultural workers to the United States on a temporary basis as farm laborers because of the difficulty of finding workers for this seasonal low-paid labor. The program was terminated in 1964 because of public outrage over the poor treatment of such workers. Immigration laws routinely give special priority to workers who have skills that are in demand among American employers. Immigrants with nursing degrees, for example, have long received special priority. In recent years, Silicon Valley employers have lobbied hard to open immigration quotas to allow more highly skilled workers in high-tech fields, such as computer programmers, to work in the United States.

Today, a productive workforce is a highly educated workforce. Education, as we will see in Chapter 18, is primarily the responsibility of state and local governments. The federal government, however, supports the development of a productive workforce with a variety of programs to support higher education, such as the educational grants, tax breaks, and loans discussed at the beginning of this chapter. The federal government also sponsors a limited array of job-training programs that focus primarily on low-skilled workers. Some analysts argue that the federal government must do much more to support the development of a highly skilled workforce if the United States is to sustain economic growth in the future.

Full Employment Before the 1930s, neither the federal nor the state governments sought to promote full employment. Unemployment was widely viewed as an unfortunate occurrence that government could do little to alter. The New Deal response to the prolonged and massive unemployment of the Great Depression changed that. The federal government put millions of people back to work on public projects sponsored by such programs as the Works Progress Administration (WPA). The bridges, walkways, and buildings they created can still be seen across the United States today. The federal government viewed these programs as temporary measures, however. As the buildup for World War II boosted the economy and unemployment melted away, the employment programs were dismantled.

The New Deal and government wartime spending, however, showed that government could help ensure full employment. Public expectations changed as well: Americans looked to the federal government to reduce unemployment after the war. Moreover, economic theory now supported their expectations. Keynes's theories that government could boost employment by stimulating demand had become very influential.

Federal policy placed the most emphasis on achieving full employment in the 1960s. Keynesian economists in the Council of Economic Advisers convinced President Kennedy to enact the first tax cut designed to stimulate the economy and promote full employment.[7] The policy was widely seen as a success and unemployment declined to a low of 3.4 percent in 1968. For economists, full employment is a technical term, it does not mean literally zero percent unemployment. It means the rate at which further employment will set off inflation. During the 1960s, economic advisers contended over whether the

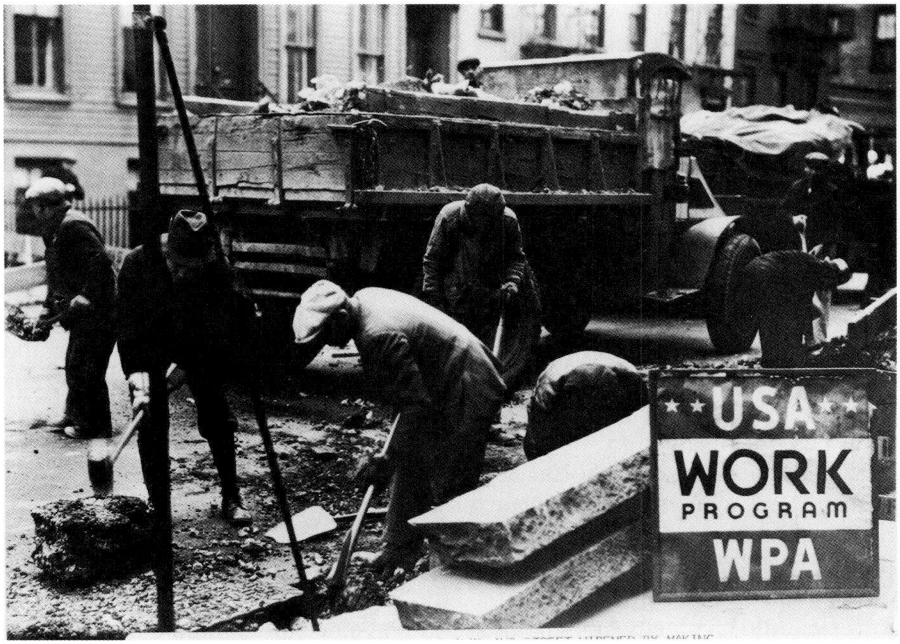

During the Depression, the WPA program put unemployed people to work on a wide range of public projects, from construction to the arts.

economy was at "full employment" at 4 percent or at 3 percent unemployment. This question became a critical problem for economic policy making during the late 1960s and the 1970s, when stubbornly high rates of inflation plagued the American economy. Many economists argued that the economy could not support an unemployment rate that was lower than 6 percent. In the trade-off between unemployment and inflation, the definition of full employment was revised upward.

Favorable economic conditions in the 1990s reduced unemployment to record lows once again. Many analysts characterize the transformation as the "new economy." They contend that the economy has changed so much that the old trade-offs between inflation and unemployment no longer exist. Even in these favorable conditions, many proponents of full employment argue that the government could do much more to promote employment. The official measure of unemployment counts only those people who are defined as "actively seeking work." It does not include those discouraged workers who have dropped out of the labor force. For this reason, some analysts argue that the real rate of unemployment is about 9 percentage points higher than official figures.[8]

inflation
a consisitent increase in the general level of prices

Low Inflation During the 1970s and early 1980s, **inflation,** a consistent increase in the general level of prices, was one of America's most vexing problems. There was much disagreement over what to do about it—what public policies were most appropriate and effective. The first effort, beginning in 1971, was the adoption of strict controls over wages, prices, dividends, and rents—that is, authorizing an agency in the executive branch to place limits on what wage people could be paid for their work, what rent their real estate could bring, and what interest they could get on their money. After two years of effort, these particular policies were fairly well discredited, and the search resumed for one or more other policies to fight inflation. Since oil prices had become so clearly a major source of inflation in the late 1970s, President Carter experimented with the licensing of imports of oil from the Middle East, with tariffs and excise taxes on unusually large oil profits made by producers, and with sales taxes on gasoline at the pump to discourage all casual consumption of gasoline. President Carter also attempted to reduce consumer spending in general by raising income taxes, especially Social Security taxes on employees.

The continuing high rate of inflation paved the way to an entirely different approach by President Reagan in the early 1980s. In place of oil import licensing and selective tax increases, President Reagan proposed and got a general tax cut. The Reagan theory was that if tax cuts were deep enough and were guaranteed to endure, they would increase the "supply" of money, would change people's psychology from pessimism to optimism and would thereby encourage individuals and corporations to invest enough and produce enough to get us out of inflation. At the same time, President Reagan supported the continuation of the high Social Security taxes enacted during the Carter administration, which probably went further than any other method to fight inflation by discouraging consumption. As we have said, inflation is caused by too many dollars chasing too few goods, bidding up prices. Any tax will take dollars out of consumption, but since the Social Security tax hits middle and lower-middle-income people the heaviest, and since these middle-income people are the heaviest consumers, such a tax reduces consumer dollars. Another policy supported by the Reagan administration was restraining the amount of credit in the economy by pushing up interest rates.

Inflation was finally reduced from its historic highs of nearly 20 percent down toward 2 and 3 percent each year. But no one is absolutely certain which policy, if any, contributed to this reduction. After all, the two-year recession of 1981–1982 produced such significant increases in unemployment that consumption was cut, and any cut in consumption—whether from a tax policy or a loss of wages—will reduce prices. At the same time, the international price of oil dropped, independently of our policies. Consequently, we do not know exactly what policy to adopt the next time inflation becomes a problem. But no government will stand by and permit inflation or unemployment or global economic competition to become a problem without trying to do something about it.

PROMOTE BUSINESS DEVELOPMENT

During the nineteenth century, the national government was a promoter of markets. National roads and canals were built to tie states and regions together. National tariff policies promoted domestic markets by restricting imported goods; a tax on an import raised its price and weakened its ability to compete with similar domestic products. The national government also heavily subsidized the railroad system. Until the 1840s, railroads were thought to be of limited commercial value. But between 1850 and 1872, Congress granted over 100 million acres of public domain land to railroad interests, and state and local governments pitched in an estimated $280 million in cash and credit. Before the end of the century, 35,000 miles of track existed—almost half the world's total.

Railroads were not the only clients of federal support for the private markets. Many sectors of agriculture began receiving federal subsidies in the

In addition to land on which to lay tracks, railroad companies were provided financial aid by federal, state, and local governments to construct the railroads.

nineteenth century. Some still are: despite significant cuts in the agriculture budget in the 1980s, federal subsidies still amount to nearly $10 billion per year, for commodities such as sugar ($1.4 billion) and for the agricultural market in general, through programs such as rural electrification ($2 billion).

In the twentieth century, the national government promoted business development indirectly through **categorical grants** (see Chapter 4), in which the national government offers grants to states on condition that the state (or local) government undertake a particular activity. Thus, in order to use motor transportation to improve national markets, a 900,000-mile national highway system was built during the 1930s, based on a formula whereby the national government would pay 50 percent of the cost if the state would provide the other 50 percent. Over twenty years, beginning in the late 1950s, the federal government constructed nearly 45,000 miles of interstate highways. This was brought about through a program whereby the national government agreed to pay 90 percent of the construction costs on the condition that each state provide 10 percent of the costs of any portion of a highway built within its boundaries.[9] The tremendous growth of highways was a major boon to the automobile and to the trucking industries.

categorical grants
congressional grants given to states and localities on the condition that expenditures be limited to a problem or group specified by the law

The federal government also supports specific business sectors with direct subsidies, loans, and tax breaks. In 1953, the Small Business Administration (SBA) was created to offer loans, loan guarantees, and disaster assistance to small businesses. Recognizing that such businesses often find it harder to obtain financing and to recover from unexpected events such as fires, the federal government has provided assistance where the market would not. Today, the SBA provides more than $45 billion in such assistance to small businesses.

Among the many contemporary examples of policies promoting private industry, Sematech may be the most instructive. Sematech is a nonprofit, research and development (R&D) consortium of major U.S. computer microchip manufacturers, set up in 1987 to work with government and academic institutions to reestablish U.S. leadership in semiconductor manufacturing. (The United States appeared to be in danger of losing out to the Japanese in this area in the 1980s.) The results of its research are distributed among the fourteen consortium members.[10] For nine years industry and government together spent $1.7 billion to make the American microchip industry the leader in the world. The government contributed about half of the total expenditures. In 1997, federal funding was phased out. Industry leaders, convinced they no longer needed federal support, themselves initiated the break with government. At a critical moment, the federal government had stepped in to save the chip industry; it stepped out once that goal had been achieved.

One of the Clinton administration's economic goals was to promote international trade through treaties and direct negotiation. President Clinton is shown here visiting a Chrysler dealership in Japan to reassure American companies that he represents their interests abroad.

Although Republicans officially opposed the Sematech subsidies, most support for the high-tech industry is bipartisan, in response to arguments that development of this infant industry is in the national interest. Of course, a certain amount of promotion of "infant industries" is justified today, just as tariffs were justified in the late-nineteenth century to support infant industries.

PROMOTE INTERNATIONAL TRADE

The promotion and advertising of American goods and services abroad is a long-standing goal of U.S. trade policy, and is one of the major obligations of the Department of Commerce. Yet modern trade policy involves a complex arrangement of treaties, tariffs, and other mechanisms of policy formation. The support for Sematech and the "infant" computer industry with an eye on foreign competition is an example of a type of national public policy—promoting the private economy—that goes all the way back to the Founding. For example, there exists the long-standing U.S. policy of granting **most favored nation status** to other countries—that is, the United States offers to another country the same tariff rate it already gives to its most favored trading partner, in return for trade (and sometimes other) concessions. In 1998, to avoid any suggestion that "most favored nation" implied some special relationship with an undemocratic country (China, for example), President Clinton changed the term from "most favored nation" to "normal trade relations."[11]

most favored nation status
agreement to offer a trading partner the lowest tariff rate offered to other trading partners

The most important international organization for promoting free trade is the **World Trade Organization (WTO)**, which officially came into being in 1995. The WTO grew out of the **General Agreement on Tariffs and Trade (GATT)**. Since World War II, GATT had brought together a wide range of nations for regular negotiations designed to reduce barriers to trade. Such barriers, many believed, had contributed to the breakdown of the world economy in the 1930s and had helped to cause World War II. The WTO has over 130 members worldwide; decisions about trade are made by the Ministerial Conference, which meets every two years. Similar policy goals are pursued in regional arrangements, such as the **North American Free Trade Agreement (NAFTA)**, a trade treaty between the United States, Canada, and Mexico.

World Trade Organization (WTO)
international trade agency promoting free trade that grew out of the General Agreement on Tariffs and Trade

General Agreement on Tariffs and Trade (GATT)
international trade organization, in existence from 1947 to 1995, that set many of the rules governing international trade

North American Free Trade Agreement (NAFTA)
trade treaty between the United States, Canada, and Mexico to lower and eliminate tariffs between the three countries

Working toward freer trade has been an important goal of each presidential administration since World War II. President Clinton made the passage of NAFTA one of the central objectives of his first term. Yet as globalization has advanced, concerns about free trade and about the operation of the WTO, in particular, have grown. The WTO meetings held in Seattle in 1999 witnessed unprecedented protests by groups that included environmentalists and labor unions. Protesters denounced the undemocratic decision-making process of the WTO, which, they charged, was dominated by the concerns of business. These critics believe that the WTO does not pay sufficient attention to such issues as environmental degradation, human rights, and labor practices, including use of child labor in many countries. If such practices go unchecked, they believe, trade will force Americans to loosen labor standards and environmental regulations. Until now, the conditions have centered on business concerns, such as protection of intellectual property rights on software and CDs, which are easy to pirate. After the upheaval in Seattle, President Clinton, a strong supporter of free trade, spoke for the first time in favor of incorporating labor and environmental issues into trade negotiations. However, this will present a formidable challenge for free trade because developing countries are likely to resist such conditions.[12]

Globalization and free trade is likely to be a contentious political issue in the future. Labor unions, environmental organizations, and human rights groups, with little history of cooperation in the past, have joined together to challenge established patterns of trade negotiation. Yet many political leaders strongly support free trade as the best route to growth and prosperity. American trade policy, once a relatively consensual area of policy in which decisions could be made behind closed doors, has moved out into the arena of public conflict, where it is likely to stay.

REGULATE INDUSTRIAL RELATIONS

Stable relations between business and labor are important elements of a productive economy. In the latter half of the nineteenth century, strikes over low wages or working conditions became a standard feature of American economic life. In fact, the United States has one of the most violent histories of labor relations in the world. Yet for most of American history, the federal government did little to regulate relations between business and labor. Local governments and courts often weighed in on the side of business by prohibiting strikes and arresting strikers.

As the economic depression enveloped the United States in the 1930s, massive strikes for union recognition and plummeting wages prompted the federal government to take action. Congress passed the 1935 National Labor Relations Act, which set up a new framework for industrial relations. The new law created a permanent agency, the National Labor Relations Board (NLRB), charged with overseeing union elections and collective bargaining between labor and industry. The federal government weighed in further on the side of organized labor in 1938, when it passed the Fair Labor Standards Act, which created the minimum wage. Because it is not indexed to inflation, the value of the minimum wages declines if it is not raised periodically. Since 1938, conflicts over increasing the minimum wage have been a regular feature of American politics.

In the 1950s and 1960s, the federal government played an active role in industrial relations. The Department of Labor and, occasionally, even the president directly intervened in labor-management disputes to ensure peaceful industrial relations. Although Democrats were generally seen as more supportive to labor, both parties sought to achieve a balance between business and labor that would promote a strong stable economy.

President Reagan made a decisive break with this tradition of compromise in 1981, when he fired striking air traffic controllers and hired permanent replacements to take their jobs. Since that time, organized labor has grown weaker and the mechanisms of collective bargaining have become less effective. Politicians are much less likely to intervene in labor relations. There are occasional exceptions, such as in the early 1990s, when President Clinton brought labor and management together to avert an airline strike. But, with the exception of the minimum wage, the federal government has significantly reduced its involvement in industrial relations.

PROTECT THE ENVIRONMENT

In 1969, the Cayuhoga River in Cleveland, long a dumping ground for industrial waste, caught fire. Images of the burning river provided a vivid reminder that America's industrial prosperity had come at a cost to the natural environment and to the health of urban America. At the same time, a more affluent America, with more time for leisure, grew concerned about the quality of the environment and the need to preserve natural beauty. The first "Earth Day" in 1970 celebrated this new set of concerns that would become a major feature of American politics in the coming decades.[13]

A wave of new laws wrote environmental goals into policy. The 1969 National Environmental Policy Act (NEPA), the Clean Air Act Amendments of

1970, the 1972 Clean Water Act, and the 1974 Safe Drinking Water Act together established a new set of goals and procedures for protecting the environment. They are properly considered as part of economic policy because they regulate the activities of virtually every aspect of the economy. NEPA, for example, requires federal agencies to prepare an environmental impact statement for every major development project that they propose. In this way, environmental impacts routinely become factored into considerations about whether a particular project is feasible or desirable.

Environmental disasters have often served to draw attention to new environmental hazards and prompt greater federal regulation. For example, in the mid-1970s the residents of the Love Canal neighborhood in Buffalo, New York, discovered that their neighborhood had been built on a toxic waste dump. Many of the chemicals in the soil were suspected carcinogens. At federal and state cost, residents were moved to new homes. Partly as a result of this highly publicized incident, Congress passed legislation to facilitate cleanup of hazardous waste sites. Yet government action and corporate liability are often bitterly contested issues in this area. As the book and film *A Civil Action*—about toxic waste in a Massachusetts community—demonstrated, identifying the sources of toxic pollution and linking such pollution to health hazards can be very difficult.[14]

Protecting the environment presents policy makers with difficult trade-offs. Compliance with environmental regulations can be very costly. Moreover critics maintain that federal standards are sometimes too high. How clean should the air be? What is the difference between pure drinking water and safe drinking water? Who should bear the costs of providing environmental benefits? Not only do citizens, consumers, and businesses take different perspectives on these questions, the goals themselves often present a moving target. As new scientific evidence shows (or fails to find evidence for) new or suspected environmental hazards, conflicts over the proper government role emerge. Global warming is an example of an issue that has attracted more attention as mounting scientific evidence shows that our climate has grown hotter.

In the decades since environmental goals first became incorporated into public policy, presidents have placed more or less emphasis on these goals and federal agencies have experimented with different methods for promoting environmental objectives. But despite such shifts, there has never been any doubt that Americans now expect the federal government to play a leading role in preserving natural beauty and promoting a clean and healthful environment.

Student Perspectives

Americans have a long and sordid history of placing their pocketbooks before ecosystems.

Case in point—the Snake River dams. For some time, many citizens of the Palouse have extolled the virtues of the dams on the Columbia and Snake rivers.

The dams do have their benefits. Electricity rates are lowered and opportunities for recreation [are] created by [them]. They [also] create jobs in many sectors.

[But] cheap electricity is no excuse for the destruction of an ecosystem. [Indeed,] despite efforts to resuscitate the Snake, [its] traditional salmon runs are already gone, and any further attempts would be tantamount to beating a dead fish.

Today, with prices of petroleum products sky-high, many wallet-weary consumers are [now] calling for drilling in ecologically sensitive and federally protected oil [reserves] in Alaska. These reserves lie beneath tundra ecosystems.

It is time to cast aside our economic tunnel vision and to forget about spoiling one of our precious wilderness areas.

If developed, the wilderness would be slashed with access roads and smothered by people. The oil extraction itself would leave the area irreparably degraded.

Tundra ecosystems are especially susceptible to ecological damage. The minimal growing season and bitter conditions provide many organisms a meager existence. The areas being considered for development would become even more hostile after being pillaged and cast aside.

The wildernesses of Alaska can be our living testament to the future. That is, if we think of something other than our wallets.

SOURCE: Jacov Smulkowski, "Choose Ecosystem Over Economics," *Daily Evergreen* (Washington State University), March 29, 2000.

An official from the Consumer Product Safety Commission demonstrates the potential danger of some types of baby cribs. In areas of consumer safety, the national government regularly plays a protective role.

PROTECT CONSUMERS

A final goal of economic policy is to protect consumers. The idea that the federal government should protect consumers emerged in the first decade of the 1900s. Upton Sinclair's graphic exposé about the unsanitary practices of the meatpacking industry, *The Jungle,* published in 1906, galvanized public concern about unsanitary food processing. These concerns prompted the U.S. Department of Agriculture to inspect packing plants and the meat they produced, stamping approved meats with the now familiar "USDA" certification. Similar concern about food and drug safety led to the creation of the Food and Drug Administration in 1927.

The movement for consumer protection took off again in the 1960s. Consumer advocate Ralph Nader's 1965 book *Unsafe at Any Speed* helped spark new demands for federal action. Nader's book showed that design flaws in the Corvair, a popular car model, had caused deaths that could have been prevented. Nader's book not only led to the demise of the Corvair, it galvanized calls for more federal action to protect consumers. The first response was the 1966 National Traffic and Motor Vehicle Safety Act, which gave the Department of Transportation responsibility for ensuring vehicle safety. Federal responsibility for consumer safety expanded in 1972 when Congress created the Consumer Product Safety Commission. The Commission, which is an independent agency, informs consumers about hazards associated with products and works with industry to set product standards. In cases where safety concerns are severe, it will see that such products are recalled. Through the Consumer Product Safety Commission, the Department of Transportation, and the Food and Drug Administration (which regulates food, drugs, and cosmetics), the federal government continues to play an active role in protecting the public from unsafe products.

What Are the Tools of Economic Policy?

- How can we classify the broad set of tools used by the government to accomplish its economic policy goals? More specifically, what are these tools called?

The U.S. economy is no accident; it is the result of specific policies that have expanded American markets and sustained massive economic growth. The Constitution provides that Congress shall have the power

> To lay and collect Taxes, . . . to pay the Debts and provide for the common Defence and general Welfare; . . . To borrow Money; . . . To coin Money [and] regulate the Value thereof. . . .

These clauses of Article I, Section 8, are the constitutional sources of the fiscal and monetary policies of the national government. Nothing is said, however, about *how* these powers can be used, although the way they are used shapes the economy. As it works to meet the multiple goals of economic policy outlined above, the federal government relies on a broad set of tools that have evolved over time. Let us now turn to the actual tools designed to accomplish the goals of economic policy.

MONETARY POLICIES

Monetary policies manipulate the growth of the entire economy by controlling the availability of money to banks. With a very few exceptions, banks in the United States are privately owned and locally operated. Until well into the twentieth century, banks were regulated, if at all, by state legislatures. Each bank was granted a charter, giving it permission to make loans, hold deposits, and make investments within that state. Although more than 25,000 banks continue to be state-chartered banks, they are less important than they used to be in the overall financial picture, as the most important banks now are members of the federal banking system.

monetary policies
efforts to regulate the economy through the manipulation of the supply of money and credit. America's most powerful institution in this area of monetary policy is the Federal Reserve Board

But banks did not become the core of American capitalism without intense political controversy. The Federalist majority in Congress, led by Alexander Hamilton, did in fact establish a Bank of the United States in 1791, but it was vigorously opposed by agrarian interests led by Thomas Jefferson, based on the fear that the interests of urban, industrial capitalism would dominate such a bank. The Bank of the United States was terminated during the administration of Andrew Jackson, but the fear of a central, public bank still existed eight decades later, when Congress in 1913 established an institution—the **Federal Reserve System**—to integrate private banks into a single national system. The Federal Reserve System did not become a central bank in the European tradition, but rather is composed of twelve Federal Reserve banks, each located in a major commercial city. The Federal Reserve banks are not ordinary banks; they are banker's banks, which make loans to other banks, clear checks, and supply the economy with currency and coins. They also play a regulatory role over the member banks. Every national bank must be a member of the Federal Reserve System; each must follow national banking rules and must purchase stock in the Federal Reserve System (which helps make the system self-financing). State banks and savings and loan associations may also join if they accept national rules. At the top of the system is the Federal Reserve Board—"the Fed"—comprising seven members appointed by the president (with Senate confirmation) for fourteen-year terms. The chairman of the Fed is selected by the president from among the seven members of the board for a four-year term. In all other concerns, however, the Fed is an independent agency (see Chapter 15) inasmuch as its members cannot be removed during their terms except "for cause," and the president's executive power does not extend to them or their policies.

Federal Reserve System
a system of twelve Federal Reserve Banks that facilitates exchanges of cash, checks, and credit; regulates member banks; and uses monetary policies to fight inflation and deflation

The major advantage that a bank gains from being in the Federal Reserve System is that it can borrow from the system, using as collateral notes on loans that it already holds. This enables banks to expand their loan operations continually, as long as there is demand for loans in the economy. On the other hand, it is this very access of member banks to the Federal Reserve System that gives the Fed its power: the ability to expand and contract the *amount of credit* available in the United States.

President Clinton and Federal Reserve Board Chair Alan Greenspan. Although the Fed is meant to remain independent, presidents do use subtle pressure to try to shape the Fed's policies.

The Fed can affect the total amount of credit through the interest (called the discount rate) it charges on the loans it extends to member banks. If the Fed significantly decreases the discount rate, it can give a boost to a sagging economy. If the Fed raises the discount rate, it can put a brake on the economy, because the higher discount rate also increases the general interest rates charged by leading private banks to their customers.

reserve requirement
the amount of liquid assets and ready cash that banks are required to hold to meet depositors' demands for their money

A second power of the Fed is control over the **reserve requirement**—the amount of cash and negotiable securities every bank must hold readily available to cover withdrawals and checks written by their depositors. Generally the rule is that a bank must hold at least 20 percent of all of its outstanding loans as its reserve requirement. When the Fed decides to increase the reserve requirement, it can decrease significantly the amount of money banks have to lend; conversely, if the Fed lowers the reserve requirement, banks can be more liberal in extending more loans.[15]

open-market operations
method by which the Open Market Committee of the Federal Reserve System buys and sells government securities, etc., to help finance government operations and to reduce or increase the total amount of money circulating in the economy

A third power of the Fed is called **open-market operations,** whereby the Fed buys and sells government securities in order to increase or decrease the supply of money in the economy. When the Fed buys government securities in the open market, it increases the amount of money available to consumers to spend or invest; when it sells securities, it is reducing the money supply.

Finally, a fourth power is derived from one of the important services rendered by the Federal Reserve System, which is the opportunity for member banks to borrow from each other. One of the original reasons for creating a Federal Reserve System was to balance regions of the country that might be vigorously expanding with other areas that might be fairly dormant: the national system would enable the banks in a growing region, facing lots of demand for credit, to borrow money from banks in regions of the country where the demand for credit is much lower. This exchange is called the "federal funds market," and the interest rate charged by one bank to another, the **federal**

funds rate, can be manipulated just like the discount rate, to expand or contract credit.[16]

The federal government also provides insurance to foster credit and encourage private capital investment. The Federal Deposit Insurance Corporation (FDIC) insures bank deposits up to $100,000. Another important promoter of investment is the federal insurance of home mortgages through the Department of Housing and Urban Development (HUD). By guaranteeing mortgages, the government can reduce the risks that banks run in making such loans, thus allowing banks to lower their interest rates and make such loans more affordable to middle- and lower-income families. Such programs have enabled millions of families who could not have otherwise afforded it to finance the purchase of a home.

federal funds rate
the interest rate on loans between banks that the Federal Reserve Board influences by affecting the supply of money available

FISCAL POLICIES

Fiscal policies include the government's taxing and spending powers. Personal and corporate income taxes, which raise most of the U.S. government's revenues, are the most prominent examples. While the direct purpose of an income tax is to raise revenue, each tax has a different impact on the economy, and government can plan for that impact. For example, President Clinton's commitment in his 1992 campaign to a "middle-class tax cut" was motivated by the goal of encouraging economic growth through increased consumption. Soon after the election, upon learning that the deficit would be far larger than had been earlier reported to him, he confessed he would have to break his promise of such a tax cut. Nevertheless, the idea of a middle-class tax cut is an example of a fiscal policy aimed at increased consumption, because of the theory that people in middle-income brackets tend to spend a high proportion of unexpected earnings or windfalls, rather than saving or investing them.[17]

fiscal policies
the use of taxing, monetary, and spending powers to manipulate the economy

Taxation During the nineteenth century, the federal government received most of its revenue from a single tax, the **tariff.** It also relied on excise taxes, which are taxes levied on specific products, such as tobacco and alcohol. As federal activities expanded in the 1900s, the federal government added new sources of tax revenue. The most important was the income tax, proposed by Congress in 1909, ratified by the states, and added to the Constitution in 1913 as the Sixteenth Amendment. The income tax is levied on individuals as well as corporations. With the creation of the Social Security system in 1935, social insurance taxes became an additional source of federal revenue.

tariff
a tax on imported goods

Before World War II, excise taxes were by far the most important source of revenue, accounting for 49 percent of federal revenues in 1934. Relatively few Americans paid income taxes, and income taxes contributed only modestly to federal coffers. In 1934 individual income taxes accounted for only 14 percent of federal revenues.[18] The need to raise revenue for World War II made the income tax much more important. Congress expanded the base of the income tax so that most Americans paid income taxes after World War II. In addition, income tax withholding was introduced, ensuring an efficient collection system. Table 17.1 on the next page shows several notable shifts that have occurred in taxes since 1960. Social insurance taxes now comprise a much greater share of federal revenues, rising from 15.9 percent of revenues in 1960

Table 17.1

FEDERAL REVENUES BY TYPE OF TAX AS PERCENTAGE OF TOTAL RECEIPTS, 1960–2000

Year	Individual Income Tax	Corporation Income Tax	Social Insurance and Retirement Receipts	Excise Taxes	Other
1960	44.0	23.2	15.9	12.6	4.2
1970	46.9	17.1	23.0	8.1	4.9
1980	47.2	12.5	30.5	4.7	5.1
1990	45.2	9.1	36.8	3.4	5.4
2000 (est.)	48.6	9.8	33.2	3.5	4.8

SOURCE: Office of Management and Budget, *The Budget for Fiscal Year 2001, Historical Tables,* Table 2.2.

to 33.2 percent in 2000. Receipts from corporate income taxes have declined over the same time period, dropping from 23.2 percent of receipts in 1960 to an estimated 9.8 in 2000. The share of the federal individual income tax has risen only modestly from 44 percent in 1960 to 48.6 percent in 2000.

progressive/regressive taxation

taxation that hits the upper income brackets more heavily (progressive) or the lower income brackets more heavily (regressive)

One of the most important features of the American income tax is that it is a "progressive" or a "graduated" tax, with the heaviest burden carried by those most able to pay. A tax is called **progressive** if the rate of taxation goes up with each higher income bracket. A tax is called **regressive** if people in lower income brackets pay a higher proportion of their income toward the tax than people in higher income brackets. For example, a sales tax is deemed regressive because everybody pays at the same rate, so that the proportion of total income paid in taxes goes down as the total income goes up (assuming, as is generally the case, that as total income goes up the amount spent on sales-taxable purchases increases at a lower rate). The Social Security tax is another example of a regressive tax. In 2000, Social Security law applied a tax of 6.2 percent on the first $76,2000 of income for the retirement program and an additional 1.45 percent on all income (without limit) for Medicare benefits, for a total of 7.65 percent in Social Security taxes. This means that a person earning an income of $76,200 pays $5,829.30 in Social Security taxes, a rate of 7.65 percent. But someone earning twice that income, $130,800, pays a total of $6,621 in Social Security taxes, a rate of 5.1 percent. As one's income continues to rise, the amount of Social Security taxes also rises, but the rate, or the percentage of one's income that goes to taxes, declines.

redistribution

a policy whose objective is to tax or spend in such a way as to reduce the disparities of wealth between the lowest and the highest income brackets

Although the primary purpose of the graduated income tax is, of course, to raise revenue, an important second objective is to collect revenue in such a way as to reduce the disparities of wealth between the lowest and the highest income brackets. We call this a policy of **redistribution.** Table 17.2 examines whether the policy of redistribution has been effective. Note first that the gap between the lowest fifth and the highest fifth (i.e., between the poorest and the richest Americans) was growing during the years before truly progressive income taxation was implemented—from a gap of 37.9 percentage points in 1910 to a gap of 45.9 percentage points twenty years later, just before the stock market crash of 1929 and the beginning of the Great Depression. The gap continued to grow for another six years, until the mid-1930s, when a genuine progressive income tax was adopted by Congress. During the next forty years, the gap between the poorest and the richest was reduced from a high of 47.6 percentage points to around 36 percentage points, where it remained until 1980. After 1980 the gap began slowly to spread again. What happened?

First, most of the taxes in the United States are regressive taxes—such as Social Security taxes, state sales taxes, many federal excise taxes, and tariffs—and these taxes tend to neutralize the redistributive impact of the federal and state progressive income taxes. Second, another policy objective of the income tax is the encouragement of the capitalist economy by rewarding investment. The tax laws allow individuals or companies to deduct from their taxable income any money they can justify as an investment or a "business expense"; this gives an incentive to individuals and companies to spend money to expand their production, their advertising, or their staff, and reduces the income taxes businesses have to pay. These kinds of deductions are called incentives or "equity" by those who support them; others call them **"loopholes."** The tax laws of the 1980s actually closed a number of important loopholes in U.S. tax laws. But others still exist—on home mortgages and on business expenses, for example—and others will return, because there is a strong consensus among

loophole
incentive to individuals and businesses to reduce their tax liabilities by investing their money in areas that the government designates

INCOME DISTRIBUTION IN THE UNITED STATES, 1910–99 — Table 17.2

Family income bracket	1910	1929	1935	1944	1950	1960	1970	1980	1990	1995	1999
Lowest fifth	8.3	5.4	4.1	4.9	4.5	4.8	5.4	5.1	4.6	4.4	3.6
Second fifth	11.5	10.1	9.2	10.9	12.0	12.2	12.2	11.6	10.7	10.1	8.9
Third fifth	15.0	14.4	14.1	16.2	17.4	17.8	17.6	17.5	16.7	15.8	14.9
Fourth fifth	19.0	18.8	20.9	22.2	23.5	24.0	23.8	24.3	24.0	23.2	23.2
Highest fifth	46.2	51.3	51.7	45.8	42.6	41.3	41.4	41.6	44.3	46.5	49.4
Gap between lowest and highest fifths	37.9	45.9	47.6	40.9	38.1	36.5	36.0	36.5	39.7	42.1	45.8

Figures are not strictly comparable because of differences in calculating procedures.
SOURCES: Data for 1910–29 and 1944–50 are from Allan Rosenbaum, "State Government, Political Power, and Public Policy: The Case of Illinois" (Ph.D. diss., University of Chicago, 1974), chaps. 10–11. Used by permission. Data for 1935 are from U.S. Department of Commerce, Bureau of the Census, "Family Personal Income Received by Each Fifth and Top 5 Percent of Families and Unattached Individuals, 1929–1964," *Historical Statistics of the United States, Colonial Times to 1970, Bicentennial Edition, Part 2,* Series G319-336 (Washington, D.C.: Government Printing Office, 1975), p. 301. Data for 1960–99 are from U.S. Department of Commerce, Bureau of the Census, *Current Population Reports,* Series P-60 (Washington, D.C.: Government Printing Office), various issues.

members of Congress, both Democrats and Republicans, that businesses often need such incentives. The differences between the two parties focus largely on which incentives are justifiable.[19]

Finally, the tax reform laws of 1981 and 1986 significantly reduced the progressiveness of the federal income tax. Drastic rate reductions were instituted in 1986, and as of 1995, there were five tax brackets, ranging from a 15 percent tax on those in the lowest income bracket to 39.6 percent on those in the highest income bracket. Prior to the 1980s, the highest tax brackets sometimes were taxed at a rate of 90 percent on the last $1 million of taxable income earned in a given year. Meanwhile, Social Security taxes—the most regressive taxes of all—remain high and are likely to be increased.[20]

In every presidential election year, both Democrats and Republicans try to woo voters with pledges of tax cuts. In 2000, presidential candidate George W. Bush proposed a major tax cut, which aimed to reduce the taxes of all Americans. Yet critics charged that his plan would help the wealthiest taxpayers the most, with one third of the tax benefit going to the richest 1 percent of taxpayers. Al Gore put less emphasis on tax cuts. Instead of a large across the board reduction in taxes, he proposed several smaller cuts designed to help taxpayers save for specific purposes, such as education.[21] The projected budget surplus and the relative (if unequally shared) economic prosperity meant that tax cuts did not attract as much voter interest as they had in the 1990s.

Spending and Budgeting The federal government's power to spend is one of the most important tools of economic policy. Decisions about how much to spend affect the overall health of the economy. They also affect every aspect of American life from the distribution of income to the availability of different modes of transportation to the level of education in society. Not surprisingly, the fight for control over spending is one of the most contentious in Washington, as interest groups and politicians strive to create a healthy economy and determine the priorities and appropriate levels of spending. Decisions about spending are made as part of the annual budget process. During the 1990s, when the federal **budget deficit** became a major political issue and when parties were deeply split on spending, the budget process became the focal point of the entire policy making process. Even though the budget deficit has disappeared, the budget continues to dominate the attention of policy makers.

budget deficit
amount by which government spending exceeds government revenue in a fiscal year

The president and Congress have each created institutions to assert control over the budget process. The Office of Management and Budget (OMB) in the Executive Office of the President is responsible for preparing the president's budget. This budget contains the president's spending priorities and the estimated costs of the president's policy proposals. It is viewed as the starting point for the annual debate over the budget. When different parties control the presidency and Congress, the president's budget may have little influence on the budget that is ultimately adopted. For example, when President Clinton presented his budget for fiscal year 2001 to Congress, he found little interest among congressional Republicans who believed the plan called for too much spending and not enough tax cuts.

Congress has its own budget institutions. Congress created the Congressional Budget Office (CBO) in 1974 so that it could have reliable information about the costs and economic impact of the policies it considers. At the same time, Congress established a budget process designed to establish spending priorities and to consider individual expenditures in light of the entire budget. A key element of the process is the annual budget resolution, which designates broad targets for spending. By estimating the costs of policy proposals, Congress hoped to control spending and to reduce deficits. When the congressional budget process proved unable to hold down deficits in the 1980s, Congress established stricter measures to control spending, including "spending caps" that limit spending on some types of programs.

A very large and growing proportion of the annual federal budget is **mandatory spending** or, in the words of the OMB, "relatively uncontrollable." Interest payments on the national debt, for example, are determined by the actual size of the national debt. Legislation has mandated payment rates for such programs as retirement under Social Security, retirement for federal employees, unemployment assistance, Medicare, and farm price supports (see Figure 17.2). These payments increase with the cost of living; they increase as the

mandatory spending
federal spending that is made up of "uncontrollables," budget items that cannot be controlled through the regular budget process

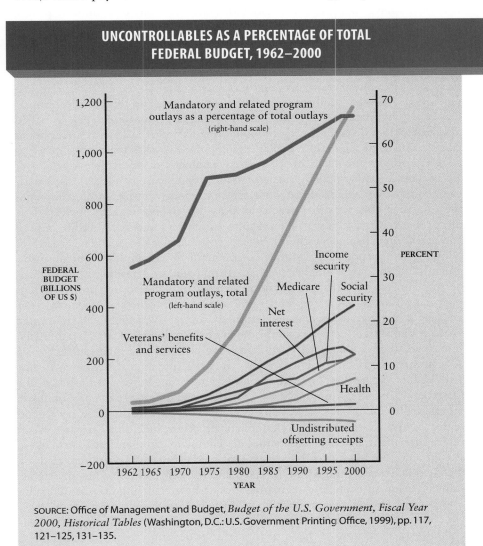

UNCONTROLLABLES AS A PERCENTAGE OF TOTAL FEDERAL BUDGET, 1962–2000

Figure 17.2

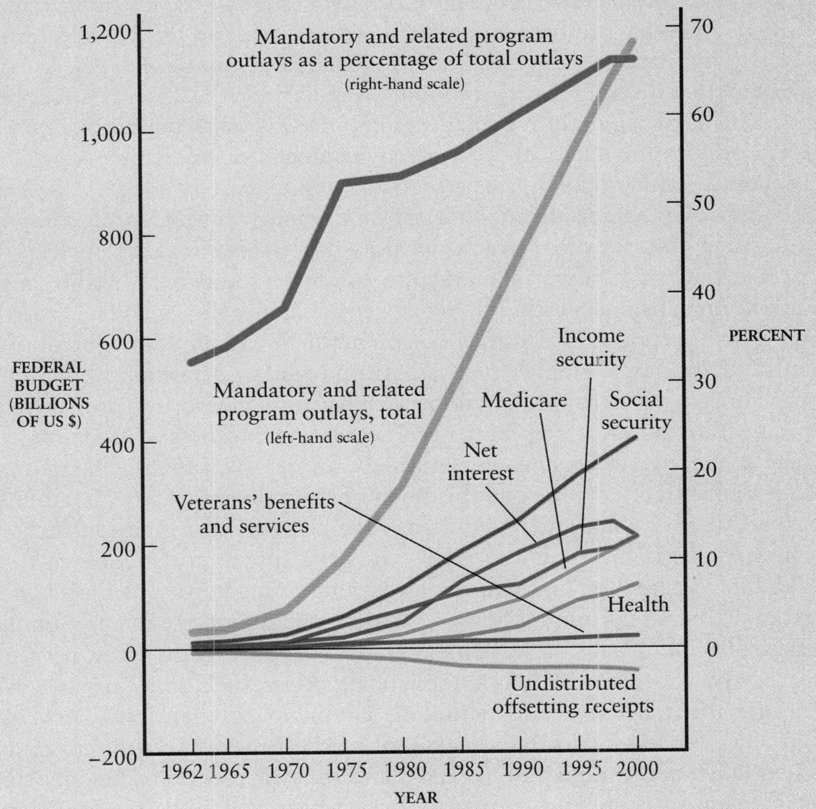

SOURCE: Office of Management and Budget, *Budget of the U.S. Government, Fiscal Year 2000, Historical Tables* (Washington, D.C.: U.S. Government Printing Office, 1999), pp. 117, 121–125, 131–135.

uncontrollables

budgetary items that are beyond the control of budgetary committees and can be controlled only by substantive legislative action in Congress. Some uncontrollables are beyond the power of Congress, because the terms of payments are set in contracts, such as interest on the debt

discretionary spending

federal spending on programs that are controlled through the regular budget process

monopoly

the existence of a single firm in a market that controls all the goods and services of that market; absence of competition

antitrust policy

government regulation of large businesses that have established monopolies

average age of the population goes up; they increase as national and world agricultural surpluses go up. In 1970, 38.6 percent of the total federal budget was made up of these **uncontrollables;** in 1975, 52.5 percent fell into that category; and by 2000, around 66.5 percent was in the uncontrollable category. This means that the national government now has very little **discretionary spending** to increase or decrease spending to counteract fluctuations in the business cycle.

Government spending as a fiscal policy works fairly well when deliberate deficit spending is used to stop a recession and to speed up the recovery period, but it does not work very well in fighting against inflation, because elected politicians are politically unable to make the drastic expenditure cuts necessary to balance the budget, much less to produce a budgetary surplus.

REGULATION AND ANTITRUST POLICY

Americans have long been suspicious of concentrations of economic power. Federal economic regulation aims to protect the public against potential abuses by concentrated economic power in two ways. First, the federal government can establish conditions that govern the operation of big businesses to ensure fair competition. For example, it can require business to make information about its activities and account books available to the public. Second, the federal government can force large businesses to break up into smaller companies if it finds that the company has established a **monopoly.** This is called **antitrust policy.** In addition to economic regulation, the federal government engages in social regulation. Social regulation establishes conditions on businesses in order to protect workers, the environment, and consumers.

Federal regulatory policy was a reaction to public demands. As the American economy prospered throughout the nineteenth century, some companies grew so large that they were recognized as possessing "market power." This meant that they were powerful enough to eliminate competitors and to impose conditions on consumers rather than cater to consumer demand. The growth of billion-dollar corporations led to collusion among companies to control prices, much to the dismay of smaller businesses and ordinary consumers. Small businesses, laborers, farmers, and consumers all began to clamor for protective regulation. Although the states had been regulating businesses in one way or another all along, interest groups turned toward Washington as economic problems appeared to be beyond the reach of the individual state governments. If markets were national, there would have to be national regulation.[22]

The first national regulatory policy was the Interstate Commerce Act of 1887, which created the first national independent regulatory commission, the Interstate Commerce Commission (ICC), designed to control the monopolistic practices of the railroads. Two years later, the Sherman Antitrust Act extended regulatory power to cover all monopolistic practices, including "trusts" or any other agreement between companies to eliminate competition. These were strengthened in 1914 with the enactment of the Federal Trade Act (creating the Federal Trade Commission, or FTC) and the Clayton Act. The only significant addition of economic regulatory policy beyond regulation of interstate trade, however, was the establishment of the Federal Reserve System in 1913, which was given powers to regulate the banking industry along with its general monetary powers. At the same time, public demands to protect consumers led the federal government to enact a more limited number of social regula-

In 1906, Congress passed the New Meat Inspection Act, which required that all meat intended for interstate commerce meet federal health standards. This photo shows a Chicago slaughterhouse immediately following the passage of the act.

tions. As we have seen, Upton Sinclair's best-seller about the meatpacking industry, *The Jungle,* led to the federal meat inspection program in 1906. Two decades later the Food and Drug Administration was set up to test and regulate products viewed as essential to public health.

The modern epoch of comprehensive national regulation began in the 1930s. Most of the regulatory programs of the 1930s were established to regulate the conduct of companies within specifically designated sectors of American industry. For example, the jurisdiction of one agency was the securities industry; the jurisdiction of another was the radio (and eventually television) industry. Another was banking. Another was coal mining; still another was agriculture. At this time Congress also set the basic framework of American labor regulation, including the rules for collective bargaining and the minimum wage.

When Congress turned once again toward regulatory policies in the 1970s, it became still bolder, moving beyond the effort to regulate specific sectors of industry toward regulating some aspect of the entire economy. The scope or jurisdiction of such agencies as the Occupational Safety and Health Administration (OSHA), the Consumer Product Safety Commission (CPSC), and the Environmental Protection Agency (EPA) is as broad and as wide as the entire economy, indeed the entire society.

The most important recent example of federal economic regulation was the government's case against Microsoft. Faced with strong competition from Netscape's Navigator browser software, Microsoft used its near-monopoly of the market for personal computer operating systems "to displace Netscape's

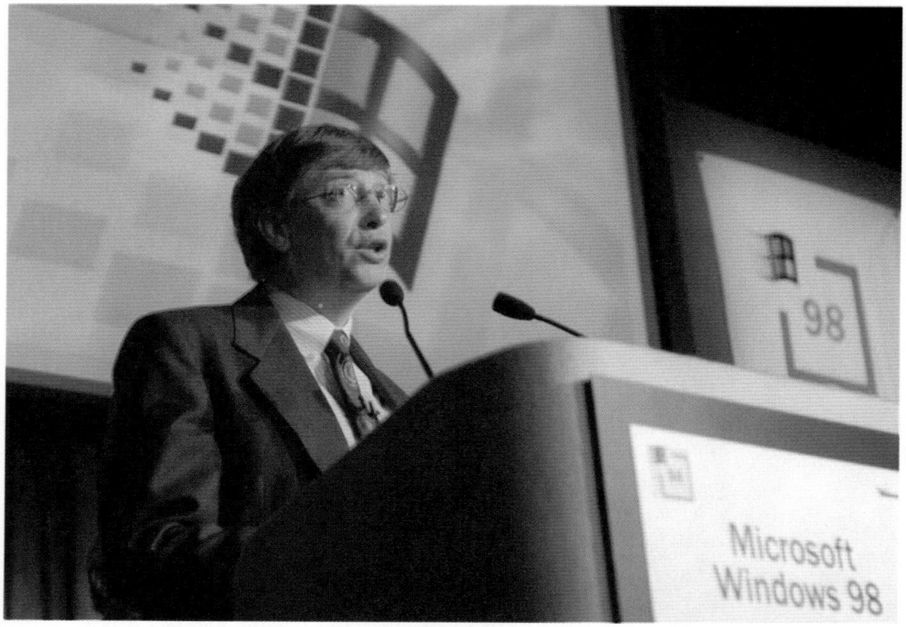

Microsoft chairman Bill Gates discusses his company's operating system, Windows 98. In 1999, the U.S. Justice Department argued that Microsoft's packaging of its Web browser, Internet Explorer, with Windows 98 restricts consumer choice.

Navigator with its own Internet Explorer browser" by requiring that computers run by Microsoft's Windows 98 operating system present users with a preloaded icon for Internet Explorer. Computer manufacturing companies would have to comply or they would "lose their Windows license and thus lose their business. . . ."[23] Such a practice—forcing a vendor to take Explorer in order to carry Windows 98—constitutes "product tying," a violation of antitrust law (the oldest of federal economic regulations). The Justice Department's Antitrust Division went to court and got an injunction to stop Microsoft's strong-arming. Microsoft chairman Bill Gates chose to bargain with the Justice Department in order to hold off further government action.

In November 1999, the federal court ruled that Microsoft had used its monopoly power to harm the consumer by reducing competition and thereby stifling innovation. The judge charged that "Microsoft has demonstrated that it will use its prodigious market power and immense profits to harm any firm that insists on pursuing initiatives that could intensify competition against one of Microsoft's core products."[24] Although Attorney General Janet Reno hailed the ruling as a victory for consumers, some analysts believed it would stifle innovation. The Justice Department recommended that Microsoft be split into two companies, one for the Windows operating system and another for other software applications. Not surprisingly, Microsoft vehemently contested this plan.

deregulation
a policy of reducing or eliminating regulatory restraints on the conduct of individuals or private institutions

By the late 1970s, a reaction against regulation set in. Businesses complained about the burden of the new regulations they confronted and many economists began to argue that excessive regulation was hurting the economy. Congress and the president responded with a wave of **deregulation.** For example, President Reagan went about the task of changing the direction of regulation by way of "presidential oversight." One of his first actions after taking

POLICY DEBATE

Should the Government Regulate Microsoft?

When the giant computer software firm Microsoft came under government scrutiny in the late 1990s for what critics charged were anticompetitive practices, the classic debate over free enterprise versus government regulation reemerged. Throughout the nineteenth century, the prevailing government laissez-faire economic philosophy prevented interference with market forces, resulting in the exercise of unprecedented economic and political power by a handful of corporate giants in such areas as oil, steel, and railroads. The rise of the Progressive era early in the twentieth century ushered in the modern era of government regulation of market practices, as the country came to support the principle of government regulation to protect citizens and reduce market chaos. In the Microsoft case, the Justice Department and nineteen states sued in 1998, charging that the company, headed by Bill Gates, had tied its Internet web browser to its Windows operating system in order to unfairly undercut its competition. Microsoft argued that the browser software was integral to Windows operation and was not a separate product. In November 1999, after almost a year and a half of testimony, a federal judge issued a finding of fact that mostly supported the government's claim of monopolistic practices, but considerable further legal wrangling lay ahead.

Throughout the dispute, Microsoft has maintained that the development of computer software differed from monopolistic practices covered by the Sherman Antitrust Act of 1890—which was used most importantly to break up Standard Oil in 1911—because the computer industry was fast-paced, fluid, and extremely competitive. Too much government interference could squelch critical product development. In addition, Microsoft's copyright on Windows could be compromised by an unfavorable antitrust ruling by forcing the company to alter its product design or reveal design secrets. Further, those whom the government has an interest in protecting—consumers—have been happy with the Microsoft system. Indeed, their interest is in having smooth and uncomplicated access to the Internet, a goal achieved by Microsoft's system. Before this development, consumers faced a chaotic and confusing series of choices that benefited neither the companies nor the consumers. Above all, Microsoft asserted that it must be free to innovate, a process that can only be hampered by government intrusion. If the courts ultimately decide to break Microsoft up into three to five separate companies, the result will be an arbitrary solution to a problem that does not exist, and it will only degrade the computer services so highly sought by industry, government, and consumers.

Government prosecutors argued that the browser software was obviously a separate product from Windows, and the fact that Microsoft gave the browser away for free when its competitors had to charge a fee to turn a profit underscored Microsoft's effort to drive its competition out of the business. While different in particulars, the Microsoft case was the same as past antitrust cases involving widely different sectors of the economy, the government argued, because the company engaged in classic monopolistic practices, including collusion, bribery, exclusionary contracts, and other predatory practices all centering on how Microsoft competed in the marketplace. And, as the federal judge noted in 1999, copyright law did not protect this, or any company, from charges of monopoly. In particular, Microsoft sought to drive its main competitor, Netscape Communications, from the marketplace by designing a product that forced users to use only the Microsoft system. Prosecutors argued that a system like Netscape's could be as technologically compatible with Windows as that of Microsoft. Beyond arguments over technology, a detailed examination of Microsoft e-mails, internal corporate documents, and eyewitness testimony generally supported prosecution claims of arm-twisting monopolistic practices.

In June 2000, federal judge Thomas Penfield Jackson issued his final ruling, in which he sided with the government prosecutors. He ordered the breakup of Microsoft into two companies, one for its Windows operating system, and one for other computer programs and its Internet businesses. He also imposed additional restrictions to make sure that Microsoft would not continue to use its operating systems monopoly to stifle competition. Bill Gates immediately vowed to appeal the ruling.

STUDENT DEBATE

Should the Government Regulate Microsoft?

Yes

For nearly fifteen years, Microsoft has led innovations in computer technology, readily supplying consumers with PC operating systems like Windows 95 and 98. These systems, highly praised for their user-friendliness, have made company chairman and CEO Bill Gates an eye-popping $75 billion fortune, and allowed his stock portfolio to go platinum. Last May, however, the Justice Department, in conjunction with twenty states, initiated an anti-trust lawsuit against his plum operation.

According to the 1890 Sherman Anti-Trust Act, on which the suit takes its basis, no corporation may monopolize any part of the trade or commerce among the several states, or with foreign nations. In other words, it's illegal for any single business to dominate the market for a particular product. In a free market economy, consumers always have the liberty to choose among several manufacturers to supply their product demands. This forces companies to price their merchandise competitively, thus contributing to a healthy economy. A monopoly occurs when a certain manufacturing body grows too large to facilitate this type of fair competition.

After assessing the current evidence, District Court Judge Thomas Penfield Jackson determined that, more likely than not, Gates' firm is guilty of just such an offense. Microsoft enjoys so much power that "it could charge a price for Windows substantially above [that elicited by the existence of] a competitive market," he said. The key to Microsoft's power, Jackson reasoned, lies in the nearly 70,000 software applications the Windows operating system supports. It seems everything finds a home (and an icon) on Gates' desktop, from the simplest card game to any number of word-processing programs, audio players, and Internet browsers. By contrast, Apple's Mac-OS can accommodate only about 12,000 applications—and this is Microsoft's biggest current competition. Something is very wrong with this picture.

Gates, of course, denies all accusations of anticompetitive conduct, maintaining his company competes legally with rival corporations. Um, right. Of course Microsoft is a monopoly. The fact that Windows boasts so many software possibilities makes it impossible for other companies to compete. In Jackson's words, it is "prohibitively costly" for companies like Apple to develop new applications to compete with Windows. As it stands, Microsoft is under no legal obligation to share its technology. This effectively stifles the industry—how many of us can name another PC or Mac operating system on par with Windows? Failing that, who can name another PC or Mac operating system, period?

A court decision against Microsoft could force the software giant to publish the intimate specifications of certain programs. Freely circulating this information would help rival companies produce similar operating systems to eclipse Gates' much-touted applications. The competition will encourage Microsoft to set fairer prices, and perhaps even develop more innovative software applications in an effort to stay one step ahead. In the end, the computing industry will advance significantly.

And why not? After all, communication facilitates both science and business. The truth is, Microsoft has had too solitary a ride on the information superhighway it helped pave. Introducing a little healthy competition to the mix only will benefit the corporation and, of course, the consumers who fuel the computing industry with their hard-earned dollars. With all the genius Bill Gates displays, he'll come up with some way to maintain himself and his company in the technological race. For now, however, he must give the little people a fair chance to succeed.

SOURCE: Kiki Petrosino, "Creating Better Computers by Ending Microsoft Monopoly," *Cavalier Daily* (University of Virginia), November 17, 1999.

No

Charles E. Wilson, Secretary of Defense during the Eisenhower Administration, is best remembered for the quote, "What's good for the country is good for General Motors, and vice versa."

Today, that quote could best be applied to the computer company Microsoft, a company that provides thousands of jobs, billions of dollars in taxes and has revolutionized the computer industry in this country and throughout the world.

Yet despite all the good Microsoft does, it is now under attack from the Department of Justice for antitrust violations. This is not a good thing.

Microsoft is being demonized for daring to market its Internet browser, Internet Explorer, as part of its Windows 98 operating system. This is considered restraint of trade because about 90 percent of the computers on this planet run off of Windows.

Both the federal government and most of Microsoft's major competitors believe that if Microsoft is allowed to market an Internet browser with Windows, no one will have any incentive to buy a competing browser.

This is of course a baseless fear. Microsoft's main competitor in the browser industry, Netscape, already controls 40 percent of the market and its browser is available free on the Internet.

The browser industry is open to competition, which means the company that produces the best product at the cheapest price is going to win.

Microsoft is by no means all powerful. Its main strength is software for personal computers, an important market but one that is declining in importance. This means if Microsoft wants to continue the aggressive expansionist policies that have made it so successful, it is going to have to enter new markets.

Computer industry specialists believe the next major markets will be servers, information appliances, and embedded software systems. These are all markets with established companies that are more than capable of defending themselves and Microsoft has been floundering in its attempts to compete with them.

Microsoft's Win2000 product is already over two years behind schedule (crippling Microsoft's efforts to compete in the critical business server market), Microsoft Network only has two million customers compared to the 16 million held by America On-Line and then there is Microsoft's Web TV, the biggest commercial flop since New Coke. Microsoft is still an immensely powerful company but it faces ferocious competition in most of the markets it will need to expand in to survive.

It is appropriate to expect Microsoft to fight for its life in the marketplace, it is not appropriate to expect it to fight for its life in the courts.

Microsoft provides good products at reasonable prices and in doing so has made computers widely available across the whole country. It pumps billions of dollars into the economy every year, making the entire country richer. It helps facilitate the development of new technologies that improve the lives of everyone.

In other words, Microsoft is good for the country. Which means this antitrust suit has to be bad for the country. Microsoft has achieved its prominence by beating its competition on the open market; it should not be punished for being successful.

With the net value of Microsoft stock currently valued around 400 billion dollars, can the country afford to risk damaging a company that plays that vital of a role in the national economy? Gates is a smart man; he knows if he gets lazy and complacent he will get crushed in the marketplace, which is precisely why he has never gotten lazy and complacent.

His competitors are understandably frustrated and are trying to use the power of the federal government to beat the man they have found to be unbeatable.

Maybe they should work on improving their own products instead? Microsoft makes this country richer, stronger, and better; it should be allowed to continue to do this.

SOURCE: Brendan Guy, "Monopoly Madness," *The Battalion* (Texas A&M University), February 26, 1999.

office was Executive Order 12291, issued February 17, 1981, which gave the OMB the authority to review all proposals by all executive branch agencies for new regulations to be applied to companies or people within their jurisdiction. By this means, Reagan succeeded in reducing the total number of regulations issued by federal agencies to such an extent that the number of pages in the *Federal Register* dropped from 87,000 in 1980 to 49,600 in 1987.[25] Although Presidents Bush and Clinton also favored deregulation as a principle, the number of pages crept up steadily after 1987, reaching 69,680 by 1993. This had dropped slightly to 68,101 by 1994, and by 1996 President Clinton was claiming an additional reduction of 16,000 pages of "unnecessary regulations." These might not show up as 16,000 reduced pages in the *Federal Register,* but they do amount to a substantial reduction in regulation.

In 1993, President Clinton and Vice President Al Gore criticized the vast number of federal regulations, pointing especially to regulations on purchasing everything from aspirin to insect repellent as "outrageous" rules that wasted taxpayers' money. Despite the president's rhetoric, it was the Republicans who sought most vigorously to cut the number of regulations.

Yet, as impressive as the deregulation movement has been, few regulatory programs have actually been terminated. Except for finally fulfilling Reagan's wish to abolish the Interstate Commerce Commission, Congress does not seem to be seriously committed to terminating any major regulatory program or activity.

Is deregulation good economic policy? It depends. In the late 1980s, some states opened the electrical-power industry to competition, which resulted in lower prices. But during the heat wave of summer 1998, electricity prices in cities such as Chicago and Akron, Ohio, fluctuated wildly, producing widespread consumer dissatisfaction. This made some people yearn for a return to traditional regulation; others defended the free market, believing that after a period of adjustment the prices would stabilize.

It is quite unlikely that any president will significantly reduce the level of government regulation for long. There will be cycles of regulation and deregulation because legislators and administrators are responsive to changes in attitudes and sentiments about what needs regulating and by how much. But it is truly unlikely that the overall amount of state and national government regulation in the United States will be significantly reduced.

SUBSIDIES AND CONTRACTING

Subsidies and contracting are the carrots of economic policy. Their purpose is to encourage people to do something they might not otherwise do or to get people to do more of what they are already doing. Sometimes the purpose is merely to compensate people for something done in the past.

subsidies
government grants of cash or other valuable commodities, such as land, to individuals or organizations; used to promote activities desired by the government, to reward political support, or to buy off political opposition

Subsidies **Subsidies** are simply government grants of cash or other valuable commodities, such as land. Although subsidies are often denounced as "giveaways," they have played a fundamental role in the history of government in the United States. Subsidies were the dominant form of public policy of the national government and the state and local governments throughout the nineteenth century. They continue to be an important category of public policy at all levels of government. The first planning document ever written for the national government, Alexander Hamilton's *Report on Manufactures,* was based almost entirely on Hamilton's assumption that American industry could be encouraged by federal subsidies and that these were not only desirable but constitutional.

The thrust of Hamilton's plan was not lost on later policy makers. Subsidies in the form of land grants were given to farmers and to railroad companies to encourage western settlement. Substantial cash subsidies have traditionally been given to shipbuilders to help build the commercial fleet and to guarantee the use of their ships as military personnel carriers in time of war. Policies using the subsidy technique continued to be plentiful in the twentieth century, even during the 1990s when there was widespread public and official hostility toward subsidies. For example, through 1994, the total annual value of subsidies to industry alone was estimated at $53 billion, based on relatively conservative Congressional Budget Office figures.[26] Crop subsidies alone, implemented by the Department of Agriculture, amount to about $6 billion annually.

Subsidies have always been a technique favored by politicians because subsidies can be treated as "benefits" that can be spread widely in response to many demands that might otherwise produce profound political conflict. Subsidies can, in other words, be used to buy off the opposition.

Another secret of the popularity of subsidies is that those who receive the benefits do not perceive the controls inherent in them. In the first place, most of the resources available for subsidies come from taxation. (In the nineteenth century, there was a lot of public land to distribute, but that is no longer the case.) Second, the effect of any subsidy has to be measured somewhat indirectly in terms of what people *would be doing* if the subsidy had not been available. For example, many thousands of people settled in lands west of the Mississippi only because land subsidies were available. Similarly, hundreds of research laboratories exist in universities and corporations only because certain types of research subsidies from the government are available.

Between 1851 and 1871, railroad companies were given more than two hundred million acres of public land by the federal government. The railroads then sold the land at low prices to attract settlers to build along their lines.

Contracting Like any corporation, a government agency must purchase goods and services by contract. The law requires open bidding for a substantial proportion of these contracts because government contracts are extremely valuable to businesses in the private sector and because the opportunities and incentives for abuse are very great. But contracting is more than a method of buying goods and services. Contracting is also an important technique of policy because government agencies are often authorized to use their **contracting power** as a means of encouraging corporations to improve themselves, as a means of helping to build up whole sectors of the economy, and as a means of encouraging certain desirable goals or behavior, such as equal employment opportunity. For example, the infant airline industry of the 1930s was nurtured by the national government's lucrative contracts to carry airmail. A more recent example is the use of government contracting to encourage industries, universities, and other organizations to engage in research and development.

contracting power
the power of government to set conditions on companies seeking to sell goods or services to government agencies

Government-by-contract has been around for a long time, and has always been seen by business as a major source of economic opportunity. In the Pentagon alone, nearly $94 billion was spent in 1994 on contracts with the twenty top defense companies in the United States and abroad. The top company, in terms of the value of its defense contracts, was Lockheed Martin, whose revenues from those defense contracts amounted to $14.4 billion. This represented nearly 63 percent of Lockheed Martin's total annual revenues.

McDonnell Douglas came in second with slightly over $9 billion in 1994. Revenues from defense contracts represented nearly 64 percent of these companies' total annual revenues.[27]

The Politics of Economic Policy Making

- How do political leaders disagree about what the priorities of economic policy should be? What groups have the most influence on economic policy making?
- Does economic policy serve the public interest or special interests?
- How does the debate over economic policy reflect the broader debate over American political values?

Political leaders care deeply about maintaining a healthy economy. As presidents from Herbert Hoover (who presided over the beginning of the Great Depression of the 1930s) to Jimmy Carter (who faced double-digit inflation) discovered, voters will punish politicians for poor economic performance. Yet, even though all politicians want a healthy economy, they often differ in their views about how to attain it. Moreover, politicians disagree about what the priorities of economic policy should be. Democrats and Republicans alike want to promote economic growth but Democrats are generally more concerned about equality and unemployment than are Republicans. Republicans stress the importance of economic freedom for maintaining a healthy economy, whereas Democrats are often more willing to support economic regulation to attain social or environmental objectives. Such differences along party lines are not hard and fast divisions, however. The politics of economic policy making are also greatly influenced by economic ideas.

As we have seen, Keynesian ideas, which used spending and tax policy to promote growth and low unemployment, dominated economic policy in the 1960s and in the first half of the 1970s. The Council of Economic Advisers (CEA) played a central role in economic policy during that time because the president relied on its advice about whether to stimulate or depress the economy. As Keynesian prescriptions became less effective, however, the CEA began to lose its central role. Since the late 1970s, when President Carter began to emphasize monetary policy, the Chairman of the Federal Reserve has occupied the pivotal position in economic policy making. The long run of economic prosperity in the 1990s made longtime Fed Chairman Alan Greenspan into something of a cult figure. Universally praised by Democrats and Republicans alike for his management of the economy, Greenspan has served four four-year terms as head of the Federal Reserve. In addition to the Federal Reserve, the Department of the Treasury plays an important role in making economic policy. Clinton's second Secretary of the Treasury, Robert Rubin, came to Washington from Wall Street and was widely regarded as essential in maintaining investor confidence in the administration. The Treasury Secretary is also an important actor in international trade policy, working to open markets around the world to American products.

The groups that influence decisions about economic policy are as wide ranging as the objectives of policy. Consumer groups, environmentalists, businesses, and labor all attempt to shape economic policy. Of these groups, organized labor and business are the most consistent actors who weigh in across the spectrum of policies. In the past, organized labor was much more important in influencing economic policy than it is today. At the height of their strength in the 1950s, unions represented some 35 percent of the labor force. Newspapers covered the "labor beat" as a critical element of economic reporting and presidents of both parties listened attentively to the views of union leaders. Today, labor unions, representing 13 percent of the labor force, are much less powerful in influencing economic policy. Newspapers no longer routinely cover their activities. Democratic presidents continue to court labor because unions control resources and votes important to Democratic politicians, but labor's overall power has waned. On particular issues, organized labor can still exercise significant influence. For example, labor played a key role in Congress's decision to increase the minimum wage in 1996. Labor has recently sought to boost its political profile and has particularly sought to influence trade policy. Labor and environmentalists, long-time antagonists, have joined to challenge free trade with countries that use unfair labor practices (such as child labor or prison labor) and that degrade their environments. Protesting at the WTO meetings in Seattle in 1999, they proclaimed the new alliance in a banner that read "Teamsters and Turtles, Together At Last!"[28] The protests in Seattle mark trade policy as an area of political contention for the future.

Business organizations are the most consistently powerful actors in economic policy. Business groups are most united around the goal of reducing government regulation. Organizations such as the U.S. Chamber of Commerce, which represents small business, and the Business Roundtable and the National Association of Manufacturers, which represent big business, actively worked to roll back government regulation in the 1970s and 1980s. Big and small business often have different priorities, however. Small businesses are much more opposed to any government regulation that might increase their costs. Big businesses are often more willing to work with government to achieve their goals. When Clinton proposed universal health coverage in 1993, for example, some big businesses supported the plan because they were already providing health insurance to their employees. Small businesses, which are less likely to provide such benefits, strenuously opposed the plan.[29]

In the past decade, small business organizations, such as the National Federation of Independent Business (NFIB) and the Small Business Survival Committee, have become very active politically. Moreover, the number of associations representing small businesses has mushroomed. Small business groups enjoy close ties with congressional Republicans, which gave them unprecedented access to power when Republicans took control of Congress in 1995. They used their influence in Congress to press for decreased regulation and reduced taxes. Such access was not enough to guarantee success but it did ensure that the concerns of small business became factored into policy making. For example, small business bitterly opposed the increased minimum wage passed in 1996, so in order to gain their support for the measure, congressional Republicans inserted a variety of tax cuts for small business into the final bill.

ECONOMIC POLICY AND THE PUBLIC INTEREST

With so many groups seeking to influence economic policy, it is important to ask, does economic policy serve the public interest or does it serve special interests? The answer is not simple because many specific interests, such as business, labor, environmentalists, and consumer groups claim to act in the public interest. The old saying that "What's good for General Motors is good for America," is echoed today by consumer and environmental groups that call themselves public interest groups. Complicating matters further is the fact that the public has an interest in being protected from unregulated markets but it also has an interest in promoting a vibrant and prosperous economy. Decisions about when protection from the market is warranted and when such protection unacceptably impedes markets are at the heart of economic policy making.

Historically, Americans have been more concerned with ensuring economic liberty than with promoting economic equality. The widespread perception of openness and opportunity in American society has made Americans more tolerant of economic inequality than Europeans. American economic policy has rarely aimed to promote economic equality. Instead, economic policy has sought to ensure fairness in the marketplace and protect against the worst side effects of the free market. One of the central ways to ensure fair markets is to guard against the emergence of businesses so large that they can control markets. As we have seen, antitrust policy aims to break up such concentrations of power in the name of free and fair competition. The laws designed to strengthen labor in the 1930s likewise aimed to limit the power of big business by creating a countervailing power; they did not attempt directly to create equality. Consumer and environmental regulations are key ways that economic policy protects against the worst side effects of the free market. Over time, as Americans have grown more concerned about the quality of life, policies in these areas have placed greater restrictions on the market. In a sense, economic prosperity and market success laid the foundation for such restrictions. As Americans felt more economically secure, they could afford to worry about how the economy affected the nonmaterial aspects of their lives, such as the environment. It is no accident that social regulation of the economy took off after the unprecedented prosperity of the 1960s.

Today, the boom in high technology has made the American economy the envy of the world, and free trade has created markets for American products across the globe. Yet, challenges to unrestricted markets have emerged in each domain. The federal government, as we have seen, slapped the Microsoft Corporation with antitrust violations, charging that it is a market-inhibiting monopoly. Although many foes of Microsoft applauded the move, others worry that such government action will actually undermine the free market that it claims to preserve. Similar tensions characterize the free trade debate. Those proposing more restrictions on trade fear that unregulated trade will drive American labor and environmental standards down to the level of their worst competitors. Should American workers have to compete directly with child labor in China or India? they ask. Proponents of free trade argue that restrictions will hurt American workers by restricting markets. American products will not find buyers if we restrict trade, they argue. As these cases show, debates about the appropriate balance between economic liberty and protection

AMERICAN DEMOCRACY IN COMPARATIVE PERSPECTIVE

Two Visions of Western Capitalism

Among the wealthiest and most industrially developed democracies of the world, there have traditionally been two competing visions of capitalism: *Anglo-American* and *continental European.* While both visions encompass the espoused virtues of profit, property, and free enterprise, and while both grow from a core liberal philosophy that views capitalism as the base from which personal liberty and freedom arise, the two visions differ with respect to how they weight the relative values of wealth and distribution. Anglo-American capitalism traditionally values wealth over distribution, while continental European capitalism has historically been buffeted and shaped by struggles over distributional justice. Following from their respective visions of capitalism is the role of government in the market economy.

Anglo-American capitalism is built on a system of values that attributes personal liberty and political democracy to economic prosperity and opportunities for personal wealth. These goals are best achieved through self-interested activities of consumers and producers in an environment fostering maximum personal economic choice, entrepreneurial activity, free trade, and unrestricted markets. According to [this] liberal version of capitalism, a social harmony evolves from the unfettered competition of individuals. Consumers dictate efficient information to producers as to what to supply. In return, producers collect a profit—capital—and in turn invest the profit in even more efficient and diverse ways of producing yet more goods and services for the sovereign and rational consumer, thereby receiving yet more profit for yet more future investment. Wealth is [seen as] a by-product of the harmonious mechanisms of the market, all built upon the rational actions of the consumer in a free society. In [contrast,] government is seen as a force that distorts the efficient harmony of the marketplace. The countries most closely identified with the Anglo-American capitalism model are those countries that trace their lineage to Great Britain, especially the United States, Canada, New Zealand, Ireland, and Australia, and Britain itself.

Continental European capitalism, [on the other hand, grew out of social democracy, a nineteenth-century philosophy that emphasized] building a just system of economic distribution in society, not merely a wealthy society. This entailed a commitment to equalize wealth, control and ultimately diffuse capital's concentration, and empower the working class with their own political parties and labor unions. [Continental European] capitalism was indeed much influenced by a strong social democratic presence in such countries as Germany, France, Italy, Norway, Belgium, Sweden, Austria, and the Netherlands. By the twentieth century, though all continental European democracies were capitalist, the vestiges of social democracy remained visible on the landscape of politics as well as deeply embedded in the social fabric of several countries.

The core logic of social democracy entails a much more salient and active role of government within the market. In theory, the individual and sovereign consumer does not stand alone as in the Anglo-American version of capitalism. Rather, "workers" and individuals in general are part of a community, a society, where responsibilities are shared, risk is diffused, and the virtue of private property, while the centerpiece of all democratic capitalist systems, remains an item to be regulated through government in order to ensure a just market that does not concentrate economic power so starkly as in the Anglo-American democracies. Continental western Europe is, to be sure, capitalist, driven by private competition, individualism, and a free spirit for entrepreneurship and the advancement of private good. Nevertheless, social insurance, publicly controlled benefits, a degree of corporatism (see Chapter 10), and the protection of society from the uncertainties of capitalist competition are central tenets of the social democratic logic of capitalism. Government is seen as a necessary and legitimate partner in the economy and its market—for better or worse.

The degree of [government] regulation [in social democratic economies] has led some critics to argue that social democracy carries with it a heavy cost for its citizens. One such cost is the difficulty of reforming the economy when the world market demands cheaper and different goods than social democratic economies traditionally produce. Not only has this recently led to high unemployment challenges for governments in continental European democracies, but it has meant that many of the unemployed remain so for a much longer period of time than those in the Anglo-American countries.

SOURCES: David Landes, *The Wealth and Poverty of Nations* (New York: Norton, 1998); Adam Przeworski, *Capitalism and Social Democracy* (New York: Cambridge University Press, 1985); Robert Heilbronner, *The Nature and Logic of Capitalism* (New York: Norton, 1985).

from markets are an ongoing feature of American economic policy. Chances of addressing the public interest are greatest when all voices can participate in that debate.

The Citizen's Role

Economic policy is often viewed as the domain of experts. Disputes over economic decision making can appear to be obscure debates conducted in a complicated technical language. Ordinary citizens may feel that they have no way to enter such debates and they may feel unsure about what their real interests are. Yet no area of policy is more fundamental to the lives of the majority of American citizens. Decisions about the economy affect such basic concerns as whether a student can afford to attend college and whether a family can afford to buy a home. How can citizens influence economic policy making?

Despite the often technical nature of economic policy, many major shifts in policy have occurred as a result of citizen action. The initial creation of antitrust laws at the turn of the last century was a response to a widespread public fear that business had grown too big and that its power would hurt consumers. Likewise, the social regulation of the 1960s emerged from the movement of environmental and consumer groups that pressed the government to incorporate new objectives into economic policy making. Politicians are extremely sensitive to what voters think about many aspects of the economy, in particular taxes and inflation. The "tax revolt" that started in California in the late 1970s was launched by ordinary citizens. For the next two decades politicians at all levels of government became very cautious about suggesting new taxes.

If citizens are to be effective actors in economic policy they must evaluate how economic policy proposals affect them. But such judgments are often not straightforward: they involve at least three different dimensions. First, and most simply, is the impact on the individual wallet: does policy hurt or help my budget? Second, citizens must ask, what is the impact of policy on the public services that I rely on? Taxpayers may dislike paying the IRS but they depend on the roads and national defense that government provides and they enjoy the national parks that their taxes support. Finally, citizens must think about how policy reflects their values and their vision about how they want the nation to develop over the long-term. The majority of Americans who earn well above the minimum wage support increases in the minimum wage because such policy is in accordance with their ideas about fairness. They believe in rewarding people who are working and trying to take responsibility for their lives. Such ideas about what is fair are one of the most important ways that public beliefs influence economic policy.

The work of politics is to translate fundamental values into policy. Even though economic policy debates are strewn with often hard-to-grasp technical decisions, citizens can exercise a powerful impact on policy when they partici-

Politics on the Web

In the 1950s, the federal government built a national highway system to promote the nation's growing economy. In the 1970s, the federal government created a new system for communication called the Arpanet, which eventually became the Internet. What future public policies will be needed to foster continued Internet development? If the World Wide Web is to become as widespread as the telephone or the television, the government has an interest in extending Internet access. The national government will likely pay for wiring in areas that might otherwise be ill-served, such as elementary schools, poor communities, and rural areas. Some of these initiatives may be promotional in nature—giving incentives to companies for extending access—whereas others may be regulatory—managing access fees or requiring a certain level of coverage even if it's unprofitable in some areas. Internet issues will occupy a growing piece of the political agenda, in economic as well as other issue areas. The puzzle will be how to regulate the Internet without limiting its economic potential.

www.wwnorton.com/wtp3e

pate. Policy makers rely on citizen participation to clarify the full range of competing objectives that economic policy must try to balance.

GET INVOLVED Shaping Economic Policies Closer to Home

While the views of the citizenry as a whole can influence the direction of economic policy, as an individual you can participate in shaping important economic policies that are decidedly closer to home. Here is one example:

An important arena of economic policy that local governments control is community zoning—the determination of land use in different zones or areas of the community. Some zones may be reserved for residential use, others for commercial and industrial use, still others for mixed use. Local officials may limit the height of buildings in some areas, require space for parks and recreation in other areas, and limit growth and development elsewhere. Local zoning decisions have an immense impact on the economic, social, and cultural life of communities.

Suppose that some developers want to build a ten-story luxury hotel in a residential zone where all buildings are limited to two stories in height. The developers must apply for a zoning variance, which is legal permission to ignore zoning restrictions. They will likely have to defend their application for a variance at public hearings of the zoning board, planning commission, or city council. There, they may argue that the proposed ten-story hotel will be beneficial to the city because it will replace an old dilapidated structure with a modern one, provide jobs and income for local residents, and attract convention and tourist dollars. Often, developers win approval for variances because no one opposes them at public hearings.

If you oppose the construction of a ten-story luxury hotel in your residential neighborhood, you have options. As an individual, you can attend the public hearings, ask questions, and make counterarguments. Unless someone does this, officials may be unaware of residents' concern, for example, that this development will cause traffic congestion and erode the human-scale quality of neighborhood life. As a member or representative of a homeowners association or a tenants organization, you can warn developers that they are being scrutinized and alert public officials that objectionable decisions will become issues during the next election.

Once you have the attention of the policy makers, consider three strategies. One is to oppose the proposed zoning variance. You will have to give reasons why granting it would be a mistake. Also, it will help your cause to publicize your reasons and mobilize broad local support for them. A second strategy is delay. Request that city officials commission a study of the environmental impact of the proposed development on the community. This could help decision makers recognize that the development is a mistake. It also could buy you time to garner greater public support. A third strategy is to lobby for trade-offs. You may suggest that your group will give up its opposition to the zoning variance if the developers (a) reduce the hotel to five stories and (b) pay the costs of converting a nearby empty lot into a neighborhood park. If developers and residents agree, policy makers will likely approve the compromise.

Summary

The study of public policy is necessary for the understanding of government in action. *Policy* is the purposive and deliberate aspect of government in action. The federal government is involved in the economy for four main reasons. First, government action seeks to manage the economy in order to prevent recessions and other major disruptions of economic life. Second, the government acts to protect the welfare and property of individuals. Third, government strives to regulate competition in order to ensure fair and free markets. Finally, the government intervenes to provide public goods, facilities—such as highways—that the state provides because no single market participant can afford to provide those facilities itself.

Views about whether government should be involved in the economy vary widely. Three main schools of economic thought have influenced the beliefs of policy makers about how and how much the federal government should become involved in the economy. The oldest school of thought, the laissez-faire approach, is associated with the Scottish economist Adam Smith. Smith argued that government should leave the economy alone. Laissez-faire ideas dominated American economic policy until the Great Depression of the 1930s. At that time, the prolonged economic slump and high rates of unemployment prompted the federal government to provide jobs for those out of work and to launch other spending programs designed to assist the needy. Rationale for such actions were found in Keynesian ideas. The British economist John Maynard Keynes argued that when the economy declined government could play a positive role by spending or taxing to stimulate the economy. By putting money in the hands of workers who would spend it on their daily needs, the economy could be revived. The third school of thought is called the monetarist school of thought. Often linked to American economist Milton Friedman, this school of thought argues that government should limit its actions to manipulating the supply of money.

Economic policy strives to achieve a variety of often conflicting goals. These include creating a strong and stable economy with high rates of growth, full employment, and low inflation. In addition, economic policy seeks to assist particular business sectors, such as housing and small business. Throughout our nation's history, promotion of international trade has been an important objective of the federal government. Economic policy is also used to achieve social goals. These include the protection of labor, the environment, and consumers. The federal government relies on a diverse assortment of tools in economic policy. Most central today in managing the overall health of the economy are monetary policies. This makes the Federal Reserve Bank's decisions about whether to raise or lower interest rates the most closely watched actions in economic policy. Also of central importance are fiscal policies, which include taxing and spending. Concern about deficits during the 1990s made the federal budget the focus of all policy making in Congress. Regulation and antitrust policy implemented through the Justice Department and various independent regulatory authorities are another widely used tool of economic policy. Finally, the government provides subsidies and issues contracts in order to achieve economic objectives.

Economic policy making is a highly political activity. Many groups are organized to influence economic policy, including organized labor, environmentalists, and consumer advocates. Business lobbies are very influential in debates about economic policy but they are not always in agreement with one another. Big business and small business often have different priorities in economic policy. Reaching the public interest in economic policy making is not a simple matter. The public wants the prosperity that free markets can create but it also wants to be protected from the harms that unregulated markets can inflict.

FOR FURTHER READING

Bryner, Gary C. *Blue Skies, Green Politics: The Clean Air Act of 1990,* revised edition. Washington, D.C.: Congressional Quarterly, 1995.

Friedman, Milton, and Walter Heller. *Monetary versus Fiscal Policy.* New York: Norton, 1969.

Greider, William. *Secrets of the Temple: How the Federal Reserve Runs the Country.* New York: Simon & Schuster, 1987.

Harris, Richard A., and Sidney M. Milkis. *The Politics of Regulatory Change,* 2nd ed. New York: Oxford University Press, 1996.

Kettl, Donald F. *Deficit Politics: Public Budgeting in Its Institutional and Historical Context.* New York: Macmillan, 1992.

Krugman, Paul. *Peddling Prosperity: Economic Sense and Nonsense in the Age of Diminished Expectations.* New York: Norton, 1994.

Schick, Alan. *The Federal Budget: Politics, Policy, Process.* Washington, D.C.: Brookings Institution Press, 1995.

Stein, Robert M., and Kenneth N. Bickers. *Perpetuating the Pork Barrel: Policy Subsystems and American Democracy.* New York: Cambridge University Press, 1995.

Weir, Margaret. *Politics and Jobs: The Boundaries of Employment Policy in the United States.* Princeton, N.J.: Princeton University Press, 1992.

STUDY OUTLINE

1. Public policy is an officially expressed intention backed by a sanction, which can be a reward or a punishment.

Why Is Government Involved in the Economy?

1. At the most basic level, government makes it possible for markets to function efficiently by setting the rules for economic exchange and punishing those who violate the rules.
2. Since the Great Depression of the 1930s, the public has held the government responsible for maintaining a healthy economy.
3. Government protects the welfare and property of individuals by maintaining law and order, creating protection for consumers, and providing protection of private property.
4. Government helps protect markets by regulating competition.
5. Government makes the market economy possible by providing public goods.

Should Government Be Involved in the Economy?

1. There are different theories about whether, how much, and in what ways government should be involved in the economy.
2. Proponents of laissez-faire argue that the economy will flourish if the government leaves it alone.
3. Proponents of Keynesianism argue for an ongoing role for government in the economy by redistributing money and stimulating consumer demand.
4. Proponents of monetarism argue that the role of government in the economy should be limited to regulating the supply of money.

What Are the Goals of Economic Policy?

1. Government strives to achieve multiple economic goals, some of which may conflict with one another.
2. A strong and stable economy is the basic goal of all economic policy. But the key elements of a strong economy—

economic growth, full employment, and low inflation—often appear to conflict with one another.

3. Government promotes business development indirectly through categorical grants and supports specific business sectors with direct subsidies, loans, and tax breaks.
4. The promotion of American goods and services abroad is a long-standing goal of U.S. policy. The most important international organization for promoting free trade today is the World Trade Organization.
5. From the 1930s to the 1980s, the government regulated industrial relations by overseeing union elections and collective bargaining between labor groups and management. But more recently, with the exception of the minimum wage, the government has significantly reduced its involvement in industrial relations.
6. Environmental protection laws are part of economic policy because they regulate the activity of virtually every aspect of the economy.
7. The federal government plays an active role in protecting consumers from unsafe products.

What Are the Tools of Economic Policy?

1. Monetary policies manipulate the growth of the entire economy by controlling the availability of money to banks through the Federal Reserve System.
2. Fiscal policies include the government's taxing and spending powers.
3. During the nineteenth century, the federal government received most of its revenue from a single tax, the tariff. Since then, the federal government added new sources of tax revenue, the most important being the income tax and social insurance taxes. One of the most important features of the American income tax is that it is a progressive tax.
4. The federal government's power to spend is one of the most important tools of economic policy because spending decisions affect every aspect of the economy. These decisions, which are typically contentious, are made as part of the annual budget process involving the president and Congress.
5. The federal government can establish conditions that govern the operation of big businesses to ensure fair competition and can force large monopolies to break up into smaller companies. In addition to economic regulation, the federal government can also impose conditions upon businesses in order to protect workers, the environment, and consumers.
6. By the late 1970s, a reaction against regulation set in. Though the deregulation movement has resulted in a reduction in the amount of regulatory laws, few regulatory programs have actually been terminated.
7. Subsidies and contracting are the carrots of economic policy. Their purpose is to encourage people to do something they might not otherwise do or to get people to do more of what they are already doing.

The Politics of Economic Policy Making

1. Politicians disagree about what the priorities of economic policy should be. While both Democrats and Republicans want to promote economic growth, Republicans stress the importance of maintaining economic freedom while Democrats are more willing to support economic regulation to attain social or environmental objectives.
2. Consumer groups, environmentalists, businesses, and labor all attempt to shape economic policy, though business groups are the most consistently influential today.
3. Historically, Americans have been more concerned about ensuring economic liberty than with promoting economic equality, though debates about the appropriate balance between the two are an ongoing feature of economic policy in the United States.

PRACTICE QUIZ

1. The argument for laissez-faire was first elaborated by
   a) James Madison.
   b) Adam Smith.
   c) Alan Greenspan.
   d) Milton Friedman.
2. Which of the following economic perspectives argues for an ongoing role for government in the economy?
   a) laissez-faire
   b) Keynesianism
   c) monetarism
   d) rational expectations
3. The theories of which economist were used to help justify the increase in government spending during the New Deal?
   a) John Maynard Keynes
   b) Milton Friedman
   c) Robert Lucas
   d) Alan Greenspan
4. Monetary policy is handled largely by
   a) Congress.
   b) the president.
   c) the Department of the Treasury.
   d) the Federal Reserve System.

5. Monetary policy seeks to influence the economy through
   a) taxing and spending.
   b) the availability of credit and money.
   c) foreign exchange of currency.
   d) administrative regulation.
6. A situation in which the government attempts to affect the economy through taxing and spending is an example of
   a) an expropriation policy.
   b) a monetary policy.
   c) a fiscal policy.
   d) eminent domain.
7. A tax that places a greater burden on those who are better able to afford it is called
   a) regressive.
   b) progressive.
   c) a flat tax.
   d) voodoo economics.
8. Which groups currently have the most political influence in economic policy making?
   a) consumer groups
   b) labor unions
   c) business groups
   d) environmental groups
9. Which of the following is *not* a reason that government forms and changes regulatory policies?
   a) public opinion
   b) politics
   c) morality
   d) budget surplus
10. Which of the following is *not* one of the reasons why government is involved in the economy?
    a) to guarantee economic equality
    b) to protect property
    c) to regulate competition
    d) to provide public goods

CRITICAL THINKING QUESTIONS

1. Think about a specific instance of government intervention in the American economy since the New Deal. What economic policy tool was used? What other tools might have been used? More generally, think about different economic perspectives about the role of government in the economy. In your opinion, when is government action in the economy necessary?
2. One of the chief functions of government is the collection of revenue. Describe the system of taxation used by the federal government. What are the multiple goals of tax policy in America? How else might some of these goals be achieved? In what ways is the tax system in the United States progressive? In what ways is it regressive? Is tax reform necessary? Why or why not?

KEY TERMS

antitrust policy (p. 684)
budget deficit (p. 682)
categorical grants (p. 672)
contracting power (p. 691)
deregulation (p. 686)
discretionary spending (p. 684)
federal funds rate (p. 679)
Federal Reserve System (p. 677)
fiscal policies (p. 679)
General Agreement on Tariffs and Trade (GATT) (p. 673)
Gross Domestic Product (GDP) (p. 666)
inflation (p. 670)
Keynesianism (p. 664)
laissez-faire capitalism (p. 663)
loophole (p. 681)
mandatory spending (p. 683)
monetarism (p. 665)
monetary policies (p. 677)
monopoly (p. 684)
most favored nation status (p. 673)
North American Free Trade Agreement (NAFTA) (p. 673)
open-market operations (p. 678)
progressive/regressive taxation (p. 680)
public goods (p. 662)
public policy (p. 658)
redistribution (p. 680)
reserve requirement (p. 678)
subsidies (p. 690)
tariff (p. 679)
uncontrollables (p. 684)
World Trade Organization (WTO) (p. 673)

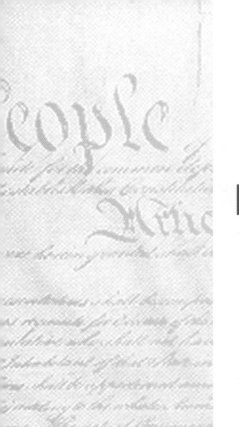

18 Social Policy

★ The Welfare State

What type of welfare system existed before the creation of the welfare state in the 1930s?

What are some important examples of contributory and noncontributory welfare programs?

What two major welfare programs were created in 1965? What were the long-term effects of these programs?

Has welfare reform been successful? Why or why not?

How do we pay for the welfare state?

★ Who Gets What from Social Policy?

Which groups receive the most benefits from social policies? Which groups receive the fewest?

How effectively does social policy reach the groups that are most likely to be poor?

★ Breaking the Cycle of Poverty

What policies are aimed at helping the poor break out of poverty?

Which policies have been most successful?

★ The Welfare State and American Values

How has the formation of social policy reflected the debate over liberty, equality, and democracy?

STUDENTS AND POLITICS

SINCE the time of the Founding, Americans have been sharply divided about the power of the government. Conflict over the role and policies of the national government remains at the heart of American politics today. For instance, X-PAC, a political action committee that aims to represent the economic and political needs of "Generation X," has made reform of Social Security its primary goal. Arguing that Social Security reform "is the single most pressing issue facing our generation," leaders of the group believe the current system will saddle young people with high taxes throughout their working lives but will not provide security for them when it is their turn to retire. Indeed, another youth organization opposed to Social Security in its present form, Third Millennium, sponsored a poll that showed that more eighteen- to thirty-four-year-olds believe UFOs exist (46 percent) than believe Social Security will exist by the time they retire (28 percent).

The 2030 Center, another youth organization, sees the matter very differently. Pressing for "stronger bonds between generations," this organization argues that Social Security requires only minor reforms. It believes that generational tension over Social Security has been mostly manufactured by private interests that stand to gain if Social Security is radically reformed. Declaring that "we are all in it together," the 2030 Center argues instead that greater public investment will provide a more prosperous future for Americans of all ages.[1]

These sharp divisions among groups claiming to represent young people reveal how difficult it is to reach agreement around social policies even for groups that claim to represent the same constituency. And even when fundamental ideals are widely shared, there is rarely consensus on how those ideals should be reflected in social policy.

If there is one widely shared American ideal, it is the belief in **equality of opportunity:** the freedom to use whatever talents and wealth one has to reach one's fullest potential. This ideal is enshrined in the Declaration of Independence:

equality of opportunity
a widely shared American ideal that all people should have the freedom to use whatever talents and wealth they have to reach their fullest potential

> We hold these truths to be self-evident, that all men are created equal, that they are endowed by their Creator with certain unalienable Rights, that among these are Life, Liberty, and the pursuit of Happiness.

What Thomas Jefferson, the Declaration's author, meant is that all individuals have the right to pursue happiness, in fact, an *equal* right to pursue happiness. But what does the equal right to pursue happiness mean in practice and what role should the government play in securing it? These questions are at the heart of debates about social policy.

Social policies promote a range of public goals. The first is to protect against the risks and insecurities that most people face over the course of their lives. These include illness, disability, temporary unemployment, and the reduced earning capability that comes with old age. Most spending on social welfare in the United States goes to programs, such as Social Security and medical insurance for the elderly, that serve these purposes. These are widely regarded as successful and popular programs. They are the least controversial areas of social spending, although the debates about funding Social Security reveal that even widely agreed upon policies can generate conflict. Such conflicts over how to achieve security against risks has prevented the United States from adopting universal health insurance. Despite the fact that most Americans support a public role in guaranteeing health coverage, disputes over how this should be done have blocked repeated efforts at health reform.

More controversial have been the second two goals of social policy: promoting equality of opportunity and assisting the poor. Americans admire the ideal of equal opportunity; in practice it poses problems because equality of opportunity inevitably means *in*equality of results or outcomes. One of the obvious reasons for this is inequalities in talent. But in the real world, talent is not the only differentiating factor. Another explanation is past inequality—the inequality of past generations visited on the present one. This is generally called social class, or the class system.

Finally, there is prejudice pure and simple. This includes racial and religious bias, ethnocentrism, and traditionalist attitudes toward the roles of women. Some of these prejudices are caused by the class system, because social class separates people, and their ignorance of each other breeds anxiety and stereotyping.

What should government do to address such past inequalities that hinder equality of opportunity today? What kind of assistance is fair? There is no general agreement: groups that have suffered from past inequality generally support much more extensive government action to promote equality of opportunity than do others. Yet most Americans support some government action, especially those that involve education.

The third goal of social policy—to alleviate poverty—has long generated controversy in the United States. Americans take pride in the strong work ethic and prize the value of self-sufficiency. As a result, the majority of Americans express suspicions that the able-bodied poor will not try hard enough to support themselves if they are offered too much assistance or if they receive the wrong kind of assistance. Yet, there is also recognition that poverty may be the product of past inequality of opportunity. People in the bottom income brackets are disproportionately composed of members of groups who have been deprived of opportunities to pursue their interests and their happiness. And, it is undeniably true as well that in today's America, millions of people are born, live, and will die in poverty, and may realistically expect their children to do the same.

For example, although many African Americans have improved their economic situations over the past few decades, *as a group* African Americans remain economically deprived. In 1998, the per capita income for white Americans was $21,394, but the per capita income for blacks was more than $8,000 less, just $12,957.[2] For Latinos, who had a per capita income of $11,434, the difference was even greater. In 1998, one eighth of the U.S. population—34.5 million people—lived in what the government defines as poverty (for a family of four, an income of about $16,660). Looked at according to race, the figures were strikingly different: 8.2 percent of whites lived below the poverty level, but 26.1 percent of all African Americans and 25.6 percent of all Latinos lived in poverty (see Figure 18.1). The connection between poverty and equal opportunity complicates decisions about how to address poverty. How can we reconcile our desire to promote self-sufficiency with our ideals of fairness and equal opportunity?

Such questions become even more troublesome when we realize that 39 percent of the poor are children. In 1998, nearly one-fifth of all children in America—18.9 percent—lived in poverty. When broken down by race the numbers reveal that while one in ten white children lives in poverty, more than one in three of all black and Latino children live in officially defined poverty. Surely children cannot be faulted for failing to support themselves. How can we assist poor children in ways that are consistent with our values?

Since the 1960s, a variety of educational programs and income assistance policies have sought to end poverty and promote equal opportunity. Much progress has been made toward these goals. However, the disproportionate rates of poverty among minorities suggest that our policies have not solved the problem of unequal opportunity. Likewise, the high rates of child poverty challenge us to find new ways to assist the poor.

There is no way to know precisely when the government ought to be called upon and what the government ought to do to help individuals secure the right to pursue their own happiness. Economic and social transformations pose new challenges and often alter public views about what government should do. In the 1930s, a deep and widespread economic depression created broad public

PERCENTAGE OF AMERICANS LIVING BELOW THE POVERTY LINE, 1998

Figure 18.1

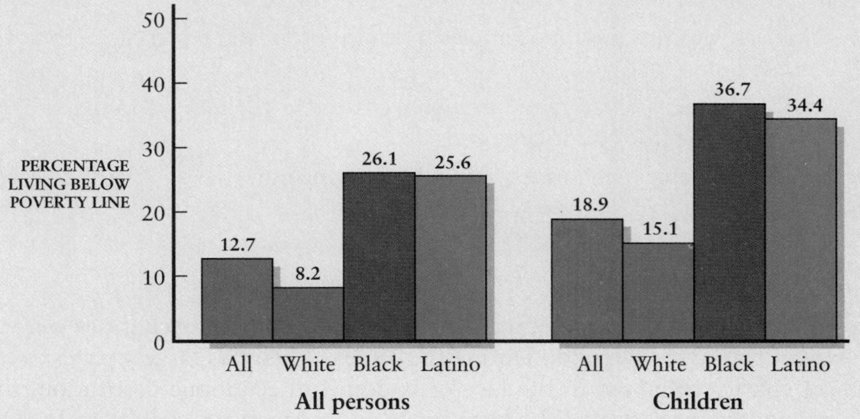

SOURCE: U.S. Bureau of the Census, Current Population Reports, Series P 60–207, *Poverty in the United States: 1998* (U.S. Government Printing Office, 1999).

support for new programs such as federal unemployment insurance. Today, the increased numbers of women in the labor force and the growth in single-parent households have prompted calls for more government assistance to help people combine work and family responsibilities more effectively. Yet there is no agreement on what government should do. Likewise, as the economy has changed, inequality among working people has grown. Should the government address such inequality? If so, with what measures? Shifting patterns of risk and opportunity provoke new demands from citizens and, in so doing, place social policy issues at the center of national politics.

- ***The first section of this chapter will deal with policies concerned with economic insecurity.*** Most of these come under the conventional label of "social welfare policy" or "the welfare state." We will also look at how the welfare state is financed.
- ***The second section analyzes who benefits from social policies.*** In this section, we also assess how effectively welfare policies help the poor.
- ***The third section looks at policies aimed at permanently changing the status of America's poorest citizens.*** Through education, job training, housing assistance, and health care, governments in America help the poor break the cycle of poverty.
- ***Last, we will consider how the welfare state in America reflects (or does not reflect) the values of liberty, equality, and democracy.*** Citizens have an opportunity to influence the debate over social policies, although most Americans tend to take a pragmatic perspective that strikes a balance among these core political ideals.

The Welfare State

- What type of welfare system existed before the creation of the welfare state in the 1930s?
- What are some important examples of contributory and noncontributory welfare programs?
- What two major welfare programs were created in 1965? What were the long-term effects of these programs?
- Has welfare reform been successful? Why or why not?
- How do we pay for the welfare state?

For much of American history, local governments and private charities were in charge of caring for the poor. During the 1930s, when this largely private system of charity collapsed in the face of widespread economic destitution, the federal government created the beginnings of an American welfare state. The idea of the welfare state was new; it meant that the national government would oversee programs designed to promote economic security for all Americans—not just for the poor. The American system of social welfare comprises many different policies enacted over the years since the Great Depression. Because each program is governed by distinct rules, the kind and level of assistance available varies widely.

THE HISTORY OF THE WELFARE SYSTEM

There has always been a welfare system in America. But until 1935, it was almost entirely private, composed of an extensive system of voluntary philanthropy through churches and other religious groups, ethnic and fraternal societies, communities and neighborhoods, and philanthropically inclined rich individuals. Most often it was called "charity," and although it was private and voluntary, it was thought of as a public obligation.

There were great variations in the generosity of charity from town to town, but one thing seems to have been universal: the tradition of distinguishing between two classes of poverty—the "deserving poor" and the "undeserving poor." The deserving poor were the widows and orphans and others rendered dependent by some misfortune, such as the death or serious injury of the family's breadwinner in the course of honest labor. The undeserving poor were able-bodied persons unwilling to work, transients new to the community, and others of whom, for various reasons, the community did not approve. This private charity was a very subjective matter: the givers and their agents spent a great deal of time and resources examining the qualifications, both economic and moral, of the seekers of charity.

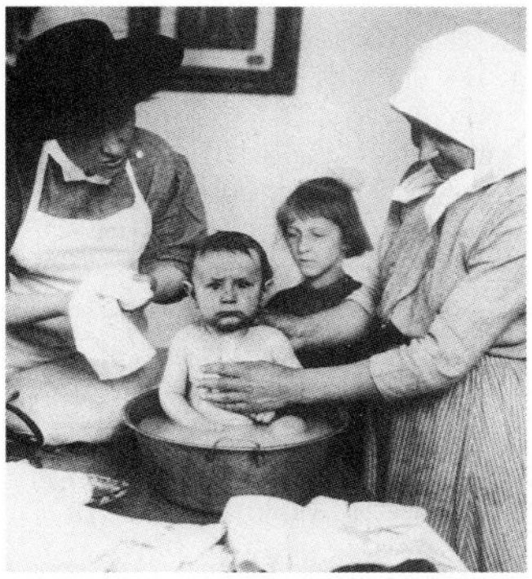

Chicago's Hull House was one of the most famous settlement houses in the early twentieth century. There, social workers instructed the poor in methods of hygiene and child rearing.

Much of the private charity was given in cash, called "outdoor relief." But because of fears that outdoor relief spawned poverty rather than relieving or preventing it, many communities set up settlement houses and other "indoor relief" institutions. Some of America's most dedicated and unselfish citizens worked in the settlement houses, and their efforts made a significant contribution to the development of the field of social work.

A still larger institution of indoor relief was the police station, where many of America's poor sought temporary shelter. But even in the severest weather, the homeless could not stay in police stations for many nights without being jailed as vagrants.[3] Indeed, the settlement houses and the police departments were not all that different in their approaches, since social workers in those days tended to consider "all social case work [to be] mental hygiene."[4] And even though not all social workers were budding psychiatrists, "it was true that they focused on counseling and other preventive techniques, obscuring and even ignoring larger structural problems."[5]

The severe limitations on financing faced by private charitable organizations and settlement houses slowly produced a movement by many groups toward public assumption of some of these charitable or welfare functions. Workers' compensation laws were enacted in a few states, for example, but the effect of such laws was limited because they benefited only workers injured on the job, and of them, only those who worked for certain types of companies. A more important effort, one that led more directly to the modern welfare state, was public aid to mothers with dependent children. Beginning in Illinois in 1911, the movement for mother's pensions spread to include forty states by 1926. Initially, such aid was viewed as simply an inexpensive alternative to providing "indoor relief" to mothers and their children. Moreover, applicants not only had to pass a rigorous means test, but also had to prove that they were deserving, because the laws provided that assistance would be provided only to individuals who were deemed to be "physically, mentally, and morally fit." In most states, a mother was deemed unfit if her children were illegitimate.[6]

In effect, these criteria proved to be racially discriminatory. Many African Americans in the South and ethnic immigrants in the North were denied benefits on the grounds of "moral unfitness." Furthermore, local governments were allowed to decide whether to establish such pension programs. In the South, many counties with large numbers of African American women refused to implement assistance programs.

In the early days of the Depression, much of the available assistance for the destitute was provided by private groups, through projects such as this soup kitchen in New York City.

Despite the spread of state government programs to assume some of the obligation to relieve the poor, the private sector remained dominant until the 1930s. Even as late as 1928, only 11.6 percent of all relief granted in fifteen of the largest cities came from public funds.[7] Nevertheless, the various state and local public experiences provided guidance and precedents for the national government's welfare system, once it was developed.

The traditional approach, dominated by the private sector with its severe distinction between deserving and undeserving poor, crumbled in 1929 before the stark reality of the Great Depression. During the Depression, misfortune became so widespread and private wealth shrank so drastically that private charity was out of the question and the distinction between deserving and undeserving became impossible to draw. Around 20 percent of the workforce immediately became unemployed; this figure grew as the Depression stretched into years. Moreover, few of these individuals had any monetary resources or any family farm on which to fall back. Banks failed, wiping out the savings of millions who had been prudent enough or fortunate enough to have any savings at all. Thousands of businesses failed as well, throwing middle-class Americans onto the bread lines along with unemployed laborers, dispossessed farmers, and those who had never worked in any capacity whatsoever. The Great Depression proved to Americans that poverty could be a result of imperfections in the economic system as well as of individual irresponsibility. It also forced Americans to alter drastically their standards regarding who was deserving and who was not.

Once poverty and dependency were accepted as problems inherent in the economic system, a large-scale public policy approach was not far away. By the time the Roosevelt administration took office in 1933, the question was not whether there was to be a public welfare system, but how generous or restrictive that system would be.

FOUNDATIONS OF THE WELFARE STATE

If the welfare state were truly a state, its founding would be the Social Security Act of 1935. This act created two separate categories of welfare: contributory and noncontributory. Table 18.1 lists the key programs in each of these categories, with the year of their enactment and the most recent figures on the number of Americans they benefit and their cost to the federal government.

contributory programs
social programs financed in whole or in part by taxation or other mandatory contributions by their present or future recipients. The most important example is Social Security, which is financed by a payroll tax

Contributory Programs The category of welfare programs that are financed by taxation can justifiably be called "forced savings"; these programs force working Americans to set aside a portion of their current earnings to provide income and benefits during their retirement years. These **contributory pro-**

Table 18.1

PUBLIC WELFARE PROGRAMS

Type of Program	Year enacted	Number of recipients in 1998 (in millions)	Federal outlays in 1998 (in billions)
Contributory (Insurance) System			
Old Age, Survivors, and Disability Insurance	1935	44.2	$375.0
Medicare*	1965	38.4	$214.0
Unemployment Compensation*	1935	7.3	$19.7
Noncontributory (Public Assistance) System			
Medicaid*	1965	33.6	$123.6
Food Stamps	1964	19.8	$16.9
Supplemental Security Income (cash assistance for aged, blind, disabled)	1974	6.5	$29.0
Housing Assistance to low-income families**	1937	5.0†	$25.1
School Lunch Program	1946	26.6	$5.1
Temporary Assistance to Needy Families*	1996	6.8***	$16.5

†Number of households
*1997
**1996
***June 1999
SOURCE: All data (except TANF expenditure) is from U.S. Census Bureau, Statistical Abstract of the United States 1999 (US GPO, 1999). TANF expenditure is from Budget of the United States Government, Fiscal Year 1999, pp. 223–227, www.access.gpo.gov (accessed January 21, 2000).

Social Security
a contributory welfare program into which working Americans contribute a percentage of their wages, and from which they receive cash benefits after retirement

grams are what most people have in mind when they refer to **Social Security** or social insurance. Under the original contributory program, old-age insurance, the employer and the employee were each required to pay equal amounts, which in 1937 were set at 1 percent of the first $3,000 of wages, to be deducted from the paycheck of each employee and matched by the same amount from the employer. This percentage has increased over the years; the contribution is now 7.65 percent subdivided as follows: 6.20 percent on the first $72,600 of income for Social Security benefits, plus 1.45 percent on all earnings for Medicare.[8]

Social Security may seem to be a rather conservative approach to welfare. In effect, the Social Security tax, as a forced saving, sends a message that people cannot be trusted to save voluntarily in order to take care of their own needs. But in another sense, it is quite radical. Social Security is not real insurance; workers' contributions do not accumulate in a personal account, like they would in an annuity. Consequently, contributors do not receive benefits in proportion to their own contributions, and this means that there is a redistribution of wealth occurring. In brief, Social Security mildly redistributes wealth

Medicare
a form of national health insurance for the elderly and the disabled

indexing
periodic process of adjusting social benefits or wages to account for increases in the cost of living

cost-of-living adjustments (COLAs)
changes made to the level of benefits of a government program based on the rate of inflation

noncontributory programs
social programs that provide assistance to people based on demonstrated need rather than any contribution they have made

Aid to Families with Dependent Children (AFDC)
federal funds, administered by the states, for children living with parents or relatives who fall below state standards of need. Replaced in 1996 by TANF

Temporary Assistance to Needy Families (TANF)
a federal block grant that replaced the AFDC program in 1996

means testing
a procedure by which potential beneficiaries of a public assistance program establish their eligibility by demonstrating a genuine need for the assistance

from higher- to lower-income people, and it quite significantly redistributes wealth from younger workers to older retirees.

Congress increased Social Security benefits every two or three years during the 1950s and 1960s. The biggest single expansion in contributory programs since 1935 was the establishment in 1965 of **Medicare,** which provides substantial medical services to elderly persons who are already eligible to receive old-age, survivors', and disability insurance under the original Social Security system. In 1972, Congress decided to end the grind of biennial legislation to increase benefits by establishing **indexing,** whereby benefits paid out under contributory programs would be modified annually by **cost-of-living adjustments** (**COLAs**) designed to increase benefits to keep up with the rate of inflation. But, of course, Social Security taxes (contributions) also increased after almost every benefit increase. This made Social Security, in the words of one observer, "a politically ideal program. It bridged partisan conflict by providing liberal benefits under conservative financial auspices."[9] In other words, conservatives could more readily yield to the demands of the well-organized and ever-growing constituency of elderly voters if benefit increases were automatic; liberals could cement conservative support by agreeing to finance the increased benefits through increases in the regressive Social Security tax rather than out of the general revenues coming from the more progressive income tax. (See Chapter 17 for a discussion of regressive and progressive taxes.)

Noncontributory Programs Programs to which beneficiaries do not have to contribute—**noncontributory programs**—are also known as "public assistance programs," or, derisively, as "welfare." Until 1996, the most important noncontributory program was **Aid to Families with Dependent Children** (**AFDC**)—originally called Aid to Dependent Children, or ADC—which was founded in 1935 by the original Social Security Act. In 1996, Congress abolished AFDC and replaced it with the **Temporary Assistance to Needy Families** (**TANF**) block grant. Eligibility for public assistance is determined by **means testing,** a procedure that requires applicants to show a financial need for assistance. Between 1935 and 1965, the government created programs to provide housing assistance, school lunches, and food stamps to other needy Americans.

As with contributory programs, the noncontributory public assistance programs also made their most significant advances in the 1960s and 1970s. The largest single category of expansion was the establishment in 1965 of **Medicaid,** a program that provides extended medical services to all low-income persons who have already established eligibility through means testing under AFDC or TANF. Noncontributory programs underwent another major transformation in the 1970s in the level of benefits they provide. Besides being means tested, noncontributory programs are federal rather than national; grants-in-aid are provided by the national government to the states as incentives to establish the programs (see Chapter 4). Thus, from the beginning there were considerable disparities in benefits from state to state. The national government sought to rectify the disparities in levels of old-age benefits in 1974 by creating the **Supplemental Security Income** (**SSI**) program to augment benefits for the aged, the blind, and the disabled. SSI provides uniform minimum benefits across the entire nation and includes mandatory COLAs. States are allowed to be more generous if they wish, but no state is permitted to provide

VARIATIONS IN STATE SPENDING ON TANF BENEFITS — **Figure 18.2**

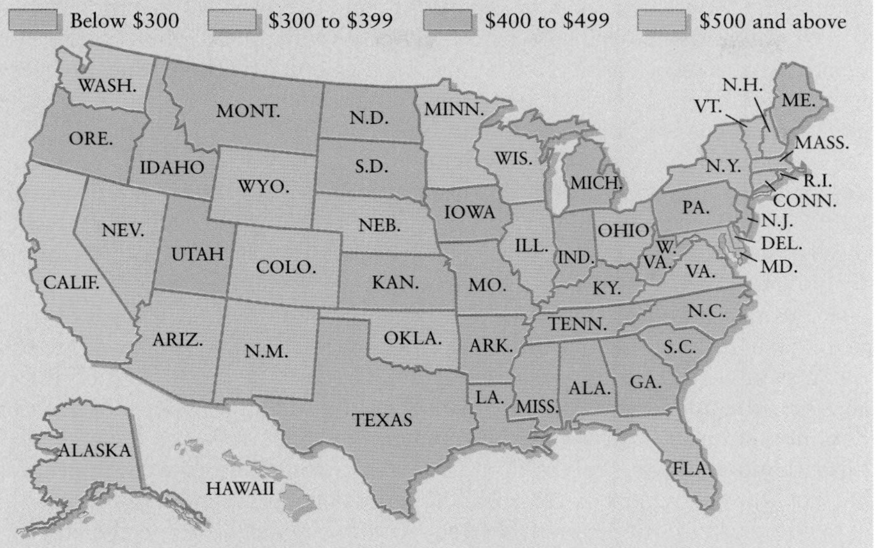

SOURCE: Ways and Means Committee Print, WMCP:105-7, *1998 Green Book* from U.S. GPO Online via GPO Access at http://access.gpo.gov/congress/wm001.html (accessed June 19, 1998).

benefits below the minimum level set by the national government. As a result, twenty-five states increased their own SSI benefits to the mandated level.

The new TANF program is also administered by the states and, like the old-age benefits just discussed, benefit levels vary widely from state to state (see Figure 18.2). For example, although the median national "standard of need" for a family of three was $542 per month (55 percent of the poverty-line income) in 1998, the states' monthly TANF benefits varied from $170 in Mississippi to $923 in Alaska.[10]

The number of people receiving AFDC benefits expanded in the 1970s, in part because new welfare programs had been established in the mid-1960s: Medicaid (discussed earlier) and **food stamps,** which are coupons that can be exchanged for food at most grocery stores. These programs provide what are called **in-kind benefits**—noncash goods and services that would otherwise have to be paid for in cash by the beneficiary. In addition to simply adding on the cost of medical services and food to the level of benefits given to AFDC recipients, the possibility of receiving Medicaid benefits provided an incentive for poor Americans to establish their eligibility for AFDC, which would also establish their eligibility to receive Medicaid. At the same time, the government significantly expanded its publicity efforts to encourage the dependent unemployed to establish their eligibility for these various programs.

Another, more complex reason for the growth of AFDC in the 1970s was that it became more difficult for the government to terminate people's AFDC

Medicaid
a federally financed, state-operated program providing medical services to low-income people

Supplemental Security Income (SSI)
a program providing a minimum monthly income to people who pass a "means test" and who are sixty-five or older, blind, or disabled. Financed from general revenues rather than from Social Security contributions

food stamps
coupons that can be exchanged for food at most grocery stores; the largest in-kind benefits program

in-kind benefits
goods and services provided to needy individuals and families by the federal government

entitlement
eligibility for benefits by virtue of a category of benefits defined by legislation

benefits for lack of eligibility. In the 1970 case of *Goldberg v. Kelly,* the Supreme Court held that the financial benefits of AFDC could not be revoked without due process—i.e., a hearing at which evidence is presented, etc.[11] This ruling inaugurated the concept of the **entitlement,** a class of government benefits with a status similar to that of property (which, according to the Fourteenth Amendment, cannot be taken from people "without due process of law"). *Goldberg v. Kelly* did not provide that the beneficiary had a "right" to government benefits; it provided that once a person's eligibility for AFDC was established, and as long as the program was still in effect, that person could not be denied benefits without due process. The decision left open the possibility that Congress could terminate the program and its benefits by passing a piece of legislation. If the welfare benefit were truly a property right, Congress would have no authority to deny it by a mere majority vote.

Thus the establishment of in-kind benefit programs and the legal obstacles involved in terminating benefits contributed to the growth of the welfare state. But it is important to note that real federal spending on AFDC itself did not rise after the mid-1970s. Unlike Social Security, AFDC was not indexed to inflation; without cost of living adjustments, the value of AFDC benefits fell by more than one-third. Moreover, the largest noncontributory welfare program, Medicaid (as shown by Table 18.1), actually devotes less than one-third of its expenditures to poor families; the rest goes to the disabled and the elderly in nursing homes.[12] Together, these programs have significantly increased the security of the poor and the vulnerable and must be included in a genuine assessment of the redistributive influence and the cost of the welfare state today.

WELFARE REFORM

The federally funded school lunch program provides nutritious lunches for needy children. In many schools in poor neighborhoods, a majority of the students rely on the school lunch program.

The Republicans controlling the White House and the Senate in the 1980s initially had welfare reform very high on their agenda. They proceeded immediately, with the cooperation of many Democrats, to cut the rate of increase of all the major social welfare programs, including the contributory social insurance programs and the noncontributory, "need-based" programs. However, very little was actually cut in either type of program, and the welfare state quickly began to expand again (see Figure 18.3). After 1984, expenditures for public assistance programs began to increase at a rate about equal to the rate of general economic growth (called the gross domestic product, or GDP). Moreover, no public assistance programs were terminated, despite Republican railings against them. Having discovered how extremely popular Social Security was in the United States, President Ronald Reagan thought it necessary to make frequent public promises not to alter what he himself called the "safety net." President George Bush joined in, adding to his defense of the safety net his promise of a "kinder, gentler nation."

President Bill Clinton was elected on a platform of "putting people first," but deficit realities significantly revised the meaning of that promise. Clinton's most positive achievement in the welfare field was his 1994 increase in the Earned Income Tax Credit, by which working parents whose annual income falls below approximately $25,000 can file through their income tax returns for an income supplement of up to $2,500. Yet aside from this one benefit increase, Clinton's campaign to "end welfare as we know it" had led to no new, concrete policies by 1995. By 1994, Clinton had proposed a new welfare plan

SOCIAL WELFARE EXPENDITURES FOR PUBLIC PROGRAMS, 1970–95 **Figure 18.3**

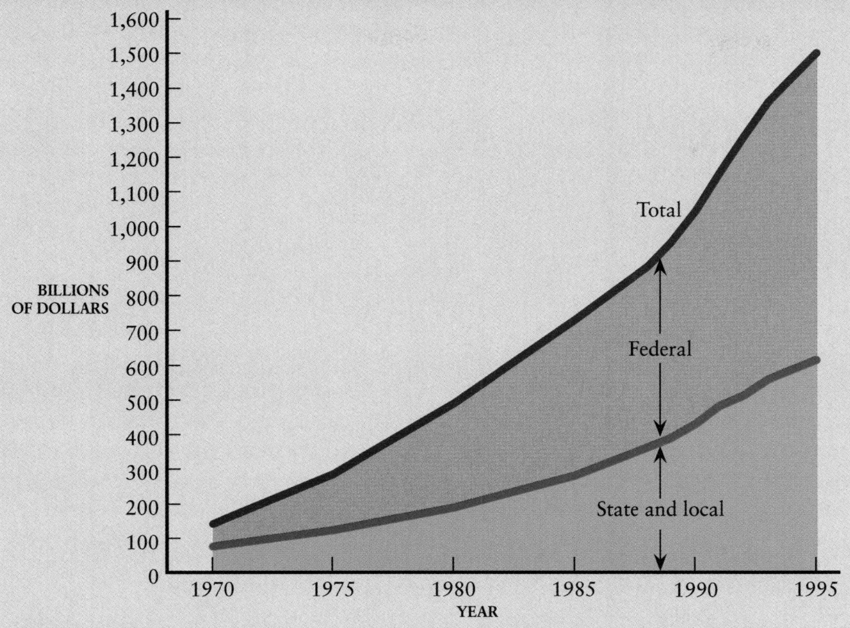

SOURCE: U.S. Bureau of the Census, *Statisical Abstract of the United States, 1999* (Washington, D.C.: Government Printing Office, 1999), p. 386.

that would have required four hundred thousand welfare recipients to find jobs by 2000 and would have limited benefits to two years for those who refused to work or to join job-training programs. But the 1994 Republican congressional triumph moved President Clinton to the periphery of policy making, especially in welfare and other social policy matters. His reform proposal died.

The Republicans brought with them their "Contract with America," which included a promise to introduce a bill to "reduce illegitimacy, control welfare spending, and reduce welfare dependence." The Republican welfare bill was far more radical than anything Clinton had in mind: removing the federal guarantee of assistance, forcing 1.5 million welfare recipients to work by 2000, denying public aid to legal immigrants who are not citizens, and granting states wide discretion in administering welfare programs. In fact, the Republican plan would return full discretion and implementation to the states, eliminating the national standards referred to earlier. The Republicans would achieve this by replacing the existing welfare programs with direct-to-the-state cash programs, called block grants.

During the 104th Congress (1995–96), President Clinton twice vetoed proposals for welfare reform, arguing that they would harm children. However, in August 1996, the president signed a third bill similar to the previous proposals. This major reform of welfare abolished AFDC and replaced the federal guarantee of assistance to the poor with block grants to the states through the new TANF program. This program allows states to deny assistance to legal immigrants and requires the head of each family receiving welfare to work

Figure 18.4 SHRINKING WELFARE ROLLS, 1993–99

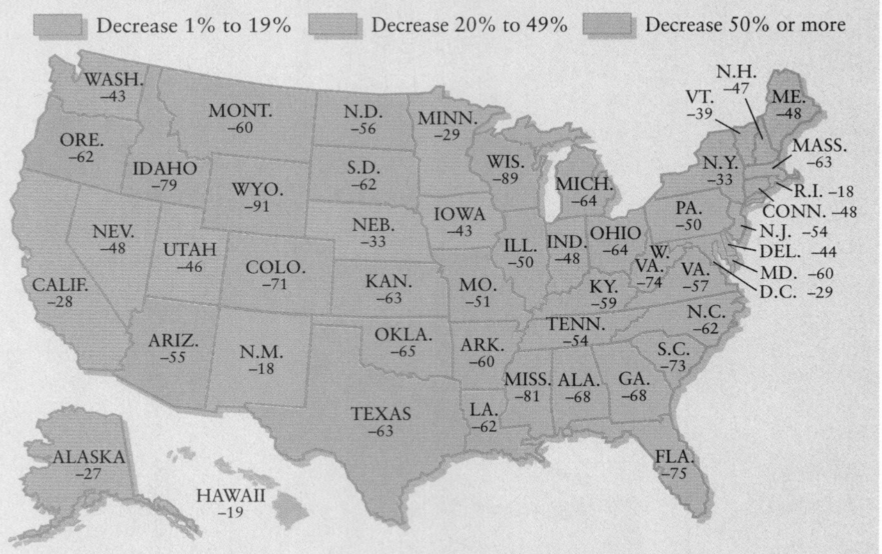

SOURCE: U.S. Department of Health and Human Services Administration for Children and Families, December 3, 1999.

within two years or lose assistance. The legislation also establishes a lifetime limit of five years on the receipt of assistance.

Since this new welfare law was enacted, the number of families receiving assistance dropped by 51 percent nationwide (see Figure 18.4).[13] Some observers take this as a sign that welfare reform is working; indeed, former welfare recipients have been more successful at finding and keeping jobs than many critics of the new law predicted. Other evidence suggests more caution in declaring welfare reform a success. Early studies show that welfare recipients are not paid enough to pull their families out of poverty and that child care and transportation continue to cause many problems for people seeking to leave welfare.[14] Moreover, one big question remains unanswered. What will happen to former welfare recipients and other low-income workers when there is an economic downturn and fewer jobs available? Welfare reform has been implemented in a time of record low unemployment levels; when employers are less desperate for workers, welfare recipients are more likely to have difficulty finding jobs. These concerns suggest that the 1996 law may not mark the end of welfare reform but may be a prelude to a round of future reforms.

HOW DO WE PAY FOR THE WELFARE STATE?

Since the 1930s, when the main elements of the welfare state were first created, spending on social policy has grown dramatically. Most striking has been the growth of entitlement programs, the largest of which are Social Security and Medicare. The costs of entitlement programs grew from 20 percent of the total

POLICY DEBATE

Does Social Security Need to Be Saved?

Since its creation in 1935, the Social Security system has provided retirement, survivor, and disability benefits to millions of Americans. Up until now, the system has run "in the black"—that is, it has collected more money than it has given out. In 1998, 44 million Americans received a total of $375 billion in Social Security benefits, given to 27 million retirees, 6 million spouses and children, 7 million survivors of deceased workers, and 5 million disabled workers. Even today, more than half of all American workers do not have a private pension plan; they will have to rely solely on Social Security for their retirement. If there were no Social Security, half of all senior citizens would be living below the poverty line. Thus, Social Security guarantees a measure of equality.

Nearly all wage earners and self-employed individuals pay into Social Security. Yet many fear that the system cannot sustain itself. When the baby boomer generation—a relatively large percentage of Americans, born between 1946 and 1964—reaches retirement age, their large numbers and longer life expectancies may place too great a demand on the system, forcing today's young people to pay ever more into a system that may be bankrupt by the time they retire.

Those who argue for a major change in Social Security point out that Social Security benefits are not drawn from an interest-bearing account; rather, they are paid for from taxes collected from current workers. Therefore, current workers carry the primary financial burden for the system. When baby boomers retire, their political and economic clout will be so great that they will be able to push aside any effort to limit benefits or relieve the financial burden on a much smaller number of younger wage earners. For Social Security to continue, it may have to borrow, or draw money from the federal Treasury, leaving younger generations with a staggering debt. If no changes are made in the current system, the Social Security Trust Fund (the account where surplus monies are held) will, according to projections, go bankrupt by 2034.

Contrary to popular impressions, Social Security benefits are not a simple repayment, plus interest, of money contributed by workers. The average retiree receives back the equivalent of all the money he or she contributed over a lifetime of work, plus interest, in the space of four to eight years. Most retirees receive far more than they put in. Why should today's student-age population provide subsidies to retirees who do not need the extra income? Several reform ideas have been suggested. One proposes an investment shift from the current low-yield, conservative, U.S. government securities to private investment in higher-yield stocks and bonds. Another proposal urges a shift to means testing, to reduce or eliminate benefits for those who already have ample income. A third proposal calls for raising the minimum retirement age. The current payroll tax for raising funds could also be altered. As of 2000, income is taxed only up to $72,600, so that a worker making a million dollars a year pays the same Social Security taxes as a worker making $73,000. If action is not taken soon, the system will likely be pushed to extinction by the burdens of the vast number of baby boomers.

Although nearly all observers favor some reform, defenders of the system argue that critics vastly overstate the problem. First, estimates of a looming Social Security crisis are based on very conservative economic projections that assume a far slower rate of growth in the nation's economy than has occurred up until now. Given the nation's history of growth, such projections are unduly pessimistic. Yet even if they are accurate, other factors will minimize the financial burden on younger workers when the baby boomers retire. In the year 2030, for example, at the height of boomer retirement, the overall workforce will be larger than during the height of the baby boom. The reasons for this surge in the twenty-first-century workforce include an increase in births and changing work patterns.

As for proposals to radically alter the distribution of benefits, system supporters point out that Social Security was created to serve several purposes. While the system provides a vital safety net to protect the elderly from poverty, it was also intended to be a universal system, entitling every worker to receive benefits from past work. It was also designed to be a progressive system by awarding greater benefits to those who earned more, and a hedge against inflation by including cost-of-living increases. Moreover, "generational sharing," whereby current workers would provide benefits for retirees, was part of the system's design. These purposes are as valid today as they were in 1935.

STUDENT DEBATE

Should Social Security Be Privatized?

Yes

There is much talk about reforming Social Security. As college students, we should be scared. We face the prospect of paying taxes far in excess of current levels into a system that may not exist when we retire. While that does not have to be the case, Clinton's proposal in the State of the Union address to use excess revenue to save Social Security fails to scratch the surface of the necessary changes. The only thing that can keep the system solvent is privatization.

The first thing that must be understood is that the Social Security "trust fund" cannot be shored up with excess government revenue because the trust fund does not exist. Social Security is a pay-as-you-go system. Taxes collected from workers are immediately paid out to recipients. Any money leftover is lent to the rest of the federal government, and in return, the trust fund receives IOUs from the treasury.

Unfortunately, these IOUs have absolutely no value. When payouts begin to exceed taxes in approximately 2013, the Social Security system must ask the treasury to redeem its IOUs. The treasury can get the money through tax revenues or borrowing.

In the State of the Union, Clinton proposed to use a portion of the excess revenues to pay off part of the national debt. The logic is that if the government has less outstanding debt, it will be easier to borrow from the private sector down the road.

Unfortunately, there is no reason to believe that the benefits reaped from this will be used to save Social Security. Congress could just as easily borrow money for new spending programs, there could be a war, or most likely, the extraordinarily rosy budget projections currently being used (which are the basis for Clinton's plan) will simply not hold.

The only way to make Social Security solvent over the long term is some form of privatization. What we need to do is move from a pay-as-you-go system to a wealth-based system under which individuals contribute to individual accounts under their control.

This would accomplish two important goals. First, it would increase the rate of return on each worker's contribution. Today, the average return on Social Security is 2.2 percent—in 20 years, it will be negative. Compare this to the nine percent average return historically achieved by funds investing in stocks and bonds.

Second, it would reduce payroll taxes. Given the higher rate of return on private retirement account contributions, benefits equivalent to those provided today could be financed with a payroll tax one-fifth the size of the current one.

It is time for serious reform. Although many people are concerned about the uncertainty of switching to a private system, Chile, the United Kingdom, and Sweden all have enacted similar reforms with great success. Few of us should want to be forced into a failing system—and there is no reason for that to happen. Privatization is a viable and tested alternative.

SOURCE: Ryan Sager, "Privatization Is the Only Way to Save Social Security," *The Hatchet*, (George Washington University), February 11, 1999.

No

Why does America need to strengthen Social Security? The answer is simple: For nearly half of Americans, Social Security is the only pension they have. The program has worked to relieve poverty among the old, disabled workers, women, and minorities. It prevents social inequality among the rich and poor. For young families, it prevents their in-laws from moving in for support.

Social Security has worked so well because all working Americans contribute to the program and all Americans receive a guaranteed benefit. Ryan Sager, president of GW Libertarians, proposed investing 2 percent of the current Social Security tax in private accounts.

What that means is the guaranteed benefits so many Americans rely on will be cut dramatically. The idea behind this scheme is that the investments will cover the difference.

This two-percent contribution from the average wage earner will only be $540 per year, which equals $21 every two weeks that a worker will contribute. For one-third of all workers, the contribution every two weeks would be $6.50. These deposits are not significant for any broker or even a mutual fund to accept. Individual accounts are too great of a risk to sacrifice over Social Security's guaranteed benefits.

The amount of risk in the stock market for an individual is so large that poor investments will leave many Americans worse off. The cost of supplying information to workers to inform them of good stocks and mutual funds will be enormous not to mention potentially misleading.

Finally, the cost of having brokers or mutual funds conduct trades will be equal to 20 percent of the paid benefits from individual accounts, according to Professor Peter Diamond of the Massachusetts Institute of Technology. These costs are Wall Street's gain.

President Clinton's plan on the other hand, is designed to maintain and continue the guaranteed benefits of the Social Security system. Reserving the surplus for Social Security preserves the system so that when Americans who are in their twenties retire, they not only are entitled to, but they will receive the same benefits as their parents and grandparents did.

The president's plan maintains the fairness and stability Social Security was designed to have. Many may argue that because the president has proposed investing part of the surplus in investments other than U.S. Treasury bills, politicians such as senators Lott and Daschle and representatives Gephardt and Hastert will make the Social Security investment decisions.

They are wrong.

A board of governors similar to the Federal Reserve Board will be established to pick investors. These expert investors will decide how to diversify and invest about 15 percent of the Social Security trust fund, which is equal to the assets of Fidelity or Merrill Lynch.

The final issue is how to increase the wealth and savings of all Americans. The president has proposed USA accounts to do this. Unlike individual retirement accounts, these accounts promote savings and do not replace the guaranteed benefits of Social Security. Social Security is not a retirement issue, but rather it is an issue that will affect the lives of every student at [George Washington University].

SOURCE: Adam Streisfeld, "Privatization Will Not Aid Security," *The Hatchet* (George Washington University), February 18, 1999.

federal budget in 1962 to nearly 57 percent by 1998. Funds to pay for these social programs have come disproportionately from increases in payroll taxes. In 1970, social insurance taxes accounted for 23 percent of all federal revenues; in 1998 they had grown to 33 percent of all federal revenues.[15] During the same time period corporate taxes fell from 17 percent to 10.1 percent of all federal revenues. Because the payroll tax is regressive, low- and middle-income families have carried the burden for funding increased social spending.

Perspectives on Politics

THE FUTURE OF MEDICARE

"Faith in Medicare's long-term solvency has shriveled to the point that a majority of Americans 18-to-34 believe that the TV soap opera *General Hospital* will outlast the Medicare system....

"And, remarkably, 60 percent of young Americans would drop out of the Medicare system completely and save for their own healthcare needs if given the opportunity....

"The survey ... tells the sorry tale of young people convinced that the government's largest health care program will come crashing down on them. Asked 'Do you think Medicare will exist by the time you retire?,' only one-third (34 percent) said yes.

"'Remarkably, young adults have more faith in the endurance of a fictional medical program than in a huge, real-life government program,' says Third Millennium Executive Director Richard Thau. 'This poll should act as a clarion call to candidates of all parties: fix this system now or you'll permanently lose the support of this jaded generation.'"

SOURCE: Third Millennium press release, available at http://thirdmil.org/pub/press/medbail.html.

Although much public attention has centered on welfare and other social spending programs for the poor, such as food stamps, these programs account for only a small proportion of social spending. AFDC, for example, even at its height made up only 1 percent of the federal budget. In recent years, Congress has tightly controlled spending on most means-tested programs, and currently lawmakers and government officials express little concern that spending on such programs is out of control. The biggest spending increases have come in social insurance programs that provide broad-based benefits. Such expenditures are hard to control because these programs are entitlements, and the government has promised to cover all people who fit the category of beneficiary. So, for example, the burgeoning elderly population will require that spending on Social Security automatically increase in the future. Furthermore, because Social Security benefits are indexed to inflation, there is no easy way to reduce benefits. Spending on medical programs—Medicare and Medicaid—has also proven difficult to control, in part because of the growing numbers of people eligible for the programs but also because of rising health care costs. Health care expenditures have risen much more sharply than inflation in recent years.

Concern about social spending has centered on Social Security because the aging of the baby-boom generation will force spending up sharply in the coming decades. Critics of the present system make several charges.[16] One of the most important is that the Social Security trust fund—the special government account from which Social Security payments are made—will go bankrupt. Indeed, in 1998, the Board of Trustees of the Social Security system projected that by 2032, the Social Security trust fund would no longer have enough money to pay the full benefits due retirees. Recent budget surpluses have pushed that date back by a few years but they have not eliminated the problem. A second criticism is that Americans are not getting their money's worth from Social Security and that they would be better off if they could take at least part of the payroll tax that currently pays for Social Security and invest it themselves. Supporters of this view advocate establishing private retirement accounts that individuals would control.

Supporters of the current system challenge each of these criticisms.[17] First, they question the accuracy of forecasting the size of the trust fund so far into the future and charge that projections of future shortfalls are based on highly conservative assumptions. And in any case, they argue, the current projection is not that Social Security will become bankrupt in 2032, but rather that its revenues will be sufficient to cover only 70 to 75 percent of the benefits promised. Thus, supporters believe that minor changes in benefits, taxes, and retirement age, if made soon, will easily ensure that the current system remains sound. Second, they argue that setting up private accounts would expose retirees to unacceptable risks. Although the stock market has risen dramatically in recent years, opponents of private accounts caution that stock markets can also decline for prolonged periods, a fact that Americans familiar only with recent trends have not experienced. Moreover, supporters of the present system emphasize that Social Security is not just a retirement account, it is a social insurance program that provides "income protection to workers and their families if the wage earner retires, becomes disabled or dies."[18] Because it provides this social insurance protection, supporters argue, Social Security's returns should not be compared to those of a private retirement account.

Even though the federal budget is now in surplus, conflicts about financing social policy expenditures are likely to continue. In part this is because the retirement of the baby-boom generation and the escalating costs of health care are expected to force budgets out of balance again in the not-distant future. But conflicts about financing social policy are also driven by fundamental divisions about whether and how the federal government should help provide security for Americans.[19] As the social policies established during the Great Depression are challenged, Americans once again face basic questions about how best to shape social policy in ways that support our national values.

Who Gets What from Social Policy?

- Which groups receive the most benefits from social policies? Which groups receive the fewest?
- How effectively does social policy reach the groups that are most likely to be poor?

The two categories of social policy—contributory and noncontributory—generally serve different groups of people. We can understand much about the development of social policy by examining which constituencies benefit from different policies.

The strongest and most generous programs are those in which the beneficiaries are widely perceived as deserving of assistance and also are politically powerful. Because Americans prize work, constituencies who have "earned" their benefits in some way or those who cannot work because of a disability are usually seen as most deserving of government assistance. Politically powerful constituencies are those who vote as a group, lobby effectively, and mobilize to protect the programs from which they benefit.

When we study social policies from a group perspective, we can see that the elderly and the middle class receive the most benefits from the government's social policies and that children and the working poor receive the fewest. (In addition, America's social policies do little to change the fact that minorities and women are more likely to be poor than white Americans and men.

THE ELDERLY

The elderly are the beneficiaries of the two strongest and most generous social policies: old-age pensions (what we call Social Security) and Medicare (medical care for the elderly). As these programs have grown, they have provided most elderly Americans with economic security and have dramatically reduced the poverty rate among the elderly. In 1959, before very many people over the age of sixty-five received social insurance, the poverty rate for the elderly was 35 percent; by 1998, it had dropped to 10.5 percent.[20] Because of this progress, many people call Social Security the most effective antipoverty program in the United States.[21] This does not mean that the elderly are rich, however; in 1998, the median income of elderly households was $21,729, well below the national median income. The aim of these programs is to provide security and prevent poverty, rather than to assist people once they have become poor. And they succeeded in preventing poverty among most of the aged.

One reason that Social Security and Medicare are politically strong is that the elderly are widely seen as a deserving population. They are not expected to work, because of their age. Moreover, both programs are contributory, and a work history is a requirement for receiving a Social Security pension. But these programs are also strong because they serve a constituency that has become quite powerful. The elderly are a very large group: in 1998, there were 34.4 million Americans over the age of sixty-five. Because Social Security and Medicare are not means-tested, they are available to all former workers and their spouses over the age of sixty-five, whether they are poor or not. The size of this group is of such political importance because the elderly turn out to vote in higher numbers than the rest of the population.

In addition, the elderly have developed strong and sophisticated lobbying

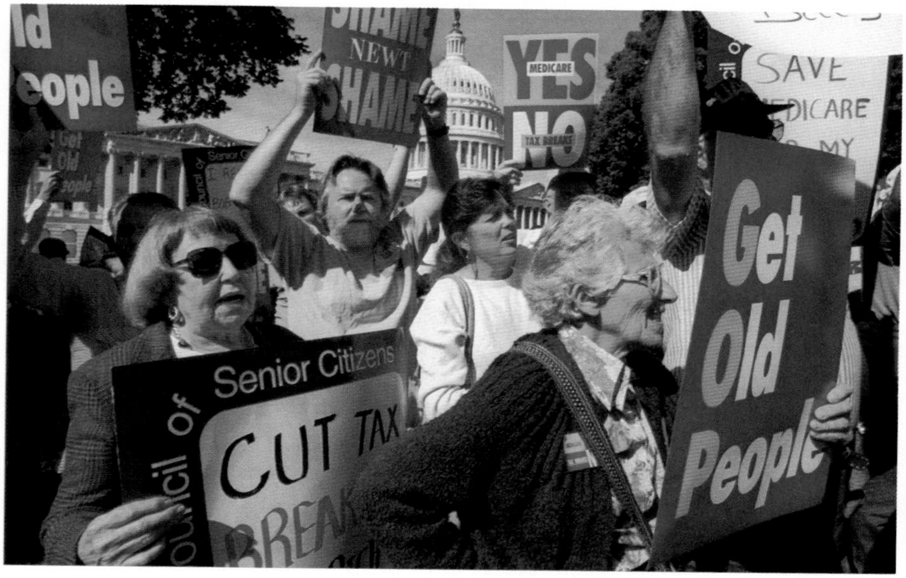

Senior citizens vigorously protested cuts in Medicare that were proposed by the Republican Congress in 1995. Fearing negative political repercussions, Congress retreated from its efforts to overhaul the Medicare system.

organizations that can influence policy making and mobilize elderly Americans to defend these programs against proposals to cut them. One important and influential organization that defends the interests of old people in Washington is the American Association of Retired Persons (AARP). The AARP had 33 million members in 1998, amounting to one-fifth of all voters. It also has a sophisticated lobbying organization in Washington, which employs 28 lobbyists and a staff of 165 policy analysts.[22] (See Chapter 12 for more discussion of the AARP's lobbying efforts.) Although the AARP is the largest and the strongest organization of the elderly, other groups, such as the National Council of Senior Citizens, to which many retired union members belong, also lobby Congress on behalf of the elderly.

When Congress considers changes in programs that affect the elderly, these lobbying groups pay close attention. They mobilize their supporters and work with legislators to block changes they believe will hurt the elderly. Because of the tremendous political strength of the elderly, Social Security has been nicknamed the "third rail of American politics: touch it and you die."[23] In 1995, the power of the elderly lobby appeared on the wane as congressional Republicans proposed significant changes in Medicare. Ultimately, however, Congress dropped these proposals in the face of public disapproval—much of it stimulated by senior citizens' organizations.

THE MIDDLE CLASS

Americans don't usually think of the middle class as benefiting from social policies, but government action promotes the social welfare of the middle class in a variety of ways. First, medical care and pensions for the elderly help the middle class by relieving them of the burden of caring for elderly relatives. Before these programs existed, old people were more likely to live with and depend financially on their adult children. Many middle-class families whose parents and grandparents are in nursing homes rely on Medicaid to pay nursing-home bills.

In addition, the middle class benefits from what some analysts call the **"shadow welfare state."**[24] These are the social benefits that private employers offer to their workers: medical insurance and pensions, for example. The federal government subsidizes such benefits by not taxing the payments that employers and employees make for health insurance and pensions. These **tax expenditures,** as they are called, are an important way in which the federal government helps ensure the social welfare of the middle class. (Such programs are called "tax expenditures" because the federal government helps finance them through the tax system rather than by direct spending.) Another key tax expenditure that helps the middle class is the tax exemption on mortgage interest payments: taxpayers can deduct the amount they have paid in interest on a mortgage from the income they report on their tax return. By not taxing these payments, the government makes homeownership less expensive.

People often don't think of these tax expenditures as part of social policy because they are not as visible as the programs that provide direct payments or services to beneficiaries. But tax expenditures represent a significant federal investment: They cost the national treasury some $300 billion a year and make it easier and less expensive for working Americans to obtain health care, save for retirement, and buy homes. These programs are very popular with the middle class and Congress rarely considers reducing them. On the few

shadow welfare state
social benefits that private employers offer to their workers, such as medical insurance and pensions

tax expenditures
government subsidies provided to employers and employees through tax deductions for amounts spent on health insurance and other benefits; these represent one way the government helps to ensure the social welfare of the middle class

occasions when public officials have tried to limit these programs—with proposals to limit the amount of mortgage interest that can be deducted, for example—they have quickly retreated. These programs are simply too popular among Americans whose power comes from their numbers at the polling booth.

THE WORKING POOR

People who are working but are poor or are just above the poverty line receive only limited assistance from government social programs. This is somewhat surprising, given that Americans value work so highly. But the working poor are typically employed in jobs that do not provide pensions or health care; often they are renters because they cannot afford to buy homes. This means they cannot benefit from the shadow welfare state that subsidizes the social benefits enjoyed by most middle-class Americans. At the same time, however, they cannot get assistance through programs such as Medicaid and TANF, which are largely restricted to the nonworking poor.

Two government programs do assist the working poor: the Earned Income Tax Credit (EITC) and food stamps. The EITC was implemented in 1976 to provide poor workers some relief from increases in the taxes that pay for Social Security. As it has expanded, the EITC has provided a modest wage supplement for the working poor, allowing them to catch up on utility bills or pay for children's clothing. Poor workers can also receive food stamps. These two programs help supplement the income of poor workers, but they offer only modest support. Because the wages of less-educated workers have declined significantly over the past fifteen years and minimum wages have not kept pace with inflation, the problems of the working poor remain acute.

Even though the working poor may be seen as deserving, they are not politically powerful because they are not organized. There is no equivalent to the AARP for the poor. Nonetheless, because work is highly valued in American society, politicians find it difficult to cut the few social programs that help the working poor. In 1995, efforts to cut the EITC were defeated by coalitions of Democrats and moderate Republicans, although Congress did place new restrictions on food stamps and reduced the level of spending.

THE NONWORKING POOR

The only nonworking, able-bodied poor people who receive federal cash assistance are parents who are caring for children. The primary source of cash assistance for these families was AFDC and now is the state-run TANF program, but they also rely on food stamps and Medicaid. Able-bodied adults who are not caring for children are not eligible for federal assistance other than food stamps. Many states provide small amounts of cash assistance to such individuals through programs called "general assistance," but in the past decade, many states have abolished or greatly reduced their general assistance programs in an effort to encourage these adults to work. Thus, the primary reason the federal government provides any assistance to able-bodied adults is because they are caring for children. Although Americans don't like to subsidize adults who are not working, they do not want to harm children.

AFDC was the most unpopular social spending program, and as a result, spending on it declined after 1980. Under TANF, states receive a fixed amount of federal funds, whether the welfare rolls rise or fall. Because the numbers of people on welfare have declined so dramatically since 1994—by over 50 percent—states have had generous levels of federal resources for the remaining welfare recipients. Many states, however, have used the windfall of federal dollars to cut taxes and indirectly support programs that benefit the middle class, not the poor.[25] Welfare recipients have little political power to resist cuts in their benefits. In the late 1960s and early 1970s, the short-lived National Welfare Rights Organization sought to represent the interests of welfare recipients. But it proved difficult to keep the organization operating because its members and its constituents had few resources and were difficult to organize.[26] Because welfare recipients are widely viewed as undeserving, and because they are not politically organized, they have played little part in recent debates about welfare.

MINORITIES, WOMEN, AND CHILDREN

We saw at the beginning of this chapter that minorities, women, and children are disproportionately poor. Much of this poverty is the result of disadvantages that stem from the position of these groups in the labor market. As we saw from the statistics in the introduction to this chapter, African Americans and Latinos tend to be economically less well off than the rest of the American population. Much of this economic inequality stems from the fact that minority workers tend to have low-wage jobs. Minorities are also more likely to become unemployed and to remain unemployed for longer periods of time than are white Americans. African Americans, for example, typically have experienced twice as much unemployment than other Americans have. The combination of low-wage jobs and unemployment often means that minorities are less likely to have jobs that give them access to the shadow welfare state. They are more likely to fall into the precarious categories of the working poor or the nonworking poor.

In the past several decades, policy analysts have begun to talk about the "feminization of poverty," or the fact that women are more likely to be poor than men are. This problem is particularly acute for single mothers, who are more than twice as likely to fall below the poverty line than the average American (see Figure 18.5 on the next page). When the Social Security Act was passed in 1935, the main programs for poor women were Aid to Dependent Children (ADC) and survivors' insurance for widows. The framers of the act believed that ADC would gradually disappear as more women became eligible for survivors' insurance. The social model behind the Social Security Act

Student Perspectives

Every time the welfare issue comes up, you hear the same old stereotypical remarks:

Why are we paying for teenaged mothers to keep having babies? Why should we support people who are too lazy to work? Their parents were on welfare, they're on welfare, and their kids are going to be on welfare, so what good is it doing?

I've even heard some people go so far as to suggest that people on welfare were all less intelligent than everyone else and should be shipped off to an island somewhere. They're probably kidding, but in every joke there lies some seriousness.

Too bad the witty jokesters never realize they are in the same room with a guy whose family was once on welfare.

The stereotypical welfare recipient profiled on the nightly news represents a small minority. Most people on welfare really need it. It's not that they can't always find a job, but when you are a single mother trying to raise a few kids while flipping burgers, you might need a little extra help to get you through tough times.

When my mother applied for welfare, she had little choice. She was single and trying to feed four children with little or no support from my father. Shortly after my parents split up, the bank took the house I grew up in. We had to put most of our stuff in a rented storage garage while we moved in with my grandparents.

With no college education under her belt, my mom worked the night shift at a plastics factory and eventually started taking classes during the day at Akron University. I don't know how she managed, but after eighteen months, we got another house. Then, on the day I left for Penn State, my mom got her associate's degree from Akron.

We were only on welfare and food stamps for a few years, but without those resources, the rest of my family would still be living with my grandparents.

SOURCE: Don Stewart, "Stereotypes Don't Apply to Every Welfare Recipient," *Daily Collegian* (Pennsylvania State University), June 15, 1999.

Figure 18.5 POVERTY LEVEL IN THE UNITED STATES, 1959–98

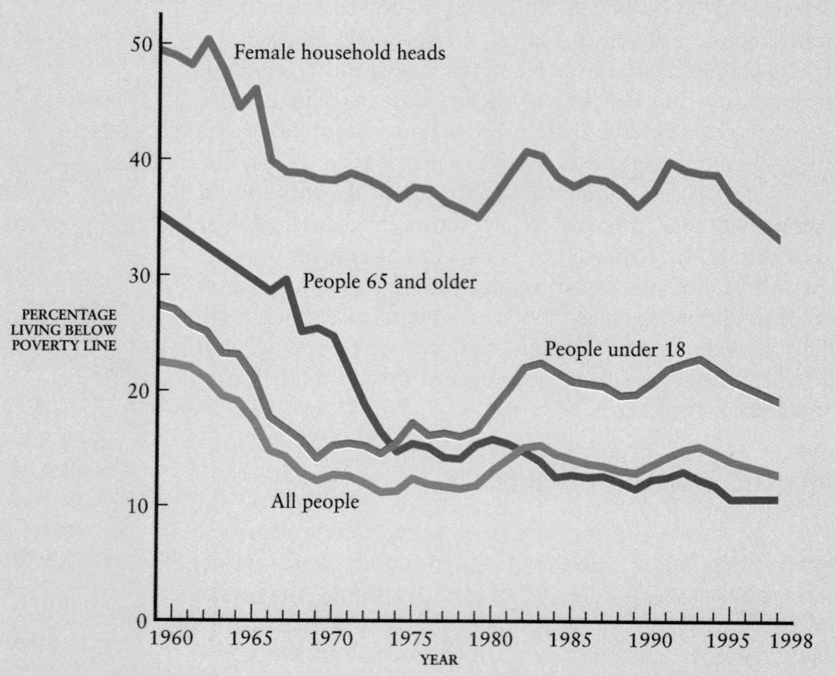

SOURCE: U.S. Bureau of the Census, *Statistical Abstract of the United States: 1997* (Washington, D.C.: Government Printing Office, 1997), p. 476. 1998 data from U.S. Bureau of the Census, Historical Poverty Tables (www.census.gov/income/histpov/).

was that of a male breadwinner with a wife and children. Women were not expected to work, and if a woman's husband died, ADC or survivors' insurance would help her stay at home and raise her children. The framers of Social Security did not envision today's large number of single women heading families. At the same time, they did not envision that so many women with children would also be working. This combination of changes helped make AFDC (the successor program to ADC) more controversial. Many people asked, Why shouldn't welfare recipients work, if the majority of women who are not on welfare work? Such questions led to the welfare reform of 1996, which created TANF, specifically meant as a means of temporary assistance to families.

The need to combine work and childcare is a problem for most single parents. This problem is more acute for single mothers than for single fathers, because on average, women still earn less than men, and because working creates new expenses such as childcare and transportation costs. Many women working in low-wage jobs do not receive health insurance as a benefit of their jobs; they must pay the cost of such insurance themselves. As a result, many poor women found that once they were working, the expenses of childcare, transportation, insurance, etc., left them with less cash per month than they would have received if they had not worked and had instead collected AFDC and

Medicaid benefits. These women concluded that it was not "worth it" for them to leave AFDC and work. Some states are now experimenting with programs to encourage women to work by allowing them to keep some of their welfare benefits even when they are working. Although Americans want individuals to be self-sufficient, research suggests that single mothers with low-wage jobs are likely to need continuing assistance to make ends meet.[27]

One of the most troubling issues related to American social policy is the number of American children who live in poverty. The rate of child poverty in 1998 was 18.9 percent—6.2 percent higher than that of the population as a whole. These high rates of poverty stem in part from the design of American social policies. Because these policies do not generously assist able-bodied adults who aren't working, and because these policies offer little help to the working poor, the children of these adults are likely to be poor as well.

As child poverty has grown, several lobbying groups have emerged to represent children's interests; the most well known of these is the Children's Defense Fund. But even with a sophisticated lobbying operation, poor children do not have much political power. Although their numbers are large, children do not vote and therefore cannot wield much political power.[28]

Breaking the Cycle of Poverty

- What policies are aimed at helping the poor break out of poverty?
- Which policies have been most successful?

Poverty is a cycle. Many individuals break out of it, but they have to overcome heavy odds. Although many policies may aim at breaking the cycle and others have a beneficial effect on the redistribution of opportunities, four types of policies stand out as most significant: education policies, employment policies, health policies, and housing policies.

EDUCATION POLICIES

Those who understand American federalism from Chapter 4 already are aware that most of the education of the American people is provided by the public policies of state and local governments. What may be less appreciated is the fact that these education policies—especially the policy of universal compulsory public education—are the most important single force in the distribution and redistribution of opportunity in America.

Compared to state and local efforts, the role of national education policy pales in comparison. With but three exceptions, the national government did not involve itself at all in education for the first century of its existence as an independent republic (see Table 18.2 on the next page). The first two of these exceptions were actually prior to the Constitution—the Land Ordinance of 1785 and the Northwest Ordinance of 1787. These provided for a survey of all the public lands in the Northwest Territory and required that four sections of the thirty-six sections in each township be reserved for public schools and their

Table 18.2 GROWTH OF THE WELFARE STATE

	Welfare	Education	Health and housing
State era (1789–1935)	Private and local charity State child labor laws State unemployment and injury compensation State mothers' pensions	Northwest Ordinance of 1787 (federal) Local academies Local public schools State compulsory education laws Federal Morrill Act of 1862 for land-grant colleges	Local public health ordinances
Federal era (1935–present)	Federal Social Security System Disability insurance VISTA, OEO* Supplemental Security Income Cost of living adjustment (indexing)	GI Bill National Defense Education Act of 1958 Elementary and Secondary Education Act of 1965 School desegregation Head Start	Public housing Hospital construction School lunch program Food stamps Medicare Medicaid

*VISTA = Volunteers in Service to America; OEO = Office of Economic Opportunity

maintenance. It was not until 1862, with adoption of the Morrill Act, that Congress took a third step, establishing the land-grant colleges and universities. Later in the nineteenth century, more federal programs were created for the education of farmers and other rural residents. But the most important national education policies have come only since World War II: the GI Bill of Rights of 1944, the National Defense Education Act (NDEA) of 1958, the Elementary and Secondary Education Act of 1965 (ESEA), and various youth and adult vocational training acts since 1958. Note, however, that since the GI Bill was aimed almost entirely at postsecondary schooling, the national government did not really enter the field of elementary education until after 1957.[29]

What finally brought the national government into elementary education was embarrassment over the fact that the Soviet Union had beaten the United States into space with the launching of Sputnik. The national policy under NDEA was aimed specifically at improving education in science and mathematics. General federal aid for education did not come until ESEA in 1965, which allocated funds to school districts with substantial numbers of children from families who were unemployed or earning less than $2,000 a year. By the early 1970s, federal expenditures for elementary and secondary education were running over $4 billion per year, and rose to a peak in 1980 at $4.8 billion.[30] Cuts by the Reagan administration of over 10 percent were substantial but not anywhere near the administration's goals. President Bush vowed time after time to be the "education president," and the Democratic majority in Congress was more than ready to help him. In truth, however, all of Bush's plans for improving elementary and secondary education depended on private financing or on state and local governments.

President Clinton's education program had a more national and public orientation, as might be expected of a Democratic president. It included more federal aid for preschool programs for needy children, national education standards coupled with teachers' incentives, and, at the postsecondary level, scholarships for minorities and an ambitious national service program available to all students to earn credit toward college tuition. Clinton's most concrete achievement in education policy was the Improving America's Schools Act of 1994, also known as Goals 2000, which aimed to reverse federal policies dating back to the 1960s that set lower academic standards for schools in poorer school districts than for those in wealthier ones. Goals 2000, in keeping with the rest of Clinton's education agenda, set uniform national standards for educational achievement from the wealthiest to the poorest school districts, and committed $400 million in federal funds to help establish these standards. The logic of the old system was that it was unfair to expect disadvantaged children to have to perform at the same level as children from wealthier backgrounds. But the result, not surprisingly, was to discourage children in poor school districts from achieving academic excellence. President Clinton's education secretary, Richard Riley, assessed the consequences in a 1994 speech: "About the fastest way I know to create an unthinking, angry 18-year-old who is spiritually numb and heading down the road to violence is to give that young person a watered-down curriculum from first grade on."[31]

One of the hottest areas of controversy in education is school choice. For over two hundred years, schools have been public institutions in the United States, and many name public schooling as the most important social policy in America. Today, however, there are serious challenges to the public monopoly on education. Some critics of public schools argue that government should simply provide parents with vouchers that they can use to attend the school of their choice, public or private. Supporters of vouchers claim that the public education system is too bureaucratic to provide quality education and does not allow parents enough control over their children's education. Although

Student Perspectives

Republican presidential candidates in the forefront are getting in line to support school vouchers as a means of fixing America's educational problems, despite the disastrous results of the charter experiments in Ohio. When asked if he supported vouchers, Republican presidential candidate Gary Bauer answered, "Yes, the Milwaukee and Cleveland pilot projects have been very encouraging, and if activist judges allow them to continue and expand, will increase the pressure on urban public schools to improve their performance." The actual results are the complete opposite.

* * *

The initial proficiency test results of the charter schools are abysmal. In Ohio charter schools, only 2 percent of fourth graders and 1 percent of sixth graders passed all sections of the test compared to 32 percent of fourth graders and 33 percent of sixth graders in public schools.

One example of disastrous beginning is Columbus' own Riser Military Academy, a bootcamp-styled charter school which opened without textbooks, no working telephone, no bathrooms, and unfinished classrooms. The school has been ordered to close this summer.

Young voters should keep in mind the presidential candidates supporting the disastrous voucher experiments in Ohio. Front runner George W. Bush has said, "My proposal says any school that receives federal Title I funds must measure student improvement. If, after three years, student performance does not improve, the federal funds should be given directly to the parents to use as they see fit, including private education. Under my plan, the federal government will no longer pay schools to cheat poor children."

But Bush gives no reason why private schools run by entrepreneurs would be any better at teaching our children than current publicly run ones. He also has never given a solution to the lack of private alternatives for handicapped and very poor children whose families cannot afford the private costs that vouchers do not cover. These are the children being cheated the most already in public schools. America needs to focus on improving our public schools, rather than handing the baton over to the entrepreneurs.

SOURCE: Martha Knox, "Candidates, Vouchers Cheating Students," *The Lantern* (Ohio State University), February 4, 2000).

voucher plans have so far only been implemented on a very small scale in a few places (Cleveland, Milwaukee, and Florida), wealthy supporters of vouchers have funded private voucher plans across the country. In Congress, Republicans have sought to use federal influence to spread the use of vouchers. Supporters of public education believe that vouchers will inevitably lead to greater inequalities in education, preventing schools from offering equal opportunity.

Pressures to change the organization of schooling have led to the creation of charter schools across the country. Charter schools are publicly funded schools that are free from the bureaucratic rules and regulations of the school district in which they are located. Charter schools are free to design specialized curricula and to use resources in ways they think most effective. Since the creation of the first charter schools in Minnesota in 1990, states across the country have passed legislation to allow charter schools. The great popularity of such schools suggests that reforms allowing more flexibility and responsiveness to parents may well be possible within the existing public system.

EMPLOYMENT AND TRAINING PROGRAMS

Considering the importance that Americans attach to work and the high value they place on education, it is somewhat surprising that the United States does not have a strong system for employment and job training. Such programs have two goals. One is to prepare entry-level workers for new jobs or to retrain workers whose jobs have disappeared. A second goal is to provide public jobs during economic downturns when sufficient private employment is not available. Since the 1930s, the American employment and training systems have fared poorly in terms of expenditures, stability, and results.[32]

The first public employment programs were launched during the New Deal. These programs were created to use the power of the federal government to get people back to work again. An "alphabet soup" of federal programs sought to employ those who did not have jobs: the Civilian Conservation Corps (CCC) put young men to work on environmental projects in rural areas; and the Works Progress Administration (WPA) employed many different kinds of workers, from writers and artists to manual laborers. In the despairing circumstances of the Great Depression, these public employment programs enjoyed widespread support. But by the end of the 1930s, questions about corruption and inefficiency in employment programs reduced support for them.

Students and Politics

"For the estimated 300 welfare recipients at [San Francisco] State [University], getting a college degree may be a better alternative to working full-time or enrolling in job training. . . .

"As changes in welfare programs across the nation are beginning to take effect, people on public assistance need to choose whether or not to pursue a college degree. New reforms in welfare laws will give students a chance to finish school while working and still receive public assistance.

"'Research shows 90 percent of parents receiving welfare get jobs making enough money to leave the welfare program one year after graduating,' said Diana Spatz, . . . the executive director of LIFETimE.

"Low-Income Families Empowerment Through Education is a Bay Area nonprofit organization that advocates higher education opportunities for parents on welfare. It is also one of many support groups emerging around the country that monitors welfare reform and educates welfare recipients about the changes coming their way. . . .

"People on welfare now have more accessible resources, like LIFETimE, that can guide them and teach them how to sever their reliance on government assistance.

"Many of these resource groups operate at a college or university helping people get back into school. For many of the directors, who benefited from government aid themselves, the groups are providing services that they did not have when they wanted to leave the welfare system. Now they want to be mentors for others.

"For years, Cheryl Cronin worked as a carpenter and raised her son alone. But when she injured both her arms and doctors told her that her career was over, she felt her only alternative was to go back to school. A former high school dropout, Cronin entered college at age 37, when her son had just completed high school.

"'What I personally want to be able to do is to hold out one of my hands and help a woman up,' said Cronin. . . . 'At the same time, I want to hold out my other hand and have someone pull me up,' she adds. 'That is what I call a bridge to the 21st century.'"

SOURCE: Anthony Chu, "Students on Welfare Find Future in School," *Golden Gater* (San Francisco State University), June 1, 1998; reprinted on U-Wire, http://www.uwire.com/uwire/98/6/news06019808.chtml (accessed June 1998).

Not until the 1960s did the federal government try again. This time, as part of the War on Poverty, government programs were designed to train and retrain workers, primarily the poor, rather than to provide them with public employment. For the most part, the results of these programs were disappointing. It proved very difficult to design effective training policies in the federal system; lack of coordination and poor administration plagued the Great Society training programs. Concern about such administrative problems led Congress to combine funds for all the different training programs into a single block grant in 1973, via the Comprehensive Employment and Training Act (CETA). In doing this, Congress hoped that more local flexibility would create more effective programs.

CETA expanded greatly and, as unemployment rose sharply during the 1970s, became primarily a public-service employment program. The federal government provided state and local governments funds to create jobs for the unemployed. At its peak, CETA had a budget of more than $10 billion and provided jobs for nearly 739,000 workers—12 percent of the nation's unemployed. But complaints soon arose that CETA was providing jobs primarily to people who were the most job-ready and was doing little for the most disadvantaged. This practice of selecting the most well prepared as participants—called "creaming"—has been a persistent problem with other job-training programs as well. Critics also charged that localities were simply using CETA money to perform tasks they would have paid for out of their own funds if federal money had not been available. Congress abolished CETA in 1981, making it one of the only federal programs totally eliminated in the past twenty or so years.[33]

But job training has remained a popular idea, and in 1982, Congress created a new program that supported local efforts at job training. The Job Training Partnership Act (JTPA) became the primary federal program supporting job training. In addition to retraining adult workers, JTPA provides funding for summer jobs for youth. President Clinton placed an especially high value on creating a strong system of job training. Clinton's program made use of tax credits and direct subsidies to employers to set up apprentice-training jobs for young people and was to be part of a more ambitious national system that was called "lifelong learning." It was inspired by training programs that exist in some European countries, and it coupled national initiatives with community organizations and administration. Yet Clinton's initiatives in job training remained small, as budgetary pressures and congressional skepticism limited his legislative achievements. Nevertheless, as the American economy changes and many corporations transfer operations out of the country or downsize their workforces, the need for retraining has become more pressing. Such training is particularly important for the three-quarters of American workers who have not finished four years of college. Enhancing the ability of the federal government to assist American workers, who face increasing economic insecurity, is one of the most important challenges confronting policy makers today.

HEALTH POLICIES

Until recent decades, no government in the United States—national, state, or local—concerned itself directly with individual health. But public responsibility was always accepted for *public* health. After New York City's newly created

Board of Health was credited with holding down a cholera epidemic in 1867, most states followed with the creation of statewide public health agencies. Within a decade, the results were obvious. Between 1884 and 1894, for example, Massachusetts's rate of infant mortality dropped from 161.3 per 1,000 to 141.4 per 1,000.[34] Reductions in mortality rates during the late nineteenth century may be the most significant contribution ever made by government to human welfare.

The U.S. Public Health Service (USPHS) has been in existence since 1798 but was a small part of public health policy until after World War II. Established in 1937, but little noticed for twenty years, was the National Institutes of Health (NIH), an agency within the USPHS created to do biomedical research. Between 1950 and 1989, NIH expenditures by the national government increased from $160 million to $7.1 billion—two-thirds of the nation's entire expenditure on health research. NIH research on the link between smoking and disease led to one of the most visible public-health campaigns in American history. Today, NIH's focus has turned to cancer and acquired immunodeficiency syndrome (AIDS). As with smoking, this work on AIDS has resulted in massive public-health education as well as new products and regulations.

Other, more recent commitments to the improvement of public health are the numerous laws aimed at cleaning up and defending the environment (including the creation in 1970 of the Environmental Protection Agency) and laws attempting to improve the health and safety of consumer products (regulated by the Consumer Product Safety Commission, created in 1972). Health policies aimed directly at the poor include Medicaid and nutritional programs, particularly food stamps and the school lunch program.

In the fiscal year 1998 budget, federal grants to states for Medicaid totaled $95.6 billion, up from $40 billion in 1990. Federal programs for AIDS research, treatment, prevention, and income support had a budget of $13.1 billion in 1998, a major increase from the $2.9 billion spent in 1990.[35] President Clinton also put greater emphasis on AIDS by appointing an "AIDS czar" to coordinate federal AIDS policy, and by giving this position Cabinet status. However, the position has been a difficult balancing act between advocates, health care professionals, and the realities of government finances.

President Clinton's major attempt to reshape federal health policy, and the boldest policy initiative of his administration, was his effort to reform America's health care system. In September 1993, Clinton announced a plan with two key objectives: to limit the rising costs of the American health care system (1991 per capita health spending in America, $2,932, was 83 percent higher than in twenty-one other industrialized nations)[36] and to provide universal health insurance coverage for all Americans (almost 40 million Americans lack health insurance). Clinton's plan at first garnered enormous public support and seemed likely to win congressional approval in some form. But the plan, which entailed a major expansion of federal administration of the health care system, gradually lost momentum as resistance to it took root among those who feared changes in a system that worked well for them. Although Clinton had pledged to make health care the centerpiece of his 1994 legislative agenda, no health care bill even came up for a full congressional vote that year. Following the failure of President Clinton's health care initiative, some congressional Democrats continued to press for federal health programs and some Republicans, fearing the public's scorn and their chances for re-election, found room for bipartisan agreement. On August 21, 1996, the Health Insurance Portability and Accountability Act was signed into law by President Clinton. The bill, sponsored by liberal Democrat Ted Kennedy of Massachusetts and moderate Republican Nancy Kassebaum of Kansas, required insurance companies to carry over coverage to employees who lost or changed their jobs. The Kennedy-Kassebaum bill was hailed as a triumph of bipartisanship. But, as one scholar of the health care reform debate said, the Kennedy-Kassebaum bill was "incremental" progress at best and "exhibited a high ratio of hype to accomplishment."[37]

HOUSING POLICIES

Through public housing for low-income families, which originated in 1937 with the Wagner-Steagall National Housing Act, and subsidized private housing after 1950, the percent of American families living in overcrowded conditions was reduced from 20 percent in 1940 to 9 percent in 1970. Federal policies made an even greater contribution to reducing "substandard" housing, defined by the U.S. Census Bureau as dilapidated houses without hot running water and without some other plumbing. In 1940, almost 50 percent of American households lived in substandard housing. By 1950, this had been reduced to 35 percent; by 1975, to 8 percent.[38] Urban redevelopment programs and rent-supplement programs have helped in a small way to give low-income families access to better neighborhoods and, through that, to better schools and working conditions.

The Clinton administration at first showed a strong ideological commitment to encouraging housing policies and combating homelessness. For instance, in 1994, the Department of Housing and Urban Development (HUD) launched a comprehensive plan to increase emergency shelter availability, access to transitional and rehabilitative services, and the amount of affordable permanent housing. Federal appropriations nearly doubled in 1995, to $1.7 billion. But, especially after 1994, the Clinton administration began to retreat. HUD Secretary Henry Cisneros continually had to waive, virtually to the point of abandonment, a long-standing one-for-one HUD rule, which provided that for every public housing unit destroyed, another would have to be built. And he spent most of his time consolidating programs, downsizing them, and devolving their functions to the state and local governments. In the end, HUD had taken the biggest hit of all departments from Congress. Although not able to carry out its vow to abolish HUD, Congress did cut HUD's budget by more than 10 percent for 1997—from $19.8 billion to $17.8 billion.[39]

The Welfare State and American Values

▶ How has the formation of social policy reflected the debate over liberty, equality, and democracy?

The development of social policy in the United States reflects the tensions between the values of liberty, equality, and democracy. Until the 1930s, the federal government did very little in the domain of social policy. The country's major social policy was free public education, which was established by the states and administered locally. Americans placed especially strong emphasis on education because an educated citizenry was seen as an essential component of a strong democracy.[40] Given the strength of these beliefs, it is not surprising that free public education was available in the United States well before European nations established public education systems.

Other public social policies, established from the 1930s on, have stirred up much more controversy. Liberals often argue that more generous social policies are needed if America is to truly ensure equality of opportunity. Some liberals have argued that the government needs to go beyond simply providing opportunity and should ensure more equal conditions, especially where children are concerned. Conservative critics, on the other hand, often argue that social policies that offer income support take the ideal of equality too far and, in the process, do for individuals what they should be doing for themselves. From this perspective, social policies make the government too big, and big government is seen as a fundamental threat to Americans' liberties.

libertarian
the political philosophy that is skeptical of any government intervention as a potential threat against individual liberty; libertarians believe that government has caused more problems than it has solved

Yet conservatives do not agree about how best to achieve a balance between the ideals of liberty, equality, and democracy. Two different conservative perspectives can be distinguished. The **libertarian** view holds that government social policy interferes with society too much and, in the process, has created more problems than it has solved.[41] Many libertarians believe that the mere existence of social policies is an infringement on individual liberties: the government forces some citizens to pay taxes for the benefit of other citizens. The most extreme policy prescription that emerges from this perspective advocates the elimination of all social policies. For example, political scientist Charles Murray has proposed eliminating all social programs except temporary unemployment insurance. In his view, such a move would both enhance the freedom of all Americans and improve society, because individuals would recover their individual initiative if they had to take care of themselves.[42] A less sweeping approach would reduce social programs to a bare minimum or make them temporary.

Other conservatives see things differently. They want to use the power of the government to enforce certain standards of behavior among beneficiaries of government social programs. Many people with these views call themselves "new paternalists."[43] They believe that government social programs have not forced recipients to behave responsibly. They reject the idea that social programs should simply be abandoned, because they fear the consequences for our democracy. New paternalists do not believe that individuals will behave more responsibly if government programs are withdrawn; instead they fear that social disorder will simply continue. In their view, such disorder will inevitably undermine a healthy democracy, and the primary role of government social policy should be to restore the social order.

Some of the measures supported by new paternalists are also backed by many liberals. These include requiring work in exchange for welfare benefits and compelling absent parents (usually fathers) to make child support payments to the families they have abandoned. Many people from varying political perspectives applauded in 1995 when the federal government tracked down and arrested a prominent investment banker who had fled from state to

AMERICAN DEMOCRACY IN COMPARATIVE PERSPECTIVE

Government, Wealth, and Distribution in Western Democracies

As with the role of government in the economy, so goes its commitment to social policies. Anglo-American democracies (see last chapter) are generally characterized by a greater degree of skepticism toward an active role of government in shaping social policy, while continental European social democracies have historically shown a more active commitment to various contributory and public assistance programs. These respective attitudes in many instances result in distinctly different patterns of public expenditures devoted to various social policies across the two groups of democracies. They have also served to set the United States apart not only from democracies identified with the continental European pattern but frequently from the pattern common to that of the Anglo-American democracies, as well.

By comparing public opinion polls, we can see that on average, while nearly a third of respondents in Anglo-American democracies *strongly* favored cuts in government spending in the mid-1990s, over 40 percent of Americans are in favor of such cuts, a proportion closer to that of the continental European democracies. Cuts in spending seem to elicit a different response from respondents than questions dealing directly with taxes. If respondents are asked to choose between reduced taxes (even if this means cuts in social spending) or increased social spending, typically over half the respondents in the Anglo-American countries would prefer to reduce taxes. Ironically, respondents in the United States are less strident in their support of reduced taxes at the expense of social spending (40 percent). Perhaps this is because they already pay among the lowest taxes among industrial democracies (as seen in the last chapter). Indeed, the public within the continental European democracies, already paying much higher tax rates than their Anglo-American counterparts, are even more supportive of reduced taxes (57 percent).

When asked, however, whether it is the responsibility of government to provide for the health care of the sick, as well as a decent standard of living for the old, the difference between the citizens within the two traditions of capitalism diverge sharply. On average, nearly two-thirds of the respondents across the sample of twelve democracies in 1996 confirmed that it was *definitely* the responsibility of the government to provide health care for the sick, while another six in ten expressed the same attitude with respect to providing a decent standard of living for the old. These percentages were slightly higher for the continental European social democracies (71 percent and 68 percent, respectively), while they were sharply lower for the Anglo-American democracies (62 percent and 55 percent, respectively). For citizens in the United States, the respective proportions were significantly smaller. Less than 40 percent of the respondents in the United States expressed such a definite affirmative attitude toward government's obligation to provide health care for the sick or a decent standard of living for the old.

Finally, with respect to the government's role in shaping various social policies, there is virtually no difference between the degree of commitment to education and health care across the two capitalist traditions. On average, governments of both capitalist traditions spend the equivalent of 6 to 7 percent of their Gross Domestic Product on general health care and education (these are figures for all levels of government—local, regional, and national). However, social security transfers are another matter. These are primarily public assistance program expenditures that serve to redistribute income within society. These consist of benefits for sickness, old age, family allowances, social assistance grants, and welfare provisions spent by all levels of government. Such expenditures amount to 19 percent of the GDP for continental European social democracies, while only 14 percent for Anglo-American democracies (13 percent for the United States) as of the mid-1990s.

SOURCES: World Bank, *Entering the 21st Century: World Development Report, 1999/2000* (New York: Oxford University Press, 1999); United Nations Development Programme, *Human Development Report 1999* (New York: Oxford University Press, 1999); Nancy Birdsall, "Life is Unfair: Inequality in the World," *Foreign Policy,* 111 (Summer 1998), pp. 76–93.

state in order to avoid paying child support.[44] Other measures are more controversial. For example, some states have enacted reforms denying additional welfare benefits to women who bear a child while on welfare. Liberals charge that such measures violate a most basic individual liberty: the right to have children.[45] New paternalists argue that infringement of individual liberties is simply the price that beneficiaries of government programs have to pay in return for receiving public support.

Conservatives share the view that the primary problems that many social policies address are not economic in origin but instead stem from individual deficiencies. If people behaved more responsibly—if they saved for their retirement, if they did not have children they can't afford to support—there would be little need for government social policy. Liberals, in contrast, believe that the root of many social problems is economic. They believe that opportunities for economic success are not equally available to all Americans and that it is the government's responsibility to open opportunities for all. Thus, liberals are far more likely than conservatives to believe that the ideal of equality compels the state to provide social programs. But, like conservatives, liberals do not all agree: some liberals place a greater emphasis on achieving equality as a *result;* others believe that government should do all it can to provide opportunity but that it should not go beyond providing opportunity.

Some liberals who believe that the government should do more to promote equal outcomes have argued that social benefits should be provided as a right of citizenship and that all Americans should be entitled to a basic standard of living. At particular historical moments, there have been social movements arguing in favor of such approaches to social policy in the United States, but views arguing in favor of equality of result have always been disadvantaged in the American political system. The idea of "social rights," prevalent in many European nations, has no counterpart in American politics. Moreover, the Supreme Court repeatedly refused to acknowledge social or economic rights in the 1960s and 1970s, even as it was making strong efforts to ensure political and civil rights.[46]

Most liberals, then, argue that the aim of social policy should be to provide equality of opportunity. They believe that it is particularly important to ensure that all children have an equal chance to succeed. The sharpest liberal criticism of current social policy has been directed at its failure to address the growth of child poverty. This criticism stems from the belief that poor children have far less opportunity to succeed than the children of the well-off and that such inequalities are incompatible with fundamental American ideals. Liberals also believe that the government has an important role in creating opportunities for adults. President Clinton argued that new policies are needed to help workers adapt to changes in the economy. In his vision, social policy should seek to reduce inequalities and open opportunities for individuals who are trying to help themselves by working or seeking education and training. This view borrows some of the conservative emphasis on responsible individual behavior but combines it with attention to the ideal of equality.

Where do average Americans fit in all these debates? Americans are often said to be philosophical conservatives and operational liberals.[47] When asked about government social policy in the abstract, they say they disapprove of activist government—a decidedly conservative view. But when they must evalu-

Politics on the Web

The Internet is a valuable tool for the retrieval, analysis, and dissemination of information. Vast amounts of information are available on-line about current policy debates, such as welfare reform. Policy advocates such as the Children's Defense Fund, the Electronic Policy Network (a wing of *American Prospect* magazine), and the Center on Budget and Policy Priorities, on the liberal side, and conservative organizations such as the Heritage Foundation and the Christian Coalition provide arguments for and against welfare reform proposals. Even more impressive is the impact the Internet has had in promoting particular solutions to social problems. Since the passage of the welfare reform bill in 1996, dozens of nonpartisan sites have been set up as clearinghouses for information pertaining to welfare caseloads, successful or unsuccessful innovations, and current federal laws. Sites such as the Hudson Institute's Welfare Reform Center and the University of Maryland's Welfare Reform Academy are devoted to helping states implement reforms.

www.wwnorton.com/wtp3e

ate particular programs, Americans generally express support—a more liberal perspective. Some programs, of course, are preferred over others. Policies in which the recipients are regarded as deserving, such as programs for the elderly, receive more support than those that assist working-age people. Programs that have a reputation for effectiveness and programs that require people to help themselves through work are also viewed favorably.[48]

In sum, most Americans take a pragmatic approach to social welfare policies: they favor programs that work, and they want to reform those that seem not to work. By rejecting the policy extremes, Americans signal their awareness of the tensions that social policies generate among their most deeply held values of liberty, equality, and democracy. Political debates about social policy connect most closely with the public when they consider which mix of policies represents the appropriate balance among these three ideals, rather than when they ask the public to choose among them.

The Citizen's Role

Social policy directly and indirectly touches the lives of all Americans. Most working Americans pay the payroll taxes that finance Social Security and Medicare. All Americans over the age of sixty-five are covered by Medicare and most also receive Social Security. But even people who are not directly receiving benefits are affected by the federal social role: many more people would be supporting their parents or grandparents if federal social policy did not exist. In addition, many working-age Americans would be much less secure without the protections provided by unemployment insurance, workers' compensation, food stamps, and TANF. Their quality of life would decline without the mortgage deduction and other tax expenditures that assist employers in providing benefits. Citizens thus have a direct stake in the future of social policy—both on the benefit side and on the payment side.

Because social policy is woven into the fabric of daily life for most people, it is not surprising that citizens have often played an active role in debates about social policy. This is particularly evident with regard to Social Security because it is such a big program and so many people rely on its benefits. Active citizen mobilization during the Great Depression was central to establishing Social Security in the first place. The Townsend movement of the 1930s, named after Dr. Francis Townsend, the man who led it, spurred widespread interest and built an active political movement of more than 10 million supporters pressing for public pensions for the elderly. As we saw earlier in this chapter, citizen involvement continued as Social Security grew and the AARP emerged in the 1950s as a powerful lobby to defend Social Security. With a membership of over 33 million, the AARP is one of the largest and most powerful lobbies in Washington.

In recent years, citizen interest in Social Security has begun to extend beyond the elderly. Groups such as X-PAC and the 2030 Center, discussed at the beginning of this chapter, have emerged to represent the voices of youth in this debate. Yet it is often hard to tell what is a genuine citizen voice: groups on all sides of the reform issue receive money and support from interests that stand to benefit from one policy direction or another. As reform of Social Security has become a hot issue, efforts have been made to broaden and deepen the debate. For example in 1998, the Pew Charitable Trusts, a private philanthropic foundation, launched a project called "Americans Discuss Social Security," in which it set up citizen meetings across the country, video teleconferences, and other forums through which citizens can learn about and discuss future options for Social Security. The organizers have been particularly interested in finding ways to engage college students in that debate, going so far as to sponsor a college outreach program with a $100,000 reward for the best proposal on how to encourage students to participate.[49]

Many social policies involve highly technical issues: actuaries devise highly complicated formulas to estimate future Social Security expenditures; health care experts propose intricate reforms designed to reduce costs. Yet social policy is far more than a technical issue—it fundamentally engages our national values. What do we owe each other as members of society? What should government do for its people and what should be expected of them in return? Only an engaged and informed citizenry can provide the best answers to these questions. They are too important to be left to the experts.

GET INVOLVED Serving Your Community

The welfare state is composed of agencies, programs, and policies at all levels of government. They are designed to help people meet their basic needs for food, clothing, shelter, employment, and health care. The welfare state also consists of a host of community organizations (that may or may not receive government funding) as well as interest groups and activists who seek to influence social policy.

The range of support efforts carried on within most communities is usually quite remarkable. Telephone books often have a special front section listing the "Community Services" available in the local area. These might include adoption and foster care agencies, AIDS and HIV services, alcohol and drug dependency clinics, disability rights advocacy, domestic abuse counseling, employment agencies, environmental groups, family planning, financial assistance and food programs, health care agencies, homeless and housing services, legal aid, rape hotlines, recycling information, senior services, suicide prevention, and volunteer agencies. Virtually all of these community-service organizations are devoted to ensuring a basic level of welfare for people in the area.

Other groups offer an array of goods and services to people who need them. Churches and synagogues, public and private schools, charities, hospitals, retirement homes, and fraternal organizations, as well as college fraternities and sororities, often sponsor or support outreach programs intended to improve the quality of life for people in the neighborhood. How can you get involved?

- Choose an agency, organization, or program that interests you. Telephone it or drop by its offices. Express your interest. Ask if the agency can use a volunteer. Some organizations such as government welfare offices may not use volunteers; but others such as orphanages, homeless shelters, and public hospitals are likely to have many places for dependable volunteers.
- Plan a one-day volunteer outing with a group of friends or like-minded members of an organization. Call ahead to see where and when your efforts might be helpful. Can your group perform services such as providing entertainment for disabled seniors in a retirement facility? Are your friends interested in serving food in a homeless shelter or soup kitchen? Can they chaperone a group of at-risk youth on a trip to a museum?
- Organize a fund-raiser for your favorite charity. Car washes, bake sales, and book fairs, as well as arts and crafts displays, are all good ways to raise much-needed funds for the community-service organization of your choice.

If you choose to volunteer, be aware that there are a variety of tasks that you might find yourself doing. Some organizations need someone to do office work, such as stuffing envelopes and making copies. Others want someone to perform clean-up duties, such as making beds, washing dishes, and scrubbing floors. Still others desire someone to operate a cash register in a second-hand store or gift shop. However, many organizations will provide you the opportunity to work directly with the recipients of their services.

If you want to improve the quality of life in your community in a more systematic way, consider getting involved in shaping social policy. Consider housing policy. In cities where a high proportion of residents are renters, the price of rentals is rising, and the stock of rental housing is limited, community activists may seek a new law or policy to limit rent increases and prohibit the conversion of rental housing into condominiums. A typical struggle for rent control seeks to establish a community housing policy that preserves "affordable" housing for people with low or moderate incomes.

If you participate in a rent-control struggle, you will likely have to meet several challenges. First, you will have to persuade people that local government actually has the authority to regulate what a landlord does with his property. Second, even if you win passage of a rent control law or policy, property owners are likely to sue the city for denying their property rights. Third, citizens and the courts may support you but landlords may push for a state law to override local rent contol. Over time, it is likely that many community activists will drift away while most landlords will persist in their opposition. Changing social policy is a long and difficult challenge.

Nonetheless, tenant activists and their supporters have succeeded to promote policies that keep rents sufficiently stable for low income people to remain in the community (while allowing landlords modest increases in rental income to cover the costs of maintenance and improvements). Community activists can change housing policy. They also can influence policies to ensure food, employment, and health care for the neediest members of the community.

Summary

The capitalist system is the most productive type of economy on earth, but it is not perfect. Most people face some insecurity over the course of their lives; poverty amidst plenty continues. Many policies have emerged to deal with these imperfections. This chapter discussed the welfare state and gave an account of how Americans came to recognize extremes of poverty and dependency and how Congress then attempted to reduce these extremes with policies that moderately redistribute opportunity.

The first section of this chapter examined the development of social policies. These policies—and the political conflicts surrounding them—underscore the fact that Americans hold multiple ideals. Americans are truly committed to individual liberty, but they also support equality of opportunity.

Welfare state policies are subdivided into several categories. First there are the contributory programs. Virtually all employed persons are required to contribute a portion of their wages into welfare trust funds, and later on, when they retire or are disabled, they have a right, or entitlement, to draw on those contributions. Another category of welfare is composed of noncontributory programs, also called "public assistance." These programs provide benefits for people who can demonstrate need by passing a "means test." Assistance from contributory and noncontributory programs can involve either cash benefits or in-kind benefits.

Contributory and noncontributory programs generally serve different groups of people. The elderly, who are widely viewed as deserving of benefits, receive the most comprehensive and generous social programs. The middle class benefits from the "shadow welfare state," which consists of benefits offered through their jobs but supported by federal tax breaks. There are few social programs to support the working poor because many noncontributory social programs, such as Medicaid and the new Temporary Assistance to Needy Families block grant, are reserved for the nonworking poor.

The last section of the chapter considered the tensions between the welfare state and American values. Social policies represent a balance among the ideals of liberty, democracy, and equality. Although political debates often frame the issues surrounding social policies in terms that emphasize one value over others, most Americans tend to take a pragmatic perspective that strikes a balance among these core political ideals.

FOR FURTHER READING

Katz, Michael. *In the Shadow of the Poorhouse: A Social History of Welfare in America*. New York: Basic Books, 1986.

Katznelson, Ira, and Margaret Weir. *Schooling for All: Race, Class, and the Democratic Ideal*. New York: Basic Books, 1985.

Light, Paul. *Artful Work: The Politics of Social Security Reform*. New York: Random House, 1985.

Marmor, Theodore R., Jerry L. Mashaw, and Phillip L. Harvey. *America's Misunderstood Welfare State*. New York: Basic Books, 1990.

Murray, Charles. *Losing Ground: American Social Policy, 1950–1980.* New York: Basic Books, 1984.

Orfield, Gary, and Carole Ashkinaze. *The Closing Door: Conservative Policy and Black Opportunity.* Chicago: University of Chicago Press, 1991.

Patterson, James T. *America's Struggle against Poverty, 1900–1994.* Cambridge, MA: Harvard University Press, 1994.

Skocpol, Theda. *The Missing Middle: Working Families and the Future of American Social Policy.* New York: Norton, 2000.

Weir, Margaret, Ann Orloff, and Theda Skocpol. *The Politics of Social Policy in the United States.* Princeton, NJ: Princeton University Press, 1988.

Weir, Margaret, ed. *The Social Divide: Political Parties and the Future of Activist Government.* Washington, D.C.: Brookings Institution Press, 1998.

STUDY OUTLINE

1. Equality of opportunity, a widely shared American ideal, was enshrined by Thomas Jefferson in the Declaration of Independence. But there remain problems associated with this ideal.
2. The lowest income brackets are disproportionately composed of members of groups who have been deprived of opportunities.

The Welfare State

1. Prior to 1935, the welfare system in America was composed of private groups rather than government. State governments gradually assumed some of the obligation to relieve the poor.
2. The founding of the welfare state can be dated to the Social Security Act of 1935; this act provided for both contributory and noncontributory welfare programs.
3. Contributory programs—such as Social Security and unemployment compensation—provide "forced savings" for individuals who, as a consequence of making a contribution, can receive program benefits at a later time.
4. Noncontributory programs—such as food stamps and Temporary Assistance to Needy Families (TANF)—provide assistance to people based on demonstrated need rather than any contribution they may have made.
5. Spending on social policies, especially Social Security and Medicare, has increased dramatically in recent decades, raising concerns about how entitlement programs will be paid for in future decades.

Who Gets What from Social Policy?

1. The elderly are the beneficiaries of generous social policies in part because they are perceived as being a deserving population and because they have become a strong interest group.
2. The middle class benefits from social policies in many ways; one way is through the use of tax expenditures, which provide that certain payments made by employers and employees are not taxed by the government.
3. People who are working but are still poor receive limited assistance from government social programs. Although they may be seen as deserving, they receive only limited assistance because they lack organization and political power.
4. Medicaid and TANF are programs aimed at the able-bodied, nonworking poor, but they only receive assistance if they are parents caring for children. The unpopularity of such programs has prompted efforts to decrease spending in recent years.

Breaking the Cycle of Poverty

1. Education, employment, health, and housing policies are four ways to break the cycle of poverty and redistribute opportunities.
2. The education policies of state and local governments are the most important single force in the distribution and redistribution of opportunity in America.
3. Employment and job training programs have not been a consistent goal of the modern welfare state.
4. Although states also took the early lead in the arena of public health policy, the federal government began to adopt policies in the early 1900s to protect citizens from the effects of pollution and other health hazards.
5. Federal housing policy consists of many pork-barrel programs, but it also represents a commitment to improving the conditions and opportunities of the poor.

The Welfare State and American Values

1. The development of social policy in the United States reflects the tensions between the values of liberty, equality, and democracy. Various conservative and liberal perspectives attempt to reconcile these tensions with differing views on social policy. Each of these approaches seems out of step, however, with the more pragmatic view held by most Americans.

PRACTICE QUIZ

1. Which of the following is *not* an example of a contributory program?
   a) Social Security
   b) Medicare
   c) food stamps
   d) All of the above are examples of contributory programs.

2. Approximately what proportion of the United States population lives in what the government defines as poverty?
   a) 1/10
   b) 1/7
   c) 1/4
   d) 1/100

3. Prior to 1935, the private welfare system in the United States made a distinction between
   a) contributory and noncontributory programs.
   b) citizens and recent immigrants.
   c) the deserving poor and the undeserving poor.
   d) religious and secular assistance.

4. America's welfare state was constructed initially in response to
   a) World War II.
   b) political reforms of the Progressive era.
   c) the Great Depression.
   d) the growth of the military-industrial complex.

5. Which of the following are examples of in-kind benefits?
   a) Medicaid and food stamps
   b) Social Security payments and cost-of-living adjustments
   c) Medicare and unemployment compensation
   d) none of the above

6. Means testing requires that applicants for welfare benefits show
   a) that they are capable of getting to and from their workplace.
   b) that they have the ability to store and prepare food.
   c) some definite need for assistance plus an inability to provide for it.
   d) that they have the time and resources to fully take advantage of federal educational opportunities.

7. In 1996, as part of welfare reform, Aid to Families with Dependent Children was abolished and replaced by
   a) the Earned Income Tax Credit.
   b) Aid to Dependent Children.
   c) Supplemental Security Income.
   d) Temporary Assistance to Needy Families.

8. In terms of receiving benefits of social policies, what distinguishes the elderly from the working poor?
   a) The elderly are perceived as deserving, whereas the working poor are not.
   b) There is no significant difference between these two groups.
   c) The elderly are more organized and more politically powerful than are the working poor.
   d) The elderly are less organized and less politically powerful than are the working poor.

9. Who are the chief beneficiaries of the "shadow welfare state"?
   a) the rich
   b) the nonworking poor
   c) the working poor
   d) the middle class

10. Which of the following is *not* aimed at breaking the cycle of poverty?
    a) drug policies
    b) education policies
    c) employment training programs
    d) health policies

CRITICAL THINKING QUESTIONS

1. Two factors that seem to influence a particular group's ability to get what it wants from social policy are a) the perception that the group is deserving, and b) the political organization and power of the group. In some ways, it is easy to take each of these factors as an independent ingredient of social policy success. But each factor could be seen as having an impact on the other. Select a group and discuss its relative success or failure in social policy. How might the perception of a group as deserving of assistance (and the assistance it receives) help that group become organized and politically powerful? How might organization and political power help shape public opinion favorably toward the group you selected?

2. Describe the changes over time in the welfare state in the United States. What factors led to the expansion of governmental power (both state and national) over social policy? What factors might lead to a decrease of governmental activity in social policy? How do you think social policy in the United States will change in the future? Which of today's political forces and debates will be important in shaping the social policies of the future?

KEY TERMS

Aid to Families with Dependent Children (AFDC) (p. 710)
contributory programs (p. 708)
cost-of-living adjustments (COLAs) (p. 710)
entitlement (p. 712)
equality of opportunity (p. 703)
food stamps (p. 711)
indexing (p. 710)
in-kind benefits (p. 712)
libertarian (p. 732)
means testing (p. 710)
Medicaid (p. 711)
Medicare (p. 710)
noncontributory programs (p. 710)
shadow welfare state (p. 721)
Social Security (p. 709)
Supplemental Security Income (SSI) (p. 711)
tax expenditures (p. 721)
Temporary Assistance to Needy Families (TANF) (p. 710)

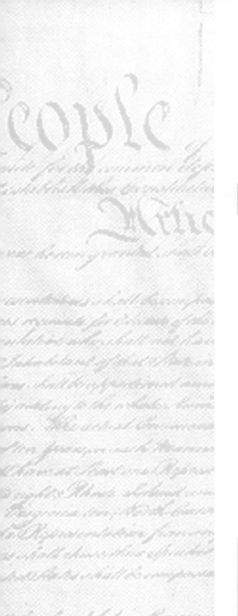

19 Foreign Policy

★ **The Players: The Makers and Shapers of Foreign Policy**

What institutions make up the foreign policy establishment?

What groups help shape foreign policy? Among these players, which are most influential?

★ **The Values in American Foreign Policy**

What are the legacies of the traditional system of foreign policy?

When and why did the traditional system of foreign policy end?

What new values guided U.S. foreign policy after World War II?

★ **The Instruments of Modern American Foreign Policy**

What are the six primary instruments of modern American foreign policy?

How does each instrument reflect a balance between the values of the traditional system of foreign policy and the values of cold war politics?

★ **Roles Nations Play**

What four traditional foreign policy roles has the United States adopted throughout its history?

Since the end of World War II, how has the role of the United States in world affairs evolved?

and Democracy

STUDENTS AND POLITICS

EVER since George Washington, in his farewell address, warned the American people "to have . . . as little political connection as possible" with foreign nations and to "steer clear of permanent alliances," Americans have been distrustful of foreign policy. Despite this distrust, the United States has been forced to pursue its national interests in the world, even if this has meant fighting a war. As a result of its foreign entanglements, the United States emerged as a world power, but not without maintaining some misgivings about foreign policy. As Alexis de Tocqueville noted in the 1830s, democracies lack the best qualities for the successful pursuit of foreign policy goals:

> Foreign policies demand scarcely any of those qualities which are peculiar to a democracy; they require, on the contrary, the perfect use of almost all those in which it is deficient. . . . A democracy can only with great difficulty regulate the details of an important undertaking, persevere in a fixed design, and work out its execution in spite of serious obstacles. It cannot combine its measures with secrecy or await their consequences with patience.[1]

The fear of foreign entanglements and the secrecy necessary to make foreign policy work formed the basis of American distrust. In some cases involving national security or fighting certain evils in the world, intervention and even cooperation with other nations was justified in the eyes of the public. Americans even learned to tolerate secrecy in the conduct of diplomacy to prevent war. But the Vietnam War shifted American sentiments back toward distrust. In 1971, *The New York Times* began publishing the "Pentagon Papers," excerpts from a secret Defense Department study of U.S. involvement in Vietnam. The Pentagon Papers revealed that U.S. officials had lied through the media to the American public about the country's entry into the war. The publication of the Pentagon Papers is but one example of how, as the American people learned more about their government, their distrust grew. And, as some elected officials discovered, the American people are a powerful force.

The American people can make or break any foreign policy. American public opinion can, as de Tocqueville warned, create barriers so that officials cannot "persevere in a fixed design . . ."; the American people can also rally to a national appeal in a way that gives greater strength to an international commitment and greater capacity to sustain that commitment—as with foreign aid, or, for that matter, the Vietnam War. It is now almost forgotten that most Americans, prior to the revelations in the Pentagon Papers, actually supported the Vietnam War substantially and consistently, despite the unusually active antiwar movement and an increasingly hostile press.[2]

A more recent, equally telling example of the power of the American people in foreign policy can be drawn from President Bill Clinton's preparations for renewed war against Iraq. At the end of 1997, Saddam Hussein, Iraq's leader, forced a standoff with the United States by ignoring the terms of surrender that had been imposed on Iraq by the United Nations after the 1991 Persian Gulf War. Saddam falsely declared that all Iraqi chemical and biological weapons had been destroyed, but then refused to allow American weapons inspectors into Iraq. Over the next weeks, the United States began a military buildup in the Persian Gulf region and sought to rebuild the coalition of nations that had easily defeated Iraq in 1991. Meanwhile, President Clinton tried valiantly to explain the Iraqi situation to the American people.

The culmination of Clinton's campaign to build public support came on the evening of February 18, 1998, with an internationally televised "town meeting" broadcast on the Cable News Network (CNN), featuring Secretary of State Madeleine Albright, Secretary of Defense William Cohen, and National Security Adviser Samuel Berger. The forum was held on the campus of Ohio State University in Columbus, Ohio. The night before the meeting, the president gave a nationally televised speech that was considered his best-ever speech on foreign policy. The president's carefully orchestrated plan to build public support for his Iraqi policy seemed to be on track. But during the town meeting the following evening, attended by 6,000 people, a relatively small number of hecklers (including some college students) opposed to any American involvement in Iraq attempted to disrupt the meeting. Even many of the well-behaved attendees displayed skepticism about the need for the military buildup in the Persian Gulf. If this forum was any indication, it was clear that the American people were not united behind the president in opposition to Iraq. Days after the Ohio State town meeting, the U.N. secretary-general negotiated an agreement with Iraq that ended the threat of an American-led air strike. The deal restored the conditions of Iraq's 1991 surrender.

Still another story of the power of a motivated minority of Americans has already been told, in Chapter 14, about the World Trade Organization (WTO). Even though the WTO exists only to implement the obligations and exchanges agreed to voluntarily by the participating countries, once WTO rulings were seen as a potential threat to American sovereignty, no amount of eloquence by President Clinton could quiet the clamor of the anti-WTO demonstrators in what came to be called "the battle of Seattle." Despite the rudeness of the demonstrators toward foreign delegates to the WTO meeting, U.S. leadership committed itself anew to linkage of labor, environmental, and human rights questions to trade agreements. There is no doubt this will make trade agreements harder to reach; but this is exactly what the demonstrators were seeking.

Both the Ohio State town meeting and the mass meeting in the Seattle streets demonstrated the power of the American people. Both cases illustrate an important fact—that public opinion polls, however influential they may be on American public policy, are not the only source of citizen influence on what the government does. Smaller segments of the American public, when sufficiently focused, can have an extraordinary impact on policy, even on foreign policy—somewhat like a magnifying glass igniting a flame by concentrating the sun's rays. And the impact of the people is considerably greater when the message is televised live on CNN and other stations, when the political leadership is indecisive, and when national objectives are poorly defined.

This extraordinary power of the American people is impressive, but it does have an ugly side: the power of the American people and their quick responsiveness to international events associated with the president (the "rallying effect" discussed in Chapter 14) force presidents and other foreign policy makers to engage in deceit. In order to manipulate the public into supporting foreign policies, high-ranking officials have on occasion actually conspired to give false or misleading information to the American public. The Pentagon Papers are perhaps the most well known example of such foreign policy deception.

This presents us with a dilemma. The American people possess an uncommon influence on what their government does, even in foreign policy. But people can make mistakes and bad decisions. In domestic policy situations a bad decision can be written off as one of the acceptable costs of democracy: bad decisions merely produce 20 or 30 percent cost overruns in a public project, or the collapse of a bridge, or the tearing down of public housing projects after only a decade of use. But a mistake in foreign policy can result in a war, and in modern warfare, most victories are achieved at great cost.

This chapter has no solution to the many foreign policy issues the United States confronts. Nonetheless, because the conduct of foreign policy is so complex and because there are particular problems facing a democracy such as the United States as it formulates and puts into effect particular foreign policies, a well-balanced analysis of foreign policy problems is essential. Such an analysis must treat at least four dimensions of foreign policy, which will make up the four main sections of this chapter.

- ***First, who makes and shapes foreign policy in the United States?*** Among these players, we will see that the president is most influential.
- ***Second, what values guide American foreign policy?*** We will look at the history of American foreign policy and see that, while the United States adopted some new values as it emerged as a world power, some legacies of the traditional system remain.
- ***Third, what tools are available for the conduct of foreign policy?*** We will examine the institutions and programs that serve to enable government to pursue America's national interests.
- ***Fourth, how does the United States conduct its foreign policy in the post–cold war world?*** We will assess the roles for America today and how well those roles uphold American political values.

The Players: The Makers and Shapers of Foreign Policy

- What institutions make up the foreign policy establishment?
- What groups help shape foreign policy? Among these players, which are most influential?

Although the power of the American people over foreign policy is impossible to overestimate, "the people" should not be given all the credit or all the blame for actual policies and their outcomes. As in domestic policy, foreign policy making is a highly pluralistic arena. First there are the official players, those who comprise the "foreign policy establishment"; these players and the agencies they head can be called the actual "makers" of foreign policy. But there are other major players, less official but still influential. We call these the "shapers."

WHO MAKES FOREIGN POLICY?

The President Although many foreign policy decisions can be made without so much as the president's fingerprint on them, these decisions must be made and implemented in the name of the president. Of course, much of the action in foreign policy takes place far from the White House and the president. But all foreign policy decisions and actions are taken to further a goal that the president wants. That all foreign policies come from the president is a necessity in making any foreign policy. All heads of state must have some confidence that each head of state has enough power and stability to negotiate, to make agreements, and to keep those agreements.

The Bureaucracy The major foreign policy players in the bureaucracy are the secretaries of the departments of State, Defense, and the Treasury; the Joint Chiefs of Staff (JCOS), especially the chair of the JCOS; and the director of the Central Intelligence Agency (CIA). A separate unit in the bureaucracy comprising these people and a few others is the National Security Council (NSC), whose main purpose is to iron out the differences among the key players and to integrate their positions in order to confirm or reinforce a decision the president wants to make in foreign policy or military policy. During the Clinton administration, the secretary of the Department of Commerce also became an increasingly important foreign policy maker, with the rise and spread of economic globalization. Clinton's first secretary of commerce, Ron Brown, was not the first to be active in promoting world trade, but he may well have been the most vigorous and successful up to now.

In addition to these top cabinet-level officials, key lower-level staff members have policy-making influence as strong as that of the Cabinet secretaries—some may occasionally exceed Cabinet influence. These include the two or three specialized national security advisers in the White House, the staff of the NSC (headed by the national security adviser), and a few other career bureaucrats in the departments of State and Defense whose influence varies according to their specialty and to the foreign policy issue at hand.

Congress In foreign policy making, Congress has to be subdivided into three parts. The first part is the Senate. For most of American history, the Senate was the only important congressional foreign policy player because of its constitutional role in reviewing and approving treaties. The treaty power is still the primary entrée of the Senate into foreign policy making. But since World War II and the continual involvement of the United States in international security and foreign aid, Congress as a whole has become a major foreign policy maker because most modern foreign policies require financing, which requires both the House of Representatives and the Senate. Congress has also become increasingly involved in foreign policy making because of the increasing use by the president of **executive agreements** to conduct foreign policy. Executive agree-

executive agreement
an agreement, made between the president and another country, that has the force of a treaty but does not require the Senate's "advice and consent"

ments have the force of treaties but do not require prior approval by the Senate. They can, however, be revoked by action of both chambers of Congress.

The third congressional player is the foreign policy and military policy committees: in the Senate these are the Foreign Relations Committee and the Armed Services Committee; in the House, the International Affairs Committee and the Armed Services Committee. Usually, a few members of these committees who have spent years specializing in foreign affairs become trusted members of the foreign policy establishment and are actually makers rather than mere shapers of foreign policy. In fact, several members of Congress have left to become key foreign affairs Cabinet members.[3]

WHO SHAPES FOREIGN POLICY?

The shapers of foreign policy are the nonofficial, informal players, but they are typically people or groups that have great influence in the making of foreign policy. Of course, the influence of any given group varies according to the party and the ideology that is dominant at a given moment.

Interest Groups Far and away the most important category of nonofficial player is the interest group—that is, the interest groups to whom one or more foreign policy issues are of long-standing and vital relevance. The type of interest group with the reputation for the most influence is the economic interest group. Yet the myths about their influence far outnumber and outweigh the realities. The actual influence of organized economic interest groups in foreign policy varies enormously from issue to issue and year to year. Most of these groups are "single-issue" groups and are therefore most active when their particular issue is on the agenda. On many of the broader and more sustained policy issues, such as the **North American Free Trade Agreement (NAFTA)** or the general question of American involvement in international trade, the larger

North American Free Trade Agreement (NAFTA)
trade treaty between the United States, Canada, and Mexico to lower and eliminate tariffs between the three countries

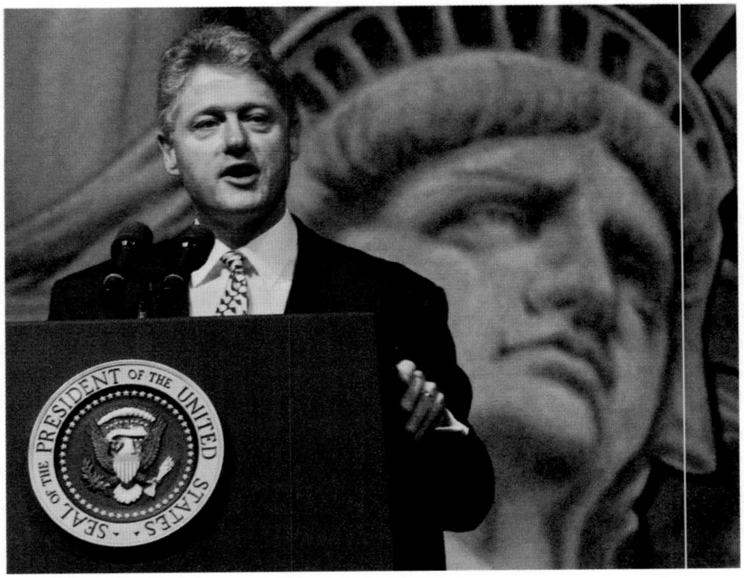

President Clinton announcing the extension of most-favored-nation status to China in 1996. The debate over China's status involved Congress, interest groups concerned about issues ranging from human rights to foreign trade, and the media, although, as in most matters of foreign policy, the president had the most important role in the debate.

Jewish-American groups, such as the Coalition for Jewish Concerns, shown demonstrating outside the United Nations in New York City, are vocal on policy matters concerning the Middle East.

interest groups, sometimes called "peak associations," find it difficult to maintain tight enough control of their many members to speak with a single voice. The most systematic study of international trade policies and their interest groups concluded that the leaders of these large, economic interest groups spend more time maintaining consensus among their members than they do actually lobbying Congress or pressuring major players in the executive branch.[4] The more successful economic interest groups, in terms of influencing foreign policy, are the narrower, single-issue groups, such as the tobacco industry, which over the years has successfully kept American foreign policy from putting heavy restrictions on international trade in and advertising of tobacco products, and the computer hardware and software industries, which have successfully hardened the American attitude toward Chinese piracy of intellectual property rights.

Another type of interest group with a well-founded reputation for influence in foreign policy is made up of people with strong attachments and identifications to their country of national origin. The interest group with the reputation for greatest influence is American Jews, whose family and emotional ties to Israel make them one of the most alert and potentially one of the most active interest groups in the whole field of foreign policy. But note once again how narrowly specialized that interest is—it focuses almost entirely and exclusively on policies toward Israel. Similarly, Americans of Irish heritage, despite having resided in the United States for two, three, or four generations, still maintain a vigilance about American policies toward Ireland and Northern Ireland; many even contribute to the terrorist activities of the Irish Republican Army. Many other ethnic and national interest groups wield similar influence over American foreign policy.

A third type of interest group, one with a reputation that has been growing in the past two decades, is the human rights interest group. Such groups are made up of people who, instead of having self-serving economic or ethnic interests in foreign policy, are genuinely concerned for the welfare and treatment of people throughout the world—particularly those who suffer under harsh political regimes. A relatively small but often quite influential example is Amnesty International, whose exposés of human rights abuses have altered the practices of many regimes around the world. In recent years, the Christian Right has also been a vocal advocate for the human rights of Christians who are persecuted in other parts of the world, most notably in China, for their religious beliefs. For example, the Christian Coalition joined groups like Amnesty International in lobbying Congress to cut trade with countries that permit attacks against religious believers.

A related type of group with a fast-growing influence is the ecological or environmental group, sometimes called the "greens." Groups of this nature, such as Greenpeace, often depend more on demonstrations than on the usual forms and strategies of influence in Washington—lobbying and using electoral politics, for example. Demonstrations in strategically located areas can have significant influence on American foreign policy. One good example of this is the opposition that relatively small environmental protection groups in the United States raised against American contracts to buy electrical power from the Canadian province of Quebec: The group opposed the ecological effect of the enlarged hydroelectric power dams that were going to have to be built in order to accommodate American demands.[5]

The Media Here again, myth may outweigh truth about media influence in foreign policy. The most important element of the policy influence of the media is the speed and scale with which the media can spread political communications. In that factor alone, the media's influence is growing—more news reaches more people faster, and people's reaction times are therefore shorter. When we combine this ability to communicate faster with the "feedback" medium of public opinion polling, it becomes clear how the media have become so influential—they enable the American people to reach the president and the other official makers of foreign policy.[6]

There is one other aspect of media influence to consider. Many unhappy politicians complain bitterly of "media bias." The complaint most often heard is that journalists have a liberal (anti-Republican) bias. Although this general complaint has never been

Students and Politics

"Anthropologist Margaret Mead said, 'Never doubt that a small group of dedicated individuals can change the world. In fact, it is the only thing that ever has.'

"This quote is on the World Wide Web site of Penn State Students for a Free Tibet and, while heading out in their cars . . . for Washington, D.C., [members of this group] may keep it in mind. While many students are still sleeping, this organization is on a mission.

"The group is rallying together in Lafayette Park with other organizations, such as Amnesty International, for a cause it strongly believes in, said Steve Marquardt, vice president of Penn State Students for a Free Tibet.

"'Tibet, a country of nomadic Buddhists, has suffered countless numbers of human rights violations,' Marquardt said. He added that the Chinese government has since killed Tibetans and committed other atrocities. China has polluted Tibet with toxic waste and burned down homes, he added.

"'Tibet is the worst case of human rights violations in the world and since the Chinese government has a strong military presence, those who speak out face imprisonment,' Marquardt said. . . .

"Tibet has been under the control of the communist Chinese government since the 1950s, said Paul Moses, the group's adviser.

"'We hope to teach people about the human rights issues in Tibet, and therefore apply public pressure to the government of China,' Moses said.

"The group's mission is educational and it hopes to promote awareness of the issue, Moses said.

"Such awareness leads to pressure that can influence China, just as pressure helped end apartheid in South Africa, he added."

SOURCE: Christopher Antonacci, "PSU students rally for Tibet's freedom," *Daily Collegian* (Pennsylvania State University), October 29, 1997; reprinted on Uwire, http://www.uwire.com/uwire/97/10/news10299705.chtml (accessed June 1998).

adequately documented, one aspect of media bias has been shown. Using survey evidence, Michael Robinson demonstrated that reliance on television as a source of news gave people negative attitudes toward public policies and especially toward government and public officials.[7] Robinson called this attitude "videomalaise." A later study found, in addition, that "television news in particular has an inherent bias toward reporting negative and critical information. In other words, 'videomalaise' [is] as much a product of the medium as of the message."[8] One probable influence of the media on foreign as well as domestic policy has been to make the American people far more cynical and skeptical than they would otherwise have been. Beyond that, however, the influence of any medium of communication or any one influential journalist or news program varies from case to case.

PUTTING IT TOGETHER

What can we say about who really makes American foreign policy? First, except for the president, the influence of players and shapers varies from case to case—this is a good reason to look with some care at each example of foreign policy in this chapter. Second, since the one constant influence is the centrality of the president in foreign policy making, it is best to evaluate other actors and factors as they interact with the president.[9] Third, the reason influence varies from case to case is that each case arises under different conditions and with vastly different time constraints: for issues that arise and are resolved quickly, the opportunity for influence is limited. Fourth, foreign policy experts will usually disagree about the level of influence any player or type of player has on policy making.

But just to get started, let's make a few tentative generalizations and then put them to the test with the substance and experience reported in the remainder of this chapter. First, when an important foreign policy decision has to be made under conditions of crisis—where "time is of the essence"—the influence of the presidency is at its strongest. Second, under those time constraints, access to the decision is limited almost exclusively to the narrowest definition of the "foreign policy establishment." The arena for participation is tiny; any discussion at all is limited to the officially and constitutionally designated players. To put this another way, in a crisis, the foreign policy establishment works as it is supposed to.[10] As time becomes less restricted, even when the decision to be made is of great importance, the arena of participation expands to include more government players and more nonofficial, informal players—the most concerned interest groups and the most important journalists. In other words, the arena becomes more pluralistic, and therefore less distinguishable from the politics of domestic policy making. Third, because there are so many other countries with power and interests on any given issue, there are severe limits on the choices the United States can make. As one author concludes, in foreign affairs, "policy takes precedence over politics."[11] Thus, even though foreign policy making in noncrisis situations may more closely resemble the pluralistic politics of domestic policy making, foreign policy making is still a narrower arena with fewer participants.

The Values in American Foreign Policy

- What are the legacies of the traditional system of foreign policy?
- When and why did the traditional system of foreign policy end?
- What new values guided U.S. foreign policy after World War II?

When President Washington was preparing to leave office in 1796, he crafted with great care, and with the help of Alexander Hamilton and James Madison, a farewell address that is one of the most memorable documents in American history. We have already had occasion to look at a portion of Washington's farewell address, because in it he gave some stern warnings against political parties (see Chapter 10). But Washington's greater concern was to warn the nation against foreign influence:

> History and experience prove that foreign influence is one of the most baneful foes of republican government. . . . The great rule of conduct for us in regard to foreign nations is, in extending our commercial relations to have with them as little *political* connection as possible. So far as we have already formed engagements let them be fulfilled with perfect good faith. Here let us stop. . . . There can be no greater error than to expect or calculate upon real favors from nation to nation. . . . Trust to temporary alliances for extraordinary emergencies, [but in all other instances] steer clear of permanent alliances with any portion of the foreign world. . . . Such an attachment of a small or weak toward a great and powerful nation dooms the former to be the satellite of the latter [emphasis in original.][12]

With the exception of a few leaders such as Thomas Jefferson and Thomas Paine, who were eager to take sides with the French against all others, Washington was probably expressing sentiments shared by most Americans. In fact, during most of the nineteenth century, American foreign policy was to a large extent no foreign policy. But Americans were never isolationist, if isolationism means the refusal to have any associations with the outside world. Americans were eager for trade and for treaties and contracts facilitating trade. Americans were also expansionists, but their vision of expansionism was limited to filling up the North American continent only (see Figure 19.1 on the next page).

LEGACIES OF THE TRADITIONAL SYSTEM

Two legacies flowed from the long tradition based on Washington's farewell address. One is the intermingling of domestic and foreign policy institutions. The other is unilateralism—America's willingness to go it alone. Each reveals much about the values behind today's conduct of foreign policy.

Intermingling of Domestic and Foreign Policy Because the major European powers once policed the world, American political leaders could treat foreign

Figure 19.1 TERRITORIAL EXPANSION BY THE UNITED STATES, 1803–53

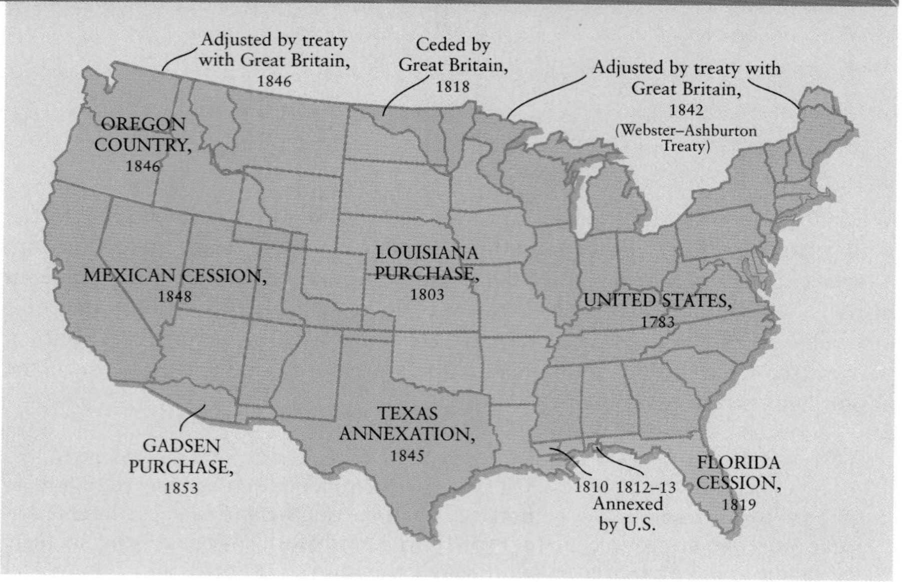

America's foreign policy during the nineteenth century was primarily focused on territorial expansion, as the nation sought to fuel its growing economy with land and natural resources.

policy as a mere extension of domestic policy. The tariff is the best example. A tax on one category of imported goods as a favor to interests in one section of the country would directly cause friction elsewhere in the country. But the demands of those adversely affected could be met without directly compromising the original tariff, by adding a tariff to still other goods that would placate those who were complaining about the original tariff. In this manner, Congress was continually adding and adjusting tariffs on more and more classes of commodities.

unilateralism
a foreign policy that seeks to avoid international alliances, entanglements, and permanent commitments in favor of independence, neutrality, and freedom of action

Unilateralism Unilateralism, not isolationism, was the American posture toward the world until the middle of the twentieth century. Isolationism means trying to cut off contacts with the outside, to be a self-sufficient fortress. America was never isolationist; it preferred **unilateralism,** or "going it alone." Americans have always been more likely to rally around the president in support of direct action rather than for a sustained, diplomatic involvement.

THE GREAT LEAP TO WORLD POWER

The traditional era of U.S. foreign policy came to an end with World War I for two important reasons. First, the "balance of power" system[13] that had kept the major European powers from world war for a hundred years had collapsed.[14] In fact, the great powers themselves had collapsed internally. The most devastating of all wars up to that time had ruined their economies, their empires, and, in most cases, their political systems. Second, the United States was suddenly one of the great powers. Yet there was no discernible change in America's approach to foreign policy in the period between World War I and

World War II. After World War I, as one foreign policy analyst put it, "the United States withdrew once more into its insularity. Since America was unwilling to use its power, that power, for purposes of foreign policy, did not really exist."[15]

The Great Leap in foreign policy was finally made thirty years after conditions demanded it and only then after another world war. Following World War II, pressure for a new tradition came into direct conflict with the old. The new tradition required foreign entanglements; the old tradition feared them deeply. The new tradition required diplomacy; the old distrusted it. The new tradition required acceptance of antagonistic political systems; the old embraced democracy and was aloof from all else.

The values of the new tradition were all apparent during the **cold war.** Instead of unilateralism, the United States pursued **multilateralism,** entering into treaties with other nations to achieve its foreign policy goals (see Figure 19.2). The most notable of these treaties is that which formed the **North Atlantic Treaty Organization (NATO)** in 1948, which allied the United States, Canada, and most of Western Europe. With its NATO allies, the United States practiced a two-pronged policy in dealing with its cold war rival, the Soviet Union:

cold war
the period of struggle between the United States and the former Soviet Union between the late 1940s and about 1990

multilateralism
a foreign policy that seeks to encourage the involvement of several nation-states in coordinated action, usually in relation to a common adversary, with terms and conditions usually specified in a multicountry treaty

COLLECTIVE DEFENSE TREATIES SIGNED BY THE UNITED STATES — **Figure 19.2**

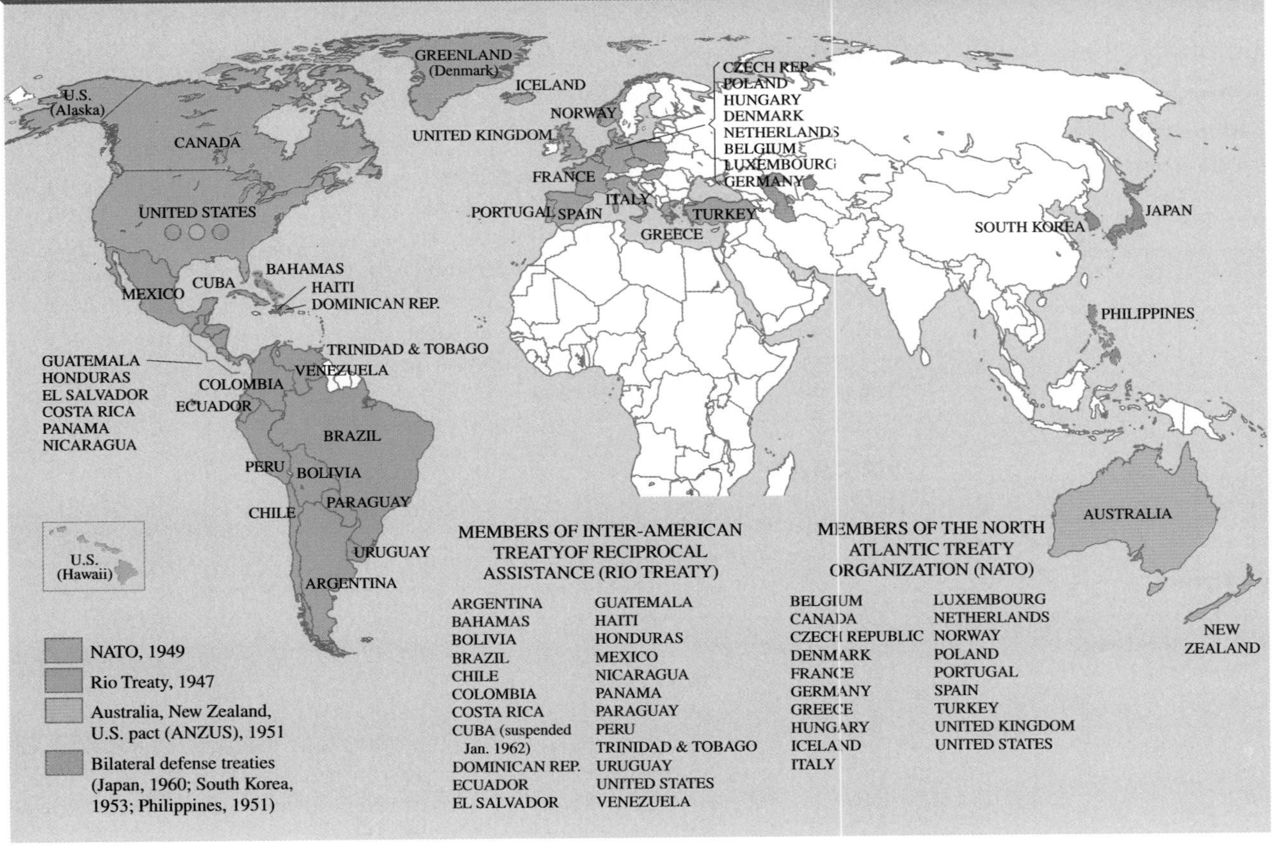

containment and **deterrence.** Fearing that the Soviet Union was bent on world domination, the United States fought wars in Korea and Vietnam to "contain" Soviet power. And in order to deter a direct attack against itself or its NATO allies, the United States developed a multi-billion-dollar nuclear arsenal capable of destroying the Soviet Union many times over. An arms race between the United States and the Soviet Union was extremely difficult if not impossible to resist because there was no way for either side to know when they had enough deterrent to continue preventing aggression by the other side. The cold war ended abruptly in 1989, after the Soviet Union had spent itself into oblivion and allowed its empire to collapse. Many observers called the end of the cold war a victory for democracy. But more importantly, it was a victory for capitalism over communism, a vindication of the free market as the best way to produce the greatest wealth of nations. Furthering capitalism has long been one of the values guiding American foreign policy and this might be more true now than at any time before.

North Atlantic Treaty Organization (NATO)
a treaty organization, comprising the United States, Canada, and most of Western Europe, formed in 1948 to counter the perceived threat from the Soviet Union

containment
the policy used by the United States during the cold war to restrict the expansion of communism and limit the influence of the Soviet Union

deterrence
the development and maintenance of military strength as a means of discouraging attack

The Instruments of Modern American Foreign Policy

- What are the six primary instruments of modern American foreign policy?
- How does each instrument reflect a balance between the values of the traditional system of foreign policy and the values of cold war politics?

Any **nation-state** has at hand certain instruments, or tools, to use in implementing its foreign policy. An instrument is neutral, capable of serving many goals. There have been many instruments of American foreign policy, and we can deal here only with those instruments we deem to be most important in the modern epoch: diplomacy, the United Nations, the international monetary structure, economic aid, collective security, and military deterrence. Each of these instruments will be evaluated in this section for its utility in the conduct of American foreign policy, and each will be assessed in light of the history and development of American values.

nation-state
a political entity consisting of a people with some common cultural experience (nation) who also share a common political authority (state), recognized by other sovereignties (nation-states)

DIPLOMACY

We begin this treatment of instruments with diplomacy because it is the instrument to which all other instruments should be subordinated, although they seldom are. **Diplomacy** is the representation of a government to other foreign governments. Its purpose is to promote national values or interests by peaceful means. According to Hans Morgenthau, "a diplomacy that ends in war has failed in its primary objective."[16]

The first effort to create a modern diplomatic service in the United States was made through the Rogers Act of 1924, which established the initial framework for a professional foreign service staff. But it took World War II and the Foreign Service Act of 1946 to forge the foreign service into a fully professional diplomatic corps.

diplomacy
the representation of a government to other foreign governments

Diplomacy, by its very nature, is overshadowed by spectacular international events, dramatic initiatives, and meetings among heads of state or their direct personal representatives. The traditional American distrust of diplomacy continues today, albeit in weaker form. Impatience with or downright distrust of diplomacy has been built not only into all the other instruments of foreign policy but also into the modern presidential system itself.[17] So much personal responsibility has been heaped upon the presidency that it is difficult for presidents to entrust any of their authority or responsibility in foreign policy to professional diplomats in the State Department and other bureaucracies.

Distrust of diplomacy has also produced a tendency among all recent presidents to turn frequently to military and civilian personnel outside the State Department to take on a special diplomatic role as direct personal representatives of the president. As discouraging as it is to those who have dedicated their careers to foreign service to have personal appointees chosen over their heads, it is probably even more discouraging when they are displaced from a foreign policy issue as soon as relations with the country they are posted in begin to heat up. When a special personal representative is sent abroad to represent the president, that envoy holds a status higher than that of the local ambassador, and the embassy becomes the envoy's temporary residence and base of operation. Despite the impressive professionalization of the American foreign service—with advanced training, competitive exams, language requirements, and career commitment—this practice of displacing career ambassadors with political appointees and with special personal presidential representatives continues. For instance, when President Clinton sought in 1994 to make a final diplomatic attempt to persuade Haiti's military dictator to relinquish power to the country's freely elected president before dispatching U.S. military forces to the island, he sent a team of three personal representatives—former president Jimmy Carter, Senator Sam Nunn, and former chairman of the Joint Chiefs of Staff Colin Powell.

The significance of diplomacy and its vulnerability to domestic politics may be better appreciated as we proceed to the other instruments. Diplomacy was an instrument more or less imposed on Americans as the prevailing method of dealing among nation-states in the nineteenth century. The other instruments to be identified and assessed below are instruments that Americans self-consciously crafted for themselves to take care of their own chosen place in the world affairs of the second half of the twentieth century. They are, therefore, more reflective of American culture and values than is diplomacy.

Students and Politics

[George Washington University] senior Anisha Lal sat in the tenth row at [the] opening ceremony of the NATO 50th Anniversary Summit.

"I really lucked out," Lal said. "There were a couple of empty seats and I got to go sit down. It was amazing. Here I was in a room with the most powerful people in the world."

For many George Washington University students, school and socializing [were] pushed aside for a chance to take part in the historic NATO conference, which ended Sunday.

Lal, an international affairs major who volunteered three weeks for the summit, said seeing leaders from around the world made the thirty-hour weeks of entering data and delivering tickets to the White House worth the effort.

"I worked with a lot of people who had definite opinions about world politics and things such as the bombing of Kosovo," she said. "Although everyone was busy, there was also time to think about the importance of NATO."

Senior international affairs major Franz Kuo spent the weekend working with NATO TV to produce footage of the conference.

"I'm really excited to be working with NATO TV because I'll get to go to all the events and really see what's going on," Kuo said. "It's been very interesting to work with lots of different government agencies. I've learned a lot about how our government deals with others."

Associate Dean Nathan Brown said student volunteers gained a greater appreciation of how international affairs works on a daily basis.

"It's a real charge to be participating in an international conference and not just watching it on TV," Brown said. "They see how an international summit works, how media plays into it, how countries try to come together and solve problems."

SOURCE: Rebecca Brink, "George Washington U. Students Make History at NATO Conference," *The Hatchet* (George Washington University), April 26, 1999.

AMERICAN DEMOCRACY IN COMPARATIVE PERSPECTIVE

Foreign Policy, NGOs, and the Internet Revolution

Diplomacy is a sober business, designed to carefully communicate the interests of the nation-state to diplomatic representatives of other nation-states in order to ensure that the passions of the respective populations do not foreclose nonviolent resolution to conflict. Thus, the practice of articulating and negotiating national interests among nations has traditionally been concentrated in the hands of a few highly trained and seasoned professionals, knowledgable in the ways of the world, adept at adjusting to a foreign culture, and fluent in foreign languages.

That, at least, is the ideal that most people have in mind when they think of foreign policy—specialists representing the political leaders of a nation-state working patiently to craft the policies of one nation-state toward another. The practice in today's world is somewhat different. To be sure, diplomacy still dominates formal relations between nation-states. However, eating away at the flesh of this system is the process of globalization. More specifically, what has changed is the ease by which actors who are not diplomats and therefore not attached to the government of the nation-state shape its foreign policy. These are not interest groups based solely in a nation-state that work simply to influence the preferences of their national leaders. Rather, these are transnational groups and coalitions that reach across borders and act to influence nation-states on a global basis. These nonformal, voluntary actors can rely on new forms of information technology to mobilize the interests of people through the articulation of common values and goals that affect populations within and across several nation-states. They have no interests per se in the power and sovereignty of the nation-state. Rather, they are far more likely to identify an issue that affects the security, health, and well being of people in general and to direct their efforts to influence the diplomacy of a nation to address those transnational concerns.

These new actors are known as *nongovernmental organizations,* or NGOs. An NGO is typically a private, voluntary, nonprofit organization. They are one of two major new actors on the international scene that influence the foreign policy environment of the nation-state; the other is the formal intergovernmental body (World Bank, International Monetary Fund, or the World Trade Organization). Intergovernmental bodies act as agents for the nation-states. In effect, they represent the nation-state and its foreign policy bureaucracy. The lines of control are more direct and formal. Nation-states dominate intergovernmental organizations.

Not so with NGOs, which are independent of the nation-state and its foreign policy bureaucracy and, as such, are much less constrained by the formalities of diplomacy and nation-state policies. NGOs are often associated with environmental groups, such as Greenpeace or Friends of the Earth. However, these groups encompass the full spectrum of policy interests of the nation-state and its population: education, research, business, law, philanthropic foundations, social services, culture, sports, human rights, health care, and, increasingly and importantly, labor.

What makes NGOs so powerful as a tool of foreign policy is the ease by which information technology allows nation-based NGOs to mobilize across international boundaries and form global coalitions, concentrating and coordinating their efforts to influence the domestic and foreign policies of nation-states. Fundamental to the success of NGOs is cheap and easily accessed Internet. The Association for Progressive Communications provides 50,000 NGOs in 133 countries access to millions of Internet users around the world at the cost of a local telephone call.

While the power of the United States and the influence of its foreign policy bureaucracy may not be as vulnerable to NGO pressure as other wealthy democracies, in an age of globalization and information connectivity, the foreign policy of the United States will nonetheless be impacted by the effect of these NGOs acting through America's most powerful trading allies. Globalization has in effect shrunk the distances between countries, and NGOs have opened the doors of the foreign policy structure to pressures previously excluded from the diplomatic activities of nation-states.

SOURCES: Jessica T. Mathews, "Power Shift," *Foreign Affairs,* January/February 1997, pp. 50–66; Curtis Runyan, "Action on the Front Lines," *World Watch,* November/December 1999, pp. 12–21; and Jayne Rodgers, "NGO Use of Computer-Mediated Communications: Opening New Spaces of Political Representation," paper presented at the 1998 International Studies Association meetings, available from *Columbia International Affairs Online,* at http://www.ciaonet.org/.

THE UNITED NATIONS

United Nations (UN)
an organization of nations founded in 1945 to serve as a channel for negotiation and a means of settling international disputes peaceably. The UN has had frequent successes in providing a forum for negotiation and on some occasions a means of preventing international conflicts from spreading. On a number of occasions, the UN has been a convenient cover for U.S. foreign policy goals

The utility of the **United Nations** (UN) to the United States as an instrument of foreign policy can too easily be underestimated. During the first decade or more after its founding in 1945, the United Nations was a direct servant of American interests. The most spectacular example of the use of the United Nations as an instrument of American foreign policy was the official UN authorization and sponsorship of intervention in Korea with an international "peacekeeping force" in 1950. Thanks to the Soviet boycott of the United Nations at that time, which deprived the USSR of its ability to use its veto in the Security Council of the UN, the United States was able to conduct the Korean War under the auspices of the United Nations.

The United States provided 40 percent of the UN budget in 1946 (its first full year of operation) and 26 percent of the $1.2 billion UN budget in 1997–98.[18] Many Americans feel that the United Nations does not give good value for the investment. But any evaluation of the United Nations must take into account the purpose for which the United States sought to create it: to achieve power without diplomacy. After World War II, when the United States could no longer remain aloof from foreign policy, the nation's leaders sought to use our power to create an international structure that could be run with a minimum of regular diplomatic involvement—so that Americans could return to their normal domestic pursuits. As one constitutional scholar characterized our Founding in 1787, so we could say of our effort to found the United Nations—we sought to create "a machine that would go of itself."[19]

The UN may have gained a new lease on life in the post–cold war era, with its performance in the Gulf War. Although President Bush's immediate reaction to Iraq's invasion of Kuwait was unilateral, he quickly turned to the UN for sponsorship. The UN General Assembly initially adopted resolutions condemning the invasion and approving the full blockade of Iraq. Once the blockade was seen as having failed to achieve the unconditional withdrawal demanded by the UN, the General Assembly adopted further resolutions authorizing the twenty-nine-nation coalition to use force if, by January 15, 1991, the resolutions were not observed. The Gulf War victory was a genuine UN victory. The cost of the operation was estimated at $61.1 billion. First authorized by the U.S. Congress, actual U.S. outlays were offset by pledges from the other participants—the largest shares coming from Saudi Arabia ($15.6 billion), Kuwait ($16 billion), Japan ($10 billion), and Germany ($6.5 billion). The final U.S. costs were estimated at a maximum of $8 billion.[20]

Whether or not the UN is able to maintain its central position in future border and trade disputes, demands for self-determination, and other provocations to war depends entirely upon the character of each dispute. The Gulf War was a special case because it was a clear instance of invasion of one country by another that also threatened the control of oil, which is of vital interest to the industrial countries of the world. But in the case of the former Yugoslavia, although the Bosnian conflict violated the world's conscience, it did not threaten vital national interests outside the country's region. When Yugoslavia's communist regime collapsed in the early 1990s, the country broke apart into historically ethnically distinct regions. In one of these, Bosnia, a fierce war broke out between Muslims, Croatians, and Serbians. From the outset, all outside parties urged peace, and United Nations troops were deployed

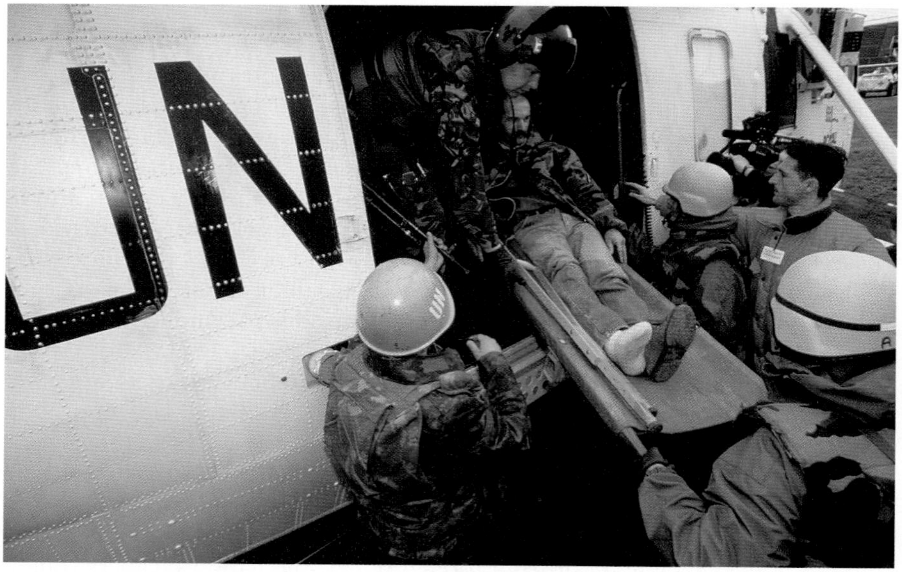

UN troops in Bosnia were stationed there for humanitarian purposes.

to create "safe havens" in several Bosnian cities and towns. Yet despite his campaign criticism of President Bush for not doing more to stop the bloodshed in Bosnia, President Clinton was also unable to muster enough support for a more active policy. Faced with resistance from NATO allies and from Russia, and with the unwillingness of the American people to risk the lives of U.S. soldiers over an issue not vital to U.S. interests, Clinton gave up his stern warnings and accepted the outcome: the international community's failure to prevent Serbs from waging a war of aggression and "ethnic cleansing." Not until November 1995, after still another year of frustration and with UN peacekeeping troops in increasingly serious danger from both sides in the Yugoslav civil war, was President Clinton able to achieve a ceasefire and a peace agreement in Dayton, Ohio, among the heads of the warring factions. (UN peacekeepers and aid workers were again present in Kosovo immediately following the pullout of hostile Serbian troops in 1999.)

Despite the difficulty of restoring peace, the UN and its peacekeeping troops did an extraordinary job in the former Yugoslavia, dealing both with the intransigence of the warring parties and with the disagreement among the European powers about how to deal with a vicious and destructive civil war in their own neighborhood. This and other recent UN interventions show the promise and the limits of the UN as an instrument of foreign policy in the post–cold war era. Although the United States can no longer control UN decisions, as it could in the UN's early days, the UN continues to function as a useful instrument of American foreign policy.[21]

THE INTERNATIONAL MONETARY STRUCTURE

Fear of a repeat of the economic devastation that followed World War I brought the United States together with its allies (except the USSR) to Bretton Woods, New Hampshire, in 1944 to create a new international economic structure for the postwar world. The result was two institutions: the International Bank for Reconstruction and Development (commonly called the World Bank) and the International Monetary Fund.

The World Bank was set up to finance long-term capital. Leading nations took on the obligation of contributing funds to enable the World Bank to make loans to capital-hungry countries. (The U.S. quota has been about one-third of the total.)

International Monetary Fund (IMF)
an institution established in 1944 which provides loans and facilitates international monetary exchange

The **International Monetary Fund (IMF)** was set up to provide for the short-term flow of money. After the war, the dollar, instead of gold, was the chief means by which the currencies of one country would be "changed into" currencies of another country for purposes of making international transactions. To permit debtor countries with no international balances to make purchases and investments, the IMF was set up to lend dollars or other appropriate currencies to needy member countries to help them overcome temporary trade deficits. For many years after World War II, the IMF, along with U.S. foreign aid, in effect constituted the only international medium of exchange.

During the 1990s, the IMF returned to a position of enhanced importance through its efforts to reform some of the largest debtor nations and formerly communist countries, to bring them more fully into the global capitalist economy. For example, in the early 1990s, Russia and thirteen other former Soviet republics were invited to join the IMF and the World Bank with the expectation of receiving $10.5 billion from these two agencies, primarily for a currency-stabilization fund. Each republic was to get a permanent IMF representative, and the IMF increased its staff by at least 10 percent to provide the expertise necessary to cope with the problems of these emerging capitalist economies.[22]

These activities of the IMF indicate just how effectively it is committed to the extension of the capitalist victory over communism. The reforms imposed on poorer countries—imposed as conditions to be met before receiving IMF loans—are reforms that commit a troubled country to joining or maintaining membership in the system of global capital exchange that allows investment to seek the highest profits, without restraint. This goal can ignite a boom—as it did in South Korea, Indonesia, Singapore, and Thailand—but that boom can terminate just as abruptly, leaving the economy in question defenseless.

Two 1997–98 financial crises in East Asia are good illustrations of the role and impact of the IMF. First came the Korea crisis. Economic failure caused great national embarrassment and suffering in South Korea in the autumn of 1997, along with great fear that the newly elected president, Kim Dae Jung,

Students and Politics

Students from around the country began arriving in the nation's capital Friday, ready to protest the actions of the World Bank and International Monetary Fund during their weekend meetings.

Outside the World Bank headquarters Friday, Peter Graif, 19, sat and watched with two friends as police barricaded the building. He traveled all night from Amherst College in Massachusetts and will be spending the weekend sleeping on a gymnasium floor.

"We just realized this is the first chance to get our voices heard," Graif said. "What the World Bank is doing isn't fair to the rest of the world."

Looren Finkelstein, an event organizer for Youth Speak Out, said the organizations protesting will highlight the concerns of students at the high school and collegiate level.

"These are some pretty incredible students that are going to be speaking," she said.

Many other student groups are protesting this weekend, each touting issues on their agenda. By protesting the meeting, organizers of the student group Free the Planet said they want to bring attention to the IMF and World Bank on a national level.

"These institutions work on a global level, but they don't answer to anybody," said Finkelstein, who also works for Free the Planet, an organization concerned with protecting the environment.

On the street outside the World Bank, as the media waited for the protests to begin, Graif and his friends sat and watched.

"I think college students are interested in issues that represent structural problems," he said. "It's a common ground for a lot of issues. There's a place for your voice to be heard here."

SOURCE: Matt Berger and Sarah Lechner, "College Students Ready to Protest IMF, World Bank," U-Wire (D.C. Bureau), April 14, 2000.

who was the first in Korea's modern history to come from outside the governing oligarchy, would be in danger of a coup d'état. Yet Kim's hand was actually strengthened because Koreans heaped the shame of economic failure on the outgoing regime.

The second case is the even deeper crisis in Indonesia, which was almost entirely attributable to the monetary reforms the IMF had imposed. To keep themselves tied to the global market, Indonesia had to negotiate an international exchange rate with the IMF that moved the value of the Indonesian currency, the rupiah, from 4,000 to the U.S. dollar up to 5,000 to the dollar (a 25 percent devaluation), and then Indonesia had to allow the rupiah to reach a free-market exchange rate. Within weeks the Indonesian rupiah fell below 10,000 to the dollar, producing at Indonesian banks long lines of panicked customers seeking to withdraw their money. Recognizing this run on Indonesian banks could cause violence, the government deployed fourteen thousand additional police officers around the Indonesian capital, Jakarta. The entire society was for a while on the verge of collapse and civil war. But out of it came the removal, after a thirty-two-year reign, of the autocratic, dictatorial president, Suharto, and his replacement by a weaker but consequently less dictatorial former aide, B. J. Habibie, who immediately issued a promise of elections within a year. This kind of suffering and sacrifice may be unreasonable and unnecessary, but the IMF is playing precisely the role for which it was designed.[23]

ECONOMIC AID

Commitment to rebuilding war-torn countries came as early as commitment to the basic postwar international monetary structure. This is the way President Franklin Roosevelt put the case in a press conference in November 1942, less than one year after the United States entered World War II:

> Sure, we are going to rehabilitate [other nations after the war]. Why? . . . Not only from the humanitarian point of view . . . but from the viewpoint of our own pocketbooks, and our safety from future war.[24]

The particular form and timing for enacting American foreign aid was heavily influenced by Great Britain's sudden decision in 1947 that it would no longer be able to maintain its commitments to Greece and Turkey. Within three weeks of that announcement, President Truman recommended a $400 million direct aid program for Greece and Turkey, and by mid-May of 1947, Congress approved it. Since President Truman had placed the Greece-Turkey action within the larger context of a commitment to help rebuild and defend all countries the world over, wherever the leadership wished to develop democratic systems or to ward off communism, the Greek-Turkish aid was followed quickly by the historically unprecedented program that came to be known as the Marshall Plan, named in honor of Secretary of State (and former five-star general) George C. Marshall.[25]

Marshall Plan
the U.S. European Recovery Plan, in which over $34 billion was spent for the relief, reconstruction, and economic recovery of Western Europe after World War II

The **Marshall Plan**—officially known as the European Recovery Program (ERP)—was essential for the rebuilding of war-torn Europe. By 1952, the United States had spent over $34 billion for the relief, reconstruction, and economic recovery of Western Europe. The emphasis was shifted in 1951, with passage of the Mutual Security Act, to building up European military capacity.

Between 1948 and 1951, the European Recovery Program, popularly known as the Marshall Plan, spent billions of dollars rebuilding Western Europe. This Berlin site was reconstructed as an office building and shopping center.

Of the $48 billion appropriated between 1952 and 1961, over half went for military assistance, the rest for continuing economic aid. Over those years, the geographic emphasis of U.S. aid also shifted, toward South Korea, Taiwan, the Philippines, Vietnam, Iran, Greece, and Turkey—that is, toward the rim of communism. In the 1960s, the emphasis shifted once again, toward what became known as the Third World. From 1962 to 1975, over $100 billion was sent, mainly to Latin America for economic assistance. Other countries of Africa and Asia were also brought in.[26]

Many critics have argued that foreign aid is really aid for political and economic elites, not for the people. Although this is to a large extent true, it needs to be understood in a broader context. If a country's leaders oppose distributing food or any other form of assistance to its people, there is little the United States, or any aid organization, can do, short of terminating the assistance. Goods have to be exchanged across national borders before they can reach the people who need them. Needy people would probably be worse off if the United States cut off aid altogether. The lines of international communication must be kept open. That is why diplomacy exists, and foreign aid can facilitate diplomacy, just as diplomacy is necessary to help get foreign aid where it is most needed.

Another important criticism of U.S. foreign aid policy is that it has not been tied closely enough to U.S. diplomacy. The original Marshall Plan was set up as an independent program outside the State Department and had its own separate missions in each participating country. Essentially, "ERP became a Second State Department."[27] This did not change until the program was reorganized as the Agency for International Development (AID) in the early 1960s. Meanwhile, the Defense Department has always had principal jurisdiction over that substantial proportion of economic aid that goes to military assistance. The Department of Agriculture administers the commodity aid programs, such as Food for Peace. Each department has in effect been able to conduct its own foreign policy, leaving many foreign diplomats to ask, "Who's in charge here?"

That brings us back to the history of U.S. efforts to balance traditional values with the modern needs of world leadership. Economic assistance is an instrument of American foreign policy, but it has been less effective than it might have been because of the inability of American politics to overcome its traditional opposition to foreign entanglements and build a unified foreign policy—something that the older nation-states would call a foreign ministry. We have undoubtedly made progress, but foreigners still often wonder who is in charge.

COLLECTIVE SECURITY

In 1947, most Americans hoped that the United States could meet its world obligations through the United Nations and economic structures alone. But most foreign policy makers recognized that it was a vain hope even as they were permitting and encouraging Americans to believe it. They had anticipated the need for military entanglements at the time of drafting the original UN Charter by insisting upon language that recognized the right of all nations to provide for their mutual defense independently of the United Nations. And almost immediately after enactment of the Marshall Plan, the White House and a parade of State and Defense Department officials followed up with an urgent request to the Senate to ratify and to Congress to finance mutual defense alliances.

At first quite reluctant to approve treaties providing for national security alliances, the Senate ultimately agreed with the executive branch. The first collective security agreement was the Rio Treaty (ratified by the Senate in September 1947), which created the Organization of American States (OAS). This was the model treaty, anticipating all succeeding collective security treaties by providing that an armed attack against any of its members "shall be considered as an attack against all the American States," including the United States. A more significant break with U.S. tradition against peacetime entanglements came with the North Atlantic Treaty (signed in April 1949), which created the North Atlantic Treaty Organization (NATO). ANZUS, a treaty tying Australia and New Zealand to the United States, was signed in September 1951. Three years later, the Southeast Asia Treaty created the Southeast Asia Treaty Organization (SEATO).

bilateral treaties

treaties made between two nations

In addition to these multilateral treaties, the United States entered into a number of **bilateral treaties**—treaties between two countries. As one author has observed, the United States has been a *producer* of security while most of its allies have been *consumers* of security.[28] Figure 19.3 demonstrates that the United States has consistently devoted a greater percentage of its gross domestic product (GDP) to defense than have its NATO allies and Japan.

This pattern has continued in the post–cold war era, and its best illustration is in the Persian Gulf War, where the United States provided the initiative, the leadership, and most of the armed forces, even though its allies were obliged to reimburse over 90 percent of the cost.

It is difficult to evaluate collective security and its treaties, because the pur-

DEFENSE SPENDING AS A PERCENTAGE OF GROSS DOMESTIC PRODUCT, 1961–95

Figure 19.3

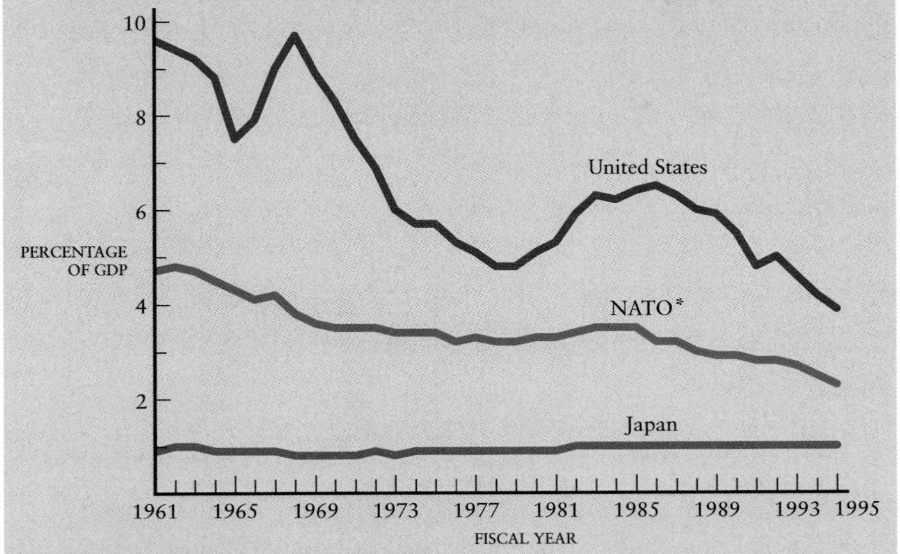

*Excluding the United States.
SOURCES: Office of Management and Budget, *Budget of the United States Government, Fiscal Year 1995, Historical Tables* (Washington, DC: Government Printing Office, 1994), pp. 39–42; *SIPRI Yearbook* (Stockholm, Sweden: Stockholm International Peace Research Institute, various years), 1979: pp. 36–37, 46–47; 1986: pp. 243–44; 1994: pp. 396, 560.

pose of collective security as an instrument of foreign policy is prevention, and success of this kind has to be measured according to what did *not* happen. The critics have argued that U.S. collective security treaties posed a threat of encirclement to the Soviet Union, forcing it to produce its own collective security, particularly the Warsaw Pact.[29] Nevertheless, no one can deny the counterargument that the world has enjoyed more than fifty years without world war.

Although the Soviet Union has collapsed, Russia has emerged from a period of confusion and consolidation signaling its determination to play once again an active role in regional and world politics. The challenge for the United States and NATO in coming years will be how to broaden membership in the alliance to include the nations of Eastern Europe and some of the former Soviet republics without antagonizing Russia, which might see such an expansion of NATO as a new era of encirclement.

In 1998 the expansion of NATO took its first steps, extending membership to Poland, Hungary, and the Czech Republic. Most of Washington embraced this expansion as the true and fitting end of the cold war, and the U.S. Senate echoed this with a resounding 80-to-19 vote to induct these three former Soviet satellites into NATO. The expansion was also welcomed among European member nations, who quickly approved the move, which was hailed as the final closing of the book on Yalta, the 1945 treaty that divided Europe into

Western and Soviet spheres of influence after the defeat of Germany. But some strong voices did not support NATO expansion. George Kennan, architect of the United State's containment policy, predicted that NATO expansion was "the beginning of a new Cold War . . . a tragic mistake. . . . Our differences in the Cold War were with the Soviet Communist regime. And now we are turning our backs on the very people [Russia's current leaders] who mounted the greatest bloodless revolution in history to remove that Soviet Regime."[30]

NATO's ability to assist in implementing the uncertain peace in the former Yugoslavia will be a genuine test of the viability of NATO and collective security in general, now that the cold war is over. NATO was put to the test in 1999 during its efforts to halt the "ethnic cleansing" in Kosovo by the Serbs, but after months of a relentless bombing campaign, NATO prevailed, though Kosovo's future seemed uncertain. NATO and the other mutual security organizations throughout the world are likely to survive. But these organizations are going to be less like military alliances and more like economic associations to advance technology, reduce trade barriers, and protect the world environment. Another form of collective security may well have emerged from the 1991 Persian Gulf War, with nations forming temporary coalitions under UN sponsorship to check a particularly aggressive nation.

MILITARY DETERRENCE

For the first century and a half of its existence as an independent republic, the United States held strongly to a "Minuteman" theory of defense: Maintain a small corps of professional officers, a few flagships, and a small contingent of marines; leave the rest of defense to the state militias. In case of war, mobilize as quickly as possible, taking advantage of the country's immense size and its separation from Europe to gain time to mobilize.

The United States applied this policy as recently as the post–World War I years and was beginning to apply it after World War II, until the new policy of preparedness won out. The cycle of demobilization-remobilization was broken, and in its place the United States adopted a new policy of constant mobilization and preparedness: deterrence, or the development and maintenance of military strength as a means of discouraging attack. After World War II, military deterrence against the Soviet Union became the fundamental American foreign policy objective, requiring a vast commitment of national resources. With preparedness as the goal, peacetime defense expenditures grew steadily over the course of the cold war.

The end of the cold war raised public expectations for a "peace dividend"—surplus federal money resulting from reductions in the defense budget—after nearly a decade of the largest peacetime defense budget increases in U.S. history. Many defense experts, liberal and conservative, feared what they called a budget "free-fall," not only because deterrence was still needed but also because severe and abrupt cuts could endanger private industry in many friendly foreign countries as well as in the United States.

The Persian Gulf War brought both points dramatically into focus. First, the Iraqi invasion of Kuwait revealed the size, strength, and advanced modern technological base not only of the Iraqi armed forces but of other countries, Arab and non-Arab, including the capability, then or soon, to make atomic weapons and other weapons of massive destructive power. Moreover, the de-

HOW THE F-16 IS PRODUCED: THE INTERNATIONAL RELATIONS OF DEFENSE

Figure 19.4

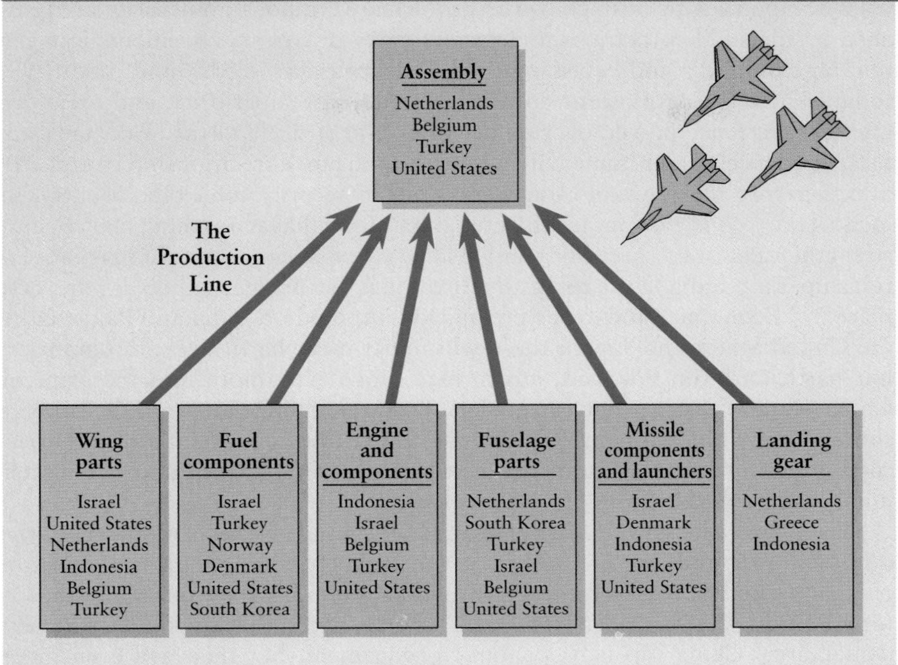

SOURCE: U.S. Congress, Office of Technology Assessment, *Arming Our Allies: Cooperation and Competition in Defense Technology*, Series OTA-ICS-449 (Washington, DC: Government Printing Office, May 1990), pp. 42–43. Information provided by the primary manufacturer, General Dynamics Corporation.

This is a summary of an elaborate diagram of at least seventy-five separate parts that go into the F-16.

mand for advanced weaponry was intensifying. The decisive victory of the United States and its allies in the Gulf War, far from discouraging the international arms trade, gave it fresh impetus. Following the Gulf War victory, *Newsweek* reported that "industry reps quickly realized that foreign customers would now be beating a path to their doors, seeking to buy the winning weaponry." The Soviet Union at one time led the list of major world arms sellers, and Russia and several other republics of the former Soviet Union have continued to make international arms sales, particularly since now there are "no ideological limitations" in the competition for customers.[31] The United States now leads the list of military weapons exporters, followed by Great Britain, France, and Russia. Thus, some shrinkage of defense expenditure has been desirable, but Democrats and Republicans alike agree that this reduction must be guided by the continuing need to maintain U.S. and allied credibility as a deterrent to post–cold war arms races.

As to the second point, domestic pressures join international demands to fuel post–cold war defense spending. Each cut in military production and each closing of a military base or plant translates into a significant loss of jobs. Moreover, the conversion of defense industries to domestic uses is not a problem faced by the United States alone. Figure 19.4 conveys a dramatic picture of the "international relations" of the production of one single weapons system, the F-16 fighter airplane.

Support for policies of deterrence and doubts about the applicability of cold war policies to post–cold war problems were both immensely strengthened by the sudden (because undetected) entry of two new members into the nuclear club: India and Pakistan tested nuclear devices in May and June 1998. India's initial five explosions gave it a few days of superiority, and therefore greater deterrence power, over its neighbor and rival, Pakistan. Pakistan's six blasts two weeks later immediately returned the power relationship to equality and therefore there was no long-term gain in security for either country. In fact, as the *Economist* put it, "By going first, India has if anything managed to strengthen Pakistan's security relationship with nuclear-armed China—a relationship that India used to justify breaking the nuclear taboo in the first place."[32] Economic sanctions were quickly imposed on India and Pakistan by the United States and Japan; these will inflict great harm on both countries, but particularly on Pakistan, which may move even more into the arms of China. But as the other nuclear powers were trying to decide what their policy should be toward deterring Pakistan and India from developing their nuclear capabilities further, both countries were already talking about improving their missile delivery capacities.

Just a few weeks after the Indian and Pakistani news, revelations about the sale of missile and satellite materials and technology to China by American companies with U.S. government approval raised more questions about the future of military deterrence. President Clinton asserted that such sales will help democratize China through economic engagement, but they will even more certainly feed worldwide fears that China is the pivot of a new, post–cold war arms race.

All of this suggests that the threat of the arms race and international conflicts persists even in the post–cold war era. It also suggests that the United States is an important part of the problem as well as the most essential part of the solution. The only real hope for a significant reduction in the international demand for arms will come from changes in the general political and economic environment. But such changes do not happen spontaneously. On the international level, genuine reduction in the demand for arms will require diplomacy; try as we might, power without diplomacy can never be a permanent solution. And this must in turn be accompanied by economic growth, not only in the United States but everywhere.

Roles Nations Play

- What four traditional foreign policy roles has the United States adopted throughout its history?
- Since the end of World War II, how has the role of the United States in world affairs evolved?

Although each president has hundreds of small foreign fires to fight and can choose whichever instruments of policy best fit each particular situation, the primary foreign policy problem any president faces is choosing an overall role for the country in foreign affairs. Roles help us to define a situation in order to control the element of surprise in international relations. Surprise is in fact the most dangerous aspect of international relations, especially in a world made smaller and more fragile by advances in and the proliferation of military technology.

CHOOSING A ROLE

The problem of choosing a role can be understood by identifying a limited number of roles played by nation-states in the past. Four such roles will be drawn from history—the Napoleonic, the Holy Alliance, the balance-of-power, and the economic expansionist roles. Although the definitions given here will be exaggerations of the real world, they do capture in broad outline the basic choices available.

The Napoleonic Role The **Napoleonic role** takes its name from the role played by postrevolutionary France under Napoleon. The French at that time felt not only that their new democratic system of government was the best on earth but also that France would not be safe until democracy was adopted universally. If this meant intervention into the internal affairs of France's neighbors, and if that meant warlike reactions, then so be it. President Woodrow Wilson expressed a similar viewpoint when he supported the U.S. declaration of war in 1917 with his argument that "the world must be made safe for democracy." Obviously such a position can be adopted by any powerful nation as a rationalization for intervening at its convenience in the internal affairs of another country. But it can also be sincerely espoused, and in the United States it has from time to time enjoyed broad popular consensus. We played the Napoleonic role most recently in ousting Philippine dictator Ferdinand Marcos (February 1986), Panamanian leader Manuel Noriega (December 1989), the Sandinista government of Nicaragua (February 1990), and the military rulers of Haiti (September 1994).

Napoleonic role
a strategy pursued by a powerful nation to prevent aggressive actions against themselves by improving the internal state of affairs of a particular country, even if this means encouraging revolution in that country

The Holy Alliance Role The concept of the **Holy Alliance role** emerged out of the defeat of Napoleon and the agreement by the leaders of Great Britain, Russia, Austria, and Prussia to preserve the social order against *all* revolution, including democratic revolution, at whatever cost. (Post-Napoleonic France also joined it.) The Holy Alliance made use of every kind of political instrument available—including political suppression, espionage, sabotage, and outright military intervention—to keep existing governments in power. The Holy Alliance role is comparable to the Napoleonic role in that each operates on the assumption that intervention into the internal affairs of other countries is justified for the maintenance of peace. But Napoleonic intervention is motivated by fear of dictatorship, and it can accept and even encourage revolution. In contrast, Holy Alliance intervention is antagonistic to any form of political change, even when this means supporting an existing dictatorship.[33] Because the Holy Alliance role became more important after the cold war ended, illustrations of this role will be given later in the chapter.

Holy Alliance role
a strategy pursued by a superpower to prevent any change in the existing distribution of power among nation-states, even if this requires intervention into the internal affairs of another country in order to keep a ruler from being overturned

The Balance-of-Power Role The **balance-of-power role** is basically an effort by the major powers to play off against each other so that no great power or combination of great and lesser powers can impose conditions on others. The

balance-of-power role
the strategy whereby many countries form alliances with one or more other countries in order to counterbalance the behavior of other, usually more powerful, nation-states

most relevant example of the use of this strategy is found in the nineteenth century, especially the latter half. The feature of the balance-of-power role that is most distinct from the two previously identified roles is that this role accepts the political system of each country, asking no questions except whether the country will join an alliance and will use its resources to ensure that each country will respect the borders and interests of all the others.[34]

economic expansionist role
the strategy often pursued by capitalist countries to adopt foreign policies that will maximize the success of domestic corporations in their dealings with other countries

The Economic Expansionist Role The **economic expansionist role,** also called the capitalist role, shares with the balance-of-power role the attitude that the political system or ideology of a country is irrelevant; the only question is whether a country has anything to buy or sell and whether its entrepreneurs, corporations, and government agencies will honor their contracts. Governments and their armies are occasionally drawn into economic expansionist relationships in order to establish, reopen, or expand trade relationships, and to keep the lines of commerce open. But the role is political, too. The point can be made that the economic expansionist role was the role consistently played by the United States in Latin and Central America, until the cold war (perhaps in the 1960s and beyond) pushed us toward the Holy Alliance role with most of those countries.

Like arms control, however, economic expansion does not happen spontaneously. In the past, economic expansion owed a great deal to military backing, because contracts do not enforce themselves, trade deficits are not paid automatically, and new regimes do not always honor the commitments made by regimes they replace. The only way to expand economic relationships is through diplomacy.

FOREIGN POLICY VALUES FOR AMERICA TODAY

Although "making the world safe for democracy" was used to justify the U.S. entry into World War I, it was taken more seriously after World War II, when at last the United States was willing to play a more sustained part in world affairs. The Napoleonic role was most suited to America's view of the postwar world. To create the world's ruling regimes in the American image would indeed give Americans the opportunity to return to their private pursuits, for if all or even most of the world's countries were governed by democratic constitutions, there would be no more war, since no democracy would ever attack another democracy—or so it has been assumed.[35]

Making the World Safe for Democracy The emergence of the Soviet Union as a superpower had an overwhelming influence on American foreign policy thinking in the post–World War II era. The distribution of power in the world was "bipolar," and Americans saw the world separated in two, with an "iron curtain" dividing the communist world from the free world. Immediately after the war, America's foreign policy goal had been "prodemocracy," a Napoleonic role dominated by the Marshall Plan and the genuine hope for a democratic world. This quickly shifted toward a Holy Alliance role, with "containment" as the primary foreign policy criterion.[36] Containment was fundamentally a Holy Alliance concept. According to foreign-policy expert Richard Barnet, during the 1950s and 1960s, "the United States used its military or paramilitary power on an average of once every eighteen months either to prevent a government deemed undesirable from coming to power or to overthrow a revolutionary or reformist government considered inimical to America's interests."[37] Although Barnet did not refer to a Holy Alliance, his description fits the model perfectly.

During the 1970s, the United States played the Holy Alliance role less frequently, not so much because of the outcome of the Vietnam War as because of the emergence of a multipolar world. In 1972, the United States accepted (and later recognized) the communist government of the People's Republic of China and broke forever its pure bipolar, cold war view of world power distribution. Other powers became politically important as well, including Japan, the European Economic Community (now the European Union), India, and, depending on their own resolve, the countries making up the Organization of Petroleum Exporting Countries (OPEC). The United States experimented with all four of the previously identified roles, depending on which was appropriate to a specific region of the world. In the Middle East, America tended to play an almost classic balance-of-power role, by appearing sometimes cool in its relations with Israel and by playing off one Arab country against another. The United States has been able to do this despite the fact that every country in the Middle East recognizes that for cultural, domestic, and geostrategic reasons, the United States has always considered Israel as its most durable and important ally in the region and has unwaveringly committed itself to Israel's survival in a very hostile environment. President Nixon introduced balance-of-power considerations in the Far East by "playing the China card." In other parts of the world, particularly in Latin America, we tended to hold to the Holy Alliance and Napoleonic roles.

This multipolar phase ended after 1989, with the collapse of the Soviet Union and the end of the cold war. Soon thereafter the Warsaw Pact collapsed too, ending armed confrontation in Europe. With almost equal suddenness, the popular demand for "self-determination" produced several new nation-states and the demand for still more. On the one hand, it was indeed good to witness the reemergence of some twenty-five major nationalities after anywhere from forty-five to seventy-five years of suppression. On the other hand, policy makers with a sense of history are aware that this new world order bears a strong resemblance to the world of 1914. Then, the trend was known as "Balkanization." Balkanization meant nationhood and self-determination, but it also meant war. The Soviet Union after World War I and Yugoslavia after World War II kept more than twenty nationalities from making war against each other for several decades. In 1989 and the years that followed, the world was caught unprepared for the dangers of a new disorder that the reemergence of these nationalities produced.

It should also be emphasized that the demand for nationhood emerged with new vigor in many other parts of the world—the Middle East, South and Southeast Asia, and South Africa. Perhaps we are seeing worldwide Balkanization; we should not overlook the reemergence of the spirit of nationhood among ethnic minorities in Canada and the United States.

Making the World Safe for Democracy and Markets The abrupt end of the cold war unleashed another dynamic factor, the globalization of markets; one could call it the globalization of capitalism. This is good news, but it has its problematic side because the free market can disrupt nationhood. Although the globalization of markets is enormously productive, countries like to enjoy its benefits while attempting at the same time to prevent international economic influences from affecting local jobs, local families, and established class and tribal relationships.

This struggle between capitalism and nationhood produces a new kind of bipolarity in the world. The old world order was shaped by *external bipolarity*—of West versus East. This seems to have been replaced by *internal bipolarity,* wherein each country is struggling to make its own hard policy choices to preserve its cultural uniqueness while competing effectively in the global marketplace.

Approval of the North American Free Trade Agreement (NAFTA) serves as the best example of this struggle within the United States. NAFTA was supported by a majority of Democrats and Republicans on the grounds that a freer, global market was in America's national interest. But even as NAFTA was being embraced by large bipartisan majorities in Congress, three important factions were rising to fight it. Former presidential candidate Pat Buchanan led a large segment of conservative Americans to fight NAFTA because, he argued, communities and families would be threatened by job losses and by competition from legal and illegal immigrant workers. Another large faction, led by Ross Perot, opposed NAFTA largely on the theory that American companies would move their operations to Mexico, where labor costs are lower. Organized labor also joined the fight against NAFTA.

Approval of NAFTA did not, however, put the issue to rest. Opposition was revived in 1997 when "fast-track" authority was up for renewal. Ever since President Ford, Congress had regularly enacted a guarantee—subject to periodic renewal—that any trade agreement negotiated by the president would receive consideration by Congress within ninety days and would be voted "up or down" with no amendments allowed. Due in large part to opposition from within his own Democratic Party (especially from organized labor) President

More than 30,000 protesters converged on Seattle to protest the World Trade Organization conference held in November 1999. The "battle in Seattle" was evidence of internal bipolarity within the United States, as Americans debated over the impact of a free-trade system on jobs and the environment.

POLICY DEBATE

Economic Prosperity versus the Environment

Economic growth and increased international trade are seen as the primary means of improving the lives of people throughout the world. Developed nations, like the United States, can provide new technologies in return for raw materials and products that can be made more cheaply in developing nations. When President Clinton won passage of the North American Free Trade Agreement (NAFTA) in 1993, his goal was to eliminate trade barriers so that all nations could benefit. Yet increased trade and development come at a price. Environmental degradation from nuclear waste, oil spills, deforestation, cropland depletion, and overuse of pesticides are just a few of the adverse consequences of development that may be accelerating such problems as pollution and global warming. Developed nations impose strict pollution guidelines, but consume most of the world's resources. Developing nations impose few or no pollution guidelines, but struggle to feed their populations and improve people's standard of living. Sharp disagreement exists over the proper balance between economic development and protection of the environment.

Supporters of greater economic development argue that threats to the environment, although a legitimate concern, have been overstated. At a time when nearly a quarter of the world's population goes to bed hungry every night, economic development must proceed in order to help all concerned. In the case of global warming, for example, scientists disagree over the degree to which global warming is occurring and whether it is primarily the product of human-produced pollution or simply the result of natural global forces. The relatively primitive computerized models used to predict global warming are imprecise and have been notoriously poor at predicting climate change in the past. Furthermore, many experts argue that global warming in the next century will likely be very gradual, and that nations will be able to adapt to changing temperatures.

Overreaction to the scare about the greenhouse effect is evidenced, according to its critics, in the 1992 Global Climate Treaty, which, if implemented, would require a 60 to 80 percent worldwide reduction in carbon dioxide emissions. This would mean a proportionate reduction in the use of fossil fuels, without any consideration of the disastrous economic effects of such a drastic change. A more reasonable goal would be the stabilization of current emissions levels. Environmental alarmists have exaggerated the problem, in part because their research support encourages it. The U.S. government spends over $2 billion a year on global change research, which has implicitly helped cultivate environmental alarmism. A moderate approach would conform most closely to the needs for development and environmental protection.

Advocates of environmental protection, on the other hand, argue that the environmental threat is both real and dire. The evidence that societies are rapidly depleting resources and polluting the environment is abundant. For example, in the former communist countries of eastern Europe and the republics of the former Soviet Union, pollution control was sacrificed to industrialization. Today we are seeing the result: residents of these areas have shorter life spans and serious health problems directly attributable to a degraded environment. Water pollution alone accounts for about 2 million deaths a year in these areas.

As for global warming, the scientific community agrees that it is occurring, that it arises from the emission of "greenhouse" gases, and that it poses a major threat to human existence. Environmental problems, by their nature, take a long time to form and a long time to stop. The great danger is that governments will do nothing until the damage becomes irreversible. Models of the earth's climate that are generally accepted by experts predict that the increase in greenhouse gases will produce an average global temperature increase of from two to seven degrees during this century. Although these numbers sound modest, they would prompt drastic changes in rainfall, flooding, droughts, heat waves, and a rise in sea level. More to the point, existing technologies offer ways or reducing greenhouse gases without abruptly halting economic development. Policies that do not take into account future ecological conditions will simply hasten the day when the world's resources will be unable to meet human needs.

STUDENT DEBATE

Is the World Trade Organization Good for America's Interests?

Yes

Maybe free trade isn't such a good idea after all—or at least that's what one might think after seeing thousands of protesters in Seattle last week. They were there to protest the World Trade Organization, which had convened a meeting for the trade ministers of all 134 member nations. While most protesters blocked intersections and chained themselves together to prevent the ministers from attending the meeting, a handful adopted a more violent approach and smashed storefronts.

They were protesting what the WTO stands for—free trade. The WTO arose from what used to be known as GATT—General Agreements on Tariffs and Trade. It was an extensive series of rules and regulations that governed trade relations, mainly for the benefit of developed nations. The most recent round of GATT negotiations—called the Uruguay Round for its host country, lasting from 1986–1994—created the WTO to oversee future trade negotiations and moderate trade disputes between members.

The premise behind the WTO is simple: The elimination of all trade barriers, enabling any nation to sell its goods in another nation. The WTO does not allow its members to construct their own barriers for labor and environmental concerns. This includes obvious barriers such as tariffs and import quotas, but it also covers any domestic regulation that discriminates against products on the basis of production methods. This means that a country may not prohibit imports that are manufactured by child labor or sweatshops or that use production methods that excessively pollute or that may pose a health risk, unless the risk has been supported by scientific evidence.

This is where the protesters come in. One might call them neoprotectionists—their primary concern with free trade is not the security of American jobs, but instead the right of individual countries to set their own standards on acceptable trade. They object to any world trading system that does not take into account labor, environmental and, to a lesser extent, health concerns.

But besides questioning the free trade policies of the WTO, they also demand reform of the WTO itself. They charge that the organization is undemocratic, that it conducts its meetings and dispute trials in secrecy and they want labor rights and environmentalist groups to have a say in WTO business.

But is the WTO all that bad? Many international organizations conduct their business behind closed doors. How can one expect the WTO to be any different? And where were these protesters five or ten years ago? True, the WTO negotiations were not conducted in this country, but the United States did participate in the negotiations and could have brought some of the same concerns to the table if protesters had made them known.

The charges that the WTO is undemocratic hold little water: It operates on complete consensus. All 134 members must agree to all changes—there is no special role for the most powerful nations. And why should the labor and environment groups have a say? How are they democratic? They are simply lobbying groups. One of the primary advantages of the WTO is that there are no lobbying groups—only nations, all of which must agree on trade policy.

This does not mean that the protesters' calls should be ignored. Issues of environmental and labor regulation are a concern for many industrialized countries, but they would represent a real threat to the economies of lesser-developed Third World countries. Granted, increased globalization means increased international trade, but it also means increased importance of global concerns.

But is the WTO the appropriate forum for environmental and labor issues? A look at a recent success in bringing together environmental concerns with Third World economic demands demonstrates there is a better alternative. The Montreal Protocol on Ozone Depletion managed to address the environmental worries of the industrialized nations with the Third World's inability to operate clean industries. This was not conducted by the WTO—it was done under the auspices of the UN.

SOURCE: Charles Newman, "To Trade, or Not to Trade?" *The Chronicle* (Duke University), December 6, 1999.

No

To put it bluntly, the global economy is failing the human race and despoiling the planet. Despite an explosion of international trade and investment over the past few decades, poverty and inequality have risen sharply and ecological deterioration has accelerated.

And yet, more trade, not more economic and environmental justice, is the prescription coming from World Trade Organization bureaucrats who will meet in Seattle from November 29 to December 3 [1999].

This powerful new body, composed of appointed (not elected) trade representatives from countries around the world, was established in 1995 following that year's General Agreement on Tariffs and Trade (GATT) negotiations.

The WTO's main charge is to remove obstacles to free trade like tariffs and quotas, but also environmental, health, consumer and worker protection laws that may be construed as "barriers" to commerce. A WTO tribunal is empowered to interpret and rule on the legitimacy of various nations' laws, based on their conformity with GATT's narrow, trade-focused framework. If found in violation, offending nations must remove or nullify such laws or face severe fines or sanctions.

Since the WTO's founding, a host of rulings have forced countries to rescind popular laws, including:

- A section of the U.S. Marine Mammal Protection Act, which required the tuna industry to adopt fishing methods that would not injure or kill dolphins.
- A key provision of the U.S. Clean Air Act, which set standards for gasoline prohibiting domestic and foreign producers from selling highly polluting formulas in the United States.
- The European Union's ban on beef injected with potentially harmful artificial hormones.

Unfortunately, rather than taking heed of popular support for fair wages, stronger environmental laws and universal health care, government leaders are increasingly touting the myth that ever-greater world trade will make most people better off and our environment cleaner and healthier. But this is a total sham.

According to the United Nations, between 1972 and 1992 when the world's combined Gross National Product grew by $20 trillion, only 15 percent flowed to less industrialized nations.

Global income trends are even more illuminating: in 1960, the richest 20 percent received 70 percent of world income, while the poorest 20 percent made only 2.3 percent (for a 30 to 1 ratio). In 1993, the richest 20 percent garnered a whopping 85 percent of world income, while the income of the poorest 20 percent fell to a mere 1.4 percent (for a 61 to 1 ratio).

Of course, the ever-widening chasm between the rich and poor and the flagrant consumption of the wealthy few also has wrought unparalleled ecological devastation.

According to World Watch Institute's "State of the World 1999," insatiable logging and ranching continue to destroy our temperate and tropical forests, species diversity is being reduced at an ever-increasing rate, freshwater is being sucked from lakes and aquifers faster than it is recharging, fish are being caught more rapidly than they can reproduce, and fertilizers are not boosting agricultural productivity as fast as food demand is rising.

Worst of all, highly industrialized and industrializing nations, with their profligate burning of fossil fuels, have brought the world's biosphere to the brink of climatic instability. To say that more free trade will resolve these problems is dangerous fantasy. Despite the utopian dreams of WTO trade bureaucrats, commerce cannot, should not, and will never be separate or immune from social values.

SOURCE: Aaron G. Lehmer, "The Protest of the Decade," *The Lumberjack Online* (Humboldt State University), October 27, 1999.

Clinton failed to get his renewal, and his commitment to advancement of international trade was going to be much more difficult to pursue.

Another form of internal bipolarity became evident in 1999 over the World Trade Organization (WTO) and its authority to impose limits and restrictions on sovereign nations, even the United States. The WTO had been around since 1994, when it was set up by the major trading nations to facilitate implementation of treaties made under the General Agreement on Tariffs and Trade (GATT). But protesters in Seattle saw the WTO as a threat to local ways of life and a contributor to job loss, environmental degradation, and violation of human rights.

These battles are examples of the "internal bipolarity" that is coming to the fore around the world. As *New York Times* foreign affairs columnist Thomas Friedman put it, ". . . now that the free market is triumphing on a global basis, the most interesting conflicts are between the winners and losers within countries. It is these internal battles that will increasingly shape international affairs."[38]

The global market is here to stay and American values have changed enough to incorporate it, despite the toll it may take on community and family tradition. Meanwhile, many of the elements of foreign policy created during the cold war still exist because they turned out to be good adjustments to the modern era. The Marshall Plan and the various forms of international economic aid that succeeded it continue to this day. Although appropriations for foreign aid have been shrinking, only a small minority of members of the Senate and the House favor the outright abolition of foreign aid programs. NATO and other collective security arrangements continue, as do some aspects of containment, even though there is no longer a Soviet Union, because collective security arrangements have, as we shall see, proven useful in dealing with new democracies and other nations seeking to join the global market. Even though the former Soviet Union is now more often an ally than an adversary, the United States still quite frequently uses unilateral and multilateral means of keeping civil wars contained within their own borders, so that conflict does not spread into neighboring states. America is practicing a new form of containment, but one that is based on the values and institutions of cold war containment.

The quest for a global market is more than a search for world prosperity. Economic globalization carries with it the hope that economic competition will displace armed conflict, perhaps even reducing if not eliminating the need for traditional diplomacy. But since there are too many instances in world history when economic competition actually led to war rather than avoided it, the United States has added democratization to the recipe of globalization because of the fairly well-supported hypothesis that democracies never go to war against each other. Thus democratization is a genuine and strongly committed goal of U.S. foreign policy, even if it is secondary to economic expansion. Meanwhile, we play the economic card in hopes that capitalism will contribute not only to world prosperity but also to the expansion of democratization.

One of the first indications of the post–cold war American foreign policy was President Bush's conciliatory approach to the dictatorial regime of the People's Republic of China after its brutal military suppression of the democratic student movement in Tiananman Square in June 1989. Subsequently, President Clinton also maintained friendly relations with the dictatorial regime, and both presidents continued to grant the Chinese "normal trade relations" status. Their policy was to separate China's trade status from its human rights record, arguing that economic growth provided the only effective means to bring about political reform in a country as large and as powerful as China.

The Holy Alliance Role in the Post–Cold War Era At first glance, it appears that America finally got what it wanted—a world that would run itself well enough without need for much U.S. foreign policy. But the United States has obviously been betrayed by events. U.S. foreign policy roles and priorities have not been shuffled very much, if at all. In fact, the Holy Alliance role seems to be more prominent than ever. There is, of course, one big difference—the absence of the Soviet Union and the current willingness of Russia to support rather than oppose American policies. During the cold war era, the purpose of the Holy Alliance role was to keep regimes in power as long as they did not espouse Soviet foreign policy goals. In the post–cold war world, the purpose of the Holy Alliance role is still to keep regimes in power, but only as long as they maintain general stability, keep their nationalities contained within their own borders, and encourage their economies to attain some level of participation in the global market.

We have already dealt with the first case of the Holy Alliance role in the post–cold war era, Iraq's invasion of Kuwait and our Desert Storm response to it. (It was used earlier in this chapter to illustrate the renewed importance of the UN.) Desert Storm is in fact a very dramatic case of the Holy Alliance role. Iraq's invasion of Kuwait occurred in July 1990, and Desert Storm was not undertaken until January 1991. In the interim, President Bush was mobilizing Congress and the American people, not only in case the United States had to intervene militarily, but also in hopes that the possibility of such action might convince Saddam Hussein to withdraw voluntarily. President Bush was also putting together a worldwide alliance of twenty-nine nations—he had no intention of leading the United States into Desert Storm without this alliance, even though most of its members did not send troops but instead sent political approval plus what amounted to a monetary subscription. Bush had initially taken a Napoleonic position, urging the people of Iraq to "take matters into their own hands" and to force Hussein to "step aside." But after America withdrew its troops, and uprisings inside Iraq began to emerge, President Bush backed away, thus revealing his real intent of leaving the existing dictatorship in power, with or without Hussein. It was enough that the Iraqis stayed within their borders.

Bosnia was another clear case of America playing the Holy Alliance role. At first, the United States refused to exert leadership, and it deferred to the European nations when civil war erupted after Croatia and Bosnia-Herzegovina declared independence from Yugoslavia. When Europe failed to address the problem adequately, the United States and the United Kingdom stepped in, again to no avail. Although our surprise bombing in 1995 to drive the warring factions to the negotiating table in Dayton, Ohio, was virtually unilateral, what emerged was a new alliance of twenty-five nations acting "in concert" to separate the warring factions from one another. And, although one-third of the sixty thousand occupying troops and virtually all the navy and air force units were American, twenty-four other nations established and maintained a physical presence in the field, all in order to maintain the status quo. Almost everything about the Bosnian operation was an acting out of the traditional Holy Alliance role.

Kosovo in 1999 is the most recent and the most spectacular case of post–cold war Holy Alliance policy—although history may prove that the United States and virtually the entire Western world stumbled into this war.[39] Throughout 1998 and early 1999, ethnic cleansing was proceeding in Kosovo, but the United States would not go it alone, and the NATO nations (except for Great Britain) were not willing to intervene in Kosovo. As late as January 1999, the CIA reported to President Clinton that "[Yugoslav President Milosevic] doesn't believe NATO is going to bomb."[40] It is clear that these delays were due less to American indecision and more to America's or President Clinton's inability to forge a European, multicountry alliance. Prospects of embarrassment at the upcoming fiftieth anniversary of NATO may have forced some European leaders to reconsider an alliance—but even so, only if the United States took the lead, and then only if it promised to limit the assault to an air war only, which guaranteed a minimum of casualties, especially on the allied side.

So the United States got its alliance—and a precedent-setting one—but without any ground troops. President Clinton deserves some blame for the delays and for the artificial restrictions that allowed Milosevic to make the eventual intervention by the alliance all more dangerous for the Kosovars, whom the United States wanted to defend and protect. The charge that Clinton's impeachment could not be "compartmentalized" seems to have had some basis to it.[41] But there are inherent limits to multinational coalitions, which President Clinton had to confront no matter what his domestic political distractions were at the time. NATO is simply a more formalized version of any multicountry alliance with the same fundamental problem of any such alliance: *The power of decision tends toward the weakest member.* This was undoubtedly in the mind of Admiral Leighton Smith, commander of NATO forces in southern Europe, 1994–1996, when he observed of Kosovo: "The lesson we've learned is that coalitions aren't good ways to fight a war."[42]

NATO was created as a multilateral defense treaty, which essentially states that an attack on any alliance member is an act of war against all members. And who but the most vulnerable is most likely to be the victim of an attack? The same principle applies now that NATO has become an offensive rather than a defensive alliance. Opposition within the NATO alliance to intervene in Kosovo came mostly from the weaker and more internally divided Italy and Greece than from Britain, France, or Germany. Once the alliance expanded to include Russia, America's hands were tied even more. Russia was instrumental in getting Milosevic to accept the retreat, but it also kept Milosevic in power as part of the price. As reconstruction was beginning in the summer of 1999, the European Union—essentially the political-economic wing of European NATO—voted to provide $1.5 billion for the three-year start-up of the reconstruction. But, as White House National Security Advisor Samuel Berger revealed, Russian objections had prevented the alliance from including in its policy statement that no funds would go to Serbia as long as Milosevic was in power.[43]

The Kosovo campaign validates what we have been observing throughout this chapter: Holy Alliance politics is the prevailing American role in the world today, and the United States draws virtually all its allies and potential allies into that role at one point or another. As *The Washington Post* put it in 1999:

> . . . Whatever the shortcomings, fighting in coalition arrangements appears to be an unavoidable fact of post–cold war life. . . . "We need partners both for political legitimacy and for risk-sharing," says . . . a senior Pentagon planner earlier in the Clinton administration.[44]

The freedom-loving, free-market magazine the *Economist* goes even further:

> If the United States were indeed going to remain the world's only great power as far ahead as the eye can see, people who like this newspaper believe in the danger of monopoly and the need for competition would draw the necessary conclusions: Europe should provide a counterbalance to this overwhelming American power. But that is not in fact what the future really holds. . . . The one-superpower world will not last. [China, Russia, and the Muslim world will all become geopolitical competitors.]
> . . . This is why the alliance of the democracies needs not only new members but also a new purpose. The alliance can no longer be just a protective American arm around Europe's shoulder; it also has to be a way for Europe and America to work together in other parts of the world. . . . This must be done—if it can be done at all—in partnership with America. . . .[45]

When leaders in a democracy engage in unilateral or multilateral alliance-based action, they must have overwhelming justification because they must be prepared with overwhelming military superiority. This very point gave rise to an historic observation made by General Douglas MacArthur, prior to his dismissal for insubordination by President Truman in 1952: "In war, there is no substitute for victory."[46] But MacArthur was overlooking the prior question—and therefore the whole purpose of foreign policy—Is there a substitute for war? The answer is a hopeful but most certain "yes." And that substitute is diplomacy.

Diplomacy seems to be even more important now than during the cold war, when the two superpowers held each other at bay through a shared strategy of "mutually assured destruction" (MAD). For example, when the Holy Alliance approach to the dissolution of Yugoslavia reached its limits in a military stalemate, diplomacy contributed to conditions that gave rise in 2000 to popular elections in Serbia, ultimately leading to the peaceful removal of Slobodan Milosevic and the installation of the first democratically elected government in modern Yugoslavian history.

Diplomacy made even more definitive contributions to two other important breakthroughs in 2000. First, there was a dramatic turnaround in Korea, which culminated in the first meeting between North Korean and South Korean heads of state since the partitioning of Korea following World War II. This commencement of negotiations between the two Koreas produced a Nobel Peace Prize in 2000 for South Korean President Kim Dae Jung. (That the Prize was not also awarded to North Korea's Kim Jong is, to some extent, questionable.) Second, in continuation of the seven-year "peace process" between Israelis and Palestinians, a fifteen-day summit meeting was held at Camp David in June 2000, with President Clinton and Secretary of State Madeleine Albright operating as "honest brokers." The summit concluded with a number of radical concessions, on the part of Israel, concerning the establishment of a genuine Palestinian state. The fact that progress toward this end was interrupted in October 2000 by a "mini–civil war," fought in the streets of Jerusalem by rock-throwing Palestinians and armed Israeli militia, does not raise any question about the value of diplomacy but only suggests its limits. Indeed, diplomacy managed to bring two profound adversaries to the bargaining table, yielding the result of genuine amity between them and showing promise of spectacular, historic success. That all this was impaired—and perhaps permanently destroyed—by the actions of radicals in both camps demonstrates not only that diplomacy is highly fragile, but that a small number of citizens can, when acting in concert, shape important foreign policy decisions. This, however, should not be thought of as a shortcoming of diplomacy. Rather, it is further confirmation that diplomacy is ultimately the only alternative to war.

Politics on the Web

In a pre-Internet world, the U.S. national security system tried to prevent military secrets from ending up in the wrong hands. The global reach of the Internet renders such control difficult, however. In 1998, an Israeli citizen was arrested for a serious attack on the Pentagon's computer network. That same year, within two weeks of atomic tests by India, a hacker broke into the Indian nuclear weapons research facility and stole classified information.

The Internet could also be a great asset for democracy, however. The very openness that causes headaches for U.S. military security promotes an exchange of political and intellectual thought. An autocratic government has a clear choice to either limit Internet access and potentially hamstring intellectual and economic growth, or open up access and expose its population to political and social change. As the example of China shows, once the democratic genie is let out of the bottle—in large part due to the Internet—it's almost impossible to put it back.

www.wwnorton.com/wtp3e

The Citizen's Role

The American people are too large and diffuse a nation to participate in making foreign policy in any truly democratic way. A people, even a free and mature people, can at best set limits, or broadly defined national interests within which policy makers and policy shapers can operate. A people can constrain power but cannot guide or direct the powerful.

If the whole American people is too broad to conduct foreign policy, the American presidency is too narrow. We need a "vital middle" player to form foreign policy in our democracy. This "vital middle" is in fact provided by the Constitution. Foreign policy was always supposed to involve the president and Congress, and, now that the cold war has ended, no time is more appropriate to revive that principle. During the cold war, a genuine foreign policy debate was carried out in Congress about once every decade. Each time it happened, it was a great moment of renewal of the Constitution and redirection and revitalization of public policy. The "Cooper/Church" debate in 1970 over the continuation of military activity in Cambodia did very little to alter the course of the Vietnam War, but in focusing on the constitutionality of the war and the legality of the U.S. incursion into Cambodia, the debate revived the strength of constitutionalism in the United States and brought America to its senses about the difference between democracy and tyranny. Almost exactly twenty years later, the Persian Gulf War did the same thing. Anticipating opposition in Congress, President Bush sought and got UN support and multilateral cooperation. When he took the issue to Congress in January 1991, he was supported by a narrow margin, but he got from the debate an enlightened and guided support that no opinion poll could have provided. Success in the Gulf War brought Bush a 90 percent popular approval rating. But that was not the true measure of his political base; Congress was.

The end of the cold war has opened Congress to opportunities in foreign-policy debates that it has not had since before the Great Depression. During the cold war, because the United States had to remain mobilized and secretive most of the time, it could not afford a substantial and public congressional role in foreign policy. But now, without the imminent threat of atomic holocaust, genuine crises are rare. Thus even important foreign policy issues permit time for debate and deliberation, which allows Congress to play its legitimate role.

During the cold war, following as it did a world war and a long domestic economic crisis, Congress developed what one expert has called "a culture of deference"—a bipartisan culture of defeat that can be summed up by a maxim shared by most influential members of the House and Senate: "We shouldn't make foreign policy."[47] But this doesn't make sense anymore. The end of the cold war did not just liberate the republics of the former Soviet Union and Eastern Europe to embrace democracy; it liberated all legislatures of the world to get involved in foreign affairs. Foreign policy making in the United States will remain the president's domain. But public deliberation and debate, in an ongoing search for the national interest, is the domain of Congress. Congress is the vital middle between a hopeless isolationist rejection of foreign policy altogether and an equally hopeless delegation of total power to the chief executive.

GET INVOLVED Voicing Your Views

The world has become a smaller place due to revolutions in transportation and communication, the globalization of the marketplace, and the growth of international organizations such as the United Nations. Moreover, the world has become a smaller place because the potential for nuclear meltdown, explosions, and fallout, for biological, chemical, and ecological disasters in peace and in war, and for a host of other threats puts people of all countries in the same precarious position. Americans are increasingly aware of what is happening in other nations and they are increasingly affected by events occurring in other nations.

Especially since World War II, the United States has become intricately involved in the cultures, economies, and politics of other nations. At the same time, American citizens have become deeply concerned about U.S. relations with other nations. Wars bring out extremely strong feelings. Many Americans protested against the Vietnam War in the 1960s and 1970s, and many citizens held rallies supporting the Persian Gulf War in 1991. Note that Americans' concerns about foreign policy reach beyond war. Many citizens have expressed intense views on the North American Free Trade Agreement and World Trade Organization policies, U.S. relations with Mexico and Israel, human rights violations in China, and UN peacekeeping efforts in Eastern Europe and Africa.

How can you voice your views on a foreign policy issue? One voice is likely to have little impact. But several hundred or several thousand voices can make an impression. One way to situate your voice among a large number of supporters is to circulate a petition stating your views. To whom should you address your petition? The key players in U.S. foreign policy are the president, the bureaucracy, and Congress. It is a strategic question whether you want to address your petition to one, two, or all three. Will your petition have an impact? You may be able to get additional support and publicity for a petition drive by making alliances with appropriate interest groups and promoting press coverage. The more signatures, allies, and coverage you get, the greater the probability that your petition will be heard, if not heeded.

To begin, write up your petition. Clearly express the issue that concerns you and briefly state your position. You must be clear and brief if you are to get people to sign your petition. Type up your petition, create blank spaces for signatures and addresses, and make multiple copies. Develop a strategy for gathering signatures. Will you do it alone? Do you have collaborators? What high-pedestrian traffic areas are good places for gathering signatures? Can you set up a table with a banner announcing your cause? Will you politely stop people, try to interest them in your cause, and solicit their signatures? Do you have money to hire people to collect signatures? Will any campus organizations or interest groups help solicit signatures among their members and extended networks? Execute your strategy; encourage people to sign your petition.

Suppose that you choose to address your petition to the president. When you have accumulated a substantial number of signatures, compose a brief cover letter, attach your petition and signature sheets, and mail the packet to the White House. Simultaneously, put together a press release. Describe your petition and its importance. Record the number of signatures gathered. Discuss the petition's potential impact. Include the name, telephone number, and e-mail address of a contact person at the bottom. Send copies of the press release to appropriate media outlets. Follow up a few days later with phone calls to see if you can schedule interviews. Even if local publicity does not get back to Washington, D.C., it might capture the attention of potential supporters as well as local members of Congress.

The cost of conducting an informal petition drive (with a few friends) is quite low. But the time commitment is quite high. Furthermore, a petition drive generates only one piece of mail for the White House to handle. Here is another option: draft postcards that express your views on a foreign policy issue, distribute them, and have individuals send them directly to the White House.

Perhaps you belong to a student organization that will sponsor the effort. With modest funding, your organization may be able to pre-print the postcards. Use cardstock-weight paper in a bright color that will attract attention. On one side of the postcard, you should have printed the president's address: The President, The White House, 1600 Pennsylvania Avenue, Washington, D.C., 20500. If you have ample resources, pre-pay postage costs. That way, people are more likely to mail them.

On the other side of the postcard, print a brief, clear summary of your issue and the action you want the president to take. You might write something like:

> Dear Mr. President: I, the undersigned registered voter, am deeply concerned about the __________ situation in __________. I strongly encourage you to __________.

At the bottom of the postcard, leave a line for a signature.

Once the cards are designed and printed, distribute them to people you think are likely to support your expressed foreign policy preference. All that they have to do is sign the card, affix a stamp (if you did not pre-pay postage), and drop it in a mailbox. Ideally, you will flood the White House mailroom with colored postcards promoting your foreign policy message and garner enough attention for a White House aide to transmit the message to presidential advisers.

More likely, you and your supporters will add your voices to the chorus of citizens who have expressed similar views to the president, or the State Department, or Congress. The louder the chorus, the more powerful the message, and the greater the likelihood that decision makers will take notice.

Summary

This chapter began by raising some dilemmas about forming foreign policy in a democracy like the United States. Skepticism about foreign entanglements and the secrecy surrounding many foreign policy issues form the basis of these dilemmas. Although we cannot provide solutions to the foreign policy issues that the United States faces, we can provide a well-balanced analysis of the problems of foreign policy. This analysis is based on the five basic dimensions of foreign policy: the players, the setting, the values, the instruments, and the roles.

The first section of this chapter looked at the players in foreign policy: the makers and the shapers. The influence of institutions and groups varies from case to case, with the important exception of the president. Since the president is central to all foreign policy, it is best to assess how other actors interact with the president. In most instances, this interaction involves only the narrowest element of the foreign policy establishment. The American people have an opportunity to influence foreign policy, but primarily through Congress or interest groups.

The next section, on values, traced the history of American values that had a particular relevance to American perspectives on the outside world. We found that the American fear of a big government applied to foreign as well as domestic governmental powers. The Founders and the active public of the Founding period all recognized that foreign policy was special, that the national government had special powers in its dealings with foreigners, and that presidential supremacy was justified in the conduct of foreign affairs. The only way to avoid the big national government and presidential supremacy was to avoid the foreign entanglements that made foreign policy, diplomacy, secrecy, and presidential discretion necessary. Americans held on to their "antistatist" tradition until World War II, long after world conditions cried out for American involvement. And even as we became involved in world affairs, we held on tightly to the legacies of 150 years of tradition: the intermingling of domestic and foreign policy institutions, and unilateralism, the tendency to "go it alone" when confronted with foreign conflicts.

We then looked at the instruments—that is, the tools—of American foreign policy. These are the basic statutes and the institutions by which foreign policy has been conducted since World War II: diplomacy, the United Nations, the international monetary structure, economic aid, collective security, and military deterrence. Although Republicans and Democrats look at the world somewhat differently, and although each president has tried to impose a distinctive flavor on foreign policy, they have all made use of these basic instruments, and that has given foreign policies a certain continuity. When Congress created these instruments after World War II, the old tradition was still so strong that it moved Congress to try to create instruments that would do their international work with a minimum of diplomacy—a minimum of human involvement.

The next section concentrated on the role or roles the president and Congress have sought to play in the world. To help simplify the tremendous variety of tactics and strategies that foreign policy leaders can select, we narrowed the field down to four categories of roles nations play, suggesting that there is a certain amount of consistency and stability in the conduct of a nation-state in its dealings with other nation-states. These were labeled according to actual roles that diplomatic historians have identified in the history of major Western nation-states: the Napoleonic, Holy Alliance, balance-of-power, and economic expansionist roles. We also attempted to identify and assess the role of the United States in the post–cold war era, essentially the Holy Alliance role. But whatever its advantages may be, the Holy Alliance approach will never allow the United States to conduct foreign policy without diplomacy. America is tied inextricably to the perils and ambiguities of international relationships, and diplomacy is still the monarch of all available instruments of foreign policy.

We concluded by returning to the dilemma we raised in the chapter's introduction: In a democracy like the United States, who should make foreign policy? The chapter provided numerous case studies to seek an answer to this question. We believe that between the extremes of isolationism and total power resting with the president resides a middle ground where the American people can express their will through the members of Congress. The national interest can be defined only through debate and deliberation, which we hope will serve as the foundations for the formation of foreign policy in the American democracy.

FOR FURTHER READING

Crabb, Cecil V., and Kevin V. Mulcahy. *Presidents and Foreign Policymaking: From FDR to Reagan.* Baton Rouge: Louisiana State University Press, 1986.

Doremus, Paul N., William W. Keller, Louis Pauly, and Simon Reich. *The Myth of the Global Corporation.* Princeton, NJ: Princeton University Press, 1998.

Gilpin, Robert. *The Political Economy of International Relations.* Princeton, NJ: Princeton University Press, 1987.

Graubard, Stephen, ed. "The Exit from Communism." *Daedalus* 121, no. 2 (Spring 1992).

———."The Quest for World Order." *Daedalus* 124, no. 3 (Summer 1995).

Greenfield, Liah. *Nationalism: Five Roads to Modernity.* Cambridge, MA: Harvard University Press, 1993.

Keller, William W. *Arm in Arm: The Political Economy of the Global Arms Race.* New York: Basic Books, 1995.

Kennan, George F. *Around the Cragged Hill: A Personal and Political Philosophy.* New York: Norton, 1993.

Kennedy, Paul M. *The Rise and Fall of the Great Powers: Economic Change and Military Conflict from 1500 to 2000.* New York: Random House, 1987.

LaFeber, Walter. *The American Age: United States Foreign Policy at Home and Abroad since 1750.* New York: Norton, 1989.

———. *The Clash: U.S.-Japanese Relations Throughout History.* New York: Norton, 1997.

Wirls, Daniel. *Buildup: The Politics of Defense in the Reagan Era.* Ithaca, NY: Cornell University Press, 1992.

STUDY OUTLINE

1. Traditionally, Americans have been skeptical and distrustful of foreign policy.
2. Public opinion can have a determinative impact on the success or failure of foreign policy. Consequently, politicians often engage in deceit in order to curry the public's favor.

The Players: The Makers and Shapers of Foreign Policy

1. All foreign policy decisions must be made and implemented in the name of the president.
2. The key players in foreign policy in the bureaucracy are the secretaries of State, Defense, and Treasury; the Joint Chiefs of Staff (especially the chair); and the Director of the Central Intelligence Agency.
3. Although the Senate traditionally has more foreign policy power than the House, since World War II, the House and the Senate have both been important players in foreign policy.
4. Many types of interest groups help shape American foreign policy. These groups include economic interest groups, ethnic or national interest groups, and human rights interest groups.
5. The media serve to communicate issues and policies to the American people, and to communicate the public's opinions back to the president. One definite influence of television on foreign policy has been to make the American people more cynical and skeptical than they otherwise would have been.
6. Individual or group influence in foreign policy varies from case to case and from situation to situation.

The Values in American Foreign Policy

1. The intermingling of domestic and foreign policy institutions and unilateralism are the two identifiable legacies of our traditional system of maintaining sovereignty.
2. The intermingling of domestic and foreign policy institutions was originally possible because the major European powers policed the world.
3. Traditionally, unilateralism, the desire to go it alone, was the American posture toward the world.
4. Although the traditional era of American foreign policy came to an end with World War I, there was no discernible change in approach to such policy until after World War II.

The Instruments of Modern American Foreign Policy

1. Diplomacy is the representation of a government to other foreign governments, and it is the foreign policy instrument to which all other instruments must be subordinated.
2. The United Nations is an instrument whose usefulness to American foreign policy can too easily be underestimated.
3. The international monetary structure, which consists of the World Bank and the International Monetary Fund, was created to avoid the economic devastation that followed World War I.
4. Economic aid has been important as an instrument of American foreign policy, but it was put together as a balance between traditional values and the modern needs of a great, imperial power.
5. After World War II, the United States recognized the importance of collective security, and subsequently entered into multilateral collective security treaties and other bilateral treaties.
6. World War II broke the American cycle of demobilization-remobilization and led to a new policy of military preparedness.

Roles Nations Play

1. There are four roles available to a nation in the conduct of its foreign policy: the Napoleonic role, the Holy Alliance role, the balance-of-power role, and the economic expansionist role.
2. Although the United States played the Napoleonic role during the postwar era and then switched to the Holy Alliance role, the United States is now beginning to adopt all four roles, playing whichever one is appropriate to a particular region and set of circumstances.

PRACTICE QUIZ

1. Who noted that a democracy such as the United States lacked the qualities best suited for successful foreign policies?
   a) George Washington
   b) Alexis de Tocqueville
   c) Woodrow Wilson
   d) Ronald Reagan

2. The making of American foreign policy is
   a) dominated entirely by the president.
   b) dominated entirely by Congress.
   c) dominated entirely by interest groups.
   d) highly pluralistic, involving a large mix of both official and unofficial players.

3. The term "unilateralism" describes
   a) an approach to foreign policy that involves complex and time-consuming negotiations between multiple powers.
   b) a "go-it-alone" approach to foreign policy.
   c) episodes in American foreign policy during which the president dominates Congress.
   d) instances when the U.S. Supreme Court refuses to approve a treaty negotiated by the president.

4. The "cold war" refers to the
   a) competition between the United States and Canada over Alaska.
   b) the years between World War I and World War II when the United States and Germany were hostile to one another.
   c) the period of struggle between the United States and the Soviet Union between the late 1940s and the late 1980s.
   d) the economic competition between the United States and Japan today.

5. The North Atlantic Treaty Organization was formed in 1948 by the United States,
   a) Canada, and most of Eastern Europe.
   b) Canada, and Mexico.
   c) Canada, and most of Western Europe.
   d) Canada, and the United Kingdom.

6. Which of the following terms best describes the American posture toward the world prior to the middle of the twentieth century?
   a) interventionist
   b) isolationist
   c) unilateralist
   d) none of the above

7. The United Nations' activity in which country points to a new humanitarian role for the UN?
   a) Pakistan
   b) Russia
   c) the former Yugoslavia
   d) the United States

8. Which of the following are important international economic institutions created after World War II?
   a) the Federal Reserve
   b) the World Bank
   c) the International Monetary Fund
   d) Both b and c are correct.

9. Which of the following terms describes the idea that the development and maintenance of military strength discourages attack?
   a) deterrence
   b) containment
   c) "minuteman" theory of defense
   d) detente

10. Which of the following was dedicated to the relief, reconstruction, and economic recovery of Western Europe?
    a) the Marshall Plan
    b) the Lend-Lease Act
    c) the General Agreement on Tariffs and Trade
    d) the North American Free Trade Agreement

CRITICAL THINKING QUESTIONS

1. In previous chapters we have learned about the political nature of most of the key players in American foreign policy. How might politics (in addition to democracy) impede the effectiveness of the United States in the international arena? Can you think of an instance in which the United States was hampered by domestic politics?

2. What is the proper balance between governmental effectiveness in international politics and the public's "right to know"? Surely, for tactical reasons the government should be able to keep some activities secret. But given the potential for abuse of governmental secrecy, how might the public hold the government accountable while preserving for the United States the tactical advantage of secrecy?

KEY TERMS

balance-of-power role (p. 767)
bilateral treaties (p. 762)
cold war (p. 753)
containment (p. 754)
deterrence (p. 754)
diplomacy (p. 754)
economic expansionist role (p. 768)
executive agreement (p. 746)
Holy Alliance role (p. 767)
International Monetary Fund (IMF) (p. 759)
Marshall Plan (p. 760)
multilateralism (p. 753)
Napoleonic role (p. 767)
nation-state (p. 754)
North American Free Trade Agreement (NAFTA) (p. 747)
North Atlantic Treaty Organization (NATO) (p. 754)
unilateralism (p. 752)
United Nations (UN) (p. 757)

PART VI

Texas Politics

20 The Political

★ **Texas Political Culture**

How would one describe Texas political culture?
What patterns of Texas politics reflect its political culture?

★ **The Land**

How has the diverse geography of Texas affected its development?

★ **Economic Change in Texas**

What are the three great periods of economic change that have defined the Texas political economy over the last 150 years?

★ **The People: Texas Demography**

How did the population of Texas change during the 1990s? What is its racial and ethnic composition? How does the population of Texas compare to the rest of the nation in terms of age and income?

★ **Urbanization**

What is the history of urbanization in Texas?
How can one describe its current urban political economy?

Culture, People, and Economy of Texas

LEGENDS die. Eras come to an end. Sometimes this happens at the same time.

On June 20, 1999, former Lieutenant Governor Bob Bullock was laid to rest in the historical Texas State Cemetery in Austin, the final resting place of eleven governors, two American Revolutionary War veterans, sixty-four Republic of Texas veterans, and about twenty-two hundred Confederate veterans and their spouses. He was eulogized by Byron Tunnell, a close personal friend and former Democratic Speaker of the Texas House of Representatives, and by the second-term Republican governor of Texas, George W. Bush.

Bullock was a towering figure in Texas politics, almost larger than life, for over forty years. He was born on July 10, 1929, in Hillsboro, a small town near Waco in central Texas. As a student at Baylor University Law School, he was elected to the Texas House of Representatives in 1957 as a Democrat. He quit before the end of his second term to go and practice law. Bullock returned to state government in the mid-1960s as an assistant to Governor Preston Smith. Later, he was appointed secretary of state by Governor Smith.

In 1974, Bullock was elected state comptroller, where he would modernize an antiquated tax collection system and establish himself as a force to be reckoned with in the state's political hierarchy. After sixteen years as comptroller, Bullock was elected lieutenant governor, a position from which he dominated state politics for the next ten years.

Like his public career, Bullock's private life was sensational. He was divorced four times, married five. Early in his political career he had been a heavy drinker, often holding political court in one of Austin's many bars. Although he had given up alcohol for abstinence in the early 1980s, he never stopped holding court. He was feared and respected by friend and foe alike. He was not afraid to intimidate others. His fierce temper was legendary, as was his willingness to use power to accomplish his objectives. He dominated people in politics more than anyone else in his generation. As the political columnist Molly Ivins explained at his retirement, "Not since Lyndon B. Johnson has there been another pol who could so dominate everyone around him by sheer force of personality."[1] But his desire for power never went beyond the state's boundaries. Others sought to nationalize their political careers, but Bullock's eyes remained focused on Austin. At his retirement, Bullock captured his commitments well when he noted, "Only death will end my love affair with Texas."

Bullock was in many ways a throwback to an earlier time. When he entered politics, the state had been dominated by a Democratic Party establishment for over eighty years. To be a successful politician, one had to be white, male, and a conservative Democrat. By the time he left politics, minorities, women, and Republicans had come to play crucial roles in the state. Bullock himself helped to bring Texas politics into this new era when, as lieutenant governor, he presided over a bipartisan Senate, demanding support not only from his fellow Democrats but Republicans as well. If one wanted to be a player in the Texas Senate, one had to play by the rules laid down by the lieutenant governor. In the 1998 gubernatorial campaign Bullock actively supported the re-election of Republican governor George W. Bush, abandoning his close friend and political protégé Garry Mauro, the Democratic candidate. When asked why he supported the opposing party's candidate, Bullock replied that he felt that Bush was the better candidate. The product of one political era, Bullock helped to lay the foundations of another.

Texas Political Culture

- How would one describe Texas political culture?
- What patterns of Texas politics reflect its political culture?

Entering the twenty-first century, Texas finds itself at the beginning of a new era. Certain myths continue to define Texas in the popular imagination. An unpopulated rural land that rolls on forever, an arid countryside that challenges the heartiest of souls, undeveloped prairies that build up into mountains, and a coastal land of inhospitable heat and humidity—such are the myths of the land that is Texas. The cowboy who challenges both Indian and Mexican rule, the rancher and farmer who cherish their economic independence, the wildcatter who is willing to risk everything for one more roll of the dice, and the independent entrepreneur who fears the needless intrusion of government into his life—such are the myths about the people. But the reality of the land and the people of Texas is a far cry from the myth.

political culture
broadly shared values, beliefs, and attitudes about how the government should function. American political culture emphasizes the values of liberty, equality, and democracy

Studies of Texas politics often begin with a discussion of the **political culture** of the state. Though the concept is somewhat open-ended and can be stretched so far as to be meaningless, states do often exhibit a distinctive culture that is the "product of their entire history." Presumably the political culture of a state has an effect on how people participate in politics and how individuals and institutions interact.[2] Daniel Elazar has created a classification scheme for state political cultures that has been used widely. He uses the concepts of *moralistic*, *individualistic,* and *traditionalistic* to describe such cultures. These three state political cultures are contemporary manifestations of the ethnic, socioreligious, and socioeconomic differences that existed among the original thirteen colonies.[3]

moralistic political culture
the belief that government should be active in promoting the public good and that citizens should participate in politics and civic activities to ensure that good

According to Elazar, **moralistic political cultures** were rooted in New England, where Puritans and other religious groups sought to create the Good Society. In such a culture, politics is the concern of everyone and government is expected to be interventionist in promoting the public good and in advancing the public welfare. Citizen participation in politics is viewed as positive and people are encouraged to pursue the public good in civic activities.

Individualistic political cultures, on the other hand, originated in the middle states, where Americans sought material wealth and personal freedom through commercial activities. A state with an individualistic political culture generally places a low value on citizen participation in politics. Politics is a matter for professionals rather than for citizens and the role of government is strictly limited. Government's role is to ensure stability so that individuals can pursue their own interests.

individualistic political culture
the belief that government should limit its role to providing order in society, so that citizens can pursue their economic self-interests

Traditionalistic political culture developed initially in the South, reflecting the values of the slave plantation economy and its successor, the Jim Crow era. Traditionalistic culture is ambivalent about the marketplace values that run through individualistic cultures and about the elitist, paternalistic views that pervade moralistic cultures. Rooted in preindustrial values that emphasize social hierarchy and close interpersonal, often familial, relations among people, traditional culture is concerned with the preservation of tradition and the existing social order. In such states, public participation is limited and government is by an established **elite.** Public policies disproportionately benefit the interests of those elites.

traditionalistic political culture
the belief that government should be dominated by political elites and guided by tradition

elite
a small group of people that dominates the political process

States can, of course, have cultures that combine these concepts. One book classified Colorado, for example, as having a "moralistic" political culture. California was classified as having a "moralistic individualistic" political culture and New York an "individualistic moralistic" culture. New Jersey was classified as "individualistic" and Georgia "traditionalistic." Florida and Kentucky were seen as "traditionalistic individualistic."

Often Texas is categorized as having a "traditionalistic individualistic" political culture.[4] Taxes are kept low and social services are minimized. Political elites, such as business leaders, have a major voice in how the state is run. In spite of the difficulty in measuring the concept of political culture in any empirical way, it is a concept widely regarded as useful in explaining the fundamental beliefs about the state and the role of state government.

Yet, the concept of political culture is not a stagnant one. The political culture of a state can change over time. Texas is undergoing dramatic changes, including some change in the state's political culture. It is also the case, however, that it is misleading to have one classification for the political culture of a state as large and as diverse as Texas. In fact, Texas has many different political cultures or subcultures within its borders. Texas has over nineteen million people with large populations of Anglo Americans, Hispanics, and African Americans. These people reside in a state that is larger in area that the combined area of the fifteen smallest states. It is a state where Texarkana, in the far northeastern corner of the state, is actually closer to Chicago than it is to El Paso. El Paso is closer to the Pacific Ocean than it is to the eastern boundary of Texas, and the eastern boundary is closer to the Atlantic Ocean than it is to El Paso. One can drive in a straight line for over eight hundred miles without leaving Texas—almost the same distance as from New York to St. Louis or from Chicago to Boston.

As Professor Donald Whisenhunt has written:

> All areas of Texas have shared a heritage from the past seventy-five to one hundred years. . . . Even in these years, however, Texas history has been heavily regionalized. Issues affecting one part of the state do not always have much to do with another part, just as events in Chicago often have little in common with events in Boston.

> To be very honest, the limited heritage shared by all is a frail thing on which to build a modern state.[5]

And the limited common heritage means as well that the idea of a common political culture throughout the state should be treated with great caution.

But regardless of the degree of one's enthusiasm for the usefulness of the concept of political culture in explaining Texas politics, it is clear that there have been three long-lasting patterns in Texas politics that do seem related to the concept of a "traditionalistic individualistic" state political culture. These patterns relate to a domination of the state by political elites interested in limited government with low taxes and few social services. It is also the case that at least some of these lasting characteristics of state politics are undergoing rapid change. These three patterns of state politics are:

THE ONE-PARTY STATE

For over one hundred years, Texas was dominated by the Democratic Party. Winning the Democratic Party primary was tantamount to winning the general election. As we will see in later chapters, this pattern no longer holds. In the 1990s, there emerged substantial competition between the parties for control of the state legislature, with Republicans actually gaining a one-vote majority in the state senate. Moreover, by the end of the decade all major statewide elected offices were controlled by Republicans. The question today is not whether the political culture of Texas will continue to be defined by a powerful Democratic Party, but how that culture will be redefined by an increasingly powerful Republican Party.

PROVINCIALISM

provincialism
a narrow, limited, and self-interested view of the world

A second pattern that has defined Texas political culture is **provincialism.** In an often-repeated anecdote, former governor Miriam Ferguson was once

Texas is no longer the one-party state. Beginning in the early 1990s, Republicans gained control of all the major statewide offices, shifting the power almost entirely from the Democratic dominance that had characterized Texas for over a hundred years.

asked about bilingual education in Texas. Her response was, "If English was good enough for Jesus Christ, it is good enough for me." That anecdote nicely describes the long-time provincialism of Texas that stressed rural values and Jeffersonian notions of limited government. The result often was an intolerance of diversity and a notion of the public interest that dismissed social services and expenditures for education. The result was that some of the more popular politicians in Texas have stressed cornpone, intolerance, and a narrow worldview rather than policies that might offer advantages to the state in its competition with other states and with other nations. Like the one-party Democratic state, Texas provincialism has faded as a defining feature of the political culture. The growing influence of minorities, women, and gays in state politics and the ongoing urbanization of the state has undercut provincialism at its roots, leaving in its place a state whose political culture is being defined by diversity and an outward looking view to the future and the world economy.

BUSINESS DOMINANCE

A third, continuing pattern that has helped to define Texas's political culture is that it has long been dominated by business. Labor unions are rare in Texas except in the oil refinery areas around Beaumont-Port Arthur. Other groups that might offer an alternative to a business perspective, such as consumer interests, are unorganized and poorly funded. The major interests in Texas politics in terms of campaign contributions, organized interest groups, and lobbyists are business groups.

This chapter will investigate the economic, social, and demographic changes that transformed Texas's political culture in the twentieth century. These changes have shaken Texas government and politics in the 1990s and will continue to shape it well into the first decade of the twenty-first century. Understanding how these factors fit together provides a first step for understanding what government and politics is all about in Texas today.

"TEXAS" — Box 20.1

Various explanations have been offered as to the origins of the word "Texas." One popular account maintains that it was derived from a number of words commonly used by Native Americans in east Texas in the seventeenth century. Words such as *tejas, tayshas, texias, techan,* and *teysas* usually meant "friends" or "allies." An early Spanish missionary, Francisco de Jesus Maria, reported that "Texias" meant "friends" and applied to a number of groups allied against the Apaches. Early Spanish documents did not apply the term to any particular geographic area, but to the Neches-Angelina group of Indians. The idea embodied in the original Native American word has been carried over into the state motto: Friendship.

SOURCE: Phillip L. Fry, "Texas, Origin of Name," *The Handbook of Texas Online,* www.tsha.utexas.edu/handbook/online/articles/view/TT/pft4.html.

Box 20.2 SIX FLAGS OVER TEXAS

Six flags have flown over Texas since Spanish rule in the sixteenth century:

- Spanish: 1519–1685 and 1690–1821
- French: 1685–1690
- Mexican: 1821–1836
- Republic of Texas: 1836–1845
- United States: 1845–1861 and 1865 to the present
- Confederacy: 1861–1865

A version of the Lone Star Flag was approved by President Mirabeau B. Lamar on January 25, 1839. The flag was to consist of a "blue perpendicular stripe of the width of one-third of the whole length of the flag, with a white star of five points in the center thereof, and two horizontal stripes of equal breadth, the upper stripe white, the lower red, of the length of two-thirds of the whole flag." It was formally adopted as the state flag in 1844 and readopted in 1933 after being mistakenly revoked by legislation in 1879. Echoing the color scheme of the national flag, the colors represent the virtues of bravery (red), purity (white), and loyalty (blue).

SOURCE: Dallas Morning News, *Texas Almanac 2000–2001* (Dallas: Dallas Morning News, 1999), pp. 9–10.

The Land

▶ How has the diverse geography of Texas affected its develpoment?

Much of Texas's history has been shaped by the relationship forged between its people and the land. Texas is the second largest state in size, next to Alaska, comprising 267,000 square miles. Of this, 261,914 square miles are land and 5,363 square miles are inland water. The longest straight-line distance across the state north-south is 801 miles, while the longest east-west distance is 773 miles.[6] To put this into perspective, the east-west distance from New York City to Chicago is 821 miles, cutting across five different states. Meanwhile, the north-south distance between New York City and Charleston, South Carolina, is 763 miles, cutting across six different states.

Distances alone do not tell the whole story of the diverse geography found in Texas. There are four distinct physical regions in Texas: the Gulf Coastal Plains, the Interior Lowlands, the Great Plains, and the Basin and Range Province (see Figure 20.1).[7]

THE COASTAL PLAINS

The Gulf Coastal Plains extend from the Louisiana border and the Gulf of Mexico, along the Rio Grande up to Del Rio, and northward to the line of the Balcones Fault and Escarpment. As one moves to the west, the climate be-

THE PHYSICAL REGIONS OF TEXAS **Figure 20.1**

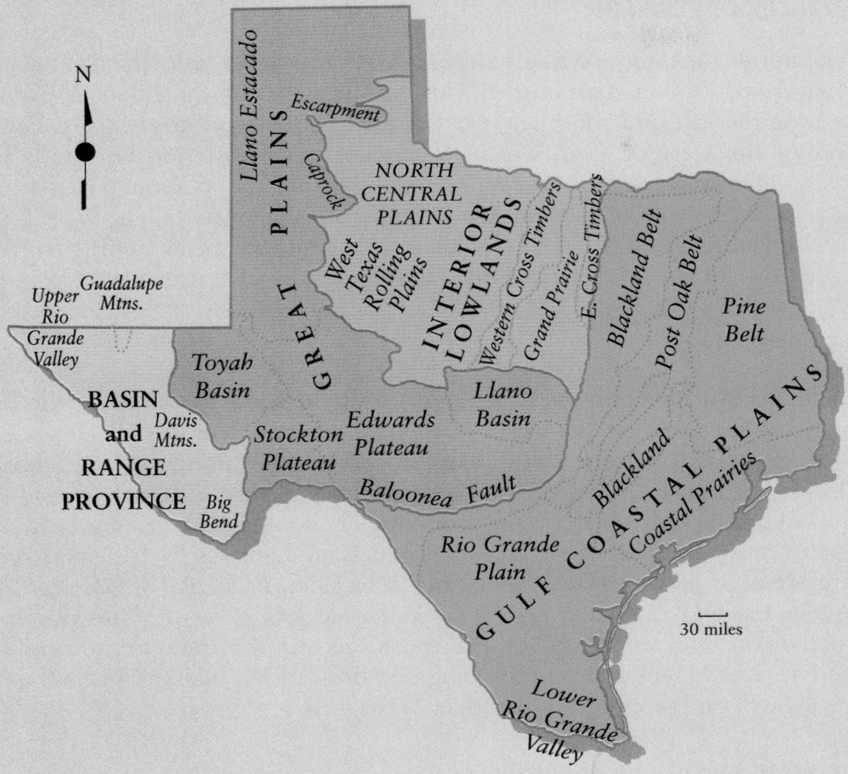

SOURCE: Dallas Morning News, *Texas Almanac 2000–2001* (Dallas: Dallas Morning News, 1999), p. 55.

comes increasingly more arid. Forests become less important as post oak trees dominate the landscape until they too are replaced by the prairies and brush lands of central Texas.

The east portion of the Gulf Coastal Plains—so-called East Texas—is characterized by hilly surfaces covered by forests of pine and hardwoods. Almost all of Texas's timber production takes place here. It is also the home of some of Texas's most famous oil fields. To the west is the Blackland Belt. A rolling prairie soil made the Blackland Belt a prime farming area in the late nineteenth and early twentieth centuries. It was a major center of cotton production in Texas. Today it is the most densely populated area of the state and has a diversified manufacturing base.

The Coastal Prairies around Houston and Beaumont were the center for the post–World War II industrial boom, particularly in the petrochemical industry. Winter vegetable and fruit production play a major role in the Lower Rio Grande Valley, while livestock becomes important in the Rio Grande

Plain, an area that receives less than twenty-four inches of rainfall on average every year and during the summer months experiences rapid evaporation.

THE INTERIOR LOWLANDS

The Interior Lowlands region is an extension of the interior lowlands that runs down from the Canadian border. They are bordered by the Balcones Escarpment on the east and south and the Caprock Escarpment on the west. Beginning to the west of Fort Worth, the eastern edge Interior Lowlands has predominantly an agricultural economy and a rural population. The western portion, meanwhile, rises from 750 to 2,000 feet in elevation. The West Texas Rolling Plains contains much level, cultivable land, and is the home to a large cattle-raising industry. Many of the state's largest ranches are located here.

THE GREAT PLAINS

Pushing down into northwest Texas from the Rocky Mountains to the Balcones Fault, the Great Plains defines the terrain in much of western Texas, rising from 2,700 feet in the east to more than 4,000 feet along the New Mexico border. The major city on the northern plains is Amarillo. Ranching and petroleum production dominate the economy. The southern plains economy centers around agriculture and cotton production. Lubbock is the major city. Large-scale irrigation from underwater reservoirs, particularly the Olgallala Aquifer, has played a major role in the economic development of this region. A recent major concern of policy makers is the fact that pumping out of the aquifer exceeds replenishment, raising questions of the viability of basing future growth on the irrigation practices of the past.[8]

THE BASIN AND RANGE PROVINCE

The fourth geographic region in Texas is the Basin and Range Province. Here one finds Texas's true mountains in the Guadeloupe Range along the border with New Mexico, which includes Guadeloupe Peak (8,749 feet) and El Capitan (8,085 feet). To the southeast is found Big Bend country, a name derived from the fact that the Rio Grande River surrounds it on three sides as it makes its southward swing. Rainfall and population are sparse in this region.

Economic Change in Texas

▶ What are the three great periods of economic change that have defined the Texas political economy over the last 150 years?

creative destruction
Joseph Schumpeter's concept that capitalism is subject to periodic waves of transformation, fueled by technological change

The famous twentieth-century economist Joseph Schumpeter characterized the capitalist economic system as being a process of **"creative destruction."**[9] By this he meant that capitalism was an economic system that underwent periodic waves of transformation fueled by technological innovations in production and distribution. These waves of technological transformation were put into place by entrepreneurs who had visions of new ways of producing and distributing goods and services and were willing to act upon those visions. The capitalist process of creative destruction not only created a new economic and social world, it also destroyed old ones. The world of railroads, steam, and steel transformed American economic and social life by nationalizing the market and making new opportunities available to businesses and individuals in the late nineteenth century. It also destroyed the local markets that had defined rural American communities since the Founding. Similarly, the technological innovation tied to gas combustion engines, electricity, and radio restructured the American economy again in the 1920s, leaving in its wake a society and economy that would never be the same.

Schumpeter's theory of creative destruction provides a useful way to think about the economic changes that have shaped and reshaped the Texas economy since the days of the Republic. There are three great waves of creative destruction that have helped to define and redefine the Texas political economy over the last 150 years. The first centered on the production of cotton and cattle and its distribution by an extensive railroad system. The second grew out of the oil industry. The third, and most recent, is tied to the development of the high-tech economy.

COTTON

Cotton is one of the oldest crops grown in Texas.[10] Missions in San Antonio in the eighteenth century are reported to have produced several thousand pounds of cotton annually, which were spun and woven by local craftsmen. Serious cultivation of cotton began in 1821 with the arrival of Anglo Americans. Political independence, statehood, and the ongoing removal of the Native American "threat" in the years prior to the Civil War promoted the development of the cotton industry. By the mid-nineteenth century, cotton production in Texas soared, placing Texas eighth among the top cotton producing states in the union. Although production fell in the years following the Civil War, by 1869 it had begun to pick up again. By 1880, Texas led all states in the production of cotton in most years.

A number of technological breakthroughs further stimulated the cotton industry in Texas. In the 1870s, barbed wire was introduced, enabling farmers to cordon off their lands and protect their cash crop. Second, the building of railroads brought Texas farmers into a national market. The earliest railroads had been located around Houston and Galveston, reinforcing traditional patterns of trade through the gulf ports. The new railroad lines extended in from the northeast, radically altering patterns of trade. Finally, a newly designed plow made it easier to dig up the prairie soil and significantly increase farm productivity.

Throughout the 1870s, immigrants from the Deep South and Europe flooded the prairies of Texas to farm cotton. Most of these newly arrived Texans farmed cotton as tenant farmers or sharecroppers. Tenants would live on farms owned by landowners, providing their own animals, tools, and seed. They would receive two-thirds of the final value of the cotton grown on the farm, while the landlords would receive the other one-third. Sharecroppers only furnished their labor but received only one-half of the value of the final product. The number of farms doubled between 1880 and 1890, and the

Land and machinery once used to farm cotton lies dormant in Texas. Although one quarter of the cotton produced in the United States comes from Texas, the state's cotton industry has been in decline since the 1920s.

number of tenants tripled. Almost half of the state farmers were tenants by the turn of the century.[11]

Two important consequences followed from the tenant and sharecropping system. First, a system of social and economic dependency was created in the rural areas that trapped many Texans. The notorious "crop-lien" system was developed to extend credit to farmers in exchange for liens on their crops. The result often was to trap farmers into a debt cycle from which they could not escape. Second, the tenant and sharecropping system helped to fuel radical political discontent in rural areas, sparking both the Grange and Populist movements. These movements would play a major role in defining the style of Texas's politics throughout much of the late nineteenth and early twentieth centuries.

Cotton production cycled up and down as farmers experienced a series of crises and opportunities in the late nineteenth and early twentieth centuries, ranging from boll weevils to an increased demand brought on by World War I to a collapse in prices following the war. Although some sharecroppers returned to the farm during the Great Depression in the thirties, the general decline of the cotton culture continued after World War II. There also was a geographical shift in the production of cotton from east and central Texas to the High Plains and Rio Grande Valley.[12]

CATTLE RANCHING

The history of ranching and the cattle industry parallels that of cotton in many ways.[13] Its origins extend back to the late seventeenth century when the Spanish brought livestock over to feed their missionaries, soldiers, and civilians.

Ranching offered an attractive alternative to farming for immigrants during the periods of Mexican and Republican rule. In the 1830s, traffic in cattle was limited to local areas. This began to change as cattle drives and railroads began opening up new markets in the east.

Following the Civil War, the cattle industry took off, expanding throughout the state. As with cotton, the invention of barbed wire helped to close off the lands used for grazing. By the end of the century, ranching had been transformed from open range to fenced pasturing. As a result, conflicts often broke out between large and small ranchers, as well as ranchers and farmers. As cattle raising became a more specialized and rationalized business, periodic conflicts broke out between employers and employees. Throughout the twentieth century, ranching remained a cyclical industry, struggling when national and international prices collapsed and thriving during bull markets.

The most famous ranch in Texas history is the King Ranch of south Texas. The King Ranch grew out of two large purchases of Spanish land grants in 1853, totaling over 68,000 acres. Initially managed as a partnership, the ranch later came under the control of the King family. Early stock on the ranch included cattle, horses, sheep, and goats. In the 1880s, longhorns were added as were shorthorns, Herefords, and Brahman bulls. By the early 1920s, the King Ranch had become a diversified enterprise that extended into activities other than ranching, included horse breeding and racing, oil and gas production, and timber. Indeed, oil may have been the salvation of the ranch as it tried to weather the downside of the cattle industry cycle in the 1920s and early 1930s. In 1945, the Borregas oilfield was discovered on the ranch. By 1953, there were over 650 oil and gas producing wells. Over the next fifty years, oil and gas royalties totaled over $1 billion.

In the 1990s, the King Ranch continued to play an important part in the state's economy. It owned over 60,000 head of cattle and maintained ranching operations in Texas, Arizona, Kentucky, Florida, and Brazil. Ranked in the top two hundred largest business enterprises in Texas, the King Ranch continues to extend its reach out in a wide array of business operations today.[14]

As we enter the twentieth-first century, cotton production and ranching remain important industries in Texas. Approximately one-quarter of the total cotton production in the United States comes from Texas. Since 1986, the annual cotton crop has averaged 4.45 million bales, worth around $1.2 billion a year. This compares favorably to 1900 production figures of 3.4 million bales. Texas generally leads the nation in the number of cattle, calves, beef cows, cattle on feed, the total value of cattle and calves, and in cash receipts. The total value of farm and ranch assets in 1997 was $93 billion. But production figures and net assets do not tell the whole story.

Neither cotton production nor ranching drives the Texas political economy as it did in the past. The number of people making a living off agriculture has dropped significantly over the last fifty years as agribusiness has pushed out the family farm and ranch. In 1940, 23 percent of the population worked on farms and ranches. Seventeen percent were suppliers to farms and ranches or helped to assemble, process, or distribute agricultural products. In 1998, less than 2 percent of the population lived on farms and ranches, with an additional 17 percent of the population providing support, processing, or distribution services to agriculture in Texas.

The gusher at Spindletop was the first major oil strike in Texas and produced 800,000 barrels in just nine days before it was capped. Spindletop's success drew many to the business, starting an oil boom throughout the state.

The nineteenth-century dominance of cotton and cattle was challenged in the early twentieth century by a new set of technological breakthroughs. These focused not upon what grew on the land, but what lay beneath it.

OIL IN THE TEXAS ECONOMY

Oil was first sighted in the mid-seventeenth century by Spanish explorers.[15] There was no market or demand for the product, and nothing was done to develop the natural resource. A century later, encouraged by a growing demand for petroleum products following the Civil War, a scattering of entrepreneurs dug wells, although they were not commercially viable. The first economically significant oil discovery was in 1894 in Navarro County near Corsicana. By 1898, the state's first modern oil refinery was operating at the site. Although production peaked in 1900, the economic viability of oil production had been proven.

What catapulted Texas into the era of oil and gas was the discovery at Spindletop on January 10, 1901. Located three miles south of Beaumont along the Gulf Coast, the Spindletop discovery produced Texas's first oil boom. Although production at the site peaked in 1902 at 17.5 million barrels, the success of Spindletop encouraged large numbers of speculators and entrepreneurs to try their luck in the new business. Within three years, three major oil fields had been discovered within 150 miles of Spindletop.

Oil fever spread throughout Texas over the next decade. In north central Texas, major discoveries took place at Brownwood, Petrolia, and Wichita Falls. In the teens, major discoveries were made in Wichita County, Limestone County near Mexia, and once again in Navarro County. In 1921, oil was found in the Panhandle, and by the end of the decade major oil fields were being developed all across the state. The biggest oil field in the state was found in October 1930 in east Texas. As Mary G. Ramos notes, "By the time the East Texas field was developed, Texas' economy was powered not by agriculture, but by petroleum."[16]

The oil and gas industry transformed the social and economic fabric of Texas in a number of important ways. By providing cheap oil and gas the industry made possible a new industrial revolution in twentieth-century America that was fueled by hydrocarbons. Cheap oil provided a new fuel for transportation and manufacturing. Railroads and steamships were able to convert from coal to oil. Manufacturing plants and farms were able to operate more efficiently with a new cheap source of energy, encouraging individuals to migrate to cities away from farms. Automobile production was encouraged, as was the building of roads. The interstate highway system that was built in the 1950s and 1960s changed fundamentally the transportation patterns that shaped the movements of people and goods in Texas. The triangle formed by I-35 from San Antonio to Dallas-Fort Worth, I-45 from Dallas-Fort Worth to Houston, and I-10 from Houston to San Antonio became the heartland of the Texas economy and the location of an increasing percentage of the state's population (see Figure 20.2).

The oil and gas industry also had a number of very specific effects on Texas. Most importantly, it sparked a rapid industrialization of the Gulf Coast region. Among the companies developing the Gulf Coast oil fields were Gulf Oil, Sun Oil, Magnolia Petroleum, the Texas Company (later Texaco), and Humble Oil (which later became Esso and then Exxon). The refineries,

THE INTERSTATE HIGHWAY SYSTEM IN TEXAS

Figure 20.2

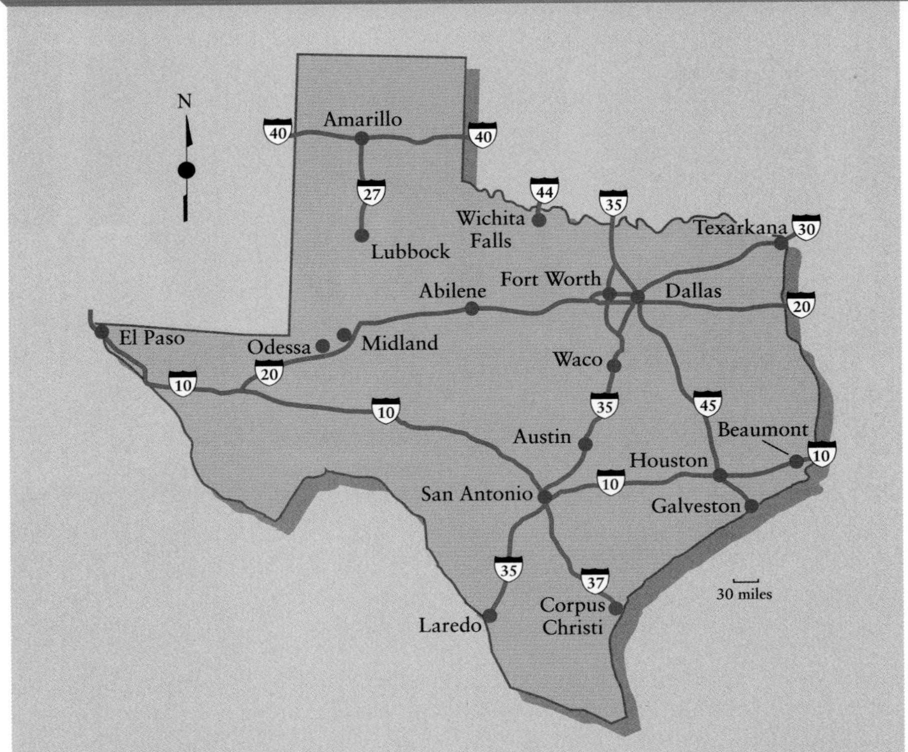

SOURCE: Dallas Morning News, *Texas Almanac 2000–2001* (Dallas: Dallas Morning News, 1999), p. 599.

pipelines, and export facilities lay the foundations for the large-scale industrialization that would take place along the Gulf Coast in the Houston-Beaumont-Port Arthur region. By 1929 in Harris County, for example, 27 percent of all manufacturing employees worked in refineries. By 1940, the capacity of all the refineries had increased fourfold.[17] The petrochemical industry continued to flourish throughout the 1960s when demand for its products grew at the rate of 10 percent a year.

One important effect of the oil and gas boom in Texas was the development of a new rhythm to economic life in the state. There had been a natural pace to the economy when it was tied to the production of cotton and cattle. Prices of products could rise and fall, bringing prosperity or gloom to local economies. But there was a bond between the land and the people and the communities that formed around them. Oil and gas, on the other hand, introduced a boom and bust mentality that carried over into the communities that

With the oil boom came boom towns—hastily constructed communities built around the oil fields of Texas.

would spring up around oil and gas discoveries. Rural areas were often unprepared for the population explosion that followed an oil or gas strike. Housing was often inadequate or nonexistent. Schools would become quickly overcrowded. General living conditions were poor as people sought to "make it big." The irony of the oil and gas business was that a major discovery that brought large amounts of new oil and gas to market could lead to a sudden collapse in prices. Prosperous economic times could quickly turn into local depressions. And when particular fields were tapped out, boom towns could quickly become ghost towns.

The oil and gas industry also transformed government and the role that it played in the economy. Following the Civil War, a series of attempts to regulate the railroads had largely failed. In 1890, after considerable controversy fueled by Populist anti-railroad sentiment, a constitutional amendment was passed to create an agency to regulate the railroads, the Texas Railroad Commission. This regulatory power was extended in 1917 to regulate energy. The Railroad Commission was empowered to see that petroleum pipelines were "common carriers" (that they transported all producers' oil and gas) and to promote well-spacing rules. In an attempt to bring stability to world oil prices brought on by the glut of oil on world markets in the 1930s, the Commission won the authority to prorate oil and determine how much every oil well in Texas might produce. Through the late 1960s, the Railroad Commission was one of the most important regulatory bodies in the nation. It was also one of the few democratically elected agencies.

Helping to expand the power of state government in the economy through the Railroad Commission was only one effect of the oil and gas industry in

Texas. There also was an important fiscal effect on state government. Beginning in 1905, the state collected oil-production taxes. These rose from $101,403 in 1906 to over $1 million in 1919 and almost $6 million in 1929. By 1996, oil-production taxes, or severance taxes, contributed $376 million to the state budget.

Much like the state coffers, higher education in Texas has benefited from the oil and gas industry. What many thought was worthless land at the time had been set aside by the state constitution of 1876 and the state legislature in 1883 to support higher education (the Permanent University Fund). As luck would have it, oil was discovered in the west Texas Permian Basin in 1923 on university lands. Soon seventeen wells were producing oil on university lands, sparking a building boom at the University of Texas. In 1931, the income of the Permanent University Fund was split between the University of Texas at Austin and Texas A&M University, with the former receiving two-thirds and the latter one-third. In 1984, the income was opened up to all University of Texas schools, not just the Austin campus. Along with the royalties from other natural resources on university land, oil and gas royalties created one of the largest university endowments in the world. Between 1923 and 1998, income from these natural resources was approximately $3.15 billion, and returns on investments were $8.16 billion.[18]

The oil and gas industry had one other effect on life in Texas that is worth noting. Fortunes were made in the industry that paved the way for an expansion of private philanthropy that would have a major influence in shaping Texas's culture. Among the most famous of these were the Meadows Foundations, established in 1948 to promote programs in health, education, visual arts, social services, and historical preservation. The Sid W. Richardson Foundation was founded in 1947 and supported health medicine and education programs, as well as the development of the arts in Fort Worth. The Bass Performance Hall, which opened in May 1998, was funded by the Bass brothers, grandnephews of independent oilman Sid Richardson.

One can trace out the rise and decline of the oil and gas industry in Texas through production figures (see Table 20.1 on the next page). In 1915, almost 25 million barrels of oil were produced in Texas, worth a little over $13 million. Production of natural gas stood at 13.3 thousand cubic feet (MCF) worth $2.6 million. By 1945 the production of oil had risen to almost 755 million barrels worth $914 million, while natural gas production rose to 1.7 million MCF worth almost $45 million. The halcyon days of oil and gas production were the early 1970s, when production peaked at 1.3 billion barrels of oil per year and 8.7 million MCF. The value of the oil and gas produced in Texas skyrocketed in the late 1970s and early 1980s as the average price of each commodity shot up due to the actions of the Middle East oil cartel (OPEC). In 1973, the average price per barrel of oil stood at $3.98. In 1981, it had risen to $34.59. Rising prices helped to mask a fact that became all too apparent to Texas oil producers in the late 1980s. Oil production was in decline. Between 1980 and 1989, it fell from 977 million barrels of oil per year to almost 680 million barrels and to just under 465 million barrels in 1996. A similar tale is found in the gas industry, as production figures fell from 7.2 million MCF in 1979 to 5.6 million MCF in 1989 to 3.7 million MCF in 1996. Oil and gas remained significant

Table 20.1 OIL PRODUCTION IN TEXAS, SELECTED YEARS

Year	Production	Value in thousands of dollars	Average price per barrel
1915	24,943,000	$13,027,000	$0.52
1945	754,710,000	$914,410,000	$1.21
1955	1,053,297,000	$2,989,330,000	$2.84
1965	1,000,749,000	$2,962,119,000	$2.96
1975	1,221,929,000	$9,336,570,000	$7.64
1980	977,436,000	$21,259,233,000	$21.75
1985	860,300,000	$23,159,286,000	$26.92
1990	672,081,000	$15,047,902,000	$22.39
1995	503,200,000	$8,177,700,000	$16.25
1997	464,900,000	$8,526,800,000	$18.32

SOURCE: Dallas Morning News, *Texas Almanac 2000–2001* (Dallas: Dallas Morning News, 1999), p. 613.

industries in the Texas economy, but they were becoming increasingly less important. As the 1980s slipped into the 1990s, the Texas economy continued to diversify and other industries and technologies began to assume significant roles in plotting the state's economic future. Among the most important of these was the burgeoning high-tech industry.

This bumper sticker from the 1980s expresses both the anxiety over decreased oil production and a confidence in the stability and wealth of the industry that characterized the times.

THE EMERGENCE OF THE HIGH-TECH ECONOMY

The jarring movement out of the era of oil and gas and into that of high tech was not an easy one.[19] World oil prices peaked in 1981 at $35 per barrel. At the time, oil related businesses accounted for 26 percent of the gross state product. From 1971 to 1981, the average rate of economic growth was 4.4 percent. Fueled by a booming oil-based economy and a rapidly increasing population, real estate prices shot up in urban areas such as Houston and Dallas. Projections were made that as oil prices rose, perhaps to $70 or $80 per barrel on the world market, future prosperity was inevitable. Indeed, there was some talk that Texas's oil-driven economy had become recession proof. Such talk proved to be premature, to say the least.

World oil prices began to collapse in 1982, bottoming out on March 31, 1986, at $10 per barrel. Other sectors of the economy began to suffer as the price of oil fell. Real estate deals and construction projects slowed down and then shut down. Speculators defaulted on their loans, and banks began to fail. Throughout the 1980s, 370 banks went under in Texas. At the same time, the state went through two major recessions, one in 1982 and another in 1986–87. The average annual economic growth slowed to 1.7 percent, the worst since World War II.

Texas emerged from the economic malaise of the eighties with a transformed state economy. While remaining an important sector in the economy, the oil and gas business was no longer the primary driving force. By 1992, the production of oil had fallen to 642 million barrels worth only $11.8 billion. This continued to fall until 1997 to just under 465 million barrels worth a little over $8.5 billion. Over 146,000 jobs had been lost in the oil industry throughout the 1980s. By the early 1990s, oil only accounted for about 12 percent of the gross state product.

In contrast to the 1980s, the 1990s were a period of rapid growth. Unlike early periods of speculative booms, such as that of the 1970s, the economy's growth was grounded on real demand in a rapidly diversifying economy. At the heart of this boom was a rapidly growing manufacturing sector tied to high tech. In the 1990s, Texas went from seventh in the nation in total manufacturing employment to second. In 1998, the gross state product from manufacturing in Texas reached over $103 billion, averaging a growth rate of 9.25 percent between 1993 and 1998. Over 25 percent of the employment in manufacturing was found in computers or electronic employment. In 1998, Texas accounted for 7 percent of the nation's manufacturing employment in electronics and computers, up from a 5.8 percent share in 1988. Over $36 billion in computers and electronics were exported from Texas in 1997, accounting for over 15 percent of total U.S. exports of these products. Forty-five percent of the state's exports were from the high-tech industry. Significantly, in 1998, oil- and gas-related manufacturing employment comprised only 21 percent of the state total and 25 percent of the total exports from the state.[20]

Two metropolitan areas stand out as national centers for the rapidly evolving high-tech industry. The Austin-San Marcos metropolitan area has become a production center for computer chips, personal computers, and other related computer hardware. Seven of the area's largest employers are part of the computer or semiconductor industry. The Dallas metropolitan area, particularly

Politics on the Web

The Internet is the latest in a series of technological revolutions that has driven Texas into the modern world economy. The Internet undercuts much of the parochialism that has dominated political culture in Texas since the Civil War. It provides citizens with a vast and still rapidly growing set of resources for understanding the local communities in which they live and how they are tied to other regional, national, and international worlds. The Internet is helping to both transform and unify Texas. It helps Texans to understand why they are part of an emerging global order and why the values that have dominated their culture must change if Texas is to prosper in the global economy.

Access to news media from across the state, the nation, and even the world means that the average citizen is no longer limited by the attitudes and opinions of local elites. What was true and good about the world for one's parents may no longer be true for one's children. A new, more outward-looking political culture will likely emerge to redefine Texas in this era of high tech.

www.wwnorton.com/wtp3e

north of the city, is the home of a number of important electronic and electronic equipment companies.

NAFTA

North American Free Trade Agreement (NAFTA)
trade treaty between the United States, Canada, and Mexico to lower and eliminate tariffs between the three countries

Another defining feature of the Texas economy in the 1990s was the **North American Free Trade Agreement (NAFTA)**. Signed on December 17, 1992, by Prime Minister Brian Mulroney of Canada, President Carlos Salinas de Gortari of Mexico, and President Bush of the United States, NAFTA sought to create a free trade zone in North America that was the largest of its kind in the world. Considerable controversy surrounded the passage of NAFTA, with many groups arguing that free trade would hurt many American workers and companies because of the cheap labor available in Mexico. After eight years, it appears that the trade agreement has had both negative and positive impacts on Texas.

According to a report released by the Texas Public Policy Foundation, 21,019 workers in Texas were certified by the U.S. Department of Labor as being negatively impacted by NAFTA through mid-1999.[21] This placed Texas second in the nation behind North Carolina in the number of affected workers. Such workers generally lost their jobs because of the stiffer competition from low-wage businesses in Mexico or because plants had been relocated to Mexico (under federal law such workers are entitled to additional unemployment compensation). In addition, between 1994 and 1998, 260 companies in Texas filed petitions claiming that they were injured by NAFTA-induced competition. This was a diverse group of companies including Levi-Strauss, Fisher Price, Continental Airlines, Lockheed, and Hagger. Significantly, not all Texas workers who filed were certified as being negatively affected by NAFTA. But of those who were, over half were from El Paso. Since 1994, over 10,000 El Paso workers have been certified by the Department of Labor as being injured by NAFTA, more than any other American city. The losses were largely in El Paso's low-

The signing of NAFTA in 1992 created a free trade zone in North America. Many workers in Texas have been adversely affected by the availability of cheaper labor in Mexico, but the overall effect of NAFTA on the state's economy remains to be seen.

skill, low-wage garment industry, an industry that could not compete with the even lower wages found south of the border.

While there were some losers in the movement toward free trade with Mexico and Canada, there were also big winners. According to the Texas Public Policy Foundation report, conservative estimates are that Texas increased exports to Canada and Mexico by over $10 billion in the first five years of NAFTA. Of the thirty-two industries in Texas that export to Mexico, twenty-four had double-digit gains. Meanwhile, twenty-seven of the thirty-one industries that exported to Canada showed gains as well. One calculation by the Department of Commerce puts the total number of jobs added to Texas's economy by NAFTA at 190,000. A second study by the Council of the Americas puts the total number of new jobs at 194,000. A few statistics put the importance of Texas's international trade, particularly with Mexico and Canada into perspective.[22] In 1998,

- Texas's $86.9 billion in exports was the second largest in the United States, following California.
- In per capita exports, Texas ranked third.
- Exports took up approximately 13.3 percent of the gross state product in Texas, ranking it fourth among U.S. states in the ratio between exports and gross state product.
- The North American market (Mexico and Canada) was the destination for over 50 percent of these exports in 1998.
- $10.2 billion of the $34.7 billion total net gain in exports (or nearly 30 percent) from Texas between 1993 and 1998 was in the high-tech sector of electronic equipment and components.

It is important to stress that Texas is only at the beginning of the era of high tech and NAFTA. The state is only beginning to feel the effects of the movement of the economy into the information age and the global economy. It is impossible to say exactly what the state's economy will look like in twenty years, or which companies will become the Texacos or Exxons of the information age. We can say, however, that it will be an economy as different from that of the oil and gas era, as the oil and gas era was from the era of cotton and cattle.

The People: Texas Demography

▶ How did the population of Texas change during the 1990s? What is its racial and ethnic composition? How does the population of Texas compare to the rest of the nation in terms of age and income?

The population in Texas has grown rapidly since the early days of the Republic. In 1850 the population stood at a little over 210,000 people, over one-quarter of whom were African American slaves. Texas in 1850 also was an overwhelmingly rural state. Only 4 percent of the population lived in urban areas. By 1900 the population had increased to over three million people, with 83 percent continuing to live in rural areas. The 1980s began as boom years for population growth, with increases running between 2.9 percent and 1.6 percent per year from 1980 through 1986. With the collapse of oil prices, however, population growth slowed significantly between 1987 and 1989 to less than 1 percent.[23]

With a recovering economy, however, population growth surged forward in the 1990s (see Table 20.2). In 1990, 17 million people resided in the state. By 1998, the number of people had reached 19.76 million people. Between 1990 and 1996 alone, Texas had added more to its total population than any other state in the union (2.14 million) and was the tenth fastest growing in percentage terms, with a population change of 12.6 percent for the period. Fifty-seven percent of the population were Anglo American in 1998, down from 61 percent in 1990. Twelve percent were African American. Twenty-nine percent were Hispanic, up from 25 percent in 1990.

Three factors account for the population growth in Texas in the 1990s: natural increase due to the difference between births and deaths; international immigration, particularly from Mexico; and domestic immigration from other states. As Table 20.3 reveals, the makeup of the growth in population shifted in significant ways over the course of the decade. In 1991, almost two-thirds of population growth was accounted for by natural increases. A little over 20 percent was due to international immigration, while under 14 percent was due to domestic immigration. By 1998, natural increases only accounted for a little over half of the population growth, while international immigration accounted for 23.6 percent and domestic immigration for over 21 percent. As the state entered the twenty-first century, Texas was being redefined not by *native-born Texans* but by individuals coming to Texas to share and contribute to the state's high-tech economic boom.

ANGLOS

For most of the nineteenth and twentieth centuries the dominant ethnic group has been white or Anglo. Anglos in Texas comprise a wide range of European ethnic groups, including English, Germans, Scots, Irish, Czechs, and European Jews. The first wave of Anglos came to Texas prior to the break with Mexico.

Table 20.2 THE CHANGING FACE OF TEXAS: 1850–1998

	1850	1900	1950	1990	1998*
Population	213,000	3,050,000	7,710,000	17,000,000	19,760,000
Anglo	72%	80%	87%	61%	57%
African American	28	20	13	12	12
Hispanic	NA	NA	NA	25	29
Other	NA	NA	NA	2	2

NA = not available
* estimated
SOURCES: *Statistical Abstract of the United States: 1994* (Washington, D.C.: U.S. Department of Commerce, Bureau of the Census, 1994); Dallas Morning News, *Texas Almanac 2000–2001* (Dallas: Dallas Morning News, 1999).

Emancipation for African Americans living in Texas came on June 19, 1865. Emancipation, however, did not bring anything approaching equality. Between 1865 and 1868, a series of Black Codes were passed by the state legislature and various cities that sought to restrict the rights of former slaves. Military occupation and Congressional Reconstruction opened up new opportunities for former slaves, who supported the Radical Wing of the Republican Party. Ten African American delegates helped to write the Texas Constitution of 1869. Forty-three served as members of the state legislature between 1868 and 1900. The end of Reconstruction and the return to power of the Demo-cratic Party in the mid-1870s reversed much of the progress made by former slaves in the state. In 1900, over 100,000 African Americans voted in Texas elections. By 1903, the number had fallen to under 5,000, largely due to the imposition of the poll tax in 1902 and the passage of a white primary law in 1903. Segregation of the races became a guiding principle of public policy, backed by the police power of the state and reinforced by lynchings and race riots against African Americans. For all intents and purposes, African Americans had become second-class citizens, disenfranchised by the political system and marginalized by the political culture.

Federal court cases in the 1940s and 1950s offered some hope of relief to African Americans living in Texas. The white primary was outlawed in 1944 in the Supreme Court decision in *Smith v. Allwright*. In 1950, African Americans were guaranteed admission to Texas's graduate and professional schools in *Sweatt v. Painter*. Finally, the segregation of public schools was outlawed by the Supreme Court in *Brown v. Board of Education* in 1954.

Political progress was much slower. The Civil Rights Act of 1964 and the Voting Rights Act of 1965 helped to open up the political system in Texas to African Americans. In 1966, a small number of African American candidates actually began to win political office in the state. In 1972, Barbara Jordan became the first African American to be elected to the United States House of Representatives from Texas.

Today the African American population is concentrated in east Texas, where the southern plantation and sharecropping systems had dominated in the nineteenth century. Large numbers had also migrated to form sizable

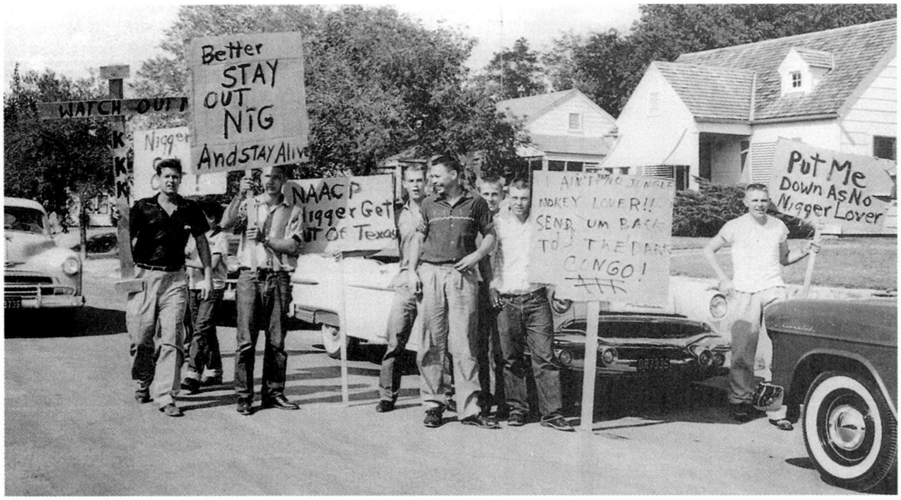

These signs appeared in Fort Worth's Riverside section in September of 1956 during a protest over a black family moving into a previously all-white block of homes.

minorities in the urban and suburban areas of Houston and Dallas. African American political leaders have come to play major roles in these areas as members of Congress, the state legislature, and city councils. African Americans were also elected mayors of Houston and Dallas in the late 1990s. The political influence of African Americans in Texas has not been extended to west Texas where few African Americans live.

AGE

When compared to the rest of the nation, the population of Texas is relatively young. In 1997, 28.7 percent of the population was under eighteen years old, compared to 26.0 percent nationally. This ranked Texas as fifth among the states in youth. Meanwhile, only 10.1 percent of the population in Texas was sixty-five years of age or older, compared to 12.7 percent nationally. Here Texas ranked forty-sixth among the fifty states. Having a relatively young population compared to other states presents Texas with a variety of problems and opportunities, as we shall see in later chapters.

POVERTY AND WEALTH

Younger populations tend to be poorer, as income and poverty statistics bear out. As noted above, the 1990s were a period of rapid economic growth in Texas. Between 1990 and 1997, personal income per capita in constant 1992 dollars rose from $18,027 to $20,990. Despite these gains, however, Texas continued to lag behind the nation as a whole (see Table 20.4). At the national level during the same period personal per capita income rose from $20,090 to $22,713. In 1997, Texas ranked only twenty-eighth among the states in per capita income, up from twenty-ninth in 1990.

A more disturbing story is revealed when one looks at changes in median household income figures. Between 1990 and 1996, median household income actually fell from $33,887 to $33,072 (in constant 1996 dollars). This paralleled a similar decline at the national level, where median household income in constant 1996 dollars fell from $35,945 to $35,492 between 1990 and 1996. During this same period, Texas dropped from twenty-ninth to thirty-second in state rankings for median household income.

The percentage of the population in Texas living below the poverty level—a level established by the federal government, which will be discussed in more

Table 20.4 PER CAPITA INCOME IN TEXAS AND THE UNITED STATES, 1980–1997 (IN CONSTANT 1992 DOLLARS)

	1980	1990	1995	1997
Texas	16,821	18,027	19,204	20,990
USA	16,991	20,090	21,188	22,713

SOURCES: *Statistical Abstract of the United States: 1996* and *1998* (Washington, D.C.: U.S. Department of Commerce, Bureau of the Census, 1996, 1998).

detail in a later chapter—also rose from 15.7 percent to 16.6 percent between 1990 and 1996. Texas continued to be ranked as the state with the eleventh-highest percentage of people living below the poverty line. The increase was over three times higher than the increase at the national level, i.e., from 13.5 percent to 13.7 percent.

Urbanization

- What is the history of urbanization in Texas?
- How can one describe its current urban political economy?

urbanization
the process by which people move from rural areas to cities

Urbanization is the process by which people move from rural to urban areas. Suburbanization is the process by which people move out of central city areas to surrounding suburban areas. Much of Texas's history is linked to ongoing urbanization. By the end of the twentieth century, this process was largely complete, as over 80 percent of the population now resides in urban areas (see Table 20.5). Suburbanization, however, continues, as city populations spill over into surrounding suburban areas.

Urbanization in Texas owes little to Native American civilization.[26] Most Texas cities are the result of European settlement and culture. The Spanish influence on urban life in Texas grew out of efforts to extend territorial control northward out of Mexico through a series of presidios (garrisons), missions (churches), and pueblos (towns). The physical organization and planning of the towns reflected this imperial mission. For example, the largest Spanish settlement was San Antonio. It was initially established as a supply depot to missions in east Texas. Later it expanded as missions were established to convert local Native Americans to Christianity and farms were cultivated to feed the local population. By the early nineteenth century, San Antonio's population had reached 2,500. Other smaller settlements were located in east Texas, along the border with French and, later, American territory.

Anglo American influence began with the arrival of Moses Austin and, later, his son, Stephen F. Austin, in 1820 in San Antonio. The Spanish offered the Austins and other impresarios grants of land to encourage the inflow of Americans into underpopulated regions of Texas. Small towns emerged as administrative units for impresario grants. There was considerably more freedom and dynamism in Anglo American urban areas than in Spanish ones.

URBANIZATION IN TEXAS, 1850–1990 — **Table 20.5**

	1850	1900	1950	1990
Urban	4%	17%	63%	80%
Rural	96	83	37	20

SOURCES: *Statistical Abstract of the United States: 1994* (Washington, D.C.: U.S. Department of Commerce, Bureau of the Census, 1994); Dallas Morning News, *Texas Almanac 2000–2001* (Dallas: Dallas Morning News, 1999).

Americans brought with them a host of new interests and ideas that would transform urban life in Texas, including a new language, slavery, Protestantism, and a commitment to free enterprise and democracy. The courthouse became a central feature of many Anglo American towns, often located in the center of the town surrounded by shops.

The expansion of Anglo American urban life initially began along the Gulf Coast and gradually expanded east to west, particularly along rivers. New technologies transformed the urban landscape of Texas. Dredging technologies helped to stimulate the growth of port cities such as Houston, Galveston, Corpus Christi, and Brownsville. Railroad construction in the second half of the nineteenth century opened up new lands, which had been difficult for populations to reach, to urban development. In 1880 there were only eleven towns of 4,000 or more people in all of Texas. Following the rapid expansion of the railroads in the 1880s and 1890s, this rose to thirty-six. By 1910, when the railroad network of 13,110 miles was completed, Texas had forty-nine towns with a population of 4,000 or more. By 1920, five cities—Dallas, El Paso, Fort Worth, Houston, and San Antonio—had populations of over 50,000. Later technological breakthroughs in transportation, such as cars and air travel, would reinforce the population grid laid out by the railroads.

THE URBAN POLITICAL ECONOMY

political economy
the complex interrelations between politics and the economy, as well as their effect upon each other

Understanding the complexity of the **political economy** of Texas today demands having some sense of how Texas's three major metropolitan areas compare to one another.

By 1929, the year this picture was taken, Houston was already a metropolis with suburbs stretching out in all directions.

Houston Houston, located in Harris County, is the largest city in Texas and the fourth largest city in the United States—with a population of 1,841,064—behind New York, Los Angeles, and Chicago. Its consolidated metropolitan area encompasses seven counties, with a population of 4,320,000 in 1997, ranking it tenth in the nation.

The city originated in 1836 out of the entrepreneurial dreams of two brothers, Augustus Chapman Allen and John Kirby Allen, who sought to create a "great interior commercial emporium of Texas."[27] The town was named after Sam Houston, the leader of Texas's army during its war of independence from Mexico, and within two years had grown from twelve people and one cabin to one-hundred houses and 1,500 people.

Early settlers came from the South, bringing with them the institution of slavery. One of the consequences of this was that segregation was built into the social structure from the outset. For the first half of the twentieth century, African Americans were either denied or given limited access to a variety of public services such as parks, schools, buses, restrooms, and restaurants. Although not enforced legally, residential segregation divided the city into a number of distinct racially divided neighborhoods for much of the twentieth century.

In the late nineteenth century, Houston's economic well being depended upon cotton and commerce. Railroads played an integral role in placing Houston at the hub of the Texas economy. The opening up of the Houston Ship Channel further enhanced Houston's place in the state economy by helping to turn it into the second or third (depending on whose ranking is used) deep-water port in the United States. But it was oil that fundamentally transformed the Houston area the most in the twentieth century. Oil refineries opened up along the Ship Channel and a petrochemical industry emerged, making Houston one of the leading energy centers in the world. Today it continues to rank first in the nation in the manufacture of petroleum equipment.

By 1930, Houston had become the largest city in Texas, with a population of around 292,000 people. Population continued to expand throughout the 1940s, 1950s, and 1960s, assisted by a liberal annexation policy that enabled the center-city to incorporate into itself many of the outlying suburban areas. Although the oil bust in the mid-1980s slowed down the city's growth, it continued unabated in the 1990s, extending out into suburban areas such as Clear Lake City and other urban areas such as Galveston.

Getting an exact count of the ethnic breakdown of Houston is difficult given the large influx of new people into the Houston area. In 1990, the U.S. Census found that 64.7 percent of the population was white, 19.2 percent was black, and 3.9 percent was Asian. Hispanics (who may designate themselves as either white or black), meanwhile, counted for 22.9 percent of the overall population. Estimates for the larger Houston-Galveston-Brazoria metropolitan areas provide a slightly different breakdown. In a population of 4,320,041, 76.5 percent were white, 18.3 percent were black, and 23.6 percent were identified as Hispanic.

In 1994, the personal per capita income of residents in the larger metropolitan area was $22,651, ranking it fortieth in the nation. This placed Houston well ahead of San Antonio's and Austin's metropolitan areas but behind Dallas-Fort Worth. Meanwhile, in 1993, 17.8 percent of the metropolitan population lived in poverty, more than in Dallas-Fort Worth and Austin, but less than in San Antonio.[28]

Dallas-Fort Worth The Metroplex is an economic region encompassing the cities of Dallas and Fort Worth, as well as a number of other suburban cities, including Arlington (population 300,000+), Mesquite (114,000+), Garland (193,000+), Richardson (90,000+), Irving (175,000+), Plano (198,000+), Carrolton (100,000+), Grand Prairie (113,000+), and Denton (78,000+). The major counties in the area are Dallas, Tarrant, and Collin. It is joined together by a number of interlocking highways running north-south (I-30W, I-30E, 75/I-45) and east-west (I-20, I-30, I-635), and a major international airport that is strategically located in the national air system.

By 1917, the first Texas rail crossroads turned Dallas into a booming business district for the markets to the east and north.

Dallas was founded as a trading post in 1841, near where two roads were to be built by the Republic.[29] By the 1850s, it had become a retail center servicing the rural areas. By 1870, the population had reached 3,000 people. The coming of the Houston and Texas Central Railroad in 1871 and the Texas and Pacific Railroad in 1873 made Dallas the first rail crossroads in Texas and transformed forever its place in the state's economy. Markets now beckoned east and north, encouraging entrepreneurs and merchants to set up shop. Cotton became a major cash crop and the population expanded over threefold to more than 10,000 people in 1880. By the turn of the century, the city had grown to over 42,000 people.

As was the case with Houston, the oil economy changed the direction and scope of the city's economic life. With the discovery of oil in east Texas in 1830, Dallas became a major center for petroleum financing. By the end of

Table 20.6 POPULATIONS OF THE LARGEST CITIES IN TEXAS

Houston (Harris County)	1,841,064
San Antonio (Bexar County)	1,123,626
Dallas (Dallas County)	1,085,614
Austin (Travis County)	608,053
El Paso (El Paso County)	600,277
Fort Worth (Tarrant County)	489,277
Arlington (Tarrant County)	301,991

World War II, the economy had diversified, making Dallas into a minor manufacturing center in the nation. In the 1950s and 1960s, technology companies such as Ling-Tempco-Vought (LTV) and Texas Instruments were added to the industrial mix, transforming Dallas into the third-largest technology center in the nation. The high-tech boom of the 1990s built off the corporate infrastructure laid down in the 1950s and 1960s.

Dallas grew from 844,401 people in 1970 to 904,078 in 1980 to 1,006,877 in 1990. According to the 1990 census, 47.77 percent of the population was white, 28.0 percent was black, 20.9 percent was Hispanic, and 2.2 percent was Asian.

Although they are locked together in important ways economically, Dallas and Fort Worth are as different as night and day. While Dallas looks to the East and embodies a more corporate white-collar business culture, Fort Worth looks to the West. It is where the West begins in Texas.

Fort Worth originated as an army post in 1849.[30] By 1953, the post had been abandoned as new forts were located to the west. Although settlers took the fort over, population growth was slow through the early 1870s. The spark

Table 20.7 ETHNIC BREAKDOWN OF LARGEST TEXAS COUNTIES (1990)

County	Population (in millions)	White	Black	Asian	Native American	Other	Hispanic
Harris	3.2 m	64.7%	19.2%	3.9%	.3%	11.9%	22.9%
Dallas	2.0	67	19.9	2.8	.5	9.7	17.0
Tarrant	1.3	78.4	12.0	2.5	.5	6.5	12.0
Bexar	1.3	74.1	7.1	1.3	.4	17.1	49.7
Travis	.7	73.3	11.0	2.9	.4	12.5	21.1
El Paso	.7	76.5	3.7	1.1	.4	18.2	69.6
Collin	.4	89.1	4.1	2.8	.4	3.5	6.9

NOTE: This table is based on the U.S. Bureau of the Census 1990 survey. Residents were asked to classify themselves as White, Black, American Indian, Eskimo and Aleut, Asian and Pacific Islander, or Other. In a separate question, residents were asked to classify their ethnic background as Hispanic. Hispanics thus could be classified as any race.
SOURCE: Dallas Morning News, *Texas Almanac 2000–2001* (Dallas: Dallas Morning News, 1999).

that enabled the town to begin to prosper was the rise of the cattle industry. Fort Worth was a convenient place for cowboys to rest on their cattle drives to Kansas. Cattle buyers established headquarters in the city. Gradually other businesses grew up around these key businesses. Transportation and communication links improved with the establishment of stage lines to the west and railroad lines to the north and east.

By 1900, Fort Worth was served by eight different railroad companies, many of them transporting cattle and cattle-related products to national markets. Two world wars encouraged further economic development in Fort Worth. Over 100,000 troops were trained at Camp Bowie during World War I. World War II brought an important airforce base and, along with it, the aviation industry. The Consolidated Vultee Aircraft Corporation, which was later bought by General Dynamics, became the largest manufacturing concern in the city. Between 1900 and 1950, the population grew from 26,668 to 277,047. By 1990, the population had reached 447,619 people.

The overall metropolitan area of Dallas-Fort Worth included 4,320,041 people as of 1996, making it the tenth largest in the nation, but well behind the Houston metropolitan area. Per capita income stands at $23,449, the twenty-ninth highest in the nation among the 273 metropolitan areas. In 1996, fewer people lived below the poverty line (14.9 percent) than in either Houston or San Antonio. Also in 1996, 81.9 percent of the population was white, 14.2 percent was black, and 15.1 percent was Hispanic.

San Antonio San Antonio is located in Bexar County, the fourth largest county in Texas today. San Antonio grew out of the Spanish presidio San Antonio de Bexar that was founded in 1718.[31] In 1773, it became the capital of Spanish Texas, with a population of around 2,100 people. Because of the threats posed by Native Americans and Mexicans after the Texas Revolution, the population declined to about 800 people by 1846. Upon Texas's entry into the Union, however, the population took off, reaching 3,488 in 1850 and 8,235 in 1860. By the Civil War, San Antonio was the largest city in Texas.

Following the Civil War, San Antonio grew rapidly, stimulated by the building of the San Antonio Railroad in 1877. By 1880, the population had reached over 20,000 people, most being Anglo Americans from southern states. Population continued to grow through the first two decades of the twentieth century, reaching 161,000 by 1920. Mexican immigration increased significantly into San Antonio following the Mexican Revolution of 1910 and the building of a city infrastructure that provided paved roads, utilities, water, telephones, and hospitals. By midcentury, San Antonio had become a unique blend of Hispanic, German, and southern Anglo American cultures. Population growth slowed down in the 1930s, but picked up again during World War II, reaching over 408,000 in 1950. Major military bases came to dot the landscape around San Antonio. By 1960, the population topped 587,000 people.

Today, San Antonio is Texas's third largest city. In 1997, the population of the city was 935,933 people, and the San Antonio metropolitan area as a whole had a population of 1,511,386, making it the twenty-fourth largest metropolitan area in the country.

San Antonio's population has become increasingly Hispanic. Approximately 55.6 percent of the people are Mexican American, 35.9 percent are

San Antonio is the third largest city in Texas. Major military bases were built around the city after World War II, increasing San Antonio's population as well as becoming an important part of the city's economy.

The Little Saigon Mall in Haltom City attests to the changing demographic landscape of Texas. The state's increasingly diverse population complicates notions of the "typical" Texan.

Anglo American, and 7 percent are African American. The remaining 1.5 percent categorize themselves as "other." In 1996, the entire metropolitan area of San Antonio was 52.1 percent Hispanic, ranking it seventh in the nation.

Unlike Houston or Dallas, San Antonio lacks high-paying manufacturing jobs. The economy rests upon four legs: national military bases, educational institutions, tourism, and a large medical research complex. As a result, average metropolitan income is low. In 1996, personal per capita income in the San Antonio metropolitan area was $18,209, placing it at 194 out of 273 areas in the United States. Meanwhile, 21.9 percent of the population lived under the poverty line, the twenty-fifth highest rate in the country.

Summary

In this chapter we have seen how the landscape of Texas has been transformed by economic and demographic shifts over the past hundred years. Economically there have been three great technological revolutions that have reshaped the economic life of the state. The first—based on the production of agricultural products like cotton and cattle and on the newly built railroad system—defined economic life in the latter decades of the nineteenth and early twentieth centuries. The second—based on the production of oil and the industries that cheap oil made possible—dominated the economy well into the second half of the twentieth century. The third—the era of high tech—has transformed the state by diversifying its economy and tying it closely to the growing international economy. Accompanying and fueling these economic revolutions has been ongoing demographic change in the state that has redefined whom the "typical" Texan is and where this person lives. No longer can it be said that this person is simply an extension of an Anglo American culture rooted in southern tradition. No longer does this person live in a small town, living life close to the land much like his or her ancestors. Like the economy, the people of Texas have been diversified. Increasing numbers of Hispanics from Mexico and Anglo Americans from other parts of the United States have created a new melting pot of cultures and concerns throughout the state. These cultures have come together in the big metropolitan areas across the state.

Since the Republican Party's challenge to the dominance of the Democrats in the 1990s, the Texas political landscape has changed dramatically. The state is now a cornerstone of the national Republican Party.

Any discussion of the changing political economy of Texas at the turn of the twenty-first century would be incomplete without drawing attention to the fundamental political transformation that has accompanied the most recent economic and demographic shifts. Texas is no longer a single-party state dominated by the Democratic Party. Beginning in 1876, the Democratic Party exerted a near monopoly on political power in the state that continued for over one-hundred years. To be effective in politics meant being effective in the Democratic Party. This one-party politics successfully weathered Texas's move from an economy based on cotton and cattle to one dominated by oil. But as the influence of oil went into decline in the eighties so did Democratic Party dominance. Accompanying the rise of the high-tech economy in the 1980s and 1990s was a triumphant Republican Party.

Table 20.8 charts out the transformation of Texas from a one-party state dominated by the Democrats into a two-party state increasingly dominated by

TEXAS ELECTION RESULTS, 1980–1998

Table 20.8

	1980	1982	1984	1986	1988	1990	1992	1994	1996	1998
U.S. House										
Democratic	19	22	17	17	19	19	21	19	16	17
Republican	5	5	10	10	8	8	9	11	14	13
U.S. Senate										
Democratic	1	1	1	1	1	1	.5*	0	0	0
Republican	1	1	1	1	1	1	.5*	2	2	2
Texas House										
Democratic	114	115	98	94	93	93	92	90	82	79
Republican	36	35	52	56	57	57	58	60	68	71
Texas Senate										
Democratic	24	26	25	25	23	23	18	17	14	15
Republican	7	5	6	6	8	8	13	14	17	16

SOURCES: Harvey J. Tucker and Gary M. Halter, *Texas Legislative Almanac 1999* (College Station: Texas A&M Press, 1999); Dallas Morning News, *Texas Almanac 2000–2001* (Dallas: Dallas Morning News, 1999).

*Republican Kay Bailey Hutcheson was elected to the Senate in a special election in mid-1993. She succeeded Democrat Robert Kreuger, who had been appointed to replace Democrat Lloyd Bentsen, who left the Senate to serve in the Clinton administration. Bentsen was re-elected to the Senate in 1998.

the Republican Party. Of the twenty-four Texas seats in the U.S. House of Representatives in 1980, nineteen were held by Democrats and only five by Republicans. By 1998, the numbers had shifted to seventeen Republicans and thirteen Democrats, and this despite redistricting that tended to favor the Democrats in the 1990s. A similar story is found in the Texas state legislature. In 1980, Democrats held an overwhelming majority over the Republicans—114 to 36 in the State House and 24 to 7 in the State Senate. By 1998, the Democratic majority had almost vanished in the House (79 to 71) and been lost in the Senate (15 to 16). More disturbingly, at least from the perspective of the Democratic Party, by 1998 all major statewide office races had been won by Republicans. Moreover, the state had not gone Democratic in a presidential election since 1976. Texas was considered by many to be a cornerstone to the national Republican coalition that took over the U.S. House and Senate in 1994.

The chapters that follow will analyze the way in which Texas politics and government works and how it has changed over the last twenty years in response to contemporary economic and demographic pressures.

FOR FURTHER READING

Barr, Alwyn. *Black Texans: A History of African Americans in Texas, 1528–1995.* Norman: University of Oklahoma Press, 1996.

Champagne, Anthony, and Edward J. Harpham, eds. *Texas at the Crossroads.* College Station: Texas A&M University Press, 1987.

Dallas Morning News. *Texas Almanac.* Dallas: Belo. Biannual publication.

Fehrenbach, T. H. *Lone Star: A History of Texas and the Texans.* New York: Macmillan, 1968.

Forman, Maury, and Robert A. Calvert. *Cartooning Texas.* College Station: Texas A&M University Press, 1993.

Montejano, David. *Anglos and Mexicans in the Making of Texas, 1836–1986*. Austin: University of Texas Press, 1987.

Menig, D. W. *Imperial Texas: An Interpretive Essay in Cultural Geography*. Austin: University of Texas Press, 1969.

STUDY OUTLINE

Texas Political Culture

1. According to Daniel Elazar's classification of state political culture, Texas is categorized as having a "traditionalistic individualistic" political culture.
2. Three patterns of Texas politics that reflect its political culture are its history as a one-party state, its provincialism, and its dominance by business.

The Land

1. Land influenced Texans and Texas politics.
2. The Coastal Plains, Interior Lowlands, Great Plains, and Basin and Range Province are the four physical regions of Texas, and each has separate and distinct features.

Economic Change in Texas

1. Land is an important influence on the political economy of Texas.
2. Cotton, cattle, and oil had great influence on Texas's politics and economy and are derived from Texas's vast land.
3. The oil industry dominated the Texas economy from early in the twentieth century to the 1980s.
4. Texas's oil-based economy began to fail in 1982 and bottomed out in 1986.
5. By 1992, the Texas economy was transformed to one based not on oil, but on high technology.
6. The North American Free Trade Agreement (NAFTA) expanded markets for goods produced in Texas.

The People: Texas Demography

1. The population of Texas grew by almost three million between 1990 and 1998.
2. This growth is due to increased birth rate, immigration, and domestic migration.
3. Texans tend to be younger and poorer than the national average.

Urbanization

1. Over 80 percent of Texas's population lives in urban areas.

The Urban Political Economy

1. Texas has three major metropolitan areas: Houston, Dallas-Fort Worth, and San Antonio.
2. Each metropolitan area has a separate and distinct economy.

Summary

1. Economic and demographic changes affect the economy and politics of Texas.
2. Three technological revolutions shaped the economic life of the state: the first centered on the production of cotton and cattle and its distribution by an extensive railroad system; the second grew out of the oil industry; the third is tied to the development of a high-tech economy.
3. Until the 1980s, Texas was a one-party state, dominated by the Democratic Party.

PRACTICE QUIZ

1. In terms of area, how does Texas rank among the fifty states?
   a) first
   b) second
   c) fifth
   d) seventh
2. Which of Texas's physical regions is characterized by the presence of many of the state's largest ranches?
   a) Coastal Plains
   b) Great Plains
   c) Interior Lowlands
   d) Basin and Range Province
3. Which of Texas's physical regions is found in west Texas?
   a) Coastal Plains
   b) Great Plains
   c) Interior Lowlands
   d) Basin and Range Province
4. Creative destruction
   a) destroys both old and new economies.

b) creates new economies and destroys old ones.
c) maintains old economies and creates new ones.
d) creates and maintains old and new economies.

5. Land and land use gave rise to which three economies?
   a) railroads, transportation, and high technology
   b) cotton, cattle, and oil
   c) oil, cattle, and transportation
   d) insurance, computers, and electronics

6. Which of the following is the most famous ranch in Texas history and, in the twenty-first century, has holdings in several states and nations?
   a) XIT
   b) Bass Brothers
   c) King Ranch
   d) Crown

7. Which industry controlled the politics and economy of Texas for most of the twentieth century?
   a) cotton
   b) cattle
   c) railroad
   d) oil

8. The Texas economy of the twenty-first century is centered on
   a) computers, electronics, and other high-tech products.
   b) transportation, oil and natural gas, and banking.
   c) insurance, construction, and banking.
   d) education, the military, and agriculture.

9. Which of the following accounts for most of Texas's population growth?
   a) immigration
   b) the positive difference between births and deaths
   c) domestic immigration
   d) movement from rural to urban areas

10. The three major metropolitan areas in Texas are
    a) Houston, Dallas-Fort Worth, and San Antonio.
    b) Houston, Dallas-Fort Worth, and El Paso.
    c) El Paso, Houston, and Austin.
    d) San Antonio, El Paso, and Brownsville-Harlingen-McAllen.

CRITICAL THINKING QUESTIONS

1. In the late 1980s, the price of oil fell from over $35 a barrel to $10 a barrel. The fall devastated government revenues and dramatically increased the state's unemployment, business collapses, personal bankruptcies, and bank failures. In short, Texas's economy was near collapse. To what extent has the economy of Texas changed so that devastation in one industry will not have the catastrophic effect that the failure of the oil industry did in the 1980s?

2. Based on the population growth, urbanization, and economic change of the last two decades, what do the next two decades hold for Texas? Which areas will grow in population, and will government be ready for that growth? What economies will remain strong and which might decline? What can/should government do to maintain and strengthen the economy of Texas?

KEY TERMS

creative destruction (p. 796)
elite (p. 791)
individualistic political culture (p. 791)
North American Free Trade Agreement (NAFTA) (p. 806)
moralistic political culture (p. 790)
political culture (p. 790)
political economy (p. 814)
provincialism (p. 792)
traditionalistic political culture (p. 791)
urbanization (p. 813)

21 The Texas

★ **The Role of a State Constitution**

What are the functions of a state constitution?

What are the similarities and differences between the U.S. and Texas constitutions?

★ **The Constitution of *Coahuila y Tejas,* 1827**

What was the historical background to the Constitution of *Coahuila y Tejas*? What were its provisions? What were the consequences of its adoption?

★ **The Constitution of the Republic of Texas, 1836**

What was the historical background to the Constitution of the Republic of Texas? What were its provisions? What were the consequences of its adoption?

★ **The Texas State Constitution of 1845**

What was the historical background to the Texas State Constitution of 1845? What were its provisions? What were the consequences of its adoption?

★ **The Constitution of 1861: Texas Joins the Confederacy**

What was the historical background to the Texas State Constitution of 1861? What were its provisions? What were the consequences of its adoption?

★ **The Constitution of 1866: Texas Rejoins the Union**

What was the historical background to the Texas State Constitution of 1866? What were its provisions? What were the consequences of its adoption?

★ **The Reconstruction Constitution of 1869**

What was the historical background to the Constitution of 1869? What were its provisions? What were the consequences of its adoption?

★ **The Constitution of 1876**

What was the historical background to the Constitution of 1876? What were its provisions? What were the consequences of its adoption?

★ **The Constitution of Texas Today**

How is the principle of limited government embodied in the Texas Constitution? How is the philosophy of republican government reflected in the Constitution today?

★ **Recent Attempts to Amend the Texas Constitution**

What was the rationale for attempting to amend the Constitution in 1974 and 1999? What changes were proposed? Why did these attempts fail?

Constitution

IN the early 1970s, there was an unsuccessful effort to create a new Texas Constitution because, it was claimed, the existing Texas Constitution "is bulky, it's wordy, it's tedious, it's tiresome." At the end of the century, a second effort to revise the constitution was undertaken. It also failed. In spite of these major reform efforts, the Texas Constitution remains a document much disparaged and not well understood by the population as a whole.

This chapter will seek to answer several questions about the Texas Constitution. What is the function of a state constitution? What is the background to constitutional government in Texas over the last 160 years? How did such a maligned document get created? What are its major themes? How does it resemble or differ from the United States Constitution today? And, why do so many politicians and academics continue to criticize the document?

The Role of a State Constitution

- What are the functions of a state constitution?
- What are the similarities and differences between the U.S. and Texas constitutions?

State **constitutions** perform a number of important functions. They legitimate state political institutions by clearly explaining from where their power and authority are derived. State constitutions also delegate power, explaining which powers are granted to particular institutions and individuals and how those powers are to be used. They prevent the concentration of political power by providing political mechanisms that check and balance the powers of one political institution or individual office holder against another. Finally, they mark out the limits of political power. Through declarations of rights, state constitutions explicitly forbid certain kinds of governmental activities intruding into the lives of individuals.

constitution
the legal structure of a government, which establishes its power and authority as well as the limits on that power

Texas has had seven constitutions in the course of its history. From the first, the idea of constitutional government in Texas has been heavily indebted to the larger American experience (see Chapter 3). Five ideas unite the U.S. and Texas constitutional experience. First, political power in both is ultimately derived from the people. Political power is something that is artificially created through the constitution by the conscious act of a people. Second, political power is divided into three separate parts and placed in separate branches of government. The legislative, executive, and judicial branches of government have their own unique powers and corresponding duties and obligations. Third, the U.S. and Texas constitutions structure political power in such a way that the power of one branch is checked and balanced by the power of the other two branches. The idea of checks and balances reflects a common concern among the framers of the U.S. Constitution and the authors of Texas's various constitutions that the intent of writing a constitution was not just to establish effective governing institutions. Its purpose was also to create political institutions that did not tyrannize the very people who established them. The concern to prevent the emergence of tyranny is also found in a fourth idea that underlies the U.S. and Texas constitutions: the idea of individual rights. Government is explicitly forbidden from violating a number of particular rights that are possessed by the people.

federalism
a system of government in which power is divided, by a constitution, between a central government and regional governments

The final idea embodied in both the U.S. and Texas constitutions is that of **federalism.** Federalism is the dividing up of government into a central government along with a series of regional governments (see Chapter 4). Both governments exercise direct authority over individual citizens of the United States and of each particular state. Article IV, Section 4, of the U.S. Constitution guarantees that every state in the Union will have a "Republican Form of Government." Curiously, no attempt is made to explain what exactly a "republican form of government" entails. The Tenth Amendment to the U.S. Constitution also recognizes the importance of the idea of federalism to the American political system. It reads: "The powers not delegated to the United States by the Constitution, nor prohibited by it to the States, are reserved to the States respectively, or to the people." According to the U.S. Constitution, there are thus enormous reservoirs of political power derived from the people that reside in the states themselves.

supremacy clause
Article VI of the Constitution, which states that laws passed by the national government and all treaties are the supreme law of the land and superior to all laws adopted by any state or any subdivision

There are, however, some important differences that distinguish the constitutional experience of Texas with that of the United States. Most important of all is the subordinate role that Texas has in the federal system. Article VI of the U.S. Constitution contains the famous **supremacy clause** declaring the Constitution and the laws of the United States to be "the supreme Law of the Land." It requires all judges in every state to be bound by the U.S. Constitution, notwithstanding the laws or constitution of their particular state. In matters of disagreement, the U.S. Constitution thus takes precedence over the Texas Constitution.

confederation
a system of government in which states retain sovereign authority except for the powers expressly delegated to the national government

One of the major issues of the Civil War was over how the federal system was to be understood. Was the United States a **confederation** of autonomous sovereign states that were ultimately independent political entities capable of withdrawing (much like the current European Union)? Was the United States a perpetual union of states that were ultimately in a subordinate relationship to the central government? The results of the war and the passage of the Fourteenth Amendment in 1868 ultimately resolved this question in terms of the latter. The idea that the United States was a perpetual union composed of subordinate states would have profound implications for constitutional government in Texas throughout the late nineteenth and twentieth centuries. The incorporation of the Bill of Rights through the Fourteenth Amendment became a dominant theme of constitutional law in the twentieth century, placing restrictions upon Texas government and public policy that went far beyond those laid out in Texas's own constitution.

Another major difference between the U.S. and Texas constitutions lies in the **"necessary and proper clause"** of Article I, Section 8. Section 8 begins by listing in detail the specific powers granted to Congress by the Constitution. The Founders thus appeared to want to limit the scope of national government activities. But Section 8 concludes by granting Congress the power that is needed to accomplish its constitutional tasks. The net effect of this clause was to provide a constitutional basis for an enormous expansion of central government activities over the next two hundred years.

necessary and proper clause
from Article I, Section 8 of the Constitution, it provides Congress with the authority to make all laws "necessary and proper" to carry out its expressed powers

Drafters of Texas's various constitutions generally have been unwilling to grant such an enormous loophole in the exercise of governmental power. While granting state government the power to accomplish certain tasks, Texas constitutions have generally denied office holders broad grants of discretionary power to accomplish their goals.

The Constitution of *Coahuila y Tejas,* 1827

▶ What was the historical background to the Constitution of *Coahuila y Tejas?* What were its provisions? What were the consequences of its adoption?

Despite the growing fears of American expansionism following the Louisiana Purchase, in 1803 Spanish Texas was still sparsely populated. In 1804, the population of Spanish Texas was estimated to be 3,605. In 1811, Juan Bautista de las Casas launched the first revolt against Spanish rule in San Antonio. The so-called Casas Revolt was successfully put down by the summer of 1811. The next year, a second challenge to Spanish rule took place along the border between Texas and the United States. After capturing Nacogdoches, La Bahía, and San Antonio, rebel forces under Jose Bernardo Gutiérrez de Lara issued a declaration of independence from New Spain and drafted a constitution. By 1813, however, this revolt had been put down and bloody reprisals had depopulated the state. Texas remained part of New Spain until the Mexican War of Independence.[1]

The Mexican War of Independence grew out of a series of revolts against Spanish rule during the Napoleonic Wars. Burdened by debts brought on by a crippling war with France, Spain sought to exact more wealth from its colonies. The forced abdication of Ferdinand VII in favor of his brother Joseph in 1808 and an intensifying economic crisis in New Spain in 1809 and 1810 worked to undermine the legitimacy of Spanish rule. Revolts broke out in Guanajuato and spread throughout Mexico and its Texas province. Although initially put down by royalist forces loyal to Spain, by 1820 local revolts and guerrilla actions had helped to undermine continued royal rule from Spain. On August 24, 1821, Mexico was formally granted independence.

The first federal constitution that Texas operated under was the Mexican Constitution. At the national level, there were to be two houses of congress. The lower house was composed of deputies serving two-year terms. The upper house of senators served four-year terms and were selected by state legislatures. The president and vice-president were elected for four-year terms by the legislative bodies of the states. There was a supreme court composed of eleven judges and an attorney general. While the Mexican Constitution mandated separate legislative, executive, and judicial branches, no attempt was made to define the scope of state rights in the Mexican confederation. Local affairs remained independent of the central government. While embodying many of the ideas found in the U.S. Constitution, there was one important difference: Catholicism was established as the state religion and supported financially by the state.[2]

Under the Mexican Constitution the state of Coahuila and the sparsely populated province of Texas were combined together into the state of Coahuila and Texas. Saltillo, Mexico, was the capital. More than two years were spent drafting a constitution for the new state. It was published finally on March 11, 1827.

unicameral
comprising one body or house, as in a unicameral legislature

The state was formally divided into three separate districts, with Texas comprising the District of Bexar. Legislative power was placed in a **unicameral** legislature composed of twelve deputies elected by the people. The people of the District of Bexar (Texas) elected two of these. Along with wide-ranging legislative powers, the legislature was also empowered to elect state officials when no majority emerged from the popular vote, to serve as a grand jury in political and military matters, and to regulate the army and militia. Executive power was vested in a governor and a vice-governor, each elected by the people for a four-year term. Judicial power was placed in state courts. While these courts could try cases, they were not supposed to interpret the law.

The Constitution of 1827 formally guaranteed citizens the right to liberty, security, property, and equality. Language in the Constitution also supported efforts to curtail the spread of slavery, an institution of vital importance to planters who were immigrating from the American south. The legislature was ordered to promote education and freedom of the press. As in the Mexican federal constitution, Catholicism was the established state religion.[3]

The Constitution of the Republic of Texas, 1836

▶ What was the historical background to the Constitution of the Republic of Texas? What were its provisions? What were the consequences of its adoption?

Texas's break with Mexico was in large part a constitutional crisis that culminated in separation. Political conventions held in San Felipe de Austin in 1832 and 1833 reflected a growing discontent among Texans over their place in the Mexican federal system. Along with other demands for a more liberal immigration policy for people from the United States and for the establishment of English- and Spanish-speaking primary schools, calls for separate statehood for Texas emerged from the conventions. The 1833 convention actually drafted a constitution for this newly proposed state modeled on the Massachusetts Constitution of 1780. Stephen F. Austin's attempt to bring the proposed constitution to the attention of the central government in Mexico City led to his imprisonment, which, in turn, pushed Texas closer to open rebellion against the central Mexican government.

On November 7, 1835, a declaration was adopted by a meeting of state political leaders at San Felipe, which stated the reasons Texans were beginning to take up arms against the Mexican government. The declaration proclaimed that Texas was rising up in defense of its rights and liberties as well as the republican principles articulated in the Mexican Constitution of 1824. This declaration was but a prelude to the formal Texas Declaration of Independence that emerged out of the convention of 1836 held at Washington-on-the-Brazos.

Of the fifty-nine delegates attending the Convention of 1836, only ten had lived in Texas prior to 1830. Two had arrived as late as 1836. Thirty-nine of the delegates were from southern slave states, six were from the border state of Kentucky, seven were from northern states, three were from Mexico (including two born in Texas), and four were from other English-speaking lands.[4] The final

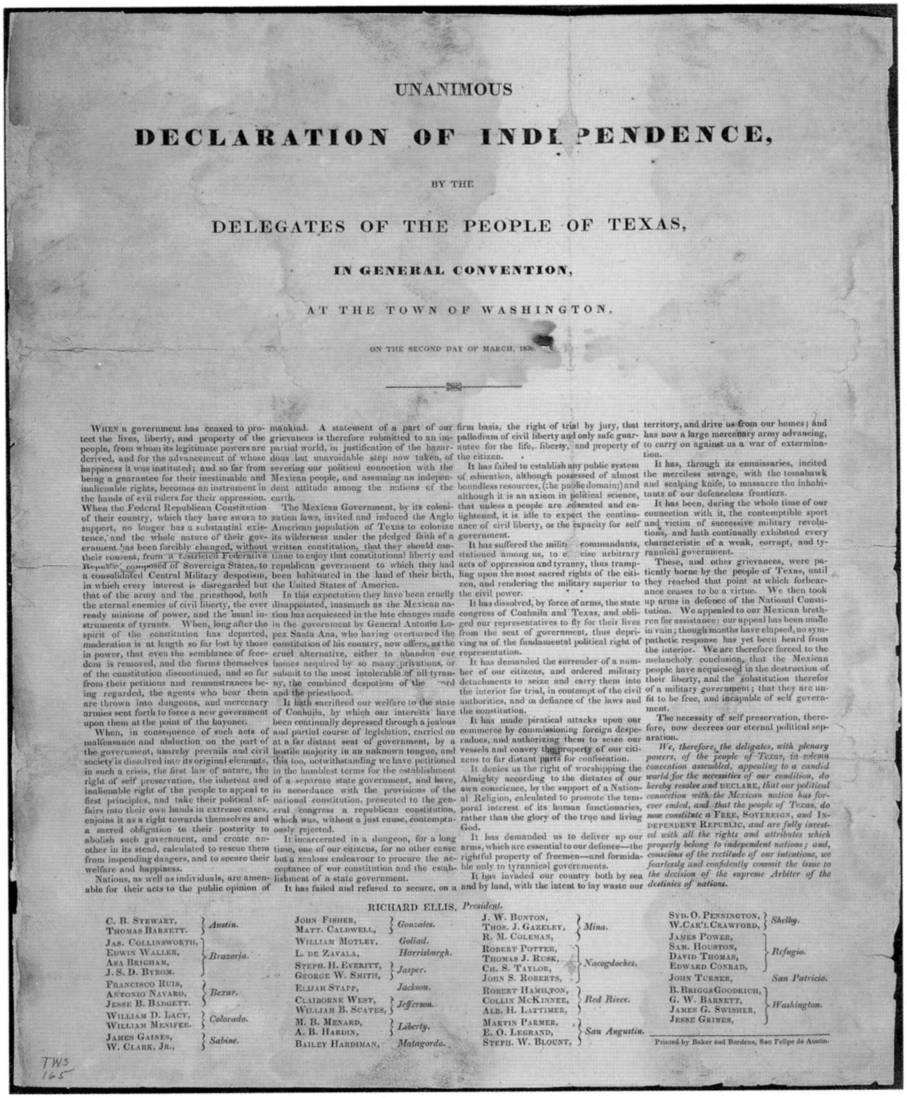

UNANIMOUS

DECLARATION OF INDEPENDENCE,

BY THE

DELEGATES OF THE PEOPLE OF TEXAS,

IN GENERAL CONVENTION,

AT THE TOWN OF WASHINGTON,

ON THE SECOND DAY OF MARCH, 1836.

WHEN a government has ceased to protect the lives, liberty, and property of the people, from whom its legitimate powers are derived, and for the advancement of whose happiness it was instituted; and so far from being a guarantee for their inestimable and inalienable rights, becomes an instrument in the hands of evil rulers for their oppression. When the Federal Republican Constitution of their country, which they have sworn to support, no longer has a substantial existence, and the whole nature of their government has been forcibly changed, without their consent, from a restricted Federative Republic, composed of Sovereign States, to a consolidated Central Military despotism, in which every interest is disregarded but that of the army and the priesthood, both the eternal enemies of civil liberty, the ever ready minions of power, and the usual instruments of tyrants. When, long after the spirit of the constitution has departed, moderation is at length so far lost by those in power, that even the semblance of freedom is removed, and the forms themselves of the constitution discontinued, and so far from their petitions and remonstrances being regarded, the agents who bear them are thrown into dungeons, and mercenary armies sent forth to force a new government upon them at the point of the bayonet.

When, in consequence of such acts of malfeasance and abduction on the part of the government, anarchy prevails and civil society is dissolved into its original elements, in such a crisis, the first law of nature, the right of self preservation, the inherent and inalienable right of the people to appeal to first principles, and take their political affairs into their own hands in extreme cases, enjoins it as a right towards themselves and a sacred obligation to their posterity to abolish such government, and create another in its stead, calculated to rescue them from impending dangers, and to secure their welfare and happiness.

Nations, as well as individuals, are amenable for their acts to the public opinion of mankind. A statement of a part of our grievances is therefore submitted to an impartial world, in justification of the hazardous but unavoidable step now taken, of severing our political connection with the Mexican people, and assuming an independent attitude among the nations of the earth.

The Mexican Government, by its colonization laws, invited and induced the Anglo American population of Texas to colonize its wilderness under the pledged faith of a written constitution, that they should continue to enjoy that constitutional liberty and republican government to which they had been habituated in the land of their birth, the United States of America.

In this expectation they have been cruelly disappointed, inasmuch as the Mexican nation has acquiesced in the late changes made in the government by General Antonio Lopez Santa Ana, who having overturned the constitution of his country, now offers, as the cruel alternative, either to abandon our homes acquired by so many privations, or submit to the most intolerable of all tyranny, the combined despotism of the sword and the priesthood.

It hath sacrificed our welfare to the state of Coahuila, by which our interests have been continually depressed through a jealous and partial course of legislation, carried on at a far distant seat of government, by a hostile majority in an unknown tongue, and this too, notwithstanding we have petitioned in the humblest terms for the establishment of a separate state government, and have, in accordance with the provisions of the national constitution, presented to the general congress a republican constitution, which was, without a just cause, contemptuously rejected.

It incarcerated in a dungeon, for a long time, one of our citizens, for no other cause but a zealous endeavour to procure the acceptance of our constitution and the establishment of a state government.

It has failed and refused to secure, on a firm basis, the right of trial by jury, that palladium of civil liberty and only safe guarantee for the life, liberty, and property of the citizen.

It has failed to establish any public system of education, although possessed of almost boundless resources, (the public domain;) and although it is an axiom in political science, that unless a people are educated and enlightened, it is idle to expect the continuance of civil liberty, or the capacity for self government.

It has suffered the military commandants, stationed among us, to exercise arbitrary acts of oppression and tyranny, thus trampling upon the most sacred rights of the citizen, and rendering the military superior to the civil power.

It has dissolved, by force of arms, the state congress of Coahuila and Texas, and obliged our representatives to fly for their lives from the seat of government, thus depriving us of the fundamental political right of representation.

It has demanded the surrender of a number of our citizens, and ordered military detachments to seize and carry them into the interior for trial, in contempt of the civil authorities, and in defiance of the laws and the constitution.

It has made piratical attacks upon our commerce by commissioning foreign desperadoes, and authorizing them to seize our vessels and convey the property of our citizens to far distant parts for confiscation.

It denies us the right of worshipping the Almighty according to the dictates of our own conscience, by the support of a National Religion, calculated to promote the temporal interest of its human functionaries, rather than the glory of the true and living God.

It has demanded us to deliver up our arms, which are essential to our defence—the rightful property of freemen—and formidable only to tyrannical governments.

It has invaded our country both by sea and by land, with the intent to lay waste our territory, and drive us from our homes; and has now a large mercenary army advancing, to carry on against us a war of extermination.

It has, through its emmissaries, incited the merciless savage, with the tomahawk and scalping knife, to massacre the inhabitants of our defenceless frontiers.

It has been, during the whole time of our connection with it, the contemptible sport and victim of successive military revolutions, and hath continually exhibited every characteristic of a weak, corrupt, and tyrannical government.

These, and other grievances, were patiently borne by the people of Texas, until they reached that point at which forbearance ceases to be a virtue. We then took up arms in defence of the National Constitution. We appealed to our Mexican brethren for assistance: our appeal has been made in vain; though months have elapsed, no sympathetic response has yet been heard from the interior. We are therefore forced to the melancholy conclusion, that the Mexican people have acquiesced in the destruction of their liberty, and the substitution therefor of a military government; that they are unfit to be free, and incapable of self government.

The necessity of self preservation, therefore, now decrees our eternal political separation.

We, therefore, the delegates, with plenary powers, of the people of Texas, in solemn convention assembled, appealing to a candid world for the necessities of our condition, do hereby resolve and DECLARE, *that our political connection with the Mexican nation has forever ended, and that the people of Texas, do now constitute a* FREE, SOVEREIGN, *and* INDEPENDENT REPUBLIC, *and are fully invested with all the rights and attributes which properly belong to independent nations; and, conscious of the rectitude of our intentions, we fearlessly and confidently commit the issue to the decision of the supreme Arbiter of the destinies of nations.*

RICHARD ELLIS, *President.*

C. B. STEWART, THOMAS BARNETT. — *Austin.*
JAS. COLLINSWORTH, EDWIN WALLER, ASA BRIGHAM, J. S. D. BYROM. — *Brazoria.*
FRANCISCO RUIS, ANTONIO NAVARO, JESSE B. BADGETT. — *Bexar.*
WILLIAM D. LACY, WILLIAM MENIFEE. — *Colorado.*
JAMES GAINES, W. CLARK, JR., — *Sabine.*
JOHN FISHER, MATT. CALDWELL, — *Gonzales.*
WILLIAM MOTLEY, — *Goliad.*
L. DE ZAVALA, — *Harrisburgh.*
STEPH. H. EVERITT, GEORGE W. SMITH, — *Jasper.*
ELIJAH STAPP, — *Jackson.*
CLAIBORNE WEST, WILLIAM B. SCATES, — *Jefferson.*
M. B. MENARD, A. B. HARDIN, — *Liberty.*
BAILEY HARDIMAN, — *Matagorda.*
J. W. BUNTON, THOS. J. GAZELEY, R. M. COLEMAN, — *Mina.*
ROBERT POTTER, THOMAS J. RUSK, CH. S. TAYLOR, JOHN S. ROBERTS, — *Nacogdoches.*
ROBERT HAMILTON, COLLIN MCKINNEE, ALB. H. LATTIMER, — *Red River.*
MARTIN PARMER, E. O. LEGRAND, STEPH. W. BLOUNT, — *San Augustin.*
SYD. O. PENNINGTON, W. CAR'L CRAWFORD, — *Shelby.*
JAMES POWER, SAM. HOUSTON, DAVID THOMAS, EDWARD CONRAD, — *Refugio.*
JOHN TURNER, — *San Patricio.*
B. BRIGGS GOODRICH, G. W. BARNETT, JAMES G. SWISHER, JESSE GRIMES, — *Washington.*

Printed by Baker and Bordens, San Felipe de Austin.

TWS 165

The Texas Declaration of Independence was written by George C. Childress and adopted at the Convention of 1836. Childress modeled the document on the American Declaration of Independence.

products of the convention—the Texas Declaration of Independence and the Constitution of 1836—reflected the interests and values of these participants.

In their own Declaration of Independence, delegates to the convention proclaimed that the federal constitutional regime that they had been invited to live under by the rulers of Mexico had been replaced by a military tyranny that combined a "despotism of the sword and the priesthood." Echoing the American Declaration of Independence, they presented a long list of grievances against the central government, including the failure to provide freedom of religion, a system of public education, and trial by jury (see Box 21.1). After declaring Texas to be a separate republic independent from Mexico, the convention proceeded to draft and pass a new constitution reflecting these republican sentiments.

bicameral
having a legislative assembly composed of two chambers or houses; opposite of unicameral

Resembling the U.S. Constitution in being brief and flexible (less than 6,500 words), the 1836 Constitution established an elected chief executive with considerable powers, a **bicameral** legislature, and a four-tiered judicial system composed of justice, county, district, and supreme courts.[5] Power was divided among these three branches and a system of checks and balances was put into place. Complicated procedures were included for amending the constitution and a bill of rights was elaborated.

A number of important provisions from Spanish-Mexican law were adapted for the Texas Republic in the constitution, including the idea of community property, homestead exemptions and protections, and debtor relief. The values of American democracy percolated through the document. White male suffrage was guaranteed. Ministers and priests were ineligible for public office. But one of the most important aspects of the Constitution of 1836, at

Box 21.1 THE TEXAS DECLARATION OF INDEPENDENCE

Like the Founders during the American Revolution, leaders of the Texas Revolution felt that it was necessary to justify their actions in print. Written by George C. Childress and adopted by the general convention at Washington-on-the-Brazos on March 2, 1836, the Texas Declaration of Independence stated why it was necessary to separate from Mexico and create an independent republic. Not surprisingly, the document draws heavily upon the ideas of John Locke and Thomas Jefferson for inspiration. The description of the role of the government, "to protect the lives, liberty, and property of the people," repeated verbatim Locke's litany of the primary reason for establishing government. Like Jefferson's Declaration, Texas's declaration catalogues a list of grievances against the Mexican regime. According to the declaration, the existing government had abdicated its duties to protect the governed and broken the trustee relationship that binds a people to those in authority. By dissolving civil society into its original elements, the government had forced the people to assert their inalienable right of self-preservation and to take political affairs into their own hands again. The "melancholy conclusion" of the declaration echoed ideas that Locke and Jefferson would have understood well: Any government that stripped a people of its liberty was unacceptable to those raised on principles of self-government. Self-preservation demanded "eternal political separation" from the very state that had invited them to settle in Texas.

least from the perspective of newly immigrated Americans from the South, may have been the defense of slavery as an institution.

The State Constitution of *Coahuila y Tejas* of 1827 had challenged, albeit unsuccessfully, the existence of slavery as an institution. Although the 1836 Constitution of the Republic of Texas outlawed the importation of slaves from Africa, it guaranteed that slaveholders could keep their property and that new slaveholding immigrants could bring their slaves into Texas with them. The results of this constitutional protection were monumental. In 1836, Texas had a population of 38,470, including 5,000 slaves. By 1850, the slave population had grown to 58,161, over one-quarter of the state's population. By 1860, there were over 182,566 slaves, accounting for over 30 percent of the state's population.[6] For all intents and purposes, the Constitution of 1836 not only saved slavery as an institution in Texas but also provided the protections needed for it to flourish.

The Texas State Constitution of 1845

▶ What was the historical background to the Texas State Constitution of 1845? What were its provisions? What were the consequences of its adoption?

Although the 1836 Constitution called for annexation by the United States, Texas remained an independent republic for nine years. There were concerns in the United States that if Texas were admitted to the union, it would be as a slave state. Texas's admission to the union could alter the delicate balance between slave and free states and further divide the nation over the sensitive subject of slavery. Additionally, it was feared that annexation by the United States

The lowering of the Republic flag marked Texas's annexation to the Union on March 1, 1845. A state constitution was drafted shortly thereafter to reflect Texas's new role.

would lead to war with Mexico. Santa Anna—the Mexican general and dictator whom Sam Houston had defeated at the battle of San Jacinto—had repudiated the Treaty of Velasco that ended the war between Texas and Mexico. Still claiming Texas as part of its own territory, Mexico undoubtedly would have gone to war to protect what it felt to be rightfully its own.

Hesitation over admitting Texas to the Union was overcome by the mid-1840s. On March 1, 1845, the United States Congress approved a resolution that would bring Texas into the Union as a state. There were a number of interesting provisions to the annexation resolution. First, the Republic of Texas ceded all military armaments, bases, and facilities pertaining to public defense to the United States. Second, Texas retained a right to all "its vacant and unappropriated lands" as well as to its public debts. This was no small matter, as Texas claimed an enormous amount of land that extended far beyond its present state boundaries. These issues were not resolved until the passage of the Compromise of 1850. Finally, Texas was given permission to break up into four additional states when population proved adequate.

On July 4, 1845, a convention was called by Governor Anson Jones to draft a state constitution in Austin. Drafters of the constitution relied heavily on the Constitution of 1836, although the final document ended up being almost twice as long. The familiar doctrines of separation of powers, checks and balances, and individual rights defined the basic design of government.

Under the Constitution of 1845, the legislature was to be composed of two houses. The House of Representatives would have between forty-five and ninety members, elected for two-year terms. Members would have to be at least twenty-one years of age. The Senate was to be composed of between nineteen and thirty-three members, elected for four-year terms. Half of the Senate would be elected every two years. As in the U.S. Constitution, revenue bills were to originate in the House. Executive vetoes could be overturned by a two-thirds vote of each house. In a separate article on education, the legislature was ordered to establish a public school system and to set aside lands to support a Permanent School Fund. Another interesting power granted to the legislature was the power to select the treasurer and comptroller in a joint session.

This constitution provided for an elected governor and lieutenant governor. The governor's term was set at two years. He could only serve four years as governor in any six-year period. Among the executive powers granted to the governor were the powers to convene and adjourn the legislature, to veto legislation, to grant pardons and reprieves, and to command the state militia. The governor also had the power to appoint the attorney general, secretary of state, and district and supreme court judges, subject to the approval of the Senate.

The Constitution of 1845 established a judicial branch consisting of a supreme court composed of three judges, district courts, and lower courts deemed necessary by the legislature. Judges on the higher courts were to be appointed to six-year terms and could be removed from office subject to a two-thirds vote of both houses of the legislature.

Amending the Constitution of 1845 was difficult. After being proposed by a two-thirds vote of each house, amendments had to be approved by a majority of the voters. In the next legislature, another two-thirds vote of each house was necessary for ratification. Only one amendment was ever made to the Constitution of 1845. In 1850, an amendment was added to provide for the election of state officials who were originally appointed by the governor or by the legislature.[7]

This constitution contained some unusual provisions. Consistent with the terms of annexation, Texas could divide itself into as many as five states. Texas itself had to pay its foreign debt. It would retain title to its public lands, which could be sold to pay its debt. There was even a provision allowing Texas to fly its flag at the same height as the U.S. flag.

The Constitution of 1861: Texas Joins the Confederacy

▶ What was the historical background to the Texas State Constitution of 1861? What were its provisions? What were the consequences of its adoption?

The issue of slavery had delayed Texas's admission into the United States for nine years until 1845. It drove Texas from the union in 1861. By 1860, slavery had become a vital institution to the Texas economy. Concentrated in east Texas and along the Gulf Coast, slaves had come to constitute 30 percent of the population. However, there were large sections of the state, particularly in the north and west where the economy was based on ranching or corn and wheat production rather than cotton. There slavery was virtually nonexistent. The question of whether Texas should secede was a controversial one that divided the state along regional and ethnic as well as party lines.

Pressure to secede mounted following the presidential election of Abraham Lincoln in November 1860. A staunch unionist, Governor Sam Houston refused to convene a special session of the legislature to discuss secession. Seeking to bypass Houston, a number of influential political leaders in the state, including the chief justice of the Supreme Court called for a special convention to be convened to consider secession in January 1861. Giving in to the pressure, Houston called a special session of the legislature in the hopes of undercutting the upcoming secession convention. The legislature, however, had other ideas, validating the call for the convention and turning its chambers over to the convention.

Governor Sam Houston opposed secession from the Union and attempted to block efforts by those wishing to secede.

Lawyers and slaveholders dominated the secession convention. Lawyers composed 40 percent of the delegates; slaveholders composed 70 percent. The Texas Ordinance of Secession, produced by the convention on February 2, 1861, reflected this pro-slavery membership. In striking language it proclaimed that the northern states had broken faith with Texas, particularly regarding the institution of slavery. Northerners had violated the very laws and constitution of the federal Union by appealing to a "higher law" that trampled upon the rights of Texans. In a language that people living in the twenty-first century find hard to understand, the Ordinance of Secession proclaimed

> We hold as undeniable truths that the governments of the various States, and of the confederacy itself, were established exclusively by the white race, for themselves and their posterity; that the African race had no agency in their establishment; that they were rightfully held and regarded as an inferior and dependent race, and in that condition only could their existence in this country be rendered beneficial and tolerable.[8]

Confederacy
the Confederate States of America, those southern states that seceded from the United States in 1861 and argued that the power of a government is based in its states

Texas voters approved secession from the union on February 23, 1861. The secession convention reconvened to enact a new constitution to guide the state as it entered the **Confederacy**. There were surprisingly few changes in the final document. This constitution was similar to the Constitution of 1845 except that references to the United States of America were replaced with references to the Confederate States of America. Public officials had to declare allegiance to the Confederacy, and slavery and states' rights were defended. A clause in the 1845 Constitution that provided for the emancipation of slaves was eliminated and freeing slaves was declared illegal. But for the most part, the document accepted the existing constitutional framework. Controversial proposals, such as resuming the African slave trade and taking a strong states' rights position, were rejected. The move out of the Union into the Confederacy may have been a radical one, but the new constitution was conservative insofar as it reaffirmed the existing constitutional order in the state.[9]

The Constitution of 1866: Texas Rejoins the Union

▶ What was the historical background to the Texas State Constitution of 1866? What were its provisions? What were the consequences of its adoption?

Defeat in the Civil War led to the institution of another state constitution in 1866. The provisional governor Andrew Jackson Hamilton called a constitutional convention on November 15, 1865, a little over six months after the surrender of Lee's army in Virginia. Delegates were elected on January 8, 1866, and the convention was convened for February 7. Few former secessionists were excluded from voting, with the result being that there were strong unionist and secessionist factions at the convention.

A number of actions were taken to bring the state into compliance with President Andrew Johnson's policy of Reconstruction, including the rejection of the right to secession, a repudiation of the war debt incurred by the state, and an acceptance of the abolition of slavery. The convention granted freedmen fundamental rights to their persons and property and gave them the right to sue and be sued as well as the right to contract with others. However, there was little support for extending suffrage to blacks, and they were banned from holding public office. The convention also made a few changes to the existing constitutional system in Texas. These changes came to be known as the Constitution of 1866.

As in the two previous constitutions, the size of the House was set at between forty-five and ninety, while that of the Senate was set at between nineteen and thirty-three. Terms of office remained the same as under the 1845 and 1861 constitutions, although salaries were increased. Reapportionment was to be based on the number of white male citizens who would be counted in a census every ten years.

The governor's salary was also increased and the term was extended to four years, with a limit of eight years in any twelve-year period. The governor was also granted, for the first time, a line-item veto on appropriations. The comptroller and the treasurer were to be elected by the voters for four-year terms.

Under the new constitution, the Supreme Court was expanded from three to five judges and terms were increased to ten years. Salaries also were increased. The chief justice was to be selected from the five judges on the Supreme Court. District court judges were to be elected for eight-year terms, and the attorney general for a four-year term.

Voters ratified the Constitution of 1866 in June in a relatively close referendum, 28,119 to 23,400. The close vote was attributed to a widespread unhappiness with the increase in salaries of the various state officers.[10]

The Reconstruction Constitution of 1869

▶ What was the historical background to the Constitution of 1869? What were its provisions? What were the consequences of its adoption?

In 1869, Texas wrote still another constitution in order to meet the requirements for the Congressional Reconstruction Acts of 1867. A vote calling for a constitutional convention was ordered by General Winfield Scott Hancock, the commander of the Texas and Louisiana Military district, in early 1868. Although Democrats were opposed to the convention, **Radical Republicans** easily won by 44,689 to 11,440. Of the ninety delegates to the convention, only six had served in the previous constitutional convention. Ten were blacks. The vast majority represented the interests of various wings in the Republican Party. The convention was a rancorous affair as delegates argued over a wide range of issues, including railroad charters, lawlessness in the state, and whether laws passed during the war years were legal. In the final days of the convention, delegates finally got down to the constitutional matters and the problems of accepting the Thirteenth and Fourteenth amendments. Although delegates never completed their task of reworking the Constitution of 1866, their efforts were published under orders by military officials and became the Constitution of 1869.

Radical Republicans
a bloc of Republicans in the U.S. Congress who pushed through the adoption of black suffrage as well as an extended period of military occupation in the South following the Civil War

A number of features of the Constitution of 1869 stand out.[11] The U.S. Constitution was declared to be the supreme law of the land. Slavery was forbidden and blacks were given the right to vote. Fourteenth Amendment guarantees of equality before the law were recognized. Additionally, the constitution altered the relationship between the three branches of government.

The House of Representatives was set at ninety and the Senate at thirty members. Senatorial terms were extended to six years, one-third of the seats to be elected every biennium. Legislative sessions were to be held annually.

The most important critical changes were in the executive and the courts. The powers of the governor were vastly expanded. Among other things, the governor was given wide-ranging appointment powers that included the power to appoint judges. The Supreme Court was reduced from five to three judges. The term of Supreme Court judges was also lowered to nine years, with one new judge to be appointed every three years. There were increased salaries for state officials.

A Republican affiliated with the Radical faction of the party and a former Union general, Edmund Davis, governed under this constitution. Davis had

Former Union general Edmund Davis governed the state of Texas under the Constitution of 1869. The constitution granted Davis vast unchecked powers and he was perceived as presiding over a corrupt administration. The example of Davis's reign motivated the revision of executive branch power in the Constitution of 1876.

vast power, since the constitution had centralized power in the executive while reducing local governmental powers. Varying interpretations exist of the government provided by Davis, though the popular perception at the time was that Davis presided over a corrupt, extravagant administration that eventually turned to the state police and the militia to attempt to maintain its regime.

In 1872, the Democrats regained control of the state government and in 1873, Democrat Richard Coke was elected governor; Davis attempted to maintain control over the governor's office by having his handpicked Supreme Court invalidate Coke's election. Davis refused to give up his office and surrounded himself with state police in the capitol. However, when Democrats slipped past guards and gathered upstairs in the capitol building to organize a government, Davis was unable to obtain federal troops to retain him in office. Democrats were able to form a government, and Davis left office.

The Constitution of 1876

▶ What was the historical background to the Constitution of 1876? What were its provisions? What were the consequences of its adoption?

Grange
a militant farmers movement of the late-nineteenth century which fought for improved conditions for farmers

To prevent another government such as Davis's, efforts were made to write a new constitution. In 1874, a constitution was proposed and later rejected by a sitting legislature.[12] Finally in 1875, a constitutional convention was called. Three delegates were selected by popular vote from each of the thirty senatorial districts. The final composition of the convention included seventy-five Democrats and fifteen Republicans, six of whom were black. Not one of the elected delegates had participated in the constitutional conventional of 1868–69. Forty of the delegates were farmers, and forty were members of the **Grange**, a militant farming organization that had emerged to improve the plight of farmers.

These framers were committed to a constitution with four major themes. First, they were committed to strong popular control of state government. Second, they believed that a constitution should seriously limit the power of state government. Third, they sought economy in government. Fourth, the framers sought to promote agrarian interests, particularly those of small farmers, who formed the basis of support for the Grange Movement.

Popular control of state government meant that the governor's vast appointment powers were to be limited by having public officials subject to election. Judges and other officials who had been appointed by the governor under the 1869 Constitution were now independently elected officials. But popular control of the government did not mean that all the electorate voted. When the framers of the 1876 Constitution thought of popular control of state government, they thought of control by white males.

In an era of agriculture when prices and incomes were low and when little was demanded or expected from government, much in the Constitution of 1876 made sense. However, one might question whether a constitution designed by white males primarily for whites in a rural agrarian society—and for the purpose of keeping the likes of Edmund Davis from ever controlling the state again—is workable in the modern era.

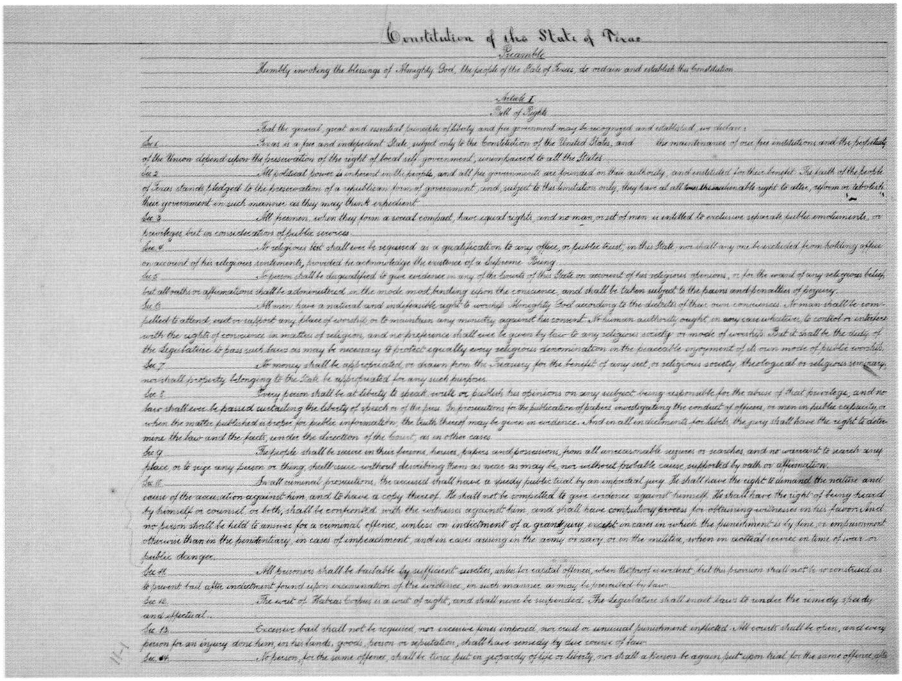

Constitution of the State of Texas

Preamble

Humbly invoking the blessings of Almighty God, the people of the State of Texas, do ordain and establish this Constitution.

Article I

Bill of Rights

That the general, great and essential principles of liberty and free government may be recognized and established, we declare:

Sec 1. Texas is a free and independent State, subject only to the Constitution of the United States, and the maintenance of our free institutions and the perpetuity of the Union depend upon the preservation of the right of local self-government, unimpaired to all the States.

Sec 2. All political power is inherent in the people, and all free governments are founded on their authority, and instituted for their benefit. The faith of the people of Texas stands pledged to the preservation of a republican form of government, and, subject to this limitation only, they have at all times the inalienable right to alter, reform or abolish their government in such manner as they may think expedient.

Sec 3. All freemen, when they form a social compact, have equal rights, and no man, or set of men, is entitled to exclusive separate public emoluments, or privileges but in consideration of public services.

Sec 4. No religious test shall ever be required as a qualification to any office, or public trust, in this State, nor shall any one be excluded from holding office on account of his religious sentiments, provided he acknowledge the existence of a Supreme Being.

Sec 5. No person shall be disqualified to give evidence in any of the Courts of this State on account of his religious opinions, or for the want of any religious belief, but all oaths or affirmations shall be administered in the mode most binding upon the conscience, and shall be taken subject to the pains and penalties of perjury.

Sec 6. All men have a natural and indefeasible right to worship Almighty God according to the dictates of their own consciences. No man shall be compelled to attend, erect or support any place of worship, or to maintain any ministry against his consent. No human authority ought, in any case whatever, to control or interfere with the rights of conscience in matters of religion, and no preference shall ever be given by law to any religious society or mode of worship. But it shall be the duty of the Legislature to pass such laws as may be necessary to protect equally every religious denomination in the peaceable enjoyment of its own mode of public worship.

Sec 7. No money shall be appropriated, or drawn from the Treasury for the benefit of any sect, or religious society, theological or religious seminary, nor shall property belonging to the State be appropriated for any such purposes.

Sec 8. Every person shall be at liberty to speak, write or publish his opinions on any subject, being responsible for the abuse of that privilege, and no law shall ever be passed curtailing the liberty of speech or of the press. In prosecutions for the publication of papers investigating the conduct of officers, or men in public capacity, or when the matter published is proper for public information, the truth thereof may be given in evidence. And in all indictments for libels, the jury shall have the right to determine the law and the facts, under the direction of the Court, as in other cases.

Sec 9. The people shall be secure in their persons, houses, papers and possessions, from all unreasonable seizures or searches, and no warrant to search any place, or to seize any person or thing, shall issue without describing them as near as may be, nor without probable cause, supported by oath or affirmation.

Sec 10. In all criminal prosecutions, the accused shall have a speedy public trial by an impartial jury. He shall have the right to demand the nature and cause of the accusation against him, and to have a copy thereof. He shall not be compelled to give evidence against himself. He shall have the right of being heard by himself or counsel, or both, shall be confronted with the witnesses against him, and shall have compulsory process for obtaining witnesses in his favor. And no person shall be held to answer for a criminal offence, unless on indictment of a grand jury, except in cases in which the punishment is by fine, or imprisonment otherwise than in the penitentiary, in cases of impeachment, and in cases arising in the army or navy, or in the militia, when in actual service in time of war or public danger.

Sec 11. All prisoners shall be bailable by sufficient sureties, unless for capital offences, when the proof is evident; but this provision shall not be so construed as to prevent bail after indictment found upon examination of the evidence, in such manner as may be prescribed by law.

Sec 12. The writ of Habeas Corpus is a writ of right, and shall never be suspended. The Legislature shall enact laws to render the remedy speedy and effectual.

Sec 13. Excessive bail shall not be required, nor excessive fines imposed, nor cruel or unusual punishment inflicted. All courts shall be open, and every person for an injury done him, in his lands, goods, person or reputation, shall have remedy by due course of law.

Sec 14. No person, for the same offence, shall be twice put in jeopardy of life or liberty, nor shall a person be again put upon trial for the same offence, after

The Constitution of 1876 was drafted in response to Edmund Davis's tyrannical leadership. The framers of the constitution sought popular control of state government which limited the appointment powers of the governor as provided by the Constitution of 1869.

State government was to be a government of limited powers. There would be a diffusion of executive powers among numerous officeholders to prevent any future governor from wielding the vast powers held by Governor Davis. Although subsequently changed by constitutional amendment, the governor initially was further limited in powers by serving only a two-year term. The legislature would be a part-time legislature, ordinarily sitting for a limited time period every other year. This was in contrast to the 1869 Constitution, which provided that the legislature meet in annual sessions. Additionally, legislators would not be highly paid. The judicial branch would be elected, rather than appointed, to further limit gubernatorial power. The constitution would place great restrictions on the actions of government, restrictions that would have to be modified through a complex constitutional amendment process.

The constitution would have restrictions on the extent of government debt and on the government's power to tax. To emphasize that Texas government was an economical one, there were even limits on the salaries of state officials, especially legislators. A major economic depression had begun in 1873 and many Texans were experiencing economic hardships. One way money was saved was to decentralize public education. Schools were segregated and compulsory education laws were eliminated. By having local control over education, white landowners could avoid paying taxes for the education of black students.

Texas at that time was an agricultural state and many of the framers of the Constitution of 1876 were farmers, often farmers involved with the Grange, a political organization of mostly small farmers. The framers wished to protect agrarian interests and wrote into the constitution laws protecting homesteads and restricting institutions that, at that time, were perceived to be harmful to farmers, such as banks and railroads. Greater responsibility was placed on local instead of state officials. There were also detailed regulations on railroad competition, freight and passenger rates, and railroad construction incentives.

Even in its earliest stages, the Texas Constitution of 1876 was a detailed document that included numerous restrictions on government power. With the U.S. Constitution, much had been left unsaid so that the document was short, flexible, and allowed lawmaking to be done by statute. With the Texas Constitution, the standard was different. It was to be lengthy, rigid, and detailed. Regulations were placed, not in statutes, but in the body of the constitution. The idea was that the Radical Republicans and E. J. Davis would never again be able to reign and spend in Texas. They, of course, never did, although the constitution over the years had become an increasingly unwieldy document.

The Constitution of Texas Today

▶ How is the principle of limited government embodied in the Texas Constitution? How is the philosophy of republican government reflected in the Constitution today?

The United States Constitution had two great virtues: brevity and flexibility. Neither of these virtues could be said to characterize the Texas Constitution. The U.S. Constitution is limited to seven short articles and twenty-seven amendments, and takes up only eight pages of *The World Almanac*. In contrast, the Texas Constitution in 1999 contained sixteen articles and has been amended over 377 times. Many of the articles are lengthy, complex affairs, taking up over sixty-seven pages of text in one edition of the *Texas Almanac*. But it is not just the length that differentiates the two constitutions. There is a difference in tone and in the fears of what government could do if the principle of **limited government** was not clearly established.

limited government
a government whose powers are defined and limited by a constitution

The Texas Constitution severely curtails executive power by limiting the power granted to the governor and decentralizing executive authority in ways unimagined by the writers of the U.S. Constitution. It also addresses a number of specific policy problems directly in the text, turning what might appear to be matters of public policy into issues of constitutional authority. By granting a variety of boards and districts a special place in the constitution, additional checks and balances were put into place that make it difficult for government to exercise power effectively without being able to maintain extraordinary majorities in a variety of political arenas. Quite unintentionally, the Texas Constitution became a place where special interests could seek to promote and protect their own interests, even in the face of considerable political opposition.

The U.S. Constitution was written to overcome the liabilities of the Articles of Confederation and create a government that could act effectively in the public welfare in a variety of policy areas. The Texas Constitution was written to prevent the expansion of governmental authority and the return of a system of political power that acted against the interests of the people.

THE PREAMBLE

The preamble to Texas's Constitution is surprisingly short: "Humbly invoking the blessings of Almighty God, the people of the State of Texas do ordain and establish this Constitution." This brevity is more than made up for in what follows.

ARTICLE I: BILL OF RIGHTS

Article I of the U.S. Constitution establishes and delegates power to the legislative branch of government. One of the overriding concerns of the Founders was to create a legislature that could act effectively in public affairs. What came to be known as the Bill of Rights—the first ten amendments to the Constitution—was added after the original Constitution was drafted and approved.

In contrast, the Texas Constitution puts its Bill of Rights up front as Article I, well before any discussion of the legislature, the executive, or the courts. From the beginning, the purpose of the Texas Constitution was not simply to create a set of institutions that could wield political power. It was to limit the way in which political power is used and to prevent political power from being abused.

The Bill of Rights embodies certain ideas captured in the U.S. Bill of Rights. All "free men" are declared to have free and equal rights that cannot be denied or abridged because of sex, race, color, creed, or national origin. Freedom of religious worship is guaranteed, and there will be no religious test for office. Liberty of speech and press are guaranteed. Individuals are protected from unreasonable search and seizure, from excessive bail, bills of attainder or ex-post facto laws, and from double jeopardy. Article I also guarantees individuals a right to trial by jury and the right to bear arms "in the lawful defense of himself or the State; but the Legislature shall have the power, by law, to regulate the wearing of arms, with a view to prevent crime" (Article I, Section 23).

Article I also contains some ideas that move well outside those guaranteed by the first ten amendments to the U.S. Constitution. The right to **republican government**, something clearly stated in the main body of the Constitution but not in the U.S. Bill of Rights, is powerfully articulated in the first two sections of Article I. According to Article I of the Texas Constitution, all political power is inherent in the people and the people of Texas have at all times the "inalienable right to alter, reform or abolish their government in such manner as they may think expedient" (Article I, Section 2).

republican government
a representative democracy, a system of government in which the people select representatives

The differences between the Texas Bill of Rights and the U.S. Bill of Rights are not simply matters of where best to articulate a philosophy of republican government. They also involve very concrete matters of public policy. Section 26, for example, forbids monopolies that are contrary to the public interest, and states that the law of primogeniture and entail (a law designed to keep large landed properties together by restricting inheritance to the first-born) will never be in effect in the state. While monopolies remain a public concern today, primogeniture and entail are not. Section 11 grapples with the complicated issue of bail and under what specific circumstances an individual can be denied bail. Significantly, Section 11 has been the subject of three major constitutional revisions: in 1955, 1977, and 1993. Section 30, adopted in 1989, provides a long list of the "rights of crime victims," including a right to be treated fairly and with dignity, a right to be protected from the accused, and a right to restitution. While important matters of public policy for Texas today, these could hardly be considered to be proper material for the U.S. Constitution.

ARTICLE II: THE POWERS OF GOVERNMENT

Like the U.S. Constitution, Article II divides the power of government in Texas into three distinct branches: the legislative, the executive, and the judicial. It also stipulates that no one in any one branch shall be attached to either of the other branches, except where explicitly permitted (as in the case of the lieutenant governor's role in the Senate). The article—one short paragraph of text—assures that a version of the **separation of powers** doctrine found in the U.S. Constitution will be embodied in Texas institutions.

separation of powers
the division of governmental power among several institutions that must cooperate in decision making

ARTICLE III: LEGISLATIVE DEPARTMENT

Article II is one of the shortest articles in the Texas Constitution. Article III is the longest, comprising almost one-third of the text. Like Article I of the U.S. Constitution, Article III of the Texas Constitution vests legislative power in two houses: a Senate of thirty-one members and a House of Representatives of no more than one-hundred-fifty members. It stipulates the terms of office and qualifications. House members serve two-year terms, while senators serve four-year terms, half being elected every two years. House members must be citizens of the United States, must be at least twenty-one years of age, and have resided in the state for two years and in their district for one year. Senators must be citizens of the United States, must be at least twenty-six years old, and must have resided in the state for five years and in their districts for one year. In addition, Article III provides for the selection of officers in both houses of the legislature, states when and for how long the legislature shall meet (Section 5), and explains how the legislative proceedings will be conducted (Sections 29–41) and how representative districts will be apportioned (Sections 25, 26, and 28).

Like Article I, Texas's Bill of Rights, Article III moves well beyond the U.S. Constitution, putting limits on what the legislature can do. For example, it puts limits on what legislators may receive in salary and makes it difficult to increase that salary. Not only does it stipulate the mileage and per diem that members will receive while serving in the legislature (Section 24), Article III also creates a bipartisan Texas Ethics Commission whose job it is to recommend salary increases for members of the legislature. Significantly, even their recommendations are subject to approval by the people in a referendum, something that has proven difficult to achieve. Article III, Section 49(a), also subjects the legislature to the actions of the Comptroller of Public Accounts, whose duty is to prepare a report prior to the legislative session on the financial condition of the state treasury and to provide estimates as to future expenditures of the state. This provision of the Constitution effectively subjects the state legislature to the financial calculations and endorsements of the Comptroller, a check on the legislature all but unimaginable to the writers of the U.S. Constitution.

Putting constraints on certain legislative actions is only part of the story. The largest portion of Article III (Sections 47–64) is dedicated to addressing a variety of policy problems, including lotteries, emergency service districts, the problem of debt creation, problems surrounding the Veterans' Land Board and the Texas Water Development Board, Texas park development, the creation of a state medical education board, and even the establishment of an economic development fund in support of the now defunct superconducting supercollider.

ARTICLE IV: EXECUTIVE DEPARTMENT

Article II of the U.S. Constitution concentrates executive power in the presidency. The desire was to create a more effective and more responsible executive than had been possible under the Articles of Confederation. In contrast, Article IV of the Texas Constitution states that the executive shall consist of six distinct offices: the Governor, who serves as the chief executive; the Lieutenant Governor, who serves as the president of the Senate; the Secretary of State, who keeps the official seals of the state; the Comptroller of Public Accounts; the Commissioner of the General Land Office; and the Attorney General, who acts as the state's chief legal officer. With the exception of the Secretary of State, who is appointed by the Governor and approved by the Senate, all other offices are elected by qualified voters every four years. Besides creating a **plural executive**, Article IV guarantees its members will have independent political bases in the electorate. This provides an additional check against any concentration of powers in the hands of any one person.

plural executive
an executive branch in which power is fragmented because the election of statewide officeholders is independent from the governor

ARTICLE V: JUDICIAL DEPARTMENT

Article III of the U.S. Constitution succinctly provides for a supreme court and empowers Congress to create any necessary lower courts. Nothing could be further from the detailed discussion of the state courts found in Article V of the Texas Constitution. Besides creating one supreme court to hear civil cases and one court of criminal appeals to hear criminal cases, Article V provides for such lesser courts as courts of appeal, district courts, commissioner's courts, and justice of the peace courts, and empowers the legislature to establish other courts as deemed necessary. It also goes into such details as the retirement and compensation of judges, the jurisdictions of the various courts, as well as the duties of judges, what to do in the case of court vacancies, and a series of discussions on particular issues involving the lower courts.

An even greater difference between the Federal Constitution's treatment of the courts and Texas's Constitution is the crucial role given to elections. Federal judges are appointed by the executive and approved by the Senate. In Texas, the people elect state judges. Nine supreme court and nine court of criminal appeals judges are elected at large in the state. Lower court positions are elected by their relevant geographic locations. Much like the U.S. Constitution, the Texas Constitution seeks to create an independent judiciary that can check and balance the other two branches of government. But it seeks an additional check as well. It wants the people to watch over the court.

ARTICLE VI: SUFFRAGE

Article VI contains a short but detailed discussion about who may vote in Texas. It also empowers the legislature to enact laws regulating voter registration and the selection of electors for president and vice president.

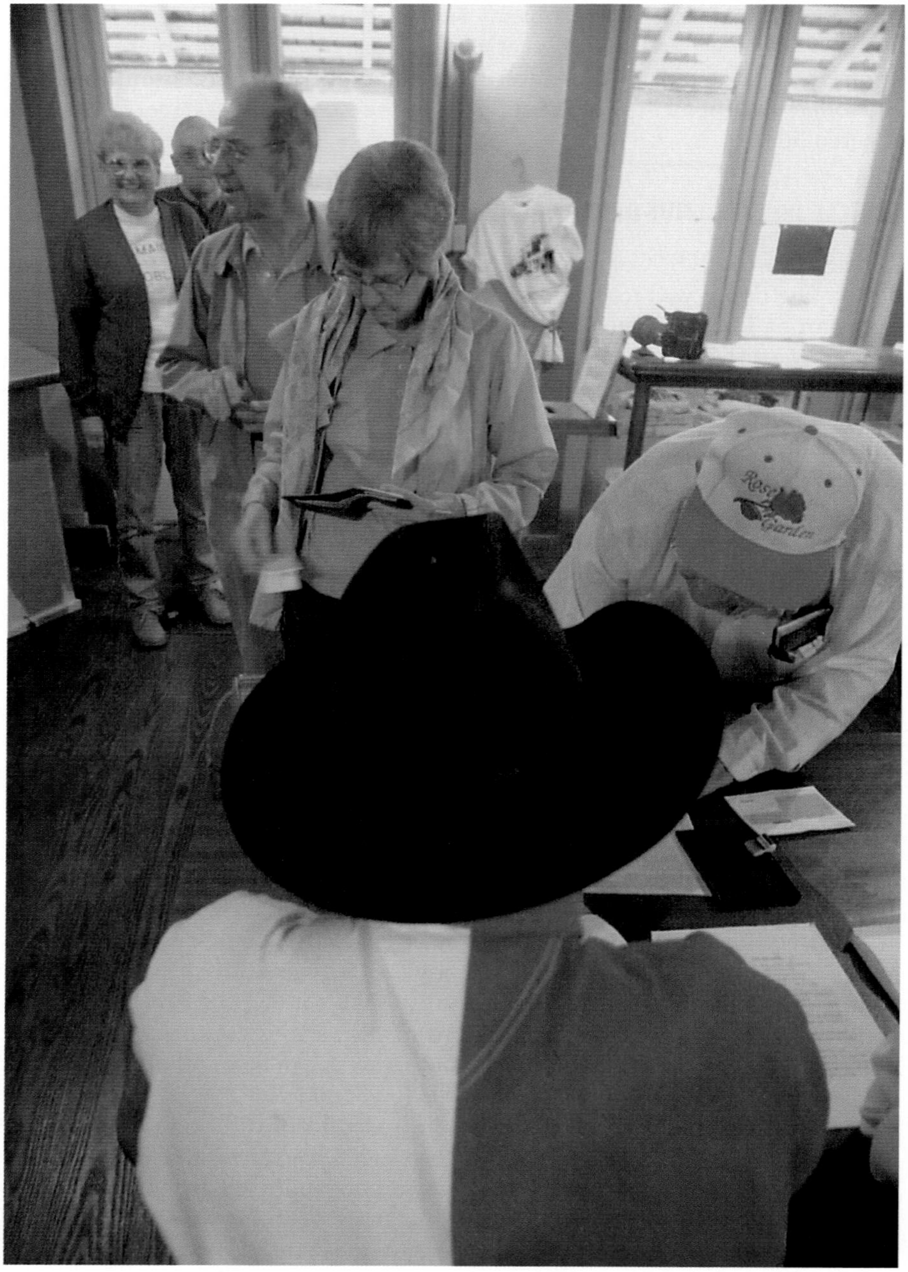

Article VI of the Texas Constitution establishes who can vote and grants the Texas legislature power to regulate voter registration and the selection of electors.

ARTICLE VII: EDUCATION

The concerns found in the Texas Declaration of Independence over the need for public schools to promote a republican form of government are directly addressed in Article VII. Section 1 makes it a duty of the state legislature to support and maintain "an efficient system of public free schools." Sections 2–8 provide for their funding and the creation of a State Board of Education to oversee the operations of elementary and secondary education in the state. State universities are the subject of over half of Article VII, where detailed discussions of the funding and operations of particular state institutions are put directly into the text.

ARTICLE VIII: TAXATION AND REVENUE

The complex issue of taxation is the subject of Article VIII. Once again we find a highly detailed account of a series of important policy issues built directly into the text of the constitution. One of the most controversial issues found in the Texas Constitution centers around the issue of the income tax. Section 1 enables the legislature to tax the income of individuals and businesses. This power, however, is subject to Section 24, which was passed by the 73rd legislature in 1993. Section 24 requires that the registered voters in the state approve a personal income tax and that the proceeds from this tax be dedicated to education and tax relief. As with other portions of the constitution, the net effect of these provisions is to seriously curtail what the state legislature can do and how it is able to do it. If Section 24 of Article VIII is any indication, the public fear of unresponsive and potentially tyrannical government was as alive in the 1990s as it was in 1876.

ARTICLES IX AND XI: LOCAL GOVERNMENT

These articles provide highly detailed discussions of the creation, organization, and operation of counties and municipal corporations.

ARTICLES X, XII, XIII, AND XIV

These heavily revised articles deal with a series of specific topics: the railroads (X), private corporations (XII), Spanish and Mexican Land Titles (XIII), and public lands (XIV). Article X empowers the state to regulate railroads and to establish the Railroad Commission. Article XII empowers the state to create general laws creating private corporations and protecting the public and individual stockholders. Article XIII, now entirely deleted from the constitution, dealt with the nineteenth-century issue of Spanish and Mexican land titles. Article XIV created a General Land Office to deal with the registration of land titles.

ARTICLE XV: IMPEACHMENT

Impeachment is, in the U.S. Constitution, one of the major checks Congress holds against both the executive and judicial branches of government. The House of Representatives holds the power to impeach an individual; the Senate is responsible for conducting trials. A two-thirds vote in the Senate following impeachment by the House leads to the removal of an individual from office.

impeachment
the formal charge by the House of Representatives that a government official has committed "Treason, Bribery, or other high Crimes and Misdemeanors"

A similar process is provided for in Article XV of the Texas Constitution. The House has the power to impeach. The Senate has the power to try the governor, lieutenant governor, attorney general, land office commissioner, and comptroller, as well as judges of the supreme court, the courts of appeal, and district courts. Conviction requires a two-thirds vote of the senators present. In contrast to the U.S. Constitution, all officers against whom articles of impeachment are preferred are suspended from their office. The governor is empowered to appoint a person to fill the vacancy until the decision on impeachment is reached.

Despite these similarities with the impeachment procedures in the U.S. Constitution, the Texas Constitution has its own caveats. The supreme court has original jurisdiction to hear and determine whether district court judges are competent to discharge their judicial duties. The governor may also remove judges of the supreme court, courts of appeal, and district courts when requested by the two-thirds vote of each legislature. Significantly, the reasons for removing a judge in this case need not rise to the level of an impeachable offense, but only involve a "willful neglect of duty, incompetence, habitual drunkenness, oppression in office, or other reasonable cause" (Article XV, Section 8). The barriers to removing a judge by political means are thus, at least on paper, much lower in Texas than in national government.

In 1980, Section 9 was added to Article XV, providing a new way to remove officials appointed by the governor. With the advice and consent of two-thirds of the members of the senate present, a governor may remove an appointed public official. If the legislature is not in session, the governor is empowered to call a special two-day session to consider the proposed removal.

ARTICLE XVI: GENERAL PROVISIONS

Article XVI is one of the lengthiest in the Texas Constitution and has no parallel in the U.S. Constitution. It is literally a catchall article grappling with a variety of issues ranging from official oaths of office to community property to banking corporations and stock laws to the election of the Texas Railroad Commission to the state retirement systems. Here, perhaps more than anywhere else, we see the complexity and confusion of the philosophy of Texas's Constitution come to the foreground.

ARTICLE XVII: AMENDING THE CONSTITUTION

Like the U.S. Constitution, the Texas Constitution explicitly delineates how it can be amended. Essentially, it establishes a four-stage process: First, the legislature must meet either in regular or special session and propose amendments. Second, these amendments must be approved by a two-thirds vote of all the members elected to each house. Third, a brief statement explaining the amendments must be published twice in each recognized newspaper in the state that meets the publication requirements for official state notices. Finally, the amendments must be approved by a majority of the state voters (see Box 21.2).

Recent Attempts to Amend the Texas Constitution

- What was the rationale for attempting to amend the Constitution in 1974 and 1999? What changes were proposed? Why did these attempts fail?

NOVEMBER 2, 1999, CONSTITUTIONAL AMENDMENT ELECTION

Box 21.2

Sample Ballot

No. 1 *"The constitutional amendment to revise the provisions for the filling of a vacancy in the office of governor or lieutenant governor."*
The proposed amendment would make clear that a lieutenant governor who becomes governor ceases to have the authority of the lieutenant governor's office. When a lieutenant governor permanently filled a vacancy in the governor's office, the state senate would elect one of its members to serve as lieutenant governor.

No. 2 *"The constitutional amendment relating to the making of advances under a reverse mortgage and payment of a reverse mortgage."*
This proposed amendment would eliminate conflicts between state law and federal guidelines regarding reverse mortgages, a device by which equity in homes can be used as supplemental income. Under current law, borrowers are not generally required to repay the money until death or moving from the home. Such a provision makes it unlikely that lenders will make reverse mortgage loans.

No. 3 *"The constitutional amendment to eliminate duplicative, executed, obsolete, archaic, and ineffective provisions of the Texas Constitution."*
This proposed amendment would revise 64 constitutional provisions and eliminate 17 others. The resolution dealing with the affected provisions is 100 pages long and includes eliminating provisions in the constitution on aid to indigent and disabled Confederate soldiers and sailors and to give authority to the governor to protect the frontier from Indians and other hostiles. A related amendment was passed in 1997 that eliminated duplicate numbers in the Constitution and some obsolete amendments.

No. 4 *"The constitutional amendment to authorize the legislature to exempt property owned by institutions engaged primarily in public charitable functions from* ad valorem *taxation."*
Currently tax-exempt status requires that property be used "exclusively" for charitable functions. This amendment would allow exemptions for property owned by institutions engaged "primarily" in charitable functions.

No. 5 *"The constitutional amendment allowing state employees to receive compensation for serving as a member of a governing body of a school district, city, town or other local governmental district."*
State employees could, with this amendment, be paid for service on a school board or other local governmental body.

No. 6 *"The constitutional amendment increasing the maximum size of an urban homestead to 10 acres, prescribing permissible uses of urban homesteads, and preventing the overburdening of a homestead."*
This proposed amendment would increase the size of lots that are eligible for home equity loans, but it would eliminate separate business owners' homestead protection and would allow liens to be valid even if only part of the property is used as collateral in an equity loan.

No. 7 *"The constitutional amendment authorizing garnishment of wages for the enforcement of court-ordered spousal maintenance."*
Wages could be garnished for court-ordered spousal maintenance under this amendment. Currently garnishment is only allowed for payment of child support.

Box 21.2 NOVEMBER 2, 1999, CONSTITUTIONAL AMENDMENT ELECTION

No. 8 *"The constitutional amendment to provide that the adjutant general serves at the pleasure of the governor."*
The adjutant general is responsible for overseeing the Texas National Guard. The amendment would allow the adjutant general to be appointed and replaced by the governor at his will. It would also remove the constitutionally mandated term limits on the office of adjutant general.

No. 9 *"The constitutional amendment authorizing the legislature to create a judicial compensation commission."*
The amendment would create a nine member commission that would make recommendations on salaries for judges. The commission would be appointed by the governor and the recommendations would become law unless rejected by a majority of either the Texas House or Senate.

No. 10 *"The constitutional amendment to provide that the commissioner of health and human services serves at the pleasure of the governor."*
Term limits on the commissioner of health and human services would be removed under this amendment and the commissioner would serve at the pleasure of the governor. This would presumably create a closer working relationship between the governor and the official responsible for one quarter of all state spending.

No. 11 *"The constitutional amendment permitting a political subdivision to purchase nonassessable property and casualty insurance from an authorized mutual insurance company in the same manner that the political subdivision purchases life, health, and accident insurance."*
In 1986 an amendment was passed allowing public funds to be used to pay for non-assessable life, health or accident insurance policies. This amendment would add property and casualty insurance to the list.

No. 12 *"The constitutional amendment to authorize the legislature to exempt from* ad valorem *taxation leased motor vehicles not held by the lessee primarily to produce income."*
The amendment would exempt leased vehicles for personal use from *ad valorem* taxes, providing the same tax break as exists for purchased vehicles.

No. 13 *"The constitutional amendment providing for the issuance of $400 million in general obligation bonds to finance educational loans to students."*
This proposed amendment would allow for the issuance of $400 million in bonds to finance student loans.

No. 14 *"The constitutional amendment authorizing the legislature to provide that a state board, commission or other agency shall be governed by a board composed of an odd number of three or more members."*
This proposed amendment would limit the possibility of tie votes by having an odd number of board and commission members.

No. 15 *"The constitutional amendment permitting spouses to agree to convert separate property to community property."*
With this amendment, spouses could convert separate property into joint property. This would offer more flexibility for managing family assets and possibly

NOVEMBER 2, 1999, CONSTITUTIONAL AMENDMENT ELECTION Box 21.2

offer better tax breaks and estate planning for married couples. At the same time, if a marriage is dissolved, the spouse who converted separate property into joint property would likely see the property divided in half.

No. 16 *"The constitutional amendment to provide that certain counties shall be divided into a specific number of precincts."*

This proposed amendment raises the population brackets used by counties to determine the number of justice of the peace and constable precincts in the county. Counties with populations between 18,000 and 50,000 would have between two and eight precincts. Counties with populations of 50,000 or more would have from between four and eight precincts.

No. 17 *"The constitutional amendment relating to the investment of the permanent university fund and the distribution from the permanent university fund to the available university fund."*

Under this amendment, fund distributions would be determined by the Board of Regents and would be governed by more flexible investment rules.

Final Results of 1999 Vote Texas Amendments

1. Succession Yes 74.1%
2. Reverse mortgages Yes 64.2%
3. Archaic provisions Yes 76.7%
4. Exemption for primarily charitable Yes 51.9%
5. Allow state employees to be paid No 54.6%
6. 10 acre homestead Yes 67.5%
7. Garnishment for alimony Yes 67.5%
8. Adjutant general at governor's discretion No 52.6%
9. Salary commission No 59.0%
10. Health and human services appointed No 52.1%
11. Insurance Yes 62.3%
12. Leased vehicles Yes 57.2%
13. College loans Yes 71.1%
14. Odd number of members Yes 73.2%
15. Community property Yes 67.4%
16. Flexibility in determining JPs and constables Yes 64.0%
17. Regents more flexible Yes 61.2%

SOURCES: "Constitutional Amendment Election, Collin County, Texas, November 2, 1999, Sample Ballot," Collin County Courthouse, McKinney, Texas. Descriptions of the proposed amendments are from Dave Simmons, "Texans Can Change Constitution," *McKinney Courier-Gazette,* Nov. 2, 1999, p. 1.

Given the difficulty of amending the state constitution, a surprising number of amendments have been proposed since 1876. A considerable number of these have been turned down in the popular vote. As Table 21.1 on the next page shows, demands for amending the Constitution have intensified in recent years, as legislators have grappled with the problem of making changes in public policy while being constrained by an unwieldy constitutional document.

Table 21.1 AMENDING THE TEXAS CONSTITUTION

The Constitution of Texas has been amended 377 times since its inception in 1876.

Years	Number proposed	Number adopted	Average number adopted per session
1879–1900	31	17	1.62
1901–1920	55	21	2.10
1921–1940	91	47	4.70
1941–1960	78	59	5.90
1961–1980	151	98	9.80
1981–1997	163	135	15.0
Totals	569	377	

SOURCE: Texas Legislative Reference Library

SHARPSTOWN AND THE FAILED CONSTITUTIONAL REFORMS OF 1974

A drive to rewrite the Texas Constitution grew out of a major stock fraud that broke in the early 1970s, involving the Sharpstown State Bank and the National Bankers Life Insurance Corporation. Following the 1970 elections, which had been dominated, as generally was the case, by the conservative wing of the Democratic Party, a suit was filed in Dallas federal court. Attorneys for the Securities and Exchange Commission alleged that a number of influential Democrats, including Governor Preston Smith, state Democratic chairman and state banking board member Elmer Baum, Speaker of the House Gus Mutscher, and others had been bribed. By the fall of 1971, Mutscher and two of his associates had been indicted. On March 15, 1972, they were convicted and sentenced to five years' probation.

The convictions fueled a firestorm in the state to "throw the rascals out." During the 1972 elections "reform" candidates dominated the Democratic primary and the general election. Conservative rancher-banker Dolph Briscoe became governor, but only by a plurality, making him the first governor in the history of the state not to receive a majority of the popular vote. Other reform-minded candidates like William P. Hobby, Jr., and John Hill were successful. Hobby won the lieutenant governor's race, while Hill became attorney general, defeating the three-term Democratic incumbent Crawford C. Martin. When the smoke had cleared, half of the House seats were occupied by new members and the Senate had witnessed a higher than normal rate of turnover. The elections had one other outcome: an amendment was passed empowering the legislature to sit as a constitutional convention whose task would be to rewrite the Constitution.[13]

The constitutional convention convened on January 8, 1974, in Austin. The idea was for the convention to draft a new constitution that would then be presented to the voters of the state for ratification. Originally scheduled to last 90 days, the convention was extended to 150 days. Even then there was not enough time. Bitter politics coupled with the intense demands of highly mobilized special interests made it impossible to reach the necessary agreement. In the end, proponents of a new constitution failed to achieve a two-thirds majority by three votes (118–62 with 1 abstention).

The movement to rewrite the constitution did not die at the convention. During the next session of the legislature, eight constitutional amendments were passed that would have effectively rewritten the Constitution through the normal amendment process. Each proposal, however, was turned down by the electorate in a special election on November 4, 1975 (see Box 21.3 on the next page). The Constitution of 1876 remained alive, if not well.

THE 1999 RATLIFF-JUNELL PROPOSAL

For the first time since the unsuccessful effort to revise the Constitution in the mid-1970s, state senator Bill Ratliff and state representative Rob Junell, both powerhouses in the state legislature, proposed a new constitution for Texas in 1999. Ratliff argued, "It's time for Texas to have a constitution that's appropriate for the twenty-first century." They were concerned that the 1876 Constitution was too restrictive and cumbersome for modern government. For example, it has over 90,000 words and has been amended 377 times. It is

Senator Bill Ratliff and Representative Rob Junell have proposed rewriting the Texas constitution.

Box 21.3 REWRITING THE 1876 CONSTITUTION

"It was 25 years ago that the sound of the gavel at 12 noon, January 8, 1974, echoed through the Texas House of Representatives Chamber. [Lieutenant Governor] Bill Hobby called to order the first constitutional convention held in almost 100 years. This was the first time the 181 members of the Texas House and Senate met as a single body as delegates to a constitutional convention.

"As I walked across the convention floor on that day to nominate my controversial friend, Price Daniel Jr., as president of the convention, I was full of hope for a new day for Texas. During the 1973 legislative session Daniel had served as speaker of the Texas House. He played a major role in passing legislation that cleaned up state government after the Sharpstown bank scandal that occurred during the 1971 legislative session. He had made a lot of enemies in the process; many sitting in the convention as delegates. Lobbyists and their legislative minions did not like Price.

"But on that day optimism prevailed. The crowded balconies, the press of people on the convention floor and the pageantry and solemnity of the opening ceremonies were, hopefully, the rising curtain on a new era of state government. Price and I were both only 33 years old and in the full spring of our lives.

"Six months later, on the last night of the convention, tempers were flaring across the convention floor. The balconies were crowded with lobbyists threatening delegates if they voted for the constitution. Additional security guards were called out, as well as Department of Public Safety patrolmen.

"At 11:31 P.M. on July 30, the last night of the convention, I stood at the front microphone and laid out the final draft of a proposed constitution. From July 11 to July 30 I had presented 32 different versions of a proposed constitution, none of which had received the necessary two-thirds vote requirement. This was our last chance. For 28 minutes, the vote was held open as we tried to secure enough votes. At 11:59 P.M., Price cracked down the gavel, crushing the dreams we had for a new constitution. The final vote of 118 to 62 was three votes shy of the two-thirds requirement.

"The following year, 1975, under the leadership of [Lieutenant Governor] Hobby and House Speaker Bill Clayton, D-Plainview, the Legislature submitted the constitution drafted by the convention to the people on an article by article basis. Immediately, the lobbyists began to organize to defeat the proposed articles. The AFL-CIO opposed two of the articles. The business lobby opposed other articles. They found it difficult to educate their followers on which specific one to vote against. They came to the conclusion that it was easier to scratch each others' backs, combine their forces and oppose all of the articles.

"Along with [Lieutenant Governor] Hobby, Attorney General John Hill and Price Daniel Jr., we organized a pro-constitution group; but we were unable to convince voters to support the new constitution. It did not cut taxes, did not bestow any financial benefit for any specific cause and did not give any goodies to any special interest. There simply was no selfish reason to be for it—only the hope for a better framework of state government.

"Twenty days before the vote, [Governor] Dolph Briscoe announced that he would vote against all 11 articles. That was the death blow. All the articles were defeated on November 4, 1975."

SOURCE: Nelson W. Woolf, "So You Want to Write a New Texas Constitution," *Houston Chronicle*, January 17, 1999, Outlook section, p. 1.

divided into 376 sections. It is a document that is lengthy, cluttered, and disorganized. The document has become so chaotic that in 1999 a constitutional amendment was proposed "to eliminate duplicative, executed, obsolete, archaic, and ineffective provisions" in the Constitution.

Among the major Ratliff-Junell proposals were that the governor would be given the authority to appoint several state officeholders who are now elected. Additionally, the executive branch would be reorganized so that the governor would have an appointed cabinet of department heads, subject to senate confirmation, much like the U.S. president. With their proposal, only the lieutenant governor, the attorney general, and the state comptroller would be elected.

The governor would get the constitutional authority to intervene in any lawsuits where the state is a party. Currently, the governor cannot commute death sentences without a recommendation from the Board of Pardons and Paroles. The proposed constitution would give the governor the power to commute death sentences. The governor would also be given the power to appoint all appellate and district judges. Afterward, the judges would be subject to voter approval in retention elections—where they have no opponent on the ballot, but where voters are asked if they wish to retain the appointed judge in office for a specified time period. Ratliff argued that the changes would make the governor more accountable for how state government works.

In reference to the legislature, it would remain part-time and would continue to meet in regular session every other year. However, a salary commission would be created that could raise legislative pay, currently $7,200 a year, without voter approval. Other salaries would also be raised. For example, the lieutenant governor's salary, also $7,200 a year, would be raised to the governor's level, which is currently $115,345 a year. The speaker of the house also has a salary of $7,200 a year and it would be set at 90 percent of the governor's salary. The speaker would then be prohibited from holding any other full-time, salaried employment.

State senators' terms are four-year terms and state representatives' terms are two-year terms. These terms would be increased to six years for state senators and four years for state representatives. For the first time, there would also be term limits so that representatives' service would be limited to eight regular sessions in the House or sixteen years in office and nine regular sessions in the Senate or eighteen years in office. Under this proposed constitution, the legislature would convene in a special fifteen-day "veto session," in order to consider overriding any gubernatorial vetoes from previous sessions.

While county government would remain as it is today, local voters would be given the authority to abolish their own obsolete offices without statewide approval through constitutional amendments.

Other parts of the proposed constitution would merge the Texas Supreme Court and the Texas Court of Criminal Appeals into a single court of fifteen justices. The merged court would have a single chief justice. Only the University of Texas at Austin, Texas A&M at College Station, and Prairie View A&M would receive funds from the Permanent University Fund. Other universities would receive funding from a separate fund. Provisions on home equity loans would be simplified. Marriage would be defined to include only heterosexual marriages.

Even as it was proposed, its sponsors realized that it would be tough to pass. And they were right—the proposed constitution did not pass, but suffered the fate of earlier efforts to change the 1876 Constitution.

Politics on the Web

The Web has opened up new sources of information, providing average citizens with information about public affairs that a generation ago was only available to professional activists inside and outside government. The Web has become a resource for educating the citizenry.

Nothing demonstrates the contributions that the Web can make to civic education in Texas better than the online introduction of the Texas Constitution. A complex and lengthy document that has been amended almost four-hundred times, the constitution is difficult to read, much less to understand. Prior to the advent of the Internet, the complete text of the constitution was printed in the *Texas Almanac,* with over sixty-seven pages and a lengthy index. Mastering the constitution was a cumbersome, if not impossible task for the average citizen. Now, instead, the text of the constitution is reproduced on a state-sponsored Web site that contains a search function that allows one to explore the various themes in the document more systematically. While the Internet may not have made the Constitution a more succinct document, it has made it a little easier for the average citizen to read and understand.

www.wwnorton.com/wtp3e

There is much to praise about the Ratliff-Junell proposal. For example, it provides more reasonable compensation for public officials, and it creates a more accountable executive branch. Yet, the Ratliff-Junell proposal operates with a mindset similar to that of the framers of the 1876 Constitution. That is the notion that it is appropriate to place solutions to immediate concerns in a constitution, rather than allowing a constitution to be a broad, flexible document that allows each generation the freedom to develop their own policies. Thus, the heterosexual marriage provision would seem inappropriate for a constitution. Similarly, it would seem that the term limits provision is a response to an immediate political issue that may not be the kind of basic concept of government needed in a fundamental document such as a constitution.

It should be added that many people see some desirable things in the Texas Constitution. Like many state constitutions, the Texas Constitution has a Bill of Rights. Nor are all the rights in the Texas Bill of Rights merely a duplication of the rights in the U.S. Constitution. To some extent, the Texas Bill of Rights provides more constitutional protections than does the U.S. Constitution. State constitutions may do this under the doctrine of independent state grounds. That is, while a state constitution may provide more rights than the U.S. Constitution, it may not take away rights granted by the U.S. Constitution. One may think of the U.S. Constitution as a baseline to which states can add, but not subtract, protections. One of the most interesting Texas rights is an amendment adopted in 1972. It states, "Equality under the law shall not be denied or abridged because of sex, race, color, creed, or national origin. This amendment is self-operative." Although not the subject of much litigation, it should be noted that this amendment provides explicit protection from sex discrimination, something that is not mentioned in the U.S. Constitution. It is, in fact, a state version of the federal Equal Rights Amendment, which was almost ratified in the 1970s, but which never quite received sufficient support from the states to become a part of the U.S. Constitution.

Still, in spite of its positive aspects, the Texas Constitution is a lengthy, confusing, and highly restrictive document. Yet, efforts to drastically change the document seem doomed to failure. There is little public outcry over the large numbers of confusing amendments on which the public regularly must cast ballots. Additionally, the Constitution provides protections for the interests of key groups in Texas society, groups that are reluctant to give up those protections in exchange for a more flexible document.

Summary

In this chapter we have explored the history of constitutional government in Texas. We have analyzed the seven constitutions under which Texas has been governed and explained the similarities and differences between the U.S. Constitution and Texas's current constitution (the Constitution of 1876). We also discussed attempts over the past thirty years to replace this constitution with a new one.

A number of themes are emphasized. First, Texas's current constitution is a lengthy document far more complex than its predecessors or the U.S. Constitution. Matters that are considered public policy in most other states often must be addressed as constitutional issues in Texas. Second, the Texas Constitution is based upon a general distrust of politicians and political power. It was originally written to prevent the expansion of political power that had taken place during Reconstruction and to make sure that political power could not be centralized in such a way that it might hurt the liberties and civil rights of the people. By limiting and decentralizing power, the Texas Constitution makes it difficult to exercise power effectively without being able to maintain extraordinary majorities in a variety of political arenas. Third, the Texas Constitution has been a difficult document to replace. Although amended almost four hundred times, it has not been replaced by a new one. It appears unlikely that it will be replaced in the future. Part of the reason for this is that it has proven difficult to mobilize support for a wholesale reworking of the constitution. Another part of the reason is that the general distrust of government and political power that gave birth to the Constitution of 1876 continues to hold sway among the citizenry.

FOR FURTHER READING

Kinkaid, John. *State Constitutions in a Federal System.* Newbury Park, CA: Sage Publications, 1988.

Maddex, Robert L. *State Constitutions in the United States*. Washington, DC: Congressional Quarterly Press, 1998.

May, Janice C. *The Texas State Constitution: A Reference Guide*. Westport, CT: Greenwood Press, 1996.

McKay, Seth S. *Seven Decades of the Texas Constitution of 1876*. Lubbock, TX: Texas Technological College Press, 1943.

Miller, Laurence. "The Texas Constitution." *Texas Politics: A Reader*, 2nd ed. Anthony Champagne and Edward J. Harpham (eds.). New York: Norton, 1998.

Tarr, G. Alan. *Understanding State Constitutions.* Princeton: Princeton University Press, 1998.

Wallace, Ernest, David M. Vigness, and George B. Ward. *Documents of Texas History*. Austin: State House Press, 1994.

STUDY OUTLINE

The Role of a State Constitution

1. State constitutions legitimize political institutions, delegate powers to agencies and institutions, and limit government.
2. Five ideas unite the U.S. and Texas political experience: political power is derived from the people, political power is divided into three separate branches of government, there is a system of checks and balances among the three branches, individual rights are guaranteed, and federalism.
3. Texas is subordinate to the national government through Article VI, the Supremacy Clause, of the U.S. Constitution.
4. Unlike the Texas Constitution, the U.S. Constitution has implied powers through the "necessary and proper clause."

The Constitution of *Coahuila y Tejas,* 1827

1. Under the Mexican Constitution local affairs were independent of the central government.
2. Texas was part of the Mexican state of Coahuila and Texas and elected two of twelve deputies to the unicameral state legislature.
3. The Constitution of 1827 guaranteed citizens' rights to liberty, security, property, and equality. It also supported efforts to limit slavery.

The Constitution of the Republic of Texas, 1836

1. This constitution closely resembles the U.S. Constitution and is known as the Constitution of the Republic of Texas.
2. Texans borrowed from Spanish-Mexican law to include the ideas of community property, homestead exemptions, and debtor relief in the new constitution.
3. Slavery flourished under this constitution.

The Texas State Constitution of 1845

1. The Constitution of 1845 was adopted when Texas was admitted to the United States.
2. Under the resolution adopted by the U.S. Congress in 1845, which admitted Texas to the Union, Texas gave all military armaments, bases, and facilities meant for public defense to the United States, retained its public land and public debts, was given permission to divide itself into four additional states (a total of five states), and was permitted to fly its state flag at the same height as the U.S. flag.
3. Slavery was permitted under this document.
4. The organization of state government was similar to that provided for in the U.S. Constitution.

The Constitution of 1861: Texas Joins the Confederacy

1. This Constitution was adopted when Texas joined the Confederacy.
2. The Constitution of 1861 was comparable to the Constitution of 1845 except that the phrase "United States of America" was changed to "Confederate States of America."

The Constitution of 1866: Texas Rejoins the Union

1. This Constitution was adopted to meet the requirements of Reconstruction set by President Andrew Johnson, but was short lived.

The Reconstruction Constitution of 1869

1. This Constitution was adopted to meet the requirements of the Congressional Reconstruction Act of 1867.
2. The constitution accepted the Thirteenth and Fourteenth amendments to the U.S. Constitution.
3. Delegates never completed the task of drafting a constitution, but their efforts were published under military orders and became known as the Constitution of 1869.
4. This constitution expanded the powers of state government. Slavery was forbidden, equality before the law was recognized, and the relationship among the three branches of government was altered.
5. The governor was given immense power.

The Constitution of 1876

1. This is the present Texas Constitution, and its adoption marked the end of Reconstruction.
2. Those who wrote this document were committed to four major ideas: strong popular control of state government, limited power of state government, economy in government, and promotion of agrarian interests.
3. The constitution is long and detailed.

The Constitution of Texas Today

1. The Texas Constitution contains sixteen articles and has been amended over 377 times.
2. Unlike previous constitutions, this constitution severely limits the power of the governor and decentralizes executive authority.
3. The present constitution was written to prevent expansion of government authority and to prevent a political system that worked against the will of the people.
4. The Texas Bill of Rights is thought to be so important that it is contained in Article I of the Texas Constitution.

Recent Attempts to Amend the Texas Constitution

1. Major state officials, including the governor and speaker of the Texas House, were accused of being involved in a major stock fraud involving Sharpstown State Bank and National Bankers Life.
2. In 1972, reform candidates replaced many state legislators, the governor, the lieutenant governor, and the attorney general.
3. The legislature called a constitutional convention, which met in 1974, but after 150 days it was unable to find the two-thirds vote necessary to submit the constitution to the people.
4. In 1975, the legislature proposed a series of eight amendments that, if adopted, would give Texas a new constitution, but all were defeated.
5. In 1999, state senator Bill Ratliff and state representative Rob Junell proposed a new constitution for Texas.
6. Under the Ratliff-Junell proposal, the governor's power was strengthened, the terms of the members of the state legislature were increased, term limits for legislators were instituted, the Texas Supreme Court and the Texas Court of Criminal Appeals were merged, and the distribution of Permanent University Fund monies beyond the University of Texas at Austin, Texas A&M at College Station, and Prairie View A&M were limited.
7. The Ratliff-Junell proposal did not pass.

PRACTICE QUIZ

1. Which idea is contained in both the U.S. and Texas Constitutions?
   a) a supremacy clause
   b) federalism
   c) laissez-faire economics
   d) *Rebus sic stantibus*

2. Which of the following is *not* an important function of a state constitution?
   a) prevents the concentration of political power
   b) delegates power to individuals and institutions
   c) allows government to intrude into the lives of businesses and individuals
   d) legitimizes political institutions

3. Which part of the U.S. Constitution reserves power to the states?
   a) Article I
   b) Article VI
   c) First Amendment
   d) Tenth Amendment

4. Under the U.S. Constitution, the government of Texas is most limited by
   a) Article IV and Article VI of the U.S. Constitution.
   b) the implied powers clause and the Tenth Amendment.
   c) the U.S. Bill of Rights.
   d) its own sense of self-importance.

5. A unique feature of the Constitution of 1869 was
   a) fewer than one percent of voters opposed it.
   b) it was less than four pages long.
   c) it was never submitted to the voters.
   d) it is considered the best of Texas's constitutions.

6. A new Texas constitution was written
   a) when Reconstruction ended.
   b) when the Compromise of 1850 was adopted.
   c) at the start of World War I.
   d) in 1999.

7. The present Texas constitution
   a) is well organized and well written.
   b) is considered to be one of the best of the fifty state constitutions.
   c) delegates a great deal of power to the governor.
   d) severely limits the power of the governor and other state officials.

8. Those who wrote the Constitution of 1876 wanted to return control of government to the people. By this they meant
   a) all adult citizens of Texas.
   b) all adult male citizens of Texas.
   c) all adult white male citizens of Texas.
   d) all citizens except carpetbaggers and scalawags.

9. Article I of the Texas Constitution
   a) contains the Texas Bill of Rights.
   b) renounces the use of the death penalty.
   c) recognizes the supremacy of the national government.
   d) accepts the principal of *rapprochement.*

10. The likelihood of the voters ratifying a new constitution for Texas is
    a) likely before 2010.
    b) scheduled for a vote in 2004.
    c) 50–50.
    d) very small.

CRITICAL THINKING QUESTIONS

1. Consider the characteristics of the constitutions adopted prior to 1876. What were the major provisions of each? Which were incorporated into the present Texas Constitution? Why does the state constitution place so many limits on state government? What changes should be made to the constitution to increase its effectiveness?

2. How does the Supremacy Clause of the United States Constitution affect Texas government?

KEY TERMS

bicameral (p. 828)
Confederacy (p. 832)
confederation (p. 824)
constitution (p. 823)
federalism (p. 824)
Grange (p. 834)
impeachment (p. 841)
limited government (p. 836)
necessary and proper clause (p. 825)
plural executive (p. 839)
Radical Republicans (p. 833)
republican government (p. 837)
separation of powers (p. 838)
supremacy clause (p. 824)
unicameral (p. 826)

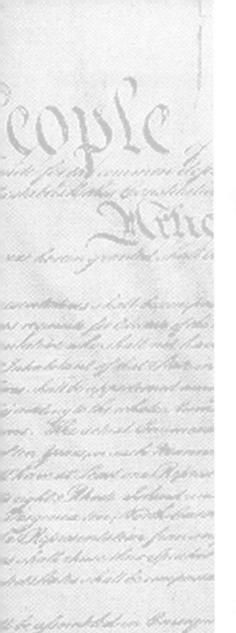

22 Parties and

★ **The Role of Political Parties in Texas Politics**

What are the important functions of political parties in Texas?
How are political parties organized in Texas?

★ **Texas's History as a One-Party State**

What is the history of the Democratic Party's dominance in Texas? How has the Republican Party's power and influence grown in recent decades? What are the current differences between Democrats and Republicans in Texas?

★ **Elections in Texas**

What are the types of elections held in Texas?

★ **Participation in Texas Elections**

Who can vote in Texas? How easy is it to register to vote? Why do few Texans vote? What will it take to increase voter participation in Texas?

★ **Campaigns**

What is the role of political parties in election campaigns in Texas?
What can candidates do to improve their chances of winning elections?

★ **Three Pivotal Elections**

What do the elections of John Tower to the U. S. Senate in 1961, William Clements to the governorship in 1978, and Ann Richards to the governorship in 1990 illustrate about changes in parties and elections in Texas?

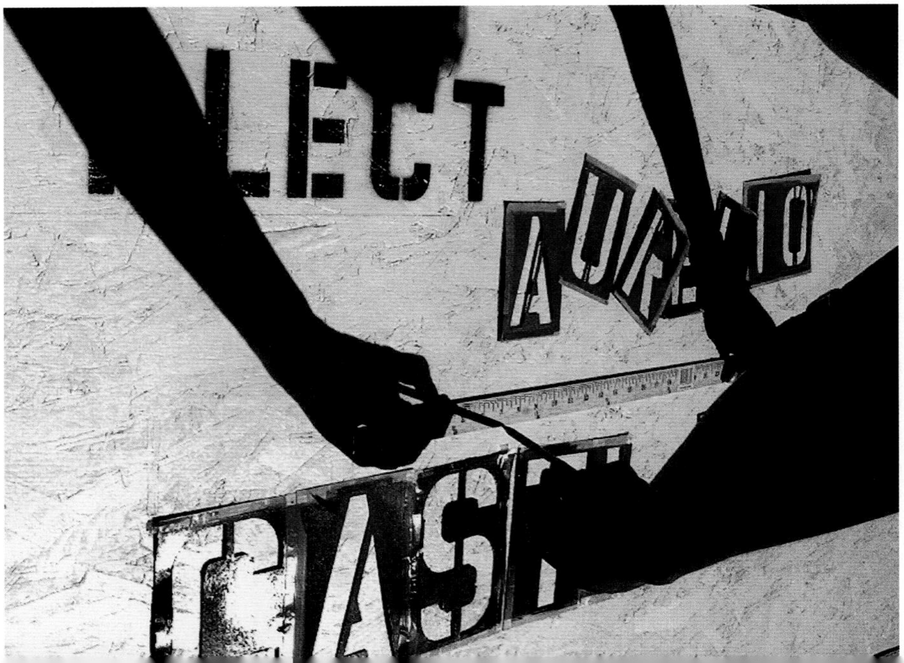

Elections in Texas

JOHN Nance Garner was one of the most important political figures Texas has ever produced. He served as a member of the House of Representatives for thirty years and was speaker of the house for two years. Following this, he served as vice president of the United States under Franklin Roosevelt for two terms.

When Garner was a congressman in 1921, he proposed that Texas be divided into several states. That could be done, he argued, because when Texas entered the Union in 1845, Congress included in its joint resolution the following provision:

> New States, of convenient size, not exceeding four in number, in addition to said State of Texas, and having sufficient population, may hereafter, by the consent of said State, be formed out of the territory thereof, which shall be entitled to admission under the provisions of the federal constitution.[1]

Texas was too big, claimed Garner, and its size affected politics in the state. Texas was so large, he said, that it would cost $12,000 "to circularize the state just once." A statewide campaign, he suggested, would cost $25,000 or even $50,000![2] Garner, of course, was talking in terms of 1921 dollars and 1921 campaigns, where television and other media costs did not exist and where most candidates only traveled by train.

He would be astounded at the costs and the effort required to run a statewide campaign in Texas today. And, he would be amazed as well that a modern statewide campaign would most likely involve Republicans—a term not mentioned in polite company in Texas politics in the Garner era.

The Role of Political Parties in Texas Politics

- What are the important functions of political parties in Texas?
- How are political parties organized in Texas?

Perhaps the most important function of parties in Texas is that they provide a label under which candidates may run and with which voters may identify. Since Texas elects very large numbers of officeholders, it is unlikely that voters will be familiar with the views or the qualifications of every candidate. However, over 60 percent of Texas voters do identify with either the Republican or

Democratic parties.[3] Those voters will use the party affiliation of the candidates as a way of deciding for whom they vote. Thus, for many voters, absent other information, the party label becomes the standard used in casting a ballot for a candidate. The party label is often used by voters as a cue to the ideology of candidates. A voter may assume that, for example, a Republican candidate is a "conservative" and may vote for or against that candidate because of the ideology that a party affiliation infers.[4]

Parties to some extent help in raising money for candidates' campaigns and in assisting candidates with legal requirements and with training for a campaign. They sometimes recruit candidates for political races, although in Texas any candidate may run in a party primary and if victorious in the primary, will become the party nominee. Parties also assist in "getting out the vote" for candidates through phone banks, door-to-door contacts, and other efforts.

Once a candidate is elected to office, party affiliation helps in organizing the government. Though the structure of the Texas legislature is largely nonpartisan, governors will usually appoint people who are members of their own party. Public officials may also feel a greater sense of loyalty and cooperation toward other public officials of their party. After all, they often campaign together and make appearances at the same political events, and their fortunes often rise and fall together based on the popularity of the party. In that sense, the banding together of officeholders with the same party affiliation provides voters an opportunity to hold the party accountable for its policies or its failures.

An election clerk waits for Republican voters to turn out for a Texas primary run-off election. When many candidates run for a party nomination it is possible that none will receive a majority vote, making a run-off between the two top vote-getters necessary.

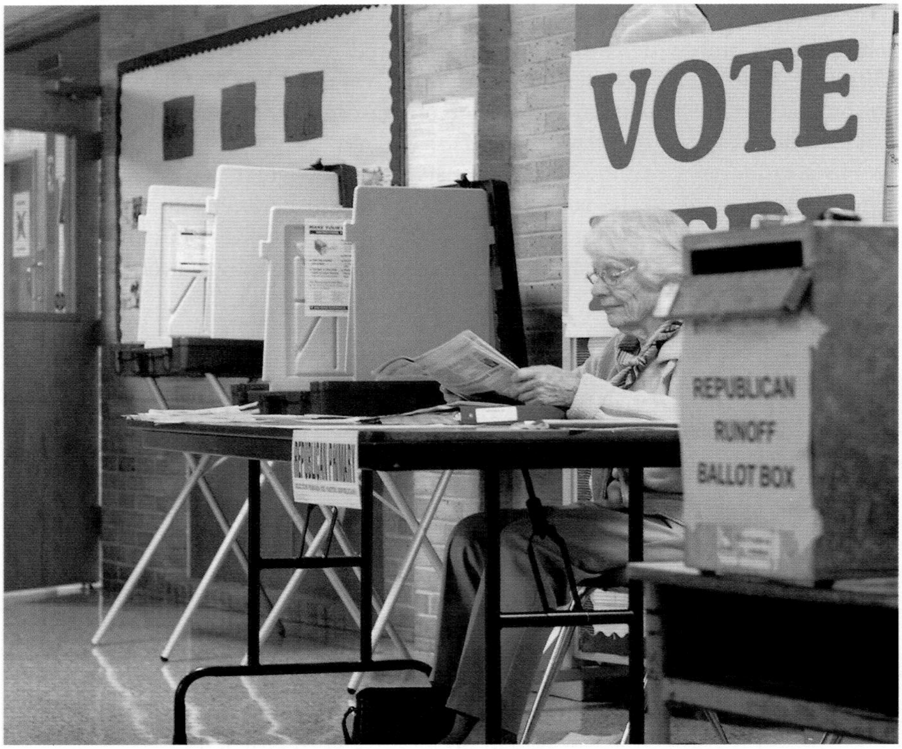

PARTY ORGANIZATION

Although it is common for Texans to proclaim that they are "registered Republicans" or "registered Democrats," Texas does not have a system of party registration for voters. Registered voters may vote in either the Democratic or Republican Party primary. When they do vote in a primary, their voter registration card will be stamped "Democrat" or "Republican" to prevent them voting in the other primary as well.

One of the most important functions of political parties is to select candidates to run for office under the party label. Today that is done through primary elections. If there are several candidates running for the party nomination in a primary election, it may be that none receive a majority vote. In that case, the party will hold a run-off election to determine who will be nominated. It was not always the case that primaries were used to select the party nominee. In the nineteenth century, candidates were nominated at party conventions, but early in this century the state moved to the primary as a way of selecting candidates.

In understanding how the parties are organized, it is best to think first in terms of the permanent organization of the party and then in terms of the temporary (campaign) organization (see Figure 22.1). In each election **precinct**, a **precinct chair** will be elected in the party primary. The precinct chair will head the precinct convention and will also serve on the party's **county executive committee**. In the primary, the **county chair** will also be elected. The county chair will head the county executive committee, which is composed of the

precinct
a local voting district

precinct chair
the local party official, elected in the party's primary election, who heads the precinct convention and serves on the party's county executive committee

county executive committee
the party group, made up of a party's county chair and precinct chairs, that is responsible for running a county's primary elections and planning county conventions

county chair
the county party official, elected in the party's primary election, who heads the county executive committee

PARTY ORGANIZATION IN TEXAS — Figure 22.1

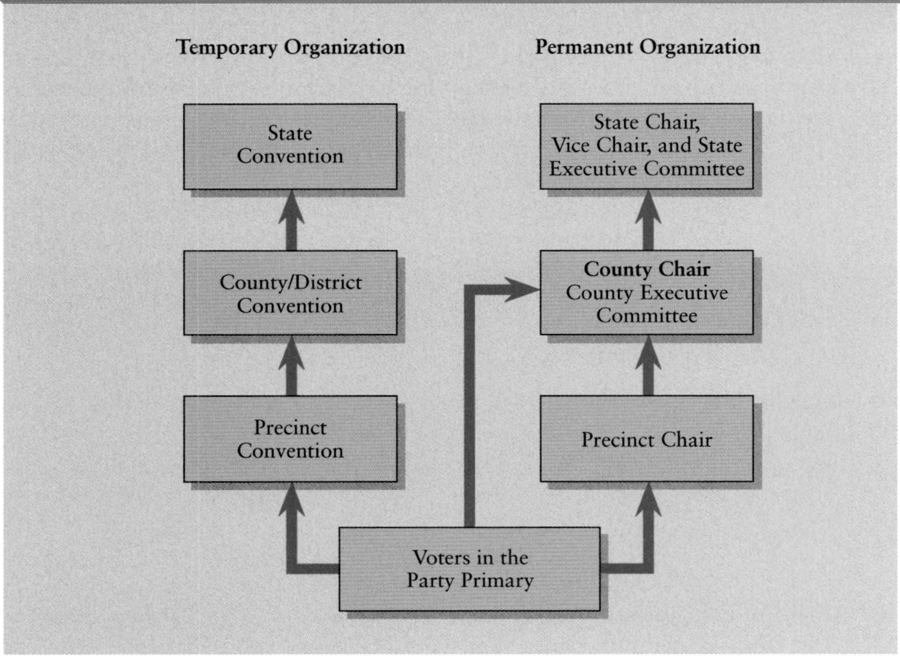

state executive committee
the committee responsible for governing a party's activities within the state, such as raising funds and establishing party policies; this committee includes the state chair and vice chair

state chair and vice chair
the party officials, elected every two years at the state convention, who serve as the top two state-level leaders in the party

precinct convention
a meeting held by a political party to select delegates for the county convention and to submit resolutions to the party's state platform; precinct conventions are held on the day of the party's primary election and are open to anyone who voted in that election

county convention
a meeting held by a political party following its precinct conventions, for the purpose of electing delegates to its state convention

state convention
a meeting held every two years by each of the major parties, for the purpose of nominating candidates for statewide office, adopting a platform, and electing the party's leadership. In presidential election years, the state convention also selects delegates for the national party convention and chooses presidential electors

chair and the precinct chairs. The main responsibility of the county executive committee is to run the county primary and plan the county conventions. There may be other district committees as well for political divisions that do not correspond to the county lines.

At the state level, there is a **state executive committee**, which includes a **state chair and vice chair**. These officers are selected every two years at the state party conventions. The state executive committee accepts filings by candidates for statewide office. It helps raise funds for the party and it helps establish party policy. Both the Democratic and Republican parties also employ professional staff to run day-to-day operations and to assist with special problems that affect the party.

The temporary organization of the party includes the **precinct conventions**. The main role of the precinct conventions is to select delegates to the **county convention** and possibly to submit resolutions that may eventually become part of the party platform.

Delegates chosen by the precinct convention then go to the county (or in urban areas, district) conventions. These conventions will elect delegates to the **state convention**. Both the Democratic and Republican parties hold state conventions every other year. These conventions certify the nominees of the party for statewide office, adopt a platform, and elect a chair, vice chair, and a state executive committee. In presidential election years, the state conventions select delegates for the national party conventions, elect delegates for the national party committee, and choose presidential electors who, if the party's choice for president carries the state in the election, will formally cast the state's electoral votes for the president in the electoral college.

Battles for control of a state party have often been fought in Texas politics, where rival ideological and other interest groups have struggled to control precinct, county, and state conventions and to elect their candidates for precinct chair, county chair, and state executive committee. In the 1950s, when loyal and liberal Democrats battled the Shivercrats for control of the Democratic Party, struggles for control of the party organization were great. There have also been calmer times in Texas politics, where involvement in the parties has been minimal and battles have been few. Sometimes, there has been such apathy that precinct conventions have been sparsely attended and offices such as precinct chair have gone unfilled.

Texas's History as a One-Party State

- What is the history of the Democratic Party's dominance in Texas?
- How has the Republican Party's power and influence grown in recent decades?
- What are the current differences betweeen Democrats and Republicans in Texas?

With the defeat of Republican governor E. J. Davis in 1873, Texas entered a period of Democratic dominance that would last for over a century. Often the Republican Party would not contest major state offices, and other parties—

such as the Populist or People's Party—though having some influence for brief periods, did not have staying power. In general elections, it was a foregone conclusion that the Democratic nominee would win. If there was a meaningful election contest, it was in the Democratic Party primary.

Republicans tended to have a limited role in Texas politics. Most commonly, people remained Republicans in the hope of gaining political patronage (usually local postmaster or rural mail carrier positions) when Republican presidents were in office. Some Republicans were business people unhappy with the liberal policies of Democratic presidents such as Franklin Roosevelt or Harry Truman. However, the Republican Party was not a threat to Democratic dominance in the state. Indeed, for Republicans interested in patronage from the national government, there may have been an incentive to keep the Republican Party small, since the fewer the Republicans, the less the competition for patronage positions. When the father of former senator Lloyd Bentsen first moved to the Rio Grande Valley, he visited with R. B. Creager, who was then state chairman of the Republican Party. Lloyd Bentsen, Sr., told Creager that he wanted to get involved in the Republican Party because his father had been a devoted Republican in South Dakota. Rather than welcoming Bentsen into the Republican Party, Creager told Bentsen, "You go back to Mission [Texas] and join the Democratic Party, because what's best for Texas is for every state in the union to have a two-party system and for Texas to be a one-party state. When you have a one-party state, your men stay in Congress longer and build up seniority."[5]

In 1952 and in 1956, however, Democratic governor Allan Shivers led a movement often known as the **Shivercrat movement,** which presaged a dramatic change in party alignments a quarter century later. Governor Shivers was a conservative Democrat and widely regarded as one of the most able Texas governors of the twentieth century. He supported the candidacy of Republican Dwight Eisenhower for the presidency against the Democratic

Shivercrat movement
a movement, led by Texas governor Allan Shivers during the 1950s, in which conservative Democrats in Texas supported Republican candidates for office because many of them believed that the national Democratic Party had become too liberal

Conservative Democratic governor Allan Shivers's party disloyalty in the 1950s expressed the philosophical differences between conservative Texas Democrats and the increasingly liberal national Democratic Party.

nominee Adlai Stevenson. Stevenson opposed the Texas position on the Tidelands, off-shore lands claimed by both Texas and the national government, which were believed to contain oil. Additionally, Stevenson was much more liberal than Shivers, and Eisenhower was a famous and popular hero of World War II. Not only did Governor Shivers support Eisenhower for the presidency, but Shivers and all statewide officeholders except the agriculture commissioner, John White, ran on the ballot as not only Democrats, but also Republicans. It was an act of party disloyalty condemned by loyal Democrats such as Speaker of the U.S. House of Representatives Sam Rayburn, and it led to much tension in the Democratic Party between liberal and conservative Democrats as well as between party loyalists and the Shivercrats.

The Shivercrat movement sent a strong message that many conservative Democrats were philosophically opposed to the national Democratic Party and, although they were unwilling to fully embrace the Republican Party, they found the Republican Party more compatible to their views. A pattern in voting known as **presidential Republicanism** was strengthening, where conservative Texas voters would vote Democratic for state offices, but vote Republican for presidential candidates. With the Shivercrat movement, those conservatives were more numerous and more closely aligned with the Republican Party.

presidential Republicanism
a voting pattern in which conservatives vote Democratic for state office, but Republican for presidential candidates

Still, in state elections, the Democratic Party was overwhelmingly the dominant party. There might be pockets of the state where Republicans showed strength. Traditionally, in the post–Civil War era, the "German counties" in the Texas Hill Country, which were settled by German immigrants, showed Republican leanings. Dallas County, whose voters were influenced by a powerful group of conservative businesspeople and a conservative newspaper, the *Dallas News*, showed early Republican strength, electing a very conservative Republican congressman in the 1950s. However, for the most part, the Democratic Party was so dominant in state elections that the Republican Party did not field opponents to the Democratic nominees.

During this era, the Democratic Party was a kind of umbrella party that held a variety of groups and interests. Liberals and conservatives belonged to the party as did members of labor unions and businesspeople, farmers and city dwellers. Often liberals and conservatives within the party battled for control of the party and its offices. But when liberals and conservatives were not engaged in periodic battles within the party, battles that occurred with considerable regularity, what political organization existed tended to be based on personal ties and personal popularity of individual candidates.

With the imposition of the poll tax and the white primary at the beginning of the century (discussed later in this chapter), stable factions ceased to exist in the Democratic Party. Earlier there were factions in Texas politics that reflected "have" and "have not" economic interests. However, until about the 1940s, Texas politics was often chaotic and confused. By about the mid-1940s, however, a liberal–conservative split developed in the Democratic Party that focused on New Deal economic policies and civil rights measures. This liberal–conservative split became a characteristic division within the Democratic Party, and liberals and conservatives battled in the party primaries. Between the mid-1940s and the mid-1970s, the victor in these primary squabbles would then go on to win the general election. However, by the late 1970s, the winner of the Democratic primary had to face a significant conservative challenge from Republicans in the general election.[6]

JAKE PICKLE* REMEMBERS THE DEMOCRATIC PARTY BATTLES OF THE 1950s

Box 22.1

Throughout the 1950s, the Texas Democratic Party was embroiled in a bitter controversy to determine who controlled the party—conservative Democrats headed by governors Allan Shivers and Price Daniel, or liberal Democrats such as Ralph Yarborough and labor leader Jerry Holleman. The controversy was so acrimonious that eventually even Speaker of the House Sam Rayburn and Senator Lyndon Johnson got involved.

"Believe it or not, back then the split between conservative and liberal Democrats was as sharp a rivalry as exists today between Democrats and Republicans. In Texas, it wasn't just a matter of political philosophy; it was a matter of loyalty. Conservative Democrats like Johnson, Rayburn, Shivers, and others intended to maintain control of 'their' party. Maintaining control was everything, because control meant votes, and votes meant legislation.

* * *

"As far as I'm concerned, in terms of acrimony the worst state Democratic convention was the one held in San Antonio in 1958. In San Antonio, Department of Public Safety officers, guns on hips, strolled the convention floor as an incentive for order. Still, when the votes were cast and the liberals lost, delegates swarmed into the convention hall orchestra pit and attempted to climb on stage. . . . [I]t fell to me to stand on stage and discourage people from breaching the ramparts! One stormer was former state senator Joe Hill from East Texas. Hill was short, portly, and had high blood pressure. There he was, huffing and puffing, his face pink as ham, trying to heave himself out of the orchestra pit onto the stage—and me. I didn't want to shove him off, or get in a fist fight. The only thing I could think to do was step on his fingers! As I scraped his fingers off the stage with my shoe I said politely, 'Sorry, Senator.'

"I consider myself a decent fellow, and although I don't think you could say I got ahead by stepping on people's toes, it *would* be accurate to say that in one instance I got ahead by stepping on people's fingers. Poor Joe Hill's, anyway."

*Jake Pickle was involved in Texas politics for much of his life. He served as a U.S. Congressman from Texas from December 1963 until his retirement in January 1995.

SOURCE: Jake Pickle and Peggy Pickle, *Jake* (Austin: University of Texas Press, 1997), pp. 70, 74–75.

THE GROWTH OF THE REPUBLICAN PARTY

One of the most important developments in Texas politics has been the growth of the Republican Party. In the 1950s, more than 60 percent of Texans identified with the Democratic Party and fewer than 10 percent identified themselves as Republicans. The remainder considered themselves independents. In the 1960s, Republican identification in Texas moved above 10 percent; Democratic identification remained above 60 percent; and identification with independents dropped slightly. The 1970s saw a decline in Democratic affiliation and an increase in Republican affiliation. That pattern of increase of Texans who identified themselves as Republicans and decline among those who identified themselves as Democrats accelerated in the 1980s. By 1994, the Texas

GROWTH OF THE REPUBLICAN PARTY IN TEXAS — Table 22.1

Year	U.S. Senate	Other statewide	U.S. House	Texas Senate	Texas House	County office	District office	School board	Total
1974	1	0	2	3	16	53	?		75+
1976	1	0	2	3	19	67	?		92+
1978	1	1	4	4	22	87	?		119+
1980	1	1	5	7	35	166	?		215+
1982	1	0	5	5	36	191	79		317
1984	1	0	10	6	52	287	90		446
1986	1	1	10	6	56	410	94		579
1988	1	5	8	8	57	485	123	5	692
1990	1	6	8	8	57	547	170	5	802
1992	1	8	9	13	58	634	183	5	911
1994	2	13	11	14	61	734	216	8	1059
1996	2	18	13	17	68	938	278	9	1343
1998	2	29	13	16	72	1098	280*	9	1519

*Estimated
SOURCE: Republican Party of Texas, www.texasgop.org/library/growth.html.

electorate was about equally divided among Democrats with 33 percent of the electorate; Republicans with 31 percent of the electorate; and independents with 36 percent.[7] The electorate may be almost equally divided between Republicans and Democrats, but Republicans have been better able than the Democrats to deliver offices to their party's candidates.

In the first quarter of the twentieth century the Republican Party was only a token party. In the state legislature, for example, Republicans never held more than one seat in the Texas Senate and never more than two seats in the Texas House from 1903–1927. From 1927–1951, there were no Republicans in the Texas legislature, and then a lone Republican was elected from Dallas to serve only one term in the Texas House. It was another decade before Republicans were again elected to the legislature, when two served in the Texas House. Then in 1962, six Republicans were elected to the House from Dallas County and one from Midland County. By 1963, there were ten Republicans in the Texas House and none in the Texas Senate.[8]

As Table 22.1 shows, as late as 1974, there were not many more than seventy-five Republican officeholders in the entire state of Texas. One of those officeholders was U.S. Senator John Tower and there were two Texas Republicans in the U.S. House of Representatives. There were no Republicans elected to state office in statewide elections. There were only three Republicans in the Texas Senate and only sixteen Republicans in the Texas House of Representatives. By 1998, both U.S. senators were Republican and thirteen members of the U.S. House of Representatives were Republican. A majority of the Texas Senate, sixteen of the thirty-one members, was Republican and seventy-two of the members of the Texas House of Representatives were Republican.

It was a record of remarkable Republican growth and Democratic Party decline. By 1998, every elected state official was Republican. That included the governor, the lieutenant governor, the attorney general, the comptroller, land

REPUBLICAN PRIMARY VOTING AS A PERCENTAGE OF DEMOCRATIC PRIMARY VOTING

Figure 22.2

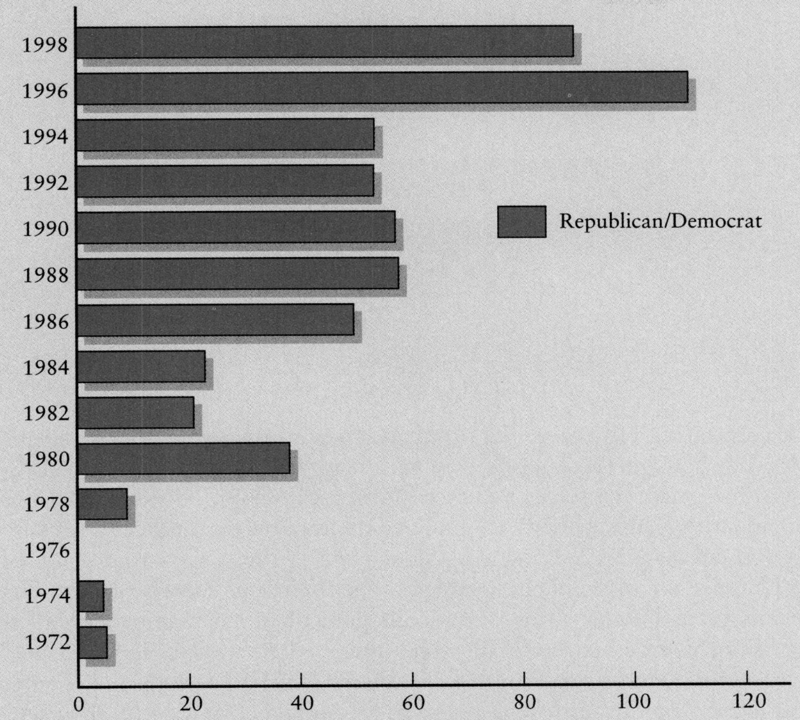

SOURCE: Republican Party of Texas, http://www.texasgop.org/library/growth.html.

commissioner, agriculture commissioner, all three members of the Texas Railroad Commission, and all nine members of both the Texas supreme court and the Texas court of criminal appeals. Only twenty years earlier, William Clements was the first state official elected as a Republican since Reconstruction. Still, as Figure 22.2 notes, more voters voted in the Democratic primary than in the Republican primary, though Republican primary participation has increased dramatically. It was only in 1996 that Republican primary participation in Texas was greater than Democratic primary participation.

CHARACTERISTICS OF REPUBLICANS AND DEMOCRATS IN TEXAS

There are significant differences between Republicans and Democrats in Texas. As Figure 22.3 on the next page shows, Texas Democrats identify themselves as significantly more liberal than do those who identify themselves as Republican or independent.

In addition, there are far more minorities who identify themselves as Democrats than identify themselves as Republicans. Only 5 percent of Texas African Americans identify themselves as Republicans and only 16 percent of Hispanics do so. On the other hand, 70 percent of Texas African Americans

Figure 22.3 IDEOLOGY OF TEXANS BY PARTY AFFILIATION

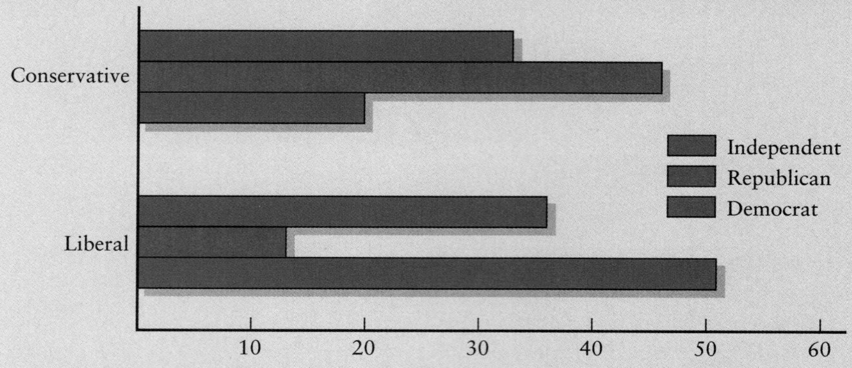

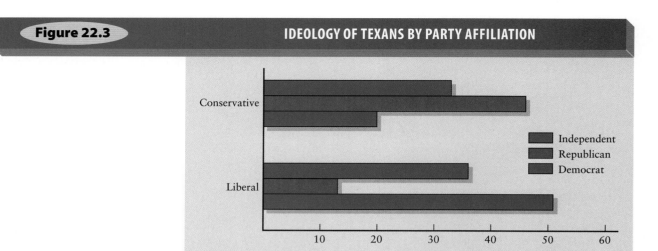

SOURCE: Dyer, Leighley, and Vedlitz, "Party Identification and Public Opinion in Texas," p. 114.

and 50 percent of Hispanics identify themselves as Democrats. Thirty-eight percent of the younger voting age population in Texas—those from eighteen to twenty-nine—see themselves as independents. However, 34 percent of this age group identify themselves as Republicans compared to only 29 percent who identify themselves as Democrats. Older people, those sixty-two years of age and older, are far more likely to identify themselves as Democrats than as Republicans or as independents. Forty-four percent of this age group call themselves Democrats compared to 30 percent who call themselves independents and 26 percent who identify as Republicans. Native Texans, perhaps in keeping with the old Democratic tradition in Texas, are more likely to identify themselves as Democrats than as Republicans or as independents: 38 percent of Native Texans call themselves Democrats; 34 percent call themselves independents; and 28 percent call themselves Republicans. On the other hand, newcomers to the state are much more likely to see themselves as either Republicans or as independents than as Democrats: 38 percent of people who have lived in Texas for less than ten years call themselves Republicans; 34 percent call themselves independents; and 27 percent call themselves Democrats. Lower income Texans are more likely to be Democrats, whereas upper income Texans are more likely to be Republicans. About 21 percent of Texans with incomes of $10,000 to $20,000 claim a Republican affiliation compared to about 38 percent who are Democrats. In contrast, nearly 46 percent of Texans with incomes over $60,000 are Republicans compared to about 20 percent who are Democrats.[9]

Within the Republican Party are two segments that have recently fought for control of the party. One segment is commonly called the Religious Right. This group includes religious conservatives who are especially concerned with social issues such as abortion, prayer in public schools and at school events, the teaching of evolution in public schools, and the perceived decline in family values. The other segment of the party is composed of economic conservatives. This group is primarily concerned with reduced government spending, lower taxes, and greater emphasis on free enterprise. These tensions have led to numerous intra-party battles, and it is this split in the Republican Party that is likely the greatest threat to continued Republican dominance of Texas politics. Professor Paul Lenchner describes well the importance of this division of the Republican Party:

> The significance of Republican fissures should not be underestimated. The party is being pulled in opposite directions. When it looks outward, the incentives are for relative moderation in trying to reach the vast pool of voters without consistent ideological views or a strong attachment to either major party. When it looks inward, there is pressure to hew firmly to the social conservative line. Somehow the party's leaders must convince the activists who control the state organization of the necessity of pragmatism in the political arena. In view of what we have seen at the party's recent state conventions, this is likely to be a daunting task.[10]

What are the implications of these data for the political parties in Texas? First, one would expect the Democratic Party in Texas to be a more "liberal" party. That is, it would be more likely to see a role for government in people's lives, to support greater regulation of the economy, and to support more social welfare legislation than would Republicans. Second, the base of the Democratic Party seems to be minorities, older Texans, and native Texans. Of this base of support, only one group is showing dramatic growth—the Hispanic population.

At the same time, the Republican Party should benefit from growth in Texas from its young population and from migration to the state. The party's weakness is in the minority population. Since it is the Hispanic population that is the large and growing minority population, one would expect the Republican Party to make a special effort to appeal to that segment of the population. Perhaps this is one reason that Governor Bush was the first Texas Republican gubernatorial candidate to broadcast commercials in south Texas in Spanish.

Elections in Texas

▶ What are the types of elections held in Texas?

In the first years of the twenty-first century, Texas is a democracy, but its government is not reflective of the characteristics of its population. Neither those who vote nor those elected are truly representative of the population as a whole. Elected officials are usually white, male, affluent, well educated, politically active, and middle aged. The population is female, less well educated, lower-middle class, and seldom politically active.

Elections are the way that the people select leaders, authorize actions by government, and borrow money on behalf of government. In Texas, there are a multitude of elections: primary elections, general elections, city elections, school board elections, special elections, elections for community college boards of regents and the boards of directors for many special districts, and bond elections for city, county, and state governments.

PRIMARY ELECTIONS

Primary elections are the first elections held. In Texas, they are held on the second Tuesday in March of even numbered years. Primary elections determine the party's nominees for the general election. They are conducted by the political party and funded jointly by the party and the state. Essentially, parties

Politics on the Web

Following national political parties, state political parties have turned to the Internet as a new place in which to exert their influence. Highly sophisticated Web sites have been developed in Texas by both major political parties to mobilize voters, to promote ideological and policy positions on key issues affecting Texas and the nation, and to raise funds. Smaller parties in Texas, such as the Libertarian Party and the Reform Party, have seen the web as an inexpensive arena in which they can present their candidates and political positions to the public. Candidates for a wide range of offices also have used the Internet as a vehicle for presenting their campaign to a larger audience throughout the state.

One of the conseqences of Web-oriented politics has been to broaden the scope of politics in the state. What used to be a local issue limited to a particular part of the state is often transformed into a state or even a national issue. The Internet gives whole new meaning to former Speaker of the U.S. House of Representatives Tip O'Neill's "All politics is local."

www.wwnorton.com/wtp3e

primary elections
elections used to select a party's candidate for the general election

collect filing fees from those seeking nomination and use these funds to pay for their share of holding the primary election.

Both parties conduct primaries in all of Texas's 254 counties. Within each county, voters cast ballots in precincts. The number of voting precincts varies depending on the population of the county. Less populated counties like Loving and Kenedy have as few as six precincts, while Harris County contains more than one-thousand voting precincts.[11]

Republicans seeking their party's nomination file papers and pay a filing fee to the Republican Party. Likewise, Democrats file papers and pay a filing fee to the Democratic Party. If four Republicans (or Democrats) seek the office of governor, they will campaign against each other and one will be chosen to run in the general election. To win the primary election requires an absolute majority. The party's nominees must have more votes than all opponents combined. If no candidate receives an absolute majority, there is a **run-off primary** held the second Tuesday in April between the two candidates receiving the most votes. Voters who participate in the Republican Party primary cannot vote in a Democratic run-off. Likewise, anyone who voted in the Democratic Party primary cannot vote in a Republican run-off; however, those who vote in neither the Democratic nor Republican primary can vote in either the Republican or Democratic run-off primary.

run-off primary
a second primary election between the two candidates who received the most votes in the first primary election

An **open primary** allows any registered voter to cast a ballot in either, but not both primaries. There are no party restrictions. One can consider oneself a Republican and vote in the Democratic primary or can leave home intending to vote in the Democratic primary, change one's mind, and vote in the Republican primary.

open primary
a primary election in which the voter can wait until the day of the primary to choose which party to enroll in to select candidates for the general election

The Texas Constitution and election laws call the Texas system a **closed primary,** since one must declare one's party affiliation before voting, but in practice it is an open primary. Before receiving a primary ballot, the voter signs a roll sheet indicating eligibility to vote and pledging to support the party's candidates. By signing the roll sheet, there is a declaration of party affiliation made prior to voting. However, since the declaration of party affiliation is only made a few moments prior to voting in the primary, the primary is closed only in the narrowest sense of the term.

closed primary
a primary election in which voters can participate in the nomination of candidates, but only of the party in which they are enrolled for a period of time prior to primary day

GENERAL ELECTION

The **general election** is held the first Tuesday following the first Monday in November of even numbered years. The Democratic Party's nominee runs against the nominee of the Republican Party. It is possible that independent and minor party candidates will also appear on the general election ballot.

general election
a decisive election which determines who is elected to office

Major state officials (governor, lieutenant governor, comptroller of public accounts, attorney general, etc.) are elected in nonpresidential election years.[12] This eliminates popular presidential candidates from influencing the outcomes of Texas races. For example, it is possible that a popular Republican presidential candidate might draw more than the usual number of Republican votes and an unusually large Republican presidential vote might swing the election for statewide candidates running under the Republican banner. Likewise, it prevents an uncommonly popular statewide candidate from influencing the presidential election. If statewide elections were held in presidential election years, a Democratic candidate for governor, for example, might influence

Texas's presidential voting by increasing the number of votes for Democratic candidates in general.

General elections are held in November to select national and state officeholders. Members of city councils, school boards, and other local government entities are also selected by general elections; however, these elections usually take place outside the traditional early November time period.

SPECIAL ELECTIONS

In Texas, **special elections** are used to fill a vacancy in office, give approval to borrow money, or to ratify amendments to the Texas Constitution. The dates for special elections are specified by the Texas legislature. If a Texas senator resigns, for example, the governor will call a special election to fill the vacancy.

special election
an election that is not held on a regularly scheduled basis; in Texas, a special election is called to fill a vacancy in office, to give approval for the state government to borrow money, or to ratify amendments to the Texas Constitution

Laws require voter approval before any governmental agency can borrow money and undertake long-term debt. If the local school district wants to borrow money to build a new high school and repair three elementary schools, a special election must be held. During the election, voters decide whether or not they will allow the school board to borrow the money.

The Texas Constitution has nearly four-hundred amendments. The legislature proposes amendments and they are ratified by the voters in a special election.

Participation in Texas Elections

- Who can vote in Texas? How easy is it to register to vote?
- Why do few Texans vote?
- What will it take to increase voter participation in Texas?

We will now focus on voting in Texas. Issues include who can vote, how easy it is to register to vote, why few Texans vote, and what it will take to increase voter participation in the state.

EARLIER RESTRICTIONS ON THE FRANCHISE

For much of the period of one-party Democratic control, there were restrictions on the franchise. Women were allowed to vote in primaries and party conventions in Texas in 1918 and obtained the right to vote in all elections as a result of the Nineteenth Amendment to the U.S. Constitution in 1920. However, some of the most influential politicians in the state were opposed to the franchise for women. Joseph Weldon Bailey, for example, who had been Democratic leader in the U.S. House of Representatives and later the informal Democratic leader in the U.S. Senate, was an eloquent opponent of women's suffrage, arguing that women could not vote because they could not perform the three basic duties of citizenship: jury service, *posse comitatus* service (citizens who are deputized to deal with an emergency), and military service. He believed that women's morals dictated their beliefs and that women would

John Nance Garner's political prominence in Texas in the 1930s was guaranteed by the political bosses that controlled the Latino votes in the south Texas region he represented.

force their beliefs on men. The result, he felt, would be prohibition.[13] Tinie Wells, the wife of Jim Wells, perhaps the most influential south Texas political leader of his day, was also an important and influential spokesperson for the anti-women's suffrage movement.[14] Governor "Farmer Jim" Ferguson was another opponent of women's suffrage, but when he was impeached, his successor, William P. Hobby, proved a key supporter of women's right to vote. It was Governor Hobby who called the legislature into special session in 1919 to consider the Nineteenth Amendment and thus Texas became the ninth state and the first state in the South to ratify the women's suffrage amendment.[15]

Minorities had an even tougher time gaining access to the ballot. In the early part of the twentieth century, powerful political bosses such as Jim Wells and Archer Parr had economic power and personal influence over Hispanic voters. This power was used to support national politicians such as John Nance Garner. Garner represented a huge part of south Texas, which stretched from Laredo to Corpus Christi and then north almost to San Antonio. A lifelong Democrat, he began his service in the House of Representatives in 1903 and served until 1933. From 1931–1933, he was speaker of the U.S. House of Representatives, and from 1933–1941, he was vice president of the United States. Garner was the first speaker from Texas and the first vice president from Texas. His south Texas political base was secured by votes that were controlled by the south Texas political bosses.[16]

One restriction on voting that affected poor people in general was the **poll tax.** Enacted in 1902, it required voters to pay a tax, presumably to cover the costs of elections. That tax was usually between $1.50 and $1.75. It was a small sum, but it had to be paid in advance of the election and, in the first third of the century, the tax could be one, two, or even more days' wages for a farm worker. Thus, it tended to disenfranchise poorer people.

poll tax
a state-imposed tax upon voters as a prerequisite for registration. Poll taxes were rendered unconstitutional in national elections by the Twenty-fourth Amendment, and in state elections by the Supreme Court in 1966

The south Texas political bosses used the poll tax, however, to great advantage. They would purchase large numbers of poll tax receipts and provide those receipts to their supporters who often depended on the bosses for jobs and other economic, legal, and political assistance, and who therefore would vote as the bosses wanted.

Although the poll tax was made illegal for federal elections in 1964 by the passage of the Twenty-fourth Amendment to the U.S. Constitution, it remained legal in Texas until 1966 when it was held unconstitutional.[17] After the elimination of the poll tax, Texas continued to require **early registration** for voting—registration more than nine months before the general election—and registration was required on a yearly basis. This requirement effectively prevented migrant workers from voting. These provisions lasted until 1971 when they, too, were voided by the federal courts.[18] Texas even allowed only property owners to vote in revenue bond and tax elections until the practice was stopped by federal courts.[19] Texas also required an unusually long period of residency for voters—voters had to have lived in the state for at least one year and to have lived in the county for at least six months prior to voting. This was another restriction on the franchise that was struck down by the federal courts.[20]

early registration
the requirement that a voter register more than nine months before the general election; in effect in Texas until 1971

The most oppressive restriction on the franchise, however, was designed to minimize the political strength of African American voters. It was the **white primary.** For this restriction on the franchise to work, it was necessary for Texas to be a one-party state, where elections were decided in the party primary. In 1923 the Texas Legislature flatly prohibited African Americans from voting in the

white primary
primary election in which only white voters are eligible to participate

Democratic primary. The effect in one-party Texas, of course, was to prevent African Americans from participating in the only "real" election contests. Texas was able to do this because of a 1921 U.S. Supreme Court decision, *Newberry v. United States,* which dealt with a federal campaign expenditures law. In interpreting the law, the Court stated that the primary election was "in no real sense part of the manner of holding the election."[21] This cleared the way for southern states, including Texas, to discriminate against African Americans in the primaries. In 1927, however, the Supreme Court struck down the Texas white primary law, claiming that the legal ban on black participation was a violation of the equal protection clause of the Constitution.[22] In response, the Texas legislature passed another law that authorized the political parties, through their state executive committees, to determine the qualifications for voting in the primaries. That law, of course, allowed the parties to create white primaries. The theory was that what a state could not do directly because of the Fourteenth Amendment, it could authorize political parties to do. However, in *Nixon v. Condon,* the U.S. Supreme Court held that the state executive committees were acting as agents of the state and were discriminating in violation of the Fourteenth Amendment.[23] As a result, the Texas Democratic Party convention, acting on its own authority and without any state law, passed a resolution that confined party membership to white citizens. That case was also appealed to the U.S. Supreme Court and, in *Grovey v. Townsend,* the Court held there was no violation of the Fourteenth Amendment. It is "state action" that violates the "equal protection of the laws" that the Fourteenth Amendment protects against. Since there was no state law authorizing the white primary, the Court believed there was no "state action," only discrimination by a private organization, the Democratic Party, which is not banned by the Fourteenth Amendment.[24] Thus, the Court upheld the white primary until 1944, in *Smith v. Allwright,* when it decided that the operation of primary elections involved so much state action and so much public responsibility that the white primary did involve unconstitutional state action.[25] Even with the *Smith* decision, at least one Texas county held unofficial primaries by the Jaybird Party. This was a Democratic political organization that excluded African Americans. The winners in the Jaybird primary then entered the regular Democratic Party primary where they were never defeated for county office and where they seldom had opposition. In *Terry v. Adams,* the U.S. Supreme Court finally ruled that the Jaybird primary was an integral, and the only effective, part of the elective process in the county. Thus, the Fifteenth Amendment (which deals with the right to vote) was applicable and the white "pre-primary" primary of the Jaybird Party was ruled unconstitutional.[26]

One can detect, at least since the 1940s, a gradual expansion of the franchise in Texas. Much of that expansion was brought about by litigation in the federal courts, often by African American and Hispanic civil rights organizations. Federal laws also played an important role in the expansion of the franchise. The most important of these laws was the 1965 Voting Rights Act that applied to Texas as a result of Congressional amendments after 1975.

If Texas had had a competitive two-party system during this era instead of a one-party system, it might have been harder for the state to impose and maintain these restrictions on the franchise. In a competitive two-party system, to obtain and retain power, both parties would have to search for ways of building and increasing their base of support in order to be the victorious party. In a one-party system, there is more of an incentive to restrict participation in the party in order to retain control over the party. Losers in a battle for control of a one-party system essentially have no place to go. If they cannot maintain a place in the dominant party's councils, then they have no other avenue for expressing their political views.

QUALIFICATIONS TO VOTE

Today meeting the qualifications to register to vote in Texas is relatively easy. A voter must be

1. 18 years of age
2. a U.S. citizen
3. a resident of Texas for 30 days
4. a resident of the county for 30 days

To be eligible to vote, you must be a registered voter for thirty days preceding the election and a resident of the voting precinct on the day of the election. There are two groups of people who cannot vote even if they meet all the above qualifications: felons and those judged by a court to be mentally incompetent.

motor voter law

a national act, passed in 1993, which requires states to allow people to register to vote when applying for a driver's license

Sixty percent of the state's population is registered to vote.[27] The **motor voter law,**[28] which allows individuals to register to vote when renewing driver's licenses, is one factor in increased registration. Public schools distribute voter registration cards as students turn eighteen. Cooperative efforts between the secretary of state's office and corporations such as Diamond Shamrock, Stop 'n' Go, and the Southland Corporation (which operates 7-Eleven stores) also increase the number of registered voters. By January 2000, Texas had more than fourteen million registered voters.[29]

LOW VOTER TURNOUT

In most elections, fewer than 50 percent of U.S. citizens vote.[30] Even fewer Texans exercise their right to vote. Historically, Texans rank in the bottom third in terms of voter participation. In the 1998 gubernatorial election only a little more than 32 percent of registered voters cast ballots. Fewer than 31 percent of Harris County voters participated in the election. Only 27 percent of voters in Bexar County went to the polls, and fewer than 30 percent of Dallas County voters voted.[31] Turnout was much worse in the special elections on constitutional amendments in August and November 1997. In the August election, about 7 percent of registered voters voted and in the November election, fewer than 11 percent voted.[32] Considering the ease of registration and the ability to vote early, voter participation should be higher. Why do so few Texans vote?

A more detailed analysis reminds us of several reasons Texans seldom vote:

1. low levels of educational attainment
2. low per capita income
3. high rate of poverty
4. ethnicity
5. residing in the South

6. young population
7. traditionalistic and individualistic political culture
8. weak political parties and interest groups
9. poor media

Income and education are the two most important factors in determining if someone votes.

Texas ranks in the bottom third of states in most comparisons of educational achievement. It ranks forty-ninth among the fifty states in per pupil expenditures by state government and thirty-seventh when considering expenditures by local and state government. Teachers' salaries consistently rank thirty-eighth in the nation. The state ranks forty-fifth in average SAT/ACT scores. Texas students drop out of school at rates exceeding the national average. A larger percentage of adult Texans cannot read or write than adults for the country as a whole.[33] Dr. Bernard Weinstein of the University of North Texas characterized public education in Texas as dismal.[34] Many Texans are not well educated, and this is reflected in their low levels of voting.

The higher an individual's income, the more likely she is to vote. The lower her income, the less likely. The state's per capita income is less than the national average. Eighteen percent of Texans live in poverty, considerably above the 12-percent poverty rate for the United States as a whole. Texas's high rate of poverty and low incomes are excellent predictors of low voter participation. Together, they hold little hope for Texans to increase their levels of voting.

Voter participation among African Americans and Hispanics is lower than that of Anglos. Slightly more than 40 percent of Texans have an ethnic heritage that predisposes them to not vote.[35] This sizable group of residents further erodes Texas's voting base. A recent study of Latino voting by the William C. Valasquez Institute indicates just how important ethnicity is as a predictor

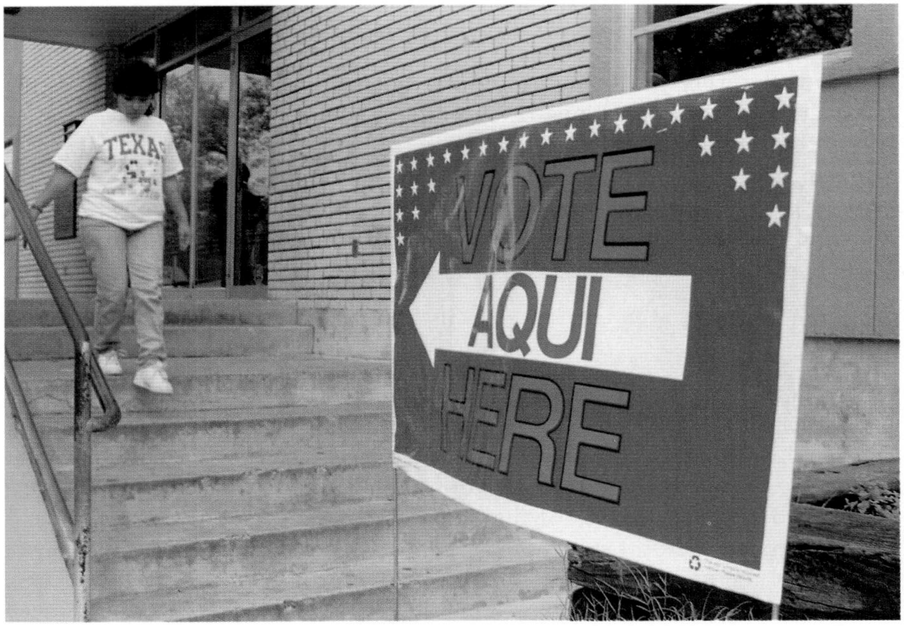

In addition to education and income level, ethnicity plays a role in voter participation. Latino voter turnout rates in Texas are considerably lower than statewide turnout rates.

of voting participation. The Institute estimated that there were 1,767,452 Latinos registered to vote in Texas, but only 472,436 cast ballots in the 1998 general election. That means that Latino voting participation was 26.7 percent.[36] Since 32.4 percent of registered voters in Texas voted in the 1998 elections, Latino participation was 5.7 percent less than that of Texas voters as a whole. Put another way, if Latino participation equaled the rate of participation for Texas voters in general, Latinos would have cast about 100,000 more votes in Texas.

In the southern states that composed the Confederacy, individuals participate in smaller numbers than other parts of the United States. Texas was part of the Confederacy and its level of participation is consistent with lower levels of voting in the south. Young people vote in smaller numbers as well and the average age of Texans is less than the national average.

According to Daniel Elazar (See Chapter 20), Texas's political culture is traditionalistic and individualistic. Low levels of voting characterize these cultures. In a traditionalistic political culture, the political and economic elite discourages voting. People choose not to vote in individualistic cultures because of real or perceived corruption in government.

Interestingly, there are still other possible explanations for low voter participation in Texas. In keeping with the Texas tradition of decentralized government, there are so many elections in Texas and so many candidates for office that voters are simply overloaded with elections and candidates. It is interesting to remember that, as previously noted, voter participation was much higher in the general election in 1998 than in the two special constitutional elections of 1997. If there were fewer elections, the ballot might be longer, but there would likely be higher voter turnout since more voters would be attracted to at least some races or issues on the ballot. Additionally, elections for major offices in Texas are scheduled to not coincide with the presidential election in order to keep the state election separate from the influence of the presidential candidates. However, there is a trade-off in having elections in non-presidential election years, because the highest voter participation tends to occur for presidential elections. A third problem is that most elections in Texas involve very low-visibility offices. Voters likely know little about the candidates for these positions or the offices themselves and such a lack of knowledge would naturally discourage voter participation. Efforts have been made in a number of states, most notably Washington, to increase voter knowledge by having the state provide biographical information about the candidates to voters, but Texas makes no such effort to enhance voter knowledge of candidates.

VOTER EDUCATION

In the fall of 1994, candidates were seeking many offices, from U.S. senator to governor, from hundreds of judicial offices to many statewide executive positions on down to inspector of hides and animals and public weigher. As part of a course assignment on voter education, students from San Jacinto College were asked to collect copies of the Texas Democratic and Texas Republican Party platforms. Several students visited the headquarters of the East Harris County Democrats to ask for a copy of the platform. Although the office was staffed by long-time party volunteers, not one person knew where a copy of

CANDIDATE INFORMATION ON THE INTERNET

Box 22.2

The Texas legislature recently attempted to place judicial candidate information on the Internet, to offer citizens more detailed background on the candidates and perhaps reduce the costs of judicial campaigns. This seemingly straightforward reform passed with no significant opposition in the Texas legislature. But it met unexpected opposition from Texas governor and Republican presidential candidate George W. Bush.

In May [1999], the bi-partisan bill sponsored by state representative Henry Cuellar, a Democrat, and state senator Robert Duncan, a Republican, breezed through both chambers of the Texas legislature. . . .

The legislation called for the Texas Secretary of State to post information distributed by judicial candidates on the Internet. Cuellar, an attorney, thought this legislation was a perfect way to increase voter understanding of judicial campaigns: "If it's hard for us in the legal system to know who the candidates are, then it's definitely going to be hard for typical voters."

But Governor George W. Bush disagreed. In June [1999], Bush vetoed the legislation, saying it would place the Secretary of State in an "inappropriate role." But that reasoning doesn't stand up to the scrutiny of others who study the problems of judicial campaigns. Anthony Champagne, a professor at the School of Social Science at the University of Texas [at Dallas] . . . says "there is nothing inappropriate about trying to get truthful information out to the public."

Champagne is not alone. The American Bar Association has recommended that states which elect judges should provide voters with candidate information as a means of making voters more aware, and also as a way to try to alleviate some of the increasing costs of campaigning for voter recognition. . . .

If the legislation had passed, Texas would not have been alone in putting information on the Internet. Washington (since 1996), Alaska, California and Oregon have web judicial voter's guides. . . .

SOURCE: Shannon Davis, "The Rise and Fall of a Reform Bill," *Frontline: Justice for Sale*, www.pbs.org/wgbh/pages/shows/justice/howshould/risefall.html/frontline.

the platform could be found. Even more shocking, no one knew what a platform was! The Republicans knew about their party's platform but wanted to charge the students $5.00 to $25.00 for a copy.

By educating the public, interest groups and parties increase understanding of candidates and issues. By failing to adequately publicize issues and candidates, by charging for platforms, and through the type of ineptitude found in the East Harris County Democrats office, parties perpetuate low levels of voting in Texas.

Many people believe political parties should offer the voters a real choice among candidates. However, in Texas, this seldom happens. In many counties, one party appears on the ballot to the exclusion of the other. Democrats will seek only a few offices, leaving the Republicans unchallenged for the majority. Often, when both Democrats and Republicans challenge each other there is little philosophical difference between the two, and candidates with similar philosophies fail to offer voters a real choice between the candidates. With only one candidate on the ballot or little difference between candidates when two names appear on the ballot, voters decide not to vote. They believe their vote really doesn't make a difference.

INCREASING PARTICIPATION

Although Texas has a long history of limited voter participation, it is possible to increase voting levels. In-migration will have a positive affect. Many newcomers are affluent and educated. These new Texans often come from states with a heritage of higher levels of participation. As people move to Texas from states that have higher levels of participation, voting activity in Texas should increase. Not only will newcomers vote; their example can induce others to vote. Some of those coming to Texas were party activists where they once lived. They will bring their experience and enthusiasm to Texas, and perhaps rejuvenate Texas's parties. A stronger media presence, and politically active in-migrants can move Texas from being a state with relatively few people voting to a state with a strong participatory base.

Another way to address this problem is for parties to make their candidates known to the public through candidate forums, mailings, and advertising. Candidates, parties, and volunteers can also diligently work to make the public aware of the candidates, their qualifications, and the parties' platforms. Print and electronic media also have a responsibility to publicize platforms, compare candidates' qualifications, analyze political advertisements, and inform the public about issues important to Texas and the local area. Media in Texas often fail in their efforts. Outside the major metropolitan areas they may lack personnel and financial resources to adequately inform the public about all the issues. Others are constrained by parent companies.

Education and income remain the two most important factors in determining whether someone will vote. Texas spends 30 percent of its income on public education. Billions of dollars more are spent by local school districts. An examination of our system of public education indicates that it is improving. Strengthening our public education system will improve voter participation in Texas.

In many states, levels of income are increasing. However, this is not the case in Texas. For Texans with middle incomes and those living with the bottom 20 percent of incomes, average incomes fell during the late 1990s. Texas is one of only ten states for which this is true. In the remaining forty states, average income of both groups increased.[37] So long as incomes in Texas fail to increase, voter participation will not increase.

EARLY VOTING

early voting
a procedure which allows voters to cast ballots during the two-week period before the regularly scheduled election date

Early voting is another way to increase participation. This is a procedure that increases the polling period from twelve hours on Election Day to an additional two weeks prior to the election. The legislature has allowed early voting in an effort to increase participation. It is designed for those who have trouble getting to the polls between 7:00 A.M. and 7:00 P.M. on election day. For most elections, early voting commences on the seventeenth day before the elections and ends four days prior to election day.

Voting early is basically the same as voting on election day. An individual appears at one of the designated polling places, presents appropriate identification, and receives and casts a ballot. Each general election has seen an increase in early voting, but overall turnout has increased only modestly. Those who normally vote on the official Election Day simply cast their ballots early. Professor James Carter has suggested that the lengthened time for voting should benefit the Democratic Party by providing it with more time to get supporters to vote. However, it appears that the Republican Party is actually the primary beneficiary of early voting.[38]

POLITIQUERAS

politiqueras
paid campaign workers in the Rio Grande Valley who are hired by political candidates to bring out the vote on their behalf

Politiqueras increase participation, especially in local elections. Found in the Rio Grande Valley, **politiqueras** are paid campaign workers hired by a candidate to produce a certain number of votes. They are women[39] who control a certain number of votes, in a manner similar to that of the political bosses of earlier eras, and can vote the people as a block. The number of votes controlled can be as few as two or three dozen individuals or more than two-hundred. Politiqueras work for several candidates (governor, lieutenant governor, candidates for the Texas House of Representatives, etc.) at one time, but never work for two opposing candidates.

Politiqueras use the motor voter law to increase the number of registered voters. This, in turn, expands the pool of voters. These women make great use of the old absentee voting law, and Texas's current early voting law is also a great boon to them. Both make it easier to deliver the promised votes.

Politiqueras are paid weekly and the size of their paycheck is directly tied to the number of votes promised. Generally, a portion of promised votes are delivered throughout the early voting period. If a payment is not made, fewer votes are found in the following week. Typically candidates employ several politiqueras because each woman controls different voters living in different voting precincts. There is a degree of trust in this system, however, with computers and other tracking devices, it is easy to determine how many votes each politiquera delivers.

For some politiqueras, working for the candidates and turning out the vote is a business. They support families with their earnings. These women work for candidates in many elections: primary and general elections, city elections, bond elections, and school board elections. Some politiqueras earn in excess of $30,000 yearly. Others supplement other income with the few thousand dollars they make. All enjoy prestige in their communities. They are seen as leaders who can accomplish what others cannot.

In one neighborhood in Brownsville, there was a huge hole in an alley and garbage had not been collected in three weeks. Calls to the city produced no results. Finally, the local politiquera was called and contacted the city council member she had assisted. That afternoon, the council member, the politiquera, and the neighbors gathered and examined the hole. Two days later the hole was repaired and the garbage collected. It was the politquera who had solved the problem with one phone call. And, in the process, she built additional political support.

Is the use of politiqueras illegal or unethical? Not really. The politiquera is a paid campaign worker, much like the press aide who distributes news releases and holds news conferences.

Campaigns

- What is the role of political parties in election campaigns in Texas?
- What can candidates do to improve their chances of winning elections?

Political campaigns are efforts of candidates to win support of the voters. The goal of the campaign is to attain sufficient support to win the primary election in March and the general election in November. Some campaigns last a year or more; however, the more accepted practice is to limit the campaign to a few weeks before the election. In Texas, campaigns to win the party primary begin in January and continue to the second Tuesday in March. Labor Day is the traditional start of the general election campaign and lasts from early September to the first Tuesday following the first Monday in November.

Campaigns involve attempts to reach the voters through print and electronic media, the mail, door-to-door campaigning, speeches to large and small groups, coffee hours, and telephone solicitation. Costs are enormous. In the 1980s and 1990s candidates for statewide races spent as much as $30 million.

There are places in the United States where the parties have a major role in the running of political campaigns. That is not the case in Texas. Here the candidates have the major responsibility for campaign strategy, for running their campaigns, and for raising money. At times, party leaders will try to recruit individuals to run for office, especially if no candidates volunteer to seek an office or the candidates appear to be weak ones. For the most part, the benefit of the party to a candidate in Texas is that the party provides the party label under which the candidate runs. That "Democrat" or "Republican" label is, of course, important to candidates because many voters use the party label in casting their votes, especially for low visibility races. The party also contains numerous activists who can be tapped by the candidate for campaign tasks such as manning phone banks, preparing mailings, and posting campaign ads. Additionally, the party does provide some support for the candidate, most commonly through campaigns to get out the vote for the party's candidates. Campaigning in Texas, however, is generally left up to the candidate and in that effort, the parties take a secondary role.

Name recognition is an important task for candidates. If voters do not recognize your name, you have little chance of winning. Incumbents hold a distinct advantage in this regard. The officeholder has many ways to get name visibility. She can mail out news releases, send newsletters to her constituents, appear on radio talk shows, and give speeches to civic clubs. Challengers have a more difficult time getting that crucial name visibility.

In 1978, William R. Clements was a political unknown. He spent thousands of dollars of his own fortune to gain name recognition. He leased hundreds of billboards throughout the state. Each had a blue background with white letters proclaiming "CLEMENTS." In the print media, early ads bore the simple message, "ELECT CLEMENTS." The unprecedented scale of this advertising effort made Clements's name better known among the voters in Texas. This, in turn, stimulated interest in his campaign's message. Clements won the race for governor, becoming the first Republican to hold that office in Texas since the end of Reconstruction.

Running for statewide office is significantly different from seeking the office of state representative from an urban area. One obvious difference is the amount of money needed for the campaign, but there are others. The statewide candidate travels tens of thousands of miles across the state to seek votes. In a more localized race, candidates spend much time traveling, but there is a difference. The local candidate will walk from house to apartment to condominium complex. She will wear out more than one pair of shoes knocking on doors and visiting with potential voters. A statewide candidate flies from city to city, gives a speech, shakes a few hands, and climbs back into the plane for another campaign stop two-hundred miles away.

Media is the most expensive item in most campaigns. In metropolitan areas, television, radio, and print advertising is very costly. Full-page ads in metropolitan newspapers can be as much as $40,000. Candidates for the Texas House of Representatives and Texas Senate who represent metropolitan areas need to reach only a small portion of the population, but they are forced to purchase ads in media sources that go to hundreds of thousands of people not represented. In rural areas, any individual ad is relatively inexpensive. However, candidates must advertise in dozens of small newspapers and radio stations and costs mount.

Texas House District 70 contains almost a dozen counties in west Texas. In a recent election, the incumbent had no opposition in either the primary election or general election yet he had almost $100,000 in media expenses. Most communities in the district had weekly newspapers, and many had radio stations that expected that the incumbent would purchase ads whether or not he had an opponent in order to maintain name recognition. Meeting this expectation for the primary and general election was expensive.

Three Pivotal Elections

▶ What do the elections of John Tower to the U.S. Senate in 1961, William Clements to the governorship in 1978, and Ann Richards to the governorship in 1990 illustrate about changes in parties and elections in Texas?

In order to understand how dramatically Texas political parties have changed in recent years, it is useful to explore three elections that illustrate the power positions of the Democratic and Republican parties in Texas. The first election we will discuss is the election of Republican John Tower to the U.S. Senate in 1961. The second is the election of Republican William Clements to the governorship in 1978. The third is the election of Democrat Ann Richards as governor in 1990.

Tower's election shows the initial success of the Republican Party in a statewide race. That success was due to a long-standing division in the Democratic Party between the liberal and conservative wings. In the 1961 senate race, the conservative wing of the party won the nomination, but the liberal wing refused to back the conservative Democrat. Some liberal Democrats, in disgust over the party's nomination of a conservative, even chose to back the Republican candidate.

In 1978, Republican Bill Clements became the first Republican governor since Reconstruction. The Republicans were again able to benefit from divisions in the Democratic Party between the moderate John Hill supporters and the conservative Dolph Briscoe supporters. Democratic nominee Hill also assumed that, like previous gubernatorial elections in Texas, the Republicans posed no real threat. Clements's financial resources, Democratic Party divisions, and Hill's arrogance led to another Republican victory in a statewide race. However, it proved a victory unlike Tower's senate victory. A senator can do little to build a state party because senators are federal, rather than state, officials. However, a governor has vast appointment power, and Clements used that power to build further Republican strength.

In 1990, it initially appeared Democratic Party divisions would again lead to their defeat. Ann Richards, a liberal Democrat, had alienated moderate-conservative former Democratic governor Mark White. Additionally, liberal Democrat Jim Mattox had also been in a bitter Democratic primary battle with Richards. The Republican nominee, Clayton Williams, like Bill Clements before him, seemed to have near-unlimited wealth to run a campaign and initially presented a colorful rural image, not unlike that of earlier successful Texas politician-entertainers. However, things were different in 1990. In the past, divisions in the Democratic Party contributed to the defeat of Democratic candidates. In 1990 Williams's words and actions proved too crude for urban Republican women. Williams came to be seen as an embarrassment and the Republican Party became divided over his candidacy. Unlike the past, when Republicans were able to take advantage of Democratic divisions and weakness in the Democratic candidates, the tide had turned. Richards took advantage of Republican division over their candidate and won. Her victory, however, was costly. The Williams-Richards campaign was the most expensive gubernatorial campaign in Texas history. Unlike previous Democratic governors, Richards faced a powerful Republican Party that was, with an urban and sophisticated candidate, able to defeat her in her bid for re-election.

THE BEACHHEAD: JOHN TOWER'S ELECTION TO THE U.S. SENATE IN 1961

John Tower held statewide office longer than any Republican in Texas history, and, between his election in 1961 and the election of William Clements in 1978, he was the only Republican in a statewide office in Texas. Tower appealed strongly to Texas conservatives. He was, for example, one of the leading opponents of the Civil Rights Act of 1964 and of the Voting Rights Act of 1965. In 1965, he opposed a measure to abolish the poll tax in Texas and in three other states. In 1983, only a few months from his retirement from the Senate, Tower opposed the creation of a national holiday honoring Martin Luther King, Jr. Chandler Davidson describes Tower's voting record as "at the right edge of his own national party."[40] And, Tower had enormous political difficulties. Not only was he a Republican when Democrats were in ascendancy, but he faced difficulties in his own party from the right. In 1976, for example, he was humiliated by his party for his support of President Ford over Ronald Reagan in a bitter primary election in Texas, which Reagan won. For that, Tower was denied an at-large position as a delegate to the Republican convention. He was also viewed by many Republicans as "part of the country club set," meaning that he seemed more concerned with economic issues than with the issues promoted by the religious right within the Republican Party.[41] Somehow, however, Tower lasted from election to the senate in 1961 until his retirement in 1985.

Yet, his election in 1961 was a fluke. From 1877 to 1961, no Republican had represented Texas in the U.S. Senate, and from 1877 through 1962 Republicans had only represented Texas in the U.S. House a total of fourteen terms.[42] Tower had served in the Navy in World War II and worked as a radio announcer and salesman in north Texas before doing graduate work at the London School of Economics and Southern Methodist University. He married the cousin of a leader of the Republican Party in Texas and became a government professor at Midwestern State College in Wichita Falls. Tower became active in Republican Party politics and ran unsuccessfully for the Texas House of Representatives in 1954. In 1960, he was the Republican sacrificial lamb against Lyndon Johnson for the U.S. Senate. Johnson was running for the U.S. Senate as well as for vice president. He was able to run for both offices because of a special law, commonly called the Johnson Law, which was passed by the Texas legislature in 1959 and allowed him the dual candidacies. Johnson's candidacy for the Senate, of course, was political insurance for him in case he failed to win national office.

John Tower was the first Republican senator from Texas. His fluke victory in a 1961 special election was partly due to a divided Democratic Party unable to offer a strong opponent.

Johnson won both offices and that required a special election in 1961 to fill the senate seat. However, perhaps partly because of irritation over Johnson's dual candidacy and because of Tower's assiduous campaigning, Tower got 41.5 percent of the vote. It was by most standards a landslide election for Johnson, but by the standards of a weak Texas Republican Party, Tower had shown remarkable strength. In 1954, the Republican nominee against Johnson for the U.S. Senate had only received 15 percent of the vote.

As a result of his 1960 race, Tower had no problem getting the Republican nomination for the 1961 special election. Texas had changed its election law so that one could no longer win the election with a plurality of the vote. Conservative Democrats had feared that a liberal Democrat or a Republican might be able to win the election by plurality, but they did not believe that possible if the requirement was a majority vote. Tower, however, was the only Republican in the race, but there were plenty of Democrats seeking the senate seat. Overall, there were more than seventy candidates on the ballot! Of these candidates, the battle was between six contenders: Tower, the only Republican, and five Democrats. Of the Democrats, William Blakely was the interim appointee to the senate seat and was a conservative Democrat. Jim Wright was a moderate-liberal Democratic congressman. Will Wilson was a moderate-conservative Democrat and was the incumbent Texas attorney general. Maury Maverick, Jr., was a liberal Democrat. Henry Gonzalez was also a liberal Democrat and was then a state senator.

There were so many names on the ballot because it was a special election and the candidates had not had to go through party primaries. Additionally, the candidates were not identified by party affiliation. Since it was a special election, voter participation was low and the Democratic candidates seriously divided the Democratic Party. Tower got 30.93 percent of the vote and Blakely received the next highest vote—18.03 percent of the vote. But Blakely was a weak candidate. He was a poor campaigner and stayed in Washington for

Box 22.3 JOHN TOWER ON BECOMING THE FIRST REPUBLICAN SENATOR FROM TEXAS SINCE RECONSTRUCTION

TOWER: . . . It occurred to me that I was really a favorite for a run-off spot anyway, whether I ran first or second. And of course the Democrats' strength was diluted by the fact that there were five major Democrat candidates and only one Republican candidate, so that made it an almost certainty that I would get into the run-off. And as it turned out, I ran first, with about 35 percent of the vote; Blakely came in second with around 20 percent (these are rough figures); and behind him was Jim Wright, and then Will Wilson, and then I believe Henry Gonzalez and Maury Maverick in that order. Then that put me in the run-off with Blakely.

INTERVIEWER: Did you have any preference of whom you faced in the run-off?

TOWER: It occurred to me that Blakely would be the best one I could run off against, because I had then figured to pick up the dissident liberal Democrat votes. I thought I would probably pick up most of the Maverick, Gonzalez votes, and probably a sizeable portion of the Wright votes.

INTERVIEWER: Did you ever feel the hand of [Lyndon] Johnson at all in this campaign?

TOWER: No, I didn't. And I don't think Lyndon really realized that I was the threat I was. . . .

. . .

TOWER: Too, Blakely, whom I think a very fine gentleman, but he had no political acumen whatsoever—absolutely none! He was not a good candidate, he didn't like crowds, he was not a particularly good speaker. So he had his problems. He was adequately funded, and again I had to really scrap for money.

But too I think my political judgment was a lot better than Blakely's. . . .

INTERVIEWER: Well, you made sense, and Blakely seemed kind of lost.

TOWER: I exploited the divisions in the Democratic party too. The dissident Democrats voted for me.

INTERVIEWER: Were you ever actually approached personally by the liberal wing [of the Democratic Party in Texas] to talk about ways and means, what they would like to do?

TOWER: I certainly had communication with them. . . .

INTERVIEWER: Has that ever caused you any problem since, the fact that you did have this support from the liberal wings?

TOWER: No, because I never had to promise them anything, you see, I never had to commit myself on a position to them. As a matter of fact, they regarded me as a Neanderthal conservative, but they also felt I was an honest one because I wore the Republican label. And their mentality was that the conservative Democrats are not really Democrats, and of course still that's their view. So in effect they put it this way—"If we're going to have a Republican senator, let's have one that calls himself a Republican." That was their rationale.

. . .

TOWER: . . . The Republican organization performed and the Democratic organization didn't perform. The Democrats always used to fight in battles at primaries centered around courthouse cliques, whereas the Republicans started the fighting in general elections. Still the Democrats are not as good at fighting general elections as the Republicans are, although they beat us pretty regularly, but that's just by virtue of sheer numbers. Again, we polled a percentage of votes way out of proportion to the people that identified themselves as Republicans.

SOURCE: Transcript, John G. Tower Oral History Interview I, August 8, 1971, by Joe B. Frantz, Internet Copy, LBJ Library, pp. 9–11.

much of the campaign season rather than campaigning against Tower. Additionally, liberal Democrats refused to support the conservative Blakely. The result was that Tower won the run-off with 50.6 percent of the vote.[43]

In a regular election, Tower would not have won and never in his political career did Tower have coattails that helped elect other Republican officeholders. But it was a first for Texas Republicans. Lyndon Johnson's senate seat was in Republican hands. It showed that with a divided Democratic Party, Republicans could win a statewide election. As Allen Duckworth, the political editor of the *Dallas Morning News* wrote, "The Republicans of Texas are a long, long way from conquering the state, but they have established a small beachhead."[44]

CREATING A TWO-PARTY STATE: THE ELECTION OF GOVERNOR BILL CLEMENTS IN 1978

When Bill Clements was considering running for governor of Texas, his wife, an astute Republican political activist, argued that while John Tower's election to the U.S. Senate had been important, one could not build a two-party state by winning federal offices. The way to build a two-party state was for a Republican to become governor. That, she felt, would translate into Republican gains at the state and local level. And, she believed, William Clements was just the person to lead the Republican Party to victory.[45]

Bill Clements was a self-made man, an enormously successful contractor who had built one of the world's most successful oil drilling companies. He was wealthy, though estimates of that wealth vary greatly. In the late 1970s it was estimated that Clements was worth between $29 and $75 million. In 1969–1970 Clements was appointed by President Nixon to a blue-ribbon committee to study Pentagon defense policies. In 1972, he was the cochairman of the Committee to Re-elect the President in Texas. Then, from 1973–1977, he was deputy secretary of defense and was responsible for billions of dollars worth of weapons development and procurement.[46]

Marrying Republican national committeewoman Rita Bass in 1975, Clements soon set his sights on the governorship of Texas. Clements had a rough, abrasive personality and was confident in his abilities and opinions—his critics thought too confident. Most importantly, he was not accustomed to losing and was willing to work and spend money to win the nomination and then the election.

Ray Hutchison, a Dallas bond attorney and the husband of current Republican senator Kay Bailey Hutchison, also sought the Republican nomination. Hutchison was the Texas Republican Party chairman and a former state legislator. Hutchison had been unsuccessful in recruiting a Republican opponent to the Democratic incumbent governor, Dolph Briscoe. He believed that Briscoe was vulnerable and, when he could get no one else to run, he decided to run himself. Others thought that Hutchison was running simply because he was state chairman and no one seemed to want to run against Briscoe. Few sensed that Briscoe could be defeated in his re-election bid. Additionally, John Tower was up for re-election and his race would soak up a great deal of Republican campaign dollars. A strong Republican candidate would have to turn to personal resources for campaign funding. Hutchison did not have the money that would be needed for a serious campaign.

Clements, who had not answered an earlier inquiry from Hutchison about his interest in the governor's race, finally decided that he could win and that he was willing to put his wealth into the race. He beat Hutchison 3–1 in the Republican primary and outspent Hutchison by ten to one. In a primary that attracted just over 158,000 voters, Clements spent $2.2 million, $1.7 million of which was borrowed money.

In the Democratic primary, the incumbent governor, multimillionaire rancher and oilman Dolph Briscoe was defeated in a three-man race. Opposing Briscoe was former governor Preston Smith and Texas attorney general John Hill. Briscoe, a conservative Democrat and a passive governor, won only 42 percent of the Democratic primary vote. John Hill received a majority of 51.5 percent. Although generally not considered a liberal,[47] Hill was to the left of Briscoe and had been an activist state attorney general since his election in 1972. He had been secretary of state under Governor John Connally and had been a hugely successful lawyer. He was not as wealthy as either Briscoe or Clements, but he was a millionaire. Hill was ambitious, very ambitious. He had run unsuccessfully for governor in 1968 and shortly after becoming attorney general had begun planning for another try at the governorship.[48]

Hill, looking at the result of every Texas governor's race since Reconstruction, assumed he was the next governor of Texas. After all, he had been victorious in the Democratic primary and had even beaten an incumbent governor. Hill and his campaign took the summer off prior to the general election. Even when Hill began campaigning in early September, he ran under the assumption that he would be the next governor. When he made speeches, he would recognize local Democrats and then talk about how he was looking forward to working with them when he took office. Hill's campaign was described as being "boldly overconfident."[49]

Hill had lost the support of many of the more conservative Democrats who were loyal to Briscoe, and while Briscoe did not endorse Clements, Briscoe's wife told the *Dallas Times Herald* that she thought Clements was better suited to be governor than was Hill. Additionally, Briscoe's three children supported Clements because, they said, he was more conservative than Hill. Nevertheless, it looked like Hill's confidence was well-grounded. On October 22, 1978, a *Texas Monthly* poll showed Hill in the lead by 11 percent. Hill's response to the poll was to say, "There is no way I will lose. It's all over. We think we have enough votes to win regardless of the turnout. The polls show I'm going straight up."[50]

Actually, Hill was going straight down. A Clements campaign newspaper was mailed to 1.5 million Texans accusing Hill of being an ambulance chasing plaintiff's lawyer. Clements aligned himself with a Corpus Christi radio evangelist, Lester Roloff, who had opposed state efforts to regulate his homes for wayward children. Hill, as attorney general, had supported the state's efforts to license and inspect the homes and Hill refused to promise Roloff that he would exempt the schools from state regulation. Clements, on the other hand, agreed to support the exemption. Roloff mounted a major literature campaign, primarily in rural churches on the Sunday before the election, in which Hill was accused of being "anti-church and anti-Christian." For the first time, Hill concluded that he might lose the election.[51]

Clements also had developed an impressive phone bank operation that contacted 20 percent of the state's voters on the day of the election. The election that night was very close, although at 2 A.M. Hill was in the lead and some media called the race for Hill. However, by 6 A.M. Clements was ahead

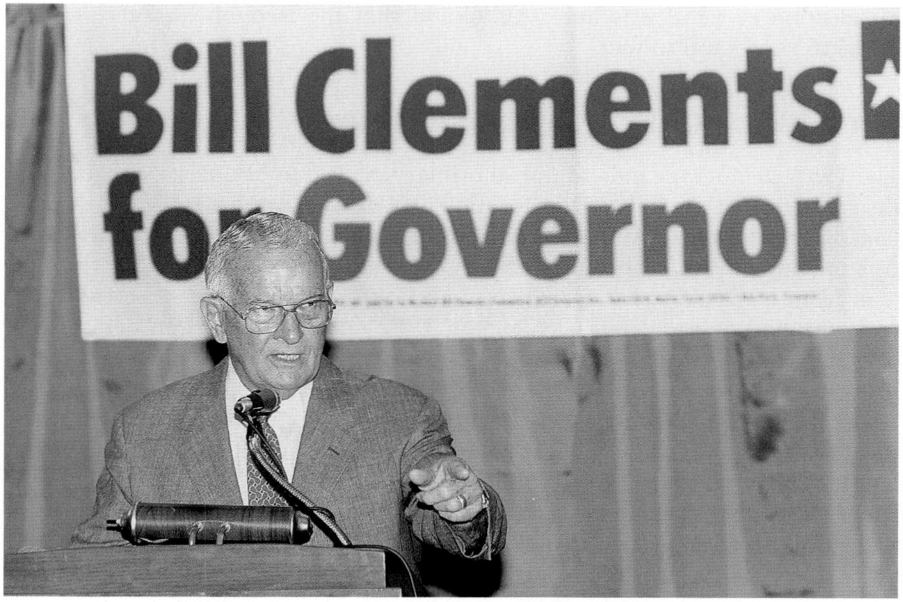

Bill Clements speaks to the press after his 1986 comeback victory.

and by 7 A.M., ABC announced Clements the winner. It was close enough for Hill to ask for a recount, but Clements had won the race by a total of 16,909 votes out of 2.2 million cast. It was not the closest statewide election—John Tower had won his race to be re-elected to the U.S. Senate over Robert Krueger by a margin of only 12,227 votes.[52]

Clements had spent $7 million to do it, the most money at the time in a nonpresidential political race, but he was the first Republican Texas governor since Reconstruction. He had built a superb campaign organization with effective media, phone banks, and polling. But he had also won because Hill had been too confident. Hill had looked to the past and assumed that a Republican could not win the governorship. But the conservative Briscoe Democrats, angry at Hill's defeat of Briscoe in the Democratic primary, abandoned Hill in droves.[53] With support of conservatives who had once been Democrats, it was clear that Republicans in Texas could win the highest executive office in the state.

In 1982, Clements was defeated in his re-election bid by Mark White, the Democratic Texas attorney general. White won with 53.2 percent of the vote even though Clements spent twice as much in the campaign. But the economy in Texas was weak at the time and White had successfully made an issue of high utility bills. Most importantly, unlike in 1978, the Democratic Party was unified. Clements was triple-teamed with a unified campaign by Democrats Lloyd Bentsen, who was running for re-election to the U.S. Senate, Bill Hobby, who was running for re-election as lieutenant governor, and Mark White.

Bill Clements and the Republicans could not be counted out, however. White was hurt by the faltering Texas economy and Clements was out for revenge. In 1986, Clements made his comeback, winning 52.7 percent of the vote. He spent $13 million in that race, only one million more than White. It was the costliest Texas governor's race up to that time.[54] Clements proved that his election in 1978 was not a fluke, and that the Republican Party was in Texas to stay—and to win.

CLAYTON WILLIAMS VERSUS ANN RICHARDS IN 1990

The 1990 Democratic gubernatorial primary proved to be a nasty one, even by the standards of the Texas Democratic Party. Its most important players were Ann Richards, the state treasurer and a former county commissioner from Austin; Jim Mattox, the state's attorney general and a former U.S. congressman from Dallas; and former Governor Mark White, the Texas attorney general who had defeated Bill Clements in 1982 and who had been defeated by Clements in 1986. All were able and tested candidates and all had run successful statewide campaigns. Richards and Mattox were the liberals in the race, White the moderate-conservative. Mattox, in particular was known as a rough campaigner. He was described by columnist Molly Ivins as "a man so mean he wouldn't spit in your ear if your brains were on fire."[55] Mattox accused Richards of drug use, a charge that White also picked up. Richards in turn attacked Mattox's and especially White's finances. In the primary, White finished third. His money had dried up, his campaign had disintegrated, and he received less than 20 percent of the primary vote. He was bitter, so bitter that just before the November election, he refused to say that he would vote for Richards. Given the Hill–Briscoe tensions of 1978, it was a bad omen; the conservatives might again jump the traces for the Republican candidate.

Prior to running in the general election, however, Richards still had to beat Mattox in the run-off primary. Richards had received only 39.2 percent of the primary vote to Mattox's 37 percent. Democrats feared that the run-off primary would create such ill feeling in the party that the winner would have no chance at the governorship. The Democratic nominee for Texas attorney general, Dan Morales, pleaded with both candidates to run a clean campaign because, he said, "a run-off marred by personal attacks and mudslinging could hurt all Democrats in the November general election." Texas Democratic Party chairman Bob Slagle met for five days with representatives of the two campaigns to try to work out a truce.[56] However, peace efforts failed and the personal attacks between the two candidates continued. The fruits of those personal attacks for the Democratic Party and its nominee were well illustrated when, in the week before the run-off primary election, Mark White called a news conference and said that he would never endorse, never support, and never vote for Ann Richards. He offered a comparison between her campaign tactics and those of Nazi storm troopers.[57]

Richards won the run-off with 57 percent of the vote, but the Democratic Party was badly wounded by the primary and the run-off campaigns. Was it a victory to nowhere? It seemed that way. The Democratic Party was divided, just as it had been when John Hill lost to Bill Clements in 1978. Worse, a liberal, Ann Richards, had won the Democratic nomination and liberal Democrats had not done well in statewide races even when Texas was a one-party Democratic state. But, Republicans were about to learn a lesson—there could be victory for Democrats, even liberal Democrats, if Republicans erred and chose a candidate who proved an embarrassment.

The early front-runner in the Republican primary was former congressman Kent Hance, an attractive and able politician who was a Democrat turned Republican. But Hance and the other Republicans in the primary were soon overwhelmed by the money and media buys of a man who had never before run for political office—a remarkably colorful and wealthy west Texan, Clayton Williams. Celia Morris offers a vivid portrait of Williams:

> He was a grinning, jug-eared, guitar-playing, high-energy guy in chaps who had come out of the Texas recession with $110 million of his own money, after paying his debts.
>
> To the amazement of bystanders, he had even ridden a horse up the capitol steps to publicize his telecommunications company's fight against AT&T. . . .
>
> With nothing short of genius, Williams exploited the cowboy myth—far and away the most powerful in Texas culture. Not only did he wear a ten-gallon hat and boots, but he said he didn't even own a pair of shoes. Admitting that he had "decked" an employee in an office dispute, he said he would do it again, and his audiences loved it. He confessed to ABC's Judd Rose that he would like to be John Wayne, of whom he had two statues and a portrait, and Rose concluded that since Williams had "brawled, boozed, and whored," he was "a throwback to the old West, not unlike the image his ads promote relentlessly." His corporate jet was even nicknamed Lonesome Dove.
>
> Williams had the gall of a daylight bank robber, as well as the zest, and journalists who went to scoff were abashed to find they really liked the guy. He spoke cowhand Spanish with gusto, teared up whenever he heard the Texas A&M fight song, and danced on tables when he was deep enough in the sauce. When he was young, he had announced that he would make a million dollars, kill a lion on an African safari, and marry a beautiful woman, and he had done all three, though not in that order.[58]

Williams had run a strong Republican primary campaign, in which he had spent about $6 million of his own funds. He had personally financed about two thirds of his primary campaign expenditures. Such wealth and willingness to spend it is a major asset in a Texas political campaign, which relies heavily on expensive media buys. A television advertisement that claimed Williams would deal with the crime and drug issue by having addicts and criminals break up rocks had remarkable political appeal and seemed to turn Williams into a serious candidate. But the popularity of "bustin' rocks" somewhat obscured Williams's tendency to make thoughtless and insensitive remarks. In March, for example, at a rainy outing on his ranch, Williams commented that "the weather's like rape. If it's inevitable, you might as well lie back and enjoy it."[59] Still, in September 1990, a *Houston Chronicle* poll showed Williams ahead of Richards 48 percent to 33 percent. Political observers did not see how she could overcome such a gap in such a short time, and Richards herself was fearful that her loss would be so enormous that she would bring down the entire Democratic ticket.[60]

However, Williams's gaffes kept coming. There were embarrassing remarks about prostitutes and ungentlemanly comments about Ann Richards. And, there were media stories of overuse of irrigation water on his properties and irregularities at a bank he owned.

In a Dallas television interview, Williams said that he could neither recall the sole constitutional amendment on the ballot or how he had voted on it. It was, unfortunately for Williams, an important amendment, especially for a governor, since it would have weakened the governor's appointment powers. Shortly after, Williams, a multimillionaire, announced that he had paid no income taxes in 1986.[61]

Ann Richards's gubernatorial victory in 1990 was due largely to the inappropriateness of her Republican opponent, Clayton Williams. Williams's public gaffes and ungentlemanly behavior toward Richards did not go over well with many Republicans, especially women, who ended up crossing party lines and voting for Richards.

Ultimately, Williams lost the election. Women in particular voted heavily for Richards, and even conservative Republican Dallas County went for Richards. Richards won 52 percent of the two-party vote. Celia Morris claims that 61 percent of women voted for Richards and 21 percent of Republican voters crossed party lines and voted for her.[62] Other data question that high proportion of votes by women and high percentage of crossover voting,[63] but it is clear that women did strongly support Richards.[64] Richards won by fewer than 100,000 votes, however, and, if Libertarian votes are counted, she won with less than 50 percent of the vote.[65] However, Ann Richards was governor, not because of a resurgence of Democratic fortunes in Texas, but because of the loss of women voters by Republicans. It was less of a Richards victory than it was a Republican defeat.

Clayton Williams was rich and colorful with a cowboy image that should have been appealing to Texans. Indeed, one is reminded of "Pappy" O'Daniel (see Chapter 25) and his colorful style and rural appeal. But something was different. Texas was no longer the provincial state that it was in the 1930s. Republican voters were educated, urban voters, and, instead of enjoying Williams's colorful personality, they were embarrassed by him. He lost the support of urban Republican women and, with that loss, even a liberal Democrat was able to win the governorship. It was, however, a different environment for Ann Richards than for previous Democratic governors. She was elected, unlike other Texas Democratic governors, not as the choice of the voters, but rather as the only alternative to a Republican candidate whose words and behavior had made him unacceptable to urban Republicans. By 1990, a Democratic governor of Texas was an anomaly, one that would be eliminated in the next election when the Republican Party would nominate an urban, more sophisticated candidate.

THE LASTING SIGNIFICANCE

These three elections—John Tower to the U.S. Senate in 1961; Bill Clements as governor in 1978; and Ann Richards as governor in 1990—offer important lessons about the nature of political parties in Texas. In 1961, John Tower became the first Republican to win statewide office in Texas since Reconstruction, but his victory was the result of special circumstances—it was a special election and the Democratic Party was deeply divided. That split in the Democratic Party, with liberals in the party refusing to support William Blakely, led to Tower's victory. In 1978, John Hill assumed that the old pattern in Texas politics would remain. That is, the victor in the Democratic gubernatorial primary would become governor. Thus, he became overconfident and did nothing to heal the breach in the Democratic Party brought about by his primary victory over Democratic governor Dolph Briscoe. Although Hill was not a liberal Democrat, he was to the left of both Briscoe and Republican Bill Clements, and conservative Briscoe Democrats voted for Clements over Hill. Thus, again the ideological breach in the Democratic Party allowed for a Republican victory. That victory was a lot more important to the Republican Party than was John Tower's earlier victory, because the main power of the governor of Texas resides in the office's appointment power, and Clements was able to build the party in Texas by using that power. In 1990, it again looked like the ideological divisions in the Democratic Party would cause a Republican victory. The moderate-conservative Mark White was alienated by Ann Richards because of the bitterness of the Democratic primary and there was intense bitterness between Richards and fellow liberal Democrat Jim Mattox. Democratic infighting almost handed the Republicans another victory, except Clayton Williams's gaffes and behavior created a gender gap that allowed Richards to be victorious. Williams created a gender division in voting in general and in the Republican Party in particular, and Richards was able to win with crossover voting by Republican women. However, the Richards victory can best be seen as a Republican defeat, rather than a Democratic victory. And, 1990 shows, unlike an earlier era in Texas politics, that Texans want sophisticated candidates rather than colorful entertainers.

It used to be that, in the absence of meaningful Republican opposition, the divisions in the Democratic Party would be fought out in the Democratic primary. The winner of the primary would win the election because the losing Democratic faction had no place else to go. Once the Republican Party became meaningful, losers in the Democratic primary did have someplace else to go. The Tower election in 1961 shows that liberals were willing to vote for a Republican conservative over a Democratic conservative if they did not get their way within the Democratic Party. Similarly, 1978 shows that conservative Democrats could now go to the Republican candidate when they lost within the Democratic Party. The 1961 U.S. Senate race and the 1978 gubernatorial race were lost by the Democratic Party rather than won by the Republicans.

And, in 1990, Republicans discovered that a two-party system allowed those disaffected members of their party to also cross over the party line and vote for the opposing candidate. Now that the Republican Party was truly competitive, 1990 was their election to lose—and they promptly did.

One effect of a two-party system is that the disaffected in one party now have someplace to go—they can vote for the candidate of the opposing party. Looking at this situation rationally, one would expect that each party would now try to avoid internal party blood-lettings in order to minimize defections from the party and in order to produce a unified front against the opposing party. Whether that is the lesson that has been learned by the parties and their candidates, however, remains to be seen.

Summary

Political parties provide a structure through which candidates strive to achieve office. Moving through that structure, however, is a massive undertaking. The candidate must first run in a party primary and then, if the candidate does not receive a majority of the votes, must run in a run-off primary. Ideally, the battles of primaries and run-off primaries will be forgotten and the party will come together in support of the nominee in order to win the election. However, what often happens is that the primaries and run-offs create enormous conflicts and divisions in the party that are not healed. The opposition then exploits those party divisions so that their candidate can win the election.

Texas is so large, so diverse, and has so many media markets that campaigns—especially statewide campaigns—are very expensive. For the most part, the candidates themselves must raise the money that is necessary to win an election. In a gubernatorial campaign, such campaigns can cost $30 million or more. One effect of the high cost of campaigns in Texas is that candidates are often very wealthy individuals who are willing to provide money to their campaigns.

Although Texas once tried to narrow the franchise, primarily by limiting the right to vote through poll taxes and white primaries, in recent years it has tried to expand the franchise through the motor voter law and through early voting. Yet, voter participation in Texas is quite low. That is probably because of the demographics of Texas voters, but it may also be due to the scheduling of elections in Texas, the vast number of elections, and the large number of low visibility candidates for office.

One of the most striking developments in Texas politics over the past twenty to twenty-five years is that the era of one-party Democratic dominance is gone from the Texas political scene. That decline in Democratic dominance corresponds to the rise of the Republican Party in Texas. Currently, every statewide elected officeholder in Texas is a Republican. Republicans were adept in John Tower's race for the senate in 1961 and Bill Clement's race for the governorship in 1978 in exploiting divisions in the Democratic Party. In 1961, the Republicans won their first statewide election since Reconstruction, and in 1978, Republicans won their first governor's race since Reconstruction. However, as the Republican Party developed into a major party in Texas, Democrats were able to exploit Republican divisions that led to Democrat Ann Richards's gubernatorial victory in 1990.

Currently, the most dangerous division in the Republican Party is the split between religious conservatives who have a social agenda and economic conservatives who have a low-taxing/low-spending agenda. Nor are Republicans secure as the dominant party. It is important that they grow and expand their base of support. One of the Republican Party's great weaknesses is its lack of support among Hispanics, the fastest growing ethnic group in Texas. If the Republicans are to continue their remarkable successes in Texas politics, they will have to make greater inroads with Hispanic voters.

Are there limits to Republican strength in Texas? It should be emphasized that people who identify with the Democratic Party still have a slight edge in Texas over those who identify with the Republican Party. Additionally, those who identify themselves as independents have a slight edge over both Republicans and Democrats. However, the success of the Republican Party in winning elections in Texas over the past twenty years has been extraordinary.

It does seem unlikely that Texas will become a one-party Republican state in the same way that it once was one-party Democratic. It is unlikely that the Democratic Party, well established in Texas for 150 years, will not suddenly dry up and mount no political challenges against Republicans. Nor is it likely that independents will move wholeheartedly into the Republican camp.

Democrats still have a significant base of support in the minority community, with older Texans, with native Texans, and with liberals. Yet, the Democratic Party clearly is in trouble. For Texas to be a competitive two-party state, the Democrats need to win some statewide elections, and yet no Democrat currently holds a statewide elected office. The party needs to regroup and redirect its appeal to Texans. Most importantly, if the Democratic Party is to do more than lose elections, it must do what parties have traditionally done in states that have political machines. That is, it must get out the vote. If Democrats voted in the same proportions as Republicans do, they would win elections, but participation among Texas Democrats is lower than participation among Texas Republicans.

FOR FURTHER READING

Anders, Evan. *Boss Rule in South Texas: The Progressive Era.* Austin: University of Texas Press, 1982.

Davidson, Chandler. *Race and Class in Texas Politics.* Princeton, NJ: Princeton University Press, 1990.

Green, George Norris. *The Establishment in Texas Politics, 1938–1957.* Westport, CN: Greenwood Press, 1979.

Key, V. O. *Southern Politics.* New York: Vintage Books, 1949.

Olien, Roger M. *From Token to Triumph: The Texas Republicans since 1920.* Dallas: SMU Press, 1982.

Tolleson-Rinehart, Sue, and Jeanie R. Stanley. *Claytie and the Lady.* Austin: University of Texas Press, 1994.

STUDY OUTLINE

The Role of Political Parties in Texas Politics

1. The most important function of Texas parties is to provide a label under which candidates run and with which voters identify those seeking office.
2. Sixty percent of Texas voters identify with either the Democratic or Republican parties.
3. Party membership helps in organizing government.
4. The Democratic and Republican parties have both temporary and permanent organizations.
5. Each party has the same organizational structure. On a state level, permanent organization includes the state executive committee, the county or district executive committee, and the precinct chairperson.
6. On a state level, temporary organization includes the state convention, the county or district convention, and the precinct convention.

Texas's History as a One-Party State

1. Starting in 1873, Texas became a one-party Democratic state in which the Republican Party seldom contested for major state offices.
2. Allan Shivers led the Shivercrat movement, which signaled that Texas Democrats were more conservative than the national Democratic Party.
3. Until the late-1970s, the winner of the Democratic Party primary usually won the general election.
4. Starting in the 1970s, the Republican Party began to strongly challenge the Democratic Party in the general election.
5. In 2000, party identification was split between the Democratic Party and the Republican Party, but Republican voters are more likely to vote.
6. The 1990s marked a dramatic growth of the Republican Party and a similar decline for the Democratic Party.
7. Democrats identify themselves as more liberal than Republicans or independents.
8. The base of support for the Democratic Party is minorities and native and older Texans. Of these groups, only the Hispanic population is growing.
9. Republicans are more conservative than Democrats and receive support from individuals 18 to 29, those who recently moved to Texas, and those with incomes over $60,000.
10. The Republican Party will benefit from Texas's young population and continued migration into the state. Its weakness is the lack of support from minorities.
11. Conflict between the religious right and economic conservatives in the Republican Party pose a threat to the party's continued dominance in Texas.

Elections in Texas

1. Texas is a democracy but its government is not reflective of the characteristics of its population.
2. Many elections are held throughout the year.
3. Primary elections are paid for by the state and political parties and determine the party's nominees for the general election.
4. To win a party's nomination, a candidate must receive an absolute majority of votes cast. If no candidate receives the required number of votes, a run-off primary is held.
5. Officially, Texas conducts a closed primary, but in reality, Texas has an open primary.
6. General elections are held the first Tuesday following the first Monday of even numbered years.
7. In Texas, major state officials are not elected in the same year as the President of the United States is elected.

8. Special elections are used to fill a vacancy in office, to borrow money, or to ratify amendments to the Texas Constitution.

Participation in Texas Elections

1. The white primary, poll tax, and early voter registration reduced voter participation.
2. Sixty percent of eligible Texans are registered to vote, yet fewer than half of registered voters cast ballots.
3. Income and education are the two most important factors in determining if people vote, and the state has low levels of educational attainment and per capita income.
4. Participation in Texas can be increased through better educational programs, increases in per capita income, parties and interest groups taking a more active role in educating the public, and better media participation in informing the public.
5. Early voting is intended to increase levels of participation.
6. *Politiqueras* are women political workers from the Rio Grande Valley who are employed by politicians to deliver a certain number of votes for a candidate.

Campaigns

1. The goal of a political campaign is to win both the primary and the general election.
2. In Texas, candidates are responsible for planning campaign strategy and raising money, and parties take a secondary role.
3. Media are the most expensive costs in most campaigns.

Three Pivotal Elections

1. The election of John Tower in 1961, the election of Bill Clements in 1978, and the election of Ann Richards in 1990 offer important lessons in the study of political parties in Texas.

PRACTICE QUIZ

1. Providing a label that helps voters identify those seeking office is an important function of
   a) the state.
   b) political parties.
   c) interest groups.
   d) regional and subregional governments.
2. In the state of Texas, the highest level of temporary party organization is the
   a) state convention.
   b) state executive committee.
   c) governor's convention
   d) civil executive committee.
3. In Texas, the Republican Party began to challenge the dominance of the Democratic Party in the
   a) 1960s.
   b) 1970s.
   c) 1980s.
   d) 1990s.
4. The first Tuesday following the first Monday in November is the day for which election?
   a) primary election
   b) run-off primary
   c) general election
   d) run-off for the general election
5. Officially, Texas has a
   a) joint primary.
   b) extended primary.
   c) open primary.
   d) closed primary.
6. Which of the following is *not* a type of election found in Texas?
   a) general
   b) primary
   c) distinguished
   d) special
7. Politiqueras are found in which part of Texas?
   a) in the metropolitan areas of central Texas
   b) in the Rio Grande Valley
   c) in the rural areas of east Texas
   d) in the trans Pecos region
8. The two most important factors in determining if someone will vote are
   a) income and education.
   b) education and family history of voting.
   c) income and gender.
   d) party membership and gender.
9. The most costly item for most political campaigns is
   a) travel.
   b) security.
   c) fund raising.
   d) media.

CRITICAL THINKING QUESTIONS

1. Parties provide labels under which candidates run for office and by which votes identify candidates. Consider how electoral decisions could be made if candidates were not identified by party membership. For example, would more people vote? Would it be more or less difficult for individuals to discover the candidates' views on the issues? Would fund raising be more or less difficult?

2. Voter participation in Texas is among the lowest in the nation. What accounts for the state's low levels of participation? What can be done to increase voter participation in the near term? In the long term?

KEY TERMS

closed primary (p. 866)
county chair (p. 857)
county convention (p. 858)
county executive committee (p. 857)
early registration (p. 868)
early voting (p. 874)
general election (p. 866)
motor voter law (p. 870)
open primary (p. 866)
politiqueras (p. 875)
poll tax (p. 868)
precinct (p. 857)
precinct chair (p. 857)
precinct convention (p. 858)
presidential Republicanism (p. 860)
primary elections (p. 865)
run-off primary (p. 866)
Shivercrat movement (p. 859)
special election (p. 867)
state chair and vice chair (p. 858)
state convention (p. 858)
state executive committee (p. 858)
white primary (p. 868)

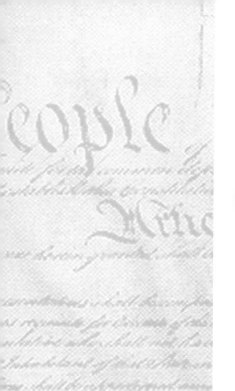

23 Interest Groups,

★ **Interest Groups in the Political Process**

How much influence do interest groups have in Texas state politics? What form does this influence take? How do lobbyists gain access to policy makers? How do lobbyists try to influence policy?

★ **The Lobbying "Bidness": Two Stories**

How do the Texas Chemical Council and the Texas Trial Lawyers Association illustrate the influence of interest groups in Texas?

Lobbying, and Lobbyists

IN the early 1970s, the Speaker of the Texas House of Representatives, Gus Mutscher, was in trouble. He was a defendant in civil cases that sought damages in a stock-fraud case. He was also being sued by the Federal Deposit Insurance Corporation for payment of a $332,000 loan from the Sharpstown State Bank, which he had used to buy stock. He had sought financial aid from other interests as well, such as the private Moody Bank in Galveston. Then Speaker Mutscher tried to excuse his financial hustling by saying that he needed an airplane and traveling money to be "more independent" of the business lobby.[1]

Could lobbyists—especially business lobbyists—be that important in Texas politics that a Speaker would admit to concerns about being dependent on them? It is to the question of lobbying, lobbyists, and interest groups and their role in Texas politics that we now turn.

Interest Groups in the Political Process

▶ How much influence do interest groups have in Texas state politics? What form does this influence take? How do lobbyists gain access to policy makers? How do lobbyists try to influence policy?

It is probably true that all of us have political interests, goals, or objectives that can be achieved with governmental intervention. Many of us, however, will never act to achieve those goals. A few of us may privately speak to a legislator or other official. However, some of us will join with others to try to convince the government to help us in achieving our interests. When that is done, we have formed an **interest group**.

interest group
a membership organization created to pursue a common interest through political participation, with the ultimate goal of getting favorable public policy decisions from government

At one time, it was often claimed that business-oriented interest groups dominated the Texas legislature. Using campaign contributions, political pressure, and sometimes corruption, it was claimed "The Lobby," as pro-business groups were called, ran Texas government. Some of the most influential business leaders of the state belonged to the "8F Crowd." 8F was the number on a suite of rooms at the Lamar Hotel in Houston, where George Brown, a founder of Brown & Root, one of the world's largest construction firms, held court. He met regularly with other fabulously wealthy Texans such as Jesse Jones of Texas Commerce Bank and Tenneco, Gus Wortham of American General Insurance, and James Elkins of the Vinson & Elkins law firm. These men socialized together and worked together to promote their political interests. It was claimed that for forty years these men were the king-makers in Texas politics and determined much of the important policy of state government.[2]

The "8F Crowd" was, of course, an interest group—an elite, wealthy, powerful pro-business interest group. Although the "8F Crowd" is long gone from the Texas political scene, much of what they did is still done in Texas politics by other interest groups, though no modern-day interest group is ascribed the influence that was alleged to be held by the "8F Crowd."

Nevertheless, Texas is known as a state that has long had powerful interest groups. Even during the Texas Constitutional Convention of 1875, an interest group played an important role. That was the Grange, a powerful farmers' organization, of which many of the framers were members. As Chapter 21 indicated, the Constitution of 1876 reflected many of the values of Grange members. It was a document for rural Texas that was pro–small farmer and opposed to a powerful state government.

With the development of a strong oil and gas industry in Texas in the first half of the twentieth century, the oil industry began playing an important role in state politics. In one-party states, interest groups often assume an important role in state politics, perhaps because one-party states tend to have a small number of important sectors in their economies and limited economic development. However, as Chapter 22 showed, Texas has in the past twenty years moved from a Democratic one-party system to a competitive two-party system and now, some argue, seems to be moving to a Republican one-party system. It also now has a strong and diversified economy. Yet interest groups maintain great influence. No single interest is as influential as the Grange was in the nineteenth century, or the oil and gas industry—or even the "8F Crowd"—was in the first half of the twentieth century, but interest groups remain unusually powerful in Texas politics.[3]

THE BOND THAT LASTS: INTEREST GROUPS AND POLICY MAKERS

Interest groups want something from policy makers—they want policy that is beneficial for their group. On the other hand, policy makers benefit from developing relationships with interest groups. From those groups, the policy maker gains information since the interest groups can provide substantial expertise in areas that are of special concern to the group. Additionally, interest groups can provide campaign funds to the policy maker. In a state as large as Texas, with numerous media markets and with competitive parties, considerable campaign funds are necessary to run in and win elections. An interest group can help raise money from its membership for a candidate sympathetic to the interest group's goals. Additionally, interest groups can supply votes to the policy maker. They can assist in mobilizing their own group and they can also supply campaign workers to distribute campaign leaflets and to operate phone banks in order to get out the vote. Interest groups can also publicize issues through press conferences, press releases, publications, conferences, hearings, and even by filing lawsuits. Finally, interest groups can engage in research and education programs. It has become increasingly common for interest groups to engage in public education programs by running advertisements in the Texas media explaining why their particular approach to a public policy problem would be more beneficial to Texans in general.

Unlike a private citizen interested in and involved in politics, an interest group has several advantages. Larger or better-funded interest groups have: (1) time; (2) money; (3) expertise; and (4) continuity.

Although concerned citizens do have an impact on public policy in Texas, organized and well-funded interest groups have an advantage in affecting the policy process. It is difficult for a concerned citizen from Houston to spend time in Austin developing relationships with policy makers and trying to convince those policy makers of the desirability of public policies that are compatible with the individual's goals. On the other hand, if that individual joins with like-minded people to create an organized interest group, there may be a greater likelihood of achieving policy goals. It might be possible to fund an office in Austin and pay a staff that could, on a daily basis, monitor events in state government and develop relationships with key policy makers. Additionally, while there are some individuals in Texas who do have the money to provide substantial campaign support to policy makers, even those individuals can get more "bang for the buck" if they join with like-minded individuals in **bundling** their contributions into a larger contribution from the interest group.[4] The creation of an organized interest group also allows for the development of a staff. The staff can gain in-depth knowledge of an area of policy far greater than could be gained by most individuals working alone. Also, an individual may be intensely concerned with an issue in one legislative session, but may find it difficult to sustain that interest over a period of many legislative sessions. At least the larger, better-funded, more successful organized interest groups have continuity. They are in Austin, developing relationships with policy makers and presenting the views of the organization day in and day out, year in and year out. The result is that legislators and other policy makers can develop long-standing relationships with the interest groups and the groups' representatives in Austin.

bundling
the interest-group practice of combining campaign contributions from several individuals into one larger contribution from the group, so as to increase the group's impact on the candidate

lobbyist
an individual employed by an interest group who tries to influence governmental decisions on behalf of that group

TYPES OF INTEREST GROUPS AND LOBBYISTS

Interest groups strive to influence public opinion, to make their views known to policy makers, and to elect and support policy makers who are friendly to their point of view. To do those things, interest groups usually maintain **lobbyists** in Austin who will try to gain access to policy makers and communicate their objectives to those policy makers. There are several different types of lobbyists. Some interest groups have full-time staffs in Austin who work as lobbyists. One form of interest group is, of course, a corporation, and companies often have government relations departments that lobby for the company's interests. Lobbyists may be employed by an interest group to deal with one issue or they may be employed by an interest group on a regular basis. Some lobbyists represent only one client; others will represent large numbers of clients. All lobbyists, however, must be able to reach and communicate with policy makers. Corporate interest groups tend to use either government relations departments or law firms to represent their interests in Austin. Often industries have broad interests that need representation in Austin. For example, an insurance company may have one specific interest they wish to have represented in Austin. However, the insurance industry as a whole also has a wide range of issues that need representation, and thus they will form an industry-wide interest group.

Nina Butts, a lobbyist with Texans Against Gun Violence, a single-issue interest group, discusses gun-control measures at a press conference in Austin.

Interest groups may also represent professional groups. One of the most influential professional groups in Austin is the Texas Medical Association, which represents the interests of the medical community in state government. Other professional groups represent accountants, chiropractors, opticians, dentists, and teachers.

That teachers are an important interest group suggests still another type of interest group in Austin—public employee interest groups. Public school teachers may be the largest and most effective of these groups, but firefighters, police officers, and even justices of the peace and constables all are represented in Austin.

Some interest groups are single-issue interest groups. For example, an interest group may be concerned about the regulation of abortion or school vouchers or tort reform or the environment. Other interest groups are concerned with multiple issues that affect the group. Public school teachers, for example, are concerned about job security, qualifications of teachers, health insurance, pensions, salaries, and other matters that affect the lives of their members.

Civil rights groups such as the National Association for the Advancement of Colored People, the League of United Latin American Citizens, or the Mexican American Legal Defense Fund are concerned about civil rights issues affecting the lives primarily of African Americans and Latinos. Interestingly, not only do these groups often try to influence public opinion and the legislature, but they have had notable success in representing their groups' interests through litigation, especially in the federal courts.

There are also public interest groups that try to promote consumer, environmental, and general public issues in Austin. Examples of these groups are Public Citizen, the Sierra Club, and Common Cause. Groups like the Sierra Club work to promote environmental interests, while groups like Public Citizen and Common Cause tend to have broader interests and work to promote more open government. These groups rarely have much funding, but they often can provide policy makers with information and expertise. In addition, they can mobilize their membership to support or oppose bills and they can publicize matters that are important to their goals.

GETTING ACCESS TO POLICY MAKERS

It is important for the interest groups' representatives, the lobbyists, to communicate with policy makers, and that need for communication means lobbyists must gain access to policy makers. Gaining access to policy makers, of course, imposes on the time of legislators and so lobbyists will often spend significant sums entertaining legislators. That entertainment is one of the most criticized aspects of lobbying, but from the lobbyists' perspective, entertainment of a legislator provides the lobbyist access to the policy maker and puts the policy maker in a congenial frame of mind. Entertainment by lobbyists can involve expensive dinners, golfing, and other entertainment.

Access to policy makers may also be gained by building support for an issue among their constituents. Constituents may be encouraged, for example, to write or call legislators about a bill and offer their opinions. Essentially, the interest group tries to mobilize interested voters to get involved in the political process on behalf of the groups' goals.

One important way of gaining access to those in government is to employ former officials as lobbyists. A lobbyist who is a former legislator often has

Politics on the Web

Interest groups, like political parties, have turned to the Internet as a vehicle for building support and raising funds, as well as for presenting their views to the public on a variety of issues in an inexpensive and timely manner. Web sites also provide interest groups with a new way for keeping their membership informed, mobilizing their membership to action, and recruiting new members.

Texas think tanks and other so-called public interest groups particularly benefit from the Internet. Before the Internet, studies on public affairs would be released and get one or two days of good press before being exiled to the shelves of a few public and personal libraries. Today, however, such studies are published online, making them available to anyone who might access them through any one of a number of keyword searches on the various search engines. As a result, citizens interested in a particularly controversial public issue no longer need depend upon the press as their sole source of information. They can go to the source and formulate their own opinions at their own speed. More importantly for interest groups, the Internet keeps their reports and studies on public affairs in the public eye.

www.wwnorton.com/wtp3e

friends in the legislature and can use that friendship to gain access. Additionally, a former legislator often is in an exceptionally good position to understand the personal relationships and informal power centers that must be contacted to accomplish a legislative objective. As a result, some of the best-paid lobbyists in Austin are former Texas state officials and often are former legislators. The issue of lobbying by former officials and their staffs is a significant one since there is a concern that policy decisions may be made with an eye toward future lucrative lobbying jobs. That concern over former public officials was significant enough that when "Pete" Laney was elected Speaker of the Texas House of Representatives in 1993, he pledged that he would not immediately seek a lobbying job after leaving office, and he placed a similar restriction on his top staff.[5]

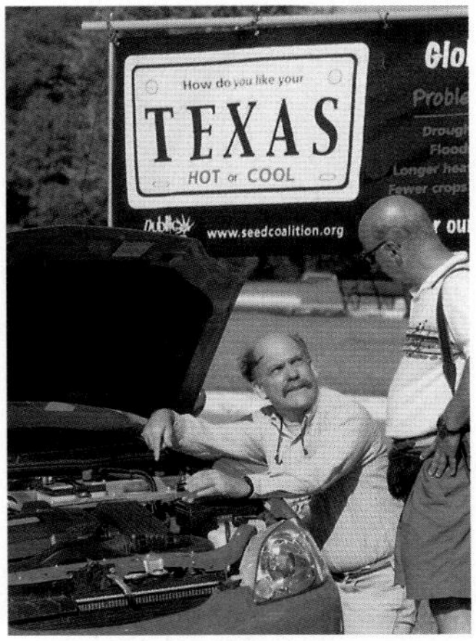

A member of Public Citizen, a consumer and environmental interest group, discusses the engine of a hybrid gas/electric automobile with a tourist visiting Austin.

At the end of 1997 there were 1,662 registered lobbyists in Texas, almost double the number registered ten years earlier. It is unclear how much these lobbyists were paid due to the nature of Texas reporting laws,[6] but they may have made up to $210 million for representing 2,304 clients. At least 110 of those lobbyists were once public officials, and at least 91 of those were former legislators, including three former Speakers, perhaps the most powerful legislators. There were also six former officers of the legislature. Although former public officials constitute only 7 percent of all registered lobbyists, they had 17 percent of all lobbying contracts and about 21 percent of all lobbying income. Reporting laws suggest that the average lobbyist has an income possibly as high as $126,062, but the average public-official-turned-lobbyist has an income about three times that amount.

Once lobbyists obtain access to policy makers, they provide information that may be useful. For example, they may explain how a bill benefits the legislator's district, or how it benefits the state, or how it is perceived as being unfair. Since the staffs of Texas legislators are small, lobbyists perform useful functions by explaining what numerous bills are intended to do. They may even write bills to be introduced by friendly legislators or write amendments to bills. Almost certainly if a bill affects the interests of a lobbyist's client and reaches a point in the process where there are hearings on the bill, the lobbyists will arrange for testimony to be given at the hearing explaining the viewpoint of the interest group on the proposed legislation.

Lobbyists do not limit their activities to the legislative process, of course. Rules proposed by the bureaucracy or the courts can affect the interests of lobbyists' clients and they will testify at hearings on rules and try to provide information to administrators in face-to-face meetings as well.

There is always a concern that lobbyists may corrupt policy makers by bribing them in order to accomplish the interest groups' policy objectives. Early in the twentieth century, the famed U.S. congressman and Speaker Sam Rayburn served in the Texas House of Representatives for six years. At that time, he was especially concerned with corruption and refused to accept free meals and entertainment from lobbyists. He called some of his fellow legislators "steak men." By that he meant that the legislators would sell their votes on a bill for a steak dinner at the Driskoll Hotel in Austin. "Steak men" (and women) may still exist in Texas politics, but, for the most part, lobbyists provide information, campaign contributions, and political support (or opposition) rather than bribes.

Still, from time to time lobbying does stoop to very low levels. In 1989, "Bo" Pilgrim, a large poultry producer, distributed $10,000 checks to state senators in the capitol while he was lobbying them on workers' compensation reform. Perhaps even more troubling, some senators accepted the checks until media attention forced them to reconsider. Yet, this practice of offering $10,000 while asking for a senator to vote on a specific bill was not illegal. A year later, the Speaker of the Texas House of Representatives, "Gib" Lewis, got in trouble for his close relationship to a law firm that specialized in collecting delinquent taxes for local governments. In 1991, Speaker Lewis was indicted for receipt of an illegal gift from the law firm. Ultimately, Lewis plea-bargained and received a minor penalty. The result of these scandals, however, was legislation that created a state Ethics Commission. There were also additional lobbying reporting requirements imposed and restrictions on speaking fees that interest groups paid legislators and pleasure trips that lobbyists provided legislators. By no means was the law a major regulation of or restriction on lobbying practices, but it did put some limits on lobbying behavior.

Texas only has weak laws dealing with lobbying by former government officials. A former member of the governing body or a former executive head of a regulatory agency cannot lobby the agency for two years after leaving office. Senior employees or former officers of Texas regulatory agencies cannot ever lobby a government entity on matters they were involved in when employed by the government. However, there are no legal restrictions on lobbying by a former governor, former lieutenant governor, former legislator, or any former aides to these officials.[7]

WHO REPRESENTS BUBBA?

Another problem with lobbying was well described by the director of a public interest lobby, Craig McDonald, "Legislators are rubbing shoulders with . . . lobbyists, almost all of whom hustle for business interests. While corporate interests dominate our legislative process, there is virtually no counterbalancing lobby to represent Bubba. Nowhere on the list of Texas' biggest lobby spenders will you find a single group dedicated to the interests of consumers, the environment or human services. No wonder these citizen interests repeatedly get steamrolled in Austin."[8]

Figure 23.1 classifies the interests represented by the registered lobbyists and estimates the value of those lobbying contracts. Although the categories are very broad, it is clear that business interests do dominate lobbying in Texas government. Of course, many issues considered by Texas government may pit one business interest against another and sometimes a business or professional organization may find itself aligned with consumer interests. For example, the Texas Trial Lawyers Association, an organization of plaintiffs' lawyers in Texas, frequently finds itself aligned with consumer interests. Many of the clients of these lawyers are consumers who sue large businesses. The interests of these lawyers and their clients are especially close since the lawyers are paid on a contingent fee basis, which means the lawyers don't receive payment unless their clients receive payment. It is also the case that lobbying is not all there is to the representation of interests in Austin. Interest groups without money may still be able to mobilize their members in order to accomplish their objectives or they may be able to influence public opinion. Still, there is no question that money does help in politics. Figure 23.1 does provide support for concern that, in this battle of mostly business interests, there may not be an

INTERESTS REPRESENTED BY TEXAS LOBBYISTS Figure 23.1

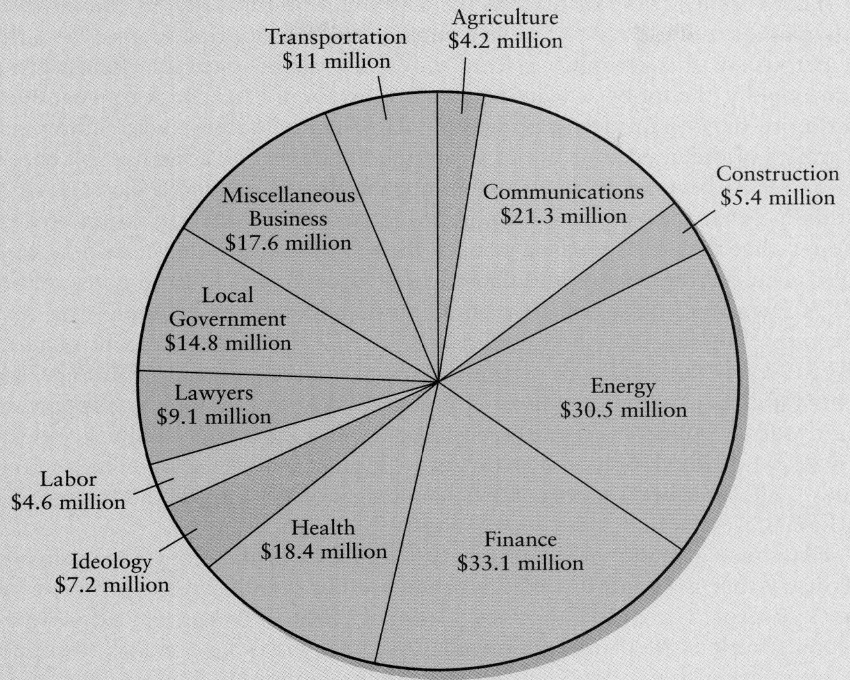

SOURCE: Texans for Public Justice, "Austin's Oldest Profession," www.tpj.org/reports/lobby/industry.html.
NOTE: The amounts in the figure are rounded. The Communications category includes Communications and Electronics. The Energy category includes Energy and Natural Resources. The Finance category is the FIRE category of the Finance, Insurance, and Real Estate Industry. The Lawyer category is the category for Lawyers and Lobbyists. Expenditures are the maximum values on the broad range of amounts in the lobbying report forms. Amounts are only for direct lobbying of government officials and do not include money for grassroots lobbying or media campaigns.

objective voice or at the very least a voice for the public interest that reaches the ears of legislators.

ANOTHER SIDE TO LOBBYING: SHOW ME THE MONEY

Lobbyists in Texas represent mostly business interests, and they are active in trying to gain access to government officials and inform them of the legislative desires of their clients. But, interest groups are not simply information channels between business and government in Texas. They also promote the political interests of elected officials who support their viewpoints and oppose the interests of those who do not. One major way that interest groups engage in this activity is by making campaign contributions. Interest groups may encourage individual members to make contributions to candidates or they may

political action committee (PAC)
a private group that raises and distributes funds for use in election campaigns

collect funds from their members, bundling those funds as a donation from the interest group. When this is done, the interest group creates a **political action committee (PAC)** to make the contribution.

There are a variety of reasons for forming a political action committee. A candidate is more likely to notice a substantial contribution from a PAC than numerous small contributions from individual members of an interest group. Additionally, the lobbyist who delivers a substantial PAC check to a candidate can more likely gain access to a politician than a lobbyist who simply asks members of the interest group to separately mail in small contribution checks.

The PAC becomes a way for the interest groups to send a message to the candidate that its members support the goals of the interest group strongly enough that they are prepared to back those goals with money. In some cases, a PAC can even serve as a middleman to provide money to candidates that the PAC's members might not want to support publicly. For example, the Texas Chemical Council PAC is known as FREEPAC. One solicitation in behalf of FREEPAC to the members of the Chemical Council noted, "FREEPAC can contribute to candidates whom company PACs would like to support but can't, due to political circumstances. Supporting the Texas chemical industry can be politically dangerous, as well as expensive for elected officials or candidates. Those who support the chemical industry need the support of FREEPAC."[9]

issue advocacy
independent spending by individuals or interest groups on a campaign issue but not directly tied to a particular candidate

PACs may give money directly to the candidate or they may engage in **issue advocacy** that is supportive of the candidate but is independent of the candidate's control. The candidate does not report these independent expenditures on contribution disclosure statements. PACs may also spend money to support an issue rather than a specific candidate or to support such activities as "get-out-the-vote" campaigns.

In 1997–98 there were 891 political action committees in Texas. Of these, 506 can be identified as business political action committees, 86 as labor

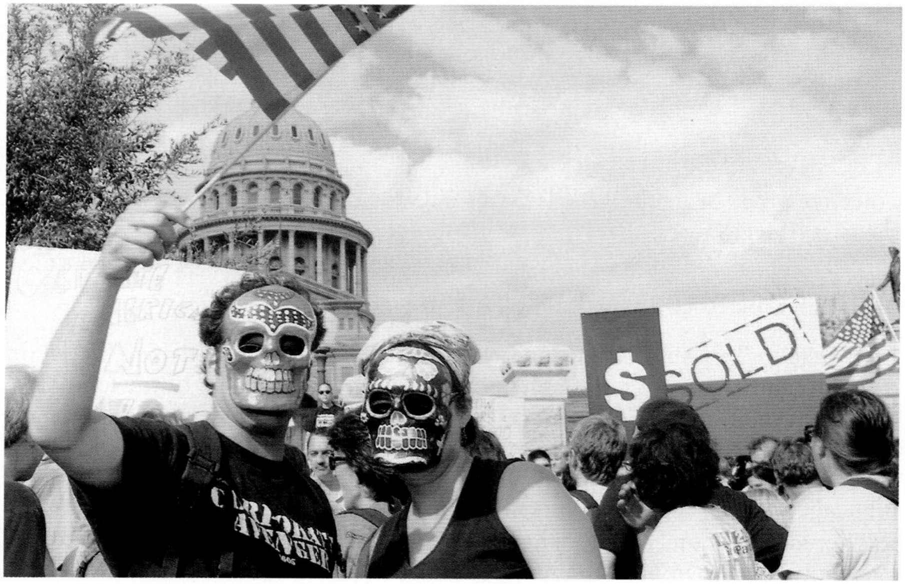

Demonstrators in front of the capitol building in Austin protest against business influence in government.

PACs, 263 as ideology-oriented or single issue PACs, and 37 could not be identified. Figure 23.2 shows that political action committee expenditures are overwhelmingly from business-related PACs. Business PACs contributed about $31.5 million to Texas political campaigns, labor PACs only about $2.3 million, and ideological or single-issue PACs about $17.7 million. Business-related interest groups clearly dominate the action in political action committee contributions.

The two largest business PACs are Vinson & Elkins, a major law firm that represents the business community, and the Texas Association of Realtors. Vinson & Elkins gave $1.2 million in the 1997–98 spending cycle and the Texas Association of Realtors gave $1.1 million. Business PACs in the finance/insurance/real estate area gave the most money, over $7.1 million; followed by the lawyer and lobbyist PACs, which gave over $6.5 million; and energy and natural resources business PACs, which gave nearly $5.2 million. Of the one hundred biggest-spending PACs in Texas in 1997–98, seventy-eight were business-related.[10]

Ideological and single-issue PACs include those that provide contributions from the Democratic and Republican parties. There are also PACs in this group that are dedicated to reform of the tort laws, support for school vouchers, abortion rights, the environment, gun laws, and minority issues. Two PACs, however, account for more than half of all the spending of ideological and single-issue political action committees. They are the Texas Democratic Party's PAC and the Texas Republican Campaign Committee. Actually, both parties have a large number of political action committees devoted to a variety of purposes. Altogether there were about 50 PACs in 1998 that spent money for the Democratic Party's interests and about 128 PACs that spent money for

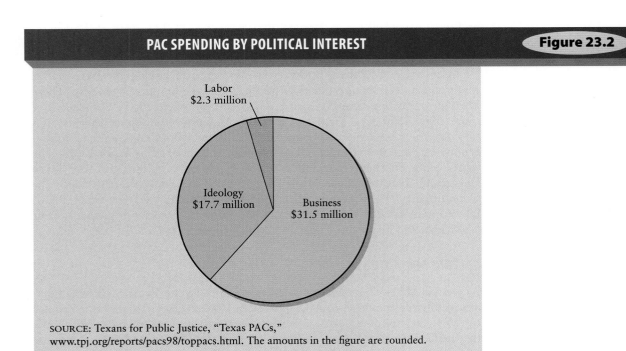

PAC SPENDING BY POLITICAL INTEREST **Figure 23.2**

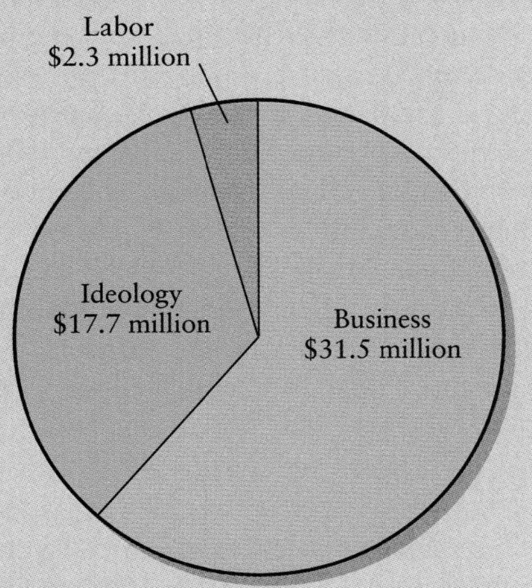

SOURCE: Texans for Public Justice, "Texas PACs," www.tpj.org/reports/pacs98/toppacs.html. The amounts in the figure are rounded.

Box 23.1

JIM HIGHTOWER MEETS THE FARM BUREAU

After I first took office as Texas agriculture commissioner in 1983—having run a headbutting, bloodletting campaign against the chemical companies, the right-wing Farm Bureau, and other forces of ignorance and arrogance—these same forces sent their lobbyists around to see me, offering big toothy smiles, cooing words of congratulations, and proffering checks to help pay off my campaign debt. It's a ritual in Texas politics called "getting well."

The Farm Bureau lobbyist, a particularly smarmy character, took me by the elbow, pulled me closer to him than I ever wanted to be, and with his hot, Binaca-tinged lobbyist's breath whispered confidentially into my ear: "Now that you're in, Hightower, we can start with a clean slate. You move over to the middle of the road and we'll get along juuusst fine."

Later I was laughing about this with a farmer I knew from Deaf Smith County. This corn farmer looked me in the eye and gave me the truest political advice I ever got: "The hell with the middle of the road," he said, "there's nothing in the middle of the road but yellow stripes and dead armadillos."

SOURCE: Jim Hightower, *There's Nothing in the Middle of the Road but Yellow Stripes and Dead Armadillos* (New York: HarperCollins, 1997), p. 246.

the Republican Party's interests. When the expenditures of all the party political action committees are counted, more than $15 million or 84 percent of the ideological and single-issue PACs were political party committees. Among political action committees devoted to single issues, the most important are Texans for Lawsuit Reform, which spent $1.2 million in the 1998 election cycle, and the Texas Civil Justice League, which spent $356,331. Both of these committees were primarily funded by business interests to promote laws sympathetic to defendants in tort suits.[11]

In contrast to business and even ideological and single-issue PACs, labor represents a very small amount of political action committee spending. There are only eighty-six labor PACs and only five of those had 1997–98 spending of more than $100,000. Two teacher political action committees that are opposed to the school voucher proposals of Governor Bush and Lieutenant Governor Perry spent one fourth of all the money expended by labor PACs. The Texas State Teachers Association spent $432,005 and the ACT for Texas Classroom Teachers Association spent $119,534. The AFL-CIO PAC, the Committee on Political Education Fund, spent $200,312. The other major labor PACs are the San Antonio Police Officers Association, which spent $188,835, and Teamsters Local 745, which spent $143,720.[12]

GETTING OUT THE VOTE

As we will see in Chapter 26 on the Texas judiciary, the Texas Medical Association constructed a grassroots campaign in 1988 to elect its slate of candidates to the Texas Supreme Court. Physicians were encouraged to give to TEXPAC, the medical association PAC. They were also encouraged to make individual contributions. Additionally, physicians were given slate cards with recommended candidates, literature endorsing candidates, and even expensively produced videotapes. They were asked to not only encourage families and friends to vote for the medical association endorsed candidates, but also to encourage their patients to vote for the association's candidates. The effort by the medical association was remarkably successful for its fund-raising success and for its success in reaching and mobilizing the grass roots.[13]

More recently, a pro-business interest group that supports restrictions on civil lawsuits, the Texans for Lawsuit Reform, has attempted with mixed success to combine campaign contributions with a grassroots campaign in favor of its tort reform agenda. Part of the grassroots campaign involves placement of highway billboards that support tort reform. When state senator Drew Nixon voted against bringing a tort reform bill to the floor of the Texas Senate, he faced the wrath of Texans for Lawsuit Reform. Nixon had received $7,500 in campaign contributions from the interest group when he ran for re-election in 1996, but Texans for Lawsuit Reform attacked him in news releases when he opposed the tort reform bill in 1999. Nixon responded in kind with news releases, but soon found himself "deluged by phone calls and faxes from angry TLR [Texans for Lawsuit Reform] members."[14]

Developer Richard Weekley organized Texans for Lawsuit Reform. When it was organized in the early 1990s, it put together a $600,000 campaign fund for legislative and judicial candidates in only three months. On its 270 member board of governors are some of the most influential businesspeople and civil defense lawyers in Texas.[15]

One of the most aggressive interest groups, it proved very successful in achieving its goals in the 1995 legislative session, but far less successful in later years. In 1997, Representative Patricia Gray proved an obstacle to the TLR program, claiming she would not let the bills out of her committee until they were amended to make sure that plaintiffs with legitimate claims were not denied their day in court. TLR attempted a grassroots campaign to counter Representative Gray's uncooperativeness. In a speech to Houston realtors, for example, a consultant who had worked for TLR urged those in attendance to complain to Gray and the other four Democrats on the committee. That speech was followed by a similar effort before the Heights Chamber of Commerce in the Houston area. That effort led to Gray's receipt of more than twenty phone calls and fifty faxes.[16]

SUPPOSE INTEREST GROUPS WANT TO DEFEAT A CANDIDATE

Generally speaking, it is difficult and risky to try to defeat an incumbent Texas legislator. Incumbency gives a legislator enormous political advantages. For example, in the 1998 primary elections there were 132 House incumbents seeking re-election and only 19 faced a challenge in their party's primary. Of those, only five challengers defeated an incumbent in a primary. In the 1998 general elections, only 36 of the 127 remaining House incumbents faced a challenger and challengers defeated only two of these incumbents. These data clearly suggest that if an incumbent runs for re-election, it is far safer for interest groups to try to work with the incumbent and to support the legislator for re-election. It does seem that is the general strategy. Campaign money, for example, overwhelmingly goes to incumbents. There were 52 incumbents in the Texas House of Representatives in 1998 who faced opposition either in the primary, the general election, or both. Those 52 incumbents raised $8.7 million, while their 71 opponents raised only $3.6 million.[17]

Money goes to incumbents even if they face no opposition. There were eighty incumbents who had no primary or general election opponent, but they raised $6.2 million for the 1998 general election anyway.[18] Why? Interests are certain of the outcome in those races and freely give to build ties with the legislator. More importantly, the legislator welcomes campaign contributions because the legislator knows that a large campaign war chest will likely frighten away political opponents, who will conclude that the incumbent's resources are so great that successful opposition is impossible.

Of course, there are times when an interest group does not want to help a candidate or even pressure a candidate—they want to defeat that candidate. It can be a risky strategy because the candidate might win and then the interest

Box 23.2 **CAMPAIGN FINANCE IN TEXAS**

Opponents of national campaign finance reform maintain that no major new laws are needed, preferring a laissez-faire approach instead. One state that provides a real-world experiment in this minimalist stance on campaign finance is ours.

Texas has no limits on campaign contributions to candidates for state legislative or executive offices. It relies only on disclosure to regulate campaigns, and those laws are weak and porous.

For example, candidates don't have to report their contributors' employers or occupations. Also, contributions made in the last ten days of a statewide campaign don't have to be reported until after the election.

Groups that engage in independent expenditures have few regulatory requirements, too. And out-of-state political action committees fare well, rarely having to disclose their contributions in Texas.

So what are the consequences of such a minimalist campaign system? Is Texas a shining model for the nation or an egregious example of special influence run amok?

Here are the facts:

Big Money Dominates. Most campaign money in state races comes from only a small number of big contributors. In state House races in 1996, 48 percent of the contributions came from only nine ZIP codes out of 2,609 in Texas. One person alone gave $3.8 million to state candidates in 1998. Gov. George W. Bush got 25 percent of his $25 million that year from just 207 donors.

Money Wins. Not surprisingly, the candidate spending the most money in Texas wins almost all of the time. Out of 66 contested state House races in 1996, 59 were won by the candidate with more money. The fabled grassroots campaign doesn't have a chance anymore in Texas.

Campaigns Aren't Competitive. Incumbents usually lock up big contributions because they have the power to assist special interests. That money imbalance has so stifled election competition that most incumbents barely break a sweat in their races anymore. . . .

SOURCE: Fred Lewis, "Laissez-faire Financing Fails Texas," *Dallas Morning News*, April 2, 2000, p. 6J.

group will be faced with not only an unfriendly public official, but also one angry at the interest group for its opposition. When that happens, the interest group will "get well" or "get on the late train." What this means is that the interest group will make a substantial political contribution to the candidate it opposed who won. Often, winning candidates have significant campaign debts after a grueling election battle and they are appreciative of the late contributions of former enemies, which are offered as a way of making amends. When Governor Bill Clements ran for re-election in 1982, he was defeated by State Attorney General Mark White. However, after White's election, he had campaign debts of nearly $5 million. Between the November 1982 election and January 1983, the "late train" givers, who were trying to make amends for supporting Clements over White, easily repaid the loans.[19]

Commonly, candidates are especially loyal to those supporters who were early backers, because without support at the very beginning of a campaign, it is hard for a candidate to build an organization and get the support necessary to make a decent campaign start. There is even a national PAC, EMILY's List (Early Money Is Like Yeast), that provides early campaign funding to female candidates. EMILY's List is a PAC funded by women on behalf of female candidates. In Texas, it was an important early contributor to Ann Richards. However, though "late train" contributors may never have the loyalty that politicians reserve for their earliest supporters, at least those debt-paying late contributions will make the official feel somewhat more positive about the interest group and its goals.

Sometimes PACs will even give to both candidates as a way to avoid alienating either candidate, though the possibility remains that such dual giving will wind up alienating both candidates. At other times, interest groups simply don't care if they alienate a candidate. In 1994, Texans for Lawsuit Reform gave $120,000 to one candidate for the Texas legislature, an enormous sum. They did not care, however, that they might alienate that candidate's opponent if the opponent won. The opponent was not only backed by the state's trial lawyers, but was a trial lawyer himself. Texans for Lawsuit Reform knew that there was no way such a candidate would ever support their objectives and so they had no fear that he would be alienated from them if he won. No matter what, such a candidate would be opposed to the objectives of the interest group. As the founder of Texans for Lawsuit Reform put it, "That's about as clear-cut as you can get."[20]

When an interest group is convinced that it cannot work with a public official, the interest group may undertake an all-out effort to defeat that official. That is what happened in 1996 and 1998 to Zeb Zbranek, a Democrat and a state representative from Liberty County. Zbranek sat on the House Committee on Civil Practices, a crucial committee for legislation dealing with tort reform. From that powerful position, Zbranek opposed the tort reform efforts of Texans for Lawsuit Reform. The result was that TLR spent $83,000 in the 1996 election opposing Zbranek. In 1998, TLR supported Zbranek's opponent in the Democratic primary with $30,000 in contributions. When Zbranek won the primary, TLR supported his Republican opponent in the general election, even paying for two of the Republican's full-time campaign managers.[21] By the end of 1998, Texans for Lawsuit Reform had spent $183,959 in three unsuccessful efforts to defeat Zbranek.[22] Such a strategy may win for TLR the lifetime enmity of Zbranek, but TLR probably figures

Putting Children First's unsuccessful attempt to oust Speaker of the Texas House, Pete Laney, hurt their credibility as a single-issue-oriented interest group as well as all but destroyed their chances of influencing legislation in a Laney-led House.

that Zbranek would never be a friend anyway. And, TLR might either defeat Zbranek or so exhaust him with difficult and expensive campaigns that Zbranek retires from office.

One of the most dangerous and most foolish efforts by an interest group in recent years was an effort by Putting Children First, a pro–school voucher organization, to oust the Speaker of the Texas House of Representatives, "Pete" Laney, by electing a Republican House majority in 1998. Putting Children First viewed Laney as unsupportive of school vouchers. In trying to accomplish their coup against Laney, they worked with Texans for Lawsuit Reform. Unfortunately for Putting Children First and Texans for Lawsuit Reform, not only did they fail to elect a Republican House and topple Laney, but then-Lieutenant Governor Bob Bullock resigned as honorary chairman of Putting Children First. Bullock, who had no desire to oust Laney, protested the partisanship of the group.[23] The result was that Putting Children First lost the friendship of Bullock and the credibility that his honorary chairmanship gave the group. Bullock, after all, was one of the most able statewide elected officials in Texas history and was highly regarded in political circles. Additionally, and more dangerous in the long-term for these interest groups, "Pete" Laney is still Speaker, and the Speaker of the Texas House is the most powerful member of the House. No doubt their activities were noted by Laney and will be remembered by him. There is a saying, "If you try to kill the king, you must succeed." The reason, of course, is that the consequences of failure are quite bad for the conspirators. The same might be said of the speakership of the Texas House, "If you try to oust the Speaker, you must succeed."

The Lobbying "Bidness": Two Stories

▶ How do the Texas Chemical Council and the Texas Trial Lawyers Association illustrate the influence of interest groups in Texas?

THE CHEMICAL LOBBY

One of the state's most influential interest groups is the Texas Chemical Council, a trade group of chemical companies with business interests in Texas. In the 1996 and 1998 election cycles, political action committees tied to the Chemical Council spent more than $2.2 million in campaign contributions. Members of the Chemical Council hired 222 lobbyists in 1999 alone, paying them as much as $8.7 million. Some draw a connection between pollution in Texas and the high level of political activity of Chemical Council members. Craig McDonald, director of Texans for Public Justice has noted, "Pollution and political clout are closely linked in Texas. The TCC is a prime example of how a special-interest group harnesses big money in order to dump on average Texas citizens. Cleaning up state politics is the first step towards cleaning up the air we breathe and the water we drink." In 1996, members of the Texas Chemical Council released 187 million pounds of toxic waste into Texas.[24]

When the Texas Chemical Council was formed in 1953, it was the first trade group that was organized to influence state government.[25] Since that time, one of the ways that the Chemical Council and its members have influenced state government is through campaign contributions. Overall, incumbents in statewide offices in Texas received $457,853 from the twenty Chemical Council member political action committees that reported contributions. Out-of-state political action committees do not have to file reports in Texas unless they spend at least 20 percent of their overall expenditures in the

The business interests of the vast chemical industry in Texas are represented to the state government by the Texas Chemical Council. Generous campaign contributions from the Chemical Council to state officials have ensured not only lax environmental regulations, but direct corporate involvement in environmental legislation through key commission appointments.

state and so these reported contributions are probably less than was actually given by Chemical Council member PACs.[26] In addition, the Chemical Council members have taken a special interest in the members of three legislative committees that handle most of the environmental legislation in the House.

While Chemical Council member PACs contributed $582,375 to incumbent members of the Texas legislature between 1995 and 1998, about 24 percent of that money was given to the twenty-five members of the Senate Natural Resources Committee, the House Natural Resources Committee, and the House Environmental Committee.

Has a good relationship with state officials benefited the chemical industry? One of the most important environmental regulatory agencies in Texas is the Texas Natural Resources Conservation Commission (TNRCC). Governor Bush appointed an oil lawyer to the TNRCC, an agri-businessman, and a thirty-year veteran of Monsanto Chemical who was once a Chemical Council lobbyist.[27] When in early 1997 TNRCC officials sought to end a provision in the 1971 Texas Clean Air Act that exempts some facilities from the law, Governor Bush requested that Exxon and Marathon draft an alternative policy, which became the basis of the Clean Air Responsibility Enterprise program. The program was determined by a DuPont representative as having ". . . no 'meat' with respect to actual emissions reductions. . . ." It was enacted into law over the opposition of environmental groups.[28]

THE TRIAL LAWYER LOBBY

Trial lawyers are also known as plaintiffs' lawyers. They represent individuals against businesses, insurance companies, physicians, and other professions. Often trial lawyers are aligned politically with labor unions and consumer groups. That is because working people and consumers are often the clients of plaintiffs' lawyers. Plaintiffs' lawyers are usually paid on a contingent fee basis, where the lawyer makes money only if the case is won, and they then collect about 33 to 40 percent of the judgment or settlement. As a result, trial lawyers have an interest in promoting laws that make it easier to sue and win against businesses, insurance companies, and professionals.

Some trial lawyers have become very wealthy, and they often will contribute money for political and lobbying campaigns. Since Texas has few well-organized labor groups, trial lawyers tend to be a major source of funds for political efforts to pass laws favorable to those who sue businesses. Often trial lawyers are seen as antibusiness and tend to be aligned with liberal Democrats, who often have labor, consumer, or environmental interests, rather than with conservative Democrats or Republicans, who tend to be aligned with the business community.

The main organization of trial lawyers in Texas is the Texas Trial Lawyers Association. As Texas has moved in a conservative direction and Republicans have increasingly come to dominate the policy process, the political fortunes of the trial lawyers have declined dramatically. Additionally, business-oriented interested groups, such as the Texas Civil Justice League and Texans for Lawsuit Reform, have organized and become successful counterweights against the political efforts of the trial lawyers.

In the 1960s, the trial lawyers were very successful in protecting their interests in the legislature. Some members of the legislature were trial lawyers, and like other interest groups, the trial lawyers were willing to provide expertise, money, and votes to legislators who supported their interests. In the 1960s, the business community was concerned about the high cost of workers' compensation insurance and organized labor was concerned about the low levels of workers' compensation benefits. In an unusual move, in 1965 a coalition of business and labor developed urging the abolition of trials *de novo*—court trials that were held to appeal workers' compensation board decisions, but that were not restricted by decisions of the workers' compensation board. Court awards were usually considerably higher than board awards and lawyers' fees for court awards were twice the fees for board awards. Reform of the system, however, was prevented until the Texas Trial Lawyers Association was able to participate in developing a compromise that did not eliminate trial *de novo* and did not impair the financial interests of the trial lawyers in the workers' compensation system.

With the formation of the Texas Civil Justice League to promote business interests in the legal system in 1986, punitive damages were attacked. Businesses were fearful of punitive damages, which can be very large and which introduce a high level of uncertainty for businesses. Punitive damages do not provide an award for actual damages caused by some injury; instead, they are damages imposed to punish the offending party. In 1987, the Texas Trial Lawyers Association compromised with the Civil Justice League, agreeing to limit punitive damages to amounts no greater than four times the actual damages. Although the provision seemed a compromise between the business community and the plaintiffs' bar, it was actually a victory for the trial lawyers. Since actual damages can include damages far beyond direct economic losses, such as loss of consortium, disfigurement, or loss of future earnings, punitive damages could still be substantial and so the business community gained little from the legislation.

In 1989, the workers' compensation system again came under attack. Business interests had begun to experience large increases in the cost of workers' compensation insurance and the Texas Civil Justice League led the charge in favor of a more pro-business compensation system. By 1989, the Republican Party was showing strength and, due to an increase in pro-business representatives, the Texas House of Representatives proved quite receptive to the pro-business reforms. The Texas senate was less sympathetic to change, but ultimately it followed the lead of then Lieutenant Governor Bill Hobby. Trial *de novo* was abolished on appeal from the workers' compensation board in most cases and, for the most part, awards made by the Workers' Compensation Commission would be final. It was a major defeat for the trial lawyers because, under the new administrative system for workers' compensation, there was no financial incentive for attorney involvement. That defeat was followed by a minor setback for trial lawyers in 1993 with the passage of the Products Liability Act. That law required plaintiffs who sued manufacturers for making an inherently dangerous product to prove that a safer alternative and economically feasible design was available at the time of manufacture.

In 1994, Texas elected George W. Bush as its second Republican governor since Reconstruction, and in the 1995–96 legislature, there were fourteen Republicans in the Texas Senate and fifty-eight in the House. A Republican had defeated a strong supporter of the trial lawyers, State Senator Ted Lyon, in 1992. In 1994, a Republican defeated another of the strongest supporters of the trial lawyers, State Senator Carl Parker. After the 1994 elections, most of the effective opponents of tort reform in the legislature were gone. And, in the early 1990s there was a new, more aggressive pro-business interest group that was less inclined to compromise with the trial lawyers—Texans for Lawsuit Reform. Remaining senate Democrats and Lieutenant Governor Bob Bullock concluded that further resistance to tort reform could be politically dangerous for them, as it had been to Lyon and Parker. At the end of the session in 1995, there were numerous bills passed that promoted a pro-business civil justice agenda. For example, limits were placed on punitive damages; there were prohibitions on frivolous lawsuits; there were restrictions on where lawsuits could be filed; and there were restrictions on liability such that defendants were liable in proportion to their responsibility for the injury rather than the wealthiest defendant being potentially liable for all the damages. Taken together, the tort reform measures were an astounding loss for the interests of the trial lawyers.

The losses of the trial lawyers were not due to any changes in their approach to government. What had worked well for them in an earlier era in Texas politics simply was not working well for them anymore. What happened? By the late 1980s, the Texas Trial Lawyers Association discovered Texas politics had become a hostile environment. The business community had mobilized against them, first with a compromise-oriented interest group—the Texas Civil Justice League. Later, in the early 1990s, parts of the business community formed a very militant, take-no-prisoners tort reform interest group—Texans for Lawsuit Reform. However, the losses of the trial lawyers reflect more than the creation of counter-interest groups. The environment was different. The Democratic Party was in decline and the Republican Party was in ascendancy, and with the growth of the Republican Party in Texas came losses for liberal Democrats and gains for pro-business Republicans.[29]

Still, in spite of losing recent political battles, the Texas Trial Lawyers Association remains formidable. Of the fourteen largest legal political action committees, twelve represent corporate interests, but two represent the interests of plaintiffs' lawyers. One is the Texas Trial Lawyers Association PAC, which spent $957,484 in 1998, and the other is a newly formed political action committee, the Constitutional Defense Fund, which spent $141,250 in 1998. The Constitutional Defense Fund was created by five lawyers who litigated the state's $17.3 billion tobacco settlement, and the PAC has been one way these lawyers have opposed efforts to limit the legal fees they received in the case. The TTLA PAC is ranked seventh of the top one hundred political action committees in terms of spending in Texas. That is the same ranking it had in 1996. Only one other lawyer PAC, the Vinson & Elkins political action committee, is larger. The Constitutional Defense Fund is much smaller, ranking seventy-one in spending in 1998 out of the top one hundred PACs.[30]

Summary

Interest groups play an important role in Texas politics even though Texas is no longer a one-party state with limited economic development. Even with two major political parties and a diverse economy, Texas politics cannot be understood without also examining the role of interest groups. Interest groups in Texas have a notable pro-business tinge. Labor is weak in Texas and its role in the political process is quite limited. Trial lawyers are an especially wealthy and important interest group that promotes liberal policies in Texas, but with the growth of the Republican Party and tort reform interest groups, the influence of the trial lawyers has waned.

Though there is no single interest group or coalition of interest groups that dominates Texas politics, the overwhelming bulk of lobbyists represent business interests and the bulk of PAC money comes from business interests. Often, of course, it is the case that businesses are pitted against businesses in the political process. It is also the case that public interest, civil rights, consumer, and environmental groups may still be successful by mobilizing public opinion and influencing the media. However, the point remains that there are limited voices among interest groups that offer alternatives to business perspectives on policy issues.

FOR FURTHER READING

Goodwyn, Lawrence R. *Texas Oil, American Dreams: A Study of the Texas Independant Producers and Royalty Owners Association.* Austin: Texas State Historical Association, 1996.

Hrebenar, Robert J., and Clive S. Thomas (eds.). *Interest Group Politics in Southern States.* Tuscaloosa: University of Alabama Press, 1992.

Marquez, Benjamin. *LULAC: The Evolution of a Mexican American Political Organization.* Austin: University of Texas Press, 1993.

Pittman, H. C. *Inside the Third House: A Veteran Lobbyist Takes a 50-Year Frolic through Texas Politics.* Austin: Eakin Press, 1992.

Presley, James. *Saga of Wealth.* Austin: Texas Monthly Press, 1983.

Rozell, Mark J., and Clyde Wilcox (eds.). *God at the Grass Roots: The Christian Right in the 1994 Elections.* Lanham, MD: Rowman & Littlefield, 1995.

STUDY OUTLINE

Interest Groups in the Political Process

1. Interest groups are formed when individuals join together in an attempt to influence government and governmental officials.
2. Texas has powerful interest groups. For example, the "8F Crowd" influenced Texas politics for many years.
3. Interest groups want government to enact policies that benefit the groups, and, in return, groups provide information, money, and votes to politicians who advance the groups' programs.
4. Interest groups have at least four advantages over individuals as they attempt to influence what government does: time, money, expertise, and continuity.
5. A lobbyist is an individual who attempts to influence what governments and officials do.
6. Interest groups can be classified as corporate or business interest groups, professional groups, public-employee interest groups, single-issue interest groups, civil rights groups, or consumer and environmental interest groups.
7. Access is essential to interest group activity because lobbyists must be able to phone and meet with policy makers if the lobbyists are to advance their causes.
8. Former government officials often make excellent lobbyists, and Texas has weak laws concerning lobbying by former public officials.
9. Lobbying takes place in all branches and at all levels of government.
10. After several scandals, the legislature created the Texas Ethics Commission, which enforces lobbying reporting requirements and restrictions on how much compensation a legislator can receive for giving a speech.
11. There are many interest groups to represent business, but few groups work for the interest of consumers.
12. Interest groups create political action committees (PACs), which donate to candidates. PACs give money

directly to candidates, and they make independant expenditures to support a candidate. Business PACs give far more money than PACs in any other category.

13. In addition to contributions, influencing lawmakers' constituents is one of the most effective ways interest groups have for influencing the outcomes of elections.
14. It is difficult for groups to defeat an incumbent legislator, and incumbents receive an overwhelming percentage of PAC contributions.

The Lobbying "Bidness": Two Stories

1. The Texas Chemical Council is one of the most powerful organizations that influence Texas politics. In 1996 and 1998 its PAC contributed more than $2 million to campaigns and employed 222 lobbyists.
2. The Texas Trial Lawyers Association, once highly influential in the Texas legislature, has seen its power decline since the mid-1980s as a result of other interest groups mobilizing against it.
3. Business interest groups are more influential than public interest, civil rights, consumer, and environmental groups.

PRACTICE QUIZ

1. The goals of interest groups include all *except*
   a) electing people to office in order to control the government.
   b) influencing those who control government.
   c) educating the public and members about issues of importance to the group.
   d) maintaining a heterogeneous membership.

2. The "8F Crowd"
   a) was a group of legislators who failed the eighth grade.
   b) was a group of extremely wealthy Texans who met in Suite 8F of the Lamar Hotel in Houston and controlled Texas politics for more than forty years.
   c) were twenty-five legislators who boycotted the eighth session of the legislature in order to prevent the legislators from taking any action because it lacked a quorum.
   d) were the eight most powerful officials in the state who met in Suite F of the Austin State Office Building.

3. Interest groups supply public officials with all the following *except*
   a) information.
   b) money.
   c) media coverage.
   d) committee assignments.

4. When PACS combine small contributions from many people to form one large contribution it is called
   a) bundling.
   b) compacting.
   c) cracking.
   d) packing.

5. The most important thing interest groups need to be effective
   a) are offices in Austin.
   b) are many issues on which to lobby.
   c) are large, paid staffs.
   d) is access to politicians.

6. Trial lawyers are which type of interest group?
   a) professional group
   b) public-employee group
   c) single-issue group
   d) consumer group

7. Lobbying takes place in the
   a) legislative branch only.
   b) legislative and executive branches only.
   c) executive and judicial branches.
   d) legislative, executive, and judicial branches.

8. PACs are used to
   a) stir the public's interest in politics.
   b) elect officers of the interest group.
   c) raise money from individuals, which is then bundled and given to candidates.
   d) create media campaigns to influence the course of government.

9. One of the most important grassroots tactics of interest groups is
   a) to get out the vote.
   b) to form political alliances with executive and legislative leaders.
   c) to lobby the judicial branch of national and state government.
   d) to interpret the needs of their members.

10. In Texas, the most powerful interest groups represent which interests?
    a) consumer
    b) civil rights
    c) business
    d) public employee

CRITICAL THINKING QUESTIONS

1. The Texas Association for the Classical Kazoo (TACK) advocates increased use of the kazoo in public school music programs, government subsidies for writing music featuring the kazoo, and subsidies for bands and orchestras playing kazoo music. You are hired as the group's principal lobbyist. What techniques might this organization use to achieve its aims?

2. Interest groups representing business issues dominate Texas politics. These groups contribute massive ammounts of money to aid their causes. Likewise, these organizations employ dozens of lobbyists to work for their issues. How can other groups compete with the business interests? How likely is it that other groups will succeed against business opposition?

KEY TERMS

bundling (p. 895)
interest group (p. 893)
issue advocacy (p. 900)
lobbyist (p. 895)
political action committee (PAC) (p. 900)

24 The Texas

★ **Structure**

How is the Texas state legislature organized? What are the constitutional requirements for becoming a member? What is the current membership like?

★ **Sessions of the Legislature**

What are the different types of sessions in the Texas legislature?

★ **Powers of the Legislature**

What are the powers of the Texas legislature? To what ends does it use these powers?

★ **How a Bill Becomes Law**

What are the steps in the legislative process?

★ **Other Players in the Legislative Process**

In addition to legislators, who else is involved in the legislative process and what role do they play?

★ **Power in the Legislature**

Who are the most important leaders in the Texas legislature? What are their powers? How does the battle over redistricting illustrate the party politics within the legislature?

Legislature

THE Texas legislature is often portrayed as a body of scoundrels and buffoons—and it does have its share. However, it is also a place of exceptional political talent and sometimes of remarkable courage and eloquence. There is no better example of that talent, courage, and eloquence than former Texas state senator Henry B. Gonzalez of San Antonio. It was May 1957, and there was resistance to desegregation of schools in Texas. Bills were being considered to maintain segregation, when Gonzalez took the floor in opposition to a measure that allowed parents who objected to integration to withdraw their children from school.

Gonzalez spoke in opposition to the bill for twenty-two hours and two minutes, even though passage of the bill was certain. Gonzalez said, "I seek to register the plaintive cry, the hurt feelings, the silent, the dumb protest of the inarticulate." In response to the argument that the bill was necessary, Gonzalez responded, "Necessity is the creed of slaves and the argument of tyrants!" It was an exceptional effort that actually forced his opponents to drop four other segregation bills in order to get him to stop talking.[1]

When Gonzalez was in the Texas Senate, the conservative Democrats dominated it and the great issue in the minds of most legislators was avoidance of public school desegregation. Power battles in the legislature tended to pit liberal Democrats against conservative Democrats. At times, the liberals would win some victories, like Gonzalez's, but these victories were rare. Republicans were insignificant as a force in legislative politics.

Less than half a century later, the Texas legislature is in change. Minorities have greater influence in the legislature, especially in the House, which has smaller districts than the Senate and allows greater chances for minority voters to elect minority candidates. Indeed, in the Texas House of Representatives, out of 150 representatives, there are now 28 Hispanic representatives and 14 African American representatives. And, in what would be a shocking development to the conservative Democrats of 1957, there are now 71 Republicans in the Texas House. Republicans have a slight majority in the Texas Senate, with 16 of the 31 state senators. Additionally, the presiding officer of the Senate—the lieutenant governor—is a Republican. It is the new power of the Republican Party in the Texas legislature that, as we shall see, is probably the most important development in contemporary Texas legislative politics.

Structure

▶ How is the Texas state legislature organized? What are the constitutional requirements for becoming a member? What is the current membership like?

bicameral legislature
a legislative assembly composed of two chambers or houses; opposite of unicameral legislature

Like the U.S. Congress and all states except Nebraska, Texas has a **bicameral legislature,** with two branches, the Texas House of Representatives and the Texas Senate. Its 31 senators and 150 House members meet for 140 days every odd-numbered year. Senators serve four-year terms and House members serve for two years. Each represents a single-member district. Members of the Texas House represent approximately 140,000 people. Senators represent almost 630,000 constituents.[2] A state senator now represents about the same number of people as does a member of the U.S. House of Representatives. Elections are held in November of even-numbered years, and senators and House members take office in January of odd-numbered years.

The constitutional requirements for becoming a member of the Texas legislature are minimal. A senator must be a U.S. citizen, a qualified voter, and a resident of the state for at least five years and of the district for at least one year. Additionally, the senator must be at least twenty-six years of age. Members of the House must be at least twenty-one, U.S. citizens, qualified voters, and residents of the state for two years and of the district for one year. These requirements are in keeping with the political philosophy of those who wrote the Constitution of 1876. They believed holding public office required little or no formal training and should be open to most citizens.

The Texas legislature is changing to better represent minorities and women; however, in 1999 there were still only three women in the Texas Senate: Senator Florence Shapiro, Senator Judith Zaffirini, and Senator Jane Nelson.

Informal qualifications of legislators are a composite or average of those serving. In Texas, the typical legislator is white, male, Protestant, college educated, affluent, and has a professional or business occupation. These qualifications do not mean that a poor, high school dropout who is a day laborer cannot be elected to the state legislature, but they do indicate individuals with most of these informal qualifications have a distinct advantage. Members of the legislature must have jobs that allow them the flexibility to campaign for office and to work in the legislature for 140 days every other year in addition to special legislative sessions and meetings of committees when the legislature is not in session. Thus, forty-nine members of the Texas House—almost one third of the members—are attorneys. It is one of the few careers that pays well and yet offers the necessary degree of time flexibility. Lawyers who serve in the legislature may even gain increased legal business due either from interests with legislative concerns or because of the enhanced community and statewide visibility of a lawyer-legislator.[3]

Legislators in Texas cannot expect to live on their legislative salaries. In keeping with the Texas constitutional tradition of a low-cost, part-time legislature, Texas representatives receive a salary of only $7,200 a year. When the legislature is in regular or special session, each member receives a $125 per diem allowance, which is equal to the amount state employees receive when traveling on state business.

Originally, both salary and per diem were set by the Texas Constitution, and a constitutional amendment was necessary to change either. In 1991, Texans adopted an amendment allowing the Texas Ethics Commission to propose changes in legislative salaries, which then require voter approval. To date, the commission has not recommended a salary increase. At the start of each regular session, the Ethics Commission sets the legislative per diem.

Table 24.1 shows the proportions of minorities and women serving in the legislature. While that number has increased over the years, it is not in proportion to their strength in the population of Texas. Civil rights laws have increased voting by minorities, and those laws provide protection for minority political districts. Thus, more minority officeholders have been elected and, as

GENDER AND MINORITY MEMBERSHIP IN THE TEXAS LEGISLATURE — **Table 24.1**

	% of Texas population	% of 1999 Texas House membership	% of 1999 Texas Senate membership
Men	49	81	94
Women	51	19	7
African American	12	9	6
Anglo	60	72	74
Hispanic	25	19	19
Other	3	0	0

SOURCES: Texas Legislature Online, "House Membership Profile," www.house.state.tx.us/common/profile.htm, and "Senate Membership Profile," www.senate.state.tx.us/common/profile.htm.

the Hispanic population in Texas increases, additional Hispanic legislators should be elected. Women have also had an increased role in politics, especially since the 1970s, and as a result, it is likely that additional women will be elected to legislative office as well.

Sessions of the Legislature

▶ What are the different types of sessions in the Texas legislature?

REGULAR SESSIONS

regular session
the 140-day period during which the Texas legislature meets to consider and pass bills; occurs only in odd-numbered years

biennial
occurring every two years

The Texas Constitution specifies that **regular sessions** of the Texas legislature meet for 140 days in odd-numbered years. The idea of **biennial** legislative sessions grew from the nineteenth-century idea that legislative service is a part-time job and a belief that short biennial sessions would limit the power of the legislature. For a few years, legislators were encouraged to end their work early by paying them for only 120 days of service.

Thousands of bills and resolutions are introduced into the legislature during a regular session, and the 140-day limitation places a considerable restriction on the legislature's ability to deal with this workload. Hundreds of bills pass in the last hours of a legislative session, most with little or no debate. More die in the end-of-session crush of business because there isn't time to consider them.

SPECIAL SESSIONS

special session
a legislative session called by the governor, that addresses an agenda set by him or her and that lasts no longer than thirty days

If the legislature does not complete its agenda before the end of the legislative session or if problems arise between regular sessions, the governor may call a **special session.** Special sessions last no more than thirty days, and the governor sets their agenda. Texas has averaged one special session a year since 1876, although years go by with no special session while in some years there may be three or four sessions.

The governor's ability to set the agenda of a special session provides him with control over which issues are discussed and what bills are passed. In many instances, the governor, Speaker of the Texas House, the lieutenant governor, and various committee chairs will meet to decide what will be done to solve the problem at hand. Once the leaders address the issue and develop solutions, the governor calls the special session.

Once the session begins, the governor can open the meeting to different issues. At times, the governor bargains for a legislator's vote in return for adding to the special session agenda an issue of importance to that legislator.

Between legislative sessions, members serve on interim committees that may require a few days of their time each month. Legislators are also frequently called on to present programs to schools, colleges, and civic clubs. They supervise the staff of their district offices and address the needs of their constituents. Special sessions, interim committee meetings, speeches, and constituent services require long hours, with little remuneration. Many members devote more than forty hours a week to legislative business in addition to full-time jobs.

When Texas was a rural, predominantly agricultural state, biennial sessions worked well; however, Texas has moved beyond this description. In the twenty-first century, Texas is a modern state with more than 80 percent of its population living in metropolitan areas. In 1999, its population grew faster than any other state. It is home to many high-tech and biotech corporations. It is a center for medical research, and Texas hosts the headquarters for NASA and the Lyndon Johnson Space Center. The state's gross domestic product exceeds that of many nations. Part-time legislators serving biennial 140-day sessions may not work well anymore in allowing the state to respond quickly and effectively to crises that arise.

Powers of the Legislature

▶ What are the powers of the Texas legislature? To what end does it use these powers?

The Texas legislature sets public policy by passing bills and resolutions, but it also supervises the state bureaucracy through the budgetary process and the Sunset Act. This is achieved using legislative and nonlegislative powers. Legislative powers consist of passing bills and resolutions. Nonlegislative powers are those functions falling outside the lawmaking function.

LEGISLATIVE POWERS

Bills Revenue bills must begin in the House of Representatives. All other bills may start in either the House or the Senate. For decades, a **bill** would be introduced in either the House or Senate and work its way through the legislative process in that chamber. A bill introduced in the Senate would be passed by the Senate prior to going to the House. Today, it is customary for a bill to be introduced into the House and the same bill, a companion bill, will be introduced in the Senate. This simultaneous consideration of bills saves time in the legislature.

There are three classifications of bills in the Texas legislature: (1) **local bills;** (2) **special bills;** and (3) **general bills.** Local bills affect only units of local government such as a city, a county, special districts, or more than one city in a county. A local bill, for example, might allow Harris County to create a sports authority or voters in a county to establish a community college. Special bills give individuals or corporations an exemption from state law. A special bill could grant compensation to an individual wrongly convicted and sentenced to prison. General bills apply to all people and/or property in the state. General bills define criminal behavior, establish standards for divorce, child custody, bankruptcy, and other matters affecting people and property throughout the state.

Resolutions There are three types of **resolutions** in the Texas legislature: (1) concurrent resolutions; (2) joint resolutions; and (3) simple resolutions.

bill
a proposed law that has been sponsored by a member of the legislature and submitted to the clerk of the House or Senate

local bill
a bill affecting only units of local government, such as a city, county, or special district

special bill
a bill which gives an individual or corporation a special exemption from state law

general bill
a bill that applies to all people and/or property in the state

resolution
a proposal, made by a member of the legislature, that generally deals with the internal workings of the government; a resolution is similar to a bill, but it has a more limited scope and lacks the force of public law

concurrent resolution
a resolution of interest to both chambers of the legislature that must pass both the House and Senate and be signed by the governor

joint resolution
a resolution, most commonly a proposed amendment to the Texas Constitution or a ratification of an amendment to the U.S. Constitution, that must pass both the House and Senate but does not require the governor's signature

simple resolution
a resolution that concerns only the Texas House or Senate, such as the adoption of a rule or the appointment of an employee, and does not require the governor's signature

Concurrent resolutions must pass both the House and Senate and, except for resolutions setting the time of adjournment, require the governor's signature. These resolutions involve issues of interest to both chambers. They may request information from a state agency or call on Congress for some action. S.C.R. 6 might, for example, call on Congress to propose an amendment requiring a balanced federal budget.

Joint resolutions require passage in both the House and Senate, but are not sent to the governor. The most common use of joint resolutions is to propose amendments to the Texas Constitution or to ratify amendments to the U.S. Constitution. Resolutions that propose amendments to the Texas Constitution require a two-thirds vote of the membership of both houses of the state legislature. Ratification of amendments to the U.S. Constitution requires a majority vote in both the U.S. House and Senate.

Simple resolutions concern only the Texas House or the Senate, and they do not require the governor's signature. They are used to adopt rules, request opinions from the attorney general, appoint employees to office in the House or Senate, or to honor outstanding achievements by Texas residents. For example, SR 27 could recognize the achievements of a Nobel Prize winner or the San Jacinto College baseball program for accomplishments in the National Junior College Athletic Association.

Resolutions of honor or recognition are done without debate and without members reading the resolution. Once the Texas House of Representatives approved a simple resolution honoring Carmen DiSalvo for his unique efforts in the fields of birth and population control. Only after the resolution was passed did its sponsor identify Mr. DiSalvo as the Boston Strangler. The resolution was quickly rescinded.

NONLEGISLATIVE POWERS

constituent powers
efforts made by a member of a legislature on behalf of his or her constituency

constituents
the district comprising the area from which an official is elected

electoral powers
the legislature's mandated role in counting election returns in the elections for governor and lieutenant governor

investigative powers
the power, exercised by the House, Senate, or both chambers jointly, to investigate problems facing the state

Nonlegislative powers include constituent powers, electoral powers, investigative powers, directive and supervisory powers, and judicial powers. These activities fall outside the scope of passing bills and resolutions; however, the passage of legislation may be necessary to fulfill these powers.

Constituent powers are those things done for or in the name of **constituents.** Efforts on behalf of constituents may involve legislative activity, such as introducing a bill or voting on a resolution. Often, however, working on behalf of constituents involves nonlegislative activity, such as arranging an appointment for a constituent with a government agency that regulates some aspect of the constituent's life, writing a letter of recommendation for a constituent, or giving a speech to a civic group in the legislator's district.

Electoral powers of the legislature consist of formally counting election returns in the elections for governor and lieutenant governor. This is accomplished during a joint session of the legislature when it is organized for the regular session.

Investigative powers can be exercised by the House of Representatives, the Senate, or jointly by both bodies. The legislature can undertake to investigate problems facing the state, the integrity of a state agency, or almost anything else it wishes. A special investigative committee is established by a simple resolution creating the committee, establishing the jurisdiction of the committee, and explaining the need for the investigation. If the special committee is formed in the House, the Speaker appoints the members of the committee. The lieutenant governor appoints members for special committees in the Senate. The Speaker and the lieutenant governor share appointments if it is a joint investigation.

Directive and supervisory powers enable the legislature to have considerable control over the executive branch of government. The legislature determines the size of the appropriation each agency has to spend for the next two years. The amount of money an agency has determines how well it can carry out its goals and objectives. A review of each agency of state government takes place each twelve years.

Judicial powers include the ability of the House to impeach members of the executive and judicial branches of state government. Upon **impeachment,** a trial takes place in the Senate. A majority vote of the House is required to bring charges, and a two-thirds vote of senators attending is necessary to convict an individual of the impeachment charges.

directive and supervisory powers
the legislature's power over the executive branch; for example, the legislature determines the size of appropriations for state agencies

judicial powers
the power of the House to impeach and of the Senate to convict members of the executive and judicial branches of state government

THE IMPEACHMENT OF JIM FERGUSON

Box 24.1

In 1917, the Texas House of Representatives impeached Governor Jim Ferguson on twenty-one charges. The Texas Senate, by a two-thirds vote, convicted Ferguson of ten of those charges. Ferguson, the Senate voted, had:

1. used Canyon City Normal College insurance funds to settle a personal obligation;
2. kept those funds in his bank for more than one year without interest at his profit;
3. deposited $60,000 of the state's money in his bank at his profit;
4. assisted in the deposit of another $250,000 in his bank at his profit;
5. refused to reveal who had loaned him $156,000;
6. diverted funds from the state adjutant general to payment to Canyon City Normal College;
7. induced his bank's officers to lend him money in excess of the legal limit;
8. sought to influence the Board of Regents of the University of Texas to do his will;
9. removed Regents of the University of Texas without good cause; and
10. sought to influence the chairman of the Board of Regents by remitting a $5,000 bail bond to him.

The Senate voted to remove Ferguson from office and to bar him from further office. That, however, did not stop Ferguson. He ran again for governor, for U.S. Senator, and for president of the United States on the Independent Party ticket. In 1924, he attempted to run for governor again and was barred by the Texas courts so he installed his wife as a stand-in candidate. Miriam Ferguson became the first woman to be elected governor of Texas. By electing his wife, it was claimed, Texas got two governors for the price of one!

SOURCE: Bruce Rutherford, *The Impeachment of Jim Ferguson* (Austin: Eakin Press, 1983), pp. vii, 107–108.

impeachment
the formal charge by the House of Representatives that a government official has committed "Treason, Bribery, or other high Crimes and Misdemeanors"

introduction
the first step in the legislative process, during which a member of the legislature gets an idea for a bill and files a copy of it with the clerk of the House or secretary of the Senate

referral
the second step in the legislative process, during which a bill is assigned to the appropriate standing committee by the Speaker (for House bills) or the lieutenant governor (for Senate bills)

consideration by standing committee
the third step in the legislative process, during which a bill is killed, amended, or heard by a standing committee

floor action
the fourth step in the legislative process, during which a bill referred by a standing committee is scheduled for floor debate by the Calendars Committee

conference committee
a joint committee created to work out a compromise on House and Senate versions of a piece of legislation

action by the governor
the final step in the legislative process, during which a bill is either signed or vetoed by the governor

Each body can compel attendance at regular and special sessions. More than once Texas Rangers handcuffed absent members and brought them to the legislature. On rare occasions a chamber will punish nonmembers who disrupt proceedings by imprisoning them for up to forty-eight hours. The House and Senate judge the qualifications of members and can expel a member for cause.

How a Bill Becomes Law

▶ What are the steps in the legislative process?

Anyone can write a bill, but only members of the legislature can introduce a bill. Revenue bills must start in the House of Representatives. Other bills can start in either the House or Senate. During the 76th Legislature that met in 1999, a total of 5,908 bills were introduced in the legislature. Of this number, 1,586 passed the legislature and the governor vetoed 31 of them.

Figure 24.1 shows the flow of a bill from the time it is introduced in the Texas House of Representatives to final passage and submission to the governor. A bill introduced in the Senate would follow the same procedure in reverse. Examining this figure suggests that the process of how a bill becomes law is long, detailed, cumbersome, and unfathomable. However, when distilled to its basic parts there are only six steps in how a bill becomes law. For a bill that starts in the House these steps are 1) **introduction;** 2) **referral;** 3) **consideration by standing committee;** and 4) **floor action.** Steps one through four are repeated in the Senate. Step five is action by a **conference committee** and, finally, 6) **action by the governor.**

INTRODUCTION IN THE HOUSE

A bill is introduced by placing copies of the bill with the clerk of the House. In the Senate, the secretary of the Senate receives the bill. The clerk numbers the bill and enrolls it by recording its number, title, caption, and sponsor in a ledger. Similar information is entered into a computer.

Rules of the legislature require the bill be read on three separate occasions. After enrollment, for the first time the bill is read by its number, title, and caption.

REFERRAL

After undergoing first reading, the bill is assigned to a standing committee by the Speaker. In the Senate, the lieutenant governor assigns it to a committee. Since committees in the Texas legislature have overlapping jurisdictions, the Speaker and lieutenant governor can assign a bill to a friendly committee or an unfriendly one. The committee to which a bill is assigned can determine whether the bill survives or dies in committee.

COMMITTEE ACTION

Every bill introduced in the Texas legislature is assigned to a **standing committee,** and the vast majority of bills die in committee. The chair of the committee

HOW A BILL BECOMES LAW IN TEXAS

Figure 24.1

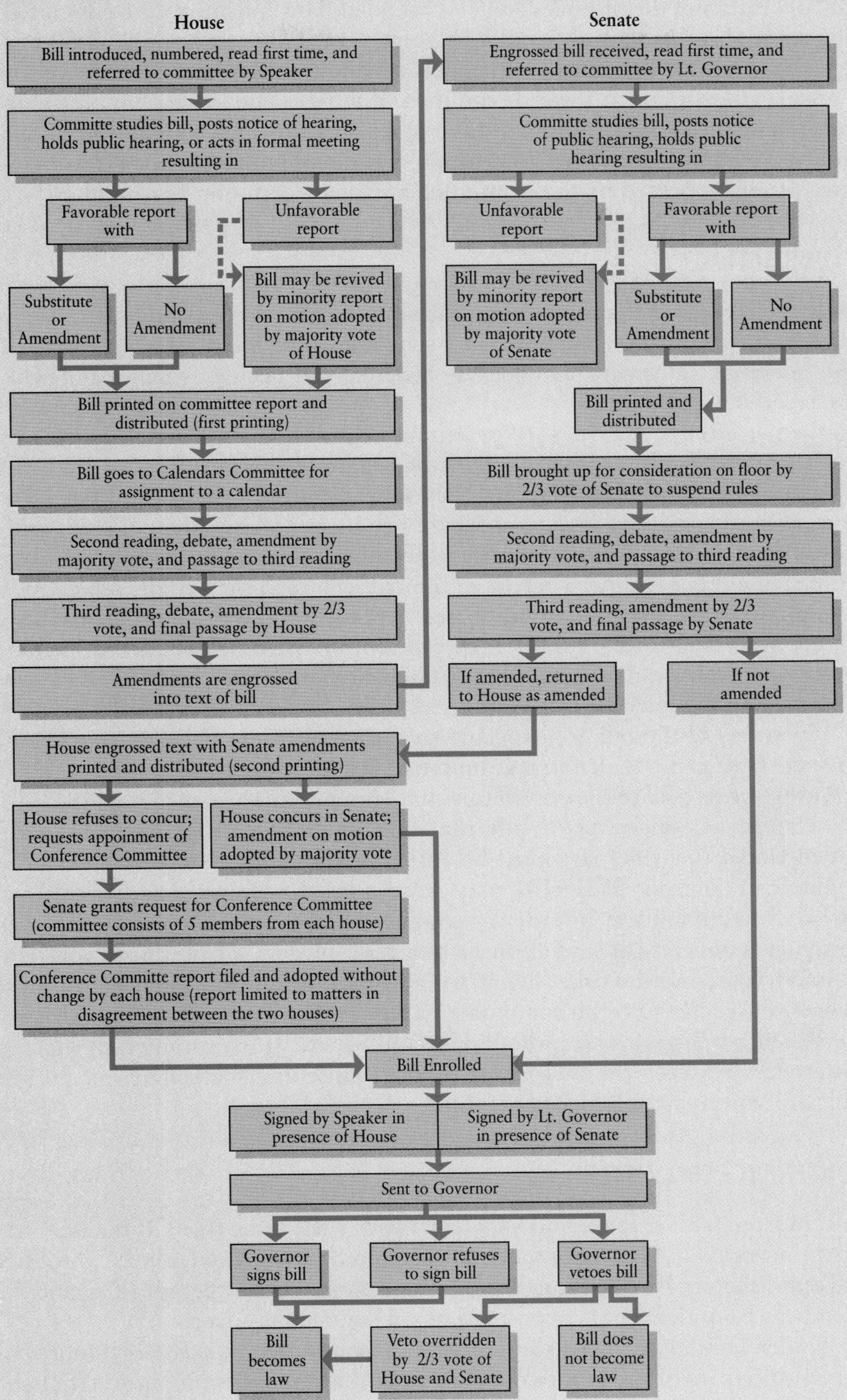

SOURCE: Citizen Handbook,"Basics [*sic*] Steps in the Texas Legislative Process," www.Senate.state.tx.us/CHBook/Chart.htm.

standing committee
a permanent committee with the power to propose and write legislation that covers a particular subject, such as finance or appropriations

pigeonholing
a step in the legislative process during which a bill is killed by the chair of the standing committee to which it was referred, as a result of his or her setting the bill aside and not bringing it before the committee

filibuster
a tactic used by members of the Senate to prevent action on legislation they oppose by continuously holding the floor and speaking until the majority backs down. Once given the floor, senators have unlimited time to speak, and it requires a vote of three-fifths of the Senate to end a filibuster

kills most by pigeonholing. **Pigeonholing** means the committee chair sets the bill aside and never brings it before the committee.

Standing committees are considered the "workhorses" of the legislature. If the bill does not die, it most likely is amended. Few bills leave the committee in the same form as they arrived. Parts of several bills can also be combined to form a single bill. Changes are made to make the bill more acceptable to the entire legislature or to meet the political desires of the leadership or members of the committee. Hearings can take place to allow experts and the public to educate committee members on the good and bad points of the bill. In the Senate, all bills reported by the committee must have a public hearing.

FLOOR ACTION

Bills referred by a standing committee go next to the Calendars Committee, which, after consulting the Speaker, schedules bills for debate. In the Senate, the lieutenant governor controls the agenda and decides when a bill will be considered.

In the House, the Speaker determines the length of debate. Customarily, each member is allowed ten minutes of debate. Early in the session when the agenda is uncrowded, debate may last longer. Later in the session when there is a crush of legislative business, debate will be more limited. Some bills will be voted on without debate; however, important or controversial bills are usually allocated adequate time. There is unlimited debate in the Senate, which means it is possible for a senator to **filibuster.** A filibuster is when a senator talks for lengthy periods of time in an effort to kill a bill or to obtain amendments or other compromises (such as Senator Gonzalez's filibuster in 1957, which was discussed in the introduction to this chapter).

Sponsors of the bill are expected to gather sufficient votes to pass the bill. In fact, before the Calendars Committee schedules the bill for floor debate, sponsors often assure the committee that enough votes exist to pass the bill.

The Texas Senate has a rule that bills shall be considered in numerical order. Under this rule, SB1 must be voted on and either pass or fail before the Senate can consider SB2. HB1 may never pass the House, and, by tradition, SB1 dies in committee. In order to conduct business, the Senate must suspend this rule requiring consideration in numerical order. A two-thirds vote is required to suspend the rules. Thus, for all practical purposes, legislation in the Senate must have two-thirds support to pass rather than a simple majority.

When a bill passes both the House and Senate, it is examined. If there are differences between the bill passed by the House and the Senate bill, the two bills are sent to a conference committee.

CONFERENCE COMMITTEE

Bills must pass the House and Senate in exactly the same form. If the bill is different in any way, it is sent to a conference committee. Conference committees have ten members: five from the House appointed by the Speaker, and five members from the Senate appointed by the lieutenant governor.

Under legislative rules, the conference committee consists of House and Senate sponsors of the bill, two members of the standing committees that considered the bill, and enough other members to make the required ten.

Each bill gets its own conference committee. The Senate members know what compromises they can make and still have the bill passed by the Senate. Likewise, the members of the committee from the House are aware of the compromises they can make and still have the bill passed in the House. Unless specifically instructed, the conference committee cannot change parts of the bill that are the same. Changes are made and compromises reached only on parts of the bill that are different.

Once a compromise is reached, the report of the conference committee goes to the House and Senate. It can be debated in each chamber, but the report cannot be changed. It must be accepted as is. If the report is agreed to in both chambers of the legislature, the next stop is the governor's desk. If either chamber fails to approve the report of the conference committee, the bill is dead. While it is possible for the conference committee to try a second time to reach a compromise, it is unusual for conference committees to do so.

Upon passage, a final copy of the bill is prepared. The Speaker of the House, the clerk of the House, the president of the Senate (lieutenant governor), and the secretary of the Senate sign the bill. The next stop is the governor's desk.

GOVERNOR

It is the governor's responsibility to sign or **veto** legislation. During the first 130 days of a regular session, he has ten days from the time a bill arrives on his desk to sign or veto the legislation. If he neither signs nor vetoes the bill in the ten days, it becomes law without his signature. In the last ten days of a session, he has twenty days from the time the bill arrives on his desk to sign or veto the legislation. Again, if he does neither, it becomes law without his signature.

veto
the governor's power to turn down legislation; can be overridden by a two-thirds vote of both the House and Senate

The governor's veto can be overridden by a two-thirds vote of both the House and Senate. Anytime the governor vetoes a bill, a message is attached explaining why it was vetoed. It is then returned to the chamber that originated the bill. If the presiding officer elects to allow a vote to override the veto, a vote is scheduled. Only two vetoes have been overridden in more than seventy years.

Many bills arrive on the governor's desk in the last few days of a session. Almost all important or controversial bills reach the governor in the waning moments of a session. If the governor wants to veto a bill that comes to him from day 131 to day 140, he simply waits until the legislature adjourns to exercise the veto. His veto cannot be overridden because the legislature has adjourned. Vetoing legislation after legislative adjournment is called a **post-adjournment veto.** The post-adjournment veto provides the governor with an excellent bargaining tool in which the veto can be threatened unless changes are made in a bill.

post-adjournment veto
a veto of a bill that occurs after the legislature adjourns, thus preventing the legislature from overriding it

The governor also has an **item veto** that allows the governor to sign a bill and draw lines through specific items. Except for the items which the governor drew a line through, the bill becomes law. In Texas, the item veto applies only to the state's omnibus appropriations bill.

item veto
the governor's power to strike specific items or lines in a bill

Other Players in the Legislative Process

▶ In addition to legislators, who else is involved in the legislative process and what role do they play?

Governor George W. Bush signs legislation lowering the legal intoxication limit for drivers. The governor of Texas may either sign or veto legislation within ten days of the time the bill arrives on his or her desk.

During regular and special sessions, members of the Texas legislature are directly involved in lawmaking. In addition to legislators there are others who are directly or indirectly involved. Two officials with direct involvement in the legislative process are the governor and the comptroller.

GOVERNOR

message power
the power deriving from the governor's State of the State message

The governor interacts with the legislature through **message power,** the ability to call special sessions, and the power to sign or veto legislation.

Message Power Early in each session, the governor delivers a State of the State message that is similar to the president's State of the Union message. In this address, the governor puts forth a vision for Texas and what legislation will accomplish that vision. If the governor chooses to submit an executive budget, a letter stating why this budget should be adopted accompanies it.

Periodically, the governor will visit with legislators urging their vote on a bill. A personal visit can be persuasive, but more and more the governor uses members of his paid staff to lobby the legislature. Like lobbyists for corporations and interest groups, the governor's representatives use their skills to encourage passage of bills the governor favors and to kill bills the governor opposes. There is a problem with the governor's use of paid lobbyists. The Texas Constitution forbids use of tax dollars to influence the legislature, but this ban is avoided by claiming that the governor's representatives are simply providing needed information to the legislators.

Calling Special Sessions Special sessions last for thirty days, but there is no limit to the number of special sessions called by the governor. They are needed

Spectators sit in the gallery and look down on the floor of the Texas House of Representatives during the State of the State address by Governor Bush.

to allow the legislature to complete business left undone at the end of a regular session or to address major problems that arise between regular sessions. When the governor calls a special session, he sets the agenda for the session. His ability to determine the agenda provides the governor with significant control over the session.

Signing and Vetoing Legislation It is the governor's responsibility to sign or veto legislation. It is his major check on the legislature, and it provides him with some of his bargaining power

COMPTROLLER OF PUBLIC ACCOUNTS

The comptroller of public accounts issues revenue estimates to inform the legislature of the amount of money it has to spend in the next two years. Texas's operating budgets must balance. The Texas Constitution forbids borrowing money to conduct the daily operations of government. The estimate provided by the comptroller sets the limit on state spending. If the legislature wants to spend more than the comptroller estimates, it must enhance revenue—that is, increase taxes and fees.

The comptroller's estimates can be political in nature. She can provide a low revenue estimate and tell the legislature that the estimate will remain low until it passes bills the comptroller wants. Upon passage of those bills, the revenue estimate increases to allow the legislature to complete its business.

MEDIA

Media can determine issues of importance by the selection of stories they cover. If the media cover more stories on crime, crime and criminal justice issues will move toward the top of the legislature's agenda. A media focus on child abuse, alcohol related traffic deaths, or poor performance by Texas pubic school students will increase legislative attention to these issues.

The media coverage of the legislature provides the public with needed information on what is going on in Austin. Stories portraying the legislature as modern, efficient, and hard working provide the public with a positive attitude toward the legislature; whereas stories about legislators sleeping at their desks or killing legislation on technicalities provide a negative image.

COURTS

Federal and state courts influence the legislative agenda. In recent years the courts' scrutiny included the prison system, the state's treatment of patients in state mental hospitals, the funding of public education, and equality of funding for colleges and universities in south Texas. The ability to rule acts of the legislature and actions of state agencies unconstitutional gives courts significant power over issues addressed by the legislature.

LOBBYISTS

During a regular session, more than 1,600 individuals register as lobbyists and attempt to influence the legislature. A lobbyist's responsibility is to convince legislators to support the interest represented by the lobbyist. Lobbyists want legislators' votes on bills. At the least, they desire access to legislators.

PUBLIC

Individuals can influence legislators. First and foremost, legislators are evaluated at each election. If the public believes they do a good job representing them, legislators are re-elected. A legislator who fails to live up to expectations may not be re-elected.

The public can serve as lobbyists. Letters, e-mail, or telephone calls urging representatives or senators to vote a certain way constitute a lobbying effort. Members of the public can also write legislation to be considered by the legislature.

Power in the Legislature

▶ Who are the most important leaders in the Texas legislature? What are their powers? How does the battle over redistricting illustrate the party politics within the legislature?

LEADERSHIP

Speaker
the chief presiding officer of the House of Representatives. The Speaker is the most important party and House leader, and can influence the legislative agenda, the fate of individual pieces of legislation, and members' positions within the House

The **Speaker** of the Texas House of Representatives and the lieutenant governor are two of the most powerful political figures in the state of Texas. James E. "Pete" Laney (D–Hale Center) was first elected Speaker in 1993. Rick Perry (R–Haskell) was elected lieutenant governor in 1998. The Texas House and Senate endow both men with considerable control over the legislative process. It is fair to say that either of them can usually kill legislation they oppose, and often they have the power to pass legislation they support.

Members of the House elect the Speaker at the beginning of the regular session. Additionally, at the start of each regular session, members of the House adopt rules that give the Speaker institutional powers sufficient to control the work of the House.

The lieutenant governor is elected statewide to a four-year term. His major responsibility is to serve as president of the Senate and to preside over the Senate. Unlike the Speaker, the lieutenant governor is not a member of the Senate, simply its presiding officer. He may only vote to break a tie.

At the start of each regular session, senators adopt rules that the Senate will follow for the next two years. These rules give the lieutenant governor enormous control of the work of the Senate.

As lieutenant governor of Texas, Rick Perry held one of the most powerful political offices in the state. The office of lieutenant governor is endowed with considerable influence over the legislative process. Furthermore, in the absence of the governor, governing falls to the lieutenant governor.

CENTRALIZING POWER: SOURCES OF THE LEADERSHIP'S POWER

The operation of the Texas legislature is significantly different from the U.S. Congress. In the U.S. Congress, the leader of the president's party in the House and the Senate is the president's spokesperson in that house of Congress. Additionally, there is a high level of partisanship, where committee appointments are made in such a way that the majority party controls every important committee and chairs of those committees are always members of the majority party. There is a party division such that each house of Congress has majority party leadership and minority party leadership. Such divisions do not exist in the Texas legislature. There is no member of the Texas legislature who is formally known as the governor's spokesperson. While there is partisanship in the Texas legislature, it is far from the level of the U.S. Congress. There is no majority and minority party leadership, for example. Committee assignments and committee chairmanship appointments cross party lines so that in the Texas House, for example, where the majority party is Democratic, a Republican may be on an important committee and successfully sponsor important legislation. A Republican may even be assigned the chairmanship of an important committee. This largely nonpartisan structure of the Texas legislature is important from the perspective of leadership. If the governor has no leader in the legislature, and if the membership does not owe allegiance to party leaders in the legislature, then leadership and power is further centralized in the Speaker and lieutenant governor. The Speaker and lieutenant governor can make appointments with limited regard for party affiliation, thus assuring that members will be loyal to them rather than to the party.

This low level of partisanship in the legislature has persisted even though the Republicans have recently gained control of both the Texas Senate and the office of the lieutenant governor. However, most of the powers of the Speaker and of the lieutenant governor are granted by the rules that are voted on by each chamber's membership at the beginning of the legislative session. There is the potential that the powers of the Speaker and of the lieutenant governor could be greatly reduced if the members of the legislature so chose. One could, for example, imagine a future Republican Senate that would reduce the powers of the lieutenant governor over the Texas Senate if a partisan Democrat were elected as lieutenant governor. Of course, one of the first rules that would have to change is the requirement of a two-thirds vote for a bill in the Senate to be voted on out of order. Such a rule requires bipartisan voting since neither party will have two-thirds control of the Texas Senate in the foreseeable future. For the time being, however, it seems likely that the current system of powerful presiding officers will continue. That would likely be the case even if the Republicans gain control

Box 24.2

BOB BULLOCK: LIEUTENANT GOVERNOR AND TEXAS POWERHOUSE

One of the most influential of all Texas lieutenant governors was Bob Bullock, who not only worked his will on the Texas Senate, but also concerned himself with the details of state government. Often, whatever Bob Bullock wanted, he was able to get as is suggested by this story of how Bullock decided that funding for state parks would be changed.

> In 1993 Lieutenant Governor Bob Bullock called Andy Sansom to his office. Andy had been the executive director of Parks and Wildlife for three years by then. Bullock, who was uncomfortable with dedicated funds and saw no connection between parks and cigarettes, said that from then on there would be no more cigarette money going to parks. Not one penny. And there would be no more undedicated revenue from the general fund. Sansom could see his budget imploding. "But what alternative do I have?" he asked.
>
> Bullock calmly said, "Suicide."
>
> Fortunately for Andy, Bullock was not against parks and had an alternative in mind after all. Parks and Wildlife would receive a portion of the sales tax that came from sporting goods. This portion was capped, however, so that parks could receive no more money than they would have received from the cigarette tax in any given year. The rest of the money would have to be made up from user fees, cuts in operating expenses, and other sources such as endowments, legacies, or gifts.

SOURCE: Gregory Curtis, "Fix the Roof," *Texas Monthly,* www.texasmonthly.com/mag/1999/mar/btl.1.html.

of the Texas House, although it is likely that if the Republicans do gain control, within a short time they will want to elect a Republican Speaker. Additionally, Republican control of both houses of the legislature would probably lead to somewhat more conservative policies, since, as Chapter 22 (on parties and elections) points out, the Democratic Party is somewhat more liberal. Some key interest groups, such as Texans for Lawsuit Reform, believe a Republican House would lead to more pro-business legislation. Another interest group, Putting

Box 24.3

DUTIES AND POWERS OF THE SPEAKER AND LIEUTENANT GOVERNOR

The formal, institutional duties of the Speaker of the House and the lieutenant governor are similar. The Speaker and lieutenant governor:

1. preside over the House and Senate.
2. call on members who wish to speak.
3. appoint members to standing committees.
4. designate the chair and vice chair of each committee.
5. assign bills to standing committees.
6. assign members to conference committees.

Children First, believes that a Republican majority in the House would lead to school vouchers as well as a Republican Speaker (see Chapter 23).

The largely nonpartisan structure of the Texas legislature and the lack of formal lines of gubernatorial authority in the legislature are very important in centralizing power in the hands of the Speaker and the lieutenant governor. However, these officials have other important sources of power as well. One of those powers—a power especially important in the Texas House—is the power of **recognition.** The Senate rule allowing unlimited debate lessens the lieutenant governor's power in this area. In the House, the Speaker controls legislative debate including who speaks and how long debate will last. On occasion, the Speaker ignores or skips a member seeking recognition to speak. This is a signal to other members of the House that this individual has fallen from the Speaker's good graces. That ability to pick and choose among those desiring to speak on the House floor, however, allows the Speaker to structure the debate and to affect the outcome of legislation.

recognition
the Speaker of the House's power to control floor debate by recognizing who can speak before the House

As mentioned earlier, in the Senate, there is a rule that for bills to be voted on, they must be taken in order and, for a bill to be taken out of order, there must be a two-thirds vote. Given the vast powers of the lieutenant governor, on issues that are important to him he can usually control the votes of at least one-third of the membership. Thus, if a bill is opposed by the lieutenant governor, he can frequently prevent it from being taken out of order for consideration.

One of the most important sources of power for the Speaker and the lieutenant governor is the committee assignment power. The committees on which legislators serve are important to individual members and to the presiding officer. For members, assignments to powerful committees increase their prestige in the legislature. It also affects how well constituents are represented. For the lieutenant governor and the Speaker, assigning members to standing committees is one of their most important duties.

Senator Judith Zaffirini is Chair of the Senate Committee on Human Services. Although a Republican, Lieutenant Governor Perry appointed Democrats to five of the thirteen Senate committee chairs.

According to rules of the Texas House, the Speaker appoints one-half the membership of each committee in the House and designates its chairperson. The remaining committee seats are filled by seniority. On the Senate side of the capitol, the lieutenant governor designates approximately 80 percent of Senate committee positions and appoints the committee chair. The remaining seats are filled by seniority.

In reality, both presiding officers directly appoint or have significant influence over each and every committee assignment. Party affiliation and seniority are of only moderate importance in committee assignments. The most important factor in committee assignments is the members' relationships with the presiding officer. In order to maintain control over the legislature, the Speaker and lieutenant governor use their committee assignment powers to appoint members who are loyal to them and who are supportive of their legislative agendas. When chairs and vice chairs of committees are appointed, only the most loyal friends and allies of the Speaker and lieutenant governor are appointed to control important committees. Although the Speaker is a Democrat, thirteen of the thirty-six standing committees in the House have Republican chairs. The lieutenant governor is a Republican, but five of the thirteen standing committee chairs in the Senate are Democrats.

Not only do the Speaker and the lieutenant governor have vast committee assignment powers, but also committees in the Texas legislature have overlapping jurisdiction. While each bill must be assigned to a standing committee,

Box 24.4

STANDING COMMITTEES OF THE TEXAS SENATE AND HOUSE (76th LEGISLATURE), THEIR CHAIRS, AND THE CHAIR'S PARTY AFFILIATION

Senate Committees

Administration—Chair: Harris (Republican)
Criminal Justice—Chair: Armbrister (Democrat)
Economic Development—Chair: Sibley (Republican)
Education—Chair: Bivins (Republican)
Finance—Chair: Ratliff (Republican)
Health Services—Chair: Nelson (Republican)
Human Services—Chair: Zaffirini (Democrat)
Intergovernmental Relations—Chair: Madla (Democrat)
Jurisprudence—Chair: Ellis (Democrat)
Natural Resources—Chair: Brown (Republican)
Nominations—Chair: Wentworth (Republican)
State Affairs—Chair: Shapiro (Republican)
Veteran Affairs and Military Installations—Chair: Truan (Democrat)

House Committees

Agriculture and Livestock—Chair: Swinford (Republican)
Appropriations—Chair: Junell (Democrat)
Business and Industry—Chair: Brimer (Republican)
Calendars—Chair: Telford (Democrat)
Civil Practices—Chair: Bosse (Democrat)
Corrections—Chair: Haggerty (Republican)
County Affairs—Chair: Ramsay (Democrat)
Criminal Jurisprudence—Chair: Hinojosa (Democrat)
Economic Development—Chair: Solis (Democrat)
Elections—Chair: Danburg (Democrat)
Energy Resources—Chair: Lewis (Democrat)
Environmental Regulation—Chair: Chisum (Republican)
Financial Institutions—Chair: Averitt (Republican)
General Investigating—Chair: Gallego (Democrat)
Higher Education—Chair: Rangel (Democrat)
House Administration—Chair: Goolsby (Republican)
Human Services—Chair: Naishtat (Democrat)
Insurance—Chair: Smithee (Republican)
Judicial Affairs—Chair: Thompson (Democrat)
Juvenile Justice and Family Issues—Chair: Goodman (Republican)
Land and Resource Management—Chair: Walker (Republican)
Licensing and Administative Procedures—Chair: Wilson (Democrat)
Local and Consent Calendars—Chair: Davis (Democrat)
Natural Resources—Chair: Counts (Democrat)
Pensions and Investments—Chair: Greenberg (Democrat)
Public Education—Chair: Sadler (Democrat)
Public Health—Chair: Gray (Democrat)
Public Safety—Chair: Turner (Democrat)
Redistricting—Chair: Jones (Republican)
Rules and Resolutions—Chair: Edwards (Democrat)
State Affairs—Chair: Wolens (Democrat)
State Recreational Resources—Chair: Kuempel (Republican)
State, Federal, and International Relations—Chair: Hunter (Republican)
Transportation—Chair: Alexander (Democrat)
Urban Affairs—Chair: Carter (Republican)
Ways and Means—Chair: Oliveira (Democrat)

SOURCES: Republican Party of Texas, "Texas State Representatives," www.texasgop.org/leadership/state_house.asp; Republican Party of Texas, "Texas State Senators," www.texasgop.org/leadership/state_senate.asp; Texas Legislative Reference Library, "Senate Committees-76th Legislature (1999)," www.lrl.state.tx.us/refdesk/ceo76/scomte76.htm; Texas Legislative Reference Library, "House Committees-76th Legislature (1999)," www.lrl.state.tx.us/refdesk/ceo76/hcomte76.htm.

there is more than one committee to which a bill can be assigned. Since the Speaker and the lieutenant governor assign a bill to committees in their respective chambers, they use the bill assignment power to influence the fate of the bill. They can, for example, assign bills they oppose to committees they believe hostile to the bill and those they support to committees they believe will favor the bill.

Since bills must pass the House and Senate in exactly the same form, the Speaker and the lieutenant governor can exercise still another important influence on policy through their power to appoint conference committees. If any differences exist in a bill passed by both the House and the Senate, the bill goes to a conference committee that works out the differences in the House and Senate versions. By appointing the conference committee members, the Speaker and lieutenant governor can affect the language and even the fate of the bill.

WHERE POWER AND PARTISANSHIP MATTER: THE REDISTRICTING BATTLE

That the Texas legislature is far less partisan than the U.S. Congress does not mean that it is completely nonpartisan. One of the most important issues facing a future session of the Texas legislature will prove very controversial and very partisan. That issue is redistricting—the redrawing of district lines for the Texas House, the Texas Senate, and the U.S. House of Representatives, which must be done every ten years after the federal census.

There are 150 Texas House districts and 31 Texas Senate districts. One senator or one member of the House represents each district. This is called representation by **single-member districts.**

After each census, the legislature draws new boundaries for each district. Drawing new boundaries for Texas House and Senate districts is called **redistricting.** Newly drawn districts must contain an almost equal number of people in order to ensure equal representation. It guarantees that each person's vote counts the same whether the vote is cast in Houston, Big Lake, El Paso, Presidio, Brownsville, or Commerce.

For almost fifty years, Texas and other states failed to draw new boundaries, and even after U.S. Supreme Court decisions, Texas did not do so willingly.

It was not until the U.S. Supreme Court's decisions in *Baker v. Carr* and *Reynolds v. Sims*[4] compelled the legislature to draw new districts that boundaries were drawn which fairly represented the population. These and subsequent decisions meant that Texas had to draw legislative districts of roughly equal populations—a concept known as the **one-person, one-vote** principle.

The Texas House redistricts itself, and the Texas Senate redistricts itself. As much as possible legislators from each region of the state draw new boundaries for their districts. Senators from the Houston metropolitan area redistrict themselves, as do senators from the Fort Worth-Dallas area, the Rio Grande Valley, west Texas, and the Panhandle. House districts are drawn in the same manner. Once the House is satisfied with its redistricting, it passes a bill to which the Senate agrees. When the Senate completes its redistricting, the House will concur. Of course, as with any bill, the governor must sign the bill for it to go into effect.

Congressional redistricting is also a responsibility of the legislature. Once Congress apportions itself, the Texas legislature divides Texas into the appropriate number of Congressional districts. According to the 1964 Supreme

single-member district
an electorate that is allowed to select only one representative from each district; the normal method of representation in the United States

redistricting
the process of redrawing election districts and redistributing legislative representatives. This happens every ten years to reflect shifts in population or in response to legal challenges to existing districts

one-person, one-vote
the principle that all citizens have the right to participate in politics on equal terms

Court case *Wesberry v Sanders,*[5] each state's congressional districts must be equal in population. During the 1990s Texas had thirty members in the U.S. House of Representatives; there were thirteen Republican members and seventeen Democratic members. Depending on how the districts are drawn, the representation of the two political parties in the U.S. House of Representatives can be significantly changed. Indeed, reapportionment can so change the division of the parties that the control of the U.S. House of Representatives can be affected. Thus, Texans can expect highly partisan maneuvering over redistricting.

If the legislature fails to redistrict the Texas House or Texas Senate at the first regular session after the census, the task falls to the Legislative Redistricting Board (LRB). The LRB has five *ex officio* members: the lieutenant governor, Speaker of the House, attorney general, commissioner of the General Land Office, and comptroller of public accounts.

When the legislature adjourns without redistricting either the House, Senate, or both, the LRB comes into existence. It must meet within ninety days of legislative adjournment and complete its responsibilities within another sixty days. Even here, the influence of the Speaker and the lieutenant governor is clearly visible.

Summary

The Texas legislature is an institution undergoing great changes. Minorities and women are increasingly being elected to the legislature, as are Republicans. Republicans now control the Texas Senate and may soon control the Texas House of Representatives. Additionally, the lieutenant governor, who is the presiding officer of the Senate, is now a Republican.

Yet, in spite of the changes in the Texas legislature, it seems an archaic institution as a result of the limitations of the 1876 Constitution. The legislature only meets once every two years for regular sessions, and then only for 140 days. Additionally, the legislature is designed to be a part-time body where compensation is limited to $7,200 a year and a $125 per diem expense account.

One of the most intriguing aspects of the Texas legislature is the vast concentration of power in the hands of the Speaker of the Texas House and the lieutenant governor, who is the presiding officer of the Texas Senate. The powers of these officers are such that either can usually prevent the passage of any legislation that he opposes and possibly bring about the passage of legislation he favors. In keeping with the traditions of the 1876 Constitution, it is also a body that emphasizes the weakness of the governor, who has no formal spokesperson such as a majority or minority leader in either chamber. To the extent that a governor has influence over policy making in Texas, that influence must be shared with the real powers in the legislature—the Speaker and the lieutenant governor.

In spite of the dramatic growth of the Republican Party in the Texas legislature, it is a far less partisan body than, for example, the U.S. Congress. The Republican lieutenant governor has appointed Democrats to committee chairmanships in the Texas Senate and the Democratic Speaker has appointed

Politics on the Web

The Internet holds the potential for radically changing the citizen's grasp of political processes. No longer does one have to depend on secondhand accounts for how the legislature works in Texas. Anyone can follow a bill from its introduction in the legislature to its referral to committee and subcommittee to its amendment and passage. Audio files of committee hearings on bills are available online. This technology brings the legislative process to life and helps citizens better experience for themselves how personalities can affect the political process.

The Web also holds representatives more accountable to their constituents for their actions in the legislature. With the information available on the Internet, it is easier for citizens to find out how a legislator voted on an issue and his or her real role in the passage of a particular piece of legislation. To be sure, the Internet has not made the legislative process less complex. It has only opened up the process to scrutiny by educated consumers of political information. This is, however, no small victory for people who believe that citizens should know—or at least be able to find out—what is going on in public affairs.

www.wwnorton.com/wtp3e

Republicans to committee chairmanships in the Texas House of Representatives. However, if the Republicans gain control of the Texas House, it seems likely that they will elect a Republican Speaker and that more conservative laws will be passed than now when Democrats retain control of the House of Representatives.

An important issue facing the legislature will be reapportionment—the redrawing of legislative district lines that reflects changes in population patterns over the past decade. It is a matter of vast importance, not only for incumbent Texas legislators and their potential challengers, but even for the partisan division of the U.S. House of Representatives since U.S. House district lines also must be redrawn.

Thus, the Texas legislature is a peculiar mix of rapid change, immense political controversy, and highly centralized power wrapped in a nineteenth-century institution.

FOR FURTHER READING

Banks, Jimmy. *Money, Marbles and Chalk: The Wondrous World of Texas Politics*. Austin: Texas Publishing Co., 1971.

Davis, William J. *There Shall Also Be a Lieutenant Governor*. Austin: Institute of Public Affairs, 1967.

Deaton, Charles. *The Year They Threw the Rascals Out*. Austin: Shoal Creek Press, 1973.

Rosenthal, Alan. *Governors and Legislatures: Contending Powers*. Washington, DC: Congressional Quarterly Press, 1990.

Rosenthal, Alan. *Legislative Life, People, Process, and Performance in the States*. New York: Harper & Row, 1981.

Tucker, Harvey J., and Gary M. Halter. *Texas Legislative Almanac 1999*. College Station: Texas A&M University Press, 1999.

STUDY OUTLINE

Structure

1. Texas has a bicameral legislature composed of a House of Representatives and a Senate.
2. The Texas House has 150 members who serve two-year terms. The Texas Senate has 31 members who serve four-year terms.
3. Members of the House represent about 140,000 people, while senators represent approximately 630,000 constituents.
4. Formal qualifications to serve in the legislature are minimal.
5. The average legislator is a college educated, white male who works as a business or professional person.
6. The annual salary of a member of the legislature is $7,200.
7. The number of minorities and women serving in the legislature increased in the past two decades.

Sessions of the Legislature

1. The Texas legislature meets in regular session 140 days every odd-numbered year.
2. The governor calls special sessions of the legislature, which last no longer than thirty days, and the governor sets the agenda for the special session.

Functions of the Legislature

1. The legislature has legislative and nonlegislative functions.
2. Legislative functions include passing bills and resolutions.
3. There are three classifications of bills: local bills, special bills, and general bills.
4. There are three types of resolutions: concurrent resolutions, joint resolutions, and simple resolutions.
5. Nonlegislative powers include constituent powers, electoral powers, investigative powers, directive and supervisory powers, and judicial powers.

How a Bill Becomes Law

1. Bills can be written by anyone, but must be introduced by a legislator.

2. A bill must pass the House and Senate in exactly the same form.
3. Every bill is assigned to a standing committee, and most bills die in committee.
4. The governor can sign a bill, allow it to become law without his signature, or veto it.

Other Players in the Legislative Process

1. In addition to legislators, two state officials, the governor and comptroller of public accounts, are directly involved in the legislative process.
2. The governor exercises the message power, signs and vetoes legislation, and calls special sessions.
3. The comptroller of public accounts issues revenue estimates that determine the amount of money the state can spend in the next two years.
4. The media, courts, lobbyists, and the public are also involved in the legislative process.

Power in the Legislature

1. The speaker of the House and the lieutenant governor are the two most powerful political figures in Texas.
2. A major source of power for the speaker and the lieutenant governor is the power to assign legislators to standing committees.
3. Party membership is much less important in the Texas legislature then in the U.S. Congress.
4. Committee membership and the chairs of standing committees cross party lines.
5. The governor lacks a formal spokesperson in the legislature.
6. The ability to appoint members of conference committees gives the Speaker and the lieutenant governor control over the final content of a bill.
7. Redistricting is a major issue for the legislature.

PRACTICE QUIZ

1. There are ____ members of the Texas Senate and Texas Senators serve a ____ year term.
   a) 31/4
   b) 100/6
   c) 150/2
   d) 435/2
2. The Texas legislature meets in regular session
   a) 90 days every year.
   b) 180 days every year.
   c) 140 days each odd-numbered year and 60 days each even-numbered year.
   d) 140 days each odd-numbered year.
3. The agenda for a special session of the Texas legislature is set by the
   a) lieutenant governor and the Speaker of the House.
   b) governor.
   c) Texas Supreme Court.
   d) chair of the Joint committee on Special Sessions.
4. If a bill fails to pass the Texas House and Texas Senate in exactly the same form, the bill
   a) dies.
   b) is returned to the standing committee in the House or Senate that originally considered the bill.
   c) is sent to a conference committee.
   d) is sent to the governor, who decides which version of the bill will be signed.
5. Which state official, in large part, determines the amount of money the legislature may appropriate?
   a) governor
   b) comptroller of public accounts
   c) lieutenant governor
   d) attorney general
6. The ____ provides the governor with a powerful tool with which to bargain with the legislature.
   a) ability to introduce five bills in a regular session
   b) post-adjournment veto
   c) pocket veto
   d) message power
7. The two most powerful political figures in the Texas legislature are the
   a) governor and the lieutenant governor.
   b) governor and the attorney general.
   c) Speaker of the House and the governor.
   d) Speaker of the House and the lieutenant governor.
8. The ability of the lieutenant governor and the Speaker of the House to control the final outcome of legislation comes from their power to
   a) appoint members of conference committees.
   b) refuse to approve the work of standing committees.
   c) exercise the legislative item veto.
   d) change up to three lines in any bill.
9. An important issue for the legislature every 10 years is
   a) adopting a budget.
   b) deciding the order of succession to the office of governor.
   c) impeaching the lieutenant governor.
   d) redistricting.

CRITICAL THINKING QUESTIONS

1. Texas is the second largest state and the second most populous state. Its population is growing faster than all but a few states. Can a legislature that meets only 140 days every other year meet the needs of this modern, urban state? Will problems arise that need full-time attention? Will changes in the economy make a full-time legislature necessary?

2. Do individuals have an opportunity to influence the legislative process? Or, is the process essentially closed to the people legislators are supposed to represent and open only to lobbyists and individuals with money?

KEY TERMS

action by the governor (p. 922)
bicameral legislature (p. 916)
biennial (p. 918)
bill (p. 919)
concurrent resolution (p. 920)
conference committee (p. 922)
consideration by standing committee (p. 922)
constituent powers (p. 920)
constituents (p. 920)
directive and supervisory powers (p. 921)
electoral powers (p. 920)
filibuster (p. 924)
floor action (p. 922)
general bill (p. 919)
impeachment (p. 921)
introduction (p. 922)
investigative powers (p. 920)
item veto (p. 925)
joint resolution (p. 920)
judicial powers (p. 921)
local bill (p. 919)
message power (p. 926)
one-person, one-vote (p. 933)
pigeonholing (p. 924)
post-adjournment veto (p. 925)
recognition (p. 931)
redistricting (p. 933)
referral (p. 922)
regular session (p. 918)
resolution (p. 919)
simple resolution (p. 920)
single-member district (p. 933)
Speaker (p. 928)
special bill (p. 919)
special session (p. 918)
standing committee (p. 922)
veto (p. 925)

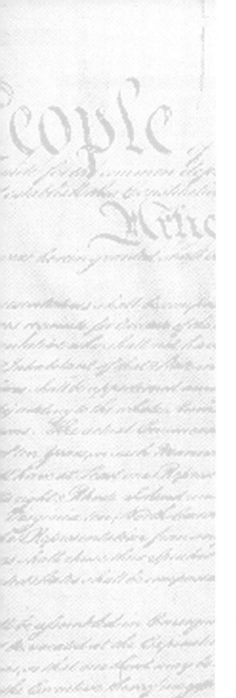

25 The Texas

★ The Governor

How are gubernatorial campaigns and elections conducted in Texas? How can a governor be removed from office? How is a governor succeeded? What resources does a governor possess?

What are the governor's formal powers? How does the governor exercise these powers?

★ The Plural Executive

What offices are comprised by the plural executive? What responsibilities does each have? How are they held accountable?

★ Boards, Commissions, and Regulatory Agencies

How can one classify agencies within the Texas bureaucracy? What are some of these important agencies and what does each do? How are they held accountable?

Executive Branch

ALTHOUGH Texas governors do not have much formal power, some have proved their value to the Texas electorate by providing enormous entertainment. In the days of Texas provincialism, no governor was more entertaining than W. Lee O'Daniel. While his political style is unimaginable in modern Texas, in the late 1930s and early 1940s, he was the most popular politician in the state.

In the mid-1920s, O'Daniel became sales and then general manager of the Burrus Mill and Elevator Company in Ft. Worth. As a way of promoting the flour sold by the company, O'Daniel had a daily radio show, which initially featured a western band led by a musician who later became famous, Bob Wills. Wills's band was known as the Lightcrust Doughboys and the show invariably opened with a woman asking O'Daniel, "Please pass the biscuits, Pappy." Thus, O'Daniel became known as "Pappy" O'Daniel. The show played at noon every day on the three most powerful radio stations in Texas, and it probably had more daily listeners than any other Texas radio program.

In 1935, O'Daniel organized his own company and began to advertise his "Hillbilly Flour" on a radio show. He even composed music for the band. The show provided listeners with hillbilly and sacred music, religious talks, lectures on morals, and stories of Texas heroes. O'Daniel even organized a safety crusade where one could get a badge if the listener walked on the lefthand side of the street facing traffic.

O'Daniel claimed that his listeners had begun asking him to run for governor so he asked them to write him about whether he should join the race. He claimed he received letters from over 54,000 people with only four suggesting he not run. In response to this poll, O'Daniel ran for governor in 1938. His platform was the Ten Commandments. His motto was the Golden Rule. He promised people over sixty-five years of age would receive pensions of $30 a month from the state and his slogan was, "Less Johnson grass and politicians, more smokestacks and businessmen." Former governor James Ferguson, himself no lightweight as a political entertainer, described O'Daniel as "a slick-haired banjo-picker . . . who crooned his way into the governor's office [and] has been giving the people of Texas a song and dance ever since."[1]

His appeal was remarkable. Along the sides of highways, crowds of 20,000 to 40,000 people would gather to see him. In passing through some communities, such crowds would gather that he would feel compelled to give unscheduled speeches. O'Daniel overwhelmed his opposition in the Democratic primary, which was then the real election in Texas. He won without a run-off and carried 231 of the state's counties. In those days, a governor's term was only two years, and O'Daniel's popularity continued in 1940 when he ran for re-election. Again, he won without a run-off.

In 1941, O'Daniel decided he wanted to be U.S. senator. Long-time Senator Morris Sheppard died and O'Daniel wanted to appoint a replacement who would fill the seat until the special senatorial election when O'Daniel would run. However, he obviously did not want to appoint someone who would prove a political threat. As a result, O'Daniel appointed eighty-seven-year-old Andrew Jackson Houston, the son of Sam Houston. Houston was in his dotage and lived only long enough to go to Washington and attend one committee meeting. But O'Daniel had accomplished his objective. Houston was certainly not a political threat to him in the special election of 1941. The person who was a political threat was Congressman Lyndon Johnson who ran as a pro-Roosevelt candidate. In an honest election, Johnson would have probably won, but with some strange vote totals appearing in east Texas, O'Daniel beat Johnson by fewer than 1,350 votes. O'Daniel then won re-election to the Senate in the regular election of 1942.

O'Daniel was pure cornpone, but a master of the radio and of entertainment for rural Texas voters. He provided them with music and fun. And, he provided them with ineffective and very conservative leadership. He supported a regressive sales tax. He opposed spending more money for orphanages and mental institutions. He cut the budget so much that the Texas Rangers had no funds for ammunition. He was adamantly antilabor and hinted darkly of communist and Nazi cells in Texas. He was an isolationist at the outbreak of World War II.[2]

Texas was to have many ineffective, ultraconservative governors and senators, but none like O'Daniel, who mastered the technology of the politics of entertainment at a time when Texans were living hardscrabble lives and were desperate for the pleasure of watching O'Daniel's political camp meetings and hearing his radio broadcasts.

One reason so few Texas governors have been effective is that they have little formal power. In 1983, a study was done of the appointment, budget, removal, and organizational powers of governors that ranked Texas's governor forty-ninth in the nation, only ahead of the governor of South Carolina. In 1990, a study was done of gubernatorial authority in the nation that also ranked Texas's governor forty-ninth, ahead of the governor of Rhode Island.[3]

While the governor of Texas is the most visible state official and is one of the highest-paid governors in the nation, Texas's governor has far less formal power than most governors. To understand the restrictions placed on the office, it is necessary to remember that the Constitution of 1876 was a reaction to the Reconstruction government that existed in Texas following the Civil War. The governor during Reconstruction was very powerful and state government was regarded as oppressive and corrupt. When a new constitution was drafted at the end of the Reconstruction era, Texans did their best to ensure that no state official had extensive power. The Texas Constitution of 1876 placed strict limits on the governor's ability to control the people appointed to office and almost eliminated the possibility that appointees to office could be removed. Power was further fragmented among other officeholders who are collectively known as the **plural executive.** Each of these officeholders is elected and has separate and distinct responsibilities. Members of major state boards, such as the Railroad Commission and the State Board of Education, are also elected and are largely outside the control of the governor.

plural executive
an executive branch in which power is fragmented because the election of statewide officeholders is independent from the governor

The Governor

- How are gubernatorial campaigns and elections conducted in Texas? How can a governor be removed from office? How is a governor succeeded? What resources does a governor possess?
- What are the governor's formal powers? How does the governor exercise these powers?

The governor of Texas is the state's chief executive, but has few formal powers with which to influence the activities of state government. Governors who are successful in pushing their programs through the legislature and seeing them implemented by the bureaucracy are able to use the limited formal powers available to them, exercise their personal political power, exploit the prestige of the office of governor, and marshal various special interests to their cause. One political writer likens the office of governor to a bronco that breaks most men and will be successfully ridden by very few. In short, successful governors are successful politicians.[4]

QUALIFICATIONS

There are only three formal constitutionally required qualifications to become governor of Texas. Article IV of the Texas Constitution requires the governor to: (1) be at least thirty years of age; (2) be a U.S. citizen; and (3) to live in Texas five years immediately before election. As a practical matter, Texas governors have tended to be male, white, Democrat, politically moderate or conservative, either personally wealthy or with access to wealth, Protestant, middle aged, and they have had considerable prior political experience.

Women compose more than 50 percent of the population of the United States and Texas, but fewer than a dozen have served as governor of any state. Only two women, Miriam Ferguson (1925–27, 1933–35) and Ann Richards (1991–95) have served as governor of Texas. No nonwhite has served as governor, and no African American or Hispanic has been nominated to run for governor by the Democratic or Republican parties.

William Clements's victory over John Hill in the gubernatorial campaign of 1978 was the first time since Reconstruction that a Republican won the office. George W. Bush is the second Republican elected governor and the first individual elected for two consecutive four-year terms. The Republican Party is strong and growing more powerful in each election and, as time goes by, it is likely that more Republicans will be elected to the governorship.

Access to money is important because it is inordinately expensive to run for governor. A campaign for the governor's office can cost $25–30 million, and few Texans have that amount of money available. In 1990, Clayton Williams loaned his campaign $8 million. It was his plan to win the governor's office and let friends, supporters, and lobbyists hold fund-raisers to pay back the money. Unfortunately for Williams, he lost the election to Ann Richards and no one contributes much to losing candidates. Williams lost his $8 million.

Sam Kinch, former editor of *Texas Weekly,* suggests that prior political experience is an important consideration in selecting a governor. Kinch maintains that while experience may not mean that someone will be a better governor, it does mean he is more likely to know how to handle the pressures of the office.[5]

ELECTION AND TERM OF OFFICE

Prior to 1974, Texas governors served two-year terms with most being elected to a maximum of two consecutive two-year terms. There have, as Table 25.1 shows, been exceptions, such as Coke Stevenson, Price Daniel, and John Connally serving for six years or Allan Shivers serving for eight years. In 1972, Texas voters adopted a constitutional amendment changing the governor's term to four years and in 1974, Dolph Briscoe was the first governor elected to a four-year term of office.

Gubernatorial elections are held in off-years (election years in which a president is not elected) to minimize the effect of presidential elections on the selection of the Texas governor. The Texas legislature, controlled at the time by Democrats, designed the off-year system to eliminate the possibility of a popular Republican presidential candidate bringing votes to a Republican candidate for governor. Likewise, party leaders wanted to negate the chances of an unpopular Democratic presidential candidate costing a Democratic gubernatorial candidate votes in the general election. Unfortunately, because of this timing, voter turnout in these gubernatorial contests is quite low.

Table 25.1 GOVERNORS OF TEXAS AND THEIR TERMS OF OFFICE SINCE 1874

Richard Coke	1874–76	Miriam Ferguson	1933–35
Richard B. Hubbard	1876–79	James V. Allred	1935–39
Oran M. Roberts	1879–83	W. Lee O'Daniel	1939–41
John Ireland	1883–87	Coke Stevenson	1941–47
Lawrence S. Ross	1887–91	Beauford H. Jester	1947–49
James S. Hogg	1891–95	Allan Shivers	1949–57
Charles A. Culberson	1895–99	Price Daniel	1957–63
Joseph D. Sayers	1899–1903	John Connally	1963–69
S. W. T. Lanham	1903–07	Preston Smith	1969–73
Thomas M. Campbell	1907–11	Dolph Briscoe	1973–79*
Oscar B. Colquitt	1911–15	William Clements	1979–83
James E. Ferguson	1915–17	Mark White	1983–87
William P. Hobby	1917–21	William Clements	1987–91
Pat. M. Neff	1921–25	Ann Richards	1991–95
Miriam Ferguson	1925–27	George W. Bush	1995–2000**
Dan Moody	1927–31	Rick Perry	2000–
Ross Sterling	1931–33		

*Term changed to four years with the 1974 general election.
**Resigned to become president of the United States.
SOURCE: Dallas Morning News, *Texas Almanac and State Industrial Guide 1998–1999* (Dallas: A. H. Belo, 1999).

CAMPAIGNS

Campaigns for governor of Texas last at least ten months. Candidates hit the campaign trail in January of an election year to win their party's primary election in March and continue campaigning until the November general election. Successful candidates spend thousands of hours and millions of dollars campaigning. The money goes to pay staff salaries, travel, opinion polls, telephone banks, direct mailings, and advertisements in print and broadcast media. Texas is so large no one newspaper, radio, or television station reaches all parts of the state. There are twenty-seven media markets in which statewide candidates must purchase print and electronic advertisements to be able to reach every corner of the state. Media costs in the 1998 gubernatorial campaign totaled more than $15 million, and this is the largest single item of spending in most campaigns.

In the 1990 gubernatorial election, Ann Richards and Clayton Williams spent more than $31 million. Williams spent approximately $20 million in his losing effort and financed $8 million of the campaign with his personal fortune. While Richards was not wealthy in her own right, she had access to a cadre of supporters who were willing to back her campaign to the tune of $11 million. High-priced campaigns illustrate that successful candidates need personal wealth or access to wealth.

REMOVAL OF A GOVERNOR

In Texas, the only constitutional method of removing a governor from office is by impeachment and conviction. **Impeachment** means to accuse or to indict, and is similar to a true bill (indictment) by a grand jury. The Texas Constitution notes the governor may be impeached but does not give any grounds for impeachment. Possible justification for impeachment includes failure to perform the duties of governor, gross incompetence, or official misconduct.

impeachment
the formal charge by the House of Representatives that a government official has committed "Treason, Bribery, or other high Crimes and Misdemeanors"

Impeachment begins in the Texas House of Representatives. A majority vote of the Texas House is required to impeach or to bring charges. If the House votes impeachment, the trial takes place in the Texas Senate. One or more members of the Texas House prosecute the case and the Chief Justice of the Supreme Court of Texas presides over the impeachment proceedings. A two-thirds vote of the senators present and voting is necessary to convict. If convicted, the penalty is removal from office and disqualification from holding any other state office.

Any member of the executive or judicial branch may be impeached. Once the House votes impeachment charges against an official, that individual is suspended from office and cannot exercise any of his duties. Governor James Ferguson is the only Texas governor to be impeached and convicted.

SUCCESSION

The Texas Constitution provides for the lieutenant governor to become governor if the office becomes vacant through impeachment and conviction, death, resignation, or the governor's absence from the state.

In December 2000 a succession occurred when Governor George W. Bush became president-elect of the United States and resigned as governor. Lieutenant Governor Rick Perry immediately took the oath to become governor of Texas. According to the *Houston Chronicle,* Rick Perry is "a politician who so looks the part that it's been joked that he was ordered straight from central casting."[6] Perry, a former state legislator from Haskell, was a conservative Democrat who switched to the Republican Party in 1990 and ran successfully for commissioner of agriculture. His six years in the Texas House, eight years as head of a major state agency, and two years as lieutenant governor and president of the Texas state Senate provide him with a great deal more experience than any other governor of the last three decades.[7]

If the governor is impeached, the lieutenant governor serves as acting governor, before and during the trial. Should the governor leave the bounds of the state, the lieutenant governor becomes acting governor. While serving as acting governor, the lieutenant governor earns the governor's daily salary of $316, which is far better than the $20 earned as lieutenant governor. (However, the governor does not forfeit his salary if he is absent from the state. Both the governor and lieutenant governor earn $316 for every day the governor is out of the state.)

When out of the state, the governor is legally entitled to Department of Public Safety protection. George W. Bush spent part of 1999 and 2000 campaigning for president of the United States. During fiscal year 1999, it cost Texans an additional $2,365,000 to provide protection for the governor while he was on the presidential campaign trail.[8] In 1992, Governor Ann Richards was often out of the state campaigning for Bill Clinton, and the Texas taxpayers picked up the cost of her security detail.

Constitutionally the governor's office is weak. Former lieutenant governor Bill Hobby noted that about the only way he knew when he was acting governor was by a note his secretary left on his daily calendar.[9] In the first three months of 2000, then–Lieutenant Governor Rick Perry served as acting governor more days than Bush was in the state to serve as governor. Perry's press secretary has commented that the added duties of being acting governor have not been very noticeable and that those duties have made little difference in Perry's schedule.[10] State government takes little notice of the governor's absences. Speaker of the Texas House Pete Laney has said that the governor's office is "holding court and cutting ribbons" and commented on Governor Bush's out-of-state campaigning by saying, "I guess we've been doing pretty well without one (a governor)."[11]

Legislation further defines succession from the governor to the lieutenant governor, to the president *pro tempore* of the Texas Senate, Speaker of the House, attorney general, and the chief judges of the Texas Courts of Appeal in ascending order.

Part of the governor's compensation includes use of an official mansion in Austin.

COMPENSATION

The governor's salary is set by the legislature. In fiscal year 2001, Texas paid its governor $115,345 annually. This salary makes George W. Bush the seventh highest-paid governor in the nation. In addition to his salary, the governor receives use of an official mansion located near the capitol grounds. Governors and the legislature often squabble about the amount of money needed for upkeep of the mansion and its grounds. The governor also receives use of a limousine, state-owned aircraft, and a personal staff. The value of the perquisites exceeds $3 million a year.

STAFF

The governor's staff consists of more than two-hundred individuals. This includes a chief of staff, deputy chief of staff, general counsel, and a press secretary. A scheduler coordinates the governor's appointments, personal appearances, and work schedule.

The staff keeps the governor informed about issues and problems facing the state, and it may suggest courses of action. In addition, during a four-year term, a governor makes hundreds of appointments to various state posts. It is impossible for a governor to be personally acquainted with each appointee. Part of his staff finds qualified individuals for each post and recommends them to the governor. Other staff members track legislation. They talk with legislators, especially key people such as committee chairpersons. His staff lets the governor know when his personal touch might make a difference in the outcome of legislation. For each bill that passes the legislature, a staff member prepares a summary of the bill with a recommendation that the governor sign or veto the bill.

Recent governors have used their staffs to be more accessible to the public. Governor Bush, like his immediate predecessors, wanted his staff to be no more than a phone call away from those who need assistance. In theory, individuals need only call a member of the governor's staff to receive help or find where to go for help. A toll-free number (1-800-252-9600) handles more than 10,000 calls each year from Texans needing assistance with their problems with state government.

EXECUTIVE POWERS OF THE GOVERNOR

Texas has a board or agency form of government. Approximately two-hundred state boards, commissions, and agencies make up the executive branch of Texas government. Agencies may be as obscure as the Texas Funeral Commission or the State Preservation Board or as well known as the Public Utilities Commission of Texas or the Texas Department of Human Services, but each is important to its constituents. These multi-member boards are the policy making body for their agencies. They employ and oversee the people who operate the agencies on a daily basis.

Appointment Power The governor's power of **appointment** is his most significant executive power. It allows him a degree of control over about two-hundred state agencies. Governor Bush appointed 334 people to office during fiscal year 1997 and 493 in fiscal year 1998.[12] If he completes his term of office, he will appoint all the members of the state boards, commissions, and agencies.

The power of appointment enables the governor to exercise the power of **patronage.** It permits him to reward his supporters by appointing them to office. Most of the offices pay very little, but they do offer supporters some prestige. The governor can also use the appointment power to repay political favors by appointing friends and associates of legislators to office. A governor can also use the appointment power to garner political IOUs from politicians. Most importantly, a governor can use the appointment power to influence agency policy. To a great degree, the effectiveness of a governor's use of the appointment power will determine the governor's success in office.

appointment
the power of the chief executive, whether the president of the United States or the governor of a state, to appoint members of the executive branch to office

patronage
the resources available to higher officials, usually opportunities to make partisan appointments to offices and to confer grants, licenses, or special favors to supporters

The governor appoints people to office, but the Texas Senate must also confirm them. However, since the Senate may not meet for almost two years, the appointee takes office immediately and does not wait for Senate confirmation. An important limitation on the power of the governor to appoint persons to office is the requirement that the individual's state senator must approve the appointment. This is known as **senatorial courtesy** and applies regardless of the party affiliation of the governor, senator, or appointee. Usually, if the appointee's senator concurs in the appointment, the remainder of the Senate will agree. However, if the appointee's senator opposes the appointment, the remainder of the Senate will also oppose the appointment.

senatorial courtesy
the practice whereby the governor, before formally nominating a person for a state judgeship, seeks the indication that the senator from the candidate's own district supports the nomination

If senatorial confirmation was required for an appointment, a governor cannot remove an appointee who refuses to resign unless the governor can show cause and get two-thirds of the Texas Senate to approve.[13] This complex procedure for the termination of members of boards and commissions along with the practice of senatorial courtesy can be a significant limitation on the governor's power to influence the policies of state agencies.

Budgetary Power Officially, the Texas governor is the state's chief budget officer. As such, governors are required to submit an **executive budget** to the legislature. This budget suggests a plan for revenue and expenditure for Texas, but more importantly, it indicates the governor's priorities for the state in the next biennium.

executive budget
the state budget prepared and submitted by the governor to the legislature, which indicates the governor's spending priorities; in recent years, the executive budget has been overshadowed in terms of importance by the legislative budget

legislative budget
the state budget prepared and submitted by the Legislative Budget Board (LBB), which is fully considered by the House and Senate

In 1949, in an effort to gain more control over the state's budget, the legislature established the Legislative Budget Board (LBB), which is responsible for preparing a **legislative budget.** Thus, two budgets are prepared and submitted to the legislature: an executive budget by the governor and a legislative budget by the LBB. As a creation of the legislature, the LBB's budget proposal receives more consideration by the House and Senate than the governor's recommendations, and in recent years the governor's budget has fallen into disuse. Legend has it that the governor's budget has been used as a doorstop, paperweight, and one diminutive legislator used two copies as a booster in his office chair. In 1989, Governor Clements recognized the futility of submitting an executive budget and simply endorsed the recommendations of the LBB. Ann Richards followed Clements's precedent, but Governor George Bush has taken a more active role in budget preparation.

The governor has some control over the final appropriations bill through the use of the line-item veto; however, the governor cannot impound funds or transfer funds from one agency to another, even if circumstances change from the time the money was appropriated. Overall, the budgetary process does not provide the governor with an effective means to control state agencies.

In the mid-1980s, then-Comptroller of Public Accounts Bob Bullock notified Governor Mark White that due to a decline in the price of oil, state revenues would fall 13 percent (about $1 billion) below projections. In an effort to avert a fiscal crisis, Governor White called on all state agencies to reduce expenditures, but he had no legal way to back the request. In order to meet the revenue shortfall, the governor had to call a special session of the legislature.

Military Power The governor is commander-in-chief of the state's National Guard units when they are not under presidential orders. These units are headed by the adjutant general, who is appointed by the governor. Under his

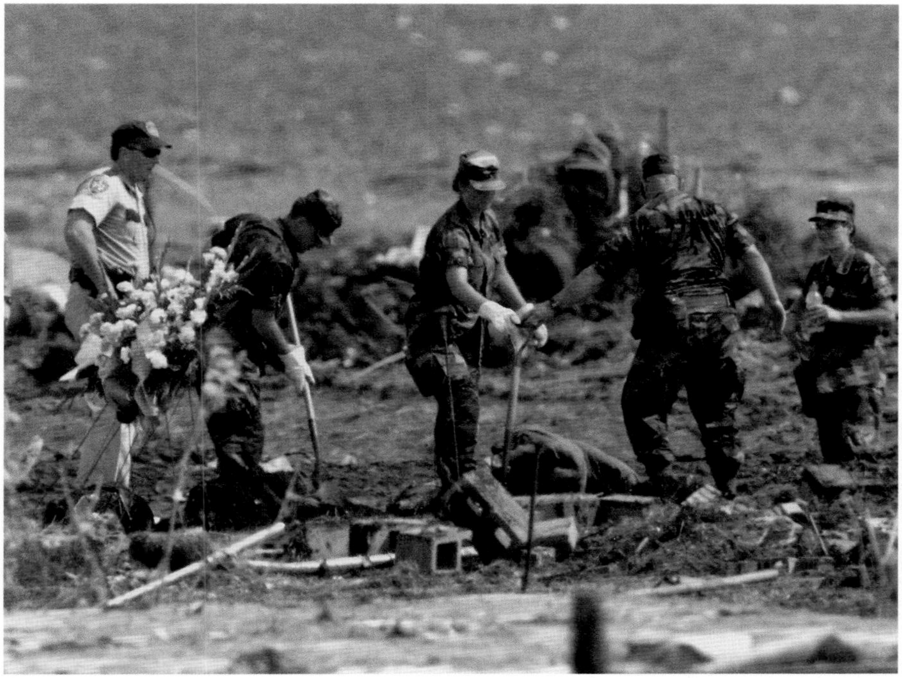

Members of the Texas National Guard dig through rubble in a tornado-damaged neighborhood in Jarell, Texas. Deployment of the state's national guard in times of emergency is one aspect of the governor's executive powers.

military power, the governor can declare martial law that suspends most civil authority and imposes military rule over an area. Martial law can be declared in the event of a riot, flood, hurricane, tornado, or other natural disaster to protect lives and property.

Police Power In Texas, law enforcement and police power is primarily a local responsibility, and the governor has few responsibilities in this area. The governor appoints, with Senate approval, the three-member Public Safety Commission that directs the work of the Department of Public Safety (DPS). The DPS is responsible for highway traffic enforcement (highway patrol), driver's licensing, motor vehicle inspection, truck weighing stations, and the Texas Rangers. When circumstances warrant, the governor can assume command of the Rangers, an elite, highly trained force of about one-hundred officers. If there is evidence of ongoing violence or corruption, the governor can use his informal powers, the prestige of the governor's office, and appeals to the media to compel appropriate action from local law enforcement officials.

LEGISLATIVE POWERS OF THE GOVERNOR

The governor's legislative powers include message power, power of the veto, and the authority to call special sessions and set their agendas. If a governor uses these powers effectively, he can have considerable control over the state's legislative business, but they do not enhance his ability to control the executive branch of state government.

message power
the power deriving from the governor's State of the State message

Message Power Any communication between the governor and the legislature is part of the **message power.** Early in each regular session, the governor delivers a state-of-the-state message. In this speech to a joint session of the legislature, the governor explains his plan for the state in the coming two years. He may propose specific programs or simply set general goals for the state. The speech is covered by most news media, and it is often broadcast on public television and radio stations.

If the governor submits an executive budget, he may address the legislature on the important items in his proposed plan of spending and revenue. At the very least, the budget proposal is forwarded to the legislature with a letter briefly explaining the budget.

Lobbying by governors is part of the message power. Governors try to pass or defeat bills important to them. For example, early in 1991, Governor Ann Richards successfully lobbied for legislation that would expand higher educational opportunities in the Rio Grande Valley and resulted in the creation of the University of Texas at Brownsville.

Although Governor Bill Clements personally lobbied the legislature, he preferred to use his five full-time paid lobbyists to influence the legislature. While not exactly part of the governor's message power, the use of lobbyists is an effective way for a governor to communicate with and influence the legislature.

veto
the governor's power to turn down legislation; can be overridden by a two-thirds vote of both the House and Senate

post-adjournment veto
a veto of a bill that occurs after the legislature adjourns, thus preventing the legislature from overriding it

line-item veto
the power of the executive to veto specific provisions (lines) of a bill passed by the legislature

Veto Power Governors of Texas can sign or **veto** legislation—but in most cases he signs legislation. In the last three sessions of the legislature, less than 5 percent of bills passed by the legislature were vetoed.

When the governor vetoes a bill after the legislature adjourns, it is called a **post-adjournment veto.** Of the 148 bills vetoed in one four-year period, 145 were post-adjournment vetoes. This veto is absolute since the legislature that passed the vetoed bills no longer exists. As a result, if the governor decides to veto a bill, it stays vetoed.

Texas governors possess the **line-item veto,** which is the ability to veto individual parts of an appropriation bill. The governor signs the bill, but strikes out particular lines in the bill. Items struck from the bill do not become law, but the reminder of the appropriations bill does. In 1999, the governor used his line-item veto on seven items in the fiscal year 2000 and fiscal year 2001 general appropriations bill. A line-item veto cannot be overridden by the legislature.

special session
a legislative session called by the governor, that addresses an agenda set by him or her and that lasts no longer than thirty days

Special Sessions Special sessions of the Texas legislature are called by the governor, last for no more than thirty days, and may consider only those items placed on the agenda by the governor. **Special sessions** are called to address critical problems that have arisen since the last regular session. The nature of special sessions allows the legislature to focus attention on specific issues.

From 1989 to 1993, the legislature met in special session at least three times a year. These sessions considered the complicated and divisive issues of reform of workers compensation laws and public school finance. During this period there were so many special sessions that the Texas Legislature, which meets in regular session only 140 days every odd-numbered year, met longer than the Congress of the United States.

JOHN CONNALLY AND THE FAILURE TO CALL A SPECIAL SESSION FOR LEGISLATION ON A $1.25-AN-HOUR TEXAS MINIMUM WAGE

Box 25.1

John Connally was one of the most able and effective governors of Texas, but he was out of touch with the needs of poorer people in Texas. In the summer of 1966, a march was held to dramatize the plight of migrant workers and to seek from the governor a special session of the legislature to enact a state $1.25-an-hour minimum wage. Governor Connally initially tried to ignore the marchers on their walk from Rio Grande City to Austin. Finally, however, he concluded the marchers could no longer be ignored.

Near New Braunfels, a Lincoln Continental pulled up next to the marchers and out stepped Governor Connally, Speaker of the Texas House Ben Barnes, and Texas Attorney General Waggoner Carr. Connally started shaking hands and speaking with the farm workers, but as time went by, he began criticizing the marchers and their needs. He told them that he would refuse to meet with them in Austin and that he would not call a special session of the legislature to consider the minimum wage. When told that people in the Rio Grande Valley did not have enough to eat and lived in substandard housing, Connally replied, "I'm sure there are people who have substandard housing—all over this state, all over this nation, all over this world. . . ." Connally lingered a little longer and then left in his Lincoln, driving away in a cloud of dust. But his patronizing behavior toward the marchers became a symbol of the indifference of the state's political establishment to the needs of migrant workers.

One biographer of Connally wrote of the incident, "The showdown at New Braunfels would be remembered for years. The image of Connally, with his limousine, his cool high fashion, and his paladins by his side, chastising the dusty and the hot, the brown and the poor under the August sun, was a lasting one. It came to be considered, even among his closest advisors like George Christian, one of the worst mistakes of his governorship."

SOURCE: James Reston, Jr., *The Lone Star: The Life of John Connally* (New York: Harper & Row, 1989), pp. 310–13, quote is from p. 313.

JUDICIAL POWER OF THE GOVERNOR

Texas elects each of its state court judges, but when vacancies occur due to the death, resignation, or retirement of the incumbent, or as a result of creation of new courts, the governor is responsible for appointing individuals to fill these vacancies.

Once appointed to office, judges tend to remain in office. More than 95 percent of incumbents win reelection. Through this power to appoint judges, the governor has considerable influence over the Texas judicial system.

THE OFFICE AND ITS OCCUPANTS

People often expect the governor to be able to do things he is not equipped to do. He is expected to be chief executive in more than name only, yet receives little in the way of formal power. Constitutionally and statutorily the

Box 25.2 **AFTER JOHN CONNALLY**

John Connally was one of Texas's most effective governors. Generally speaking, Connally was "farsighted" and "sophisticated" rather than "provincial." He served three two-year terms from 1963–69. Four years of Preston Smith and six years of Dolph Briscoe, neither of whom could be labeled effective, farsighted, or sophisticated, followed him in the governor's office, however. Smith played pool in Austin pool halls and often answered his own phone. Briscoe ran an office described as "a black hole that never got organized enough to answer mail routinely." Neither Smith nor Briscoe understood power and how to use it, and corruption flourished under Smith's administration. Neither governor was able to attract and use able people. Neither was able "to create and communicate new goals, ideas, programs, [and] philosophies. . . ." It was not only a decade of weak governors, but also the downfall of the Democratic Party's dominance in Texas. Dolph Briscoe was defeated in the Democratic primary when he sought renomination for the governorship. Bill Clements, the first Republican governor since Reconstruction, followed him in the governor's office.

SOURCE: Gregory Curtis, "Behind the Lines: The Last Whimper," *Texas Monthly*, www.texasmonthly.com/mag/1998/jan/btl.1.html.

As an office with constitutionally limited powers, the office of governor does not automatically imbue its holder with strength and leadership. John Connally was regarded as a strong governor due in part to the dynamic personality he brought to the position.

governor is ill-equipped to exert control and direction over the Texas bureaucracy.

John Connally was regarded as a strong governor, while Dolph Briscoe was regarded as weak. In part, the difference was that Connally actively sought to lead. As governor, he had a dynamic personality, while Briscoe was more retiring in his personal style and did not seek to have the impact Connally had. Allan Shivers was an imperial governor, as Richard Nixon was the imperial president, while Preston Smith was described as one of the most ordinary people ever to serve as governor. Smith is seldom given credit for doing anything as governor, yet he established the first actual planning organization in Texas government.

In large part, the office of governor is what the person holding the position makes it. Whether the governor is viewed as strong or weak depends on how the governor conducts himself in office, makes use of the formal power he has, and exercises his political influence. Governors differ considerably in terms of their strength and effectiveness, but an axiom of Texas politics is successful governors must be successful politicians.

The Plural Executive

▶ What offices are comprised by the plural executive? What responsibilities does each have? How are they held accountable?

When Texans drafted a constitution in 1876, they chose to limit executive power and disperse it through several elected officials called the plural executive. Texans elect six of the seven people who make up the plural executive: the governor, lieutenant governor, attorney general, comptroller of public accounts, commissioner of the General Land Office, and commissioner of agriculture. The governor appoints the seventh person, the secretary of state, and except for the lieutenant governor who receives the same salary as a legislator, salaries of members of the plural executive are set by the legislature. Additionally, two major regulatory agencies, the Railroad Commission of Texas and the State Board of Education, are run by officials who are independently elected. The result, suggested by Table 25.2, is vast fragmentation of responsibility for public policy in the state.

Elections are partisan and each member of the plural executive may choose to operate independently of others. At times, members of the plural executive may be in competition with one another, often due to conflicting personal ambitions. That, for example, occurred when John Hill was attorney general and sought to take the governorship from Dolph Briscoe and when Mark White was attorney general and sought the governorship from Bill Clements. Champions of the plural executive believe that it limits the power of executive officials and makes these officers more accountable to the public. Opponents assert the plural executive is inefficient and does not promote good government. The governor is a member of the plural executive, but this multipart executive limits the governor's control of the executive branch because he has little authority over this group.

SECRETARY OF STATE

Strangely, given Texas's fragmentation of power, the governor does appoint the Texas **secretary of state,** even though this office is an elected official in thirty-seven states.[14] Though once considered a "glorified keeper of certain state records," it is now an important office.[15] The secretary of state has myriad responsibilities, and the appointment of a secretary of state is one of the governor's most important tasks. The first appointment made by Governor Rick Perry was Democratic state representative Henry R. Cuellar as secretary of state. Mr. Cuellar is from Laredo and he served in the Texas House for fourteen years. He is known for his unflagging efforts to improve conditions in the state's *colonias.*[16]

secretary of state
state official, appointed by the governor, whose primary responsibility is administering elections

ELECTED OFFICIALS IN TEXAS WITH EXECUTIVE RESPONSIBILITIES — **Table 25.2**

Single Elected Executives	Multi-Elected Executives
Governor	Railroad Commission (3 members)
Lieutenant Governor	
Attorney General	
Land Commissioner	State Board of Education (15 members)
Agriculture Commissioner	
Comptroller	

As Texas's chief election official, the secretary of state conducts voter registration drives. His office works with organizations such as the League of Women Voters to increase the number of registered voters. The secretary of state's office collects election night returns from county judges and county clerks and makes results available to the media. This service provides media and voters with a convenient method of receiving the latest official election returns in Texas.

All debt and Uniform Commercial Code filings are placed with the secretary of state's office. When any individual borrows money from a financial institution, a copy of the loan agreement is placed in the secretary of state's office.

LIEUTENANT GOVERNOR

lieutenant governor
the second-highest elected official in the state and president of the state Senate

The **lieutenant governor** is a member of the plural executive and has executive responsibility such as serving as acting governor when the governor is absent from the state. However, his real power results from his duties as president of the Senate, not from any executive responsibilities he may exercise.

ATTORNEY GENERAL

attorney general
elected state official who serves as the state's chief lawyer

The **attorney general** (AG) is elected to a four-year term. John Cornyn, the first Republican elected AG since Reconstruction, is serving his first term. The AG acts as the chief lawyer for the state of Texas. He is, in effect, head of Texas's civil law firm.

The AG's office is concerned primarily with civil matters. When a lawsuit is filed against the state or by the state, the AG manages the legal activities surrounding that lawsuit. Any time a state agency needs legal representation, the AG's office represents the agency. In any lawsuit to which Texas is a party, the AG's office has full responsibility to resolve the case. His office can litigate, compromise, settle, or choose not to pursue the suit.

One of the more important powers of the AG's office comes from the opinion process. Any agency of state or local government can ask the AG's office for an advisory opinion in which it asks if some action is legal. The AG's office will rule on the question, and the ruling has the force of law unless overturned by a court or the legislature.

Probably the most controversial and criticized aspect of the work of the office of attorney general is child support collection. Almost one-half of the attorney general's two thousand employees are involved in collecting child support, and they collect more than $750 million a year. However, it is a program that is the subject of intense criticism because much child support remains uncollected.

The AG's office has little responsibility in criminal law, but may appoint a special prosecutor if a local district attorney asks the AG for assistance. This can happen when there is a conflict of interest with the district attorney. The DA may not want to prosecute one of his local officials because he is friends with or works with the official under investigation.

Generally, in Texas, criminal cases are prosecuted by district or county attorneys elected in each county. The county is usually responsible for the costs of the trial and for all appeals in state court. If a criminal case is appealed to the federal courts, the attorney general's office assumes responsibility.

Attorney General John Cornyn speaks at an event sponsored by East Texans Against Lawsuit Abuse. The office of the attorney general manages all the legal activities around lawsuits involving the state.

COMMISSIONER OF THE GENERAL LAND OFFICE

The Land Office is the oldest state agency in Texas. The commissioner of the General Land Office is elected to a four-year term. Republican David Dewhurst is serving his first term as commissioner.

land commissioner
elected state official who is the manager of most publicly owned lands

Historically the **land commissioner** gave away land. Today, the General Land Office (GLO) is the land manager for most publicly owned lands in Texas. Texas owns or has mineral interest in 20.3 million acres of land in the state plus all submerged lands up to ten miles into the Gulf of Mexico. The GLO also awards grazing and oil and gas exploration rights on this land. All but 28 of Texas's 254 counties have some of these public lands; however, eight million acres is located west of the Pecos River and four million acres is found along the Texas coast.

Thousands of producing oil and gas wells are found on state-owned land and are managed by the GLO. If the price of oil is eighteen to nineteen dollars a barrel, the Land Office raises over $300 million a year in royalties on oil and natural gas produced by these wells. A significant portion of this money goes to the Permanent School Fund and Permanent University Fund.

The commissioner also manages the Veterans' Land Program, in which the state makes low-cost loans to Texas veterans. The program includes loans for land, housing, and home improvements. Recently, the GLO was given authority over some environmental matters. The land commissioner is responsible for environmental quality on public lands and waters, especially along the Texas coast. Four million acres of submerged lands on the coast of Texas are owned by the state and managed by the Land Office. Additionally, all of Texas's Gulf Coast beaches are publicly owned and under the jurisdiction of the GLO.

The commissioner of the GLO is influential because he is the person primarily responsible for awarding the right to explore for and produce oil and natural gas on state-owned land and he has responsibility for more than 18,000 producing wells.[17]

COMMISSIONER OF AGRICULTURE

agricultural commissioner
elected state official who is primarily responsible for enforcing agricultural laws

The commissioner of agriculture is elected to a four-year term. Susan Combs is serving her first term as commissioner of agriculture. The **agricultural commissioner** is primarily responsible for enforcing agricultural laws. These include administration of animal quarantine laws, inspection of food, and enforcement of disease and pest control programs. Enforcement of the state's laws help to ensure Texas's farm products are of high quality and disease free.

The Department of Agriculture checks weights and measures. Each year a representative of the department checks each motor fuel pump to ensure it dispenses the correct amount of fuel. Scales used by grocery stores and markets are checked to guarantee they weigh products correctly.

Farming and ranching are big business in Texas. While a large number of small family farms exist in the state, large corporate farms increasingly dominate Texas agriculture. These large agribusinesses are greatly affected by the decisions of the commissioner. Decisions of the commissioner of agriculture can increase or decrease the cost of production. Changes in production costs affect the profit margins of these agribusinesses and ultimately the price consumers pay for food products.

COMPTROLLER OF PUBLIC ACCOUNTS

comptroller
elected state official who directs the collection of taxes and other revenues

Carole Keaton Rylander is serving her first term of four years as comptroller of public accounts. The **comptroller** is a powerful state official because she directs the collection of tax and nontax revenues, and before each legislative session she issues an evaluation and estimate of anticipated state revenues. Tax collection is the most visible function of the comptroller. She collects most taxes and many fees levied by Texas. These include the general sales tax, severance tax on natural resources, motor fuel tax, inheritance tax, most occupational taxes, and many minor taxes. In any given year, this office collects over $35 billion in tax revenue.

Although collecting billions in revenue is important, estimating revenues provides the comptroller with more power. These estimates, issued monthly during legislative sessions, are vital to the appropriations process because the legislature is prohibited from spending more than the comptroller estimates will be available. Final passage of any appropriations bill is contingent upon the comptroller certifying that revenues will be available to cover the monies spent in the appropriation. Since most bills require the expenditure of monies, this provides the comptroller with significant power over the legislative process. If the comptroller is unable to certify monies are available to pay for the appropriation, the legislature must reduce the appropriation or increase revenues. More than auditor, accountant, and tax collector, the comptroller is a key figure in the appropriations process.

In 1996, the office of state treasurer was eliminated and the comptroller of public accounts assumed the duties of that office. Originally the state treasurer and now the comptroller of public accounts is the official custodian of state

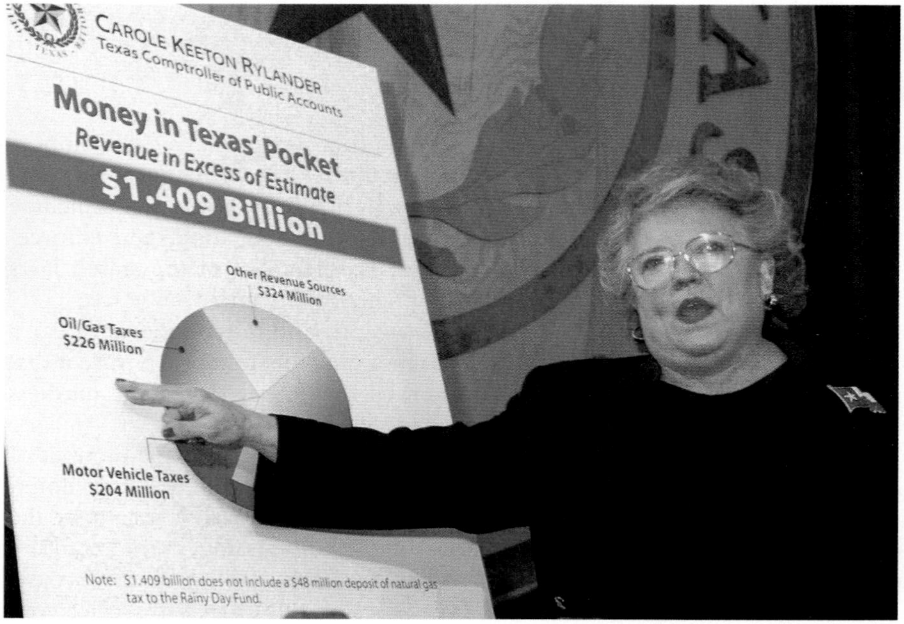

Texas comptroller of public accounts Carole Keaton Rylander announces a projected surplus in the Texas budget. In addition to collecting taxes, the comptroller provides revenue estimates to the legislature, on which it must base its appropriations budget.

funds and is responsible for the safety of the state's money and for investing that money.

To assure the safety of Texas's money, funds are deposited only in financial institutions designated by the State Depository Board as eligible to receive state monies. Deposits are required to earn as much money as possible because all money earned in this fashion does not have to be made up in tax dollars. The more money earned for Texas, the fewer tax dollars needed. From 1983–99, Texas earned more from the money it had on deposit than it had in the previous 146 years combined. The vast amounts of money handled by the comptroller and her relationship with financial institutions can provide this officeholder with considerable power.

An interesting responsibility is the comptroller's power to return abandoned money and property to its rightful owners. In October of each year, the comptroller publishes a list of individuals with unclaimed property. The 1999 list included $117,000 in a forgotten savings account, a certificate of deposit

FORMER COMPTROLLER JOHN SHARP ON THE OFFICE OF COMPTROLLER **Box 25.3**

". . . When all is said and done, however, the purpose of the comptroller's office isn't to administer high-profile programs . . . no matter how important they might be. The real job of the comptroller is to enforce the pay-as-you-go provision of the Texas constitution. That may not sound like a lot, but it isn't always an easy thing to do. The first Texas comptroller—whose name, appropriately enough, was John Money—lasted only fifteen days on the job. He took the oath of office on the day after Christmas in 1835, leaving shortly after the new year dawned in 1836. Apparently he considered running off to join Texas' revolutionary army less dangerous than serving as tax collector for the provisional government.

"He might have been right. As with every Texas comptroller since, one of Money's main tasks was to tell lawmakers how much money they could spend and remind them that they couldn't dispute the revenue estimate without a four-fifths vote of both houses, a provision many of us wish the federal government had. That doesn't always make the comptroller popular with legislators, but it provides a pretty good measure of protection for Texas taxpayers. Even though a two-thirds vote is all that's needed to override the governor's veto, it takes a four-fifths vote to override the comptroller, which has never happened. (I'm duty bound to point out how high the stakes can sometimes get. Back in 1903, comptroller Robert M. Love—whose name seemingly didn't reflect how some people felt about him—was shot to death at his desk in the Capitol. Yet even in death, Love wasn't overridden.)

"The fact is, the Legislature can't spend more than you say it can. That's important, because when it comes to spending tax dollars, the only difference between Democrats and Republicans is that though both will spend every dime in the state treasury, Republicans will tell people they feel bad about it. . . ."

SOURCE: John Sharp, "Dear Carole," *Texas Monthly*, www.texasmonthly.com/biz/1999/jun/carole.1.html.

for $104,000, gold coins, diamond rings, family photos, and rare baseball trading cards. Money that remains unclaimed goes to the state.

ACCOUNTABILITY OF THE PLURAL EXECUTIVE

Except for the secretary of state, each member of the plural executive is directly accountable to the people of Texas through elections. The plural executive is accountable to the legislature in three ways: the budgetary process, sunset review, and the impeachment process. The amount of money appropriated to an agency by the legislature can be an indication of the quality of work done by a department. Significantly increased appropriations indicate an agency in good standing with the legislature, while little or no increase in funds is an indication of legislative displeasure.

The Texas Constitution and not the legislature create most agencies of the plural executive. Therefore they would not cease to exist under the Sunset process, which will be discussed later. However, the Sunset review allows the legislature to examine the quality and nature of the work of each agency and to seek ways for that agency to better serve the people of Texas. Impeachment and conviction is the ultimate check on an elected official. The Texas House of Representatives can impeach an official for criminal activity or gross malfeasance in office. The Texas Senate then tries the official. If convicted by the Senate, the official is removed from office.

THE PLURAL EXECUTIVE AND THE GOVERNOR

The plural executive dilutes the ability of the governor to control state government. He appoints the secretary of state but has no control over other members of the plural executive. Officials are elected independently, and they do not run as a slate. They do not answer to the governor, and they do not serve as his cabinet. They tend to operate their offices as independent fiefdoms and jealously guard their turf. The plural executive makes state government appear as if it is going in several different directions at once.

With each member of the plural executive having separate and distinct responsibilities, there is a lack of cohesiveness in state government and statewide planning. However, the plural executive is a product of Texas's history and environment. Like much of Texas government, it is a product of the reaction to Governor E. J. Davis at the close of Reconstruction.

Boards, Commissions, and Regulatory Agencies

▶ How can one classify agencies within the Texas bureaucracy? What are some of these important agencies and what does each do? How are they held accountable?

Although state government in Texas has approximately two-hundred state boards and commissions and four major agencies within the plural executive, it ranks only forty-fifth among the states in the number of employees. Agencies

Politics on the Web

Just as the Web makes political leaders more vulnerable to public scrutiny, it also provides political leaders in the state with a new vehicle for communicating with their constituency. Statewide officeholders in Texas, such as the governor and the comptroller, use their Web sites not only to keep Texans informed about issues affecting the state, but also to sell their administration and initiatives. Careful projection of images and messages over the Web can help officeholders set the agenda for state politics and define what the key issues of politics and government are to be in the state over the next few years. Web sites involve a direct contact between the elected representative and the people. Interpretation is left up to the consumer. This may mean that a message gets through to the average citizen that is not contaminated by the editorial comments of the news media. But it also might mean that the average citizen is subject to considerably more manipulation without the balanced perspective of a news professional to properly interpret the message.

www.wwnorton.com/wtp3e

within the Texas **bureaucracy** can be classified as multi-member boards appointed by the governor and confirmed by the Senate, multi-member boards elected by the people, and agencies with single executives elected by the people.

bureaucracy
the complex structure of offices, tasks, rules, and principles of organization that are employed by all large-scale institutions to coordinate effectively the work of their personnel

APPOINTED OFFICIALS

Most boards and commissions in Texas are headed by members appointed by the governor and confirmed by the Senate. They serve staggered six-year terms. If an agency has nine members, three are appointed every two years. Multimember commissions with heads appointed by the governor include innocuous agencies, like the Bandera County River Authority, the State Seed and Plant Board, the Caddo Lake Compact Commission, and the Texas Funeral Commission. There are also better known agencies, such as the Texas Alcoholic Beverage Commission, the Department of Parks and Wildlife, and the Texas Department of Corrections. There are also agencies that have a direct impact on all our lives, such as the Department of Transportation and the Public Utilities Commission. What follows are two examples of these agencies—the Public Utilities Commission and the Texas Alcoholic Beverage Commission.

PUBLIC UTILITIES COMMISSION (PUC)

More than any other agency, the PUC has a direct effect on consumers' pocketbooks. Prior to 1975, cities in Texas set utility rates. The Public Utilities Commission was established in 1975, in part, to protect consumers and to curb the rate at which utility costs were increasing. The commission is responsible for setting local telephone and some electric rates.

All local telephone rates are set by the PUC. Rates vary from one part of Texas to another, but all rates in a service area are the same. The commission

Judy Walsh, a commissioner on the Texas Public Utility Commission, speaks to the Senate Economic Development Committee. The PUC is primarily responsible for telephone and electric rates.

also determines the maximum charge for pay telephones and approves additional services such as Caller-ID, call waiting, and call forwarding. In 1999, the Texas legislature approved legislation that allows the PUC to adopt rules that will lower intrastate long distance rates. A rule that took effect in September 1999 prohibits an individual's local service from being disconnected for nonpayment of long distance bills. Another regulation established by the PUC requires all calls to information to be answered by a person, not a recording with a menu. The personal touch is not yet a casualty of the computer age.

The commission sets electric rates for private companies offering service to those residing outside the city limits. Cities may continue to establish rates or allow the PUC to set the rates. If a city determines the rate and the electric company disagrees with the rate set, the company may appeal to the PUC.

TEXAS ALCOHOLIC BEVERAGE COMMISSION

The Twenty-First Amendment gives states the responsibility for making and enforcing regulations concerning the alcoholic beverage industry. In Texas, the Texas Alcoholic Beverage Commission (TABC) regulates this industry. For fiscal year 2001, the TABC's budget is $124 million. The commission's five-hundred employees enforce laws, rules, and regulations affecting the alcoholic beverage industry. These policies cover all aspects of the manufacture, importation, transportation, and sale of alcoholic beverages. Regulations include establishing the alcohol content of beer; prohibiting outdoor advertising or the manufacture of alcoholic beverages in areas that prohibit the sale of alcoholic beverages; transporting beer, wine, or liquor through a dry area; assisting in the enforcement of the minimum drinking age; and checking on hours of operation. Issuing permits and licenses, administering the selective sales tax on alcoholic beverages, and leveling fines by the agency raise more than $170 million a year.

Enforcing the twenty-one-year-old drinking age is a priority with the commission. In 1998, the last year for which figures are available, the TABC issued 48 percent more "minor in possession" citations than in the previous year. A commission spokesperson has noted that young people may not be drinking more, but the enforcement officers are catching more of them.[18]

ELECTED OFFICIALS

Members of two state agencies are elected by the voters: the State Board of Education (SBOE) and the Railroad Commission of Texas (RRC). The RRC has three members elected to six-year terms of office. One of the three members is elected every two years.

At one time the Railroad Commission was one of the most powerful state agencies in the nation. It regulated intrastate railroads, trucks, and bus transportation, and supervised the oil and natural gas industry in Texas. For most of its life, regulation of the oil and gas industry was the primary focus of the RRC.

Today, the RRC is a shadow of its former self. Court decisions, deregulation of the transportation industry, other state and federal legislation, and the decline in the nation's dependence on Texas's crude oil production have diminished the power of the commission.

STATE BOARD OF EDUCATION (SBOE)

The SBOE is a fifteen-member board elected to four-year terms from single-member districts. Policy for public education (pre-kindergarten to grade twelve programs supported by the state government) in Texas is set by the SBOE. The education bureaucracy is called the Texas Education Agency (TEA). It enforces rules and regulations affecting grades pre-kindergarten through twelve in Texas. Together these two agencies control public education in Texas by determining licensing requirements for public school teachers, setting minimum high-school graduation criteria for recommended or advanced curriculum, establishing standards for accreditation of public schools, and adopting public school textbooks.

Texas spends millions of dollars each year purchasing textbooks and furnishes these books without charge to students. Books must meet stringent criteria, and because the state buys so many textbooks, publishers print books especially for students in Texas. Often states that spend less money on textbooks than Texas does must purchase those originally printed for Texas.

The commissioner of education is appointed by the governor from a list of candidates submitted by the SBOE. He is administrative head of the TEA and serves as advisor to the State Board of Education. The commissioner of education is at the apex of the public education bureaucracy in Texas.

MAKING AGENCIES ACCOUNTABLE

In a democracy, elected officials are ultimately responsible to voters. Appointed officials are indirectly accountable to the people through the elected officials who appointed them. Both are responsible to legislatures who determine responsibilities and appropriate money to carry out those responsibilities. In Texas, the plural executive is responsible to the legislature for its biennial funding and to the voters for re-election. The myriad of state agencies look to the legislature for funding and once each twelve years must justify their existence to the **Sunset Advisory Commission** (SAC).

Sunset Advisory Commission (SAC)
a commission created in 1975 for the purpose of reviewing the effectiveness of state agencies

The ten-member Sunset Advisory Commission has four members from the Texas Senate and one public member appointed by the lieutenant governor. Four members from the Texas House and one public member are appointed by the Speaker of the Texas House.

The Sunset Review Act created the Sunset Advisory Commission in 1975. It establishes specific criteria to be considered in evaluating the continuing need for an agency. One of several laws enacted in the mid-1970s to bring more openness and accountability to Texas government, the Sunset process establishes a date on which an agency is abolished unless the legislature passes a bill for the agency to continue in operation.

Agencies are reviewed every twelve years. During its Sunset review, an agency must, among other things, document its efficiency, the extent to which it meets legislative mandates, and its promptness and effectiveness in handling complaints, and establish the continuing need for its services. The review process is lengthy, lasting almost two years.

After a thorough study of an agency, the SAC recommends one of three actions to the legislature: (1) the agency continues as is, with no change in its organization or functions; (2) the agency continues but with changes (reorganization, a new focus for the agency, or merger with other agencies); or (3) the agency is abolished.

If options one or two are recommended, specific action by the legislature is required before the deadline of the agency's abolishment. Option one requires specific legislation to re-create the agency in its existing form. The second option requires the legislature to re-create the agency with some or all the changes recommended by the SAC. If the legislature agrees the agency should be abolished, no action is necessary. It will die on the sunset deadline; the sun sets and the agency is no more.

Each state agency has been through the Sunset process at least once. The legislature has allowed the sun to set on forty-two agencies. More than a dozen agencies have also been merged with existing bodies. Since 1975, the legislature accepted the majority of recommendations of the Sunset Commission.

Summary

Executive power in Texas is segregated among many officeholders. It was the intent of those who wrote the Constitution of 1876 to give the governor only limited power and distribute remaining authority among many officials. The governor takes an oath to see that the laws of the state are carried out, but the constitution and laws of the state effectively deny him the ability to fulfull this promise.

The formal, legal, and constitutional qualifications to become governor are easily met, but there are informal qualifications that further determine who can become governor. Qualifications relating to party membership, gender, age, political philosophy, and ethnicity are not found in the constitution; however, these traits can tell us which candidate is more likely to win.

Texas governors serve a four-year term and can be re-elected an unlimited number of times. Campaigns for the governor's chair are inordinately expensive. Those without personal wealth or the ability to raise significant sums are often doomed to defeat.

A Texas governor's powers are divided into three areas: executive, legislative, and judicial. Executive powers are concerned with the governor's ability to supervise the executive branch of government. His formal powers, those specifically found in the state constitution or state laws, are limited. He appoints hundreds of people to office but often loses control over them once they are confirmed by the Senate. It is next to impossible for the governor to fire anyone, and he has almost no control over the budget. Legislators pay little attention to his budgetary recommendations, and the constitution deprives him of any budget execution authority. While the governor has the line-item veto, the amount disallowed by the governor is usually insignificant.

The governor's power over the legislature may be his most significant power, but it offers him no help in controlling the executive branch of government. His legislative powers include the message power, power to call special sessions, and authority to sign or veto legislation.

Governors assert their political power when exercising the message power. Essentially this is a form of lobbying. He may try to persuade legislators to vote for bills he favors or to vote against bills he opposes. This lobbying might involve personal calls or visits by the governor or work by lobbyists hired to focus on the governor's program.

Calling or not calling special sessions and setting their agendas provides the governor with broad control between regular sessions.

The governor may sign legislation, veto legislation, or allow it to become law without his signature. Governors sign more than 90 percent of the bills passed. Most bills vetoed are killed after the legislature adjourns. If the legislature adjourns and the governor vetoes the bill after adjournment, the legislature cannot override the veto. This is called a post-adjournment veto and is permanent.

Judicial powers of the governor include the power to fill a judicial vacancy that occurs when a sitting judge dies, retires, or resigns, and powers of clemency. Clemency normally includes the power to issue pardons, grant paroles, and issue reprieves. The state legislature severely limits the governor's power in this area because of abuses of previous governors. Pardons can be granted only on the recommendation of the Board of Pardons and Paroles. Texas governors can neither grant nor deny paroles. Governors have the ability to grant each person condemned to death one thirty-day reprieve. Additional reprieves and any other act of clemency must be recommended by the Board of Pardons and Paroles.

Texas governors have only limited formal powers with which to govern the state. To be successful, a governor must have and know how to use political power. He must be able to get his way through the gentle art of persuasion rather than with any specific power from the legislature or constitution. Governors lacking political skills do not do well in Texas; however successful politicians are successful governors.

The plural executive—composed of the governor, lieutenant governor, secretary of state, attorney general, commissioner of the general land office, commissioner of agriculture, and comptroller of public accounts—is not a formal group. It should not be considered the governor's cabinet. It does not, in fact, hold meetings, but is a way for students of Texas politics to identify several state officials who have considerable authority in the executive branch.

The secretary of state is appointed by the governor, and the remaining officials are elected to four-year terms by the voters. They do not run as a team. Each official has separate and distinct responsibilities. The authority of one does not interfere with the jurisdiction of another.

Many criticize this form of government as ineffective and inefficient, but it is unique to Texas. This format accomplishes the founders' idea that government should be limited so that no one individual can achieve too much power. It holds those officeholders accountable to the legislature for their budgets, to the legislature and the Sunset Advisory Commission for the continuation of agencies, and to the voters who control the future of the officeholder.

The bureaucracy carries out the laws passed by the legislature. It is nothing more or less than employees of government. There are approximately two hundred agencies in Texas, giving truth to the statement that Texas is an agency or commission form of government. These agencies run the prisons, set utility rates, license doctors and nurses, ensure that Texas has clean water, air, and beaches, build highways, enforce traffic laws, and carry out countless other responsibilities. Agencies are accountable to the legislature through the budgetary process and through Sunset review.

No one individual is responsible for the daily operation of Texas government. The governor takes an oath to see that the laws are faithfully executed, but he has no formal or institutional power to carry out this responsibility. So, who runs Texas? Many people do! The list includes the governor, the plural executive, and members of the bureaucracy.

FOR FURTHER READING

Barta, Carolyn. *Bill Clements: Texian to His Toenails.* Austin: Eakin Press, 1996.

Gantt, Jr., Fred. *The Chief Executive of Texas: A Study of Gubernatorial Leadership.* Austin: University of Texas Press, 1964.

Henrickson, Kenneth. *The Chief Executive of Texas: From Stephen F. Austin to John B. Connally, Jr.* College Station: Texas A&M University Press, 1995.

Morehead, Richard. *Fifty Years in Texas Politics: From Roosevelt to Reagan, from the Fergusons to Clements.* Austin: Eakin Press, 1982.

Reston, Jr., James. *Lone Star: The Life of John Connally.* New York: Harper & Row, 1989.

Sabato, Larry. *Goodbye to Good-time Charlie: The American Governorship Transformed*, 2nd ed. Washington, DC: Congressional Quartely Press, 1983.

STUDY OUTLINE

The Governor

1. The governor of Texas has few formal powers to influence what happens in state government.
2. Governors are selected in off-year elections so that presidential elections will not influence the outcome of statewide elections.
3. The only constitutional method of removing a governor from office before the end of his term is impeachment and conviction.
4. The governor's power of appointment is his most effective means of controlling the executive branch of state government, but his power of removal and control over the budget provide him with little control over the executive branch.
5. The governor's powers vis-à-vis the legislature are mostly negative and include his ability to exercise the veto, post-adjournment veto, and line-item veto.
6. Governors control special sessions by deciding if and when to call them, and by setting the sessions' agendas.
7. Judges in Texas are officially elected, not appointed, to office. However, governors can appoint judges to vacant seats.
8. The governor has only limited power of clemency.

The Plural Executive

1. The plural executive, by fragmenting power among several state officials, illustrates Texans' distrust of a centralized government.
2. Each member of the plural executive is accountable to the voters and the legislature.
3. Members of the plural executive often operate independently of each other and the governor.

Boards, Commissions, and Regulatory Agencies

1. The Texas bureaucracy can be divided into those headed by appointed officials and those headed by elected officials.
2. Appointed officials are indirectly accountable to the people through the elected officials who appointed them and to the legislature.
3. Elected officials are directly accountable to the people and to the legislature.
4. Once every twelve years, the Sunset Advisory Commission investigates the performance of each agency and makes recommendations to continue the agency with no changes, continue the agency with changes, or abolish the agency.

PRACTICE QUIZ

1. Which of the following is *not* a qualification to become governor of Texas?
   a) A candidate must be thirty years of age.
   b) A candidate must have lived in Texas for five years.
   c) A candidate must be a U.S. citizen.
   d) A candidate must be literate.

2. The election for governor of Texas is held in an off-year in order to
   a) increase voter participation in elections in odd-numbered years.
   b) influence the presidential vote in Texas.
   c) prevent the presidential vote in Texas from influencing the election of state officials.
   d) decrease the likelihood of voter fraud.
3. The only constitutional method of removing the governor is
   a) *quo warranto* proceedings.
   b) *ex post facto* removal.
   c) impeachment.
   d) impeachment and conviction.
4. The governor's most effective power in controlling the executive branch of state government is his power
   a) of appointment.
   b) of removal.
   c) of judicial review.
   d) to create a state budget.
5. the governor's veto is absolute when it is a
   a) line-item veto.
   b) special veto.
   c) post-adjournment veto.
   d) select veto.
6. The governor can grant
   a) pardons.
   b) suspended sentences.
   c) probation.
   d) parole.
7. Which member of the plural executive is appointed?
   a) secretary of state
   b) lieutenant governor
   c) comptroller of public accounts
   d) attorney general
8. Members of the plural executive are accountable to the
   a) voters and the governor.
   b) legislature.
   c) legislature and voters.
   d) constitution.
9. Which agency investigates the performance of state agencies and recommends if an agency should be abolished, continued as is, or continued with changes?
   a) Legislative Budget Board
   b) Legislative Research Bureau
   c) Texas Research League
   d) Sunset Advisory Commission
10. Who runs state government?
   a) the governor alone
   b) the governor and the plural executive
   c) the executive directors of various state agencies
   d) numerous elected and appointed officials

CRITICAL THINKING QUESTIONS

1. Texas has a weak executive form of government. Many people are responsible for some part of government, but no one individual is "in charge." How responsive is state government to the people? How effective is state government? Would state government work better if there was one person with the power and responsibility for the operation of state government? Explain your answer.
2. The commissioner of agriculture, commissioner of the General Land Office, comptroller of public accounts, and the attorney general are part of the plural executive. Each heads an agency that has significant responsibility for the operation of state government. To what extent is the public aware of these agencies and the major role they play in government? Explain your answer.

KEY TERMS

agricultural commissioner (p. 953)
appointment (p. 945)
attorney general (p. 952)
bureaucracy (p. 957)
comptroller (p. 954)
executive budget (p. 946)
impeachment (p. 943)
land commissioner (p. 953)
legislative budget (p. 946)
lieutenant governor (p. 952)
line-item veto (p. 948)
message power (p. 948)
patronage (p. 945)
plural executive (p. 940)
post-adjournment veto (p. 948)
secretary of state (p. 951)
senatorial courtesy (p. 946)
special session (p. 948)
Sunset Advisory Commission (SAC) (p. 959)
veto (p. 948)

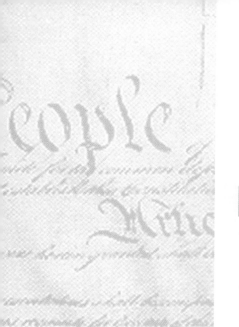

26 The Texas

★ **Court Structure**

How can one describe the large and complex structure of the Texas court system? What is the jurisdiction and authority of each level of court?

★ **The Legal Process**

What are differences between civil law and criminal law in Texas? How is the legal process different in civil and criminal cases?

★ **How Judges Are Selected**

What is the most important feature of how judges are selected in Texas? What does this feature reveal about Texas politics more broadly? How does the selection process influence who becomes a judge in Texas? What alternatives or reforms to the current selection process are available?

★ **The Importance of the Texas Courts**

What are some of the ways that courts in Texas have an important impact upon the lives of all Texans?

Judiciary

IT is often a surprise to people to learn that Texas has two supreme courts—one for civil cases, which is called the Supreme Court of Texas, and one for criminal cases, which is called the Texas Court of Criminal Appeals. Each court is a nine-judge court that hears cases across the corridor from each other in the Tom C. Clark Building in Austin. All eighteen judges on these courts are elected.

Because the Texas Court of Criminal Appeals only deals with criminal cases where little money is involved, judicial campaigns for those offices tend to be inexpensive. A candidate can file and take a chance. With the right sounding name, a good placement on the ballot (first is preferable), and a popular party affiliation, the candidate, regardless of experience or ability, has a chance at winning.

That is what happened in 1994. Steve Mansfield, a lawyer with minimal criminal law experience, inflated his resume and ran as a Republican. He defeated a highly respected incumbent judge, who was running as a Democrat in a year when Democrats did poorly in Texas judicial elections. Once he was on the state's highest criminal court, Judge Mansfield was arrested on criminal trespass charges for allegedly trying to scalp complimentary tickets for a University of Texas–Texas A&M football game. The State Commission on Judicial Conduct reprimanded him.

Judge Mansfield's inexperience when he was elected to the bench and his behavior on the bench made him a poster judge for judicial reform. He won, it was argued, because voters knew little about the Texas Court of Criminal Appeals and about candidates for the office. What voters knew was that Mansfield was a Republican running in a Republican year.[1]

In 2000, after considerable waffling back and forth, Mansfield decided not to run for re-election. Nevertheless, his story tells us much about the Texas judiciary. As the following chapter illustrates, the Texas court structure is complex and confusing. Perhaps the most controversial aspect of the Texas judiciary is that judges are chosen in partisan elections, where the ability of the judicial candidate is often irrelevant to whether the candidate is elected or not.

Court Structure

- How can one describe the large and complex structure of the Texas court system?
- What is the jurisdiction and authority of each level of court?

Texas Supreme Court
the highest court in Texas; consists of nine justices and has final appellate authority over all civil cases

Texas Court of Criminal Appeals
the highest criminal court in Texas; consists of nine justices and has final appellate authority over all criminal cases

courts of appeal
the fourteen intermediate-level appellate courts which hear appeals from district and county courts, to determine if the decisions of these lower courts followed legal principle and court procedure

district courts
the major trial courts in Texas, which have general jurisdiction over a broad range of civil and criminal cases

county judge
the person in each of Texas's 254 counties who presides over the county court and county commissioners court, with responsibility for the administration of county government

Texas has a large and complex court structure consisting of a hodge-podge of courts with overlapping jurisdiction (see Figure 26.1). Additionally, some courts have specialized jurisdiction, whereas others have broad authority to handle a variety of cases. At the highest level is the **Texas Supreme Court,** which consists of nine justices, including a chief justice. This court hears civil cases only. The chief justice is paid $115,000 yearly and associate justices are paid $113,000. The only requirements for being a Texas Supreme Court justice is that a justice must be a citizen of the United States and a resident of Texas, at least thirty-five years of age, and either a practicing lawyer or judge for at least ten years. The term of a justice is six years with at least three justices being elected every two years.

The **Texas Court of Criminal Appeals** is the highest court in the state for criminal cases. This court also has nine judges, including a presiding judge. The pay, terms, and qualifications of Court of Criminal Appeals judges are the same as for the Texas Supreme Court. Perhaps the most important task of the Court of Criminal Appeals is to have jurisdiction over automatic appeals in death penalty cases.

Both the Supreme Court and Court of Criminal Appeals have appellate jurisdiction. This means that they have the authority to review the decisions of lower courts to determine if legal principles and court procedures were followed correctly. This authority also provides the power to order that a case be retried if mistakes were made. Texas has fourteen other appellate courts, located in various parts of the state, which have both criminal and civil jurisdiction. These courts are intermediate appellate courts and hear appeals from the trial courts. Usually, before the Supreme Court or the Court of Criminal Appeals hears a case, the initial appeal has been heard by one of the **courts of appeal.** Presently, there are eighty judges who serve on the fourteen courts of appeal, which range in size from three to thirteen judges. Although there are occasions when every judge on a court of appeal will hear a case, mostly appeals at this level are heard by panels of three judges.

Like the higher appellate judges, a courts of appeal justice must be a citizen of the United States and a resident of Texas, at least thirty-five, and a lawyer or judge for at least ten years. Each of the fourteen courts has one chief justice. The salaries of these justices are capped at $1,000 less than a Supreme Court justice or $500 less in the case of a chief justice, but they make at least $107,350, with the chief justice making $500 a year more.

The major trial courts in Texas are the **district courts.** Each county has at least one district court, although rural parts of Texas may have several counties that are served by one district court. In contrast, urban counties have many district courts. Harris County (Houston), for example, has fifty-nine district courts. District courts usually have general jurisdiction, meaning that they hear a broad range of civil and criminal cases. However, in urban counties, there are some district courts with specialized jurisdiction that will hear only civil, criminal, juvenile, or family law matters. Those district courts having general jurisdiction would hear felonies, divorces, land disputes, election contests, and civil lawsuits. Currently, there are 396 district judges.

Texas is unusual in having the office of **county judge** in each of its 254 counties. Not only does the county judge preside over the county commissioners court and thus has responsibilities for administration of county government, but

THE STRUCTURE OF THE TEXAS COURT SYSTEM — **Figure 26.1**

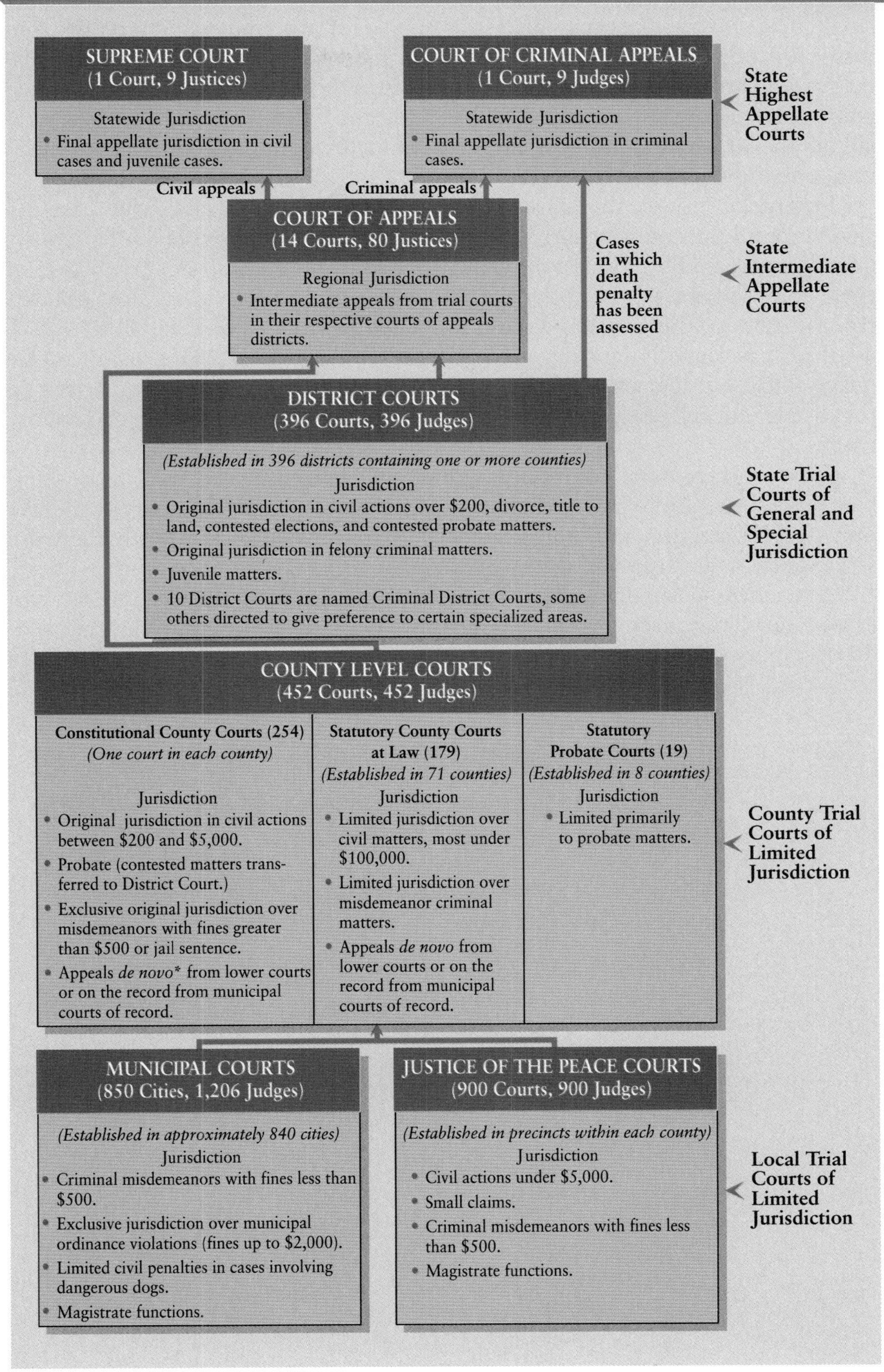
SUPREME COURT
(1 Court, 9 Justices)
Statewide Jurisdiction
• Final appellate jurisdiction in civil cases and juvenile cases.
COURT OF CRIMINAL APPEALS
(1 Court, 9 Judges)
Statewide Jurisdiction
• Final appellate jurisdiction in criminal cases.
State Highest Appellate Courts
Civil appeals
Criminal appeals
COURT OF APPEALS
(14 Courts, 80 Justices)
Regional Jurisdiction
• Intermediate appeals from trial courts in their respective courts of appeals districts.
Cases in which death penalty has been assessed
State Intermediate Appellate Courts
DISTRICT COURTS
(396 Courts, 396 Judges)
(Established in 396 districts containing one or more counties)
Jurisdiction
• Original jurisdiction in civil actions over $200, divorce, title to land, contested elections, and contested probate matters.
• Original jurisdiction in felony criminal matters.
• Juvenile matters.
• 10 District Courts are named Criminal District Courts, some others directed to give preference to certain specialized areas.
State Trial Courts of General and Special Jurisdiction
COUNTY LEVEL COURTS
(452 Courts, 452 Judges)
Constitutional County Courts (254)
(One court in each county)
Jurisdiction
• Original jurisdiction in civil actions between $200 and $5,000.
• Probate (contested matters transferred to District Court.)
• Exclusive original jurisdiction over misdemeanors with fines greater than $500 or jail sentence.
• Appeals de novo* from lower courts or on the record from municipal courts of record.
Statutory County Courts at Law (179)
(Established in 71 counties)
Jurisdiction
• Limited jurisdiction over civil matters, most under $100,000.
• Limited jurisdiction over misdemeanor criminal matters.
• Appeals de novo from lower courts or on the record from municipal courts of record.
Statutory Probate Courts (19)
(Established in 8 counties)
Jurisdiction
• Limited primarily to probate matters.
County Trial Courts of Limited Jurisdiction
MUNICIPAL COURTS
(850 Cities, 1,206 Judges)
(Established in approximately 840 cities)
Jurisdiction
• Criminal misdemeanors with fines less than $500.
• Exclusive jurisdiction over municipal ordinance violations (fines up to $2,000).
• Limited civil penalties in cases involving dangerous dogs.
• Magistrate functions.
JUSTICE OF THE PEACE COURTS
(900 Courts, 900 Judges)
(Established in precincts within each county)
Jurisdiction
• Civil actions under $5,000.
• Small claims.
• Criminal misdemeanors with fines less than $500.
• Magistrate functions.
Local Trial Courts of Limited Jurisdiction

county courts
courts (one per Texas county) with limited jurisdiction over probate cases, minor criminal offenses, and minor civil cases

statutory county courts at law
courts which are designed to assist the judicial functions of the county courts in larger counties

statutory probate courts
courts which are designed to assist the judicial functions of the county courts in larger urban areas; the jurisdiction of these courts is limited to probate matters

the county judge presides over the county court. Often these **county courts** have jurisdiction over probate cases and over the more serious misdemeanor criminal offenses as well as over civil cases where the amounts in dispute are relatively small. The county court may also hear appeals from municipal courts or from justice of the peace courts. Thus, the county judge combines political-administrative functions with some judicial functions. However, in the more populated counties, there are county courts at law and sometimes probate courts. As a result, in the larger counties most, and sometimes all, of the county judges' judicial duties are now performed by other courts.

In larger counties, there are **statutory county courts at law,** which are designed to aid the county court in its judicial functions. Since the county courts at law are created by statute, often at widely different times, the jurisdiction of these courts varies significantly. Usually, the county courts at law hear appeals from justices of the peace and from municipal courts. In civil cases, they usually hear cases involving sums greater than would be heard by a justice of the peace court, but less than would be heard by district courts. In comparison to the district courts, less serious criminal offenses would be heard by the county courts at law.

Some of the county courts at law have specialized jurisdiction, most commonly these are in the most urban counties, where some of the courts will have only civil jurisdiction and others only criminal jurisdiction. Currently there are 179 county court at law judges.

In the most urban areas of the state, the legislature has created courts known as **statutory probate courts.** These courts are highly specialized in that their primary activity involves probate matters that relate to the disposition of property

Box 26.1 COURT STRUCTURE

"Texas has no uniform judicial framework to guarantee the just, prompt and efficient disposition of a litigant's complaint. The framers of our current Constitution deliberately designed a system to 'localize justice,' establishing a multiplicity of largely autonomous conveniently located courts across the state. With the passage of time, the organization of the courts has become more, not less, cumbersome. A case may frequently be eligible for filing in more than one court, either because of overlapping geographical boundaries or overlapping subject matter jurisdiction. Courts with the same name may have different responsibilities and similar places may have quite dissimilar court structures. Finally, those charged with administering the court structure frequently lack essential authority to effect meaningful solutions. One study has concluded that '[b]ecause the courts are so decentralized and because individually they are quite independent, it is difficult to call the Texas judiciary a system.'

"Perhaps this fragmented, decentralized structure served Texas well when means of communication were limited and methods of transportation uncertain. Twentieth century technology, however, has made the justification for much of our current court structure obsolete. . . ."

SOURCE: Citizens' Commission on the Texas Judicial System, *Report and Recommendations: Into the Twenty-First Century* (1993), p. 3.

of deceased persons. They may also deal with matters relating to guardianship of people unable to handle their own affairs, and they may handle mental health commitments. In other parts of the state, depending on the statute, probate matters may be heard by the county court, the county court at law, or the district court. Currently, there are nineteen statutory probate court judges.

Each county in Texas has between one and eight justice of the peace precincts, depending on population. Within each precinct are either one or two **justice of the peace courts.** There are about nine hundred justice of the peace courts in Texas. These courts hear class C misdemeanors, which are less serious minor crimes. They also have jurisdiction over minor civil matters and they function as small claims courts. Justices may issue search and arrest warrants. In counties without medical examiners, justices may serve the administrative functions of coroners.

Municipal courts have been created by the legislature in each of the incorporated cities of the state. Approximately 850 cities and towns in Texas have these courts, and larger cities have multiple courts. Municipal courts have jurisdiction over violations of city **ordinances** and, concurrent with justice of the peace courts, have jurisdiction over class C misdemeanors where the punishment is a fine. Municipal judges may issue search and arrest warrants, but they have only limited civil jurisdiction.[2]

justice of the peace courts
local trial courts with limited jurisdiction over small claims and very minor criminal misdemeanors

municipal courts
local trial courts with limited jurisdiction over violations of city ordinances and very minor criminal misdemeanors. Municipal courts are located in each of Texas's incorporated cities and towns

ordinance
a regulation enacted by a city government

The Legal Process

- What are differences between civil law and criminal law in Texas?
- How is the legal process different in civil and criminal cases?

Just as the Texas Supreme Court hears civil cases and the Texas Court of Criminal Appeals hears criminal cases, it is useful to think of the law as divided into these parts. **Civil law** involves a dispute, usually between private individuals over relationships, obligations, and responsibility. Though there are exceptions with a violation of the civil law, the remedy is often for the offending party to pay compensation to the injured party.

In contrast, **criminal law** involves the violation of concepts of right and wrong as defined by criminal statutes. In criminal law, the state accuses individuals of violations and, if found guilty, the violator is subject to punishment. In some cases, that punishment may involve loss of liberty or even loss of life.

In civil law, an aggrieved person will usually obtain a lawyer and file a petition that details the **complaint** against the person accused of causing the harm. The petition is filed with the clerk of court, who issues a citation against the defendant. The defendant will usually file an **answer** explaining why the allegations are not valid. Depending on the issue, the amounts of money that may be awarded as damages, and the probability of success, the aggrieved person may be able to obtain the services of a lawyer on a **contingent fee** basis. This means that the lawyer will not charge the individual if the case is lost but will obtain a portion of the damages awarded if the case is won. It is not unusual for such contingent fee arrangements to involve one third or more of the damages award plus expenses. Lawyers who handle cases on contingent fee

civil law
a system of jurisprudence, including private law and governmental actions, to settle disputes that do not involve criminal penalties

criminal law
the branch of law that deals with disputes or actions involving criminal penalties (as opposed to civil law); it regulates the conduct of individuals, defines crimes, and provides punishment for criminal acts

complaint
the presentation of a grievance by the plaintiff in a civil case

answer
the presentation of a defendant's defense against an allegation in a civil case

contingent fee
a fee paid to the lawyer in a civil case, which is contingent on winning the case

agreements often handle personal injury cases and are known as trial lawyers. Traditionally, these lawyers will contribute money to judicial candidates who are sympathetic to plaintiffs. The reason is that they only make money if they win and so they have a strong economic interest in supporting the election efforts of judicial candidates who are sympathetic to plaintiffs and to the award of large damages.

The person being sued will either have to hire an attorney on his own or, if insured, the individual will be represented by an attorney paid for by the insurance company. Fee arrangements vary for civil defense lawyers, but often they are paid by the hour. Civil defense lawyers also like to win cases, of course, but since they are often paid by the hour whether they win or lose a case, they may not have the same economic incentives to contribute money to judicial campaigns.

The court to which a civil case is taken depends on the type of case and the amount of money involved. Most commonly, a civil case will settle, where the dispute is resolved without going to court. Settlements may, however, occur during trial, sometimes immediately before a jury renders its decision. If a case does not settle and goes to trial, it may be heard by either a judge or, if requested by either side, by a jury. While civil jury cases do not have to be unanimous in Texas, the burden of proof is on the plaintiff. The standard of proof that the plaintiff must meet is **preponderance of the evidence.** That means that the plaintiff must show that is more likely than not that the defendant is the cause of the harm suffered by the plaintiff.

preponderance of the evidence
the standard of proof in a civil jury case, by which the plaintiff must show that the defendant is the cause of the harm suffered by the plaintiff

Civil cases may involve tiny amounts of damages or they may involve billions of dollars, which have the potential of breaking huge corporations, such as what happened in the 1980s when Pennzoil sued Texaco in a dispute over the takeover of the Getty Oil Company.[3]

Civil case verdicts may, of course, be appealed. Appeals are usually from the trial court to the intermediate court of appeal and perhaps further to the state supreme court. Given the cost of appeals and the delay that is involved, it

The boxes of evidence that the State of Texas prepared for the trial against tobacco companies in 1997 occupies an entire gym in Texarkana. In a civil case, the plaintiff bears the burden of proof and must demonstrate that the defendant is more likely than not responsible for the harm suffered by the plaintiff.

is not unusual for some settlement to be reached after the verdict, but before the case goes through the appellate process. For example, a plaintiff might agree to settle for much less than the verdict in the case in order to avoid the expense and delay of further appeals.

In criminal cases, the state alleges a violation of a criminal law and is usually represented in court by a prosecutor. Some prosecutors are career prosecutors with vast trial experience. These people will often prosecute the most difficult and complex cases, such as felonies and **capital cases.** However, because the pay of prosecutors is often much lower than lawyers who do litigation in the private sector, it is common for most prosecutors to be quite young and inexperienced. Once trial experience is gained, it is common for prosecutors to move into the private sector.

Defendants may hire criminal defense attorneys, who usually charge a flat fee to handle the case. Criminal defense lawyers, of course, do not work on a contingent fee basis and, since most criminal defendants are found guilty, criminal defense lawyers often prefer to obtain as much of their fee as possible in advance of the verdict.

In Texas, indigent criminal defendants are often represented by court-appointed lawyers. These are lawyers appointed by the judge to represent a defendant. Often the fee charged is less than would usually be charged non-indigent defendants. Thus, some lawyers are reluctant to do court appointments; others may not put the time and energy into a court-appointed case that they would if they were privately paid; others take court appointments because they have a limited number of paying clients; and still others take court appointments to gain experience. In 1995 in Texas there were 98,804 appointments of attorneys to handle felony criminal cases.[4]

Serious crimes are **felonies** and in those cases, as well as many lesser offenses known as **misdemeanors,** prior to the trial there will be an indictment by a grand jury. In Texas a **grand jury** consists of twelve persons who sit for from two to six months. Depending on the county, a grand jury may meet only once or twice or it may meet several times a week. Although sometimes grand juries are selected randomly from qualified citizens, mostly Texas grand jurors are chosen by a commissioner system. A district judge will appoint several grand jury commissioners who will then select fifteen to twenty citizens of the county. The first twelve who are qualified become the grand jury.[5]

Grand juries can inquire into any criminal matter but usually spend most of their time on felony crimes. They work in secret and rely heavily on the information provided by the prosecutor, though in some cases grand juries will work quite independently of the prosecutor. These grand juries are called runaway grand juries because the prosecutor has lost control of them, but such cases are very rare. If nine of the grand jurors decide a trial is warranted, they will indict a suspect. An **indictment** is also known as a "true bill." On the other hand, sometimes a grand jury does not believe a trial is warranted. In those cases, the grand jury decides to "no bill."

Although a suspect has the right to trial by jury, he may waive that right and undergo a **bench trial** before the judge only. Most commonly, the suspect will engage in a **plea bargain.** With plea bargaining, a suspect agrees to plead guilty in exchange for a lighter sentence than might be imposed if the suspect were found guilty at trial. Approximately 97 percent of criminal convictions in Texas are the result of plea bargains.[6] If the suspect does choose trial by jury,

capital case
a criminal case that involves murder or calls for the death penalty

felony
a serious criminal offense, punishable by a prison sentence or a fine

misdemeanor
a minor criminal offense, usually punishable by a small fine or a short jail sentence

grand jury
jury that determines whether sufficient evidence is available to justify a trial; grand juries do not rule on the accused's guilt or innocence

indictment
a written statement issued by a grand jury that charges a suspect with a crime and states that a trial is warranted

bench trial
a trial held without a jury and before only a judge

plea bargains
negotiated agreements in criminal cases in which a defendant agrees to plead guilty in return for the state's agreement to reduce the severity of the criminal charge the defendant is facing

felony juries will have twelve members; misdemeanor juries will have six members. There must be a unanimous verdict of guilty or not guilty. If there is not unanimity, the result is a hung jury and a mistrial is declared. The prosecutor may then choose to re-try the suspect. In addition to the requirement of unanimity in jury decisions, another important difference between civil and criminal cases is the standard of proof. In criminal cases, rather than the standard of preponderance of the evidence, the standard is **beyond a reasonable doubt.** This means that the prosecutor must prove the charges against the defendant and they must be proven to a very high standard so that a reasonable doubt of innocence must not exist.

beyond a reasonable doubt
the legal standard in criminal cases, which requires the prosecution to prove that a reasonable doubt of innocence does not exist

If a guilty verdict is returned, there will be a separate hearing on the sentence, which in Texas is sometimes also determined by the jury. At the sentencing hearing, factors such as prior record and background will be considered even though it is likely these factors could not be considered at the trial portion of the proceeding.

There may of course also be appeals of a verdict. Usually the appeals are by a convicted defendant who alleges an error at the trial that may have affected the case's outcome. In rare cases a prosecutor may also appeal. For the most part, however, criminal defendants will appeal their convictions to an intermediate appeals court and perhaps further to the Court of Criminal Appeals. In capital cases, however, the appeal will be directly to the Texas Court of Criminal Appeals.

How Judges Are Selected

- What is the most important feature of how judges are selected in Texas? What does this feature reveal about Texas politics more broadly?
- How does the selection process influence who becomes a judge in Texas?
- What alternatives or reforms to the current selection process are available?

Although there are still generalist lawyers who handle all sorts of cases, much of the practice of law is very specialized. Thus, in the civil process trial lawyers and civil defense lawyers tend to back opposing candidates for judgeships. It is not unusual for trial lawyers to support one candidate, often the Democrat, who is more likely to be the more "liberal" or pro-plaintiff candidate, and for the civil defense lawyers to support the Republican, who is more likely to be the "conservative" or pro-defendant candidate. The civil defense lawyers will often align themselves with business groups and with professional groups, such as medical doctors, to support judges inclined to favor the civil defense side.

In the criminal process, it is sometimes possible to see criminal defense lawyers backing one candidate and prosecutors backing the other. Some prosecutors' offices are quite political and will publicly support pro-prosecution judicial candidates. They will often be aligned with victims' rights groups. Criminal defense lawyers, on the other hand, will often back one of their own in contested criminal court races.

One big difference in the campaigns of civil court judges versus criminal court judges is the amounts of money involved. Enormous amounts can be involved in civil cases and so it is worth lots of money to trial lawyers and civil defense interests to elect candidates favorable to their point of view. On the other hand, with the exception of a relatively few highly paid criminal defense lawyers, the practice of criminal law is not very lucrative. Prosecutors are on salary, and usually the salaries are not large. Criminal defense lawyers often represent clients with little money. And, most criminal cases are plea-bargained. The economic incentives to contribute large sums to criminal court races don't exist. The result is that a strong candidate for the Texas Supreme Court may raise in the neighborhood of $1,000,000 for a campaign while a strong candidate for the Texas Court of Criminal Appeals may raise $100,000.

INITIAL APPOINTMENT OF JUDGES BY THE GOVERNOR

A notable aspect of the Texas judiciary is that, with the exception of municipal judges, who tend to be appointed by local governments, all judges are elected in partisan elections. Still, because the governor appoints district and appellate judges to the bench to fill vacancies prior to an election or to fill judgeships on new courts, large percentages of judges initially get to the bench through appointment. Although there has been some controversy over the relatively small number of appointments of minorities made by some governors, gubernatorial appointment has generated little additional controversy.[7] Table 26.1 shows that there has been some decline over the years in the percentage of district and appellate judges who have initially gained their seats through appointment by the governor. Currently only about 40 percent of appellate judges and less than half of the trial judges initially got to the bench through appointment.[8] Still, the controversial issue in Texas judicial politics deals with how the remaining judges obtained their seats and how all judges retain their seats if they wish to remain in office. That controversy involves the partisan election of judges in Texas.

PERCENTAGE OF JUDGES OBTAINING THEIR POSITION INITIALLY THROUGH APPOINTMENT

Table 26.1

Year	Trial Courts[a]	Appellate Courts[b]
1962	57%	50%
1984	67%	51%
1998	46%	40%

[a] Trial courts are the district and criminal district courts. Lower courts are not appointed by the governor.
[b] Appellate courts are the Supreme Court, the Court of Criminal Appeals, and the courts of appeal.
SOURCE: Anthony Champagne, "The Selection and Retention of Judges in Texas," *Southwestern Law Journal*, 40 (May 1986), p. 66; and "Profile of Appellate and Trial Judges as of September 1, 1998," Texas Judiciary Online, www.courts.state.tx.us.

THE ELECTIONS BECOME REALLY PARTISAN

Until 1978, the selection of judges in partisan elections did not create much concern. Texas was overwhelmingly a Democratic state and judges were elected as Democrats. The only real competition occurred in the Democratic primary and, with the political advantage of incumbency, judges were rarely defeated even in the primary. The only real competition in judicial races occurred in those relatively rare cases where there was an open seat in which no incumbent sought office. Beginning in 1978, however, changes began to occur in Texas judicial politics. William Clements, the first Republican governor since Reconstruction, was elected. The governor has the power to appoint judges to the district and higher courts when new courts have been created or where a judicial vacancy occurs as a result of death, resignation, or retirement. Unlike the previous Democratic governors, who appointed members of the Democratic Party, Clements began appointing Republicans. With that advantage of incumbency, some of the Republican judges began to win re-election.

Additionally, helped by the popularity of Ronald Reagan in Texas, other Republicans began seeking judicial offices and winning. Thus, by the early 1980s, in statewide elections and in several counties in Texas, there began to be competition in judicial races. With that competition in judicial races, incumbent judges began to be defeated. Sensing the growth of Republican strength, a number of Democratic judges changed to a Republican Party affiliation. From 1980 through July 24, 1985, thirteen district and appellate judges changed from the Democratic to the Republican Party; eleven county court judges switched; and five justices of the peace changed parties. Judge Don Koons switched parties in early 1985 and explained his move to the Republican Party by saying: "I ran as a Democrat in 1982. It was a long, tough year, but we won. On the other hand, it cost a lot more money and time away from the bench to run as a Democrat. The work suffers some, and you've got to be always hustling money." Koons apparently believed that with the emerging strength of the Republican Party, a switch in party affiliation would make his job more secure. That point was made especially clear by Judge Richard Mays, who changed to the Republican Party in August 1985. He described the political realities as follows: "My political philosophy about general things has nothing to do with me [sic] being a judge. That's not the reason I'm switching parties. The reason I'm switching is that to be a judge in Dallas County you need to be a Republican."[9]

Additionally, judicial elections became more expensive because judicial candidates needed money to run meaningful campaigns. In particular, campaigns that used television advertising became very expensive because of high media costs.

Judicial candidates needed money because judicial races tend to be low-visibility campaigns where voters are unaware of the candidates and where the races tend to be overshadowed by higher visibility races such as the race for governor or U.S. senator. Money was needed to give judicial candidates some degree of name visibility to voters. However, in general, Texas voters do not give much money to judicial campaigns. Instead, it is lawyers, interest groups, and potential litigants who tend to be donors in judicial races.[10] That has raised concerns about the neutrality of Texas judges who are deciding cases that involve the financial interests of persons who have given them campaign funds. A recent Texas poll found that 83 percent of the respondents thought that judges were strongly or somewhat influenced by contributions in their decisions; only 7 percent of the respondents did not.[11]

Contributions for judicial races in Texas can sometimes amount to several hundred thousand dollars, especially for hotly contested district court races or appellate races. In general, however, the most expensive races are for the Texas Supreme Court, since they are statewide races and because the Court sets the tone of tort law throughout the state. Table 26.2 on the next page shows the average contributions to Texas Supreme Court candidates for each election period from 1980 through 1998. The actual dollar amounts of campaign contributions are listed, but those amounts are also standardized to 1998 dollars to control for the effects of inflation over this lengthy time period.

In spite of judicial campaigns, however, voters often know little about judicial candidates. As a result, they vote not for the best-qualified person to be a judge, but for the party label. As the Republican Party has become increasingly dominant in statewide races, it is the Republican label, rather than the qualifications or experience of judicial candidates that has determined the outcome of judicial races. Related to the importance of party label in judicial races is the effect of top-of-the-ticket voting. In 1984, the popularity of Ronald Reagan seemed to help Texas judicial candidacies in that many voters

COMPLAINT FOR DECLARATORY AND INJUNCTIVE RELIEF — Box 26.2

"This action challenges the constitutionality of the system by which judges of the Texas state courts are elected. Under that system, any person—including lawyers who regularly appear before the judges, individuals who are frequent parties to judicial proceedings, or special interest political action committees—can contribute thousands of dollars to the campaigns of judicial candidates. No judge is precluded from sitting on a case in which a contributor has an interest, regardless of the amount that contributor gave to the judge's campaign. As a result, recent surveys conducted by the Texas Supreme Court showed that 83 percent of the Texas public, 79 percent of Texas lawyers, and 48 percent of Texas state judges believe that campaign contributions have a significant influence on judicial decisions. Only one percent of lawyers and 14 percent of judges believe that campaign contributions have *no* influence. . . .

"The inevitable result of this system of financing judicial elections is that, in some cases, judicial decisions are influenced by, or based on the fact of, one lawyer's or one party's financial contributions to the judge's election. Even when a judicial decision is not affected by a contribution to the judge's campaign, there is an appearance that such contributions were a factor in the decisional process. . . .

. . . [T]he present system of judicial elections, including the method of financing them and the absence of any requirement that a judge not participate in a case in which a significant contributor has an interest, violates the rights of plaintiffs under the Due Process Clause of the Fourteenth Amendment to the United States Constitution. . . ."

SOURCE: "Complaint for Declaratory and Injunctive Relief," *Public Citizen, Inc., et al. v. Elton Bomer, Secretary of State,* filed in the United States District Court for the Western District of Texas, Austin Division, April 3, 2000.

Table 26.2 AVERAGE CONTRIBUTIONS TO TEXAS SUPREME COURT CANDIDATES[a]

Year	Average For All Candidates[b]	Average For Winning Candidates[b]
1980	$155,033	$298,167
	($301,973)	($580,770)
1982[c]	$173,174	$332,998
	($288,023)	($553,842)
1984[c]	$967,405	$1,922,183
	($1,494,447)	($2,969,388)
1986	$519,309	$1,024,817
	($760,476)	($1,500,742)
1988	$859,413	$842,148
	($1,165,966)	($1,142,542)
1990	$970,154	$1,544,939
	($1,191,349)	($1,897,185)
1992	$1,096,001	$1,096,687
	($1,253,825)	($1,254,610)
1994	$1,499,577	$1,627,285
	($1,624,042)	($1,762,350)
1996	$656,190	$1,277,127
	($671,217)	($1,306,373)
1998	$521,519	$829,794

[a] Averages are reported for candidates from contested races featuring both a Republican and Democratic candidate.
[b] Averages reported without parentheses are for nominal dollar amounts received, while those in parentheses are in 1998 dollars.
[c] The 1982 and 1984 elections each featured only one contested race with both a Democratic and Republican candidate.
SOURCE: Kyle Cheek and Anthony Champagne, "Money in Texas Supreme Court Elections," *Judicature* (forthcoming).

cast straight or almost straight Republican ballots. In that year, Reagan received nearly 64 percent of the presidential vote in Texas. All four Republican incumbent district judges who were challenged by Democrats won. There were sixteen Democratic incumbent district judges who were challenged by Republicans. Only three of those Democrats won. In contrast, in 1982, U.S. Senator Lloyd Bentsen ran for re-election. Bentsen was a very popular senator and a Democrat. His candidacy on the Democratic ballot seems to have encouraged voters to cast ballots for Democrats further down on the ticket. Bentsen received slightly more than 59 percent of the vote in Texas. In that year there were twenty-six Republican incumbent district judges who faced Democratic opposition and only fourteen won. Yet, there were sixteen Democratic district judges who faced opposition and fourteen won.[12]

Even voters who try to make a serious effort to learn about judicial candidates can have a hard time. In Houston, for example, voters are faced with ballots loaded with so many judicial candidates that it becomes nearly impos-

JUDICIAL POLITICS: DECLARATION OF RECUSAL* IN *ROGERS V. BRADLEY* [909 SW2D 872 (1995)]

Box 26.3

Justice Gammage (Associate Justice, Supreme Court of Texas):

"The problem is the perception created by a nineteen-minute video produced by TEX-PAC, the political action committee of the Texas Medical Association. A parody of Star Wars entitled Court Wars III, the video was intended to garner support for TEX-PAC's favored candidates for the Texas Supreme Court in the 1992 general election. By analogizing the Texas Trial Lawyers' Association to Darth Vader's evil empire and a 'bipartisan coalition of medicine, business, agriculture and industry' to the champions of 'fairness, impartiality and reform,' the video sought to persuade viewers that the election of certain candidates to the Texas Supreme Court was important in their professional and personal lives. The video urged physicians not only to contribute money, but also to 'conduct grass roots efforts . . . from . . . slate cards to office displays, voter information materials and handouts, to sample letters to communicate with your patients, colleagues and friends, to signature-styled newspaper ads. . . .'

* * *

"In an effort to drive home the importance of the Court races, the video goes beyond general statements to focus on the consequences of one particular medical malpractice case. Pointing to this case, the narrator alleges that '[a]n unjust legal system that punishes the innocent, along with the guilty, still flourishes in Texas, and medicine will always be a prime target.' The defendant doctor is described as being 'faced with bankruptcy, all for coming to the rescue of a patient in desperate need of his help.' This 'tragic situation' is called 'a classic exercise [example] in Texas justice where no good deed goes unpunished.' Although a similar situation could 'happen anytime in any place,' the doctor is not without hope, as '[he] has a Supreme Court he can appeal to, if we prevail in November. Without that, he would have no chance, and his career would be ruined as a practicing physician.' . . . The doctor himself then appears on the video, stating in part:

> And for me personally, it is absolutely vital that I have a fair Supreme Court. The issues that came up in this case pertain to every doctor, and every doctor in the state suffers the same gross, how shall I say, reversal of what would be commonly thought of as justice. And, therefore, it's absolutely vital to me that we need to know who is on the Supreme Court and where they're coming from. . . .

"The doctor whose case is highlighted and who appears on the video is Brian Bernard Bradley, the respondent in the matter before us. . . .

"I believe that (1) where a person or entity has sought to engender support, financial or otherwise, for a judicial candidate or group of candidates, and (2) where that effort is made through a medium which is intended to be widely circulated, and (3) where that effort ties the success of the person's or entity's chosen candidate or candidates to the probable result in a pending or impending case, a judge should recuse from participation in that case. . . ."

Justice Enoch (Associate Justice, Supreme Court of Texas), responding to the declaration of recusal:

* * *

Box 26.3

JUDICIAL POLITICS: DECLARATION OF RECUSAL* IN *ROGERS V. BRADLEY* [909 SW2D 872 (1995)]

"I conclude with a final comment. I am not critical of those who raise money for and campaign on behalf of judicial candidates. Those parties should be commended for their involvement in the political process. The vice lies rather in the Texas judicial selection system, which places intolerable tensions between the process by which judges are chosen and the obligations they must discharge once in office. This Court has unanimously supported efforts to reform judicial elections in Texas. It is the Texas Legislature that has failed to respond, and judges in this State continue to be faced with partisan contested election campaigns. To establish recusal as proper under the facts of this case would seriously jeopardize their ability to perform the duties of their office. For candidates and their supporters alike, the fine line of conducting a campaign which draws public interest and attention without eroding public confidence in judicial neutrality is hard to hew. But, as we expect citizens to be knowledgeable about the political realities of judicial elections, we must expect them to know where that line should be drawn."

*Recusal means a judge withdraws from deciding a case.
SOURCE: Excerpted from *Rogers v. Bradley,* 909 SW2nd 872 (1995).

sible to be an informed voter. A typical Harris County election ballot will have three seats on the Supreme Court, as many as fifteen seats on other appellate courts, thirty-seven seats on the district court bench, and seventeen on the county courts.[13] In 1994, voters in Harris County were faced with forty-five judicial elections that were primary elections and then eight run-off primary elections. In the general election, there were fifty-nine contested judicial elections and sixteen more elections where the judicial candidate was unopposed.

THE NAME GAME

Voters who are casual in the balloting for judgeships have been known to cast ballots based on the "name-game." That is, voters will vote for candidates who have a name they recognize, although not necessarily because of the ability or qualifications of the judicial candidate. Some candidates are blessed with politically appealing names. In recent years judges have been elected with names such as Sam Houston Clinton, Ira Sam Houston, John Marshall, and Sam Bass. If one is not born with an attractive name, it can sometimes be created by listing a nickname on the ballot and running as "Bill" instead of "William," "Bob" instead of "Robert," or "Joe" instead of "Joseph." Some judges have established name identification with the voters by having held previous offices such as Price Daniel, who had been governor and U.S. senator, or John Hill, who had been Texas attorney general and an unsuccessful gubernatorial candidate. Others can rely on being the namesake of famous Texas political figures, such as Martin Dies, whose father had been a well-known Texas congressman. Still others benefit from having a name that is similar to another well-known person or institution. Former Chief Justice Joe Greenhill believed that he gained votes in Dallas because of the well-known Greenhill School, even though he had no relationship to the school. Similarly, he believed that the candidacy of a person named Greenwood in the Houston area unintentionally gained him votes because of the similarity of their names. Former Chief Justice Robert Calvert thought that he benefited from having a name that was identical to that of the state comptroller, a long-time Texas officeholder whose name appeared on all state warrants,[14] and that Calvert's Whiskey advertising campaigns also helped with its newspaper advertising that said "Switch to Calvert." Perhaps the most famous instance of voter name confusion was the successful effort of Don Yarbrough to win a seat on the Texas Supreme Court. His name was apparently confused with the well-known gubernatorial candidate Don Yarbrough, or possibly with the long-time Texas senator, Ralph Yarborough. The result was that Don Yarbrough defeated a respected judge, even though Yarbrough was the subject of numerous lawsuits and a disbarment proceeding. Don Yarbrough left the Supreme Court and was convicted of a crime. He escaped to Grenada where he attended medical school, but subsequently was returned to Texas when disorders in Grenada and a U.S. Marine invasion forced him to leave the island nation.

At times a name can create political difficulties for a judge. It was widely believed that Judge Charles Dally's name was a political liability since voters might identify the name with judicial delay. When Tom Price decided to run for a judgeship in 1974, one of the reasons that he chose to oppose Judge Carl Friedlander was because the judge's name was a difficult one. Similarly, one of the state's most respected judges, St. John Garwood, was nearly defeated by a candidate whose name, Jefferson Davis Smith, was more folksy and who had developed name identification with voters by his frequent tries for office.[15] Gene Kelly was a great actor and dancer. That name is shared by a frequent candidate for high judicial offices who has not yet won office, although he has often been able to gain the Democratic nomination for Texas Supreme Court.

There has also been scholarly research on name recognition of judges. One study consisted of telephone interviews with one thousand Dallas County voters. The voters were asked if they recognized the names of a listing of public officials who are shown in Table 26.3 on the next page. At the time Lloyd Bentsen was a U.S. senator from Texas and Annette Strauss was the mayor of Dallas. Raul Gonzales was a justice on the Texas Supreme Court. The other persons were district court judges in Dallas County.

Lloyd Bentsen had very high name recognition as did Mayor Annette Strauss. Justice Gonzales had moderately high recognition as did Larry Baraka, who at the time had been involved in a visible and controversial case that had been the subject of a movie. Jack Hampton had been the subject of nationwide controversy over remarks he had made about gay murder victims in a trial he had conducted. No other district court judge had high name recognition except for Ron Chapman, who had remarkably high name recognition, almost as high as Lloyd Bentsen and Annette Strauss and far higher than any other judge. The voters were then asked to recall the "public office" that these individuals held. Overwhelmingly in reference to Ron Chapman the respondents stated that Chapman's public office was "disk jockey." At the time, there was another Ron Chapman who *was* a disk jockey and was the most popular radio personality in Dallas County. Judge Ron Chapman seemed to be benefiting from the high name recognition created by disk jockey

Table 26.3 NAME RECOGNITION IN DALLAS COUNTY (N = 1000)

Candidate	% Recognizing Name
Lloyd Bentsen	98.6
Annette Strauss	96.5
Raul Gonzales	46.1
Larry Baraka	41.7
Joe B. Brown	29.2
Adolph Canales	12.6
Ron Chapman	85.8
Jack Hampton	41.0
Jesse Oliver	28.7

SOURCE: Anthony Champagne and Greg Thielemann, "Awareness of Trial Court Judges," *Judicature,* 75 (1991), pp. 271–76.

Ron Chapman. That probably explained why Chapman was the last Democrat in Dallas County who was able to win elections to its trial courts.[16]

MINORITY REPRESENTATION IN THE TEXAS JUDICIARY

Minority groups have been concerned that countywide and larger partisan judicial races make it difficult for minorities to get elected to judgeships. It is the case that Texas judges do not reflect the diversity of the state. Chief Justice Tom Phillips has stated that only 8 percent of Texas judges are Hispanic and less than 3 percent are African American.[17] Table 26.4 lists the ethnicity of Texas judges as of April 13, 2000. The data are incomplete since many judges

Table 26.4 RACE AND ETHNICITY OF TEXAS JUDGES (APRIL 13, 2000)

Percent Race and Ethnic Status	Appeals Courts	District Courts	County Courts at Law	Probate Courts	County Courts	Municipal Courts	Justice of the Peace Courts
Percent White	85%	85%	83%	91%	92%	86%	81%
Percent Black	0%	3%	2%	0%	0%	3%	3%
Percent Hispanic	9%	10%	13%	9%	7%	10%	15%
Percent Other	6%	2%	2%	0%	1%	1%	1%
Total Number	52	323	133	11	193	469	539

SOURCE: Personal correspondence from the Texas Office of Court Administration, April 13, 2000.

did not comply with a request to supply information on their ethnicity and only those that reported their ethnicity are reported in the table. Nevertheless, this is the most complete data currently available, and it also shows that the numbers of minority judges are very low at all levels of the Texas court system.

While women do not comprise 50 percent of the judiciary as they do in the population, there is a higher proportion of women in the Texas judiciary than minorities. Women were at one time a great rarity on the bench. In 1970 only 1 percent of the nation's judiciary was female. As late as 1979 only 4 percent of the nation's judges were women.[18] In Texas, the first woman to serve as a state judge was Sarah Hughes, who was appointed in 1935 and who served as a district judge until 1961 when she was appointed to the federal bench. Famous for a number of her decisions, including one that forced Dallas County to build a new jail, she is probably best known as the judge who swore in Lyndon Johnson as president after the assassination of John F. Kennedy. In April 2000, however, 29 percent of appellate judges in Texas were women, 25 percent of district judges were women, 32 percent of county court-at-law judges were female, as were 27 percent of the probate judges. Ten percent of county judges, 33 percent of municipal judges, and 31 percent of justices of the peace were women.[19]

Different interpretations have been offered for the low numbers of minorities on the bench. One is that white voters dominate countywide and larger districts and will vote against minority judicial candidates. Civil rights organizations representing Hispanics and African Americans have argued that for

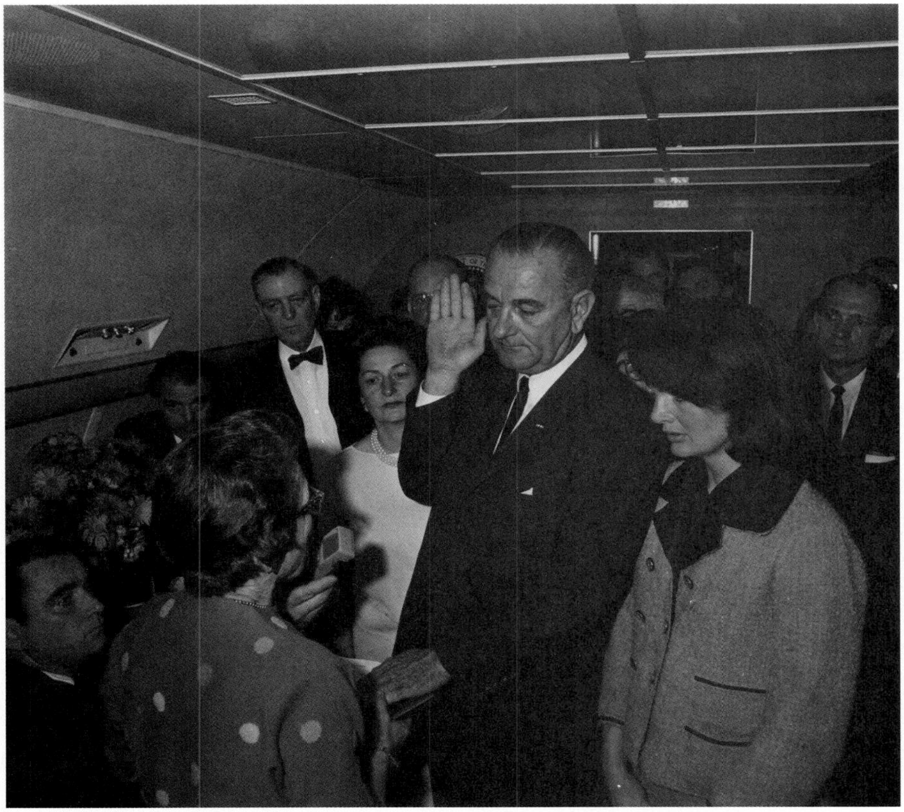

Best known as the judge who swore in Lyndon Johnson as president after the assassination of John F. Kennedy, Sarah Hughes was the first woman to serve as a state judge in Texas.

minorities to get elected to office, there must be smaller judicial districts where minority voters comprise the majority.

An alternative argument is that minority candidates, like minority voters, tend to be Democrats at a time when Republicans increasingly are winning judicial races. Thus, minorities do not get elected to judicial office because they run as Democrats.[20] Still another argument is that there are few minority judges because there are few minority lawyers and, with the exception of county judges and justices of the peace, judges in Texas must be lawyers.

The issue of minority representation on the bench has been the subject of major concern by minority and civil rights leaders in Texas. It was also the subject of prolonged federal litigation. In 1989 a case was tried in federal court in Midland. The case, *League of United Latin American Citizens v. Mattox,*[21] was a suit against countywide election of judges in ten of the larger counties in Texas. The suit, filed by minority plaintiffs, argued that countywide election of judges diluted the strength of minority voters and violated the Voting Rights Act. The trial judge agreed with the plaintiffs and after a political solution failed, ordered that judges be elected in nonpartisan elections from smaller judicial districts. The trial court order, however, was blocked by the Fifth Circuit, which is the federal Court of Appeals for the region that includes Texas.[22] The case was then appealed to the U.S. Supreme Court, along with a Louisiana case, and the Supreme Court held that the Voting Rights Act did apply to judicial elections.[23] The case was then returned to the Fifth Circuit to examine whether minority voting strength was diluted and to determine the state's interest in maintaining countywide elections. Ordinarily the federal courts of appeal do not sit as an entire group to hear cases; instead, they hear cases in panels of three judges. Such a panel decided in favor of the minority plaintiffs and a settlement seemed to be reached with the state to have elections of judges from smaller districts in the larger counties. However, in important cases, it is sometimes possible to appeal a decision of a panel of three judges to the entire court of appeal. When this happens, the court is said to sit ***en banc.*** That happened when some of the defendants in the suit were unhappy with the settlement and the entire Fifth Circuit voted in 1993 that party affiliation of minority candidates explained the failure of minority judicial candidates to win election rather than the candidates' minority status. Thus, countywide election of judges was not illegal and there was no legal need to reduce the size of districts from which judges were elected.[24]

en banc
as a panel, with all judges participating

Since that decision, minority leaders and minority groups have continued to express concerns about the small numbers of minority judges, but any solution that would involve smaller districts would have to result from an act of the legislature rather than the actions of a federal court. One of the most influential minority leaders is state senator Rodney Ellis, a Democrat from Houston. Ellis argued that the *en banc* decision of the Fifth Circuit ". . . radically reinterpreted voting rights law to fit its need. In order to preserve the status quo," Ellis wrote, "the court eviscerated the meaning and intent of the Voting Rights Act."[25] In contrast, David Godbey, one of the attorneys for a defendant in the litigation and now a state district judge in Dallas, wrote that the reason the Fifth Circuit decided as it did was because there was no proof of violation of the Voting Rights Act. The plaintiffs, Godbey wrote, ". . . failed to prove racial discrimination in voting. The evidence for Dallas County showed simply that Republican candidates usually win—whether they are white, black or brown—and that most African-American voters prefer Democratic candidates. The Fifth Circuit ruled that losing elections because of partisan politics, rather than race, does not establish a Voting Rights Act violation and that the people of Texas are entitled to continue electing their judges free from federal interference."[26]

There have been judicial reform bills in the legislature in the mid- and late-1990s that have included provisions for smaller judicial districts, but those bills have not passed. Perhaps the strongest judicial reform bill was one backed by then Lieutenant Governor Bob Bullock who created a task force to try to develop an acceptable compromise on the judicial selection issue. The proposed constitutional amendment designed by the task force passed the Texas Senate in 1995, but failed to pass the Texas House. Under the plan, all appellate judges would be appointed by the governor. District judges, on the other hand, would be elected from county commissioner precincts and they would be elected in nonpartisan elections. After serving for a time, they would run countywide in **retention elections** where there would be a "yes" or "no" vote on their retention in office and where they would face no opponent on the ballot.

retention election
an election in which voters decide "yes" or "no" regarding whether to keep an incumbent in office

On the surface, the compromise seemed to offer something for almost everyone. Because the governor appointed appellate judges, judges would have greater career security and no worries about campaign funding. The business community, recognizing that Texas tended to elect conservative governors and was increasingly likely to elect conservative Republican governors, got appointed appellate judges. Nonpartisan elections would protect trial judges from party sweeps where judges are voted out of office solely because of their party affiliation. Minorities would get smaller judicial districts for the major trial courts. But what looked like a great compromise fell through. Although African Americans were supportive of the compromise, Hispanics were not. The two largest counties in Texas—Harris and Dallas—elected a total of 96 of the 386 district judges then chosen in Texas. Under the compromise one-fourth of Harris and Dallas County judges would be elected from each of the county commissioners precincts in that county. Both Dallas and Harris Counties had three white county commissioners and one African American. Hispanics, on the other had, elected no county commissioner and believed that the compromise would not promote the election of more Hispanic judges. They believed that to elect Hispanic judges, considerably smaller districts would be needed. As a result, much Hispanic support was not forthcoming. Additionally, the political parties opposed the compromise. Nonpartisan elections might protect the interests of judges, but they weakened the political parties. Additionally, an appointive system for appellate judges reduced the number of elective offices and so reduced the role of the political parties. Governor George W. Bush, although his powers would benefit from an appointed appellate judiciary, opposed the compromise, probably because he did not want to oppose the Republican Party. Because the plan had the support of Lieutenant Governor Bob Bullock and because he gave the legislation priority on his legislative agenda that year, the Bullock proposal was probably the best hope for judicial change for a long time to come.[27]

State senator Rodney Ellis disagreed with the Fifth Circuit's decision about the lack of minority judges being due to party affiliation rather than minority status. He has emerged as a prominent leader seeking a solution to the small numbers of minority judges.

One of the underlying concerns about smaller districts within the business community seems to be a fear that small districts might create a narrower electorate for judges. That narrow electorate might in some areas prove unduly sympathetic to plaintiffs who file suit against businesses. Additionally, at a time when the Republican Party is increasingly successful in judicial races, smaller judicial districts may increase the strength of the Democratic Party. While Republicans can win elections countywide in urban areas such as Dallas and Harris County, for example, they cannot win all elections when the political boundaries are less than countywide, such as those based on county commissioner precincts, state representatives' districts, or justice of the peace precincts. Indeed, David Godbey claimed that his client in the litigation by civil rights lawyers to create smaller judicial districts, Republican judge Harold Entz, intervened in the case as a defendant because he feared that the Democratic attorney general would not ably defend the case and would try to settle it in ways that would create Democratically-advantageous smaller judicial districts.[28]

Whatever the cause of the low number of minority judges, the lack of diversity on the bench, along with the role of money in judicial races, the defeat of incumbents, the importance of party label, top-of-the-ticket voting, and the "name-game" have all created support for alternative judicial selection systems.

ALTERNATIVE MEANS OF SELECTION

There are a variety of ways that judges are selected in the United States. One way is through appointment by the governor and approval by the state senate. This method is used in Texas to select judges to new courts or courts where there has been a death, resignation, or retirement during a judicial term. It is also similar to the system for selecting federal judges, who are appointed by the president and confirmed by vote of the U.S. Senate. However, this method of judicial selection is contrary to Texas's traditional distrust of a powerful chief executive. At a time when it seems increasingly likely that Texas governors will be Republicans, it also is not a system that Democrats tend to favor.

Another system for selecting judges is nonpartisan election. Such a system for selecting judges in Texas would eliminate much of the partisan politics, but, at the same time, it would make it more difficult for candidates to reach voters since in a truly nonpartisan election, judicial candidates would have to run for office without the benefit of political parties. In some states that have ostensibly nonpartisan elections, such as Ohio, the parties continue to take an active role to the point that it is difficult to distinguish that type of nonpartisan system from a partisan election system. If Texas instituted a truly nonpartisan system, however, candidates would require even more campaign money in order to reach voters they could no longer reach though the mechanisms of the political parties.

merit selection
a judicial reform under which judges would be nominated by a blue-ribbon committee, appointed by the governor, and, after a brief period in office, forced to run in a retention election

Most commonly, however, judicial reformers argue for a system of judicial selection that is commonly called **merit selection** of judges. With this system, a blue-ribbon committee consisting of lawyers and lay people supply the names of a small number of candidates for a judgeship to the governor. The governor makes the judicial appointment from this list and, after the judge serves for a brief time, she runs in a retention election. In a retention election, the incumbent does not have an opponent. Instead, a question is posed to the voters as to whether the incumbent should be retained for a term of office. The voters then vote "yes" or "no" on the question of the judge's retention. As might be expected in an election where one does not have an opponent, the incumbent usually wins. One study of retention elections found that only 1.6 percent of incumbent judges were defeated in retention elections.[29] Yet, from time to time, interest groups will organize against a judge in a retention election and spend a great deal of money trying to defeat him, and sometimes those efforts have been successful. One of the great concerns about retention elections is the nature of the merit selection commission, since those commissioners filter out all but a handful of prospective judges. Some are quite fearful of this centralized method of determining who should be judges and, although there is much support for merit selection in Texas, there is also much opposition.[30]

In recent years one of the most popular reform proposals is known as "appoint-elect-retain." Under this system, the governor would appoint a judge with confirmation by two-thirds of the state Senate. The gubernatorial nominee would not assume office until confirmed by the Senate, which would meet year-round for the purpose of dealing with judicial confirmations. In the first election thereafter, the judge would run in a contested nonpartisan election and in subsequent elections would run in retention elections. This is, of course, a hybrid plan that encompasses aspects of gubernatorial appointment, nonpartisan election, and merit selection.

Another popular reform plan would have appellate vacancies filled by gubernatorial appointment with senatorial confirmation. The appellate judges would then run in nonpartisan elections followed by retention election. Additionally, in Dallas, Tarrant, and Bexar counties, district court judges would be elected from county commissioner precincts rather than countywide. Additionally, in Harris County, district judges would be elected from smaller geographic regions than county commissioner precincts. Supporters of this plan tend to believe that it would increase the number of minority judges, especially trial court judges in urban areas. Again, of course, it is a hybrid plan designed to combine various reform proposals in order to gain sufficient support to become the new way Texas selects its judges.

At least for the time being, however, it seems likely that not much will change in the way Texas selects its judges. Such a change would be a major structural change, and major changes are always difficult to initiate. Changing the way Texas selects its judges might upset many voters, who like being able to vote for judges, and would surely upset the political parties, who like having large numbers of judicial candidates running under their party label. It might also upset lawyers accustomed to the traditional ways of selecting judges and even judges who have benefited from the present system. That has led some to argue that judicial reform needs to be less drastic and more incremental. These reformers have suggested lengthening judicial terms of office on the grounds that longer terms mean fewer election contests and therefore less need for campaign money, less chance for defeat of incumbents, and less involvement of judges in politics. Another proposed incremental reform is to remove judges from the straight party vote. This means that a voter would actually have to cast a ballot for the judicial candidate rather than simply voting for everyone on the Republican or Democratic column by casting a straight party vote. Such a reform would remove judicial candidates from the effects of top-of-the-ticket voting. It would, of course, also reduce the votes that judges receive and lessen their dependence and reliance on the political parties. Still another suggested reform is to increase the levels of experience needed to serve on the bench. The idea is that even if judicial races are subject to the whims of voters, high qualifications for judges would mean that there would be experienced judges rather than highly inexperienced judges who simply won because they were good campaigners or because they had the right party affiliation in that election year.

Judicial Campaign Fairness Act

a judicial reform under which campaign contributions are limited by the amount that a judicial candidate can receive from an individual donor

Perhaps the most significant judicial reform in Texas is the **Judicial Campaign Fairness Act.** Essentially, if a judicial candidate agrees to abide by the act, she may use that compliance in political advertising. Among the most important aspects of compliance with the act are campaign contribution limitations. For example, statewide judicial candidates limit themselves to contributions of no more than $5,000 from any individual in any election. Thus, if a candidate runs in a party primary, a run-off primary, and a general election, she can receive no more than $15,000 from any individual donor. Additionally, statewide candidates can receive no more than $30,000 per election from any law firm. While the amounts of money that can be donated are still quite high, there has been a significant reduction from contribution amounts in the 1980s when, prior to the Act, some donors would give candidates $25,000, $50,000, and even more in campaign contributions. A recent strengthening of campaign contribution limits requires that if a judge receives campaign contributions from a party to a lawsuit or if the party's lawyer had made contributions in excess of the limits in the Judicial Campaign Fairness Act, the judge would be recused from the case.[31]

For many, it is the role of money in judicial campaigns that is the most troubling issue in Texas judicial politics. In November 1999, a *Frontline* television show was broadcast by PBS entitled *Justice for Sale*. The program focused on judicial politics, especially fund-raising, in Pennsylvania, Louisiana, and Texas. One of the major themes of the broadcast was that campaign fund-raising by judges at least created the appearance of impropriety, and, in some cases, campaign contributions suggested that judicial decisions were being bought. An alternative viewpoint, however, is that money is necessary if judges campaign for office in order to enhance their visibility among voters. What judicial campaign contributors are doing is contributing money to present those candidates to voters whose judicial philosophy is most compatible with the philosophy of the contributors. That, it can be argued, is what free speech and the democratic process are about. Nevertheless, the concern remains that there is something questionable about the contribution of money to judges who then decide cases of interest to contributors. As long as judges are elected, however, money will be necessary to run judicial campaigns and, where elections are competitive, a great deal of campaign money will be necessary. One of the most expensive, hard fought, and most intense battles by interest groups in Texas judicial elections occurred in 1988 in a battle over Texas Supreme Court races that resulted in a change in the tone of tort law in the state.

THE 1988 TEXAS SUPREME COURT RACES

John Hill, Jr., a former secretary of state of Texas, attorney general of Texas, and unsuccessful 1978 Democratic gubernatorial nominee was elected chief justice of Texas in 1984. As chief justice, he began to express concerns about the judiciary, perhaps influenced by a scandal involving Justice C. L. Ray that, among other matters, involved close relationships between Ray and major campaign contributors. Justice William Kilgarlin was swept into the scandal as well, although for far less serious reasons. On May 10, 1986, Chief Justice

Hill called for judges in Texas to be chosen through a merit selection type of system and offered himself as the leader of a movement for judicial reform.

That advocacy of selection system changes was not treated kindly by his colleagues on the court. One of his colleagues, Justice Franklin Spears, took a leadership role in an organization whose purpose was to oppose Hill's merit selection reforms. By November 1986, there was unprecedented conflict on the court, and Hill began to appear more and more as an outcast. Spears charged that "[the Chief Justice] goes his merry way and says, 'I am the Supreme Court.'" Spears suggested that Hill had not been able to adjust to membership in a collegial body.

On August 26, 1987, Chief Justice Hill issued a surprise announcement. He stated that he would resign the chief justiceship after serving half of the six-year term for which he had been elected. He noted at the August press conference that he believed he could be more effective as a private citizen working toward judicial reform than if he remained as chief justice. With Hill's departure from the court, the other justices purchased as their gift for him a silver tray that cost each justice $6.89. Nevertheless, Hill would soon be able to afford more expensive gifts. He was to be a named partner in the firm of Liddell, Sapp, Zivley, Hill & LaBoon at a reported salary of $700,000 a year.

On January 4, 1988, Hill swore in his replacement, Tom Phillips, a Houston Republican and state district judge. The swearing-in ceremony provided another forum for Hill to plead for merit selection. One consequence of the speech was an attack on Hill by Justice Robert Campbell, who resigned on January 6 so that, Campbell claimed, he could campaign against Hill's merit selection proposals. Justice Oscar Mauzy expressed surprise over Campbell's resignation, but he could not avoid adding a remark criticizing Hill: "I think he [Campbell] went out of this with a lot more class than the preceding member of this court that resigned."

The result of Hill's reform efforts was extraordinary conflict on the Texas Supreme Court and, as a result of his resignation during the administration of a Republican governor, the provision of an opening wedge for Republican penetration of the court.[32]

By the time of the 1988 elections, two thirds of the Texas Supreme Court was up for grabs. Associate Justice Ted Z. Robertson chose to run against Phillips for chief justice. Bill Kilgarlin, under an ethics cloud because of an admonition from the State Commission on Judicial Conduct, was opposed by Republican Nathan Hecht. Democratic incumbent Raul Gonzalez was opposed by Republican Charles Ben Howell. New appointee to the court Barbara Culver was opposed by Democrat Jack Hightower. New appointee Eugene Cook was opposed by Democrat Karl Bayer. There was also a race where there was no incumbent—an open seat—between Democrat Lloyd Doggett and Republican Paul Murphy.

In the early 1980s, the Court had moved strongly in the plaintiffs' direction. This was an opportunity for the civil defense interests to recoup their losses. It turned into an all-out battle between plaintiff and civil defense interests. Tom Phillips raised about $1,000,300, much of it from civil defense interests. His opponent, Ted Z. Robertson, raised $1,883,690, much of it from trial lawyers. Lloyd Doggett raised $658,135, much of it from trial lawyers; whereas Paul Murphy raised $438,013 from civil defense interests, 11.4 percent of the money coming from the Texas Medical Association. Bill Kilgarlin received strong plaintiffs' lawyer backing and raised $2,038,902 to the $653,254 raised by Nathan Hecht, who had civil defense backing. Barbara Culver raised $548,425 to challenger Jack Hightower's $449,290, but this was not clearly a plaintiff–defense battle. Culver had opposed capping medical malpractice claims, and Hightower had strong Medical Association support. Eugene Cook raised $460,867 to Karl Bayer's $130,589. Bayer got off to a late start due to Wallace's late resignation. Gonzalez had strong defense interest backing and raised $826,038, but his opponent, Republican Charles Ben Howell, had almost no financial backing.

Altogether the twelve major candidates for the Texas Supreme Court raised $10,092,955. Additionally, a political action committee primarily funded by trial lawyers raised another $1.4 million in independent contributions for television commercials and get-out-the-vote campaigns. The Texas Medical Association political action committee gave $181,355 in direct contributions to candidates and encouraged individual doctors to give at least $250,000 more.

When the dust settled, three Republicans had been elected to the Texas Supreme Court—Tom Phillips, Nathan Hecht, and Eugene Cook. Phillips and Hecht had beaten the most heavily funded plaintiff-backed candidates, and Eugene Cook was a pro–civil defense Republican. Raul Gonzalez, a Democrat, was pro–civil defense and he defeated grossly underfunded Charles Ben Howell. Jack Hightower, a moderate, defeated Culver. Only one strongly pro-plaintiff justice, Lloyd Doggett, emerged from this battle over the Supreme Court.[33]

The result was the beginning of Republican domination of the Court. The pattern of continued Republican electoral victories on the Texas Supreme Court began in 1988. And, the civil defense side learned that in head-on battles with heavily funded plaintiff-backed candidates such as Kilgarlin and Robertson, the civil defense backed candidates could win. It was the beginning of the end of the pro-plaintiff court of the 1980s. The 1990s would see a court that, as some wags put it, ". . . never saw an insurance company it did not like."

JUDICIAL DISCIPLINE

Elections do not necessarily remove judges who have committed ethical or other improprieties and, even if they did so, since trial judges have four-year terms and appellate judges have six-year terms, the judges would not necessarily be removed in a timely fashion. As a result, in 1965, an amendment to the Texas Constitution created the Commission on Judicial Conduct. The commission consists of eleven members serving six-year staggered terms. Five are judges appointed by the Texas Supreme Court and represent appellate, district, county court-at-law, justice of the peace, and municipal judges. Two members are attorneys appointed by the State Bar. Four are citizen members appointed by the governor. The commission members receive no pay and meet at least six times a year.[34]

The commission has the responsibility of policing the behavior of 3,335 judges in Texas. In fiscal year 1998, there were 922 complaints against Texas judges, and the commission disposed of 910 of them. Most complaints lack merit—often complaints are filed by disappointed litigants, for example. However, when a complaint is found to be meritorious, the commission has a variety of disciplinary tools. It can privately or publicly admonish, warn, or

DISCIPLINE AGAINST A JUSTICE **Box 26.4**

". . . On February 9, 1984, San Antonio attorney Pat Maloney, Sr., made a $10,000 contribution to Justice Ray's campaign account, and again on June 7, 1984, Mr. Maloney made another $10,000 contribution to Justice Ray's campaign. Justice Ray is the Justice on the Supreme Court who is charged with the duty of managing transfers of Courts of Appeals cases (periodically equalizing dockets among the fourteen Courts of Appeals).

"Between September and December, 1985, Mr. Maloney sent Justice Ray at least five letters requesting that specific cases in which he (Maloney) represented litigants be transferred from various Courts of Appeals to other Courts of Appeals. One of Mr. Maloney's letters dated November 18, 1985, requested that *Anthony Paul Cropper v. Caterpillar Tractor Company, Inc.*, . . . be transferred. Another letter dated December 17, 1985, again requested that such case be transferred and also requested that *Cardenas et al v. Garcia*, . . . be transferred.

* * *

"On March 6, 1986, Mr. Judice furnished sworn testimony to the House Judicial Affairs Committee stating that during the preparation of the list of cases to be transferred, Justice Ray advised Mr. Judice, 'Just get me a list of all 143 cases.' He further said, 'Wait a minute, by the way, make sure you get me the information on these two cases (the two cases referred to above) because I have a letter or letters of complaint concerning the pendency of these two cases, the length of pendency of these two cases.' Mr. Judice further testified to the House Committee that the two cases were included in a proposed Order of Transfer submitted to the Supreme Court for action; however, prior to the order being finalized, it was discovered that one of the cases (the *Garcia* case) was not ripe for transfer and such case was not included by the Supreme Court in the final Order of Transfer.

"It has been alleged that Justice Ray acted improperly in considering private entreaties from Mr. Maloney requesting that the two cases be transferred, and that he showed favoritism to Mr. Maloney by attempting to secure the selective transfer of the two cases.

* * *

". . . Although the Commission recognizes that campaign contributions from attorneys are legitimate, the appearance of partiality in this case was especially significant in the light of the substantial contributions which Justice Ray had received from Mr. Maloney."

Justice Ray was given a reprimand by the State Commission on Judicial Conduct.

SOURCE: Excerpted from State Commission on Judicial Conduct, "Findings, Conclusions, and Public Reprimand Relating to Certain Activities of Justice C. L. Ray of the Supreme Court of Texas" (mimeographed, June 8, 1987).

reprimand a judge. It can also order further education for a judge, and it may even order a physical or psychiatric evaluation. In serious cases, there may be formal proceedings against a judge, where there is a hearing before the commission or a special master appointed by the commission. After the hearing, the commission may determine that the judge should be removed and, if so,

Table 26.5 DISCIPLINARY ACTION BY THE STATE COMMISSION ON JUDICIAL CONDUCT (FISCAL YEAR 1998)

Resignation	11
Removal by tribunal	1
Public reprimand	1
Public warning	1
Public admonition	1
Private reprimand	2
Private warning	9
Private admonition	4
Additional education	14
Additional education and sanction	1
Formal proceedings voted	5
Suspensions	1

SOURCE: State of Texas, State Commission on Judicial Conduct, 1998 Annual Report, p. 16.

the Supreme Court will appoint a seven-judge review tribunal. That tribunal may remove, censure, or prohibit the judge from ever again holding judicial office. The commission may also request that the Supreme Court suspend the judge or may suspend a judge itself if the judge is indicted for a felony or charged with a misdemeanor involving his office. In order to avoid publicity, expense, and the possible loss of a judicial pension, a judge will sometimes resign while under investigation by the commission.[35]

In fiscal year 1998, the commission's work led to disciplinary actions against fifty judges (see Table 26.5).

The Importance of the Texas Courts

▶ What are some of the ways that courts in Texas have an important impact upon the lives of all Texans?

The Texas courts have an important impact upon the lives of Texans in all sorts of ways, whether it involves the adjudication of a traffic accident, determination of child support, imposition of a jail sentence, or imposition of the most serious punishment of all, the death penalty.

THE DEATH PENALTY

The most serious aspect of the judicial system in Texas, and one of the most controversial, is the death penalty. Texas has led the nation in the number of executions since the death penalty was reinstated in 1976. Since 1977, lethal injection has been the means for execution in Texas. Beginning in 1923, the state ordered that executions be done in Huntsville by electrocution. Prior to that time, each county was responsible for carrying out executions.[36]

Although California has the largest death row population, it has not carried out many executions. Texas, on the other hand, has executed as many as thirty-seven people in one year and, with the exception of 1996, has executed at least twelve people in every year since 1992. In 1999, there were thirty-five executions, and twelve in the first quarter of 2000.[37] Fourteen more executions were scheduled through August 2000.[38] As of mid-March 2000, there were 454 people on death row.[39]

In Texas, one is subject to the death penalty for the murder of a public safety officer, fireman, or correctional employee; murder during commission of a kidnapping, burglary, robbery, aggravated rape, or arson; murder for hire; multiple murders; murder during a prison escape; murder by a prison inmate serving a life sentence; or murder of a child under the age of six.

A stay on death row can be a lengthy one, even in Texas. The average time spent on death row prior to execution is 10.39 years, although the time varies considerably. One inmate under a death sentence waived his appeals and spent only a little more than eight months on death row prior to execution. On the other hand, Robert Excell White, who was executed in March 1999, was convicted of murdering three men in 1974.[40] It was a death sentence carried out in February 1998, however, which initiated the greatest controversy over the death penalty. Karla Faye Tucker, a convicted axe murderer, created national demands for clemency. Tucker was widely believed to have undergone a religious conversion since her 1983 conviction. She was also attractive and articulate and was the first woman in modern times to be executed in Texas.

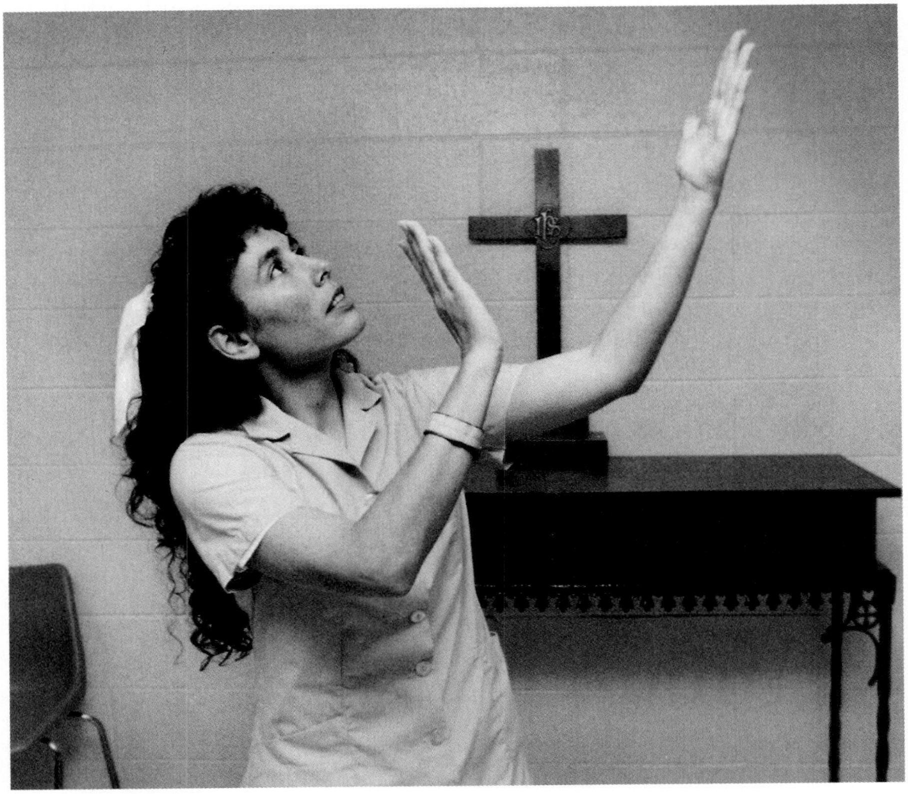

Karla Faye Tucker's execution—Texas's first modern execution of a woman—was especially controversial.

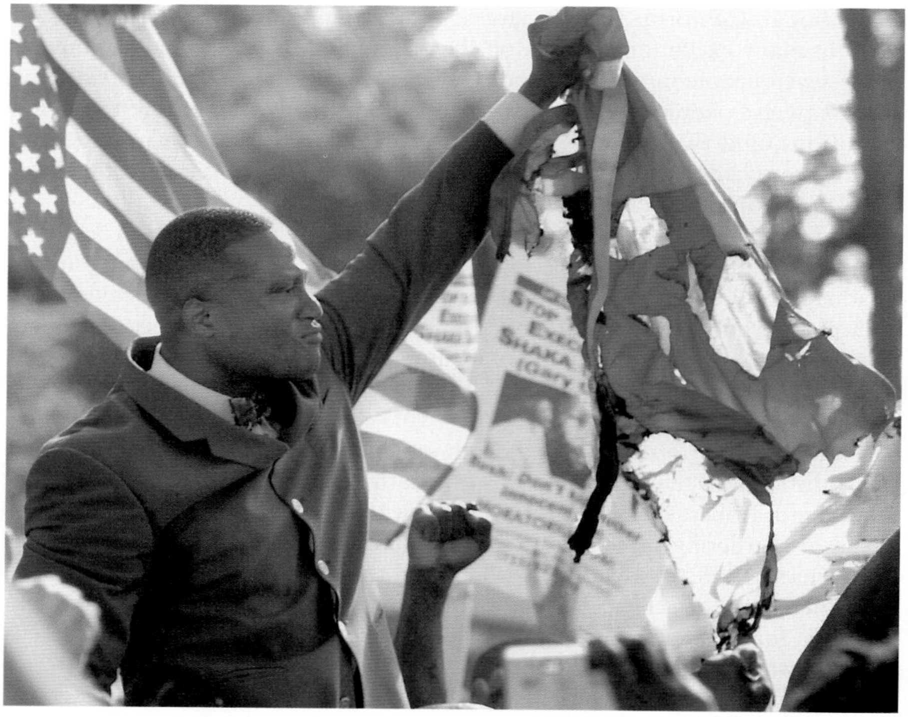

A demonstrator burns a Texas state flag outside a prison in Huntsville as part of a protest against a scheduled execution and the Texas criminal justice system's disproportionate application of the death penalty on African Americans.

Supporters of her execution argued that her gender, appearance, articulateness, and possible religious conversion were irrelevant to the fact that she was a convicted murderer who should be treated like others in similar situations.

One of the issues involving the death penalty is whether offenders are treated in the same way. There is a racial/ethnic disparity such that minorities, especially African Americans, are disproportionately represented on death row. As of mid-March 2000, there were 186 African Americans on death row, 101 Hispanics, 163 whites, and 4 of "other" racial/ethnic classifications.[41] Since 1982, 108 whites have been executed, 69 African Americans, 32 Hispanics, and 2 "other."[42] It may be that there is a bias in the criminal justice system such that minorities are disproportionately subject to the death penalty. There has been considerable argument at the national level that minorities are unfairly subjected to the death penalty more than are whites; however, the U.S. Supreme Court has refused to strike down the death penalty on the basis of statistical generalizations.[43]

It is the Texas Board of Pardons and Paroles that votes on clemency to death row inmates. Recently, the board has been subject to intense criticism because of its secrecy and, most importantly, because contrary to every other state, the Board votes by fax on clemency petitions rather than meeting to discuss and vote on petitions.[44] Both a federal and a state judge have been highly critical of this process.[45] Oddly, this board was originally considered to be a remedy for possible corruption in granting clemency by the governor. Prior to 1936, the governor essentially had unlimited power to grant clemency and the power was often abused, especially by Governor Miriam Ferguson, who granted four thousand requests for commutations of sentences in 1922 alone. It was widely believed that payments were made for many of these acts of ex-

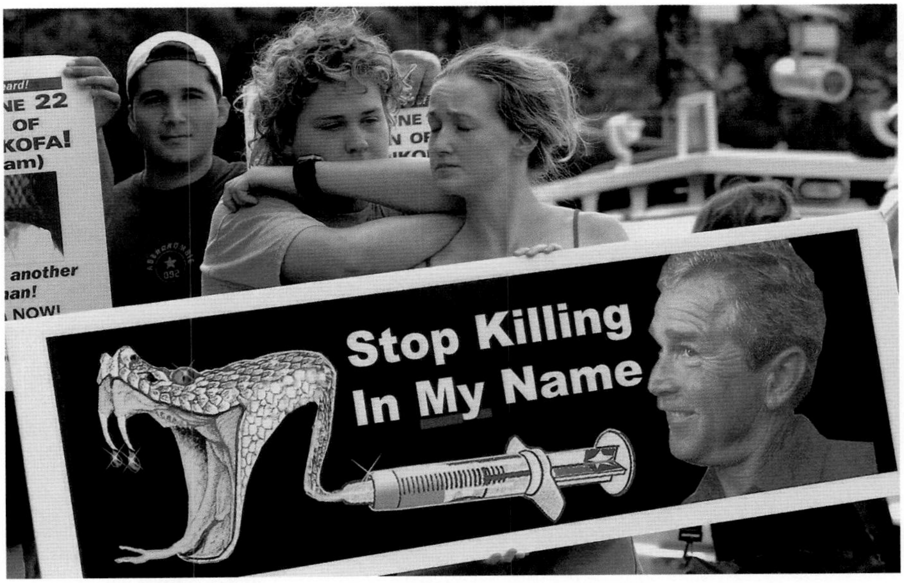

Students at Sam Houston State University protest at a prison in Huntsville. While the governor's direct power over clemency may be limited, the Texas Board of Pardons and Paroles is comprised of governor's appointees.

ecutive clemency. In reaction, a constitutional amendment was passed in 1936 that charged the board with giving the governor recommendations on clemency. Without such a recommendation, the governor can only grant a single thirty-day reprieve. No other state so limits the powers of the governor.

The Board has eighteen members in seven regions of the state and that, claims the board, is why board members are limited in their ability to have face-to-face meetings even in death penalty cases. Recently, however, Governor Bush appointed six new members of the Board, a large enough number that significant changes in how the Board functions may be in the offing. Although the governor may not be trying to affect the policies of the Board by making a large number of new appointments, it is the governor's power to appoint members of state boards and commissions that is one of the most important ways that a Texas governor can affect state policies.

OTHER CRIMINAL PUNISHMENTS

Although the death penalty is the most significant punishment that can be imposed, the Texas courts impose other deprivations of liberty as well. By August 2000, for example, Texas was projected to have over 146,000 adults in state facilities.[46] In terms of both federal and state prisoners per 10,000 population, Texas ranked eighteenth in the country in 1990, but second in the nation in 1996.[47] Texas ranked tenth in the nation in the violent crime rate per 100,000 population in 1990 and thirteenth in the nation in 1996,[48] suggesting that the increased incarceration rate is more of a political response for action against crime, rather than required by a high-crime rate.

Figure 26.2 on the next page shows the numbers of criminal cases disposed of by the courts of appeal and by the trial courts from 1990 and 1998. As can be seen from the figure, Texas judges dispose of large numbers of criminal cases, and it is a caseload that is increasing over time.

Figure 26.2 CRIMINAL CASES DISPOSED OF BY TEXAS COURTS IN 1990 AND 1998

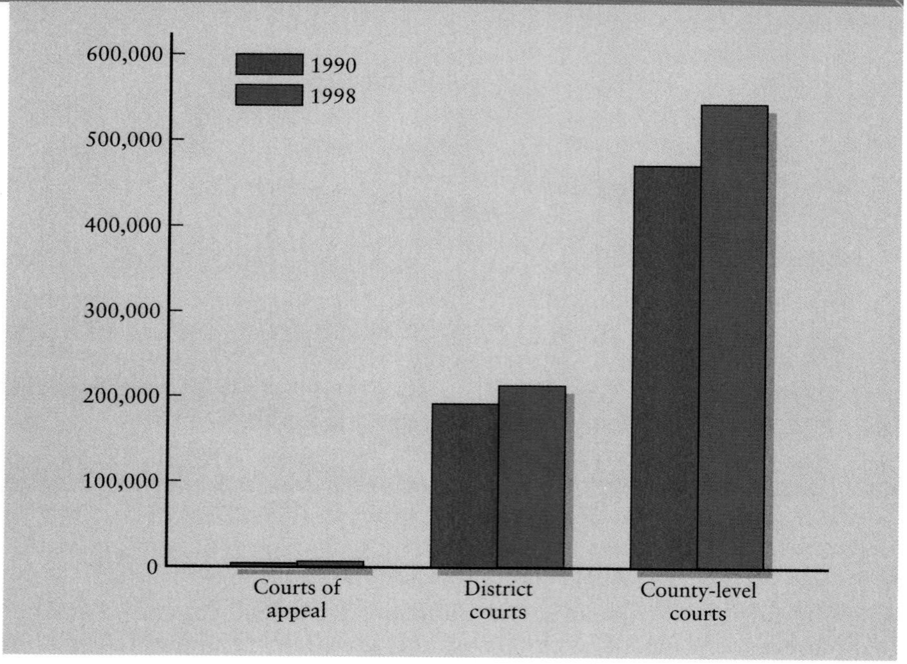

Before the Internet, one of the biggest problems facing citizens interested in judicial affairs was direct access to court decisions. One either had to be affiliated with a law firm or a library that subscribed to expensive law publishing services, such as Lexis-Nexis, or one had to rely upon newspapers for their accounts of judicial rulings. The Internet changed this situation entirely by making legal rulings directly available to everyone as soon as they are available to the press. The two highest courts in Texas—the Supreme Court and the Court of Criminal Appeals—both maintain excellent Web sites that provide up-to-date information on the operations of the courts and on their membership as well as online transcripts of all recent decisions rendered by the courts.

www.wwnorton.com/wtp3e

CIVIL CASES

Figure 26.3 shows the numbers of civil cases disposed of by the courts of appeal and the trial courts from 1990 and 1998. The Texas court system is overloaded and would not be able to adequately function without the aid of visiting judges, retired or defeated judges who continue hearing cases in order to assist with the growing caseloads.

It is the Texas Supreme Court that sets the tone for civil cases throughout the state. Most important of those types of cases, because of the large amounts of money involved, is tort law. In the early- to mid-1980s, the Court tended to be sympathetic to the plaintiffs' positions in tort cases. That is, they tended to support the side in a case that was suing businesses, professionals, and insurance companies. However, in 1988, more justices began to be elected who favored the defendants in civil lawsuits. One reason for this change was that in 1988, Republican justices began to be elected, and they were more conservative than many of the previous justices who were Democrats. Another explanation is that interest groups that were harmed by the pro-plaintiff tendencies of the Court began to organize, raise and spend money, and elect justices more sympathetic to their perspective. In the 1980s, plaintiffs lawyers, lawyers who sue businesses, professionals, and insurance companies, had worked to elect pro-plaintiff justices. The tide turned and business, professional, and insurance interests were now electing pro-defense justices. In 1996–97, civil defendants won three-fourths of the time and insurance companies won almost all their substantive cases. Physicians, hospitals, and pharmaceutical companies won all

CIVIL CASES DISPOSED OF BY TEXAS COURTS IN 1990 AND 1998

Figure 26.3

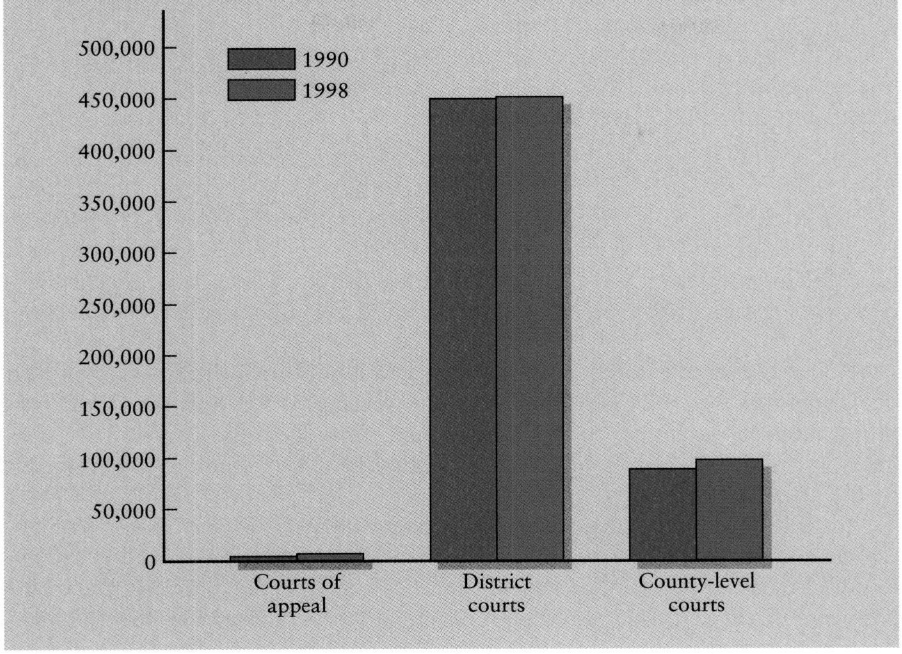

seven of their cases before the Texas Supreme Court. In 1997–98, civil defendants won 69 percent of the time.[49] However, in 1998–99, the Court was not as strongly pro-defendant, perhaps because of several new justices on the Court who were regarded as somewhat moderate in their judicial philosophy. In insurance cases, defendants won 40 percent of the time; plaintiffs 40 percent of the time; and the decision of the Court was a split decision 20 percent of the time. Defendants in medical cases, however, still won 100 percent of the time.[50] It is this power of the Texas Supreme Court to set the tone in civil cases that makes that court a political battleground, since millions—even billions of dollars—can be at stake as a result of the Court's decisions.

Summary

Texas elects its judges in partisan judicial elections. For many years, when the Democratic Party was dominant, Texas judicial elections were staid, low-budget, noncompetitive events. However, with the growth of the Republican Party, judicial elections have become highly political, and large amounts of money have been raised for judicial candidates, especially in Texas Supreme Court races. Often these judicial races pit business interests against candidates backed by the plaintiffs bar because the Supreme Court sets the tone of tort law in the state.

There have been problems in Texas judicial races, in large part because voters often don't know much about judicial candidates. As a result, ballots are often cast based on the candidate's party affiliation or the candidate's name appeal. The result has been the election of several judicial candidates who lacked significant qualifications for the job.

There have been numerous efforts to change the way judges are selected in Texas. There have been efforts to change the system of selection to "merit selection" and to nonpartisan election. Minority groups have pushed to reduce the size of judicial districts in order to increase the election of minority judges. However, efforts to change the system of selection have so far been unsuccessful. No majority coalition can agree on appropriate changes in the judicial selection system, and there is significant opposition to change from groups such as the political parties and business interests. Additionally, Texans seem satisfied with the current system of selection and seem to prefer to elect their judges.

Texas, like many states, has a State Commission on Judicial Conduct that deals with some of the more egregious improprieties of Texas judges and disciplines them for unethical conduct. To some extent, it can be argued, the Commission provides controls over Texas judicial behavior that are not provided by the election process.

Texas courts handle large caseloads of both civil and criminal cases. The highest civil court in the state is the Texas Supreme Court, currently an all-Republican court elected with strong support from business interests. The Court has been heavily criticized for being too sympathetic to those interests. The highest criminal court in the state is the Texas Court of Criminal Appeals. That court is also an all-Republican court, which was elected with strong support from prosecutors and victims-rights groups. Perhaps its most important function is as the appellate court for the death penalty in the state. It is a strongly pro–death penalty court, and Texas ranks first in the nation in executions.

Because the Texas court system affects the liberty and especially the pocketbooks of Texans, it will continue to be an area of concern and controversy. And the most controversial area of Texas justice will continue to be the process by which judges are selected.

FOR FURTHER READING

American Bar Association. *Report and Recommendations of the Task Force on Lawyers' Political Contributions.* Chicago: ABA, 1998.

Anderson, Ken. *Crime in Texas: Your Complete Guide to the Criminal Justice System.* Austin: University of Texas Press, 1997.

Champagne, Anthony, and Judith Haydel (eds.). *Judicial Reform in the States.* Lanham, MD: University Press of America, 1993.

DuBois, Philip. *Judicial Elections and the Quest for Accountability.* Austin: University of Texas Press, 1980.

Texas Commission on Judicial Efficiency. *Governance of the Texas Judiciary: Independence and Accountability.* Austin: State of Texas, 1996.

Watson, Richard, and Robert Downing, *The Politics of the Bench and the Bar.* New York: Wiley, 1969.

STUDY OUTLINE

Court Structure

1. The highest court in Texas with civil jurisdiction is the Texas Supreme Court.
2. The Court of Criminal Appeals is the highest criminal court in Texas.
3. Texas has fourteen intermediate appellate courts, which have both civil and criminal jurisdiction.
4. District courts have original civil and original criminal jurisdiction and are considered the major trial courts in the state.
5. County courts were created by the Texas Constitution, hear relatively minor civil cases, and have original jurisdiction over many misdemeanors.
6. Statutory county courts are created by the legislature to handle the caseloads of urban counties.
7. Justice of the peace courts hear some misdemeanors and function as small claims courts.
8. Municipal courts have jurisdiction over violations of city ordinances and some misdemeanors.

The Legal Process

1. The legal process is divided into civil law and criminal law. Civil cases are disputes between individuals, and these cases are decided by a preponderance of evidence. Criminal cases allege violations of law, are disputes between the state government and an individual, and guilt is determined based on evidence beyond a reasonable doubt.
2. When a person is found guilty, a separate hearing is held to determine the person's punishment.

How Judges Are Selected

1. All state court judges are elected in partisan elections; however, many judges originally obtain office by being appointed by the governor. By 2000, fewer than one-half of judges were originally appointed to office.
2. For a century, judicial elections were won by Democrats with virtually no opposition from the Republican Party. In 1978, a Republican, William Clements, was elected governor of Texas, and this triggered competition between the two parties for judgeships. As the Republican Party gained strength, some Democratic judges switched parties. The growth of competition increased the cost of running for office.
3. Running as a Republican candidate is now more important than qualifications or judicial experience. Judicial races receive very little publicity, making it difficult for voters to learn about the candidates. The number of judicial races in metropolitan areas such as Harris County require voters to cast ballots in dozens of judicial contests. Candidates with familiar names have a distinct advantage in elections.
4. Countywide and larger partisan judicial races may make it difficult for minorities to win elections. There are substantially more female judges than minority judges. The U.S. Supreme Court ruled that the Voting Rights Act does not apply to judicial elections. Losing elections due to partisan politics rather than race does not violate federal law.
5. Retention elections allow voters to cast a yes or no ballot on the question of retaining a particular judge.
6. There are several ways state court judges are selected throughout the United States, including appointment by the governor with approval by the state senate. Another system is selecting judges with nonpartisan elections. The merit selection of judges combines appointment with input from an independent commission and retention elections. A recent reform proposal is known as "appoint-elect-retain." Texas is unlikely to change its method of judicial selection.
7. The Judicial Campaign Fairness Act provides for voluntary limits on judicial candidates. It places limits on individual contributions and contributions from law firms.
8. The Texas Constitution creates an eleven-member Commission on Judicial Conduct, which has the responsibility of policing the behavior of more than three thousand judges. Many complaints against judges are without merit, but when complaints are justified the commission has a variety of remedies.

The Importance of the Texas Courts

1. Texas courts affect the lives of Texans by adjudicating issues from speeding tickets to traffic accidents and imposing child support payments to imposing the death penalty.
2. There is a racial/ethnic disparity of death-row cases, with African Americans more likely to be subject to the death penalty.
3. The Texas Board of Pardons and Paroles, which votes on clemency issues for death-row inmates, is under criticism because of its secrecy and its policy of voting on issues by fax rather than holding face-to-face meetings to discuss and vote on petitions. In 1996, Texas ranked second in the nation in terms of prisoners per 10,000 population.
4. The Texas court system is overloaded and must use visiting judges—retired judges, and judges who were defeated for reelection—to hear cases.
5. Texas courts, especially the appellate courts, are more conservative than a decade ago.

PRACTICE QUIZ

1. The highest criminal court in the state of Texas is the
   a) Texas Supreme Court.
   b) Texas Court of Appeals.
   c) Texas Court of Criminal Appeals.
   d) district court.
2. To reduce the caseload of county courts, the legislature created
   a) justice of the peace courts.
   b) regional courts.
   c) district courts.
   d) statutory county courts.
3. Upon conviction, the criminal's punishment is determined
   a) by the judge.
   b) in a separate hearing by the jury that determined the person's guilt.
   c) by the prosecuting attorney.
   d) by the prosecuting and defense attorneys.
4. Which of the following represents the largest number of judges?
   a) African American judges
   b) Asian American judges
   c) female judges
   d) Hispanic judges
5. In civil cases, defense lawyers often align themselves with
   a) business and industry.
   b) labor groups.
   c) groups that support workers.
   d) judges supported by the Democratic Party.
6. Elections lost due to party membership rather than race or ethnicity do not violate
   a) the Fifth Amendment to the U.S. Constitution.
   b) Article I of the Texas Constitution.
   c) *Clements v. Maddox.*
   d) The Voting Rights Act.
7. Which of the following sets voluntary campaign limits for judicial candidates in Texas?
   a) Judicial Campaign Fairness Act
   b) Judicial Campaign Act
   c) Voting Rights Act
   d) Civil Rights Act
8. In Texas, which event marked the rise of the Republican Party and partisan judicial elections?
   a) the election of President Ronald Reagan
   b) the impeachment of William Jefferson Clinton
   c) the appointment of Tom Phillips as Chief Justice of the United States
   d) the election of William Clements as governor of Texas
9. How likely is Texas to change its method of selecting judicial candidates?
   a) Texas is scheduled to change to the Missouri Plain in January 2002.
   b) extremely likely in the next two decades
   c) likely in the next decade
   d) unlikely
10. Philosophically, in past few years, Texas courts became
    a) less likely to impose the death penalty.
    b) more liberal.
    c) more concerned with civil rights.
    d) more conservative.

CRITICAL THINKING QUESTIONS

1. During 1999 and 2000, Governor George W. Bush issued pardons to six prison inmates who were cleared by DNA testing. In June of 2000, Attorney General John Cornyn reported that at least six death-row inmates were sentenced to death based on racially biased testimony. What can the state do to ensure that Texans receive equal treatment under the law? Can the judicial system ever truly ensure that only the guilty are convicted? Explain.

2. Few minorities hold judicial office in Texas. Although African Americans and Hispanics make up over 40 percent of the Texas population, only about 10 percent of state court judges belong to these groups. Offer at least three suggestions, including alternative election methods, to increase the number of minorities holding judicial office in Texas.

KEY TERMS

answer (p. 969)
bench trial (p. 971)
beyond a reasonable doubt (p. 972)
capital case (p. 971)
civil law (p. 969)
complaint (p. 969)
contingent fee (p. 969)
county courts (p. 968)
county judge (p. 966)
courts of appeal (p. 966)
criminal law (p. 969)
district courts (p. 966)
en banc (p. 982)
felony (p. 971)
grand jury (p. 971)
indictment (p. 971)
Judicial Campaign Fairness Act (p. 986)
justice of the peace courts (p. 969)
merit selection (p. 984)
misdemeanor (p. 971)
municipal courts (p. 969)
ordinance (p. 969)
plea bargains (p. 971)
preponderance of the evidence (p. 970)
retention election (p. 983)
statutory county courts at law (p. 968)
statutory probate courts (p. 968)
Texas Court of Criminal Appeals (p. 966)
Texas Supreme Court (p. 966)

27 Local Government

★ **County Government in Texas**

How is county government in Texas a form of checks and balances? Does this system make it more difficult to govern?

What explains the variation in the types of public offices at the county level?

What are the primary functions of county government?

★ **City Government in Texas**

What are the three major forms of city government in Texas? How do they vary?

★ **Special Districts**

What are the types of special districts in Texas? What functions do each perform?

How are special districts created, governed, and financed?

What are regional councils of government and what do they do?

in Texas

IN 1956, a young African American nurse moved to Dallas to begin work at the Dallas Veterans Hospital. When she showed up for work, her coworkers were shocked. They were unaware that there were black professionals in Dallas. Due to race, she was unable to find housing in nurses' residences or apartment buildings, and she had to move to a roominghouse. When she went to downtown stores, she found she could not try on clothes because nothing that had touched the skin of a black person could be sold to a white person.

At the time, the local government was dominated by wealthy white businessmen who controlled the local political structure through an organization called the Dallas Citizens Council, described by one author as "a collection of dollars represented by men." African Americans and other minorities had no voice in running Dallas, but by the 1960s there was change in the air. In the 1960s, the nurse began organizing boycotts of downtown stores by African Americans, forcing those stores to open their shelves and their jobs to blacks. Later, the nurse ran for the Texas Legislature and won. Now that nurse is a congresswoman from Dallas—Eddie Bernice Johnson. Her story is a story of vast change in local government and in community practices. While race remains an issue in local government now, the theme of Texas cities over the past forty years has been one of increased inclusiveness of the populace—especially of minorities—in the governance of their communities.[1]

At the heart of American democracy lies the idea of local self-government. The nineteenth-century French political theorist Alexis de Tocqueville recognized the importance of local government to republican forms of government when he wrote in his monumental work *Democracy in America,* "The strength of free peoples resides in the local community. Local institutions are to liberty what primary schools are to science; they put it within the people's reach; they teach the people to appreciate its peaceful enjoyment and accustom them to make use of it. Without local institutions a nation may give itself a free government, but it has not got the spirit of liberty."[2]

Local government institutions play a major role in Texas. In 1997, there were 4,700 local governments, an average of 18.5 per county. Of these local governments, 1,431 were *general purpose* governments, including 254 county governments and 1,177 municipal governments. There were also 3,269 *special purpose* governments, including 1,087 public school systems and 2,182 special district governments.[3] Local government is everywhere in Texas, providing water, electricity, and sewer services, as well as police protection and public education.

The problem of local government in Texas, as elsewhere across the country, has been how to balance the demands of democracy with those of efficiency.

What is the most efficient way to deliver public services to people at the local level? How can efficient public institutions be made accountable to the people?

In this chapter, we will investigate three aspects of local government in Texas: county government, city government, and special district government. Our goal will be to understand how local governments work and how they have been shaped by the social, political, and economic changes of recent decades. If Tocqueville is right and local government holds the key to democratic self-government, we must understand the institutions and processes that structure local government if we want to understand Texas.

County Government in Texas

- How is county government in Texas a form of checks and balances? Does this system make it more difficult to govern?
- What explains the variation in the types of public offices at the county level? What are the primary functions of county government?

All but two states have governmental units known as counties (or parishes), but Texas has 254 counties, more counties than any other state.[4] County government in Texas is primarily a way of governing rural areas, and because Texas is so vast, with huge areas that are sparsely populated, county government remains an important aspect of local government. As was discussed in previous chapters, the Texas Constitution places numerous restrictions on government, and there are numerous provisions of the Constitution which place restrictions on counties. Indeed, in Texas, counties have very constricted governmental powers. Unlike city governments, they usually do not have powers to legislate. Given that they lack much of the power of self-government, they often primarily function as an administrative arm of the state government.

Texas counties have their origins in "municipality," which was the local governmental unit under Spanish and Mexican rule. These municipalities were large and included settlements and surrounding rural territories. In 1835, Texas was divided into three departments and twenty-three municipalities. With the Republic of 1836, the twenty-three municipalities became counties. By the time Texas became a state in 1845, there were thirty-six counties, and when Texas entered the Confederacy in 1861, there were 122 counties. The number of counties increased steadily until 1921 when the 254th county was created. The initial idea behind counties was that each citizen could travel to the county seat, by horseback, of course, and return home in a day. Given the sparse population of west Texas, in particular, that initial idea for county organization was eventually rejected, but it does show that Texans believed the local center of government, the county seat, should be accessible to the people.[5]

NUMEROUS COUNTY OFFICES: CHECKS AND BALANCES OR BUILT-IN PROBLEMS?

Like the state government, one of the characteristics of county government in Texas is a multiplicity of elected governmental officials. Some argue that the large number of public officials at the county level is desirable because it creates a strong system of checks and balances, where no official can dominate county government.[6] However, that system of checks and balances comes at a high price. There are problems of coordination of governmental activity, much like what occurs at the state level. One of the most important bodies of county elected officials is the **county commissioners' court,** which is the main governing unit in the county. Although the commissioners' court is not really a judicial court, it may have gotten its name from the Republic of Texas Constitution (1836–45) when the county governing unit consisted of the chief justice of the county court and the justices of the peace within the county.[7]

The structure of the current arrangement for the county commissioners' court, shown in Figure 27.1, consists of a **county judge** who is elected countywide and whose term of office is four years. The county judge presides over the meetings of the commissioners' court and has administrative powers as well as judicial powers in rural counties. In those counties, the county judge hears minor criminal cases and handles some civil matters such as probate matters. In larger counties, the county judge is an administrator only, with the judicial duties of the office removed by the creation of judgeships, such as probate judges and county court-at-law judges.

Each commissioners' court also has four **county commissioners;** each of these officials is elected from precincts that are about the size of one-fourth the population of the county. In the late 1960s, one of the great issues in constitutional law involved the issue of malapportionment, the notion that election districts did not represent equal population groupings but other types of groupings such as equal land areas. The malapportionment of Texas's county commissioners' courts became an important case before the U.S. Supreme Court because the commissioners' precincts tended to be drawn to represent fairly equal land areas within the county rather than equal population groupings. In *Avery v. Midland County* (1968), the U.S. Supreme Court held that the principle of one person-one vote applied to commissioners' courts just like it applied to legislative districts. The result was that commissioners' precincts must now be drawn to reflect equal population groupings within counties.[8]

county commissioners' court
the main governing body of each county; has the authority to set the county tax rate and budget

county judge
the person in each of Texas's 254 counties who presides over the county court and county commissioners' court; is responsible for the administration of county government

county commissioners
government officials (four per county) on the county commissioners' court, whose main duty is the construction and maintenance of roads and bridges

THE COUNTY COMMISSIONERS' COURT — **Figure 27.1**

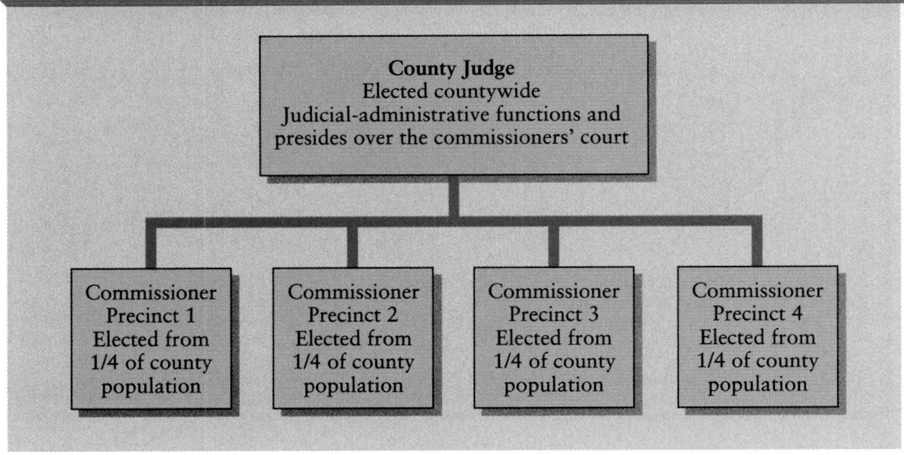

The main duty of county commissioners is the construction and the maintenance of roads and bridges; usually each commissioner provides for roadwork within his precinct. That aspect of the commissioners' work is, of course, very important to rural residents and can be politically controversial and sometimes tinged with corruption. In 1980, a federal probe of county commissioners began over the issue of kickbacks on road and bridge supplies. The investigation centered on about eight counties in east Texas, but when news of the federal investigation surfaced, prices paid for road and bridge supplies in some Texas counties suddenly dropped as much as 20 percent at a time when inflation was running about 12 percent.[9]

The commissioners' court also sets the county tax rate and the county budget. Related to its taxing and budgeting powers is its power to make contracts and pay bills. Perhaps the most important expenditure of most county commissioners' courts, other than road and bridge expenditures, is the cost of building and maintaining county jail facilities. Indigent health care can be a significant cost for counties as well, along with, in some cases, fire protection and sanitation. Some counties also have costs associated with the maintenance of libraries and hospitals and costs for emergency welfare expenditures, such as those brought on by natural disasters or fires. There are county officials that it can appoint, and it can hire personnel as well as fill vacancies in county offices. It also administers elections in the county.

However, as earlier noted, there are numerous elected officials in Texas counties, each with an independent power base. As the box on the conflict between the Tarrant County sheriff and the Tarrant County commissioners shows, it seems nearly inevitable that tensions would develop between the budgetary powers of the commissioners' courts and the needs and desires of other elected county officials.

The commissioners' court oversees outdoor burning bans, county budgets and tax rates, bridge and road maintenance, and numerous other county interests.

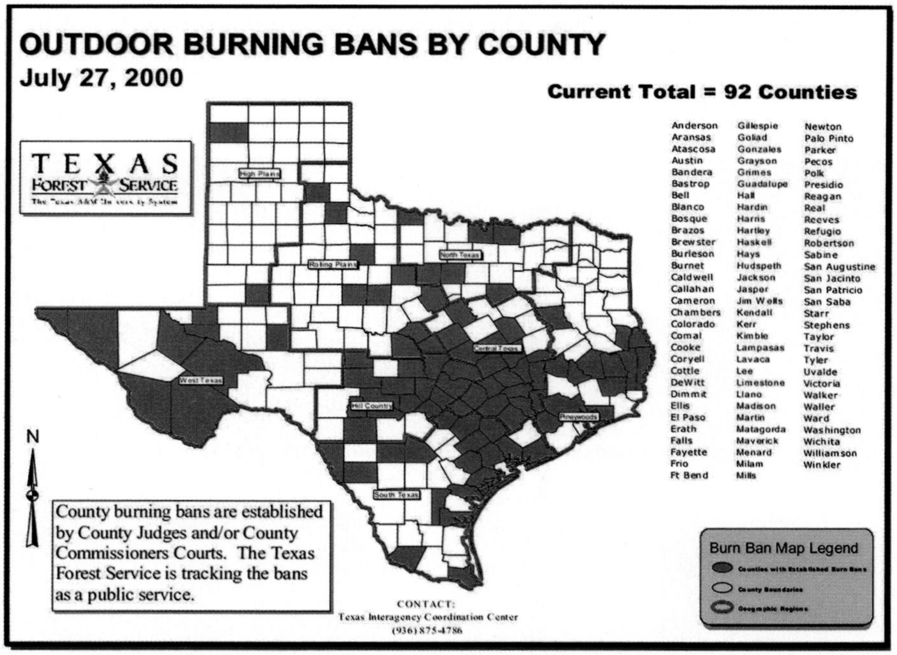

THE PROBLEM OF MULTIPLE OFFICEHOLDERS AT THE COUNTY LEVEL

Box 27.1

Tarrant County Sheriff David Williams has apparently given up at least part of his battle against county commissioners.

State District Judge Bob McGrath said Thursday that Williams has dropped his lawsuit aimed at blocking the county from enacting part of its $240 million 1999 budget.

Williams filed the case in November after commissioners allotted his department $54.2 million, about $2 million more than last year but noticeably less than the $65 million he requested.

Commissioners angrily branded the lawsuit frivolous and accused Williams of "grandstanding" on one hand and wasting taxpayers' money on the other.

Tarrant County Judge Tom Vandergriff said Thursday he was surprised but pleased that Williams had dropped his claim.

The sheriff, who routinely ignores media requests for comment, issued no statement on Thursday.

In his lengthy and bitter battle with commissioners, Williams has claimed the County is withholding essential funding that is both disrupting his office and illegally usurping his powers.

The sheriff blames commissioners for mass defections and plunging morale and challenges their authority over the county budget.

Commissioners argue it is their duty to hold the sheriff's department fiscally accountable.

SOURCE: "Fort Worth Sheriff Drops Lawsuit against Tarrant County Commissioners," *Corpus Christi Caller Times,* February 19, 1999, http://callertimes.com/autoconv/newstexmex99/newstexmex129.html.

As is pointed out in Table 27.1, other officeholders are elected at the county level and still others at the precinct level of the county. There is some variation in the numbers of officeholders depending on the county. For example, there will be more justices of the peace and more **constables** in larger counties than in smaller ones. In some counties, constables serve legal papers;

constable
precinct-level county official involved with serving legal papers and, in some counties, enforcing the law

COUNTY AND PRECINCT-LEVEL ELECTED OFFICIALS

Table 27.1

Countywide Officials	Precinct-Level Officials
County judge	County commissioners
Possibly county court at law judges, probate judges, and district judges	Justices of the peace
County, criminal district, and district attorney	Constables
Sheriff	
County and district clerk	
Possibly county treasurer	
Tax assessor-collector	

in others, constables not only serve legal papers, but also have a law enforcement role in which they patrol, give tickets, and make arrests. Bastrop, Travis, and Harris counties even use constables to check on truants from school. In Bastrop County alone, they handle 2,400 cases a year and seem to have found a niche area that others in law enforcement do not want.[10]

Larger counties may have probate judges, numerous district judges, and county court-at-law judges. Smaller counties may not have probate judges or even county court-at-law judges. Some of the smaller counties may share district judges with other counties. Laws setting up various offices often vary from county to county as well. As a result, some counties have county attorneys and others have criminal district attorneys. Some counties have county clerks and district clerks; smaller counties may combine the offices in one person. Some counties have county treasurers; others do not have such an office.

ARE SOME COUNTIES TOO SMALL?

The reason for the variation in offices is not simply that laws were passed at different times, thus sacrificing uniformity in the laws. It is also the case that Texas is a large, diverse state with great variation among its counties. The result is that there is great variation in the numbers of government officials, the duties of officials, and the services provided by the different county governments. Harris County, for example, in 1996 had 3,126,966 people compared to Loving County, which had 141 residents. Brewster County has a population of only 9,221, but it has 6,204 square miles of territory, about the size of Connecticut and Rhode Island combined. Rockwall County, in contrast, has only 147 square miles and a population of 34,153.

One of the medium-size Texas counties is Jasper County in east Texas, though it only has a population of a bit more than 30,000. However, while a small population may create a sense of community and closeness to local government, citizens of Jasper County have learned that when unusual events occur in a small county, it can place a terrific strain on county resources. Three white men were charged with the torture and death of a black man in Jasper County, and in unrelated murders, two other men faced capital murder charges. Capital murder cases are very expensive to try and Jasper County was faced with the prospect of five such trials. The total county budget was only $6 million and the district attorney went before the commissioners' court and estimated that it would cost $1 million to try the cases. The court raised property taxes from 39.20 cents to 43.815 cents and three cents of that was to pay for the trials. And, there were other costs, such as the security costs to monitor demonstrations by the Ku Klux Klan and New Black Panthers, that Jasper has incurred as a result of the hate crime. Efforts have been undertaken by those in county government to get federal funds for the extraordinary expense, other counties have volunteered law enforcement assistance, and the FBI has absorbed the costs of forensics testing. Nevertheless, the expense for the small county is enough that the county judge suggested the commissioners' court might issue certificates of obligation to pay expenses.[11]

In 1996, Jasper County had a population of 32,954. There were 170 Texas counties with populations less than 30,000, and 145 of those counties had populations less than 20,000. Of those 170 counties, 89 counties had populations less than 10,000 people. Seventeen of those counties had populations less than 2,000.

Politics on the Web

Despite Tocqueville's belief that local government is the bedrock upon which American democracy rests, large numbers of people are unaware of who actually represents them in city or county government. The Internet provides local government with a unique opportunity to change this by educating citizens as to how their local government works and who is responsible for making key political decisions.

Over the past five years, city and county governments across Texas have developed Web sites to provide information about local government and to open up new lines of contact between citizens and their elected representatives. Some sites, such as Houston's, are quite sophisticated, providing detailed historical information on local government and politics as well as on current public officials. Others simply provide the names and phone numbers of key public officials. The increasing number of local governments feeling the need to have a presence on the Web suggests that the Web will play a larger role in tying people more closely (and perhaps interactively) to local political institutions.

www.wwnorton.com/wtp3e

Members of the Texas Department of Public Safety stand guard as the Ku Klux Klan holds a rally in Jasper. After a racially motivated hate crime, Jasper county commissioners had to adjust property taxes to help defray the costs associated with the five capital murder cases that resulted and the extra security needed for them.

At the other end of the scale, only 19 counties had a population greater than 200,000, and only 7 of those counties had a population greater than 500,000.

Counties exist as they do for a variety of reasons. One reason commonly given, but which offers only a partial explanation, is that counties were intended to be compact enough that people could ride a horse to the county seat and back in one day. Whatever value that reason had for the development of counties is, of course, long gone. Other reasons are political. For example, wealthy landowners may have urged the legislature to create counties so that they could control county government and hence the amount of property taxes they might pay. Still one must wonder if so many small counties are needed, and the Jasper County situation suggests that even moderate-size counties by Texas standards may be too small to function adequately in unusual situations.

THE FUNCTIONS OF COUNTY GOVERNMENT

What then are the main functions of Texas county government? Table 27.2 on the next page lists them. Like most other things about county government in Texas, these five primary functions are performed with great variation among the counties.

County road and bridge construction and maintenance has traditionally been such an important function of the commissioners' court that often county commissioners are called "road commissioners." County commissioners maintain more than one half of the roads in the state.[12] Although a 1947 law gave counties the authority to place the road system under the authority of a county engineer, in most counties roads and bridges remain one of the most important responsibilities of the commissioners.

Table 27.2 **PRIMARY FUNCTIONS OF COUNTY GOVERNMENT**

- Road and bridge maintenance
- Law enforcement
- Dispute resolution
- Record-keeping
- Social services

Road and bridge construction is one of the most important jobs of the county commissioners.

county attorney
county official who prosecutes lesser criminal cases in the county court

district attorney
public official who prosecutes the more serious criminal cases in the district court

county clerk
public official who is the main record-keeper of the county

Law enforcement is another important responsibility of county government. This job is undertaken by constables and by the sheriff. It is the sheriff who is the chief law enforcement officer within county government, and in rural counties where there are few city police departments the sheriff may be the major law enforcement official in the county. In addition to law enforcement and the provision of deputies for the district[13] and county courts, sheriffs are responsible for the county jail. In many counties, operating a county jail is an expensive and major undertaking. On November 1, 1999, for example, Harris County was guarding and supervising 8,771 inmates in its county jail, Dallas County had 7,184 inmates in its jail, Tarrant County had 3,416. On the other hand, fourteen counties had no jails. Glasscock County had room for twelve inmates in its jail, but no residents; Sterling County had room for five inmates, but no residents. Real County had a jail capacity of three and one inmate, and Terrell County had a capacity of five and one inmate.

Although the law enforcement budget is passed by the county commissioners' court, sheriffs often have considerable influence in county government and develop their own law enforcement styles. The sheriff of Smith County, for example, not only has a SWAT team, but two armored personnel carriers, each of which weighs thirteen tons, moves on tracks, can float, can move up 60-degree grades, and can go forty miles per hour.[14]

County and **district attorneys** also perform a law enforcement role. They prosecute criminal cases. Usually, the district attorneys prosecute the more serious criminal cases in the district courts; whereas, the county attorneys prosecute the lesser criminal cases in the county courts.

Record-keeping is an important function of county government. **County clerks** keep vital statistics for the county and issue licenses; they maintain records for the commissioners' court and the county courts. Most importantly, the county clerk is responsible for records relating to property transactions. Sometimes the county clerk maintains election and voting records. If there is a **district clerk,** he maintains records for the district courts, though in small counties this office is combined with the office of the county clerk. Tax records are maintained by the **county tax assessor-collector** who also collects taxes, though in the smaller counties this job is often performed by the sheriff. Although constitutional amendments have eliminated the office of county treasurer in many counties, where the office does exist, the treasurer is responsible for receiving and expending county funds. The **county auditor** now does much of the work of the county treasurer. There are now about two-hundred county auditors in Texas. Auditors are not elected, but instead are appointed by the county's district judges. Not only do they audit the county's funds, but in large counties they will often prepare the county budget for the commissioners' court.

Counties also have an important role in dispute resolution through their court system. The civil law is a way of resolving disputes between people, and the justice of the peace court and the county and district courts deal with large numbers of civil disputes as well as criminal matters. County and district attorneys may also represent the interests of the county or state in disputes that involve governmental interests.

Finally, counties may perform a social service function. The social services provided will vary from county to county. However, the most important social services will be the provision of emergency welfare assistance to individuals. This may include the provision of food, housing, rental assistance, or shelter to needy individuals. Larger counties have health departments to work on the prevention and control of communicable diseases. Some counties operate mental health services. Some counties provide parks, airports, fire protection, and sanitation facilities. One of the most important social services provided by counties is the provision of indigent health care. Texas counties had medical expenditures in 1997 of over $40 million.[15]

district clerk
public official who is the main record-keeper of the district court

county tax assessor-collector
public official who maintains the county tax records and collects the taxes owed to the county

county auditor
public official, appointed by the county district judge, who receives and disburses county funds; in large counties, this official also prepares the county budget

COUNTY GOVERNMENTS IN PESPECTIVE

County government occupies an important role in Texas local government, although the powers of county government are greatly restricted by the Texas legislature. One of the most notable features of Texas counties are their great variation in geographical size, population, and even in county offices, duties of county officials, and services provided by county government. Additionally, like the state government, county government has a large number of elected county officials. Although this may limit the power of any one county official, it also produces disagreement, conflict, and difficulty in accomplishing objectives.

Many of Texas's counties are very small, possibly too small to meet the needs of Texans in the 2000s, although there is no serious effort now to change the current structure of counties. Counties do perform important and often expensive functions. Some of those functions of county government and the costs associated with them—for example, road and bridge construction and maintenance, jail construction and operation, and indigent health care—are likely to significantly increase in the future.

City Government in Texas

▶ What are the three major forms of city government in Texas? How do they vary?

According to a 1997 U.S. Census Bureau study, there are 1,177 municipal governments incorporated in Texas, ranging in size from 24 residents to over 1.7 million (see Table 27.3 on the next page). Like county governments, municipal governments are creations of the state of Texas. In the early years of the Republic of Texas, the Texas Congress was responsible for enacting laws that incorporated cities. The number of urban areas grew in the state in the late nineteenth and

Table 27.3 MUNICIPAL GOVERNMENTS IN TEXAS

Size	Number
300,000+	6
200,000–299,999	2
100,000–199,999	15
50,000–99,999	21
25,000–49,999	42
10,000–24,999	101
5,000–9,999	106
2,500–4,999	163
1,000–2,499	284
less than 1,000	437
Total	1,177

SOURCE: U.S. Census Bureau, *1997 Census of Governments. Volume 1, Government Organizations.* August 1999, p. 9.

early twentieth centuries, making the management of local affairs a growing burden on the state legislature. In 1912, the legislature passed a constitutional home-rule amendment that enabled cities of more than 5,000 inhabitants to adopt home-rule charters with a majority vote of qualified voters.

home-rule charter
the rules under which a city operates

Home-rule charters essentially lay down the rules under which a city will operate.[16] They provide for the form of government found in the city and specify the number of members serving on the city's governing body. They also may provide the governing body the power to annex land adjacent to the city as well as set property tax rates up to $2.50 per $100 valuation. Home-rule cities are also constitutionally authorized to borrow money in ways not available to smaller municipal entities. Home-rule charters must be consistent with the state constitution and any other statutory provisions. For example, the state has mandated that most city elections take place on a date provided by the Texas Election Code. City elections must be conducted under the general guidelines set by the state. Nevertheless, home rule in Texas has delegated enormous power to local city governments. According to a report by the Advisory Commission on Intergovernmental Relations, the Texas Constitution leaves cities more "home rule" in Texas than in any other state. According to Terrell Blodgett, in the mid-1990s there were 310 home-rule cities in Texas.[17] Table 27.4 lists the eleven largest of these.

Cities and towns of less than 5,000 people are chartered by general statute, as was the case for all cities and towns prior to the passage of the Home Rule Charter Amendments in 1912. These "general law" cities and towns may only act or organize themselves as explicitly permitted by statutory law passed by the state legislature. They are also limited in what they can do by the constitution. For example, general law cities may levy, assess, and collect taxes as authorized by statute. But the constitution sets a maximum property tax rate of $1.50 per $100 valuation, compared to $2.50 per $100 valuation for home-rule cities.

THE LARGEST HOME-RULE CITIES

Table 27.4

Name	Population	Form of Government	First Charter	Present Form Adopted
Houston	1,841,064	Mayor-council	1905	1994
San Antonio	1,123,626	Council-manager	1914	1951
Dallas	1,085,614	Council-manager	1889	1907
Austin	608,053	Council-manager	1919	1994
El Paso	600,277	Mayor-council	1873	1907
Fort Worth	489,277	Council-manager	1924	1985
Arlington	301,991	Council-manager	1920	1990
Corpus Christi	276,712	Council-manager	1926	1993
Plano	198,186	Council-manager	1961	1993
Garland	193,475	Council-manager	1951	1994
Lubbock	192,732	Council-manager	1917	1988

FORMS OF GOVERNMENT IN TEXAS CITIES

In Texas there have been three major forms of city government: the mayor-council form, the commissioner form, and the council-manager form. The **mayor-council form of government** is the oldest. It consists of an elected mayor and city council. The mayor is elected from the city at large. The council may be elected either at large or from a series of **single-member districts,** or a mixture of the two. In the mayor-council form of government, the mayor is the chief executive officer of the city. He presides over council meetings and has a variety of appointment powers. The city council, meanwhile, serves as the legislative body in the city, passing local laws and watching over the executive departments.

In Texas there have been both strong mayor-council systems and weak ones, depending on the powers given to the mayor by the city charter or state statute. In the *strong mayor-council* variation, various executive powers, such as appointive and removal powers to boards and departments or veto powers, are strong. These powers enable the mayor to establish effective control over various executive departments in the city and to control the legislative agenda of the city council. In the *weak mayor-council* variation, these executive powers are much more limited, fragmenting power between the mayor and other elected or appointed officials.

In the 1990s, the mayor-council form of government was the dominant form of government in most of the incorporated cities in Texas, particularly among general-law cities. However, among home-rule cities the mayor-council government was not popular. According to a 1995 survey of 284 home-rule cities conducted by the *Texas Almanac*, only 31 had adopted the mayor-council form of government.

A second form of city government found in Texas is the **commissioner form of government.**[18] Under the commissioner system, the city is run by a small commission, composed of between five and seven members generally elected on an at-large basis. The commission acts in both a legislative and an

mayor-council form of government
a form of city government in which the mayor is the chief executive and the city council is the legislative body; in the *strong mayor-council* variation, the mayor's powers enable him or her to control executive departments and the agenda of the city council; in the *weak mayor-council* variation, the mayor's power is more limited

single-member district
an electorate that is allowed to select only one representative from each district

commissioner form of government
a form of city government in which the city is run by a small group of elected commissioners who act in both legislative and executive capacities

executive capacity. As a group, commissioners pass laws for the city. As individuals, individual commissioners are in charge of one of a variety of departments. One also is designated as the mayor to preside at meetings.

The commission plan was developed as a response to the devastating hurricane that hit Galveston in 1900, claiming an estimated 6,000 lives. It reflected a desire to bring good business practices to city government that would somehow escape the squabbles and inefficiency of traditional local government found in the mayor-council form. The commission plan was adopted by Houston in 1905 and by a number of other Texas cities in 1907, including Dallas, Fort Worth, and El Paso. Republicans and Democratic Progressives across the country supported the plan and other reform principles often integrated with it, including nonpartisan elections, merit selection of employees, and such direct democracy techniques as the initiative, referendum, and recall. At its peak in 1918, the commission form was used by approximately five hundred cities across the country and seventy-five cities in Texas. Following World War I, the number of commission-form cities went into decline. By 2000, no city in Texas used a pure commission form of government, although twenty-six still claimed to be using some variation of a commission-manager form of government.[19] In practice, none of the "commissioners" in these cities exercised executive control over specific city departments as envisioned in the original commission system. Instead, they functioned more like council members under the council-manager form of city government.[20]

council-manager form of government
a form of city government in which public policies are developed by the city council and executive and administrative functions are assigned to a professional city manager

at-large election
an election in which officials are selected by voters of the entire geographical area, rather than from smaller districts within that area

The third form of city government found in Texas is the **council-manager form of government.**[21] As originally envisioned, a city council elected in an **at-large election** was to be the policy-making body. Council members generally received little or no pay and were thought to be publicly motivated citizens interested in serving the public good, rather than professional politicians. A mayor was selected from among council members. The city manager was to be the chief executive and administrative official in the city. As in the commissioner form of government the goal of the council-manager form of government was twofold: to free local government from the seamier side of politics and to bring administrative expertise to local government.

Amarillo was the first city to abandon the commissioner form of government for the council-manager system in 1913. In 1914, Taylor and Denton followed suit. By 1947, there were 47 council-manager systems in Texas. By the mid-1990s, 251 of the home-rule cities were council-manager. Across the United States, it has become the most popular form of government for American cities of over 10,000 residents.

Today council-manager systems vary across the state in a number of ways. The desire for professional administration of local government remains high. Most city managers have graduate degrees and are paid high salaries like other executive officers in the private sector. But a desire for more political accountability through traditional democratic processes has introduced some changes. The growing ethnic and racial diversity of some Texas cities has forced many political leaders to question the wisdom of freeing local government too much from democratic controls. In most cities, mayors now are elected at large from the population as a whole, rather than from just the council. Many cities also elect council members from single-member districts, rather than just at-large districts. At-large districts are seen by many as undercutting minority representation by diluting their votes. Only when Dallas moved from an at-large council to a council elected from single-member districts in 1991 did minorities come to play a major role in the decision-making processes of city government. But most cities and towns under the council-manager system continue to view local political offices as part-time jobs. Mayoral and council salaries remain low. A few cities, such as Austin, offer considerably higher salaries. The demand for more democratic accountability in local government will likely continue to lead to more changes in the council-manager system of government across Texas. Balancing an efficient city government run by professionals with democratic political processes will continue to be a problem as Texas's metropolitan areas continue to grow and diversify in the early twenty-first century.

A TALE OF THREE CITIES

Houston is the largest city in Texas with over 1.7 million people. It has a strong mayor form of government. There are sixteen elected officials in the city serving concurrent two-year terms, including a mayor, a controller, and fourteen council members. The mayor serves as the chief executive official in the city and is the city's chief administrator and official representative. Much of his power follows from his power to appoint department heads and people serving on advisory boards, subject to council approval. The mayor also presides over the city council with voting privileges. The fourteen-member council is a legislative body composed of five at-large seats and nine single-member district seats.

In contrast to most other cities, the city controller in Houston is an elected position.[22] The **city controller** is the city's chief financial officer. Besides investing city funds, conducting internal audits of city departments, and operating the city's financial management system, the controller is also responsible for certifying the availability of funds for city council initiatives. In the end, the office of the controller is both a professional position and a political position. Not surprisingly, the controller often comes into conflict with the mayor and the council over important policy issues.

city controller
the chief financial officer of a city

Although local politics in Houston is nominally nonpartisan, in recent years it has taken on a partisan flavor. The election of Lee Brown in 1997, Houston's first minority mayor, came after a hard-fought campaign where Democrats, including President Clinton, endorsed Brown's candidacy. His challenger, Rob Mosbacher, had run numerous times in statewide elections as a Republican. He was endorsed by leading state Republicans, including former President George Bush.

Texas's second largest city, San Antonio, has a council-manager form of government. The council is composed of members elected from ten single-member districts on a nonpartisan basis. The mayor is the eleventh member of the council and is selected at large. All members of the council serve for two-year terms and receive largely honorific salaries. The mayor's salary is a paltry $3,000 per year, while other council members are paid $20 per meeting, not to exceed $1,040 per year. Members are subject to recall if 10 percent of the qualified voters in a district sign a petition of recall and a recall election is successful. The city charter also provides for initiatives and referendums that emerge from the voters.

The city manager in San Antonio serves at the pleasure of the council as the chief executive and administrative official in the city. He has wide-ranging

Lee Brown's campaign for mayor of Houston was markedly more partisan than Houston politics tends to be.

appointment and removal authority over officers and employees in the administrative service of the city. In 2000, the city manager was Alexander E. Briseno. Beginning his career as an assistant to the city manager in 1977, Briseno rose through the professional hierarchy in the city. He supervised almost every city department before becoming city manager in April 1990. In 2000, he supervised the activities of all city departments, including over 11,000 employees.

Like San Antonio, Dallas operates under a council-manager form of government. For years, city politics had been dominated by the white business community. At-large nonpartisan elections tended to elect a council that was relatively united in its understanding of the problems facing the city and its vision of where the city should go. A bitter struggle over rewriting the city charter divided the city along racial lines in the late 1980s and early 1990s. The new charter put into place in 1991 called for a fourteen-member council elected from single-member districts and a mayor elected at large. Members are limited to serving four two-year terms consecutively. Under the new charter, membership on the council was transformed as a significant number of African Americans and Hispanics were elected to the council. In 1995, Ronald Kirk was elected as the first African American mayor of Dallas with over 62 percent of the popular vote.

As in other council-manager systems, the power of the mayor in Dallas is weak. The mayor presides over council meetings, creates council committees, and appoints members, chairs, and co-chairs. In many ways, however, he is only first among equals on the council. The council as a whole is the legislative body for the city, approving budgets, determining the tax rate, and appointing key public officials, including the city manager, city attorney, city auditor, city secretary, municipal court judges, and various citizen boards and commissions. The city manager serves at the will of the council and is removable by a two-thirds vote of the council. As in San Antonio, the city manager's powers in Dallas are large. As the chief administrative officer, the city manager has the power to appoint and remove all heads of departments and subordinate officers and employees in the city, subject to civil service provisions. Despite the attempt to remove the city manager from the pressures of political life in Dallas, recent city managers have found themselves forced to accommodate the reality of an increasingly politicized city council. The political pressures emerging from Dallas's single-member district council may ultimately compel the city to reexamine the wisdom of remaining a council-manager system. As Dallas has learned in the 1990s, efficient government and democratic governance are not as easy to balance as advocates of the council-manager system once thought.

Special Districts

- What are the types of special districts in Texas? What functions do each perform?
- How are special districts created, governed, and financed?
- What are regional councils of government and what do they do?

A **special district** is a unit of local government that performs a single service in a limited geographical area. These governments solve problems that cross borders of existing units of government. Special districts can be created to serve an entire county, part of a county, all of two or more counties, or parts of two or more counties. The number of special districts increased dramatically in the last fifty years. In the United States, the number increased 400 percent,[23] and in Texas, the number increased more than 600 percent.[24] By the year 2000, there were more special districts than any other form of local government.

special district
a unit of local government that performs a single service, such as education or sanitation, within a limited geographical area

Districts can be created to do almost anything that is legal. Some districts are formed to provide hospital care, others to furnish pure water to cities who, in turn, sell it to their residents. Mosquito control, navigation, flood control, sanitation, drainage, and law enforcement are a few more examples of special districts.

TYPES OF SPECIAL DISTRICTS

There are two types of special districts in Texas. The first is the **school district**, which consists of independent school districts in the state. These districts offer public education from pre-kindergarten through twelfth grade. Almost all school districts offer the full range of educational opportunities; however, some small, rural schools provide education only through the eighth grade. Others limit their programs to the sixth grade, and still others end with the

school district
a specific type of special district that provides public education in a designated area

fourth grade. Those with limited offerings contract with nearby districts to complete the education of their students.

The second classification of special districts is the **nonschool special district.** Everything except the school districts are included in this category. Municipal utility districts (MUDs), water districts, community college districts, and hospital districts are the most common examples in this category.

nonschool special district
any special district other than a school district; examples include municipal utility districts (MUDs) and hospital districts

SCHOOL DISTRICTS

Every inch of land in Texas is part of a school district, and there are slightly more than 1,000 school districts in Texas. Some districts in east and west Texas cover an entire county. In metropolitan counties there may be a dozen or more districts. Each is governed by an elected board of trustees composed of five to nine members. The board employs a superintendent to oversee the daily operation of the district. On the recommendation of the superintendent, the trustees,

- sit over all policy for the school district
- adopt the budget for the district
- set the tax rate for the district (The maximum tax rate for a district is $1.50 for each $100 the property is worth. A rate higher than $1.50 requires voter approval.)
- adopt textbooks for classroom use
- hire principals, faculty, and support staff
- set the school calendar
- determine salaries and benefits for employees

Educating millions of students is a daunting task. By localizing public education, the state places much of the burden on the local school districts. This allows local residents to participate in governing the school districts. Unfortunately few people vote in elections to select members of the board of trustees. Even fewer individuals attend meetings of the school board.

NONSCHOOL SPECIAL DISTRICTS

Municipal Utility Districts **Municipal utility districts** (MUDs) offer electricity, water, sewer, and sanitation services outside the city limits. These governments might offer all utility services or only one or two. It depends on the needs of the special district. While located throughout Texas, the vast majority are found in the Houston metropolitan area.

municipal utility district (MUD)
a special district that offers services such as electricity, water, sewage, and sanitation outside the city limits

MUDs can be a financial blessing for developers. Entrepreneurs build housing additions outside the city limits. These builders must furnish utilities to the homes they build, but few developers can afford to do this over a long period of time.

Banks and finance companies, legislators, and land developers maintain a warm and snug relationship with each other. Banks and finance companies willingly loan land developers millions of dollars to establish residential subdivisions, build new homes, and run water and sewer services to these houses.

When a few houses are sold, the developer asks the residents to establish a municipal utility district. The enabling legislation is seldom a problem because of the close relationship between developers and local legislators.

Once the MUD is up and running, the board of directors sets a tax rate and determines how much to charge residents for its services. One of its first activities is to borrow money by issuing bonds. The bond proceeds are used to purchase the utilities from the developer, often at a premium. Using the proceeds from the sale of the utilities the developer is able to repay his loans. By establishing the MUD, residents agree to pay a property tax to retire the bonded indebtedness. In addition to the property tax, residents pay a monthly fee for the water, sewer, and sanitation services.

Flood control districts, which can be composed of several counties, regulate flooding and minimize the potential damage caused by flooding.

Flood Control Districts Flooding is seldom confined to a single county, and a flood control district can be created to solve a multicounty flood control problem.

Community College Districts Community college districts are classified as nonschool special districts because they do not offer public education from prekindergarten through grade twelve. Community colleges offer post secondary academic and vocational programs. They are governed by an elected board of regents. Residents of the district pay a property tax to the district. In return, residents pay lower tuition. The board employs a president or chancellor who operates the college on a daily basis. The regents set policy on the recommendation of the president/chancellor. Among the regents' responsibilities are:

- set overall policy for the district
- set the tax rate
- set the cost of tuition and fees
- build new buildings and repair older ones
- hire teachers, counselors, administrators, and nonprofessional staff
- set the school calendar
- determine salaries and benefits for employees

Creating a Special District Special districts are created by voters of the area to be served. Creating a special district requires

- a petition signed by the residents of the area to be served requesting the legislature to authorize an election to create a special district
- enabling legislation in the form of a law that authorizes a special election to create the district
- a positive vote of those voting in the special election

Governing a Special District Most special districts are governed by boards elected by the voters of the district. The board of a school district is called the board of trustees, the governing board of a community college is the board of regents, and the governing boards of other special districts are known as boards of directors. Each board is the policy-making group for its district. The directors set the tax rate and establish rules and policy for the operation of the district. It employs an individual who runs the district on a day-to-day basis.

property tax
a tax based on an assessment of the value of one's property, which is used to fund the services provided by local governments, such as education

Revenues **Property taxes** are the primary source of revenue for special districts, and the second largest source of income are **user fees.** For some districts the property tax comprises as much as 90 percent of revenues. In 1949, school districts received 80 percent of their income from the state and the school

user fee
a fee paid for public goods and services, such as water or sewage

district furnished 20 percent of necessary funds, primarily from property taxes. Today the largest source of revenue for most districts is the property tax, with state and federal aid furnishing the remainder.

Property tax rates and actual user fees are set by governing boards. User fees are raised from providing goods and services. Water districts, for example, sell water, sewer, and, possibly, sanitation services.

Hospital districts set fees for room occupancy, medicine dispensed, use of surgical suites, X-rays taken and evaluated, nursing and laboratory service, and a myriad of other charges. The board of trustees of a school district sets the local property tax rate. Tuition paid by in-district and out-of-district students, building fees, student fees, and technology and lab fees are determined by the board of regents of a community college district.

Hidden Governments There are more special districts than any other form of local government. Everyone in Texas lives in a least one special district, the school district. Most people live in several, have the opportunity to vote for people to represent them on the governing board of the districts, and pay property taxes to these agencies of government. Yet, few people are aware these agencies exist, thus their reputation as "**hidden governments.**"

hidden government
a concept that refers to special districts, since many citizens are not aware that they exist

Special districts provide a needed service in a specific geographic area. Existing governments may lack authority to provide the service or the necessary funds to finance the project. Using a special district, recipients of the services pay for them through property taxes and user fees. Special districts are an example of democracy working. Districts are created by a vote of the residents of the area to be served. The boards are elected by the voters. Decisions on policy, taxing, and fees are made by the board, in an open meeting attended by interested residents. Although democratic in theory, less than 10 percent of eligible voters cast ballots in special district elections. Fewer than 1 percent of district residents ever attend a board meeting.

COUNCILS OF GOVERNMENT (COGS)

One of the greatest problems facing local governments in Texas today is coordination across legal boundaries. The Regional Planning Act of 1965 initially provided for the creation of regional **councils of government** (COGs) to promote coordination and planning across all local governments in a particular region. There are twenty-four regional councils in Texas today, each with its own bylaws or articles of agreement. The governing body of a regional council must consist of at least two-thirds of local elected officials of cities and counties, and may include citizen members and representatives of other groups.

council of government (COG)
a regional planning board composed of local elected officials and some private citizens from the same area

The basic responsibilities of regional councils include planning for the economic development of an area, helping local governments carry out regional projects, contracting with local governments to provide certain services, and reviewing applications for state and federal financial assistance. Originally COGs focused considerable attention on meeting federal mandates for water and sewer provision, open space, and housing planning. More recently, activities have focused on comprehensive planning and service delivery in such policy areas as aging, employment and training, criminal justice, economic development, environmental quality, and transportation.[25]

Summary

In this chapter we have investigated the role of local government in Texas government and politics. In many ways, local government affects the average citizen's life much more than the activities of either the federal or the state government proper. Sadly, local government may not be functioning as well as we might hope. Part of the problem may lie in the conflicting demands we have come to place upon it. On the one hand, Texans want local government of all kinds to provide an efficient delivery of services to all in a fair and equitable manner. On the other hand, Texans have also wanted to keep local government under some sort of democratic control. But what sort of local controls are the best? The demands of efficiency and democracy are not easily balanced. The social, political, and economic changes of the last twenty years may spark a rethinking of local government in Texas for the first time since the early decades of the twentieth century.

FOR FURTHER READING

Brooks, David B. *Texas Practice: County and Special District Law*. St. Paul, MN: West Publishing, 1989.

Hazel, Michael V. *Dallas: A History of Big D*. Austin: Texas State Historical Association, 1997.

Hill, Patricia Evridge. *Dallas: The Making of a Modern City*. Austin: University of Texas Press, 1988.

Gourney, Luke. *Texas Boundaries: Evolution of the State's Counties*. College Station: Texas A&M University Press, 1995.

Humphrey, David. *Austin: A History of the Capital City*. Austin: Texas State Historical Association, 1997.

Orum, Anthony M. *Power, Money and the People: The Making of Modern Austin*. Austin: Texas Monthly Press, 1987.

Schutze, Jim. *The Accommodation*. Secaucus, NJ: Citadel Press, 1986.

Miller, Char, and Haywood T. Sanders, eds. *Urban Texas: Politics and Development*. College Station: Texas A&M University Press, 1990.

STUDY OUTLINE

County Government in Texas

1. County government is primarily a way of governing rural areas.
2. The state constitution places many restrictions on county government.
3. A large number of elected officials at the county level creates a system of checks and balances where no one individual can control county government.
4. The county commissioners' court is the primary governing unit of the county.
5. Each county has four county commissioners who represent precincts equal in population. Each is responsible for building and maintaining county roads and bridges in his or her precinct.
6. All Texas counties have the same governmental structure, but more populous counties have more employees, judges, and attorneys.
7. Counties vary widely in size and population.
8. Counties exist for a variety of reasons. Historically counties were compact in size so that government would be close to the people, but this reason is no longer valid. Politically, the large number of low population counties has in the past allowed large landowners an opportunity to control county government.
9. The situation in Jasper County, which was faced with the prospect of five expensive capital murder trials, suggests a need for larger counties that would provide additional revenues.

10. There are five primary functions of county government in Texas: (1) build and maintain county roads and bridges; (2) provide law enforcement through the sheriff and constables and the county courts and jails; (3) record keeping by the county clerk, district clerk, and county tax assessor and collector; (4) resolve civil disputes through the justice of the peace, county, and district courts; and (5) provide social services.

City Government in Texas

1. The two legal forms of municipal government in Texas are general-law cities and home-rule cities.
2. In Texas there are three major forms of city government: mayor-council, commissioner, and council-manager.
3. The mayor-council form of government can be either weak or strong.
4. Most general-law cities use the weak mayor-council form of government.
5. The commissioner form of government was formed to bring good business practices to city government, but in 2001, no Texas city uses the pure form of commissioner government.
6. The council-manager form of government was designed to free local government from the seamier side of politics and to bring administrative expertise to local government.
7. Most home-rule cities use the council-manager form of government.
8. Houston is Texas's largest city and uses the strong mayor-council form of government.
9. The city comptroller is often at odds with the mayor and council.
10. San Antonio and Dallas both use a council-manager form of government.
11. In San Antonio and Dallas the mayor is weak. In these cities, the power of the mayor comes from his political skills and ability to influence council members and various constituencies in the city.
12. Dallas's use of single-member districts politicizes the council and puts extreme pressure on the city manager.

Special Districts

1. A special district is a unit of local government that provides a single service not provided by any other local government.
2. There are two types of special districts in Texas: school districts and nonschool special districts.
3. School districts are commonly known as independent school districts or ISDs. The districts provide public education for pre-kindergarten through grade twelve.
4. All other special districts, including community college districts, are known as nonschool special districts.
5. A special district is created by the voters of the area served and is governed by a board elected by the voters. Their major source of revenue is the property tax.
6. Regional councils of governments are used to plan and coordinate activities of local governments. Originally designed to meet federal government mandates, more recently COGs have focused on comprehensive planning and service delivery.

PRACTICE QUIZ

1. Which of the following is *not* a type of local government found in Texas?
   a) city
   b) council of government
   c) county
   d) special district
2. The basic governing body of a county is known as
   a) a council of government.
   b) a county council.
   c) a county commissioners' court.
   d) a county governing committee.
3. Which county official(s) are responsible for the jail and the safety of the prisoners?
   a) sheriff
   b) county council
   c) county commissioners court
   d) council of mayors
4. Each county commissioner's precinct must be equal in population according to
   a) the Civil Rights Act of 1964.
   b) the Voting Rights Act of 1975.
   c) *Avery v. Midland.*
   d) *Marbury v. Madison.*
5. The two legal classifications of Texas cities are
   a) local and regional.
   b) general law and home rule.
   c) tax and non-tax.
   d) charter and non-charter.
6. The form of city government that allows the mayor to establish control over most of the city's government is called the
   a) commissioner form of city government.
   b) manager-council form of city government.
   c) council of government form of city government.
   d) strong mayor-council form of city government.

7. To adopt a home-rule charter, a city must have a minimum population of
   a) 201.
   b) 5,000.
   c) 10,000.
   d) 50,000.

8. Which local government provides a single service not provided by any other local government?
   a) special district
   b) council of government
   c) city
   d) county

9. What are the two types of special district found in Texas?
   a) school and non-school
   b) home rule and general law
   c) tax and non-tax
   d) statutory and constitutional

10. Comprehensive planning and service delivery in a specific geographic area is the function of a
   a) special district.
   b) council of government.
   c) city.
   d) county.

CRITICAL THINKING QUESTIONS

1. Local government affects your life more directly than state or national government. Whether or not the police and fire departments come when called is a function of local government. Whether you have water when you turn on the faucet is a function of local government. Whether those accused of a crime are tried quickly is a function of local government. For potholes to be filled, streets paved, or trash picked up, local government must be working correctly. The quality of public education is a function of local government. These and other activities directly affect the quality of your life, yet few people vote in local elections. What can be done to increase participation at this important level of government?

2. Examine a telephone directory for a large city and find a list of government offices (usually in the "Blue Pages" section). Consider all activities that government undertakes. Which do you believe should be excluded from the scope of government? In which areas should government's power be increased? Other than those functions you discovered, what else should government do? Explain and discuss your answers.

KEY TERMS

at-large election (p. 1012)
city controller (p. 1013)
commissioner form of government (p. 1011)
constable (p. 1005)
council-manager form of government (p. 1012)
council of government (COG) (p. 1018)
county attorney (p. 1008)
county auditor (p. 1009)
county clerk (p. 1008)
county commissioners (p. 1003)
county commissioners' court (p. 1003)
county judge (p. 1003)
county tax assessor-collector (p. 1009)
district attorney (p. 1008)
district clerk (p. 1009)
hidden government (p. 1018)
home-rule charter (p. 1010)
mayor-council form of government (p. 1011)
municipal utility district (MUD) (p. 1016)
nonschool special district (p. 1016)
property tax (p. 1017)
school district (p. 1015)
single-member district (p. 1011)
special district (p. 1015)
user fee (p. 1017)

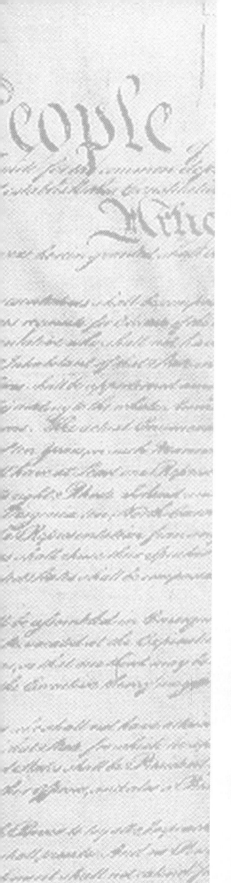

28 Public Policy

★ **Taxing and Spending in Texas**

Is Texas's reputation as a low-tax state a deserved one?

How does the Texas Constitution affect the budget process? How does this process work in practice today?

What are the sources for funding the state government in Texas? What other sources have been considered?

What are the primary expenditures of the Texas state government?

★ **Crime and Corrections Policy**

What is the history of the prison system in Texas?

What are the important issues and trends regarding the incarceration of criminals in Texas?

★ **Education Policy in Texas**

What is the history of public education in Texas?

What are the most important issues that have shaped education policy in Texas over the past fifty years? Have these issues been resolved?

★ **Welfare Policy**

What is the nature of poverty in Texas? How have welfare policies sought to remedy it?

In the past ten years, what attempts have been made to reform the welfare system? How successful have these attempts been?

in Texas

LIKE other states, Texas is involved in a broad range of public policy initiatives. Some of these activities, such as crime and corrections or public education, are largely state responsibilities. While the national government may contribute some funds and regulate various aspects of these public policy areas, they remain for the most part the duty and responsibility of the state of Texas. Other public policy areas, however, have involved considerable intermingling of state and federal government responsibilities. The balance of power between the state and federal governments in these areas has shifted over time.

For the nineteenth and early twentieth centuries, most public policy initiatives related to education, police, and welfare originated in state legislatures and were implemented by state agencies. With the New Deal and the passage of the Social Security Act of 1935, the federal government came to play an increasingly important role in public policy making. Federal projects such as the Works Progress Administration and the Civilian Conservation Corps originated out of Washington, D.C., and were funded by federal dollars in the 1930s. Aid for Dependent Children (later to become Aid for Families with Dependent Children), Unemployment Insurance, Old Age Assistance, and Aid for the Blind were established under the Social Security Act of 1935 as state-federal programs. States were responsible for establishing and implementing the programs under federal guidelines. Financial responsibilities were divided between the national and state governments.

Federal involvement in a variety of policy areas intensified throughout the 1960s and 1970s as the federal government assumed more responsibility for setting the direction of public policy in the country. With the passage of such programs as the National Defense Education Act (1957), the Civil Rights Act of 1964, the Elementary and Secondary Education Act of 1965, Medicare and Medicaid (1965), and the Supplemental Security Income Act (1972), the federal government assumed a central role in a variety of public policy areas traditionally the responsibility of states, including welfare and health-care financing.

As the century drew to a close, questions were raised about the wisdom of further nationalization and centralization of public policy, particularly with regard to welfare and education. Discontent over the failure of the traditional state/federal welfare system spread to both political parties. For the first time since the New Deal, states like Texas began to assume a larger responsibility in addressing the problems of poverty. With the welfare reforms of 1996, the federal government effectively delegated primary responsibility for making welfare policy back to the states for the first time since the 1930s.

This chapter will assess the role that the state of Texas plays in a number of important policy arenas today. It will begin with an analysis of the state budget. The state budget lies at the heart of public policy making in Texas. Understanding how revenue is raised and allocated across all state programs provides a special insight into the constraints and opportunities facing policy makers in Texas. This will be followed by a detailed analysis of three important policy areas in which the state is actively involved: crime and corrections, public education, and welfare. Appreciating the evolution of public policy in these areas will enable us to assess the important role Texas political institutions and political processes play in the policy making process.

Taxing and Spending in Texas

- Is Texas's reputation as a low-tax state a deserved one?
- How does the Texas constitution affect the budget process? How does this process work in practice today?
- What are the sources for funding the state government in Texas? What other sources have been considered?
- What are the primary expenditures of the Texas state government?

A LOW-TAX STATE?

Texas has a reputation of being a "low tax–low service" state that seeks to maintain a favorable environment for business. For the most part, this reputation is well earned. Texas is one of four states that still does not have a personal income tax. There is a high sales tax in Texas of 6.25 percent, the sixth highest in the nation.[1] But state taxes per capita in 1997 were $1,184, ranking Texas forty-eighth among the fifty states. This was well below the national average of state taxes per capita of $1,657. Texas state taxes as a percentage of gross state product are also low at 4.48 percent in 1995, ranking Texas forty-seventh in the nation.

While Texas taxes are low when compared to other states' taxes, local taxes are a slightly different story. Texas ranks nineteenth among the states in terms of local property taxes paid per capita at $755 per person, above the national average of $738 per capita. As a percent of gross state product, local property taxes are 2.76 percent in Texas, again above the national average of 2.68 percent. Similarly, Texas ranks seventeenth when considering all local taxes per capita, at $979, below the national average of $994 per capita. Local taxes in Texas take up 3.58 percent of the gross state budget, ranking Texas twentieth among the fifty states.

When state and local taxes are taken together, Texas's low-tax image is slightly tarnished. Combined state and local taxes were $2,099 per capita in 1995, ranking Texas fortieth in the nation. Meanwhile state and local taxes were 7.52 percent of the gross state product, well below the national average of 9.14 percent. Despite the fact that tax revenue took a larger share of the state economy in the 1990s than the 1980s (7.52 percent versus 6.59 percent), it is hard to argue that Texas has shed its low-tax reputation.

The 1970s and early 1980s were boom years for the Texas economy. Rising inflation coupled with high oil prices and rapid economic growth drove the economy forward.[2] Tax increases were unnecessary as tax revenues soared. The problem facing the legislature was not how to balance the budget, but how to spend revenue windfalls. There were no tax increases in Texas during this time.

The collapse of oil prices and a sputtering state economy in the mid-1980s, particularly severe in real estate and construction, brought on a serious budget crisis. As projected deficits mounted, tax increases became commonplace. Between 1985 and 1986, state tax collections fell. Income from the **oil severance tax** alone dropped 28 percent. Tax rates were increased and the tax base was broadened in almost every year between 1984 and 1991. As the state's economy turned around in the early 1990s, the budgetary situation brightened considerably. Renewed budget surpluses did not bring a return to the spending patterns of pre–oil crash years. Business and political leaders from both parties expressed an ongoing concern that taxes were becoming burdensome, perhaps placing the state at a disadvantage with other states in trying to create a favorable environment for business. Additionally, a growing concern that state government was growing too fast sparked demands for making government more efficient. In 1991 the Texas **comptroller of public accounts** instituted the Texas Performance Review. Over the next decade a series of reports appeared presenting proposals to make Texas government more efficient and to bring more rigorous analysis of spending priorities in the budget. As the decade came to a close, the budget situation was much brighter than it had been at the outset. Policy makers remained cautious, however, about launching any spending initiatives that might push the state back into a budget crisis. The catch phrase of the day became making government more efficient, not larger.

oil severance tax
a tax levied on oil production, at a rate of 4.6 percent of the value of the oil; until the mid-1980s, this tax accounted for 30 percent of the state's revenues, but it now accounts for only 5 percent

comptroller of public accounts
the elected state official who directs the collection of taxes and other revenues

THE CONSTITUTION AND THE BUDGET

A number of constitutional factors affect the way the budget is made in Texas. First, the legislature is compelled to write a two-year or a **biennial budget** because of the constitutional provision that the legislature may only meet in regular session once every two years. One of the effects of this is to force government agencies to project their budgetary needs well in advance of any clear understanding of the particular problems that they may be facing during the biennium. Second, the legislature can only meet for 140 days in regular session. This seriously limits the amount of time that the legislature can spend analyzing the budget or developing innovative responses to pressing matters of public importance.

Third, a large portion of the biennial budget is dedicated for special purposes by federal law or by the Texas Constitution or state statute. These **dedicated funds** include federal monies earmarked for financing health care for the poor (Medicaid), as well as state funds for highways, education, teachers' retirement, and numerous other purposes. The purpose of dedicated funds is not difficult to understand. Supporters of particular programs want to create a stable revenue source for priority programs. But in protecting their own programs, supporters encourage other interests to do likewise, the end result being that the legislature loses control of a large portion of the budget.

biennial
occurring every two years

dedicated funds
a portion of the state budget that is dedicated to mandatory spending on programs like health care for the poor

Fourth, there are a number of specific constitutional provisions that constrain the legislature's control of the budget.[3]

appropriations
the amounts of money approved by the state legislature in statutes (bills) that each unit or agency of government can spend

The Pay-as-You-Go Limit Article III, Section 49a, requires the state to maintain a balanced budget. All bills making **appropriations** must be sent to the comptroller of public accounts to certify that they are within available limit projections. One of the most important consequences of the **pay-as-you-go limit** is to put the comptroller at the heart of the budget process.

pay-as-you-go limit
a rule in the Texas Constitution that prohibits the state government from borrowing money

The Welfare Spending Limit Article III, Section 51a, provides that the amount of money that the state pays for assistance to or on behalf of needy dependent children and their caretakers shall not exceed 1 percent of the state budget in any biennium. This article sets a constitutional limit on the amount of money that the state may pay out to welfare beneficiaries under the Temporary Assistance for Needy Families program. For the 1998–99 biennium, this restriction was not particularly important. The total state budget for the biennium was over $87.1 billion, setting a welfare ceiling of $871 million. However, the legislature only appropriated $274.2 million for the Temporary Assistance for Needy Families program, $597 million below the 1 percent constitutional limit.

The Limit on the Growth of Certain Appropriations Article VIII, Section 22, limits the biennial rate of growth of appropriations from state revenue not dedicated by the Constitution to the estimated growth of the state's economy. In the 1998–99 biennium, appropriations from state taxes not dedicated by the Constitution were $38.9 billion, $825 million below that set by the Article VIII limit.

debt service
the amount of a budget spent by a government on paying interest on its debt

Limitation on Debt Payable from the General Revenue Fund Under a 1997 Amendment to Article III of the Texas Constitution, the legislature is prohibited from authorizing additional state debt if the resulting **debt service** from the general revenue exceeded 5 percent of the average amount of the General Revenue Fund revenue for the three preceding fiscal years. Going into the 1998–99 biennium, the debt service on outstanding debt as a percentage of unrestricted general revenue was 1.8 percent, well below the constitutional restriction.

THE BUDGETARY PROCESS

In theory, Texas has a "dual-budget" system. This means that responsibility for preparing an initial draft of the budget is shared by the governor and the legislature. In practice, the budget is the responsibility of the legislature.

Prior to 1949, there was little coordination in public budgeting. Financial procedures varied and state agencies were funded by individual appropriations. In 1949, a law passed establishing a ten-member Legislative Budget Board (LBB), whose primary job would be to recommend appropriations for all agencies of state government. The board is chaired by the lieutenant governor. The vice-chair is the speaker of the House. Other members include the chairs of the House Appropriations Committee, the House Committee on Ways and Means, the Senate Finance Committee, and the Senate State Affairs

Committee. Two additional members from the Senate and the House are chosen by the lieutenant governor and the Speaker, respectively.

The Legislative Budget Board appoints a budget director, who brings together budgeting requests from the various state agencies and prepares appropriation bills for them. Since 1973, the Legislative Budget Board has also been responsible for evaluating agency programs and developing estimates as to the probable costs of implementing legislation introduced in a legislative session. The LBB's draft budget, not the governor's, serves as the basis for final legislation.

The budgetary process involves two stages.[4] In the first stage, the Legislative Budgeting Board develops a draft budget based on requests supplied by state agencies. Hearings are conducted well before the legislature goes into session. Since 1992, each agency has been required to develop a five-year plan, which includes goals, objectives, strategies, and performance measures. This information provides the basis for LBB funding recommendations for each agency.

While the draft budgets are being prepared, the Comptroller's Office prepares the Biennial Revenue Estimate (BRE). The BRE is a detailed forecast of the total revenue that the state is expected to take in over the next two-year biennium. The comptroller effectively sets a ceiling on what the state legislature may spend. Although the legislature can override the comptroller's estimates with a four-fifths vote of each house, this has never happened. The BRE is updated when economic conditions change significantly and for special sessions of the legislature.

The second stage of the budget process involves the legislative process. Budgets are submitted to the House Appropriations Committee and the Senate Finance Committee. They then work their way through the committee system and are subject to hearings, debates, and revisions. If new revenue is called for, the bills must originate in the House and are generally referred to the House Ways and Means Committee. Fiscal notes that estimate a bill's effect on state finances are prepared by the LBB. These accompany bills through the legislative process and are revised when necessary. Final versions of the budget are prepared by the House Appropriations Committee and the Senate Finance Committee. Differences are reconciled in a conference committee.

The comptroller then formally "certifies" the budget. Certification means that the comptroller's office has analyzed the bill's contents and concluded that it is within the current revenue estimates. After certification, the budget moves on to the governor, who decides whether or not to veto certain items.

REVENUE IN TEXAS

Government and public policy in Texas is funded from a variety of sources, including sales tax, severance taxes on oil and natural gas produced in the state, licensing income, interest and dividends, and federal aid. In 1999, 49 percent of government revenues came from taxes of one sort or another. Many of these taxes are based on complex formulas. People often are unaware that they are paying them. But they are important sources of state revenue (see Table 28.1 on the next two pages).

Sales and Use Tax The most important single tax financing Texas government is the sales tax. Today, the sales tax in Texas is 6.25 percent of the retail sales price of tangible personal property and selected services. Together county, city,

Table 28.1 ANNUAL TEXAS STATE BUDGET BY YEAR AND REVENUE BY SOURCE (ROUNDED TO THE NEAREST MILLION $)

	1980		1985		1990		1995	
Sales tax	$2,521	(23.649%)	$4,192	(24.689%)	$7,589	(32.592%)	$10,259	(26.521%)
Oil production and regulation	$786	(7.373%)	$1,040	(6.125%)	$516	(2.216%)	$375	(0.969%)
Natural gas production tax	$734	(6.886%)	$1,123	(6.614%)	$568	(2.439%)	$512	(1.324%)
Motor fuels tax	$481	(4.512%)	$987	(5.813%)	$1,515	(6.506%)	$2,235	(5.778%)
Motor vehicle sales and rental	$438	(4.109%)	$895	(5.271%)	$1,092	(4.690%)	$1,788	(4.622%)
Corporation franchise	$341	(3.199%)	$856	(5.042%)	$587	(2.521%)	$1,423	(3.679%)
Cigarette and tobacco taxes	$322	(3.021%)	$374	(2.203%)	$432	(1.855%)	$639	(1.652%)
Alcoholic beverage tax	$200	(1.876%)	$333	(1.961%)	$335	(1.439%)	$407	(1.052%)
Insurance company taxes	$176	(1.651%)	$368	(2.167%)	$526	(2.259%)	$608	(1.572%)
Utility taxes	$112	(1.051%)	$210	(1.237%)	$198	(0.850%)	$241	(0.623%)
Inheritance tax	$76	(0.713%)	$148	(0.872%)	$131	(0.563%)	$172	(0.445%)
Hotel and Motel tax			$61	(0.359%)	$115	(0.494%)	$171	(0.442%)
Other taxes	$157	(1.473%)	$135	(0.795%)	$28	(0.120%)	$28	(0.072%)
Total Tax Revenue	$6,344	(59.512%)	$10,722	(63.149%)	$13,632	(58.544%)	$18,858	(48.751%)
Federal funds	$2,613	(24.512%)	$3,470	(20.437%)	$5,930	(25.467%)	$11,408	(29.492%)
Interest income	$536	(5.028%)	$1,001	(5.896%)	$1,340	(5.755%)	$1,715	(4.434%)
Licenses and fees	$478	(4.484%)	$933	(5.495%)	$1,590	(6.828%)	$3,768	(9.741%)
Contributions to employee benefits			$37	(0.218%)	$82	(0.352%)	$122	(0.315%)
Sales of goods and services			$152	(0.895%)	$138	(0.593%)	$173	(0.447%)
Land income	$550	(5.159%)	$526	(3.098%)	$279	(1.198%)	$201	(0.520%)
Settlement of claims			$3	(0.018%)	$16	(0.069%)	$6	(0.016%)
Other revenue sources	$139	(1.304%)	$135	(0.795%)	$278	(1.194%)	$769	(1.988%)
Net lottery proceeds							$1,662	(4.297%)
Total Revenue Other Sources	$4,316	(40.488%)	$6,257	(36.851%)	$9,653	(41.456%)	$19,824	(51.249%)
Total Net Revenue	$10,660		$16,979		$23,285		$38,682	

SOURCE: Texas Comptroller of Public Accounts, www.cpa.state.tx.us/misc/revenue.html.

and metropolitan transit authorities are authorized to impose an additional 2 percent sales and use tax. In 1999, the 6.25 percent sales and use tax accounted for over 27 percent of state revenues and over 55 percent of state tax revenues.

Oil Production and Regulation Taxes The oil severance tax is 4.6 percent of the market value of oil produced in the state. As late as 1980, the state took in $786 million in oil production taxes, over 6 percent of total state revenues. By 1999, this once vital revenue source had fallen to $211 million, only .44 percent of state revenues.

Natural Gas Production Tax There is a 7.5 percent tax on the market value of all natural gas produced in the state. As in the case of the oil production tax, revenues have fallen significantly from $734 million or 6.9 per-

ANNUAL TEXAS STATE BUDGET BY YEAR AND REVENUE BY SOURCE (ROUNDED TO THE NEAREST MILLION $)—CONTINUED

Table 28.1

1996		1997		1998		1999	
$10,791	(26.652%)	$11,340	(26.589%)	$12,459	(27.998%)	$13,069	(27.244%)
$377	(0.931%)	$429	(1.006%)	$304	(0.683%)	$211	(0.440%
$447	(1.104%)	$712	(1.669%)	$575	(1.292%)	$489	(1.019%)
$2,321	(5.733%)	$2,383	(5.587%)	$2,506	(5.632%)	$2,593	(5.405%)
$1,965	(4.853%)	$2,050	(4.807%)	$2,277	(5.117%)	$2,483	(5.176%)
$1,639	(4.048%)	$1,797	(4.213%)	$1,938	(4.355%)	$2,078	(4.332%)
$567	(1.400%)	$655	(1.536%)	$561	(1.261%)	$624	(1.301%)
$419	(1.035%)	$432	(1.013%)	$456	(1.025%)	$483	(1.007%)
$627	(1.549%)	$706	(1.655%)	$747	(1.679%)	$812	(1.693%)
$241	(0.595%)	$258	(0.605%)	$242	(0.544%)	$266	(0.555%)
$160	(0.395%)	$208	(0.488%)	$327	(0.735%)	$256	(0.534%)
$176	(0.435%)	$186	(0.436%)	$207	(0.465%)	$220	(0.459%)
$32	(0.079%)	$33	(0.077%)	$36	(0.081%)	$32	(0.067%)
$19,762	(48.810%)	$21,189	(49.681%)	$22,635	(50.866%)	$23,616	(49.231%)
$11,658	(28.794%)	$12,128	(28.436%)	$12,632	(28.387%)	$13,926	(29.031%)
$2,076	(5.127%)	$1,860	(4.361%)	$1,565	(3.517%)	$1,576	(3.285%)
$3,841	(9.487%)	$3,866	(9.064%)	$4,113	(9.243%)	$4,182	(8.718%)
$95	(0.235%)	$89	(0.209%)	$93	(0.209%)	$100	(0.208%)
$198	(0.489%)	$237	(0.556%)	$256	(0.575%)	$329	(0.686%)
$223	(0.551%)	$294	(0.689%)	$340	(0.764%)	$226	(0.471%)
$15	(0.037%)	$6	(0.014%)	$10	(0.022%)	$1,117	(2.329%)
$902	(2.228%)	$1,124	(2.635%)	$1,205	(2.708%)	$1,477	(3.079%)
$1,718	(4.243%)	$1,857	(4.354%)	$1,650	(3.708%)	$1,421	(2.962%)
$20,726	(51.190%)	$21,461	(50.319%)	$21,864	(49.134%)	$24,354	(50.769%)
$40,488		$42,650		$44,499		$47,970	

cent of state revenues in 1980 to $489 million or a little over 1 percent of state revenues.

Motor Fuels Tax The motor fuels tax in Texas is 20 cents per gallon of gasoline and diesel fuel. There is a 15 cents per gallon tax on liquefied gas. In 1999, the motor fuels tax took in approximately $2.6 billion, 5.4 percent of all state revenues.

Motor Vehicle Sales and Rentals and Manufactured Home Sales Tax There is a 6.25 percent tax on the sales price of all motor vehicles in the state. There is also a 10 percent tax on all rental vehicles up to thirty-five days and 6.25 percent thereafter. Newly manufactured homes are also taxed at 5 percent of 65 percent of the sales price. In 1999, these taxes took in $2.5 billion, 5.2 percent of total state revenues.

Sales tax is an important source of revenue for Texas. In 1999 it accounted for over 27 percent of total state revenues.

Corporate Franchise Tax Prior to 1991, the Franchise Tax applied only to the capital of a corporation. Service industries were taxed much more lightly than capital intensive industries like petrochemicals. In 1991, the legislature expanded this tax to apply to income or assets, making the tax something of a franchise and a corporate income tax. All domestic and foreign corporations, banks, savings and loans, and limited liability companies, unless specifically exempted, must pay the state $2.50 per $1,000 capital and the amount by which a tax of 4.5 percent on earned surplus exceeds the tax on capital. In 1999, the Corporate Franchise Tax took in a little over $2 billion, roughly 5.2 percent of state revenues.

Tobacco Taxes Texas imposes a variety of taxes on cigarettes and tobacco products. For example, every pack of twenty cigarettes has a 41-cent tax included in the purchase price. In 1999, $624 million came to the state in the form of taxes on tobacco products.

Alcoholic Beverage Taxes As with tobacco there are a variety of taxes imposed on alcoholic beverages. For example, beer is taxed at the rate of $6.00 per 31-gallon barrel. Liquor is taxed at the rate of $2.40 per gallon. Mixed drinks are taxed at 14 percent of gross receipts. This tax took in $483 million in 1999 and accounted for a little over 1 percent of state revenues.

Insurance Premium Taxes There is a complex schedule of tax rates applied to insurance premiums. For example, life, health, and accident insurance is taxed at the rate of 1.75 percent on gross premium receipts. For life insurance premiums, there is a half-rate applied to the first $450,000 in premiums. In 1999, insurance premium taxes came to $812 million or 1.7 percent of state revenue.

Utility Taxes There is a tax of one-sixth of 1 percent on the gross receipts of public utilities. For gas, electric, and water utilities there is a tax on gross receipts ranging from .581 percent in towns of less than 2,500 people, 1.07 percent in cities of between 2,500 and 9,999 people, and 1.997 percent in cities of 10,000 or more. There is also a tax on gas utility administration of half of 1 percent of the gross income of gas utilities.

Hotel and Motel Tax This state tax is 6 percent of the hotel and motel occupancy bill paid by the occupant. In 1999, $220 million were collected through the hotel and motel tax, approximately .5 percent of total state revenues.

Insurance Tax This state tax is equal to the amount of the federal credit that is imposed on the transfer of property at death. In 1999, the state insurance tax accounted for $256 million or .5 percent of total state revenues.

THE QUESTION OF THE INCOME TAX IN TEXAS

Many commentators have complained that the tax system in Texas is too **"regressive."**[5] By this they mean that the tax burden in the state falls more heavily upon lower income individuals. Sales and use taxes like those found in Texas are generally considered to be regressive. There have been occasional calls for the institution of a state income tax in Texas. Supporters argue that the income tax is not only a more reliable source of revenue for the state, but it can also be made fairer. Unlike sales and use taxes, which are equally applied to everyone whatever their income, income taxes can be made **"progressive."** A progressive income tax is one where people with lower income pay a lower tax rate than people of higher income. Progressive income taxes thus place a higher tax burden on the rich than they do on the poor.

progressive/regressive taxation
taxation that hits the upper income brackets more heavily (progressive) or the lower income brackets more heavily (regressive)

For the past forty years, few politicians were willing to support an income tax. One of the attractive features of Texas to business had always been the fact that there was no income tax. But in the early 1990s, the first serious attempt to put into place a state income tax was undertaken. Responding to mounting budgetary pressures, retiring Lieutenant Governor Bill Hobby came out in favor of an income tax in late 1989. Bob Bullock, Hobby's successor, announced in early 1991 that he would actively campaign for an income tax. A blue-ribbon panel chaired by former governor John Connally was charged with looking into new revenue sources for the state. The committee ended up recommending to the legislature both a corporate and a personal income tax but not without generating an enormous amount of controversy. Chairman Connally himself opposed the income-tax recommendations, as did Governor Ann Richards. By the 1993 legislative session Lieutenant Governor Bullock was backing off. Bullock proposed that a constitutional amendment be enacted requiring voter approval of any personal income tax. Moreover, it specified that funds raised under the personal income tax be used to support public education. The amendment quickly passed the 73rd legislature and was overwhelmingly approved by voters on November 2, 1993. Given the constitutional impediments, it is unlikely that Texans will have a personal income tax in the foreseeable future.[6]

E-COMMERCE AND STATE TAXES

The rapid expansion of the Internet (the World Wide Web) and the growth of electronic commerce (e-commerce) has raised serious questions for the future of tax policy in Texas and other states dependent upon a state sales tax. Consumer sales over the Internet are expected to grow from about $10 billion in 1998 to $100 billion in 2003. Business-to-business transactions are expected to grow from $43 billion to $1 trillion in 2003.[7] The problem is that most commercial transactions over the Internet escape state sales taxes.

In Texas, Internet sales are supposed to be treated like a mail-order sale. Companies physically located in Texas must collect the state sales tax. For example, Texans buying a computer or a book from a company located in Texas must pay the sales tax. However, they are not taxed if the company is located in another state. Instead, Texas consumers are supposed to pay a "use tax" on products purchased from out-of-state companies. The use tax is the same rate as the sales tax. The problem is that few people voluntarily pay or even know about the use tax. With the exception of expensive purchases that are easier to trace, the state has a difficult time collecting a use tax.

E-commerce thus presents state policy makers with two troubling issues. On the one hand, there is the economic development issue. Both traditional "brick and mortar" business and newly emerging Internet companies located in the state find themselves at a comparative disadvantage with businesses located in other states that sell to Texans over the Internet. Policy makers do not want to do anything that might impede Texas's businesses in e-commerce. On the other hand, there is the tax issue. Given the sales tax's central place in the state's tax system, policy makers cannot afford to let the sales tax be undermined without providing for some alternative source of revenue.

For now, the question of e-commerce and the sales tax remains a troubling one facing state policy makers. A national advisory commission was established to look into the problem for the U.S. Congress. Its report is due on October 1, 2001.

OTHER STATE REVENUE

matching funds
federal monies given to a state to match the state's funding on a joint program

Next to taxes, the second largest source of revenue for Texas is the federal government. Historically, Texas spends relatively little compared to other states for state-federal programs. As a result, the federal **matching funds** (federal monies going to a state based upon state spending for a program) also have been relatively low. Nevertheless, federal aid to Texas skyrocketed in the 1980s because of the expansion of transportation and human-services programs. In recent years, the growth of federal dollars going into the state has slowed down as welfare caseloads have fallen and Medicaid (health care financing for the poor) have grown less than expected. In 1999, over $13.9 billion, or 29 percent of state revenues came from Washington. This is up from 25.5 percent in 1990. Federal monies are concentrated in three areas: health care and human services, transportation funds, and education aid. In 1998, over $7.7 billion came from the federal government to support health care and human-services programs in Texas. The federal government sent $1.79 billion for education in the state, and $1.16 billion for transportation (see Table 28.2).

In addition to federal monies, there are a number of other revenue sources, including interest income, licenses and fees, the sales of goods and services provided by the state, and land income. Two other sources in recent years have

Table 28.2 FEDERAL REVENUE BY STATE AGENCY, 1998 (ROUNDED TO THE NEAREST MILLION $)

Texas Health and Human Services Commission	$6,347
Texas Department of Health	$457
Department of Human Services	$929
Texas Education Agency	$1,790
Texas Department of Transportation	$1,155
Texas Workforce Commission	$679
Department of Protective and Regulatory Services	$158
Texas Rehabilitation Commission	$237
Texas Department of Housing and Community Affairs	$192
All Other Agencies	$687
Total All Agencies	$12,631

SOURCE: *Texas Almanac 2000–2001* (Dallas: Dallas Morning News, 1999), p. 460.

THE LOTTERY IN TEXAS

Box 28.1

Attitudes about the appropriateness of using gambling as a source of state revenues are mixed. Some argue that the lottery unfairly takes money from people who can least afford to give it up by fooling them into thinking that they, too, can make it rich if they only have a little luck. However, there was overwhelming support for instituting the lottery as a source of state revenue. The lottery passed a November 1991 referendum, by a vote of 1,326,154 to 728,994. According to a study by the Texas Lottery Commission in 1998, playing the lottery does not appear to be limited to any one group or class, although some differences do emerge.

- Sixty-eight percent of Texans had purchased a lottery ticket in the previous year.
- Forty-two percent had played scratch-off games.
- Seventy-six percent of Texans between the ages of forty-six and sixty-four had played the lottery, but only 50 percent of those over sixty-five.
- Sixty-five percent of college graduates played the lottery, while only 57 percent of those with less than a high school education did.
- Seventy-two percent of individuals making over $50,000 a year played the lottery, while 64 percent of those making under $10,000 did.
- Approximately 71 percent of men and 64 percent of women played the lottery.

SOURCE: Dallas Morning News, *Texas Almanac 2000–2001* (Dallas: Dallas Morning News, 1999), p. 460.

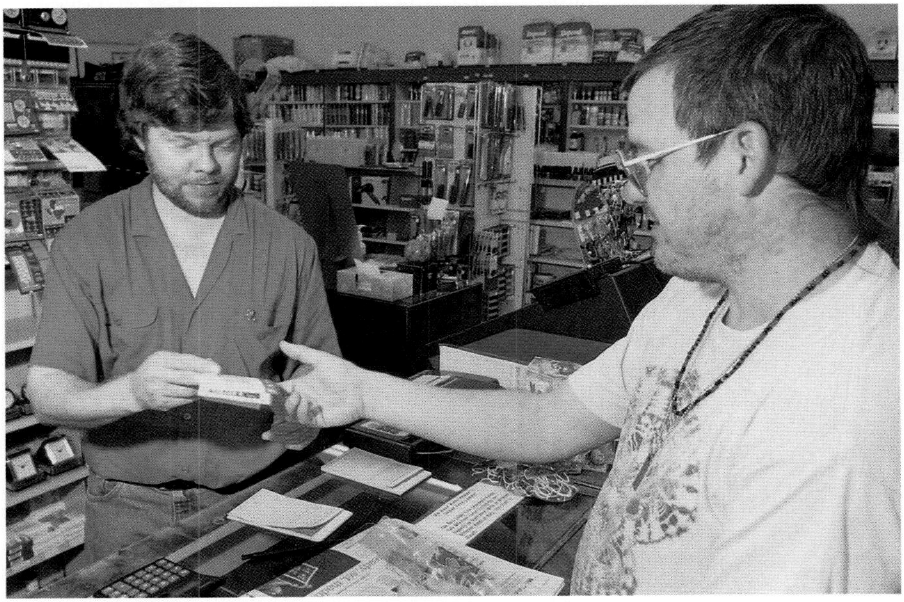

The lottery, approved by voters in 1991, generates over one billion dollars in state revenue each year.

had a major impact on monies flowing into the state budget. A state lottery was passed by the state legislature in July 1991 and approved by the voters in November. In 1992, the Texas lottery awarded $1.25 billion to players, while adding $657 million to state revenues. This rose to almost $1.65 billion in awards and $1.4 billion in state revenues in 1998. Despite its success, revenues generated by the lottery are still only 2.96 percent of the total state revenue.

A second major source of nontax revenue is a result of the settlement that the state reached with tobacco companies in 1999. Under the settlement, Texas will receive over $17.3 billion over the next twenty-five years, and an additional $580 million every year thereafter from the tobacco industry. The largest payment—$3.3 billion—comes up front, while the remainder will be spread out over the remaining twenty-five years. Nationwide, states received a total of $246 billion in the final settlement reached with the tobacco industry. The annualized payout from the tobacco settlement in Texas equals about 2 percent of the budget, approximately the same amount collected by cigarette taxes.[8]

EXPENDITURES IN TEXAS

In 1999, Texas government spent over $45.6 billion. The largest expenditure was on public education and higher education. In 1999, over $17.2 billion or almost 37.7 percent of the state budget went to education programs. Public edu-

Box 28.2 **WHERE IS THE TOBACCO MONEY GOING?**

Like other states participating in the tobacco settlement, Texas has formulated a strategy for spending the financial windfall. Some of the money that comes to Texas from the tobacco settlement has already been spent by the legislature. During the 1999 session, the legislature appropriated $180 million to the Children's Health Insurance Program (CHIP) to provide health insurance for 500,000 children eighteen years old or younger who are not eligible for Medicaid (health insurance provided by Texas and the federal government for the poor). The CHIP program is viewed by many as an investment of sorts, as the federal government will reimburse the state 74 cents for every state dollar spent on the program.

Most of the money, however, is going to a series of permanent endowment funds established for a variety of purposes. One group of thirteen funds totaling $595 million will be controlled by state universities and medical schools. A second made up of five funds totaling $474 million will be managed by the comptroller and go to programs relating to tobacco education and improving rural health-care facilities. A third group of funds capitalized with $420 million will be used by state medical schools and higher-education institutions. Finally, a local governments' permanent fund will be established with an initial capitalization of $1.05 billion that will rise to $2 billion. Most of the earnings from this fund will go directly to local entities such as public hospitals to reimburse them for unpaid health-care costs.

SOURCE: Texas Comptroller of Public Accounts, "Who Wants to Be a Billionaire? Texas Spending Tobacco Money on Health Care, Endowments," *Fiscal Notes* (January 2000), www.window.state.tx.us/comptrol/fnotes/fn0001/fna.html.

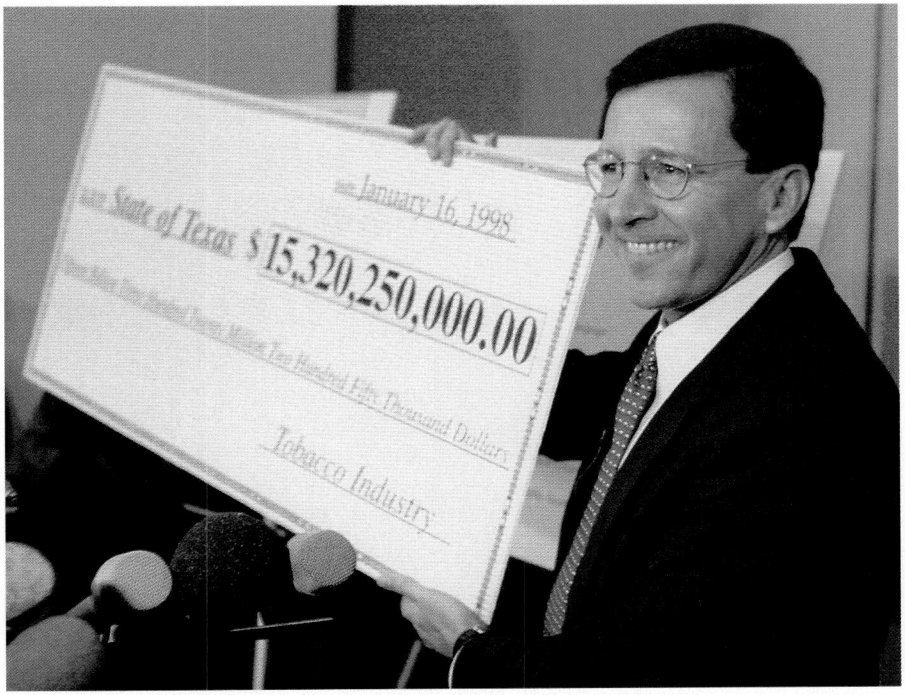

The money awarded by the Texas tobacco settlement is a major source of non-tax revenue for the state.

cation and higher education were followed closely by health and human services programs, which spent over $16 billion or approximately 35 percent of the state budget. Transportation was the third largest expenditure of the state budget, receiving over $3.7 billion or almost 8.2 percent of the state budget. Public safety and corrections programs were the fourth largest in terms of expenditures, taking up almost $2.9 billion or a little over 6.3 percent of the state budget. Total expenditures for the 1998–99 biennium stood at $88.9 billion (see Table 28.3 on the next page).

Curtailing government spending or even limiting increases in that spending is not an easy task. One of the charges launched by George W. Bush, in his race against Democratic incumbent Ann Richards in 1994, was her administration's inability to control rising state expenditures. During her four-year term in office state expenditures rose 47 percent. Bush pledged to stop this "explosive growth of state spending." This was easier said than done. According to a report by the *Dallas Morning News*, the Texas state budget continued to grow well into Bush's second term in office. Following the 1999 legislative session, the third under a Bush administration, it was shown that state spending had grown during the Bush years by 36 percent. The projected budget for the biennium 2000–2001 is for over $98 billion.

A number of factors lay behind the state spending increases. The cost of living had risen by 11 percent during the Bush years and the population had grown by 7 percent. In addition, new revenue had become available to the state through the tobacco settlement as well as through the federal government. The new revenues became tied to new expenditures. The Bush administration had supported the passage of tax cuts in Texas, in contrast to the tax increases that took place under the Richards administration. But the fact

Table 28.3 ANNUAL TEXAS STATE BUDGET BY YEAR AND EXPENDITURES BY FUNCTION, 1990–99 (ROUNDED TO THE NEAREST MILLION $)

	1990		1995		1996		1997		1998		1999	
General Government												
Executive departments	$953	(4.202%)	$1,298	(3.300%)	$1,257	(3.169%)	$1,283	(3.095%)	$1,371	(3.172%)	$1,433	(3.136%)
Legislative	$54	(0.238%)	$83	(0.211%)	$80	(0.202%)	$97	(0.234%)	$91	(0.211%)	$100	(0.219%)
Judicial	$72	(0.317%)	$92	(0.234%)	$104	(0.262%)	$111	(0.268%)	$124	(0.287%)	$132	(0.289%)
Total General Government	$1,079	(4.757%)	$1,473	(3.745%)	$1,442	(3.635%)	$1,491	(3.596%)	$1,586	(3.669%)	$1,665	(3.644%)
Health and human services	$5,657	(24.943%)	$13,540	(34.421%)	$13,593	(34.266%)	$15,026	(36.242%)	$14,700	(34.009%)	$16,043	(35.114%)
Public safety and corrections	$1,036	(4.568%)	$2,260	(5.745%)	$2,292	(5.778%)	$2,445	(5.897%)	$2,671	(6.179%)	$2,879	(6.301%)
Transportation	$2,582	(11.384%)	$2,741	(6.968%)	$3,364	(8.480%)	$3,021	(7.287%)	$3,292	(7.616%)	$3,718	(8.138%)
Natural resources and recreation	$250	(1.102%)	$953	(2.423%)	$666	(1.679%)	$712	(1.717%)	$733	(1.696%)	$740	(1.620%)
Education	$10,057	(44.343%)	$14,510	(36.886%)	$14,779	(37.256%)	$15,317	(36.944%)	$16,607	(38.421%)	$17,215	(37.679%)
Regulatory services	$157	(0.692%)	$166	(0.422%)	$171	(0.431%)	$174	(0.420%)	$184	(0.426%)	$188	(0.411%)
Lottery winnings paid			$454	(1.154%)	$381	(0.960%)	$430	(1.037%)	$388	(0.898%)	$324	(0.709%)
Employee benefits	$1,131	(4.987%)	$1,732	(4.403%)	$1,785	(4.500%)	$1,712	(4.129%)	$1,767	(4.088%)	$1,789	(3.916%)
Debt service	$315	(1.389%)	$463	(1.177%)	$526	(1.326%)	$553	(1.334%)	$529	(1.224%)	$479	(1.048%)
Capital outlay	$414	(1.825%)	$1,045	(2.657%)	$671	(1.691%)	$580	(1.399%)	$767	(1.774%)	$648	(1.418%)
Total Net Expenditures	$22,680		$39,337		$39,669		$41,460		$43,224		$45,688	

SOURCE: Texas Comptroller of Public Accounts, www.cpa.state.tx.us/misc/expend.html.

remained that, in the end, all the Bush administration could do was limit, and that only modestly, increases in state spending.

To understand better the pressures on government spending as well as the constraints and opportunities facing state governmental leaders, it is necessary to look more closely at three major areas of public policy in which the state is involved: crime and corrections, education, and public welfare.

Crime and Corrections Policy

- What is the history of the prison system in Texas?
- What are the important issues and trends regarding the incarceration of criminals in Texas?

HISTORY OF THE PRISON SYSTEM

Shortly after Texas joined the Union, construction was authorized for a state penitentiary in Huntsville. The 225-cell facility opened in 1849 and confined prisoners in single cells at night and congregated inmates during the day to work in silence. From 1870 to 1883, the entire prison system was leased to private contractors who used the labor of inmates in exchange for providing maintenance and security for prisoners. After 1883, convicts in the Texas prison system were leased to railroads, planters, and others who provided the prisoner with food, clothing, and a stipend to the state. These leasing arrangements were abandoned in 1910 due to scandals and abuses of the system.[9]

Although Texas moved to a state-run system, abuses continued. In 1924, for example, an investigation of the system found cruel and brutal treatment of prisoners, inefficient management, and inadequate care of inmates. That investigation led to the creation of a state prison board, which oversaw the work of a general prison manager. Still, however, the abuses continued. By the mid-1940s, the Texas prison system was considered one of the worst in the United States. In 1974, the Joint Committee on Prison Reform submitted findings to the legislature that were very critical of the Texas prison system. It criticized numerous aspects of the prison system's operation from living and working conditions for inmates to classification of inmates to medical care to staff training. Still nothing much happened.[10]

The event that had the most dramatic effect on the operation of the Texas prison system in modern times was a federal court case, *Ruiz v. Estelle*.[11] Lawsuits filed by prisoners are nothing new. During the tenure of W. J. Estelle, Jr., the prison director from 1973–83 and the defendant in the *Ruiz* case, prisoners filed 19,696 cases in the federal courts, a caseload amounting to about 20 percent of the federal court docket during that period.[12] However, the *Ruiz* case was exceptional. It was a class action on behalf of inmates, which initially began in 1972, and it focused on issues of crowding in the system, security and supervision, health care, discipline, and access to the courts. In 1980, the federal court concluded that there had been a violation of inmates' constitutionally guaranteed rights, and Texas joined several other states in having its prison system declared unconstitutional.

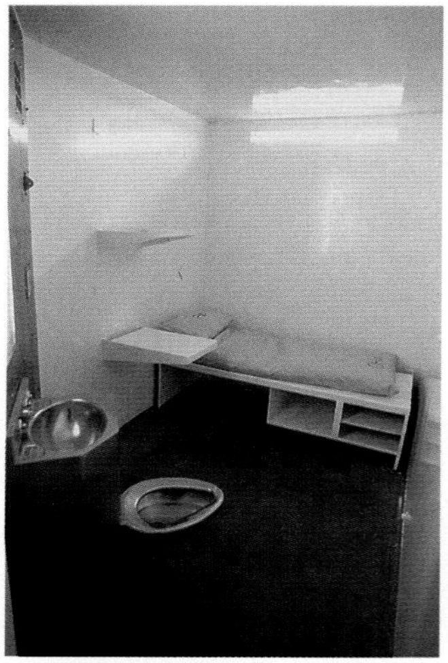

A new death row cell in Huntsville. After *Ruiz v. Estelle* in 1980, federal courts mandated vast improvements in Texas's prisons.

The result was the appointment by the court of a special master, a court officer, to oversee the Texas prison system to eliminate the constitutional problems such as overcrowding, improper supervision of inmates, and improper care of inmates. It was a massive reform of the system, one that had to be imposed from without—from the federal courts—since the state seemed unwilling or unable to reform its own prison system. That court oversight of the prison system may end in 2001. A federal appeals court is currently considering Texas's request to end the involvement of federal courts in the prison system's operation.

For a long time, many in Texas government were resistant to federal court supervision of the prison system, arguing, for example, that the *Ruiz* decision involved federal court judicial activism and was an interference with the rights of the state. In order to reduce the overcrowding in state prisons to comply with *Ruiz*, the decision also encouraged the early release of prisoners who then re-entered society and committed further crimes. *Ruiz* did, however, help to turn the criminal justice system into a major public policy issue in Texas.

TEXAS CRIME AND CORRECTIONS

It has long been claimed that Texas does things in a big way and that is certainly true of its levels of crime and the way it deals with criminals. In the 1998–99 biennium, there were 138,635 adults incarcerated in the state's correctional institutions and another 163,648 adult felony offenders on probation. There were also 2,943 juveniles incarcerated in state institutions. These numbers exclude those incarcerated in municipal and county facilities. Texas keeps building more and more jails to house its criminal-offender population. In the 1998–99 biennium alone, bond funding was provided for an additional 5,440 state prison beds. A total of $7,036.4 million was expected to be spent

Figure 28.1 TEXAS PRISON COSTS (IN MILLIONS OF $)

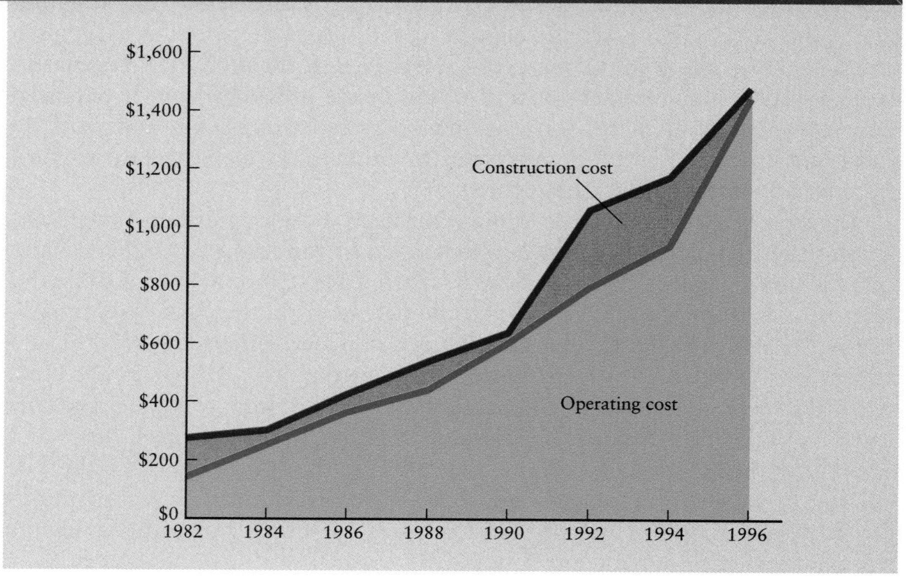

out of the state budget alone for the 1998–99 biennium for public safety and criminal justice.[13]

Texas incarcerates far more criminals than does any other state, although in 1997 only 22 percent of supervised offenders were in prison or in state jails. The remainder were on parole or probation. It is, of course, expensive to incarcerate an offender. It costs about $39 a day to keep an inmate in prison and only about $2 a day to supervise an offender on parole. Figure 28.1 shows the dramatic increases in the costs of prison construction and prison maintenance in Texas over time. Operating costs of Texas prisons moved from $147 million in 1982 to $609 million in 1990 to $1,446 million in 1996. While there has been a steady increase in prison operating costs, prison construction costs have varied from year to year. In 1982, $126 million was spent on prison construction, but in 1990 only $24 million was spent. The greatest period of prison construction was from 1991 through 1995. During those years, $1,375 million was spent on prison construction.[14]

However, in recent years the state government has significantly increased the incarceration of offenders by building more prisons. From 1976 to 1990, the rate of property crime in Texas rose 38 percent and the violent crime rate rose 113 percent. During the same time period, prison expansion did not keep up with the increase in the crime rate. Instead, generous early-release policies were used to move prisoners out of prison to allow room for newly convicted prisoners. With prison expansion, however, early-release polices were reduced. In 1990, for example, 38,000 prisoners were given early release from prison; however, even with a much larger prison population in 1997, only a little more than 28,000 prisoners were given early release.[15]

As is shown by Figure 28.2, the Texas prison population has soared, especially since about 1992. In 1980, at the time of *Ruiz*, the Texas prison population consisted of fewer than 30,000 inmates. A decade later, in 1990, there

TEXAS INMATE POPULATION, 1980–97 **Figure 28.2**

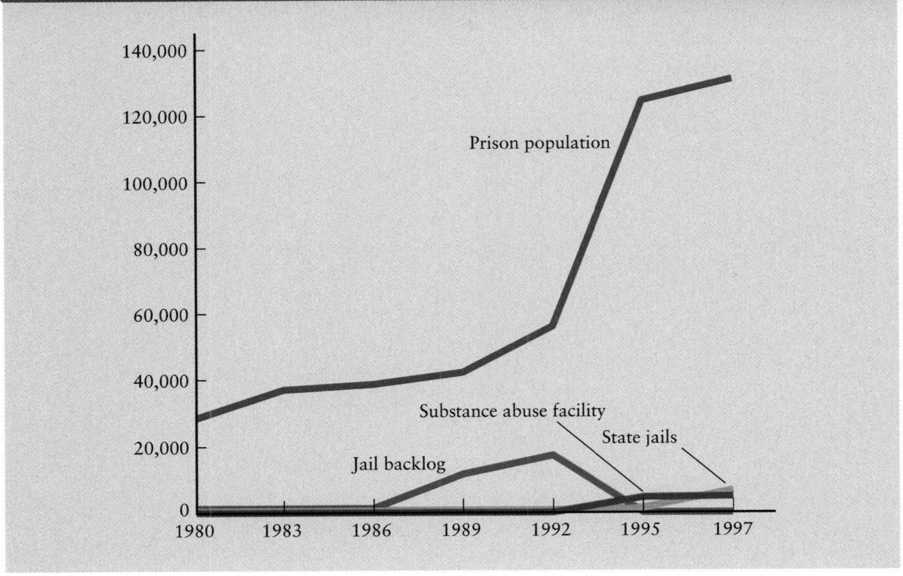

were slightly more than 49,000 inmates in Texas prisons and another 6,439 in jail awaiting transfer to state prison. Only seven years later, there were almost 130,000 inmates in state prisons. While there was no backlog of prisoners in jails awaiting transfer, there were 6,288 additional inmates in state jails and another 4,569 prisoners in substance abuse facilities. Put another way, there were 4.9 inmates in state correctional facilities in 1997 for every inmate in state correctional facilities in 1980.[16]

For much of the 1980s the rate of violent and property crime in Texas was higher than the national average. By the mid-1990s, however, those rates of crimes were close to the rates for the nation as a whole. It may be argued that the reduction in the crime rate is caused by the increased incarceration of offenders.[17] There may also be other causes, however, such as an improved economy in the 1990s. Others have suggested demographic change determines the size of the prison population. The most prison prone group in society are males between the ages of twenty and twenty-nine. If that demographic group is large, then one would expect the prison population to also be large.[18] Indeed, 94 percent of Texas prisoners are male and 34.4 percent of the prison population is between the ages of twenty and twenty-nine.[19] Of course, changes in laws and treatment practices also affect the crime rate and the incarceration rate. Long sentences for habitual criminals, for example, are relatively new as are long sentences for the use of a firearm in the commission of a crime.[20] Interestingly, Texas's rate of incarceration of offenders is far higher than other urban states and far higher than the national average, even though its crime rates are at about the level of the national average. Figure 28.3 shows that the number of prison inmates per 100,000 population in Texas in January 1994 was 539. The national average was 370. No state comes close to Texas in its rate of incarceration of criminals. The next closest rate of incarceration is Georgia, which incar-

Figure 28.3 PRISON INMATES PER 100,000 POPULATION, 1994

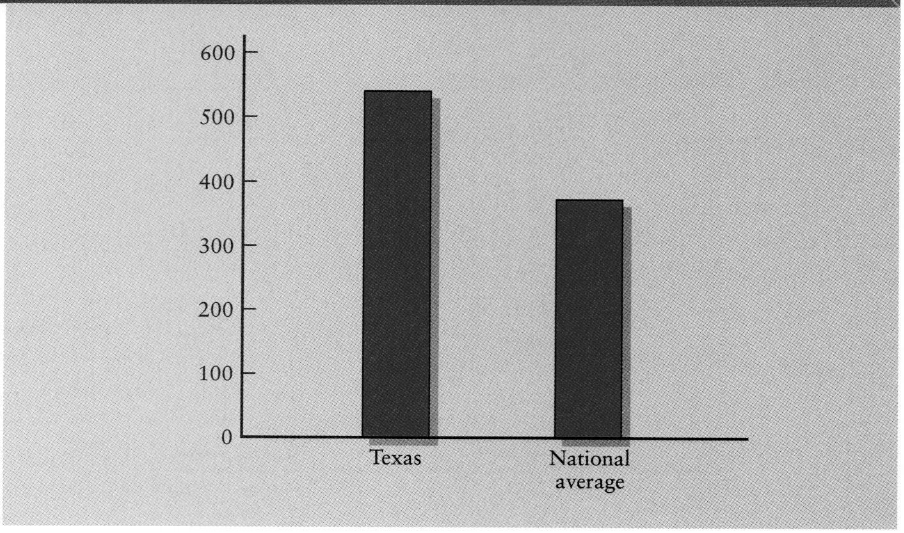

cerates 432 per 100,000 population and Michigan, which incarcerates 405. California and New York, the closest states in population to Texas, incarcerate 369 per 100,000 population and 359 per 100,000, respectively.[21]

As Figure 28.4 shows, Texas does imprison mostly violent offenders. In August 1997, 43 percent of Texas inmates had been convicted of violent offenses and 27 percent had been convicted of property offenses. Twenty-three percent of the inmate population was convicted of drug offenses. Whether imprisonment for drug offenses is an appropriate remedy for the drug problem is, of course, a debatable point, but it is interesting that more than one in five people in Texas prisons are there because of drugs.[22]

During the administration of Governor Ann Richards, there was recognition that very large proportions of prisoners were involved with alcoholism, drug addiction, and drug-related crimes.[23] Some effort was made to create alcohol and drug abuse treatment programs within the prison system to help alleviate these problems, although these problems remain severe.

In Texas, however, there is little indication that there will be a change in prison policies. In spite of the great expense associated with incarcerating prisoners, Texans seem to support a "tough on crime" approach that is much harsher than that of the rest of the nation. The result is that we may expect continued high levels of incarceration, continued prison construction, and higher and higher costs for prison building and maintenance.

Education Policy in Texas

- What is the history of public education in Texas?
- What are the most important issues that have shaped education policy in Texas over the past fifty years? Have these issues been resolved?

PRISON POPULATION BY OFFENSE, AUGUST 1997 — **Figure 28.4**

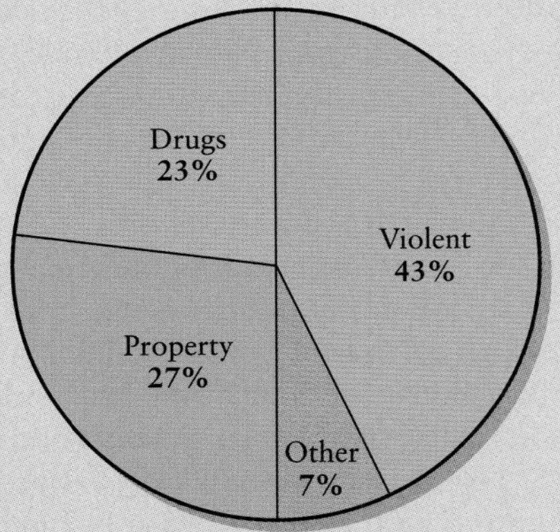

The debate over public education in Texas extends back to the break with Mexico.[24] One of the indictments of the Mexican regime contained in the Texas Declaration of Independence was that the government had failed to establish a public system of education. Although the Constitution of the Republic of Texas mandated Congress to establish a public system of education, a bill actually establishing a public school system did not pass the legislature until 1854. Public education was to be financed with a special school fund funded with $2 million of the $10 million given to Texas by the United States government upon admission to the Union to settle outstanding land claims on parts of what is now New Mexico, Colorado, and Oklahoma. Unfortunately, the fund was used for a variety of other purposes in the following years, including the purchase of railroad stock and the building of prisons. When Democrats returned to power following Reconstruction, an effort was made to protect the fund and commit its use solely to education. Under the Constitution of 1876, the Special School Fund became the Permanent School Fund and restrictions were placed upon how the money could be used and invested.[25] Provisions were also made in the Constitution of 1876 to support public education through one-fourth of the occupation tax, a $1 poll tax, and local taxation.

Throughout much of the late nineteenth and early twentieth centuries, public education remained largely a local affair. Many of the school systems were chronically short of funds, finding themselves facing such problems as a shortage of supplies and textbooks, inadequate facilities, and poorly trained teachers. In 1949, the state legislature tried to address some of these problems by passing the **Gilmer-Aikin Laws.** Under the Gilmer-Aikin Laws, school districts were consolidated into 2,900 administrative units, state equalization funding was provided to supplement local taxes, teacher salaries were raised, and a minimum school year was established. In addition, the laws established the Texas Education Agency to supervise public education in the state.

Gilmer-Aikin Laws

education reform legislation passed in 1949 that equalized funding across the state, raised teachers' salaries, mandated a minimum length for the school year, and provided more supervision over public education

The Gilmer-Aikin Laws also established bureaucratic institutions responsible for public education in the state. Previously, public education had been run by a nine-member State Board of Education that was appointed by the governor for six-year terms and an elected state superintendent of public instruction. This was replaced by an elected twenty-one-member board from each of the congressional districts in Texas. The State Board of Education became the policy-making body for public education in the state, adopting budgets, establishing regulations for school accreditation, executing contracts for the purchase of textbooks, and investing in the Permanent School Fund. The board also had the power to appoint a commissioner of education, subject to confirmation by the Texas Senate. The commissioner of education served a four-year term and became the chief executive officer for the State Department of Education, later renamed the Texas Education Agency (TEA). The TEA was responsible for setting standards for public schools, for supervising the public schools of the state, and for handling federal funds related to public education. For the next fifty years, educational policy in the state would work through the institutional framework established by the Gilmer-Aikin Laws.[26]

Since 1949, the State Board of Education has undergone occasional restructuring. Membership was expanded to twenty-four members in 1973 and to twenty-seven in 1981. Following a special legislative session, the board became a fifteen-member appointed body in 1984. But in 1988, it reverted back to an elected body composed of fifteen members serving four-year terms.

Three issues have played a major role in shaping educational policy over the last fifty years: desegregation, equity in funding, and promoting excellence in education.

DESEGREGATION

Few issues have troubled educational policy in Texas as much as desegregation. Segregation of the races was provided for under the Texas Constitution of 1876. In *Plessy v. Ferguson* (1896), the U.S. Supreme Court upheld the validity of segregated schools through the now infamous "separate but equal" doctrine. In Texas, as elsewhere across the South, segregated schools may have been separate, but they were far from equal. In the 1920s and 1930s, for example, the length of the school term for black schools was only about four days shorter than that for white schools, but Texas spent an average of $3.39 less per student (about one-third less) on the education of African American students than on white students.[27]

The United States Supreme Court overturned *Plessy v. Ferguson* in the 1954 case *Brown v. Board of Education,* ruling that segregated schools violated the equal protection clause of the Fourteenth Amendment. Schools districts were ordered to desegregate their schools systems "with all due speed." In some cases, "all due speed" was quite quick. The San Antonio school district, for example, became one of the first school districts in the nation to comply with the Supreme Court's order. Other school districts in the state, such as Houston's, were much slower in implementing the court's desegregation ruling.

The desegregation of public schools was hampered further by hostile political opposition at both the local and state levels. In 1957, the Texas state legislature passed laws encouraging school districts to resist federally ordered desegregation, although then governor Price Daniel, Sr. chose to ignore such laws.[28] By the 1960s, legally segregated schools were a thing of the past. Nevertheless, **de facto** segregation remained a problem, particularly in urban areas with large minority populations. As in many other urban areas across the country, a large number of middle and upper income whites in Texas abandoned urban public school systems for suburban public schools or private schools.

de facto
literally, "by fact"; practices that occur even when there is no legal enforcement, such as school segregation in much of the United States today

EQUITY IN THE PUBLIC SCHOOL SYSTEM

Federal court cases like *Brown v. Board of Education* played a major role in shaping educational policy regarding the desegregation of schools. Two other important court cases played a major role in shaping education policy and politics in Texas over the last thirty years: *Rodriguez v. San Antonio ISD* and *Edgewood v. Kirby.*

Rodriguez v. San Antonio *Rodriguez v. San Antonio ISD* was a landmark case involving the constitutionality of using property taxes to fund public schools.[29] At the heart of the case lay the question of the equitable funding of public schools. Lawyers for Rodriguez and seven other children in the poor Edgewood school district argued that the current system of financing public schools in Texas was unfair. The Edgewood school district had one of the highest property tax rates in the country, but could raise only $37 per pupil.

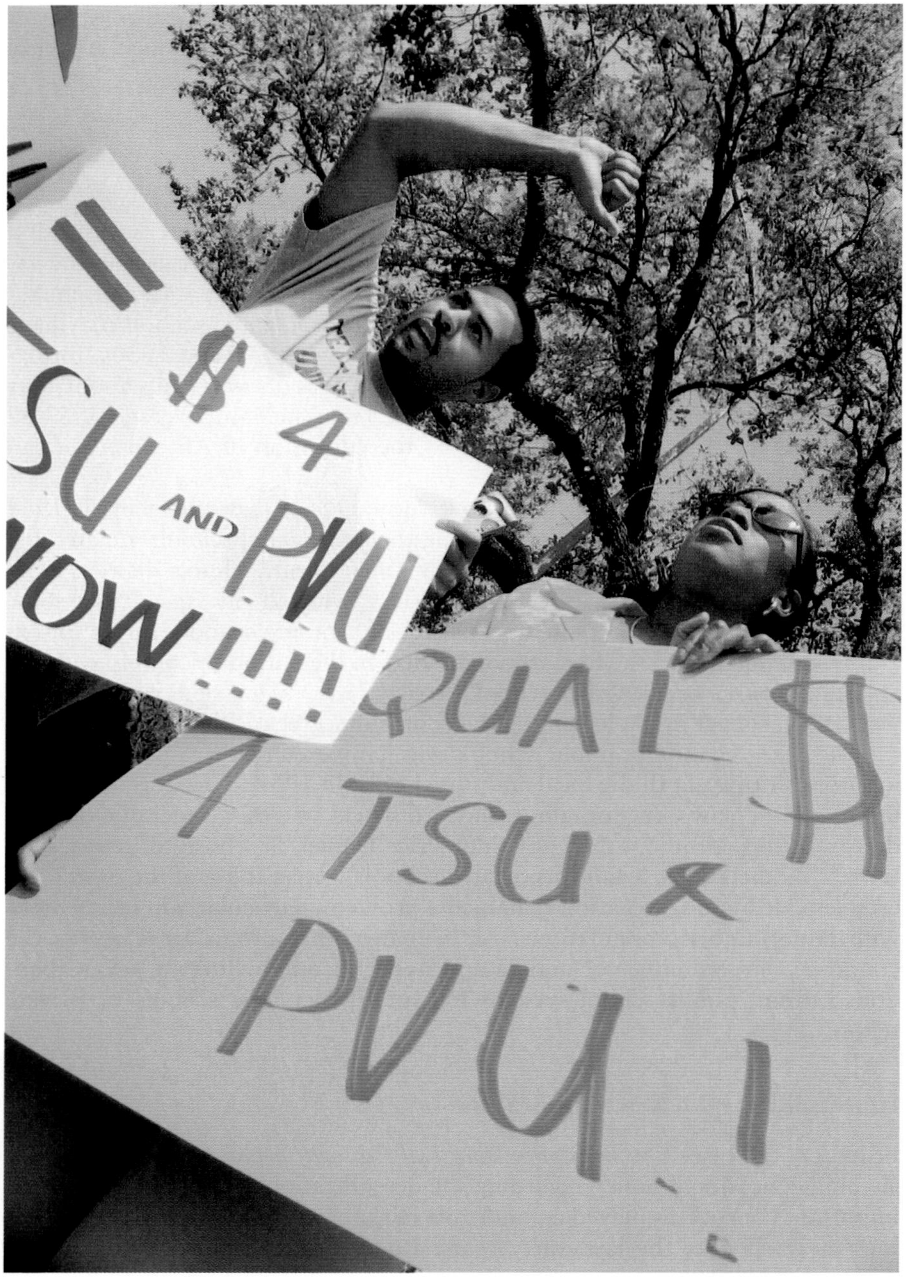

Texas Southern University students demonstrate to highlight the funding discrepancies between Texas Southern and the University of Houston.

Meanwhile the neighboring school district of Alamo Heights was able to raise $413 per pupil with a much lower property tax rate. The difference was that the value of the property subject to taxation in Alamo Heights far exceeded that in Edgewood. Equalizing educational funding would require Edgewood to tax at the rate of $5.76 per $100 property value while Alamo Heights could tax at a rate of $0.68 per $100 property value.

A three-judge federal district court was impaneled to hear the case in January 1969. The district court initially delayed action, giving the 1971 Texas legislature time to address the funding issue. When the legislature failed to address the issue during its regular session, the court took action. On December 23, 1971, it ruled that the Texas school finance system was unconstitutional under the **equal protection clause** of the Fourteenth Amendment of the U.S. Constitution. However, on appeal to the U.S. Supreme Court, the decision was overturned. On March 21, 1973, the Supreme Court ruled 5–4 that states such as Texas were not required to subsidize poorer school districts under the equal protection clause of the Constitution. The question of equity in public school funding would have to be addressed later in terms of Texas's state constitution and in Texas courts.

equal protection clause
provision of the Fourteenth Amendment guaranteeing citizens "the equal protection of the laws." This clause has served as the basis for the civil rights of African Americans, women, and other groups

Edgewood v. Kirby The second landmark case involving the financing of public schools was *Edgewood ISD v. Kirby.* Unlike *Rodriguez, Edgewood* considered the equity of funding public schools by the existing property tax system in terms of the Texas state constitution. Much of the litigation over the next few years would center around Article 7, Section 1, of the 1876 Constitution, which read:

> A general diffusion of knowledge being essential to the preservation of the liberties and rights of the people, it shall be the duty of the Legislature of the State to establish and make suitable provision for the support and maintenance of an efficient system of free public schools.

A key constitutional issue would be exactly what constituted an "efficient system of free public schools."

On behalf of the Edgewood Independent School District, the Mexican American Legal Defense and Education Fund (MALDEF) sued William Kirby, the State Commissioner of Education, on May 23, 1984. Initially only eight districts were represented in the case. By the time the case was finally decided, sixty-seven other school districts had joined the original plaintiffs in the case. The plaintiffs argued that the state's reliance on local property taxes to fund public education discriminated against poor children by denying them equal opportunities in education. A month after the original case was filed, the legislature passed House Bill 72, a modest reform measure that increased state aid to poor districts. In 1985, plaintiffs filed an amended lawsuit, arguing that the legislature's action was far from satisfactory.

The amended case was heard early in 1987 by a state district judge, who ruled on April 29, 1987, in favor of the plaintiffs. He found the state's system for financing public education unconstitutional, violating both the "equal protection" (Article 1, Section 3) and "efficient system" (Article 7, Section 1) clauses of the Texas Constitution. The judge called for the institution of a new system of public school funding by September 1989.

In a 2–1 vote, a state appeals court reversed this decision in December 1988, finding that the funding system was constitutional. Appealing this decision to the Texas Supreme Court, plaintiffs finally won on July 5, 1989. In a 9–0 decision, the Texas Supreme Court held that the funding system was, indeed, in violation of the state constitution. The court held that education was a fundamental right under the Texas Constitution and that the "glaring disparities" between rich and poor schools violated the efficiency clause of the constitution. In its ruling the court did not demand "absolute equality" in per pupil spending. But it did require a standard of "substantially equal access to similar revenues per pupil at similar levels of tax effort."[30] It ordered the legislature to implement an equitable system by the 1990–91 school year.

The Supreme Court's ruling touched off a political firestorm that would sweep through Texas politics throughout the early 1990s. The legislature failed to pass appropriate legislation in four special sessions called to address the funding problem. Finally, on June 1, 1990, a master appointed by the Texas Supreme Court announced an equity financing plan that would be implemented if the legislature failed to develop one of its own. Essentially the plan called for wealthy school districts to transfer funds to poorer districts in order to equalize funds available to all public schools across the state. The so-called "Robin Hood" plan finally shook the legislature into action. During a sixth special session, the legislature passed Senate Bill 1 (SB 1), which, among other things, implemented funding adjustments to further assist poor school districts. Significantly, the bill did not restrict the ability of wealthier districts to enrich themselves through their higher property tax bases.

The new system of funding was found to be unconstitutional by a state district court in a case that came to be known as *Edgewood II*. The Supreme Court upheld the lower court ruling, arguing that SB 1 failed to restructure the overall funding system. The court was particularly critical of the ability of wealthy school systems to accumulate funds outside the system and hinted that a solution might lie in the creation of consolidated countywide tax bases. The legislature responded by passing Senate Bill 351 (SB 351), creating 188 "county education districts," which would equalize wealth across districts by broadening the tax base. Property taxes funding schools were to be collected by both the county education district and the local school district.

This time wealthier districts challenged the legislative initiatives to settle the equity problem in public schools. In January 1992, the state Supreme Court held 7–2 in *Edgewood III* that SB 351 violated two constitutional provisions: first, it had failed to get the required local voter approval of school property tax levies (Article 7, Section 3). Second, it had violated Article 7, Sections 1–3, which had prohibited a state property tax since 1980. Interestingly, the court did not rule on the nature of the tax itself or whether it adequately addressed the equity question. The state was given until June 1993 to devise a new system for funding public education that was equitable and constitutional.

The legislature met in special session and during regular session in an attempt to meet the court-imposed deadline. A constitutional amendment to allow for a statewide property tax was put before the voters on May 1, 1993, and soundly defeated. The legislature responded by quickly passing Senate Bill 7. The key difference between SB 7 and earlier attempts to address the equity issue was its equalization and recapture provisions. Seeking to redress the imbalance between wealthier and poorer districts, the bill set a $280,000 cap on the per student taxable property value base in all districts. Districts with property values exceeding this limit had to choose one of a variety of methods to reduce their taxable wealth. Among these methods were consolidating with a poorer district, ceding property tax base to another poorer district, writing a check to the state, partnering with a poorer district, and consolidating with one or more other districts.

Senate Bill 7 was challenged in *Edgewood IV*, but was upheld as being constitutional by the state Supreme Court. The court noted that additional work

Politics on the Web

Often the key to public policy making is acquiring control over information. One who controls the flow of information about a policy issue can often define what a particular policy problem is and how it should be considered in the policy making process. The Internet makes it increasingly difficult for individuals to control the flow of information. It places in the hands of the average citizen policy reports and data that used to be available only to professional policy experts. Indeed, the problem facing policy makers and citizens alike in the age of the Internet might not be getting enough information, but information overload. How is information provided over the Internet going to be used to understand and address policy problems? How are we to differentiate good information from bad, or insightful policy reports from hack jobs? Learning to utilize properly the vast new information resources available may be one of the greatest problems facing policy makers and concerned citizens alike in the information age.

www.wwnorton.com/wtp3e

The Edgewood cases challenged the property tax–based funding system that made for inferior facilities and impoverished resources for schools in poor districts while schools in wealthy districts thrived.

was still needed on equalizing and improving school facilities across the state. These concerns were addressed by the legislature in the 1995 legislative session. Although it took seven years, the public school system in Texas was at last in compliance with the demands of the state constitution.

The struggle to rework the funding mechanism for public education was only one dimension of educational policy in Texas in the 1980s and 1990s. Concerns over the quality of education in the state and how best to promote educational excellence also helped to redefine educational policy in the late twentieth century.

EDUCATIONAL EXCELLENCE AND ACCOUNTABILITY IN TEXAS

The equity issue in public education had been touched off by litigation. Only when forced by the courts to rethink how schools were being funded was the legislature finally willing to act. A different set of factors has driven the debate over education excellence and accountability.

The issue of education reform came to a head in the early 1980s in Texas. The Texas debate was actually part of a larger national debate over the state of education in the United States.[31] A 1983 report by the National Commission on Excellence in Education, *A Nation at Risk,* identified a number of crises that were beginning to grip the nation's educational system. Test scores were declining and functional illiteracy was on the rise. Students were simply not equipped with the intellectual skills that were required in the modern world. If something were not done soon to reform education in the United States, the report argued, the nation was at risk of falling behind other competitors in the rapidly changing world of international competition.[32]

Educational reform was put on the state agenda when at the end of the 1983 regular session the legislature established the Select Committee on Public Education (SCOPE). Earlier in the session Democratic Governor Mark White had hoped to put into place a commission that he could appoint concerned with the narrow issue of pay raises for teachers. What he got, as Clark D. Thomas has noted, was something very different. SCOPE was created as a twenty-two-member committee to which the governor would have only five appointments.[33] The remaining seats were filled by appointments made by the House and Senate leadership and by three members of the State Board of Education. The intent of the legislature in creating SCOPE was not just to figure out how to fund pay raises for teachers but to evaluate the entire system of public education in the state.

One of the most important decisions made by Governor White was deciding that Dallas businessman Ross Perot should chair the committee. Perot had supported White's opponent in the 1982 gubernatorial race. It was felt that his participation in the process would help broaden support for the committee across party lines as well as bring in needed support from the business community. At the time of his selection, however, few knew how important Perot would be to the process of educational reform. To the surprise of many, Perot took an active role in SCOPE, mobilizing the committee in private and public to take on what he saw to be abuses in the public education system. Perot was particularly scornful of athletic programs and what he saw to be the misplaced priorities of the existing educational system. In the end SCOPE presented 140 recommendations for reforming the education system in Texas in its final report on April 19, 1984. Among the most controversial of the proposed reforms was "no pass, no play." Students who failed to earn a passing grade of 70, raised from 60, would be unable to participate in any extracurricular activities for the next grading period of six weeks. But "no pass, no play" was only the tip of the iceberg. Among other reform proposals were the setting of new standards for students' attendance and performance, the development of annual performance reports and the tightening of accreditation standards, the cutting off of state funds to schools that could not meet those standards, the lengthening of the school year from 175 to 180 days, and the development of a professional career ladder for teachers, tying pay raises to performance.[34] Many of the reform proposals were put into place in a 266-page education reform bill and the necessary accompanying tax increases in early July 1984.

The so-called "Perot reforms" were but the first round in the debate over excellence and accountability in the public school system. A second round opened during the 1995 legislative session. There were some important differences in the reform package finally signed by Republican Governor George W. Bush. The Perot reforms had generally tended to centralize control over education policy in the state. The Bush reforms, in contrast, gave more discretion to local school districts to achieve the educational goals being mandated by the state. Some of the reforms put through were symbolic. The controversial "no pass, no play" rule was relaxed, cutting the period of nonparticipation from six to three weeks and lifting a ban on practicing while on scholastic probation. But other changes were more substantive. Local control of public schools was increased by limiting the power of the Texas Education Agency. Local voters were empowered to adopt home charters that could free their school districts from many state requirements, including class-size caps at lower grades. The 1995 reforms also enabled students, under certain circumstances, to transfer from low-performing schools to high-performing schools in their districts, thus promoting competition among the schools by holding them accountable for the performance of their students.[35]

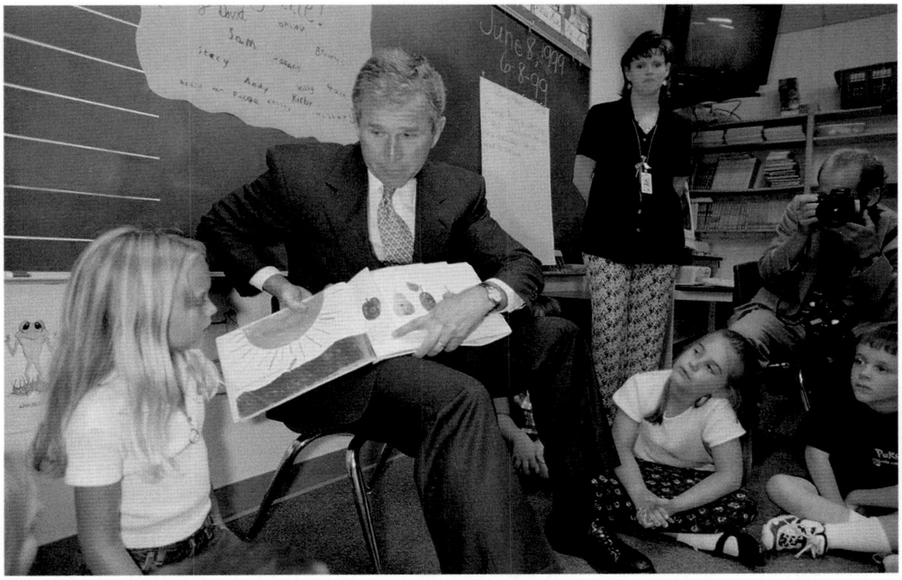

Governor Bush reads *The Very Hungry Caterpillar* to a first-grade class after a symbolic signing of several education reform bills.

Reforming public schools remained high on the legislative agenda during the 1999 legislative session. Calling public schools the number one funding priority of the 1999 legislative session, Governor Bush signed into law a \$3.8 billion school plan that provided for a \$3,000 teacher raise as well as \$1.35 billion in school property tax cuts. In addition, the bill sought to curb social promotion (advancement to the next grade regardless of classroom performance) and to create incentives for school districts to expand kindergarten and pre-kindergarten programs.[36] The booming economy of the 1990s was enabling state politicians to have their cake and eat it, too, something politicians in the 1980s would have thought unimaginable.

EDUCATION POLICY IN PERSPECTIVE

It is probably too early to judge whether or not the reforms instituted in the 1980s and 1990s have been successful in improving the overall equity and excellence of public education in Texas. Statistics taken from the mid-1990s suggested that the state still had a long way to go in turning its public school system into one of the best in the nation. In 1995, Texas led the nation in the number of public school districts (1,044) and number of public school teachers (240,207). Texas ranked fifteenth among the states in terms of education spending as a percentage of all state and local expenditures. But overall state expenditures in Texas are low, and other disturbing numbers indicate that all may not be well. The high-school dropout rate in Texas in 1990 was 12.5 percent of all sixteen- to nineteen-year-olds, eleventh in the nation. The pupil-teacher ratio in public schools was 15.7 to 1, thirty-first in the nation. Per capita state spending in 1996 was \$448, thirty-sixth in the nation, while the average classroom teacher salary stood at \$32,000, thirty-fifth in the nation. Reforming education with a concern for equity and excellence will continue to be a major policy issue in the state well into the twenty-first century.

Welfare Policy

- What is the nature of poverty in Texas? How have welfare policies sought to remedy it?
- In the past ten years, what attempts have been made to reform the welfare system? How successful have these attempts been?

POVERTY IN TEXAS

Poverty has never been a popular subject in Texas. The idea that there are individuals who have trouble taking care of themselves or meeting the basic needs of their families seems to fly in the face of Texas's individualistic culture. Given the booming Texas economy of the late 1990s, one might hope that the poverty problem would go away. It hasn't. Between 1988 and 1997, the percentage of Texans living in poverty fell from 18.01 percent to 16.75 percent, but it rose again in 1998 to 17.8 percent. The absolute number of people living in poverty fluctuated from 3,005,548 in 1988 to 2,964,658 in 1991, but rose again to 3,296,780 in 1997 and 3,497,098 in 1998.[37] Despite the economic boom fostered by the age of high tech, poverty remains one of the most intractable problems facing the state.

Policy makers define poverty in very specific terms. Poverty is the condition under which individuals or families do not have the resources to meet their basic needs, including food, shelter, health care, transportation, and clothing. The U.S. Department of Health and Human services developed a "poverty index" in 1964. This index was revised in 1969 and 1980. The index calculates the consumption requirements of families based on their size and composition. The poverty index is adjusted every year to account for the rate of inflation. Although there is considerable controversy as to whether or not it adequately measures the minimal needs of a family, the poverty index is the generally accepted standard against which poverty is measured.

In 1997, the poverty level for a family of four was $16,050. This meant that any family of four individuals was considered to be living in poverty if the family income was less than $16,050. For a family of five, the poverty level was $19,660, and for a family of six it was $21,490. The poverty line for a family of four in 1999 was projected to be $16,800, $750 more than in 1997.

Table 28.4 on the next two pages sheds much light on the nature of poverty in Texas. More women are poor than men (44.66 percent versus 55.34 percent). The vast majority of poor people are minorities. Hispanics compose 53.17 percent of all people living below the poverty line, while blacks compose 20.70 percent and Anglos 26.13 percent. More disturbingly, over one out of every four African Americans or Hispanics in Texas lives in poverty. Poverty in Texas is largely a metropolitan problem, with over 80 percent of poor people living in metropolitan areas. Not surprisingly, poor people are generally less well educated than more economically well-off people. Indeed, one-third of those adults with less than a high school education live in poverty. Another troubling statistic worth noting is that just under 50 percent of children living in poverty live only with their mother. Equally troubling is the fact the 46.24 percent of all single-mother families are impoverished in Texas.

DEMOGRAPHIC PROFILE OF POVERTY IN TEXAS, 1997 — Table 28.4

Category	Number Living in Poverty	Percentage of Poverty Population
Sex		
Male	1,472,227	44.66%
Female	1,824,553	55.34%
Race/Ethnicity		
Anglo and other	861,397	26.13%
Black	682,453	20.70%
Hispanic	1,752,930	53.17%
Age		
Under 18	1,378,033	41.80%
18-64	1,605,406	48.70%
65+	313,341	9.50%
U.S. Citizenship Status		
Native citizen	2,681,823	81.35%
Naturalized citizen	91,356	2.77%
Not U.S. citizen	523,601	15.88%
Residence		
Metropolitan	2,662,861	80.77%
Nonmetropolitan	633,919	19.23%
Totals	3,296,780	100%
Adult Educational Attainment		
Less than high school	1,052,975	54.88%
High school	504,240	26.28%
Some college	281,942	14.69%
College or higher	79,590	4.15%
Total	1,918,747	100%
Nonretired Adult Labor Force Status		
Employed	711,719	43.68%
Unemployed	135,083	8.29%
Not in labor force	1,629,456	48.03%
Total	1,629,456	100%
Adult Marital Status		
Married	764,324	39.83%
Widowed	227,410	11.85%
Divorced/separated	389,306	20.29%
Single, never married	537,707	28.02%
Total	1,918,747	100%

Table 28.4 DEMOGRAPHIC PROFILE OF POVERTY IN TEXAS, 1997 (CONTINUED)

Category	Number Living in Poverty	Percentage of Poverty Population
Presence of Parents		
(Children under 18)		
Both parents present	556,097	41.46%
Only mother present	645,430	48.12%
Only father present	59,057	4.40%
Neither parent present	80,703	6.02%
Total	1,341,287	100%

SOURCE: Health and Human Services Commission, "Demographic Profile of the Texas Population Living in Poverty in 1997," www.hhsc.state.tx.us/cons_bud/dssi/dempov97.htm.

There is also a regional component to poverty in Texas. In 1998, poverty was relatively low in north central Texas (Dallas-Fort Worth) and the central Gulf Coast regions, at 12.2 percent and 13.4 percent respectively. In sharp contrast, however, the border regions had some of the poorest counties in the nation. In south Texas, the area around Edinburgh, 40.2 percent of the population was poor. In far west Texas, in the region around El Paso, poverty stood at 31.6 percent. In San Antonio the poverty rate was 21.3 percent.

New Deal
President Franklin D. Roosevelt's 1930s program of stimulating the national economy and providing relief to victims of the Great Depression

WELFARE IN TEXAS, 1935–96

The origins of modern welfare policy lie in President Roosevelt's **New Deal.**[38] Prior to the 1930s, welfare was considered to be a state and local responsibility. The Great Depression overwhelmed many of the state and local welfare

Hispanics compose the majority of people living below the poverty line in Texas. The border counties in west Texas are by far the poorest counties in the state.

arrangements, causing the federal government to expand its role in addressing the needs of the poor and the unemployed. The Social Security Act of 1935 transformed the way in which welfare policy was implemented in the United States. Along with two social insurance programs (Old Age Insurance and Unemployment Insurance), the Social Security Act established a number of state-federal public assistance programs: Aid for Dependent Children (ADC, later **Aid to Families with Dependent Children** or AFDC), Old Age Assistance (OAA), and Aid for the Blind (AB). States administered and determined the benefit levels for these programs. In exchange for federal assistance in funding, state programs had to meet certain minimum federal guidelines.

Aid to Families with Dependent Children (AFDC)
federal funds, administered by the states, for children living with parents or relatives who fall below state standards of need. Replaced in 1996 by TANF

The Department of Public Welfare was established in Texas in 1939 to run the state's various public assistance programs. It was to be supervised by a state board of welfare, composed of three members appointed by the governor for six-year terms. The board appointed an executive director who, in turn, was the chief administrative officer of the department.[39]

Through the early 1960s, the basic strategy adopted by welfare policy makers in Texas was to minimize the cost to the state while maximizing federal dollars. Some programs were expanded during these years. In 1950, ADC became AFDC as mothers were included in the program. Other new social-service programs were also added. Much of the initiative for the expansion of welfare came from the federal government. One of the major issues in Texas was the problem of the constitutional ceiling on welfare spending. This had to be raised from $35 million in 1945 to $52 million in 1961, and again to $60 million in 1963. Between 1945 and 1965, state AFDC expenditures rose from $1.495 million to $3.899 million. At the same time, federal expenditures in Texas rose from $1.242 million to $16.594 million.[40]

Welfare policy in Texas was transformed fundamentally in the 1960s. Federal court decisions between 1968 and 1971 effectively ended a series of practices such as man-in-the-house rules and residency requirements, which had been used by states to keep welfare rolls low. In 1965, Congress established **Medicaid,** a state-federal program to finance health care for the poor. Lyndon Johnson's "War on Poverty" also expanded the number of social service programs available to the poor. Increasingly, it was argued, the solution to alleviating poverty was through an expanded federal control over welfare programs.

Medicaid
a federally financed, state-operated program providing medical services to low-income people

In 1965, the Department of Public Welfare was authorized to work with the federal government's new antipoverty programs. The welfare ceiling was raised to $80 million in 1969. Among the welfare programs administered by the Department were four public assistance programs: Aid for Families with Dependent Children, Aid for the Blind, Aid to the Permanently and Totally Disabled, and Old Age Assistance. The latter three programs were taken over by the federal government in 1972 in the form of the new national Supplemental Security Income program. Along with these programs the Department ran the Texas Medical Assistance Program (Medicaid), the national food stamp program, and a series of social-service programs.

In 1977, the Department of Public Welfare became the Department of Human Resources. It was renamed again in 1985 as the Texas Department of Human Services. Symbolically, the name reflected an ongoing desire on the part of policy makers to think of the agency less as a welfare agency and more as a service agency to the poor. By 1980, the department was reorganized to focus upon the major client groups being served: families with children and aged and disabled people. In 1981, the constitutional ceiling on welfare spending was replaced with a more flexible standard. Instead of a flat cap of $80 million, welfare expenditures could not exceed 1 percent of the total state budget. In 1989, the board was expanded from three to six members.[41]

Between 1967 and 1973, participation rates and welfare expenditures in Texas exploded. The number of children on AFDC during this time rose from 79,914 to 325,244, while the number of families on AFDC went from 23,509 to 120,254. Rates leveled off in the late 1970s, but they began to push upward again in the 1980s. Liberal attempts to reform welfare by nationalizing AFDC (turning the state-federal program into a national program as with Supplemental Security Income) failed throughout the 1970s. Conservative attempts to compel welfare recipients to participate in job training programs, such as the Work Incentive Program of 1967, were of limited success. A frustrating political stalemate set in. Few were happy with welfare policy as currently conducted. But no consensus had emerged as to what was a better alternative. Meanwhile, welfare rolls expanded and expenditures continued to increase in both Texas and the nation.

THE IDEA OF DEPENDENCY AND WELFARE REFORM

By the mid-1980s, a new critique of welfare programs had begun to emerge. At its heart lay the idea that the well-intentioned policies of the 1960s had backfired, creating a dysfunctional underclass of people dependent upon welfare. Welfare programs, like AFDC, may have helped people financially in the short run, but in the long run they had robbed people of the character traits and the moral values that would enable them to succeed in a market economy.[42] Skyrocketing illegitimacy rates, particularly among minorities and the poor, were seen as the partial result of a perverse set of incentives put into place by the state supposedly to help the poor. Under the existing welfare system, the more children you had, the higher the welfare check. Because some states did not provide welfare to families with fathers in the home, fathers were actually being encouraged to abandon their families so that they might qualify for welfare. According to critics, the poor needed the encouragement and proper incentives to become independent workers, not a permanent source of income from the state.

At the national level, the deadlock over welfare reform was broken with the passage of the Family Support Act in 1988. In the attempt to stem the rising tide of illegitimacy rates and single-parent families among the poor, the act mandated two-parent coverage for all state AFDC programs. It also established a number of new "workfare" programs whose goals were to get people off welfare and into the workforce. New standards were also developed that demanded parents participate in these workfare programs or lose their benefits.[43]

Much hyperbole surrounded the passage of the Family Support Act. While the Act did break new ground in formulating programs transitioning people from welfare to work, it also was an important expansion of the existing AFDC system. Far from declining, welfare roles expanded unabated in the early 1990s. In Texas, welfare programs expanded rapidly. By 1994, there were on average 786,400 people receiving AFDC in Texas. Total federal and state expenditures rose from $188.3 million in 1984 to $544.9 million in

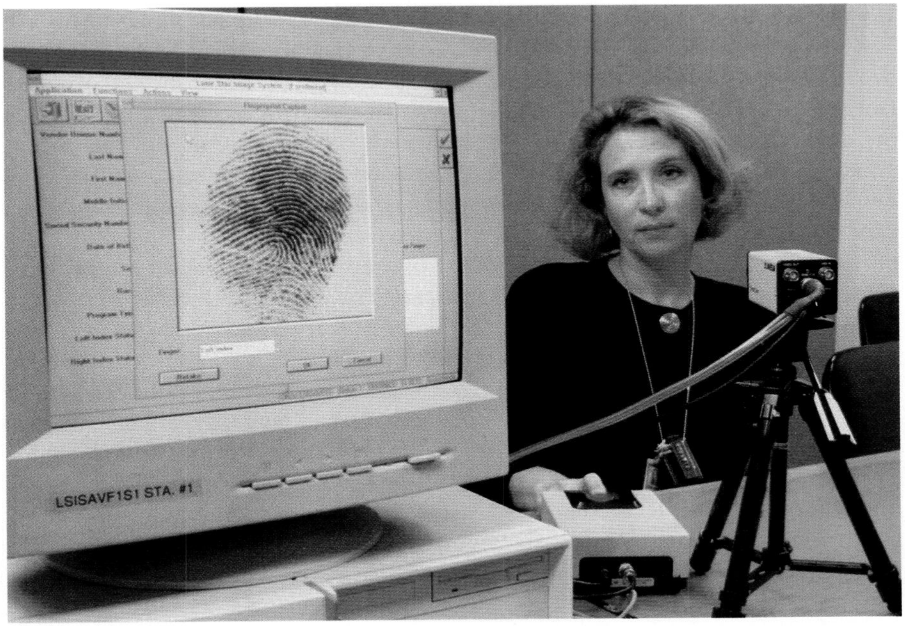

The fingerprinting of welfare recipients to discourage fraud is one way in which Texas is experimenting with welfare reform.

1994. Food stamp costs also rose rapidly during this period, from $664.9 million to $2.2 billion. But AFDC and Food stamps were only part of the problem. Medicaid—the state-federal program to finance health care for the poor—was escalating at a rate of more than 20 percent a year. During the 1994–95 biennium, $18.6 billion in state and federal funds was being spent on Medicaid. This was 13 percent of the state budget or $6.7 billion. Escalating costs of AFDC, food stamps, and Medicaid provided the backdrop to the welfare reforms that would be put into place by Texas policy makers in 1995.

Growing discontent over welfare policy across the country encouraged many states to seek **waivers** from federal regulations so that they, too, might experiment with welfare reform.[44] Some states sought to modify AFDC rules to eliminate some of the perverse incentive structures in the welfare system. Other states set caps on benefits and how long one could continue to receive welfare. Welfare became a state issue during the 1994 elections. George W. Bush echoed the ideas of conservative critics of the welfare system, arguing that the existing system was robbing people of their independence. Among the changes that he called for were

waiver
an exemption from a federal requirement

- strengthening child-support procedures and penalties
- imposing a two-year limit on benefits for recipients able to work
- requiring individuals receiving welfare to accept a state-sponsored job if after two years they were unable to find work
- creating new child-care and job-training programs
- requiring unwed mothers to live with their parents or grandparents
- moving family support systems from the state to the local level.

Data released by the comptroller's office lent support to the Bush contention that there were serious problems with the existing system of welfare in

Texas. Over one-quarter of all welfare recipients in 1993 were "long-term" recipients, who had remained on the rolls for five years or more. The publication of *A Partnership for Independence: Welfare Reform in Texas,* by the office of Democratic comptroller John Sharp, helped to set the legislative agenda for the debate over welfare policy. Agreeing with other critics across the nation unhappy with the current state of welfare policy, the report documented how welfare often failed to help those most in need or to encourage those dependent on welfare to become independent of government largess. Among the report's one hundred proposals were many of the reforms that had been put into place by conservative reformers in other states or by the Bush campaign.

A bipartisan legislative coalition ultimately supported major welfare reform in Texas. On May 26, 1995, the vote on House Bill 1863 in the House was 128–9 and in the Senate 30–1. The law provided a number of "carrot and stick" incentives that sought to mold the character of welfare recipients in positive ways and wean them off welfare. Among the carrots were expanded education and job-training programs, as well as a select number of pilot studies involving transitional child care and medical benefits. Among the sticks were a limitation on benefits to thirty-six months, alimony for spouses who couldn't support themselves, and the institution of a five-year ban on reapplying for benefits once benefits ran out. In order to implement the state reforms, Texas secured a waiver from the federal government freeing the state from various federal regulations regarding welfare programs. In granting the waivers to Texas and other states, the Clinton administration hoped to stimulate innovative reforms that might be repeated elsewhere.

Texas was ahead of the welfare reform curve in 1995. In 1996, President Bill Clinton signed into law the most important reform in federal welfare policy since the New Deal. The Personal Responsibility and Work Opportunity Reconciliation Act essentially rethought the assumptions that had guided the expansion of welfare programs for sixty years. Under the legislation, AFDC, JOBS (a work-related training program), and the Emergency Assistance Program were combined into one block grant entitled **Temporary Assistance for Needy Families (TANF).** As with the welfare reforms instituted in Texas and in other states across the country, the primary purpose of TANF was to make families self-sufficient by ending the cycle of dependency on government benefits. States like Texas were given great flexibility in setting benefit levels, eligibility requirements, and other program details.

Temporary Assistance for Needy Families (TANF)

a federal block grant that replaced the AFDC program in 1996

Today in Texas TANF-Basic provides temporary financial assistance to families with needy children where one or both of the parents are missing or disabled.[45] TANF-Unemployed Parents (TANF-UP) provides assistance to two-parent needy families where the principal wage earner is unemployed or underemployed. The one-time TANF program provides a $1,000 payment to individuals in certain crisis situations. To qualify, a recipient's income must be below 17 percent of the poverty income limit based on family size. In addition, the combined equity of the family may not exceed $2,000 ($3,000 for the elderly and disabled). People participating in TANF-Basic and TANF-UP receive a monthly assistance payment based on the size of their family. They cannot receive benefits for more than thirty-six months. They are also eligible for Medicaid benefits, food stamps, and child day-care services. Unless legally exempt, recipients are also required to participate in an employment services program.

The client profile of participants in TANF-Basic provides a good insight into the population that is currently being served by the program.

- The average TANF-Basic family comprises 2.7 people.
- In 96 percent of the cases, the family caretaker is female.
- On average, the caretaker is thirty-one years old.
- Only 4.6 percent of the caretakers have jobs.
- Forty-three percent of TANF children are under six years old.
- The family is black or Hispanic in 79 percent of the cases.
- The average gross earnings of employed TANF-Basic families is $2,354.

EVALUATING WELFARE REFORM

The recent welfare reforms in Texas will probably be evaluated along two dimensions. First, they will be measured in terms of the number of people receiving welfare assistance from the state. To the degree to which the reforms contribute to lowering the number of welfare recipients in Texas, they will be deemed a success. To the degree to which they do not lighten the welfare rolls, they likely will be considered a failure. A second measure of success will be the degree to which the reforms help to take people off welfare and transition them into the workforce as productive independent members of society.

In terms of changes in the number of people on welfare, the welfare reforms appear to be a success. Certain major state leaders, such as Governor Bush, view them this way. The average monthly number of people on welfare in Texas rose from a little over half a million in 1989 to a peak of more than three-quarters of a million in 1994, but then began to fall in 1995. Time limits and work requirements were put into place by the state legislature in 1995, one year before similar measures were passed nationally by the U.S. Congress. The decline continued over the next three years in the number of people on welfare. During the 1999 state legislature, it was estimated that the welfare rolls had dropped 47 percent to 340,000. Two-thirds of the people who have left the rolls have been children.[46]

In terms of the second measure—the number of people being transitioned from welfare to work—preliminary indications also seem to be that the welfare reforms of 1995 are accomplishing their objectives. Early findings of a study conducted by the Texas Department of Human Services seems to indicate that a considerable number of former welfare recipients (45 percent of the 1,396 surveyed) had found work and that many of those were working in jobs that offered possible advancement (41 percent of the 1,396 surveyed). Further, it was estimated that as of October 1998, the Department of Human Services had helped more than 16,000 families choose work over welfare.[47]

One qualifier must be made before we trumpet the success of welfare reform in the 1990s. Current reforms have all taken place under conditions of a booming economy and a rising demand for all types of labor. There seem to be jobs available for people who are willing and able to work. But how will the new welfare policies work when the economy goes into recession, as it must sooner or later? When labor markets tighten and jobs are difficult to find, will Texas policy makers be satisfied with the welfare reforms that have been put into place? How far will unemployment be allowed to go before policy makers demand that we reconsider the incentive structure created to get people off the public dole? These are questions that policy makers concerned with welfare reform will have to consider one day. Only then will we be able to fully evaluate exactly how successful the welfare reforms of the mid-1990s actually were.

Summary

In this chapter we examined various aspects of public policy making in Texas. We focused particular attention on the complex tax and spending issues surrounding the budget and the issues that have driven policy making in crime and corrections, public education, and welfare. In earlier chapters we saw how Texas's economy was transformed in the 1980s and 1990s with the high-tech revolution. We also traced out how social and political changes have restructured the political party system in the state and the increasing power of the Republican Party. In this chapter we have seen how many of these changes resulted in important changes in public policy in the 1990s. The reforms in budgetary policy as well as crime and corrections, public education, and welfare are part a larger shift in the Texas political economy away from an oil, cattle, and cotton economy into an era of computers, high tech, and globalization. We can't be sure exactly where public policy in Texas will be going in the next decade. We can be sure that changes we have witnessed in the last decade will intensify as the Texas political system tries to meet the challenges and opportunities of the twenty-first century.

FOR FURTHER READING

Champagne, Anthony, and Edward J. Harpham, eds. *Texas at the Crossroads.* College Station: Texas A&M University Press, 1987.

Champagne, Anthony, and Edward J. Harpham, eds. *Texas Politics: A Reader,* 2nd edition. New York: Norton, 1998.

San Miguel, Jr., Guadalupe. *Let Them Take Heed: Mexican Americans and the Campaign for Educational Equality in Texas, 1910–1981.* Austin: University of Texas Press, 1987.

Mead, Lawrence. *The New Politics of Poverty: The Nonworking Poor in America.* New York: Basic, 1992.

Parrish, James R. *A Two-Headed Monster: Crime and Texas Prisons.* Austin: Eakin Pess, 1989.

Toch, Thomas. *In the Name of Excellence: The Struggle to Reform the Nation's Schools, Why It's Failing and What Should Be Done.* New York: Oxford University Press, 1991.

Walker, Donald R. *Penalogy for Profit: A History of the Texas Prison System, 1867–1912.* College Station: Texas A&M University Press, 1988.

STUDY OUTLINE

Taxing and Spending in Texas

1. Texas is correctly perceived as a low-tax, low-service state.
2. The 1990s brought efforts to make state government more efficient.
3. The Texas Constitution affects budget making by limiting the state legislature to biennial sessions and forcing agencies and the legislature to project spending needs more than two years into the future. Dedicated funds further limit the legislature's ability to prepare effective and efficient budgets. Specific constitutional provisions such as pay-as-you-go and the welfare spending limit also handicap the legislature.

4. Although the governor is responsible for preparing a budget, in practice, the legislature fulfills all budgetary responsibilities.
5. The Legislative Budget Board (LBB) was established in 1949 to recommend levels of state spending for all government agencies.
6. The budgetary process involves two stages. First, the LBB develops a draft budget based on agency requests, and the Office of the Comptroller of Public Accounts prepares a Biennial Revenue Estimate (BRE). The BRE sets a ceiling on state spending. The second stage of the process involves the legislature. The House Ways and Means Committee and the Senate Finance Committee consider the budget prepared by the LBB, weigh requests for additional monies from agencies, and eventually draft an appropriations bill.
7. In 1999, slightly less than one-half of the state's revenue came from tax sources.
8. The general sales and use tax is the largest source of tax revenue. Currently, the state collects a general sales tax of 6.25 percent.
9. Texas collects more than a dozen selective sales taxes, including the motor fuel tax, motor vehicle sales and rental tax, alcoholic beverage tax, and tobacco tax.
10. *Ad valorem taxes,* known as property taxes, are a major source of revenue for counties, cities, and special districts.
11. Although extremely complicated, Texas's "truth in taxation" laws give taxpayers a voice in determining property tax rates.
12. Texas's reliance on various sales and use taxes produces a system of regressive taxation in which the tax burden falls on those with lower incomes. Supporters of a state income tax believe it would be more fair by shifting the burden to individuals with higher incomes. An income tax would produce a more reliable source of revenue.
13. It is unlikely Texas will enact any income tax because the state Constitution requires voter approval for an income tax to take effect.
14. Products purchased over the Internet from companies in Texas escape the state sales tax; however, products purchased over the Internet from businesses in Texas are taxed. This loss of tax revenue is significant, but policy makers must balance the desire for more revenue against the possibility of placing Texas companies at a comparative disadvantage.
15. Next to taxes, the largest source of revenue for Texas is the federal government. Federal monies are concentrated in three areas: health care and human services, transportation, and education.
16. Dollars generated by the state lottery and money from the tobacco settlement are two more important sources of state revenue. The state's share of the lottery goes directly to public education, and tobacco settlement money goes to programs for anti-tobacco education programs, research in medical schools, and the Children's Health Insurance Program (CHIP).
17. Public and higher education are the largest item of expenditure for the state. Education spending is followed closely by health and human services, transportation, and public safety and corrections.
18. It is difficult for the state to cut spending or even limit increases in outlays.

Crime and Corrections Policy

1. According to court cases and independent studies, from the earliest days of the state prison system, prisoners were abused and treated in a cruel and brutal manner. Meaningful reforms did not occur until the decision in *Ruiz v. Estelle,* which declared the Texas prison system unconstitutional.
2. Texas incarcerates an ever-growing number of people, which increases its penal construction and operating costs. The state's crime rate is comparable to the national average, but Texas's rate of incarceration exceeds the national average. Many Texans support the state's "tough on crime" policy and its associated costs.

Education Policy in Texas

1. The government's responsibility to establish a public system of education was acknowledged as early as 1836; however, establishment and funding of public schools were primarily local concerns until the early twentieth century. Inadequate facilities, lack of textbooks and other supplies, and poorly trained teachers were problems faced by many schools.
2. The Gilmer-Aikin Laws established the bureaucratic institutions responsible for public education in Texas.
3. The State Board of Education is an elected body composed of fifteen members who serve four-year terms.
4. Three issues have dominated educational policy in Texas for the last half-century: desegregation, equity in funding, and promoting excellence in education.
5. Segregation of the races was specified in the Constitution of 1876, and during the 1920s and 1930s, the state spent one-third less educating African American than white students.
6. San Antonio was one of the first school districts in the nation to comply with *Brown v. Board of Education,* which ruled segregated schools violated the U.S. Constitution. *De facto* segregation remained a problem.
7. In the last thirty years, two court cases, *Rodriguez v. San Antonio ISD* and *Edgewood v. Kirby* played an important role in the formation of education policy.
8. Lower federal courts ruled in *Rodriguez v. San Antonio ISD* that the Texas system of financing public education violated the Fourteenth Amendment to the U.S.

Constitution; however, the U.S. Supreme Court ruled that the state was not required to subsidize poorer school districts.

9. In the 1980s and early 1990s, the issue of equity was addressed by the Texas Supreme Court in the case of *Edgewood v. Kirby,* in which plaintiffs maintained the state was in violation of the "efficiency" clause of Article 7, Section 1, of the Texas Constitution. The Texas Supreme Court held that "glaring disparities" existed between property-poor and property-wealthy districts and required the legislature to develop a system that guaranteed "substantially equal access to similar revenues per pupil at similar levels of tax effort."
10. After seven years, several special sessions, and three regular sessions, the legislature implemented a new method of financing public education that was upheld by the Texas Supreme Court.
11. Serious efforts at educational reform began in 1983 with the creation of the Select Committee on Public Education (SCOPE), chaired by Ross Perot. SCOPE presented 140 recommendations for reforming Texas's educational system. SCOPE reforms of 1984 centralized responsibility and administration of public education, but changes in 1995 decentralized authority and returned some responsibility to local districts and the public.
12. An expanding Texas economy enabled the state to pay for reforms it could not afford a decade earlier.
13. Texas has the largest number of school districts and the largest number of school teachers of any state, but the pupil-teacher ratio remains high and the state has an exceptionally high drop-out rate. A concern for quality and excellence in the classroom will remain a major policy issue for the state.

Welfare Policy

1. Poverty is one of the most persistent problems facing Texas.
2. Policy makers use a very specific definition for poverty and set a definitive income level for those living in poverty.
3. Slightly less than one-half of children in poverty live with only their mother, and 46 percent of single-mother families live in poverty.
4. The Great Depression overwhelmed most state and local welfare arrangements, and the national government expanded its role.
5. The basic state approach to welfare through the 1960s was to reduce state cost and optimize the use of federal monies. In the 1960s, federal court decisions and federal legislation significantly changed Texas's welfare policy, and in the late 1960s and early 1970s, the number of Texans on welfare dramatically increased.
6. The first significant attempt at welfare reform was the Family Support Act of 1988, but it actually increased the number of Texans receiving benefits from the Aid to Families with Dependent Children (AFDC, now called Temporary Assistance for Needy Families, TANF) and those qualifying for food stamps.
7. Welfare reform in Texas began in 1995 with the expansion of education and job training programs, a thirty-six-month limit on benefits, a limited alimony system for spouses who couldn't support themselves, and a five-year ban on reapplying for benefits.
8. Contemporary welfare reform at the national level began in 1996 when President Bill Clinton signed the Personal Responsibility and Work Opportunity Reconciliation Act.
9. The success of welfare reform is evaluated in two areas: (a) Is there a decrease in the number of people receiving benefits? and (b) are people able to stay off welfare? From 1994–98, the number of people on welfare rolls in Texas declined 47 percent. Forty-five percent of former welfare recipients surveyed said they had found work in which there is a possibility for advancement.
10. Success in moving from welfare to work may be due more to a strong and robust economy than any change in the welfare system.

PRACTICE QUIZ

1. One result of Texas being a low-tax state is that
   a) it is continually in need of more money.
   b) it is also a low-service state.
   c) the state continually asks businesses to self-assess their taxes.
   d) citizens never lack for services

2. The Texan Constitution
   a) severely limits the budgetary process.
   b) makes little mention of monetary concerns.
   c) places no restrictions on state spending for welfare.
   d) prohibits the state receiving money from the federal government.

3. What is the major source of tax revenue for the state?
   a) federal funds
   b) selective sales tax on motor fuel
   c) selective sales tax on alcoholic beverages
   d) general sales tax

4. The most costly item in the Texas budget is
   a) public safety and corrections.
   b) public and higher education.
   c) transportation.
   d) human services.

5. The Texas prison system
   a) is considered a model of an effective and efficient state prison system.
   b) has space for at least 10,000 more inmates.
   c) is often overcrowded, fails to rehabilitate prisoners, and is subject to rising costs.
   d) is the most costly part of the state budget.

6. Which of the following best describes corrections policy in Texas?
   a) Spare no expense to rehabilitate those in prison.
   b) Lock up some prisoners, then lock up some more prisoners, and build more prisons if necessary.
   c) Create as many drug and alcohol abuse rehabilitation, and educational programs as are necessary.
   d) Place more emphasis on parole and probation and less on incarceration.

7. Public education in Texas is jointly controlled by
   a) the state and local school boards.
   b) local school boards and county government.
   c) county government and the state.
   d) the state and federal government.

8. Which of the following is *not* one of the three most important education policy issues of the last fifty years?
   a) desegregation
   b) equity in funding
   c) no pass, no play
   d) excellence in education and accountability

9. The real test of welfare reform will come
   a) when 90 percent of Texans can graduate from high school.
   b) if it works during a recession.
   c) if it is able to continue to wisely use its increased level of federal funds.
   d) if Texas maintains its status as the least welfare-dependent state.

CRITICAL THINKING QUESTIONS

1. Some public schools and some school districts provide an excellent education, but on the whole, Texas's system of public education is dismal. In most categories of educational achievement, Texas's public schools rank near the bottom, despite the fact that the state budget allocates more for education than any other item.

   Call on your experience as a public or private school student, textbook readings, class discussion, and current events to propose a series of changes to enhance the state's educational system. While cost need not be a major factor in your consideration, you should not propose unreasonably costly programs.

2. Is the current tax system in Texas fair? Why or why not? How would the proposals for new forms of taxation affect the majority of Texans? What concerns should be kept in mind when proposing changes to the tax system?

KEY TERMS

Aid to Families with Dependent Children (AFDC) (p. 1053)
appropriations (p. 1026)
biennial (p. 1025)
comptroller of public accounts (p. 1025)
debt service (p. 1026)
dedicated funds (p. 1025)
de facto (p. 1043)
equal protection clause (p. 1045)
Gilmer-Aikin Laws (p. 1042)
matching funds (p. 1032)
Medicaid (p. 1053)
New Deal (p. 1052)
oil severance tax (p. 1025)
pay-as-you-go limit (p. 1026)
progressive/regressive taxation (p. 1031)
Temporary Assistance for Needy Families (TANF) (p. 1056)
waiver (p. 1055)

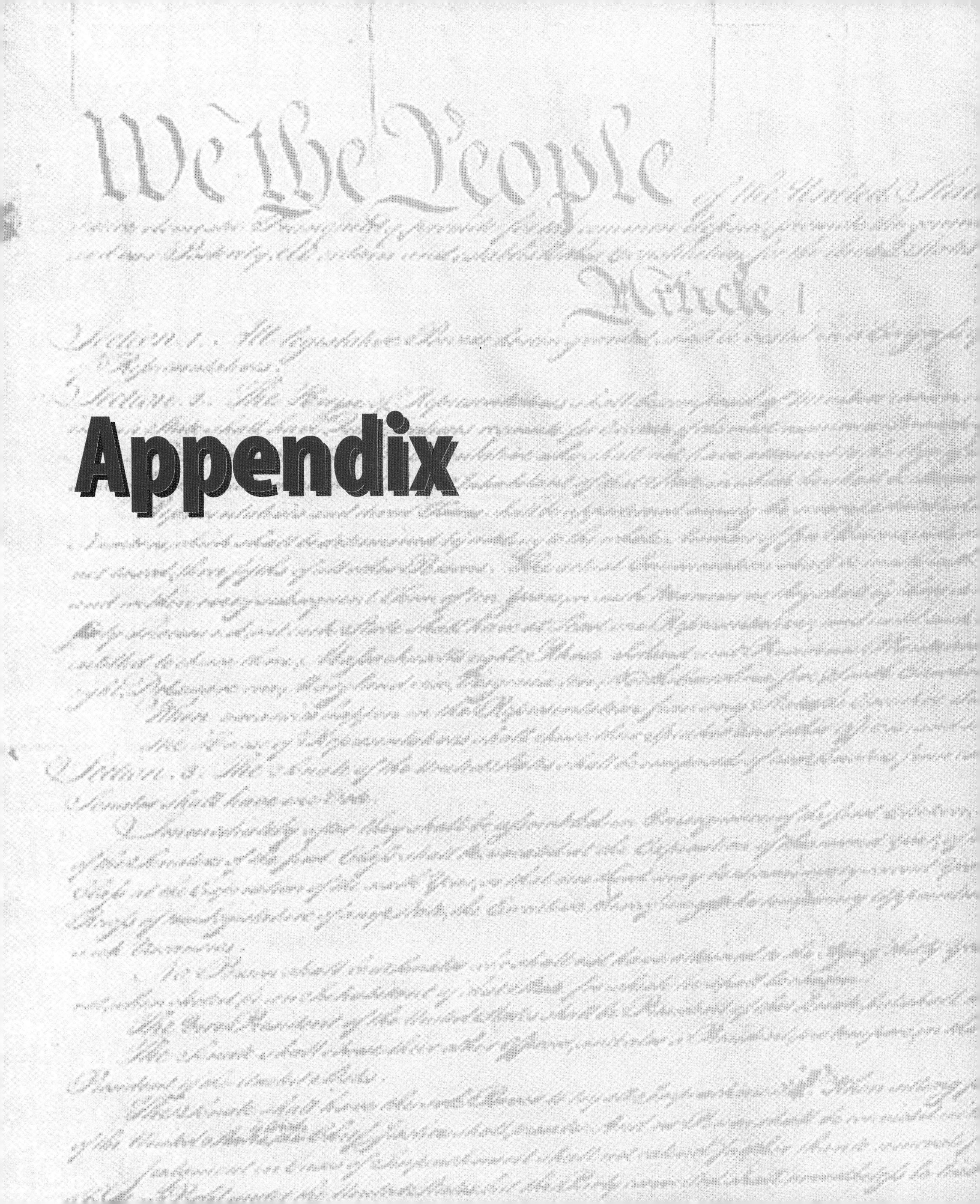

Appendix

The Declaration of Independence

In Congress, July 4, 1776

The unanimous Declaration of the thirteen united States of America,

When in the Course of human events, it becomes necessary for one people to dissolve the political bands which have connected them with another, and to assume among the powers of the earth, the separate and equal station to which the Laws of Nature and of Nature's God entitle them, a decent respect to the opinions of mankind requires that they should declare the causes which impel them to the separation.

We hold these truths to be self-evident, that all men are created equal, that they are endowed by their Creator with certain unalienable Rights, that among these are Life, Liberty and the pursuit of Happiness.—That to secure these rights, Governments are instituted among Men, deriving their just powers from the consent of the governed. —That whenever any Form of Government becomes destructive of these ends, it is the Right of the People to alter or to abolish it, and to institute new Government, laying its foundation on such principles and organizing its powers in such form, as to them shall seem most likely to effect their Safety and Happiness. Prudence, indeed, will dictate that Governments long established should not be changed for light and transient causes; and accordingly all experience hath shewn, that mankind are more disposed to suffer, while evils are sufferable, than to right themselves by abolishing the forms to which they are accustomed. But when a long train of abuses and usurpations, pursuing invariably the same Object evinces a design to reduce them under absolute Despotism, it is their right, it is their duty, to throw off such Government, and to provide new Guards for their future security.—Such has been the patient sufferance of these Colonies; and such is now the necessity which constrains them to alter their former Systems of Government. The history of the present King of Great Britain is a history of repeated injuries and usurpations, all having in direct object the establishment of an absolute Tyranny over these States. To prove this, let Facts be submitted to a candid world.

He has refused his Assent to Laws, the most wholesome and necessary for the public good.

He has forbidden his Governors to pass Laws of immediate and pressing importance, unless suspended in their operation till his Assent should be obtained; and when so suspended, he has utterly neglected to attend to them.

He has refused to pass other Laws for the accommodation of large districts of people, unless those people would relinquish the right of Representation in the Legislature, a right inestimable to them and formidable to tyrants only.

He has called together legislative bodies at places unusual, uncomfortable, and distant from the depository of their public Records, for the sole purpose of fatiguing them into compliance with his measures.

He has dissolved Representative Houses repeatedly, for opposing with manly firmness his invasions on the rights of the people.

He has refused for a long time, after such dissolutions, to cause others to be elected; whereby the Legislative powers, incapable of Annihilation, have returned to the People at large for their exercise; the State remaining in the mean time exposed to all the dangers of invasion from without, and convulsions within.

He has endeavoured to prevent the population of these States; for that purpose obstructing the Laws for Naturalization of Foreigners; refusing to pass others to encourage their migrations hither, and raising the conditions of new Appropriations of Lands.

He has obstructed the Administration of Justice, by refusing his Assent to Laws for establishing Judiciary powers.

He has made Judges dependent on his Will alone, for the tenure of their offices, and the amount and payment of their salaries.

He has erected a multitude of New Offices, and sent hither swarms of Officers to harrass our people, and eat out their substance.

He has kept among us, in times of peace, Standing Armies without the Consent of our legislatures.

He has affected to render the Military independent of and superior to the Civil power.

He has combined with others to subject us to a jurisdiction foreign to our constitution, and unacknowledged by our laws; giving his Assent to their Acts of pretended Legislation:

For Quartering large bodies of armed troops among us:

For protecting them, by a mock Trial, from punishment for any Murders which they should commit on the Inhabitants of these States:

For cutting off our Trade with all parts of the world:

For imposing Taxes on us without our Consent:

For depriving us in many cases, of the benefits of Trial by Jury:

For transporting us beyond Seas to be tried for pretended offences:

For abolishing the free System of English Laws in a neighboring Province, establishing therein an Arbitrary government, and enlarging its Boundaries so as to render it at once an example and fit instrument for introducing the same absolute rule into these Colonies:

For taking away our Charters, abolishing our most valuable Laws, and altering fundamentally the Forms of our Governments:

For suspending our own Legislatures, and declaring themselves invested with power to legislate for us in all cases whatsoever.

He has abdicated Government here, by declaring us out of his Protection and waging War against us.

He has plundered our seas, ravaged our Coasts, burnt our towns, and destroyed the lives of our people.

He is at this time transporting large Armies of foreign Mercenaries to compleat the works of death, desolation and tyranny, already begun with circumstances of Cruelty & perfidy scarcely paralleled in the most barbarous ages, and totally unworthy the Head of a civilized nation.

He has constrained our fellow Citizens taken Captive on the high Seas to bear Arms against their Country, to become the executioners of their friends and Brethren, or to fall themselves by their Hands.

He has excited domestic insurrections amongst us, and has endeavoured to bring on the inhabitants of our frontiers, the merciless Indian Savages, whose known rule of warfare, is an undistinguished destruction of all ages, sexes and conditions.

In every stage of these Oppressions We have Petitioned for Redress in the most humble terms: Our repeated Petitions have been answered only by repeated injury. A Prince whose character is thus marked by every act which may define a Tyrant, is unfit to be the ruler of a free people.

Nor have We been wanting in attentions to our Brittish brethren. We have warned them from time to time of attempts by their legislature to extend an unwarrantable jurisdiction over us. We have reminded them of the circumstances of our emigration and settlement here. We have appealed to their native justice and magnanimity, and we have conjured them by the ties of our common kindred to disavow these usurpations, which, would inevitably interrupt our connections and correspondence. They too have been deaf to the voice of justice and of consanguinity. We must, therefore, acquiesce in the necessity, which denounces our Separation, and hold them, as we hold the rest of mankind, Enemies in War, in Peace Friends.

We, Therefore, the Representatives of the United States of America, in General Congress, Assembled, appealing to the Supreme Judge of the world for the rectitude of our intentions, do, in the Name, and by Authority of the good People of these Colonies, solemnly publish and declare, That these United Colonies are, and of Right ought to be Free and Independent States; that they are Absolved from all Allegiance to the British Crown, and that all political connection between them and the State of Great Britain, is and ought to be totally dissolved; and that as Free and Independent States, they have full Power to levy War, conclude Peace, contract Alliances, establish Commerce, and to do all other Acts and Things which Independent States may of right do. And for the support of this Declaration, with a firm reliance on the protection of divine Providence, we mutually pledge to each other our Lives, our Fortunes and our sacred Honor.

The foregoing Declaration was, by order of Congress, engrossed, and signed by the following members:

John Hancock

NEW HAMPSHIRE
Josiah Bartlett
William Whipple
Matthew Thornton

MASSACHUSETTS BAY
Samuel Adams
John Adams
Robert Treat Paine
Elbridge Gerry

RHODE ISLAND
Stephen Hopkins
William Ellery

CONNECTICUT
Roger Sherman
Samuel Huntington
William Williams
Oliver Wolcott

NEW YORK
William Floyd
Philip Livingston
Francis Lewis
Lewis Morris

NEW JERSEY
Richard Stockton
John Witherspoon
Francis Hopkinson
John Hart
Abraham Clark

PENNSYLVANIA
Robert Morris
Benjamin Rush
Benjamin Franklin
John Morton
George Clymer
James Smith
George Taylor
James Wilson
George Ross

DELAWARE
Caesar Rodney
George Read
Thomas M'Kean

MARYLAND
Samuel Chase
William Paca
Thomas Stone
Charles Carroll, of Carrollton

VIRGINIA
George Wythe
Richard Henry Lee
Thomas Jefferson
Benjamin Harrison
Thomas Nelson, Jr.
Francis Lightfoot Lee
Carter Braxton

NORTH CAROLINA
William Hooper
Joseph Hewes
John Penn

SOUTH CAROLINA
Edward Rutledge
Thomas Heyward, Jr.
Thomas Lynch, Jr.
Arthur Middleton

GEORGIA
Button Gwinnett
Lyman Hall
George Walton

Resolved, That copies of the Declaration be sent to the several assemblies, conventions, and committees, or councils of safety, and to the several commanding officers of the continental troops; that it be proclaimed in each of the United States, at the head of the army.

The Articles of Confederation

Agreed to by Congress November 15, 1777; ratified and in force March 1, 1781

To all whom these Presents shall come, we the undersigned Delegates of the States affixed to our Names, send greeting. Whereas the Delegates of the United States of America, in Congress assembled, did, on the fifteenth day of November, in the Year of Our Lord One thousand Seven Hundred and Seventy seven, and in the Second Year of the Independence of America, agree to certain articles of Confederation and perpetual Union between the States of Newhampshire, Massachusetts-bay, Rhodeisland and Providence Plantations, Connecticut, New-York, New-Jersey, Pennsylvania, Delaware, Maryland, Virginia, North-Carolina, South-Carolina and Georgia in the words following, viz. "Articles of Confederation and perpetual Union between the states of Newhampshire, Massachusetts-bay, Rhodeisland and Providence Plantations, Connecticut, New-York, New-Jersey, Pennsylvania, Delaware, Maryland, Virginia, North-Carolina, South-Carolina and Georgia.

Art. I. The Stile of this confederacy shall be "The United States of America."

Art. II. Each state retains its sovereignty, freedom and independence, and every Power, Jurisdiction and right, which is not by this confederation expressly delegated to the United States, in Congress assembled.

Art. III. The said states hereby severally enter into a firm league of friendship with each other, for their common defence, the security of their Liberties, and their mutual and general welfare, binding themselves to assist each other, against all force offered to, or attacks made upon them, or any of them, on account of religion, sovereignty, trade, or any other pretence whatever.

Art. IV. The better to secure and perpetuate mutual friendship and intercourse among the people of the different states in this union, the free inhabitants of each of these states, paupers, vagabonds and fugitives from Justice excepted, shall be entitled to all privileges and immunities of free citizens in the several states; and the people of each state shall have free ingress and regress to and from any other state, and shall enjoy therein all the privileges of trade and commerce, subject to the same duties, impositions and restrictions as the inhabitants thereof respectively, provided that such restriction shall not extend so far as to prevent the removal of property imported into any state, to any other state, of which the Owner is an inhabitant; provided also that no imposition, duties or restriction shall be laid by any state, on the property of the united states, or either of them.

If any Person guilty of, or charged with treason, felony, or other high misdemeanor in any state, shall flee from Justice, and be found in any of the united states, he shall, upon demand of the Governor or executive power, of the state from which he fled, be delivered up and removed to the state having jurisdiction of his offence.

Full faith and credit shall be given in each of these states to the records, acts and judicial proceedings of the courts and magistrates of every other state.

Art. V. For the more convenient management of the general interests of the united states, delegates shall be annually appointed in such manner as the legislature of each state shall direct, to meet in Congress on the first Monday in November, in every year, with a power reserved to each state, to recall its delegates, or any of them, at any time within the year, and to send others in their stead, for the remainder of the Year.

No state shall be represented in Congress by less than two, nor by more than seven Members; and no person shall be capable of being a delegate for more than three years in any term of six years; nor shall any person, being a delegate, be capable of holding any office under the united states, for which he, or another for his benefit receives any salary, fees or emolument of any kind.

Each state shall maintain its own delegates in a meeting of the states, and while they act as members of the committee of the states.

In determining questions in the united states, in Congress assembled, each state shall have one vote.

Freedom of speech and debate in Congress shall not be

impeached or questioned in any Court, or place out of Congress, and the members of congress shall be protected in their persons from arrests and imprisonments, during the time of their going to and from, and attendance on congress, except for treason, felony, or breach of the peace.

Art. VI. No state without the Consent of the united states in congress assembled, shall send any embassy to, or receive any embassy from, or enter into any conference, agreement, or alliance or treaty with any King, prince or state; nor shall any person holding any office or profit or trust under the united states, or any of them, accept of any present, emolument, office or title of any kind whatever from any king, prince or foreign state; nor shall the united states in congress assembled, or any of them, grant any title of nobility.

No two or more states shall enter into any treaty, confederation or alliance whatever between them, without the consent of the united states in congress assembled, specifying accurately the purposes for which the same is to be entered into, and how long it shall continue.

No state shall lay any imposts or duties, which may interfere with any stipulations in treaties, entered into by the united states in congress assembled, with any king, prince or state, in pursuance of any treaties already proposed by congress, to the courts of France and Spain.

No vessels of war shall be kept up in time of peace by any state, except such number only, as shall be deemed necessary by the united states in congress assembled, for the defence of such state, or its trade; nor shall any body of forces be kept up by any state, in time of peace, except such number only, as in the judgment of the united states, in congress assembled, shall be deemed requisite to garrison the forts necessary for the defence of such state; but every state shall always keep up a well regulated and disciplined militia, sufficiently armed and accoutred, and shall provide and constantly have ready for use, in public stores, a due number of field pieces and tents, and a proper quantity of arms, ammunition and camp equipage.

No state shall engage in any war without the consent of the united states in congress assembled, unless such state be actually invaded by enemies, or shall have received certain advice of a resolution being formed by some nation of Indians to invade such state, and the danger is so imminent as not to admit of a delay, till the united states in congress asssembled can be consulted; nor shall any state grant commissions to any ships or vessels of war, nor letters of marque or reprisal, except it be after a declaration of war by the united states in congress assembled, and then only against the kingdom or state and the subjects thereof, against which war has been so declared, and under such regulations as shall be established by the united states in congress assembled, unless such state be infested by pirates; in which case vessels of war may be fitted out for that occasion, and kept so long as the danger shall continue, or until the united states in congress assembled shall determine otherwise.

Art. VII. When land-forces are raised by any state for the common defence, all officers of or under the rank of colonel, shall be appointed by the legislature of each state respectively, by whom such forces shall be raised, or in such manner as such state shall direct, and all vacancies shall be filled up by the state which first made the appointment.

Art. VIII. All charges of war, and all other expences that shall be incurred for the common defence or general welfare, and allowed by the united states in congress assembled, shall be defrayed out of a common treasury, which shall be supplied by the several states in proportion to the value of all land within each state, granted to or surveyed for any Person, as such land and the buildings and improvements thereon shall be estimated according to such mode as the united states in congress assembled, shall from time to time direct and appoint.

The taxes for paying that proportion shall be laid and levied by the authority and direction of the legislatures of the several states within the time agreed upon by the united states in congress assembled.

Art. IX. The united states in congress assembled, shall have the sole and exclusive right and power of determining on peace and war, except in the cases mentioned in the sixth article—of sending and receiving ambassadors—entering into treaties and alliances, provided that no treaty of commerce shall be made whereby the legislative power of the respective states shall be restrained from imposing such imposts and duties on foreigners, as their own people are subjected to, or from prohibiting the exportation of any species of goods or commodities whatsoever—of establishing rules for deciding in all cases, what captures on land or water shall be legal, and in what manner prizes taken by land or naval forces in the service of the united states shall be divided or appropriated—of granting letters of marque and reprisal in times of peace—appointing courts for the trial of piracies and felonies committed on the high seas and establishing courts for receiving and determining finally appeals in all cases of captures, provided that no member of congress shall be appointed a judge of any of the said courts.

The united states in congress assembled shall also be the last resort on appeal in all disputes and differences now subsisting or that hereafter may arise between two or more states concerning boundary, jurisdiction or any other cause whatever; which authority shall always be exercised in the manner following. Whenever the legislative or executive authority or lawful agent of any state in controversy with another shall present a petition to congress stating the matter in question and praying for a hearing, notice thereof shall be given by order of congress to the legislative or executive authority of the other state in controversy, and a day assigned for the appearance of the parties by their lawful agents, who shall then be directed to appoint by joint consent, commissioners or judges to constitute a court for hearing and determining the matter in question: but if they cannot agree, congress shall name three persons out of each of the united states, and from the list of such persons each party shall alternately strike out one, the petitioners beginning, until the number shall be reduced to thirteen; and from that number not less than seven, nor more than nine names as congress shall direct, shall in the presence of congress be drawn out by lot, and the persons whose names shall be so drawn or any five of them, shall be commissioners or judges, to hear and finally determine the controversy, so always as a major part of the judges who shall hear the cause shall agree in the determination: and if either party shall neglect to attend at the day appointed, without shewing reasons, which congress shall judge sufficient, or being present shall refuse to strike, the congress shall proceed to nominate three persons out of each state, and the secretary of congress shall strike in behalf of such party absent or refusing; and the judgment and sentence of the court to be appointed, in the manner before prescribed, shall be final and conclusive; and if any of the parties shall refuse to submit to the authority of such court, or to appear to defend their claim or cause, the court shall nevertheless proceed to pronounce sentence, or judgment, which shall in like manner be final and decisive, the judgment or sentence and other proceedings being in either case transmitted to congress, and lodged among the acts of congress for the security of the parties concerned: provided that every commissioner, before he sits in judgment, shall take an oath to be administered by one of the judges of the supreme or superior court of the state, where the cause shall be tried, "well and truly to hear and determine the matter in question, according to the best of his judgment, without favour, affection or hope of reward:" provided also, that no state shall be deprived of territory for the benefit of the united states.

All controversies concerning the private right of soil claimed under different grants of two or more states, whose jurisdictions as they may respect such lands, and the states which passed such grants are adjusted, the said grants or either of them being at the same time claimed to have originated antecedent to such settlement of jurisdiction, shall on the petition of either party to the congress of the united states, be finally determined as near as may be in the same manner as is before prescribed for deciding disputes respecting territorial jurisdiction between different states.

The united states in congress assembled shall also have the sole and exclusive right and power of regulating the alloy and value of coin struck by their own authority, or by that of the respective states—fixing the standard of weights and measures throughout the united states—regulating the trade and managing all affairs with the Indians, not members of any of the states, provided that the legislative right of any state within its own limits be not infringed or violated—establishing and regulating post-offices from one state to another, throughout all the united states, and exacting such postage on the papers passing thro' the same as may be requisite to defray the expences of the said office—appointing all officers of the land forces, in the service of the united states, excepting regimental officers—appointing all the officers of the naval forces, and commissioning all officers whatever in the service of the united states—making rules for the government and regulation of the said land and naval forces, and directing their operations.

The united states in congress assembled shall have authority to appoint a committee, to sit in the recess of congress, to be denominated "A Committee of the States," and to consist of one delegate from each state; and to appoint such other committees and civil officers as may be necessary for managing the general affairs of the united states under their direction—to appoint one of their number to preside, provided that no person be allowed to serve in the office of president more than one year in any term of three years; to ascertain the necessary sums of Money to be raised for the service of the united states, and to appropriate and apply the same for defraying the public expenses—to borrow money, or emit bills on the credit of the united states, transmitting every half year to the respective states an account of the sums of money so borrowed or emitted,—to build and equip a navy—to agree upon the number of land forces, and to make requisitions from each state for its quota, in proportion to the number of white inhabitants in such state; which requisition shall be binding, and thereupon the legislature of each state shall appoint the regimental officers, raise the men and cloath, arm and equip then in a soldier like manner, at the expense of the united states; and the officers and men so cloathed, armed and equipped shall march to the place appointed, and within the time agreed on by the united states in congress assembled: But if the united states in congress assembled shall, on consideration of circumstances judge proper that any state should not raise men, or should raise a smaller number than its quota, and that any other state should raise a greater number of men than the quota thereof, such extra number shall be raised, officered, cloathed, armed and equipped in the same manner as the quota of such state, unless the legislature of such state shall judge that such extra number cannot be safely spared out of the same, in which case they shall raise officer, cloath, arm and equip as many of such extra number as they judge can be safely spared. And the officers and men so cloathed, armed and equipped, shall march to the place appointed, and within the time agreed on by the united states in congress assembled.

The united states in congress assembled shall never engage in a war, nor grant letters of marque and reprisal in time of peace, nor enter into any treaties or alliances, nor coin money, nor regulate the value thereof, nor ascertain the sums and expenses necessary for the defence and welfare of the united states, or any of them, nor emit bills, nor borrow money on the credit of the united states, nor appropriate money, nor agree upon the number of vessels of war, to be built or purchased, or the number of land or sea forces to be raised, nor appoint a commander in chief of the army or navy, unless nine states assent to the same: nor shall a question on any other point, except for adjourning from day to day be determined, unless by the votes of a majority of the united states in congress assembled.

The congress of the united states shall have power to adjourn to any time within the year, and to any place within the united states, so that no period of adjournment be for a longer duration than the space of six Months, and shall publish the Journal of their proceedings monthly, except such parts thereof relating to treaties, alliances or military operations, as in their judgment require secrecy; and the yeas and nays of the delegates of each state on any question shall be entered on the Journal, when it is desired by any delegate; and the delegates of a state, or any of them, at his or their request shall be furnished with a transcript of the said Journal, except such parts as are above excepted, to lay before the legislatures of the several states.

Art. X. The committee of the states, or any nine of them, shall be authorised to execute, in the recess of congress, such of the powers of congress as the united states in congress assembled, by the consent of nine states, shall from time to time think expedient to vest them with; provided that no power be delegated to the said committee, for the exercise of which, by the articles of confederation, the voice of nine states in the congress of the united states assembled is requisite.

Art. XI. Canada acceding to this confederation, and joining in the measures of the united states, shall be admitted into, and entitled to all the advantages of this union: but no other colony shall be admitted into the same, unless such admission be agreed to by nine states.

Art. XII. All bills of credit emitted, monies borrowed and debts contracted by, or under the authority of congress, before the assembling of the united states, in pursuance of the present confederation, shall be deemed and considered as a charge against the united states, for payment and satisfaction whereof the said united states and the public faith are hereby solemnly pledged.

Art. XIII. Every state shall abide by the determinations of the united states in congress assembled, on all questions which by this confederation are submitted to them. And the Articles of this confederation shall be inviolably observed by every state, and the union shall be perpetual; nor shall any alteration at any time hereafter be made in any of them; unless such alteration be agreed to in a congress of the united states, and be afterwards confirmed by the legislatures of every state.

And Whereas it hath pleased the Great Governor of the World to incline the hearts of the legislatures we respectively represent in congress, to approve of, and to authorize us to ratify the said articles of confederation and perpetual union. Know Ye that we the undersigned delegates, by virtue of the power and authority to us given for that purpose, do by these presents, in the name and in behalf of our respective constituents, fully and entirely ratify and confirm each and every of the said articles of confederation and perpetual union, and all and singular the matters and things therein contained: And we do further solemnly plight and engage the faith of our respective constituents, that they shall abide by the determinations of the united states in congress assembled, on all questions, which by the said confederation are submitted to them. And that the articles thereof shall be inviolably observed by the states we respectively represent, and that the union shall be perpetual. In Witness whereof we have hereunto set our hands in Congress. Done at Philadelphia in the state of Pennsylvania the ninth day of July, in the Year of our Lord one Thousand seven Hundred and Seventy-eight, and in the third year of the independence of America.

The Constitution of the United States of America

[PREAMBLE]
We the People of the United States, in Order to form a more perfect Union, establish Justice, insure domestic Tranquility, provide for the common defence, promote the general Welfare, and secure the Blessings of Liberty to ourselves and our Posterity, do ordain and establish this Constitution for the United States of America.

Article I

Section 1

[LEGISLATIVE POWERS]

All legislative Powers herein granted shall be vested in a Congress of the United States, which shall consist of a Senate and House of Representatives.

Section 2

[HOUSE OF REPRESENTATIVES, HOW CONSTITUTED, POWER OF IMPEACHMENT]

The House of Representatives shall be composed of Members chosen every second Year by the People of the several States, and the Electors in each State shall have the Qualifications requisite for Electors of the most numerous Branch of the State Legislature.

No Person shall be a Representative who shall not have attained to the Age of twenty five Years, and been seven Years a Citizen of the United States, and who shall not, when elected, be an Inhabitant of that State in which he shall be chosen.

Representatives and *direct Taxes*[1] shall be apportioned among the several States which may be included within this Union, according to their respective Numbers, *which shall be determined by adding to the whole Number of free Persons, including those bound to Service for a Term of Years,* and excluding Indians not taxed, *three fifths of all other Persons.*[2] The actual Enumeration shall be made within three Years after the first Meeting of the Congress of the United States, and within every subsequent Term of ten Years, in such Manner as they shall by Law direct. The Number of Representatives shall not exceed one for every thirty Thousand, but each State shall have at Least one Representative; *and until such enumeration shall be made, the State of New Hampshire shall be entitled to chuse three, Massachusetts eight, Rhode-Island and Providence Plantations one, Connecticut five, New-York six, New Jersey four, Pennsylvania eight, Delaware one, Maryland six, Virginia ten, North Carolina five, South Carolina five, and Georgia three.*[3]

When vacancies happen in the Representation from any State, the Executive Authority thereof shall issue Writs of Election to fill such Vacancies.

The House of Representatives shall chuse their Speaker and other Officers; and shall have the sole Power of Impeachment.

Section 3

[THE SENATE, HOW CONSTITUTED, IMPEACHMENT TRIALS]

The Senate of the United States shall be composed of two Senators from each State, *chosen by the Legislature thereof,*[4] for six Years; and each Senator shall have one Vote.

[1]Modified by Sixteenth Amendment.

[2]Modified by Fourteenth Amendment.

[3]Temporary provision.

[4]Modified by Seventeenth Amendment.

Immediately after they shall be assembled in Consequence of the first Election, they shall be divided as equally as may be into three Classes. The Seats of the Senators of the first Class shall be vacated at the Expiration of the second Year, of the second Class at the Expiration of the fourth Year, and of the third Class at the Expiration of the sixth Year, so that one third may be chosen every second Year; *and if Vacancies happen by Resignation, or otherwise, during the Recess of the Legislature of any State, the Executive thereof may make temporary Appointments until the next Meeting of the Legislature, which shall then fill such Vacancies.*[5]

No Person shall be a Senator who shall not have attained to the Age of thirty Years, and been nine Years a Citizen of the United States, and who shall not, when elected, be an Inhabitant of that State for which he shall be chosen.

The Vice President of the United States shall be President of the Senate, but shall have no Vote, unless they be equally divided.

The Senate shall chuse their other Officers, and also a President pro tempore, in the Absence of the Vice President, or when he shall exercise the Office of President of the United States.

The Senate shall have the sole Power to try all Impeachments. When sitting for that Purpose, they shall be on Oath or Affirmation. When the President of the United States is tried, the Chief Justice shall preside: And no Person shall be convicted without the Concurrence of two thirds of the Members present.

Judgment in Cases of Impeachment shall not extend further than to removal from Office, and disqualification to hold and enjoy any Office of honor, Trust or Profit under the United States: but the Party convicted shall nevertheless be liable and subject to Indictment, Trial, Judgment and Punishment, according to Law.

Section 4

[ELECTION OF SENATORS AND REPRESENTATIVES]

The Times, Places and Manner of holding Elections for Senators and Representatives, shall be prescribed in each State by the Legislature thereof; but the Congress may at any time by Law make or alter such Regulations, except as to the Places of chusing Senators.

The Congress shall assemble at least once in every Year, and such Meeting shall be on the first Monday in December, unless they shall by Law appoint a different Day.[6]

[5]Modified by Seventeenth Amendment.

[6]Modified by Twentieth Amendment.

Section 5

[QUORUM, JOURNALS, MEETINGS, ADJOURNMENTS]

Each House shall be the Judge of the Elections, Returns and Qualifications of its own Members, and a Majority of each shall constitute a Quorum to do Business; but a smaller Number may adjourn from day to day, and may be authorized to compel the Attendance of absent Members, in such Manner, and under such Penalties as each House may provide.

Each House may determine the Rules of its Proceedings, punish its Members for disorderly Behaviour, and, with the Concurrence of two thirds, expel a Member.

Each House shall keep a Journal of its Proceedings, and from time to time publish the same, excepting such Parts as may in their Judgment require Secrecy; and the Yeas and Nays of the Members of either House on any questions shall, at the Desire of one fifth of those Present, be entered on the Journal.

Neither House, during the Session of Congress, shall, without the Consent of the other, adjourn for more than three days, nor to any other Place than that in which the two Houses shall be sitting.

Section 6

[COMPENSATION, PRIVILEGES, DISABILITIES]

The Senators and Representatives shall receive a Compensation for their Services, to be ascertained by Law, and paid out of the Treasury of the United States. They shall in all Cases, except Treason, Felony and Breach of the Peace, be privileged from Arrest during their Attendance at the Session of their respective Houses, and in going to and returning from the same; and for any Speech or Debate in either House, they shall not be questioned in any other Place.

No Senator or Representative shall, during the Time for which he was elected, be appointed to any civil Office under the Authority of the United States, which shall have been created, or the Emoluments whereof shall have been encreased during such time; and no Person holding any Office under the United States, shall be a Member of either House during his Continuance in Office.

Section 7

[PROCEDURE IN PASSING BILLS AND RESOLUTIONS]

All Bills for raising Revenue shall originate in the House of Representatives; but the Senate may propose or concur with Amendments as on other Bills.

Every Bill which shall have passed the House of Representatives and the Senate, shall, before it become a Law, be presented to the President of the United States: If he approve he shall sign it, but if not he shall return it, with his Objections to that House in which it shall have originated, who shall enter the Objections at large on their Journal, and proceed to reconsider it. If after such Reconsideration two thirds of that House shall agree to pass the Bill, it shall be sent, together with the Objections, to the other House, by which it shall likewise be reconsidered, and if approved by two thirds of that House, it shall become a Law. But in all such Cases the Votes of both Houses shall be determined by yeas and Nays, and the Names of the Persons voting for and against the Bill shall be entered on the Journal of each House respectively. If any Bill shall not be returned by the President within ten Days (Sundays excepted) after it shall have been presented to him, the Same shall be a Law, in like Manner as if he had signed it, unless the Congress by their Adjournment prevent its Return, in which Case it shall not be a Law.

Every Order, Resolution, or Vote to which the Concurrence of the Senate and House of Representatives may be necessary (except on a question of Adjournment) shall be presented to the President of the United States; and before the Same shall take Effect, shall be approved by him, or being disapproved by him, shall be repassed by two thirds of the Senate and House of Representatives, according to the Rules and Limitations prescribed in the Case of a Bill.

Section 8

[POWERS OF CONGRESS]

The Congress shall have Power

To lay and collect Taxes, Duties, Imposts and Excises, to pay the Debts and provide for the common Defence and general Welfare of the United States; but all Duties, Imposts and Excises shall be uniform throughout the United States;

To borrow Money on the credit of the United States;

To regulate Commerce with foreign Nations, and among the several States, and with the Indian Tribes;

To establish an uniform Rule of Naturalization, and uniform Laws on the subject of Bankruptcies throughout the United States;

To coin Money, regulate the Value thereof, and of foreign Coin, and fix the Standard of Weights and Measures;

To provide for the Punishment of counterfeiting the Securities and current Coin of the United States;

To establish Post Offices and post Roads;

To promote the Progress of Science and useful Arts, by securing for limited Times to Authors and Inventors the exclusive Right to their respective Writings and Discoveries;

To constitute Tribunals inferior to the supreme Court;

To define and punish Piracies and Felonies committed on the high Seas, and Offences against the Law of Nations;

To declare War, grant Letters of Marque and Reprisal, and make Rules concerning Captures on Land and Water;

To raise and support Armies, but no Appropriation of Money to that Use shall be for a longer Term than two Years;

To provide and maintain a Navy;

To make Rules for the Government and Regulation of the land and naval Forces;

To provide for calling forth the Militia to execute the Laws of the Union, suppress Insurrections and repel Invasions;

To provide for organizing, arming, and disciplining, the Militia, and for governing such Part of them as may be employed in the Service of the United States, reserving to the States respectively, the Appointment of the Officers, and the Authority of training the Militia according to the discipline prescribed by Congress;

To exercise exclusive Legislation in all Cases whatsoever, over such District (not exceeding ten Miles square) as may, by Cession of particular States, and the Acceptance of Congress, become the Seat of the Government of the United States, and to exercise like Authority over all Places purchased by the Consent of the Legislature of the State in which the Same shall be, for the Erection of Forts, Magazines, Arsenals, dock-Yards, and other needful Buildings;—And

To make all Laws which shall be necessary and proper for carrying into Execution the foregoing Powers, and all other Powers vested by this Constitution in the Government of the United States, or in any Department or Officer thereof.

Section 9

[SOME RESTRICTIONS ON FEDERAL POWER]

The Migration or Importation of such Persons as any of the States now existing shall think proper to admit, shall not be prohibited by the Congress prior to the Year one thousand eight hundred and eight, but a Tax or duty may be imposed on such Importation, not exceeding ten dollars for each Person.[7]

The Privilege of the Writ of Habeas Corpus shall not be suspended, unless when in Cases of Rebellion or Invasion the public Safety may require it.

No Bill of Attainder or ex post facto Law shall be passed.

No Capitation, or other direct, Tax shall be laid, unless in Proportion to the Census or Enumeration herein before directed to be taken.[8]

No Tax or Duty shall be laid on Articles exported from any State.

No Preference shall be given by any Regulation of Commerce or Revenue to the Ports of one State over those of another; nor shall Vessels bound to, or from, one State, be obliged to enter, clear, or pay Duties in another.

[7]Temporary provision.

[8]Modified by Sixteenth Amendment.

No Money shall be drawn from the Treasury, but in Consequence of Appropriations made by Law; and a regular Statement and Account of the Receipts and Expenditures of all public Money shall be published from time to time.

No Title of Nobility shall be granted by the United States: And no Person holding any Office of Profit or Trust under them, shall, without the Consent of the Congress, accept of any present, Emolument, Office, or Title, of any kind whatever, from any King, Prince, or foreign State.

Section 10

[RESTRICTIONS UPON POWERS OF STATES]

No State shall enter into any Treaty, Alliance, or Confederation; grant Letters of Marque and Reprisal; coin Money; emit Bills of Credit; make any Thing but gold and silver Coin a Tender in Payment of Debts; pass any Bill of Attainder, ex post facto Law, or Law impairing the Obligation of Contracts, or grant any Title of Nobility.

No State shall, without the Consent of the Congress, lay any Imposts or Duties on Imports or Exports, except what may be absolutely necessary for executing it's inspection Laws: and the net Produce of all Duties and Imposts, laid by any State on Imports or Exports, shall be for the Use of the Treasury of the United States; and all such Laws shall be subject to the Revision and Controul of the Congress.

No State shall, without the Consent of Congress, lay any Duty of Tonnage, keep Troops, or Ships of War in time of Peace, enter into any Agreement or Compact with another State, or with a foreign Power, or engage in War, unless actually invaded, or in such imminent Danger as will not admit of delay.

ARTICLE II

Section 1

[EXECUTIVE POWER, ELECTION, QUALIFICATIONS OF THE PRESIDENT]

The executive Power shall be vested in a President of the United States of America. *He shall hold his Office during the Term of four Years, and, together with the Vice President, chosen for the same Term, be elected, as follows*[9]

Each State shall appoint, in such Manner as the Legislature thereof may direct, a Number of Electors, equal to the whole Number of Senators and Representatives to which the State may be entitled in the Congress: but no Senator or Representative, or Person holding an Office of Trust or Profit under the United States, shall be appointed an Elector.

The electors shall meet in their respective States, and vote by ballot for two Persons, of whom one at least shall not be an Inhabitant of the same State with themselves. And they shall make a List of all the Persons voted for, and of the Number of Votes for each; which List they shall sign and certify, and transmit sealed to the Seat of the Government of the United States, directed to the President of the Senate. The President of the Senate shall, in the Presence of the Senate and House of Representatives, open all the Certificates, and the Votes shall then be counted. The Person having the greatest Number of Votes shall be the President, if such Number be a Majority of the whole Number of Electors appointed; and if there be more than one who have such Majority, and have an equal Number of Votes, then the House of Representatives shall immediately chuse by Ballot one of them for President; and if no Person have a Majority, then from the five highest on the List the said House shall in like Manner chuse the President. But in chusing the President, the Votes shall be taken by States, the Representation from each State having one Vote; A quorum for this Purpose shall consist of a Member or Members from two thirds of the States, and a Majority of all the States shall be necessary to a Choice. In every Case, after the Choice of the President, the person having the greatest Number of Votes of the Electors shall be the Vice President. But if there should remain two or more who have equal Votes, the Senate shall chuse from them by Ballot the Vice President.[10]

The Congress may determine the Time of chusing the Electors, and the Day on which they shall give their Votes; which Day shall be the same throughout the United States.

No Person except a natural born Citizen, or a Citizen of the United States, at the time of the Adoption of this Constitution, shall be eligible to the Office of President; neither shall any Person be eligible to that Office who shall not have attained to the Age of thirty five Years, and been fourteen Years a Resident within the United States.

In Case of the Removal of the President from Office, or his Death, Resignation, or Inability to discharge the Powers and Duties of the said Office, the Same shall devolve on the Vice President, and the Congress may by Law provide for the Case of Removal, Death, Resignation or Inability, both of the President and Vice President, declaring what Officer shall then act as President, and such Officer shall act accordingly, until the Disability be removed, or a President shall be elected.

The President shall, at stated Times, receive for his Services, a Compensation, which shall neither be increased nor diminished during the Period for which he shall have been elected, and he shall not receive within that Period any other Emolument from the United States, or any of them.

[9]Number of terms limited to two by Twenty-second Amendment.

[10]Modified by Twelfth and Twentieth Amendments.

Before he enter on the Execution of his Office, he shall take the following Oath or Affirmation:—"I do solemnly swear (or affirm) that I will faithfully execute the Office of President of the United States, and will to the best of my Ability, preserve, protect and defend the Constitution of the United States."

Section 2

[POWERS OF THE PRESIDENT]

The President shall be Commander in Chief of the Army and Navy of the United States, and of the Militia of the several States, when called into the actual Service of the United States; he may require the Opinion, in writing, of the principal Officer in each of the executive Departments, upon any Subject relating to the Duties of their respective Offices, and he shall have Power to grant Reprieves and Pardons for Offences against the United States, except in Cases of Impeachment.

He shall have Power, by and with the Advice and Consent of the Senate, to make Treaties, provided two thirds of the Senators present concur; and he shall nominate, and by and with the Advice and Consent of the Senate, shall appoint Ambassadors, other public Ministers and Consuls, Judges of the supreme Court, and all other Officers of the United States, whose Appointments are not herein otherwise provided for, and which shall be established by Law: but the Congress may by Law vest the Appointment of such inferior Officers, as they think proper, in the President alone, in the Courts of Law, or in the Heads of Departments.

The President shall have Power to fill up all Vacancies that may happen during the Recess of the Senate, by granting Commissions which shall expire at the End of their next Session.

Section 3

[POWERS AND DUTIES OF THE PRESIDENT]

He shall from time to time give to the Congress Information of the State of the Union, and recommend to their Consideration such Measures as he shall judge necessary and expedient; he may, on extraordinary Occasions, convene both Houses, or either of them, and in Case of Disagreement between them, with Respect to the Time of Adjournment, he may adjourn them to such Time as he shall think proper; he shall receive Ambassadors and other public Ministers; he shall take Care that the Laws be faithfully executed, and shall Commission all the Officers of the United States.

Section 4

[IMPEACHMENT]

The President, Vice President and all civil Officers of the United States, shall be removed from Office on Impeachment for, and Conviction of, Treason, Bribery, or other high Crimes and Misdemeanors.

ARTICLE III

Section 1

[JUDICIAL POWER, TENURE OF OFFICE]

The judicial Power of the United States, shall be vested in one supreme Court, and in such inferior Courts as the Congress may from time to time ordain and establish. The Judges, both of the supreme and inferior Courts, shall hold their Offices during good Behaviour, and shall, at stated Times, receive for their Services, a Compensation, which shall not be diminished during their Continuance in Office.

Section 2

[JURISDICTION]

The judicial Power shall extend to all Cases, in Law and Equity, arising under this Constitution, the Laws of the United States, and Treaties made, or which shall be made, under their Authority;—to all Cases affecting Ambassadors, other public Ministers and Consuls;—to all Cases of admiralty and maritime Jurisdiction;—to Controversies to which the United States shall be a Party;—to Controversies between two or more States;—*between a State and Citizens of another State;*—between Citizens of different States,—between Citizens of the same State claiming Lands under Grants of different States, *and between a State,* or the Citizens thereof, *and foreign States, Citizens or Subjects.*[11]

In all Cases affecting Ambassadors, other public Ministers and Consuls, and those in which a State shall be Party, the supreme Court shall have original Jurisdiction. In all the other Cases before mentioned, the supreme Court shall have appellate Jurisdiction, both as to Law and Fact, with such Exceptions, and under such Regulations as the Congress shall make.

The Trial of all Crimes, except in Cases of Impeachment, shall be by Jury; and such Trial shall be held in the State where the said Crimes shall have been committed; but when not committed within any State, the Trial shall be at such Place or Places as the Congress may by Law have directed.

Section 3

[TREASON, PROOF, AND PUNISHMENT]

Treason against the United States, shall consist only in levying War against them, or in adhering to their Enemies, giving them Aid and Comfort. No Person shall be con-

[11]Modified by Eleventh Amendment.

victed of Treason unless on the Testimony of two Witnesses to the same overt Act, or on Confession in open Court.

The Congress shall have Power to declare the Punishment of Treason, but no Attainder of Treason shall work Corruption of Blood, or Forfeiture except during the Life of the Person attainted.

ARTICLE IV

Section 1

[FAITH AND CREDIT AMONG STATES]

Full Faith and Credit shall be given in each State to the public Acts, Records, and judicial Proceedings of every other State. And the Congress may by general Laws prescribe the Manner in which such Acts, Records and Proceedings shall be proved, and the Effect thereof.

Section 2

[PRIVILEGES AND IMMUNITIES, FUGITIVES]

The Citizens of each State shall be entitled to all Privileges and Immunities of Citizens in the several States.

A Person charged in any State with Treason, Felony or other Crime, who shall flee from Justice, and be found in another State, shall on Demand of the executive Authority of the State from which he fled, be delivered up, to be removed to the State having Jurisdiction of the Crime.

No person held to Service or Labour in one State, under the Laws thereof, escaping into another, shall, in Consequence of any Law or Regulation therein, be discharged from such Service or Labour, but shall be delivered up on Claim of the Party to whom such Service or Labour may be due.[12]

Section 3

[ADMISSION OF NEW STATES]

New States may be admitted by the Congress into this Union; but no new State shall be formed or erected within the Jurisdiction of any other State; nor any State be formed by the Junction of two or more States, or Parts of States, without the Consent of the Legislatures of the States concerned as well as of the Congress.

The Congress shall have Power to dispose of and make all needful Rules and Regulations respecting the Territory or other Property belonging to the United States; and nothing in this Constitution shall be so construed as to Prejudice any Claims of the United States, or of any particular State.

Section 4

[GUARANTEE OF REPUBLICAN GOVERNMENT]

The United States shall guarantee to every State in this Union a Republican Form of Government, and shall protect each of them against Invasion; and on Application of the Legislature, or of the Executive (when the Legislature cannot be convened), against domestic Violence.

ARTICLE V

[AMENDMENT OF THE CONSTITUTION]

The Congress, whenever two thirds of both Houses shall deem it necessary, shall propose Amendments to this Constitution, or, on the Application of the Legislatures of two thirds of the several States, shall call a Convention for proposing Amendments, which, in either Case, shall be valid to all Intents and Purposes, as Part of this Constitution, when ratified by the Legislatures of three fourths of the several States, or by Conventions in three fourths thereof, as the one or the other Mode of Ratification may be proposed by the Congress; *Provided that no Amendment which may be made prior to the Year One thousand eight hundred and eight shall in any Manner affect the first and fourth Clauses in the Ninth Section of the first Article;*[13] and that no State, without its Consent, shall be deprived of its equal Suffrage in the Senate.

ARTICLE VI

[DEBTS, SUPREMACY, OATH]

All Debts contracted and Engagements entered into, before the Adoption of this Constitution, shall be as valid against the United States under this Constitution, as under the Confederation.

This Constitution, and the Laws of the United States which shall be made in Pursuance thereof; and all Treaties made, or which shall be made, under the Authority of the United States, shall be the supreme Law of the Land; and the Judges in every State shall be bound thereby, any Thing in the Constitution or Laws of any State to the Contrary notwithstanding.

The Senators and Representatives before mentioned, and the Members of the several State Legislatures, and all executive and judicial Officers, both of the United States and of the several States, shall be bound by Oath or Affirmation, to support this Constitution; but no religious Test shall be required as a Qualification to any Office or public Trust under the United States.

[12]Repealed by the Thirteenth Amendment.

[13]Temporary provision.

ARTICLE VII

[RATIFICATION AND ESTABLISHMENT]

The Ratification of the Conventions of nine States, shall be sufficient for the Establishment of this Constitution between the States so ratifying the Same.[14]

Done in Convention by the Unanimous Consent of the States present the Seventeenth Day of September in the Year of our Lord one thousand seven hundred and Eighty seven and of the Independence of the United States of America the Twelfth. *In Witness* whereof We have hereunto subscribed our Names,

G:° WASHINGTON—
Presidt. and deputy from Virginia

NEW HAMPSHIRE
John Langdon
Nicholas Gilman

MASSACHUSETTS
Nathaniel Gorham
Rufus King

CONNECTICUT
Wm. Saml. Johnson
Roger Sherman

NEW YORK
Alexander Hamilton

NEW JERSEY
Wil: Livingston
David Brearley
Wm. Paterson
Jona: Dayton

PENNSYLVANIA
B Franklin
Thomas Mifflin
Robt. Morris
Geo. Clymer
Thos. FitzSimons
Jared Ingersoll
James Wilson
Gouv Morris

DELAWARE
Geo: Read
Gunning Bedford jun
John Dickinson
Richard Bassett
Jaco: Broom

MARYLAND
James McHenry
Dan of St Thos. Jenifer
Danl. Carroll

VIRGINIA
John Blair—
James Madison Jr.

NORTH CAROLINA
Wm. Blount
Richd. Dobbs Spaight
Hu Williamson

SOUTH CAROLINA
J. Rutledge
Charles Cotesworth Pinckney
Charles Pinckney
Pierce Butler

GEORGIA
William Few
Abr Baldwin

[14]The Constitution was submitted on September 17, 1787, by the Constitutional Convention, was ratified by the conventions of several states at various dates up to May 29, 1790, and became effective on March 4, 1789.

Amendments to the Constitution

Proposed by Congress and Ratified by the Legislatures of the Several States, Pursuant to Article V of the Original Constitution.

Amendments I-X, known as the Bill of Rights, were proposed by Congress on September 25, 1789, and ratified on December 15, 1791.

Amendment I

[FREEDOM OF RELIGION, OF SPEECH, AND OF THE PRESS]

Congress shall make no law respecting an establishment of religion, or prohibiting the free exercise thereof; or abridging the freedom of speech, or of the press; or the right of the people peaceably to assemble, and to petition the Government for a redress of grievances.

Amendment II

[RIGHT TO KEEP AND BEAR ARMS]

A well regulated Militia, being necessary to the security of a free State, the right of the people to keep and bear Arms, shall not be infringed.

Amendment III

[QUARTERING OF SOLDIERS]

No Soldier shall, in time of peace be quartered in any house, without the consent of the Owner, nor in time of war, but in a manner to be prescribed by law.

Amendment IV

[SECURITY FROM UNWARRANTABLE SEARCH AND SEIZURE]

The right of the people to be secure in their persons, houses, papers, and effects, against unreasonable searches and seizures, shall not be violated, and no Warrants shall issue, but upon probable cause, supported by Oath or affirmation, and particularly describing the place to be searched, and the persons or things to be seized.

Amendment V

[RIGHTS OF ACCUSED PERSONS IN CRIMINAL PROCEEDINGS]

No person shall be held to answer for a capital, or otherwise infamous crime, unless on a presentment or indictment of a Grand Jury, except in cases arising in the land or naval forces, or in the Militia, when in actual service in time of War or in public danger; nor shall any person be subject for the same offence to be twice put in jeopardy of life or limb; nor shall be compelled in any criminal case to be a witness against himself, nor be deprived of life, liberty, or property, without due process of law; nor shall private property be taken for public use, without just compensation.

Amendment VI

[RIGHT TO SPEEDY TRIAL, WITNESSES, ETC.]

In all criminal prosecutions, the accused shall enjoy the right to a speedy and public trial, by an impartial jury of the State and district wherein the crime shall have been committed, which district shall have been previously ascertained by law, and to be informed of the nature and cause of the accusation; to be confronted with the witnesses against him; to have compulsory process for obtaining witnesses in his favor, and to have the Assistance of Counsel for his defence.

Amendment VII

[TRIAL BY JURY IN CIVIL CASES]

In suits at common law, where the value in controversy shall exceed twenty dollars, the right of trial by jury shall be preserved, and no fact tried by a jury, shall be otherwise reexamined in any Court of the United States, than according to the rules of the common law.

Amendment VIII

[BAILS, FINES, PUNISHMENTS]

Excessive bail shall not be required, nor excessive fines imposed, nor cruel and unusual punishments inflicted.

Amendment IX

[RESERVATION OF RIGHTS OF PEOPLE]

The enumeration in the Constitution, of certain rights, shall not be construed to deny or disparage others retained by the people.

Amendment X

[POWERS RESERVED TO STATES OR PEOPLE]

The powers not delegated to the United States by the Constitution, nor prohibited by it to the States, are reserved to the States respectively, or to the people.

Amendment XI

[Proposed by Congress on March 4, 1794; declared ratified on January 8, 1798.]

[RESTRICTION OF JUDICIAL POWER]

The Judicial power of the United States shall not be construed to extend to any suit in law or equity, commenced or prosecuted against one of the United States by Citizens of another State, or by Citizens or Subjects of any Foreign State.

Amendment XII

[Proposed by Congress on December 9, 1803; declared ratified on September 25, 1804.]

[ELECTION OF PRESIDENT AND VICE PRESIDENT]

The Electors shall meet in their respective states and vote by ballot for President and Vice-President, one of whom, at least, shall not be an inhabitant of the same state with themselves; they shall name in their ballots the person voted for as President, and in distinct ballots the person voted for as Vice-President, and they shall make distinct lists of all persons voted for as President, and of all persons voted for as Vice-President, and of the number of votes for each, which lists they shall sign and certify, and transmit sealed to the seat of the government of the United States, directed to the President of the Senate;—the President of the Senate shall, in presence of the Senate and House of Representatives, open all the certificates and the votes shall then be counted;—The person having the greatest number of votes for President, shall be the President, if such number be a majority of the whole number of Electors appointed; and if no person have such majority, then from the persons having the highest numbers not exceeding three on the list of those voted for as President, the House of Representatives shall choose immediately, by ballot, the President. But in choosing the President, the votes shall be taken by states, the representation from each state having one vote; a quorum for this purpose shall consist of a member or members from two-thirds of the states, and a majority of all the states shall be necessary to a choice. And if the House of Representatives shall not choose a President whenever the right of choice shall devolve upon them, before the fourth day of March next following, then the Vice-President shall act as President, as in the case of the death or other constitutional disability of the President.—The person having the greatest number of votes as Vice-President, shall be the Vice-President, if such number be a majority of the whole number of Electors appointed, and if no person have a majority, then from the two highest numbers on the list, the Senate shall choose the Vice-President; a quorum for the purpose shall consist of two-thirds of the whole number of Senators, and a majority of the whole number shall be necessary to a choice. But no person constitutionally ineligible to the office of President shall be eligible to that of Vice-President of the United States.

Amendment XIII

[Proposed by Congress on January 31, 1865; declared ratified on December 18, 1865.]

Section 1

[ABOLITION OF SLAVERY]

Neither slavery nor involuntary servitude, except as a punishment for crime whereof the party shall have been duly convicted, shall exist within the United States, or any place subject to their jurisdiction.

Section 2

[POWER TO ENFORCE THIS ARTICLE]

Congress shall have power to enforce this article by appropriate legislation.

AMENDMENT XIV

[Proposed by Congress on June 13, 1866, declared ratified on July 28, 1868.]

Section 1

[CITIZENSHIP RIGHTS NOT TO BE ABRIDGED BY STATES]

All persons born or naturalized in the United States, and subject to the jurisdiction thereof, are citizens of the United States and of the State wherein they reside. No State shall make or enforce any law which shall abridge the privileges or immunities of citizens of the United States; nor shall any State deprive any person of life, liberty, or property, without due process of law; nor deny to any person within its jurisdiction the equal protection of the laws.

Section 2

[APPORTIONMENT OF REPRESENTATIVES IN CONGRESS]

Representatives shall be apportioned among the several States according to their respective numbers, counting the whole number of persons in each State, excluding Indians not taxed. But when the right to vote at any election for the choice of electors for President and Vice- President of the United States, Representatives in Congress, the Executive and Judicial officers of a State, or the members of the Legislature thereof, is denied to any of the male inhabitants of such State, being twenty-one years of age, and citizens of the United States, or in any way abridged, except for participation in rebellion, or other crime, the basis of representation therein shall be reduced in the proportion which the number of such male citizens shall bear to the whole number of male citizens twenty-one years of age in such State.

Section 3

[PERSONS DISQUALIFIED FROM HOLDING OFFICE]

No person shall be a Senator or Representative in Congress, or elector of President and Vice-President, or hold any office, civil or military, under the United States, or under any State, who, having previously taken an oath, as a member of Congress, or as an officer of the United States, or as a member of any State legislature, or as an executive or judicial officer of any State, to support the Constitution of the United States, shall have engaged in insurrection or rebellion against the same, or given aid or comfort to the enemies thereof. But Congress may by a vote of two-thirds of each House, remove such disability.

Section 4

[WHAT PUBLIC DEBTS ARE VALID]

The validity of the public debt of the United States, authorized by law, including debts incurred for payment of pensions and bounties for services in suppressing insurrection or rebellion, shall not be questioned. But neither the United States nor any State shall assume or pay any debt or obligation incurred in aid of insurrection or rebellion against the United States, or any claim for the loss or emancipation of any slave; but all such debts, obligations and claims shall be held illegal and void.

Section 5

[POWER TO ENFORCE THIS ARTICLE]

The Congress shall have power to enforce, by appropriate legislation, the provisions of this article.

AMENDMENT XV

[Proposed by Congress on February 26, 1869; declared ratified on March 30, 1870.]

Section 1

[NEGRO SUFFRAGE]

The right of citizens of the United States to vote shall not be denied or abridged by the United States or by any State on account of race, color, or previous condition of servitude.

Section 2

[POWER TO ENFORCE THIS ARTICLE]

The Congress shall have power to enforce this article by appropriate legislation.

AMENDMENT XVI

[Proposed by Congress on July 2, 1909; declared ratified on February 25, 1913.]

[AUTHORIZING INCOME TAXES]

The Congress shall have power to lay and collect taxes on incomes, from whatever source derived, without apportionment among the several States, and without regard to any census or enumeration.

Amendment XVII

[Proposed by Congress on May 13, 1912; declared ratified on May 31, 1913.]

[POPULAR ELECTION OF SENATORS]

The Senate of the United States shall be composed of two Senators from each State, elected by the people thereof, for six years; and each Senator shall have one vote. The electors in each State shall have the qualifications requisite for electors of the most numerous branch of the State legislatures.

When vacancies happen in the representation of any State in the Senate, the executive authority of such State shall issue writs of election to fill such vacancies: *Provided,* That the legislature of any State may empower the executive thereof to make temporary appointments until the people fill the vacancies by election as the legislature may direct.

This amendment shall not be so construed as to affect the election or term of any Senator chosen before it becomes valid as part of the Constitution.

Amendment XVIII

[Proposed by Congress December 18, 1917; declared ratified on January 29, 1919.]

Section 1

[NATIONAL LIQUOR PROHIBITION]

After one year from the ratification of this article the manufacture, sale, or transportation of intoxicating liquors within, the importation thereof into, or the exportation thereof from the United States and all territory subject to the jurisdiction thereof for beverage purposes is hereby prohibited.

Section 2

[POWER TO ENFORCE THIS ARTICLE]

The Congress and the several States shall have concurrent power to enforce this article by appropriate legislation.

Section 3

[RATIFICATION WITHIN SEVEN YEARS]

This article shall be inoperative unless it shall have been ratified as an amendment to the Constitution by the legislatures of the several States, as provided in the Constitution, within seven years from the date of the submission hereof to the States by the Congress.[1]

Amendment XIX

[Proposed by Congress on June 4, 1919; declared ratified on August 26, 1920.]

[WOMAN SUFFRAGE]

The right of citizens of the United States to vote shall not be denied or abridged by the United States or by any State on account of sex.

Congress shall have power to enforce this article by appropriate legislation.

Amendment XX

[Proposed by Congress on March 2, 1932; declared ratified on February 6, 1933.]

Section 1

[TERMS OF OFFICE]

The terms of the President and Vice President shall end at noon on the 20th day of January, and the terms of Senators and Representatives at noon on the 3d day of January, of the years in which such terms would have ended if this article had not been ratified; and the terms of their successors shall then begin.

Section 2

[TIME OF CONVENING CONGRESS]

The Congress shall assemble at least once in every year, and such meeting shall begin at noon on the 3d day of January, unless they shall by law appoint a different day.

Section 3

[DEATH OF PRESIDENT-ELECT]

If, at the time fixed for the beginning of the term of the President, the President elect shall have died, the Vice President elect shall become President. If a President shall not have been chosen before the time fixed for the beginning of his term, or if the President elect shall have failed to qualify, then the Vice President elect shall act as President until a President shall have qualified; and the Congress may by law provide for the case wherein neither

[1]Repealed by the Twenty-first Amendment

a President elect nor a Vice President elect shall have qualified, declaring who shall then act as President, or the manner in which one who is to act shall be selected, and such person shall act accordingly until a President or Vice President shall have qualified.

Section 4

[ELECTION OF THE PRESIDENT]

The Congress may by law provide for the case of the death of any of the persons from whom the House of Representatives may choose a President whenever the right of choice shall have devolved upon them, and for the case of the death of any of the persons from whom the Senate may choose a Vice President whenever the right of choice shall have devolved upon them.

Section 5

[AMENDMENT TAKES EFFECT]

Sections 1 and 2 shall take effect on the 15th day of October following the ratification of this article.

Section 6

[RATIFICATION WITHIN SEVEN YEARS]

This article shall be inoperative unless it shall have been ratified as an amendment to the Constitution by the legislatures of three-fourths of the several States within seven years from the date of its submission.

AMENDMENT XXI

[Proposed by Congress on February 20, 1933; declared ratified on December 5, 1933.]

Section 1

[NATIONAL LIQUOR PROHIBITION REPEALED]

The eighteenth article of amendment to the Constitution of the United States is hereby repealed.

Section 2

[TRANSPORTATION OF LIQUOR INTO "DRY" STATES]

The transportation or importation into any State, Territory, or Possession of the United States for delivery or use therein of intoxicating liquors, in violation of the laws thereof, is hereby prohibited.

Section 3

[RATIFICATION WITHIN SEVEN YEARS]

This article shall be inoperative unless it shall have been ratified as an amendment to the Constitution by conventions in the several States, as provided in the Constitution, within seven years from the date of the submission hereof to the States by the Congress.

AMENDMENT XXII

[Proposed by Congress on March 21, 1947; declared ratified on February 27, 1951.]

Section 1

[TENURE OF PRESIDENT LIMITED]

No person shall be elected to the office of President more than twice, and no person who has held the office of President or acted as President, for more than two years of a term to which some other person was elected President shall be elected to the office of the President more than once. But this Article shall not apply to any person holding the office of President when this Article was proposed by the Congress, and shall not prevent any person who may be holding the office of President, or acting as President, during the term within which this Article becomes operative from holding the office of President or acting as President during the remainder of such term.

Section 2

[RATIFICATION WITHIN SEVEN YEARS]

This article shall be inoperative unless it shall have been ratified as an amendment to the Constitution by the legislatures of three-fourths of the several States within seven years from the date of its submission to the States by the Congress.

AMENDMENT XXIII

[Proposed by Congress on June 16, 1960; declared ratified on March 29, 1961.]

Section 1

[ELECTORAL COLLEGE VOTES FOR THE DISTRICT OF COLUMBIA]

The District constituting the seat of Government of the United States shall appoint in such manner as the Congress may direct:

A number of electors of President and Vice President equal to the whole number of Senators and Representatives in Congress to which the District would be entitled if it were a State, but in no event more than the least populous State; they shall be in addition to those appointed by the

States, but they shall be considered, for the purposes of the election of President and Vice President, to be electors appointed by a State; and they shall meet in the District and perform such duties as provided by the twelfth article of amendment.

Section 2

[POWER TO ENFORCE THIS ARTICLE]

The Congress shall have power to enforce this article by appropriate legislation.

AMENDMENT XXIV

[Proposed by Congress on August 27, 1962; declared ratified on January 23, 1964.]

Section 1

[ANTI-POLL TAX]

The right of citizens of the United States to vote in any primary or other election for President or Vice President, for electors for President or Vice President, or for Senator or Representative of Congress, shall not be denied or abridged by the United States or any State by reason of failure to pay any poll tax or other tax.

Section 2

[POWER TO ENFORCE THIS ARTICLE]

The Congress shall have power to enforce this article by appropriate legislation.

AMENDMENT XXV

[Proposed by Congress on July 6, 1965; declared ratified on February 10, 1967.]

Section 1

[VICE PRESIDENT TO BECOME PRESIDENT]

In case of the removal of the President from office or his death or resignation, the Vice President shall become President.

Section 2

[CHOICE OF A NEW VICE PRESIDENT]

Whenever there is a vacancy in the office of the Vice President, the President shall nominate a Vice President who shall take the office upon confirmation by a majority vote of both houses of Congress.

Section 3

[PRESIDENT MAY DECLARE OWN DISABILITY]

Whenever the President transmits to the President pro tempore of the Senate and the Speaker of the House of Representatives his written declaration that he is unable to discharge the powers and duties of his office, and until he transmits to them a written declaration to the contrary, such powers and duties shall be discharged by the Vice President as Acting President.

Section 4

[ALTERNATE PROCEDURES TO DECLARE AND TO END PRESIDENTIAL DISABILITY]

Whenever the Vice President and a majority of either the principal officers of the executive departments, or of such other body as Congress may by law provide, transmit to the President pro tempore of the Senate and the Speaker of the House of Representatives their written declaration that the President is unable to discharge the powers and duties of his office, the Vice President shall immediately assume the powers and duties of the office as Acting President.

Thereafter, when the President transmits to the President pro tempore of the Senate and the Speaker of the House of Representatives his written declaration that no inability exists, he shall resume the powers and duties of his office unless the Vice President and a majority of either the principal officers of the executive department, or of such other body as Congress may by law provide, transmit within four days to the President pro tempore of the Senate and the Speaker of the House of Representatives their written declaration that the President is unable to discharge the powers and duties of his office. Thereupon Congress shall decide the issue, assembling within forty eight hours for that purpose if not in session. If the Congress, within twenty one days after receipt of the latter written declaration, or, if Congress is not in session, within twenty one days after Congress is required to assemble, determines by two-thirds vote of both Houses that the President is unable to discharge the powers and duties of his office, the Vice President shall continue to discharge the same as Acting President; otherwise, the President shall resume the powers and duties of his office.

Amendment XXVI

[Proposed by Congress on March 23, 1971; declared ratified on July 1, 1971.]

Section 1

[EIGHTEEN-YEAR-OLD VOTE]

The right of citizens of the United States, who are eighteen years of age or older, to vote shall not be denied or abridged by the United States or by any State on account of age.

Section 2

[POWER TO ENFORCE THIS ARTICLE]

The Congress shall have power to enforce this article by appropriate legislation.

Amendment XXVII

[Proposed by Congress on September 25, 1789; declared ratified on May 8, 1992.]

[CONGRESS CANNOT RAISE ITS OWN PAY]

No law varying the compensation for the services of the Senators and Representatives, shall take effect, until an election of representatives shall have intervened.

The Federalist Papers

No. 10: Madison

Among the numerous advantages promised by a well constructed Union, none deserves to be more accurately developed than its tendency to break and control the violence of faction. The friend of popular governments never finds himself so much alarmed for their character and fate, as when he contemplates their propensity to this dangerous vice. He will not fail therefore to set a due value on any plan which, without violating the principles to which he is attached, provides a proper cure for it. The instability, injustice, and confusion introduced into the public councils have, in truth, been the mortal diseases under which popular governments have everywhere perished, as they continue to be the favorite and fruitful topics from which the adversaries to liberty derive their most specious declamations. The valuable improvements made by the American constitutions on the popular models, both ancient and modern, cannot certainly be too much admired; but it would be an unwarrantable partiality to contend that they have as effectually obviated the danger on this side, as was wished and expected. Complaints are everywhere heard from our most considerate and virtuous citizens, equally the friends of public and private faith and of public and personal liberty, that our governments are too unstable, that the public good is disregarded in the conflicts of rival parties, and that measures are too often decided, not according to the rules of justice and the rights of the minor party, but by the superior force of an interested and overbearing majority. However anxiously we may wish that these complaints had no foundation, the evidence of known facts will not permit us to deny that they are in some degree true. It will be found, indeed, on a candid review of our situation, that some of the distresses under which we labor have been erroneously charged on the operation of our governments; but it will be found, at the same time, that other causes will not alone account for many of our heaviest misfortunes; and, particularly, for that prevailing and increasing distrust of public engagements and alarm for private rights which are echoed from one end of the continent to the other. These must be chiefly, if not wholly, effects of the unsteadiness and injustice with which a factious spirit has tainted our public administration.

By a faction I understand a number of citizens, whether amounting to a majority or minority of the whole, who are united and actuated by some common impulse of passion, or of interest, adverse to the rights of other citizens, or to the permanent and aggregate interests of the community.

There are two methods of curing the mischiefs of faction: the one, by removing its causes; the other, by controlling its effects.

There are again two methods of removing the causes of faction: the one, by destroying the liberty which is essential to its existence; the other, by giving to every citizen the same opinions, the same passions, and the same interests.

It could never be more truly said than of the first remedy, that it is worse than the disease. Liberty is to faction what air is to fire, an aliment without which it instantly expires. But it could not be a less folly to abolish liberty, which is essential to political life, because it nourishes faction, than it would be to wish the annihilation of air, which is essential to animal life, because it imparts to fire its destructive agency.

The second expedient is as impracticable, as the first would be unwise. As long as the reason of man continues fallible, and he is at liberty to exercise it, different opinions will be formed. As long as the connection subsists between his reason and his self-love, his opinions and his passions will have a reciprocal influence on each other; and the former will be objects to which the latter will attach themselves. The diversity in the faculties of men, from which the rights of property originate, is not less an insuperable obstacle to a uniformity of interests. The protection of these faculties is the first object of Government. From the protection of different and unequal faculties of acquiring property, the possession of different degrees and kinds of property immediately results; and from the influence of these on the sentiments and views of the respective proprietors, ensues a division of the society into different interests and parties.

The latent causes of faction are thus sown in the nature of man; and we see them everywhere brought into different degrees of activity, according to the different circumstances of civil society. A zeal for different opinions concerning religion, concerning Government, and many other points, as well of speculation as of practice; an attachment to different leaders ambitiously contending for pre-eminence and power; or to persons of other descriptions whose fortunes have been interesting to the human passions, have in turn divided mankind into parties, inflamed them with mutual animosity, and rendered them much more disposed to vex and oppress each other, than to co-operate for their common good. So strong is this propensity of mankind to fall into mutual animosities, that where no substantial occasion presents itself, the most frivolous and fanciful distinctions have been sufficient to kindle their unfriendly passions, and excite their most violent conflicts. But the most common and durable source of factions has been the various and unequal distribution of property. Those who hold and those who are without property have ever formed distinct interests in society. Those who are creditors, and those who are debtors, fall under a like discrimination. A landed interest, a manufacturing interest, a mercantile interest, a moneyed interest, with many lesser interests, grow up of necessity in civilized nations, and divide them into different classes, actuated by different sentiments and views. The regulation of these various and interfering interests forms the principal task of modern Legislation, and involves the spirit of party and faction in the necessary and ordinary operations of Government.

No man is allowed to be judge in his own cause, because his interest would certainly bias his judgment and, not improbably, corrupt his integrity. With equal, nay with greater reason, a body of men are unfit to be both judges and parties at the same time; yet what are many of the most important acts of legislation but so many judicial determinations, not indeed concerning the rights of single persons, but concerning the rights of large bodies of citizens; and what are the different classes of legislators but advocates and parties to the causes which they determine? Is a law proposed concerning private debts? It is a question to which the creditors are parties on one side and the debtors on the other. Justice ought to hold the balance between them. Yet the parties are, and must be, themselves the judges; and the most numerous party, or in other words, the most powerful faction must be expected to prevail. Shall domestic manufacturers be encouraged, and in what degree, by restrictions on foreign manufacturers? are questions which would be differently decided by the landed and the manufacturing classes, and probably by neither with a sole regard to justice and the public good. The apportionment of taxes on the various descriptions of property is an act which seems to require the most exact impartiality; yet there is, perhaps, no legislative act in which greater opportunity and temptation are given to a predominant party to trample on the rules of justice. Every shilling with which they overburden the inferior number is a shilling saved to their own pockets.

It is in vain to say that enlightened statesmen will be able to adjust these clashing interests and render them all subservient to the public good. Enlightened statesmen will not always be at the helm. Nor, in many cases, can such an adjustment be made at all without taking into view indirect and remote considerations, which will rarely prevail over the immediate interest which one party may find in disregarding the rights of another or the good of the whole.

The inference to which we are brought is that the *causes* of faction cannot be removed and that relief is only to be sought in the means of controlling its *effects*.

If a faction consists of less than a majority, relief is supplied by the republican principle, which enables the majority to defeat its sinister views by regular vote. It may clog the administration, it may convulse the society; but it will be unable to execute and mask its violence under the forms of the Constitution. When a majority is included in a faction, the form of popular government, on the other hand, enables it to sacrifice to its ruling passion or interest both the public good and the rights of other citizens. To secure the public good and private rights against the danger of such a faction, and at the same time to preserve the spirit and the form of popular government, is then the great object to which our enquiries are directed. Let me add that it is the great desideratum by which alone this form of government can be rescued from the opprobrium under which it has so long labored and be recommended to the esteem and adoption of mankind.

By what means is this object attainable? Evidently by one of two only. Either the existence of the same passion or interest in a majority at the same time must be prevented, or the majority, having such co-existent passion or interest, must be rendered, by their number and local situation, unable to concert and carry into effect schemes of oppression. If the impulse and the opportunity be suffered to coincide, we well know that neither moral nor religious motives can be relied on as an adequate control. They are not found to be such on the injustice and violence of individuals, and lose their efficacy in proportion to the number combined together, that is, in proportion as their efficacy becomes needful.

From this view of the subject it may be concluded that a pure Democracy, by which I mean a Society consisting of a small number of citizens, who assemble and administer the Government in person, can admit of no cure for the mischiefs of faction. A common passion or interest will, in almost every case, be felt by a majority of the whole; a communication and concert results from the form of Government itself; and there is nothing to check the inducements to sacrifice the weaker party or an obnoxious individual. Hence it is that such Democracies have ever been spectacles of turbulence and contention; have ever been found incompatible with personal security or the rights of property; and have in general been as short in their lives as they have been violent in their deaths. Theoretic politicians, who have patronized this species of Government, have erroneously supposed that by reducing mankind to a perfect equality in their political rights, they would at the same time be perfectly equalized and assimilated in their possessions, their opinions, and their passions.

A Republic, by which I mean a Government in which the scheme of representation takes place, opens a different prospect and promises the cure for which we are seeking. Let us examine the points in which it varies from pure Democracy, and we shall comprehend both the nature of the cure and the efficacy which it must derive from the Union.

The two great points of difference between a Democracy and a Republic are: first, the delegation of the Government, in the latter, to a small number of citizens elected by the rest; secondly, the greater number of citizens and greater sphere of country over which the latter may be extended.

The effect of the first difference is, on the one hand, to refine and enlarge the public views by passing them through the medium of a chosen body of citizens, whose wisdom may best discern the true interest of their country and whose patriotism and love of justice will be least likely to sacrifice it to temporary or partial considerations. Under such a regulation it may well happen that the public voice, pronounced by the representatives of the people, will be more consonant to the public good than if pronounced by the people themselves, convened for the purpose. On the other hand, the effect may be inverted. Men of factious tempers, of local prejudices, or of sinister designs, may, by intrigue, by corruption, or by other means, first obtain the suffrages, and then betray the interests of the people. The question resulting is, whether small or extensive Republics are most favorable to the election of proper guardians of the public weal; and it is clearly decided in favor of the latter by two obvious considerations.

In the first place it is to be remarked that however small the Republic may be, the Representatives must be raised to a certain number in order to guard against the cabals of a few; and that however large it may be they must be limited to a certain number in order to guard against the confusion of a multitude. Hence, the number of Representatives in the two cases not being in proportion to that of the Constituents, and being proportionally greatest in the small Republic, it follows that if the proportion of fit characters be not less in the large than in the small Republic, the former will present a greater option, and consequently a greater probability of a fit choice.

In the next place, as each Representative will be chosen by a greater number of citizens in the large than in the small Republic, it will be more difficult for unworthy candidates to practise with success the vicious arts by which elections are too often carried; and the suffrages of the people being more free, will be more likely to centre on men who possess the most attractive merit and the most diffusive and established characters.

It must be confessed that in this, as in most other cases, there is a mean, on both sides of which inconveniencies will be found to lie. By enlarging too much the number of electors, you render the representative too little acquainted with all their local circumstances and lesser interests; as by reducing it too much, you render him unduly attached to these, and too little fit to comprehend and pursue great and national objects. The Federal Constitution forms a happy combination in this respect; the great and aggregate interests being referred to the national, the local and particular to the State legislatures.

The other point of difference is the greater number of citizens and extent of territory which may be brought within the compass of Republican than of Democratic Government; and it is this circumstance principally which renders factious combinations less to be dreaded in the former than in the latter. The smaller the society, the fewer probably will be the distinct parties and interests composing it; the fewer the distinct parties and interests, the more frequently will a majority be found of the same party; and the smaller the number of individuals composing a majority, and the smaller the compass within which they are placed, the more easily will they concert and execute their plans of oppression. Extend the sphere and you take in a greater variety of parties and interests; you make it less probable that a majority of the whole will have a common motive to invade the rights of other citizens; or if such a common motive exists, it will be more difficult for all who feel it to discover their own strength and to act in unison with each other. Besides other impediments, it may be remarked, that where there is a consciousness of unjust or dishonorable purposes, communication is always checked by distrust in proportion to the number whose concurrence is necessary.

Hence, it clearly appears that the same advantage which a Republic has over a Democracy in controlling the effects of faction is enjoyed by a large over a small republic—is enjoyed by the Union over the States composing it. Does this advantage consist in the substitution of representatives whose enlightened views and virtuous sentiments render them superior to local prejudices and to schemes of injustice? It will not be denied that the representation of the Union will be most likely to possess these requisite endowments. Does it consist in the greater security afforded by a greater variety of parties, against the event of any one party being able to outnumber and oppress the rest? In an equal degree does the increased variety of parties comprised within the Union increase this security? Does it, in fine, consist in the greater obstacles opposed to the concert and accomplishment of the secret wishes of an unjust and interested majority? Here again the extent of the Union gives it the most palpable advantage.

The influence of factious leaders may kindle a flame within their particular States but will be unable to spread a general conflagration through the other States: a religious sect may degenerate into a political faction in a part of the Confederacy; but the variety of sects dispersed over the entire face of it must secure the national Councils against any danger from that source: a rage for paper money, for an abolition of debts, for an equal division of property, or for any other improper or wicked project, will be less apt to pervade the whole body of the Union than a particular member of it; in the same proportion as such a malady is more likely to taint a particular county or district than an entire State.

In the extent and proper structure of the Union, therefore, we behold a republican remedy for the diseases most incident to Republican Government. And according to the degree of pleasure and pride we feel in being republicans ought to be our zeal in cherishing the spirit and supporting the character of federalist.

PUBLIUS

No. 51: Madison

To what expedient, then, shall we finally resort, for maintaining in practice the necessary partition of power among the several departments as laid down in the constitution? The only answer that can be given is that as all these exterior provisions are found to be inadequate the defect must be supplied, by so contriving the interior structure of the government as that its several constituent parts may, by their mutual relations, be the means of keeping each other in their proper places. Without presuming to undertake a full development of this important idea I will hazard a few general observations which may perhaps place it in a clearer light, and enable us to form a more correct judgment of the principles and structure of the government planned by the convention.

In order to lay a due foundation for that separate and distinct exercise of the different powers of government, which to a certain extent is admitted on all hands to be essential to the preservation of liberty, it is evident that each department should have a will of its own; and consequently should be so constituted that the members of each should have as little agency as possible in the appointment of the members of the others. Were this principle rigorously adhered to, it would require that all the appointments for the supreme executive, legislative, and judiciary magistracies should be drawn from the same fountain of authority, the people, through channels having no communication whatever with one another. Perhaps such a plan of constructing the several departments would be less difficult in practice than it may in contemplation appear. Some difficulties, however, and some additional expense would attend the execution of it. Some deviations, therefore, from the principle must be admitted. In the constitution of the judiciary department in particular, it might be inexpedient to insist rigorously on the principle: first, because peculiar qualifications being essential in the members, the primary consideration ought to be to select that mode of choice which best secures these qualifications; second, because the permanent tenure by which the appointments are held in that department must soon destroy all sense of dependence on the authority conferring them.

It is equally evident that the members of each department should be as little dependent as possible on those of the others for the emoluments annexed to their offices. Were the executive magistrate, or the judges, not independent of the legislature in this particular, their independence in every other would be merely nominal.

But the great security against a gradual concentration of the several powers in the same department consists in giving to those who administer each department the necessary constitutional means and personal motives to resist encroachments of the others. The provision for defence must in this, as in all other cases, be made commensurate to the danger of attack. Ambition must be made to counteract ambition. The interest of the man must be connected with the constitutional rights of the place. It may be a reflection on human nature that such devices should be necessary to control the abuses of government. But what is government itself but the greatest of all reflections on human nature? If men were angels, no government would be necessary. If angels were to govern men, neither external nor internal controls on government would be necessary. In framing a government which is to be administered by men over men, the great difficulty lies in this: You must first enable the government to control the governed; and in the next place oblige it to control itself. A dependence on the people is, no doubt, the primary control on the government; but experience has taught mankind the necessity of auxiliary precautions.

This policy of supplying, by opposite and rival interests, the defect of better motives, might be traced through the whole system of human affairs, private as well as public. We see it particularly displayed in all the subordinate distributions of power, where the constant aim is to divide and arrange the several offices in such a manner as that each may be a check on the other; that the private interest of every individual may be a sentinel over the public rights. These inventions of prudence cannot be less requisite in the distribution of the supreme powers of the State.

But it is not possible to give to each department an equal power of self-defense. In republican government, the legislative authority necessarily predominates. The remedy for this inconveniency is to divide the legislature into different branches; and to render them, by different modes of election and different principles of action, as little connected with each other as the nature of their common functions and their common dependence on the society will admit. It may even be necessary to guard against dangerous encroachments by still further precautions. As the weight of the legislative authority requires that it should be thus divided, the weakness of the executive may require, on the other hand, that it should be fortified. An absolute negative on the legislature appears, at first view, to be the natural defense with which the executive magistrate should be armed. But perhaps it would be neither altogether safe nor alone sufficient. On ordinary occasions it might not be exerted with the requisite firmness, and on extraordinary occasions it might be perfidiously abused. May not this defect of an absolute negative be supplied by some qualified connection between this weaker branch of the stronger department, by which the latter may be led to support the constitutional rights of the former, without being too much detached from the rights of its own department?

If the principles on which these observations are founded be just, as I persuade myself they are, and they be applied as a criterion to the several State constitutions, and to the federal Constitution, it will be found that if the latter does not perfectly correspond with them, the former are infinitely less able to bear such a test.

There are, moreover, two considerations particularly applicable to the federal system of America, which place that system in a very interesting point of view.

First. In a single republic, all the power surrendered by the people is submitted to the administration of a single government; and usurpations are guarded against by a division of the government into distinct and separate departments. In the compound republic of America, the power surrendered by the people is first divided between two distinct governments, and then the portion allotted to each subdivided among distinct and separate departments. Hence a double security arises to the rights of the people. The different governments will control each other, at the same time that each will be controlled by itself.

Second. It is of great importance in a republic not only to guard the society against the oppression of its rulers, but to guard one part of the society against the injustice of the other part. Different interests necessarily exist in different classes of citizens. If a majority be united by a common interest, the rights of the minority will be insecure. There are but two methods of providing against this evil: The one by creating a will in the community independent of the majority—that is, of the society itself; the other, by comprehending in the society so many separate descriptions of citizens as will render an unjust combination of a majority of the whole very improbable, if not impracticable. The first method prevails in all governments possessing an hereditary or self-appointed authority. This, at best, is but a precarious security; because a power independent of the society may as well espouse the unjust views of the major as the rightful interests of the minor party, and may possibly be turned against both parties. The second method will be exemplified in the federal republic of the United States. Whilst all authority in it will be derived from and dependent on the society, the society itself will be broken into so many parts, interests and classes of citizens, that the rights of individuals, or of the minority, will be in little danger from interested combinations of the majority. In a free government the security for civil rights must be the same as that for religious rights. It consists in the one case in the multiplicity of interests, and in the other in the multiplicity of sects. The degree of security in both cases will depend on the number of interests and sects; and this may be presumed to depend on the extent of country and number of people comprehended under the same government. This view of the subject must particularly recommend a proper federal system to all the sincere and considerate friends of republican government: Since it shows that in exact proportion as the territory of the Union may be formed into more circumscribed Confederacies, or States, oppressive combinations of a majority will be facilitated; the best security, under the republican form, for the rights of every class of citizens, will be diminished; and consequently the stability and independence of some member of the government, the only other security, must be proportionally increased. Justice is the end of government. It is the end of civil society. It ever has been and ever will be pursued until it be obtained, or until liberty be lost in the pursuit. In a society under the forms of which the stronger faction can readily unite and oppress the weaker, anarchy may as truly be said to reign as in a state of nature, where the weaker individual is not secured against the violence of the stronger: And as, in the latter state, even the stronger individuals are prompted, by the uncertainty of their condition, to submit to a government which may protect the weak as well as themselves: So, in the former state, will the more powerful factions or parties be gradually induced, by a like motive, to wish for a government which will protect all parties, the weaker as well as the more powerful. It can be little doubted that if the State of Rhode Island was separated from the Confederacy and left to itself, the insecurity of rights under the popular form of government within such narrow limits would be displayed by such reiterated oppressions of factious majorities that some power altogether independent of the people would soon be called for by the voice of the very factions whose misrule had proved the necessity of it. In the extended republic of the United States, and among the great variety of interests, parties, and sects which it embraces, a coalition of a majority of the whole society could seldom take place on any other principles than those of justice and the general good; and there being thus less danger to a minor from the will of the major party, there must be less pretext, also, to provide for the security of the former, by introducing into the government a will not dependent on the latter, or, in other words, a will independent of the society itself. It is no less certain than it is important, notwithstanding the contrary opinions which have been entertained, that the larger the society, provided it lie within a practicable sphere, the more duly capable it will be of self-government. And happily for the *republican cause,* the practicable sphere may be carried to a very great extent by a judicious modification and mixture of the *federal principle.*

PUBLIUS

Presidents and Vice Presidents

	President	Vice President
1	George Washington (Federalist 1789)	John Adams (Federalist 1789)
2	John Adams (Federalist 1797)	Thomas Jefferson (Dem.-Rep. 1797)
3	Thomas Jefferson (Dem.-Rep. 1801)	Aaron Burr (Dem.-Rep. 1801) George Clinton (Dem.-Rep. 1805)
4	James Madison (Dem.-Rep. 1809)	George Clinton (Dem.-Rep. 1809) Elbridge Gerry (Dem.-Rep. 1813)
5	James Monroe (Dem.-Rep. 1817)	Daniel D. Tompkins (Dem.-Rep. 1817)
6	John Quincy Adams (Dem.-Rep. 1825)	John C. Calhoun (Dem.-Rep. 1825)
7	Andrew Jackson (Democratic 1829)	John C. Calhoun (Democratic 1829) Martin Van Buren (Democratic 1833)
8	Martin Van Buren (Democratic 1837)	Richard M. Johnson (Democratic 1837)
9	William H. Harrison (Whig 1841)	John Tyler (Whig 1841)
10	John Tyler (Whig and Democratic 1841)	
11	James K. Polk (Democratic 1845)	George M. Dallas (Democratic 1845)
12	Zachary Taylor (Whig 1849)	Millard Fillmore (Whig 1849)
13	Millard Fillmore (Whig 1850)	

	President	Vice President
14	Franklin Pierce (Democratic 1853)	William R. D. King (Democratic 1853)
15	James Buchanan (Democratic 1857)	John C. Breckinridge (Democratic 1857)
16	Abraham Lincoln (Republican 1861)	Hannibal Hamlin (Republican 1861) Andrew Johnson (Unionist 1865)
17	Andrew Johnson (Unionist 1865)	
18	Ulysses S. Grant (Republican 1869)	Schuyler Colfax (Republican 1869) Henry Wilson (Republican 1873)
19	Rutherford B. Hayes (Republican 1877)	William A. Wheeler (Republican 1877)
20	James A. Garfield (Republican 1881)	Chester A. Arthur (Republican 1881)
21	Chester A. Arthur (Republican 1881)	
22	Grover Cleveland (Democratic 1885)	Thomas A. Hendricks (Democratic 1885)
23	Benjamin Harrison (Republican 1889)	Levi P. Morton (Republican 1889)
24	Grover Cleveland (Democratic 1893)	Adlai E. Stevenson (Democratic 1893)
25	William McKinley (Republican 1897)	Garret A. Hobart (Republican 1897) Theodore Roosevelt (Republican 1901)
26	Theodore Roosevelt (Republican 1901)	Charles W. Fairbanks (Republican 1905)

	President	Vice President
27	William H. Taft (Republican 1909)	James S. Sherman (Republican 1909)
28	Woodrow Wilson (Democratic 1913)	Thomas R. Marshall (Democratic 1913)
29	Warren G. Harding (Republican 1921)	Calvin Coolidge (Republican 1921)
30	Calvin Coolidge (Republican 1923)	Charles G. Dawes (Republican 1925)
31	Herbert Hoover (Republican 1929)	Charles Curtis (Republican 1929)
32	Franklin D. Roosevelt (Democratic 1933)	John Nance Garner (Democratic 1933) Henry A. Wallace (Democratic 1941) Harry S. Truman (Democratic 1945)
33.	Harry S. Truman (Democratic 1945)	Alben W. Barkley (Democratic 1949)
34.	Dwight D. Eisenhower (Republican 1953)	Richard M. Nixon (Republican 1953)

	President	Vice President
35	John F. Kennedy (Democratic 1961)	Lyndon B. Johnson (Democratic 1961)
36	Lyndon B. Johnson (Democratic 1963)	Hubert H. Humphrey (Democratic 1965)
37	Richard M. Nixon (Republican 1969)	Spiro T. Agnew (Republican 1969) Gerald R. Ford (Republican 1973)
38	Gerald R. Ford (Republican 1974)	Nelson Rockefeller (Republican 1974)
39	James E. Carter (Democratic 1977)	Walter Mondale (Democratic 1977)
40	Ronald Reagan (Republican 1981)	George H. W. Bush (Republican 1981)
41	George H. W. Bush (Republican 1989)	J. Danforth Quayle (Republican 1989)
42	William J. Clinton (Democrat 1993)	Albert Gore, Jr. (Democrat 1993)
43	George W. Bush, Jr. (Republican 2001)	Richard Cheney (Republican 2001)

Glossary

access the actual involvement of interest groups in the decision-making process

administrative adjudication applying rules and precedents to specific cases to settle disputes with regulated parties

administrative regulation rules made by regulatory agencies and commissions

affirmative action government policies or programs that seek to address past injustices against specified groups by making special efforts to provide members of these groups with access to educational and employment opportunities

agencies of socialization social institutions, including families and schools, that help to shape individuals' basic political beliefs and values

agency representation the type of representation by which representatives are held accountable to their constituency if they fail to represent that constituency properly. This is the incentive for good representation when the personal backgrounds, views, and interests of the representative differ from those of his or her constituency

agenda setting the power of the media to bring public attention to particular issues and problems

Aid to Families with Dependent Children (AFDC) federal funds, administered by the states, for children living with parents or relatives who fall below state standards of need. Replaced in 1996 by TANF

amendment a change added to a bill, law, or constitution

American political community citizens who are eligible to vote and participate in American political life

amicus curiae literally, "friend of the court"; individuals or groups who are not parties to a lawsuit but who seek to assist the Supreme Court in reaching a decision by presenting additional briefs

Antifederalists those who favored strong state governments and a weak national government and who were opponents of the constitution proposed at the American Constitutional Convention of 1787

antitrust policy government regulation of large businesses that have established monopolies

appellate court a court that hears the appeals of trial court decisions

appropriations the amounts of money approved by Congress in statutes (bills) that each unit or agency of government can spend

Articles of Confederation America's first written constitution; served as the basis for America's national government until 1789

attitude (or opinion) a specific preference on a particular issue

authoritarian government a system of rule in which the government recognizes no formal limits but may nevertheless be restrained by the power of other social institutions

autocracy a form of government in which a single individual—a king, queen, or dictator—rules

balance-of-power role the strategy whereby many countries from alliances with one or more other countries in order to counterbalance the behavior of other, usually more powerful, nation-states

bandwagon effect a shift in electoral support to the candidate that public opinion polls report as the front-runner

benign gerrymandering attempts to draw district boundaries so as to create districts made up primarily of disadvantaged or underrepresented minorities

bicameral having a legislative assembly composed of two chambers or houses; opposite of unicameral

bilateral treaties treaties made between two nations

bill a proposed law that has been sponsored by a member of Congress and submitted to the clerk of the House or Senate

Bill of Rights the first ten amendments to the Constitution, which guarantee certain rights and liberties to the people

bills of attainder laws that decree a person guilty of a crime without a trial

block grants federal grants-in-aid that allow states considerable discretion in how the funds should be spent

briefs written documents in which attorneys explain, using case precedents, why the court should find in favor of their client

Brown v. Board of Education the 1954 Supreme Court decision that struck down the "separate but equal" doctrine as fundamentally unequal. This case eliminated state power to use race as a criterion of discrimination in law and provided the national government with the power to intervene by exercising strict regulatory policies against discriminatory actions

budget deficit amount by which government spending exceeds government revenue in a fiscal year

bureaucracy the complex structure of offices, tasks, rules, and principles of organization that are employed by all large-scale institutions to coordinate effectively the work of their personnel

Cabinet the secretaries, or chief administrators, of the major departments of the federal government. Cabinet secretaries are appointed by the president with the consent of the Senate

campaign an effort by political candidates and their staffs to win the backing of donors, political activists, and voters in the quest for political office

capture an interest's acquisition of substantial influence over the government agency charged with regulating its activities

categorical grants congressional grants given to states and localities on the condition that expenditures be limited to a problem or group specified by the law

caucus (congressional) an association of members of Congress based on party, interest, or social group such as gender or race

caucus (political) a normally closed meeting of a political or legislative group to select candidates, plan strategy, or make decisions regarding legislative matters

checks and balances mechanisms through which each branch of government is able to participate in and influence the activities of the other branches. Major examples include the presidential veto power over congressional legislation, the power of the Senate to approve presidential appointments, and judicial review of congressional enactments

chief justice justice on the Supreme Court who presides over the Court's public sessions

citizenship informed and active membership in a political community

civic engagement a sense of concern among members of the political community about public social and political life, expressed through participation in social and political organizations

civil law a system of jurisprudence, including private law and governmental actions, to settle disputes that do not involve criminal penalties

civil liberties areas of personal freedom with which governments are constrained from interfering

civil penalties regulatory techniques in which fines or another form of material restitution is imposed for violating civil laws or common law principles, for example through negligence

civil rights legal or moral claims that citizens are entitled to make upon government

class action suit a legal action by which a group or class of individuals with common interests can file a suit on behalf of everyone who shares that interest

"clear and present danger" test test to determine whether speech is protected or unprotected, based on its capacity to present a "clear and present danger" to society

closed caucus a presidential nominating caucus open only to registered party members

closed primary a primary election in which voters can participate in the nomination of candidates, but only of the party in which they are enrolled for a period of time prior to primary day

closed rule a provision by the House Rules Committee limiting or prohibiting the introduction of amendments during debate

cloture a rule allowing a majority of two-thirds or three-fifths of the members in a legislative body to set a time limit on debate over a given bill

coalition a group in interests that join together for the purpose of influencing government

coattail effect the result of voters casting their ballot for president or governor and "automatically" voting for the remainder of the party's ticket

cold war the period of struggle between the United States and the former Soviet Union between the late 1940s and about 1990

collective goods benefits, sought by groups, that are broadly available and cannot be denied to nonmembers

commander in chief the power of the president as commander of the national military and the state national guard units (when called into service)

commerce clause Article I, Section 8, of the Constitution, which delegates to Congress the power "to regulate commerce with foreign nations, and among the several States and with the Indian tribes." This clause was interpreted by the Supreme Court in favor of national power over the economy

concurrent powers authority possessed by both state and national governments, such as the power to levy taxes

confederation a system of government in which states retain sovereign authority except for the powers expressly delegated to the national government

conference a gathering of House Republicans every two years to elect their House leaders. Democrats call their gathering the caucus

conference committee a joint committee created to work out a compromise on House and Senate versions of a piece of legislation

conservative today this term refers to those who generally support the social and economic status quo and are suspicious of efforts to introduce new political formulae and economic arrangements. Conservatives believe that a large and powerful government poses a threat to citizens' freedom

constituency the district comprising the area from which an official is elected

constitutional government a system of rule in which formal and effective limits are placed on the powers of the government

containment the policy used by the United States during the cold war to restrict the expansion of communism and limit the influence of the Soviet Union

contracting power the power of government to set conditions on companies seeking to sell goods or services to government agencies

contributory programs social programs financed in whole or in part by taxation or other mandatory contributions by their present or future recipients. The most important example is Social Security, which is financed by a payroll tax

cooperative federalism a type of federalism existing since the New Deal era in which grants-in-aid have been used strategically to encourage states and localities (without commanding them) to pursue nationally defined goals. Also known as intergovernmental cooperation

cost of living adjustments (COLAs) changes made to the level of benefits of a government program based on the rate of inflation

criminal law the branch of law that deals with disputes or actions involving criminal penalties (as opposed to civil law); it regulates the conduct of individuals, defines crimes, and provides punishment for criminal acts

criminal penalties regulatory techniques in which imprisonment or heavy fines and the loss of certain civil rights and liberties are imposed

de facto literally, "by fact"; practices that occur even when there is no legal enforcement, such as school segregation in much of the United States today

de jure literally, "by law"; legally enforced practices, such as school segregation in the South before the 1960s

defendant the one against whom a complaint is brought in a criminal or civil case

delegate the role of a representative who votes according to the preferences of his or her constituency

delegated powers constitutional powers that are assigned to one governmental agency but that are exercised by another agency with the express permission of the first

delegates political activists selected to vote at a party's national convention

democracy a system of rule that permits citizens to play a significant part in the governmental process, usually through the election of key public officials

department the largest subunit of the executive branch. The secretaries of the fourteen departments form the Cabinet

deregulation a policy of reducing or eliminating regulatory restraints on the conduct of individuals or private institutions

deterrence the development and maintenance of military strength as a means of discouraging attack

devolution a policy to remove a program from one level of government by delegating it or passing it down to a lower level of government, such as from the national government to the state and local governments

diplomacy the representation of a government to other foreign governments

direct democracy a system of rule that permits citizens to vote directly on laws and policies

direct-action politics a form of politics, such as civil disobedience or revolutionary action, that takes place outside formal channels

discount rate the interest rate charged by the Federal Reserve System when commercial banks borrow in order to expand their lending operations; an effective tool of monetary policy

discretionary spending federal spending on programs that are controlled through the regular budget process

discrimination use of any unreasonable and unjust criterion of exclusion

dissenting opinion a decision written by a justice in the minority in a particular case in which the justice wishes to express his or her reasoning in the case

divided government the condition in American government wherein the presidency is controlled by one party while the opposing party controls one or both houses of Congress

double jeopardy the Fifth Amendment right providing that a person cannot be tried twice for the same crime

dual federalism the system of government that prevailed in the United States from 1789 to 1937, in which most fundamental governmental powers were shared between the federal and state governments

due process of law the right of every citizen against arbitrary action by national or state governments

economic expansionist role the strategy often pursued by capitalist countries to adopt foreign policies that will maximize the success of domestic corporations in their dealings with other countries

elastic clause Article I, Section 8, of the Constitution (also known as the necessary and proper clause), which enumerates the powers of Congress and provides Congress with the authority to make all laws "necessary and proper" to carry them out

electoral college the presidential electors from each state who meet after the popular election to cast ballots for president and vice president

electoral realignment the point in history when a new party supplants the ruling party, becoming in turn the dominant political force. In the United States, this has tended to occur roughly every thirty years

eminent domain the right of government to take private property for public use

entitlement eligibility for benefits by virtue of a category of benefits defined by legislation

equal protection clause provision of the Fourteenth Amendment guaranteeing citizens "the equal protection of the laws." This clause has served as the basis for the civil rights of African Americans, women, and other groups

equal time rule the requirement that broadcasters provide candidates for the same political office an equal opportunity to communicate their messages to the public

equality of opportunity a widely shared American ideal that all people should have the freedom to use whatever talents and wealth they have to reach their fullest potential

establishment clause the First Amendment clause that says that "Congress shall make no law respecting an establishment of religion." This law means that a "wall of separation" exists between church and state

ex post facto laws laws that declare an action to be illegal after it has been committed

exclusionary rule the ability of courts to exclude evidence obtained in violation of the Fourth Amendment

executive agreement an agreement, made between the president and another country, that has the force of a treaty but does not require the Senate's "advice and consent"

Executive Office of the President the permanent agencies that perform defined management tasks for the president. Created in 1939, the EOP includes the Office of Management and Budget, the Council of Economic Advisers, the National Security Council, and other agencies

executive order a rule or regulation issued by the president that has the effect and formal status of legislation

executive privilege the claim that confidential communications deemed vital to the national interest between the president and close advisers should not be revealed without the consent of the president

expressed powers specific powers granted to Congress under Article I, Section 8, of the Constitution

expropriation confiscation of property with or without compensation

fairness doctrine a Federal Communications Commission (FCC) requirement for broadcasters who air programs on controversial issues to provide time for opposing views. The FCC ceased enforcing this doctrine in 1985

federal funds rate the interest rate on loans between banks that the Federal Reserve Board influences by affecting the supply of money available

Federal Reserve Board (Fed) the governing board of the Federal Reserve System, comprising a chair and six other members, all appointed by the president with the consent of the Senate

Federal Reserve System a system of twelve Federal Reserve Banks that facilitates exchanges of cash, checks, and credit; regulates member banks; and uses monetary policies to fight inflation and deflation

federal system a system of government in which the national government shares power with lower levels of government, such as states

federalism a system of government in which power is divided, by a constitution, between a central government and regional governments

Federalist Papers a series of essays written by James Madison, Alexander Hamilton, and John Jay supporting the ratification of the Constitution

Federalists those who favored a strong national government and supported the constitution proposed at the American Constitutional Convention of 1787

fighting words speech that directly incites damaging conduct

filibuster a tactic used by members of the Senate to prevent action on legislation they oppose by continuously holding the floor and speaking until the majority backs down. Once given the floor, senators have unlimited time to speak, and it requires a vote of three-fifths of the Senate to end a filibuster

fiscal policy the use of taxing, monetary, and spending powers to manipulate the economy

food stamps coupons that can be exchanged for food at most grocery stores; the largest in-kind benefits program

formula grants grants-in-aid in which a formula is used to determine the amount of federal funds a state or local government will receive

framing the power of the media to influence how events and issues are interpreted

free exercise clause the First Amendment clause that protects a citizen's right to believe and practice whatever religion he or she chooses

free riders those who enjoy the benefits of collective goods but did not participate in acquiring them

full faith and credit clause provision from Article IV, Section 1 of the Constitution, requiring that the states normally honor the public acts and judicial decisions that take place in another state

gender gap a distinctive pattern of voting behavior reflecting the differences in views between men and women

General Agreement on Tariffs and Trade (GATT) international trade organization, in existence from 1947 to 1995, that set many of the rules governing international trade

gerrymandering apportionment of voters in districts in such a way as to give unfair advantage to one racial or ethnic group or political party

going public a strategy that attempts to mobilize the widest and most favorable climate of public opinion

government institutions and procedures through which a territory and its people are ruled

government corporation a government agency that performs a service normally provided by the private sector

grand jury jury that determines whether sufficient evidence is available to justify a trial; grand juries do not rule on the accused's guilt or innocence

grants-in-aid programs through which Congress provides money to state and local governments on the condition that the funds be employed for purposes defined by the federal government

grassroots mobilization a lobbying campaign in which a group mobilizes its membership to contact government officials in support of the group's position

Great Compromise the agreement reached at the Constitutional Convention of 1787 that gave each state an equal number of senators regardless of its population, but linked representation in the House of Representatives to population

Gross Domestic Product (GDP) index of the total output of goods and services produced in the economy

habeas corpus a court order demanding that an individual in custody be brought into court and shown the cause for detention

Holy Alliance role a strategy pursued by a superpower to prevent any change in the existing distribution of power among nation-states, even if this requires intervention into the international affairs of another country in order to keep a ruler from being overturned

home rule power delegated by the state to a local unit of government to manage its own affairs

illusion of saliency the impression conveyed by polls that something is important to the public when actually it is not

impeachment the formal charge by the House of Representatives that a government official has committed "Treason, Bribery, or other high Crimes and Misdemeanors"

implementation the efforts of departments and agencies to translate laws into specific bureaucratic routines

implied powers powers derived from the "necessary and proper" clause of Article I, Section 8, of the Constitution. Such powers are not specifically expressed, but are implied through the expansive interpretation of delegated powers

in-kind benefits goods and services provided to needy individuals and families by the federal government

incumbency holding a political office for which one is running

incumbent a candidate running for a position that he or she already holds

independent agency an agency that is not part of a Cabinet department

independent counsel an official appointed to investigate criminal misconduct by members of the executive branch

indexing periodic process of adjusting social benefits or wages to account for increases in the cost of living

inflation a consistent increase in the general level of prices

infomercial a lengthy campaign advertisement on television

informational benefits special newsletters, periodicals, training programs, conferences, and other information provided to members of groups to entice others to join

inherent powers powers claimed by a president that are not expressed in the Constitution, but are inferred from it

institutional advertising advertising designed to create a positive image of an organization

intermediate scrutiny test, used by the Supreme Court in gender discrimination cases, which places the burden of proof partially on the government and partially on the challengers to show that the law in question is constitutional

International Monetary Fund (IMF) an institution established in 1944 at Bretton Woods, New Hampshire, which provides loans and facilitates international monetary exchange

iron triangle the stable, cooperative relationships that often develop between a congressional committee, an administrative agency, and one or more supportive interest groups. Not all of these relationships are triangular, but the iron triangle is the most typical

issue network a loose network of elected leaders, public officials, activists, and interest groups drawn together by a specific policy issue

issue advocacy independent spending by individuals or interest groups on a campaign issue but not directly tied to a particular candidate

joint committee a legislative committee formed of members of both the House and the Senate

judicial activism judicial philosophy that posits that the Court should go beyond the words of the Constitution or a statute to consider the broader societal implications of its decisions

judicial restraint judicial philosophy whose adherents refuse to go beyond the clear words of the Constitution in interpreting its meaning

judicial review the power of the courts to declare actions of the legislative and executive branches invalid or unconstitutional. The Supreme Court asserted this power in *Marbury v. Madison*

jurisdiction the sphere of a court's power and authority

Keynesianism economic theory, based on the ideas of British economist John Maynard Keynes, that argues that the government can stimulate the economy by increasing public spending or by cutting taxes

Kitchen Cabinet an informal group of advisers to whom the president turns for counsel and guidance. Members of the official Cabinet may or may not also be members of the Kitchen Cabinet

laissez-faire capitalism an economic system in which the means of production and distribution are privately owned and operated for profit with minimal or no government interference

legislative initiative the president's inherent power to bring a legislative agenda before Congress

***Lemon* test** a rule articulated in *Lemon v. Kurtzman* that government action toward religion is permissible if it is secular in purpose, does not lead to "excessive entanglement" with religion, and neither promotes nor inhibits the practice of religion

libel a written statement made in "reckless disregard of the truth" that is considered damaging to a victim because it is "malicious, scandalous, and defamatory"

liberal a liberal today generally supports political and social reform; extensive governmental intervention in the economy; the expansion of federal social services; more vigorous efforts on behalf of the poor, minorities, and women; and greater concern for consumers and the environment

libertarian the political philosophy that is skeptical of any government intervention as a potential threat against individual liberty; libertarians believe that government has caused more problems than it has solved

liberty freedom from government control

license permission to engage in some activity that is otherwise illegal, such as hunting or practicing medicine

limited government a government whose powers are defined and limited by a constitution

line-item veto the power of the executive to veto specific provisions (lines) of a bill passed by the legislature

litigation a lawsuit or legal proceeding; as a form of political participation, an attempt to seek relief in a court of law

lobbying a strategy by which organized interests seek to influence the passage of legislation by exerting direct pressure on members of the legislature

logrolling a legislative practice wherein agreements are made between legislators in voting for or against a bill. Unlike bargaining, parties to logrolling have nothing in common but their desire to exchange support

loophole incentive to individuals and businesses to reduce their tax liabilities by investing their money in areas that the government designates

machines strong party organizations in late-nineteenth- and early-twentieth-century American cities. These machines were led by "bosses" who controlled party nominations and patronage

majority leader the elected leader of the majority party in the House of Representatives or in the Senate. In the House, the majority leader is subordinate in the party hierarchy to the Speaker of the House

majority party the party that holds the majority of legislative seats in either the House or the Senate

majority rule/minority rights the democratic principle that a government follows the preferences of the majority of voters but protects the interests of the minority

majority system a type of electoral system in which, to win a seat in the parliament or other representative body, a candidate must receive a majority of all the votes cast in the relevant district

mandate a claim by a victorious candidate that the electorate has given him or her special authority to carry out promises made during the campaign

mandatory spending federal spending that is made up of "uncontrollables," budget items that cannot be controlled through the regular budget process

marketplace of ideas the public forum in which beliefs and ideas are exchanged and compete

Marshall Plan the U.S. European Recovery Plan, in which over $34 billion was spent for the relief, reconstruction, and economic recovery of Western Europe after World War II

material benefits special goods, services, or money provided to members of groups to entice others to join

means testing a procedure by which potential beneficiaries of a public assistance program establish their eligibility by demonstrating a genuine need for the assistance

Medicaid a federally financed, state-operated program providing medical services to low-income people

Medicare a form of national health insurance for the elderly and the disabled

membership association an organized group in which members actually play a substantial role, sitting on committees and engaging in group projects

merit system a product of civil service reform, in which appointees to positions in public bureaucracies must objectively be deemed qualified for the position

midterm elections congressional elections that do not coincide with a presidential election; also called off-year elections

minority district a gerrymandered voting district that improves the chances of minority candidates by making selected minority groups the majority within the district

minority leader the elected leader of the minority party in the House or Senate

minority party the party that holds a minority of legislative seats in either the House or the Senate

***Miranda* rule** the requirement, articulated by the Supreme Court in *Miranda v. Arizona*, that persons under arrest must be informed prior to police interrogation of their rights to remain silent and to have the benefit of legal counsel

mobilization the process by which large numbers of people are organized for a political activity

monetarism economic theory that contends that the role of the government in the economy should be limited to regulating the supply of money

monetary policies efforts to regulate the economy through manipulation of the supply of money and credit. America's most powerful institution in the area of monetary policy is the Federal Reserve Board

monopoly the existence of a single firm in a market that controls all the goods and services of that market; absence of competition

mootness a criterion used by courts to screen cases that no longer require resolution

most favored nation status agreement to offer a trading partner the lowest tariff rate offered to other trading partners

multilateralism a foreign policy that seeks to encourage the involvement of several nation-states in coordinated action, usually in relation to a common adversary, with terms and conditions usually specified in a multi-country treaty

multiple-member district an electorate that selects all candidates at large from the whole district; each voter is given the number of votes equivalent to the number of seats to be filled

Napoleonic role a strategy pursued by a powerful nation to prevent aggressive actions against themselves by improving the internal state of affairs of a particular country, even if this means encouraging revolution in that country

nation-state a political entity consisting of a people with some common cultural experience (nation) who also share a common political authority (state), recognized by other sovereignties (nation-states)

national convention a national party political institution that serves to nominate the party's presidential and vice presidential candidates, establish party rules, and write and ratify the party's platform

National Security Council (NSC) a presidential foreign-policy advisory council composed of the president; the vice president; the secretaries of state, defense, and the treasury; the attorney general; and other officials invited by the president

necessary and proper clause from Article I, Section 8 of the Constitution, it provides Congress with the authority to make all laws "necessary and proper" to carry out its expressed powers

New Deal coalition the coalition of northern urban liberals, southern white conservatives, organized labor, and blacks that dominated national politics until the 1960s

New Federalism attempts by Presidents Nixon and Reagan to return power to the states through block grants

New Jersey Plan a framework for the Constitution, introduced by William Paterson, which called for equal state representation in the national legislature regardless of population

New Politics movement a political movement that began in the 1960s and 1970s, made up of professionals and intellectuals for whom the civil rights and antiwar movements were formative experiences. The New Politics movement strengthened public-interest groups

nomination the process through which political parties select their candidates for election to public office

noncontributory programs social programs that provide assistance to people based on demonstrated need rather than any contribution they have made

North American Free Trade Agreement (NAFTA) trade treaty between the United States, Canada, and Mexico to lower and eliminate tariffs between the three countries

North Atlantic Treaty Organization (NATO) a treaty organization, comprising the United States, Canada, and most of western Europe, formed in 1948 to counter the perceived threat from the Soviet Union

oligarchy a form of government in which a small group—landowners, military officers, or wealthy merchants—controls most of the governing decisions

open caucus a presidential nominating caucus open to anyone who wishes to attend

open market operations method by which the Open Market Committee of the Federal Reserve System buys and sells government securities, etc., to help finance government operations and to loosen or tighten the total amount of money circulating in the economy

open primary a primary election in which the voter can wait until the day of the primary to choose which party to enroll in to select candidates for the general election

open rule a provision by the House Rules Committee that permits floor debate and the addition of new amendments to a bill

opinion the written explanation of the Supreme Court's decision in a particular case

oral argument stage in Supreme Court procedure in which attorneys for both sides appear before the Court to present their positions and answer questions posed by justices

original jurisdiction the authority to initially consider a case. Distinguished from appellate jurisdiction, which is the authority to hear appeals from a lower court's decision

oversight the effort by Congress, through hearings, investigations, and other techniques, to exercise control over the activities of executive agencies

party activists partisans who contribute time, energy, and effort to support their party and its candidates

party identification an individual voter's psychological ties to one party or another

party organization the formal structure of a political party, including its leadership, election committees, active members, and paid staff

party vote a roll-call vote in the House or Senate in which at least 50 percent of the members of one party take a particular position and are opposed by at least 50 percent of the members of the other party. Party votes are rare today, although they were fairly common in the nineteenth century

patronage the resources available to higher officials, usually opportunities to make partisan appointments to offices and to confer grants, licenses, or special favors to supporters

per curiam decision by an appellate court, without a written opinion, that refuses to review the decision of a lower court; amounts to a reaffirmation of the lower court's opinion

permanent campaign description of presidential politics in which all presidential actions are taken with re-election in mind

plaintiff the individual or organization who brings a complaint in court

platform a party document, written at a national convention, that contains party philosophy, principles, and positions on issues

plea bargains negotiated agreements in criminal cases in which a defendant agrees to plead guilty in return for the state's agreement to reduce the severity of the criminal charge the defendant is facing

pluralism the theory that all interests are and should be free to compete for influence in the government. The outcome of this competition is compromise and moderation

plurality system a type of electoral system in which, to win a seat in the parliament or other representative body, a candidate need only receive the most votes in the election, not necessarily a majority of the votes cast

pocket veto a presidential veto that is automatically triggered if the president does not act on a given piece of legislation passed during the final ten days of a legislative session

police power power reserved to the government to regulate the health, safety, and morals of its citizens

policy entrepreneur an individual who identifies a problem as a political issue and brings a policy proposal into the political agenda

policy of redistribution a policy whose objective is to tax or spend in such a way as to reduce the disparities of wealth between the lowest and the highest income brackets

political action committee (PAC) a private group that raises and distributes funds for use in election campaigns

political culture broadly shared values, beliefs, and attitudes about how the government should function. American political culture emphasizes the values of liberty, equality, and democracy

political efficacy the ability to influence government and politics

political equality the right to participate in politics equally, based on the principle of "one person, one vote"

political ideology a cohesive set of beliefs that form a general philosophy about the role of government

political institution an organization that connects people to politics, such as a political party, or a governmental organization, such as the Congress or the courts

political machines local party organizations that controlled local politics in the late nineteenth and early twentieth centuries through patronage and control of nominations

political participation political activities, such as voting, contacting political officials, volunteering for a campaign, or participating in a protest, whose purpose is to influence government

political parties organized groups that attempt to influence the government by electing their members to important government offices

political socialization the induction of individuals into the political culture; learning the underlying beliefs and values that the political system is based on

politics conflict over the leadership, structure, and policies of governments

poll tax a state-imposed tax upon voters as a prerequisite for registration. Poll taxes were rendered unconstitutional in national elections by the Twenty-fourth Amendment, and in state elections by the Supreme Court in 1966

popular sovereignty a principle of democracy in which political authority rests ultimately in the hands of the people

pork barrel appropriations made by legislative bodies for local projects that are often not needed but that are created so that local representatives can win re-election in their home districts

power influence over a government's leadership, organization, or policies
precedents prior cases whose principles are used by judges as the bases for their decisions in present cases
preemption the principle that allows the national government to override state or local actions in certain policy areas
primary elections elections used to select a party's candidate for the general election
prior restraint an effort by a governmental agency to block the publication of material it deems libelous or harmful in some other way; censorship. In the United States, the courts forbid prior restraint except under the most extraordinary circumstances
private bill a proposal in Congress to provide a specific person with some kind of relief, such as a special exemption from immigration quotas
privatization removing all or part of a program from the public sector to the private sector
privileges and immunities clause provision from Article IV, Section 2 of the Constitution, that a state cannot discriminate against someone from another state or give its own residents special privileges
procedural liberties restraints on how the government is supposed to act; for example, citizens are guaranteed the due process of law
progressive/regressive taxation taxation that hits the upper income brackets more heavily (progressive) or the lower income brackets more heavily (regressive)
project grants grant programs in which state and local governments submit proposals to federal agencies and for which funding is provided on a competitive basis
proportional representation a multiple-member district system that allows each political party representation in proportion to its percentage of the total vote
prospective voting voting based on the imagined future performance of a candidate
protest participation that involves assembling crowds to confront a government or other official organization
public goods goods that are provided by the government because they either are not supplied by the market or are not supplied in sufficient quantities
public interest groups groups that claim they serve the general good rather than their own particular interest
public law cases in private law, civil law, or criminal law in which one party to the dispute argues that a license is unfair, a law is inequitable or unconstitutional, or an agency has acted unfairly, violated a procedure, or gone beyond its jurisdiction
public opinion citizens' attitudes about political issues, leaders, institutions, and events
public opinion polls scientific instruments for measuring public opinion
public policy a law, rule, statute, or edict that expresses the government's goals and provides for rewards and punishments to promote their attainment
public relations an attempt, usually through the use of paid consultants, to establish a favorable relationship with the public and influence its political opinions
purposive benefits selective benefits of group membership that emphasize the purpose and accomplishments of the group
push polling a polling technique in which the questions are designed to shape the respondent's opinion

rallying effect the generally favorable reaction of the public to presidential actions taken in foreign policy, or more precisely, to decisions made during international crises
redistributive programs economic policies designed to control the economy through taxing and spending, with the goal of benefiting the poor
redistricting the process of redrawing election districts and redistributing legislative representatives. This happens every ten years to reflect shifts in population or in response to legal challenges to existing districts
redlining a practice in which banks refuse to make loans to people living in certain geographic locations
referendum the practice of referring a measure proposed or passed by a legislature to the vote of the electorate for approval or rejection
regulated federalism a form of federalism in which Congress imposes legislation on states and localities, requiring them to meet national standards
regulation a technique of control in which the government adopts rules imposing restrictions on the conduct of private citizens
regulatory agencies departments, bureaus, or independent agencies whose primary mission is to impose limits, restrictions, or other obligations on the conduct of individuals or companies in the private sector
regulatory tax a tax whose primary purpose is not to raise revenue but to influence conduct: e.g. a heavy tax on gasoline to discourage recreational driving
representative democracy/republic a system of government in which the populace selects representatives, who play a significant role in governmental decision making
reserve requirement the amount of liquid assets and ready cash that banks are required to hold to meet depositors' demands for their money
reserved powers powers, derived from the Tenth Amendment to the Constitution, that are not specifically delegated to the national government or denied to the states
responsible party government a set of principles that idealizes a strong role for parties in defining their stance on issues, mobilizing voters, and fulfilling their campaign promises once in office

retrospective voting voting based on the past performance of a candidate

revenue agencies agencies responsible for collecting taxes. Examples include the Internal Revenue Service for income taxes, the U.S. Customs Service for tariffs and other taxes on imported goods, and the Bureau of Alcohol, Tobacco, and Firearms for collection of taxes on the sales of those particular products

revenue sharing the process by which one unit of government yields a portion of its tax income to another unit of government, according to an established formula. Revenue sharing typically involves the national government providing money to state governments

right of rebuttal a Federal Communications Commission regulation giving individuals the right to have the opportunity to respond to personal attacks made on a radio or television broadcast

right to privacy the right to be let alone, which has been interpreted by the Supreme Court to entail free access to birth control and abortions

roll-call vote a vote in which each legislator's yes or no vote is recorded as the clerk calls the names of the members alphabetically

rulemaking a quasi-legislative administrative process that produces regulations by government agencies

salient interests attitudes and views that are especially important to the individual holding them

sample a small group selected by researchers to represent the most important characteristics of an entire population

select committee a (usually) temporary legislative committee set up to highlight or investigate a particular issue or address an issue not within the jurisdiction of existing committees

selective incorporation the process by which different protections in the Bill of Rights were incorporated into the Fourteenth Amendment, thus guaranteeing citizens protection from state as well as national government

senatorial courtesy the practice whereby the president, before formally nominating a person for a federal judgeship, seeks the indication that senators from the candidate's own state support the nomination

seniority priority or status ranking given to an individual on the basis of length of continuous service on a committee in Congress

separate but equal rule doctrine that public accommodations could be segregated by race but still be equal

separation of powers the division of governmental power among several institutions that must cooperate in decision making

shadow welfare state social benefits that private employers offer to their workers, such as medical insurance and pensions

single-member district an electorate that is allowed to select only one representative from each district; the normal method of representation in the United States

slander an oral statement, made in "reckless disregard of the truth," which is considered damaging to the victim because it is "malicious, scandalous, and defamatory"

Social Security a contributory welfare program into which working Americans contribute a percentage of their wages, and from which they receive cash benefits after retirement

socioeconomic status status in society based on level of education, income, and occupational prestige

sociological representation a type of representation in which representatives have the same racial, ethnic, religious, or educational backgrounds as their constituents. It is based on the principle that if two individuals are similar in background, character, interests, and perspectives, then one could correctly represent the other's views

soft money money contributed directly to political parties for voter registration and organization

solicitor general the top government lawyer in all cases before the Supreme Court where the government is a party

solidary benefits selective benefits of a group membership that emphasize friendship, networking, and consciousness-raising

Speaker of the House the chief presiding officer of the House of Representatives. The Speaker is elected at the beginning of every Congress on a straight party vote. The Speaker is the most important party and House leader, and can influence the legislative agenda, the fate of individual pieces of legislation, and members' positions within the House

speech-plus speech accompanied by conduct such as sit-ins, picketing, and demonstrations; protection of this form of speech under the First Amendment is conditional, and restrictions imposed by state or local authorities are acceptable if properly balanced by considerations of public order

split-ticket voting the practice of casting ballots for the candidates of at least two different political parties in the same election

spot advertisement a fifteen-, thirty-, or sixty-second television campaign commercial that permits a candidate's message to be delivered to a target audience

staff agency a legislative support agency responsible for policy analysis

staff organization a type of membership group in which a professional staff conducts most of the group's activities

standing the right of an individual or organization to initiate a court case

standing committee a permanent committee with the power to propose and write legislation that covers a particular subject, such as finance or appropriations

stare decisis literally, "let the decision stand." The doctrine that a previous decision by a court applies as a precedent in similar cases until that decision is overruled

states' rights the principle that the states should oppose the increasing authority of the national government. This principle was most popular in the period before the Civil War

straight-ticket voting the practice of casting ballots for candidates of only one party

strict scrutiny test, used by the Supreme Court in racial discrimination cases and other cases involving civil liberties and civil rights, which places the burden of proof on the government rather than on the challengers to show that the law in question is constitutional

subsidies government grants of cash or other valuable commodities such as land to individuals or organizations; used to promote activities desired by the government, to reward political support, or to buy off political opposition

substantive liberties restraints on what the government shall and shall not have the power to do

suffrage the right to vote; also called franchise

superdelegate a convention delegate position, in Democratic conventions, reserved for party officials

Supplemental Security Income (SSI) a program providing a minimum monthly income to people who pass a "means test" and who are sixty-five or older, blind, or disabled. Financed from general revenues rather than from Social Security contributions

supremacy clause Article VI of the Constitution, which states that laws passed by the national government and all treaties are the supreme law of the land and superior to all laws adopted by any state or any subdivision

supreme court the highest court in a particular state or in the United States. This court primarily serves an appellate function

tariff a tax on imported goods

tax expenditures government subsidies provided to employers and employees through tax deductions for amounts spent on health insurance and other benefits; these represent one way the government helps to ensure the social welfare of the middle class

Temporary Assistance to Needy Families (TANF) a federal block grant that replaced the AFDC program in 1996

term limits legally prescribed limits on the number of terms an elected official can serve

third parties parties that organize to compete against the two major American political parties

Three-fifths Compromise the agreement reached at the Constitutional Convention of 1787 that stipulated that for purposes of the apportionment of congressional seats, every slave would be counted as three-fifths of a person

totalitarian government a system of rule in which the government recognizes no formal limits on its power and seeks to absorb or eliminate other social institutions that might challenge it

town meeting a media format in which candidates meet with ordinary citizens. Allows candidates to deliver messages without the presence of journalists or commentators

trial court the first court to hear a criminal or civil case

trustee the role of a representative who votes based on what he or she thinks is best for his or her constituency

turnout the percentage of eligible individuals who actually vote

two-party system a political system in which only two parties have a realistic opportunity to compete effectively for control

tyranny oppressive and unjust government that employs cruel and unjust use of power and authority

uncontrollables budgetary items that are beyond the control of budgetary committees and can be controlled only by substantive legislative action in Congress. Some uncontrollables are beyond the power of Congress, because the terms of payments are set in contracts, such as interest on the debt

unfunded mandates regulations or conditions for receiving grants that impose costs on state and local governments for which they are not reimbursed by the federal government

Uniform Commercial Code code used in many states in the area of contract law to reduce interstate differences in judicial decisions

unilateralism a foreign policy that seeks to avoid international alliances, entanglements, and permanent commitments in favor of independence, neutrality, and freedom of action

unit rule the convention voting system under which a state delegation casts all of its votes for the candidate supported by the majority of the state's delegates

unitary system a centralized government system in which lower levels of government have little power independent of the national government

United Nations an organization of nations founded in 1945 to serve as a channel for negotiation and a means of settling international disputes peaceably. The UN has had frequent successes in providing a forum for negotiation and on some occasions a means of preventing international conflicts from spreading. On a number of occasions, the UN has been a convenient cover for U.S. foreign policy goals

values (or beliefs) basic principles that shape a person's opinions about political issues and events

veto the president's constitutional power to turn down acts of Congress. A presidential veto may be overridden by a two-thirds vote of each house of Congress

Virginia Plan a framework for the Constitution, introduced by Edmund Randolph, which called for representation in the national legislature based upon the population of each state

War Powers Resolution a resolution of Congress that the president can send troops into action abroad only by authorization of Congress, or if American troops are already under attack or serious threat

whip system a communications network in each house of Congress; whips take polls of the membership in order to learn their intentions on specific legislative issues and to assist the majority and minority leaders in various tasks

white ethnics white immigrants to the United States whose culture differs from that of WASPs

White House staff analysts and advisers to the president, often given the title "special assistant"

white primary primary election in which only white voters are eligible to participate

winner-take-all system a system in which all of a state's presidential nominating delegates are awarded to the candidate who wins the most votes, while runners-up receive no delegates

World Trade Organization (WTO) international trade agency promoting free trade that grew out of the General Agreement on Tariffs and Trade

writ of *certiorari* a decision of at least four of the nine Supreme Court justices to review a decision of a lower court; from the Latin "to make more certain"

writ of *habeas corpus* a court order that the individual in custody be brought into court and shown the cause for detention. *Habeas corpus* is guaranteed by the Constitution and can be suspended only in cases of rebellion or invasion

Endnotes

Chapter 1

1. Gary Orren, "Fall from Grace: The Public's Loss of Trust in Government," in *Why People Don't Trust Government,* ed. Joseph S. Nye, Jr., Philip D. Zelikow, and David C. King (Cambridge, MA: Harvard University Press, 1997), pp. 80–81.

2. Robert J. Blendon et al., "Changing Attitudes in America," in *Why People Don't Trust Government,* ed. Nye, Zelikow, and King, pp. 207–8.

3. Blendon et al., "Changing Attitudes in America," pp. 210–11.

4. On the role of the media see Orren, "Fall from Grace."

5. Richard Morin and Claudia Deane, "Poll Shows More Citizens Satisfied with Government," *Washington Post,* January 21, 1998, p. A6.

6. Diana Owen, "Mixed Signals: Generation X's Attitudes toward the Political System," in *After the Boom: The Politics of Generation X,* ed. Stephen C. Craig and Stephen Earl Bennett (Lanham, MD: Rowman and Littlefield, 1997), p. 95.

7. Joseph S. Nye, Jr., "Introduction: The Decline of Confidence in Government," in *Why People Don't Trust Government,* ed. Nye, Zelikow, and King, p. 4.

8. Orren, "Fall from Grace," p. 81.

9. Owen, "Mixed Signals," p. 98.

10. Michael Walzer, *Spheres of Justice* (New York: Basic Books, 1983), p. 304.

11. This definition is taken from Norman H. Nie, Jane Junn, and Kenneth Stehlik-Barry, *Education and Democratic Citizenship in America* (Chicago: University of Chicago Press, 1996).

12. See Eugen Weber, *Peasants into Frenchmen: The Modernization of Rural France, 1870–1914* (Stanford, CA: Stanford University Press, 1976), chap. 5.

13. See V. O. Key, *Politics, Parties, and Pressure Groups* (New York: Crowell, 1964), p. 201.

14. Harold Lasswell, *Politics: Who Gets What, When, How* (New York: Meridian Books, 1958).

15. Herbert McClosky and John Zaller, *The American Ethos: Public Attitudes toward Capitalism and Democracy* (Cambridge, MA: Harvard University Press, 1984), p. 19.

16. J. R. Pole, *The Pursuit of Equality in American History* (Berkeley: University of California Press, 1978), p. 3.

17. See Judith N. Shklar, *American Citizenship: The Quest for Inclusion* (Cambridge, MA: Harvard University Press, 1991).

18. Cindy Skrzycki, "OSHA Abandons Rules Effort on Repetitive Injury," *Washington Post,* June 13, 1995, p. D1.

19. See Rogers M. Smith, *Liberalism and American Constitutional Law* (Cambridge, MA: Harvard University Press, 1985), chap. 6.

20. The case was *San Antonio Independent School District v. Rodriguez,* 411 U.S. 1 (1973). See the discussion in Smith, *Liberalism and American Constitutional Law,* pp. 163–64.

21. See the discussion in Eileen McDonagh, "Gender Political Change," in *New Perspectives on American Politics,* ed. Lawrence C. Dodd and Calvin Jillson (Washington, DC: Congressional Quarterly Press, 1994), pp. 58–73. The argument for moving women's issues into the public sphere is made by Jean Bethke Elshtain, *Public Man, Private Woman* (Princeton, NJ: Princeton University Press, 1981).

22. On current differences in wealth, see Keith Bradsher, "Gap in Wealth in U.S. Called Widest in West," *New York Times,* April 17, 1995, p. A1; on income inequality, see Gary Burtless and Timothy Smeeding, "America's Tide Lifting the Yachts, Swamping the Rowboats," *Washington Post,* June 25, 1995, p. C3.

23. Kevin Phillips, *The Politics of Rich and Poor: Wealth and the American Electorate in the Reagan Aftermath* (New York: Random House, 1994); and Thomas Byrne Edsall, *The New Politics of Inequality* (New York: Norton, 1984).

24. Kevin Phillips, *Arrogant Capital: Washington, Wall Street, and the Frustration of American Politics* (Boston: Little, Brown, 1994).

Chapter 2

1. Only 11 million (42 percent) of eighteen- to twenty-year-olds actually registered to vote. See Congressional Quarterly, *Presidential Elections: 1789–1996* (Washington, DC: Congressional Quarterly Press, 1997), p. 80.

2. Although we discuss each of these groups separately, it is important to note that these identities are not mutually exclusive. Members of different racial and ethnic groups also have class, gender, and religious allegiances. At times these overlapping affinities make it easier to reach consensus in politics because it means that individuals have cross-cutting identities; they can see much in common with many different people. In other cases, however, a single identity, such as race, can determine so much about a person's life that it draws a sharp line of difference.

3. Richard A. Easterlin, "Economic and Social Characteristics of the Immigrants," *Immigration,* ed. Richard A. Easterlin, David Ward, William S. Bernard, and Reed Ueda (Cambridge, MA: Harvard University Press, 1982), pp. 16–17.

4. It is important to note, however, that many European immigrants did not stay in the United States. Half of the southern Italians and over two-thirds of some groups from eastern Europe

who came to the United States between 1890 and 1910 returned home. See Richard Oestreicher, "Urban Working-Class Political Behavior and Theories of American Electoral Behavior," *Journal of American History* 74 (March 1988), p. 1274. On naturalization and citizenship, see Reed Ueda, "Naturalization and Citizenship," *Immigration,* ed. Easterlin et al., pp. 106–54.

5. Reed Ueda, "Naturalization and Citizenship," p. 118.

6. Nathan Glazer and Daniel P. Moynihan, *Beyond the Melting Pot* (Cambridge, MA: MIT Press, 1970), pp. 301–10.

7. August Meier and Elliot Rudwick, *From Plantation to Ghetto* (New York: Hill and Wang, 1976), pp. 184–88.

8. On the growth of black political power and the more limited progress on social and economic change in the South after the civil rights movement, see James W. Button, *Blacks and Social Change: The Impact of the Civil Rights Movement in Southern Communities* (Princeton, NJ: Princeton University Press, 1993).

9. See William Julius Wilson, *The Truly Disadvantaged: The Inner City, the Underclass, and Public Policy* (Chicago: University of Chicago Press, 1987); and Douglas Massey and Nancy Denton, *American Apartheid: Segregation and the Making of the American Underclass* (Cambridge, MA: Harvard University Press, 1993).

10. See Michael C. Dawson, *Behind the Mule: Race and Class in African-American Politics* (Princeton, NJ: Princeton University Press, 1994), chaps. 5 and 6.

11. Ibid.

12. U.S. Census Bureau, *Statistical Abstract of the United States: 1998* (U.S. Government Printing Office, 1998), p. 54.

13. New Mexico had a different history because not many Anglos settled there initially. ("Anglo" is the term for a non-Hispanic white generally of European background.) Mexican Americans had considerable power in territorial legislatures between 1865 and 1912. See Lawrence H. Fuchs, *The American Kaleidoscope* (Hanover, NH: University Press of New England, 1990), pp. 239–40.

14. On La Raza Unida Party, see "La Raza Unida Party and the Chicano Student Movement in California," in *Latinos in the American Political System,* ed. F. Chris Garcia (Notre Dame, IN: University of Notre Dame Press, 1988), pp. 213–35.

15. Glazer and Moynihan, *Beyond the Melting Pot,* p. 101.

16. U.S. House of Representatives, Committee on the Judiciary, Hearings on the Immigration and Nationality Act, 104th Cong., 1st sess. (May 1995), Serial no. 1, p. 596.

17. Dick Kirschten, "Hispanics: Beyond the Myths," *National Journal,* August 14, 1999, p. 2356.

18. William Branigin, "Latino Voters Gaining Political Clout," *Washington Post,* November 9, 1998, p. A8.

19. *United States v. Wong Kim Ark,* 169 U.S. 649 (1898).

20. Only 1,428 Chinese were let in to the United States between 1944 and 1952. See Ronald Takaki, *A Different Mirror: A History of Multicultural America* (Boston: Little, Brown, 1993), p. 387.

21. U.S. House of Representatives, Committee on the Judiciary, Hearings on the Immigration and Nationality Act, 104th Cong., 1st sess. (May 1995), Serial no. 1, p. 596.

22. Ibid.

23. James Sterngold, "For Asian-Americans, A New Political Resolve," *New York Times,* September 22, 1999, p. A1.

24. Not all Indian tribes agreed with this, including the Navajos. See Takaki, *A Different Mirror,* pp. 238–45.

25. On the resurgence of Indian political activity, see Stephen Cornell, *The Return of the Native: American Indian Political Resurgence* (New York: Oxford University Press, 1990); and Dee Brown, *Bury My Heart at Wounded Knee* (New York: Holt, 1971).

26. Dirk Johnson, "Economic Pulse: Indian Country; Economics Come to Life on Indian Reservations," *New York Times,* July 3, 1994, p. 1.

27. Maria Puente, "The New Immigrants: Is the Latest Wave a Drain or Boon to Society?" *USA Today,* June 30, 1995, p. A1.

28. Cited in Maria Puente, "The New Immigrants."

29. See Robert Pear, "Deciding Who Gets What in America," *New York Times,* November 27, 1994, sec. 4, p. 5.

30. David Jackson, "Citizen Plan May Have Aided Felons; Proper Background Checks Not Done," *Chicago Tribune,* February 25, 1997, p. 3. On differences between immigration now and in the past see Nathan Glazer, "Immigration and the American Future," *Public Interest,* no. 118 (winter 1995), pp. 45–60.

31. Maria Puente, "Immigrants Favor ID Card," *USA Today,* July 5, 1995, p. 1A.

32. In fact, some students of immigration worry that Americanization may be harmful to immigrants, especially for the children of nonwhite immigrants. These immigrants may find it difficult to enter middle-class white society; instead they may adopt values adversarial to the mainstream. In this case, remaining in immigrant circles may be the best strategy. See Alejandro Portes and Min Zhou, "Should Immigrants Assimilate?" *Public Interest,* no. 116 (summer 1994), pp. 18–33.

33. On the Knights of Labor, see Leon Fink, *Workingmen's Democracy: The Knights of Labor and American Politics* (Urbana: University of Illinois Press, 1985).

34. Clay Chandler, "It's Getting Awfully Crowded in the Middle," *Washington Post,* December 18, 1994, p. H1.

35. See Edward N. Wolff, *Top Heavy: A Study of Increasing Inequality of Wealth in America* (New York: Twentieth Century Fund, 1995).

36. Cited in Benjamin DeMott, *The Imperial Middle: Why Americans Can't Think Straight about Class* (New York: Morrow, 1990), pp. 9–10.

37. On politics and women, see Paula Baker, "The Domestication of Politics: Women and American Political Society, 1780–1920," *American Historical Review* 89 (June 1984), pp. 620–47. On women's separate sphere, see Sheila M. Rothman, *Woman's Proper Place* (New York: Basic Books, 1978).

38. See Thomas B. Edsall, "Pollsters View Gender Gap as Political Fixture," *Washington Post,* August 15, 1995, p. A11.

39. Richard L. Berke, "Defections among Men to G.O.P. Helped Insure Rout of Democrats," *New York Times,* November 11, 1994, p. A1.

40. "Fact Sheet: Women in Elective Office," Center for the American Woman and Politics, Eagleton Institute of Politics, Rutgers University, January 2000.

41. David S. Broder, "Key to Women's Political Parity: Running," *Washington Post,* September 8, 1994, p. A17.

42. "The Impact of Women in Public Office: Findings at a Glance," Center for the American Woman and Politics (New Brunswick, NJ: Rutgers University, n.d.).

43. Gwen Ifill, "The Louisiana Election; Female Lawmakers Wrestle with New Public Attitudes on 'Women's' Issues," *New York Times,* November 18, 1991, p. B7.

44. *Engel v. Vitale,* 370 U.S. 421 (1962); *Abington School Dis-*

trict v. Schempp, 374 U.S. 203 (1963); *Roe v. Wade,* 410 U.S. 113 (1973).

45. David von Drehle, "Life of the Grand Old Party; Energized Coalition Enters Another Political Phase," *Washington Post,* August 14, 1994, p. A1.

46. Rene Sanchez, "Survey of College Freshmen Finds Rise in Volunteerism," *Washington Post,* January 13, 1997, p. A1.

47. See the discussion in Craig A. Rimmerman, *The New Citizenship: Unconventional Politics, Activism, and Service* (Boulder, CO: Westview, 1997), pp. 97–113.

48. Noah Bilenker, interview with the author, March 23, 1998.

Chapter 3

1. Herbert Storing, *What the Antifederalists Were For* (Chicago: University of Chicago Press, 1981).

2. The social makeup of colonial America and some of the social conflicts that divided colonial society are discussed in Jackson Turner Main, *The Social Structure of Revolutionary America* (Princeton, NJ: Princeton University Press, 1965).

3. George B. Tindall and David E. Shi, *America: A Narrative History,* 3rd ed. (New York: Norton, 1992), p. 194.

4. For a discussion of events leading up to the Revolution, see Charles M. Andrews, *The Colonial Background of the American Revolution* (New Haven, CT: Yale University Press, 1924).

5. See Carl Becker, *The Declaration of Independence* (New York: Knopf, 1942).

6. See Merrill Jensen, *The Articles of Confederation* (Madison: University of Wisconsin Press, 1970).

7. Reported in Samuel E. Morrison, Henry Steele Commager, and William Leuchtenberg, *The Growth of the American Republic,* vol. 1 (New York: Oxford University Press, 1969), p. 244.

8. Quoted in Morrison et al., *The Growth of the American Republic,* vol. 1, p. 242.

9. Charles A. Beard, *An Economic Interpretation of the Constitution of the United States* (New York: Macmillan, 1913).

10. Madison's notes along with the somewhat less complete records kept by several other participants in the convention are available in a four-volume set. See Max Farrand, ed., *The Records of the Federal Convention of 1787,* 4 vols., rev. ed. (New Haven, CT: Yale University Press, 1966).

11. Farrand, ed., *The Records of the Federal Convention of 1787,* vol. 1, p. 476.

12. Farrand, ed., *The Records of the Federal Convention of 1787,* vol. 2, p. 10.

13. E. M. Earle, ed., *The Federalist* (New York: Modern Library, 1937), No. 71.

14. Earle, ed., *The Federalist,* No. 62.

15. Earle, ed., *The Federalist,* No. 70.

16. Max Farrand, *The Framing of the Constitution of the United States* (New Haven, CT: Yale University Press, 1962), p. 49.

17. Richard E. Neustadt, *Presidential Power* (New York: Wiley, 1960), p. 33.

18. Melancton Smith, quoted in Storing, *What the Anti-Federalists Were For,* p. 17.

19. "Essays of Brutus," No. 1, in Herbert Storing, ed., *The Complete Anti-Federalist* (Chicago: University of Chicago Press, 1981).

20. Earle, ed., *The Federalist,* No. 57.

21. "Essays of Brutus," No. 15, in Storing, ed., *The Complete Anti-Federalist.*

22. Earle, ed., *The Federalist,* No. 10

23. "Essays of Brutus," No. 7, in Storing, ed., *The Complete Anti-Federalist.*

24. "Essays of Brutus," No. 6, in Storing, ed., *The Complete Anti-Federalist.*

25. Storing, *What the Anti-Federalists Were For,* p. 28.

26. Earle, ed., *The Federalist,* No. 51.

27. Quoted in Storing, *What the Anti-Federalists Were For,* p. 30.

28. Observation by Colonel George Mason, delegate from Virginia, early during the convention period. Quoted in Farrand, ed., *The Records of the Federal Convention of 1787,* vol. 1, pp. 202–3.

29. Clinton Rossiter, ed., *The Federalist Papers* (New York: New American Library, 1961), No. 43, p. 278.

30. See Marcia Lee, "The Equal Rights Amendment: Public Policy by Means of a Constitutional Amendment," in *The Politics of Policy-Making in America,* ed. David Caputo (San Francisco: Freeman, 1977); Jane Mansbridge, *Why We Lost the ERA* (Chicago: University of Chicago Press, 1986); and Donald Mathews and Jane Sherron DeHart, *Sex, Gender, and the Politics of the ERA* (New York: Oxford University Press, 1990).

31. The Fourteenth Amendment is included in this table as well as in Table 3.4 because it seeks not only to define citizenship but *seems* to intend also that this definition of citizenship included, along with the right to vote, all the rights of the Bill of Rights, regardless of the state in which the citizen resided. A great deal more will be said about this in Chapter 5.

32. Earle, ed., *The Federalist,* No. 10.

Chapter 4

1. Andre Henderson, "Cruise Control," *Governing,* February 1995, p. 39. Unemployment benefit figures are from U.S. House of Representatives, Committee on Ways and Means, *1998 Green Book* (Washington, DC: U.S. Government Printing Office, 1998), p. 340.

2. Ken I. Kersch, "Full Faith and Credit for Same-Sex Marriages?" *Political Science Quarterly,* 112 (Spring 1997), pp. 117–36; Joan Biskupic, "Once Unthinkable, Now Under Debate," *Washington Post,* September 3, 1996, p. A1.

3. Linda Greenhouse, "Supreme Court Weaves Legal Principles

from a Tangle of Legislation," *New York Times,* June 30, 1988, p. A20.

4. *Hicklin v. Orbeck,* 437 U.S. 518 (1978).

5. *Sweeny v. Woodall,* 344 U.S. 86 (1953).

6. Marlise Simons, "France Won't Extradite American Convicted of Murder," *New York Times,* December 5, 1997, p. A9.

7. A good discussion of the constitutional position of local governments is in York Willbern, *The Withering Away of the City* (Bloomington: Indiana University Press, 1971). For more on the structure and theory of federalism, see Thomas R. Dye, *American Federalism: Competition among Governments* (Lexington, MA: Lexington Books, 1990), chap. 1; and Martha Derthick, "Up-to-Date in Kansas City: Reflections on American Federalism" (the 1992 John Gaus Lecture), *PS: Political Science & Politics* 25 (December 1992), pp. 671–75.

8. For a good treatment of the contrast between national political stability and social instability, see Samuel P. Huntington, *Political Order in Changing Societies* (New Haven, CT: Yale University Press, 1068), chap. 2.

9. *McCulloch v. Maryland,* 4 Wheaton 316 (1819).

10. *Gibbons v. Ogden,* 9 Wheaton 1 (1824).

11. The Sherman Antitrust Act, adopted in 1890, for example, was enacted not to restrict commerce, but rather to protect it from monopolies, or trusts, so as to prevent unfair trade practices, and to enable the market again to become self-regulating. Moreover, the Supreme Court sought to uphold liberty of contract to protect businesses. For example, in *Lochner v. New York,* 198 U.S. 45 (1905), the Court invalidated a New York law regulating the sanitary conditions and hours of labor of bakers on the grounds that the law interfered with liberty of contract.

12. The key case in this process of expanding the power of the national government is generally considered to be *NLRB v. Jones & Laughlin Steel Corporation,* 301 U.S. 1 (1937), in which the Supreme Court approved federal regulation of the workplace and thereby virtually eliminated interstate commerce as a limit on the national government's power.

13. *U.S. v. Darby Lumber Co.,* 312 U.S. 100 (1941).

14. W. John Moore, "Pleading the 10th," *National Journal,* July 29, 1995, p. 1940.

15. *Printz v. United States,* 117 S.Ct. 2365 (1997).

16. *Seminole Indian Tribe v. Florida,* 116 S.Ct. 1114 (1996).

17. *United States v. Lopez,* 115 S.Ct. 1624 (1995).

18. See the poll reported in Guy Gugliotta, "Scaling Down the American Dream," *Washington Post,* April 19, 1995, p. A21.

19. Kenneth T. Palmer, "The Evolution of Grant Policies," in *The Changing Politics of Federal Grants,* by Lawrence D. Brown, James W. Fossett, and Kenneth T. Palmer (Washington, DC: Brookings, 1984), p. 15.

20. Palmer, "The Evolution of Grant Policies," p. 6.

21. Morton Grozdins, *The American System,* ed. Daniel J. Elazar (Chicago: Rand McNally, 1966).

22. See Terry Sanford, *Storm Over the States* (New York: McGraw-Hill, 1967).

23. James L. Sundquist with David W. Davis, *Making Federalism Work* (Washington, DC: Brookings, 1969), p. 271. George Wallace was mistrusted by the architects of the War on Poverty because he was a strong proponent of racial segregation. He believed in "states' rights," which meant that states, not the federal government, should decide what liberty and equality meant.

24. See Don Kettl, *The Regulation of American Federalism* (Baton Rouge: Louisiana State University Press, 1983).

25. Eliza Newlin Carney, "Power Grab," *National Journal,* April 11, 1998, p. 798.

26. See Advisory Commission on Intergovernmental Relations, *Federal Regulation of State and Local Governments: The Mixed Record of the 1980s* (Washington, DC: Advisory Commission on Intergovernmental Relations, July 1993).

27. Advisory Commission on Intergovernmental Relations, *Federal Regulation of State and Local Governments,* p. iii.

28. Statement of James L. Blum, Acting Director of the Congressional Budget Office, before the Subcommittee on Rules and Organization of the House and the Subcommittee on Legislative and Budget Process, Committee on Rules, U.S. House of Representatives, February 2, 1999 (http://www.cbo.gov).

29. Quoted in Timothy Conlon, *New Federalism: Intergovernmental Reform from Nixon to Reagan* (Washington, DC: Brookings, 1988), p. 25.

30. For the emergence of complaints about federal categorical grants, see Palmer, "The Evolution of Grant Policies," pp. 17–18. On the governors' efforts to gain more control over federal grants after the 1994 congressional elections, see Dan Balz, "GOP Governors Eager to Do Things Their Way," *Washington Post,* November 22, 1994, p. A4.

31. Advisory Commission on Intergovernmental Relations, *Federal Regulation of State and Local Governments,* p. 51.

32. Dan Balz, "Governors Press Congress for Power to Manage Programs at State Level," *Washington Post,* December 11, 1994, p. A6; Robert Pear, "Attention Is Turning Governors' Heads: But Some Still Worry that Congress Will Shift Burden to the States," *New York Times,* January 30, 1995, p. A14.

33. Robert Frank, "Proposed Block Grants Seen Unlikely to Cure Management Problems," *Wall Street Journal,* May 1, 1995, p. 1.

34. Judith Havemann, "Scholars Question Whether Welfare Shift Is Reform," *Washington Post,* April 20, 1995, p. A8.

35. Dennis Chaptman, "Tax Rebate Bill Gets Governor's Blessing," *Milwaukee Journal Sentinel,* November 17, 1999, p. 1

36. U.S. Committee on Federalism and National Purpose, *To Form a More Perfect Union* (Washington, DC: National Conference on Social Welfare, 1985). See also the discussion in Paul E. Peterson, *The Price of Federalism* (Washington, DC: Brookings, 1995), esp. chap. 8.

37. Malcolm Gladwell, "In States' Experiments, a Cutting Contest," *New York Times,* March 10, 1995, p. 6.

38. The phrase "laboratories of democracy" was coined by Supreme Court justice Louis Brandeis in his dissenting opinion in *New State Ice Co. v. Liebman,* 285 U.S. 262 (1932).

39. Jason DeParle, "Life After Welfare," *New York Times,* August 29, 1999, p. 1.

40. "Motor Vehicle Fatalities in 1996 were 12 Percent Higher on Interstates, Freeways in 12 States that Raised Speed Limits," Press Release of the Insurance Institute for Highway Safety, October 10, 1997.

41. See Stephen Barr, "Americans Gain a Small Measure of Confidence in Government," *Washington Post,* March 24, 1997, p. A17.

42. Sidney Verba, Kay Lehman Schlozman, and Henry E. Brady, *Voice and Equality: Civic Voluntarism in American Politics* (Cambridge, MA: Harvard University Press, 1995), pp. 66–67.

CHAPTER 5

1. *Reno, Attorney General of the United States, et al. v. American Civil Liberties Union et al.,* 117 S.Ct. 2329 (1997).

2. Amy Harmon, "Ideological Foes Meet on Web Decency," *New York Times,* December 1, 1997, p. D1.

3. Bennett Haselton, telephone interview by author, February 12, 1998; PEACEFIRE web site, http://www.peacefire.org.

4. Clinton Rossiter, ed., *The Federalist Papers* (New York: New American Library, 1961), No. 84, p. 513.

5. Rossiter, ed., *The Federalist Papers,* No. 84, p. 513.

6. Clinton Rossiter, *1787: The Grand Convention* (New York: Norton, 1987), p. 302.

7. Rossiter, *1787,* p. 303. Rossiter also reports that "in 1941 the States of Connecticut, Massachusetts and Georgia celebrated the sesquicentennial of the Bill of Rights by giving their hitherto withheld and unneeded assent."

8. Let there be no confusion about the words "liberty" and "freedom." They are synonymous and interchangeable. "Freedom" comes from the German, *Freiheit.* "Liberty" is from the French, *liberté.* Although people sometimes try to make them appear to be different, both of them have equal concern with the absence of restraints on individual choices of action.

9. For some recent scholarship on the Bill of Rights and its development, see Geoffrey Stone, Richard Epstein, and Cass Sunstein, eds. *The Bill of Rights and the Modern State* (Chicago: University of Chicago Press, 1992); and Michael J. Meyer and William A. Parent, eds., *The Constitution of Rights* (Ithaca, NY: Cornell University Press, 1992).

10. *Barron v. Baltimore,* 7 Peters 243, 246 (1833).

11. The Fourteenth Amendment also seems designed to introduce civil rights. The final clause of the all-important Section 1 provides that no state can "deny to any person within its jurisdiction the equal protection of the laws." It is not unreasonable to conclude that the purpose of this provision was to obligate the state governments as well as the national government to take *positive* actions to protect citizens from arbitrary and discriminatory actions, at least those based on race. This will be explored in Chapter 6.

12. For example, *The Slaughterhouse Cases,* 16 Wallace 36 (1883).

13. *Chicago, Burlington and Quincy Railroad Company v. Chicago,* 166 U.S. 226 (1897).

14. *Gitlow v. New York,* 268 U.S. 652 (1925).

15. *Near v. Minnesota,* 283 U.S. 697 (1931); *Hague v. C.I.O.,* 307 U.S. 496 (1939).

16. *Palko v. Connecticut,* 302 U.S. 319 (1937).

17. All of these were implicitly included in the *Palko* case as "not incorporated" into the Fourteenth Amendment as limitations on the powers of the states.

18. There is one interesting exception, which involves the Sixth Amendment right to public trial. In the 1948 case *In re Oliver,* 33 U.S. 257, the right to the public trial was, in effect, incorporated as part of the Fourteenth Amendment. However, the issue in that case was put more generally as "due process," and public trial itself was not actually mentioned in so many words. Later opinions, such as *Duncan v. Louisiana,* 391 U.S. 145 (1968), cited the *Oliver* case as the precedent for more explicit incorporation of public trials as part of the Fourteenth Amendment.

19. For a lively and readable treatment of the possibilities of restricting provisions of the Bill of Rights, without actually reversing prior decisions, see David G. Savage, *Turning Right: The Making of the Rehnquist Supreme Court* (New York: Wiley, 1992). For an indication that the Supreme Court in the 1990s may in fact be moving toward more restrictions on the Bill of Rights, see Richard Lacayo, "The Soul of a New Majority," *Time,* July 10, 1995, pp. 46–48.

20. *Abington School District v. Schempp,* 374 U.S. 203 (1963).

21. *Engel v. Vitale,* 370 U.S. 421 (1962).

22. *Wallace v. Jaffree,* 472 U.S. 38 (1985).

23. *Lynch v. Donnelly,* 465 U.S. 668 (1984).

24. *Lemon v. Kurtzman,* 403 U.S. 602 (1971). The *Lemon* test is still good law, but as recently as the 1994 Court term, four justices have urged that the *Lemon* test be abandoned. Here is a settled area of law that may soon become unsettled.

25. *Rosenberger v. Rector and Visitors of the University of Virginia,* 115 S.Ct. 2510 (1995).

26. *Agostini v. Felton,* 117 S.Ct. 1997 (1997). The case being overruled was *Aguilar v. Felton,* 473 U.S. 402 (1985).

27. For good coverage of voucher and charter school experiments, see Peter Schrag, "The Voucher Seduction," *American Prospect,* November 23, 1999, pp. 46–52.

28. *West Virginia State Board of Education v. Barnette,* 319 U.S. 624 (1943). The case it reversed was *Minersville School District v. Gobitus,* 310 U.S. 586 (1940).

29. *Employment Division, Department of Human Resources of Oregon v. Smith,* 494 U.S. 872 (1990).

30. *City of Boerne v. Flores,* 117 S.Ct. 293 (1996).

31. *Wisconsin v. Yoder,* 406 U.S. 205 (1972).

32. *U.S. v. Carolene Products Company,* 304 U.S. 144 (1938), note 4. This footnote is one of the Court's most important doctrines. See Alfred H. Kelly, Winfred A. Harbison, and Herman Belz, *The American Constitution: Its Origins and Development,* 7th ed. (New York: Norton, 1991), Vol. 2, pp. 519–23.

33. *Schenk v. U.S.,* 249 U.S. 47 (1919).

34. *Brandenburg v. Ohio,* 395 U.S. 444 (1969).

35. *Stromberg v. California,* 283 U.S. 359 (1931).

36. *Texas v. Johnson,* 488 U.S. 884 (1989).

37. *United States v. Eichman,* 496 U.S. 310 (1990).

38. For a good general discussion of "speech plus," see Louis Fisher, *American Constitutional Law* (New York: McGraw-Hill, 1990), pp. 544–46. The case upholding the buffer zone against the abortion protesters is *Madsen v. Women's Health Center,* 114 S.Ct. 2516 (1994).

39. *Buckley v. American Constitutional Law Foundation,* 119 S.Ct. 636 (1999).

40. *Near v. Minnesota,* 283 U.S. 697 (1931).

41. *New York Times v. U.S.,* 403 U.S. 731 (1971).

42. *Cable News Network v. Noriega,* 111 S.Ct. 451 (1990); *Turner Broadcasting System v. Federal Communications Commission,* 114 S.Ct. 2445 (1994).

43. *New York Times v. Sullivan,* 376 U.S. 254 (1964).

44. *Masson v. New Yorker Magazine,* 111 S.Ct. 2419 (1991).

45. *Hustler Magazine v. Falwell,* 108 S.Ct. 876 (1988).

46. *Roth v. U.S.,* 354 U.S. 476 (1957).

47. Concurring opinion in *Jacobellis v. Ohio,* 378 U.S. 184 (1964).

48. *Miller v. California,* 413 U.S. 15 (1973).

49. *Reno v. American Civil Liberties Union,* 117 S.Ct. 2329 (1997).

50. *Reno v. ACLUII,* No. 98-0002; *U.S. v. Playboy Entertainment Group,* No. 98-1682. For a good discussion of these issues, see Wendy Kaminer, "The Politics of Sanctimony," *American Prospect,* November 23, 1999, pp. 15–16.

51. *Chaplinsky v. State of New Hampshire,* 315 U.S. 568 (1942).

52. *Dennis v. United States,* 341 U.S. 494 (1951), which upheld the infamous Smith Act of 1940, which provided criminal penalties for those who "willfully and knowingly conspire to teach and advocate the forceful and violent overthrow and destruction of the government."

53. *Bethel School District No. 403 v. Fraser,* 478 U.S. 675 (1986).

54. *Hazelwood School District v. Kuhlmeier,* 108 S.Ct. 562 (1988).

55. "The Penn File: An Update," *Wall Street Journal,* April 11, 1994, p. A14.

56. *Meritor Savings Bank, FBD v. Vinson,* 477 U.S. 57 (1986).

57. Charles Fried, "The New First Amendment Jurisprudence: A Threat to Liberty," in *The Bill of Rights and the Modern State,* ed. Stone, Epstein, and Sunstein, p. 249.

58. *Broadcasting Company v. Acting Attorney General,* 405 U.S. 1000 (1972).

59. *Board of Trustees of the State University of New York v. Fox,* 109 S.Ct. 3028 (1989).

60. *City Council v. Taxpayers for Vincent,* 466 U.S. 789 (1984).

61. *Posadas de Puerto Rico Associates v. Tourism Company of Puerto Rico,* 479 U.S. 328 (1986).

62. Fisher, *American Constitutional Law,* p. 546.

63. *Bigelow v. Virginia,* 421 U.S. 809 (1975).

64. *Virginia State Board of Pharmacy v. Virginia Citizens Consumer Council,* 425 U.S. 748 (1976). Later cases restored the rights of lawyers to advertise their services.

65. *44 Liquormart, Inc. and Peoples Super Liquor Stores Inc., Petitioners v. Rhode Island and Rhode Island Liquor Stores Association,* 116 S.Ct. 1495 (1996).

66. *United States v. Miller,* 307 U.S. 174 (1939). A good, albeit brief, treatment of this will be found in Edward Corwin and J. W. Peltason, *Corwin & Peltason's Understanding the Constitution,* 13th ed. (Fort Worth, TX: Harcourt Brace, 1994), pp. 248–49.

67. *Printz v. United States,* 117 S.Ct. 2365 (1997), and *Mack v. United States,* 116 S.Ct. 2521 (1996).

68. The Supreme Court itself provides an intriguing suggestion for a criterion to distinguish between appropriate and inappropriate regulation of the right to bear arms. In 1939 the Supreme Court upheld a federal law making it a crime to ship sawed-off shotguns in interstate commerce, on the grounds that such weapons had no reasonable relationship "to the preservation or efficiency of a well-regulated militia." *U.S. v. Miller,* 307 U.S. 174 (1939). However, that does not make the current issues any easier to settle. The following are two treatments of the Second Amendment by two scholars who both favor handgun control but differ fundamentally on how to treat the issue and the general constitutional problem: Sanford Levinson, "The Embarrassing Second Amendment," *Yale Law Journal* 99 (1989), pp. 637–59; and Robert Spitzer, *The Politics of Gun Control* (Chatham, NJ: Chatham House, 1995).

69. See Corwin and Peltason, *Understanding the Constitution,* pp. 283–86.

70. *In re Winship,* 397 U.S. 361 (1970). An outstanding treatment of due process in issues involving the Fourth through Seventh Amendments will be found in Fisher, *American Constitutional Law,* chap. 13.

71. *Horton v. California,* 496 U.S. 128 (1990).

72. *Mapp v. Ohio,* 367 U.S. 643 (1961). Although Ms. Mapp went free in this case, she was later convicted in New York on narcotics trafficking charges and served nine years of a twenty-year sentence.

73. For a good discussion of the issue, see Fisher, *American Constitutional Law,* pp. 884–89.

74. *National Treasury Employees Union v. Von Raab,* 39 U.S. 656 (1989).

75. *Skinner v. Railroad Labor Executives Association,* 489 U.S. 602 (1989).

76. *Vernonia School District 47J v. Acton,* 115 S.Ct. 2386 (1985).

77. *Chandler et al. v. Miller, Governor of Georgia et al.,* 117 S.Ct. 1295 (1997).

78. Corwin and Peltason, *Understanding the Constitution,* p. 286.

79. *Miranda v. Arizona,* 348 U.S. 436 (1966).

80. *Berman v. Parker,* 348 U.S. 26 (1954). For a thorough analysis of the case see Benjamin Ginsberg, "*Berman v. Parker:* Congress, the Court, and the Public Purpose," *Polity* 4 (1971), pp. 48–75. For a later application of the case that suggests that "just compensation"—defined as something approximating market value—is about all a property owner can hope for protection against a public taking of property, see Theodore Lowi et al., *Poliscide; Big Government, Big Science, Lilliputian Politics,* 2nd ed. (Lanham, MD: University Press of America, 1990), pp. 267–70.

81. *Gideon v. Wainwright,* 372 U.S. 335 (1963). For a full account of the story of the trial and release of Clarence Earl Gideon, see Anthony Lewis, *Gideon's Trumpet* (New York: Random House, 1964). See also David O'Brien, *Storm Center,* 2nd ed. (New York: Norton, 1990).

82. For further discussion of these issues, see Corwin and Peltason, *Understanding the Constitution,* pp. 319–23.

83. *Congressional Quarterly Weekly Report,* October 21, 1995, p. 3212.

84. *Furman v. Georgia,* 408 U.S. 238 (1972).

85. *Gregg v. Georgia,* 428 U.S. 153 (1976).

86. *Minerville School District v. Gobitis,* 310 U.S. 586 (1940).

87. *West Virginia State Board of Education v. Barnette,* 319 U.S. 624 (1943)

88. *NAACP v. Alabama ex rel. Patterson,* 357 U.S. 449 (1958).

89. *Griswold v. Connecticut,* 381 U.S. 479 (1965).

90. *Griswold v. Connecticut,* concurring opinion. In 1972, the Court extended the privacy right to unmarried women: *Eisenstadt v. Baird,* 405 U.S. 438 (1972).

91. *Roe v. Wade,* 410 U.S. 113 (1973).

92. *Webster v. Reproductive Health Services,* 109 S.Ct. 3040 (1989), which upheld a Missouri law that restricted the use of public medical facilities for abortion. The decision opened the way for other states to limit the availability of abortion.

93. *Planned Parenthood of Southeastern Pennsylvania v. Casey,* 112 S.Ct. 2791 (1992).

94. *Stenberg v. Carhart,* 120 S.Ct. 2597 (2000).

95. *Bowers v. Hardwick,* 478 U.S. 186 (1986).

96. The dissenters were quoting an earlier case, *Olmstead v. United States,* 27 U.S. 438 (1928), to emphasize the nature of their disagreement with the majority in the *Bowers* case.

97. *Washington v. Glucksberg,* 117 S.Ct. 2258 (1997).

98. *Washington v. Glucksberg.*

99. *Washington v. Glucksberg.*

100. For an excellent discussion, see David M. O'Brien, *Supreme Court Watch* 1997 (New York: Norton, 1998), pp. 117–30.

101. *Roe v. Wade.*

102. *Rosenberger v. University of Virginia.*

Chapter 6

1. William Booth, "U. of Calif. Ends Racial Preferences," *Washington Post,* July 21, 1995, p. A1.

2. The *Slaughterhouse Cases,* 16 Wallace 36 (1873).

3. See *Civil Rights Cases,* 109 U.S. 3 (1883).

4. Anatole France, *Le lys rouge* (1984), chap. 7.

5. *Plessy v. Ferguson,* 163 U.S. 537 (1896).

6. The prospect of a Fair Employment Practices law tied to the commerce power produced the Dixiecrat break with the Democratic Party in 1948. The Democratic Party organization of the States of the Old Confederacy seceded from the national party and nominated its own candidate, the then-Democratic governor of South Carolina, Strom Thurmond, who is now a Republican senator. This almost cost President Truman the election.

7. This was based on the provision in Article VI of the Constitution that "all treaties made, . . . under the authority of the United States," shall be the "supreme law of the land." The committee recognized that if the U.S. Senate ratified the Human Rights Covenant of the United Nations—a treaty—then that power could be used as the constitutional umbrella for effective civil rights legislation. The Supreme Court had recognized in *Missouri v. Holland,* 252 U.S. 416 (1920), that a treaty could enlarge federal power at the expense of the states.

8. *Missouri ex rel. Gaines v. Canada,* 305 U.S. 337 (1938).

9. *Sweatt v. Painter,* 339 U.S. 629 (1950).

10. *Smith v. Allwright,* 321 U.S. 649 (1944).

11. *Shelley v. Kraemer,* 334 U.S. 1 (1948).

12. Kermit L. Hall, *The Magic Mirror: Law in American History* (New York: Oxford University Press, 1989), pp. 322–24. See also Richard Kluger, *Simple Justice* (New York: Random House, Vintage Edition, 1977), pp. 530–37.

13. The District of Columbia case came up too, but since the District of Columbia is not a state, this case did not directly involve the Fourteenth Amendment and its "equal protection" clause. It confronted the Court on the same grounds, however—that segregation is inherently unequal. Its victory in effect was "incorporation in reverse," with equal protection moving from the Fourteenth Amendment to become part of the Bill of Rights. See *Bolling v. Sharpe,* 347 U.S. 497 (1954).

14. *Brown v. Board of Education of Topeka, Kansas,* 347 U.S. 483 (1954).

15. The Supreme Court first declared that race was a suspect classification requiring strict scrutiny in the decision *Korematsu v. United States,* 323 U.S. 214 (1944). In this case, the Court upheld President Roosevelt's executive order of 1941 allowing the military to exclude persons of Japanese ancestry from the West Coast and to place them in internment camps. It is one of the few cases in which classification based on race survived strict scrutiny.

16. The two most important cases were *Cooper v. Aaron,* 358 U.S. 1 (1958), which required Little Rock, Arkansas, to desegregate; and *Griffin v. Prince Edward County School Board,* 377 U.S. 218 (1964), which forced all the schools of that Virginia county to reopen after five years of closing to avoid desegregation.

17. In *Cooper v. Aaron,* the Supreme Court ordered immediate compliance with the lower court's desegregation order and went beyond that with a stern warning that it is "emphatically the province and duty of the judicial department to say what the law is."

18. *Shuttlesworth v. Birmingham Board of Education,* 358 U.S. 101 (1958), upheld a "pupil placement" plan purporting to assign pupils on various bases, with no mention of race. This case interpreted *Brown* to mean that school districts must stop explicit racial discrimination but were under no obligation to take positive steps to desegregate. For a while black parents were doomed to case-by-case approaches.

19. For good treatments of this long stretch of the struggle of the federal courts to integrate the schools, see Paul Brest and Sanford Levinson, *Processes of Constitutional Decision-Making: Cases and Materials,* 2nd ed. (Boston: Little, Brown, 1983), pp. 471–80; and Alfred Kelly et al., *The American Constitution: Its Origins and Development,* 6th ed. (New York: Norton, 1983), pp. 610–16.

20. Pierre Thomas, "Denny's to Settle Bias Cases," *Washington Post,* May 24, 1994, p. A1.

21. See Hamil Harris, "For Blacks, Cabs Can Be Hard to Get," *Washington Post,* July 21, 1994, p. J1.

22. For a thorough analysis of the Office for Civil Rights, see Jeremy Rabkin, "Office for Civil Rights," in *The Politics of Regulation,* ed. James Q. Wilson (New York: Basic Books, 1980).

23. This was an accepted way of using quotas or ratios to determine statistically that blacks or other minorities were being excluded from schools or jobs, and then on the basis of that statistical evidence to authorize the Justice Department to bring suits in individual cases and in "class action" suits as well. In most segregated situations outside the South, it is virtually impossible to identify and document an intent to discriminate.

24. *Swann v. Charlotte-Mecklenberg Board of Education,* 402 U.S. 1 (1971).

25. *Milliken v. Bradley,* 418 U.S. 717 (1974).

26. For a good evaluation of the Boston effort, see Gary Orfield, *Must We Bus? Segregated Schools and National Policy* (Washington: Brookings Institution, 1978), pp. 144–46. See also Bob Woodward and Scott Armstrong, *The Brethren: Inside the Supreme Court* (New York: Simon and Schuster, 1979), pp. 426–27; and J. Anthony Lukas, *Common Ground* (New York: Random House, 1986).

27. *Board of Education v. Dowell,* 498 U.S. 237 (1991).

28. *Missouri v. Jenkins,* 115 S.Ct. 2038 (1995).

29. See especially *Katzenbach v. McClung,* 379 U.S. 294 (1964). Almost immediately after passage of the Civil Rights Act of 1964, a case was brought challenging the validity of Title II, which covered discrimination in public accommodations. Ollie's Barbecue was a neighborhood restaurant in Birmingham, Alabama. It was located eleven blocks away from an interstate highway and even farther from railroad and bus stations. Its table service was for whites only; there was only a take-out service for blacks. The Supreme Court agreed that Ollie's was strictly an intrastate restaurant, but since a substantial proportion of its food and other supplies were bought from companies outside the state of Alabama, there was a sufficient connection to interstate commerce; therefore, racial discrimination at such restaurants would "impose commercial burdens of national magnitude upon interstate commerce." Although this case involved Title II, it had direct bearing on the constitutionality of Title VII.

30. *Griggs v. Duke Power Company,* 401 U.S. 24 (1971). See also Allan Sindler, *Bakke, DeFunis, and Minority Admissions* (New York: Longman, 1978), pp. 180–89.

31. For a good treatment of these issues, see Charles O. Gregory and Harold A. Katz, *Labor and the Law* (New York: Norton, 1979), chap. 17.

32. In 1970, this act was amended to outlaw for five years literacy tests as a condition for voting in all states.

33. Joint Center for Political Studies, *Black Elected Officials: A National Roster—1988* (Washington, DC: Joint Center for Political Studies Press, 1988), pp. 9–10. For a comprehensive analysis and evaluation of the Voting Rights Act, see Bernard Grofman and Chandler Davidson, eds., *Controversies in Minority Voting: The Voting Rights Act in Perspective* (Washington, DC: Brookings, 1992).

34. See Douglas S. Massey and Nancy A. Denton, *American Apartheid: Segregation and the Making of the Underclass* (Cambridge, MA: Harvard University Press, 1993), chap. 7.

35. See Jane J. Mansbridge, *Why We Lost the ERA* (Chicago: University of Chicago Press, 1986); and Gilbert Steiner, *Constitutional Inequality* (Washington, DC: Brookings, 1985).

36. *See Frontiero v. Richardson,* 411 U.S. 677 (1973).

37. See *Craig v. Boren,* 423 U.S. 1047 (1976).

38. *Franklin v. Gwinnett County Public Schools,* 503 U.S. 60 (1992).

39. Jennifer Halperin, "Women Step Up to Bat," *Illinois Issues* 21 (September 1995), pp. 11–14.

40. Joan Biskupic and David Nakamura, "Court Won't Review Sports Equity Ruling," *Washington Post,* April 22, 1997, p. A1.

41. *U.S. v. Virginia,* 116 S.Ct. 2264 (1996).

42. Judith Havemann, "Two Women Quit Citadel over Alleged Harassment," *Washington Post,* January 13, 1997, p. A1.

43. *Meritor Savings Bank v. Vinson,* 477 U.S. 57 (1986).

44. *Harris v. Forklift Systems, Inc.,* 510 U.S. 17 (1993).

45. *Burlington Industries v. Ellerth,* 118 S.Ct. 2257 (1998); *Faragher v. City of Boca Raton,* 118 S.Ct. 2275 (1998).

46. *Lau v. Nichols,* 414 U.S. 563 (1974).

47. Dick Kirschten, "Not Black and White," *National Journal,* March 2, 1991, p. 497.

48. See the discussion in Robert A. Katzmann, *Institutional Disability: The Saga of Transportation Policy for the Disabled* (Washington, DC: Brookings, 1986).

49. For example, after pressure from the Justice Department, one of the nation's largest rental-car companies agreed to make special hand-controls available to any customer requesting them. See "Avis Agrees to Equip Cars for Disabled," *Los Angeles Times,* September 2, 1994, p. D1.

50. The case and the interview with Stephen Bokat was reported in Margaret Warner, "Expanding Coverage," *The NewsHour with Jim Lehrer Transcript,* June 30, 1998, online NewsHour, http://webcro5.pbs.org.

51. *Bowers v. Hardwick,* 478 U.S. 186 (1986).

52. Quoted in Joan Biskupic, "Gay Rights Activists Seek a Supreme Court Test Case," *Washington Post,* December 19, 1993, p. A1.

53. *Romer v. Evans,* 116 S.Ct. 1620 (1996).

54. For excellent coverage of the political and constitutional issues surrounding the actions of states on same-sex marriage, see Kenneth Kersch, "Full Faith and Credit for Same-Sex Marriages?" *Political Science Quarterly,* 112, 117–36. (Spring 1997).

55. From Lyndon B. Johnson, *The Vantage Point* (New York: Holt, Rinehart, and Winston, 1971), p. 166.

56. The Department of Health, Education, and Welfare (HEW) was the cabinet department charged with administering most federal social programs. In 1980, when education programs were transferred to the newly created Department of Education, HEW was renamed the Department of Health and Human Services.

57. *Regents of the University of California v. Bakke,* 438 U.S. 265 (1978).

58. See, for example, *United Steelworkers v. Weber,* 443 U.S. 193 (1979); and *Fullilove v. Klutznick,* 100 S.Ct. 2758 (1980).

59. *Ward's Cove v. Atonio,* 109 S.Ct. 2115 (1989).

60. *Griggs v. Duke Power Company,* 401 U.S. 24 (1971).

61. *Martin v. Wilks,* 109 S.Ct. 2180 (1989). In this case, some white firefighters in Birmingham challenged a consent decree mandating goals for hiring and promoting blacks. This was an affirmative action plan that had been worked out between the employer and aggrieved black employees and had been accepted by a federal court. Such agreements become "consent decrees" and are subject to enforcement. Chief Justice Rehnquist held that the white firefighters could challenge the legality of such programs, even though they had not been parties to the original litigation.

62. *St. Mary's Honor Center v. Hicks,* 113 S.Ct. 2742 (1993).

63. *Adarand Constructors v. Pena,* 115 S.Ct. 2097 (1995).

64. Ann Devroy, "Clinton Study Backs Affirmative Action," *Washington Post,* July 19, 1995, p. A1.

65. *Hopwood v. State of Texas,* 78 F3d 932 (5th Cir., 1996).

66. See Lydia Lum, "Applications by Minorities Down Sharply," *Houston Chronicle,* April 8, 1997, p. A1; R. G. Ratcliffe, "Senate Approves Bill Designed to Boost Minority Enrollments," *Houston Chronicle,* May 8, 1997, p. A1.

67. Linda Greenhouse, "Settlement Ends High Court Case on Preferences," *New York Times,* November 22, 1997, p. A1; Barry Bearak, "Rights Groups Ducked a Fight, Opponents Say," *New York Times,* November 22, 1997, p. A1.

68. Michael A. Fletcher, "Opponents of Affirmative Action Heartened by Court Decision," *Washington Post,* April 13, 1997, p. A21.

69. See Sam Howe Verhovek, "Houston Vote Underlined Complexity of Rights Issue," *New York Times,* November 6, 1997, p. A1.

70. There are still many genuine racists in America, but with the exception of a lunatic fringe, made up of neo-Nazis and members of the Ku Klux Klan, most racists are too ashamed or embarrassed to take part in normal political discourse. They are not included in either category here.

71. *Slaughterhouse Cases,* 16 Wallace 36 (1873).

72. See Paul M. Sniderman and Edward G. Carmines, *Reaching beyond Race* (Cambridge, MA: Harvard University Press, 1997).

Chapter 7

1. Alexander Astin et al., "The American Freshman: National Norms for Fall 1994," Cooperative Institutional Research Program of the American Council on Education and the Higher Education Research Institute of the University of California at Los Angeles, 1994.

2. Quoted in the *Tampa Tribune,* January 9, 1995, p. 1.

3. Henry K. Lee, "Tentative Pact Between UC, Hunger Strikers," *San Francisco Chronicle,* May 8, 1999, p. A15.

4. For a discussion of the political beliefs of Americans, see Harry Holloway and John George, *Public Opinion* (New York: St. Martin's, 1986). See also Paul R. Abramson, *Political Attitudes in America* (San Francisco: Freeman, 1983).

5. See Louis Hartz, *The Liberal Tradition in America* (New York: Harcourt, Brace, 1955).

6. See Paul M. Sniderman and Edward G. Carmines, *Reaching beyond Race* (Cambridge, MA: Harvard University Press, 1997).

7. Ben Gose, "Penn to Replace Controversial Speech Code; Will No Longer Punish Students for Insults," *Chronicle of Higher Education,* June 29, 1994, p. A30.

8. See Angus Campbell et al., *The American Voter* (New York: Wiley, 1960), p. 147.

9. Richard Morin, "Poll Reflects Division over Simpson Case," *Washington Post,* October 8, 1995, p. A31.

10. "Middle-Class Views in Black and White," *Washington Post,* October 9, 1995, p. A22.

11. For data see Rutgers University, Eagleton Institute of Politics, Center for the American Woman in Politics, "Sex Differences in Voter Turnout," August 1994.

12. Pamela Johnston Conover, "The Role of Social Groups in Political Thinking," *British Journal of Political Science* 18 (1988), pp. 51–78.

13. See Michael C. Dawson, "Structure and Ideology: The Shaping of Black Opinion," paper presented to the 1995 annual meeting of the Midwest Political Science Association, Chicago, Illinois, April 7–9, 1995. See also Michael C. Dawson, *Behind the Mule: Race, Class, and African American Politics* (Princeton, NJ: Princeton University Press, 1994).

14. Elisabeth Noelle-Neumann, *The Spiral of Silence* (Chicago: University of Chicago Press, 1984).

15. Ole R. Holsti, "A Widening Gap Between the Military and Civilian Society?" John M. Olin Institute for Strategic Studies.

16. Michael X. Delli Carpini and Scott Keeter, *What Americans Know about Politics and Why It Matters* (New Haven, CT: Yale University Press, 1996).

17. Sniderman and Carmines, *Reaching beyond Race,* ch. 4.

18. For an interesting discussion of opinion formation, see John Zaller, *The Nature and Origins of Mass Opinion* (New York: Cambridge University Press, 1992).

19. Gerald F. Seib and Michael K. Frisby, "Selling Sacrifice," *Wall Street Journal,* February 5, 1993, p. 1.

20. Michael K. Frisby, "Clinton Seeks Strategic Edge with Opinion Polls," *Wall Street Journal,* June 24, 1996, p. A16.

21. John M. Broder, "Clinton Eager to Veto Tax Cut, Aide Says," *New York Times,* September 2, 1999, p. A22.

22. Eric Convey and Ed Hayward, "Campaign Strategy Seen Behind Hillary's Remarks," *Boston Herald,* August 2, 1999, p. 6.

23. James Carney, "Playing by the Numbers," *Time,* April 11, 1994, p. 40.

24. See Gillian Peele, *Revival and Reaction* (Oxford, U.K.: Clarendon, 1985). Also see Connie Paige, *The Right-to-Lifers* (New York: Summit, 1983).

25. See David Vogel, "The Power of Business in America: A Reappraisal," *British Journal of Political Science* 13 (January 1983), pp. 19–44.

26. See David Vogel, "The Public Interest Movement and the American Reform Tradition," *Political Science Quarterly* 96 (winter 1980), pp. 607–27.

27. Jason DeParle, "The Clinton Welfare Bill Begins Trek in Congress," *New York Times,* July 15, 1994, p. 1.

28. Joe Queenan, "Birth of a Notion," *Washington Post,* September 20, 1992, p. C1.

29. Zaller, *The Nature and Origins of Mass Opinion.*

30. See Shanto Iyengar, *Is Anyone Responsible? How Television Frames Political Issues* (Chicago: University of Chicago Press, 1991); and Shanto Iyengar, *Do the Media Govern?* (Thousand Oaks, CA: Sage, 1997).

31. Michael Kagay and Janet Elder, "Numbers Are No Problem for Pollsters, Words Are," *New York Times,* August 9, 1992, p. E6.

32. See Richard Morin, "Is Bush's Bounce a Boom or a Bust?" *Washington Post National Weekly Edition,* August 31–September 6, 1992, p. 37.

33. See Thomas E. Mann and Gary Orren, eds., *Media Polls in American Politics* (Washington, DC: Brookings, 1992).

34. For an excellent and reflective discussion by a journalist, see Richard Morin, "Clinton Slide in Survey Shows Perils of Polling," *Washington Post,* August 29, 1992, p. A6.

35. See Michael Traugott, "The Impact of Media Polls on the Public," in *Media Polls in American Politics,* Mann and Orren, eds., pp. 125–49.

36. Michael Barone, "Why Opinion Polls Are Worth Less," *U.S. News & World Report,* December 9, 1996, p. 52.

37. Carl Cannon, "A Pox on Both Our Parties," in David C. Canon et. al., eds., *The Enduring Debate* (New York: Norton, 2000), p. 389.

38. Donn Tibbetts, "Draft Bill Requires Notice of Push Polling," *Manchester Union Leader,* October 3, 1996, p. A6.

39. "Dial S for Smear," *Memphis Commercial Appeal,* September 22, 1996, p. 6B.

40. Amy Keller, "Subcommittee Launches Investigation of Push Polls," *Roll Call,* October 3, 1996, p. 1.

41. For a discussion of the growing difficulty of persuading people to respond to surveys, see John Brehm, *Phantom Respondents* (Ann Arbor: University of Michigan Press, 1993).

42. Benjamin I. Page and Robert Y. Shapiro, "Effects of Public Opinion on Policy," *American Political Science Review* 77 (March 1983), pp. 175–90.

43. Robert A. Erikson, Gerald Wright, and John McIver, *Statehouse Democracy: Public Opinion and Democracy in the American States* (New York: Cambridge University Press, 1994).

44. The results of separate studies by the political scientists Lawrence Jacobs, Robert Shapiro, and Alan Monroe were reported by Richard Morin in "Which Comes First, the Politician or the Poll?" *Washington Post National Weekly Edition,* February 10, 1997, p. 35.

45. Delli Carpini and Keeter. *What Americans Know about Politics and Why It Matters.*

Chapter 8

1. Nat Hentoff, "Students Learning to Burn Newspapers," *Washington Post,* August 16, 1997, p. A21.

2. Richard Daigle, "Collegiate Censorship by Theft," *Atlanta Journal and Constitution,* March 6, 1994, p. F1.

3. "Daily Cal Papers Stolen from Campus," *San Francisco Chronicle,* October 16, 1997, p. C14.

4. John O'Conner, "Wheatbread Editor Has Court Date with Dean," *Telegram and Gazette* (Worcester, MA), February 12, 1997, p. B8.

5. "Promoting Free Speech," *Indianapolis Star,* October 7, 1996, p. A6.

6. Daigle, "Collegiate Censorship by Theft."

7. Benjamin Ginsberg and Martin Shefter, *Politics by Other Means* (New York: Basic Books, 1990), p. 24.

8. U.S. Bureau of the Census, *Statistical Abstract of the United States: 1994* (Washington, DC: Department of Commerce, 1994), pp. 567, 576.

9. For a criticism of the increasing consolidation of the media, see the essays in Patricia Aufderheide et al., *Conglomerates and the Media* (New York: New Press, 1997).

10. See Leo Bogart, "Newspapers in Transition," *Wilson Quarterly,* special issue, 1982; and Richard Harwood, "The Golden Age of Press Diversity," *Washington Post,* July 22, 1994, p. A23.

11. See Benjamin Ginsberg, *The Captive Public* (New York: Basic Books, 1986).

12. Michael Dawson, "Structure and Ideology: The Shaping of Black Public Opinion," paper presented to the 1995 meeting of the Midwest Political Science Association, Chicago, Illinois, April 7, 1995.

13. *Red Lion Broadcasting Company v. FCC,* 395 U.S. 367 (1969).

14. See the discussions in Gary Paul Gates, *Air Time* (New York: Harper & Row, 1978); Edward Jay Epstein, *News from Nowhere* (New York: Random House, 1973); Michael Parenti, *Inventing Reality* (New York: St. Martin's, 1986); Herbert Gans, *Deciding What's News* (New York: Vintage, 1980); and W. Lance Bennett, *News: The Politics of Illusion* (New York: Longman, 1986).

15. See Edith Efron, *The News Twisters* (Los Angeles: Nash Publishing, 1971).

16. Rowan Scarborough, "Leftist Press? Reporters Working in Washington Acknowledge Liberal Leanings in Poll," *Washington Times,* April 18, 1996, p. 1.

17. David Firestone, "Steven Brill Strikes a Nerve in News Media," *New York Times,* June 20, 1998, p. 4.

18. See Tom Burnes, "The Organization of Public Opinion," in *Mass Communication and Society,* ed. James Curran (Beverly Hills, CA: Sage, 1979), pp. 44–230. See also David Altheide, Creating Reality (Beverly Hills, CA: Sage, 1976).

19. David Garrow, *Protest at Selma* (New Haven, CT: Yale University Press, 1978).

20. Garrow, *Protest at Selma.*

21. See Todd Gitlin, *The Whole World Is Watching* (Berkeley, CA: University of California Press, 1980).

22. Quoted in George Brown Tindall and David E. Shi, *America: A Narrative History,* 4th ed. (New York: Norton, 1996), p. 1429.

23. See Dan Balz, "Bradley Offers Antipoverty Plan," *Washington Post,* October 22, 1999, p. A13.

24. For a discussion of framing, see Amy Jasperson, et al., "Framing and the Public Agenda," *Political Communication,* vol. 15, no. 2, pp. 205–224.

25. William S. Klein, "Inside the Spin Machine: How Political News Is Made," *Washington Post,* August 8, 1999, p. B4.

26. See Martin Linsky, *Impact: How the Press Affects Federal Policymaking* (New York: Norton, 1986).

27. Carl Allen, "UB Paper Prints Apology for Story on Student Poll," *Buffalo News,* November 15, 1997, p. 1B.

28. For a good discussion of how to evaluate media biases see Don Hazen and Julie Winokur, eds., *We the Media* (New York: New Press, 1997).

Chapter 9

1. See Craig A. Rimmerman, *The New Citizenship: Unconventional Politics, Activism, and Service* (Boulder, CO: Westview, 1997), pp. 40–45.

2. Waltrina Middleton, "Volunteers," *Washington Post,* May 6, 1999, p. M4.

3. Mary Maushard, "Community Service Duties Unfulfilled by About 30," *Baltimore Sun,* June 13, 1998, p. 2B.

4. Karlene Hanko, "College, University Presidents Pledge to Encourage Participation in Politics," *Daily Pennsylvanian,* July 13, 1999.

5. For a discussion of the decline of voting turnout over time, see Ruy A. Teixeira, *The Disappearing American Voter* (Washington, DC: Brookings, 1992). On the 1994 elections, see Paul Taylor, "Behind the Broom of '94: Wealthier, Educated Voters," *Washington Post,* June 8, 1995, p. A12.

6. Sidney Verba, Kay Lehman Schlozman, and Henry E. Brady, *Voice and Equality: Civic Voluntarism in American Politics* (Cambridge, MA: Harvard University Press, 1995), chap. 3, for kinds of participation, and pp. 66–67 for prevalence of local activity.

7. For a discussion of citizen lobbying, see Jeffrey M. Berry, *The New Liberalism: The Rising Power of Citizen Groups* (Washington, DC: Brookings, 1999).

8. Verba, Schlozman, and Brady, *Voice and Equality,* p. 51.

9. Steven J. Rosenstone and John Mark Hansen, *Mobilization, Participation, and Democracy in America* (New York: Macmillan, 1993), chap. 3; and Verba, Schlozman, and Brady, *Voice and Equality,* pp. 71–74.

10. Benjamin Ginsberg, *The Consequences of Consent* (New York: Random House, 1982), p. 39.

11. The University of the State of New York, State Education Department, Bureau of Elementary Curriculum Development, *Social Studies—Grade 1, A Teaching System* (Albany, NY: 1971), p. 32.

12. Robert Jackman, "Political Institutions and Voter Turnout in the Democracies," *American Political Science Review* 81 (June 1987), p. 420.

13. See Thomas B. Edsall, "Huge Gains in South Fueled GOP Vote in '94," *Washington Post,* September 27, 1995, p. A8.

14. See Richard A. Brody, "The Puzzle of Political Participation in America," in *The New American Political System,* ed. Anthony King (Washington, DC: American Enterprise Institute, 1978), chap. 8.

15. On the nineteenth century, see Michael E. McGerr, *The Decline of Popular Politics: The American North, 1865–1928* (New York: Oxford University Press, 1986).

16. Verba, Schlozman, and Brady, *Voice and Equality.*

17. See Alexis de Tocqueville, *Democracy in America* (New York: Vintage, 1945).

18. Robert D. Putnam, "Bowling Alone: America's Declining Social Capital," *Journal of Democracy* 6, no. 1 (January 1995), pp. 65–78.

19. On television see Robert D. Putnam, "Tuning In, Tuning Out: The Strange Disappearance of Social Capital in America," *PS: Political Science and Politics* 28, no. 4 (December 1995), pp. 664–83; for a reply see Pippa Norris, "Does Television Erode Social Capital? A Reply to Putnam," *PS: Political Science and Politics* 29, no. 3 (September 1996), pp. 474–80.

20. Michael Schudson, "What If Civic Life Didn't Die?" *American Prospect* 25 (March–April 1996), pp. 17–20.

21. Rosenstone and Hansen, *Mobilization, Participation, and Democracy in America,* p. 59.

22. Robert A. Jackson, Robert D. Brown, and Gerald C. Wright, "Registration, Turnout and the Electoral Representativeness of U.S. State Electorates," *American Politics Quarterly,* vol. 26, no. 3 (July 1998), pp. 259–87. Also, Benjamin Highton, "Easy Registration and Voter Turnout," *Journal of Politics,* vol. 59, no. 2 (April 1997), pp. 565–87.

23. Connie Cass, "'Motor Voter' Impact Slight," *Chattanooga News-Free Press,* June 20, 1997, p. A5. On the need to motivate voters see Marshall Ganz, "Motor Voter or Motivated Voter?" *American Prospect,* no. 28 (September–October 1996), pp. 41–49. On the hopes for Motor Voter see Frances Fox Piven and Richard A. Cloward, "Northern Bourbons: A Preliminary Report on the National Voter Registration Act," *PS: Political Science and Politics* 29, no. 1 (March 1996), pp. 39–42. On turnout in the 1996 election, see Barbara Vobejda, "Just under Half of Possible Voters Went to the Polls," *Washington Post,* November 7, 1996, p. A3.

24. Lawrence Bobo and Franklin D. Gilliam, "Race, Sociopolitical Participation, and Black Empowerment," *American Political Science Review* 24, no. 2 (June 1990), pp. 377–93.

25. Rosenstone and Hansen, *Mobilization, Participation, and Democracy in America,* p. 59.

26. Erik Austin and Jerome Chubb, *Political Facts of the United States since 1789* (New York: Columbia University Press, 1986), pp. 378–79.

27. Kenneth N. Weine, "Campaigns without a Human Face," *Washington Post,* October 27, 1996, p. C1.; see also Margaret Weir and Marshall Ganz, "Reconnecting People and Politics," *The New Majority: Toward Popular Progressive Politics,* ed. Stanley B. Greenberg and Theda Skocpol (New Haven, CT: Yale University Press, 1997), pp. 149–71.

Chapter 10

1. Agence France Presse wire service report, December 20, 1994.

2. Pan Xiaozhu, Xinhua News Agency report, July 30, 1994.

3. Jack Dennis and Diana Owen, "The Partnership Puzzle: Identification and Attitudes of Generation X," in *After the Boom: The Politics of Generation X,* ed. Stephen C. Craig and Stephen E. Bennett (Lanham, MD: Rowman and Littlefield, 1997).

4. See Richard Hofstadter, *The Idea of a Party System* (Berkeley: University of California Press, 1969).

5. John Aldrich, *Why Parties: The Origin and Transformation of Political Parties in America* (Chicago: University of Chicago Press, 1995).

6. See Walter Dean Burnham, *Critical Elections and the Mainsprings of American Electoral Politics* (New York: Norton, 1970). See also James L. Sundquist, *Dynamics of the Party System* (Washington, DC: Brookings, 1983).

7. Benjamin Ginsberg, *The Consequences of Consent* (New York: Random House, 1982), chap. 4.

8. For a discussion of third parties in the United States, see Daniel Mazmanian, *Third Parties in Presidential Election* (Washington, DC: Brookings, 1974).

9. See Maurice Duverger, *Political Parties* (New York: Wiley, 1954).

10. See Harold Gosnell, *Machine Politics Chicago Model,* rev. ed. (Chicago: University of Chicago Press, 1968).

11. For a useful discussion, see John Bibby and Thomas Holbrook, "Parties and Elections," in *Politics in the American States,* ed. Virginia Gray and Herbert Jacob (Washington, DC: Congressional Quarterly Press, 1996), pp. 78–121.

12. Alan Greenblatt, "With Major Issues Fading, Capitol Life Lures Fewer," *Congressional Quarterly Weekly Report,* October 25, 1997, p. 2625.

13. For an excellent analysis of the parties' role in recruitment, see Paul Herrnson, *Congressional Elections: Campaigning at Home and in Washington* (Washington, DC: Congressional Quarterly Press, 1995).

14. Ceci Connolly and Dan Baily, "Democrats Echo Themes in Face-Off," *Washington Post,* October 28, 1999, p. 1.

15. Duverger, *Political Parties,* p. 426.

16. Duverger, *Political Parties,* chap. 1.

17. Stanley Kelley, Jr., Richard E. Ayres, and William Bowen, "Registration and Voting: Putting First Things First," *American Political Science Review* 61 (June 1967), pp. 359–70.

18. David H. Fischer, *The Revolution of American Conservatism* (New York: Harper & Row, 1965), p. 93.

19. Fischer, *The Revolution of American Conservatism,* p. 109.

20. Henry Jones Ford, *The Rise and Growth of American Politics* (New York: Da Capo Press, 1967 reprint of the 1898 edition), chap. 9.

21. Ford, *The Rise and Growth of American Politics,* p. 125.

22. Ford, *The Rise and Growth of American Politics,* p. 125.

23. Ford, *The Rise and Growth of American Politics,* p. 126.

24. Mark Barabak, "Los Angeles Times Interview: Cruz Bustamente: On Surviving a Bruising First Term as Assembly Speaker," *Los Angeles Times,* August 24, 1997, p. M3.

Chapter 11

1. "Court Upholds GU Students' Voting Rights," *Washington Post,* September 18, 1998, p. B2.

2. B. G. Gregg, "Proposed Voting Law Angers Students: Lansing Legislation Would Have Them Vote in Home Districts," *Detroit News,* April 19, 1999, p. C1.

3. Gregg, "Proposed Voting Law," p. C1.

4. Clinton Rossiter, ed., *The Federalist Papers* (New York: New American Library, 1961), No. 57, p. 352.

5. *League of United Latin American Citizens v. Wilson,* CV-94-7569 (C.D. Calif.), 1995.

6. *Gray v. Sanders,* 372 U.S. 368 (1963); *Wesberry v. Sanders,* 376 U.S. 1 (1964); *Reynolds v. Sims,* 377 U.S. 533 (1964).

7. *Thornburg v. Gingles,* 478 U.S. 613 (1986).

8. *Shaw v. Reno,* 509 U.S. 113 (1993).

9. State legislatures determine the system by which electors are selected and almost all states use this "winner-take-all" system. Maine and Nebraska, however, provide that one electoral vote goes to the winner in each congressional district and two electoral votes go to the winner statewide.

10. Mary McGrory, "The Lost Leader," *Washington Post,* October 26, 1995, p. A2.

11. Larry J. Sabato, *The Rise of Political Consultants* (New York: Basic Books, 1981).

12. Larry J. Sabato, *The Rise of Political Consultants,* p. 250.

13. M. Ostrogorski, *Democracy and the Organization of Political Parties* (New York: Macmillan, 1902).

14. Timothy Clark, "The RNC Prospers, the DNC Struggles as They Face the 1980 Election," *National Journal,* October 27, 1980, p. 1619.

15. For discussions of the consequences, see Thomas Edsall, *The New Politics of Inequality* (New York: Norton, 1984). Also see Thomas Edsall, "Both Parties Get the Company's Money—But the Boss Backs the GOP," *Washington Post National Weekly Edition,* September 16, 1986, p. 14; and Benjamin Ginsberg, "Money and Power: The New Political Economy of American Elections," in *The Political Economy,* ed. Thomas Ferguson and Joel Rogers (Armonk, NY: M. E. Sharpe, 1984).

16. Jonathan Salant, "Million-Dollar Campaigns Proliferate in 105th," *Congressional Quarterly Weekly Report,* December 21, 1996, pp. 3448–51.

17. U.S. Federal Election Commission, "Financing the 1996 Presidential Campaign," Internet Release, April 28, 1998.

18. *Buckley v. Valeo,* 424 U.S. 1 (1976); *Colorado Republican Party v. Federal Election Commission,* 64 U.S.L.W. 4663 (1996).

19. FEC reports.

20. FEC reports.

21. David Broder and Ruth Marcus, "Wielding Third Force in Politics," *Washington Post,* September 20, 1997, p. 1.

22. Broder and Marcus, "Wielding Third Force in Politics."

23. Jill Abramson and Leslie Wayne, "Nonprofit Groups Were Partners to Both Parties in Last Election," *New York Times,* October 24, 1997, p. 1.

24. Leslie Wayne, "Papers Detail GOP Ties to Tax Group," *New York Times,* November 10, 1997, p. A27.

25. Andy Dabilis, "Two New Senators Begin Their Terms as Mavericks," *Boston Globe,* January 10, 1993, p. 2.

Chapter 12

1. Richard Appelbaum and Peter Dreier, "The Campus Anti-Sweatshop Movement," *American Prospect,* September–October 1999, p. 71.

2. Ibid., p. 77.

3. bid., p. 77.

4. Alexis de Tocqueville, *Democracy in America* (New York: Random House, 1955), vol. 1, chap. 12; vol. 2, chap. 5.

5. Clinton Rossiter, ed., *The Federalist Papers* (New York: New American Library, 1961), No. 10, p. 83.

6. Rossiter, ed., *Federalist Papers,* No. 10.

7. The best statement of the pluralist view is in David Truman, *The Governmental Process* (New York: Knopf, 1951), chap. 2.

8. E. E. Schattschneider, *The Semisovereign People* (New York: Holt, Rinehart, and Winston, 1960), p. 35.

9. Betsy Wagner and David Bowermaster, "B.S. Economics," *Washington Monthly,* November 1992, pp. 19–21.

10. Mancur Olson, *The Logic of Collective Action* (Cambridge, MA: Harvard University Press, 1965).

11. Timothy Penny and Steven Schier, *Payment Due: A Nation in Debt, A Generation in Trouble* (Boulder, CO: Westview, 1996), pp. 64–65.

12. Kay Lehman Schlozman and John T. Tierney, *Organized Interests and American Democracy* (New York: Harper & Row, 1986), p. 60.

13. John Herbers, "Special Interests Gaining Power as Voter Disillusionment Grows," *New York Times,* November 14, 1978.

14. Saundra Torry, "Army of Lobbyists Has Drawn $8 Million on Tobacco Fight," *Washington Post,* September 11, 1997, p. A4.

15. Thomas B. Edsall, "Liberal Lobby Snared in Campaign Probes," *Washington Post,* November 3, 1997, p. A9.

16. For discussions of lobbying, see Allan J. Cigler and Burdett A. Loomis, eds., *Interest Group Politics* (Washington, DC: Congressional Quarterly Press, 1983). See also Jeffrey M. Berry, *Lobbying for the People* (Princeton, NJ: Princeton University Press, 1977).

17. "The Swarming Lobbyists," *Time,* August 7, 1978, p. 15.

18. Ruth Marcus, "Lobbying's Big Hitters Go to Bat," *Washington Post,* August 3, 1997, p. 1.

19. Michael Weisskopf, "Lobbyists Rally around Their Own Cause: Clinton Move to Eliminate Tax Break Sparks Intense Hill Campaign," *Washington Post,* May 14, 1993, p. A16.

20. Phil Kuntz, "Ticket to a Better Image?" *Congressional Quarterly Weekly Report,* May 7, 1994, p. 1105.

21. See especially Marver Bernstein, *Regulating Business by Independent Commission* (Princeton, NJ: Princeton University Press, 1955). See also George J. Stigler, "The Theory of Economic Regulation," *Bell Journal of Economics and Management Science* 2 (1971), pp. 3–21.

22. Quoted in John E. Chubb, *Interest Groups and the Bureaucracy: The Politics of Energy* (Stanford, CA: Stanford University Press, 1983).

23. John P. Heinz, Edward O. Laumann, Robert L. Nelson, and Robert H. Salisbury, *The Hollow Core: Private Interests in National Policy Making* (Cambridge, MA: Harvard University Press, 1993), p. 96. See also Schlozman and Tierney, *Organized Interests and American Democracy,* chap. 13.

24. The famous and prophetic movie *The China Syndrome* portrayed some dramatic moments at a public hearing involving an administrative agency's decision to build or expand an atomic energy plant.

25. *Roe v. Wade,* 93 S.Ct. 705 (1973).

26. *Webster v. Reproductive Health Services,* 109 S.Ct. 3040 (1989)

27. *Brown v. Board of Education of Topeka, Kansas,* 74 S.Ct. 686 (1954).

28. See, for example, *Duke Power Co. v. Carolina Environmental Study Group,* 438 U.S. 59 (1978).

29. E. Pendleton Herring, *Group Representation before Congress* (New York: McGraw-Hill, 1936).

30. Ann Devroy, "Gay Rights Leaders Meet President in Oval Office: White House Tries to Play Down Session," *Washington Post,* April 17, 1993, p. 1.

31. Michael Weisskopf and Steven Mufson, "Lobbyists in Full Swing on Tax Plan," *Washington Post,* February 17, 1993, p. 1.

32. Michael Weisskopf, "Energized by Pulpit or Passion, the Public is Calling," *Washington Post,* February 1, 1993, p. 1.

33. Stephen Engelberg, "A New Breed of Hired Hands Cultivates Grass-Roots Anger," *New York Times,* March 17, 1993, p. A1.

34. "The K Street crowd" is a reference to the street where most law firms that mainly engage in lobbying are located.

35. Unlike spending on lobbying, these expenditures do not have to be reported; they therefore need to be reported voluntarily by each group, or estimated.

36. James C. Benton, "Money and Power: The Fight Over Electricity Deregulation," *Congressional Quarterly Weekly Report,* August 12, 2000, pp. 1964–69.

37. Jane Fritsch, "The Grass Roots, Just a Free Phone Call Away," *New York Times,* June 23, 1995, pp. A1 and A22.

38. Ruth Marcus, "Campaign Finance Proposal Drawing Opposition from Diverse Groups," *Washington Post,* May 1, 1996, p. A12.

39. Leslie Wayne, "Business Is Biggest Campaign Spender, Study Says," *New York Times,* October 18, 1996, p. 1.

40. Thomas B. Edsall, "Dole Outlines Changes for Political Financing," *New York Times,* October 21, 1996, p. 1.

41. David Sanger and James Sterngold, "Fund Raiser for Democrats Now Faces Harsh Spotlight," *New York Times,* October 21, 1996, p. 1.

42. Filed as *Colorado Republican Federal Campaign Committee v. Jones,* 95-489 (1996).

43. Ruth Marcus, "Outside Groups Pushing Election Laws into Irrelevance," *Washington Post,* August 8, 1996, p. A9.

44. Richard L. Burke, "Religious-Right Candidates Gain as GOP Turnout Rises," *New York Times,* November 12, 1994, p. 10.

45. John Harwood, "Dole Presses Hot-Button Issues to Try to Rouse GOP Activists Missing from Campaign So Far," *Wall Street Journal,* October 16, 1996, p. A22.

46. Some Americans and even more Europeans would stress only the negative aspect of the softening and adulterating effect of the two-party system on class and other basic subdivisions of society. For a discussion of how the working class was divided and softened, with native workers joining the Democratic Party and new immigrant workers becoming Republicans, see Gwendolyn Mink, *Old Labor and New Immigrants in American Political Development: Union, Party, and State, 1875–1920* (Ithaca, NY: Cornell University Press, 1986).

47. Rossiter, ed., *The Federalist Papers,* No. 10.

48. Olson, *The Logic of Collective Action.*

49. Steve Ma, telephone interview by author, February 12, 1998.

50. Steve Ma, interview, February 12, 1998.

51. Steve Ma, interview, February 12, 1998.

CHAPTER 13

1. See Cara Tanamachi, "Groups Give Voice to Generation X," *Austin-American Statesman,* October 22, 1996, p. A1.

2. Herb Asher and Mike Barr, "Popular Support for Congress and Its Members," and Karlyn Borman and Everett Carll Ladd, "Public Opinion toward Congress: A Historical Look," in *Congress, the Press, and the Public,* ed. Thomas E. Mann and Norman J. Ornstein (Washington DC: American Enterprise Institute and Brookings Institution, 1994), pp. 34, 51, 53.

3. John R. Hibbing and Elizabeth Theiss-Morse, *Congress as Public Enemy: Public Attitudes toward American Political*

Institutions (New York: Cambridge University Press, 1995), p. 100.

4. This argument is developed in Hibbing and Theiss-Morse, *Congress as Public Enemy.* For more on the institutionalization of Congress, see Nelson Polsby, "The Institutionalization of the US House of Representatives," *American Political Science Review* 62 (1968): 144–68; on professionalization see Alan Ehrenhalt, *The United States of Ambition: Politicians, Power, and the Pursuit of Office* (New York: Times Books, 1991).

5. For data on religious affiliations of the members of the 105th Congress, see *Congressional Quarterly Weekly Report,* January 4, 1997.

6. For data on occupational backgrounds of the members of the 105th Congress, see *Congressional Quarterly Weekly Report,* January 4, 1997.

7. Marian D. Irish and James Prothro, *The Politics of American Democracy,* 5th ed. (Englewood Cliffs, NJ: Prentice-Hall, 1971), p. 352.

8. For a discussion, see Benjamin Ginsberg, *The Consequences of Consent* (New York: Random House, 1982), chap. 1.

9. For some interesting empirical evidence, see Angus Campbell, Philip Converse, Warren Miller, and Donald Stokes, *Elections and the Political Order* (New York: Wiley, 1966), chap. 11.

10. Congressional Quarterly, *Guide to the Congress of the United States,* 3rd ed. (Washington, DC: Congressional Quarterly Press, 1982), p. 599.

11. John S. Saloma, *Congress and the New Politics* (Boston: Little, Brown, 1969), pp. 184–85. A 1977 official report using less detailed categories came up with almost the same impression of Congress's workload. Commission on Administrative Review, *Administrative Reorganization and Legislative Management,* House Doc. #95-232 (September 28, 1977), vol. 2, especially pp. 17–19.

12. See Linda Fowler and Robert McClure, *Political Ambition: Who Decides to Run for Congress* (New Haven, CT: Yale University Press, 1989); and Alan Ehrenhalt, *The United States of Ambition.*

13. See Barbara C. Burrell, *A Woman's Place Is in the House: Campaigning for Congress in the Feminist Era* (Ann Arbor: University of Michigan Press, 1994), chap. 6; and the essays in Elizabeth Adell Cook, Sue Thomas, and Clyde Wilcox, eds., *The Year of the Woman: Myths and Realities* (Boulder, CO: Westview, 1994).

14. Ruth Marcus and Juliet Eilperin, "Battle for House Fuels Cash Race," *Washington Post,* August 11, 1999, p. A1; Alison Mitchell, "Congress Chasing Campaign Donors Early and Often," *New York Times,* June 14, 1999, p. A1; Gilbert Craig, "Kohn Vows to Win Dairy Price Fight," *Milwaukee Journal Sentinel,* November 21, 1999, p. 1.

15. See Burrell, *A Woman's Place Is in the House;* and David Broder, "Key to Women's Political Parity: Running," *Washington Post,* September 8, 1994, p. A17.

16. "Did Redistricting Sink the Democrats?" *National Journal,* December 17, 1994, p. 2984.

17. *Miller v. Johnson,* 115 S.Ct. 2475 (1995).

18. *Congressional Quarterly Weekly Report,* October 17, 1998, p. 2792; Jeff Plungis, "The Driving Force of Bud Schuster," *Congressional Quarterly Weekly Report,* August 7, 1999, p. 1916.

19. http:.www.house.gov/stark/services.html

20. Congressional Quarterly, *Guide to the Congress of the United States,* 2nd ed. (Washington, DC: Congressional Quarterly Press, 1976), pp. 229–310.

21. Richard Fenno, Jr., *Home Style: House Members in Their Districts* (Boston: Little, Brown, 1978).

22. On the agenda activities of the Democratic leadership, see Paul S. Herrnson and Kelly D. Patterson, "Toward a More Programmatic Democratic Party? Agenda-Setting and Coalition-Building in the House of Representatives," *Polity 27* (summer 1995) pp. 607–28.

23. Richard C. Fenno, *Congressmen in Committees* (Boston: Little, Brown, 1973), p. 1; Richard L. Hall, "Participation, Abdication, and Representation in Congressional Committees," in *Congress Reconsidered,* 5th ed., ed. Lawrence C. Dodd and Bruce I. Oppenheimer (Washington DC: Congressional Quarterly Press, 1993), p. 164.

24. See Thomas E. Mann and Norman J. Ornstein, *Renewing Congress: A First Report of the Renewing Congress Project* (Washington, DC: American Enterprise Institute and Brookings Institution, 1992). See also the essays in Roger H. Davidson, ed., *The Postreform Congress* (New York: St. Martin's, 1992).

25. Richard E. Cohen, "Crackup of the Committees," *National Journal,* July 31, 1999, p. 2210–16.

26. Jeff Plungis, "The Driving Force of Bud Schuster," *Congressional Quarterly Weekly Report,* August 7, 1999, p. 1919.

27. Kenneth Cooper, "GOP Moves to Restrict Office Funds," *Washington Post,* December 7, 1994, p. 1.

28. Susan Webb Hammond, "Congressional Caucuses in the 104th Congress," in *Congress Reconsidered,* 6th ed., ed. Lawrence C. Dodd and Bruce I. Oppenheimer (Washington, DC: Congressional Quarterly Press, 1996).

29. Richard Sammon, "Panel Backs Senate Changes, But Fights Loom for Floor," *Congressional Quarterly Weekly Report,* June 18, 1994, pp. 1575–76.

30. See Robert Pear, "Senator X Kills Measure on Anonymity," *New York Times,* November 11, 1997, p. 12.

31. See John W. Kingdon, *Congressmen's Voting Decisions* (New York: Harper & Row, 1973), chap. 3; and R. Douglas Arnold, *The Logic of Congressional Action* (New Haven, CT: Yale University Press, 1990).

32. Jane Fritsch, "The Grass Roots, Just a Free Phone Call Away," *New York Times,* June 23, 1995, p. A1.

33. Daniel Franklin, "Tommy Boggs and the Death of Health Care Reform," *Washington Monthly,* April 1995, p. 36.

34. Peter H. Stone, "Follow the Leaders," *National Journal,* June 24, 1995, p. 1641.

35. Holly Idelson, "Signs Point to Greater Loyalty on Both Sides of the Aisle," *Congressional Quarterly Weekly Report,* December 19, 1992, p. 3849.

36. "GOP Leadership PACs' Fundraising Far Outstrips 1997–98," *Congressional Quarterly Weekly Report,* August 15, 1999, p. 1991.

37. Alison Mitchell, "Underlying Tensions Kept Congress Divided to the End," *New York Times,* November 21, 1999, p. 1.

38. James J. Kilpatrick, "Don't Overlook Corn for Porn Plot," *Chicago Sun-Times,* January 3, 1992, p. 23.

39. Dennis McDougal, "Cattle Are Bargaining Chip of the NEA," *Los Angeles Times,* November 2, 1991, p. F1.

40. David Broder, "At 6 Months, House GOP Juggernaut still Cohesive.

41. *U.S. v. Pink,* 315 U.S. 203 (1942). For a good discussion of

the problem, see James W. Davis, *The American Presidency* (New York: Harper & Row, 1987), chap. 8.

42. Carroll J. Doherty, "Impeachment: How It Would Work," *Congressional Quarterly Weekly Report,* January 31, 1998, p. 222.

43. See Kenneth A. Shepsle. "Representation and Governance: The Great Legislative Trade-off," *Political Science Quarterly* 103:3 (1988), pp. 461–84.

44. Role of the Public in Government Decisions Survey, January 1999, Roper Center Public Opinion Online, Accession number 0325495; Role of the Public in Government Decisions Survey, January 1999, Roper Center Public Opinion Online, Accession number 0325490.

45. See Hibbing and Theiss-Morse, *Congress as Public Enemy,* p. 105.

46. Jeffrey H. Birnbaum, "Washington's Power 25," *Fortune,* December 8, 1997, p. 144.

47. Birnbaum, "Washington's Power 25."

48. Marilyn Werber Serafini, "Biomedical Warfare," *National Journal,* February 1, 1997, p. 220.

CHAPTER 14

1. Editorial, *New York Times,* December 2, 1999, p. A34.

2. "President Chides World Trade Body in Stormy Seattle, *New York Times,* December 2, 1999, p. 1.

3. CNN/*Time* polls, January 23 and 30, 1998.

4. E. S. Corwin, *The President: Office and Powers,* 3rd rev. ed. (New York: New York University Press, 1957), p. 2.

5. *In re Neagle,* 135 U.S. 1 (1890). Neagle, a deputy U.S. marshal, had been authorized by the president to protect a Supreme Court justice whose life had been threatened by an angry litigant. When the litigant attempted to carry out his threat, Neagle shot and killed him. Neagle was then arrested by the local authorities and tried for murder. His defense was that his act was "done in pursuance of a law of the United States." Although the law was not an act of Congress, the Supreme Court declared that it was an executive order of the president, and the protection of a federal judge was a reasonable extension of the president's power to "take care that the laws be faithfully executed."

6. The Supreme Court did in fact disapprove broad delegations of legislative power by declaring the National Industrial Recovery Act of 1933 unconstitutional on the grounds that Congress did not accompany the broad delegations with sufficient standards or guidelines for presidential discretion (*Panama Refining Co. v. Ryan,* 293 U.S. 388 [1935], and *Schechter Poultry Corp. v. United States,* 295 U.S. 495 [1935]). The Supreme Court has never reversed those two decisions, but it has also never really followed them. Thus, broad delegations of legislative power from Congress to the executive branch can be presumed to be constitutional.

7. Arthur Schlesinger, Jr., *The Imperial Presidency* (Boston: Houghton Mifflin, 1973).

8. In *United States v. Pink,* 315 U.S. 203 (1942), the Supreme Court confirmed that an executive agreement is the legal equivalent of a treaty, despite the absence of Senate approval. This case approved the executive agreement that was used to establish diplomatic relations with the Soviet Union in 1933. An executive agreement, not a treaty, was used in 1940 to exchange "fifty overage destroyers" for ninety-nine-year leases on some important military bases.

9. These statutes are contained mainly in Title 10 of the United States Code, Sections 331, 332, and 333.

10. The best study covering all aspects of the domestic use of the military is that of Adam Yarmolinsky, *The Military Establishment* (New York: Harper & Row, 1971). Probably the most famous instance of a president's unilateral use of the power to protect a state "against domestic violence" was in dealing with the Pullman Strike of 1894. The famous Supreme Court case that ensued was *In re Debs,* 158 U.S. 564 (1895).

11. There is a third source of presidential power implied from the provision for "faithful execution of the laws." This is the president's power to impound funds—that is, to refuse to spend money Congress has appropriated for certain purposes. One author referred to this as a "retroactive veto power" (Robert E. Goosetree, "The Power of the President to Impound Appropriated Funds," *American University Law Review,* January 1962). This impoundment power was used freely and to considerable effect by many modern presidents, and Congress occasionally delegated such power to the president by statute. But in reaction to the Watergate scandal, Congress adopted the Budget and Impoundment Control Act of 1974 and designed this act to circumscribe the president's ability to impound funds by requiring that the president must spend all appropriated funds unless both houses of Congress consent to an impoundment within forty-five days of a presidential request. Therefore, since 1974, the use of impoundment has declined significantly. Presidents have either had to bite their tongues and accept unwanted appropriations or had to revert to the older and more dependable but politically limited method of vetoing the entire bill.

12. For a different perspective, see William F. Grover, *The President as Prisoner: A Structural Critique of the Carter and Reagan Years* (Albany: State University of New York Press, 1988).

13. For more on the veto, see Chapter 13 and Robert J. Spitzer, *The Presidential Veto: Touchstone of the American Presidency* (Albany: State University of New York Press, 1989).

14. For a good review of President Clinton's legislative leadership in the first session of his last Congress, see *Congressional Quarterly Weekly,* November 13, 1999, especially the cover story by Andrew Taylor, "Clinton Gives Republicans a Gentler Year-End Beating," pp. 2698–2700.

15. *New York Times,* December 23, 1992, p. 1.

16. A substantial portion of this section is taken from Theodore J. Lowi, *The Personal President* (Ithaca, NY: Cornell University Press, 1985), pp. 141–50.

17. All the figures since 1967, and probably 1957, are understated, because additional White House staff members were on "detail" service from the military and other departments (some secretly assigned) and are not counted here because they were not on the White House payroll.

18. See Donna K. H. Walters, "The Disarray at the White House Proves Clinton Wouldn't Last as a Fortune 500 CEO," *Plain Dealer,* July 10, 1994, p. 1C; and Paul Richter, "The Battle for Washington: Leon Panetta's Burden," *Los Angeles Times Sunday Magazine,* January 8, 1995, p. 16.

19. The actual number is difficult to estimate because, as with

White House staff, some EOP personnel, especially in national security work, are detailed to EOP from outside agencies.

20. Article I, Section 3, provides that "The Vice-President . . . shall be President of the Senate, but shall have no Vote, unless they be equally divided." This is the only vote the vice president is allowed.

21. Richard Neustadt, *Presidential Power* (New York: Wiley, 1960), p. 26.

22. A wider range of group phenomena was covered in Chapter 11. In that chapter the focus was on the influence of groups *upon* the government and its policy-making processes. Here our concern is more with the relationship of groups to the presidency and the extent to which groups and coalitions of groups become a dependable resource for presidential government.

23. For a more detailed review of the New Deal coalition in comparison with later coalitions, see Thomas Ferguson and Joel Rogers, *Right Turn: The Decline of the Democrats and the Future of American Politics* (New York: Hill & Wang, 1986), chap. 2. For updates on the group basis of presidential politics, see Thomas Ferguson, "Money and Politics," in *Handbooks to the Modern Worlds: The United States,* vol. 2, ed. Godfrey Hodgson (New York: Facts on File, 1992), pp. 1060–84; and Lucius J. Barker, ed., "Black Electoral Politics," *National Political Science Review,* vol. 2 (New Brunswick, NJ: Transaction Publishers, 1990).

24. See George Edwards III, *At the Margins: Presidential Leadership of Congress* (New Haven, CT: Yale University Press, 1989), chap. 7; and Robert Locander, "The President and the News Media," in *Dimensions of the Modern Presidency,* ed. Edward Kearney (St. Louis: Forum Press, 1981), pp. 49–52.

25. Study cited in Ann Devroy, "Despite Panetta Pep Talk, White House Aides See Daunting Task," *Washington Post,* January 8, 1995, p. A4.

26. This very useful distinction between pow*er* and pow*ers* is inspired by Richard Neustadt, *Presidential Power* (New York: Wiley, 1960), p. 28.

CHAPTER 15

1. U.S. Bureau of the Census, *Statistical Abstract of the United States, 1997* (Washington, DC: U.S. Government Printing Office, 1997), pp. 348, 355.

2. Arnold Brecht and Comstock Glaser, *The Art and Techniques of Administration in German Ministries* (Cambridge, MA: Harvard University Press, 1940), p. 6.

3. This account is drawn from Alan Stone, *How America Got On-Line: Politics, Markets, and the Revolution in Telecommunications* (Armonk, NY: M. E. Sharpe, 1997), pp. 184–87.

4. Gary Bryner, *Bureaucratic Discretion* (New York: Pergamon, 1987).

5. There are historical reasons why American cabinet-level administrators are called "secretaries." During the Second Continental Congress and the subsequent confederal government, standing committees were formed to deal with executive functions related to foreign affairs, military and maritime issues, and public financing. The heads of those committees were called "secretaries" because their primary task was to handle all correspondence and documentation related to their areas of responsibility.

6. 32 Stat. 825; 15 U.S.C. 1501.

7. See William Keller, *The Liberals and J. Edgar Hoover* (Princeton, NJ: Princeton University Press, 1989). See also Victor Navasky, *Kennedy Justice* (New York: Atheneum, 1971), chap. 2 and p. 8.

8. For more detail, consult John E. Harr, *The Professional Diplomat* (Princeton, NJ: Princeton University Press, 1972), p. 11; and Nicholas Horrock, "The CIA Has Neighbors in the 'Intelligence Community,'" *New York Times,* June 29, 1975, sec. 4, p. 2. See also Roger Hilsman, *The Politics of Policy Making in Defense and Foreign Affairs,* 3rd ed. (Englewood Cliffs, NJ: Prentice Hall, 1993).

9. Daniel Patrick Moynihan, "The Culture of Secrecy," *Public Interest,* Summer 1997, pp. 55–71.

10. Sean Paige, "A Sunshine Law Still in Shadows," *Insight on the News* 14 (December 28, 1998), p. 14.

11. See Daniel P. Moynihan, *Secrecy: The American Experience* (New Haven, CT: Yale University Press, 1998).

12. See Paul Peterson, *The Price of Federalism* (Washington, DC: Brookings, 1995) for a recent argument that "redistribution" is the distinctive function of the national government in the American federal system.

13. *Budget of the United States Government, FY 1998: Analytical Perspectives* (Washington, DC: U.S. Government Printing Office, 1997), Table 12-2, p. 219.

14. For an excellent political analysis of the Fed, see Donald Kettl, *Leadership at the Fed* (New Haven, CT: Yale University Press, 1986).

15. George E. Berkley, *The Craft of Public Administration* (Boston: Allyn & Bacon, 1975), p. 417. Emphasis added.

16. Correspondent Kelli Arena, "Overhauling the IRS," CNN Financial Network, March 7, 1997.

17. Robert Cohen, "IRS, Ordered to Treat U.S. Taxpayers Better, Collects Billions Less," *Seattle Times,* December 2, 1999, p. A18.

18. Eric Schmitt, "Washington Talk: No $435 Hammers, But Questions," *New York Times,* October 23, 1990, p. A16.

19. See National Performance Review Savings, http://www.npr.gov/library/announce/040700.html (accessed on June 13, 2000).

20. National Performance Review, *Putting Customers First '97,* October 1997, p. 2.

21. Much of this discussion draws on Don F. Kettl, *Reinventing Government: A Fifth-Year Report Card* (Washington, DC: Center for Public Management, Brookings Institution, September 1998), p. 28.

22. Kettl, *Reinventing Government,* p. 28

23. A thorough review of the first session of the 104th Congress will be found in "Republican's Hopes for 1996 Lie in Unfinished Business," *Congressional Quarterly Weekly Report,* January 6, 1996, pp. 6–18.

24. Public Law 101-510, Title XXIX, Sections 2,901 and 2,902 of Part A (Defense Base Closure and Realignment Commission).

25. Donald F. Kettl and John I. DiIulio, *Fine Print,* Center for Public Management Report no. 95-1 (Washington, DC: Brookings, 1995).

26. The title was inspired by a book by Charles Hyneman,

Bureaucracy in a Democracy (New York: Harper, 1950). For a more recent effort to describe the federal bureaucracy and to provide some guidelines for improvement, see Patricia W. Ingraham and Donald F. Kettl, eds., *Agenda for Excellence: Public Service in America* (Chatham, NJ: Chatham House, 1992).

27. Clinton Rossiter, ed., *The Federalist Papers* (New York: New American Library, 1961), No. 51, p. 322.

28. The title of this section was inspired by Peri Arnold, *Making the Managerial Presidency* (Princeton, NJ: Princeton University Press, 1986).

29. See Richard Nathan, *The Plot that Failed: Nixon and the Administrative Presidency* (New York: Wiley, 1975), pp. 68–76.

30. For more details and evaluations, see David Rosenbloom, *Public Administration* (New York: Random House, 1986), pp. 186–221; Levine and Kleeman, "The Quiet Crisis"; and Patricia Ingraham and David Rosenbloom, "The State of Merit in the Federal Government," in *Agenda for Excellence,* ed. Ingraham and Kettl.

31. Lester Salamon and Alan Abramson, "Governance: The Politics of Retrenchment," in *The Reagan Record,* ed. John Palmer and Isabel Sawhill (Cambridge, MA: Ballinger, 1984), p. 40.

32. Colin Campbell, "The White House and the Presidency under the 'Let's Deal' President," in *The Bush Presidency: First Appraisals,* ed. Colin Campbell and Bert A. Rockman (Chatham, NJ: Chatham House, 1991), pp. 185–222.

33. See John Micklethwait, "Managing to Look Attractive," *New Statesman* 125, November 8, 1996, p. 24.

34. Quoted in I. M. Destler, "Reagan and the World: An 'Awesome Stubborness,'" in *The Reagan Legacy: Promise and Performance,* ed. Charles O. Jones (Chatham, NJ: Chatham House, 1988), pp. 244 and 257. The source of the quote is *Report of the President's Special Review Board* (Washington, DC: U.S. Government Printing Office, 1987).

35. Data from Norman Ornstein et al., *Vital Statistics on Congress, 1987–1988* (Washington, DC: Congressional Quarterly Press, 1987), pp. 161–62. See also Lawrence Dodd and Richard Schott, *Congress and the Administrative State* (New York: Wiley, 1979), p. 169. For a valuable and skeptical assessment of legislative oversight of administrations, see James W. Fesler and Donald F. Kettl, *The Politics of the Administrative Process* (Chatham, NJ: Chatham House, 1991), chap. 11.

36. Richard E. Cohen, "Crackup of the Committees," *National Journal* (July 31, 1999), p. 2214.

37. See Aaron Wildavsky, *The New Politics of the Budgetary Process,* 2d ed. (New York: HarperCollins, 1992), pp. 15–16.

38. National Performance Review, *From Red Tape to Results: Creating a Government That Works Better and Costs Less* (Washington, DC: U.S. Government Printing Office, 1993), p. 42.

39. The Office of Technology Assessment (OTA) was a fourth research agency serving Congress until 1995. It was one of the first agencies scheduled for elimination by the 104th Congress. Until 1983, Congress had still another tool of legislative oversight: the legislative veto. Each agency operating under such provisions was obliged to submit to Congress every proposed decision or rule, which would then lie before both chambers for thirty to sixty days. If Congress took no action by one-house or two-house resolution explicitly to veto the proposed measure during the prescribed period, it became law. The legislative veto was declared unconstitutional by the Supreme Court in 1983 on the grounds that it violated the separation of powers—the resolutions Congress passed to exercise its veto were not subject to presidential veto, as required by the Constitution. See *Immigration and Naturalization Service v. Chadha,* 462 U.S. 919 (1983).

Chapter 16

1. Martha Brant, "Last Chance Class," *Newsweek,* May 31, 1999, p. 32.

2. As reported in Pam Belluck, "Death Row Lessons and One Professor's Mission," *New York Times,* March 6, 1999, p. A7.

3. James Langton, "International: U.S. Students Win Reprieve for Men on Death Row," *Daily Telegraph* (London), February 6, 2000, p. 27.

4. Governor Ryan Press Release, January 31, 2000.

5. Bob Herbert, "Criminal Justice Breakdown," *New York Times,* February 14, 2000, p. A21.

6. Ibid.

7. See Richard Neely, *How Courts Govern America* (New Haven, CT: Yale University Press, 1981).

8. U.S. Bureau of the Census, *Statistical Abstract of the United States* (Washington, DC: Government Printing Office, 1995).

9. C. Herman Pritchett, *The American Constitution* (New York: McGraw-Hill, 1959), p. 138.

10. *Marbury v. Madison,* 1 Cr. 137 (1803).

11. *Clinton v. City of New York,* 55 U.S.L.W. 4543 (1998).

12. This review power was affirmed by the Supreme Court in *Martin v. Hunter's Lessee,* 1 Wheat. 304 (1816).

13. *Brown v. Board of Education,* 347 U.S. 483 (1954); *Loving v. Virginia,* 388 U.S. 1 (1967).

14. *Griswold v. Connecticut,* 381 U.S. 479 (1965).

15. *Brandenburg v. Ohio,* 395 U.S. 444 (1969).

16. Oliver Wendell Holmes, Jr., "The Path of the Law," *Harvard Law Review* 10 (1897), p. 457.

17. *Shelley v. Kraemer,* 334 U.S. 1 (1948).

18. *Gideon v. Wainwright,* 372 U.S. 335 (1963).

19. *Burlington Industries v. Ellerth,* 97-569 (1998).

20. *Engel v. Vitale,* 370 U.S. 421 (1962); *Gideon v. Wainwright,* 372 U.S. 335 (1963); *Escobedo v. Illinois,* 378 U.S. 478 (1964); and *Miranda v. Arizona,* 384 U.S. 436 (1966).

21. *Baker v. Carr,* 369 U.S. 186 (1962).

22. Walter F. Murphy, "The Supreme Court of the United States," in *Encyclopedia of the American Judicial System,* ed. Robert J. Janosik (New York: Scribner's, 1987).

23. *Adarand Constructors v. Pena,* 115 S.Ct. 2097 (1995); *Missouri v. Jenkins,* 115 S.Ct. 2573 (1995); *Miller v. Johnson,* 115 S.Ct. 2475 (1995).

24. Robert Scigliano, *The Supreme Court and the Presidency* (New York: Free Press, 1971), p. 162. For an interesting critique of the solicitor general's role during the Reagan administration, see Lincoln Caplan, "Annals of the Law," *New Yorker,* August 17, 1987, pp. 30–62.

25. Edward Lazarus, *Closed Chambers* (New York: Times Books, 1998), p. 6.

26. *Plyler v. Doe,* 457 U.S. 202 (1982).

27. *NAACP v. Button,* 371 U.S. 415 (1963). The quotation is from the opinion in this case.

28. *Smith v. Allwright,* 321 U.S. 649 (1994).

29. See John E. Morris, "Boalt Hall's Affirmative Action Dilemma," *American Lawyer,* November 1997, p. 4.

30. *Chicago Daily Law Bulletin,* October 5, 1994.

31. R. W. Apple, Jr., "A Divided Government Remains, and with It the Prospect of Further Combat," *New York Times,* November 7, 1996, p. B6.

32. For limits on judicial power, see Alexander Bickel, *The Least Dangerous Branch* (Indianapolis, IN: Bobbs-Merrill, 1962).

33. *Worcester v. Georgia,* 6 Pet. 515 (1832).

34. See Walter Murphy, *Congress and the Court* (Chicago: University of Chicago Press, 1962).

35. Robert Dahl, "The Supreme Court and National Policy Making," *Journal of Public Law* 6 (1958), p. 279.

36. Martin Shapiro, "The Supreme Court: From Warren to Burger," in *The New American Political System,* ed. Anthony King (Washington, DC: American Enterprise Institute, 1978).

37. *Citizens to Preserve Overton Park v. Volpe,* 401 U.S. 402 (1971).

38. Toni Locy, "Bracing for Health Care's Caseload," *Washington Post,* August 22, 1994, p. A15.

39. See "Developments in the Law—Class Actions," *Harvard Law Review* 89 (1976), p. 1318.

40. *In re Agent Orange Product Liability Litigation,* 100 F.R.D. 718 (D.C.N.Y. 1983).

41. See Donald Horowitz, *The Courts and Social Policy* (Washington, DC: Brookings, 1977).

42. *Moran v. McDonough,* 540 F2d 527 (1 Cir., 1976; *cert. denied,* 429 U.S. 1042 [1977]).

43. Clinton Rossiter, ed., *The Federalist Papers* (New York: New American Library, 1961), No. 10, p. 78.

44. Probably the best study of the role of interest groups in the judicial process is that of Clement Vose, "Litigation as a Form of Pressure Group Activity," *Annals of the American Academy of Political and Social Science,* 319 (1958); this was expanded in his book *Caucasians Only: The Supreme Court, the NAACP and the Restrictive Covenant Cases* (Berkeley: University of California Press, 1959).

45. A full account of this role of the CBC and an assessment of its effectiveness will be found in Christina Rivers, unpublished doctoral dissertation, Cornell University, 2000. For an excellent account and assessment of the role of the CBC in Congress, see Paul Frymer, *Uneasy Alliances—Race and Party Competition in America* (Princeton, NJ: Princeton University Press, 1999), chap. 6.

46. Account will be found in David O'Brien, *Storm Center,* pp. 46–48. Other accounts of *amicus* briefs in other cases are also provided there.

47. Bree Bisnette, "Students Fulfill Civic Duties, Serve Justice on Jury Duty," *Kansas State Collegian,* August 30, 1996, p. 5.

Chapter 17

1. Compare with Gabriel Kolko, *The Triumph of Conservatism* (New York: Free Press, 1963), chap. 6.

2. For a good summary of Keynes's ideas see Robert Lekachman, *The Age of Keynes* (New York: McGraw-Hill, 1966).

3. Milton Friedman, *Free to Choose* (New York: Harcourt, Brace, Jovanovich, 1980).

4. Louis Uchitelle, "107 Months, and Counting," *New York Times,* January 30, 2000, sec. 3, p. 1.

5. Bob Woodward, *The Agenda* (New York: Simon & Schuster, 1994), p. 165.

6. See David M. Hart, *Forged Consensus: Science, Technology and Economic Policy in the United States, 1921–1953* (Princeton, NJ: Princeton University Press, 1998).

7. See Margaret Weir, *Politics and Jobs: The Boundaries of Employment Policy in the United States* (Princeton, NJ: Princeton University Press, 1992).

8. See Lester Thurow, "The Crusade That's Killing Prosperity," *The American Prospect,* March–April 1996.

9. The act of 1955 officially designated the interstate highways as the National System of Interstate and Defense Highways. It was indirectly a major part of President Dwight Eisenhower's defense program. But it was just as obviously a "pork barrel" policy as any rivers and harbors legislation.

10. The members are AMD, Digital, Hewlett-Packard, Intel, IBM, Lucent, Motorola, National Semiconductor, Rockwell, and Texas Instruments. What the two hundred other companies in this industry do in regard to the support given to Sematech is another story.

11. This was done quietly in an amendment to the Internal Revenue Service Reform Act (PL 105-206), June 22, 1998. But it was not accomplished easily. See Bob Gravely, "Normal Trade with China Wins Approval," *Congressional Quarterly Weekly Report,* July 25, 1998; and Richard Dunham, "MFN by any other name is . . . NTR?," Business Week on-line news flash, June 19, 1997.

12. Joseph Kahn, "Clinton Shift on Trade: 'Wake-Up Call,'" *New York Times,* January 31, 2000, p. A6.

13. See Samuel P. Hays, *Beauty, Health, and Permanence: Environmental Politics in the United States, 1955–1985* (Cambridge: Cambridge University Press, 1987).

14. Jonathan Harr, *A Civil Action* (New York: Vintage, 1996).

15. As a rule of thumb, in a growing economy where there is demand for credit, and assuming a reserve requirement of 20 percent, a deposit of $100 will create nearly $500 of new credit. This is called the "multiplier effect," because the bank can loan out $80 of the original $100 deposit to a new borrower; that becomes another $80 deposit, 20 percent of which ($64) can be loaned out to another borrower, and so on until the original $100 grows to approximately $500 of new credit.

16. Good treatments of the Federal Reserve System and monetary policy can be found in Donald Kettl, *Leadership at the Fed* (New Haven, CT: Yale University Press, 1986); and Albert T. Sommers, *The U.S. Economy Demystified* (Lexington, MA: Lexington Books, 1988), especially chap. 5.

17. For a fascinating behind-the-scenes look at how and why President Clinton abandoned his campaign commitment to tax

cuts and economic stimulus, and instead accepted the fiscal conservatism advocated by the Federal Reserve and its chairman, Alan Greenspan, see Bob Woodward, *The Agenda: Inside the Clinton White House* (New York: Simon & Schuster, 1994).

18. Office of Management and Budget, *The Budget for Fiscal Year 2001, Historical Tables,* Table 2.2 (Washington, DC: Government Printing Office, 2000).

19. For a systematic account of the role of government in providing incentives and inducements to business, see C. E. Lindblom, *Politics and Markets* (New York: Basic Books, 1977), chap. 13. For a detailed account of the dramatic Reagan tax cuts and reforms, see Jeffrey Birnbaum and Alan Murray, *Showdown at Gucci Gulch: Lawmakers, Lobbyists, and the Unlikely Triumph of Tax Reform* (New York: Random House, 1987).

20. For further background, see David E. Rosenbaum, "Cutting the Deficit Overshadows Clinton's Promise to Cut Taxes," *New York Times,* January 12, 1993, p. A1; and "Clinton Weighing Freeze or New Tax on Social Security," *New York Times,* January 31, 1993, p. A1.

21. Richard W. Stevenson, "Our Taxes: How the 2000 Ballot Could Amend Form 1040," *New York Times,* February 27, 2000, section 3, p. 21.

22. For an account of the relationship between mechanization and law, see Lawrence Friedman, *A History of American Law* (New York: Simon & Schuster, 1973), pp. 409–29.

23. Quotes are drawn from the *Economist,* January 31, 1998, pp. 65–6.

24. Joel Brinkley, "U.S. Versus Microsoft: The Overview," *New York Times,* November 6, 1999, p. A1.

25. The *Federal Register* is the daily publication of all official acts of Congress, the president, and the administrative agencies. A law or executive order is not legally binding until published in the *Federal Register.*

26. Congressional Budget Office, *Federal Financial Support of Business* (July 1995), http://www.cbo.gov (accessed March 5, 2000).

27. "The Arms Industry—Markets and Maginot Lines," *Economist,* October 28, 1995, pp. 23–25.

28. Marc Cooper, "Teamsters and Turtles: They're Together at Last," *Los Angeles Times,* December 2, 1999, p. B11.

29. Cathie Jo Martin, "Inviting Business to the Party," in *The Social Divide,* ed. Margaret Weir (Washington, DC: Brookings, 1998), pp. 230–67.

Chapter 18

1. Materials about all these organizations can be accessed through the website http://www.americansdiscuss.org, a site devoted to discussions about Social Security.

2. The income and poverty data in this section are all from the U.S. Census Web site: http://www.census.gov/hhes/income/histinc/index.html (accessed January 2000).

3. A good source of pre-1930s welfare history is James T. Patterson, *America's Struggle against Poverty, 1900–1994* (Cambridge, MA: Harvard University Press, 1994), chap. 2.

4. Quoted in Patterson, *America's Struggle against Poverty,* p. 26.

5. Patterson, *America's Struggle against Poverty,* p. 26.

6. Patterson, *America's Struggle against Poverty,* p. 27.

7. This figure is based on a WPA study by Ann E. Geddes, reported in Merle Fainsod et al., *Government and the American Economy,* 3rd. ed. (New York: Norton, 1959), p. 769.

8. The figures cited are for 1997.

9. Edward J. Harpham, "Fiscal Crisis and the Politics of Social Security Reform," in *The Attack on the Welfare State,* ed. Anthony Champagne and Edward Harpham (Prospect Heights, IL: Waveland, 1984), p. 13.

10. House Ways and Means Committee Print, WMCP: 105-7, *1998 Green Book,* from U.S. GPO Online via GPO Access at http://www.access.gpo.gov/congress/wm001.html (accessed June 1998). 1999 cash assistance figures are from the State Policy Documentation Project of the Center for Law and Social Policy, available at http://www.spdp.org/tanf/cat-fin.htm#fin (accessed January 21, 2000).

11. *Goldberg v. Kelly,* 397 U.S. 254 (1970).

12. See U.S. House of Representatives, Committee on Ways and Means, *Where Your Money Goes: The 1994–95 Green Book* (Washington, DC: Brassey's, 1994), pp. 325, 802.

13. Ways and Means Committee Print, WMCP:105-7, *1998 Green Book,* from U.S. GPO Online via GPO Access at http://www.access.gpo.gov/congress/wm001.html (accessed June 1998).

14. See National Conference of State Legislatures, "Tracking Recipients after They Leave Welfare," at http://www.ncsl.org/statefed/welfare/followup.htm (accessed June 1998).

15. Congressional Budget Office, *The Economic and Budget Outlook: Fiscal Years 1999–2008,* Appendix E, Table E-6, posted on the Congressional Budget Office website, http://www.cbo.gov (accessed June 1998).

16. See the analysis of these arguments in Jill Quadagno, "Social Security Policy and the Entitlement Debate," *Social Policy and the Conservative Agenda,* Clarence Y. H. Lo and Michael Schwartz, eds. (Malden, MA: Blackwell, 1998), pp. 95–117; and Richard W. Stevenson, "Bipartisan Group Urges Big Changes in Social Security," *New York Times,* May 19, 1998, p. A1.

17. See, for example, Kilolo Kijakazi, Wendell Primus, and Robert Greenstein, "Understanding the Financial Status of the Social Security System in Light of the 1998 Trustees Report," report of the Center on Budget and Policy Priorities, Washington, DC, April 28, 1998; and Henry J. Aaron, "To Fix Social Security," *Washington Post,* April 8, 1998, p. A23.

18. Quoted in Quadagno, "Social Security Policy and the Entitlement Debate," p. 111.

19. See the essays in Margaret Weir, ed., *The Social Divide: Political Parties and the Future of Activist Government* (Washington, DC, and New York: Brookings Institution Press and the Russell Sage Foundation, 1998).

20. U.S. Bureau of the Census, *Statistical Abstract of the United States, 1997* (Washington, DC: U.S. Government Printing Office, 1997), p. 45.

21. See, for example, Theodore R. Marmor, Jerry L. Mashaw, and Philip L. Harvey, *America's Misunderstood Welfare State* (New York: Basic Books, 1990), p. 156.

22. Burdett A. Loomis and Allen J. Cigler, "Introduction: The Changing Nature of Interest Group Politics," in *Interest Group Politics,* 4th ed., ed. Burdett A. Loomis and Allan J. Cigler (Washington, DC: Congressional Quarterly Press, 1995), p. 12.

23. See Senator Bob Kerrey's remarks quoted in David S. Broder, "Deficit Doomsday," *Washington Post,* August 7, 1994, p. C9.

24. See Beth Stevens, "Blurring the Boundaries: How the Federal Government Has Influenced Welfare Benefits in the Private Sector," in *The Politics of Social Policy in the United States,* ed. Margaret Weir, Ann Orloff, and Theda Skocpol (Princeton, NJ: Princeton University Press, 1988), pp. 122–48.

25. Raymond Hernandez, "Federal Welfare Overhaul Allows Albany to Shift Money Elsewhere," *New York Times,* April 23, 2000, p. 1.

26. Frances Fox Piven and Richard Cloward, *Poor People's Movements* (New York: Pantheon, 1977), chap. 5.

27. See Christopher Jencks and Kathryn Edin, "Do Poor Women Have the Right to Bear Children?" *American Prospect* 20 (winter 1995), pp. 43–52.

28. For an argument that children should be given the vote, see Paul E. Petersen, "An Immodest Proposal," *Daedalus* 121 (fall 1992), pp. 151–74.

29. There were a couple of minor precedents. One was the Smith-Hughes Act of 1917, which made federal funds available to the states for vocational education at the elementary and secondary levels. Second, the Lanham Act of 1940 made federal funds available to schools in "federally impacted areas," that is, areas with an unusually large number of government employees and/or where the local tax base was reduced by large amounts of government-owned property.

30. Office of Management and Budget, *Budget of the United States Government, Fiscal Year 1982* (Washington, DC: Government Printing Office, 1981), p. 427.

31. Quoted in Rochelle L. Stanfield, "Education: An A for Effort—and Achievement," *National Journal,* October 22, 1994, p. 2485.

32. For an analysis of employment and training initiatives since the 1930s, see Margaret Weir, *Politics and Jobs* (Princeton, NJ: Princeton University Press, 1992).

33. On CETA, see Donald C. Baumer and Carl E. Van Horn, *The Politics of Unemployment* (Washington, DC: Congressional Quarterly Press, 1985).

34. Morton Keller, *Affairs of State: Public Life in Nineteenth Century America* (Cambridge, MA: Belknap Press of Harvard University Press, 1977), p. 500.

35. Office of Management and Budget, *Budget of the United States Government* (Washington, DC: Government Printing Office, 1990, 1998).

36. U.N. Development Program, Organization for Economic Cooperation and Development, cited in Paul Spector, "Failure, by the Numbers," *New York Times,* September 24, 1994.

37. Theda Skocpol, *Boomerang: Health Care Reform and the Turn against Government* (New York: Norton, 1997), pp. 194–95.

38. John E. Schwarz, *America's Hidden Success,* 2nd ed. (New York: Norton, 1988), pp. 41–42.

39. Jonathan Weisman, "True Impact of GOP Congress Reaches Well Beyond Bills," *Congressional Quarterly Weekly Report,* September 7, 1996, pp. 2515–17.

40. On the relationship between education and democracy in the United States, see Ira Katznelson and Margaret Weir, *Schooling for All: Race, Class, and the Democratic Ideal* (New York: Basic Books, 1985).

41. For a description of these different views among conservatives, see David Frum, *Dead Right* (New York: Basic Books, 1994).

42. See, for example, Charles Murray, *Losing Ground* (New York: Basic Books, 1984).

43. See, for example, Lawrence Mead, *Beyond Entitlement: The Social Obligations of Citizenship* (New York: Free Press, 1986).

44. See James C. McKinley, Jr., "Father Faces U.S. Charges over Support," *New York Times,* August 9, 1995, p. B1.

45. Jencks and Edin, "Do Poor Women Have the Right to Bear Children?"

46. See Elizabeth Bussiere, "The Failure of Constitutional Welfare Rights in the Warren Court," *Political Science Quarterly* 109 (winter 1994), pp. 105–31.

47. See L. Free and Hadley Cantril, *The Political Beliefs of Americans* (New York: Simon & Schuster, 1968).

48. See Fay Lomax Cook and Edith Barrett, *Support for the American Welfare State* (New York: Columbia University Press, 1992), and Hugh Heclo, "The Political Foundations of Antipoverty Policy," in *Fighting Poverty: What Works and What Doesn't,* ed. Sheldon H. Danziger and Daniel H. Weinberg (Cambridge, MA: Harvard University Press, 1986), pp. 312–40.

49. See the Americans Discuss website at http://Americansdiscuss.org (accessed June 1998).

Chapter 19

1. Alexis de Tocqueville, *Democracy in America,* trans. Phillips Bradley (New York: Vintage, 1945; original published 1835), Vol. 1, p. 243.

2. Bruce Russett, "Doves, Hawks, and U.S. Public Opinion," *Political Science Quarterly* 105, no. 4 (winter 1990–91), pp. 515–38. See also David W. Levy, *The Debate over Vietnam* (Baltimore, MD: Johns Hopkins University Press, 1991), pp. 95–98, 111, and 159.

3. Under President Bush, for example, Dick Cheney left the House to become secretary of defense; under President Clinton, Senator Lloyd Bentsen and Representative Les Aspin left Congress to become the secretaries of the treasury and defense, respectively.

4. Raymond A. Bauer, Ithiel de Sola Pool, and Lewis Anthony Dexter, *American Business and Public Policy: The Politics of Foreign Trade,* 2nd ed. (Chicago: Aldine-Atherton, 1972).

5. Brenda Holzinger, "Power Politics: Public Policy, Federalism, and Hydroelectric Power," unpublished Ph.D. dissertation, Cornell University, 1997.

6. For further discussion of the vulnerability of modern presidents to the people through the media, see Theodore Lowi, *The Personal President: Power Invested, Promise Unfulfilled* (Ithaca, NY: Cornell University Press, 1985); Jeffrey K. Tulis, *The Rhetorical Presidency* (Princeton, NJ: Princeton University Press, 1987);

Samuel Kernell, *Going Public: New Strategies of Presidential Leadership* (Washington, DC: Congressional Quarterly Press, 1986); Richard Rose, *The Postmodern President: The White House Meets the World* (Chatham, NJ: Chatham House, 1988); and George C. Edwards, *The Public Presidency: The Pursuit of Popular Support* (New York: St. Martin's, 1983).

7. Michael J. Robinson, "Public Affairs Television and the Growth of Political Malaise: The Case of 'TV Selling of the Pentagon,'" *American Political Science Review* 70, no. 2 (June 1976), p. 425.

8. Seymour Martin Lipset and William Schneider, *The Confidence Gap: Business, Labor, and Government in the Public Mind* (New York: Free Press, 1983), p. 405.

9. A very good brief outline of the centrality of the president in foreign policy will be found in Paul E. Peterson, "The President's Dominance in Foreign Policy Making," *Political Science Quarterly* 109, no. 2 (summer 1994), pp. 215, 234.

10. One confirmation of this will be found in Theodore Lowi, *The End of Liberalism,* 2nd ed. (New York: Norton, 1979), pp. 127–30; another will be found in Stephen Krasner, "Are Bureaucracies Important?" *Foreign Policy* 7 (summer 1972), pp. 159–79. However, it should be added that Krasner was writing his article in disagreement with Graham T. Allison, "Conceptual Models and the Cuban Missile Crisis," *American Political Science Review* 63, no. 3 (September 1969), pp. 689–718.

11. Peterson, "The President's Dominance in Foreign Policy," p. 232.

12. A full version of the text of the farewell address, along with a discussion of the contribution to it made by Hamilton and Madison, will be found in Daniel J. Boorstin, ed., *An American Primer* (Chicago: University of Chicago Press, 1966), vol. 1, pp. 192–210. This editing is by Richard B. Morris.

13. "Balance of power" was the primary foreign policy role played by the major European powers during the nineteenth century, and it is a role available to the United States in contemporary foreign affairs, a role occasionally adopted but not on a world scale. This is the third of the four roles identified and discussed later in this chapter.

14. The best analysis of what he calls the "100 years' peace" will be found in Karl Polanyi, *The Great Transformation* (New York: Rinehart, 1944; Beacon paperback edition, 1957), pp. 5ff.

15. John G. Stoessinger, *Crusaders and Pragmatists: Movers of Modern American Foreign Policy* (New York: Norton, 1985), pp. 21, 34.

16. Hans Morgenthau, *Politics among Nations,* 2nd ed. (New York: Knopf, 1956), p. 505.

17. See Lowi, *The Personal President,* pp. 167–69.

18. In 1997, the next five biggest contributors were Japan (16.0 percent), Germany (9 percent), France (6.7 percent), the United Kingdom (5.6 percent), and the Russian federation (4.4 percent). These figures do not include many specific UN operations and organizations, nor the U.S. contributions to these programs. *1998 Information Please Almanac* (Boston: Information Please LLC, 1998), pp. 348–49.

19. Michael Kammen, *A Machine That Would Go of Itself: The Constitution in American Culture* (New York: Knopf, 1986).

20. There was, in fact, an angry dispute over a "surplus" of at least $2.2 billion, on the basis of which Japan and others demanded a rebate. *Report of the Secretary of Defense to the President and Congress* (Washington, DC: U.S. Government Printing Office, 1992), p. 26.

21. Not all American policy makers agree that the UN is a worthy instrument of American foreign policy. The UN is on the verge of bankruptcy, no thanks to the United States, which owes the UN nearly $1.5 billion in dues. For a review, see Barbara Crossette, "U.N., Facing Bankruptcy, Plans to Cut Payroll by Ten Percent," *New York Times,* February 6, 1996, p. A3.

22. "IMF: Sleeve-Rolling Time," *Economist,* May 2, 1992, pp. 98–99.

23. For a thorough, critical assessment of the current conduct of the IMF, see William Greider, *One World, Ready or Not: The Manic Logic of Global Capitalism* (New York: Simon & Schuster, 1997), esp. chap. 12. On the Indonesia situation, see Seth Mydans, "Indonesia Currency Falls Hard, Clouding Recovery," *New York Times,* January 23, 1998, p. D1. For other good treatments of Indonesia and of Korea, see *Financial Times* (London), March 23, 1998, p. 4; and *Financial Times* (London), May 11, 1998, p. 15.

24. Quoted in John Lewis Gaddis, *The United States and the Origins of the Cold War* (New York: Columbia University Press, 1972), p. 21.

25. The best account of the decision and its purposes will be found in Joseph Jones, *The Fifteen Weeks* (New York: Viking, 1955).

26. Robert A. Pastor, *Congress and the Politics of U.S. Foreign Economic Policy* (Berkeley: University of California Press, 1980), pp. 256–80.

27. Quoted in Lowi, *The End of Liberalism,* 2nd ed., p. 162.

28. George Quester, *The Continuing Problem of International Politics* (Hinsdale, IL: Dryden Press, 1974), p. 229.

29. The Warsaw Pact was signed in 1955 by the Soviet Union, the German Democratic Republic (East Germany), Poland, Hungary, Czechoslovakia, Romania, Bulgaria, and Albania. Albania later dropped out. The Warsaw Pact was terminated in 1991.

30. Quoted in Thomas Friedman, "NATO Expansion Starting New Cold War?" *Times-Picayune,* May 5, 1998, p. B5. See also *Baltimore Sun,* May 2, 1998, p. 12A.

31. "Arms for Sale," *Newsweek,* April 8, 1991, pp. 22–27.

32. "A Bomb in Every Backyard?" *Economist,* June 6, 1998, p. 17.

33. For a thorough and instructive exposition of the original Holy Alliance pattern, see Paul M. Kennedy, *The Rise and Fall of the Great Powers: Economic Change and Military Conflict from 1500 to 2000* (New York: Random House, 1987), pp. 159–60. And for a comparison of the Holy Alliance role with the balance-of-power role, to be discussed next, see Polanyi, *The Great Transformation,* pp. 5–11 and 259–62.

34. Felix Gilbert et al., *The Norton History of Modern Europe* (New York: Norton, 1971), pp. 1222–24.

35. For a summary of the entire literature about the "democratic peace," see Henry S. Farber and Joanne Gowa, "Politics and Peace," *International Security* 20, no. 2 (fall 1995), pp. 123–46. See also Jack Levi, "Domestic Politics and War," *Journal of Interdisciplinary History* 18, no. 4 (spring 1988), pp. 653–73.

36. The original theory of containment was articulated by former ambassador and scholar George Kennan in a famous article published under the pseudonym Mr. X, "The Sources of Soviet Conduct," *Foreign Affairs* 25 (1947), p. 556.

37. Richard Barnet, "Reflections," *New Yorker,* March 9, 1987, p. 82.

38. Thomas L. Friedman, "14 Big Macs Later . . . ," *New York Times,* December 31, 1995, sec. 4, p. 9.

39. See, for example, the cover story of the *Economist,* "Stumbling into War," March 27–April 2, 1999, pp. 17, 27, 49, 50.

40. Quoted in Elaine Sciolino and Ethan Bronner, "How a President, Distracted by Scandal, Entered Balkan War," *New York Times,* April 18, 1999, p. 12.

41. Note once again the title of the previously cited article, "How a President, Distracted by Scandal, Entered Balkan War."

42. Bradley Graham and Dana Priest, "'No Way to Fight a War': The Limits of Coalitions," *Washington Post National Weekly Edition,* June 14, 1999, p. 8.

43. Roger Cohen, "Kosovars to Get European Help for Rebuilding," *New York Times,* June 20, 1999, p. 1.

44. Quoted in "'No Way to Fight a War': The Limits of Coalitions," op cit., p. 8.

45. Editorial, "When the Snarling's Over," *Economist,* March 13, 1999, p. 17.

46. Address, joint meeting of Congress, April 10, 1951.

47. Stephen R. Weissman, *A Culture of Deference* (New York: Basic Books, 1995), p. 17.

CHAPTER 20

1. Molly Ivins quoted in Jon Thurber, "Obituaries; Bob Bullock; Colorful Longtime Politician in Texas," *Los Angeles Times,* June 20, 1999.

2. Alan Rosenthal, "On Analyzing States," in Alan Rosenthal and Maureen Moakley eds., *The Political Life of the American States* (New York. Praeger, 1984), pp. 11–12.

3. Daniel Elazar, *American Federalism: A View from the States,* 2nd ed. (New York: Crowell, 1971), pp. 84–126. See also John Kincaid, "Introduction," in John Kincaid, ed., *Political Culture, Public Policy and the American States* (Philadelphia: Center for the Study of Federalism, Institute for the Study of Human Issues, 1982), pp. 1–24.

4. Rosenthal, p. 13.

5. Donald W. Whisenhunt, *The Five States of Texas: An Immodest Proposal* (Austin: Eakin Press, 1987), pp. 2–3.

6. See Dallas Morning News, *Texas Almanac 2000–2001* (Dallas: Dallas Morning News, 1999), p. 53.

7. The following is drawn from Dallas Morning News, *Texas Almanac 2000–2001* (Dallas: Dallas Morning News, 1999), pp. 55–58.

8. See Ibid, p. 62.

9. See Joseph A. Schumpeter, *Capitalism, Socialism, and Democracy,* 3rd ed. (New York: Harper & Brothers, 1950), Chapter 6.

10. The following is drawn from Karen Gerhardt Britton, Fred C. Elliott, and E. A. Miller, "Cotton Culture," *The Handbook of Texas Online,* www.tsha.utexas.edu/handbook/online/articles/view/CC/afc3.html.

11. Dallas Morning News, *Texas Almanac 2000–2001* (Dallas: Dallas Morning News, 1999), p. 51.

12. Ibid, pp. 567–68.

13. See "Ranching" in *The Handbook of Texas Online,* www.tsha.utexas.edu/handbook/online/articles/view/RR/azr2.html.

14. This paragraph was drawn from the King Ranch entry in *The Handbook of Texas Online,* www.tsha.utexas.edu/handbook/online/articles/view/RR/azr2.html.

15. The following is drawn from Mary G. Ramos, "Oil and Texas: A Cultural History," Dallas Morning News, *Texas Almanac 2000–2001,* pp. 29–35, and Roger M. Olien, "Oil and Gas Industry," *The Handbook of Texas Online,* www.tsha.utexas.edu/handbook/online/articles/view/RR/azr2.html.

16. Mary G. Ramos, "Oil and Texas: A Cultural History," p. 31.

17. Roger M. Olien, "Oil and Gas Industry," *The Handbook of Texas Online,* www.tsha.utexas.edu/handbook/online/articles/view/RR/azr2.html.

18. Mary G. Ramos, "Oil and Texas: A Cultural History," p. 33.

19. The following is drawn from Anthony Champagne and Edward J. Harpham, "The Changing Political Economy of Texas," in Anthony Champagne and Edward J. Harpham, eds., *Texas Politics: A Reader,* 2nd ed. (New York: Norton, 1998), pp. 4–6. Production figures are drawn from Dallas Morning News, *Texas Almanac 1994–95* (Dallas: Belo, 1993), and John Sharp, *Forces of Change: Shaping the Future of Texas* (Austin: Texas Comptroller of Public Accounts, 1993).

20. Dallas Morning News, *Texas Almanac 2000–2001,* p. 578.

21. Paul Kengor, "The Effect of NAFTA on Texas" (Austin: Texas Public Policy Foundation, 1999).

22. These are drawn from "Highlights of 1998 Texas Exports" at www.bidc.state.tx.us/booksummary/1999TE–execsum.htm (note that this URL is for 1999 highlights; 1998 data is no longer available).

23. See "Estimated Population by Year for Texas, 1980–94" at txsdc.tamu.edu/txnypop.html.

24. See Arnoldo De Leon, "Mexican Americans," *The Handbook of Texas Online,* www.tsha.utexas.edu/handbook/online/articles/view/MM/pqmue.html.

25. See W. Marvin Dulaney, "African Americans," *The Handbook of Texas Online,* www.tsha.utexas.edu/handbook/online/articles/view/AA/pkaan.html, and Chandler Davidson, "African Americans and Politics," *The Handbook of Texas Online,* www.tsha.utexas.edu/handbook/online/articles/view/AA/wmafr.html.

26. The following is based on David G. McComb, "Urbanization," *The Handbook of Texas Online,* www.tsha.utexas.edu/handbook/online/articles/view/RR/azr2.html.

27. The following is drawn from David G. McComb, "Houston, Texas," *The Handbook of Texas Online,* www.tsha.utexas.edu/handbook/online/articles/view/RR/azr2.html.

28. These statistics are taken from the Metropolitan Area rankings from the Bureau of the Census website at www.census.gov.

29. The following is drawn from Jackie McElhaney and Michael V. Hazel, "Dallas, Texas," *The Handbook of Texas Online,* www.tsha.utexas.edu/handbook/online/articles/view/RR/azr2.html.

30. The following is drawn from Janet Schmelzer, "Fort Worth, Texas," *The Handbook of Texas Online,* www.tsha.utexas.edu/handbook/online/articles/view/RR/azr2.html.

31. The following is drawn from T. R. Fehrenbach, "San Antonio, Texas," *The Handbook of Texas Online,* www.tsha.utexas.edu/handbook/online/articles/view/RR/azr2.html.

Chapter 21

1. Donald E. Chipman, "Spanish Texas," *The Handbook of Texas Online,* www.tsha.utexas.edu/handbook/online/articles/view/SS/nps1.html; Donald E. Chipman, *Spanish Texas, 1519–1821* (Austin: University of Texas Press, 1992).

2. S. S. McKay, "Constitution of 1824," *The Handbook of Texas Online,* www.tsha.utexas.edu/handbook/online/articles/view/CC/ngc2.html.

3. S. S. McKay, "Constitution of Coahuila and Texas," *The Handbook of Texas Online,* www.tsha.utexas.edu/handbook/online/articles/CC/ngc1.html.

4. See Ralph W. Steen, "Convention of 1836," *The Handbook of Texas Online,* www.tsha.utexas.edu/handbook/online/articles/view/CC/mjc12.html.

5. The following is drawn from Joe E. Ericson, "Constitution of the Republic of Texas," *The Handbook of Texas Online,* www.tsha.utexas.edu/handbook/online/articles/view/CC/mhc1.html.

6. Randolph B. Campbell, "Slavery," *The Handbook of Texas Online,* www.tsha.utexas.edu/handbook/online/articles/view/SS/yps1.html.

7. S. S. McKay, "Constitution of 1845," *The Handbook of Texas Online,* www.tsha.utexas.edu/handbook/online/articles/view/CC/mhc3.html.

8. "The Texas Ordinance of Secession. February 2, 1861," www.lsjunction.com/docs/secesson.htm.

9. See Walter L. Buenger, "Secession Convention," *The Handbook of Texas Online,* www.tsha.utexas.edu/handbook/online/articles/view/SS/mjs1.html; Walter L. Buenger, *Secession and the Union in Texas* (Austin: University of Texas Press, 1984).

10. See Claude Elliott, "Constitutional Convention of 1866," *The Handbook of Texas Online,* www.tsha.utexas.edu/handbook/online/articles/view/tmjc3.html.; S. S. McKay, "Constitution of 1866," *The Handbook of Texas Online,* www.tsha.utexas.edu/handbook/online/articles/view/CC/mhc5.html; Charles W. Ramsdell, *Reconstruction in Texas* (New York: Columbia University Press, 1970).

11. See S. S. McKay, "Constitution of 1869," *The Handbook of Texas Online,* www.tsha.utexas.edu/handbook/online/articles/view/CC/mhc6.html; Charles W. Ramsdell, *Reconstruction in Texas.*

12. See John Walker Mauer, "Constitution Proposed in 1874," *The Handbook of Texas Online,* www.tsha.utexas.edu/handbook/online/articles/view/CC/mhc12.html; John Walker Mauer, "State Constitutions in a Time of Crisis: The Case of the Texas Constitution of 1876," *Texas Law Review 68* (June 1990).

13. See Sam Kinch, Jr., "Sharpstown Stock-Fraud Scandal," *The Handbook of Texas Online,* www.tsha.utexas.edu/handbook/online/articles/view/SS/mqs1.html; Charles Deaton, *The Year They Threw the Rascals Out* (Austin: Shoal Creek, 1973).

Chapter 22

1. Quoted in Donald W. Whisenhunt, *The Five States of Texas: An Immodest Proposal* (Austin: Eakin Press, 1987), p. xi.

2. Whisenhunt, p. 11.

3. James A. Dyer, Jan E. Leighley, and Arnold Vedlitz, "Party Identification and Public Opinion in Texas, 1984–1994," in Anthony Champagne and Edward J. Harpham (eds.), *Texas Politics: A Reader,* 2nd ed. (New York: Norton, 1998), p. 110.

4. Use of party affiliation as an ideological cue is discussed in Philip L. Dubois, *From Ballot to Bench* (Austin: University of Texas Press, 1980).

5. Quoted in Chandler Davidson, *Race and Class in Texas Politics* (Princeton, NJ: Princeton University Press, 1990), p. 198.

6. Davidson, pp. 24–25.

7. Dyer, Leighley, and Vedlitz, pp. 111–13.

8. James R. Soukup, Clifton McClesky, and Harry Holloway, *Party and Factional Division in Texas* (Austin: University of Texas Press, 1964), p. 22.

9. Dyer, Leighly, and Vedlitz, pp. 107–122, and Thomas R. Dye with L. Tucker Gibson and Clay Robison, *Politics in America,* 3rd ed., Texas ed. (Upper Saddle River, NJ: Prentice Hall, 1999), pp. 751–53.

10. Paul Lenchner, "The Party System in Texas," in Champagne and Harpham, *Texas Politics,* p. 174.

11. Texas Secretary of State's Report on Voting Precincts, www.sos.state.tx./elections/historical/70-92.shtml. Dallas and Harris counties have more voting precincts than are found in the entire state of New Hampshire.

12. U.S. senators are elected to a six-year term of office. Occasionally a senatorial term expires in a presidential election year, but this is the exception to the rule.

13. Sam Acheson, *Joe Bailey: The Last Democrat* (New York: Macmillan, 1932), p. 354.

14. Joe Robert Baulch, "James B. Wells: State Economic and Political Leader," Ph.D. dissertation, Texas Tech University, 1974, pp. 358–59.

15. Sue Tolleson-Rinehart and Jeanie R. Stanley, *Claytie and the Lady* (Austin: University of Texas Press, 1994), pp. 18–19.

16. O. Douglas Weeks, "The Texas-Mexican and the Politics of South Texas 34," *American Political Science Review* (1930), pp. 625–26; Anthony Champagne, "John Nance Garner," in Roger H. Davidson, Susan Webb Hammond, and Raymond W. Smock (eds.), *Masters of the House* (Boulder, CO: Westview, 1998), pp. 145–80.

17. *U.S. v. Texas*, 384 U.S. 155 (1966).

18. *Beare v. Smith*, 321 F. Supp. 1100 (1971).

19. *Kramer v. Union Free School District No. 15*, 395 U.S. 621 (1969); *Hill v. Stone*, 421 U.S. 289 (1975).

20. *Dunn v. Blumstein*, 405 U.S. 330 (1972).

21. *Newberry v. United States*, 256 U.S. 232 (1921).

22. *Nixon v. Herndon*, 273 U.S. 536 (1927).

23. *Nixon v. Condon*, 286 U.S. 73 (1932).

24. *Grovey v. Townsend*, 295 U.S. 45 (1935).

25. *Smith v. Allwright,* 321 U.S. 649 (1944).

26. *Terry v. Adams*, 345 U.S. 461 (1953).

27. Dallas Morning News, *Texas Almanac 2000–2001* (Dallas: Dallas Morning News, 1999), p. 426.

28. The motor voter law is a federal statute that requires states to allow voter registration when individuals apply for or renew their driver's licenses.

29. Texas Secretary of State, Voter Registration Projects, www.sos.state.tx.us.

30. Thomas R. Patterson, *The American Democracy* (New York: McGraw Hill, 1999), p. 188.
31. *Texas Almanac 2000–2001*, pp. 5, 288.
32. Texas Secretary of State, Election Results,www.sos.state.tx/elections/nov2000.shtml.
33. Richard H. Kraemer, Charldean Newell, and David Prindle, *Texas Politics*, 7th ed. (Minneapolis–St. Paul, MN: West, 1998), p. 28; *Texas Almanac 2000–2001*, pp. 8, 533–54.
34. Dallas County Community College District, *Texas: It's Land and People, A Telecourse* (Dallas: Dallas County Community College, 1990).
35. *Texas Almanac 2000–2001*, pp. 5, 288.
36. William C. Valasquez Institute, Newsflash, www.wcvi.org/pdf/98_tx_newsletter.pdf.
37. Dick Lavine, "King Would Abhor the Wealth Gap in Today's Texas," *Houston Chronicle*, January 16, 2000, p. C1.
38. James Carter, "Texas Elections," in Champagne and Harpham (eds.), *Texas Politics,* pp. 133–35.
39. A *politiquero* is a man who promises to deliver a set number of votes in return for weekly compensation. Of the more than three dozen politiqueras identified in the Brownsville, Harlingen, McAllen area, fewer than half a dozen were male.
40. Davidson, p. 202, 234–35.
41. Davidson, pp. 201, 235.
42. Carolyn Barta, *Bill Clements: Texian to His Toenails* (Austin: Eakin Press, 1996), pp. 6–7.
43. Soukup, McCleskey, and Holloway, pp. 26–29.
44. Quoted in Soukup, et al., p. 27.
45. Barta, p. 7.
46. Davidson, p. 74.
47. Davidson, for example, provides a table of support for all liberal gubernatorial or U.S. senatorial candidates in Texas primary elections between 1946 and 1984; Hill does not make that list. See, Davidson, p. 26.
48. Barta, p. 200.
49. Barta, p. 209.
50. Barta, p. 211.
51. Barta, pp. 214–15.
52. Barta, p. 216.
53. Barta, p. 216.
54. Barta, p. 334.
55. Celia Morris, *Storming the Statehouse: Running for Governor with Ann Richards and Diane Feinstein* (New York: Macmillan, 1992), p. 61.
56. Morris, p. 97.
57. Morris, p. 99.
58. Morris, pp. 106–07.
59. Tolleson-Rinehart and Stanley, p. 69.
60. Tolleson-Rinehart and Stanley, p. 97.
61. Tolleson-Rinehart and Stanley, pp. 102–03.
62. Morris, p. 175.
63. Dyer, Leighley, and Vedlitz, p. 121.
64. Jeanie R. Stanley, "Gender and the Campaign for Governor," in Champagne and Harpham (eds.), *Texas Politics*, p. 154.
65. Morris, p. 288.

Chapter 23

1. Sam Kinch, Jr., and Ben Procter, *Texas Under a Cloud* (Austin: Jenkins Publishing, 1972), p. 124.
2. James W. Lamare, *Texas Politics: Economics, Power and Policy,* 3rd ed. (St. Paul, MN: West, 1988), p. 82.
3. Kenneth R. Mladenka and Kim Quaile Hill, *Texas Government: Politics and Economics* (Belmont, CA: Wadsworth, 1986), pp. 80–82.
4. An example of an individual who gives more in political contributions than do most interest groups is Dr. James Leininger, whose political spending by March of 1998 was at least $595,000. Even Dr. Leininger, however, often joins with other people to make contributions. Along with two others, for example, he guaranteed a $1.1 million loan to Rick Perry's campaign for lieutenant governor, and he often makes contributions through political action committees. See, Texans for Public Justice, "Leininger's Lieutenant?" www.tpj.org/Lobby__Watch/perryll.html.
5. Lyle C. Brown, et al., *Practicing Texas Politics: A Brief Survey,* 6th ed. (Boston: Houghton-Mifflin, 1999), p. 138.
6. The payment data is not reported in precise figures, but in broad ranges of dollar amounts.
7. Texans for Public Justice, "Texas Revolvers," www.tpj.org/reports/revolver/rev__cover.html.
8. Texans for Public Justice, "Special-Interests Spend Up to $180 Million on Lobby Services in 1999 Legislative Session," www.tpj.org/press__releases/oldest.html.
9. Texans for Public Justice, "Toxic Exposure," www.tpj.org/reports/toxic/meet.html.
10. Texans for Public Justice, "Texas PACs," www.tpj.org/reports/pacs98/compare.html.
11. Texans for Public Justice, "Texas PACs," www.tpj.org/reports/pacs98/ideological.html.
12. Texans for Public Justice, "Texas PACs," www.tpj.org/reports/pacs98/labor.html.
13. Anthony Champagne, "Campaign Contributions in Texas Supreme Court Races," *Crime, Law & Social Change,* 17 (1992), pp. 91–106.
14. Mary Flood, "Tort-Reform Group Blasts an Old Ally Who Didn't Toe Line—Sen. Drew Nixon Is Swamped With Phone Calls, Faxes About Vote on Liability Bill," *Wall St. Journal*, May 5, 1999, p. T1.
15. Texans for Public Justice, "TLR Floods Close Races with Special Interest PAC Money," www.tpj.org/Lobby__Watch/tlrflood.html.
16. Michael Totty, "Galveston Democrat at Eye of Tort-Reform Storm," *Wall Street Journal*, April 23, 1997, p. T1.
17. Texans for Public Justice, "The Gated Community," www.tpj.org/reports/gated/summary.html.
18. Texans for Public Justice, "The Gated Community."
19. Mladenka and Hill, pp. 82–83.
20. Michael Totty, "Tort Reformers Emerge as Influential Force—Business Group Uses Big War Chest in Bid to Affect Key Races," *Wall St. Journal*, November 2, 1994, p. T1.
21. Nate Blakeslee, "Election 98: $$$Market-Driven Elections," www.texasobserver.org/feature4b.html.

22. Texans for Public Justice, "TLR: Long on Cash, Short on Wins," www.tpj.org/Lobby__Watch/tlrflops.html.
23. Texans for Public Justice, "Leininger's Lieutenant?" www.tpj.org/Lobby_Watch/perryll.html.
24. Texans for Public Justice, "Texas Chemical Council Members Dump: 187 Million Pounds of Toxins in Texas Up to $10 Million into State Politics," www.tpj.org/press_releases/toxic_exp.html.
25. Texans for Public Justice, "Toxic Exposure," www.tpj.org/reports/oxic/introduction.html.
26. Texans for Public Justice, "Toxic Exposure," www.tpj.org/reports/toxic/political__rel.html.
27. Texans for Public Justice, "Toxic Exposure," www.tpj.org/reports/toxic/statewide.html.
28. Texans for Public Justice, "Toxic Exposure," www.tpj.org/reports/toxic/grandfather.html.
29. This discussion of the decline in the influence of the trial lawyers is taken from Charles P. Elliott, Jr., "The Texas Trial Lawyers Association: Interest Group Under Siege," in Champagne and Harpham (eds.), pp. 177–94.
30. Texans for Public Justice, "Texas PACS," www.tpj.org/reports/pacs98/toppacs.html and www.tpj.org/reports/pacs98/business.html.

Chapter 24

1. Jan Jarboe Russell, "Filibuster of the Century," *Texas Monthly,* December 1999, www.texasmonthly.com/mag/1999/dec/filibuster.html. Gonzalez was later elected to the U.S. House of Representatives, where he served from 1961 until his retirement in 1998.
2. Texas Legislature Online, www.capitol.state.tx.us/.
3. Anthony Champagne and Rick Collis, "Texas," in Alan Rosenthal and Maureen Moakley (eds.), *The Political Life of the American States* (New York: Praeger, 1984), p. 138.
4. *Baker v. Carr,* 369 U.S. 186 (1962); *Reynolds v. Sims,* 377 U.S. 533 (1964).
5. *Wesberry v. Sanders,* 376 U.S. 1 (1964).

Chapter 25

1. Quoted in Pamela Colloff, "Fluke of the Century," *Texas Monthly*, December 1999, www.texasmonthly.com/mag/1999/dec/fluke.html.
2. This discussion of W. Lee O'Daniel is taken from George Norris Green, *The Establishment in Texas Politics: The Primitive Years, 1938–1957* (Westport, CT: Greenwood, 1979), pp. 22–44.
3. See the discussion of gubernatorial power in Cheryl D. Young and John J. Hindera, "The Texas Governor: Weak or Strong?" in Anthony Champagne and Edward J. Harpham (eds.), *Texas Politics: A Reader* (New York: Norton, 1998), p. 53.
4. Sam Kinch, in *Government by Consent—Texas, A Telecourse* (Dallas: Dallas County Community College District, 1990).
5. Kinch, *Government by Consent.*
6. Polly Ross Hughes, "Farewell to a Yalie, Howdy to an Aggie," *Houston Chronicle,* December 14, 2000, p. 1A.
7. Hughes, p. 26A.
8. George Kuempel, "The Tab Texas Taxpayers are Picking up for Security Protection," *Dallas Morning News*, February 2, 2000, p. 25A.
9. William P. Hobby, in *Government By Consent.*
10. Christy Hoppe, "Lt. Gov. Rick Perry, Honoring the Economic Generators of Texas Tourism," *Dallas Morning News*, February 28, 2000, p. 13A.
11. Hoppe, p. 13A.
12. Hoppe, p. 13A.
13. Young and Hindera, p. 62.
14. Young and Hindera, p. 61.
15. Young and Hindera, p. 61.
16. Polly Ross Hughes, "Perry Names Democrat to Post," *Houston Chronicle,* December 16, 2000, p. 35A.
17. Texas General Land Office, "About the Land Office," www.glo.state.tx.us/landoffice.html.
18. Stephen Power, "Underage Drinker Citations Increase," *Dallas Morning News*, May 25, 1998, p. 31A.

Chapter 26

1. "Editorial: Mansfield Calls it Quits; State Court Will Benefit," *Amarillo Globe-News,* July 26, 1999, www.amarillonet.com/stories/072699/opi_calls.shtml.
2. Much of this material is from *Texas Judiciary Online,* www.courts.state.tx.us/.
3. Thomas Petzinger, Jr., *Oil and Honor: The Texaco-Pennzoil Wars* (New York: Putnam, 1987).
4. Ken Anderson, *Crime in Texas* (Austin: University of Texas Press, 1997), p. 41.
5. Anderson, p. 40.
6. Anderson, p. 44.
7. Of the seventy-nine judicial appointments made by Governor William Clements, only six were either African American or Hispanic. In contrast, one-third of Governor Ann Richards' judicial appointees were minorities. See Michael Totty, "Is This Any Way to Choose a Judge? *Wall Street Journal,* August 3, 1994, pp. T1, T4.
8. *Texas Judiciary Online,* www.courts.state.tx.us/, and Anthony Champagne, "The Selection and Retention of Judges in Texas," *Southwestern Law Journal,* 40 (1986), p. 66.
9. Champagne, pp. 79–80.

10. Texans for Public Justice, "Payola Justice: How Texas Supreme Court Justices Raise Money from Court Litigants," www.tpj.org/reports/payola/intro.html.

11. Thomas R. Phillips, "State of the Judiciary," address to the Seventy-sixth Legislature, March 29, 1999.

12. L. Douglas Kiel, Carole Funk, and Anthony Champagne, "Two-party Competition and Trial Court Elections in Texas," *Judicature,* 77 (1994), p. 291.

13. Champagne, pp. 78–79.

14. Texas used to pay its obligations with state warrants that were much like checks.

15. The discussion of the "name-game" is taken from Champagne, pp. 100–102.

16. Anthony Champagne and Greg Thielemann, "Awareness of Trial Court Judges," *Judicature,* 74 (1991), pp. 271–76.

17. Phillips, March 29, 1999.

18. Elliott Slotnik, "Gender, Affirmative Action, and Recruitment to the Federal Bench," *Golden Gate University Law Review,* 14 (1984), p. 524.

19. Personal correspondence, Texas Office of Court Administration, April 13, 2000.

20. One report is that 90 percent of African American voters and 60–79 percent of Hispanic voters vote Democratic. See Ronald W. Chapman, "Judicial Roulette: Alternatives to Single-Member Districts as a Legal and Political Solution to Voting-Rights Challenges to At-Large Judicial Elections," 48 *SMU Law Review* (1995), p. 482.

21. The trial court opinion was unpublished.

22. *League of United Latin American Citizens v. Clements,* 902 F2d 293 (1990), and *League of United Latin American Citizens v. Clements,* 914 F2d 620 (1990).

23. *Houston Lawyers' Association v. Attorney General of Texas,* 501 U.S. 419 (1991).

24. *League of United Latin American Citizens Council v. Clements,* 999 F2d 831 (1993).

25. Rodney Ellis, "Supreme Court Ruling Mocks Civil Rights," *Dallas Morning News,* January 28, 1994, p. 25A.

26. David Godbey, "People, Not Courts, Should Determine System," *Dallas Morning News,* January 28, 1994, p. 25A.

27. A discussion of the Bullock plan and the politics surrounding it is in Anthony Champagne, "Judicial Selection in Texas," in Anthony Champagne and Edward J. Harpham (eds.), *Texas Politics: A Reader,* 2nd ed. (New York: Norton, 1998), pp. 99–103.

28. Godbey, p. 25A.

29. Susan Carbon and Larry Berkson, *Judicial Retention Elections in the United States* (Chicago: American Judicature Society, 1980), p. 21.

30. A discussion of these general systems of selection is found in Champagne, "Judicial Selection in Texas," pp. 88–104.

31. The discussion of the hybrid and incremental reforms is from the "Final Report of the Judicial Selection Task Force to the Commission on Judicial Efficiency," www.tomphillips.com/task.htm.

32. Much of this material is taken from Anthony Champagne, "The Role of Personality in Judicial Reform," *State Constitutional Commentaries and Notes,* 2 (1991), pp. 5–9.

33. This material is taken from Anthony Champagne, "Campaign Contributions in Texas Supreme Court Races," *Crime, Law & Social Change,* 17 (1992), pp. 91–106.

34. State of Texas, State Commission on Judicial Conduct, *1998 Annual Report* (Austin: State of Texas, 1998), p. 11.

35. State Commission of Judicial Conduct, pp. 12, 16.

36. "Texas Death Row Facts," Texas Department of Criminal Justice, www.tdcj.state.tx.us/stat/drow~facts.htm.

37. "Texas Annual Executions," Texas Department of Criminal Justice, www.tdcj.state.tx.us/stat/annual.htm.

38. "Scheduled Executions," Texas Department of Criminal Justice, www.tdcj.state.tx.us/stat/scheduledexecutions.htm.

39. "Gender and Racial Statistics of Death Row Offenders," Texas Department of Criminal Justice, www.tdcj.state.tx.us/stat/racial.htm.

40. "Execution Statistics," Texas Department of Criminal Justice, www.tdcj.state.tx.us/stat/execstats.htm.

41. "Gender and Racial Statistics of Death Row Offenders," Texas Department of Criminal Justice, www.tdcj.state.state.tx.us/stat/racial.htm.

42. "Executed Offenders," Texas Department of Criminal Justice, www.tdcj.state.tx.us/stat/executedoffenders.htm.

43. *McCleskey v. Kemp,* 481 U.S. 279 (1987).

44. *Faulder v. Texas Board of Pardons and Paroles,* 990 SW2d 944 (1999).

45. Janet Elliott, "Judge Upholds Meetings-by-Fax for Parole Board," *TexLaw,* www.texlaw.com/today/parolebd.htm.

46. Criminal Justice Policy Council, Report to the Governor and Legislature, *Projection of Adult and Juvenile Correctional Population and Capacity, FY 1999 to FY 2003,* September 1998, unpaginated.

47. U.S. Bureau of the Census, *1998 Statistical Abstract of the United States,* Table 378, www.ojp.usdoj.gov/bjs/correct.htm.

48. 1998 Statistical Abstract of the United States, Table 378.

49. Phil Hardberger, "Juries Under Siege," *St. Mary's Law Journal,* 30 (1998), pp. 6–7.

50. "High Court Voting Patterns," *Texas Lawyer,* September 6, 1999, p. 5, based on information supplied by Court Watch.

Chapter 27

1. Jim Schutze, *The Accommodation* (Seacaucus, N.J.: Citadel Press, 1986), pp. 58 and 87.

2. Alexis de Tocqueville, *Democracy in America,* ed. J. P. Mayer, trans. George Lawrence (New York: Harper Perennial, 1988).

3. U.S. Census Bureau, *1997 Census of Governments. Volume 1, Government Organization.* August 1997, pp. 1–2.

4. The two states that don't use counties as units of local government are Connecticut and Rhode Island. See Richard L. Cole and Delbert A. Taebel, *Texas: Politics and Public Policy* (Fort Worth: Harcourt, Brace, Jovanovich, 1987), p. 151.

5. Texas Association of Counties, "Texas Counties: A Brief History," www.county.org/TXcounties/history.html.

6. Texas Association of Counties, "Texas Counties, A Brief History."

7. Cole and Taebel, *Texas Politics and Public Policy*, p. 152.
8. *Avery v. Midland County*, 88 S. Ct. 1114 (1968).
9. Anthony Champagne and Rick Collis, "Texas," in Alan Rosenthal and Maureen Moakley (eds.), *The Political Life of the American States* (Washington, D.C.: Congressional Quarterly Press, 1984), p. 140.
10. Graham Baker, "Constables Arrest Truancy Rate," *County Magazine*, November/December 1997, www.county.org/publications/county/096/truancy.html.
11. "Jasper County Scrambles for Trial Funds," www.county.org/publications/county/106/jasper.html.
12. Cole and Taebel, *Texas: Politics and Public Policy,* p. 155.
13. Texas Commission on Jail Standards, "County Jail Population Percentages," www.tcjs.state.tx.us/jailpop.html.
14. "Knock! Knock! Smith County Sheriff's Office Goes Armored," *County Magazine*, July/August 1997, www.county.org/publications/county/094/knock.html.
15. Texas Association of Counties, "1998 Indigent Health Care Survey," www.county.org/publications/county/106/survey.html.
16. Article XI, Section 5, of the Texas Constitution is concerned with home rule. For a further discussion of home rule in Texas see Terrell Blodgett, *Texas Home Rule Charters* (Austin: Texas Municipal League, 1994); "Home Rule Charters" in the *Handbook of Texas Online,* www.tsha.utexas.edu/handbook/online/articles/view/HH/mvhek.html.
17. Correspondence with Terrell Blodgett, Wednesday, February 3, 2000.
18. The following is drawn from Bradley R. Rice, "Commission Form of Government," *The Handbook of Texas Online,* www.tsha.utexas.edu/handbook/online/articles/view/CC/moc1.html.
19. Dallas Morning News, *Texas Almanac 1996–97,* (Dallas: Dallas Morning News, 1995), p. 513.
20. Correspondence with Terrell Blodgett, Wednesday, February 3, 2000.
21. For a further discussion, see Terrell Blodgett, "Council-Manager Form of Government," *The Handbook of Texas Online*, www.tsha.utexas.edu/handbook/online/articles/view/CC/moc2.html; *Texas Home Rule Charters* (Austin: Texas Municipal League, 1994).
22. For a history of the Office of Controller in Houston, see www.ci.houston.tx.us/citygovt/controller/history.html.
23. Jack C. Plano and Milton Greenberg, *The American Political Dictionary,* 10th ed. (Fort Worth: Harcourt Brace, 1997).
24. *Texas Almanac and State Industrial Guide, 2000–2001* (Dallas: Dallas Morning News, LP, 1999), p. 533. *Statistical Abstract of the United States* (Washington D.C.: Bureau of the Census, 1998), p. 496.
25. See "What is a COG?" www.txregionalcouncil.org/what.htm.

Chapter 28

1. The following numbers are drawn from *The Texas Tax System: A Presentation to the House Committee on Ways and Means,* February 17, 1999, www.window.state.tx.us/taxbud/overview.
2. See Bernard L. Weinstein, "Taxes in Texas," in Anthony Champagne and Edward J. Harpham, *Texas Politics: A Reader* (New York: Norton, 1998), chapter 12.
3. The following discussion is drawn from Texas Legislative Budget Board, *Texas Facts Book,* (Austin: State of Texas, 1998).
4. For a discussion of the budgetary process, see Texas Comptroller of Public Accounts, *Disturbing the Peace,* Appendix I (Austin: State of Texas, 1996), www.window.state.tx.us/tpr/tpr4/vol1/v13app12.html.
5. For a discussion of these issues, see Weinstein "Taxes in Texas," chapter 12.
6. See Kim Quaile Hill and Kenneth R. Mladenka, *Texas Government* (Belmont, CA: Wadsworth Publishing Company, 1993), pp. 269–70. James MacGregor Burns et al., *Government by the People. Texas Version* (Englewood Cliffs: Prentice Hall, 1995), pp. 746–48.
7. See Julie Cummins, "Re-weaving the Web Tax: State Tries to Protect Tax Base, Encourage Electronic Commerce," Texas Comptroller of Public Accounts, *Fiscal Notes* (September 1999).
8. See James LeBas, "Who Wants to Be a Billionaire? Texas Spending Tobacco Money on Health Care, Endowments," Texas Comptroller of Public Accounts, *Fiscal Notes* (January 2000).
9. Harry Mika and Lawrence J. Redlinger, "Crime and Correction," in Anthony Champagne and Edward J. Harpham (eds.), *Texas at the Crossroads* (College Station: Texas A&M University Press, 1987), pp. 245–46.
10. Mika and Redlinger, "Crime and Correction," p. 246.
11. *Ruiz v. Estelle,* 503 F. Supp. 1265 (1980).
12. Mika and Redlinger, "Crime and Correction," p. 247.
13. 1998–99 Budget for the State of Texas.
14. See the Associated Texans Against Crime Annual Report, 1998, reprinted at www.todayfoundation.org/atac/report.html.
15. Ibid.
16. Ibid.
17. Ibid.
18. Mika and Redlinger, "Crime and Correction," p. 245.
19. Associated Texans Against Crime, Annual Report, 1998.
20. Mika and Redlinger, "Crime and Correction," p. 245.
21. See www.lbb.state.tx.us/lbb/members/reports/summary/inmatep.htm, citing the Criminal Justice Institute, *Corrections Yearbook,* 1994.
22. Associated Texans Against Crime, Annual Report, 1998.
23. L. Tucker Gibson, Jr., and Clay Robison, *Government and Politics in the Lone Star State,* 2nd Edition (Upper Saddle River, NJ: Prentice Hall, 1995).
24. For a discussion of the history of public education in Texas from which the following is drawn, see Max Berger and Lee Wilborn, "Education," *The Texas Handbook Online,* www.tsha.utexas.edu/handbook/online/articles/view/EE/khe1.html; Dallas Morning News, "Public Schools," *Texas Almanac 2000–2001,* Millennium Edition (Dallas: Dallas Morning News, 1999), pp. 533–34.
25. See Lewis B. Cooper, *The Permanent School Fund of Texas* (Fort Worth: Texas State Teachers Association, 1934); Michael E. McClellan, "Permanent School Fund," *The Handbook of Texas Online,* www.tsha.utexas.edu/handbook/online/articles/view/PP/khp1.html.
26. See Oscar Mauzy, "Gilmer-Aikin Laws," *The Handbook of Texas Online,* www.tsha.utexas.edu/handbook/online/articles/

view/GG/mlg1.html; Dick Smith and Richard Allen Burns, "Texas Education Agency," *The Handbook of Texas Online,* www.tsha.utexas.edu/handbook/online/articles/view/TT/met2.ht-ml. Berger and Wilborn, "Education."

27. See Anna Victoria Wilson, "Education for African Americans," *The Handbook of Texas Online,* www.tsha.utexas.edu/handbook/online/articles/view/EE/kde2.html.

28. Arnoldo De Leon and Robert A. Calvert, "Segregation," *The Handbook of Texas Online,* www.tsha.utexas.edu/handbook/online/articles/view/SS/pks1.html.

29. The following discussion of the *Rodriguez* and *Edgewood* cases is drawn from Legislative Budget Board Staff, "Financing Public Education in Texas: Kindergarten through Grade 12," *Legislative Handbook* (February 1999); Berger and Wilborn, "Education"; Cynthia E. Orozco, "Rodriguez v. San Antonio ISD," *The Handbook of Texas Online,* www.tsha.utexas.edu/handbook/online/articles/view/RR/jrrht.html; Teresa Palomo Acosta, "Edgewood ISD v. Kirby," *The Handbook of Texas Online,* www.tsha.utexas.edu/handbook/online/articles/view/EE/jre2.html.

30. See Legislative Budget Board Staff, "Financing Public Education in Texas: Kindergarten through Grade 12," *Legislative Handbook* (February 1999), pp. 26–27.

31. See Clark D. Thomas, "Education Reform in Texas," in Champagne and Harpham (eds.), *Texas Politics,* Chapter 13.

32. National Commission on Excellence in Education, *A Nation at Risk: The Imperative for Educational Reform.* (Washington DC: Department of Education, 1983).

33. See Thomas, "Education Reform in Texas," p. 218.

34. See Thomas, "Education Reform in Texas," p. 221.

35. See Thomas, "Education Reform in Texas," p. 231; Dallas Morning News, "Public Schools," *Texas Almanac 2000–2001,* Millennium Edition (Dallas: Dallas Morning News, 1999), p. 533. See also Terrence Stutz, "State's List Cites Sub-par Schools in Transfer Plan," *Dallas Morning News,* December 24, 1999, p. 1.

36. See Terrence Stutz and Christopher Lee, "$3.8 billion School Plan Is Approved," *Dallas Morning News,* May 31, 1999, www.dallasnews.com/specials/legislature/0531leg1budget.htm.

37. Statistics on poverty in Texas are drawn from three sources: Health and Human Services Commission, "Texas Poverty Statistics for Selected Groups: 1988-97," www.hhsc.state.tx.us/cons_bud/dssi/txpov88_97.htm; "Demographic Profile of the Texas Population Living in Poverty in 1997," www.hhsc.state.tx.us/cons_bud/dssi/dempov97.htm; Texas Department of Human Services, "DHS at a Glance—Spring 1998," www.dhs.state.tx.us/publications/refguide/98Spring/TXPOPAGI.htm.

38. The following is drawn from Edward J. Harpham, "Welfare Reform and the New Paternalism in Texas," in Champagne and Harpham (eds.), *Texas Politics* (New York: Norton, 1998), Chapter 14.

39. See Vivian Elizabeth Smyrl, "Texas Department of Human Services," *The Handbook of Texas Online,* www.tsha.utexas.edu/handbook/online/articles/view/TT/mct6.html.

40. Harpham, "Welfare Reform and the New Paternalism in Texas," p. 238.

41. See Smyrl, "Texas Department of Human Services."

42. See Charles Murray, *Losing Ground* (New York: Basic Books, 1984).

43. For a discussion of these programs, see Lawrence Mead, *The New Politics of Poverty: The Nonworking Poor in America* (New York: Basic Books, 1992).

44. The following paragraphs are drawn from Harpham, "Welfare Reform and the New Paternalism in Texas," pp. 244–47.

45. The following information is drawn from Texas Department of Human Services, "Temporary Assistance for Needy Families (TANF) Reference Guide, 1999," www.dhs.state.tx.us/publications/refguide/sec2-7.html.

46. Christopher Lee, "Texas Continues Welfare System Reform," *Dallas Morning News,* May 31, 1999, www.dallasnews.com/specials/legislature/0531leg3welfare.htm.

47. Texas Department of Human Services, "Texas Families in Transition: The Impact of Welfare Reform Changes in Texas: Early Findings," December 1998.

Illustration Credits

2 © Kirk Condyles/Impact Visuals/PictureQuest; **13, 23, 24, 32, 38 (bottom), 44, 46, 68, 89, 98, 100, 110, 116, 120 (top), 129, 132 (top), 135, 148, 158, 161, 162, 165, 168, 171, 172, 174, 175, 179, 185, 186, 194, 200 (both), 202, 204, 207, 216, 218, 225, 230, 242, 248, 269, 278, 285 (top), 289, 296, 295, 299, 301, 303, 304, 306, 316, 319, 322, 333, 346, 358, 363, 371, 376, 388, 403, 407, 421, 436, 439, 442, 443, 450, 446, 452, 456 (both), 457, 463, 464, 465, 468, 480, 485, 491, 498, 503, 506, 507, 513, 555, 570, 574 (top), 579, 591, 593, 598, 604, 605, 607, 612, 635, 639, 642, 646, 647, 664, 672, 676, 678, 686, 690, 702, 708, 712, 720, 715, 742, 747, 748, 771, 788, 792, 811, 818, 840, 847, 854, 856, 871, 886, 892, 895, 897, 900, 906, 907, 916, 926, 927, 929, 931, 947, 952, 954, 957, 970, 983, 991, 992, 993, 1000, 1004, 1007, 1014, 1017, 1030, 1033, 1035, 1038, 1044, 1047, 1049, 1052, 1055** AP/Wide World Photos; **17** From the art collection of the Boatman's National Bank of St. Louis; **19, 38 (top), 73, 76, 96, 199, 305, 536, 624, 665, 669, 691, 800, 802, 804, 806, 810, 814, 831, 859, 879** Corbis-Bettmann; **20, 177, 176, 213, 221, 267, 323, 368, 638, 685, 761** UPI/Corbis-Bettmann; **27, 411** LBJ Library Collection, Austin, TX; **37, 43, 53, 80, 123, 352** Library of Congress; **41** © B. Daemmrich/The Image Works; **50, 354, 395, 671** The Granger Collection, New York; **54** © Rick Reinhard/Impact Visuals/Picture Quest; **58** Courtesy of The Christian Coalition of New York; **83, 216, 246, 530, 551, 574** Reuters/Corbis-Bettmann; **93** Eastern National Park and Monument Association/Corbis; **120** Collection of New York Historical Society; **125** PEMCO Webster and Stevens Collection, Museum of History and Industry, Seattle/Corbis; **126** Billy E. Barnes/Stock, Boston; **132** Philip Gould/Corbis; **149** Courtesy of Peacefire and Bennet Hasselton; **170** Nik Wheeler/Corbis; **206, 964** The Warder Collection; **208** Stanley J. Forman, Pulitzer Prize 1977; **210** Magnum Photos; **243** Dan Habib/Impact Visuals; **236** Carey Terry/*Daily Californian*; **260** By permission of Bob Gorrell and Creators Syndicate; **285, 687, 770** Reuters NewMedia Inc./Corbis; **292** Stock Montage, Inc.; **298** © 1963 Charles Moore/Black Star; **319 (top), 420, 538, 561** AFP/Corbis; **324** © Bob Daemmrich/Stock, Boston/PictureQuest; **369** Courtesy Brett Morgan; **426** © Cynthia Carris/Impact Visuals; **445** Courtesy Alen MacWeeney and *Modern Maturity*; **487** Courtesy of Carolyn Maloney; **492, 501, 508** © Paul S. Conkin; **540** © 1957 Burt Glinn/Magnum Photos, Inc.; **550** Photo by Alan F. Singer © CBS 1995; **583** Courtesy of IMC, Global Inc.; **615** New Jersey Newsphotos; **620** Joe Sohm/Chromo Sohm Inc./Corbis; **621** Collection, The Supreme Court of the United States, courtesy The Supreme Court Historical Society. Photo by Richard Strauss, Smithsonian Institution; **633** © 1986, Ken Heinen; **626** © *Providence Journal-Bulletin* Photo; **637** Photo by Erich Solomon; **656** © 1994 Jerome Friar/Impact Visuals; **663** © Hulton Deutsch/Corbis; **707** The Chicago Historical Society (ICHi-20216); **758** © Chris Rainier/Corbis; **798** © Ted Spiegel/Corbis; **815, 868, 1022** © Corbis; **817** © Buddy Mays/Corbis; **827, 829, 834, 835, 883, 938,** Texas State Library and Archives Commission; **914** © Tim Thompson/Corbis; **944** © David Muench/Corbis; **950** © Wally McNamee/Corbis; **981** Lyndon Baines Johnson Library, Photo by Cecil Stoughton; **1008** © Keith Wood/Corbis.

Answer Key

Chapter 1
1. d
2. b
3. c
4. d
5. c
6. d
7. d
8. a
9. a
10. a

Chapter 2
1. b
2. a
3. c
4. d
5. d
6. a
7. b
8. c
9. d
10. a

Chapter 3
1. b
2. b
3. b
4. d
5. c
6. c
7. d
8. d
9. d
10. a

Chapter 4
1. b
2. c
3. d
4. c
5. c
6. b
7. a
8. d
9. c
10. d

Chapter 5
1. a
2. c
3. c
4. a
5. d
6. d
7. b
8. a
9. a
10. c

Chapter 6
1. b
2. a
3. b
4. b
5. c
6. b
7. d
8. d
9. d
10. a

Chapter 7
1. c
2. a
3. d
4. c
5. d
6. b
7. d
8. b
9. a
10. b

Chapter 8
1. c
2. b
3. d
4. c
5. d
6. a
7. b
8. a
9. d
10. a

Chapter 9
1. d
2. d
3. a
4. c
5. d
6. d
7. a
8. c
9. c
10. d

Chapter 10
1. a
2. d
3. c
4. d
5. b
6. c
7. c
8. a
9. c
10. d

Chapter 11
1. a
2. b
3. c
4. d
5. a
6. a
7. b
8. a
9. d
10. c

Chapter 12
1. a
2. d
3. c
4. a
5. a
6. c
7. d
8. d
9. b
10. a

Chapter 13
1. a
2. d
3. c
4. c
5. a
6. c
7. b
8. a
9. a
10. c

Chapter 14
1. b
2. a
3. a
4. b
5. a
6. c
7. a
8. d
9. b
10. c

Chapter 15
1. b
2. a
3. c
4. d
5. a
6. a
7. d
8. d

Chapter 16
1. a
2. b
3. d
4. d
5. a
6. c
7. c
8. a
9. d
10. a

Chapter 17
1. b
2. b
3. a
4. d
5. b
6. c
7. b
8. c
9. d
10. a

Chapter 18
1. c
2. b
3. c
4. c
5. a
6. c
7. d
8. c
9. d
10. a

Chapter 19
1. b
2. d
3. b
4. c
5. c
6. c
7. c
8. d
9. a
10. a

Chapter 20
1. b
2. c
3. b
4. b
5. b
6. c
7. d
8. a
9. b
10. a

Chapter 21
1. b
2. c
3. d
4. c
5. c
6. a
7. d
8. c
9. a
10. d

Chapter 22
1. b
2. a
3. c
4. c
5. d
6. c
7. b
8. a
9. d

Chapter 23
1. d
2. b
3. d
4. a
5. d
6. a
7. b
8. c
9. a
10. c

Chapter 24
1. a
2. d
3. b
4. c
5. b
6. b
7. d
8. a
9. d

Chapter 25
1. d
2. c
3. d
4. a
5. c
6. a
7. a
8. c
10. d
10. d

Chapter 26
1. c
2. d
3. b
4. c
5. a
6. d
7. a
8. d
9. d
10. d

Chapter 27
1. b
2. c
3. a
4. c
5. b
6. d
7. b
8. a
9. a
10. b

Chapter 28
1. b
2. a
3. d
4. b
5. c
6. b
7. a
8. c
9. b

Index

Page numbers in *italics* refer to figures and illustrations.